"No other guide has as much to offer . . . these books are a pleasure to read."   Gene Shalit on the *Today Show*

". . . Excellently organized for the casual traveler who is looking for a mix of recreation and cultural insight."
Washington Post

★ ★ ★ ★ ★ (5-star rating) "Crisply written and remarkably personable. Cleverly organized so you can pluck out the minutest fact in a moment. Satisfyingly thorough."
Réalités

"The information they offer is up-to-date, crisply presented but far from exhaustive, the judgments knowledgeable but not opinionated."   *New York Times*

"The individual volumes are compact, the prose succinct, and the coverage up-to-date and knowledgeable . . . The format is portable and the index admirably detailed."
John Barkham Syndicate

". . . An abundance of excellent directions, diversions, and facts, including perspectives and getting-ready-to-go advice — succinct, detailed, and well organized in an easy-to-follow style."   *Los Angeles Times*

"They contain an amount of information that is truly staggering, besides being surprisingly current."
Detroit News

"These guides address themselves to the needs of the modern traveler demanding precise, qualitative information . . . Upbeat, slick, and well put together."
Dallas Morning News

". . . Attractive to look at, refreshingly easy to read, and generously packed with information."   *Miami Herald*

"These guides are as good as any published, and much better than most."   *Louisville* (Kentucky) *Times*

Stephen Birnbaum Travel Guides

Acapulco
Bahamas, and Turks & Caicos
Barcelona
Bermuda
Boston
Canada
Cancun, Cozumel & Isla Mujeres
Caribbean
Chicago
Disneyland
Eastern Europe
Europe
Europe for Business Travelers
Florence
France
Great Britain
Hawaii
Honolulu
Ireland
Italy
Ixtapa & Zihuatanejo
Las Vegas
London
Los Angeles
Mexico
Miami & Ft. Lauderdale
Montreal & Quebec City
New Orleans
New York
Paris
Portugal
Puerto Vallarta
Rome
San Francisco
South America
Spain
Toronto
United States
USA for Business Travelers
Vancouver
Venice
Walt Disney World
Washington, DC
Western Europe

CONTRIBUTING EDITORS

Susan Heller Anderson, Lynn Angell, Barbara Bell, Janet Bennett, Colette Boulard, Frederick H. Brengelman, Rebecca Brite, Bernard Cartier, Kevin Causey, Ron Clason, Roger Collis, Charles Cupic, Karen Cure, Stephanie Curtis, Les Daly, Diane Darrow, Jeff Davidson, Linda Davidson, Vicky Elliott, Emily Emerson-Le Moing, John Foy, Carol Frankel, Carolyn Friday, Alice Garrard, Edward Guiliano, Mireille Guiliano, Kathy Gunst, Jeffrey C. Haight, Ben Harte, Jill Herbers, Amy Hollowell, David Howley, Catherine Lauge, Harriet Leins, Will MacAdam, Maguy Macario, Anne Manderson, Carole Martin, Michael Moynihan, Jill Newman, Marilyn Newton, Carol Offen, Rosemary Perkins, Sam Perkins, H. W. Rochefort, Margery Safir, Tracy Smith, Nancy Solomon, Marcie Stamper, David Stevens, Nick Stout, Phoebe Tait, Catherine Temerson, Pat Wells, David Wickers

MAPS B. Andrew Mudryk   SYMBOLS   Gloria McKeown

A Stephen Birnbaum Travel Guide

Birnbaum's FRANCE 1993

Alexandra Mayes Birnbaum
EDITOR

Lois Spritzer
EXECUTIVE EDITOR

Laura L. Brengelman
Managing Editor

Mary Callahan
Jill Kadetsky
Susan McClung
Beth Schlau
Dana Margaret Schwartz
Associate Editors

Gene Gold
Assistant Editor

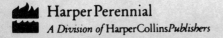

HarperPerennial
A Division of HarperCollins*Publishers*

To Stephen, who merely made all this possible.

BIRNBAUM'S FRANCE 1993. Copyright © 1992 by HarperCollins Publishers. All rights reserved. Printed in the United States of America. No part of this book may be used or reproduced in any manner whatsoever without written permission except in the case of brief quotations embodied in critical articles and reviews. For information address HarperCollins*Publishers*, 10 East 53rd Street, New York, NY 10022.

FIRST EDITION

ISSN 0749-2561 (Stephen Birnbaum Travel Guides)
ISSN 0749-2553 (France)
ISBN 0-06-278047-6 (pbk.)

92 93 94 95 96 CC/WP 10 9 8 7 6 5 4 3 2 1

Contents

GETTING READY TO GO

All the practical travel data you need to plan your vacation down to the final detail.

When and How to Go

Preparing

On the Road

PERSPECTIVES

A cultural and historical survey of France's past and present, its people, politics, and heritage.

THE CITIES

Thorough, qualitative guides to each of the 16 cities most often visited by vacationers and businesspeople. Each section, a comprehensive report of the city's most appealing attractions and amenities, is designed to be used on the spot. Directions and recommendations are immediately accessible because each guide is presented in a consistent form.

DIVERSIONS

A selective guide to more than 20 active and cerebral vacations, including the places to pursue them where your quality of experience is likely to be highest.

For the Experience

For the Body

For the Mind

DIRECTIONS

The most spectacular routes and roads, most arresting natural wonders, and most magnificent châteaux, manor houses, and gardens—all organized into 18 specific driving tours.

A Word from the Editor

To tell the truth, it sometimes seems easier to deal with France as just a chapter in a guidebook that deals with all of Europe than to try to treat this extraordinary country adequately all by itself. In a more general guidebook, it's possible to maintain the fiction that France is a truly homogeneous nation, with a single face and similar sensitivities in every corner of the country.

But the fact is that the diversity that flourishes across the Gallic landscape is extraordinarily broad, and in trying to provide a guide to each separate region it sometimes feels as if there are at least a dozen different countries demanding attention, rather than several areas of a single sovereign nation. Trying somehow to connect the dour visages found along the Brittany coast with the exuberant Mediterranean mentality of Marseilles is quite a task; no less irreconcilable is the Teutonic temperament of Alsatians when compared to the gentle demeanor of the denizens of the Dordogne.

In very practical terms, it's these very broad differences that provide the most compelling reason for the creation of this detailed guide to French life and landscape. Where travelers once routinely visited only Paris and said they'd seen France, there's a far broader recognition nowadays that Paris is no more a mirror of France than New York is an accurate image of the many faces of the United States. Just one tangible manifestation that travel suppliers are finally acknowledging this fact is the host of transatlantic flights that now head directly to such regional centers as Lyons, Nice, Nantes, Marseilles, Bordeaux, Strasbourg, and others, ignoring Paris entirely. This annually revised guide to France continues our own recognition of the increasing need to treat the world's most popular travel destinations in considerably greater depth.

Such thorough treatment only mirrors an increasingly pervasive trend among travelers — the frequent return to treasured foreign travel spots. Once upon a time, even the most dedicated travelers would visit distant parts of the world no more than once in a lifetime — usually as part of that fabled Grand Tour. But greater numbers of would-be sojourners are now availing themselves of the opportunity to visit favored parts of the world over and over again.

So where once it was routine to say you'd "seen" a particular country after a very superficial, once-over-lightly encounter, the more perceptive travelers of today recognize that it's entirely possible to have only skimmed the surface of a specific destination even after having visited that place more than a dozen times. Similarly, repeated visits to a single site permit true exploration of special interests, whether they be sporting, artistic, or intellectual in nature.

For those of us who spent several years working out the special system under which we present information in this series, the luxury of being able to devote nearly as much space as we'd like to just a single country is as close to paradise for guide writers and editors as any of us expects to come. But clearly this is not the first guide to the glories of France — one suspects that guides of one sort or another have existed at least since Caesar's legions began their exercise in tripartite division. Guides to France have existed literally for centuries, so a traveler might logically ask why another is necessary.

Our answer is that the nature of travel to France — and even of the travelers who now routinely make the trip — has changed dramatically. For the past 2,000 years or so, travel to and through France was an extremely elaborate undertaking, one that required extensive advance planning. Even as recently as the 1950s, a person who had actually been to Paris, Lyons, Marseilles, or Nice could dine out on his or her experiences for years, since such adventures were quite extraordinary and usually the province of the privileged alone.

With the advent of jet air travel in the late 1950s, however, and of increased-capacity, wide-body aircraft during the 1960s, travel to and around these once distant lands became extremely common. In fact, in more than 2 decades of nearly unending inflation, airfares — erratic though they are — may be the only commodity in the world that have actually gone down in price.

Attitudes as well as costs have also changed significantly in the last couple of decades. Beginning with the so-called flower children of the 1960s, international travel lost much of its aura of mystery. Whereas their parents might have been happy with just a superficial sampling of Paris and Versailles, these young people simply picked up and settled in various parts of Europe for an indefinite stay. While living as inexpensively as possible, they adapted to the local lifestyle, and generally immersed themselves in things European.

Thus began an explosion of travel to and through France. And over the years, the development of inexpensive charter flights and packages fueled the new American interest in and appetite for more extensive exploration.

Now, in the 1990s, those same flower children who were in the forefront of the modern travel revolution have undeniably aged. While it may be impolite to point out that they are probably well into their untrustworthy 30s and (some) 40s, their original zeal for travel remains undiminished. For them it's hardly news that the way to get to the Côte d'Azur is to head toward the Mediterranean, make a left, and then wait for the pebbled beachfronts to appear. Such experienced and knowledgeable travelers know precisely where they want to go and are more often searching for ideas and insights to expand their already sophisticated travel consciousnesses. Expansion of the routes of France's high-speed *TGV* trains have made their roamings around the French countryside far easier and more efficient, and broadly increased transatlantic gateways within France mean an easier time mapping regional itineraries.

Obviously, any guidebook to France must keep pace with and answer the real needs of today's travelers. That's why we've tried to create a guide that's specifically organized, written, and edited for the more demanding modern traveler, one for whom qualitative information is infinitely more desirable than mere quantities of unappraised data. We think that this book, along with all the other guides in our series, represents a new generation of travel guides — one that is especially responsive to modern needs and interests.

For years, dating back as far as Herr Baedeker, travel guides have tended to be encyclopedic, seemingly much more concerned with demonstrating expertise in geography and history than with a real analysis of the sorts of things that actually concern a typical modern tourist. But today, when it is hardly necessary to tell a traveler where Paris is (in many cases, the traveler has been to a given French destination nearly as often as the guidebook editors), it becomes the responsibility of those editors to provide new perspectives and to suggest new directions in order to make the guide genuinely valuable.

That's exactly what we've tried to do in this series. I think you'll notice a different, more contemporary tone to the text, as well as an organization and focus that are distinctive and more functional. And even a random reading of what follows will demonstrate a substantial departure from the standard guidebook orientation, for we've not only attempted to provide information of a more compelling sort, but we also have tried to present the data in a format that makes it particularly accessible.

Needless to say, it's difficult to decide just what to include in a guidebook of this size — and what to omit. Early on, we realized that giving up the encyclopedic approach precluded our listing every single route and restaurant, a realization that helped define our overall editorial focus. Similarly, when we discussed the possibility of presenting certain information in other than strict geographic order, we found that the new format enabled us to arrange data in a way we feel best answers the questions travelers typically ask.

Large numbers of specific questions have provided the real editorial skeleton for this book. The volume of mail we regularly receive emphasizes that modern travelers want very precise information, so we've tried to organize our material in the most responsive way possible. Readers who want to know the best restaurants around Lyons or the best places to find inexpensive couture fashions in Paris will have no trouble extracting that data from this guide.

Travel guides are, understandably, reflections of personal taste, and putting one's name on a title page obviously puts one's preferences on the line. But I think I ought to amplify just what "personal" means. Like my husband Steve Birnbaum, I don't believe in the sort of personal guidebook that's a palpable misrepresentation on its face. It is, for example, hardly possible for any single travel writer to visit thousands of restaurants (and nearly as many hotels) in any given year and provide accurate appraisals of each. And even if it were physically possible for one human being to survive such an itinerary, it would of necessity have to be done at a dead sprint, and the perceptions derived therefrom would probably be less valid than those of any other intelligent individual visiting the same establishments. It is, therefore, impossible (especially in a large, annually revised and updated guidebook *series* such as we offer) to have only one person provide all the data on the entire world.

I also happen to think that such individual orientation is of substantially less value to readers. Visiting a single hotel for just one night or eating one hasty meal in a random restaurant hardly equips anyone to provide appraisals that are of more than passing interest. No amount of doggedly alliterative or oppressively onomatopoeic text can camouflage a technique that is essentially specious. We have, therefore, chosen what I like to describe as the "thee and me" approach to restaurant and hotel evaluation and, to a somewhat more limited degree, to the sites and sights we have included in the other sections of our text. What this really reflects is a personal sampling tempered by intelligent counsel from informed local sources, and these additional friends-of-the-editor are almost always residents of the city and/or area about which they are consulted.

Despite the presence of several editors, writers, researchers, and local contributors, very precise editing and tailoring keep our text fiercely subjective. So what follows is the gospel according to Birnbaum, and it represents as much of our own taste and instincts as we can manage. It is probable, therefore, that if you like your cities stylish and your mountainsides uncrowded, prefer hotels with personality to high-rise anonymities, and recognize chocolate as the real reason for remaining alive, we're likely to have a long and meaningful relationship. Readers with dissimilar tastes may be less enraptured.

I also should point out something about the person to whom this guidebook is directed. Above all, he or she is a "visitor." This means that such elements as restaurants have been specifically picked to provide the visitor with a representative, enlightening, stimulating, and above all, pleasant experience. Since so many extraneous considerations can affect the reception and service accorded a regular restaurant patron, our choices can in no way be construed as an exhaustive guide to resident dining. We think we've listed all the best places, in various price ranges, but they were chosen with a visitor's enjoyment in mind.

Other evidence of how we've tried to tailor our text to reflect modern travel habits is most apparent in the section we call DIVERSIONS. Where once it was common for travelers to spend a foreign visit in a determinedly passive state, the emphasis is far more active today. So we've organized every activity we could reasonably evaluate and arranged the material in a way that is especially accessible to activists of either athletic or cerebral bent. It is no longer necessary, therefore, to wade through a pound or two of superflous prose just to find the very best crafts shop or the quaintest country inn within a reasonable distance of your destination.

If there is a single thing that best characterizes the revolution in and evolution of current holiday habits, it is that most travelers now consider travel a right rather than a privilege. No longer is a family trip to the far corners of the world necessarily a once-in-a-lifetime thing; nor is the idea of visiting exotic, faraway places in the least worrisome. Travel today translates as the enthusiastic desire to sample all of the world's opportunities, to find that elusive quality of experience that is not only enriching but comfortable. For that reason, we've tried to make what follows not only helpful and enlightening, but the sort of welcome companion of which every traveler dreams.

Finally, I also should point out that every good travel guide is a living enterprise; that is, no part of this text is carved in stone. In our annual revisions, we refine, expand, and further hone all our material to serve your travel needs better. To this end, no contribution is of greater value to us than your personal reaction to what we have written, as well as information reflecting your own experiences while using the book. We earnestly and enthusiastically solicit your comments about this guide *and* your opinions and perceptions about places you have recently visited. In this way, we will be able to provide the most current information — including the actual experiences of recent travelers — and to make those experiences more readily available to others. Please write to us at 10 E. 53rd St., New York, NY 10022.

We sincerely hope to hear from you.

ALEXANDRA MAYES BIRNBAUM

How to Use This Guide

A great deal of care has gone into the special organization of this guidebook, and we believe it represents a real breakthrough in the presentation of travel material. Our aim is to create a new, more modern generation of travel books and to make this guide the most useful and practical travel tool available today.

Our text is divided into five basic sections in order to present information in the best way on every possible aspect of a vacation to France. This organization itself should alert you to the vast and varied opportunities available, as well as indicate all the specific data necessary to plan a successful visit. You won't find much of the conventional "swaying palms and shimmering sand" text here; we've chosen instead to deliver more useful and practical information. Prospective French itineraries tend to speak for themselves, and with so many diverse travel opportunities, we feel our main job is to highlight what's where and to provide basic information — how, when, where, how much, and what's best — to assist you in making the most intelligent choices possible.

Here is a brief summary of the five basic sections and what you can expect to find in each. We believe that you will find both your travel planning and en-route enjoyment enhanced by having this book at your side.

GETTING READY TO GO

This mini-encyclopedia of practical travel facts is a sort of know-it-all companion with all the precise information necessary to create a successful journey to and through France. There are entries on more than 2 dozen separate topics, including how to get where you're going, what preparations to make before leaving, how to deal with possible emergencies while traveling, what to expect in the different regions of France, what your trip is likely to cost, and how to avoid prospective problems. The individual entries are specific, realistic, and where appropriate, cost-oriented.

We expect you to use this section most in the course of planning your trip, for its ideas and suggestions are intended to simplify this often confusing period. Entries are intentionally concise, in an effort to get to the meat of the matter with the least extraneous prose. These entries are augmented by extensive lists of specific sources from which to obtain even more specialized data, plus some suggestions for obtaining travel information on your own.

PERSPECTIVES

Any visit to an unfamiliar destination is enhanced and enriched by an understanding of the cultural and historical heritage of that area. We have, therefore, provided just such an introduction to France, its history, people and politics, architecture, literature, and food and drink.

THE CITIES

Individual reports on the 16 cities most visited by travelers and businesspeople have been created with the assistance of researchers, contributors, professional journalists, and experts who live in the cities. Although useful at the planning stage, THE CITIES is really designed to be taken along and used on the spot. Each report offers a short-stay guide to its city, including an essay introducing the city as a historic entity and as a place to visit. *At-a-Glance* material is actually a site-by-site survey of the most important, interesting, and sometimes most eclectic sights to see and things to do. *Sources and Resources* is a concise listing of pertinent tourist information, meant to answer myriad potentially pressing questions as they arise — from simple things such as the address of the local tourist office, how to get around, which sightseeing tours to take, and when special events and holidays occur to something more difficult like where to find the best nightspot, where to hail a taxi, which are the shops that have the finest merchandise and/or the most irresistible bargains, and where the best skiing, golf, tennis, fishing, and swimming, as well as the best museums and theaters, are to be found. *Best in Town* lists our collection of cost-and-quality choices of the best places to eat and sleep on a variety of budgets.

DIVERSIONS

This section is designed to help travelers find the best places in which to engage in a wide range of physical and cerebral activities, without having to wade through endless pages of unrelated text. This very selective guide lists the broadest possible range of activities, including all the best places to pursue them.

We start with a list of special places to stay and eat, and move to activities that require some perspiration — sports preferences and other rigorous pursuits — and go on to report on a number of more spiritual vacation opportunities. In every case, our suggestion of a particular location — and often our recommendation of a specific resort or hotel — is intended to guide you to that special place where the quality of experience is likely to be the highest. Whether you seek golf courses or tennis courts, want to go fishing or bicycling, or are searching for romantic château hotels or inspiring cooking schools, each category is the equivalent of a comprehensive checklist of the absolute best in France.

DIRECTIONS

Here are 18 itineraries that range all across France, along the most beautiful routes and roads, past the most spectacular natural wonders, through the most historic cities and countryside. DIRECTIONS is the only section of this book that is organized geographically, and its itineraries cover the touring highlights of France in short, independent journeys of 5 to 7 days' duration. Itineraries can be "connected" for longer sojourns or used individually for short, intensive explorations.

Each entry includes a guide to sightseeing highlights; a cost-and-quality guide to accommodations and food along the road (small inns, châteaux, and country hotels); and hints and suggestions for activities.

Although each of the book's sections has a distinct format and a special function, they have all been designed to be used together to provide a complete inventory of travel information. To use this book to full advantage, take a few minutes to read the table of contents and random entries in each section to get a firsthand feel for how it all fits together.

Pick and choose needed information. Assume, for example, that you have always wanted to take that typically French vacation, an eating tour of the country's temples of gastronomy — but you never really knew how to organize it or where to go. Turn first to the chapter entitled *Food and Drink* in the PERSPECTIVES section, where you will find a discussion of the food specialties and wines of the various regions, a glossary of food terms, and advice on French menus, manners, and methods. Next, choose specific restaurants from the selections offered in each city chapter in THE CITIES, in each tour route in DIRECTIONS, and in the roundup of the best in the country called *Haute Gastronomie* in the DIVERSIONS section. Then, refer to *Useful Words and Phrases,* GETTING READY TO GO, and *Food and Drink,* PERSPECTIVES, to help you with everything from making reservations to deciphering the menu. We've even provided instructions on how to write a letter requesting reservations (an important prelude to visiting many of France's great restaurants, which are often booked weeks — or months — in advance), as well as a discussion of special food and wine tours and some of their suppliers.

In other words, the sections of this book are building blocks designed to help you put together the best possible trip. Use them selectively as a tool, a source of ideas, a reference work for accurate facts, and a guidebook to the best buys, the most exciting sights, the most pleasant accommodations, the tastiest food — *the best travel experience* that you can possibly have.

GETTING READY
TO GO

When and How to Go

When to Go

 There really isn't a "best" time to visit France. For North Americans, as well as Europeans, the period from mid-May to mid-September has long been — and remains — the peak travel period, traditionally the most popular vacation time. As far as weather is concerned, France also is at its best then, warmer than Great Britain or Ireland, but more comfortable than many destinations farther south on the Continent, where heat waves are inevitable.

It is important to emphasize that France is hardly a single-season destination; more and more travelers who have a choice are enjoying the substantial advantages of off-season travel. Though many lesser tourist attractions may close during the off-season — roughly November to *Easter* — the major ones remain open and tend to be less crowded, as are some cities and other parts of the country. During the off-season, people relax and French life proceeds at a more leisurely pace, and a lively social and cultural calendar flourishes. What's more, travel generally is less expensive.

For some, the most convincing argument in favor of off-season travel is the economic one. Getting there and staying there is more affordable during less popular travel periods, as airfares, hotel rooms, and car rental rates go down and less expensive package tours become available; the independent traveler can go farther on less, too. Europe is not like the Caribbean, where high season and low season are precisely defined and rates drop automatically on a particular date. But many French hotels reduce rates during the off-season, and on the Riviera and at other seaside resorts savings can be as much as 30%. Although smaller establishments may close during the off-season in response to reduced demand, there still are plenty of alternatives, and, in cities, cut-rate "mini-break" packages — for stays of more than 1 night, especially over a weekend (when business travelers traditionally go home) — are more common.

A definite bonus to visiting during the off-season is that even the most basic services are performed more efficiently. In theory, off-season service is identical to that offered during high season, but the fact is that the absence of demanding crowds inevitably begets much more thoughtful and personal attention. The very same staff that barely can manage to get fresh towels onto the racks during the height of summer at coastal resort areas has the time to chat pleasantly in the spring or fall. And it is not only hotel service that benefits from the absence of the high-season mobs.

There are, however, some notable exceptions to this rule. The general tourism off-season is high season for skiers in the Alps, meaning higher prices and crowds everywhere there is snow. Even during the off-season, high-season rates also may prevail because of an important local event. Spring and fall are favored times for major international trade fairs — Bordeaux, Dijon, Lille, Lyons, Marseilles, Metz, Nantes, Nice, Rennes, Strasbourg, and Toulouse, as well as Paris, all have several each year. Particularly in the larger cities, such major trade shows or conferences held at the time of your visit are sure to affect the availability not only of discounts, but even of a place to stay.

It also should be noted that the months immediately before and after the peak summer months — what the travel industry refers to as shoulder seasons — often are sought out because they offer fair weather and somewhat smaller crowds. But be aware that very near high-season prices can prevail, notably in certain popular resort areas such as the French Riviera.

In short, like many other popular places, France's vacation appeal has become multi-seasonal. But the noted exceptions notwithstanding, most travel destinations are decidedly less trafficked and less expensive during the winter.

CLIMATE: Even though the northern French city of Calais is at approximately the same latitude as Vancouver, Canada, and the southern city of Perpignan is at approximately the same latitude as Detroit, France has a relatively mild climate most of the year, generally fair and warm in the summertime and not too cold in winter. But there's more to it than that; the climate of so large a country is hardly uniform. *Please note that although temperatures usually are recorded on the Celsius scale in France, for purposes of clarity we use the more familiar Fahrenheit scale.*

To the west, the influences of the Atlantic Ocean soften extremes of temperature and create a pattern of precipitation characterized by a high percentage of days year-round with at least some drizzle. This tempering is most pronounced near Cherbourg at Cap de la Hague, the northern tip of Normandy's Cotentin Peninsula, which projects into the English Channel and which, because of the Gulf Stream, often has winter temperatures as warm as those in Nice. Moving east, the climate becomes more and more of the traditional continental type, with colder winters, hotter summers, and rain tending to fall more distinctly in an alternation of definitely wet and definitely dry days. In the Mediterranean zone of the south, where there generally is less rain, what precipitation there is occurs mostly in the spring and fall. There is more sun, too, making winters milder and summers hotter than anywhere else in France — but less humid.

Mountains further contribute to variations in the climate. There are snow-covered peaks all year in the Pyrénées and the Alps, and parts of the Massif Central remain snow-covered until late in the spring. Mountains also affect the weather in surrounding regions. The Alps shelter the nearby Côte d'Azur, reinforcing the effects of the Mediterranean and giving the area a distinct southern exposure. The Vosges Mountains accentuate the continental climate of Alsace, making it penetratingly cold in winter and comfortably warm to stiflingly hot in summer.

Paris has about the same weather as the Middle Atlantic states in the US, though it's usually not warmer than the middle to upper 70s F in summer or colder than 30F in winter. The weather is most pleasant late spring through early fall (May through September or October), but since there are a nearly infinite number of reasons to go to Paris — the majority of them totally independent of any considerations about weather — it is probable that quite a few travelers will visit at other times. During the winter, when France is warm compared to North American cities in the same latitude, it frequently is overcast or actually raining (there is precipitation during about 15 days of each winter month). Central heating is widely available, but be forewarned that thermostats usually are set too low to effectively warm up drafty and damp historic buildings. Most travelers will find it damp and chilly not only in the dead of winter but also in the early spring and late fall. The lyricist of "April in Paris" clearly hadn't spent many early spring days under the consistently leaden Parisian skies. Even in summer, the city averages 12 or 13 days of rain per month.

Lyons, in central France, is at once a northern city and the gateway to both the Alps and the Mediterranean. It can be colder than Paris in the winter, though temperatures rarely drop below freezing for long and it is less damp than Paris. In summer, temperatures do not rise much above the high 70s F. Spring and winter can be rainy, and thick fogs are an occasional late fall and winter phenomenon.

The Mediterranean climate in Marseilles is dry and joyously sunny almost 300 days a year, with summer days in the mid-80s F and winter days that rarely go below 40 F. It rains in the spring and fall in brief but heavy downpours. Marseilles, along with the rest of Provence, can be windy when the capricious *mistral* (a cold, dry wind from the north) whips down the Rhône — fall, winter, or spring — at up to 65 miles an hour, for anywhere from a few hours to a few days. Farther east along the coast, on the Côte d'Azur, Nice is a bit warmer in winter and slightly cooler in summer, and has approximately the same number of days of sunshine (though tourist officials would have you believe it has a lot less rain than it does). It, too, is subject to sudden visitations by the *mistral.* In general, you can go swimming on the Côte d'Azur from May (and sometimes from April) through September, and those who live there often begin sunbathing on their terraces, or in other sheltered spots, as early as February.

The following chart lists average low and high temperatures in major French cities at different times of the year to help in planning.

AVERAGE TEMPERATURES (in °F)

	January	April	July	October
Aix-en-Provence	34–50	44–64	62–83	49–67
Ajaccio	37–55	45–64	61–81	52–72
Avignon	34–49	45–67	61–87	49–68
Biarritz	39–52	46–61	61–73	52–66
Bordeaux	36–48	43–63	57–77	46–64
Cannes	37–54	46–63	63–81	52–68
Chartres	33–43	39–56	53–72	44–59
Cognac	35–47	43–62	58–78	47–64
Dijon	28–39	41–61	57–77	43–59
Grenoble	27–43	41–61	57–79	45–61
Limoges	30–45	39–61	54–77	43–63
Lyons	30–41	43–61	59–81	45–61
Marseilles	36–50	46–64	63–84	50–68
Monte Carlo	46–54	54–61	72–79	61–68
Montpellier	34–52	46–64	61–84	50–68
Nancy	28–39	39–59	55–75	41–59
Nantes	36–46	43–59	57–75	46–61
Nice	39–55	48–63	64–81	54–70
Paris	34–43	43–61	59–77	46–61
Perpignan	39–54	50–66	66–84	54–68
Reims	30–41	39–59	55–75	43–59
Rouen	32–43	39–59	54–73	45–59
Strasbourg	28–37	41–61	55–77	43–57
Toulouse	34–48	43–63	59–81	46–64

Travelers can get current readings and extended forecasts through the *Weather Channel Connection,* the worldwide weather report center of the *Weather Channel,* a cable television station. By dialing 900-WEATHER and punching in either the first four letters of the city name or the area code for over 600 cities in the US, an up-to-date recording will provide such information as current temperature, barometric pressure, relative humidity, and wind speed, as well as a general 2-day forecast. Beach, boating, and highway reports are also provided for some locations. Weather information for over 225 international destinations can be obtained by punching in the first four letters of the city (or island) name. For instance, to hear the weather report for Paris, punch in PARI. (To find out which cities or locations in a given country are covered, enter the first four letters of the *country* name.) Callers also can access information on the weather patterns for any time of the year in the area requested, as well as international travel information such as visa requirements, US State Department travel advisories, tipping, and voltage requirements. French destinations included in this service are: Bordeaux, Brest, Cannes, Cherbourg, Lyons, Paris, Strasbourg, and Toulouse. This 24-hour service can be accessed from any touch-tone phone in the US, and costs 95¢ per minute. The charge will show up on your phone bill. For additional information, contact the *Weather Channel Connection,* 2600 Cumberland Pkwy., Atlanta, GA 30339 (phone: 404-434-6800).

SPECIAL EVENTS: Travelers may want to schedule a visit to France to coincide with some special event. The highlight of a sports lover's trip may be attending the French championships of a favorite game. For a music lover, a concert in a great cathedral or in a splendid natural setting may be an especially thrilling experience, and much more memorable than seeing the same place on an ordinary sightseeing itinerary. A folklore or harvest festival can bring nearly forgotten traditions alive or underscore their continuing significance in modern life.

In France, the calendar of such events is a busy one from spring through fall, with the notable exception of August, when most of the country is on vacation. In winter, too, a great deal is happening. In Paris, the cultural season proceeds at a pace few other cities can match. Museums and galleries mount special exhibitions; opera, ballet, and musical comedy take place at *L'Opéra,* the new *L'Opéra Bastille,* the *Salle Favart–Opéra Comique,* the *Théâtre de la Ville,* and the *Théâtre Musical de Paris Châtelet;* concerts are held at the *Salle Pleyel,* the *Salle Gaveau,* the *Théâtre des Champs-Elysées,* and the *Palais des Congrès;* and there is theater everywhere, from the *Comédie-Française* to cabarets and *cafés-théâtres.* Other cities and towns of all sizes promote their own smaller cultural programs.

The events noted below are the major ones, but they are only a sampling. Among the many *not* mentioned are flower shows in the spring, numerous additional music festivals that proliferate as spring progresses into summer, midsummer festivities, and more. Most towns with St-Jean in their names celebrate the *Feast Day of John the Baptist* on or near June 24. Some regions are known for their own kinds of festivals — for instance, in Brittany, where every town or village has a day of religious observance and pilgrimage known as a *pardon.* Some of the more colorful *pardons* — which date back to the days when penitents received indulgences on saints' days and *Ascension Thursday,* and which may be the only occasions left for visitors to see the characteristic Breton costumes in large numbers — are the *Pardon de St-Yves* (mid May) in Tréguier, the *Pardon de Ste-Anne* (the last weekend in July) in the region of Morbihan, the *Pardon de Nôtre Dame de la Clarté* (mid August) in the region of Côtes d'Armor, and the *Pardon de Ste-Anne-La-Palud* (last Sunday in August) in the region of Finistère. There are over 30 *pardons* held every year in Brittany from May to September.

A further cause for celebration not exhausted by the list below is the harvesting of the grape. Almost every district that makes wine also makes merry about it, and while two of the most important wine festivals are mentioned (in Burgundy, in September and November), there are many more — sometimes in the most unexpected places. Even Paris has one, the *Fête des Vendanges à Montmartre,* early in October, to celebrate the harvest in the city's last remaining vineyard on Montmartre.

The following special events are listed according to the months in which they usually occur. Where possible, we have indicated the exact dates for the festivities this year. However, for those events for which specific dates were not yet available as we went to press, and to guard against inevitable scheduling changes, it is best to check with the French Government Tourist Office for the exact dates of anything that may be of interest and for current schedules of festivals, fairs, and other events. Also keep in mind that some events, particularly festivals, may vary by a few days to several weeks from town to town and province to province; again, it's best to check with the tourist authorities for the most up-to-date information (see *Tourist Information,* in this section, for addresses).

January

Monte Carlo Rallye: The dean of European motor rallies. Monaco has been the finish line since the first competitors made it to the principality in 1911. Monaco.

February

Carnival: Torchlight processions, parades of floats, flower battles, masked balls, and other revelry begin 3 weekends before *Lent* and end when King Carnival is burned in effigy on *Shrove Tuesday.* Nice.

International Television Festival: Several nights of competition among the best shows from TV producers around the world. Monaco.

March

European Ski Jumping Cup: One of the major events on the slopes of Chamonix in the Haute Savoie. Mont-Blanc.

April

Prix du Président de la République: Horse race at *Auteuil Racecourse,* usually held on *Easter* Sunday. Paris.

Paris Marathon: A mid-month opportunity to see 42 kilometers of the French capital — on the run. Paris.

Lyons International Fair: A major European trade fair for 2 weeks that continues a business tradition with origins in the 15th century. Lyons.

International Tennis Championships: The big event at the *Monte Carlo Country Club.* Monaco.

May

Son et Lumière: Sound and light shows and costumed pageantry illuminate the châteaux of the Loire and their history. May through September at some castles; from June through August, the season is in full swing. Loire Valley.

Festival of the Camargue Mounted Herdsmen: Celebration by the cowboy-herdsmen of the Camargue, with parades and blessing of horses. First week in May. Arles.

Joan of Arc Commemorations: Pageants and processions in honor of the most beloved of French saints. Among the cities celebrating is the one she led to victory against the English on May 7 and 8, 1429; the one to which she accompanied the dauphin to be crowned as Charles VII; and the one that remembers her on the weekend nearest May 30, the anniversary of the day she was burned at the stake there in 1430. Orléans, Reims, Rouen.

International Film Festival: The world's most famous film festival. Two weeks of starlets splashing, photographers flashing, nonstop screenings, business dealing, and the awarding of the Golden Palm. Cannes.

Musical May: Two weeks of opera, symphony, chamber concerts, and solo recitals in theaters, churches, and country châteaux. Bordeaux.

Grande Bravade: Three days of religious processions and folkloric frolics in mid-May in honor of St-Tropez. The *Bravade des Espagnoles* a month later celebrates a victory over the Spanish and is less rowdy. St-Tropez.

Feria de la Pentecôte: Five days of bullfights, bull races, folk dancing, and flamenco in an ancient southern town. Mid May. Nîmes.

Gypsies' Pilgrimage: A gathering of Gypsies from all over Europe to honor their patron saint, Sarah, and others. The celebration in a Camargue village begins on May 23 with a candlelight vigil and ends on May 25 with a procession to the sea. The repeat in October is not as showy. Saintes-Maries-de-la-Mer.

Monaco Grand Prix: A major Formula I motor race in late May or early June. Run since 1929 right through the streets of Monaco.

French Open Tennis Championships: The first of the *Grand Slam* tournaments, bridging the months of May and June at *Roland Garros Stadium.* Paris.

June

Paris International Air Show: Aviation fair held in odd-numbered years at Le Bourget Airport. Paris.

Lyons Second Symphony Evenings: Two weeks of classical music by world re- nowned ensembles and internationally known soloists.

Strasbourg International Music Festival: Five weeks of first-rate music, some of it soaring in the city's superb Gothic cathedral. From June through July. Strasbourg.

Festival du Paris: Music, dance, opera. Each year the culture of a different foreign country is highlighted. Paris.

Grand Steeplechase de Paris: Major horse race and opening event of the *Grande Semaine* (Big Week). Next to last Sunday of the month at *Auteuil* racecourse. Paris.

Grand Prix de Paris: The original grand prix — a horse race, not a motor race — first run in 1863. Part of the *Grande Semaine,* this classic test for 3-year-olds takes place the last Sunday of the month at *Longchamp* racecourse. Paris.

The 24 Hours of Le Mans: The grueling 2-day event along one of the most famous motor racing circuits in the world. Le Mans.

July

Grand Jazz Parade: A 10-day (and night) jazz festival–jam session attracting top performers from the US and the Continent. Nice.

Bastille Day: July 14, the anniversary of the storming of the Bastille prison in 1789; France's national holiday. Celebrated everywhere with parades, fireworks, and dancing in the streets, but nowhere more colorfully than in Paris, where it all began, or in the medieval town of Carcassonne, which goes up in mock flames. Nationwide.

Tour de France: Arrival on the Champs-Elysées of the most famous bicycle race of them all, some 3 weeks (starts late June to early July) and 2,000-plus miles from the starting point. All Paris turns out for the late July finish. Paris.

Festival d'Avignon: France's theater and dance festival par excellence, presenting the classic, the contemporary, the French, and the foreign in an early July to early August wrap-up of the state of the stage art. Avignon.

International Arts and Music Festival: About 3 weeks of high-caliber music mak- ing, especially by the vocal cords, from mid-July to early August. Aix-en- Provence.

Chorégies d'Orange: A 3-week festival of opera and choral works. Three or four productions are staged beautifully each year. Mid-July to early August. Orange.

International Jazz Festival: Also known as "Jazz in Juan," it's one of the most celebrated jazz events in Europe. This 10-day bash attracts musicians and participants from around the world. Antibes.

Festival Estival: Concerts of classical music, from ancient to very modern, in churches, museums, concert halls, and in great quantity, filling the mid-July to late-September gap between the capital's *Festival du Paris* and the *Festival d'Automne* to come. Paris.

August

Basque Folk Festival: A week of singing, dancing, *pelote* games, and bullfights, which bridges the end of July and the beginning of August in Bayonne, the chief town of French Basque country.

September

Music Festival of Besançon and Franche-Comté: Almost a month of classical, particularly chamber, music, highlighted by a contest for young conductors. Besançon, Doubs.

Fête de la Vigne–Fête Folklorique Internationale: A grape harvest–cum–folklore festival that sings (in a medley of tongues), dances, and tastes its way along a Burgundy wine route. Dijon, Côte d'Or.

Berlioz Festival: A 10-day celebration of the music of Hector Berlioz in his hometown and in a city where he performed. The festival also features performances of compositions by Debussy, Franck, and Ravel. Lyons.

Festival d'Automne: Music, dance, and theater festival, stressing the contemporary in these arts. Mid-September to December. Paris.

October

Prix de l'Arc de Triomphe: Horse race at *Longchamp* racecourse run since 1920; the stakes are high. First Sunday of the month. Paris.

November

International Gastronomic Fair: A major trade fair showcasing the finest food and wine from all over the world. Dijon.

Les Trois Glorieuses: Three glorious days of wine-related merrymaking including the most important wine auction of the year. The third Saturday, Sunday, and Monday of the month at three sites in Burgundy. Clos-de-Vougeot, Beaune, Meursault.

December

International Crib-Makers' Fair: Christmas crib figures on display in crèches and for sale. Early December through mid January. Arles.

Shepherd's Festival: A centuries-old tradition at *Christmas:* midnight mass in a tiny hilltop village in Provence. Istres.

Traveling by Plane

 Flying is the most efficient way to get to France, and it is the quickest, most convenient means of travel between different parts of the country once you are there. (Cruise ships that call at French ports generally function as hotels for passengers cruising European waters, rather than as especially efficient transportation to a single country or between individual destinations.)

The air space between North America and Europe is the most heavily trafficked in the world. It is served by dozens of airlines, almost all of which sell seats at a variety of prices, under a vast spectrum of requirements and restrictions. Since you probably will spend more for your airfare than for any other single item in your travel budget, try to take advantage of the lowest fares offered by either scheduled airlines or charter companies. You should know what kinds of flights are available, the rules under which air travel operates, and all the special package options.

SCHEDULED AIRLINES: Among the dozens of airlines serving Europe from the United States, those offering regularly scheduled flights to France, many on a daily basis, are *Air France, American, British Airways, Continental, Delta, Egypt Air, Lufthansa, Northwest, Pakistan International, SAS, SwissAir, Tower Air, TWA, United, USAir,* and *UTA.*

Gateways – At present, nonstop flights to France depart from Atlanta, Boston, Chicago, Cincinnati, Dallas/Fort Worth, Detroit, Houston, Los Angeles, Miami, New York, Newark, Philadelphia, Raleigh, St. Louis, San Francisco, and Washington, DC.

Additional direct flights (meaning, usually, that there is no change of flight number between the originating and terminating cities, though there may be one or more stops en route and perhaps a change of plane) depart from some of the above cities and a few others as well.

Nonstop or direct, the majority of these flights land in Paris, either at Charles de Gaulle or Orly airports. A number of carriers fly between the US and other destinations in France. *Delta* flies nonstop to Nice; *SAS* flies direct (via Copenhagen) to Nice; and *SwissAir* has direct service to Marseilles, Nice, and Toulouse.

Tickets – When traveling on one of the many regularly scheduled flights, a full-fare ticket provides maximum travel flexibility (although at considerable expense) because there are no advance booking requirements. A prospective passenger can buy a ticket for a flight right up to the minute of takeoff — if a seat is available. If your ticket is for a round trip, you can make the return reservation whenever you wish — months before you leave, or the day before you return. Assuming the foreign immigration requirements are met, you can stay at your destination for as long as you like. (Tickets generally are good for a year and can be renewed if not used.) You also can cancel your flight at any time without penalty. However, while it is true that this category of ticket can be purchased at the last minute, it is advisable to reserve well in advance during popular vacation periods and around holiday times.

Fares – Airfares continue to change so rapidly that even the experts find it difficult to keep up with them. This ever-changing situation is due to a number of factors, including airline deregulation, volatile labor relations, increasing fuel costs, and vastly increased competition.

Perhaps the most common misconception about fares on scheduled airlines is that the cost of the ticket determines how much service will be provided on the flight. This is true only to a certain extent. A far more realistic rule of thumb is that the less you pay for your ticket, the more restrictions and qualifications are likely to come into play before you board the plane (as well as after you get off). These qualifying aspects relate to the months (and the days of the week) during which you must travel, how far in advance you must purchase your ticket, the minimum and maximum amount of time you may or must remain away, your willingness to decide on a return date at the time of booking — and your ability to stick to that decision. It is not uncommon for passengers sitting side by side on the same wide-body jet to have paid fares varying by hundreds of dollars, and all too often the traveler paying more would have been equally willing (and able) to accept the terms of the far less expensive ticket.

In general, the great variety of fares between the US and France can be reduced to four basic categories, including first class, coach (also called economy or tourist class), and excursion or discount fares. A fourth category, called business class, has been added by many airlines in recent years. In addition, Advance Purchase Excursion (APEX) fares offer savings under certain conditions.

In a class by itself is the *Concorde,* the supersonic jet developed jointly by France and Great Britain, which cruises at speeds of 1,350 miles an hour (twice the speed of sound) and makes transatlantic crossings in half the time of conventional, subsonic jets. *Air France* offers *Concorde* service from New York to Paris; *British Airways* flies from New York and Washington, DC to London. (Those taking a *British Airways' Concorde* flight from New York or Washington can buy the ticket in conjunction with a ticket for a connecting flight to Paris — on a regular, subsonic jet). Service is "single" class (with champagne and caviar all the way) and the fare is expensive, about 20% more than a first class ticket on a subsonic aircraft. Some discounts have been offered, but time is the real gift of the *Concorde:* It makes a New York to Paris run in 3¾ hours.

A **first class** ticket is your admission to the special section of the aircraft, with larger seats, more legroom, sleeperette seating on some wide-body aircraft, better (or at least more elaborately served) food, free drinks and headsets for movies and music channels, and above all, personal attention. First class fares are about twice those of full-fare economy, although both first class passengers and those paying full economy fares are entitled to reserve seats and are sold tickets on an open reservation system. An additional advantage of a first class ticket is that if you're planning to visit several cities within France or elsewhere in Europe, you may include any number of stops en route to or from your most distant destination, provided that certain set, but generous restrictions regarding maximum mileage limits and flight routes are respected.

Not too long ago, there were only two classes of air travel, first class and all the rest, usually called economy or tourist. Then **business class** came into being — one of the most successful recent airline innovations. At first, business class passengers were merely curtained off from the other economy passengers. Now a separate cabin or cabins — usually toward the front of the plane — is the norm. While standards of comfort and service are not as high as in first class, they represent a considerable improvement over conditions in the rear of the plane, with roomier seats, more leg and shoulder space between passengers, and fewer seats abreast. Free liquor and headsets, a choice of meal entrées, and a separate counter for speedier check-in are other inducements. As in first class, a business class passenger may travel on any scheduled flight he or she wishes, may buy a one-way or round-trip ticket, and have the ticket remain valid for a year. There are no minimum or maximum stay requirements, no advance booking requirements, and no cancellation penalties, and the fare allows the same free stopover privileges as first class. Airlines often have their own names for their business class service — such as Le Club on *Air France,* Medallion Class on *Delta,* and Ambassador Class on *TWA.*

The terms of the **coach** or **economy** fare may vary slightly from airline to airline, and in fact from time to time airlines may be selling more than one type of economy fare. Coach or economy passengers sit more snugly, as many as 10 in a single row on a wide-body jet, behind the first class and business class sections. Normally, alcoholic drinks are not free, nor are the headsets (except on *British Airways,* which does offer these free of charge). If there are two economy fares on the books, one (often called "regular economy") still may include a number of free stopovers. The other, less expensive fare (often called "special economy") may limit stopovers to one or two, with a charge (typically $25) for each one. Like first class passengers, however, passengers paying the full coach fare are subject to none of the restrictions that usually are attached to less expensive excursion and discount fares. There are no advance booking requirements, no minimum stay requirements, and no cancellation penalties. Tickets are sold on an open reservation system: They can be bought for a flight right up to the minute of takeoff (if seats are available), and if the ticket is round-trip, the return reservation can be made anytime you wish. Both first class and coach tickets generally are good for a year, after which they can be renewed if not used, and if you ultimately decide not to fly at all, your money will be refunded. The cost of economy and business class tickets does not vary much in the course of the year between the US and France, though on some transatlantic routes they vary from a basic (low-season) price in effect most of the year to a peak (high-season) price during the summer.

Excursion and other **discount** fares are the airlines' equivalent of a special sale and usually apply to round-trip bookings only. These fares generally differ according to the season and the number of travel days permitted. They are only a bit less flexible than full-fare economy tickets and are, therefore, often useful for both business and holiday travelers. Most round-trip excursion tickets include strict minimum and maximum stay requirements and reservations can be changed only within the specified time limits. So don't count on extending a ticket beyond the prescribed time of return or staying less time than required. Different airlines may have different regulations concerning the number of stopovers permitted, and sometimes excursion fares are less expensive during midweek. The availability of these reduced-rate seats is most limited at busy times such as holidays. Discount or excursion fare ticket holders sit with the coach passengers, and, for all intents and purposes, are indistinguishable from them. They receive all the same basic services, even though they may have paid anywhere between 30% and 55% less for the trip. Obviously, it's wise to make plans early enough to qualify for this less expensive transportation if possible.

These discount or excursion fares may masquerade under a variety of names, they may vary from city to city (from the East Coast to the West Coast, especially), but they invariably have strings attached. A common requirement is that the ticket be purchased a certain number of days — usually no fewer than 7 or 14 days — in advance of departure, though it may be booked weeks or months in advance (it has to be "ticketed," or paid for, shortly after booking, however). The return reservation usually has to be made at the time of the original ticketing and cannot be changed later than a certain number of days (again, usually 7 or 14 days) before the return flight. If events force a passenger to change the return reservation after the date allowed, the difference between the round-trip excursion rate and the round-trip coach rate probably will have to be paid, though most airlines allow passengers to use their discounted fares by standing by for an empty seat, even if they don't otherwise have standby fares. Another common condition is a minimum and maximum stay requirement; for example, 1 to 6 days or 6 to 14 days (but including at least a Saturday night). Last, cancellation penalties of up to 50% of the full price of the ticket have been assessed — check the specific penalty in effect when you purchase your discount/excursion ticket — so careful planning is imperative.

Of even greater risk — and bearing the lowest price of all the current discount fares — is the ticket where no change at all in departure and/or return flights is permitted, and where the ticket price is totally nonrefundable. If you do buy a nonrefundable ticket, you should be aware of a new policy followed by many airlines that may make it easier to change your plans if necessary. For a fee — set by each airline and payable at the airport when checking in — you *may* be able to change the time or date of a return flight on a nonrefundable ticket. However, if the nonrefundable ticket price for the replacement flight is higher than that of the original (as often is the case when trading in a weekday for a weekend flight), you will have to pay the difference. Any such change must be made a certain number of days in advance — in some cases as little as 2 days — of either the original or the replacement flight, whichever is earlier; restrictions are set by the individual carrier. (Travelers holding a nonrefundable or other restricted ticket who must change their plans due to a family emergency should know that some carriers may make special allowances in such situations; for further information, see *Staying Healthy,* in this section.)

There also is a newer, often less expensive type of excursion fare, the **APEX,** or **Advanced Purchase Excursion,** fare. As with traditional excursion fares, passengers paying an APEX fare sit with and receive the same basic services as any other coach or economy passengers, even though they may have paid up to 50% less for their seats. In return, they are subject to certain restrictions. In the case of most flights to Europe, the ticket usually is good for a minimum of 7 days abroad and a maximum, currently, of 2 to 3 months (depending on the airline and the destination); and as its name implies, it must be "ticketed," or paid for in its entirety, a certain period of time before departure — usually 14 or 21 days.

The drawback to an APEX fare is that it penalizes travelers who change their minds — and travel plans. The return reservation must be made at the time of the original ticketing, and if for some reason you change your schedule while abroad, you will have to pay a penalty of $100 or 10% of the ticket value, whichever is greater, as long as you travel within the validity period of your ticket. But if you change your return to a date less than the minimum stay or more than the maximum stay, the difference between the round-trip APEX fare and the full round-trip coach rate will have to be paid. There also is a penalty of anywhere from $50 to $100 or more for canceling or changing a reservation *before* travel begins — check the specific penalty in effect when you purchase your ticket. No stopovers are allowed on an APEX ticket, but it is possible to create an open-jaw effect by buying an APEX on a split-ticket basis; for example, flying to Paris and returning from Nice. The total price would be half the price of an APEX to Paris plus half the price of an APEX to Nice. APEX tickets to France are sold at basic and peak rates (peak season is around May through September) and may include surcharges for weekend flights.

There also is a Winter or Super APEX fare, which may go under different names for different carriers (for instance, *Air France* and some other airlines call it "Euro-saver,"). Similar to the regular APEX fare, it costs slightly less, but is more restrictive. Depending on the airline and destination, it usually is available only for off-peak winter travel and is limited to a stay of between 7 and 21 days. Advance purchase still is required (currently 30 days prior to travel), and ticketing must be completed within 48 hours of reservation. The fare is nonrefundable except in cases of hospitalization or death.

Another type of fare that sometimes is available is the **youth fare**. At present, most airlines flying to France are using a form of APEX fare as a youth fare for those through age 25. The maximum stay is extended to a year, and the return booking must be left open. Seats usually can be reserved no more than 3 days before departure, and tickets must be purchased when the reservation is made. The return is booked from France in the same manner, no more than 3 days before flight time. On most airlines, there is no cancellation penalty, but the fare is subject to availability, so it may be difficult to book a return during peak travel periods, and as with the regular APEX fare, it may not even be available for travel to or from France during high season and may be offered only on selected routes.

Standby fares, at one time the rock-bottom price at which a traveler could fly to Europe, have become elusive. At the time of this writing, most major scheduled airlines did not regularly offer standby fares on direct flights to France. Because airline fares and their conditions constantly change, however, bargain hunters should not hesitate to ask if such a fare exists at the time they plan to travel. Travelers to France also should inquire about the possibility of connecting flights through other European countries that may be offered on a standby basis.

While the definition of standby varies somewhat from airline to airline, it generally means that you make yourself available to buy a ticket for a flight (usually no sooner than the day of departure), then literally stand by on the chance that a seat will be empty. Once aboard, however, a standby passenger has the same meal service and frills (or lack of them) enjoyed by others in the economy class compartment.

Something else to check is the possibility of qualifying for a **GIT** (Group Inclusive Travel) fare, which requires that a specific dollar amount of ground arrangements be purchased, in advance, along with the ticket. The requirements vary as to number of travel days and stopovers permitted, and the minimum number of passengers required for a group. The actual fares also vary, but the cost will be spelled out in brochures distributed by the tour operators handling the ground arrangements. In the past, GIT fares were among the least expensive available from the established carriers, but the prevalence of discount fares has caused group fares to all but disappear from some air routes. Travelers reading brochures on group package tours to France will find that, in almost all cases, the applicable airfare given as a sample (to be added to the price of the land package to obtain the total tour price) is an APEX fare, the same discount fare available to the independent traveler.

The major airlines serving France from the US also may offer individual excursion fare rates similar to GIT fares, which are sold in conjunction with ground accommodation packages. Previously called ITX, and sometimes referred to as individual tour-basing fares, these fares generally are offered as part of "air/hotel/car/transfer packages," and can reduce the cost of an economy fare by more than a third. The packages are booked for a specific amount of time, with return dates specified; rescheduling and cancellation restrictions and penalties vary from carrier to carrier. At the time of this writing, these fares were offered to popular destinations throughout France — including Bordeaux, Nice, and Paris — by *Air France, American, British Airways, Continental, Delta, KLM, Northwest, TWA,* and *United,* and although their offers did not represent a substantial savings over the standard economy fare, check at the time you plan to travel. (For further information on package options, see *Package Tours,* in this section.)

Travelers looking for the least expensive possible airfares should, finally, scan the pages of their hometown newspapers (especially the Sunday travel section) for announcements of special promotional fares. Most airlines offer their most attractive special fares to encourage travel during slow seasons, and to inaugurate and publicize new routes. Even if none of these factors applies, prospective passengers can be fairly sure that the number of discount seats per flight at the lowest price is strictly limited, or that the fare offering includes a set expiration date — which means it's absolutely necessary to move fast to enjoy the lowest possible price.

Among other special airline promotional deals for which you should be on the lookout are discount or upgrade coupons sometimes offered by the major carriers and found in mail-order merchandise catalogues. For instance, airlines sometimes issue coupons that typically cost around $25 each and are good for a percentage discount or an upgrade on an international airline ticket — including flights to France. The only requirement beyond the fee generally is that a coupon purchaser must buy at least one item from the catalogue. There usually are some minimum airfare restrictions before the coupon is redeemable, but in general these are worthwhile offers. Restrictions often include certain blackout days (when the coupon cannot be used at all), usually imposed during peak travel periods. These coupons are particularly valuable to business travelers who tend to buy full-fare tickets, and while the coupons are issued in the buyer's name, they can be used by others who are traveling on the same itinerary.

It's always wise to ask about discount or promotional fares and about any conditions that might restrict booking, payment, cancellation, and changes in plans. Check the prices from neighboring cities. A special rate may be offered in a nearby city but not in yours, and it may be enough of a bargain to warrant your leaving from that city. Ask if there is a difference in price for midweek versus weekend travel, or if there is a further discount for traveling early in the morning or late at night. Also be sure to investigate package deals, which are offered by virtually every airline. These may include a car rental, accommodations, and dining and/or sightseeing features, in addition to the basic airfare, and the combined cost of packaged elements usually is considerably less than the cost of the exact same elements when purchased separately.

If in the course of your research you come across a deal that seems too good to be true, keep in mind that logic may not be a component of deeply discounted airfares — there's not always any sane relationship between miles to be flown and the price to get there. More often than not, the level of competition on a given route dictates the degree of discount, and don't be dissuaded from accepting an offer that sounds irresistible just because it also sounds illogical. Better to buy that inexpensive fare while it's being offered and worry about the sense — or absence thereof — while you're flying to your desired destination.

When you're satisfied that you've found the lowest possible price for which you can conveniently qualify (you may have to call the airline more than once, because different airline reservations clerks have been known to quote different prices), make your booking. Then, to protect yourself against fare increases, purchase and pay for your ticket as soon as possible after you've received a confirmed reservation. Airlines generally will honor their tickets, even if the operative price at the time of your flight is higher than the price you paid; if fares go up between the time you *reserve* a flight and the time you *pay* for it, you likely will be out of luck. Finally, with excursion or discount fares, it is important to remember that when a reservations clerk says that you must purchase a ticket by a specific date, this is an absolute deadline. Miss the deadline and the airline may automatically cancel your reservation without telling you.

■**Note:** Another wrinkle in the airfare scene is that if the fares go *down* after you purchase your ticket, you *may* be entitled to a refund of the difference. However, this is only possible in certain situations — availability and advance purchase restrictions pertaining to the lower rate are set by the airline. If you suspect that you may be able to qualify for such a refund, check with your travel agent or the airline.

Frequent Flyers – The leading US carriers serving France — including *American, Continental, Delta, Northwest, TWA, United,* and *USAir* — offer a bonus system to frequent travelers. After the first 10,000 miles, for example, a passenger might be eligible for a first class seat for the coach fare; after another 10,000 miles, he or she might receive a discount on his or her next ticket purchase. The value of the bonuses continues to increase as more miles are logged. Once you are signed up for such a program, if flying to Europe on *Air France, British Airways, SAS, SwissAir,* or another European airline, ask if the miles to be flown may be applied toward your collective bonus mileage account with the US carrier.

Bonus miles also may be earned by patronizing affiliated car rental companies or hotel chains, or by using one of the credit cards that now offer this reward. In deciding whether to accept such a credit card from one of the issuing organizations that tempt you with frequent flyer mileage bonuses on a specific airline, first determine whether the interest rate charged on the unpaid balance is the same as (or less than) possible alternate credit cards, and whether the annual "membership" fee also is equal or lower. If these charges are slightly higher than those of competing cards, weigh the difference against the potential value in airfare savings. Also ask about any bonus miles awarded just for signing up — 1,000 is common, 5,000 generally the maximum.

For the most up-to-date information on frequent flyer bonus options, you may want to send for the monthly newsletter *Frequent.* Issued by Frequent Publications, it provides current information about frequent flyer plans in general, as well as specific data about promotions, awards, and combination deals to help you keep track of the profusion — and confusion — of current and upcoming availabilities. For a year's subscription, send $33 to Frequent Publications, 4715-C Town Center Dr., Colorado Springs, CO 80916 (phone: 800-333-5937).

There also is a monthly magazine called *Frequent Flyer,* but unlike the newsletter mentioned above, its focus is primarily on newsy articles of interest to business travelers and other frequent flyers. Published by Official Airline Guides (PO Box 58543, Boulder, CO 80322-8543; phone: 800-323-3537), *Frequent Flyer* is available for $24 for a 1-year subscription.

Low-Fare Airlines – Increasingly, the stimulus for special fares is the appearance of airlines associated with bargain rates. On these airlines, all seats on any given flight generally sell for the same price, which is somewhat below the lowest discount fare offered by the larger, more established airlines. It is important to note that tickets offered by the smaller airlines specializing in low-cost travel frequently are not subject to the same restrictions as the lowest-priced ticket offered by the more established carriers. They may not require advance purchase or minimum and maximum stays, may involve no cancellation penalties, and may be available one way or round trip. A disadvantage to some low-fare airlines, however, is that when something goes wrong, such as delayed baggage or a flight cancellation due to equipment breakdown, their smaller fleets and fewer flights mean that passengers may have to wait longer for a solution than they would on one of the equipment-rich major carriers.

One airline offering a consistently low fare to Europe is *Virgin Atlantic Airways* (phone: 800-862-8621 or 212-242-1330), which flies from Boston, Los Angeles, Miami, Newark, and New York to London's Gatwick and Heathrow Airports. The airline sells tickets in several categories, including business or "Upper Class", economy, APEX, and nonrefundable variations on standby. Fares from New York to London include Late Saver fares — which must be booked, or purchased, no more than 20 days prior to travel — and Late Late Saver fares — which must be booked, or bought, no more than 3 days prior to travel. Travelers to France will have to take a short second flight from London to Paris, but still may save money. To determine the potential savings, add the cost of the transatlantic fare and the cost of connecting flights to come up with the total ticket price. Remember, too, that since France is such a popular holiday destination with the British, ultra-low-priced package programs are frequently available from British-based tour operators and bucket shops.

In a class by itself is *Icelandair,* a scheduled airline long known as a good source of low-cost flights to Europe. From early April to late October, *Icelandair* flies from Baltimore/Washington, New York, and Orlando to Paris, as well as to Luxembourg (just across the border from the Lorraine region in northeastern France and less than an hour by train from Metz, about 2½ hours from Strasbourg, or an average of 4 hours from Paris). At other times of the year, only the flights to Luxembourg are offered, although the airline increases the options for its passengers by offering "thru-fares" on connecting flights from Luxembourg to various European cities, including Paris and Nice. (The price of the intra-European flights — aboard Luxembourg's *Luxair* — is included in the price *Icelandair* quotes for the transatlantic portion of the travel to these additional destinations).

Icelandair sells tickets in a variety of categories, from unrestricted economy fares to a sort of standby "3-days-before" fare (which functions just like the youth fares described above but has no age requirement). Travelers should be aware, however, that all *Icelandair* flights stop in Reykjavik for 45 minutes en route to and from Luxembourg — a minor delay for most, but one that further prolongs the trip for passengers who will wait again in Luxembourg to board connecting flights to their ultimate destination in France. For reservations and tickets, contact a travel agent or *Icelandair* (phone: 800-223-5500 or 212-967-8888).

Intra-European Fares – The cost of the round trip across the Atlantic is not the only expense to be considered. Flights between European cities, when booked in Europe, can be quite expensive. Note that discounts recently have been introduced on routes between some European cities.

Recent Common Market moves toward airline deregulation are expected to lead gradually to a greater variety of budget fares. In the meantime, however, the high cost of fares between most European cities can be avoided by careful use of stopover rights on the higher-priced transatlantic tickets — first class, business class, and full-fare economy. If your ticket doesn't allow stopovers, ask about APEX, and other excursion fares. If you are able to comply with applicable restrictions and can use them, you may save as much as 35% to 50% off full-fare economy. Note that these fares, which once could be bought only after arrival in Europe, are now sold in the US and can be bought before departure.

It is not easy to inform yourself about stopover possibilities by talking to most airline reservations clerks. More than likely, an inquiry concerning any projected trip will prompt the reply that a particular route is nonstop aboard the carrier in question, thereby precluding stopovers completely, or that the carrier does not fly to all the places you want to visit. It may take additional inquiries, perhaps with the aid of a travel agent, to determine the full range of options regarding stopover privileges.

Travelers might be able to squeeze in visits to Amsterdam, Brussels, Dublin, or London on a first class ticket to Paris, for instance; and Paris might only be the first of many free European stopovers possible on a one-way or round-trip ticket to a city in Eastern Europe or points beyond. The airline that flies you on the first leg of your trip across the Atlantic issues the ticket, though you may have to use several different airlines in order to complete your journey. There is no time limit on the validity of a first class ticket, so there's no rush.

Discounts currently are available on routes between some European countries and do exist for air travel within France. *Air Inter,* the country's major domestic airline, offers reduced rates to families, married couples, senior citizens, students, youths, and children of various ages — all of which are available to French citizens as well as foreign visitors buying their tickets after arrival in France. In addition, for foreigners only, the airline offers discounted "Visit France" fares, which must be bought in the US in conjunction with a transatlantic ticket to France (both the international flight, which can be aboard any carrier, and the intra-France flight must be issued on the same ticket). *Air Inter* also offers a discount pass, the France Pass, which permits unlimited travel for any 7-day period within a given month. The pass can be used on all of the airline's routes with the exception of certain peak-hour flights (the "red flights" used mostly by business travelers). Further information on ticketing for *Air Inter*'s current airfare packages is available from *Air France* (*Air Inter*'s general sales agent in the US) or from *Jet Vacations* (phone: 800-JET-0999 or 212-247-0999).

Another French airline, *Air Littoral,* which flies to over 20 cities in France, offers a similar arrangement. Their See France Pass entitles passengers to unlimited travel over a 7- or 10-day period. For information and reservations, contact *Air France,* their general sales agent in the US (phone: 800-237-2747).

Taxes and Other Fees – Travelers who have shopped for the best possible flight at the lowest possible price should be warned that a number of extras will be added to that price and collected by the airline or travel agent who issues the ticket. In addition to the $6 International Air Transportation Tax — a departure tax paid by all passengers flying from the US to a foreign destination — there is a $10 US Federal Inspection Fee levied on all air and cruise passengers who arrive in the US from outside North America (those arriving from Canada, Mexico, the Caribbean, and US territories are exempt). Payable at the time a round-trip or incoming ticket is purchased, it combines a $5 customs inspection fee and a $5 immigration inspection fee, both instituted in 1986 to finance additional inspectors to reduce delays at gateways.

Still another fee is charged by some airlines to cover more stringent security procedures, prompted by recent terrorist incidents. The 10% Federal US Transportation Tax applies to travel within the US or US territories. It does not apply to passengers flying between US cities or territories en route to a foreign destination, unless the trip includes a stopover of more than 12 hours at a US point. Someone flying from Los Angeles to New York and stopping in New York for more than 12 hours before boarding a flight to France, for instance, would pay the 10% tax on the domestic portion of the trip. Note that these taxes *usually* (but not always) are included in advertised fares and in the prices quoted by airline reservations clerks.

Reservations – For those who don't have the time or patience to investigate personally all possible air departures and connections for a proposed trip, a travel agent can be of inestimable help. A good agent should have all the information on which flights go where and when, and which categories of tickets are available on each. Most have computerized reservation links with the major carriers, so that a seat can be reserved and confirmed in minutes. An increasing number of agents also possess fare-comparison computer programs, so they often are very reliable sources of detailed competitive price data. (For more information, see *How to Use a Travel Agent,* in this section.)

When making plane reservations through a travel agent, ask the agent to give the airline your home phone number, as well as your daytime business phone number. All too often the agent uses the agency number as the official contact for changes in flight plans. Especially during the winter, weather conditions hundreds or even thousands of miles away can wreak havoc with flight schedules. Aircraft are constantly in use, and a plane delayed in the Orient or on the West Coast can miss its scheduled flight from the East Coast the next morning. The airlines are fairly reliable about getting this sort of information to passengers if they can reach them; diligence does little good at 10 PM if the airline has only the agency's or an office number.

Reconfirmation is strongly recommended for all international flights (though it is not usually required on US domestic flights) and, in the case of flights to France, it is essential to confirm your round-trip reservations — especially the return leg — as well as any point-to-point flights within Europe. Some (though increasingly fewer) reservations to and from international destinations are automatically canceled after a required reconfirmation period (typically 72 hours) has passed — even if you have a confirmed, fully paid ticket in hand. It always is wise to call ahead to make sure that the airline did not slip up in entering your original reservation, or in registering any changes you may have made since, and that it has your seat reservation and/or special meal request in the computer. If you look at the printed information on your ticket, you'll see the airline's reconfirmation policy stated explicitly. Don't be lulled into a false sense of security by the "OK" on your ticket next to the number and time of the flight. This only means that a reservation has been entered; a reconfirmation still may be necessary. If in doubt — call.

If you plan not to take a flight on which you hold a confirmed reservation, by all means inform the airline. Because the problem of "no-shows" is a constant expense for airlines, they are allowed to overbook flights, a practice that often contributes to the threat of denied boarding for a certain number of passengers (see "Getting Bumped," below).

Seating – For most types of tickets, airline seats usually are assigned on a first-come, first-served basis at check-in, although some airlines make it possible to reserve a seat at the time of ticket purchase. Always check in early for your flight, even with advance seat assignments. A good rule of thumb for international flights is to arrive at the airport *at least* 2 hours before the scheduled departure to give yourself plenty of time in case there are long lines.

Most airlines furnish seating charts, which make choosing a seat much easier, but there are a few basics to consider. You must decide whether you prefer a window, aisle, or middle seat. On flights where smoking is permitted, you also should indicate if you prefer the smoking or nonsmoking section.

The amount of legroom provided (as well as chest room, especially when the seat in front of you is in a reclining position) is determined by something called "pitch," a measure of the distance between the back of the seat in front of you and the front of the back of your seat. The amount of pitch is a matter of airline policy, not the type of plane you fly. First class and business class seats have the greatest pitch, a fact that figures prominently in airline advertising. In economy class or coach, the standard pitch ranges from 33 to as little as 31 inches — downright cramped.

The number of seats abreast, another factor determining comfort, depends on a combination of airline policy and airplane dimensions. First class and business class have the fewest seats per row. Economy generally has 9 seats per row on a DC-10 or an L-1011, making either one slightly more comfortable than a 747, on which there normally are 10 seats per row. Charter flights on DC-10s and L-1011s, however, often have 10 seats per row and can be noticeably more cramped than 747 charters, on which the seating normally remains at 10 per row.

Airline representatives claim that most aircraft are more stable toward the front and midsection, while seats farthest from the engines are quietest. Passengers who have long legs and are traveling on a wide-body aircraft might request a seat directly behind a door or emergency exit, since these seats often have greater than average pitch, or a seat in the first row of a given section, which offers extra legroom — although these seats are increasingly being reserved for passengers who are willing (and able) to perform certain tasks in the event of emergency evacuation. It often is impossible, however, to see the movie from these seats, which are directly behind the plane's exits. Be aware that the first row of the economy section (called a "bulkhead" seat) on a conventional aircraft (not a widebody) does *not* offer extra legroom, since the fixed partition will not permit passengers to slide their feet under it, and that watching a movie from this first-row seat can be difficult and uncomfortable. These bulkhead seats do, however, provide ample room to use a bassinet or safety seat and often are reserved for families traveling with children.

A window seat protects you from aisle traffic and clumsy serving carts and also provides a view, while an aisle seat enables you to get up and stretch your legs without disturbing your fellow travelers. Middle seats are the least desirable, and seats in the last row are the worst of all, since they seldom recline fully. If you wish to avoid children on your flight or if you find that you are sitting in an especially noisy section, you usually are free to move to any unoccupied seat — if there is one.

If you are overweight, you may face the prospect of a long flight with special trepidation. Center seats in the alignments of wide-body 747s, L-1011s, and DC-10s are about 1½ inches wider than those on either side, so larger travelers tend to be more comfortable there.

Despite all these rules of thumb, finding out which specific rows are near emergency exits or at the front of a wide-body cabin can be difficult because seating arrangements on two otherwise identical planes vary from airline to airline. There is, however, a quarterly publication called the *Airline Seating Guide* that publishes seating charts for most major US airlines and many foreign carriers as well. Your travel agent should have a copy, or you can buy the US edition for $39.95 per year and the international edition for $44.95. Order from Carlson Publishing Co., Box 888, Los Alamitos, CA 90720 (phone: 800-728-4877 or 310-493-4877).

Simply reserving an airline seat in advance, however, actually may guarantee very little. Most airlines require that passengers arrive at the departure gate at least 45 minutes (sometimes more) ahead of time to hold a seat reservation. *American,* for example, may cancel seat assignments and may not honor reservations of passengers who have not checked in some period of time — usually between 30 and 45 minutes, depending on the airport — before the scheduled departure time, and they *ask* travelers to check in at least 1 hour before all domestic flights and 2 hours before international flights. It pays to read the fine print on your ticket carefully and plan ahead.

A far better strategy is to visit an airline ticket office (or one of a select group of travel agents) to secure an actual boarding pass for your specific flight. Once this has been issued, airline computers show you as checked in, and you effectively own the seat you have selected (although some carriers may not honor boarding passes of passengers arriving at the gate less than 10 minutes before departure). This also is good — but not foolproof — insurance against getting bumped from an overbooked flight and is, therefore, an especially valuable tactic at peak travel times.

Smoking – One decision regarding choosing a seat has been taken out of the hands of many travelers who smoke. Effective February 25, 1990, the US government imposed a ban that prohibits smoking on all flights scheduled for 6 hours or less within the US and its territories. The new regulation applies to both domestic and international carriers serving these routes.

In the case of flights to France, these rules do not apply to nonstop flights from the US to Europe, or those with a *continuous* flight time of over 6 hours between stops in the US or its territories. Smoking is not permitted on segments of international flights where the time between US landings is under 6 hours — for instance, flights that include a stopover (even with no change of plane), or connecting flights. To further complicate the situation, several individual carriers are banning smoking altogether on certain routes (although as we went to press these bans had not yet extended to carriers flying between the US and France — for instance, *Air France* allows smoking on all transatlantic flights.)

On those flights that do permit smoking, the US Department of Transportation has determined that nonsmoking sections must be enlarged to accommodate all passengers who wish to sit in one. The airline does not, however, have to shift seating to accommodate nonsmokers who arrive late for a flight or travelers flying standby, and in general not all airlines can guarantee a seat in the nonsmoking section on international flights. Cigar and pipe smoking are prohibited on all flights, even in the smoking sections.

For a wallet-size guide, which notes in detail the rights of nonsmokers according to these regulations, send a self-addressed, stamped envelope to *ASH (Action on Smoking and Health),* Airline Card, 2013 H St. NW, Washington, DC 20006 (phone: 202-659-4310).

Meals – If you have specific dietary requirements, be sure to let the airline know well before departure time. The available meals include vegetarian, seafood, kosher, Muslim, Hindu, high-protein, low-calorie, low-cholesterol, low-fat, low-sodium, diabetic, bland, and children's menus (not all of these may be available on every carrier). There is no extra charge for this option. It usually is necessary to request special meals when you make your reservations — check-in time is too late. It's also wise to reconfirm that your request for a special meal has made its way into the airline's computer — the time to do this is 24 hours before departure. (Note that special meals generally are not available on intra-European flights on small local carriers. If this poses a problem, try to eat before you board, or bring a snack with you.)

Baggage – Travelers from the US face two different kinds of rules. When you fly on a US airline or on a major international carrier, US baggage regulations will be in effect. Though airline baggage allowances vary slightly, in general, all passengers are allowed to carry on board, without charge, one piece of luggage that will fit easily under a seat of the plane or in an overhead bin and whose combined dimensions (length, width, and depth) do not exceed 45 inches. A reasonable amount of reading material, camera equipment, and a handbag also are allowed. In addition, all passengers are allowed to check two bags in the cargo hold: one usually not to exceed 62 inches when length, width, and depth are combined, the other not to exceed 55 inches in combined dimensions. Generally no single bag may weigh more than 70 pounds. Weight restrictions may vary, however, on some European airlines, ranging from as much as 88 pounds permitted for first class passengers to as little as 50 pounds for economy class — so check with the specific carrier in advance. (For instance, on its international flights, *Air France* adheres to the standard 70-pound limit per bag, whereas on its intra-European flights, the carrier permits 88 pounds in first class, 66 pounds in business class, and 50 pounds in economy class.)

On many intra-European flights, including domestic service in France, baggage allowances may be subject to the old weight determination, under which each economy or discount passenger is allowed only a total of 50 pounds of luggage without additional charge. First class or business class passengers are allowed a total of 66 to 88 pounds. (If you are flying from the US to Europe and connecting to a domestic flight, you generally will be allowed the same amount of baggage as on the transatlantic flight. If you break your trip and then take a domestic flight, the local carrier's weight restrictions apply.)

Charges for additional, oversize, or overweight bags usually are made at a flat rate; the actual dollar amount varies from carrier to carrier. If you plan to travel with any special equipment or sporting gear, be sure to check with the airline beforehand. Most have specific procedures for handling such baggage, and you may have to pay for transport regardless of how much other baggage you have checked. Golf clubs and skis may be checked through as luggage (most airlines are accustomed to handling them), but tennis rackets should be carried onto the plane. Some airlines require that bicycles be partially dismantled and packaged (see *Camping and Caravanning, Hiking and Biking,* in this section).

Airline policies regarding baggage allowances for children vary and usually are based on the percentage of full adult fare paid. Although on many US carriers children who are ticket holders are entitled to the same baggage allowance as a full-fare passenger, some carriers allow only one bag per child, which sometimes must be smaller than an adult's bag (around 39 to 45 inches in combined dimensions). Often there is no luggage allowance for a child traveling on an adult's lap or in a bassinet. Particularly for international carriers, it's always wise to check ahead. (For more information, see *Hints for Traveling with Children,* in this section.)

To reduce the chances of your luggage going astray, remove all airline tags from previous trips, and label each bag inside and out — with your business address rather than your home address on the outside, to prevent thieves from knowing whose house might be unguarded. Lock everything and double-check the tag that the airline attaches to make sure that it is correctly coded for your destination: CDG for Charles de Gaulle, ORY for Orly in Paris, or NCE for Nice, for instance.

If your bags are not in the baggage claim area after your flight, or if they're damaged, report the problem to airline personnel immediately. Keep in mind that policies regarding the specific time limit within which you have to make your claim vary from carrier to carrier. Fill out a report form on your lost or damaged luggage and keep a copy of it and your original baggage claim check. If you must surrender the check to claim a damaged bag, get a receipt for it to prove that you did, indeed, check your baggage on the flight. If luggage is missing, be sure to give the airline your destination and/or a telephone number where you can be reached. Also take the name and number of the person in charge of recovering lost luggage.

Most airlines have emergency funds for passengers stranded away from home without their luggage, but if it turns out that your bags are truly lost and not simply delayed, do not then and there sign any paper indicating you'll accept an offered settlement. Since the airline is responsible for the value of your bags within certain statutory limits ($1,250 per passenger for lost baggage on a US domestic flight; $9.07 per pound or $20 per kilo for checked baggage, and up to $400 per passenger for unchecked baggage, on an international flight), you should take some time to assess the extent of your loss (see *Insurance,* in this section). It's a good idea to keep records indicating the value of the contents of your luggage. A wise alternative is to take a Polaroid picture of the most valuable of your packed items just after putting them in your suitcase.

Considering the increased incidence of damage to baggage, it's now more than ever a good idea to keep the sales slips that confirm how much you paid for your bags. These are invaluable in establishing the value of damaged luggage and eliminate any arguments. A better way to protect your precious gear from the luggage-eating conveyers is to try to carry it on board wherever possible.

Be aware that airport security increasingly is an issue all over Europe, and the French take it very seriously. Heavily armed police patrol the airports, and unattended luggage of any description may be confiscated and quickly destroyed. Passengers checking in at European airports may undergo at least two separate inspections of their tickets, passports, and luggage by courteous, but serious, airline personnel — who ask passengers if their baggage has been out of their possession between packing and the airport or if they have been given gifts or other items to transport — before checked items are accepted.

Airline Clubs – Some US and foreign carriers have clubs for travelers who pay for membership. These clubs are not solely for first class passengers, although a first class ticket *may* entitle a passenger to lounge privileges. Membership entitles the traveler to use of the private lounges at airports along their route, to refreshments served in these lounges, and to check-cashing privileges at most of their counters. Extras include special telephone numbers for individual reservations, embossed luggage tags, and a membership card for identification. Airlines serving France that offer membership in such clubs include the following:

American: The *Admiral's Club.* Single yearly membership $225; $125 yearly thereafter; spouse an additional $70 per year.

Continental: The *President's Club.* Single yearly membership $150 for the first year; $100 yearly thereafter; spouse an additional $50 per year.

Delta: The *Crown Club.* Single yearly membership $150, spouse an additional $50 per year; 3-year and lifetime memberships also available.

Northwest: The *World Club.* Single yearly membership $140 (plus a onetime $50 initiation fee); spouse an additional $50 per year; 3-year and lifetime memberships available.

TWA: The *Ambassador Club.* Single yearly membership $150 for the first year (spouse an additional $25); $125 yearly per couple thereafter; lifetime memberships also available.

United: The *Red Carpet Club.* Single yearly membership $125 (plus a onetime $100 initiation fee); spouse an additional $70; 3-year and lifetime memberships also available.

USAir: The *USAir Club.* Single yearly membership $125; spouse an additional $25 per year; 3-year and lifetime membership available.

Note that such companies do not have club facilities in all airports. Other airlines also offer a variety of special services in many airports.

Getting Bumped – A special air travel problem is the possibility that an airline will accept more reservations (and sell more tickets) than there are seats on a given flight. This is entirely legal and is done to make up for "no-shows," passengers who don't show up for a flight for which they have made reservations and bought tickets. If the airline has oversold the flight and everyone does show up, there simply aren't enough seats. When this happens, the airline is subject to stringent rules designed to protect travelers.

In such cases, the airline first seeks ticket holders willing to give up their seats voluntarily in return for a negotiable sum of money or some other inducement, such as an offer of upgraded seating on the next flight or a voucher for a free trip at some other time. If there are not enough volunteers, the airline may bump passengers against their wishes.

Anyone inconvenienced in this way, however, is entitled to an explanation of the criteria used to determine who does and does not get on the flight, as well as compensation if the resulting delay exceeds certain limits. If the airline can put the bumped passengers on an alternate flight that is *scheduled to arrive* at their original destination within 1 hour of their originally scheduled arrival time, no compensation is owed. If the delay is more than 1 hour but less than 2 hours on a domestic US flight, they must be paid denied-boarding compensation equivalent to the one-way fare to their destination (but not more than $200). If the delay is more than 2 hours beyond the original arrival time on a domestic flight or more than 4 hours on an international flight, the compensation must be doubled (not more than $400). The airline also may offer bumped travelers a voucher for a free flight instead of the denied-boarding compensation. The passenger may be given the choice of either the money or the voucher, the dollar value of which may be no less than the monetary compensation to which the passenger would be entitled. The voucher is not a substitute for the bumped passenger's original ticket; the airline continues to honor that as well.

Keep in mind that the above regulations and policies are only for flights leaving the US, and do *not* apply to charters or to inbound flights originating abroad, even on US carriers. Airlines carrying passengers between foreign destinations are free to determine what compensation they will pay to passengers who are bumped because of overbooking. They generally spell out their policies on airline tickets. Some foreign airline policies are similar to the US policy; however, don't assume all carriers will be as generous.

To protect yourself as best you can against getting bumped, arrive at the airport early, allowing plenty of time to check in and get to the gate. If the flight is oversold, ask immediately for the written statement explaining the airline's policy on denied-boarding compensation and its boarding priorities. If the airline refuses to give you this information, or if you feel it has not handled the situation properly, file a complaint with both the airline and the appropriate government agency (see "Consumer Protection," below).

Delays and Cancellations – The above compensation rules also do not apply if the flight is canceled or delayed, or if a smaller aircraft is substituted due to mechanical problems. Each airline has its own policy for assisting passengers whose flights are delayed or canceled or who must wait for another flight because their original one was overbooked. Most airline personnel will make new travel arrangements if necessary. If the delay is longer than 4 hours, the airline may pay for a phone call or telegram, a meal, and, in some cases, a hotel room and transportation to it.

■**Caution:** If you are bumped or miss a flight, be sure to ask the airline to notify other airlines on which you have reservations or connecting flights. When your name is taken off the passenger list of your initial flight, the computer usually cancels all of your reservations automatically, unless *you* take steps to preserve them.

CHARTER FLIGHTS: By booking a block of seats on a specially arranged flight, charter operators offer travelers air transportation for a substantial reduction over the full coach or economy fare. These operators may offer air-only charters (selling transportation alone) or charter packages (the flight plus a combination of land arrangements such as accommodations, meals, tours, or car rentals). Charters are especially attractive to people living in smaller cities or out-of-the-way places, because they frequently leave from nearby airports, saving travelers the inconvenience and expense of getting to a major gateway.

From the consumer's standpoint, charters differ from scheduled airlines in two main respects: You generally need to book and pay in advance, and you can't change the itinerary or the departure and return dates once you've booked the flight. In practice, however, these restrictions don't always apply. Today, although most charter flights still require advance reservations, some permit last-minute bookings (when there are unsold seats available), and some even offer seats on a standby basis.

Though charters almost always are round-trip, and it is unlikely that you would be sold a one-way seat on a round-trip flight, on rare occasions one-way tickets on charters are offered. Although it may be possible to book a one-way charter in the US, giving you more flexibility in scheduling your return, note that US regulations pertaining to charters may be more permissive than the charter laws of other countries. For example, if you want to book a one-way charter back to the US, you may find advance booking rules in force.

Some things to keep in mind about the charter game:

1. It cannot be repeated often enough that if you are forced to cancel your trip, you can lose much (and possibly all) of your money unless you have cancellation insurance, which is a *must* (see *Insurance,* in this section). Frequently, if the

cancellation occurs far enough in advance (often 6 weeks or more), you may forfeit only a $25 or $50 penalty. If you cancel only 2 or 3 weeks before the flight, there may be no refund at all unless you or the operator can provide a substitute passenger.

2. Charter flights may be canceled by the operator up to 10 days before departure for any reason, usually underbooking. Your money is returned in this event, but there may be too little time for you to make new arrangements.

3. Most charters have little of the flexibility of regularly scheduled flights regarding refunds and the changing of flight dates; if you book a return flight, you must be on it or lose your money.

4. Charter operators are permitted to assess a surcharge, if fuel or other costs warrant it, of up to 10% of the airfare up to 10 days before departure.

5. Because of the economics of charter flights, your plane almost always will be full, so you will be crowded, though not necessarily uncomfortable. (There is, however, a new movement among charter airlines to provide flight accommodations that are more comfort-oriented, so this situation may change in the near future.)

To avoid problems, *always* choose charter flights with care. When you consider a charter, ask your travel agent who runs it and carefully check the company. The Better Business Bureau in the company's home city can report on how many complaints, if any, have been lodged against it in the past. Protect yourself with trip cancellation and interruption insurance, which can help safeguard your investment if you, or a traveling companion, are unable to make the trip and must cancel too late to receive a full refund from the company providing your travel services. (This is advisable whether you're buying a charter flight alone or a tour package for which the airfare is provided by charter or scheduled flight.)

Bookings – If you do fly on a charter, read the contract's fine print carefully and pay particular attention to the following:

Instructions concerning the payment of the deposit and its balance and to whom the check is to be made payable. Ordinarily, checks are made out to an escrow account, which means the charter company can't spend your money until your flight has safely returned. This provides some protection for you. To ensure the safe handling of your money, make out your check to the escrow account, the number of which must appear by law on the brochure, though all too often it is on the back in fine print. Write the details of the charter, including the destination and dates, on the face of the check; on the back, print "For Deposit Only." Your travel agent may prefer that you make out your check to the agency, saying that it will then pay the tour operator the fee minus commission. It is perfectly legal to write the check as we suggest, however, and if your agent objects too vociferously (he or she should trust the tour operator to send the proper commission), consider taking your business elsewhere. If you don't make your check out to the escrow account, you lose the protection of that escrow should the trip be canceled. Furthermore, recent bankruptcies in the travel industry have served to point out that even the protection of escrow may not be enough to safeguard a traveler's investment. More and more, insurance is becoming a necessity. The charter company should be bonded (usually by an insurance company), and if you want to file a claim against it, the claim should be sent to the bonding agent. The contract will set a time limit within which a claim must be filed.

Specific stipulations and penalties for cancellations. Most charters allow you to cancel up to 45 days in advance without major penalty, but some cancellation dates are 50 to 60 days before departure.

Stipulations regarding cancellation and major changes made by the charterer. US rules say that charter flights may not be canceled within 10 days of departure except when circumstances — such as natural disasters or political upheavals — make it physically impossible to fly. Charterers may make "major changes," however, such as in the date or place of departure or return, but you are entitled to cancel and receive a full refund if you don't wish to accept these changes. A price increase of more than 10% at any time up to 10 days before departure is considered a major change; no price increase at all is allowed during the 10 days immediately before departure.

Among the charter operators flying between the US and France is *Air France*'s subsidiary, *Jet Vacations* (888 7th Ave., New York, NY 10106; phone: 800-JET-0999 or 212-247-0999), which offers spring and summer service between New York and Paris. Other charter operators serving France include *American Trans Air* (7337 W. Washington St., Indianapolis, IN 46251; phone: 800-225-9920 or 317-243-4150).

For the full range of possibilities at the time you plan to travel, you may want to subscribe to the travel newsletter *Jax Fax*, which regularly features a list of charter companies and packagers offering seats on charter flights and may be a source for charter flights to France. For a year's subscription send a check or money order for $12 to *Jax Fax* (397 Post Rd., Darien, CT 06820; phone: 203-655-8746).

DISCOUNTS ON SCHEDULED FLIGHTS: Promotional fares often are called discount fares because they cost less than what used to be the standard airline fare — full-fare economy. Nevertheless, they cost the traveler the same whether they are bought through a travel agent or directly from the airline. Tickets that cost less if bought from some outlet other than the airline do exist, however. While it is likely that the vast majority of travelers flying to France in the near future will be doing so on a promotional fare or charter rather than on a "discount" air ticket of this sort, it still is a good idea for cost-conscious consumers to be aware of the latest developments in the budget airfare scene. Note that the following discussion makes clear-cut distinctions among the types of discounts available based on how they reach the consumer; in actual practice, the distinctions are not nearly so precise.

Courier Travel – There was a time when traveling as a courier was a sort of underground way to save money and visit otherwise unaffordable destinations, but more and more, this once exotic idea of traveling as a courier is becoming a very "establishment" exercise. Being a courier means no more than accompanying freight of one sort or another, and typically that freight replaces what otherwise would be the traveler's checked baggage. Be prepared, therefore, to carry all your own personal travel gear in a carry-on bag. In addition, the so-called courier usually pays only a portion of the total airfare — the freight company pays the remainder — and the courier also may be assessed a small registration fee. Note that many courier flights can be booked in advance (sometimes as much as 3 months) and that flights often are round trip.

There are dozens of courier companies operating actively around the globe, and several publications provide information on courier opportunities:

> *A Simple Guide to Courier Travel,* by Jesse L. Riddle, is a particularly good reference guide to courier travel. Published by the Carriage Group (PO Box 2394, Lake Oswego, OR 97035; phone: 800-222-3599), it's available for $14.95, including postage and handling.
>
> *Travel Secrets* (PO Box 2325, New York, NY 10108; phone: 212-245-8703). Provides information useful to those considering traveling as a courier and often lists specific US and Canadian courier companies. Monthly; a year's subscription costs $33.
>
> *Travel Unlimited* (PO Box 1058, Allston, MA 02134-1058; no phone). Lists courier companies and agents worldwide. Monthly; for a year's subscription send $25.

World Courier News (PO Box 77471, San Francisco, CA 94107; no phone). Provides information on courier opportunities, as well as useful tips. Each issue highlights a different destination. Monthly; for a year's subscription send $20.

Among the companies that regularly send couriers to France are the following:

Courier Travel Service (530 Central Ave., Cedarhurst, NY 11516; phone: 800-922-2FLY or 516-374-2299).

Discount Travel International (152 W. 72nd Street, Suite 223, New York, NY 10023; phone: 212-362-3636).

Travelers to France also may want to consider contacting *Excaliber International Courier Inc.*, as this company often sends couriers to London (where you can catch a connecting flight to Paris). For information, contact *Excaliber*'s representative, *Way to Go Travel* (6679 Sunset Blvd., Hollywood, CA 90028; phone: 213-466-1126). In addition, *Now Voyager* (74 Varick St., Suite 307, New York, NY 10013; phone: 212-431-1616) is a referral agency that matches up would-be couriers with courier companies.

Net Fare Sources – The newest notion for reducing the costs of travel services comes from travel agents who offer individual travelers "net" fares. Defined simply, a net fare is the bare minimum amount at which an airline or tour operator will carry a prospective traveler. It doesn't include the amount that normally would be paid to the travel agent as a commission. Traditionally, such commissions amount to about 10% on domestic fares and from 10% to 20% on international fares — not counting significant additions to these commission levels that are paid retroactively when agents sell more than a specific volume of tickets or trips for a single supplier. At press time, at least one travel agency in the US was offering travelers the opportunity to purchase tickets and/or tours for a net price. Instead of earning its income from individual commissions, this agency assesses a fixed fee that may or may not provide a bargain for travelers; it requires a little arithmetic to determine whether to use the services of a net travel agent or those of one who accepts conventional commissions. One of the potential drawbacks of buying from agencies selling travel services at net fares is that some airlines refuse to do business with them, thus possibly limiting your flight options.

Travel Avenue is a fee-based agency that rebates its ordinary agency commission to the customer. For domestic flights, they will find the lowest retail fare, then rebate 7% to 10% (depending on the airline selected) of that price minus a $10 ticket-writing charge. The rebate percentage for international flights varies from 5% to 16% (again depending on the airline), and the ticket-writing fee is $25. The ticket-writing charge is imposed per ticket; if the ticket includes more than eight separate flights, an additional $10 or $25 fee is charged. Customers using free flight coupons pay the ticket-writing charge, plus an additional $5 coupon-processing fee.

Travel Avenue will rebate its commissions on all tickets, including heavily discounted fares and senior citizen passes. Available 7 days a week, reservations should be made far enough in advance to allow the tickets to be sent by first class mail, since extra charges accrue for special handling. It's possible to economize further by making your own airline reservation, then asking *Travel Avenue* only to write/issue your ticket. For travelers outside the Chicago area, business may be transacted by phone and purchases charged to a credit card. For information, contact *Travel Avenue* at 641 W. Lake St., Suite 201, Chicago, IL 60606-1012 (phone: 312-876-1116 in Illinois; 800-333-3335 elsewhere in the US).

Consolidators and Bucket Shops – Other vendors of travel services can afford to sell tickets to their customers at an even greater discount because the airline has sold the tickets to them at a substantial discount (usually accomplished by sharply increasing commissions to that vendor), a practice in which many airlines indulge, albeit discreetly, preferring that the general public not know they are undercutting their own "list" prices. Airlines anticipating a slow period on a particular route sometimes sell off a certain portion of their capacity at a very great discount to a wholesaler, or consolidator. The wholesaler sometimes is a charter operator who resells the seats to the public as though they were charter seats, which is why prospective travelers perusing the brochures of charter operators with large programs frequently see a number of flights designated as "scheduled service." As often as not, however, the consolidator, in turn, sells the seats to a travel agency specializing in discounting. Airlines also can sell seats directly to such an agency, which thus acts as its own consolidator. The airline offers the seats either at a net wholesale price, but without the volume-purchase requirement that would be difficult for a modest retail travel agency to fulfill, or at the standard price, but with a commission override large enough (as high as 50%) to allow both a profit and a price reduction to the public.

Travel agencies specializing in discounting sometimes are called "bucket shops," a term once fraught with connotations of unreliability in this country. But in today's highly competitive travel marketplace, more and more conventional travel agencies are selling consolidator-supplied tickets, and the old bucket shops' image is becoming respectable. Agencies that specialize in discounted tickets exist in most large cities, and usually can be found by studying the smaller ads in the travel sections of Sunday newspapers.

Before buying a discounted ticket, whether from a bucket shop or a conventional, full-service travel agency, keep the following considerations in mind: To be in a position to judge how much you'll be saving, first find out the "list" prices of tickets to your destination. Then do some comparison shopping among agencies. Also bear in mind that a ticket that may not differ much in price from one available directly from the airline may, however, allow the circumvention of such things as the advance-purchase requirement. If your plans are less than final, be sure to find out about any other restrictions, such as penalties for canceling a flight or changing a reservation. Most discount tickets are non-endorsable, meaning that they can be used only on the airline that issued them, and they usually are marked "nonrefundable" to prevent their being cashed in for a list price refund.

A great many bucket shops are small businesses operating on a thin margin, so it's a good idea to check the local Better Business Bureau for any complaints registered against the one with which you're dealing — before parting with any money. If you still do not feel reassured, consider buying discounted tickets only through a conventional travel agency, which can be expected to have found its own reliable source of consolidator tickets — some of the largest consolidators, in fact, sell only to travel agencies.

A few bucket shops require payment in cash or by certified check or money order, but if credit cards are accepted, use that option. Note, however, if buying from a charter operator selling both scheduled and charter flights, that the scheduled seats are not protected by the regulations — including the use of escrow accounts — governing the charter seats. Well-established charter operators, nevertheless, may extend the same protections to their scheduled flights, and when this is the case, consumers should be sure that the payment option selected directs their money into the escrow account.

Among the numerous consolidators offering discount fares to France (and Europe in general) are the following:

> *Bargain Air* (655 Deep Valley Dr., Suite 355, Rolling Hills, CA 90274; phone: 800-347-2345 or 213-377-2919).
>
> *Council Charter* (205 E. 42nd St., New York, NY 10017; phone: 800-223-7402 or 212-661-0311).
>
> *Maharaja Travel/Consumer Wholesale Travel* (34 W. 33rd St., Suite 1014, New York, NY 10001; phone: 212-213-2020 in New York State; 800-223-6862 elsewhere in the US).

TFI Tours International (34 W. 32nd St., 12th Floor, New York, NY 10001; phone: 212-736-1140 in New York State; 800-825-3834 elsewhere in the US).

Travac Tours and Charters (989 Sixth Ave., New York, NY 10018; phone: 212-563-3303).

25 West Tours (2490 Coral Way, Miami, FL 33145; phone: 800-925-0250 or 305-856-0810).

Unitravel (1177 N. Warson Rd., St. Louis, MO 63132; phone: 314-569-0900 in Missouri; 800-325-2222 elsewhere in the US).

■**Note:** Although rebating and discounting are becoming increasingly common, there is some legal ambiguity concerning them. Strictly speaking, it is legal to discount domestic tickets, but not international tickets. On the other hand, the law that prohibits discounting, the Federal Aviation Act of 1958, is consistently ignored these days, in part because consumers benefit from the practice and in part because many illegal arrangements are indistinguishable from legal ones. Since the line separating the two is so fine that even the authorities can't always tell the difference, it is unlikely that most consumers would be able to do so, and in fact it is not illegal to *buy* a discounted ticket. If the issue of legality bothers you, ask the agency whether any ticket you're about to buy would be permissible under the above-mentioned act.

OTHER DISCOUNT TRAVEL SOURCES: An excellent source of information on economical travel opportunities is the *Consumer Reports Travel Letter,* published monthly by Consumers Union. It keeps abreast of the scene on a wide variety of fronts, including package tours, rental cars, insurance, and more, but it is especially helpful for its comprehensive coverage of airfares, offering guidance on all the options from scheduled flights on major or low-fare airlines to charters and discount sources. For a year's subscription send $37 ($57 for 2 years) to *Consumer Reports Travel Letter* (PO Box 53629, Boulder, CO 80322-3629; phone: 800-234-1970). For information on other travel newsletters, see *Books, Newspapers, Magazines, and Newsletters,* in this section.

Last-Minute Travel Clubs – Still another way to take advantage of bargain airfares is open to those who have a flexible schedule. A number of organizations, usually set up as last-minute travel clubs and functioning on a membership basis, routinely keep in touch with travel suppliers to help them dispose of unsold inventory at discounts of between 15% and 60%. A great deal of the inventory consists of complete package tours and cruises, but some clubs offer air-only charter seats and, occasionally, seats on scheduled flights.

Members pay an annual fee and receive a toll-free hotline telephone number to call for information on imminent trips. In some cases, they also receive periodic mailings with information on bargain travel opportunities for which there is more advance notice. Despite the suggestive names of the clubs providing these services, last-minute travel does not necessarily mean that you cannot make plans until literally the last minute. Trips can be announced as little as a few days or as much as 2 months before departure, but the average is from 1 to 4 weeks' notice.

Among the organizations regularly offering such discounted travel opportunities to France are the following:

Discount Club of America (61-33 Woodhaven Blvd., Rego Park, NY 11374; phone: 800-321-9587 or 718-335-9612). Two-year membership fee: $39 per family.

Discount Travel International (Ives Building, 114 Forrest Ave., Suite 205, Narberth, PA 19072; phone: 800-334-9294 or 215-668-7184). Annual fee: $45 per household.

Encore/Short Notice (4501 Forbes Blvd., Lanham, MD 20706; phone: 301-459-8020; 800-638-0930 for customer service). Annual fee: $36 per family for their

Short Notice program only; $48 per family to join the Encore program, which provides additional travel services.

Last Minute Travel (1249 Boylston St., Boston MA 02215; phone: 800-LAST-MIN or 617-267-9800). No fee.

Moment's Notice (425 Madison Ave., New York, NY 10017; phone: 212-486-0500). Annual fee: $45 per family.

Spur-of-the-Moment Tours and Cruises (10780 Jefferson Blvd., Culver City, CA 90230; phone: 310-839-2418 in southern California; 800-343-1991 elsewhere in the US). No fee.

Traveler's Advantage (3033 S. Parker Rd., Suite 1000, Aurora, CO 80014; phone: 800-548-1116). Annual fee: $49 per family.

Vacations to Go (1502 Augusta Dr., Suite 415, Houston, TX 77057; phone: 800-338-4962). Annual fee: $19.95 per family.

Worldwide Discount Travel Club (1674 Meridian Ave., Miami Beach, FL 33139; phone: 305-534-2082). Annual fee: $40 per person; $50 per family.

■**Note:** For additional information on last-minute travel discounts, a new "900" number telephone service called *Last Minute Travel Connection* (phone: 900-446-8292) provides recorded advertisements (including contact information) for discount offerings on airfares, package tours, cruises, and other travel opportunities. Since companies update their advertisements as often as every hour, listings are current. This 24-hour service is available to callers using touch-tone phones; the cost is $1 per minute (the charge will show up on your phone bill). For more information, contact *La Onda, Ltd.,* 601 Skokie Blvd., Suite 224, Northbrook, IL 60062 (phone: 708-498-9216).

Generic Air Travel – Organizations that apply the same flexible-schedule idea to air travel only and arrange for flights at literally the last minute also exist. The service they provide sometimes is known as "generic" air travel, and it operates somewhat like an ordinary airline standby service except that the organizations running it do not guarantee flights to a specific destination, but only to a general region, and offer seats on not one but several scheduled and charter airlines.

One pioneer of generic flights is *Airhitch* (2790 Broadway, Suite 100, New York, NY 10025; phone: 212-864-2000), which arranges flights to France from various US gateways. Prospective travelers stipulate a range of at least five consecutive departure dates and their desired destination, along with alternate choices, and pay the fare in advance. They are then sent a voucher good for travel *on a space-available basis* on flights to their destination *region* (i.e., not necessarily the specific destination requested) during this time period. The week before this range of departure dates begins, travelers must contact *Airhitch* for specific information about flights that will probably be available and instructions on how to proceed for check-in. (Return flights are arranged in the same manner as the outbound flights — a specified period of travel is decided upon, and a few days before this date range begins, prospective passengers contact *Airhitch* for details about flights that may be available.) If the client does not accept any of the suggested flights or cancels his or her travel plans after selecting a flight, the amount paid can be applied toward a future fare or the flight arrangements can be transferred to another individual (although, in both cases, an additional fee may be charged). No refunds are offered unless the prospective passenger does not ultimately get on any flight in the specified date range; in such a case, the full fare is refunded. (Note that *Airhitch*'s slightly more expensive "Target" program, which provides confirmed reservations on specific dates to specific destinations, offers passengers greater — but not guaranteed — certainty regarding flight arrangements.)

Bartered Travel Sources – Suppose a hotel buys advertising space in a newspaper. As payment, the hotel gives the publishing company the use of a number of hotel rooms in lieu of cash. This is barter, a common means of exchange among hotels, airlines, car rental companies, cruise lines, tour operators, restaurants, and other travel service companies. When a bartering company finds itself with empty airline seats (or excess hotel rooms, or cruise ship cabin space, and so on) and offers them to the public, considerable savings can be enjoyed.

Bartered travel clubs often offer discounts of up to 50% to members who pay an annual fee (approximately $50 at press time) which entitles them to select the flights, cruises, hotel rooms, or other travel services that the club obtained by barter. Members usually present a voucher, club credit card, or scrip (a dollar-denomination voucher negotiable only for the bartered product) to the hotel, which in turn subtracts the dollar amount from the bartering company's account.

Selling bartered travel is a perfectly legitimate means of retailing. One advantage to club members is that they don't have to wait until the last minute to obtain flight or room reservations.

Among the companies specializing in bartered travel, several that frequently offer members travel services to and in France include the following:

Travel Guild (18210 Redmond Way, Redmond, WA 98052; phone: 206-861-1900). Annual fee: $48 per family.

Travel World Leisure Club (225 W. 34th St., Suite 2203, New York, NY 10122; phone: 800-444-TWLC or 212-239-4855). Annual fee: $50 per family.

Another company, *IGT (In Good Taste) Services* (1111 Lincoln Rd., 4th Floor, Miami Beach, FL 33139; phone: 800-444-8872 or 305-534-7900) offers discounts on a variety of travel services and occasionally sells bartered travel arrangements as well. At press time, however, they were not offering bartered travel arrangements to France — call when planning your trip. Their annual membership fee is $48 per family.

CONSUMER PROTECTION: Consumers who feel that they have not been dealt with fairly by an airline should make their complaints known. Begin with the customer service representative at the airport where the problem occurs. If he or she cannot resolve your complaint to your satisfaction, write to the airline's consumer office. In a businesslike, typed letter, explain what reservations you held, what happened, the names of the employees involved, and what you expect the airline to do to remedy the situation. Send copies (never the originals) of the tickets, receipts, and other documents that back your claims. Ideally, all correspondence should be sent via certified mail, return receipt requested. This provides proof that your complaint was received.

Passengers with consumer complaints — lost baggage, compensation for getting bumped, violations of smoking and nonsmoking rules, deceptive practices by an airline, charter regulations — who are not satisfied with the airline's response should contact the US Department of Transportation (DOT), Consumer Affairs Division (400 Seventh St. SW, Room 10405, Washington, DC 20590; phone: 202-366-2220). DOT personnel stress, however, that consumers initially should direct their complaints to the airline that provoked them.

Travelers with an unresolved complaint involving a foreign carrier also can contact the US Department of Transportation. DOT personnel will do what they can to help resolve all such complaints, although their influence may be limited.

A more effective direction for a complaint against a French travel service supplier may be the *Ministère de l'Economie et des Finances, Direction Départementale de la Concurrence, de la Consommation et la Répression des Fraudes* (8 Rue Froissart, Paris 75153; phone: 1-40-27-16-00). Consumers with complaints can write to this agency, in French, outlining the specifics in as much detail as possible. (Keep in mind, if a translator is required, that this correspondence could get expensive.) They will try to resolve the complaint or, if it is out of their jurisdiction, will refer the matter to the proper authorities, and will notify you in writing (in French) of the result of their inquires and/or any action taken.

Remember, too, that the federal Fair Credit Billing Act permits purchasers to refuse to pay for credit card charges for services which have not been delivered, so the onus of dealing with the receiver for a bankrupt airline falls on the credit card company. Do not rely on another airline to honor the ticket you're holding, since the days when virtually all major carriers subscribed to a default protection program that bound them to do so are long gone. Some airlines may voluntarily step forward to accommodate the stranded passengers of a fellow carrier, but this is now an entirely altruistic act.

The deregulation of US airlines has meant that the traveler must find out for himself or herself what he or she is entitled to receive. The US Department of Transportation's informative consumer booklet *Fly Rights* is a good place to start. To receive a copy, send $1 to the Superintendent of Documents (US Government Printing Office, Washington, DC 20402-9325; phone: 202-783-3238). Specify its stock number, 050-000-00513-5, and allow 3 to 4 weeks for delivery.

■ **Note:** Those who tend to experience discomfort due to the change in air pressure while flying may be interested in the free pamphlet *Ears, Altitude and Airplane Travel;* for a copy send a self-addressed, stamped, business-size envelope to the *American Academy of Otolaryngology* (One Prince St., Alexandria, VA 22314; phone: 703-836-4444). And for when you land, *Overcoming Jet Lag* offers some helpful tips on minimizing post-flight stress; it is available from Berkeley Publishing Group (PO Box 506, Mail Order Dept., East Rutherford, NJ 07073; phone: 800-631-8571) for $6.95, plus shipping and handling.

Traveling by Ship

 There was a time when traveling by ship was extraordinarily expensive, time-consuming, utterly elegant, and was utilized almost exclusively for getting from one point to another. Alas, the days when steamships reigned as the primary means of transatlantic transportation are gone, days when England, France, Germany, Italy, the Netherlands, Norway, and Sweden — and the US — had fleets of passenger liners that offered week-plus trips across the North Atlantic. Only one ship (*Cunard*'s *Queen Elizabeth 2*) continues to offer this kind of service between the US and Europe with any degree of regularity; others make "positioning" cruises a few times a year at most. At the same time, the possibility of booking passage to Europe on a cargo ship is becoming less practical. Fewer and fewer travelers, therefore, first set foot on French soil with sea legs developed during an ocean voyage.

Although fewer travelers to Europe are choosing sea travel as a means of transport to a specific destination, more and more people are cruising *around* Europe. No longer primarily pure transportation, cruising currently is riding a wave of popularity as a leisure activity in its own right, and the host of new ships (and dozens of rebuilt old ones) testifies dramatically to the attraction of vacationing on the high seas. And due to the growing popularity of travel along coastal and inland waterways, more and more travelers — particularly repeat travelers — are climbing aboard some kind of waterborne conveyance once they've arrived in Europe, and are seeing France from its western coastal waters, from the banks of a river, or the towpath of a canal.

Many modern-day cruise ships seem much more like motels-at-sea than the classic liners of a couple of generations ago, but they are consistently comfortable and passengers often are pampered. Cruise prices can be quite reasonable, and since the single cruise price covers all the major items in a typical vacation — transportation, accommodations, all meals, entertainment, and a full range of social activities, sports, and recreation — a traveler need not fear any unexpected assaults on the family travel budget.

When selecting a cruise, your basic criteria should be where you want to go, the time you have available, how much you want to spend, and the kind of environment that best suits your style and taste (in which case price is an important determinant). Rely on the suggestions of a travel agent — preferably one specializing in cruises (see "A final note on picking a cruise," below) — but be honest with the agent (and with yourself) in describing the type of atmosphere you're seeking. Ask for suggestions from friends who have been on cruises; if you trust their judgment, they should be able to suggest a ship on which you'll feel comfortable.

There are a number of moments in the cruise-planning process when discounts are available from the major cruise lines, so it may be possible to enjoy some diminution of the list price almost anytime you book passage on a cruise ship. For those willing to commit early — say 4 to 6 months before sailing — most of the major cruise lines routinely offer a 10% reduction off posted prices, in addition to the widest selection of cabins. For those who decide to sail rather late in the game — say, 4 to 6 weeks before departure — savings often are even greater — an average of 20% — as steamship lines try to fill up their ships. The only negative aspect is that the choice of cabins tends to be limited, although it is possible that a fare upgrade will be offered to make this limited selection more palatable. In addition, there's the option of buying from a discount travel club or a travel agency that specializes in last-minute bargains; these discounters and other discount travel sources are discussed at the end of *Traveling by Plane,* above.

Most of the time, the inclusion of air transportation in the cruise package costs significantly less than if you were to buy the cruise separately and arrange your own air transportation to the port. If you do decide on one of these economical air/sea packages, be forewarned that it is not unusual for the pre-arranged flight arrangements to be less than convenient. The problems often arrive with the receipt of your cruise ticket, which also includes the airline ticket for the flight to get you to and from the ship dock. This is normally the first time you see the flights on which you have been booked and can appraise the convenience of the departure and arrival times. The cruise ship lines generally are not very forthcoming about altering flight schedules, and your own travel agent also may have difficulty in rearranging flight times or carriers. That means that the only remaining alternative is to ask the line to forget about making your flight arrangements and to pay for them separately by yourself. This may be more costly, but it's more likely to give you an arrival and departure schedule that will best conform to the sailing and docking times of the ship on which you will be cruising.

Cruise lines promote sailings to and around Europe as "get away from it all" vacations. But prospective cruise ship passengers will find that the variety of cruises is tremendous, and the quality, while generally high, varies depending on shipboard services, the tone of shipboard life, the cost of the cruise, and operative itineraries. Although there are less expensive ways to see Europe, the romance and enjoyment of a sea voyage remain irresistible for many, so a few points should be considered by such sojourners before they sign on for a seagoing vacation (after all, it's hard to get off in mid-ocean). Herewith, a rundown on what to expect from a cruise, a few suggestions on what to look for and arrange when purchasing passage on one, and some representative sailings to and around France.

CABINS: The most important factor in determining the price of a cruise is the cabin. Cabin prices are set according to size and location. The size can vary considerably on older ships, less so on newer or more recently modernized ones, and may be entirely uniform on the very newest vessels.

Shipboard accommodations utilize the same pricing pattern as hotels. Suites, which consist of a sitting room–bedroom combination and occasionally a small private deck that could be compared to a patio, cost the most. Prices for other cabins (interchangeably called staterooms) usually are more expensive on the upper passenger decks, less expensive on lower decks; if a cabin has a bathtub instead of a shower, the price probably will be higher. The outside cabins with portholes cost more than inside cabins without views and generally are preferred — although many experienced cruise passengers eschew the more expensive accommodations for they know they will spend very few waking hours in their cabins. As in all forms of travel, accommodations are more expensive for single travelers. If you are traveling on your own but want to share a double cabin to reduce the cost, some ship lines will attempt to find someone of the same sex willing to share quarters (also see *Hints for Single Travelers,* in this section).

FACILITIES AND ACTIVITIES: You may not use your cabin very much — organized shipboard activities are geared to keep you busy. A standard schedule might consist of swimming, sunbathing, and numerous other outdoor recreations. Evenings are devoted to leisurely dining, lounge shows or movies, bingo and other organized games, gambling, dancing, and a midnight buffet. Your cruise fare normally includes all of these activities — except the cost of drinks.

Most cruise ships have at least one major social lounge, a main dining room, several bars, an entertainment room that may double as a discotheque for late dancing, an exercise room, indoor games facilities, at least one pool, and shopping facilities, which can range from a single boutique to an arcade. Still others have gambling casinos and/or slot machines, card rooms, libraries, children's recreation centers, indoor pools (as well as one or more on open decks), separate movie theaters, and private meeting rooms. Open deck space should be ample, because this is where most passengers spend their days at sea.

Usually there is a social director and staff to organize and coordinate activities. Evening entertainment is provided by professionals. Movies are mostly first-run and drinks are moderate in price (or should be) because a ship is exempt from local taxes when at sea.

■ **Note:** To be prepared for possible illnesses at sea, travelers should get a prescription from their doctor for medicine to counteract motion sickness. All ships with more than 12 passengers have a doctor on board, plus facilities for handling sickness or medical emergencies.

Shore Excursions – These side trips almost always are optional and available at extra cost. Before you leave, do a little basic research about the French ports you'll be visiting and decide what sights will interest you. If several of the most compelling of these are some distance from the pier where your ship docks, the chances are that paying for a shore excursion will be worth the money.

Shore excursions usually can be booked through your travel agent at the same time you make your cruise booking, but this is worthwhile only if you can get complete details on the nature of each excursion being offered. If you can't get these details, better opt to purchase your shore arrangements after you're on board. Your enthusiasm for an excursion may be higher once you are on board because you will have met other passengers with whom to share the excitement of "shore leave." And depending on your time in port, you may decide to eschew the guided tour and venture out on your own.

Meals – All meals on board almost always are included in the basic price of a cruise, and the food generally is abundant and quite palatable. Evening meals are taken in the main dining room, where tables are assigned according to the passengers' preferences. Tables usually accommodate from 2 to 10; specify your preference when you book your cruise. If there are two sittings, you also can specify which one you want at the time you book or, at the latest, when you first board the ship. Later sittings usually are more leisurely. Breakfast frequently is available in your cabin, as well as in the main dining room. For lunch, many passengers prefer the buffet offered on deck, usually at or near the pool, but again, the main dining room is available.

DRESS: Most people pack too much for a cruise on the assumption that their daily attire should be chic and every night is a big event. Comfort is a more realistic criterion. Daytime wear on most ships is decidedly casual. Evening wear for most cruises is dressy-casual. Formal attire probably is not necessary for 1-week cruises, optional for longer ones. (For information on choosing and packing a basic wardrobe, see *How to Pack,* in this section.)

TIPS: Tips are a strictly personal expense, and you *are* expected to tip — in particular, your cabin and dining room stewards. The general rule of thumb (or palm) is to expect to pay from 10% to 20% of your total cruise budget for gratuities — the actual amount within this range is based on the length of the cruise and the extent of personalized services provided. Allow $2 to $5 a day for each cabin and dining room steward (more if you wish) and additional sums for very good service. (*Note:* Tips should be paid by and for each individual in a cabin, whether there are one, two, or more.) Others who may merit tips are the deck steward who sets up your chair at the pool or elsewhere, the wine steward in the dining room, porters who handle your luggage (tip them individually at the time they assist you), and any others who provide personal service. On some ships you can charge your bar tab to your cabin; throw in the tip when you pay it at the end of the cruise. Smart travelers tip twice during the trip: about midway through the cruise and at the end; even wiser travelers tip a bit at the start of the trip to ensure better service throughout.

Although some cruise lines do have a no-tipping policy and you are not penalized by the crew for not tipping, naturally, you aren't penalized for tipping, either. If you can restrain yourself, it is better not to tip on those few ships that discourage it. However, never make the mistake of not tipping on the majority of ships, where it is a common, expected practice. (For further information on calculating gratuities, see *Tipping,* in this section.)

SHIP SANITATION: The US Public Health Service (PHS) currently inspects all passenger vessels calling at US ports, so very precise information is available on which ships meet its requirements and which do not. The further requirement that ships immediately report any illness that occurs on board adds to the available data.

The problem for a prospective cruise passenger is to determine whether the ship on which he or she plans to sail has met the official sanitary standard. US regulations require the PHS to publish actual grades for the ships inspected (rather than the old pass or fail designation), so it's now easy to determine any cruise ship's status. Nearly 4,000 travel agents, public health organizations, and doctors receive a copy of each monthly ship sanitation summary, but be aware that not all travel agents fully understand what this ship inspection program is all about. The best advice is to deal with a travel agent who specializes in cruise bookings, for he or she is most likely to have the latest information on the sanitary conditions of all cruise ships (see "A final note on picking a cruise," below). To receive a copy of the most recent summary or a particular inspection report, write to Chief, Vessel Sanitation Program, Center for Environmental Health and Injury Control (1015 N. America Way, Room 107, Miami, FL 33132; phone: 305-536-4307). Note that the center requests that all inquiries be made in writing.

TRANSATLANTIC CROSSINGS: There are a number of cruise lines that sail between the US and Europe. Some include French ports as part of their European itineraries, while on others passengers may disembark at other ports on the Continent and sail, fly, or drive to France.

For seagoing enthusiasts, *Cunard*'s *Queen Elizabeth 2* is one of the largest and most comfortable vessels afloat and each year the *QE2* schedules approximately a dozen round-trip transatlantic crossings between April and, usually, December. The ship normally sets its course from New York to Southampton, England (a 5-day trip), and then sails directly back to the US, although on a few of the crossings it proceeds from Southampton to Cherbourg, France, or to other European ports before turning back across the Atlantic. Passengers whose ultimate destination is France wait several hours as Southampton-bound passengers disembark and US-bound passengers board, then continue on to Cherbourg; those returning to the US from France embark in Cherbourg and sail directly home. (Similarly, on some crossings, the ship calls at various East Coast US ports in addition to New York, thus giving passengers a choice of where to embark or disembark.)

If Cherbourg (or another French port) is not included in the applicable itinerary, travelers can take an intra-European flight from Southampton to France, and then take a transatlantic flight home. Another alternative is to take the *Sealink* ferry from Southampton to Le Havre (see "Ferries," below).

For those sailing to Europe on the *QE2* and flying home, another option for travel in France is based on the validity period of the return ticket. Following the transatlantic crossing, passengers have a specified time — up to 35 days for first class passengers and 15 days for the less expensive fares — during which they can tour France. The transatlantic flight included in these packages no longer must arrive at one of the 17 US gateways served by *British Airways; Cunard* now allows passengers to transfer free to connecting flights to another 60 gateways served by other carriers. Those who want to splurge can apply the air allowance included in such air/sea packages toward a ticket aboard *British Airways'* supersonic *Concorde,* although the difference between the basic allowance and the *Concorde* fare is substantial. The only maximum stay restriction for passengers who upgrade to a return flight on the *Concorde* is that they must return on or before the end of the calendar year of their sailing.

Cunard also offers various European tour packages applicable to the basic air/sea offer. Among the packages offered are a combination Paris/London package, including 3 days and 2 nights in each city; a 15-day Alpine Splendor package featuring a stop in Paris and other European cities; and a Best of Europe package, including a trip on the famed *Venice Simplon–Orient Express* train. (For information on this famous, luxury train, see *Package Tours,* in this section.) For further information, check with your travel agent, call *British Airways* (phone: 800-AIRWAYS), or contact *Cunard,* 555 Fifth Ave., New York, NY 10017 (phone: 800-5-CUNARD or 800-221-4770).

Positioning Cruises – Another interesting possibility for those who have the time is what the industry calls a positioning cruise. This is the sailing of a US- or Caribbean-based vessel from its winter berth to the city in Europe from which it will be offering summer cruise programs. Eastbound positioning cruises take place in the spring; westbound cruises return in the fall. Since ships do not make the return trip until they need to position themselves for the next cruise season, most lines offering positioning cruises have some air/sea arrangement that allows passengers to fly home economically — though the cruises themselves are not an inexpensive way to travel.

Typically, the ships set sail from Florida or from San Juan, Puerto Rico, and cross the Atlantic to any one of a number of European ports where the trip may be broken — including French ports such as Cherbourg and Le Havre — before proceeding to cruise European waters (for example, the Mediterranean, the Baltic Sea, the Black Sea, the Norwegian fjords). Passengers can elect to stay aboard for the basic transatlantic segment alone or for both the crossing and the subsequent European cruise. Ports of call on such crossings and subsequent itineraries may vary substantially from year to year. For the most current information on operative itineraries, ask your travel agent or contact the cruise line directly.

Among the lines that offer positioning cruises to France are the following:

Royal Cruise Line (One Maritime Plaza, Suite 1400, San Francisco, CA 94111; phone: 800-227-4534 or 415-956-7200). Offers a 21-day transatlantic positioning cruise aboard the *Golden Odyssey* from Aruba to Venice — travelers to France can disembark at Nice. This year, *Royal Cruise Line*'s *Crown Odyssey* also will make a 21-day trip from Athens to San Juan, with a stop in Monte Carlo or Nice.

Seabourn Cruise Line (55 Francisco Street, San Francisco, CA 94133; phone: 800-351-9595). The *Seabourn Pride* makes 12-day positioning cruises from Ft. Lauderdale to Bordeaux — passengers can disembark, or opt to continue on any of several subsequent Mediterranean cruises.

Windstar Cruises (PO Box C34013, Seattle, WA 98124-1013; phone: 800-258-7245 or 206-281-3535) The *Wind Star,* a 440-foot cruise ship, makes 21-day sailings between Nice and Barbados in the Caribbean.

INTRA-EUROPEAN CRUISES: In summer, the coastal waters of Europe are busy with ships offering cruises of varying lengths, and the French city of Nice in particular is frequently included as a port of call on the Mediterranean cruises, as is Monte Carlo in Monaco. But while many cruises out of continental ports include at least one stop in France and many begin or end in a French port, few regularly devote a significant portion of the cruise to exploring French territory. Those interested in including a cruise to other European waters before, during, or after their trip to France will, however, find that a number of European cruises depart from French ports — primarily Le Havre and Nice.

Costa Cruises (World Trade Center, 80 SW 8th St., Miami, FL 33130; phone: 800-462-6782 or 305-358-7330). The *Eugenio Costa* makes a 10-day round-trip cruise from Genoa (Italy)that stops in St-Tropez (France).

Crystal Cruises (2121 Ave. of the Stars, Los Angeles, CA 90067; phone 800-446-6645). Offers several European trips (generally 12 or 13 days in length) aboard the *Crystal Harmony,* most of which include either Villefranche or Le Havre in France amongst its ports of call.

Cunard (555 Fifth Ave., New York, NY 10017; phone: 800-5-CUNARD or 800-221-4770). *Cunard's Sea Goddess II,* a sleek, luxurious, yacht-like vessel, makes 7- to 11-day Mediterranean cruises leaving from Monte Carlo which call at Collioure and St-Tropez, as well as other European ports. Its shallow draft allows it to visit small, remote village ports, with access to little-known beaches, as well as even more exotic destinations. *Cunard's* 5-day Mediterranean Explorer cruises aboard the *Princess* visit France, Italy, and Spain.

Ocean Cruise Lines (1510 SE 17th St., Ft. Lauderdale, FL 33316; phone: 800-556-8850 or 800-999-0555). Offers several 7-day Mediterranean sailings from Nice, visiting ports in Greece and Italy. Another popular 10-day itinerary between Nice and Paris calls at Bordeaux and several other European ports. In addition, pre- or post-cruise city packages are available in Nice and Paris.

Princess Cruises (10100 Santa Monica Blvd., Los Angeles, CA 90067; phone: 800-421-0522). The *Royal Princess* and *Star Princess* make several 12-day Mediterranean cruises, sailing between London and Barcelona or between Barcelona and Venice. Ports of call include Le Havre, Cannes, and Corsica, as well as destinations in Greece, Italy, Morocco, Portugal, and Spain.

Royal Caribbean Cruise Line (1050 Caribbean Way, Miami, FL 33132; phone: 800-432-6559 in Florida; 800-327-6700 elsewhere in the US and Canada). Offers several 12-day sailings aboard the *Song of Norway* along the Mediterranean coasts of France, Italy, Portugal, and Spain. French ports of call include Nice and Paris.

Royal Cruise Line (One Maritime Plaza, Suite 1400, San Francisco, CA 94111; phone: 800-227-5628 or 415-956-7200). The *Crown Odyssey* makes a number of 12-day cruises between Lisbon and Venice that stop in Villefranche, as well as a 12-day sailing between London and Venice that stops in Nice and Paris. The smaller *Golden Odyssey* departs on a 12-day cruise from Venice to Nice and a sailing from Lisbon to Athens that stops in Nice and Monte Carlo.

Royal Viking Line (95 Merrick Way, Coral Gables, FL 33134; phone: 800-422-8000). Several 7- to 14-day European cruises are offered aboard the *Royal Viking Queen.* Ports of call include Bordeaux, Cannes, Monte Carlo, Paris, and St-Tropez, with additional stops in Great Britain, Greece, Italy, Portugal, Spain, and Turkey. In addition, the *Royal Viking Sun* makes two 14-day sailings — from Copenhagen to Rome and from Barcelona to London — with stops in Bordeaux and Cannes.

Seabourn Cruise Line (55 Francisco Street, San Francisco, CA 94133; phone: 800-351-9595). The *Seabourn Spirit* makes several 7- and 14-day cruises between Lisbon and Nice, and between Nice and Venice, all of which include Collioure among the ports of call. A number of 7- and 14-day Mediterranean cruises also are offered aboard the *Seabourn Pride,* which travels from Nice to either Lisbon or Venice, with stops at Collioure and Monte Carlo.

SeaQuest Cruises (600 Corporate Dr., Suite 410, Ft. Lauderdale, FL 33334; phone: 800-223-5688 or 305-772-7552). Specializes in exploratory cruises along some of Europe's less-traveled routes. The MS *Caledonian Star* sails from Malta to Dartmouth (Great Britain), calling at Bordeaux and making several stops at remote Mediterranean islands along the way.

Sun Line Cruises (1 Rockefeller Center, Suite 315, New York, NY 10020; phone: 800-872-6400 or 212-397-6400). The *Stella Maris* makes a 7-day Mediterranean cruise that begins in Nice, sails around Italy, and ends in Venice.

Swan Hellenic Cruises (c/o *Esplanade Tours,* 581 Boylston St., Boston, MA 02116; phone: 800-426-5492 or 617-266-7465). Offers 15- and 17-day educational cruises aboard the MTS *Orpheus* that call at Nice or Nantes, as well as destinations in Great Britain, Greece, Ireland, Italy, Morocco, Portugal, and Spain.

FREIGHTERS: An alternative to conventional cruise ships is travel by freighter. These are cargo ships that also take a limited number of passengers (usually about 12) in reasonably comfortable accommodations. The idea of traveling by freighter has long appealed to romantic souls, but there are a number of drawbacks to consider before casting off. Once upon a time, a major advantage of freighter travel was its low cost, but this is no longer the case. Though freighters usually are less expensive than cruise ships, the difference is not as great as it once was. Accommodations and recreational facilities vary, but freighters were not designed to amuse passengers, so it is important to appreciate the idea of freighter travel itself. Schedules are erratic, and travelers must fit their timetable to that of the ship. Passengers have found themselves waiting as long as a month for a promised sailing, and because freighters follow their cargo commitments, it is possible that a scheduled port could be omitted at the last minute or a new one added.

Anyone contemplating taking a freighter from a US port across the Atlantic should be aware that at press time only a few freighter lines were carrying passengers on such crossings. Among these were the following:

Container Ships Reederi (c/o *Freighter World Cruises, Inc.,* 180 S. Lake Ave., Suite 335, Pasadena, CA 91101; phone: 818-449-3106). Two ships carrying 5 and 7 passengers, respectively, depart from Long Beach, California approximately once every two months and travel via the Panama Canal to Felixstowe (Great Britain), Le Havre (France), and Rotterdam (Holland). Trips take from 23 to 24 days.

Lykes Lines (300 Poydras, New Orleans, LA 70130; phone: 800-535-1861 or 504-523-6611). Offers 14- to 19-day sailings from New Orleans and Norfolk (Virginia) to Antwerp, Bremerhaven, Felixstowe, and Le Havre, carrying up to 6 passengers. Ships leave every two weeks year-round.

Mediterranean Shipping Co. (c/o *Sea the Difference,* 96 Morton St., New York,

NY 10014; phone 800-666-9333 or 212-691-3760). Freighters accommodating 12 passengers each depart twice a month from Baltimore, Boston, Port Elizabeth (New Jersey) and Newport News (Virginia) on 18- to 19-day voyages to Antwerp (Belgium), Bremen and Hamburg (Germany), Felixstowe (Great Britain), and Le Havre (France). Prices vary substantially, based on departure point and destination.

Polish Ocean Lines (1001 Durham Ave., South Plainfield, NJ 07080; phone: 908-412-6000). Once a week, freighters travel from Port Newark, New Jersey on 8- to 10-day voyages to Le Havre (France), Rotterdam (Holland), and Bremerhaven (Germany). Passengers also can board in Baltimore, Maryland, or Wilmington, North Carolina (for a supplement). Each ship accommodates 6 passengers in 3 double cabins.

The following specialists deal only (or largely) in freighter travel. They provide information, schedules, and, when you're ready to sail, booking services.

Freighter World Cruises, Inc. (180 S. Lake Ave., Suite 335, Pasadena, CA 91101; phone: 818-449-3106). A freighter travel agency that acts as general agent for several freighter lines. Publishes the twice-monthly *Freighter Space Advisory*, listing space available on sailings worldwide. A subscription costs $27 a year, $25 of which can be credited toward the cost of a cruise.

Pearl's Travel Tips (9903 Oaks La., Seminole, FL 34642; phone: 813-393-2919). Run by Ilse Hoffman, who finds sailings for her customers and sends them off with all kinds of valuable information and advice.

TravLtips Cruise and Freighter Travel Association (PO Box 218, Flushing, NY 11358; phone: 800-872-8584 or 718-939-2400 throughout the US; 800-548-7823 from Canada). A freighter travel agency and club ($15 per year or $25 for 2 years) whose members receive the bimonthly *TravLtips* magazine of cruise and freighter travel.

Those interested in freighter travel also may want to subscribe to *Freighter Travel News,* a publication of the *Freighter Travel Club of America.* A year's subscription to this monthly newsletter costs $18. To subscribe, write to the club at 3524 Harts Lake Rd., Roy, WA 98580.

Another monthly newsletter that may be of interest to those planning to cruise French waters is *Ocean and Cruise News,* which offers comprehensive coverage of the latest on the cruise ship scene. A year's subscription costs $24. Contact *Ocean and Cruise News,* PO Box 92, Stamford, CT 06904 (phone: 203-329-2787).

INLAND WATERWAYS: Cruising the canals and rivers of Europe is becoming more and more popular, probably in reaction to the speed of jet travel and the normal rush to do as much as possible in as little time as possible. A cabin cruiser or converted barge averages only about 5 miles an hour, covering in a week of slow floating the same distance a car would travel in a few hours of determined driving. Passengers see only a small section of countryside, but they see it in depth and with an intimacy simply impossible any other way.

France's 25,000 miles of rivers are connected and paralleled by 3,000 miles of canals, making the country ideal for inland cruising. One choice area is Burgundy, where the network of rivers and canals happens to be especially dense. Here the rivers of the north and west of France — the Seine, the Loire, and the Marne — are connected to the rivers of the south and east — the Saône, the Rhône, and eventually the Rhine and even the Garonne — and cruising possibilities are limited only by time. The Canal de Briare, begun in the early 17th century and one of the oldest in France; the 19th-century Canal Latéral à la Loire, running along the middle section of the Loire; the Canal du Nivernais, the Canal du Centre, and the Canal de Bourgogne, in the heart of Burgundy; as well as the Canal de la Marne à la Saône and the Saône itself all provide wonderfully tranquil vantage points from which to view rural France. Waterside scenes range from cattle grazing in fertile pastures, to forests, orchards, and vineyards, not to mention old abbeys and châteaux (though the most famous châteaux of the Loire are to the west of this nexus of waterways) and such historic and picturesque towns as Sancerre, Nevers, Auxerre, Langres, and Dijon, once the capital of the Dukes of Burgundy.

Another choice area for inland waterway cruising is in the south of France, especially along the Canal du Midi, the technical tour de force of a 17th-century tax collector and amateur engineer, Pierre-Paul Riquet. The canal, which opened in 1681 to create a link between the Atlantic and the Mediterranean, runs an especially scenic 160-mile course across the Languedoc region, beginning at Toulouse on the Garonne River and climbing to a high point near Castelnaudary, then descending toward its Mediterranean terminal at Sète. En route, it passes the medieval walled city of Carcassonne, the equally ancient city of Béziers, and such marvels of 17th-century engineering as the world's oldest canal tunnel and the lock staircase of Fontsérannes, which carries the canal down a level of 80 feet in a distance of 350 yards. Adjacent canals include the Canal Latéral à la Garonne, running alongside the Garonne west of Toulouse and extending into the wine region of Bordeaux, and the Canal du Rhône à Sète, skirting the wild, marshy expanse of the Camargue from Sète to the Rhône River.

A third, less frequented cruising area is in northern France — in Brittany, where the rivers Vilaine and Erdre, the Canal d'Ille et Rance, and the Canal de Nantes à Brest cut through the peaceful Breton countryside and connect such old towns as Rennes, the historic capital of the duchy of Brittany, Dinan, and Josselin, the site of a magnificent, turreted castle right at the water's edge. A fourth area, no less picturesque, is in the northeast corner of the country, on the Grand Canal d'Alsace, which weaves in and out of the Rhine and runs along the Alsatian wine route south of Strasbourg, and on adjoining canals such as the Canal de la Marne au Rhin, which leads from Strasbourg into Lorraine, and the Canal du Rhône au Rhin, which crosses the region of Franche-Comté on its way to Burgundy.

There are two ways to cruise the inland waterways: by renting your own self-drive boat or by booking aboard a hotel boat. If you choose to skipper your own diesel-powered cruiser, you will be shown how to handle the craft and told whom to call if you break down. But once you cast off, you and your party — the boats sleep from 2 to 10 people — will be on your own. You help lockkeepers (*éclusiers*) operate the gates and do your own cooking (in addition to village markets, the lockkeepers themselves often have fresh provisions) or eat at cafés and restaurants along the way. The cost of the rental can vary considerably, depending on the size of the boat, the season, and the area. (And note that fuel is not included.)

The alternative is to cruise on a hotel-boat — often a converted barge, or *péniche*. These can carry anywhere from 6 to 24 guests, occasionally even more, as well as the crew. You can charter the boat and have it all to yourself or join other guests aboard. Cruises usually last from 3 days to a week; accommodations can be simple or quite luxurious, and most meals usually are included. When reading the brochure, note the boat's facilities (most cabins have private washbasins, showers, and toilets, but bathrooms also can be separate and shared), as well as the itinerary and any special features, such as sightseeing excursions, that may be offered. Many of the cruises have a special emphasis such as French food and include wine tasting excursions to vineyards and wine cellars; others make a point of visiting historic spots. Again, prices can vary substantially, depending on the season, operative itinerary, and level of luxury.

The travel firms listed below, including the operators of hotel-boat cruises and representatives of self-drive boat suppliers, can provide information or arrange your whole holiday afloat in France.

   Abercrombie & Kent/Continental Waterways (1520 Kensington Rd., Suite 212, Oak Brook, IL 60521; phone: 708-954-2944 in Illinois; 800-323-7308 elsewhere in the US). Runs hotel-boat cruises in Bordeaux, Burgundy, the Loire Valley, and Provence.

B&D de Vogue Travel Services (1830 S. Mooney Blvd., Suite 203, Box 1998, Visalia, CA 93279; phone: 800-727-4748 or 209-733-7119). Books hotel cruises in Alsace-Lorraine, the Loire Valley, and along the Canal du Midi.

Bargain Boating, Morgantown Travel Service (PO Box 757, Morgantown, WV 26507-0757; phone: 800-637-0782 or 304-292-8471). Books self-skippered boats in Alsace and Lorraine, Brittany, Burgundy, the Cognac area of Poitou-Charentes, and the south of France.

Blakes Vacations (4918 Dempster St., Skokie, IL 60077; phone: 708-982-0561 in Illinois; 800-628-8118 elswhere in the US). Books self-skippered boats in Alsace, Brittany, Burgundy, Charente, and on the Lot River.

Carlisle Cruises (22411 NE 209th Ave., Battleground, WA 98604; phone: 800-426-9297). Offers luxury barge cruises along the Canal de Bourgogne and Canal du Nivernais, between Montbard and Châtel-Censor, in Burgundy.

Esplanade Tours (581 Boylston St., Boston, MA 02116; phone: 800-628-4893 or 617-266-7465). This company which has often booked hotel-boat cruises along the Canal du Midi and elsewhere in the south of France, was not offering such cruises at press time; however, call for current itineraries when planning your trip.

Etoile de Champagne (89 Broad St., Boston, 02110; phone: 800-666-1620 or 617-426-1776). Offers four luxury chartered hotel-boat cruises thoughout the inland waterways of France. Itineraries include a trip from Amsterdam (the Netherlands) to Paris, and trips between Morez and Auxerre, Paris and Tours, and Paris and Rouen.

French Country Waterways, Ltd. (PO Box 2195, Duxbury, MA 02331; phone: 800-222-1236 or 617-934-2454 throughout the continental US). Books hotel-boat cruises that traverse the canals in the Ile-de-France and Burgundy areas. Included in the 7-day, 6-night trips are all meals and table wines, all side tours and excursions, and even bicycles. Also available on all the trips are hot-air balloon rides.

French Cruise Lines (FCL) (701 Lee St., Des Plaines, IL 60016; phone: 800-222-8664). Offers inland cruises on the Rhône and Seine rivers aboard two 100-passenger ships, the *Arlène* and the *Normandy*. Ports of call include Paris, Rouen, and Villequier. Round-trip fares for the 6- and 7-night river cruises include all meals, but not wine — only the finest French vintages are served.

French Experience (370 Lexington Ave., Suite 812, New York, NY 10017; phone: 800-28-FRANCE or 212-986-3800). Books self-skippered boats in Alsace and Lorraine, the Aquitaine, Brittany, Burgundy, the Camargue, the Midi, Nivernais, and the Upper Loire.

Frontiers International (PO Box 959, Pearce Hill Rd., Wexford, PA 15090; 800-245-1950 or 412-935-1577). Offers luxury barge cruises on the Canal du Midi, the Nivernais Canal, and the Rhône and Saône rivers.

Hideaways International (15 Goldsmith St., PO Box 1270, Littleton, MA 01460; phone: 800-843-4433 or 508-486-8955). Books skippered barge trips on inland waterways throughout France, as well as Belgium and the Netherlands.

Hoseasons Holidays Ltd. (Sunway House, Lowestoft, Suffolk NR32 3LT England; phone: 44-502-500505). Offers self-skippered boats in Alsace, Burgundy, and other areas throughout France.

KD German Rhine Line (contact *Rhine Cruise Agency*, 170 Hamilton Ave., White Plains, NY; phone: 914-948-3600 or 800-346-6525 in the eastern US; or 323 Geary St., San Francisco, CA 94102; phone: 415-392-8817 or 800-858-8587 in the western US, including Alaska and Hawaii). Books numerous hotel-boat cruises throughout France, many in combination with trips to neighboring countries such as Germany, the Netherlands, and Switzerland.

Skipper Travel Services (210 California Ave., Palo Alto, CA 94306; phone: 415-321-5658). Books hotel boats and self-drive boats in Alsace, Brittany, Burgundy, the Loire, and the south of France. Also offers hotel-boat cruises in some of these regions, as well as in Charente.

■ **A final note on picking a cruise:** A "cruise-only" travel agency can best help you choose a cruise ship and itinerary. Cruise-only agents are best equipped to tell you about a particular ship's "personality," the kind of person with whom you'll likely be traveling on a particular ship, what dress is appropriate (it varies from ship to ship), and much more. Travel agencies that specialize in booking cruises usually are members of the *National Association of Cruise Only Agencies (NACOA).* For a listing of the agencies in your area (requests are limited to three states), send a self-addressed, stamped envelope to *NACOA,* PO Box 7209, Freeport, NY 11520, or call 516-378-8006.

FERRIES: Numerous ferries link France with its largest island, Corsica, and with Great Britain and Ireland and other countries. Nearly all of them carry both passengers and cars — you simply drive on and drive off in most cases — and most routes are in service year-round. Some operators offer reduced rates for round-trip excursions, mid-week travel, or off-season travel. Space for cars should be booked as early as possible, especially for July and August crossings, even though most lines schedule more frequent departures during the summer months. Note that long journeys, of 8 to 10 hours or more, tend to be scheduled overnight.

The shipping line *Société Nationale Maritime Corse-Méditerranée (SNCM)* operates passenger and car carrying ferries between Marseilles, Nice, and Toulon on the French mainland and the Corsican ports of Bastia, Ile-Rousse, and Calvi (northern Corsica) and Ajaccio and Propriano (southwestern Corsica). Sailings vary from almost daily to two or three times a week or less, depending on the route and the season, with some of the routes served in summer only. The crossing takes from 5 to 6 hours (Nice to Calvi or Ile-Rousse, the shortest routes) up to 10 or 12 hours (Marseilles to Bastia, the longest route), and there are day as well as night ferries, the latter with cabins or *couchettes* available. *SNCM* also operates international sailings between Marseilles and Tunis (Tunisia) every sixth or seventh day depending on the season, between Marseilles and Algiers roughly once a week, and between Toulon and Porto Torres, Sardinia, about once a week, also depending on the season. Reservations can be made only in France through *SNCM* offices in Paris, Marseilles, Nice, Toulon, and other French cities. Anyone planning to transport a car by ferry in high season should make the reservation well in advance — as early as February if possible.

Ferries between France and Great Britain include the fleet of *Sealink* ships connecting Calais with Dover; Boulogne with Folkestone; Dieppe with Newhaven; and Cherbourg with Southampton (no winter service). For information write or call the central office, *Sealink British Ferries Limited* (Southern House, Lord Warden Square, Dover, Kent, CT179DH England; phone: 44-304-203203). *P&O European Ferries* (Channel House, Channel View Rd., Dover, Kent, CT179TJ England; phone: 44-304-203-388) also operates ferry services to Great Britain, from Calais and Boulogne to Dover, and from Le Havre and Cherbourg to Portsmouth. Other service is available from Le Havre to Southampton, St-Malo to Portsmouth and the Channel Islands, and from Roscoff to Plymouth. Ferries to Ireland leave from Le Havre and Cherbourg en route to Rosslare Harbour and from Le Havre and Roscoff en route to Cork.

Hoverspeed Hovercraft (*Hoverspeed LTD,* Maybrook House, Queens Gardens, Dover, Kent CT179UQ; phone: 304-24-02-41) carry both cars and passengers on a cushion of air across the English Channel between Calais and Boulogne and Dover. Since *Hovercraft* travel a few feet above the water, they can be affected by waves and are grounded when the Channel is rough. When the weather is good, however, they make the trip in an average of 35 minutes (compared to the ferry's 1¼ to 1¾ hours).

Most ferry arrivals and departures are well served by connecting passenger trains or buses, and passengers can buy through train tickets between Paris and London that include the sea portion of the trip. The Paris to London route on through services by train/*Hovercraft*/train, for example, takes an average 5½ hours; from Paris to London on through services by train/ferry/train can take from 7 to 9 hours by day, depending on the route, or about 9½ to 10½ hours overnight. *Hoverspeed* (see above) also operates a fleet of even faster catamaran ferries (between Boulogne or Calais and Dover), which cut the channel crossing time down even further — by another 15 to 20 minutes. (At the time of this writing, the effect of the pending completion of the Eurotunnel between France and Great Britain on such connecting service remained to be seen.)

There also are ferry links between France and Morocco, Algeria, and Tunisia. Corsica also can be reached by ferry from the Italian mainland and from the island of Sardinia.

Traveling by Train

Perhaps the most economical, and often the most satisfying, way to see a lot of a foreign country in a relatively short time is by rail. It certainly is the quickest way to travel between two cities up to 300 miles apart (beyond that, a flight normally would be quicker, even counting the time it takes to get to and from the airport). But time isn't always the only consideration. Traveling by train is a way to keep moving and to keep seeing at the same time. The fares usually are reasonable, and with the special discounts available to visitors, it can be an almost irresistible bargain. You only need to get to a station on time; after that, put your watch in your pocket and relax. You may not get to your destination exactly at the appointed hour (although French trains are quite punctual for the most part), but you'll have a marvelous time looking out the window and enjoying the ride.

TRAINS: While North Americans have been raised to depend on their cars, Europeans have long been able to rely on public transportation. The government-owned and -operated French railway system is one of the world's most extensive. *Société Nationale des Chemins de Fer Français (SNCF),* which is known to the English-speaking world as the *French National Railways,* operates the rail system and handles all passenger services in France. In North America, bookings on *SNCF* trains (as well as on other French and European railways) can be made through *Rail Europe* (formerly known as *FrenchRail Inc.*). It also is one of the world's most modern systems — so modern, in fact, that anyone whose knowledge of French trains was acquired before September 27, 1981, cannot be said to be truly *au courant.* On that day, the opening of the first section of a new high-speed rail line between Paris and Lyons ushered in a new railway era in France, making possible the inauguration of passenger service aboard the world's fastest train, the *TGV (Train à Grande Vitesse).* Though *TGV*s are capable of speeds of up to 317 mph (or 511 kmh) — per the world record set by a *TGV* train on May 9, 1990 — their maximum speed in commercial operation is limited to 186 mph. Yet even at that relative snail's pace, the *TGV* in one fell swoop cut the travel time between France's two largest cities from 4 hours to 2 hours and 40 minutes, and when a second section of new track opened in 1983, the time dropped again to a mere 2 hours.

At present, travelers who want to experience *TGV* service can choose from numerous daily departures from Paris to Lyons or vice versa. But because the trains are capable of running on conventional track, as well as on their own special track, it is not necessary to be traveling strictly between Paris and Lyons in order to ride them. If you're traveling between Paris and Avignon, Besançon, Chambéry, Dijon, Grenoble, Montpellier, Marseilles, Nice, Nîmes, or Toulon, or the Swiss cities of Bern, Geneva, or Lausanne — as well as a number of other cities en route — you can travel via *TGV,* riding at top speed along one or both portions of the special track and then proceeding more slowly along the old track toward your final destination. It also is possible to board a *TGV* train at an intermediate stop and ride it a short way, say from Avignon to Marseilles, though in this case you will experience *TGV*'s rolling stock but not its top speed. The *TGV* line to the Atlantic Coast serves points south and west of Paris, including Bordeaux, Nantes, Quimper, Rennes, Tours, and the Spanish border, and provides added convenience for wide-ranging day trips to western cities. A recently completed line runs between Paris and the Tarentaise Valley, near where the *1992 Winter Olympics* were held. In addition, at press time, a *TGV* line north from Paris to Arras, Calais, Hazebrouck, and Lille was under construction and should be running by the summer of this year. This line will connect at Calais to the new trans-Channel tunnel, or "Chunnel," which also is scheduled to open later this year. And finally, a *TGV* line to the new *EuroDisneyland* is due to be completed in 1994. In short, traveling through the Gallic countryside is becoming easier than ever.

As a matter of policy — the French refer to it as the *démocratisation de la vitesse* — *TGV* trains carry both first and second class passengers, and a trip between any two cities by *TGV* costs no more than a trip between the same two cities by conventional train and track. In practice, however, a supplement is charged for traveling at rush hours and on peak days, and these departures account for a good portion of the *TGV* schedule. In addition, reservations are obligatory. On the Paris–Lyons line, each train carries 275 second class passengers and 111 first class passengers, with no standees allowed. The Atlantic line carries 369 in second class and 116 in first class, and the new line to the Tarentaise Valley carries 250 and 125, respectively.

Reservations can be made following the same procedures as for any other train or, provided you already have a ticket to your destination, by using the last-minute *TGV* Réservation Rapide machines in the station. These will reserve a seat (if one is available) on any *TGV* departing within 1½ hours of a request. You cannot specify a smoking or nonsmoking car or an aisle or a window seat by machine, and meals cannot be reserved this way either, but the machine can be instructed to restrict its search to only those trains not requiring payment of a supplement. Otherwise, the necessary surcharge must be dropped into the machine in coin.

Besides the *TGV,* other categories of trains the visitor is likely to encounter in France include the *Euro City (EC)* trains, *Intercité (IC)* trains, *rapides,* and expresses. The first of these, as their name implies, are largely international trains operated by several of Europe's national railway companies, including *SNCF.* The *EC* network, introduced in May 1987, has by now all but replaced the *Trans-Europe Express (TEE),* which provided the European Economic Community with efficient, luxurious train service between major cities since the 1950s.

While it is the *TGV* system that represents the state of the art in train technology, *EC*s are the prestige trains of Europe and maintain high standards. They use modern, air conditioned coaches, are punctual and clean, and travel at a minimum speed of 54 miles per hour (the average includes time for station stops). With the exception of some first class–only trains running between Paris and Brussels, the *EC*s generally offer both first and second class service and require payment of a supplement for all departures. The supplement includes the price of a reserved seat. *Intercité (IC)* trains are similar to *EC*s in that they provide a high standard of service, have both first and second class cars, and require payment of a supplement.

A *rapide* is a fast train making limited stops. More and more, this category is becoming synonymous with the type of equipment used on the routes: *Turbotrains* and *Corail* trains. Both are examples of the latest in French railway technology, both were developed to run at speeds up to 125 mph, and both provide such amenities as air conditioned, soundproofed coaches, and the announcement of stations over a public address system. No supplement is required and seat reservations are optional. Express trains, the next category, make many more intermediate stops along main lines than do *rapides,* though they can be the fastest trains on secondary or transverse routes where *rapides* are rare and where slower trains — in the direct or omnibus categories — abound. In fact, the French railway system resembles something of a giant spider web or a wheel, with most of the main lines radiating like spokes from Paris at the center. Service between provincial cities on the same spoke is fast and frequent, but in the case of towns on different spokes, it is sometimes faster and easier to get from one to the other by going the long way around — via Paris.

A word about the many train stations in Paris: There are six main ones, each the starting point for trains to a particular region:

> **Gare d'Austerlitz:** The departure point for trains to the southwest, including Bordeaux and Toulouse in France, and Spain.
>
> **Gare de l'Est:** The departure point for eastbound trains to Alsace in France, and Austria, Luxembourg, southern Germany, and Switzerland.
>
> **Gare de Lyon:** The departure point for trains to the southeast, including the Côte d'Azur, Grenoble, Lyons, and Marseilles in France, and Italy and Switzerland.
>
> **Gare Montparnasse:** The departure point for south- and westbound trains to Bordeaux, Brittany, Chartres, Le Mans, and Nantes.
>
> **Gare du Nord:** The departure point for northbound trains to Boulogne, Calais, and Lille in France, and Belgium, the Netherlands, and northern Germany.
>
> **Gare St-Lazare:** The departure point for westbound trains to Cherbourg, Dieppe, Le Havre, and the rest of Normandy.

These stations are anywhere from a half mile to 4 miles apart, but they are connected by an interstation shuttle bus or by the Paris métro (subway), which usually is faster. If you are taking a trip that requires a transfer from station to station with little time to spare, be sure to find out beforehand exactly how to make the connection and how long it will take. Note, also, that Paris is not the only city in France with more than one railroad station.

RESERVATIONS, DINING AND SLEEPING CARS, OTHER SERVICES: Both first and second class seats on most of the better trains can be reserved in advance, either before you leave home or after your arrival in France. Reservations reduce flexibility, but they are advisable during the summer on popular routes, particularly those leading to the Atlantic or Mediterranean coasts and onward into Spain or Italy. They also are advisable at any time of the year if it is imperative that you be on a particular train.

In France, seats can be reserved as much as 6 months in advance by mail, 2 months in advance in person, or 9 days in advance by phone, with the reservation period closing anywhere from the night before to 2 or 3 hours before the departure of the train (the obligatory *TGV* reservation can be made up to a few minutes before departure). In the US, the reservation period usually runs from 2 months to 15 days before departure. The reservation fee is a flat amount per seat ($8 including communications charges if made in the US).

Dining facilities on French trains vary. On *EC* trains, passengers still can take meals in the traditional way, in a separate dining car. On *TGV* trains, meals in first class are served airline-style, at the passenger's seat, but each train also carries a bar car, which sells sandwiches, cold plates, and other simple meals to both classes. *Corail* trains and *Turbotrains* tend to offer the same possibilities as the *TGV,* while other trains may have a self-service *Gril Express* cafeteria car or no more than an ambulatory vendor dispensing sandwiches and beverages from a cart. If you're sure you will want to eat en route, it's a good idea to inquire beforehand exactly what meal service is offered on the train you'll be taking. Reservations for the dining car and for meals served at your seat should be made at the same time you make your seat reservation.

Sleeping accommodations are found on overnight trains going long distances, such as between Paris and Biarritz, Bordeaux, Grenoble, the Tarentaise Valley, Toulouse, and points along the Mediterranean, as well as on the Atlantic line. Two types of arrangements are possible: *couchettes* and sleepers.

Couchettes, available in both first and second class versions, basically are the coach seats of a compartment converted to sleeping berths, with pillows, sheets, and blankets. First class compartments contain four *couchettes* (an upper and a lower on each side of the aisle); second class compartments contain six (an upper, middle, and lower on each side). Since *couchettes* cost only a standard supplement per person (at present, about $20 in either class if reserved in the US) above the first or second class fare, they are a relatively inexpensive way to get a night's rest aboard the train. However, they provide privacy only for those traveling with a family or other group that can use the whole compartment; individual travelers are mixed with strangers of either sex.

Sleepers are actual bedroom compartments providing one to three beds with a mattress, pillow, sheets, and blanket, plus a washbasin with hot and cold water. Several kinds of compartments are available, though not always on every train. Singles, specials, and doubles are all first class accommodations. The special is the least expensive, and is a slightly smaller individual compartment than the single; the double is for two people who have booked it together. Tourist compartments (T2 and T3) are second class compartments for two and three people traveling together or for strangers, though unlike *couchette* accommodations, strangers of the opposite sex are segregated. Sleeper accommodations, in France, require payment of the basic first or second class fare plus a supplement that varies with the type of compartment (and beyond French borders, with the type of compartment and the distance traveled). From the least to the most expensive, sleeper arrangements can cost anywhere from twice the price of a *couchette* to as much as eight times more.

Naturally, it is best to travel light. More and more modern trains (such as *TGV* and *Corail*) are equipped with a place to put luggage just inside the doors, but otherwise you will have to hoist your suitcase up onto the overhead rack. If you have too much luggage to handle yourself, it can be sent as registered baggage, which is limited to three pieces per person, up to 30 kilos (approximately 66 pounds) each, for a set fee per piece. But do not expect registered baggage to travel on the same train as you do, because this possibility is limited to only a few trains. In many stations, you'll find self-service luggage carts at your disposal, and most stations have either a baggage checkroom *(consigne)* or 24-hour luggage lockers *(consigne automatique)* where you can temporarily free yourself of surplus bags. Due to recent bomb scares, however, lockers are increasingly less common in railroad stations in most European countries — France included.

Drivers should be aware of a variety of *SNCF* services. One of particular interest to foreign visitors is *Train + Auto,* a car-rental service available in more than 230 French cities. Using *Train + Auto,* passengers can reserve a car 24 hours in advance and find it waiting for them at their destination station. Car carrying trains, called *Trains Autos-Couchettes (TAC)* or *Motorail,* are another convenience. These operate principally between northern points of entry (i.e., Boulogne, Calais, Strasbourg) and the Atlantic and Mediterranean, as well as between Paris and numerous points southeast to southwest (from the Alps to the Riviera, across the Pyrénées to the Atlantic, and into neighboring countries). This service allows car owners to take to the rails for long distances while their car travels with them on the same train. Bookings should be made well in advance, especially in summer. *SNCF* also provides parking lots at reasonable prices in the vicinity of stations throughout France. To find them, look for the "Parco-train" signs.

Similar services exist for bicyclists. Some 280 stations in cities throughout France offer *Train + Vélo,* through which traditional or 10-speed bikes can be rented by the half-day, the day, or longer. Travelers with their own bicycles can ship them as registered baggage for a fee (bicycle and owner do not necessarily ride the same train), but there are many short- and medium-distance trains on which bicycles are accepted as free baggage provided their owners load them onto and take them off the baggage car themselves. (For further information on renting and transporting bicycles, see *Camping and Caravanning, Hiking and Biking* in this section.)

Special Tours and Connecting Service – *SNCF* offers a number of combination sightseeing ventures, which are either afternoon outings or excursions of one or a few days aboard *Services de Tourisme SNCF* buses. These operate out of some 250 French cities, but as they are designed mainly for the local traveler, they are conducted in French. For information on these and other tours, inquire at any *Rail Europe* office in the US (see "Further Information," below), or at rail stations in France.

Sealink ships, operated by *SNCF* with British partners, cross the Channel to Great Britain from the French ports of Calais, Boulogne, Cherbourg, St-Malo, Dunkerque, and Dieppe. Travelers can buy through train tickets from Paris to London, with no need to make separate arrangements for the sea portion of the journey. Travel is by rail to the water, where the ship waits, equipped or not with sleeping cabins depending on the length of the trip. Passengers walk to the ship and, on the other shore, board a waiting train to complete the journey. *Hoverspeed Hovercraft,* also run jointly by *SNCF* and British partners, skim across the surface of the water with their cargo of passengers and autos, crossing the Channel from Boulogne or Calais to Dover in about 35 minutes. (For additional information on current rail/ship/rail connections between France and Great Britain, see *Traveling by Ship,* in this section.)

The next step in the development of this network is a link across the English Channel. The Eurotunnel (also referred to as the "Chunnel") was still under construction as we went to press, and the official scheduled completion date (and current popular estimate) was fall of this year. This addition will connect the French railway (and other continental service) with that of the British; the underwater portion of the trip will take approximately 35 minutes.

Other Railroads – A few trains in France have nothing to do with *SNCF.* Minor railways include the privately owned, narrow-gauge *Chemins de Fer de Provence,* or *Provence Railways,* which operates over a scenic route between Nice and Digne. The limited system of *Corsican Railways* on the island of Corsica connects Bastia to Ajaccio, with an offshoot to the towns of Ile-Rousse and Calvi.

The *Orient Express* also passes through France. The legendary *Orient Express* of old, the luxury hotel on wheels that carried tourists and tycoons, kings and conspirators, from London and Paris to Istanbul, made its final run in 1977 but has since been revived as the *Venice Simplon–Orient Express.* It leaves London for Paris and Venice twice weekly from mid-February to mid-November, giving passengers a nostalgic taste of the golden age of rail aboard sumptuously restored carriages of the 1920s. Information on these deluxe trips, which can be taken all the way or in part in either direction, is available from *Venice Simplon–Orient Express,* 1155 Ave. of the Americas, New York, NY 10036 (phone: 800-524-2420).

TICKETS AND FARES: French train fares are based on a combination of the distance traveled and the quality of accommodations chosen. Most trains have both first and second class cars, with a ticket in first class generally costing 50% more than a ticket in second class. Because of this, first class generally is less crowded. It also is more spacious. On *TGV, Corail* trains, and *Turbotrains,* for instance, second class passengers sit four in a row — two abreast on either side of the aisle — while first class passengers sit three in a row. Anyone electing to travel second class, however — as most French travelers do — probably will find it perfectly satisfactory, with service that can be compared favorably to that found anywhere in North America.

A round-trip ticket between any two points, as a rule, simply costs double the price of a one-way ticket. The exception is the *billet séjour,* which allows a reduction of 25% for round trips or circle trips (which do not have to return to the point of origin) of at least 1,000 kilometers (620 miles) total distance with a stay of at least 5 days before the return portion is begun. The *billet séjour,* which can be bought only in France, is one of several ways the French economize on train travel. Other methods include the Couple Card and the Family Card, both technically open to foreigners though not easily used by the short-term visitor (a *livret de famille* or *certificat de concubinage* — which are only available through *SNCF* offices in Europe — must be presented to apply for them). Another card, the Carte Vermeil, provides 60% discounts on tickets for off-peak travel (either first or second class) for senior citizens, and is more easily obtained. (This card is available at railway stations throughout France; the only restriction is that the tickets must be bought in France for the discount to be applied.) Most visitors who plan to do a lot of train travel, however, will find that a rail pass (see below) is an equally good bargain. Passes generally are meant for foreigners only, and often must be bought in the US (or some other foreign location) prior to arrival in France.

Tickets can be bought at train stations, at auxiliary *SNCF* offices where they exist, at travel agencies displaying the *SNCF* sign, and, if necessary, aboard the train, though they'll cost more that way. They also can be bought before you go at *Rail Europe* offices, where, given fluctuations in exchange rates, they may cost a bit more or less than they would if bought in France. Tickets bought in France are valid for any train, any day — pending the payment of supplements and reservations fees necessary for some trains; the period of validity is 2 months or, in the case of a ticket bought with a reservation, for 2 months counted from the day of the intended trip. Tickets bought in North America are valid for 6 months and include fees for supplements.

Tickets purchased in Europe cannot be used until they are stamped with a date, and reminders to this effect — *compostez votre billet* — are posted in stations throughout France. Before proceeding to the platform, look for the bright orange ticket stamping machine *(composteur)* usually found just at the gate and insert your ticket until a click is heard. Failure to do so can be an expensive mistake, because the presentation of an unstamped ticket aboard the train will cost its bearer a 20% fine. A ticket stamped with any date but the date of departure will be considered null and void, costing the bearer a fine plus the price of a new ticket. The penalties are so severe because tickets on French trains are merely spot-checked; an unstamped ticket is no different from an unused ticket, for which you may request a refund. Only rail passes bought outside France — which must be validated by an information clerk (see below) — are exempt from this requirement. Round-trip tickets must be stamped both for the departure and the return, and if any trip is interrupted en route, the ticket must be stamped again before resuming travel if the stopover has been overnight.

PASSES: Rail passes are offered by most European railroad companies. They allow unlimited train travel within a set time period, frequently include connecting service via other forms of transportation, and can save the traveler a considerable amount of money, as well as time. The only requirement is validation of the pass by an information clerk on the day of your first rail trip; thereafter, there is no need to stand in line — and lines can be very long during peak travel periods — to buy individual tickets for subsequent trips. Designed primarily for foreign visitors, these passes generally must be bought in the US (or some other foreign location) prior to arrival in Europe. Although these passes can be among the best bargains around, be sure to look into the comparable cost of individual train tickets which — depending on the number of days you plan to travel — may work out to be less expensive.

France's own pass, the France Railpass, offers unlimited train travel on the *SNCF* network throughout the country. Flexibility and economy are the primary advantages of the Railpass, which can be purchased for either first or second class and for periods of 4 to 9 days, to be used within a 1-month period. These passes also include a free round trip by rail between Orly or Charles de Gaulle airports and downtown Paris, unlimited travel on the Paris métro and bus systems for 1 day, discounts at museums, and regional tourist attractions, as well as sightseeing excursions (by *SNCF* bus), and a ride on the privately owned *Chemins de Fer de Provence* railway. Passholders should contact the regional tourist offices in the areas they plan to visit to obtain a booklet entitling them to additional local discounts.

Holders of the pass are exempt from paying the supplements required on certain fast trains such as *TGV*s, *IC*s, and *EC*s (although those with a second class pass still have to pay the difference between classes to ride the first class *EC*). Children ages 4 through 11 are entitled to their own passes at a bit more than half the adult price (children under 4 travel free on French trains provided they do not occupy a seat). The France Railpass is meant for non-residents of France only and, therefore, must be bought before going abroad either from a travel agent or through *Rail Europe* offices.

The France Rail 'N Drive Pass combines rail travel and car rental through *Avis*. Designed for in-depth tourism, it provides 4 days of unlimited train travel, plus 3 days of car rental (including unlimited mileage, taxes, and drop-off charges). The total 7 days' transportation may be used during a 1-month period. The *Avis* network includes 450 locations throughout France, more than 200 of them in railway stations. Reservations from the US should be made at least 7 days in advance by calling *Avis* (phone: 800-331-1084), although, depending on availability, reservations may be made through any *Avis* office in France as little as 24 hours ahead. The France Rail 'N Drive Pass can be upgraded with 1 day air travel within France on *Air-Inter,* the French domestic airline, for $79. This program is called Fly, Rail & Drive.

The Eurailpass, the first and best known of all rail passes, also is valid in France, as well as in 16 other countries — Austria, Belgium, Denmark, Finland, Germany, Greece, Holland, Hungary, Ireland, Italy, Luxembourg, Norway, Portugal, Spain, Sweden, and Switzerland. It entitles holders to 15 or 21 days or 1, 2, or 3 months of unlimited first class travel, plus many extras, including free travel or substantial reductions on Danube and Rhine river trips, lake steamers, some ferry crossings (within and between countries in the Eurail network), and transportation by bus and private railroads, as well as scheduled *Europabus* services, and aiport to city center rail connections. Since the Eurailpass is a first class pass, Eurail travelers can ride just about any European train they wish, including special express trains, and as with France Railpassholders, they are exempt from all supplements. The only extras are the nominal reservation fee, meals, and sleeper and couchette costs.

A Eurailpass for children under 12 is half the adult price (children under 4 travel free) but includes the same features. The Eurail Youthpass, for travelers under 26 years of age, is slightly different, in that it is valid for travel in second class only.

The Eurail Saverpass resembles the basic Eurailpass, except that it provides 15 days of unlimited first class travel for three people traveling together during peak season; two people traveling together qualify if travel takes place entirely between October 1 and March 31. The Saverpass provides savings of approximately $100 per ticket as compared to the price of a 15-day Eurailpass.

Another option is the Eurail Flexipass, which can be used for first class travel for any 5 days within a 15-day period, 9 days within a 21-day period, or 14 days within a 30-day period. All of these passes must be bought before you go, either from travel agents or from the US offices of the French, German, or Italian railway companies. A *Eurail Aid* office in Europe will replace lost passes when proper documentation is provided; a reissuance fee is charged. (A list of *Eurail Aid* offices throughout Europe is provided when you buy a Eurailpass; you also can ask at any *SNCF* office in France for the nearest location.)

As with the France Rail 'N Drive Pass, both the 7-day Eurailpass and the 9-day Eurail Flexipass can be combined with 3 to 8 days of car rental through *Hertz.* The program, marketed under the name EurailDrive Pass, includes a car rental with unlimited mileage, basic insurance, and taxes, as well as some drop-off options within most of the countries of rental. Reservations must be made in the US at least 7 days in advance by calling *Hertz* at 800-654-3001.

■ **Eurailpass Insurance:** When buying a Eurailpass, you may want to consider Pass Replacement Insurance, recently introduced by *Rail Europe* and *Travel Assistance International.* In the event of loss or theft of your Eurailpass en route, you will be reimbursed for the cost of purchasing a replacement pass valid for the remaining days of travel. The fee for this insurance policy is 3% of the price of the original Eurailpass. Note that the cost of the EurailDrive program and other special services are *not* covered. For further information, contact *Rail Europe* (see below for addresses and phone numbers of regional offices) or *Travel Asssistance International,* 1133 15th St. NW, Suite 400, Washington DC 20005 (phone: 202-331-1609 in Washington, DC; 800-821-2828 elsewhere in the US).

For those planning to travel throughout both Great Britain and France, however, there is a pass covering train travel in just these two countries. (The Eurailpass is not valid in Great Britain.) Called the BritFrance Railpass, it comes in two versions, a 5-day pass that is valid for travel during any 5 days out of 15 consecutive days, and a 10-day pass, valid for any 10 days out of any 30-day period. The BritFrance Railpass includes a round-trip ticket aboard *Hoverspeed Hovercraft* across the English channel, plus certain supplements aboard *SNCF (French National Railways)* trains, including the high-speed *TGV* trains and peak-hour travel. The passes are available either from any *Rail Europe* or *BritRail* office in the US.

FURTHER INFORMATION: *Rail Europe* offices in the US make reservations, sell tickets and rail passes, and provide information on all *SNCF* services. They distribute brochures on the France Railpass and the Eurailpass which provide a good start in adding up the fares of trips you think you might take, in order to judge whether a rail pass would be worth your while.

Rail Europe also distributes the *Eurail* booklet *Through Europe by Train,* which gives timetables of the main rail services between cities all over Europe as well as between the most important cities in France. Another booklet, *Trains d'Affaires,* gives the schedules of selected trains within France. A summary of *TGV* schedules also is available.

Rail Europe is the North American representative of the *Société Nationale des Chemins de Fer Français (SNCF; French National Railways).* Although this company has administrative offices throughout the US and Canada, all information, reservations, tickets, and rail passes are available through their central North American office. For information on French railway travel, as well as connecting service to other European countries, contact *Rail Europe* at 226-230 Westchester Ave., White Plains, NY 10604 (phone: 914-682-5172 in Connecticut, New Jersey, and New York State; 800-345-1990 elsewhere in the US and Canada).

In France, there is no dearth of information sources, beginning with the information desk found in main stations. The myriad blue and orange, nearly wallet-size, city-to-city timetables — *fiches-horaires* — that can be picked up from the display racks in most stations are particularly handy and extremely portable. Also very useful — if you read French — is the *Guide Pratique du Voyageur,* a booklet explaining everything you need to know about French trains from how to travel with *petits animaux* (they must have a ticket) to how to find your *voiture.* Its companion *Guide du Voyageur TGV* explains the new high-speed trains.

Particularly if France is only a part of a more extensive trip through Europe or even farther afield, you may want to consult broader sources before finalizing plans. Both the *Eurail Traveler's Guide* (which contains a railroad map) and the *Eurail Timetable* are free from Eurailpass (Box 10383, Stamford, CT 06904-2383), as well as from the Eurail Distribution Centre (PO Box 4000, Station A, Mississauga, Ontario L5A 9Z9, Canada). The *Eurail Guide*, by Kathryn Turpin and Marvin Saltzman, is available in most travel bookstores; it also can be ordered from Eurail Guide Annuals (27540 Pacific Coast Hwy., Malibu, CA 90265; phone: 213-457-7286) for $13.95, plus shipping and handling. *Europe by Eurail*, by George Wright Ferguson, is available from Globe Pequot Press (PO Box Q, Chester, CT 06412; phone: 203-526-9571) for $14.95, plus shipping and handling. The latter two guides discuss train travel in general, contain information on France and other countries included in the Eurail network (the Saltzman book also discusses Eastern Europe and the rest of the world), and suggest numerous sightseeing excursions by rail from various base cities.

You also may want to buy the *Thomas Cook European Timetable*, a weighty and detailed compendium of European international and national rail services that constitutes the most revered and accurate railway reference in existence. The *Timetable* comes out monthly, but because most European countries — including France — switch to summer schedules at the end of May (and back to winter schedules at the end of September), the June edition offers the first complete summer schedule (and October the first complete winter schedule). The February through May editions, however, contain increasingly more definitive supplements on upcoming summer schedules that can be used to plan a trip. The *Thomas Cook European Timetable* is available in some travel bookstores or can be ordered from the *Forsyth Travel Library* (PO Box 2975, Shawnee Mission, KS 66201-1375; phone: 800-367-7984 or 913-384-3440) for $23.95, plus shipping and handling; credit card orders also are accepted by phone.

Finally, although any travel agent can assist you in making arrangements to tour France by rail, you may want to consult a train travel specialist, such as *Accent on Travel*, 1030 Curtis St., Suite 201, Menlo Park, CA 94025 (phone: 415-326-7330 in California; 800-347-0645 elsewhere in the US).

Traveling by Car

Driving certainly is the most flexible way to explore out-of-the-way regions of France. The privacy, comfort, and convenience of touring by car can't be matched by any other form of transport. Trains often whiz much too fast past too many enticing landscapes, pass between France's hills and mountains rather than climb up and around them for a better view, frequently deposit passengers in an unappealing part of town, and don't permit many spur-of-the moment stops and starts. In a car you go where you want when you want, and can stop along the way as often as you like for a meal, a photograph, or a particularly appealing view.

France is the largest country in Western Europe, yet it is still small enough to be an ideal area to cover by car. The distance from Calais in the north to Nice in the southeast is approximately 760 miles (1,216 km); from Strasbourg in the northeast to Biarritz in the southwest is roughly the same. Within these extremes, distances between points of interest are reasonably short, and the historical and cultural density is such that the flexibility of a car can be used to maximum advantage. A visitor can cover large amounts of territory, visiting major cities and sites, or spend the same amount of time motoring from one small village to another while exploring the countryside. (See DIRECTIONS for our choices of the most interesting driving routes.)

Travelers who wish to cover France from end to end can count on a good system of highways to help them make time, while those choosing to explore only one region will find that the secondary and even lesser roads are well surfaced and generally in good condition; even farther off the beaten track, this usually is the case. Either way, there is plenty of satisfying scenery en route, because — except for some predictably unlovely spots in the industrial north — la belle France is just that.

But driving isn't an inexpensive way to travel. Gas prices are far higher in Europe than in North America, and car rentals seldom are available at bargain rates. Keep in mind, however, that driving becomes more economical with more passengers. Because the price of getting wheels abroad will be more than an incidental expense, it is important to investigate every alternative before making a final choice. Many travelers find this expense amply justified when considering that rather than just the means to an end, a well-planned driving route also can be an important part of the adventure.

Before setting out, make certain that everything you need is in order. If possible, discuss your intended trip with someone who already has driven the route to find out about road conditions and available services. If you can't speak to someone personally, try to read about others' experiences. Automobile clubs (see below) and French Government Tourist Offices in the US can be good sources of driving information, although when requesting brochures and maps, be sure to specify the areas you are planning to visit. (Also see "Roads and Maps," below.)

DRIVING: A valid driver's license from his or her own state of residence enables a US citizen to drive in France. Although not required, an International Driving Permit (IDP), which is a translation of the US license in 9 languages, is recommended — particularly if you are considering driving across the border into other European countries.

You can obtain your IDP before you leave from most branches of the *American Automobile Association (AAA)*. Applicants must be at least 18 years old, and the application must be accompanied by two passport-size photos (some *AAA* branches have a photo machine available), a valid US driver's license, and a fee of $10. The IDP is good for 1 year and must be accompanied by your US license to be valid.

Proof of liability insurance also is required and is a standard part of any car rental contract. (To be sure of having the appropriate coverage, let the rental staff know in advance about the national borders you plan to cross.) If buying a car and using it abroad, the driver must carry an International Insurance Certificate, known as a Green Card (called a *Carte Verte* in France). Your insurance agent or carrier at home can arrange for a special policy to cover you in Europe, and will automatically issue your Green Card.

The French drive on the right, like Americans, and obey somewhat similar traffic rules. For the most part, the basic rule of the road in France is *priorité à droite* (priority to the right), which means that unless there is some indication to the contrary, the car coming from the right has the right of way, even if coming from a minor side street or if entering a traffic circle from an approach road. However, *priorité à gauche* (priority to the left) has been introduced at selected traffic circles. These are marked by a sign showing arrows going around in a circle, meaning that cars already in those circles have priority over cars entering. In built-up areas, priority to the right is the norm with few exceptions; in rural areas, most principal roads have the right of way, the priority indicated by a sign reading *passage protégé* or by a sign with a yellow square (standing on one of its angles, like a diamond). When the yellow square appears with a black bar, the road loses its priority and the right of way reverts to those coming from the right. This usually is the case at the entrance to a town, but not always, so keep an eye on the signs.

As in the rest of continental Europe, distances are measured in kilometers (1 mile equals 1.6 kilometers; 1 kilometer equals .62 mile) and are registered as kilometers per hour (kmh) on the speedometer. French speed limits are 130 kmh (81 mph) on toll autoroutes (superhighways), 110 kmh (68 mph) on dual carriageways (4-lane highways) and free autoroutes, and 90 kmh (56 mph) on other roads outside built-up areas. In towns, unless otherwise indicated, the speed limit is 50 kmh (30 mph); on the *périphériques* around Paris the speed limit is 80 kmh (48 mph).

Keep in mind, when touring along France's scenic roadways, that it is all too easy to inch up over the speed limit. And use alcohol sparingly prior to getting behind the wheel. Despite their casual attitude and lack of restrictions regarding the sale of wine and liquor, the French are most zealous in prosecuting those who commit infractions under the influence. Police also have the power to levy on-the-spot fines for other violations such as speeding, failure to stop at a red light, and failure to wear seat belts. Seat belts are compulsory for the driver and front-seat passenger. In addition, children under 10 must travel in the back seat — and, again, seat belts always are recommended. Use the horn sparingly — only in emergencies and when approaching blind mountain curves. In Paris and some other cities, honking is forbidden; at night, flash your headlights instead.

Pictorial direction signs are standardized according to the International Roadsign System and their meanings are indicated by their shapes — triangular signs indicate danger; circular signs give instructions; and rectangular signs are informative. Driving in French and other European cities can be a tricky proposition, since many of them do not have street signs at convenient corners, but instead identify their byways with plaques attached to the walls of corner buildings. These often are difficult to spot until you've passed them, and since most streets don't run parallel to one another, taking the next turn can lead you astray. Fortunately most European cities and towns post numerous signs pointing the way to the center of the city, and plotting a course to your destination from there may be far easier. Look for the signs that read CENTRE VILLE.

■ **Note:** Pay particular attention to parking signs in large cities throughout Europe, especially those indicating "control zones," where an unattended parked car presents a serious security risk. If you park in a restricted zone, unlike in the US (where you chance only a ticket or being towed), you may return to find that the trunk and doors have been blown off by overly cautious security forces. (More likely, however, you'll return to find one of the car's wheels "clamped," a procedure that renders your car inoperable and involves a tedious — and costly — process to get it freed.)

Roads and Maps – Western Europe's network of highways is as well maintained as any in North America, with a system comparable to the American highway system: expressways, first class roads, and well-surfaced secondary roads. France maintains its own highway system.

Except for stretches of free autoroutes in the vicinity of cities, most of the autoroutes (designated by A) in France are *autoroutes à péage,* or toll roads, and they are fairly expensive. They save time, gas, and wear and tear on the car, but they are obviously not the roads to take if you want to browse and linger along the way. The other main roads, the *routes nationales* (designated by N), and the secondary, or regional, *routes départementales* (designated by D) are free, well maintained, and much more picturesque; and undesignated minor roads may offer the most charming scenery of all.

Traffic congestion is at its worst on main roads (particularly those radiating from Paris and other major cities) on the days before and after public holidays, on the first and last days of July and August, and, above all, on the days surrounding August 15

(*Assumption Day*), the date on which every French family that has not already done so sets out on vacation. At these times, look for signs pointing out detours or alternative routes to popular holiday destinations. Service stations, information points, and tourist offices distribute free maps of the alternate routes, which, although technically longer, will probably get you to your goal faster in the end by bypassing the bottlenecks.

Be aware that in recent years, numerous changes have been taking place in the numbering of French roads. Many N roads have become D roads, some merely changing their prefix from N to D, some changing numbers as well. Another recent development is a new, Europe-wide road-numbering system. The European designations, prefaced by an E, appear together with the individual country's road numbers, so, for example, autoroute A1 in France also could be called E5, but Germany's A1 would have a different E number. Although some single-country maps use only a national number, both designations appear on Michelin's and other European maps, but expect discrepancies between the old and new numbers to appear in maps, guidebooks, and brochures for some time to come.

The most comprehensive and up-to-date road maps of France are published by Michelin, the French tire company (one of whose founders also was a cartographer). Besides all the other information pertinent to motorists that they contain, Michelin maps also plot (in yellow) a network of alternate *routes de dégagement* selected to bypass major cities and avoid congestion (mostly D roads paralleling N roads), while especially scenic stretches are further highlighted in green. These are often the choicest travel routes in the country. Michelin's red map 989 covers the entire country in considerable detail (the scale is 1:1,000,000; 1 cm equals 10 km) and should be sufficient for the needs of most motorists, but for those traveling extensively in one region, Michelin also publishes a series of 17 regional maps and a series of about 40 "detailed" or sectional maps (the scale of both series is 1:200,000; 1 cm equals 2 km). Michelin maps are readily available all over France, in bookstores and map shops around the US, and also can be ordered from the company's US headquarters, Michelin Guides and Maps (PO Box 3305, Spartanburg, SC 29304-3305; phone: 803-599-0850 in South Carolina; 800-423-0485 elsewhere in the US). A new edition of each map appears every year; if you're not buying directly from the publisher, make sure that the edition you buy is no more than 2 years old by opening one fold and checking the publication date, given just under the black circle with the map number.

The Hallwag Road Map of France is another good source of information for travelers choosing to make their way through France by car. Like their American counterparts, these maps provide regional maps of the country that include both major and secondary roads, with information on emergency assistance and highway laws and regulations. They are available in any *Rand McNally Map and Travel Bookstore,* or can be ordered through their main warehouse (8255 N. Central Park, Skokie, IL 60076; phone: 800-627-2897) for $9.95, plus shipping and handling.

Freytag & Berndt's excellent series of 28 road maps ($8.95 each) covers most major destinations throughout Europe, including France. As the publisher is Austrian, this series is best ordered from the US distributor, *Map Link* (25 E. Mason St., Suite 201, Santa Barbara, CA 93101; phone 805-965-4402), which also is a good source of just about any other kind of map of just about anywhere in the world. You may want to order their comprehensive guide to maps worldwide, *The World Map Directory* ($29.-95). If they don't have the map you want in stock, they will do their best to get it for you. Their selection of French maps includes several country maps and a wide range of city, topographical, and special-interest maps such as wine and cheese maps, and an "Artistic Treasures" map.

Road maps also are sold at gas stations throughout France. Stateside, some free maps can be obtained from the national tourist office. The French Government Tourist Office has a free map of France that indicates the location of key sites and tourist attractions, campsites, gas stations, and so on. *Avis,* the car rental company (see below), offers "Personally Yours," a travel packet complete with maps and information on places to see and things to do while driving through France.

The *American Automobile Association (AAA)* also provides a number of useful reference sources, including several regional maps of France, the 600-page *Travel Guide to Europe* , and the 64-page *Motoring in Europe* ($7.25). These are available through local *AAA* offices (see below — note that the price and availability of these publications, both for members and non-members, vary from branch to branch). Another invaluable guide, *Euroad: The Complete Guide to Motoring in Europe,* is available for $8.95, including postage and handling, from *VLE Limited,* PO Box 444, Ft. Lee, NJ 07024 (phone: 201-585-5080 or 212-580-8030).

Automobile Clubs and Breakdowns – Most European automobile clubs offer emergency assistance to any breakdown victim, whether a club member or not; however, only members of these clubs or affiliated clubs may have access to certain information services and receive discounted or free towing and repair services.

Members of the *American Automobile Association (AAA)* often are automatically entitled to a number of services from foreign clubs. With over 31 million members in chapters throughout the US and Canada, the *AAA* is the largest automobile club in North America. *AAA* affiliates throughout the US provide a variety of travel services to members, including a travel agency, trip planning, fee-free traveler's checks, and *sometimes* — if no reciprocal service agreement exists between a local French automobile club and the *AAA* — reimbursement for foreign roadside assistance. They will help plan an itinerary, send a map with clear routing directions, and even make hotel reservations. These services apply to travel in both the US and Europe. Although *AAA* members receive maps and brochures for no charge or at a discount, non-members also can order from an extensive selection of highway and topographical maps at most *AAA* branches. You can join the *AAA* through local chapters (listed in the telephone book under *AAA*) or contact the national office at 1000 AAA Dr., Heathrow, FL 32746-5063 (phone: 407-444-8544).

Although reciprocal service arrangements between US and French automobile clubs are less common than in other countries, the *Association Française des Auto Clubs* (9 Rue Anatole de la Forge, 75017 Paris; phone: 1-42-27-82-00) will provide travel information to members of US auto clubs such as the *AAA*. The main French automobile club is the *Automobile Club de France* (6-8 Pl. de la Concorde, Paris 75008; phone: 1-42-65-34-70); however, this club is more of an automobile enthusiasts association rather than the American type of "on the road assistance" organization. Motorists may not find it particularly helpful in an emergency.

If you break down on the road, immediate emergency procedure is to get the car off the road. If the road has a narrow shoulder, try to get all the way off, even if you have to hang off the shoulder a bit. Better yet, try to make it to an area where the shoulder is wider — if you are crawling along well below the speed limit, use your emergency flashers to warn other drivers. Once you've pulled off the road, raise the hood as a signal that help is needed, and tie a white handkerchief or rag to the door handle or radio antenna. Don't leave the car unattended, and don't try any major repairs on the road.

French motor patrols usually drive small cars painted white with an orange stripe. Orange emergency phones are located along major autoroutes for stranded travelers to dial for roadside assistance. They are not, however, normally found on secondary roads or rural routes.

Aside from these options, a driver in distress will have to contact the nearest service center by pay phone. And, although English is spoken in France, if language is a barrier in explaining your dilemma, your best bet may be to reach an international operator who can stay on the line as an interpreter. (For further information on calling for help, see *Mail, Telephone, and Electricity, Staying Healthy,* and *Legal Aid and Consular Services,* all in this section.) Car rental companies also make provisions for breakdowns, emergency service, and assistance; ask for a number to call when you pick up the vehicle.

Gasoline – Called *essence* in France, gasoline is sold by the liter. A liter is slightly more than 1 quart; approximately 3.8 liters equal 1 US gallon. Regular or leaded gas generally is sold in two grades — *ordinaire* and *super* (in French). Diesel (called *diesel*) also is widely available. Unleaded fuel *(sans plomb),* until recently often difficult — if not impossible — to find in some areas, is now much more readily available, and some US car rental companies in France (such as *Avis* and *National*) now offer cars that take *only* unleaded gas.

Gas prices everywhere rise and fall depending on the world supply of oil, and an American traveling overseas is further affected by the prevailing rate of exchange, so it is difficult to say exactly how much fuel will cost when you travel. It is not difficult to predict, however, that gas prices will be substantially higher than you are accustomed to paying in the US.

Particularly when traveling in rural areas, fill up whenever you come to a gas station. It may be a long way to the next open station. (Even in more populated areas, it may be difficult to find an open station on Sundays or holidays.) You don't want to get stranded on an isolated stretch — so it is a good idea to bring along an extra few gallons in a steel container. (Plastic containers tend to break when a car is bouncing over rocky roads. This, in turn, creates the danger of fire should the gasoline ignite from a static electricity spark. Plastic containers also may burst at high altitudes.)

Considering the cost of gas in France relative to US prices, gas economy is of particular concern. The prudent traveler should plan an itinerary and make as many reservations as possible in advance in order not to waste gas figuring out where to go, stay, or eat. Drive early in the day, when there is less traffic. Then leave your car at the hotel and use local transportation whenever possible after you arrive at your destination.

Although it may be as dangerous to drive at a speed much below the posted limit as it is to drive above it — particularly on toll autoroutes, superhighways where the speed limit is 130 kmh (81 mph) — at 88 kmh (55 mph) a car gets 25% better mileage than at 112 kmh (70 mph). The number of miles per liter or gallon also is increased by driving smoothly.

RENTING A CAR: Although there are other options, such as leasing or outright purchase, most travelers who want to drive in Europe simply rent a car. Travelers to France can rent a car through a travel agent or international rental firm before leaving home, or from a local company once they are in Europe. Another possibility, also arranged before departure, is to rent the car as part of a larger travel package (see "Fly/Drive Packages," below, as well as *Package Tours,* in this section).

Renting a car in France is not inexpensive, but it is possible to economize by determining your own needs and then shopping around among the car rental companies until you find the best deal. As you comparison shop, keep in mind that rates vary considerably, not only from city to city, but also from location to location within the same city. For instance, it might be less expensive to rent a car in the center of a city rather than at the airport. Ask about special rates or promotional deals, such as weekend or weekly rates, bonus coupons for airline tickets, or 24-hour rates that include gas and unlimited mileage.

Rental car companies operating in Europe can be divided into three basic categories:

large international companies; national or regional companies; and smaller local companies. Because of aggressive local competition, the cost of renting a car can be less expensive once a traveler arrives in France, compared to the prices quoted in advance in the US. Local companies usually are less expensive than the international giants.

Given this situation, it's tempting to wait until arriving to scout out the lowest-priced rental from the company located the farthest from the airport high-rent district and offering no pick-up services. But if your arrival coincides with a holiday or a peak travel period, you may be disappointed to find that even the most expensive car in town was spoken for months ago. Whenever possible, it is best to reserve in advance, anywhere from a few days in slack periods to a month or more during the busier seasons.

Renting from the US – Travel agents can arrange foreign rentals for clients, but it is just as easy to call and rent a car yourself. Listed below are some of the major international rental companies represented in France that have information and reservations numbers that can be dialed toll-free from the US:

Avis (phone: 800-331-1084). Has nearly 400 locations in France.

Budget (phone: 800-527-0700). Has nearly 200 locations in France.

Dollar Rent A Car (known throughout most of Europe as *Eurodollar Rent A Car;* phone: 800-800-6000). Has 76 locations in France.

Hertz (phone: 800-654-3001). Has over 350 locations in France.

National (known in Europe as *Europcar;* phone: 800-CAR-EUROPE). Has nearly 400 locations in France.

Thrifty (phone: 800-367-2277). Has over 30 locations in France.

Note that *Avis* also offers two helpful free services for customers traveling in France, as well as in other European countries: the "Know Before You Go" US hotline (phone: 914-355-AVIS); and an "On Call Service" for customers calling once in Europe. Both provide travelers with tourist information on France, as well as numerous other European countries. Topics may range from questions about driving (distances, gasoline prices, and license requirements) to queries about currency, customs, tipping, and weather. (Callers to the US number then receive a personal letter confirming the information discussed.) For the European service, there is a different toll-free number in each country; the numbers are given to you when you rent from *Avis* (personnel at these numbers speak English).

Another special service is *Avis*'s Europe Message Center, which operates like any answering service in that it will take phone messages any time of the day or night for *Avis* customers. *Avis* renters are given a telephone number in Europe that they can leave with anyone who wants to contact them while they are touring; if your rental car comes with a car phone, *Avis* will give this number to callers (with your permission). The tourers themselves can call a toll-free number to pick up messages or leave word for family, friends, or business colleagues. To utilize the service, a renter picks up his or her car at an *Avis* outlet in Europe, and then simply calls the Message Center and registers with the rental agreement number. It's even possible to leave an itinerary — which can be altered later if necessary — making messages easy to leave and/or pick up.

It also is possible to rent a car before you go by contacting any of a number of smaller or less well known US companies that do not operate worldwide. These organizations specialize in European auto travel, including leasing and car purchase in addition to car rental, or actually are tour operators with well-established European car rental programs. These firms, whose names and addresses are listed below, act as agents for a variety of European suppliers, offer unlimited mileage almost exclusively, and frequently manage to undersell their larger competitors by a significant margin.

There are legitimate bargains in car rentals provided you shop for them. Call all the familiar car rental names whose toll-free numbers are given above (don't forget to ask about their special discount plans), and then call the smaller companies listed below. In the recent past, the latter have tended to offer significantly lower rates, but it always pays to compare. Begin your comparison shopping early, because the best deals may be booked to capacity quickly and may require payment 14 to 21 days or more before picking up the car.

Auto Europe (PO Box 1097, Camden, ME 04843; phone: 207-236-8235; 800-223-5555 throughout the US; 800-458-9503 in Canada). Offers rentals at over 75 locations throughout France.

Europe by Car (One Rockefeller Plaza, New York, NY 10020; phone: 212-581-3040 in New York State; 800-223-1516 elsewhere in the US; and 9000 Sunset Blvd., Los Angeles, CA 90069; phone: 800-252-9401 in California only or 213-272-0424). Offers rentals at over 200 locations throughout France.

European Car Reservations (349 W. Commercial St., Suite 2950, East Rochester, NY 14445; phone: 800-535-3303). Offers rentals at over 100 locations throughout France.

Foremost Euro-Car (5430 Van Nuys Blvd., Suite 306, Van Nuys, CA 91401; phone: 800-272-3299 or 818-786-1960). Offers rentals at almost 200 locations throughout France.

Kemwel Group (106 Calvert St., Harrison, NY 10528; phone: 800-678-0678 or 914-835-5555). Offers rentals at 25 locations throughout France.

Meier's World Travel (6033 W. Century Blvd., Suite 1080, Los Angeles, CA 90045; phone: 800-937-0700). In conjunction with a number of major car rental companies (such as *Hertz*), they arrange economical rentals throughout France.

One of the ways to keep the cost of car rentals down is to deal with a car rental consolidator, such as *Connex International* (23 N. Division St., Peekskill, NY 10566; phone: 800-333-3949 or 914-739-0066). *Connex*'s main business is negotiating with virtually all of the major car rental agencies for the lowest possible prices for its customers. This company arranges rentals throughout Europe, including over 200 locations in cities and towns throughout France.

Local Rentals – It has long been common wisdom that the least expensive way to rent a car is to make arrangements in Europe. This is less true today than it used to be. Many medium to large European car rental companies have become the overseas suppliers of stateside companies such as those mentioned previously, and often the stateside agency, by dint of sheer volume, has been able to negotiate more favorable rates for its US customers than the European firm offers its own. Still, lower rates may be found by searching out small, strictly local rental companies overseas, whether at less than prime addresses in major cities or in more remote areas. But to find them you must be willing to invest a sufficient amount of vacation time comparing prices on the scene. You also must be prepared to return the car to the location that rented it; drop-off possibilities are likely to be limited.

The brochures of some of the smaller car rental companies, often available from French Government Tourist Offices in the US, can serve as a useful basis for comparison. Once overseas, local tourist authorities may be able to supply the names of local rental companies, and the local phone book (if you can read French) is another good place to begin. (For further information on local rental companies, see the individual city reports in THE CITIES.)

Travelers intending to rent a car only occasionally, relying mainly on other means of transportation, should be aware of three major French car rental companies: *Citroën* (phone: 1-43-55-39-63), *Dergi Location* (phone: 1-45-87-27-04), and *Mattei,* (phone: 1-43-46-11-50). Also bear in mind that *French National Railways (SNCF)* offers a car rental service in conjunction with *Avis* at more than 230 locations throughout France. The car is reserved at least 24 hours in advance, is available by the day or longer, and is waiting for you at the station of your destination. Note that the rates are comparable to those charged by *Avis* for cars reserved in France: That is, if you know beforehand that you will want the car for more than a few days (for 5 days, for example, the minimum rental period on *Avis*'s discount plan), you will do better to reserve it before leaving the US. The France Rail 'N Drive Pass is another joint offering of *Avis* and *French National Railways* and a similar rail-and-drive program offered by *Hertz*, EurailDrive Escape, is valid in France and in all the other countries of the Eurail network. (For further information on rail-and-drive packages, see *Traveling by Train*, above.)

Requirements – Whether you decide to rent a car in advance from a large international rental company with European branches or wait to rent from a local company, you should know that renting a car is rarely as simple as signing on the dotted line and roaring off into the night. If you are renting for personal use, you must have a valid driver's license and will have to convince the renting agency that (1) you are personally creditworthy, and (2) you will bring the car back at the stated time. This will be easy if you have a major credit card; most rental companies accept credit cards in lieu of a cash deposit, as well as for payment of your final bill. If you prefer to pay in cash, leave your credit card imprint as a "deposit," then pay your bill in cash when you return the car.

If you are planning to rent a car once in France, *Avis, Budget, Hertz,* and other US rental companies usually *will* rent to travelers paying in cash and leaving either a credit card imprint or a substantial amount of cash as a deposit. This is not necessarily standard policy, however, as some of the other international chains, and a number of local and regional European companies will *not* rent to an individual who doesn't have a valid credit card. In this case, you may have to call around to find a company that accepts cash.

Also keep in mind that although the minimum age to drive a car in France is 18 years, the minimum age to rent a car is set by the rental company. (Restrictions vary from company to company, as well as at different locations.) Many firms have a minimum age requirement of 21 years, some raise that to between 23 and 25 years, and for some models of cars it rises to 30 years. The upper age limit at many companies is between 69 and 75; others have no upper limit or may make drivers above a certain age subject to special conditions.

Costs – Finding the most economical car rental will require some telephone shopping on your part. As a *general* rule, expect to hear lower prices quoted by the smaller, strictly local companies than by the well-known international names, with those of the national French companies falling somewhere between the two.

Comparison shopping always is advisable, however, because the company that has the least expensive rentals in one country may not have the least expensive cars in another, and even the international giants offer discount plans whose conditions are easy for most travelers to fulfill. For instance, *Budget* and *National* offer discounts of anywhere from 10% to 30% off their usual rates (according to the size of the car and the duration of the rental), provided that the car is reserved a certain number of days before departure (usually 7 to 14 days, but it can be less), is rented for a minimum period (5 days or, more often, a week), is paid for at the time of booking, and, in most cases, is returned to the same location that supplied it or to another in the same country. Similar discount plans include *Hertz*'s Affordable Europe and *Avis*'s Supervalue Rates Europe.

If driving short distances for only a day or two, the best deal may be a per-day, per-mile (or per-kilometer) rate: You pay a flat fee for each day you keep the car, plus a per-mile (or per-kilometer) charge. An increasingly common alternative is to be granted a certain number of free miles or kilometers each day and then be charged on a per-mile or per-kilometer basis over that number.

A better alternative for touring the countryside may be a flat per-day rate with unlimited free mileage; this certainly is the most economical rate if you plan to drive over 100 miles (160 km). Make sure that the low, flat daily rate that catches your eye, however, is indeed a per-day rate: Often the lowest price advertised by a company turns out to be available only with a minimum 3-day rental — fine if you want the car that long, but not the bargain it appears if you really intend to use it no more than 24 hours for in-city driving. Flat weekly rates also are available, as are some flat monthly rates that represent a further saving over the daily rate. (Note: When renting a car in France, the term "mileage" may refer either to miles or kilometers.)

Another factor influencing cost is the type of car you rent. Rentals generally are based on a tiered price system, with different sizes of cars — variations of budget, economy, regular, and luxury — often listed as A (the smallest and least expensive) through F, G, or H, and sometimes even higher. Charges may increase by only a few dollars a day through several categories of subcompact and compact cars — where most of the competition is — then increase by great leaps through the remaining classes of full-size and luxury cars and passenger vans. The larger the car, the more it costs to rent and the more gas it consumes, but for some people the greater comfort and extra luggage space of a larger car (in which bags and sporting gear can be safely locked out of sight) may make it worth the additional expense. Be warned, too, that relatively few European cars have automatic transmissions, and those that do are more likely to be in the F than the A group. Similarly, cars with air conditioning are likely to be found in the more expensive categories only. Most expensive are sleek sports cars, but, again, for some people the thrill of driving such a car — for a week or a day — may be worth it.

Electing to pay for collision damage waiver (CDW) protection will add considerably to the cost of renting a car. You may be responsible for the *full value* of the vehicle being rented, but you can dispense with the possible obligation by buying the offered waiver at a cost of about $10 to $13 a day. Before making any decisions about optional collision damage waivers, check with your own insurance agent and determine whether your personal automobile insurance policy covers rented vehicles; if it does, you probably won't need to pay for the waiver. Be aware, too, that increasing numbers of credit cards automatically provide CDW coverage if the car rental is charged to the appropriate credit card. However, the specific terms of such coverage differ sharply among individual credit card companies, so check with the credit card company for information on the nature and amount of coverage provided. Business travelers also should be aware that, at the time of this writing, *American Express* had withdrawn its automatic CDW coverage from some corporate *Green* card accounts — watch for similar cutbacks by other credit card companies.

Overseas, the amount renters may be liable for should damage occur has not risen to the heights it has in the US. In addition, some European car rental agreements include collision damage waiver coverage. In this case, the CDW supplement frees the renter from liability for the *deductible* amount — as opposed to the standard CDW coverage, described above, which releases the driver from liability for the full value of the car. In France, this deductible typically ranges anywhere from $1,500 to $2,500, but can be higher for some luxury car groups. As with the full collision damage waiver, the cost of waiving this liability — which can be as high as $25 a day — is far from negligible, however. Drivers who rent cars in the US often are able to decline the CDW because many personal car insurance policies (subject to their own deductibles) extend to rental cars; unfortunately, such coverage usually does not extend to cars rented for use outside the US and Canada. Similarly, CDW coverage provided by some credit cards if the rental is charged to the card may be limited to cars rented in the US or Canada.

When inquiring about CDW coverage and costs, you should be aware that a number of the major international car rental companies now are automatically including the cost of this waiver in their quoted prices. This does not mean that they are absorbing this cost and you are receiving free coverage — total rental prices have increased to include the former CDW charge. The disadvantage of this inclusion is that you probably will not have the option to refuse this coverage, and will end up paying the added charge — even if you already are adequately covered by your own insurance policy or through a credit card company.

Additional costs to be added to the price tag include drop-off charges or one-way service fees. The lowest price quoted by any given company may apply only to a car that is returned to the same location from which it was rented. A slightly higher rate may be charged if the car is to be returned to a different location (even within the same city), and a considerably higher rate may prevail if the rental begins in one country and ends in another.

A further consideration: Don't forget that all car rentals are subject to Value Added Tax (VAT). This tax rarely is included in the rental price that's advertised or quoted, but it always must be paid — whether you pay in advance in the US or pay it when you drop off the car. In France, the VAT rate on car rentals currently is 22%.

There is a wide variation in this tax rate from country to country. One-way rentals bridging two countries used to be exempt from tax, but this is no longer the case. In general, the tax on one-way rentals is determined by the country in which the car has been rented, so even if you intend to visit only France, you still might consider a nearby country as the pick-up point — the tax rate in Belgium is 20% (no great bargain), but in Germany it is 14%; in Spain, 13%; in Luxembourg, 15%; and in Switzerland, no tax is charged. For a tourer planning to explore Alsace and/or Burgundy, Lyons, and Provence, therefore, there's a strong financial incentive to pick up his or her rental car in Switzerland and then drive across the nearby French border (at a 22% car rental cost saving!).

Some rental agencies that do not maintain their own fleets use a contractor, whose country of registration determines the rate of taxation. An example is *Kemwel Group,* whose one-way rentals from all countries are taxed at the Danish rate of 25%. *Kemwel*'s special programs offer savings to the client planning to tour Europe (particularly through countries where the tax rate is higher). Their UltraSaver and UltraSaver Plus tariffs offer inclusive rentals in some 35 cities across Europe, including all the major cities in France. These programs offer full insurance coverage (with a $100 deductible) and all European VAT, plus unlimited mileage. If part of a fly/drive package (see below) booked through *Kemwel,* rates may be even lower. Bookings must be reserved and paid for at least 14 days before delivery of the car, and the vehicle must be returned to the *Kemwel* garage from which it was originally rented. For further information, contact *Kemwel Group,* 106 Calvert St., Harrison, NY 10528 (phone: 800-678-0678 or 914-835-5555).

Also, don't forget to factor in the price of gas. Rental cars usually are delivered with a full tank of gas. (This is not always the case, however, so check the gas gauge when picking up the car, and have the amount of gas noted on your rental agreement if the tank is not full.) Remember to fill the tank before you return the car or you will have to pay to refill it, and gasoline at the car rental company's pump always is much more expensive than at a service station. This policy may vary for smaller local and regional companies; ask when picking up the vehicle. Before leaving the lot, also check that the rental car has a spare tire and jack in the trunk.

Finally, currency fluctuation is another factor to consider. Most brochures quote rental prices in US dollars, but these dollar amounts frequently are only guides; that is, they represent the prevailing rate of exchange at the time the brochure was printed. The rate may be very different when you call to make a reservation, and different again when the time comes to pay the bill (when the amount owed may be paid in cash in foreign currency or as a charge to a credit card, which is recalculated at a still later date's rate of exchange). Some companies guarantee rates in dollars (often for a slight surcharge), but this is an advantage only when the value of the dollar is steadily declining overseas. If the dollar is growing stronger overseas, you may be better off with rates guaranteed in French francs.

Fly/Drive Packages – Airlines, charter companies, car rental companies, and tour operators have been offering fly/drive packages for years, and even though the basic components of the package have changed somewhat — return airfare, a car waiting at the airport, and perhaps a night's lodging all for one inclusive price used to be the rule — the idea remains the same. You rent a car *here* for use *there* by booking it along with other arrangements for the trip. These days, the very minimum arrangement possible is the result of a tie-in between a car rental company and an airline, which entitles customers to a rental car for less than the company's usual rates, provided they show proof of having booked a flight on that airline. For information about available packages, check with the airline or your travel agent.

Slightly more elaborate fly/drive packages are listed under various names (go-as-you-please, self-drive, or, simply, car tours) in the independent vacations sections of tour catalogues. Their most common ingredients are the rental car plus some sort of hotel voucher plan, with the applicable airfare listed separately. You set off on your trip with a block of prepaid accommodations vouchers, a list of hotels that accept them (usually members of a hotel chain or association), and a reservation for the first night's stay, after which the staff of each hotel books the next one for you or you make your own reservations. Naturally, the greater the number of establishments participating in the scheme, the more freedom you have to range at will during the day's driving and still be near a place to stay for the night.

The cost of these combination packages generally varies according to the size of the car and the quality of the hotels; there usually is an additional drop-off charge if the car is picked up in one city and returned in another. Most packages are offered at several different price levels, ranging from a standard plan covering stays in hotels to a budget plan using accommodations such as small inns, farmhouses, or bed and breakfast establishments. Airlines also have special rental car rates available when you book their flights, often with a flexible hotel voucher program.

Less flexible car tours provide a rental car, a hotel plan, and a set itinerary that permits no deviation because the hotels all are reserved in advance. The deluxe car tours packaged by *AutoVenture* (425 Pike St., Suite 502, Seattle, WA 98101; phone: 800-426-7502 or 206-624-6033), whose tours come in either self-drive or chauffeured versions and feature some or many of the overnight stays in châteaux-hotels and inns belonging to France's first-rate *Relais & Châteaux* association, are of this type. The *French Experience* (370 Lexington Ave., Suite 812, New York, NY 10017; phone: 212-986-3800 or 212-986-1115 for car tours) also offers packaged self-drive tours featuring château accommodations in various regions of France, including Brittany and the Wine Country. For information on other packagers of car tours, see *Package Tours,* in this section.

LEASING: Anyone planning to be in Europe for 3 weeks or more should compare the cost of renting a car with that of leasing one for the same period. While the money saved by leasing — rather than renting for a 23-day (the minimum) or 30-day period — may not be great, what is saved over the course of a long-term lease — 45, 60, 90 days, or more — amounts to hundreds, even thousands, of dollars. Part of the saving is due to the fact that leased cars are exempt from the stiff taxes applicable to rented cars. In addition, leasing plans provide for collision insurance with no deductible amount, so there is no need to add the daily cost of collision damage waiver protection (an option offered by rental companies — see above). A further advantage of a car lease — actually, a financed purchase/repurchase plan — is that you reserve your car by specific make and model rather than by group only, and it is delivered to you fresh from the factory.

Leasing as described above is offered only in France and Belgium, and the savings it permits can be realized to the fullest only if cars are picked up and returned in these countries. Even in France, pick-up and drop-off locations are likely to be limited, and the charge for delivery to another location can be high, and on top of this must be added an identical return charge. If you don't intend to keep the car very long, the two charges can nullify the amount saved by leasing rather than renting, so you will have to do some arithmetic.

One of the major car leasing companies is *Renault,* offering leases of new cars for 23 days to 6 months. The cars are exempt from tax, all insurance is included, and there is no mileage charge. *Renault* offers free pick-up/drop-off at *Renault* branch offices in most major French cities; the car also may be picked up and returned at the airport (for an additional pick-up/drop-off charge). Variable charges apply to other locations elsewhere in Europe. For further information and reservations, ask your travel agent or contact *Renault USA,* 650 First Ave., New York, NY 10016 (phone: 212-532-1221 in New York State; 800-221-1052 elsewhere in the US).

Peugeot also offers a similar arrangement, called the "Peugeot Vacation Plan." In acccordance with the standard type of financed purchase/repurchase plan, travelers pick up the car in France, paying at the time of pick-up to use the car for a specified period of time (anywhere between 23 and 175 days), and at the end of this pre-arranged period return it to *Peugeot.* The tax-free temporary "purchase" includes unlimited mileage, factory warranty, full collision damage waiver coverage (no deductible), and 24-hour towing and roadside assistance. Pick-up and drop-off locations and charges are similar to *Renault*'s. *Peugeot*'s "European Delivery" program is a full-purchase program, including shipment of the car to the US, as discussed below. For further information, contact *Peugeot Motors of America* (1 Peugeot Plaza, PO Box 607, Lyndhurst, NJ 07071; phone: 201-935-8400). Some of the car rental firms listed above — *Auto-Europe, Europe by Car, Foremost Euro-Car,* and *Kemwel* — also arrange European car leases.

BUYING A CAR: If your plans include both buying a new car of European make and a driving tour of Europe, it's possible to combine the two ventures and save some money on each. By buying the car abroad and using it during your vacation, you pay quite a bit less for it than the US dealer would charge and at the same time avoid the expense of renting a car during your holiday. There are two basic ways to achieve this desired end, but one, factory delivery, is far simpler than the other, direct import.

Factory delivery means that you place an order for a car in the US, then pick it up in Europe, often literally at the factory gate. It also means that your new car is built to American specifications, complying with all US emission and safety standards. Because of this, only cars made by manufacturers who have established a formal program for such sales to American customers may be bought at the factory. At present, the list includes Audi, BMW, Jaguar, Mercedes-Benz, Porsche, Saab, Volkswagen, and Volvo, among others (whose manufacturers generally restrict their offerings to those models they ordinarily export to the US). The factory delivery price, in US dollars, usually runs about 5% to 15% below the sticker price of the same model at a US dealership and sometimes (depending on the manufacturer) includes the cost of shipping the car home. All contracts include US customs duty, but the cost of the incidentals and the insurance necessary for driving the car around Europe are extra, except in BMW's plan.

One of the few disadvantages of factory delivery is that car manufacturers make only a limited number of models available each year, and for certain popular models you may have to get in line early in the season. Another is that you must take your trip when the car is ready, not when you are, although you usually will have 8 to 10 weeks' notice. The actual place of delivery can vary; it is more economical to pick up the car at the factory, but arrangements sometimes — but not always — can be made to have it delivered elsewhere for an extra charge. For example, Jaguars (now owned by Ford) must be ordered through a US dealer and picked up at the factory in Coventry, England, although they also can be dropped off for shipment home in any number of European cities. For information, write to *Jaguar Cars,* 555 MacArthur Blvd., Mahwah, NJ 07430 (phone: 201-818-8500).

Cars for factory delivery usually can be ordered either through one of the manufacturer's authorized dealers in the US or through companies — among them *Europe by Car, Foremost Euro-Car,* and *Kemwel Group* (see above for contact information) — that specialize in such transactions. (Note that *Foremost Euro-Car* serves all of the US for rentals and leasing, but they arrange *sales* only for California residents.) Another company arranging car sales abroad is *Ship Side Tax Free World on Wheels BV,* 600B Lake St., Suite A, Ramsey, NJ 07446 (phone: 201-818-0400).

Occasionally an auto manufacturer offers free or discounted airfare in connection with a European delivery program. This year, Mercedes-Benz has a program including discounted round-trip airfare ($500 for two economy fare seats or one business class seat) from any US gateway served by *Delta, KLM,* or *Lufthansa* to Stuttgart (where the buyer picks up the car), plus a 2-night stay at the local *Hilton* or *Ramada* hotel, and 15 days' free comprehensive road insurance. For details, contact *Mercedes-Benz of North America,* 7700 Wisconsin Ave., Suite 1100, Bethesda, MD 20814 (phone: 800-458-8202).

The other way to buy a car abroad, **direct import**, sometimes is referred to as "gray market" buying. It is perfectly legal, but not totally hassle-free. Direct import means that you buy abroad a car that was meant for use abroad, not one built according to US specifications. It can be new or used, and may even include — if made for use in Ireland or Great Britain — a steering wheel on the right side. The main drawback to direct import is that the process of modification to bring the car into compliance with US standards is expensive and time-consuming; it typically costs from $5,000 to $7,000 in parts and labor and takes from 2 to 6 months. In addition, the same shipping, insurance, and miscellaneous expenses (another $2,000 to $5,000, according to estimates) that would be included in the factory delivery price must be added to the purchase price of the car, and the considerable burden of shepherding it on its journey from showroom to home garage usually is borne by the purchaser. Direct import dealers do exist (they are not the same as your local, factory-authorized foreign car dealer, with whom you are now in competition), but even if you use one, you still need to do a great deal of paperwork yourself.

Once upon a time, the main advantage of the direct import method — besides the fact that it can be used for makes and models not available in factory delivery programs — was that much more money could be saved importing an expensive car. Given today's exchange rates, however, the method's potential greater gain is harder to realize and must be weighed against its greater difficulties. Still, if direct importing interests you, you can obtain a list of those makes and models approved for conversion in this country, and of the converters licensed to bring them up to US specifications, by contacting the Environmental Protection Agency, Manufacturers' Operations Division, EN-340-F, Investigations/Imports Section, 401 M Street SW, Washington, DC 20460 (phone: 202-382-2479).

If you have special problems getting your car into the US, you might consider contacting a specialist in vehicle importation, such as Daniel Kokal, an independent regulatory consultant. His address is 15014 Kamputa Dr., Centerville, VA 22020 (phone: 703-818-9009).

Package Tours

If the mere thought of buying a package for travel to and through France conjures up visions of a race through ten cities in as many days in lockstep with a horde of frazzled fellow travelers, remember that packages have come a long way. For one thing, not all packages necessarily are escorted tours, and the one you buy does not have to include any organized touring at all — nor will it necessarily include traveling companions. If it does, however, you'll find that people of all sorts — many just like yourself — are taking advantage of packages today because they are economical and convenient, save you an immense amount of planning time, and exist in such variety that it's virtually impossible not to find one that suits at least the majority of your travel preferences. Given the high cost of travel these days, packages have emerged as a particularly wise buy.

In essence, a package is just an amalgam of travel services that can be purchased in a single transaction. A package (tour or otherwise) to and through France may include any or all of the following: round-trip transatlantic transportation, local transportation (and/or car rentals), accommodations, some or all meals, sightseeing, entertainment, transfers to and from the hotel at each destination, taxes, tips, escort service, and a variety of incidental features that might be offered as options at additional cost. In other words, a package can be any combination of travel elements, from a fully escorted tour offered at an all-inclusive price to a simple fly/drive booking allowing you to move about totally on your own. Its principal advantage is that it saves money: The cost of the combined arrangements invariably is well below the price of all of the same elements if bought separately, and particularly if transportation is provided by charter or discount flight, the whole package could cost less than just a round-trip economy airline ticket on a regularly scheduled flight. A package provides more than economy and convenience: It releases the traveler from having to make individual arrangements for each separate element of a trip.

Tour programs generally can be divided into two categories — "escorted" (or locally hosted) and "independent." An escorted tour means that a guide will accompany the group from the beginning of the tour through to the return flight; a locally hosted tour means that the group will be met upon arrival at each location by a different local host. On independent tours, there generally is a choice of hotels, meal plans, and sightseeing trips in each city, as well as a variety of special excursions. The independent plan is for travelers who do not want a totally set itinerary, but who do prefer confirmed hotel reservations. Whether choosing an escorted or independent tour, always bring along complete contact information for your tour operator in case a problem arises, although US tour operators often have European affiliates who can give additional assistance or make other arrangements on the spot.

To determine whether a package — or, more specifically, *which* package — fits your travel plans, start by evaluating your interests and needs, deciding how much and what you want to spend, see, and do. Gather whatever package tour information is available for your schedule. Be sure that you take the time to read the brochure *carefully* to determine precisely what is included. Keep in mind that travel brochures are written to entice you into signing up for a package tour. Often the language is deceptive and devious. For example, a brochure may quote the lowest prices for a package tour based on facilities that are unavailable during the off-season, undesirable at any season, or just plain nonexistent. Information such as "breakfast included" (as it often is in packages to France) or "plus tax" (which can add up) should be taken into account. Note, too, that the prices quoted in brochures almost always are based on double occupancy: The rate listed is for each of two people sharing a double room, and if you travel alone, the supplement for single accommodations can raise the price considerably (see *Hints for Single Travelers,* in this section).

In this age of erratic airfares, the brochure most often will *not* include the price of an airline ticket in the price of the package, though sample fares from various gateway cities usually will be listed separately as extras to be added to the price of the ground arrangements. Before figuring your actual cost, check the latest fares with the airlines, because the samples invariably are out of date by the time you read them. If the brochure gives more than one category of sample fares per gateway city — such as an individual tour-basing fare, a group fare, an excursion, APEX, or other discount ticket — your travel agent or airline tour desk will be able to tell you which one applies to the package you choose, depending on when you travel, how far in advance you book, and other factors. (An individual tour-basing fare is a fare computed as part of a package that includes land arrangements, thereby entitling a carrier to reduce the air portion almost to the absolute minimum. Though it always represents a saving over full-fare coach or economy, lately the individual tour-basing fare has not been as inexpensive as the excursion and other discount fares that also are available to individuals. The group fare usually is the least expensive fare, and it is the tour operator, not you, who makes up the group.) When the brochure does include round-trip transportation in the package price, don't forget to add the cost of round-trip transportation from your home to the departure city to come up with the total cost of the package.

Finally, read the general information regarding terms and conditions and the responsibility clause (usually in fine print at the end of the descriptive literature) to determine the precise elements for which the tour operator is — and is not — liable. Here the tour operator frequently expresses the right to change services or schedules as long as equivalent arrangements are offered. This clause also absolves the operator of responsibility for circumstances beyond human control, such as floods, or injury to you or your property. While reading, ask the following questions:

1. Does the tour include airfare or other transportation, sightseeing, meals, transfers, taxes, baggage handling, tips, or any other services? Do you want all these services?
2. If the brochure indicates that "some meals" are included, does this mean a welcoming and farewell dinner, two breakfasts, or every evening meal?
3. What classes of hotels are offered? If you will be traveling alone, what is the single supplement?
4. Does the tour itinerary or price vary according to the season?
5. Are the prices guaranteed; that is, if costs increase between the time you book and the time you depart, can surcharges unilaterally be added?
6. Do you get a full refund if you cancel? If not, be sure to obtain cancellation insurance.
7. Can the operator cancel if too few people join? At what point?

One of the consumer's biggest problems is finding enough information to judge the reliability of a tour packager, since individual travelers seldom have direct contact with the firm putting the package together. Usually, a retail travel agent is interposed between customer and tour operator, and much depends on his or her candor and cooperation. So ask a number of questions about the tour you are considering. For example:

- Has the travel agent ever used a package provided by this tour operator?
- How long has the tour operator been in business? Check the Better Business Bureau in the area where the tour operator is based to see if any complaints have been filed against it.
- Is the tour operator a member of the *United States Tour Operators Association*

(*USTOA;* 211 E. 51st St., Suite 12B, New York, NY 10022; phone: 212-944-5727)? The *USTOA* will provide a list of its members on request; it also offers a useful brochure, *How to Select a Package Tour.*

● How many and which companies are involved in the package?
● If air travel is by charter flight, is there an escrow account in which deposits will be held; if so, what is the name of the bank?

This last question is very important. US law requires that tour operators place every charter passenger's deposit and subsequent payment in a proper escrow account. Money paid into such an account cannot legally be used except to pay for the costs of a particular package or as a refund if the trip is canceled. To ensure the safe handling of your money, make your check payable to the escrow account — by law, the name of the depository bank must appear in the operator-participant contract, and usually is found in that mass of minuscule type on the back of the brochure. Write the details of the charter, including the destination and dates, on the face of the check; on the back, print "For Deposit Only." Your travel agent may prefer that you make your check out to the agency, saying that it will then pay the tour operator the fee minus commission. But it is perfectly legal to write your check as we suggest, and if your agent objects too strongly (the agent should have sufficient faith in the tour operator to trust him or her to send the proper commission), consider taking your business elsewhere. If you don't make your check out to the escrow account, you lose the protection of that escrow should the trip be canceled or the tour operator or travel agent fail. Furthermore, recent bankruptcies in the travel industry have served to point out that even the protection of escrow may not be enough to safeguard your investment. Increasingly, insurance is becoming a necessity (see *Insurance,* in this section), and payment by credit card has become popular since it offers some additional safeguards if the tour operator defaults.

■ **A word of advice:** Purchasers of vacation packages who feel they're not getting their money's worth are more likely to get a refund if they complain in writing to the operator — and bail out of the whole package immediately. Alert the tour operator or resort manager to the fact that you are dissatisfied, that you will be leaving for home as soon as transportation can be arranged, and that you expect a refund. They may have forms to fill out detailing your complaint; otherwise, state your case in a letter. Even if the difficulty in arranging immediate transportation home detains you, your dated, written complaint should help in procuring a refund from the operator.

SAMPLE PACKAGES TO FRANCE: There are so many packages available to France today that it's probably safe to say that just about any arrangement anyone might want is available for as long as it is wanted, whether it's to hit the highlights from Le Mont St-Michel to Monte Carlo, to explore a selected region in depth, or to visit only Paris. The keynote is flexibility.

Escorted Tours – Those seeking the maximum in structure will find that the classic sightseeing tour by motorcoach, fully escorted and all-inclusive (or nearly), has withstood the test of time and still is well represented among the programs of the major tour operators. Typically, these tours begin in Paris and take 2 weeks — or more — to trace a rough loop westward through Normandy and Brittany, south to the Loire Valley, the Dordogne, the Bordeaux region, and the Pyrénées, then east across Languedoc to Provence and the French Riviera, with excursions to Monaco possible from the final stopping place at Nice. Tours that trace the half circle in reverse, beginning in Nice and finishing in Paris, are equally common. Longer programs may make a full circle around the whole of France, adding the Alps, the Burgundy wine region, Alsace, Lorraine, and more to the itinerary. Shorter programs — some as short as 1 week — tend to explore a selected region — for instance, the châteaux country — in depth.

Hotel accommodations in these packages usually are characterized as first class or better, with private baths or showers accompanying all rooms, although more than a few tour packagers offer less expensive alternatives by providing more modest lodgings. These packages tend to be all-inclusive, although the number of included meals may vary considerably. Among such packages are the following:

Abercrombie & Kent (1520 Kensington Rd., Oak Brook, IL 60521; phone: 708-954-2944 in Illinois; 800-323-7308 elsewhere in the US). Offers all-inclusive package tours that take care of just about everything — right down to a traveling bellhop to handle your baggage. The Great France Express, a 12-day rail tour, allows its participants to see Aix-en-Provence, Avignon, Dijon, Monte Carlo, Nice, Paris, and many other great French cities at a leisurely pace.

AESU (248 W. Quadrangle, Village of Cross Keys, Baltimore, MD 21210; phone: 800-638-7640 or 410-323-4416). This tour operator, which specializes in accommodating travelers between the ages of 18 and 35, offers a wide variety of European packages. Ranging from 18 to 50 days in length, almost all include a 2- to 3-day excursion to Paris.

American Express Travel Related Services (offices throughout the US; phone: 800-241-1700 for information and local branch offices). On their motorcoach tours of Europe, travelers can choose from a number of different itineraries, including a 16-day Tour de France that circles the country, visiting Bordeaux, Cannes, Dijon, Mont St-Michel, Nice, and Paris. Another 16-day tour, La Belle France, takes in the capital, as well as Bordeaux, Cannes, Carcassonne, Normandy, and St-Malo in Brittany. Their 10-day French Impressions tour stops in Caen, Mont St-Michel, Orléans, and Paris. This company also offers tours that include visits to France as part of broader European itineraries and which visit some of the country's major cities.

DER Tours (11933 Wilshire Blvd., Los Angeles, CA 90025; phone: 800-937-1234). This company's 14-day Wonderful France tour visits more than 10 cities.

English Homes and Country Tours (Coombe House, Sharnden, Mayfield, East Sussex, TN20 6QA; phone: 44-435-872097). A British company that offers a 14-day escorted tour from Paris to Burgundy and the Loire Valley.

Especially France (1398 Diamond Mountain Rd., Calistoga, CA 94515; phone: 800-FRANCE-X or 707-942-4582). Aside from their regularly offered escorted tours of France, this company offers trips with a more specialized focus, such as a photographic expedition through the country.

Globus-Gateway and *Cosmos* (95-25 Queens Blvd., Rego Park, NY 11374; phone: 800-221-0090; or 150 S. Los Robles Ave., Pasadena, CA 91101; phone: 818-449-2019 or 800-556-5454). These affiliated agencies offer numerous tours of Europe, including an 11-day tour of Brittany, the châteaux country, Normandy, and Paris that begins in London; a 14-day La France tour that travels throughout the country, taking in Cannes, the Loire Valley, Lyons, Nice, Normandy, and Paris; and a 23-day Treasures of France, Spain, and Portugal tour that visits Avignon, Bordeaux, and Paris. (Bookings for both agencies must be made through travel agents; however, both can be contacted for information.)

Grandtravel (6900 Wisconsin Ave., Suite 706, Chevy Chase, MD 20815; phone: 301-986-0790 in Maryland; 800-247-7651 elsewhere in the US). This company specializes in grandparents traveling with grandchildren and offers itineraries suitable for those from ages 7 to 90. The 15-day Glories of France program covers Paris and over 14 other French cities.

In Quest of the Classics (316 Mission Ave., Oceanside, CA 92054; phone: 800-227-1393 or 619-721-1123 in California; 800-221-5246 elsewhere in the US). Customizes packages for groups with specialized interests, such as French history, culture, or fashion.

Maupintour (PO Box 807, Lawrence, KS 66044; phone: 800-255-4266). Offers a 12-day France Highlights tour that begins in Paris and travels to the Loire

Valley, Mont St-Michel, and elsewhere in Normandy, before returning to Paris. Another 14-day trip from Paris visits Brittany, Britain's Channel Islands, and Mont St-Michel.

Odyssey Adventures (89 Auburn St., Suite 1199, Portland, ME 04103; phone: 800-544-3216 or 207-878-8650). Specializes in cultural adventures for teenagers, and offers a 7-day train and biking tour from Paris to Brittany, which ends in Grindelwald (Switzerland).

Olson Travelworld (1334 Parkview Ave., Suite 210, Manhattan Beach, CA 90266; phone: 213-546-8400; 800-421-5785 in California; 800-421-2255 elsewhere in the US). Offers escorted, highly structured packages, including a 21-day Treasures of France tour that covers Avignon, Bordeaux, Burgundy, Cannes, Carcassonne, Dijon, Grenoble, Normandy, Paris, and the Riviera, with a special excursion to view some of France's prehistoric cave sites in the Dordogne. Also offered is a 16-day French Masters tour, visiting many of the cities mentioned above.

Pleasure Break (1350 E. Touhy Ave., Des Plaines, IL 60018; phone: 708-297-5738 in Illinois; 800-777-1885 elsewhere in the US). Offers a 16-day Windmills, Canals, Castles, and Capitals tour of Europe, including stays in Paris and other French cities. The company is a wholesaler, so contact your travel agent.

Solrep International (3271 W. Alabama St., Houston, TX 77098; phone: 713-529-5547 in Texas; 800-231-0985 elsewhere in the US). Offers several motorcoach tours throughout France, some of which visit other European countries as well.

Student Travel International (STI) (8619 Reseda Blvd., Suite 103, Northridge, CA 91324; phone: 800-525-0525). Offers 16- to 63-day comprehensive tours of Europe, all of which include visits to popular French destinations like Paris and the Riviera.

Tauck Tours (PO Box 5027, Westport, CT 06881-5027; phone: 203-226-6911). Offers 13-day escorted tours of France, Belgium, and the Netherlands.

Thomas Cook (Headquarters: 45 Berkeley St., Piccadilly, London W1A 1EB, England; phone: 44-71-499-4000). The best known of all British tour operators, its name is practically synonymous with the Grand Tour of Europe, but *Cook*'s wide range of itineraries spans the world. Among the packages to France is a 15-day Grand Tour of France, an escorted motorcoach tour visiting Avignon, Bordeaux, Burgundy, the Loire Valley, Mont St-Michel and elsewhere in Normandy, Nice, and Paris. (Note that although this company is a wholesaler, you can book a tour directly through any of its offices in major cities in North America, as well as through travel agents.)

Trafalgar Tours (11 E. 26th St., New York, NY 10010; phone: 212-689-8977 in New York City; 800-854-0103 elsewhere in the US). Offers numerous first class (as well as some budget) motorcoach itineraries of the Continent. Among the regular itineraries is a 14-day, 9-city Best of France motorcoach tour and a 9-day Châteaux and Champagne package, visiting Cannes, the Loire Valley, Mont St-Michel, and Reims. (As this operator is a wholesaler, bookings must be made through a travel agent.)

Travcoa (PO Box 2630, Newport Beach, CA 92658; phone: 714-476-2800; 800-992-2004 in California; 800-992-2003 elsewhere in the US). Offers a lineup of escorted motorcoach tours, including 17-, 19-, or 30-day packages in France that include all meals. Among its 17-day packages are the Vive La France tour, visiting all the major cities in France, and a Normandy, Brittany, and Châteaux tour. In addition, their Exotic France tour, ranging in length from 19 to 24 days, takes in some of the less traveled destinations in France.

TWA Getaway Tours (phone: 800-GETAWAY). Offers a wide variety of motorcoach tours throughout Europe, including a 15-day escorted tour of France and Monaco.

X.O. Travel Consultants (38 W. 32nd St., Suite 1009, New York, NY 10001; phone: 800-262-9682 or 212-947-5530). This special-interest expert offers customized group tours to France, focusing on French wine, food, gardens, and manor houses.

Independent Tours – Less restrictive arrangements for travelers who prefer more independence than that found on escorted tours are listed in the semi-escorted and hosted sections of tour catalogues. These may combine some aspects of an escorted tour, such as moving from place to place by motorcoach, with longer stays in one spot, where participants are at liberty but a host or hostess — that is, a representative of the tour company — is available at a local office or even in the hotel to answer questions and assist in arranging activities and optional excursions.

Another equally common type of package to France is the car tour or fly/drive arrangement, often described in brochures as a self-drive or go-as-you-please tour. These are independent vacations, geared to travelers who want to cover as much ground as they might on an escorted group sightseeing tour but who prefer to do it on their own. The most flexible plans include no more than a map, a rental car, and a block of as many prepaid hotel vouchers as are needed for the length of the stay (the packages typically are 4 or 7 days long, extendable by individual extra days or additional package segments), along with a list of participating hotels at which the vouchers are accepted. In most cases, only the first night's accommodation is reserved; from then on, travelers book their rooms one stop ahead as they drive from place to place, creating their own itinerary as they go. When the hotels are members of a chain or association — which they usually are — the staff of the last hotel will reserve the next one for you. In other cases, there may be a choice of reserving all accommodations before departure — usually for a fee. Operators offering these packages usually sell vouchers in more than one price category; travelers may have the option of upgrading accommodations by paying a supplement directly to more expensive establishments or can economize by choosing to stay in a modest inn, guesthouse, or bed and breakfast establishment. Another type of fly/drive arrangement is slightly more restrictive in that the tour packager supplies an itinerary that must be followed day by day, with a specific hotel to be reached each night. Often these plans are more deluxe as well.

Fly/drive packages to and around France include the following:

Abercrombie & Kent (1520 Kensington Rd., Oak Brook, IL 60521; phone: 708-954-2944 in Illinois; 800-323-7308 elsewhere in the US). Their independent itineraries include 7-day to 10-day self-drive or chauffeured tours of France, including stays in hotels that are converted manor houses, castles, and other stately homes.

AutoVenture (425 Pike Street, Suite 502, Seattle, WA 98101; phone: 206-624-6033 in Washington State; 800-426-7502 elsewhere in the US). This company's deluxe car tours feature overnight stays in hotels that are elegant converted castles or manor houses or old and distinctive country inns, most of them members of the prestigious *Relais & Châteaux* association, known for its overall high standards. Any of *AutoVenture*'s six French itineraries, 6 to 14 days in length, can be bought in either a self-drive or a chauffeured version.

David B. Mitchell & Company (200 Madison Ave., New York, NY 10016; phone: 800-372-1323 or 212-889-4822). Also offers luxurious self-drive or chauffeured tours, including 7- to 14-day tours of central France and along the Riviera.

DER Tours (11933 Wilshire Blvd., Los Angeles, CA 90025; phone: 800-937-1234). Offers fly/drive packages in and around Paris.

DMI Tours (14340 Memorial Dr., Suite 117, Houston, TX 77079; phone: 800-553-

5090 or 713-558-9933). The US representative of *Château-Accueil,* a French association of châteaux-hotels, *DMI* offers fly/drive packages featuring stays at member establishments, all of which are historical châteaux properties.

Extra Value Travel (683 S. Collier Blvd., Marco Island, FL 33937; phone: 800-336-4668). In conjunction with international car rental companies, offers week-long fly/drive bookings throughout France.

The French Experience (370 Lexington Ave., New York, NY 10017; phone: 212-986-1115). Offers fly/drive programs throughout France. Travelers can choose from among different kinds of accommodations, such as condominiums, cottages, and villas.

Marsans International Travel (19 W. 34th St., Suite 302, New York, NY 10001; phone: 212-239-3880 in New York State; 800-777-9110 elsewhere in the US). Packages 3- to 7-day car rental packages that can be booked along with airfare and accommodations for a custom fly/drive package.

Unitours (8 S. Michigan Ave., Chicago, IL 60603; phone: 312-782-1590). Offers 7-day fly/drive packages throughout France. (This company is a wholesaler, so contact your travel agent.)

■ **Custom-Made France:** Travelers interested in creating their own personalized itineraries now can take advantage of a new service offered by the French Government Tourist Board through its "France On Call" hotline (900-990-0040; 50¢ a minute throughout the US). Callers can obtain customized travel itineraries, including maps and detailed driving instructions, as well as answers over the phone to any questions they may have about their proposed trip. Callers also can request the following publications: the 1993 *France Discovery Guide,* which includes profiles of nine regions in France, with suggested excursions and lists of noteworthy sites (as well as exact mileage from one destination to another); a listing of 1,000 *"hotels de charm,"* throughout France; and the *AT&T France Fun Book,* which has 100 free coupons for discounts on shopping, restaurants, museums, and other tourist attractions. Once in France, continued assistance is available from the more than 1,000 *American Express* Welcome Centers located throughout the country, as well as through the company's toll-free hotline (phone: 05-201-202 from anywhere in France), where they can obtain information and answers to their questions (in English).

Stay-Put City and Resort Packages – A further possibility for independent travelers is a "stay put" package in France. These appeal to travelers who want to be on their own and remain in one place for the duration of their vacation, although it is not unusual for travelers to buy more than one package at a time.

Not surprisingly, since Paris is of such great interest to visitors, the Paris city package is the most popular. Basically, a city package — no matter what the city — includes round-trip transfers between airport and hotel, a choice of accommodations (usually including continental breakfast) in several price ranges, plus any of a number of other features you may not need or want but would lose valuable time arranging if you did. Common package features are 1 or 2 half-day guided tours of the city; in Paris, a boat cruise on the Seine; passes for unlimited travel by métro (subway) or bus; discount cards for shops, museums, and restaurants; temporary membership in and admission to clubs, casinos, discotheques, or other nightspots; and car rental for some or all of your stay. Other features may be anything from a souvenir travel bag to a tasting of local wines or dinner and a show.

These packages usually are a week long — although 4-day and 14-day packages also are available, amd most packages can be extended by extra days — and often are hosted; that is, a representative of the tour company may be available at a local office or even in the hotel to answer questions, handle problems, and assist in arranging activities and optional excursions. A similar stay-put resort package generally omits the sightseeing tour and may offer some sort of daily meal plan if accommodations are in hotels; accommodations in apartment hotels with kitchenettes are another common alternative.

Among the stay-put packages offered in France are the following:

American Express Travel Related Services (offices throughout the US; phone: 800-241-1700 for information and local branch offices). Offers 2-night city packages in Lyons, Monte Carlo, Nice, and Paris that can be added to many of their longer packages.

AutoVenture (425 Pike St., Suite 502, Seattle, WA 98101; phone: 206-624-6033 in Washington; 800-426-7502 elsewhere in the US). Offers city packages in Paris with sightseeing by chauffeured luxury car.

Brendan Tours (15137 Califa St., Van Nuys, CA 91411; phone: 800-421-8446 or 818-785-9696). Offers 8-day, locally hosted city tours in Paris. (This company is a wholesaler, so arrangements must be made through a travel agent.)

British Airways Holidays (phone: 800-AIRWAYS). Offers a 6-night combination Paris/London city package and an 11-day combination city package in London, Paris, and Rome.

Cavalcade Tours (2200 Fletcher Ave., Ft. Lee, NJ 07024; phone: 800-356-2405 or 201-346-9061). Offers 7-night packages in Paris. (As this tour operator is a wholesaler, bookings must be made through a travel agent.)

Châteaux Accueil (c/o *DMI Tours,* 14340 Memorial Dr., Houston, TX 77079; phone: 800-553-5090). Offers stay-put packages at private châteaux. Owners are in residence, often functioning as hosts, and in many cases English is spoken.

Continental Grand Destinations (PO Box 1460, Milwaukee, WI 53201-1460; phone: 800-634-5555). Offers 4- or 8-day city packages in Paris.

David B. Mitchell & Company (200 Madison Ave., New York, NY 10016; phone: 800-372-1323 or 212-889-4822). Offers luxury city programs in Paris and other major cities in France, featuring select deluxe hotels.

Delta's Dream Vacations (PO Box 1525, Fort Lauderdale, FL 33302; phone: 800-872-7786). Paris city packages with a 3-night minimum stay, offered by *Delta Airlines.*

DER Tours (11933 Wilshire Blvd., Los Angeles, CA 90025; phone: 800-937-1234). Offers city packages with a 3-night minimum stay in Paris and other cities in France.

DMI Tours (14340 Memorial Dr., Suite 117, Houston, TX 77079; phone: 800-553-5090 or 713-558-9933). The US representative of *Château Accueil,* a French association of châteaux hotels, *DMI* offers independent city packages all over France featuring members of the association, all of which are historical châteaux properties.

Five Star Touring (60 E. 42nd St., New York, NY 10165; phone: 800-792-7827 or 212-818-9140). Offers customized city packages to Paris, some including a private chauffeur-guide and car.

H.S.A. Voyages (formerly *H.S. & Associates,* 160 E. 26th St., Suite 5H, New York, NY 10010; phone: 800-927-4765 or 212-689-5400). Offers independent packages to Paris and other cities in France, most including a choice of half- or full-day sightseeing tours.

In Quest of the Classics (316 Mission Ave., Oceanside, CA 92054; phone: 800-227-1393 or 619-721-1123 in California; 800-221-5246 elsewhere in the US). Offers independent city packages in Paris.

Jet Vacations (1775 Broadway, New York, NY 10019; phone: 212-247-0999 or

800-JET-0999). Offers Paris city packages with a wide range of hotel choices, as well as stay-put packages along the Riviera in Cannes, La Napoule, Monte Carlo, or Nice.

Petrabax Tours (97-45 Queens Blvd., Suite 505, Rego Park, NY 11374; phone: 718-897-7272 in New York State; 800-367-6611 elsewhere in the US). Offers 6-night packages in Paris.

Solrep International (2524 Nottingham, PO Box 6799, Houston TX 77265; phone: 800-231-0985 or 713-529-5547). Offers independent city packages in Paris featuring accommodations in first class and luxury hotels in the city and historic châteaux in its suburbs.

Take-A-Guide (11 Uxbridge St., London W8 7TQ, England; in US call 800-825-4946). Offers packages in Paris that include a private, chauffeured car.

Thomas Cook (Headquarters: 45 Berkeley St., Piccadilly, London W1A 1EB, England; phone: 44-71-499-4000). Offers independent city packages to the island of Corsica.

TWA Getaway Tours (phone: 800-GETAWAY). Offers numerous city packages throughout Europe, including a 7-day, 6-night Paris Rendezvous package.

Another good example of a stay-put vacation is the resort package offered by *Club Med*, which operates its own resort villages around the world and has 12 resorts in France (9 in the Alps, 1 in Nice, and the other two in central France). For further information, contact *Club Med* (40 W. 57th St., New York, NY 10019; phone: 800-CLUB-MED) or ask a travel agent.

Special-Interest Packages – Special interest tours are a growing sector of the travel industry. Programs focusing on food and wine are prominent among the packages of this sort put together for visitors to France. Note, though, that they tend to be quite structured arrangements rather than independent ones, and they rarely are created with the budget traveler in mind. Also note that inclusive as they may be, few food and wine tours include *all* meals in the package price. This is not necessarily a cost cutting technique on the part of the packager; rather, because of the lavishness of some of the meals, others may be left to the discretion of the participants, not only to allow time for leisure, but also to allow for differing rates of metabolism. Similarly, even on wine tours that spend entire days in practically full-time tasting, unlimited table wine at meals may not always be included in the package price. The brochures usually are clear about what comes with the package and when.

Among the various food and wine tours are *Bacchants' Pilgrimages'* annual 3-week Southern France Classic tour, which visits châteaux, vineyards, and wine cellars from the Loire Valley to Cognac, Bordeaux, the Cotes du Rhône, Burgundy, Champagne, and Paris, tasting all the way. Included are winery-hosted luncheons, picnics, dinners in three-star restaurants, and other luncheons and dinners in restaurants of lesser renown. Bookings are through travel agents or *Bacchants' Pilgrimages* (475 Sansome St., Suite 840, San Francisco, CA 94111; phone: 415-981-8518). And for groups of 10 or more travelers, *Travel Concepts* (62 Commonwealth Ave., Suite 3, Boston, MA 02116; phone: 617-266-8450) offers a variety of custom-designed food and wine tours throughout Europe. Although there is no pre-planned itinerary in France, they can design one.

There also are special-interest packages catering to travelers particularly interested in the arts and/or cultural studies. Among these are the packages for classical music and opera lovers offered by *Dailey-Thorp* (330 W. 58th St., New York, NY 10019-1817; phone: 212-307-1555), which visit various French musical events, including the *Aix-en-Provence International Festival of Lyric Art and Music,* the *Orange Festival,* and the *Biennale de la Musique Française* in Lyons.

For art enthusiasts, *Prospect Art Tours* (454-458 Chiswick High Rd., London

W45TT, England; phone: 44-81-995-2151 or 44-81-995-2163) offers 5- to 15-day packages visiting key museums, private galleries, and art collections throughout Europe, including France. Artwork of France's earliest inhabitants can be explored through the Cave Art of France package offered by *Past Time Tours* (800 Larch La., Sacramento, CA 95864-5042; phone: 916-485-8140). The 14- to 21-day tours include educational lectures and a look at some of the world's most intriguing prehistoric ritual art and symbols. Leaving from Paris, the tour begins in Toulouse and continues on to Foix and Les Eyzies.

Inland waterway trips on canal or river barges outfitted as hotels are another type of special-interest package in France. Because the pace is slow, these trips frequently appeal to second-time visitors as a way to see a very small section of the country in depth. Hotel barges can carry as few as 6 to 8 or as many as 24 passengers in addition to crews of 3 to 8 people, and while the atmosphere and dress aboard are casual, the accommodations (most have cabins with private bathrooms) and attention paid to food (all meals usually are included, with unlimited table wine common) make many of the cruises quite luxurious. Packages usually are by the week, though shorter and longer ones exist. Among companies offering such packages are the following:

Abercrombie & Kent/Continental Waterways (1520 Kensington Rd., Suite 212, Oakbrook, IL 60521; phone: 708-954-2944 in Illinois; 800-323-7308 elsewhere). Offers 3- to 9-day cruise packages through Bordeaux, Burgundy, and the Loire and Rhône valleys.

French Country Waterways (PO Box 2195, Duxbury, MA 02331; phone: 800-222-1236 or 617-934-2454). Their waterway cruises of Burgundy include a week-long Wine Cruise and a Gourmet Cruise; both feature shore excursions to Michelin-starred restaurants.

The French Experience (370 Lexington Ave., New York, NY 10017; phone: 800-28-FRANCE or 212-986-1115). This company represents the *Crown Blue Line,* a European inland waterway cruising specialist, and offers 8 different itineraries in regions throughout France. Passengers can choose between weekend mini-cruises and longer sailings of up to 3 weeks.

French Cruise Lines (701 Lee St., Des Plaines, IL 60016; phone: 800-222-8664). Offers cruises on the rivers Rhône, Saône, and Seine, all on board its fleet of luxury yachts.

Skipper Travel Service (210 California Ave., Palo Alto, CA 94306; phone: 415-321-5658). Represents 6 different barging companies in Europe, most of which offer cruises exclusively in France.

For further information on companies booking self-drive boats, as well as passage on hotel-boat cruises, see *Traveling by Ship,* in this section.

For travelers interested in touring by rail, the plush *Venice Simplon–Orient Express* includes a stop in Paris on its deluxe excursions. Although it spends only a brief time on French soil, it provides a fine add-on to either the beginning or end of a Paris stay. For information, contact *Venice Simplon–Orient Express* (1155 Ave. of the Americas, 30th Floor, New York, NY 10036; phone: 800-524-2420 or 212-302-5055). For further information, see *Traveling by Train,* in this section.

The *Bombard Society* (6727 Curran St., McLean, VA 22101; phone: 800-862-8537 or 703-448-9407) offers aerial tours of the French countryside. Their Great Balloon Adventure, offered in 4- or 5-day programs in Burgundy and the Loire Valley from spring through fall, includes daily flights via hot-air balloon (flown by pilots, not tour participants), sightseeing, hotel accommodations, and meals, many of which are candlelit buffets served after the day's flight.

Sports Packages – Ski packages are foremost among the sports-related packages to France. The foundation of the package usually is a week or two of hotel or condominium accommodations at a ski resort (Avoriaz, Chamonix, Courchevel, Les Menuires, Tignes, and Val d'Isère are the common destinations), and for those choosing the hotel rather than the apartment, the price often includes a meal plan of breakfast and dinner daily. The other features of a ski vacation — round-trip bus, train, or rental car transportation between the airport and the resort, ski passes, baggage handling, taxes, and tips — are included in varying combinations according to the packager. If transatlantic transportation is by charter flight (not unusual on ski packages), airfare, too, may be included in the price. If not, the applicable "group ski" or other fare will be listed separately. The following companies offer ski packages in France:

Adventures on Skis (815 North Rd., Westfield, MA 01085; phone: 800-628-9655 or 413-568-2855). Offers 7-day packages at 12 different ski resorts in the French Alps.

Alpine Skiing and Travel (534 New State Hwy., Raynham, MA 02767; phone: 508-823-7707; 800-551-8822 in Massachusetts; 800-343-9676 elsewhere in the US). Offers 7-day packages in resorts throughout the Alps.

American Express Travel Related Services (offices throughout the US; phone: 800-241-1700 for information and local branch offices). Offers 9-day packages in Mont Blanc, with accommodations in the mountain village of Chamonix.

Club Med (40 W. 57th St., New York, NY 10019; phone: 800-CLUB-MED). There are club hotels in a number of French ski resorts, and vacation packages there include lessons at the club's private ski schools.

Donna Franca Tours (470 Commonwealth Ave., Boston, MA 02215; phone: 617-227-3111 in Massachusetts; 800-225-6290 elsewhere in the US). Offers ski packages in Les Deux Alpes, Mont Blanc, and Val Cenis.

Powder Ski Adventures (24196 Alicia Parkway, Mission Viejo, CA 92691; phone: 800-888-6262 or 714-859-7919). Offers 1- to 2-week ski packages throughout the Alps.

Steve Lohr's Skiworld and Travel (206 Central Ave., Jersey City, NJ, 07307; phone: 201-798-3900 in New Jersey; 800-223-1306 elsewhere). Offers 7-day packages at most of the major ski resorts in France.

Golf courses in many European countries are a fairly new addition; however, the courses in France have been around for quite some time. The following companies all offer custom golf tours throughout France (they recommend courses and a basic itinerary and you design the package):

Adventure Golf Holiday (815 North Rd., Westfield, MA 01085; phone: 800-628-9655 or 413-568-2855).

Adventures in Golf (29 Valencia Dr., Nashua, NH 03062; phone: 603-882-8367).

Golf Intercontinental/Marsans (19 W. 34 St., New York, NY 10001; phone: 212-239-3880 in New York State; 800-223-6114 elsewhere in the US).

Golf International (275 Madison Ave., New York, NY 10016; phone: 212-986-9176).

Golfing Holidays (231 E. Millbrae Ave., Millbrae, CA 94030; phone: 415-697-0230).

InterGolf (745 Atlantic Ave., Suite 730, Boston, MA 02111; phone: 617-426-6383).

ITC Golf Tours (4134 Atlantic Ave., Suite 205, Long Beach, CA 90807; phone: 800-257-4981 or 310-595-6905).

Wide World of Golf (PO Box 5217, Carmel, CA 93921; phone: 408-624-6667).

Tennis and golf tours operated in conjunction with canal cruises are organized by *Grand Slam Tennis Tours* (PO Box 5132, La Quinta, CA 92253; phone: 619-340-3166). The latest additions to their programs are two Tennis Experience tours. The first, from the last week of May through mid-June, includes center-court seats to the *French Open International Tennis Championship* in Paris; the second, Château Tennis, a week-long program, runs several times between May and October, and includes stays at three different châteaux (2 nights at each). The company also arranges independent tours to the *French Open*. And *Jet Vacations* (address above) takes groups to the *French Open* via the *Concorde*.

Horseback riding holidays (for accomplished riders) in France — in the regions of Beaujolais, Brittany, the Dordogne, the Loire Valley, Provence, and the Pyrénées for 1 or 2 weeks — are arranged by *FITS Equestrian* (685 Lateen Rd., Solvang, CA 93463; phone: 805-688-9494). *Equitour* (PO Box 807, Dubois, WY 82513; phone: 307-455-3363 in Wyoming; 800-545-0019 elsewhere in the US) also offers packages — not for beginners — that include 7 days discovering the Loire Valley and Provence on horseback.

Fisherfolk might enjoy the opportunity to fish private waterways along the Rilse River offered by *Fishing International* (PO Box 959, Pearce Mill Rd., Wexford, PA 15090; phone: 412-935-1577 in Pennsylvania; 800-245-1950 elsewhere in the US). These week-long packages include accommodations in small country inns and breakfast daily, and the opportunity to exchange fish stories about the Gallic one that got away with fellow enthusiasts. This company also designs custom fishing packages.

Special-interest tours for practitioners and spectators of other sports include many bicycle and hiking tours of varying levels of difficulty. For the names and addresses of their organizers, see *Camping and Caravanning, Hiking and Biking,* below.

Camping and Caravanning, Hiking and Biking

CAMPING: France welcomes campers, whether they come alone or with a group, with tents or in recreational vehicles-generally known in Europe as "caravans" (a term that technically refers to towable campers as opposed to fully motorized vehicles, known as "minibuses" or "minivans"). Camping probably is the best way to enjoy the French countryside. And fortunately, campgrounds in France are plentiful — there are over 8,500 of them.

Where to Camp – Caravanning is extremely popular with European vacationers, and many parks cater more to the caravanner than to the tent dweller. Some campgrounds have minimal facilities, and others are quite elaborate, with a variety of amenities on the premises. Most sites are open from about *Easter* through October.

Although there may be an occasional language barrier, directors of campgrounds often have a great deal of information about their region, and some even will arrange local tours or recommend sports facilities or attractions in the immediate area. Campgrounds also provide the atmosphere and opportunity to meet other travelers and exchange useful information. Too much so, sometimes — the popularity of European campgrounds causes them to be quite crowded during the summer, and campsites can be so close together that any attempt at privacy or getting away from it all is sabotaged. As campgrounds fill quickly throughout the season, and the more isolated sites always go first, it's a good idea to arrive early in the day and reserve your chosen spot — which leaves you free to explore the area for the rest of the day. (Whenever possible, try to call ahead and arrange a "pitch" in advance. At the height of the season, if you do not have advance reservations, you may be lucky to get even a less desirable site.)

In some communities, it is possible to camp free on public grounds. Ask the local police or local tourism information office about regulations. To camp on private property you first must obtain the permission of the landowner or tenant — and assume the responsibility of leaving the land exactly as you found it in return for the hospitality.

Most French campgrounds are well marked. Still, it's best to have a map or check the information available in one of the numerous comprehensive guides to sites across the Continent and/or the sources listed below. It may not be easy to find camping facilities open before June or after September, so a guide that gives this information comes in particularly handy off-season. When in difficulty, remember that tourist information offices throughout France can direct visitors to sites in the areas they serve.

The following organizations and publications will help in planning camping excursions in France:

Association Camping Club de France (218 Bd. St-Germain, Paris 75008; phone: 1-45-48-30-03). Provides specific information on member campgrounds.

Association Camping Qualité France (105 Rue Lafayette, Paris 75010; phone: 1-48-78-13-77). Publishes a guide rating campgrounds by stars.

Camping et Caravaning France is a comprehensive Michelin guide covering more than 2,000 campgrounds throughout France; unfortunately it currently is published only in French. It is available for $14.95 in bookstores throughout France and in some travel bookstores and French-language bookstores in the US, and can be ordered from Michelin Guides and Maps, PO Box 3305, Spartanburg, SC 29304-3305 (phone: 803-599-0850 in South Carolina; 800-423-0485 elsewhere in the US).

Fédération Française de Camping et de Caravaning (78 Rue de Rivoli, Paris 75004; phone: 1-42-72-84-08). This national federation of campgrounds will provide a list of its members upon request.

Fédération Nationale des Gîtes Ruraux de France (35 Rue Godot-de-Mauroy, Paris 75009; phone: 1-47-42-25-43). Issues a list of farms where camping is permitted.

French for Travellers is a pocket-size guide which devotes five pages to camping vocabulary, including such phrases as *"Pouvons-nous camper dans votre champ?"* ("May we camp in your field?"). It is available for $5.95 from Macmillan Publishing, Front and Brown Sts., Riverside, NJ 08075 (phone: 800-257-5755).

Union Nationale des Associations de Tourisme (8 Rue César-Franck, Paris 75015; phone: 1-43-06-88-21). This organization of tourism-related service associations can direct you to appropriate sources of information, including data on campgrounds.

The *American Automobile Association (AAA)* also offers a number of useful resources, including its 600-page *Travel Guide to Europe* and the 64-page *Motoring Europe*, as well as a variety of useful maps; contact the nearest branch of *AAA* or the national office (see *Traveling by Car*, in this section). In addition, the *Automobile Association of Great Britain (AA)* publishes a comprehensive guide, *Camping and Caravanning in Europe* ($14.95), which lists about 4,000 sites throughout Europe, inspected and rated by the *AA*, and provides other information of interest to campers. It is available from AA Publishing (Fanum House, Basingstoke, Hampshire RG21 2EA, England; phone: 44-256-20123). In addition, almost all local tourist offices can provide brochures about camping in their respective areas.

The French international camping organization *Fédération Internationale de Camping et Caravaning* issues a pass, called a *carnet*, that entitles the bearer to a modest discount on camping fees at many campgrounds throughout France (and elsewhere in Europe). It is available in the US from the *National Campers and Hikers Association* (4804 Transit Rd., Bldg. 2, Depew, NY 14043; phone: 716-668-6242) for a fee of $30, which includes membership in the organization, as well as camping information.

For those campers flying to Paris who need a piece of ground immediately on which to pitch their tent, nearby possibilities include *Camping du Bois de Boulogne, Allée du Bord de l'Eau,* beside the Seine near the Suresnes Bridge (phone: 1-45-24-30-00). In Versailles, try *Camping Municipal* (31 Rue Berthelot in Porchefontaine; phone: 1-39-51-23-61); it's just 5 minutes on foot from the train station. As with any accommodations in or around Paris, it's wisest to call ahead.

Those who want to combine camping and caravanning with a little trout fishing need permission to do so (see *Gone Fishing,* DIVERSIONS). To learn how to get clearance to slap some big ones on the griddle, write to the *Conseil Supérieur de la Pêche,* 134 Ave. Malakoff, Paris 75016 (phone: 1-45-01-20-20).

Most experienced campers prefer to bring their own tried and true equipment, but camping equipment is available for sale or rent throughout France. For information on outfitters, consult the above-mentioned guides to camping and caravanning or contact the national tourist offices in the US which may be able to refer you to reliable French dealers.

Keep in mind that accessible food will lure scavenging wildlife, which may invade tents and vehicles. Also, even if you are assured that the campground where you are staying provides potable water, it is safer to use bottled, purified, or boiled water for drinking. To purify tap water, either use a water purification kit (available at most camping supply stores) or bring the water to a full, *rolling* boil over a campstove. It also is generally inadvisable to use water from streams, rivers, or lakes — even purified.

Organized Camping Trips – A packaged camping tour abroad is a good way to have your cake and eat it, too. The problems of advance planning and day-to-day organizing are left to someone else, yet you still reap the benefits that shoestring travel affords and can enjoy the insights of experienced guides and the company of other campers. Be aware, however, that these packages usually are geared to the young, with ages 18 to 35 as common limits. Transfer from place to place is by bus or van (as on other sightseeing tours), overnights are in tents or shelters, and meal arrangements vary. Often there is a kitty that covers meals in restaurants or in the camps; sometimes there is a chef, and sometimes the cooking is done by the participants themselves. When considering a packaged camping tour, be sure to find out if equipment is included and what individual participants are required to bring.

Also note that a number of packagers listed below under "Hiking" and "Biking" may offer these pursuits in combination with camping — it pays to call and ask when planning your trip.

Recreational Vehicles – Known in Europe as caravans and in France as "camping-cars," recreational vehicles (RVs) will appeal most to the kind of person who prefers the flexibility of accommodations — there are countless campgrounds throughout France and a number of them provide RV hookups — and enjoys camping with a little extra comfort.

An RV undoubtably saves a traveler a great deal of money on accommodations; in-camp cooking saves money on food as well. However, it is important to remember that renting an RV is a major expense; also, any kind of RV increases gas consumption considerably.

Although the term "recreational vehicle" is applied to all manner of camping vehicles, whether towed or self-propelled, generally the models available for rent in France and nearby countries are either towable campers (caravans) or motorized RVs. The motorized models usually are minivans or minibuses — vans customized in various ways for camping, often including elevated roofs — or larger, coach-type, fully equipped homes on wheels, requiring electrical hookups at night to run the TV set, air conditioning, and kitchen appliances. Although most models are equipped with standard shift, occasionally automatic shift vehicles may be available for an additional charge.

Towed vehicles can be hired overseas, but usually are not offered by US companies. Motorized models, however, are available from international and regional car rental companies in the major cities (see *Traveling by Car,* earlier in this section), although you probably will have to do some calling around to find one. Considering the relatively high Value Added Tax charged on rented vehicles in France (22%), you might consider renting an RV in another European country and driving across the border into France (see below). In this event, inform the rental company of your plans.

If you are planning to caravan all over Europe, make sure that the appliances in the vehicle you choose are equipped to deal with the electrical and gas standards of all the countries on your itinerary. There are differences, for instance, between the bottled stove gas supplied in various countries. You should have either a sufficient supply of the type of gas your camper requires or equipment that can use more than one type. When towing a camper, note that nothing towed is automatically covered by the liability insurance of the primary vehicle, so the driver's Green Card must carry a specific endorsement that covers the towed vehicle. (For further information, see *Traveling by Car,* above).

Whether driving a camper or towing, it is essential to have some idea of the terrain you'll be encountering en route. Not only are numerous mountain passes closed in winter, but grades often are too steep and winding for certain vehicles to negotiate. Car tunnels or "piggyback" services on trains can help bypass those summits too difficult to climb, but they also impose dimensions limitations and often charge high fees. The *AAA* and some of the guides noted above provide detailed information on the principal European passes and tunnels. Local tourist offices should have information about existing conditions and whether or not a particular pass is closed.

Among the companies offering RV rentals in France or in neighboring countries (which can be driven into France) are the following:

Auto-Europe (PO Box 1907, Camden, ME 04843; phone: 207-236-8235 in Maine; 800-223-5555 elsewhere in the US). Offers minibus rentals in over 30 cities in France, as well as Germany and Great Britain.

Avis Car Away (15 Rue Fournier, Clichy 92110; phone: 1-47-30-14-04). Affiliated with *Avis* car rentals, this company rents fully equipped motorhomes throughout Europe. Pick-up and drop-off locations in France include Brest, Nice, and Paris; one-way rentals are available for an additional charge.

Avis Rent-A-Car (4500 S. 129 East Ave., Suite 100, Tulsa, OK 74134; phone: 800-331-1084). Offers minibus rentals at nearly all their locations in France; larger RVs also can be rented at 12 locations in France, as well as in the Netherlands and Switzerland.

Connex International (23 N. Division St., Peekskill, NY 10566; phone: 800-333-3949 or 914-739-0066). Rents minibuses in France and motorized RVs in Germany, Great Britain, and the Netherlands.

Europe by Car (One Rockefeller Plaza, New York, NY 10020; phone: 212-581-3040 in New York State; elsewhere in the US except California, call 800-223-1516; or 9000 Sunset Blvd., Los Angeles, CA 90069; phone: 800-252-9401 or 213-272-0424 in California; elsewhere in the US except New York State, call 800-223-1516). Rents minivans and minibuses in Austria, Belgium, Denmark, France, Germany, Great Britain, Greece, Hungary, Ireland, Italy, Luxembourg, the Netherlands, Portugal, Spain, and Switzerland.

FCI Location (Zone Industrielle de St-Brendan, Quentin 22800, France; phone: 96-74-08-36). Rents motorized RVs in France.

Kemwel Group (106 Calvert St., Harrison, NY 10528; phone: 800-678-0678 or 914-835-5555). Offers minibus rentals in 15 cities in France.

Trois Soleils (Maison Trois Soleils, 2 Rte. de Paris, Ittenheim 67117, France;

phone: 88-69-17-17). Rents motorized RVs, as well as some basic campers throughout France; a number of pick-up and drop-off locations are offered.

The general policy with the above agencies is to make reservations far enough in advance to receive a voucher required to pick up the vehicle at the designated location in Europe. RV rentals also may be arranged on arrival from a number of other European companies. For additional rental sources, ask at local car rental companies and national tourist board offices. Whether arranging the rental before leaving the US or once in Europe, make reservations as early as possible as the supply of RVs is limited and the demand great.

The French-language magazine for RV enthusiasts, *Le Monde du Camping-Car,* includes recommendations on routes and campgrounds, itineraries, feature articles, and other general RV information, including local sales and rental companies. A 1-year subscription of 10 issues costs 220F (approximately $37 US at press time); this must be paid in francs by international money order, available at US banks and post offices. To subscribe, write to Service d'Abonnement, *Le Monde du Camping-Car,* 15/17 Quai de l'Oise, Paris 75019 (phone: 1-40-34-22-07).

Useful information on RVs is available from the following sources:

Living on Wheels, by Richard A. Wolters. Provides useful information on how to choose and operate a recreational vehicle. As it's currently out of print, check your library.

Recreational Vehicle Industry Association (RVIA; PO Box 2999, Reston, VA 22090-0999). Issues a useful complimentary package of information on RVs, as well as a 24-page magazine-size guide, *Set Free in an RV* ($3), and a free catalogue of RV sources and consumer information. Write to the association for these and other publications.

Recreational Vehicle Rental Association (RVRA; 3251 Old Lee Hwy., Suite 500, Fairfax, VA 22030; phone: 800-336-0355 or 703-591-7130). This RV dealers group publishes an annual rental directory, *Who's Who in RV Rentals* ($7.50).

TL Enterprises (29901 Agoura Rd., Agoura, CA 91301; phone: 818-991-4980) publishes two monthly magazines for RV enthusiasts: *Motorhome* ($17.98 for a year's subscription) and *Trailer Life* ($14.98 for a year's subscription). Members of the *TL Enterprises' Good Sam Club* can subscribe to these magazines at discounted rates ($12 and $11, respectively), and also receive discounts on a variety of RV services. Membership costs $19 per year.

Trailblazer (1000 124th Ave. NE, Bellevue, WA 98005; phone: 206-455-8585). A recreational-vehicle and motorhome magazine. A year's subscription costs $24.

Although most RV travelers head off independently, traveling in a "caravan" where several RVs travel together offers the best of both worlds for an RV trip: Since caravan members are provided with detailed itineraries and directions, they can, if they wish, travel independently — or with one or two other RVs — to and from pre-arranged destinations, yet when the full caravan convenes, they can enjoy the fellowship of the group and participate in planned activities. Caravans usually include from 20 to 40 vehicles, which are lead by a "wagonmaster," who functions as tour escort, keeping things running smoothly and on schedule. His assistant, the "tailgunner," brings up the rear and handles any mechanical problems. The caravan tour operator takes care of trip planning and routing, insurance, campground reservations and fees, and so forth. Besides the planned sightseeing, social activities can include group dinners, shows and other entertainment, cookouts at campsites, and more, but again, caravan members always have the option of spending as much time by themselves as they wish. One operator of such RV caravan trips is *Creative World Rallies and Caravans* (606 N. Carrollton Ave., New Orleans, LA 70119; phone: 800-732-8337 or 504-486-7259), which arranges trips throughout Europe, including France.

HIKING: If you would rather eliminate all the gear and planning and take to the outdoors unencumbered, park the car and go for a day's hike. By all means, cover as much area as you can by foot; you'll see everything in far more detail than you would from the window of any conveyance. And trails abound in France — 18,600 miles of them — as does specific information on how to find them. (For information on suggested hikes throughout France, see *Great Walks and Mountain Rambles* in DIVERSION.)

For those who are hiking on their own, without benefit of a guide or group, a map of the trail is a must. Preliminary information on where to hike is available from the French Government Tourist Office in the US, and local tourist authorities often distribute information sheets on popular trails in their respective regions upon request. (Even those tourist offices that do not have literature on hand — or have little in English — may be able to direct you to associations in their areas that supply maps, guides, and further information.)

Mountaineering and hiking clubs are a particularly good source of trail information for the average hiker. Information about France's vast trail network, as well as maps and guidebooks for specific regions, are available (mostly in French) from the *Fédération Française de la Randonnée Pédestre* (*FFRP;* 64 Rue de Gergovie, Paris 75014; phone: 1-45-45-31-02). Those whose hiking enters the realm of mountain climbing can get information from *Club Alpin Français, Commission des Randonnées* (24 Av. de Laumière, Paris 75019; phone: 1-42-02-68-64).

Serious hikers may want to check at their library for the very comprehensive but out-of-print *On Foot through Europe: A Trail Guide to France & the Benelux Nations* by Craig Evans. More than 200 pages are devoted to France alone, including information about guides and guidebooks, weather, lodgings, equipment, useful addresses, long-distance footpaths, cross-country skiing possibilities, national and regional parks, and 20 individual provinces and the resources specific to each.

Other books devoted to hiking in France are *Walking in France* by Rob Hunter (Oxford Illustrated Press paperback; $9.95) and *Long Walks in France* by Adam Nicolson (Harmony Books; out of print but check your library). Both feature a variety of walks of various intensities in areas throughout the countryside and are helpful in pointing out other resources for hikers. A useful set of guidebooks is the *Walking Through* series, which covers 12 European cities (including Paris), and is available from VLE Limited (PO Box 444, Ft. Lee, NJ 07024; phone: 201-585-5080) for $3; these guides also may be found at select bookstores.

A British company that specializes in maps and other publications for hikers and climbers, and that publishes English translations of the *Topo-Guides* of the *FFRP,* is *MacCarta* (15 Highbury Pl., London N5 1QP, England; phone: 71-354-1616). And an excellent walking tour by Robertson MacCarta himself is *Walking in the Footpath of Europe: Dordogne; Pyrénées; Provence* (Seven Hills Book Distributor; $19.95 each).

Also particularly helpful for those heading out afoot are the Topographical Series maps, which are on a detailed scale of 1:100,000. There are 90 maps of France and they are available for $6.95 each, plus postage and handling, from *Map Link,* 25 E. Mason St., Santa Barbara, CA 93101 (phone: 805-965-4402).

BIKING: For young and/or fit travelers, the bicycle offers a marvelous tool for exploring France, especially in those regions conducive to easy cycling, such as Normandy, the Loire Valley, or the Médoc wine region north of Bordeaux. The French, from ages 8 to 85, have long depended on bicycles for transportation, and they typically respect foreigners who arrive in their communities *à vélo*. Biking does have its drawbacks: Little baggage can be carried, travel is slow, and cyclists are exposed to the elements. However, should a cyclist need rest or refuge from the weather, there always is a welcoming tavern or comfortable inn around the next bend.

Besides being a viable way to tour France — and to burn calories to make room for larger portions of fabulous French food — biking is a great way to meet people. Remember, however, that although many residents of France do speak some English, this is less likely to be true in rural areas, so pack a copy of a good French-English phrase book if your command of French is not up to par. (For a list of helpful terms and basic expressions, see *Useful Words and Phrases,* in this section.)

A good book to help you plan a trip is *Bicycle Touring in Europe,* by Karen and Gary Hawkins (Pantheon Books; $11.95); it offers information on buying and equipping a touring bike, useful clothing and supplies, and helpful techniques for the long-distance biker. Another good general book is *Europe by Bike,* by Karen and Terry Whitehall (Mountaineers Books; $10.95). Also look for *Expeditions in France: Bicycle Tours of the Wine Country* by Sally Taylor (Sally Taylor & Friends; $9) in travel bookstores and *Bicycling in France* in your library (it's currently out of print). The *International Youth Hostel Handbook, Volume One: Europe and the Mediterranean* ($10.95) is a guide to all the hostels of Europe to which *AYH* members have access; a map of their locations is included. (For information on joining *American Youth Hostels,* see *Hints for Single Travelers,* in this section.)

Detailed maps will infinitely improve a biking tour and are available from a number of sources. Comprehensive Michelin maps (1:200,000) covering Europe, including France, are available from Michelin Guides and Maps (PO Box 3305, Spartanburg, SC 29304-3305; phone: 803-599-0850 in South Carolina; 800-423-0485 elsewhere in the US).

One of the best sources for detailed topographical maps and just about any other type of map (of just about anywhere in the world) is *Map Link* (25 E. Mason St., Santa Barbara, CA 93101; phone: 805-965-4402). Their comprehensive guide *The World Map Directory* ($24.95) includes a wealth of sources, and if they don't stock a map of the area in which you are interested (or the type of map best suited to your outdoor exploration), they will order it for you. But it is likely that they'll have something to suit your needs — they stock numerous maps of France.

A list of suggested itineraries also may be obtained on request from the French Government Tourist Office (see *Tourist Information,* in this section, for addresses) In addition, this office now provides a telephone service, "France on Call" (900-900-0040), which enables callers to obtain personalized travel itineraries. (For further information, see *Package Tours,* earlier in this section.) Information is also available locally from the Syndicats d'Initiative. The Comité Régional du Tourisme des Pays de la Loire is particularly good at this. Contact them at Maison du Tourisme, Place du Commerce, Nantes 44000 (phone: 40-48-15-45).

Choosing, Renting, and Buying a Bike – Although many bicycling enthusiasts choose to take along their own bikes, bicycles can be rented throughout Europe. Long and short rentals are available; however, in France, particularly in rural areas, it is recommended that you check ahead.

SNCF (French National Railways) also offers a *Train + Vélo* special, whereby in some 280 French cities bicycles with ten or fewer speeds can be rented right in the train station for as little as half a day and as many as 10 or more. Rates start at about $8 a day and decrease with the number of days; group rates are negotiable. A deposit — refunded when you return the bike — is required; travelers with a valid credit card can leave an imprint in lieu of cash. The bicycle may be returned to the same station or to another that also rents bikes; ask at the ticket window for the *Guide du Train et du Vélo,* a brochure listing participating stations.

As an alternative to renting, you might consider buying a bicycle in France. Bicycle shops in France that rent bikes also sell them and buying a used bike might be even less expensive than a long-term rental. Bike shops in Paris that rent bicycles and sometimes sell used ones include *Bicyclub de France* (8 Pl. de la Porte-Champerret,

Paris 75017; phone: 1-47-66-55-92) and *Paris-Vélo* (4 Rue du Fer-à-Moulin, Paris 75905; phone: 1-43-37-59-22). For further details on bicycle rental shops in French cities, see *Sources and Resources* in the individual city reports of THE CITIES.

If you do buy a bike and plan on taking it home, remember that it will be subject to an import duty by US Customs if its price (or the total of all purchases made abroad) exceeds $400. (A European bicycle purchased in the US should have proof-of-purchase papers to avoid potential customs problems.) Even the smallest towns usually have a bike shop, so it's not difficult to replace or add to gear; however, because tires and tubes are sized to metric dimensions in France, when riding your own bike, bring extras from home.

Airlines going from the US (or elsewhere) to Europe generally allow bicycles to be checked as baggage; they require that the pedals be removed, handlebars be turned sideways, and the bike be in a shipping carton (which some airlines provide, subject to availability — call ahead to make sure). If buying a shipping carton from a bicycle shop, check the airline's specifications and also ask about storing the carton at the destination airport so that you can use it again for the return flight. Although some airlines charge only a nominal fee, if the traveler already has checked two pieces of baggage, there may be an excess baggage charge of $40 to $80 for the bicycle. As regulations vary from carrier to carrier, be sure to call well before departure to find out your airline's specific regulations. As with other baggage, make sure that the bike is thoroughly labeled with your name, a business address and phone number, and the correct airport destination code.

When the going gets rough, remember that arduous parts of the journey can be avoided by loading your bicycle on the luggage van of a train. Travelers can check their bicycles as baggage for a fee or carry them on and off the train as hand baggage on a short- or medium-length journey. In some instances, the bicycle can be checked on a train independently of its owner and can be picked up at the station upon arrival there; a number of stations provide a plastic or cardboard cover for the bicycle for a nominal fee, and a few will actually pick it up at or deliver it to a designated address. Bicycle insurance also is available — and advisable.

Biking Tours – A number of organizations offer bike tours in France. Linking up with a bike tour is more expensive than traveling alone, but with experienced leaders, an organized tour often becomes an educational, as well as a very social, experience.

One of the attractions of a bike tour is that the shipment of equipment — the bike — is handled by organizers, and the shipping fee is included in the total tour package. Travelers simply deliver the bike to the airport, already disassembled and boxed; shipping cartons can be obtained from most bicycle shops with little difficulty. Bicyclists not with a tour must make their own arrangements with the airline, and there are no standard procedures for this (see above). Although some tour organizers will rent bikes, most prefer that participants bring a bike with which they are already familiar. Another attraction of *some* tours is the existence of a "sag wagon" to carry extra luggage, fatigued cyclists, and their bikes, too, when pedaling another mile is impossible.

Most bike tours are scheduled from May to October, last 1 or 2 weeks, are limited to 20 or 25 people, and provide lodging in inns or hotels, though some use hostels or even tents. Tours vary considerably in style and ambience, so request brochures from several operators in order to make the best decision. When contacting groups, be sure to ask about the maximum number of people on the trip, the maximum number of miles to be traveled each day, and the degree of difficulty of the biking; these details should determine which tour you join and can greatly affect your enjoyment of the experience. Planning ahead is essential because trips often fill up 6 months or more in advance.

SAMPLE PACKAGE TOURS: A number of companies offer tours that feature camping, hiking, and biking, as well as other outdoor activites. While many of them specialize in outdoor adventure packages, others include these activities as part of broader tour programs. Among such companies are the following:

Alternative Travel Groups (69-71 Banbury Rd., Oxford, England 0X2 6PE; phone: 800-527-5997). The motto of this company is "The best way to see a country is on foot," and among their numerous itineraries worldwide are 9- and 11-day walking tours in the Basque region of Cévennes and in the Dordogne.

Autotours (20 Craven Ter., London W2, England; phone: 44-71-258-0272). Offers camping tours which range in length from 3 to 10 weeks. France is included in many of their itineraries, and their packages visit Bordeaux, Dijon, Paris, and the Riviera; all packages depart from London.

Backroads (1516 Fifth St., Berkeley, CA 94710-1740; phone: 510-527-1555 in California; 800-245-3874 elsewhere in the US). Offers superior food and accommodations on its 8-day Loire Valley biking tour. Geared to beginning and intermediate riders, it features stays in châteaux. Also offered is an 8-day biking/camping trip through Bordeaux and the Dordogne Valley.

Bike Tours France (334 Belton St., Charlotte, NC 28209-1831; phone: 704-527-0955). Offers customized biking itineraries for any groups (of 1 up to 24).

Blue Marble Travel (c/o *Odyssey Adventures,* 89 Auburn St., Suite 1199, Portland, ME 04103; phone: 800-544-3216 or 207-878-8650). This company, specializing in active, cultural trips for those aged between 20 and 45, offers 16- and 24-day biking trips in France, covering Paris, Burgundy, Champagne, and the Loire Valley. For those in superb physical shape, there's a 37-day transcontinental biking trip from Paris, taking in Austria, Burgundy, Italy, and Switzerland.

Brooks Country Cycling (140 W. 83rd St., New York, NY 10024; phone: 212-874-5151 in New York, New Jersey, and Connecticut; 800-284-8954 elsewhere in the US). Offers 8- and 9-day itineraries in Brittany, the Dordogne Valley, the Loire Valley, Normandy, and Perigord.

Butterfield & Robinson (70 Bond St., Suite 300, Toronto, Ontario M5B 1X3, Canada; phone: 800-678-1147 or 416-864-1354). For those seeking a deluxe tour package, the company offers a number of sophisticated 5- to 9-day bike trips to France each year, with many meals taken in Michelin-starred restaurants and overnights frequently spent in prestigious *Relais & Châteaux* hotels. Recent itineraries included visits to to Alsace, Brittany, the Dordogne, the Loire Valley, Normandy, and Provence and wine tasting trips through the vineyards of Bordeaux and Burgundy; another regular offering is a Tour de France. Bikes are provided, though you can take your own, and there are many departure dates for each itinerary. Trips are open to anyone age 18 or older; biking tours are rated at three levels of difficulty. Also offered are several walking tours — although fewer than its biking tours — including the finest in French food and accommodations in Alsace, Bordeaux, Burgundy, Dordogne, and the Pyrénées.

Distant Journeys (PO Box 1211, Camden, ME 04843; phone: 207-772-5548 from June 1 to October 15; 207-236-9788 during the rest of the year). Offers a 12-day hiking tour of Mont-Blanc, the highest peak in the Alps.

Earth Ventures (2625 N. Meridian St., Suite 612, Indianapolis, IN 46208-7705; phone: 317-926-0453). Itineraries to France include four 8- to 12-day biking tours, which comprise a combination of either ballooning, canoeing, or sailing, in Burgundy, the Loire Valley, Provence, and the Riviera.

Eurobike (PO Box 40, DeKalb, IL 60115; phone: 815-758-8851). Among its offerings is a 10-day biking trip in Bordeaux and Dordogne.

Europeds (883 Sinex Ave., Pacific Grove, CA 93950; phone: 408-372-1173). Offers 5- to 7-day inn-to-inn walking tours in Alsace, the Dordogne, and Provence, as well as several 7- to 10-day biking tours through the Dordogne, Paris and surrounding areas, and Provence, and a 10-day Tour de France trip with accommodations ranging from small country inns to 3-star hotels

Forum Travel International (91 Gregory La., #21, Pleasant Hill, CA 94523; phone: 510-671-2900). Offers enticing hiking itineraries throughout the French countryside, including Alsace, the Auvergne, Brittany, Burgundy, the Dordogne, the Loire Valley, and Upper Languedoc. All programs are classified in four grades of difficulty — the most energetic of which covers as much as 20 miles (32 km) a day and is geared to those already accustomed to hard mountain walking. The company also offers a variety of biking itineraries, each with a specific theme, such as their Hunting Castles of the French Court and In the Footsteps of Joan of Arc tours.

Himalayan Travel (112 Prospect St., 2nd Floor, Stamford, CT 06901; phone: 800-225-2380). Offers a variety of tours throughout Europe. Packages in France include a 14-day hiking and camping trip through the Loire Valley, a 9-day hiking adventure in the Cerdagne region of the Pyrénées, and a leisurely 12- to 16-day tour around the island of Corsica.

Mountain Travel-Sobek (6420 Fairmount Ave., El Cerrito, CA 94530; phone: 510-527-8100 in California; 800-227-2384 elsewhere in the US). This adventure-trip specialist offers a variety of hiking trips throughout Europe, including an unhurried 12-day hike from village to village in Provence. Also offered is a climb of intermediate difficulty in the Alps, and the classic Tour du Mont-Blanc (a 13- to 15-day trek), as well as a moderate-to-strenuous sojourn called Across the Pyrénées. Their tours range from leisurely hikes that can be taken by anyone in good health to tours only for experienced (and very fit) hikers/climbers.

New England Bicycle Tours (Box D, Randolph, VT 05060; phone: 802-728-3261). The US representative of Baumeler Tours in France, this company offers 8- and 9-day itineraries in the Bordeaux, Camargue, Dordogne, and Loire valleys, and in Provence. Trips range from leisurely to moderately strenuous, and some feature accommodations in historic châteaux.

Nouvelles Frontières (12 E. 33rd St., 11th Floor, New York, NY 10016; phone: 212-779-0600; or 87 Bd. de Grenelle, Paris 75015; phone: 1-42-73-05-68). A French agency that specializes in adventure travel–hiking and canoe/kayak trips, as well as sailing, diving, and horseback riding vacations, most of which include camping. For the most part, these leave from Paris for locations outside France. All packages can be booked through their New York office.

Progressive Travel (224 W. Galer St., Seattle, WA 98119; phone: 800-245-2229 or 206-443-4225). Their 7- to 9-day inn-to-inn biking trips cover the Dordogne Valley and Provence.

Rocky Mountain Cycling Tours (PO Box 1978, Canmore, Alberta, T0L 0M0 Canada; phone: 800-661-2453 or 403-678-6770). Organizes several biking trips throughout Provence.

Travent International (PO Box 305, Waterbury Center, VT 05677; phone: 800-325-3009 or 802-244-5153). Offers a variety of 4- to 7-day inn-to-inn bike tours in Burgundy and the Beaujolais region, the Dordogne Valley, the Loire Valley, and Provence.

Wilderness Travel (801 Allston Way, Berkeley, CA 94710; phone: 800-368-2794 or 510-548-0420). This adventure specialist offers 13- and 14-day hiking trips in the Basque Country, Mont-Blanc, and the Pyrénées. Its itineraries range from leisurely outings to hikes designed for the truly physically fit. Some trips feature cozy country inn accommodations.

World Tracks Limited (12 Abingdon Rd., London, England W8 6AF; phone: 44-71-937-3028; or contact their US rep, *Himalayan Travel,* address above)

Offers a number of European motorcoach/camping trips ranging in length from 21 to 45 days, all of which travel extensively through France.

Yamnuska (PO Box 1920, 1316 Railway Ave., Canmore, Alberta, Canada T0L 0M0; phone: 403-678-4164). Offers a 13-day Mont-Blanc hiking tour in the French Alps.

An alternative to dealing directly with the above companies is to contact *All Adventure Travel,* a specialist in hiking and biking trips worldwide. This company, which acts as a representative for numerous special tour packagers offering such outdoor adventures, can provide a wealth of detailed information about each packager and programs offered. They also will help you design and arrange all aspects of a personalized itinerary. This company operates much like a travel agency, collecting commissions from the packagers. Therefore, there is no additional charge for these services. For information, contact *All Adventure Travel,* PO Box 4307, Boulder, CO 80306 (phone: 800-537-4025 or 303-499-1981).

■ **Note:** The *Specialty Travel Index* (305 San Anselmo Ave., Suite 313, San Anselmo, CA 94960; phone: 415-459-4900 in California; 800-442-4922 elsewhere in the US) is a directory of special-interest travel and an invaluable resource. Listings include tour operators specializing in camping, as well as myriad other interests that combine nicely with a camping trip, such as biking, motorcycling, horseback riding, ballooning, and boating. It costs $6 per copy, $10 for a year's subscription of two issues.

ADDITIONAL RESOURCES: Other useful sources of information on camping, hiking, and biking in France include the following organizations, most of which also sponsor tours of their own.

American Youth Hostels (PO Box 37613, Washington, DC 20013-7613; phone: 202-783-6161). This nonprofit organization and its local chapters regularly sponsor a number of foreign hiking and biking tours. Its popular itineraries include those that combine France with neighboring European countries. They also sometimes offer hiking tours of France; itineraries vary from year to year. Membership is open to all ages, and departures are geared to various age groups and levels of skill and frequently feature accommodations in hostels — along with hotels for adults and campgrounds for younger participants.

Cyclists' Touring Club (*CTC;* Cotterell House, 69 Meadrow, Godalming, Surrey GU7 3HS, England; phone: 44-0483-41-7217). Britain's largest cycling association, this group organizes tours of numerous countries, including France. *CTC* has a number of planned routes available in pamphlet form for bikers on their own and helps members plan their own tours. The club also publishes a yearly handbook, as well as magazines.

International Bicycle Touring Society (*IBTS;* PO Box 6979, San Diego, CA 92106-0979; phone: 619-226-TOUR). Regularly sponsors low-cost bicycle tours led by member volunteers. Participants must be over 21. For information, send $2 plus a self-addressed, stamped envelope.

League of American Wheelmen (190 W. Ostend St., Suite 1208, Baltimore, MD 21230; phone: 301-539-3399 or 301-944-3399). This organization publishes *Tourfinder,* a list of organizations that sponsor bicycle tours worldwide. The list is free with membership ($25 individual, $30 family) and can be obtained by non-members who send $5. The *League* also can put you in touch with biking groups in your area.

Sierra Club (Outing Department, 730 Polk St., San Francisco, CA 94109; phone:

415-776-2211). Dedicated to preserving and protecting the natural environment, this nonprofit organization also offers numerous trips each year, including both walking tours and trips that combine hiking and biking. Some are backpacking trips, moving to a new camp each day; others make day hikes from a base camp. Recent itineraries included a 10-day hiking tour of the Dordogne, focusing on the history, culture, and natural beauty of the region.

Preparing

Calculating Costs

$ A realistic appraisal of travel expenses is the most crucial bit of planning you will undertake before any trip. It also is, unfortunately, one for which it is most difficult to give precise, practical advice.

After several years of living relatively high on the hog, travel from North America to Europe dropped off precipitously in 1987 in response, among other considerations, to the relative weakness of the US dollar on the Continent. Many Americans, who had enjoyed bargain prices while touring through Europe only a couple of years before, found that disadvantageous exchange rates really put a crimp in their travel planning. But even though the halcyon days of dollar domination seem over for the present, discount fares and the availability of charter flights can greatly reduce the cost of a European vacation. Package tours can even further reduce costs, as European providers of travel services try to win back their American clients in the 1990s.

France always has been one of the most popular European countries with both the first-time and the seasoned traveler, and while it has never been one of Europe's less expensive destinations, it is certainly one where the competition for American visitors often works to inspire surprisingly affordable travel opportunities. Nevertheless, most travelers still have to plan carefully before they go and manage their travel funds prudently.

In France, estimating travel expenses depends on the mode of transportation you choose, the part or parts of the country you plan to visit, how long you will stay, and in some cases, what time of year you plan to travel. In addition to the basics of transportation, hotels, meals, and sightseeing, you have to take into account seasonal price changes that apply on certain air routings and at popular vacation destinations, as well as the vagaries of currency exchange.

In general, it's usually also a good idea to organize your trip so that you pay for as much of it as you can in France, using francs purchased from French banks (which, barring interim variations, generally offer a more advantageous rate of exchange than US sources). That means minimizing the amount of advance deposits paid in US greenbacks and deferring as many bills as possible until you arrive in Europe, although the economies possible through prepaid package tours and other special deals may offset the savings in currency exchange. (For further information on managing money abroad, see *Credit and Currency*, in this section.)

DETERMINING A BUDGET: When calculating costs, start with the basics, the major expenses being transportation, accommodations, and food. However, don't forget such extras as local transportation, shopping, and such miscellaneous items as laundry and tips. The reasonable cost of these items usually is a positive surprise to your budget. Ask about special discount passes that provide tourists with unlimited or cut-rate travel by the day or the week on regular city or local transportation.

Entries in the individual city reports in THE CITIES give helpful information on local transportation options.

Other expenses, such as the cost of local sightseeing tours and excursions, will vary from city to city. Tourist information offices are plentiful throughout France, and most of the better hotels will have someone at the front desk to provide a rundown on the costs of local tours and full-day excursions in and out of the city.

The French Government Tourist Office and *Air France* — both well aware that they need to entice cost-conscious Americans to consider a French vacation these days — offer a free brochure filled with special offers, at rates guaranteed in dollars. This year it will be reissued as *The France Discovery Guide* and is available from either *Air France* or from one of the French Government Tourist Offices listed in *Tourist Information,* in this section. Entries in the individual city reports in THE CITIES also give specific information on these activities.

Budget-minded families can take advantage of some of the more economical accommodations options to be found in France (see our discussion of accommodations in *On the Road,* in this section). Campgrounds are particularly inexpensive, and they are located throughout the country (see *Camping and Caravanning, Hiking and Biking,* in this section). Picnicking is another way to cut costs, and France abounds with well-groomed parks and idyllic pastoral settings. A stop at a local market can provide a feast of regional specialties at a surprisingly economical price compared to the cost of a restaurant lunch. (Do, however, read our warnings about seafood in *Staying Healthy,* in this section.)

In planning any travel budget, it also is wise to allow a realistic amount for both entertainment and recreation. Are you planning to spend time sightseeing and visiting local museums? Do you intend to spend your days skiing at a popular resort? Is daily golf, tennis, or horseback riding a part of your plan? Will your children be disappointed if they don't take a *bateau-mouche* on the Seine? Finally, don't forget that if haunting clubs, discotheques, or other nightspots is an essential part of your vacation, or you feel that one performance of the *Orchestre de Paris* at the *Salle Pleyel* may not be enough, allow for the extra cost of nightlife.

If at any point in the planning process it appears impossible to estimate expenses, consider this suggestion: The easiest way to put a ceiling on the price of all these elements is to buy a package tour. A totally planned and escorted one, with almost all transportation, rooms, meals, sightseeing, local travel, tips, and a dinner show or two included and prepaid, provides a pretty exact total of what the trip will cost beforehand, and the only surprise will be the one you spring on yourself by succumbing to some irresistible, expensive souvenir. And keep in mind, particularly when calculating the major expenses, that costs vary according to fluctuations in the exchange rate — that is, how many francs a dollar will buy.

Also note that a sales tax or VAT (value added tax) is added to both goods and services in many European countries. In France, the rate ranges from lows of 5.5% and 7% on food to a high of 33.33% on luxury items. The VAT is buried in the prices of hotel rooms and restaurant meals, so you won't even notice it. It also is included in the amount shown on the price tag of retail goods. There is no escaping the tax on services, but for foreigners the tax on purchases, typically 18.6%, frequently can be reimbursed. Another alternative is to have the goods sent directly to your home address — if the store is willing to do so. For a full discussion of VAT refunds, see *Duty-Free Shopping, and Value Added Tax,* in this section.

■ **Note:** The volatility of exchange rates means that between the time you originally make your hotel reservations and the day you arrive, the price in US dollars may vary substantially from the price originally quoted. To avoid paying more than you expected, it's wise to confirm rates by writing directly to hotels or by calling their representatives in the US.

Planning A Trip

123 Travelers fall into two categories: those who make lists and those who do not. Some people prefer to plot the course of their trip to the finest detail, with contingency plans and alternatives at the ready. For others, the joy of a voyage is its spontaneity; exhaustive planning only lessens the thrill of anticipation and the sense of freedom.

For most travelers, however, any week-plus trip to France can be too expensive for an "I'll take my chances" type of attitude. Even perennial gypsies and anarchistic wanderers have to take into account the time-consuming logistics of getting around, and even with minimal baggage, they need to think about packing. Hence, at least some planning is crucial.

This is not to suggest that you work out your itinerary in minute detail before you go; but it's still wise to decide certain basics at the very start: where to go, what to do, and how much to spend. These decisions require a certain amount of consideration. So before rigorously planning specific details, you might want to establish your general travel objectives:

1. How much time will you have for the entire trip, and how much of it are you willing to spend getting where you're going?
2. What interests and/or activities do you want to pursue while on vacation? Do you want to visit one, a few, or several different places?
3. At what time of year do you want to go?
4. What kind of topography or climate would you prefer?
5. Do you want peace and privacy or lots of activity and company?
6. How much money can you afford to spend for the entire vacation?

You now can make almost all of your own travel arrangements if you have time to follow through with hotels, airlines, tour operators, and so on. But you'll probably save considerable time and energy if you have a travel agent make arrangements for you. The agent also should be able to advise you of alternate arrangements of which you may not be aware. Only rarely will a travel agent's services cost a traveler any money, and they may even save you some (see *How to Use a Travel Agent,* below).

If it applies to your schedule and destination, pay particular attention to the dates when off-season rates go into effect. In major tourism areas, accommodations may cost less during the off-season (and the weather often is perfectly acceptable at this time). Off-season rates frequently are lower for car rentals and other facilities, too. In general, it is a good idea to be aware of holiday weeks, as rates at hotels generally are higher during these periods and rooms normally are heavily booked.

Make plans early. During the summer season and other holiday periods, make hotel reservations at least a month in advance in all major cities. If you are flying at peak times, and want to benefit from savings of discount fares or charter programs, purchase tickets as far ahead as possible. (Charter flights to Paris and other popular destinations may be completely sold out months in advance.) The less flexible your schedule requirements, the earlier you should book. Many French hotels require deposits before they will guarantee reservations, and this most often is the case during peak travel periods. (Be sure you have a receipt for any deposit or use a credit card.) Religious and national holidays also are times requiring reservations well in advance in France.

Before your departure, find out what the weather is likely to be at your destination. Consult *When to Go,* in this section, for information on climatic variations and a chart of average temperatures. See *How to Pack,* also in this section, for some suggestions on how to decide what clothes to take. Also see *When to Go,* as well as the individual city reports in THE CITIES, for information on special events that may occur during your stay. The city chapters also provide essential information on local transportation and other services and resources.

Make a list of any valuable items you are carrying with you, including credit card numbers and the serial numbers of your traveler's checks. Put copies in your purse or pocket, and leave other copies at home. Put a label with your name and home address on the inside of your luggage for identification in case of loss. Put your name and business address — *never your home address* — on a label on the outside of your luggage. (Those who run businesses from home should use the office address of a friend or relative.)

Review your travel documents. If you are traveling by air, check that your ticket has been filled in correctly. The left side of the ticket should have a list of each stop you will make (even if you are only stopping to change planes), beginning with your departure point. Be sure that the list is correct, and count the number of copies to see that you have one for each plane you will take. If you have confirmed reservations, be sure that the column marked "status" says "OK" beside each flight. Have in hand vouchers or proof of payment for any reservation for which you've paid in advance; this includes hotels, transfers to and from the airport, sightseeing tours, car rentals, and tickets to special events.

Although policies vary from carrier to carrier, it's still smart to reconfirm your flight 48 to 72 hours before departure, both going and returning; reconfirmation is particularly recommended for point-to-point flights within Europe. If you will be driving while in France, bring your driver's license, International Driving Permit (which is recommended), and any other necessary documentation — such as proof of insurance.

Before traveling to France, you should consider learning some basic French. Although you can get by in France speaking only English if you stick to the major resort areas and other popular tourist destinations, your trip will be much more rewarding and enjoyable (and, in some instances, safer) if you can communicate with the people who live in the areas you will be visiting. The French will openly appreciate your efforts if you do try to converse.

Some adult education programs and community colleges offer courses in French. Berlitz, among others, has a series of teach-yourself language courses on audiocassette tapes, which are available for $15.95 (plus postage and handling) from Macmillan Publishing Co. (100 Front St., Riverside, NJ 08075; phone: 800-257-5755). For information on pronunciation and a list of common travel terms, see *Useful Words and Phrases,* in this section; an introduction to a number of native drinks and dishes that you may encounter can be found in *Food and Drink,* in PERSPECTIVES.

Finally, you always should bear in mind that despite the most careful plans, things do not always occur on schedule. If you maintain a flexible attitude and try to accept minor disruptions as less than cataclysmic, you will enjoy yourself a lot more.

How to Use a Travel Agent

 A reliable travel agent remains the best source of service and information for planning a trip abroad, whether you have a specific itinerary and require an agent only to make reservations or you need extensive help in sorting through the maze of airfares, tour offerings, hotel packages, and the scores of other arrangements that may be involved in a trip to France.

Know what you want from a travel agent so that you can evaluate what you are getting. It is perfectly reasonable to expect your agent to be a thoroughly knowledgeable travel specialist, with information about your destination and, even more crucial, a command of current airfares, ground arrangements, and other wrinkles in the travel scene.

Most travel agents work through computer reservations systems (CRS). These are used to assess the availability and cost of flights, hotels, and car rentals, and through them they can book reservations. Despite reports of "computer bias," in which a computer may favor one airline over another, the CRS should provide agents with the entire spectrum of flights available to a given destination and the complete range of fares in considerably less time than it takes to telephone the airlines individually — and at no extra cost to the client.

Make the most intelligent use of a travel agent's time and expertise; understand the economics of the industry. As a client, traditionally you pay nothing for the agent's services; with few exceptions, it's all free, from hotel bookings to advice on package tours. Any money the travel agent makes on the time spent arranging your itinerary — booking hotels or flights, or suggesting activities — comes from commissions paid by the suppliers of these services — the airlines, hotels, and so on. These commissions generally run from 10% to 15% of the total cost of the service, although suppliers often reward agencies that sell their services in volume with an increased commission called an override. In most instances, you'll find that travel agents make their time and experience available to you at no cost, and you do not pay more for an airline ticket, package tour, or other product bought from a travel agent than you would for the same one bought directly from the supplier.

Exceptions to the general rule of free service by a travel agent are the agencies beginning to practice net pricing. In essence, such agencies return their commissions and overrides to their customers and make their income by charging a flat fee per transaction instead (thus adding a charge after a reduction for the commissions has been made). Net fares and fees are a growing practice, though hardly widespread.

Even a conventional travel agent sometimes may charge a fee for special services. These chargeable items may include long-distance telephone or cable costs incurred in making a booking, for reserving a room in a place that does not pay a commission (such as a small, out-of-the-way hotel), or for a special attention such as planning a highly personalized itinerary. A fee also may be assessed in instances of deeply discounted airfares.

Choose a travel agent with the same care with which you would choose a doctor or lawyer. You will be spending a good deal of money on the basis of the agent's judgment, so you have a right to expect that judgment to be mature, informed, and interested. At the moment, unfortunately, there aren't many standards within the travel agent industry to help you gauge competence, and the quality of individual agents varies enormously.

At present, only nine states have registration, licensing, or other forms of travel agent–related legislation on their books. Rhode Island licenses travel agents; Florida, Hawaii, Iowa, and Ohio register them; and California, Illinois, Oregon, and Washington have laws governing the sale of transportation or related services. While state licensing of agents cannot absolutely guarantee competence, it can at least ensure that an agent has met some minimum requirements.

Perhaps the best-prepared agents are those who have completed the CTC Travel Management program offered by the *Institute of Certified Travel Agents (ICTA)* and carry the initials CTC (Certified Travel Counselor) after their names. This indicates a relatively high level of expertise. For a free list of CTCs in your area, send a self-addressed, stamped, #10 envelope to *ICTA,* 148 Linden St., Box 82-56, Wellesley, MA 02181 (phone: 617-237-0280 in Massachusetts; 800-542-4282 elsewhere in the US).

An agent's membership in the *American Society of Travel Agents (ASTA)* can be a useful guideline in making a selection. But keep in mind that *ASTA* is an industry organization, requiring only that its members be licensed in those states where required;

be accredited to represent the suppliers whose products they sell, including airline and cruise tickets; and adhere to its Principles of Professional Conduct and Ethics code. *ASTA* does not guarantee the competence, ethics, or financial soundness of its members, but it does offer some recourse if you feel you have been dealt with unfairly. Complaints may be registered with *ASTA* (Consumer Affairs Dept., 1101 King St., Alexandria, VA 22314; phone: 703-739-2782). First try to resolve the complaint directly with the supplier. For a list of *ASTA* members in your area, send a self-addressed, stamped, #10 envelope to *ASTA,* Public Relations Dept., at the address above.

There also is the *Association of Retail Travel Agents (ARTA),* a smaller but highly respected trade organization similar to *ASTA.* Its member agencies and agents similarly agree to abide by a code of ethics, and complaints about a member can be made to *ARTA*'s Grievance Committee, 1745 Jeff Davis Hwy., Arlington, VA 22202-3402 (phone: 800-969-6069 or 703-553-7777).

Perhaps the best way to find a travel agent is by word of mouth. If the agent (or agency) has done a good job for your friends over a period of time, it probably indicates a certain level of commitment and competence. Always ask not only for the name of the company, but also for the name of the specific agent with whom your friends dealt, for it is that individual who will serve you, and quality can vary widely within a single agency. There are some superb travel agents in the business, and they can facilitate vacation or business arrangements.

Entry Requirements and Documents

A valid US passport is the only document a US citizen needs to enter France or Monaco, and that same passport also is needed to re-enter the US. However, immigration officers in French airports *may* want to see that you have sufficient funds for your trip (for example, traveler's checks, credit cards, etc.) and a return ticket to the US. As a general rule, a US passport entitles the bearer to remain in either France or Monaco for up to 90 days as a tourist. Resident aliens of the US should inquire at the nearest French consulate to find out what documents they need to enter either France or Monaco (there is no frontier between the two countries, and French regulations pertain); similarly, US citizens intending to work, study, or reside in France or Monaco should address themselves to the consulate.

Vaccination certificates are required only if the traveler is entering from an area of contagion as defined by the World Health Organization and, as the US is considered an area "free from contagion," an international vaccination certificate no longer is required for entering France for a short period of time. Because smallpox is considered eradicated from the world, only a few countries continue to require visitors to have a smallpox vaccination certificate. You certainly will not need one to travel to France or Monaco or return to the US.

VISAS: Visas are required for study, residency, work, or stays of more than 3 months, and US citizens should address themselves to the French embassy or consulate well in advance of a proposed trip. Visas of this type are available for stays in France of up to 1 year. Note that although visas for study often are issued, it is much more difficult to get a visa permitting you to work in the country. The ready processing of a visa application also may be based on the duration of the visa you are requesting — visas for studying in France for several months are likely to be processed more quickly than residency visas good for 1 year or longer. Proof of substantial means of independent financial support during the stay also is pertinent to the acceptance of any long-term–stay application.

At least two items are necessary to apply for a visa: a valid passport and a completed visa form. (These forms may be obtained by sending a self-addressed, stamped envelope to any French consulate with a written request.) Depending on the type of visa you are requesting, additional documentation may be required; the processing fee also varies for different types of visas. Cash or a money order may be used for payment if applying in person; a money order only, if applying by mail. Application can be made through the mail or at the French embassy or consulate (see *The French Embassy and Consulates in the US,* in this section, for addresses). If applying in person, it is a good idea to call ahead to check during what hours and days visa requests are accepted.

PASSPORTS: While traveling in France, carry your passport with you at all times (for an exception to this rule, see our note "When Checking In," below). If you lose your passport while abroad, immediately report the loss to the nearest US embassy or consulate (see *Legal Aid and Consular Services,* in this section, for locations in France). You can get a 3-month temporary passport directly from the consulate, but you must fill out a "loss of passport" form and follow the same application procedure — and pay the same fees — as you did for the original (see below). It's likely to speed things up if you have a record of your passport number and the place and date of its issue (a photocopy of the first page of your passport is perfect). Keep this information separate from your passport — you might want to give it to a traveling companion to hold or put it in the bottom of your suitcase.

US passports are now valid for 10 years from the date of issue (5 years for those under age 18). The expired passport itself is not renewable, but must be turned in along with your application for a new and valid one (you will get it back, voided, when you receive the new one). Normal passports contain 24 pages, but frequent travelers can request a 48-page passport at no extra cost. Every individual, regardless of age, must have his or her own passport. Family passports no longer are issued.

Passports can be renewed by mail with forms obtained at designated locations only if the expired passport was issued no more than 12 years before the date of application for renewal and it was not issued before the applicant's 16th birthday. The rules for renewal regarding teens under 16 and younger applicants may vary depending on age and when their previous passport was issued. Those who are eligible to apply by mail must send the completed form with the expired passport, two photos (see description below), and $40 (which includes a $10 execution fee) to the nearest passport agency office. Delivery can take as little as 2 weeks or as long as 6 weeks during the busiest season — from approximately mid-March to mid-September.

Adults applying for the first time and younger applicants who must apply for a passport in person (as well as those who cannot wait for mail application turnaround) can do so at one of the following places:

1. The State Department passport agencies in Boston, Chicago, Honolulu, Houston, Long Beach (California), Miami, New Orleans, New York City, Philadelphia, San Francisco, Seattle, Stamford, CT, and Washington, DC.
2. A federal or state courthouse.
3. Any of the 1,000 post offices across the country with designated acceptance facilities.

Application blanks are available at all these offices and must be presented with the following:

1. Proof of US citizenship. This can be a previous passport or one in which you were included. If you are applying for your first passport and were born in the United States, an original or certified birth certificate is the required proof. If you were born abroad, a Certificate of Naturalization, a Certificate of Citizenship, a Report of Birth Abroad of a Citizen of the United States, or a Certification of Birth is necessary.

2. Two 2-by-2-inch, front-view photographs in color or black and white, with a light, plain background, taken within the previous 6 months. These must be taken by a photographer rather than a machine.

3. A $65 passport fee ($40 for travelers under 16) which includes a $10 execution fee. *Note:* Your best bet is to bring the exact amount in cash (no change is given), or a separate check or money order for each passport (although a family can combine several passport fees on one check or money order.)

4. Proof of identity. Again, this can be a previous passport, a Certificate of Naturalization or of Citizenship, a driver's license, or a government ID card with a physical description or a photograph. Failing any of these, you should be accompanied by a blood relative or a friend of at least 5 years' standing who will testify to your identity. Credit cards or social security cards do not suffice as proof of identity — but note that since 1988, US citizens *must* supply their social security numbers.

As getting a passport — or international visa — through the mail can mean waiting as much as 6 weeks or more, a new mini-industry has cropped up in those cities where there is a US passport office. The yellow pages currently list quite a few organizations willing to wait on line to expedite obtaining a visa or passport renewal; there's even one alternative for those who live nowhere near the cities mentioned above. In the nation's capital there's an organization called the *Washington Passport and Visa Service.* It may be the answer for folks in need of special rapid action, since this organization can get a passport application or renewal turned around in a single day. What's more, their proximity to an embassy or consulate of every foreign country represented in the US helps to speed the processing of visa applications as well. The fee for a 5- to 7-day turnaround is $30; for next-day service the charge is $50; for same-day service they charge $90. For information, application forms, and other prices, contact *Washington Passport and Visa Service,* 2318 18th St. NW, Washington, DC 20009 (phone: 800-272-7776). Another company in Washington providing a similar service is *Travisa* (2122 P St. NW, Washington, DC 20037; phone: 800-222-2589). They charge $30 for an 8- to 10-day turnaround on passport applications.

If you need an emergency passport, it also is possible to be issued a passport in a matter of hours by going directly to your nearest passport office (there is no way, however, to avoid waiting in line). Explain the nature of the emergency, usually as serious as a death in the family; a ticket in hand for a flight the following day also will suffice. Should the emergency occur outside of business hours, all is not lost. There's a 24-hour telephone number in Washington, DC (phone: 202-647-4000) that can put you in touch with a State Department duty officer who may be able to expedite your application. Note that if a passport is obtained after regular business hours, a nominal charge will be added to the standard passport fee.

■**When Checking In:** It is not at all unusual for a French hotel to ask you to surrender your passport for 24 hours. While we all get a little nervous when we're parted from our passports, the US State Department's passport division advises that it's a perfectly acceptable procedure. The purpose usually is to check the validity of the passport and ascertain whether the passport holder is a fugitive or has a police record. Many hotels merely will ask that you enter your passport number on your registration card. If a hotel does take your passport, make sure it's returned to you the next day.

DUTY AND CUSTOMS: As a general rule, the requirements for bringing the majority of items into France is that they must be in quantities small enough not to imply commercial import.

Among the items that may be taken into France duty-free are 200 cigarettes or 250 grams of tobacco, 50 cigars, up to 2 liters of wine, either 2 liters of alcohol under 38.8

proof or 1 liter above 38.8 proof, 50 grams of perfume, a quarter of a liter of cologne, 500 grams of coffee, 40 grams of tea, and on items designated as gifts valued at less than 300F (or approximately $55 per item).

If you are bringing along a computer, camera, or any other electronic equipment for your own use that you will be taking back to the US, you should register the item with the US Customs Service in order to avoid paying duty both entering and returning from France. (Also see *Customs and Returning to the US,* in this section.) For information on this procedure, as well as for a variety of informative pamphlets on US customs regulations, contact the local office of the US Customs Service or the central office, PO Box 7407, Washington, DC 20044 (phone: 202-566-8195).

Additional information regarding customs regulations is available from the French Government Tourist Office. See *Tourist Information Offices,* in this section, for addresses of offices in the US.

■ **One rule to follow:** When passing through customs, it is illegal not to declare dutiable items; penalties range from stiff fines and seizure of the goods to prison terms. So don't try to sneak anything through — it just isn't worth it.

Insurance

 It is unfortunate that most decisions to buy travel insurance are impulsive and usually are made without any real consideration of the traveler's existing policies. Therefore, the first person with whom you should discuss travel insurance is your own insurance broker, not a travel agent or the clerk behind the airport insurance counter. You may discover that the insurance you already carry — homeowner's policies and/or accident, health, and life insurance — protects you adequately while you travel and that your real needs are in the more mundane areas of excess value insurance for baggage or trip cancellation insurance.

TYPES OF INSURANCE: To make insurance decisions intelligently, however, you first should understand the basic categories of travel insurance and what they cover. Then you can decide what you should have in the broader context of your personal insurance needs, and you can choose the most economical way of getting the desired protection: through riders on existing policies; with onetime short-term policies; through a special program put together for the frequent traveler; through coverage that's part of a travel club's benefits; or with a combination policy sold by insurance companies through brokers, automobile clubs, tour operators, and travel agents.

There are seven basic categories of travel insurance:

1. Baggage and personal effects insurance
2. Personal accident and sickness insurance
3. Trip cancellation and interruption insurance
4. Default and/or bankruptcy insurance
5. Flight insurance (to cover injury or death)
6. Automobile insurance (for driving your own or a rented car)
7. Combination policies

Baggage and Personal Effects Insurance – Ask your insurance agent if baggage and personal effects are included in your current homeowner's policy, or if you will need a special rider to cover you for the duration of a trip. The object is to protect your bags and their contents in case of damage or theft anytime during your travels, not just while you're in flight and covered by the airline's policy. Furthermore, only limited protection is provided by the airline. Baggage liability varies from carrier to carrier, but generally speaking, on domestic flights, luggage usually is insured to $1,250 —

that's per passenger, not per bag. For most international flights, including domestic portions of international flights, the airline's liability limit is approximately $9.07 per pound or $20 per kilo (which comes to about $360 per 40-pound suitcase) for checked baggage and up to $400 per passenger for unchecked baggage. These limits should be specified on your airline ticket, but to be awarded any amount, you'll have to provide an itemized list of lost property, and if you're including new and/or expensive items, be prepared for a request that you back up your claim with sales receipts or other proof of purchase.

If you are carrying goods worth more than the maximum protection offered by the airline, bus, or train company, consider excess value insurance. Additional coverage is available from airlines at an average, currently, of $1 to $2 per $100 worth of coverage, up to a maximum of $5,000. This insurance can be purchased at the airline counter when you check in, though you should arrive early to fill out the necessary forms and to avoid holding up other passengers.

Major credit card companies also provide coverage for lost or delayed baggage — and this coverage often is over and above what the airline will pay. The basic coverage usually is automatic for all cardholders who use the credit card to purchase tickets, but to qualify for additional coverage, cardholders generally must enroll.

American Express: Provides $500 coverage for checked baggage; $1,250 for carry-on baggage; and $250 for valuables, such as cameras and jewelry.

Carte Blanche and Diners Club: Provide $1,250 free insurance for checked or carry-on baggage that's lost or damaged.

Discover Card: Offers $500 insurance for checked baggage and $1,250 for carry-on baggage — but to qualify for this coverage cardholders first must purchase additional flight insurance (see "Flight Insurance," below).

MasterCard and Visa: Baggage insurance coverage set by the issuing institution.

Additional baggage and personal effects insurance also is included in certain of the combination travel insurance policies discussed below.

■ **A note of warning:** Be sure to read the fine print of any excess value insurance policy; there often are specific exclusions, such as cash, tickets, furs, gold and silver objects, art, and antiques. And remember that insurance companies ordinarily will pay only the depreciated value of the goods rather than their replacement value. The best way to protect the items you're carrying in your luggage is to take photos of your valuables and keep a record of the serial numbers of such items as cameras, typewriters, laptop computers, radios, and so on. This will establish that you do, indeed, own the objects. If your luggage disappears en route or is damaged, deal with the situation immediately. If an airline loses your luggage, you will be asked to fill out a Property Irregularity Report before you leave the airport. If your property disappears at other transportation centers, tell the local company, but also report it to the police (since the insurance company will check with the police when processing the claim). When traveling by train, if you are sending excess luggage as registered baggage, remember that some trains may not have provisions for extra cargo; if your baggage does not arrive when you do, it may not be lost, just on the next train!

Personal Accident and Sickness Insurance – This covers you in case of illness during your trip or death in an accident. Most policies insure you for hospital and doctors' expenses, lost income, and so on. In most cases, it is a standard part of existing health insurance policies, though you should check with your broker to be sure that your policy will pay for any medical expenses incurred abroad. If not, take out a separate vacation accident policy or an entire vacation insurance policy that includes health and life coverage.

Two examples of such comprehensive health and life insurance coverage are the travel insurance packages offered by *Wallach & Co:*

HealthCare Global: This insurance package, which can be purchased for periods of 10 to 180 days, is offered for two age groups: Men and women up to age 75 receive $25,000 medical insurance and $50,000 death benefit; those from age 76 to 84 are eligible for $12,500 medical insurance and $25,000 death benefit. For either policy, the cost for a 10-day period is $25, with decreasing rates up to 75 days, after which the rate is $1.50 a day.

HealthCare Abroad: This program is available to individuals up to age 75. For $3 per day (minimum 10 days, maximum 90 days), policy holders receive $100,000 medical insurance and $25,000 death benefit.

Both of these basic programs also may be bought in combination with trip cancellation and baggage insurance at extra cost. For further information, write to *Wallach & Co.,* 107 W. Federal St., Box 480, Middleburg, VA 22117-0480 (phone: 703-687-3166 in Virginia; 800-237-6615 elsewhere in the US).

Trip Cancellation and Interruption Insurance – Most charter and package tour passengers pay for their travel well before departure. The disappointment of having to miss a vacation because of illness or any other reason pales before the awful prospect that not all (and sometimes none) of the money paid in advance might be returned. So cancellation insurance for any package tour is a must.

Although cancellation penalties vary (they are listed in the fine print of every tour brochure, and before you purchase a package tour you should know exactly what they are), rarely will a passenger get more than 50% of this money back if forced to cancel within a few weeks of scheduled departure. Therefore, if you book a package tour or charter flight, you should have trip cancellation insurance to guarantee full reimbursement or refund should you, a traveling companion, or a member of your immediate family get sick, forcing you to cancel your trip or *return home early.*

The key here is *not* to buy just enough insurance to guarantee full reimbursement for the cost of the package or charter in case of cancellation. The proper amount of coverage should be sufficient to reimburse you for the cost of having to catch up with a tour after its departure or having to travel home at the full economy airfare if you have to forgo the return flight of your charter. There usually is quite a discrepancy between a charter fare and the amount charged to travel the same distance on a regularly scheduled flight at full economy fare.

Trip cancellation insurance is available from travel agents and tour operators in two forms: as part of a short-term, all-purpose travel insurance package (sold by the travel agent); or as specific cancellation insurance designed by the tour operator for a specific charter tour. Generally, tour operators' policies are less expensive, but also less inclusive. Cancellation insurance also is available directly from insurance companies or their agents as part of a short-term, all-inclusive travel insurance policy.

Before you decide on a policy, read each one carefully. (Either type can be purchased from a travel agent when you book the charter or package tour.) Be certain that your policy includes enough coverage to pay your fare from the farthest destination on your itinerary should you have to miss the charter flight. Also, be sure to check the fine print for stipulations concerning "family members" and "pre-existing medical conditions," as well as allowances for living expenses if you must delay your return due to bodily injury or illness.

Default and/or Bankruptcy Insurance – Although trip cancellation insurance usually protects you if *you* are unable to complete — or begin — your trip, a fairly recent innovation is coverage in the event of default and/or bankruptcy on the part of the tour operator, airline, or other travel supplier. In some travel insurance packages, this contingency is included in the trip cancellation portion of the coverage; in others, it is a separate feature. Either way, it is becoming increasingly important. Whereas sophisticated travelers have long known to beware of the possibility of default or bankruptcy when buying a charter flight or tour package, in recent years more than a few respected scheduled airlines unexpectedly have revealed their shaky financial condition, sometimes leaving hordes of stranded ticket holders in their wake. Moreover, the value of escrow protection of a charter passenger's funds has been unreliable lately. While default/bankruptcy insurance will not ordinarily result in reimbursement in time to pay for new arrangements, it can ensure that you will get your money back, and even independent travelers buying no more than an airplane ticket may want to consider it.

Flight Insurance – Airlines have carefully established limits of liability for injury to or the death of passengers on international flights. For all international flights to, from, or with a stopover in the US, all carriers are liable for up to $75,000 per passenger. For all other international flights, the liability is based on where you purchase the ticket: If booked in advance in the US, the maximum liability is $75,000; if arrangements are made abroad, the liability is $10,000. But remember, these liabilities are not the same thing as insurance policies; every penny that an airline eventually pays in the case of injury or death may be subject to a legal battle.

But before you buy last-minute flight insurance from an airport vending machine, consider the purchase in light of your total existing insurance coverage. A careful review of your current policies may reveal that you are already amply covered for accidental death, sometimes up to three times the amount provided for by the flight insurance you're buying at the airport.

Be aware that airport insurance, the kind typically bought at a counter or from a vending machine, is among the most expensive forms of life insurance coverage, and that even within a single airport, rates for approximately the same coverage vary widely. Often policies sold in vending machines are more expensive than those sold over the counter, even when they are with the same national company.

If you buy your plane ticket with a major credit card, you generally receive automatic insurance coverage at no extra cost. Additional coverage usually can be obtained at extremely reasonable prices, but a cardholder must sign up for it in advance. (Note that rates vary slightly for residents of some states.) As we went to press, the travel accident and life insurance policies of the major credit cards were as follows:

> *American Express:* Automatically provides $100,000 in insurance to its *Green, Gold,* and *Optima* cardholders, and $500,000 to *Platinum* cardholders. With *American Express,* $4.50 per ticket buys an additional $250,000 worth of flight insurance; $7.50 buys $500,000 worth; and $14 provides an added $1 million worth of coverage.
>
> *Carte Blanche:* Automatically provides $150,000 flight insurance.
>
> *Diners Club:* Provides $350,000 free flight insurance. An additional $250,000 worth of insurance is available for $4; $500,000 costs $6.50.
>
> *Discover Card:* Provides $500,000 free flight insurance. An additional $250,000 worth of insurance is available for $4.50; $500,000 costs $6.50.
>
> *MasterCard and Visa:* Insurance coverage set by the issuing institution.

Automobile Insurance – Public liability and property damage (third-party) insurance is compulsory in Europe, and whether you drive your own car or a rental you must carry insurance. Car rentals in France usually include public liability, property damage, fire, and theft coverage and, sometimes (depending on the rental company), collision damage coverage with a deductible.

In your car rental contract, you'll see that for about $9 to $15 a day, you may buy optional collision damage waiver (CDW) protection. (If partial coverage with a deductible is included in the rental contract, the CDW will cover the deductible in the event of an accident, and can cost as much as $25 per day.)

If you do not accept the CDW coverage, you may be liable for as much as the full retail value of the rental car, and by paying for the CDW you are relieved of all responsibility for any damage to the car. Before agreeing to this coverage, however, check with your own broker about your existing personal automobile insurance policy. It very well may cover your entire liability exposure without any additional cost, or you automatically may be covered by the credit card company to which you are charging the cost of your rental. To find out the amount of rental car insurance provided by major credit cards, contact the issuing institutions.

You also should know that an increasing number of the major international car rental companies automatically are including the cost of the CDW in their basic rates. Car rental prices have increased to include this coverage, although rental company ad campaigns may promote this as a new, improved rental package "benefit." The disadvantage of this inclusion is that you may not have the option to turn down the CDW — even if you are already adequately covered by your own insurance policy or through a credit card company.

Your rental contract (with the appropriate insurance box ticked off) as well as proof of your personal insurance policy, if applicable, are required as proof of insurance. If you will be driving your own car in France, you must carry an International Insurance Certificate (called a Green Card — *Carte Verte* in France), available through insurance brokers in the US.

Combination Policies – Short-term insurance policies, which may include a combination of any or all of the types of insurance discussed above, are available through retail insurance agencies, automobile clubs, and many travel agents. These combination policies are designed to cover you for the duration of a single trip.

Policies of this type include the following:

Access America International: A subsidiary of the Blue Cross/Blue Shield plans of New York and Washington, DC, now available nationwide. Contact *Access America,* PO Box 90310, Richmond, VA 23230 (phone: 800-424-3391 or 804-285-3300).

Carefree: Underwritten by The Hartford. Contact *Carefree Travel Insurance,* Arm Coverage, PO Box 310, Mineola, NY 11501 (phone: 800-645-2424 or 516-294-0220).

NEAR Services: In addition to a full range of travel services, this organization offers a comprehensive travel insurance package. An added feature is coverage for lost or stolen airline tickets. Contact *NEAR Services,* 450 Prairie Ave., Suite 101, Calumet City, IL 60409 (phone: 708-868-6700 in the Chicago area; 800-654-6700 elsewhere in the US and Canada).

Tele-Trip: Underwritten by the Mutual of Omaha Companies. Contact *Tele-Trip Co.,* 3201 Farnam St., Omaha, NE 68131 (phone: 402-345-2400 in Nebraska; 800-228-9792 elsewhere in the US).

Travel Assistance International: Provided by Europ Assistance Worldwide Services, and underwritten by Transamerica Occidental Life Insurance. Contact *Travel Assistance International,* 1333 15th St. NW, Suite 400, Washington, DC 20005 (phone: 202-331-1609 in Washington, DC; 800-821-2828 elsewhere in the US).

Travel Guard International: Underwritten by the Insurance Company of North America, it is available through authorized travel agents, or contact *Travel Guard International,* 1145 Clark St., Stevens Point, WI 54481 (phone: 715-345-0505 in Wisconsin; 800-826-1300 elsewhere in the US).

Travel Insurance PAK: Underwritten by The Travelers. Contact *The Travelers Companies,* Ticket and Travel Plans, One Tower Sq., Hartford, CT 06183-5040 (phone: 203-277-2319 in Connecticut; 800-243-3174 elsewhere in the US).

How to Pack

 No one can provide a completely foolproof list of precisely what to pack, so it's best to let common sense, space, and comfort guide you. Keep one maxim in mind: Less is more. You simply won't need as much clothing as you think, and you are far more likely to need a forgotten accessory — or a needle and thread or scissors — than a particular piece of clothing.

As with almost anything relating to travel, a little planning can go a long way.

1. Where are you going — city, country, or both?
2. How many total days will you be gone?
3. What's the average temperature likely to be during your stay?

The goal is to remain perfectly comfortable, neat, clean, and fashionable, but to pack as little as possible. Learn to travel light by following two firm packing principles:

1. Organize your travel wardrobe around a single color — blue or brown, for example — that allows you to mix, match, and layer clothes. Holding firm to one color scheme will make it easy to eliminate items of clothing that don't harmonize.
2. Never overpack to ensure a supply of fresh clothing — shirts, blouses, underwear — for each day of a long trip. Use hotel laundries to wash and dry clean clothes. There are self-service laundries (called *lavomatique* or *blanchisseries automatiques*) in most towns of any size.

CLIMATE AND CLOTHES: Exactly what you pack on your trip will be a function of where you are going and when and the kinds of things you intend to do. A few degrees can make all the difference between being comfortably attired and very real suffering, so your initial step should be to find out what the general weather conditions are likely to be in the areas you will visit.

Although most of France is farther north than the US — Paris (sitting astride latitude 48 ° 52') is about even with Quebec's Gaspé Peninsula — the climate generally is milder. Residents of the US will find that the same wardrobe they would wear in the Middle Atlantic United States will, with a few adjustments, also be appropriate for most parts of France in the same season.

Anyone going to France from the late fall through the early spring, however, should take into account that while central heating is prevalent, interiors often are not heated to the same degree they would be in the US. Thus, although there is no need to prepare for sub-zero winters, most people probably will feel more comfortable wearing heavier clothing indoors than they might at home — for instance, sweaters rather than lightweight shirts and blouses.

In the south of France, warm clothes — even some kind of topcoat — are needed in winter in addition to lighter clothing. While the average coastal temperature in January is a pleasant 48F, the hills above the coast are cold and sometimes covered in snow. Even on the warmest day on the Riviera, moreover, the thermometer drops considerably after sunset. Rain gear is advisable most of the year, especially from fall through spring. A raincoat with a zip-out lining — and a hood or rain hat — is a versatile choice. If you do decide to take an umbrella, a compact telescoping model is best.

More information about the climate in France, along with a chart of average low and high temperatures for specific cities, is given in *When to Go,* in this section.

Keeping temperature and climate in mind, consider the problem of luggage. Plan on one suitcase per person (and in a pinch, remember it's always easier to carry two small suitcases than to schlepp one that is roughly the size of downtown Detroit). Standard 26- to 28-inch suitcases can be made to work for 1 week or 1 month, and unless you are going for no more than a weekend, never cram wardrobes for two people into one suitcase. Hanging bags are best for dresses, suits, and jackets.

FASHION: On the whole, France is no more formal than North America, but the celebrated French sense of style — a subject apart from the question of formality versus informality — is a genuine thing. This knack for knowing almost intuitively what is smart is most evident in Paris and in the more glamorous resorts of the Côte d'Azur. But since chic as the Parisians possess it is something one either has or has not, and, in the latter case, is acquired slowly rather than on the eve of a trip, the best rule to follow in choosing a travel wardrobe is to be guided by your own taste. On the Left Bank in Paris, anything goes; on the Right Bank, wear what you would in any cosmopolitan American city. Although the French do enjoy dressing up, formal attire is necessary only for the most elegant occasions — such as Friday dinner at *Maxim's,* a ball, or an *Opéra* opening night.

The advice to follow your own taste and wear what you would in similar situations at home also applies to the Côte d'Azur, the other part of France that is very sensitive to the dictates of fashion. To attempt to live up to the chic of St-Tropez, for instance, can be difficult, because St-Tropez to some extent sets the style for summer fashions all over Europe. If you wish to try, the advice might be to be stylishly casual by day and anything from stylishly casual to dressy to *outré* at night, depending on the resort.

Before packing, lay out every piece of clothing you think you might want to take. Select clothing on the basis of what can serve several functions (wherever possible, clothes should be chosen that can be used for both daytime and evening wear). Pack clothes that have a lot of pockets for traveler's checks, documents, and tickets. Eliminate items that don't mix, match, or coordinate with your color scheme. If you can't wear it in at least two distinct incarnations, leave it at home. Accessorize everything beforehand so you know exactly what you will be wearing with what.

Layering is the key to comfort — particularly when touring in parts of the countryside where mornings and evenings can be chilly even when the days are mild. No matter where you are traveling in France, however, layering is a good way to prepare for atypical temperatures or changes in the weather and even in a heat wave, an extra layer will be welcome for exploring caves and champagne cellars. Recommended basics are a lightweight wool or heavy cotton turtleneck, which can be worn under a shirt and perhaps a third layer, such as a pullover sweater, jacket, or windbreaker. In warmer weather, substitute T-shirts and lightweight cotton shirts or sweaters for the turtleneck and wool layers. As the weather changes, you can add or remove clothes as required.

And finally — since the best touring of France's castles, churches, and countryside is done on foot — it is essential to bring comfortable shoes (often this means an old pair, already broken in).

Your carry-on luggage should contain a survival kit with the basic things you will need in case your luggage gets lost or stolen: a toothbrush, toothpaste, all medications, a sweater, nightclothes, and a change of underwear. With these essential items at hand, you will be prepared for any sudden, unexpected occurrence that separates you from your suitcase. If you have many 1- or 2-night stops scheduled, you can live out of your survival case without having to unpack completely at each hotel.

Sundries – If you are traveling in the heat of summer and will be spending a lot of time outdoors, be sure to take along a sun hat (to protect hair as well as skin) and sunscreen. Also, if you are heading for a vacation on skis, do not underestimate the effect of the sun's glare off snowy slopes, especially in higher altitudes — your face and neck are particularly susceptible to burning.

Other items you might consider packing are a pocket-size flashlight with extra batteries, a small sewing kit, a first-aid kit (see *Staying Healthy,* in this section, for recommended components), binoculars, and a camera or camcorder (see *Cameras and Equipment,* also in this section).

■**Note:** For those on the go, *Travel Mini Pack* offers numerous products — from toilet articles to wrinkle-remover spray — in handy travel sizes, as well as travel accessories such as money pouches, foreign currency calculators, and even a combination hair dryer/iron. For a catalogue, contact *Travel Mini Pack,* PO Box 571, Stony Point, NY 10980 (phone: 914-429-8281). *Pacific Traveler's Supply* (529 State St., Santa Barbara, CA 93101; phone: 805-963-4438) also carries a variety of similar items, as well as an extensive collection of travel guides and maps.

PACKING: The basic idea of packing is to get everything into the suitcase and out again with as few wrinkles as possible. Simple, casual clothes — shirts, jeans and slacks, permanent press skirts — can be rolled into neat, tight sausages that keep other packed items in place and leave the clothes themselves amazingly unwrinkled. However, for items that are too bulky or delicate for even careful rolling, a suitcase should be packed with the heaviest items on the bottom, toward the hinges, so that they will not wrinkle more perishable clothes. Candidates for the bottom layer include shoes (stuff them with small items to save space), a toilet kit, handbags (stuff them to help keep their shape), and an alarm clock. Fill out this layer with things that will not wrinkle or will not matter if they do, such as sweaters, socks, a bathing suit, gloves, and underwear.

If you get this first, heavy layer as smooth as possible with the fill-ins, you will have a shelf for the next layer — the most easily wrinkled items, like slacks, jackets, shirts, dresses, and skirts. These should be buttoned and zipped and laid along the whole length of the suitcase with as little folding as possible. When you do need to make a fold, do it on a crease (as with pants), along a seam in the fabric, or where it will not show (such as shirttails). Alternate each piece of clothing, using one side of the suitcase, then the other, to make the layers as flat as possible. Make the layers even and the total contents of your bag full and firm to keep things from shifting around during transit. On the top layer put the things you will want at once: nightclothes, a bathing suit, an umbrella or raincoat, a sweater.

With men's two-suiter suitcases, follow the same procedure. Then place jackets on hangers, straighten them out, and leave them unbuttoned. If they are too wide for the suitcase, fold them lengthwise down the middle, straighten the shoulders, and fold the sleeves in along the seam.

While packing, it is a good idea to separate each layer of clothes with plastic cleaning bags, which will help preserve pressed clothes while they are in the suitcase. Unpack your bags as soon as you get to your hotel. Nothing so thoroughly destroys freshly cleaned and pressed clothes as sitting for days in a suitcase. Finally, if something is badly wrinkled and can't be professionally pressed before you must wear it, hang it for several hours in a bathroom where the bathtub has been filled with very hot water; keep the bathroom door closed so the room becomes something of a steamroom. It really works miracles.

SOME FINAL PACKING HINTS: Apart from the items you pack as carry-on luggage (see above), always keep all necessary medicine, valuable jewelry, and travel or business documents in your purse, briefcase, or carry-on bag — *not in the luggage you will check.* Tuck a bathing suit into your handbag or briefcase, too; in the case of lost baggage, it's frustrating to be without one. And whether in your overnight bag or checked luggage, cosmetics and any liquids should be packed in plastic bottles or at least wrapped in plastic bags and tied.

Golf clubs and skis may be checked through as luggage (most airlines are accustomed to handling them), but tennis rackets should be carried onto the plane. Some airlines require that bicycles be partially dismantled and packaged (see *Camping and Caravanning, Hiking and Biking,* in this section). Check with the airline before departure to see if there is a specific regulation concerning any special equipment or sporting gear you plan to take.

Hints for Handicapped Travelers

 From 40 to 50 million people in the US alone have some sort of disability, and over half this number are physically handicapped. Like everyone else today, they — and the uncounted disabled millions around the world — are on the move. More than ever before, they are demanding facilities they can use comfortably, and they are being heard.

PLANNING: Collect as much information as you can about your specific disability and facilities for the disabled in France. Make your travel arrangements well in advance and specify to all services involved the exact nature of your condition or restricted mobility, as your trip will be much more comfortable if you know that there are accommodations and facilities to suit your needs. The best way to find out if your intended destination can accommodate a handicapped traveler is to write or call the local tourist authority or hotel and ask specific questions. If you require a corridor of a certain width to maneuver a wheelchair or if you need handles on the bathroom walls for support, ask the hotel manager. A travel agent or the local chapter or national office of the organization that deals with your particular disability — for example, the *American Foundation for the Blind* or the *American Heart Association* — will supply the most up-to-date information on the subject. The following organizations offer general information on access:

ACCENT on Living (PO Box 700, Bloomington, IL 61702; phone: 309-378-2961). This information service for persons with disabilities provides a free list of travel agencies specializing in arranging trips for the disabled; for a copy send a self-addressed, stamped envelope. Also offers a wide range of publications, including a quarterly magazine ($10 per year; $17.50 for 2 years) for persons with disabilities.

Comité National Français de Liaison pour la Réadaptation des Handicapés (*CNFLRH;* 38 Bd. Raspail, Paris 75007; phone: 1-45-48-90-13). A French organization affiliated with *Mobility International USA* (see listing below), the *CNFLRH* is a central source of information to contact both before and during your trip (if you visit in person, call beforehand for an appointment). The *CNFLRH* also publishes, in French, *Touristes Quand Même!,* a city-by-city listing of local services accessible to the handicapped such as banks, churches, pharmacies, and pools, as well as some tourist sites, medical specialists for the physically disabled — physical therapists, orthopedists, and so on — and sources of wheelchair rental and repair. Updated regularly, it has recently been augmented by a third volume covering Paris alone. To obtain a copy, contact a branch of the French Government Tourist Office or the *CNFLRH.*

Information Center for Individuals with Disabilities (Fort Point Pl., 1st Floor, 27-43 Wormwood St., Boston, MA 02210; phone: 800-462-5015 in Massachusetts; 617-727-5540/1 elsewhere in the US; both numbers provide voice and TDD — telecommunications device for the deaf). The center offers information and referral services on disability-related issues, publishes fact sheets on travel agents, tour operators, and other travel resources, and can help you research your trip.

Mobility International USA (*MIUSA;* PO Box 3551, Eugene, OR 97403; phone: 503-343-1284; both voice and TDD). This US branch of *Mobility International* (the main office is at 228 Borough High St., London SE1 1JX, England; phone: 44-71-403-5688), a nonprofit British organization with affiliates worldwide, offers members advice and assistance — including information on accommodations and other travel services, and publications applicable to the traveler's disability. *Mobility International* also offers a quarterly newsletter and a comprehensive sourcebook, *A World of Options for the 90s: A Guide to International Education Exchange, Community Service and Travel for Persons with Disabilities* ($14 for members; $16 for non-members). Membership includes the newsletter and is $20 a year; subscription to the newsletter alone is $10 annually.

National Rehabilitation Information Center (8455 Colesville Rd., Suite 935, Silver Spring, MD 20910; phone: 301-588-9284). A general information, resource, research, and referral service.

Paralyzed Veterans of America (*PVA;* PVA/ATTS Program, 801 18th St. NW, Washington, DC 20006; phone: 202-416-7708 in Washington, DC; 800-424-8200 elsewhere in the US). The members of this national service organization all are veterans who have suffered spinal cord injuries, but it offers advocacy services and information to all persons with a disability. *PVA* also sponsors *Access to the Skies, (ATTS),* a program that coordinates the efforts of the national and international air travel industry in providing airport and airplane access for the disabled. Members receive several helpful publications, as well as regular notification of conferences on subjects of interest to the disabled traveler.

Royal Association for Disability and Rehabilitation (*RADAR;* 25 Mortimer St., London W1N 8AB, England; phone: 44-71-637-5400). Offers a number of publications for the handicapped, including *Holidays and Travel Abroad 1993/94 — A Guide for Disabled People,* a comprehensive guidebook focusing on international travel. This publication can be ordered by sending payment in British pounds to *RADAR.* As we went to press, it cost just over £3; call for current pricing before ordering.

Society for the Advancement of Travel for the Handicapped (*SATH;* 347 Fifth Ave., Suite 610, New York, NY 10016; phone: 212-447-7284). To keep abreast of developments in travel for the handicapped as they occur, you may want to join *SATH,* a nonprofit organization whose members include consumers, as well as travel service professionals who have experience (or an interest) in travel for the handicapped. For an annual fee of $45 ($25 for students and travelers who are 65 and older) members receive a quarterly newsletter and have access to extensive information and referral services. *SATH* also offers two useful publications: *Travel Tips for the Handicapped* (a series of informative fact sheets) and *The United States Welcomes Handicapped Visitors* (a 48-page guide covering domestic transportation and accommodations that includes useful hints for travelers with disabilities abroad); to order, send a self-addressed, #10 envelope and $1 per title for postage.

Travel Information Service (Moss Rehabilitation Hospital, 1200 W. Tabor Rd., Philadelphia, PA 19141-3099; phone: 215-456-9600 for voice; 215-456-9602 for TDD). This service assists physically handicapped people in planning trips and supplies detailed information on accessibility for a nominal fee.

Blind travelers should contact the *American Foundation for the Blind* (15 W. 16th St., New York, NY 10011; phone: 800-829-0500 or 212-620-2147) and *The Seeing Eye* (Box 375, Morristown, NJ 07963-0375; phone: 201-539-4425); both provide useful information on resources for the visually impaired. *Note:* In France, Seeing Eye dogs must be accompanied by a certificate of inoculation against rabies, issued within the previous year and certified by the attending veterinarian within 5 days before arrival. *The American Society for the Prevention of Cruelty to Animals* (*ASPCA,* Education Dept., 441 E. 92 St., New York, NY 10128; phone: 212-876-7700) offers a useful booklet, *Traveling With Your Pet,* which lists inoculation and other requirements by country. It is available for $5 (including postage and handling).

In addition, there are a number of publications — from travel guides to magazines — of interest to handicapped travelers. Among these are the following:

Access to the World, by Louise Weiss, offers sound tips for the disabled traveler. It is available for $16.95 from Facts on File (460 Park Ave. S., New York, NY 10016; phone: 212-683-2244 in New York State; 800-322-8755 elsewhere in the US; 800-443-8323 in Canada). Check with your local bookstore; it also can be ordered by phone with a credit card.

The Diabetic Traveler (PO Box 8223 RW, Stamford, CT 06905; phone: 203-327-5832) is a useful quarterly newsletter. Each issue highlights a single destination or type of travel and includes information on general resources and hints for diabetics. A 1-year subscription costs $15. When subscribing, ask for the free fact sheet including an index of special articles; back issues are available for $4 each.

Guide to Traveling with Arthritis, a free brochure available by writing to the Upjohn Company (PO Box 307-B, Coventry, CT 06238), provides lots of good, commonsense tips on planning your trip and how to be as comfortable as possible when traveling by car, bus, train, cruise ship, or plane.

Handicapped Travel Newsletter is regarded as one of the best sources of information for the disabled traveler. It is edited by wheelchair-bound Vietnam veteran Michael Quigley, who has traveled to 93 countries around the world. Issued every 2 months (plus special issues), a subscription is $10 per year. Write to *Handicapped Travel Newsletter,* PO Box 269, Athens, TX 75751 (phone: 903-677-1260).

Handi-Travel: A Resource Book for Disabled and Elderly Travellers, by Cinnie Noble, is a comprehensive travel guide full of practical tips for those with disabilities affecting mobility, hearing, or sight. To order this book, send $12.95, plus shipping and handling, to the *Canadian Rehabilitation Council for the Disabled,* 45 Sheppard Ave. E., Suite 801, Toronto, Ontario M2N 5W9, Canada (phone: 416-250-7490; both voice and TDD).

The Itinerary (PO Box 2012, Bayonne, NJ 07002-2012; phone: 201-858-3400). This quarterly travel magazine for people with disabilities includes information on accessibility, listings of tours, news of adaptive devices, travel aids, and special services, as well as numerous general travel hints. A subscription costs $10 a year.

The Physically Disabled Traveler's Guide, by Rod W. Durgin and Norene Lindsay, rates accessibility of a number of travel services and includes a list of organizations specializing in travel for the disabled. Published by *Resource Directories,* it has recently gone out of print; check your local library.

Ticket to Safe Travel offers useful information for travelers with diabetes. A reprint of this article is available free from local chapters of the *American Diabetes Association.* For the nearest branch, contact the central office at 1660 Duke St., Alexandria, VA 22314 (phone: 800-232-3472 or 703-549-1500.

Travel for the Patient with Chronic Obstructive Pulmonary Disease, a publication of the George Washington University Medical Center, provides some sound practical suggestions for those with emphysema, chronic bronchitis, asthma, or other lung ailments. To order, send $2 to Dr. Harold Silver, 1601 18th St. NW, Washington, DC 20009 (phone: 202-667-0134).

Traveling Like Everybody Else: A Practical Guide for Disabled Travelers, by Jacqueline Freedman and Susan Gersten, offers the disabled tips on traveling by car, cruise ship, and plane, as well as lists of accessible accommodations, tour operators specializing in tours for disabled travelers, and other resources. It is available for $11.95, plus postage and handling, from Modan Publishing, PO Box 1202, Bellmore, NY 11710 (phone: 516-679-1380).

Travel Tips for Hearing-Impaired People, a free pamphlet for deaf and hearing-impaired travelers, is available from the *American Academy of Otolaryngology* (One Prince St., Alexandria, VA 22314; phone: 703-836-4444). For a copy, send a self-addressed, stamped, business-size envelope to the academy.

Travel Tips for People with Arthritis, a 31-page booklet published by the *Arthritis Foundation,* provides helpful information regarding travel by car, bus, train, cruise ship, or plane, planning your trip, medical considerations, and ways to conserve your energy while traveling. It also includes listings of helpful resources, such as associations and travel agencies that operate tours for disabled travelers. For a copy, contact your local *Arthritis Foundation* chapter, or send $1 to the national office, PO Box 19000, Atlanta, GA 30326 (phone: 404-872-7100).

A few more basic resources to look for are *Travel for the Disabled,* by Helen Hecker ($19.95), and by the same author, *Directory of Travel Agencies for the Disabled* ($19.95). *Wheelchair Vagabond,* by John G. Nelson, is another useful guide for travelers confined to a wheelchair (hardcover, $14.95; paperback, $9.95). All three titles are published by Twin Peaks Press, PO Box 129, Vancouver, WA 98666 (phone: 800-637-CALM or 206-694-2462). The publisher offers a catalogue (the cost is $2) of 26 other books on travel for the disabled.

Other good sources of information are branches of the French Government Tourist Office, although brochures specifically for the handicapped may not be in English. (For the US addresses of these government tourist authorities, see *Tourist Information Offices,* in this section.)

Two organizations based in Great Britain offer information for handicapped persons traveling throughout Europe, including France. *Tripscope* (63 Esmond Rd., London W4 1JE, UK; phone: 44-81-994-9294) is a telephone-based information and referral service (not a booking agent) that can help with transportation options for journeys throughout Europe. It may, for instance, be able to recommend outlets leasing small family vehicles adapted to accommodate wheelchairs. *Tripscope* also provides information on cassettes for blind or visually-impaired travelers, and accepts written requests for information from those with speech impediments. And for general information, there's *Holiday Care Service* (2 Old Bank Chambers, Station Rd., Horley, Surrey RH6 9HW, UK; phone: 44-293-774535), a first-rate, free advisory service on accommodations, transportation, and holiday packages throughout Europe for disabled visitors.

Regularly revised hotel and restaurant guides use the symbol of access (person in a wheelchair; see the symbol at the beginning of this section) to point out accommodations suitable for wheelchair-bound guests. The red *Michelin Guide to France* (Michelin; $19.95), found in general and travel bookstores, is one such publication (Michelin Guides and Maps, PO Box 3305, Spartanburg, SC 29304-3305; phone: 803-599-0850 in South Carolina; 800-423-0485 elsewhere in the US).

PLANE: The US Department of Transportation (DOT) has ruled that US airlines must accept all passengers with disabilities. As a matter of course, US airlines were pretty good about accommodating handicapped passengers even before the ruling, although each airline has somewhat different procedures. Foreign airlines also generally are good about accommodating the disabled traveler, but again, policies vary from carrier to carrier. Most carriers can accommodate passengers in wheelchairs, although advance notice usually is required. Ask for specifics when you book your flight.

Disabled passengers should always make reservations well in advance, and should provide the airline with all relevant details of their condition. These details include information on mobility and equipment that you will need the airline to supply — such as a wheelchair for boarding or portable oxygen for in-flight use. Be sure that the person to whom you speak fully understands the degree of your disability — the more details provided, the more effective help the airline can give you.

On the day before the flight, call back to make sure that all arrangements have been prepared, and arrive early on the day of the flight so that you can board before the rest of the passengers. It's a good idea to bring a medical certificate with you, stating your specific disability or the need to carry particular medicine.

Because most airports have jetways (corridors connecting the terminal with the door of the plane), a disabled passenger usually can be taken as far as the plane, and sometimes right onto it, in a wheelchair. If not, a narrow boarding chair may be used to take you to your seat. Your own wheelchair, which will be folded and put in the baggage compartment, should be tagged as escort luggage to assure that it's available at planeside upon landing rather than in the baggage claim area. Travel is not quite as simple if your wheelchair is battery-operated: Unless it has non-spillable batteries, it might not be accepted on board, and you will have to check with the airline ahead of time to find out how the batteries and the chair should be packaged for the flight. Usually people in wheelchairs are asked to wait until other passengers have disembarked. If you are making a tight connection, be sure to tell the attendant.

Passengers who use oxygen may not use their personal supply in the cabin, though it may be carried on the plane as cargo (the tank must be empty) when properly packed and labeled. If you will need oxygen during the flight, the airline will supply it to you (there is a charge) provided you have given advance notice — 24 hours to a few days, depending on the carrier.

Useful information on every stage of air travel, from planning to arrival, is provided in the booklet *Incapacitated Passengers Air Travel Guide.* To receive a free copy, write to the *International Air Transport Association* (Publications Sales Department, 2000 Peel St., Montreal, Quebec H3A 2R4, Canada; phone: 514-844-6311). Another helpful publication is *Air Transportation of Handicapped Persons,* which explains the general guidelines that govern air carrier policies. For a copy of this free booklet, write to the US Department of Transportation (Distribution Unit, Publications Section, M-443-2, Washington, DC 20590) and ask for "Free Advisory Circular #AC-120-32." *Access Travel: A Guide to the Accessibility of Airport Terminals,* a free publication of the *Airport Operators Council International,* provides information on more than 500 airports worldwide — including major airports throughout Europe — and offers ratings of 70 features, such as wheelchair accessible bathrooms, corridor width, and parking spaces. For a copy, contact Consumer Information Center (Pueblo, CO 81009; phone: 719-948-3334). And for additional information on accessibility in Paris airports, contact the *Paris Airport Authority,* 10 E. 21st St., Suite 600, New York, NY 10010 (phone: 212-529-8484).

Among the major carriers serving France, the following airlines have TDD toll-free lines in the US for the hearing-impaired:

American: 800-582-1573 in Ohio; 800-543-1586 elsewhere in the US.
Continental: 800-343-9195 (from 8 AM to 1 AM, eastern standard time).
Delta: 800-831-4488 throughout the US.
Northwest: 800-692-2105 in Minnesota; 800-328-2298 elsewhere in the US.
TWA: 800-252-0622 in California; 800-421-8480 elsewhere in the US.
United: 800-942-8819 in Illinois; 800-323-0170 elsewhere in the US.
USAir: 800-242-1713 in Pennsylvania; 800-245-2966 elsewhere in the US.

SHIP: Among the ships calling at French ports, *Cunard*'s *Queen Elizabeth 2, Crystal Cruises*' *Crystal Harmony,* and *Royal Cruise Line*'s *Crown Odyssey* are considered the best-equipped vessels for the handicapped. Handicapped travelers are advised to book reservations at least 90 days in advance to reserve specialized cabins.

For those in wheelchairs or with limited mobility, one of the best sources for evaluating a ship's accessibility is the free chart issued by the *Cruise Lines International Association* (500 Fifth Ave., Suite 1407, New York, NY 10110; phone: 212-921-0066). The chart lists accessible ships and indicates whether they accommodate standard-size or only narrow wheelchairs, have ramps, wide doors, low or no doorsills, handrails in the rooms, and so on. (For information on ships cruising around France, see *Traveling by Ship,* in this section.)

GROUND TRANSPORTATION: Perhaps the simplest solution to getting around is to travel with an able-bodied companion who can drive. Another alternative in France is to hire a driver/translator with a car — be sure to get a recommendation from a reputable source. The organizations listed above may be able to help you make arrangements — another source is your hotel concierge.

If you are accustomed to driving your own hand-controlled car and determined to rent one, you may have to do some extensive research, as in France it is difficult to find rental cars fitted with hand controls. If agencies do provide hand-controlled cars, they are apt to be offered only on a limited basis in major metropolitan areas and usually are in high demand. The best course is to contact the major car rental agencies listed in *Traveling by Car,* in this section, well before your departure, but be forewarned, you still may be out of luck. Other sources for information on vehicles adapted for the handicapped are the organizations discussed above.

The *American Automobile Association (AAA)* publishes a useful book, *The Handicapped Driver's Mobility Guide.* Contact the central office of your local *AAA* club for availability and pricing, which may vary at different branch offices.

Although taxis and public transportation also are available in France, accessibility for the disabled varies and may be limited in rural areas, as well as in some cities. Check with a travel agent or the French tourist authorities for information.

TRAIN: Train travel in France is well organized and increasingly accessible to travelers in wheelchairs. All *TGV* trains — France's very high speed trains, which happen to be the fastest trains in the world — have doors at platform level so that passengers can roll on and off, and spaces have been set aside where they can travel in their own wheelchairs. It is possible to take the *TGV* from Paris to Lyons, Dijon, Avignon, Nîmes, Montpellier, Marseilles, and the Tarentaise Valley. The Atlantic *TGV* line sweeps through Tours, Nantes, Quimper, and Bordeaux. (For detailed information, see *Traveling by Train,* in this section.) Other trains in France are not as well adapted to wheelchairs, but timetables for each route specify which departures are accessible. A booklet describing *Société Nationale des Chemins de Fer Français (SNCF; French National Railways)* services for the handicapped can be picked up in major railroad stations in France, primarily those in Paris. Unfortunately, it is issued in French only. Ask for *Le Supplément au Guide Pratique du Voyageur à l'Attention des Personnes à Mobilité Réduite.* Another useful booklet is the *Guide des Transports à l'Usage des Personnes à Mobilité Réduite,* available from the *Comité National Français de Liaison pour la Réadaptation des Handicapés (CNFLRH),* 38 Bd. Raspail, Paris 75007 (phone: 1-45-48-90-13).

BUS: In general, bus travel is not recommended for travelers who are totally wheelchair-bound unless they have someone along who can lift them on and off or they are members of a group tour designed for the handicapped that is using a specially outfitted bus. If you have some mobility, however, you'll find local personnel usually quite happy to help you board and exit.

TOURS: Programs designed for the physically impaired are run by specialists who have researched hotels, restaurants, and places of interest to be sure they present no insurmountable obstacles. The following travel agencies and tour operators specialize in making group and individual arrangements for travelers with physical or other disabilities.

> *Access: The Foundation for Accessibility by the Disabled* (PO Box 356, Malverne, NY 11565; phone: 516-887-5798). A travelers' referral service that acts as an intermediary with tour operators and agents worldwide, and provides information on accessibility at various locations.

Accessible Journeys (412 S. 45th St., Philadelphia, PA 19104; phone: 215-747-0171). Arranges for traveling companions who are medical professionals — registered or licensed practical nurses, therapists, or doctors (all are experienced travelers). Several prospective companions' profiles and photos are sent to the client for perusal, and if one is acceptable, the "match" is made. The client usually pays all travel expenses for the companion, plus a set fee to compensate for wages the companion would be earning at his or her usual job. This company also offers tours and cruises for people with special needs, although you don't have to take one of their tours in order to hire a companion through them.

Accessible Tours/Directions Unlimited (720 N. Bedford Rd., Bedford Hills, NY 10507; phone: 914-241-1700 in New York State; 800-533-5343 elsewhere in the continental US). Arranges group or individual tours for disabled persons traveling in the company of able-bodied friends or family members. Accepts the unaccompanied traveler if completely self-sufficient.

Dialysis at Sea Cruises (611 Barry Place, Indian Rocks Beach, FL 34635; phone: 800-544-7604 or 813-596-7604). Offers cruises that include the medical services of a nephrologist (a specialist in kidney disease) and a staff of dialysis nurses. Family, friends, and companions are welcome to travel on these cruises, but the number of dialysis patients usually is limited to roughly ten travelers per trip.

Evergreen Travel Service (4114 198th St. SW, Suite 13, Lynnwood, WA 98036-6742; phone: 800-435-2288 or 206-776-1184). Offers worldwide tours and cruises for the disabled (Wings on Wheels Tours), sight-impaired/blind (White Cane Tours), and hearing-impaired/deaf (Flying Fingers Tours). Most programs are first class or deluxe, and include a trained escort.

Flying Wheels Travel (143 W. Bridge St., Box 382, Owatonna, MN 55060; phone: 800-535-6790 or 507-451-5005). Handles both tours and individual arrangements.

The Guided Tour (613 W. Cheltenham Ave., Suite 200, Melrose Park, PA 19126; phone: 800-783-5841 or 215-782-1370). Arranges tours for people with developmental and learning disabilities, and sponsors separate tours for those who also are physicaly disabled or who simply need a slower pace.

Sprout (893 Amsterdam Ave., New York, NY 10025; phone: 212-222-9575). Arranges travel programs for mildly and moderately disabled teens and adults.

USTS Travel Horizons (11 E. 44th St., New York, NY 10017; phone: 800-487-8787 or 212-687-5121). Travel agent and registered nurse Mary Ann Hamm designs trips for individual travelers requiring all types of kidney dialysis and handles arrangements for the dialysis.

Whole Person Tours (PO Box 1084, Bayonne, NJ 07002-1084; phone: 201-858-3400). Owner Bob Zywicki travels the world with his wheelchair and offers a lineup of escorted tours (many conducted by him) for the disabled. *Whole Person Tours* also publishes *The Itinerary,* a quarterly magazine for disabled travelers (see the publication source list above).

Travelers who would benefit from being accompanied by a nurse or physical therapist also can hire a companion through *Traveling Nurses' Network,* a service provided by Twin Peaks Press (PO Box 129, Vancouver, WA 98666; phone: 800-637-CALM or 206-694-2462). For a $10 fee, clients receive the names of three nurses, whom they can then contact directly; for a $125 fee, the agency will make all the hiring arrangements for the client. Travel arrangements also may be made in some cases — the fee for this further service is determined on an individual basis.

A similar service is offered by *MedEscort International* (ABE International Airport, PO Box 8766, Allentown, PA 18105; phone: 800-255-7182 in the continental US; elsewhere, call 215-791-3111). Clients can arrange to be accompanied by a nurse, paramedic, respiratory therapist, or physician through *MedEscort*. The fees are based on the disabled traveler's needs. This service also can assist in making travel arrangements.

Hints for Single Travelers

Just about the last trip in human history on which the participants were neatly paired was the voyage of Noah's Ark. Ever since, passenger lists and tour groups have reflected the same kind of asymmetry that occurs in real life, as countless individuals set forth to see the world unaccompanied (or unencumbered, depending on your outlook) by spouse, lover, friend, or relative. Unfortunately, traveling alone can turn a traveler into a second-class citizen.

The truth is that the travel industry is not very fair to people who vacation by themselves. People traveling alone almost invariably end up paying more than individuals traveling in pairs. Most travel bargains, including package tours, accommodations, resort packages, and cruises, are based on *double-occupancy* rates. This means that the per-person price is offered on the basis of two people traveling together and sharing a double room (which means they will each spend a good deal more on meals and extras). The single traveler will have to pay a surcharge, called a single supplement, for exactly the same package. In extreme cases, this can add as much as 35% — and sometimes more — to the basic per-person rate.

Don't despair, however. Throughout France, there are scores of smaller hotels and other hostelries where, in addition to a cozier atmosphere, prices are still quite reasonable for the single traveler. Some ship lines have begun to offer special cruises for singles, and some resorts cater to the single traveler.

The obvious, most effective alternative is to find a traveling companion. Even special "singles' tours" that promise no supplements usually are based on people sharing double rooms. Perhaps the most recent innovation along these lines is the creation of organizations that "introduce" the single traveler to other single travelers, somewhat like a dating service. Some charge fees, others are free, but the basic service offered is the same: to match an unattached person with a compatible travel mate, often as part of the company's own package tours. Among such organizations are the following:

Odyssey Network (118 Cedar St., Wellesley, MA 02181; phone: 617-237-2400). Originally founded to match single women travelers, this company now includes men in its enrollment. *Odyssey* offers a quarterly newsletter for members who are seeking a travel companion, and occasionally organizes small group tours. A newsletter subscription is $50.

Partners-in-Travel (PO Box 491145, Los Angeles, CA 90049; phone: 213-476-4869). Members receive a list of singles seeking traveling companions; prospective companions make contact through the agency. The membership fee is $40 per year and includes a chatty newsletter (6 issues per year).

Singleworld (401 Theodore Fremd Ave., Rye, NY 10580; phone: 800-223-6490 or 914-967-3334). For a yearly fee of $25, this club books members on tours and cruises and arranges shared accommodations, allowing individual travelers to avoid the single supplement charge; members also receive a quarterly newsletter. *Singleworld* also offers its own package tours for singles with departures categorized by age group: 35 or younger, or for all ages.

Travel Companion Exchange (PO Box 833, Amityville, NY 11701; phone: 516-454-0880). This group publishes a newsletter for singles and a directory of individuals looking for travel companions. On joining, members fill out a lengthy questionnaire and write a small listing (much like an ad in a personal column). Based on these listings, members can request copies of profiles and contact prospective traveling companions. It is wise to join well in advance of your planned vacation so that there's enough time to determine compatibility and plan a joint trip. Membership fees, including the newsletter, are $36 for 6 months or $60 a year for a single-sex listing; $66 and $120, respectively, for a complete listing. Subscription to the newsletter alone costs $24 for 6 months or $36 per year.

Also note that certain cruise lines offer guaranteed share rates for single travelers, whereby cabin mates are selected on request. For instance, two cruise lines that provide guaranteed share rates are *Cunard* (phone: 800-221-4770) and *Royal Cruise Line* (phone: 415-956-7200 or 800-622-0538 in California; 800-227-4534 elsewhere in the US).

In addition, a number of tour packagers cater to single travelers. These companies offer packages designed for individuals interested in vacationing with a group of single travelers or in being matched with a traveling companion. Among the better established of these agencies are the following:

Club Europa/VET (802 W. Oregon St., Urbana, IL 61801; phone: 800-331-1882 or 217-344-5863). Specializes in travel for 18- to 30-year-olds. Offers multi-country escorted tours ranging from 2 weeks to 2 months, including itineraries in France.*Contiki Holidays* (1432 E. Katella Ave., Anaheim, CA 92805; phone: 800-466-0610 or 714-937-0611). Specializes in vacations for 18- to 35-year-olds. Packages to France frequently are offered. As this packager is a wholesaler, reservations must be booked through a travel agent.

Cosmos: This tour operator offers budget motorcoach tours of Europe — including France — with a guaranteed-share plan whereby singles who wish to share rooms (and avoid paying the single supplement) are matched by the tour escort with individuals of the same sex and charged the basic double-occupancy tour price. Contact the firm at one of its three North American branches: 95-25 Queens Blvd., Rego Park, NY 11374 (phone: 800-221-0090); 5301 S. Federal Circle, Littleton, CO 80123-2980 (phone: 800-556-5454 or 303-797-6000); 1801 Eglinton Ave. W., Suite 104, Toronto, Ontario M6E 2H8, Canada (phone: 416-787-1281).

Gallivanting (515 E. 79th St., Suite 20F, New York, NY 10021; phone: 800-933-9699 or 212-988-0617). Offers 1- to 2-week tours for singles age 25 through 55, including cruises and outdoor activities such as hiking, rafting, hot-air ballooning, snorkeling, and sailing. *Gallivanting* also matches singles of the same sex willing to share accommodations in order to avoid paying single supplement charges, and the agency guarantees this arrangement if bookings are paid for at least 75 days in advance.

Insight International Tours (745 Atlantic Ave., Boston MA 02111; phone: 800-582-8380 or 617-482-2000). Offers a matching service for single travelers. Several tours are geared for travelers in the 18 to 35 age group.

Marion Smith Singles (611 Prescott Pl., North Woodmere, NY 11581; phone: 516-791-4852, 516-791-4865, or 212-944-2112). Specializes in tours for singles age 20 to 50, who can choose to share accommodations to avoid paying single supplement charges.

Saga International Holidays (222 Berkeley St., Boston MA 02116; phone: 800-343-0273 or 617-451-6808). A subsidiary of a British company specializing in older travelers, many of them single, *Saga* offers a broad selection of packages for people age 60 and over or those 50 to 59 traveling with someone 60 or older. Anyone can book a *Saga* trip, but a club membership (no fee) includes a subscription to their newsletter, as well as other publications and travel services — such as a matching service for single travelers.

Singles in Motion (545 W. 236th St., Suite 1D, Riverdale, NY 10463; phone: 718-884-4464). Offers a number of packages for single travelers, including tours, cruises, and excursions focusing on outdoor activities such as hiking and biking.

Solo Flights (127 S. Compo Rd., Westport, CT 06880; phone: 203-226-9993). Represents a number of packagers and cruise lines and books singles on individual and group tours.

Suddenly Single Tours (161 Dreiser Loop, Bronx, NY 10475; phone: 718-379-8800). Specializes in group tours for singles; many participants are over 40.

Travel in Two's (239 N. Broadway, Suite 3, N. Tarrytown, NY 10591; phone: 914-631-8409). This company books solo travelers on packages offered by a number of companies (at no extra cost to clients), offers its own tours, and matches singles with traveling companions. Many offerings are listed in their quarterly *Singles Vacation Newsletter,* which costs $7.50 per issue or $20 per year.

A good book for single travelers is *Traveling On Your Own* by Eleanor Berman, which offers tips on traveling solo and includes information on trips for singles, ranging from outdoor adventures to educational programs. Available in bookstores, it also can be ordered by sending $12.95, plus postage and handling, to Random House, Order Dept., 400 Hahn Rd., Westminster, MD 21157 (phone: 800-733-3000).

Single travelers also may want to subscribe to *Going Solo,* a newsletter that offers helpful information on going on your own. Issued eight times a year, a subscription costs $36. Contact Doerfer Communications, PO Box 1035, Cambridge, MA 02238 (phone: 617-876-2764).

An attractive alternative for the single traveler who is particularly interested in meeting the French is *Club Med,* which operates scores of resorts in more than 37 countries worldwide and caters to the single traveler, as well as couples and families. Though the clientele often is under 30, there is a considerable age mix: the average age is 37. *Club Med* has 12 French resorts (9 in the Alps, 1 in Nice, and 2 in central France) — and most of the guests at its resorts are European. *Club Med* offers single travelers package-rate vacations including airfare, food, wine, lodging, entertainment, and athletic facilities. The atmosphere is relaxed, the dress informal, and the price reasonable. For information, contact *Club Med* (3 E. 54th St., New York, NY 10022; phone: 800-CLUB-MED). For further information on *Club Med* and other alternatives suitable for singles, see our discussions of accommodations in *On the Road,* in this section.

Not all single travelers are looking for a swinging scene. Some take vacations to rest and relax, and they prefer being by themselves. Generally, people who want this quieter mode of travel have to accept that their accommodations will cost more than if they were part of a couple.

Those interested in a particularly cozy type of accommodation should consider staying in a bed and breakfast establishment or guesthouse. Though a single person will likely pay more than half of the rate quoted for a couple even at these smaller places, the prices still are quite reasonable, and the homey atmosphere will make you feel less conspicuously alone.

And there's always camping. Many areas along the coast, as well as some sites around the countryside, have a place to pitch a tent and enjoy the scenery. (For more information, see *Camping and Caravanning, Hiking and Biking,* in this section.)

WOMEN AND STUDENTS: Two specific groups of single travelers deserve special mention: women and students. Countless women travel by themselves in France, and such an adventure need not be feared. Recommended is Linda White's *The Independent*

Woman's Guide to Europe (Fulcrum Publishing; $13.95), which discusses subjects from tipping to transportation, as well as coping with illness, accidents, and crime.

One lingering inhibition many female travelers still harbor is that of eating alone in public places. The trick here is to relax and enjoy your meal and surroundings; while you may run across the occasional unenlightened waiter, dining solo is no longer uncommon.

Studying Abroad – A large number of single travelers are students. Travel *is* education. Travel broadens a person's knowledge and deepens his or her perception of the world in a way no media or "armchair" experience ever could. In addition, to study a country's language, art, culture, or history in one of its own schools is to enjoy the most productive method of learning.

By "student" we do not necessarily mean a person who wishes to matriculate at a foreign university to earn an academic degree. Nor do we necessarily mean a younger person. A student is anyone who wishes to include some sort of educational program in a trip to France.

There are many benefits for students abroad, and the way to begin to discover them is to consult the *Council on International Educational Exchange (CIEE)*. This organization, which runs a variety of well-known work, study, and travel programs for students, is the US sponsor of the International Student Identity Card (ISIC). Reductions on airfare, other transportation, and entry fees to most museums and other exhibitions are only some of the advantages of the card. To apply for it, write to *CIEE* at one of the following addresses: 205 E. 42nd St., New York, NY 10017 (phone: 212-661-1414); 312 Sutter St., Suite 407, San Francisco, CA 94108 (phone: 415-421-3473); and 919 Irving St., Suite 102, San Francisco, CA 94122 (phone: 415-566-6222). Mark the letter "Attn. Student ID." Application requires a $14 fee, a passport-size photograph, and proof that you are a matriculating student (this means either a transcript or a letter or bill from your school registrar with the school's official seal; high school and junior high school students can use their report cards). There is no maximum age limit, but participants must be at least 12 years old. The *International Student Travel Guide,* which gives details of the discounts country by country, is free with membership. Another free publication of *CIEE* is the informative, annual, 72-page *Student Travel Catalog,* which covers all aspects of youth-travel abroad for vacation trips, jobs, or study programs, and also includes a list of other helpful publications. You can order the catalogue from the Information and Student Services Department at the New York address given above.

Another card of value in Europe, and also available through *CIEE,* is the Federation of International Youth Travel Organizations (FIYTO) card, which provides many of the benefits of the ISIC card. In this case, cardholders need not be students, merely under age 26. To apply, send $14 with a passport-size photo and proof of birth date to *CIEE* at one of the addresses above.

CIEE also sponsors charter flights to Europe that are open to students and non-students of any age. Flights between New York and Paris (with budget-priced add-ons available from Boston, Chicago, Denver, El Paso, Los Angeles, Las Vegas, Minneapolis, St. Louis, Salt Lake City, San Diego, San Francisco, Seattle, and several other US cities) arrive and depart daily from Kennedy (JFK) or Newark airports during the high season. Regularly scheduled direct flights also are offered from Boston to Brussels. Youth fares also may be offered by some scheduled airlines offering transatlantic service to France. To find out about current discounts and restrictions, contact the individual carriers. (Also see *Traveling by Plane,* in this section.)

SNCF (French National Railways) also offers discounts to students and youths. While the France Railpass, good for unlimited travel on the *SNCF* network, is sold only in adult and children's (ages 4 to 12) versions, there is a version of the Eurailpass restricted to travelers (including non-students) under 26 years of age. The Eurail

Youthpass entitles the bearer to either 1 or 2 months of unlimited second class rail travel in 17 countries, including France. In addition, it is honored on many European steamers and ferries (including ferry crossings between Ireland and France on the *Irish Continental Line*) and on railroad connections between the airport and the center of town in various cities. The pass also entitles the bearer to reduced rates on some bus lines in several countries. The Eurail Youthpass can be purchased only by those living outside Europe or North Africa, and it must be purchased before departure. Eurailpasses can be bought from a US travel agent, from the national railway offices of the countries in the Eurail network, or from *Rail Europe* (for further information and addresses, see *Traveling by Train,* in this section).

Students and singles in general should keep in mind that youth hostels exist in many cities throughout France. They are always inexpensive, generally clean and well situated, and they are a sure place to meet other people traveling alone. Hostels are run by the hosteling associations of 68 countries that make up the *International Youth Hostel Federation* (*IYHF*); membership in one of the national associations affords access to the hostels of the rest. To join the American affiliate, *American Youth Hostels (AYH),* contact the national office (PO Box 37613, Washington, DC 20013-7613; phone: 202-783-6161), or the local *AYH* council nearest you. As we went to press, the following membership rates were in effect: $25 for adults (between 18 and 54), $10 for youths (17 and under), $15 for seniors (55 and up), and $35 for family membership. *Hosteling North America,* which lists hostels in the US and Canada, comes with your *AYH* card (non-members can purchase this book for $5, plus postage and handling); the *Guide to Budget Accommodations,* Volume 1 covers hostels in Europe (Volume 2 covers North and South America, as well as Africa, Asia, and Australia), and must be purchased ($10.95 each, plus postage and handling).

Those who go abroad without an *AYH* card may purchase youth hostel International Guest Cards and obtain information on local youth hostels by contacting *Ligue Française pour les Auberges de la Jeunesse* (38 Bd. Raspail, Paris 75007; phone: 1-45-48-69-84). (The Guest Cards are sold in packages of up to six for approximately $3 per card; each one is good for 1 night's stay.) This association also provides information on hostels throughout France. Another source of information is the tourist boards, which may provide information sheets on hostels in their areas (see the individual city reports in THE CITIES for locations).

Those interested in campus stays should know about the *U.S. and Worldwide Travel Accommodations Guide,* which lists colleges and universities throughout Europe — including France — that offer simple, but comfortable, accommodations in their residence halls, primarily during the summer season. The accommodations vary from single and double rooms to full apartments and suites with kitchens, and the rooms can be booked by the day, week, or month. Prices range from $12 to $24 per night, with an average of about $20. An added bonus of this type of arrangement is that visitors usually are free to utilize various campus sport and recreation facilities. For a copy of the guide, which describes services and facilities in detail, send $14.50 to *Campus Travel Service,* PO Box 8355, Newport Beach, CA 92660 (phone: 714-720-3729).

Opportunities for study range from summer or academic-year courses in the language and civilization of France designed specifically for foreigners (including those whose school days are well behind them) to long-term university attendance by those intending to take a French degree.

The Cultural Services of the French Embassy provides information on university study in France and is responsible for distributing and reviewing application forms for those wishing to take a degree in France. It also can supply a list of the large number of summer and academic-year language and civilization courses given by universities and other cultural institutions. Contact the French Cultural Services at one of the following locations:

Boston: 126 Mt. Auburn St., Cambridge, MA 02138 (phone: 617-354-3464).

Chicago: 737 N. Michigan Ave., Chicago, IL 60611 (phone: 312-664-3525).

Houston: 2727 Allen Pkwy., Suite 951, Houston, TX 77019 (phone: 713-528-2231).

Miami: 1 Biscayne Tower, Suite 1710, 2 S. Biscayne Blvd., Miami, FL 33131 (phone: 305-372-1376).

New Orleans: Lykes Center Bldg., 300 Poydras St., Suite 2105, New Orleans, LA 70130 (phone: 504-523-5394).

New York: 972 Fifth Ave., New York, NY 10021 (phone: 212-439-1400).

San Francisco: 540 Bush St., San Francisco, CA 94108 (phone: 415-397-4330).

Washington, DC: 4101 Reservoir Rd. NW, Washington, DC 20007 (phone: 202-944-6000).

Language schools of particular interest include those of the *Alliance Française.* Exams at this venerable institution dedicated to the diffusion of French culture are a universal standard of French proficiency. The school in Paris is in the heart of the student quarter, but there also are schools in Bordeaux, Lyons, Marseilles, Nancy, Nice, Rouen, and Toulouse. The *Alliance Française* offers year-round courses of various duration and at varying levels, from elementary to highly advanced and for special needs (commercial French, translation, corrective phonetics). For information and application forms, write to the main headquarters: *Alliance Française de Paris* (101 Bd. Raspail, Paris 75006; phone: 1-45-44-38-28). The *Institut Catholique de Paris* (21 Rue d'Assas, Paris 75006; phone: 1-42-22-41-80) also has courses at all levels in French language and civilization, with considerable use of audiovisual methods.

Eurocentres (13 Passage Dauphine, Paris 75006; phone: 1-43-25-81-40) is an international foundation with headquarters in Zurich and schools of language and civilization in several European countries. Classes at the Paris branch, open year-round, take place in a classical building equipped with the latest in multimedia learning aides; in summer, classes also are offered at centers in Amboise and La Rochelle.

The *Chambre de Commerce et d'Industrie de Paris* sponsors programs and exams in commercial French (not for beginners), with emphasis on understanding the French business world. For details and a list of schools that give preparatory courses for the tests, contact the *Chambre de Commerce et d'Industrie de Paris,* Service des Examens, 2 Rue du Viarmes, Paris 75001 (phone: 1-42-89-78-36).

Then there's the Sorbonne. The University of Paris offers a variety of courses in French language and civilization during both the summer and the academic year. The *Cours de Civilisation Française de la Sorbonne* — a potpourri of grammar, literature, history, and fine arts — is a model for courses at a number of other French universities that offer special programs for foreigners. Since the program's creation in 1919, it has been the vehicle through which more than 100,000 students the world over have come to know France and its most illustrious universities. The course is offered for any level of proficiency. Classes run October through January; February through May; and for sessions of several different lengths over the summer. For information contact *Cours de Civilisation Française de la Sorbonne* (47 Rue des Ecoles, Paris 75005; phone: 1-40-46-22-11, Ext. 2664). Another very popular source of year-round courses in language and civilization is the *l'Université d'Eté pour les Etudiants Etrangers* at the University of Provence. The courses take place in Aix-en-Provence, one of the most gracious towns in the south of France. University-age students tend to dominate, and the town is one large, animated campus. Contact the *Office Universitaire des Relations Extérieures* (Cours d'Eté, 29 Av. Robert-Schuman, Aix-en-Provence 13621; phone: 42-59-99-30, Ext. 317; or 42-59-22-71).

Complete details on more than 3,000 available courses abroad (including at French universities) and suggestions on how to apply are contained in two books published by the *Institute of International Education* (IIE Books, Publications Office, 809 UN Plaza, New York, NY 10017; phone 212-984-5412): *Vacation Study Abroad* ($31.95, plus shipping and handling) and *Academic Year Abroad* ($39.95, plus shipping and handling). A third book, *Teaching Abroad*, is out of print; check your local library. IIE Books also offers a free pamphlet called *Basic Facts on Study Abroad.*

The *National Registration Center for Study Abroad (NRCSA;* PO Box 1393, Milwaukee, WI 53201; phone: 414-278-0631) also offers a publication called the *Worldwide Classroom: Study Abroad and Learning Vacations in 40 Countries: 1993-1994,* available for $8.50, plus shipping and handling, which includes information on over 160 schools and cultural centers that offer courses for Americans with the primary focus on foreign language and culture.

Those who are interested in a "learning vacation" abroad also may be interested in *Travel and Learn* by Evelyn Kaye. This guide to educational travel discusses a wide range of opportunities — everything from archaeology to whale watching — and provides information on organizations that offer programs in these areas of interest. The book is available in bookstores for $23.95; or you can send $26 (which includes shipping charges) to Blue Penguin Publications (147 Sylvan Ave., Leonia, NJ 07605; phone: 800-800-8147 or 201-461-6918). *Learning Vacations* by Gerson G. Eisenberg also provides extensive information on seminars, workshops, courses, and so on — in a wide variety of subjects. Available in bookstores, it also can be ordered from Peterson's Guides (PO Box 2123, Princeton, NJ 08543-2123; phone: 800-338-3282 or 609-243-9111) for $11.95, plus shipping and handling.

Work, Study, Travel Abroad: The Whole World Handbook, issued by the *Council on International Educational Exchange (CIEE),* is an informative, chatty guide on study programs, work opportunities, and travel hints, with a particularly good section on France. It is available for $10.95, plus shipping and handling, from *CIEE* (address above).

AFS Intercultural Programs (313 E. 43rd St., New York, NY 10017; phone 800-AFS-INFO or 212-949-4242) sets up exchanges between US and foreign high school students on an individual basis for a semester or whole academic year.

National Association of Secondary School Principals (NASSP; 1904 Association Dr., Reston, VA 22091; phone: 703-860-0200), an association of administrators, teachers, and state education officials, sponsors *School Partnership International,* a program in which secondary schools in the US are linked with partner schools abroad for an annual short-term exchange of students and faculty.

If you are interested in a home-stay travel program, in which you learn about another culture by living with a family, contact the *Experiment in International Living* (PO Box 676, Brattleboro, VT 05302-0676; phone: 802-257-7751 in Vermont; 800-451-4465 elsewhere in the continental US), which sponsors home-stay educational travel in more than 40 countries, including locations throughout France. The organization aims its programs at high school or college students.

Another organization specializing in travel as an educational experience is the *American Institute for Foreign Study (AIFS;* 102 Greenwich Ave., Greenwich, CT 06830; phone: 800-727-AIFS, 203-869-9090, or 203-863-6087). Although it does not specialize in travel to France, approximately a third of the participants in its hundred-some programs around the world — tours, academic year, and summer programs — choose to study in France. The programs at the University of Paris, the University of Grenoble, and the Collège International de Cannes are, naturally, most favored by those studying French. At the Sorbonne, the European Studies Program is the major course offering; in Grenoble, courses include the History of French Cinema and International Relations; in Cannes, Political Science, Business Administration, Acting, and French Cuisine are included in the prospectus. Students can enroll for the full academic year or for any number of semesters. *AIFS* caters primarily to bona fide high school or college students, but its non-credit international learning programs are open to independent travelers of all ages (approximately 20% of *AIFS* students are over 25).

WORKING ABROAD: Jobs for foreigners in France are not easy to come by and in general do not pay well enough to cover all the expenses of a trip. They do provide an invaluable learning experience, however, while helping to make a trip more affordable.

For individuals age 18 (or 16 in Germany) and up who are interested in working abroad as volunteers, the *CIEE* also publishes a helpful book, *Volunteer!,* which includes volunteer programs with nonprofit organizations worldwide, many of which are located in France. It is available for $8.95, plus shipping and handling, from the *CIEE* at one of the addresses given above. *CIEE* also may be able to provide other information or assistance to those interested in working in France.

For a complete list of programs administered by French institutions, contact the French Government Tourist Office in North America (see *Tourist Information Offices,* in this section, for addresses).

Hints for Older Travelers

Special discounts and more free time are just two factors that have given Americans over age 65 a chance to see the world at affordable prices. Senior citizens make up an ever-growing segment of the travel population, and the trend among them is to travel more frequently and for longer periods of time.

PLANNING: When planning a vacation, prepare your itinerary with one eye on your own physical condition and the other on a topographical map. Keep in mind variations in climate, terrain, and altitudes, which may pose some danger for anyone with heart or breathing problems.

Older travelers may find the following publications of interest:

The Discount Guide for Travelers Over 55, by Caroline and Walter Weintz, is an excellent book for budget-conscious older travelers. Published by Penguin USA, it is currently out of print; check your local library.

Going Abroad: 101 Tips for the Mature Traveler offers tips on preparing for your trip, commonsense precautions en route, and some basic travel terminology. This concise, free booklet is available from *Grand Circle Travel,* 347 Congress St., Boston, MA 02210 (phone: 800-221-2610 or 617-350-7500).

The International Health Guide for Senior Citizen Travelers, by Dr. W. Robert Lange, covers such topics as trip preparations, food and water precautions, adjusting to weather and climate conditions, finding a doctor, motion sickness, jet lag, and so on. Also includes a list of resource organizations that provide medical assistance for travelers. It is available for $4.95 postpaid from Pilot Books, 103 Cooper St., Babylon, NY 11702 (phone: 516-422-2225).

The Mature Traveler is a monthly newsletter that provides information on travel discounts, places of interest, useful tips, and other topics of interest for travelers 49 and up. To subscribe, send $24.50 to GEM Publishing Group, PO Box 50820, Reno, NV 89513 (phone: 702-786-7419).

Take a Camel to Lunch and Other Adventures for Mature Travelers, by Nancy O'Connell, offers offbeat and unusual adventures for travelers over 50. Available for $8.95, plus shipping and handling, at bookstores or directly from Bristol Publishing Enterprises, PO Box 1737, San Leandro, CA 94577 (phone: 800-346-4889 or 510-895-4461).

Travel Tips for Older Americans is a useful booklet that provides good, basic advice. This US State Department publication (stock number: 044-000-02270-2) can be ordered by sending a check or money order for $1 to the Superintendent of Documents (US Government Printing Office, Washington, DC 20402) or by calling 202-783-3238 and charging the order to a credit card.

Unbelievably Good Deals & Great Adventures That You Absolutely Can't Get Unless You're Over 50, by Joan Rattner Heilman, offers travel tips for older travelers, including discounts on accommodations and transportation, as well as a list of organizations for seniors. It is available for $7.95 (plus shipping and handling) from Contemporary Books, 180 N. Michigan Ave., Chicago, IL 60601 (phone: 312-782-9181).

HEALTH: Health facilities in France generally are excellent; however, an inability to speak the language can pose a serious problem, not in receiving treatment at large hospitals, where many doctors and other staff members will speak English, but in getting help elsewhere or in getting to the place where help is available. A number of organizations exist to help travelers avoid or deal with a medical emergency overseas. For information on these services, see *Staying Healthy,* in this section.

Pre-trip medical and dental checkups are strongly recommended. In addition, be sure to take along any prescription medication you need, enough to last *without a new prescription* for the duration of your trip; pack all medications with a note from your doctor for the benefit of airport authorities. If you have specific medical problems, bring prescriptions and a "medical file" composed of the following:

1. A summary of your medical history and current diagnosis.
2. A list of drugs to which you are allergic.
3. Your most recent electrocardiogram, if you have heart problems.
4. Your doctor's name, address, and telephone number.

DISCOUNTS AND PACKAGES: The *Carte Vermeil* entitles anyone over 60 to a variety of discounts, including a 50% discount on rail fares in France during off-peak hours. (This doesn't restrict you to night trains only; rather, you travel during "blue periods" — from Saturday noon to Sunday at 3 PM and from Monday noon to Friday at 3 PM, excluding holidays.) The card, which is available only in France, can be obtained by filling out a form at a major railroad station and presenting it, along with one's passport, to the designated official at the station. The cost at press time was 165F (about $29) and the card is good for a year; discounts are applicable to tickets bought in France only.

The *Carte Vermeil* or other proof of age (such as a passport) will enable older travelers to take advantage of other senior citizen discounts in France — entrance fees to monuments, museums, concerts, movies, theaters, and so on. Keep an eye out for the phrases *tarif réduit* (reduced rate) and *troisième âge* ("third age," the French version of our "senior citizen" or "golden age"). Wherever you go and whatever you do, remember to ask if there are special rates for senior citizens. The answer will frequently be yes.

Many hotel chains, airlines, cruise lines, bus companies, car rental companies, and other travel suppliers offer discounts to older travelers. For instance, *Air Inter,* the national French domestic airline, offers special rates for senior citizens on selected flights within France, including potential savings of up to 60%. US airlines such as *American, Continental, Delta, Northwest, TWA, United,* and *USAir* offer those age 62 and over (and one traveling companion per qualifying senior citizen) discounts on flights from the US to France. Other airlines also offer discounts for passengers age 60 (or 62) and over, which also may apply to one traveling companion. For information on current prices and applicable restrictions, contact the individual carriers.

Some discounts, however, are extended only to bona fide members of certain senior citizens organizations. For instance, *Sheraton* offers a 25% discount to any senior citizen and participating *Holiday Inns* offer 10% discounts for *AARP* members — in both cases, these discounts may not apply during certain "blackout" periods. (See listings below for more information on *AARP* benefits.) Because the same organizations frequently offer package tours to both domestic and international destinations, the benefits of membership are twofold: Those who join can take advantage of discounts as individual travelers and also reap the savings that group travel affords. In addition, because the age requirements for some of these organizations are quite low (or nonexistent), the benefits can begin to accrue early.

In order to take advantage of these discounts, you should carry proof of your age (or eligibility). A driver's license, membership card in a recognized senior citizens organization, or a Medicare card should be adequate.

Among the organizations dedicated to helping older travelers see the world are the following:

American Association of Retired Persons (*AARP;* 601 E St. NW, Washington, DC 20049; phone: 202-434-2277). The largest and best known of these organizations. Membership is open to anyone 50 or over, whether retired or not; dues are $8 a year, $20 for 3 years, or $45 for 10 years, and include spouse. The *AARP* Travel Experience Worldwide program, available through *American Express Travel Related Services* offers members tours, cruises, and other travel programs worldwide designed exclusively for older travelers. Members can book these services by calling *American Express* at 800-927-0111 for land and air travel, or 800-745-4567 for cruises.

Mature Outlook (Customer Service Center, 6001 N. Clark St., Chicago, IL 60660; phone: 800-336-6330). Through its *Travel Alert,* tours, cruises, and other vacation packages are available to members at special savings. Hotel and car rental discounts and travel accident insurance also are available. Membership is open to anyone 50 years of age or older, costs $9.95 a year, and includes a bimonthly newsletter and magazine, as well as information on package tours for older travelers.

National Council of Senior Citizens (1331 F St. NW, Washington, DC 20004; phone: 202-347-8800). Here, too, the emphasis is on keeping costs low. This nonprofit organization offers members a different roster of package tours each year, as well as individual arrangements through its affiliated travel agency *(Vantage Travel Service).* Although most members are over 50, membership is open to anyone (regardless of age) for an annual fee of $12 per person or couple. Lifetime membership costs $150.

Certain travel agencies and tour operators offer special trips geared to older travelers. Among them are the following:

Evergreen Travel Service (4114 198th St. SW, Suite 13, Lynnwood, WA 98036-6742; phone: 800-435-2288 or 206-776-1184). This specialist in trips for persons with disabilities recently introduced Lazybones Tours, a program offering leisurely tours for older travelers. Most programs are first class or deluxe, and include an escort.

Gadabout Tours (700 E. Tahquitz Canyon Way, Palm Springs, CA 92262; phone: 619-325-5556 or 800-521-7309 in California; 800-952-5068 elsewhere in the US). Offers escorted tours and cruises to numerous destinations worldwide, including France.

Grand Circle Travel (347 Congress St., Boston, MA 02210; phone: 800-221-2610 or 617-350-7500). Caters exclusively to the over-50 traveler and packages a large variety of escorted tours, cruises, and extended vacations. Membership, which is automatic when you book a trip through *Grand Circle,* includes discount certificates on future trips and other travel services, such as a matching service for single travelers and a helpful free booklet, *Going Abroad: 101 Tips for Mature Travelers* (see the source list above).

Grandtravel (6900 Wisconsin Ave., Suite 706, Chevy Chase, MD 20815; phone: 800-247-7651 or 301-986-0790). This agency specializes in trips for grandparents and their grandchildren (aunts and uncles are welcome, too), bringing the generations together through travel. Several itineraries coincide with school vacations and emphasize historic and natural sites. Transportation, accommodations, and activities are thoughtfully arranged to meet the needs of the young and the young-at-heart.

Insight International Tours (745 Atlantic Ave., Boston, MA 02111; phone: 800-582-8380 or 617-482-2000). Offers a matching service for single travelers. Several tours are geared for mature travelers.

Saga International Holidays (222 Berkeley St., Boston MA 02116; phone: 800-343-0273 or 617-451-6808). A subsidiary of a British company catering to older travelers, *Saga* offers a broad selection of packages for people age 60 and over or those 50 to 59 traveling with someone 60 or older. Anyone can book a *Saga* trip, but a club membership (no fee) includes a subscription to their newsletter, as well as other publications and travel services.

Many travel agencies, particularly the larger ones, are delighted to make presentations to help a group of senior citizens select destinations. A local chamber of commerce should be able to provide the names of such agencies. Once a time and place are determined, an organization member or travel agent can obtain group quotations for transportation, accommodations, meal plans, and sightseeing. Larger groups usually get the best breaks.

Another choice open to older travelers is a trip that includes an educational element. *Elderhostel,* a nonprofit organization, offers programs at educational institutions worldwide, including the University of Bordeaux, University of Burgundy, University of Caen, and the University of Lyons in France. The foreign programs generally last about 2 weeks, and include double occupancy accommodations in hotels or student residence halls and all meals. Travel to the programs usually is by designated scheduled flights, and participants can arrange to extend their stay at the end of the program. Elderhostelers must be at least 60 years old (younger if a spouse or companion qualifies), in good health, and not in need of special diets. For a free catalogue describing the program and current offerings, write to *Elderhostel* (75 Federal St., Boston, MA 02110; phone: 617-426-7788). Those interested in the program also can purchase an informational videotape for $5.

Interhostel, a program sponsored by the Division of Continuing Education of the University of New Hampshire, sends travelers back to school at cooperating institutions in 25 countries on 4 continents. Participants attend lectures on the history, economy, politics, and cultural life of the country they are visiting, go on field trips to pertinent points of interest, and take part in activities meant to introduce them to their foreign contemporaries. In France, they have a program that takes in the Basque country, along with a stay in Paris. Trips are for 2 weeks; accommodations are on campus in university residence halls or off campus in modest hotels (double occupancy). Groups are limited to 35 to 40 participants who are at least 50 years old (or at least 40 if a participating spouse is at least 50), physically active, and not in need of special diets. For further information or to receive the three free seasonal catalogues, contact *Interhostel,* UNH Division of Continuing Education, 6 Garrison Ave., Durham, NH 03824 (phone: 800-733-9753 or 603-862-1147).

Hints for Traveling with Children

 What better way to encounter the world's variety than in the company of the young, wide-eyed members of your family? Their presence does not have to be a burden or an excessive expense. The current generation of discounts for children and family package deals can make a trip together quite reasonable.

A family trip will be an investment in your children's future, making geography and history come alive to them, and leaving a sure memory that will be among the fondest you will share with them someday. Their insights will be refreshing to you; their impulses may take you to unexpected places with unexpected dividends.

PLANNING: Here are several hints for making a trip with children easy and fun.

1. Children, like everyone else, will derive more pleasure from a trip if they know something about the country before they arrive. Begin their education about a month before you leave. Using maps, travel magazines, and books, give children a clear idea of where you are going and how far away it is.
2. Children should help to plan the itinerary, and where you go and what you do should reflect some of their ideas. If they know something about the sites they'll visit, they will have the excitement of recognition when they arrive.
3. Children also will enjoy learning some French phrases — a few basics like *"bonjour"* ("hello"), *"au revoir"* ("good-bye"), and *"merci bien"* ("thanks a lot").
4. Familiarize the children with francs. Give them an allowance for the trip, and be sure they understand just how far it will or won't go.
5. Give children specific responsibilities: The job of carrying their own flight bags and looking after their personal things, along with some other light chores, will give them a stake in the journey.
6. Give each child a travel diary or scrapbook to take along.

One useful resource to which you may want to refer is the *Berlitz Jr. French* instructional series for children. The series combines an illustrated storybook with a lively 60-minute audiocassette. Each book features a character, Teddy, who goes to school and learns to count and spell and speak French phrases. The book/cassette package is available for $19.95, plus shipping and handling, from Macmillan Publishing Company, Front and Brown Sts., Riverside, NJ 08075 (phone: 800-257-5755).

Children's books about France provide an excellent introduction to the country and its culture. Some particularly good titles include the following:

Adventures of Tintin series: by Herge (Methuen Children's Books; $19.95 each). Older children can follow the reporter Tintin through his thrilling escapades.

Asterix series: by Goscinny (Hodder Dargand; $19.95 for the series). These comic-book-style illustrated stories take place in France during the Roman times.

Babar series: by Laurent De Brunhoff (Random House; $10.95). Tiny tots in kindergarten up through grade 3 will enjoy the adventures of Babar the Elephant (and friends).

Castle by David Macaulay (Houghton Mifflin; $14.95 hardcover; $6.95 paperback). Using text and drawings, this book shows how castles were built in the 13th century, and is particularly suited to helping children from kindergarten to grade 5 learn about the castles they may see in France.

Cathedral: The Story of Its Construction by the same author (Houghton Mifflin; $14.95 hardcover; $6.95 paperback). A must for those visiting Chartres, Notre-Dame, Sacré-Coeur, and other great cathedrals of France.

The French Resistance by Don Lawson (Silver Burdett & Ginn; $10.95). Suitable for advanced readers interested in both intrigue and history.

Great Painters (Putnam; $20.95). This beautifully illustrated book, by Piero Ventura, is an excellent introduction to painting for older children (ages 12 and up). It discusses French painting from the Romantic movement through Impressionism, Fauvism, and Cubism.

The Red Balloon by Albert Lamerisse (Creative Education; $14.95). This French classic is about a young boy befriended by a balloon.

The Usborne First Book of France by Louise Somerville with Beatrice Rios and Camille Pataut (EDC Publishing; $6.95). This book serves as an introduction to the culture, food, and language of France for children ages 5 through 9.

Welcome to France (Passport Books, National Textbook Company; $5.95). This tiny encyclopedia is recommended for families visiting France. It points out a variety of unfamiliar sites, from tall vineyard tractors to baguettes (there's a box to check when each thing has been spotted), suggests family activities in Paris, describes churches and châteaux, and discusses food, wine, and festivals.

These and other children's books can be found at many general bookstores and in libraries. Bookstores specializing in children's books include the following:

Books of Wonder (132 7th Ave., New York, NY 10011; phone: 212-989-3270; or 464 Hudson St., New York, NY 10014; phone: 212-645-8006). Carries both new and used books for children.

Cheshire Cat (5512 Connecticut Ave. NW, Washington, DC 20015; phone: 202-244-3956). Specializes in books for children of all ages.

Eeyore's Books for Children (2212 Broadway, New York, NY 10024; phone: 212-362-0634; or 25 E. 83rd St., New York, NY 10028; phone: 212-988-3404). Carries an extensive selection of children's books; features a special travel section.

Reading Reptile, Books and Toys for Young Mammals (4120 Pennsylvania St., Kansas City, MO 64111; phone: 816-753-0441). Carries books for children and teens to age 15.

Red Balloon (891 Grand Ave., St. Paul, MN 55105; phone: 612-224-8320). Carries both new and used books for children.

White Rabbit Children's Books (7755 Girard Ave., La Jolla, CA 92037; phone: 619-454-3518). Carries books and music for children (and parents).

Another source of children's books perfect to take on the road is *The Family Travel Guides Catalogue.* This detailed booklet contains informative and amusing titles focusing on numerous countries, including France. For instance, the *Travel Papers,* a series of short articles full of useful facts for families, covers France. The *Travel Papers* and the catalogue are available from Carousel Press (PO Box 6061, Albany, CA 94706; phone: 415-527-5849), which also is the mail-order supplier of all titles.

And for parents, *Travel With Your Children* (TWYCH; 80 Eighth Ave., New York, NY 10011; phone: 212-206-0688) publishes a newsletter, *Family Travel Times,* that focuses on families with young travelers and offers helpful hints. An annual subscription (10 issues) is $35 and includes a copy of the "Airline Guide" issue (updated every other year), which focuses on the subject of flying with children. This special issue is available separately for $10.

Another newsletter devoted to family travel is *Getaways.* This quarterly publication provides reviews of family-oriented literature, activities, and useful travel tips. To subscribe, send $25 to *Getaways,* Att. Ms. Brooke Kane, PO Box 8282, McLean, VA 22107 (phone: 703-534-8747).

Also of interest to parents traveling with their children is *How to Take Great Trips With Your Kids,* by psychologist Sanford Portnoy and his wife, Joan Flynn Portnoy.

The book includes helpful tips from fellow family travelers, tips on economical accommodations and touring by car, recreational vehicle, and train, as well as over 50 games to play with your children en route. It is available for $8.95, plus shipping and handling, from Harvard Common Press (535 Albany St., Boston, MA 02118; phone: 617-423-5803). Another title worth looking for is *Great Vacations with Your Kids,* by Dorothy Jordan (Dutton; $12.95).

A series of books called "Kidding Around" includes a Paris volume that starts with an overview of the city, along with some interesting background information, and then is divided into areas, with descriptions of the various attractions in the general order in which you might encounter them. It can be ordered directly from the publisher by sending $9.95, plus shipping, to John Muir Publications, PO Box 613, Santa Fe, NM 87504, or by calling 800-888-7504 or 505-982-4087.

Another book on family travel, *Travel with Children* by Maureen Wheeler, offers a wide range of practical tips on traveling with children, and includes accounts of the author's family travel experiences. It is available for $10.95, plus shipping and handling, from Lonely Planet Publications, Embarcadero West, 112 Linden St., Oakland, CA 94607 (phone: 510-893-8555).

Finally, parents arranging a trip with their children may want to contact *Let's Take the Kids* (1268 Devon Ave., Los Angeles, CA 90024; phone: 800-726-4349 or 213-274-7088), an information service specializing in family travel. Although they do not arrange or book trips, this organization provides parents with information and advice on questions they may have about accommodations, itineraries, transportation, and other aspects of a planned vacation. They also offer a parent travel network, whereby parents who have been to a particular destination can evaluate it for others.

GETTING THERE AND GETTING AROUND: Begin early to investigate all available discount and charter flights, as well as any package deals and special rates offered by the major airlines. Booking is sometimes required up to 2 months in advance. You may well find that charter companies offer no reductions for children, or not enough to offset the risk of last-minute delays or other inconveniences to which charters are subject. The major scheduled airlines, on the other hand, almost invariably provide hefty discounts for children. If traveling by ship, note that children under 12 usually travel at considerably reduced fares on cruise lines. When using local transportation such as a bus or train, ask about lower fares for children or family rates.

Plane – When you make your reservations, tell the airline that you are traveling with a child. Children ages 2 through 12 generally travel at about half to two-thirds of the regular full-fare adult ticket price on most international flights. This regular children's fare, however, usually is much higher than the excursion fare (which also may be even further reduced for children). On many international flights, children under 2 travel at about 10% of the adult fare if they sit on an adult's lap. A second infant without a second adult would pay the fare applicable to children ages 2 through 11.

Although some airlines will, on request, supply bassinets for infants, most carriers encourage parents to bring their own safety seat on board, which then is strapped into the airline seat with a regular seat belt. This is much safer — and certainly more comfortable — than holding the child in your lap. If you do not purchase a seat for your baby, you have the option of bringing the infant restraint along on the off chance that there might be an empty seat next to yours — in which case some airlines will let you use that seat at no charge for your baby and infant seat. However, if there is no empty seat available, the infant seat no doubt will have to be checked as baggage (and you may have to pay an additional charge), since it generally does not fit under airplane seats or in the overhead racks. The safest bet is to pay for a seat.

Be forewarned: Some safety seats designed primarily for use in cars do not fit into plane seats properly. Although nearly all seats manufactured since 1985 carry labels indicating whether they meet federal standards for use aboard planes, actual seat sizes may vary from carrier to carrier. At the time of this writing, the FAA was in the process of reviewing and revising the federal regulations regarding infant travel and safety devices — it was still to be determined if children should be *required* to sit in safety seats and whether the airlines will have to provide them.

If using one of these infant restraints, you should try to get bulkhead seats, which will provide extra room to care for your child during the flight. You also should request a bulkhead seat when using a bassinet — again, this is not as safe as strapping the child in. On some planes bassinets hook into a bulkhead wall; on others they are placed on the floor in front of you. (Note that bulkhead seats often are reserved for families traveling with children.) As a general rule, babies should be held during takeoff and landing.

Request seats on the aisle if you have a toddler or if you think you will need to use the bathroom frequently. Carry onto the plane all you will need to care for and occupy your children during the flight — formula, diapers, a sweater, books, favorite stuffed animals, and so on. Dress your baby simply, with a minimum of buttons and snaps, because the only place you may have to change a diaper is at your seat or in a small lavatory. The flight attendant can warm a bottle for you.

On most US carriers, you also can ask for a hot dog, hamburger, or even a fruit plate, instead of the airline's regular lunch or dinner, if you give at least 24 hours' notice. Some, but not all, airlines have baby food aboard. While you should bring along toys from home, also ask about children's diversions. Some carriers have terrific free packages of games, coloring books, and puzzles.

When the plane takes off and lands, make sure your baby is nursing or has a bottle, pacifier, or thumb in its mouth. This sucking will make the child swallow and help to clear stopped ears. A piece of hard candy will do the same thing for an older child.

Parents traveling by plane with toddlers, children, or young teenagers may want to consult *When Kids Fly,* a free booklet published by Massport (Public Affairs Department, 10 Park Plaza, Boston, MA 02116-3971; phone: 617-973-5600), which includes helpful information on airfares for children, infant seats, what to do in the event of overbooked or cancelled flights, and so on.

■**Note:** Newborn babies, whose lungs may not be able to adjust to the altitude, should not be taken aboard an airplane. And some airlines may refuse to allow a pregnant woman in her 8th or 9th month to fly. Check with the airline ahead of time, and carry a letter from your doctor stating that you are fit to travel — and indicating the estimated date of birth.

Ship and Train – Some shipping lines offer cruises that feature special activities for children, particularly during periods that coincide with major school holidays like *Christmas, Easter,* and the summer months. On such cruises, children may be charged special cut-rate fares, and there are youth counselors to organize activities. Occasionally, a shipping line even offers free passage during the summer months for children under age 16 occupying a stateroom with two (full-fare) adult passengers. Your travel agent should know which cruise lines offer such programs.

If you plan to travel by train when abroad, note that on *SNCF (French National Railways)* children under 4 (accompanied by an adult) travel free, provided they do not occupy a seat; children under 4 occupying a seat and from ages 4 through 11 also often travel at a lower fare. For yourself, you might consider buying a France Railpass, which offers unlimited travel on French trains for a set period of time at a reduced rate. The Eurailpass, which is good for unlimited train travel throughout Europe, including France, is half price for children ages 4 through 12. Both passes must be bought before leaving the US, so plan ahead. On some buses and subways in France, children under 4 ride free, those aged 4 to 10 for half fare. For more information, see *Traveling by Ship* and *Traveling by Train,* in thus section, as well as the individual city reports in THE CITIES.

Car – Touring by car allows the greatest flexibility for traveling and packing. Games and simple toys, such as magnetic checkerboards or drawing pencils and pads, also provide a welcome diversion. And frequent stops so that children can run around make car travel much easier.

ACCOMMODATIONS AND MEALS: Often a cot for a child will be placed in a hotel room at little or no extra charge. If you wish to sleep in separate rooms, special rates sometimes are available for families; some places do not charge for children under a certain age. In many of the larger chain hotels, the staff are more used to children. These hotels also are likely to have swimming pools or gamerooms — both popular with most youngsters. Many large resorts also have recreation centers for children. Cabins, bungalows, condominiums, and other rental options offer families privacy, flexibility, some kitchen facilities, and often lower costs.

You might want to look into accommodations along the way that will add to the color of your trip. For instance, hotels in the *Relais du Silence* group — an association of moderately priced independent hotels, mostly in the country — include old manor houses, châteaux, and inns. (If you do stay at one of these *relais,* be sure to discuss the fact that they will have to be particularly well-behaved — as the name suggests, the emphasis is on peace and quiet.) Other types of accommodations to investigate include *logis,* simple, small, family-run hotels in towns and villages; *auberges,* very simple inns in rural areas; and *gîtes,* a heading that covers several types of lodgings — a *gîte* can be a room in a private house, much like a bed and breakfast, but it also can be a self-catering accommodation in a country cottage or on a farm. These lodgings provide a delightful experience for the whole family and permit a view of French life different from that gained by staying in a conventional hotel. Children will love them.

Among the least expensive options is a camping facility; many are situated in beautiful, out-of-the-way spots, and generally are good and well equipped, and less expensive than any hotel. For further information on accommodations options for the whole family, see our discussions in *On the Road,* and for information on camping facilities, see *Camping and Caravanning, Hiking and Biking,* in this section.

Better hotels in France may be able to arrange for a sitter for the times you will want to be without the children — for an evening's entertainment or a particularly rigorous stint of sightseeing. Whether the sitter is hired directly or through an agency, ask for and check references and, unless your children speak French, ask that the candidates have at least a basic command of English.

At mealtime, don't deny yourself or your children the delights of a new style of cooking. Encourage them to try new foods. Children like to know what kind of food to expect, so it will be interesting to look up French dishes before leaving. In metropolitan and resort areas, you may be able to find American-style food, but you probably will have to settle for local fare everywhere else. And don't forget about picnics. Note that although milk is pasteurized and water is potable in France, it's wise to stick to bottled water for small children and for those with sensitive stomachs.

Things to Remember

1. If you are spending your vacation touring many places, pace the days with children in mind. Break the trip into half-day segments, with running around or "doing" time built in. Keep travel time on the road to a maximum of 4 to 5 hours a day.
2. Don't forget that a child's attention span is far shorter than an adult's. Children don't have to see every sight or all of any sight to learn something from their trip; watching, playing with, and talking to other children can be equally enlightening.
3. Let your children lead the way sometimes; their perspective is different from yours, and they may lead you to things you would never have noticed on your own.

4. Remember the places that children love to visit: aquariums, zoos, amusement parks, beaches, nature trails, and so on. Among the activities that may pique their interest are bicycling, snorkeling, boat trips, horseback riding, visiting children's museums, and viewing natural habitat exhibits. And France, the home of the puppet Guignol, is rife with Punch and Judy shows and other lively entertainments.

On the Road

Credit and Currency

 It may seem hard to believe, but one of the greatest (and least understood) costs of travel is money itself. If that sounds simplistic, consider the fact that you can lose as much as 30% of your dollar's value simply by changing money at the wrong place or in the wrong form. Your one single objective in relation to the care and retention of your travel funds is to make them stretch as far as possible. When you do spend money, it should be on things that expand and enhance your travel experience, with no buying power lost due to carelessness or lack of knowledge. This requires more than merely ferreting out the best airfare or the most charming budget hotel. It means being canny about the management of money itself. Herewith, a primer on making money go as far as possible overseas.

CURRENCY: The basic unit of currency in France is the French **franc**, which is divided into 100 **centimes**. The French franc also is the basic unit of currency in Monaco, although Monégasque coins with the same face value as French coins are in circulation there (and are fully convertible in France). The franc is distributed in coin denominations of 10F, 5F, 2F, 1F, and ½F, and 20 centimes, 10 centimes, and 5 centimes. Paper money is distributed in denominations of 500F, 200F, 100F, 50F, and 20F. The value of French currency in relation to the US dollar fluctuates daily, affected by a wide variety of phenomena.

A brief word about the French way of expressing numbers: In essence, the French use a comma where Americans use a decimal point and vice versa. Thus five thousand francs, which we express as 5,000F, will be written in France as F5.000, Ff5.000, or 5.000F (or "Fr."); fifty centimes, which we write as 50 centimes (there is no abbreviation for "centimes"), is expressed as a decimal (hundredths of a franc) and appears in France as 0,50 (often without an accompanying "F," "Ff," or "Fr."); and four francs, fifty centimes appears as F4,50, Ff4,50, or 4,50F. (Note that throughout this book we use the American decimal style.)

Although US dollars may be accepted in France (particularly at points of entry), you certainly will lose a percentage of your dollar's buying power if you do not take the time to convert it into French francs. By paying for goods and services in the local currency, you save money by not negotiating invariably unfavorable exchange rates for every small purchase, and avoid difficulty where US currency is not readily — or happily — accepted. *Throughout this book, unless specifically stated otherwise, prices are given in US dollars.*

There is no limit to the amount of US currency that can be brought into France. To avoid problems anywhere along the line, it's advisable to fill out any customs forms provided when leaving the US on which you can declare all money you are taking with you — cash, traveler's checks, and so on. US law requires that anyone taking more than $10,000 into or out of the US must report this fact on customs form No. 4790, which is available at all international airports or from any office of US Customs. If taking over $10,000 out of the US, you must report this *before* leaving the US; if returning with such an amount, you should include this information on your customs declaration. Although travelers usually are not questioned by customs officials about currency when entering or leaving, the sensible course is to observe all regulations just to be on the safe side.

FOREIGN EXCHANGE: Because of the volatility of exchange rates, be sure to check the current value of the French franc before finalizing any travel budget. And before you actually depart on your trip, be aware of the most advantageous exchange rate offered by various financial institutions — US banks, currency exchange firms (at home or abroad), or French banks.

For the best sense of current trends, follow the rates posted in the financial section of your local newspaper or in such international newspapers as the *International Herald Tribune*. You also can check with your own bank or with *Thomas Cook Foreign Exchange* (for the nearest location, call 800-972-2192 in Illinois; 800-621-0666 elsewhere in the US). *Harold Reuter and Company,* a currency exchange service in New York City (200 Park Ave., Suite 332 E., New York, NY 10166; phone: 212-661-0826), is particularly helpful in determining current trends in exchange rates. *Ruesch International* offers up-to-date foreign currency information and currency-related services (such as converting French franc VAT refund checks into US dollars; see *Duty-Free Shopping and Value Added Tax,* in this section). *Ruesch* also offers a pocket-size *Foreign Currency Guide* (good for estimating equivalents while planning) and a helpful brochure, *6 Foreign Exchange Tips for the Traveler.* Contact *Ruesch International* at one of the following addresses: 3 First National Plaza, Suite 2020, Chicago, IL 60602 (phone: 312-332-5900); 1925 Century Park E., Suite 240, Los Angeles, CA 90067 (phone: 213-277-7800); 608 Fifth Ave., "Swiss Center," New York, NY 10020 (phone: 212-977-2700); or 1350 Eye St. NW, 10th Floor and street level, Washington, DC 20005 (phone: 800-424-2923 or 202-408-1200).

In France, you will find the official rate of exchange posted in banks, airports, money exchange houses, hotels, and some shops. As a general rule, expect to get more local currency for your US dollar at banks than at any other commercial establishment. Exchange rates do change from day to day, and most banks offer the same (or very similar) exchange rates. (In a pinch, the convenience of exchanging money in your hotel — sometimes on a 24-hour basis — *may* make up for the difference in the exchange rate.) Don't try to bargain in banks or hotels — no one will alter the rates for you.

Money exchange houses *(bureaux de change)* are financial institutions that charge a fee for the service of exchanging dollars for local currency. When considering alternatives, be aware that although the rate varies among these establishments, the rates of exchange offered are bound to be slightly less favorable than the terms offered at nearby banks — again, don't be surprised if you get fewer francs for your dollar than the rate published in the papers.

That said, however, the following rules of thumb are worth remembering.

Rule number one: Never (repeat: *never*) exchange more than $10 for foreign currency at hotels, restaurants, or retail shops. If you do, you are sure to lose a significant amount of your US dollar's buying power. If you do come across a storefront exchange counter offering what appears to be an incredible bargain, there's too much counterfeit specie in circulation to take the chance (see Rule number three, below).

Rule number two: Estimate your needs carefully; if you overbuy, you lose twice — buying and selling back. Every time you exchange money, someone is making a profit, and rest assured it isn't you. Use up foreign notes before leaving, saving just enough for last-minute incidentals and tips.

Rule number three: Don't buy money on the black market. The exchange rate may be better, but it is a common practice to pass off counterfeit bills to unsuspecting foreigners who aren't familiar with the local currency. It's usually a sucker's game, and you almost always are the sucker; it also can land you in jail.

Rule number four: Learn the local currency quickly and keep abreast of daily fluctuations in the exchange rate. These are listed in the English-language *International Herald Tribune* daily for the preceding day, as well as in every major newspaper in Europe. Rates change to some degree every day. For rough calculations, it is quick and safe to use round figures, but for purchases and actual currency exchanges, carry a small pocket calculator to help you compute the exact rate. Inexpensive calculators specifically designed to convert currency amounts for travelers are widely available.

When changing money, don't be afraid to ask how much commission you're being charged, and the exact amount of the prevailing exchange rate. In fact, in any exchange of money for goods or services, you should work out the rate before making any payment.

TIP PACKS: It's not a bad idea to buy a *small* amount of French coins and banknotes before your departure. But note the emphasis on "small," because, for the most part, you are better off carrying the bulk of your travel funds to France in US dollar traveler's checks (see below). Still, the advantages of tip packs are threefold:

1. You become familiar with the currency (really the only way to guard against making mistakes or being cheated during your first few hours in a new country).
2. You are guaranteed some money should you arrive when a bank or exchange counter isn't open or available.
3. You don't have to depend on hotel desks, porters, or taxi drivers to change your money.

A "tip pack" is the only foreign currency you should buy before you leave. If you do run short upon arrival, US dollars often are accepted at points of entry. In other areas, they either *may* be accepted, or someone may accommodate you by changing a small amount — though invariably at a less than advantageous rate.

TRAVELER'S CHECKS: It's wise to carry traveler's checks while on the road instead of (or in addition to) cash, since it's possible to replace them if they are stolen or lost; you usually can receive partial or full replacement funds the same day if you have your purchase receipt and proper identification. Issued in various denominations and available in both US dollars and French francs, with adequate proof of identification (credit cards, driver's license, passport), traveler's checks are as good as cash in most hotels, restaurants, stores, and banks.

You will be able to cash traveler's checks fairly easily throughout France, but don't expect to meander into a small village and be able to get instant cash. Also, even in metropolitan areas, don't assume that restaurants, small shops, and other establishments are going to be able to change checks of large denominations. Worldwide, more and more establishments are beginning to restrict the amount of traveler's checks they will accept or cash, so it is wise to purchase at least some of your checks in small denominations — say, $10 and $20. Also, don't expect to change them into US dollars except at banks and international airports.

Although traveler's checks are available in foreign currencies such as French francs, the exchange rates offered by the issuing companies in the US generally are far less favorable than those available from banks both in the US and abroad. Therefore, it usually is better to carry the bulk of your travel funds abroad in US dollar–denomination traveler's checks.

Every type of traveler's check is legal tender in banks around the world, and each company guarantees full replacement if checks are lost or stolen. After that the similarity ends. Some charge a fee for purchase, others are free; you can buy traveler's checks at almost any bank, and some are available by mail. Most important, each traveler's check issuer differs slightly in its refund policy — the amount refunded immediately, the accessibility of refund locations, the availability of a 24-hour refund service, and the time it will take for you to receive replacement checks. For instance, *American Express* guarantees replacement of lost or stolen traveler's checks in under

3 hours at any *American Express* office — other companies may not be as prompt. (Note that *American Express*'s 3-hour policy is based on a traveler's being able to provide the serial numbers of the lost checks. Without these numbers, refunds can take much longer.)

We cannot overemphasize the importance of knowing how to replace lost or stolen checks. All of the traveler's check companies have agents around the world, both in their own name and at associated agencies (usually, but not necessarily, banks), where refunds can be obtained during business hours. Most of them also have 24-hour toll-free telephone lines, and some even will provide emergency funds to tide you over on a Sunday.

Be sure to make a photocopy of the refund instructions that will be given to you by the issuing institution at the time of purchase. To avoid complications should you need to redeem lost checks (and to speed up the replacement process), keep the purchase receipt and an accurate list, by serial number, of the checks that have been spent or cashed. You may want to incorporate this information in an "emergency packet," also including your passport number and date of issue, the numbers of the credit cards you are carrying, and any other bits of information you shouldn't be without. Always keep these records separate from the checks and the original records themselves (you may want to give them to a traveling companion to hold).

Although most people understand the desirability of carrying funds in the form of traveler's checks as protection against loss or theft, an equally good reason is that US dollar traveler's checks invariably get a better rate of exchange than cash does — usually by at least 1% (know, however, that the discrepancy has been known to be substantially higher). The reasons for this are technical, but potential savings exist and it is a fact of travel life that should not be ignored.

That 1% won't do you much good, however, if you already have spent it *buying* your traveler's checks. Several of the major traveler's check companies charge 1% for the aquisition of their checks. To receive fee-free traveler's checks you may have to meet certain qualifications — for instance, *Thomas Cook*'s checks issued in US currency are free if you make your travel arrangements through its travel agency. *American Express* traveler's checks are available without charge to members of the *American Automobile Association*. Holders of some credit cards (such as the *American Express Platinum* card) also may be entitled to free traveler's checks. The issuing institution (e.g., the particular bank at which you purchase them) may itself charge a fee. If you purchase traveler's checks at a bank in which you or your company maintains significant accounts (especially commercial accounts of some size), the bank may absorb the 1% fee as a courtesy.

■ **Note:** *American Express* cardholders now can order traveler's checks by phone through a new service called *Cheques On Call.* By dialing 800-55-FOR-TC, *Green* cardholders can order up to $1,000, *Gold* cardholders, $2,500, and *Platinum* cardholders, $10,000 of *American Express* traveler's checks during any 7-day period. In addition, the usual 1% acquisition fee is waived for *Gold* and *Platinum* cardholders. There is no postage charge if the checks are sent by first class mail; *Federal Express* delivery is available for a fee.

American Express, Bank of America, Citicorp, Thomas Cook, MasterCard, and *Visa* all offer traveler's checks. Here is a list of the major companies issuing traveler's checks and the numbers to call in the event that loss or theft makes replacement necessary:

American Express: To report lost or stolen checks in the US, call 800-221-7282. In France, call 05-908600, toll-free. In other parts of Europe, *American Express* advises travelers to call 44-273-571600 (in Brighton, England), collect. Another (slower) option is to call 801-964-6665 (in the US), collect; or contact the nearest *American Express* office.

Bank of America: To report lost or stolen checks in the US, call 800-227-3460. In France, call 05-902122, toll-free, or call 415-624-5400 or 415-622-3800, collect.

Citicorp: To report lost or stolen checks in the US, call 800-645-6556 or 800-541-8882. In France, call 05-46-93-69 (toll-free); you also can call 813-623-1709 or 813-626-4444, collect. Customers also can contact *Citicorp*'s office in England by calling 44-81-318-8950 or 44-71-982-4044, collect.

MasterCard: Note that *Thomas Cook MasterCard* (below) is now handling all *MasterCard* traveler's check inquiries and refunds.

Thomas Cook MasterCard: To report lost or stolen checks in the US, call 800-223-7373. In France, call 05-908330, toll-free, or 609-987-7300 (in the US) or 44-733-502995 (in England), collect, and they will direct you to the nearest branch of *Thomas Cook.*

Visa: To report lost or stolen checks in the continental US, call 800-227-6811. In France, call 05-908299, toll-free, or 415-574-7111, collect. In Europe, you also can call this London number collect: 44-71-937-8091.

CREDIT CARDS: Some establishments you may encounter during the course of your travels may not honor any credit cards and some may not honor all cards, so there is a practical reason to carry more than one. Most US credit cards, including the principal bank cards, are honored in France; however, keep in mind that some cards may be issued under different names in Europe. For example, *MasterCard* may go under the name *Access* or *Eurocard,* and *Visa* often is called *Carte Bleue* — wherever these equivalents are accepted, *MasterCard* and *Visa* may be used. The following is a list of credit cards that enjoy wide domestic and international acceptance:

American Express: Cardholders can cash personal checks for traveler's checks and cash at *American Express* or its representatives' offices in the US up to the following limits (within any 21-day period): $1,000 for *Green* and *Optima* cardholders; $5,000 for *Gold* cardholders; and $10,000 for *Platinum* cardholders. Check cashing also is available to cardholders who are guests at participating hotels (up to $250), and for holders of airline tickets, at participating airlines (up to $50). Free travel accident, baggage, and car rental insurance if ticket or rental is charged to card; additional insurance also is available for additional cost. For further information or to report a lost or stolen *American Express* card, call 800-528-4800 throughout the continental US; in France, contact a local *American Express* office or call 919-333-3211, collect.

Carte Blanche: Free travel accident, baggage, and car rental insurance if ticket or rental is charged to card; additional insurance also is available at additional cost. For medical, legal, and travel assistance worldwide, call 800-356-3448 throughout the US; in France, call 214-680-6480, collect. For further information or to report a lost or stolen *Carte Blanche* card, call 800-525-9135 throughout the US; in France, call 303-790-2433, collect.

Diners Club: Emergency personal check cashing for cardholders staying at participating hotels and motels (up to $250 per stay). Free travel accident, baggage, and car rental insurance if ticket or rental is charged to card; additional insurance also is available for an additional fee. For medical, legal, and travel assistance worldwide, call 800-356-3448 throughout the US; in France, call 214-680-6480, collect. For further information or to report a lost or stolen *Diners Club* card, call 800-525-9135 throughout the US; in France, call 303-790-2433, collect.

Discover Card: Offered by a subsidiary of Sears, Roebuck & Co., it provides cardholders with cash advances at numerous automatic teller machines and *Sears* stores throughout the US. For further information and to report a lost or stolen *Discover* card, call 800-DISCOVER throughout the US. Note that at press time, the *Discover* card was not yet accepted in France; call for current information when planning your trip.

MasterCard: Cash advances are available at participating banks worldwide. Check with your issuing bank for information. *MasterCard* also offers a 24-hour emergency lost card service; call 800-826-2181 throughout the US; in France and elsewhere worldwide, call 314-275-6690, collect.

Visa: Cash advances are available at participating banks worldwide. Check with your issuing bank for information. *Visa* also offers a 24-hour emergency lost card service; call 800-336-8472 throughout the US. In France, call 415-574-7700, collect.

One of the thorniest problems relating to the use of credit cards abroad concerns the rate of exchange at which a purchase is charged. Be aware that the exchange rate in effect on the date that you make a foreign purchase or pay for a foreign service has nothing at all to do with the rate of exchange at which your purchase is billed to you when you get the invoice (sometimes months later) in the US. The amount which the credit card company charges is either a function of the exchange rate at which the establishment's bank processed it or the rate in effect on the day your charge is received at the credit card center. (There is a 1-year limit on the time a hotel or other business can take to forward its charge slips.)

The principle at work in this credit card–exchange rate roulette is simple, but very hard to predict. You make a purchase at a particular dollar versus local currency exchange rate. If the dollar gets stronger in the time between purchase and billing, your purchase actually costs you less than you anticipated. If the dollar drops in value during the interim, you pay more than you thought you would. There isn't much you can do about these vagaries except to follow one very broad, very clumsy rule of thumb: If the dollar is doing well at the time of purchase, its value increasing against the local currency, use your credit card on the assumption it still will be doing well when billing takes place. If the dollar is doing badly, assume it will continue to do badly and pay with traveler's checks or cash. If you get too badly stuck, the best recourse is to complain, loudly. Be aware, too, that most credit card companies charge an unannounced, un-itemized 1% fee for converting foreign currency charges to US dollars.

SENDING MONEY ABROAD: If you have used up your traveler's checks, cashed as many emergency personal checks as your credit card allows, drawn on your cash advance line to the fullest extent, and still need money, it is possible to have it sent to you via one of the following services:

American Express (phone: 800-543-4080). Offers a service in France called "Moneygram" completing money transfers to anywhere in France in only 10 minutes. The sender can go to any *American Express Travel Office* in the US and transfer money by presenting cash, a personal check, money order, or credit card — *Discover, MasterCard, Visa,* or *American Express Optima* card. (No other *American Express* or other credit cards are accepted.) *American Express Optima* cardholders also can arrange for this transfer over the phone. The minimum transfer charge is $25, which rises with the amount of the transaction. Up to $10,000 can be transferred in each transaction (additional funds can be sent in separate transactions), but credit card users are limited to the amount of their pre-established credit line. To collect at the other end, the receiver must show identification (passport, driver's license, or other picture ID) at an *American Express Travel Office* in France (there are 14 in France, 3 in Paris alone).

Western Union Telegraph Company (phone: 800-325-4176). There are two procedures for sending money via *Western Union* to France, depending on whether funds are being sent to Paris or elsewhere in the country. If sending money to

Paris, a friend or relative can go, cash in hand, to any *Western Union* office in the US, where, for a *minimum* charge of $13 (it rises with the amount of the transaction), the funds will be sent to one of *Western Union*'s four branch offices in the city and may arrive in as little as 15 minutes. Funds sent elsewhere in France must be transferred through a participating *Crédit Commercial de France, Western Union*'s correspondent bank (with branches in over 25 cities), for which there is an additional $25 surcharge, and processing can take from 2 to 5 business days. When the money arrives in France, you will not be notified — you must go to the *Western Union* branch office or bank to inquire. The funds will be turned over in French francs, based on the rate of exchange in effect on the day of receipt. For a higher fee, the US party to this transaction may call *Western Union* with a *MasterCard* or *Visa* number to send up to $2,000, although larger transfers will be sent to a predesignated location.

If you are literally down to your last centime, and you have no other way to obtain cash, the nearest US consulate (see *Legal Aid and Consular Services,* in this section) will let you call home to set these matters in motion.

CASH MACHINES: Automatic teller machines (ATMs) are increasingly common worldwide. If your bank participates in one of the international ATM networks (most do), the bank will issue you a "cash card" along with a personal identification code or number (also called a PIC or PIN). You can use this card at any ATM in the same electronic network to check your account balances, transfer monies between checking and savings accounts, and — most important for a traveler — withdraw cash instantly. Network ATMs generally are located in banks, commercial and transportation centers, and near major tourist attractions.

Some financial institutions offer exclusive automatic teller machines for their own customers only at bank branches. At the time of this writing, ATMs (called "Mini-banques") in France that *are* connected generally belong to *CIRRUS,* an international network. The *CIRRUS* system encompasses over 70,000 automatic teller machines worldwide, including over 600 locations in France. *MasterCard* and *Visa* cardholders also may use their cards to draw cash against their credit lines. For further information on the *CIRRUS* network, call 800-4-CIRRUS.

Accommodations

From elegant, centuries-old châteaux to modern, functional high-rises and modest, inexpensive inns, it's easy to be comfortable and well cared for on almost any budget in France. Admittedly, Paris and the Riviera are full of deluxe establishments providing expensive services to people with money to burn, but more affordable alternatives always have been available, particularly in the countryside.

On the whole, deluxe and first class accommodations in France, especially in the large metropolitan centers (Paris and Lyons, for instance), are somewhat more expensive than the same types of accommodations in the US. When the dollar is strong, such top-of-the-line establishments are within the range of a great number of travelers who previously would not have been able to afford them. But lately, the generally unfavorable rate of exchange has rendered princely accommodations very pricey.

Once upon a time, such things as the superiority of New World plumbing made many of the numerous less expensive accommodations alternatives unacceptable for North Americans. Today, the gap has closed considerably, and in France the majority of hostelries catering to the tourist trade are likely to be at least adequate in their basic facilities.

Before you go, consult the brochures and booklets cited in the descriptions below, most of which are available free from the US offices of the French Government Tourist Office (for addresses, see *Tourist Information,* in this section). Other publications can be purchased from the travel bookstores listed in *Books, Newspapers, Magazines and Newsletters,* also in this section.

HOTELS AND INNS: Hotels may be large or small, part of a chain or independent, new and of the "international standard" type or well established and traditional. There are built-for-the-purposes premises and converted stately homes and villas, resort hotels offering plenty of opportunities for recreation, and smaller tourist hotels offering virtually none.

The annual *Guide des Hôtels de France,* issued by the French ministry in charge of tourism, doesn't list all the hotels in the country, but it does list all those (more than 18,000) that are considered tourist hotels and that are officially graded according to the government's star system of classification. The highest rating is four stars plus L, indicating, to use the official definition, a luxury hotel. Four stars means a top hotel; three stars a very comfortable hotel; two stars, a good average hotel; and one star or *HRT* (for *Hôtels Rattachés Tourisme;* literally, hotels linked to tourism), a plain but fairly comfortable hotel. The guide, which comes out in early spring, is too extensive to be distributed to the general public, but regional versions with the same information are available by writing to any French Government Tourist Office in the US and specifying the area of the country in which you are interested (for instance, *Paris–Ile-de-France* and *Riviera–Côte d'Azur* are two of the titles). The listing for each hotel includes its address and telephone number, number of rooms, amenities, star category, and minimum and maximum room prices; though the latter inevitably are somewhat out of date by the time of publication, they include service charges and applicable taxes and certainly serve as a valid estimate. The French Government Tourist Office also distributes a list of US representatives handling reservations for French hotels, as well as a special list of selected Paris hotels, with their ratings and the names of the US representatives.

Even without such a guide in hand, it is not difficult for visitors in France to figure out where a particular hotel fits in the scheme of things. A dark blue, octagonal "Commissariat Général au Tourisme" sign on the front of any hotel that has been classified clearly reveals the number of stars attained. Inside, a detailed rendering of prices appears by law near the reception desk. A good many hotels, in fact, actually display minimum and maximum prices on the front door, where they are easily legible from the street. The posted prices include service and, except in a few cases, all taxes, so that receiving the bill at the end of a stay is rarely a cause for shock. The prices also usually are for double rooms (since in France, as elsewhere, there are more double than single rooms), and the price of a double usually holds whether it's occupied by one or two people. The price of breakfast — which may be obligatory or optional — also must be posted by the reception desk.

Hotels earn their stars according to a variety of criteria, among them the percentage of rooms with private bathrooms. All rooms in a four-star L hotel and 90% of the rooms in a four-star hotel must have them; the required proportion drops to 30% in a two-star; and there is no requirement for one-star hotels. There may be, therefore, a number of room types in any given hotel, especially in two- and three-star establishments, where the most expensive rooms will have private bathrooms containing a tub or a shower (usually slightly less expensive) and the least expensive rooms will have only a *cabinet de toilette* (that is, a washbasin with hot and cold water and a bidet) or, simply, a washbasin. (Guests in rooms with a *cabinet de toilette* or less have access to the public bathroom in the hall.) Central heating is universal in classified tourist hotels (though it may not always be adequate by American standards), and the type of breakfast provided is nearly universal: continental, which consists of coffee, tea, or hot chocolate with bread, rolls, or croissants, butter, and jam. Also nearly universal is the bolster pillow found on a French bed; for those who prefer it, the more familiar kind of pillow usually is stashed in the closet (if not, ask for one).

As in other countries, a number of well-known hotel chains or associations have properties in France, particularly in Paris and other major cities. Among these are the following (with toll-free reservations numbers to call in the US):

Best Western (phone: 800-528-1234). Has 142 properties in France, 40 in Paris alone.

Forte Hotels International (formerly *Trusthouse Forte;* phone: 800-225-5843). Has 3 properties in Paris and 1 in Monte Carlo.

Hilton International (phone: 800-445-8667). Owned by the Ladbroke's gambling group of Great Britain, there is no proprietary connection with the US *Hilton* chain. Has 3 properties in Paris, 1 in Cannes, and 1 in Strasbourg.

Holiday Inn (phone: 800-465-4329). Has 11 properties in France: 4 in Paris, 1 each in Calais, Dijon, Lyons, Nantes, Nice, Strasbourg, and Toulouse.

Hyatt (phone: 800-233-1234). Has 1 property in Paris.

Inter-Continental (phone: 800-327-0200). Has 2 properties in Paris and 1 in Cannes.

Marriott (phone: 800-228-9290). Has 1 property in Paris.

Meridien (phone: 800-543-4300). Has 2 properties in Paris and 1 in Nice.

Sheraton (phone: 800-325-3535). Has 1 property in Paris.

Among other large European chains which have a US office that will provide information and take reservations is *Pullman Sofitel.* This group, comprising the recently merged *Pullman* and *Sofitel* chains, has over 50 properties throughout France. *Pullman Sofitel* is represented by *Resinter Reservations* (2 Overhill Rd., Scarsdale, NY 10583; phone: 800-221-4542). Reservations for all *Pullman Sofitel* properties also can be made through *Utell International* (810 N. 96th St., Omaha, NE 68114-2594; phone: 800-44-UTELL), which represents over 2,000 properties throughout Europe, including over 280 in France.

Major French hotel chains include *Ibis* and *Novotel,* which together have over 200 properties throughout France, and *Mercure,* with about 100 properties. All three are represented by *Resinter Reservations* (see above). Another well-established French hotel group is *Minotels France Accueil* (2 Chemin Renou, Lausanne, Switzerland, CH-1005; phone: 41-21-204640), with 132 member establishments in France.

Relais & Châteaux – A very special case among French hotel associations is one that, though native to France, has grown to include establishments in many other countries. Two groups of members — *Relais Châteaux* and *Relais Gourmands* — belong to the *Relais & Châteaux* association, including approximately 150 establishments throughout France.

The first group is of particular interest to travelers who wish lodgings reflecting the ambience, style, and, frequently, the history of the places they are visiting. Some properties actually are ancient castles — several dating back to the 13th century — that have been converted into hotels. Others are old inns (*relais* means a posthouse or inn), manor houses, even converted mills, convents, farmhouses, and monasteries. A few well-known city establishments are included, such as the elegant *Crillon* in Paris, but most are in quiet country settings, and frequently are graced with parks, ponds, and flowering gardens.

Members of the *Relais & Châteaux* group often are expensive, though no more than you would pay for deluxe, authentically elegant accommodations and service anywhere in the world (and many are not all that costly). Accommodations and service from one *relais* or château to another can range from simple but comfortable to elegantly deluxe (they are rated three-star, four-star, and four-star L by the government), but they all maintain very high standards in order to retain their memberships, as they are reviewed annually.

Although most *Relais & Châteaux* have good restaurants, the second *Relais* group, *Relais Gourmands,* is composed of exceptionally fine restaurants. These establishments also may have rooms for rent, but the establishments are *not* rated on the basis of their accommodations, so they may not match (or even come close to) the standards of room quality maintained by the others.

An illustrated catalogue of all the *Relais & Châteaux* properties is published annually and is available for $7 from *Relais & Châteaux* (2400 Lazy Hollow, Suite 152D, Houston, TX 77063; phone: 800-743-8033 or 713-783-8033). The association also can provide information on member properties. Reservations can be made directly with the establishments or through a travel agency.

Relais du Silence, Logis, Auberges, Gîtes – Several other French hotel associations merit consideration. One, *Relais du Silence,* is similar to the *Relais & Châteaux* group but on a more modest scale. Hotels in this group, too, are mainly former manor houses, rustic wayside inns, châteaux, and other characteristic properties in picturesque country settings or at the edges of small, quiet villages (as the name implies, a premium is placed on peaceful surroundings). Most of the *Relais du Silence* — there are more than 100 in France — correspond to two- and three-star hotels in the government classification system, though a few four-star establishments also are included, and the cost of a double room at most of them is in the moderate range. The annual *Relais du Silence* booklet, also illustrated, is available from the French Government Tourist Office.

Another group well worth knowing about is the *Fédération Nationale des Logis et Auberges de France,* whose approximately 5,000 members make it by far the largest in the country. The very great majority are *logis* (literally, lodging, dwelling, or home), which are small — anywhere from 10 to 20 rooms is the average — family-run hotels at the one-star level scattered in towns and villages throughout the countryside. The remainder are *auberges* (inns), establishments that usually are too simple to be classified in the government's star system and always are found in rural locations (they used to be known as *auberges rurales*). Each group adheres to its own quality charter, which places great store in friendly service, stresses home cooking with regional specialties on the menu, and regulates such things as the amenities provided (all rooms in both the *logis* and *auberges* have a sink with hot and cold running water). Room prices, single or double, usually are not more than $30 a night and can be a good deal less. The annual guide *Logis et Auberges de France* (in French), listing 5,000 hotels and inns, is available from the *Fédération Nationale des Logis et Auberges de France* in France, can be ordered from the *Traveller's Bookstore* (22 W. 52nd St., New York, NY 10019; phone: 212-664-0995) for $21.95, plus shipping and handling, and may be found in other travel bookstores.

Finally, a last organization, the *Fédération Nationale des Gîtes Ruraux de France,* may be of interest. This is an association of the owners of several types of holiday accommodations, the majority of which are grouped under the heading *Gîte de France* (literally, lodging or stopping place) and offer self-catering country rentals by the week or longer. (These are discussed in "Rental Options," below.)

Hotels in Monaco – Information on hotels in the Principality of Monaco is available from *SBM* (509 Madison Ave., New York, NY 10022; phone: 212-688-9890) or the Monaco Government Tourist and Convention Bureau (845 Third Ave., New York, NY 10022; phone: 212-759-5227). As in France, levels of comfort and price range from the prime four-star deluxe category down to the very economical one-star. The top hotels, including such diverse specimens as the opulent 19th-century landmark *Hôtel de Paris* and the gleaming modern sprawl of *Loews,* are resort hotels in the worldly social center of Monte Carlo, on or off the beach, but usually complete with a swimming pool and at least one of the country's most gala restaurants. Budget accommodations tend to cluster not far away in the vicinity of the train station. Monaco's hoteliers frequently offer reduced rates to travelers who stay a specified length of time during the off-season.

Reservation Services in France – Though not all travelers would face the prospect of arriving in a strange city without a reservation with equal sangfroid, in France there are services that help book empty rooms for those who risk it. To begin with, the hotel reservation board at Charles de Gaulle Airport's terminal building No. 1 provides information on more than 300 Paris hotels, showing vacancies in green (or a full house in red) at the push of a button; using the phone provided, a confirmed reservation can be made on the spot.

In addition, the tourist offices of 45 French cities (and in several of the larger airports and railway stations as well) provide an *Accueil de France* service that will reserve a room in the area for a small fee. In Paris, the service is available at the main Office du Tourisme de Paris (127 Av. des Champs-Elysées; for information, call 47-23-61-72), open daily year-round, and at branch offices in the Gare d'Austerlitz, Gare de l'Est, Gare de Lyon, and Gare du Nord train stations.

The same system also can be used by those who prefer to give full rein to their wanderlust unhampered by hotel reservations made too far in advance but who still appreciate the security of knowing where they will spend the next night. Any *Accueil de France* service can book a room ahead for you, provided the area you're going to also has an *Accueil* service. The reservation is made via telex to the *Accueil* office in the destination city; you pay a service charge plus a deposit (usually half of 1 night's stay) and receive in return a check for this amount to present to the hotel, where the sum will be deducted from your bill. The annually revised *Michelin Red Guide to France* ($24.95) lists the addresses of all the *Accueil* offices in the system. To order, contact Michelin Guides and Maps, PO Box 3305, Spartanburg, SC 29304-3305 (phone: 803-599-0850 in South Carolina; 800-423-0485 elsewhere in the US).

BED AND BREAKFAST ESTABLISHMENTS AND OTHER ACCOMMODATIONS: Across the English Channel, where they are a staple of the low-cost lodging scene, bed and breakfast establishments are found wherever there are extra rooms to let in a private home and a host or hostess willing to attend to the details of hospitality. They are not yet so commonplace in France or on the rest of the Continent, but they do exist, and not only in rural locations.

A smaller French group than those discussed above offers overnight accommodations under the heading *Gîte de France–Chambre d'Hôte.* The *gîte chambre d'hôte,* actually a room in a private house or on a farm, is the nearest French equivalent to the bed and breakfast establishments of Great Britain. At latest count, there were about 6,000 of them; many are in the countryside. The rooms provided are very modest, but their owners — like the owners of other types of *gîtes* — are governed by a charter spelling out minimum standards of comfort.

A *gîte chambre d'hôte,* or bed and breakfast establishment (commonly known as a B&B), provides precisely what the name implies. It is unusual for a bed and breakfast establishment to offer the extra services found in other hostelries, so the bed and breakfast route often is the least expensive way to go.

Beyond these two fundamentals, nothing else is predictable about bed and breakfast establishments. The bed may be in an extra room in a family home, in an apartment with a separate entrance, or in a freestanding cottage elsewhere on the host's property. In European B&Bs, private baths are the exception rather than the rule. Some homes have only one room to let, whereas others may be large enough to have another party or two in residence at the same time.

Breakfast probably will be a version of the standard continental breakfast: fruit plus juice, croissant, toast, roll, or homemade bread, with jam or marmalade, and coffee or tea; however, particularly in rural areas, the breakfast may be a heartier one, and as often as not (language barrier aside), served along with some family history to add to the local lore. If you're in a studio with a kitchenette, you may be furnished with the makings and have to prepare it for yourself. Despite their name, some B&Bs offer an evening meal as well — by prior arrangement and at extra cost.

Some hosts enjoy helping guests with tips on what to see and do and even serve as informal tour guides, while in other places your privacy won't be disturbed. Whichever the case, the beauty of bed and breakfast establishments is that you'll always have a warm reception and the opportunity to meet many more inhabitants of the region than you otherwise would, which means you'll experience their hospitality in a special fashion.

Bed and breakfast establishments range from private homes and lovely mansions to small inns and guesthouses. Although some hosts may be contacted directly, as in the US, some prefer that arrangements be made through a reservations service. The general procedure for making reservations through bed and breakfast services is that you contact them with your requirements, they help find the right place, and confirm your reservations upon receipt of a deposit. Any further information needed will be provided either by the service or the owner of the bed and breakfast establishment.

It is best to find out as much as you can before you book to avoid disappointment. The French Government Tourist Office distributes a *Gîtes Ruraux de France* brochure explaining the overall system, and a selection of about 200 *gîtes chambres d'hôte* is included in the *French Farm and Village Holiday Guide* (see below).

Regional and departmental guides to *gîtes* can be obtained in France from the *Fédération Nationale des Gîtes Ruraux de France* (35 Rue Godot-de-Mauroy, Paris 75009; phone: 1-47-42-25-43). This guide also includes two other types of *gîtes* — *gîtes camping-caravaning à la ferme* (campsites) and *gîtes d'étape* (stopovers for backpackers, cyclists, and horseback riders). With the appropriate guide in tow, those traveling by car and with a modicum of French can book rooms from *gîte* to *gîte* as they drive through France, deciding early in the morning or as late as lunch where they want to stay and calling ahead.

In addition to consulting the above-mentioned organizations and publications, travelers interested in B&B accommodations should contact *The French Experience* (370 Lexington Ave., New York, NY 10017; phone: 800-28-FRANCE or 212-986-1115), which represents the *Café Couette* bed and breakfast association of France, with member establishments throughout France. (This company also handles rental properties in France — see below).

Another useful source of information on bed and breakfast services and establishments overseas is the *Bed & Breakfast Reservations Services Worldwide,* a trade association of B&B reservations services, which provides a listing of its members for $3. To order the most recent edition, contact them at PO Box 39000, Washington, DC 20016 (phone: 800-842-1486). See also the companies listed under "Rental Options," below, a number of which make reservations for bed and breakfast establishments, as well as a variety of other types of accommodations.

Farmhouses – In the country, city people rediscover the sounds of songbirds and the smell of grass. Suburbanites get the chance to poke around an area where the nearest neighbor lives miles away. Parents can say to their children, "No, milk does not originate in a cardboard carton," and prove it. Youngsters can meet people who live differently, think differently, and have different values. But even if there were no lessons to be learned, a stay at a farm would be a decidedly pleasant way to pass a couple of weeks, so it's no wonder that throughout France there are numerous farms welcoming guests.

Farm families in France often put up guests on a bed and breakfast basis — for a night or two or by the week, with weekly half-board plans often available. Travelers can pick a traditional or a modern farm, a dairy farm over a goat farm, one with ponies to ride, or one near a river or coastline for fishing. If the peace and quiet and the coziness of the welcome are appealing, a farmhouse can be an ideal base from which to explore a region by car or by foot and an especially good idea for those traveling with children. Two good sources of information on farm stays (as well as rentals) are the *Fédération Nationale des Gîtes Ruraux de France* and *French Farm and Village Holiday Guide* (see below).

Rental Options – An attractive alternative for the visitor content to stay in one spot for a week or more is to rent one of the numerous properties available throughout France. These offer a wide range of luxury and convenience, depending on the price you want to pay. One of the advantages of staying in a house, apartment (usually called a "flat" overseas), or other rented vacation home is that you will feel much more like a visitor than a tourist.

Known to Europeans as a "holiday let" or a "self-catering holiday," a vacation in a furnished rental has both the advantages and disadvantages of living "at home" abroad. It can be less expensive than staying in a first class hotel, although very luxurious and expensive rentals are available, too. It has the comforts of home, including a kitchen, which can mean potential savings on food. Furthermore, it gives a sense of the country that a large hotel often cannot. On the other hand, a certain amount of housework is involved because if you don't eat out, you have to cook, and though some rentals (especially the luxury ones) include a cleaning person, most don't. (If the rental doesn't include daily cleaning, arrangements often can be made with a nearby service.)

For a family, two or more couples, or a group of friends, the per-person cost — even for a luxurious rental — can be quite reasonable. Weekly and monthly rates are available to reduce costs still more. But best of all is the amount of space that no conventional hotel room can equal. As with hotels, the rates for properties in some areas are seasonal, rising during the peak travel season, while for others they remain the same year-round. To have your pick of the properties available, you should begin to make arrangements for a rental at least 6 months in advance.

There are several ways of finding a suitable rental property. For those who wish to arrange a rental themselves, write or call the French Government Tourist Office (for locations in the US, see *Tourist Information,* in this section), or contact the *Fédération Nationale des Agents Immobiliers* (129 Rue du Faubourg-St-Honoré, Paris 75008; phone; 1-44-20-77-00) for a list of real estate agencies handling seasonal rentals throughout France, including many seaside resorts.

The *Fédération Nationale des Gîtes Ruraux de France* (address above), an association of, among others, the owners of 35,000 *Gîtes de France* — country cottages, farmhouses, and apartments for rent by the week or longer — is a source of strictly rural rentals. Selected *gîtes* are listed in the *French Farm and Village Holiday Guide,* available from travel bookstores for $16.95. The listings are arranged *département* by *département* (very roughly, county by county) throughout France, and each entry is accompanied by a black-and-white photo, details of the accommodations, and the price. For more comprehensive listings of the *gîtes* in any particular *département,* however, it is necessary to write to the appropriate *relais départemental* (departmental headquarters) of the federation, each of which publishes a yearly guide (some free, some for a small fee) to the properties in its area. All of the *relais départemental* addresses are in the *Gîtes Ruraux de France* brochure available from the French Government Tourist Office. Once a *gîte* is chosen, the prospective renter books it with the proprietor directly or, where it exists, through a departmental booking service.

Many tour operators regularly include a few rental packages among their offerings; these generally are available through a travel agent. In addition, a number of companies specialize in rental vacations. Their plans typically include rental of the property (or several properties, but usually for a minimum stay per location), a rental car, and airfare.

The companies listed below rent a wide range of properties in France. They handle the booking and confirmation paperwork and can be expected to provide more information about the properties than that which might ordinarily be gleaned from a short listing in an accommodations guide.

At Home Abroad (405 E. 56th St., Suite 6H, New York, NY 10022; phone: 212-421-9165). Rents villas and châteaux along the Riviera, in the Dordogne region, and in the hill towns of Provence. A free brochure and newsletter are available. Photographs of properties with detailed descriptions are available for a $50 registration fee.

B & D De Vogue International Inc. (250 Beverly Dr., Beverly Hills, CA 90212; phone: 800-727-4748 or 800-438-4748; or *La Vie de Châteaux,* 9 Rue Henri Pape, Paris 75013; phone: 1-45-80-01-01). Rents apartments and châteaux throughout France.

Blake's Vacations (4918 Dempster St., Skokie, IL 60077; phone: 800-628-8118). Rents country homes throughout France.

Castles, Cottages, and Flats (7 Faneuil Hall Market Place, Boston, MA 02109; phone: 617-742-6030). The name says it all — the company represents a variety of properties throughout France.

Chez Vous (220 Redwood Highway, Suite 129, Mill Valley, CA 94941; phone: 415-331-2535). Rents country homes and rooms at bed and breakfast establishments throughout France, as well as apartments in Paris.

Europa-Let (PO Box 3537, 92 N. Main St., Ashland, OR 97520; phone: 800-462-4486 or 503-482-5806). Offers apartments, cottages, and villas throughout France.

The French Experience (370 Lexington Ave., New York, NY 10017; phone: 212-986-1115). Rents apartments, country cottages, and houses throughout France, as well as villas on the Riviera, as well as apartments in Paris.

Hideaways International (PO Box 1270, Littleton, MA 01460; phone: 800-843-4433 or 508-486-8955). Rents apartments, châteaux, private homes, and villas throughout France.

Hometours International (1170 Broadway, New York, NY 10001; phone: 800-367-4668 or 212-689-0851). Handles apartments in Antibes, Cannes, Nice, and Paris.

Interhome (124 Little Falls Rd., Fairfield, NJ 07004; phone: 201-882-6864). Represents about 10,000 condominiums, cottages, and private houses throughout France.

International Lodging Corp. (300 1st Ave., Suite 7C, New York, NY 10009; phone: 212-228-5900). Rents apartments in Paris and cottages throughout France.

Livingstone Holidays (1720 E. Garry Ave., Suite 236, Santa Ana, CA 92705; phone: 714-476-2823). Handles over 200 properties throughout France.

Rent a Home International (7200 34th Ave. NW, Seattle, WA 98117; phone: 800-488-RENT or 206-789-9377). Rents apartments in Paris and the French Riviera, and has villas and châteaux throughout the country.

Rent a Vacation Everywhere (*RAVE;* 383 Park Ave., Rochester, NY 14607; phone: 716-256-0760). Moderate to luxurious villas and apartments throughout France.

Vacances en Campagne (PO Box 297, Falls Village, CT 06031; phone: 800-533-5405). Represents over 400 properties in France. A catalogue is available for $5.

VHR Worldwide (235 Kensington Ave., Norwood, NJ 07648; phone: 201-767-

9393 in New Jersey; 800-NEED-A-VILLA elsewhere in the US). Rents apartments, country homes, and villas throughout France.

Villas International (605 Market St., Suite 510, San Francisco, CA 94105; phone: 800-221-2260 or 415-281-0910). Handles numerous rental properties throughout Europe, including apartments in Paris; chalets in the Alps; country lodgings in Brittany, Burgundy, the Dordogne, the Loire Valley, and Provence; and villas and apartments on the Atlantic Coast and the Riviera.

And for further information, including a general discussion of all forms of vacation rentals, evaluating costs, and information on rental opportunities in France, see *A Traveler's Guide to Vacation Rentals in Europe,* by Michael and Laura Murphy (Penguin; $11.95).

In addition, a useful publication, the *Worldwide Home Rental Guide,* lists properties throughout France, as well as the managing agencies. Issued twice annually, single copies may be available at newsstands for $10 an issue. For a year's subscription, send $18 to *Worldwide Home Rental Guide,* PO Box 2842, Sante Fe, NM 87504 (phone: 505-988-5188).

When considering a particular vacation rental property, look for answers to the following questions:

- How do you get from the airport to the property?
- If the property is on the shore, how far is the nearest beach? Is it sandy or rocky and is it safe for swimming?
- What size and number of beds are provided?
- How far is the property from whatever else is important to you, such as a golf course or nightlife?
- If there is no grocery store on the premises (which may be comparatively expensive, anyway), how far is the nearest market?
- Are baby-sitters, cribs, bicycles, or anything else you may need for your children available?
- Is maid service provided daily?
- Is air conditioning and/or a phone provided?
- Is a car rental part of the package? Is a car necessary?

Before deciding which rental is for you, make sure you have satisfactory answers to all your questions. Ask your travel agent to find out or call the company involved directly.

HOME EXCHANGES: Still another alternative for travelers who are content to stay in one place during their vacation is a home exchange: The Smith family from Chicago moves into the home of the Chabrol family in Paris, while the Chabrols enjoy a stay in the Smiths' home. The home exchange is an exceptionally inexpensive way to ensure comfortable, reasonable living quarters with amenities that no hotel could possibly offer; often the trade includes a car. Moreover, it allows you to live in a new community in a way that few tourists ever do: For a little while, at least, you will become something of a resident.

Several companies publish directories of individuals and families willing to trade homes with others for a specific period of time. In some cases, you must be willing to list your own home in the directory; in others, you can subscribe without appearing in it. Most listings are for straight exchanges only, but each directory also has a number of listings placed by people interested in either exchanging or renting (for instance, if they own a second home). Other arrangements include exchanges of hospitality while owners are in residence, or youth exchanges, where your teenager is received as a guest in return for your welcoming their teenager at a later date. A few house-sitting opportunities also are available. In most cases, arrangements for the actual exchange take place directly between you and the foreign host. There is no guarantee that you will find a listing in the area in which you are interested, but each of the organizations noted below includes French homes among its hundreds or even thousands of foreign listings:

Home Base Holidays (7 Park Ave., London N13 5PG England; phone: 44-81-886-8752). For $48 a year, subscribers receive four listings, with an option to list in all four.

Intervac US/International Home Exchange Service (Box 190070, San Francisco, CA 94119; phone: 415-435-3497). For $45 (plus postage) subscribers receive copies of the three directories published yearly, and are entitled to list their home in one of them; a photograph may be included with the listing for an additional $10. A $5 discount is given to travelers over age 62.

Loan-A-Home (2 Park Lane, Apt. 6E, Mt. Vernon, NY 10552; phone: 914-664-7640). Specializes in long-term (4 months or more — excluding July and August) housing arrangements worldwide for students, professors, businesspeople, and retirees, although its two annual directories (with supplements) carry a small list of short-term rentals and/or exchanges. $35 for a copy of one directory and one supplement; $45 for two directories and two supplements.

Vacation Exchange Club (PO Box 820, Haleiwa, HI 96712; phone: 800-638-3841). Some 10,000 listings. For $50, the subscriber receives two directories — one in late winter, one in the spring — and is listed in one.

Worldwide Home Exchange Club (13 Knightsbridge Green, London SW1X 7QL, England; phone: 44-71-589-6055; or 806 Brantford Ave., Silver Spring, MD 20904; phone: 301-680-8950). Handles over 1,500 listings a year worldwide, including homes throughout France. For $25 a year, you will receive two listings yearly, as well as supplements.

Better Homes and Travel (formerly *Home Exchange International*), with offices in New York, and representatives in Los Angeles, London, Paris, and Milan, functions differently in that it publishes no directory and shepherds the exchange process most of the way. Interested parties supply the firm with photographs of themselves and their homes, information on the type of home they want and where, and a registration fee of $50. The company then works with its other offices to propose a few possibilities, and only when a match is made do the parties exchange names, addresses, and phone numbers. For this service, *Better Homes and Travel* charges a closing fee, which ranges from $150 to $500 for switches from 2 weeks to 3 months in duration, and from $300 to $600 for longer switches. Contact *Better Homes and Travel,* 33 E. 33rd St., New York, NY 10016 (phone: 212-689-6608).

HOME STAYS: If the idea of actually staying in a private home as the guest of a French family appeals to you, check with the *United States Servas Committee,* which maintains a list of hosts throughout the world (at present, there are about 512 in France) willing to throw open their doors to foreign visitors entirely free of charge.

The aim of this nonprofit cultural program is to promote international understanding and peace, and every effort is made to discourage freeloaders. *Servas* will send you an application form and the name of the nearest of some 200 interviewers around the US for you to contact. After the interview, if you're approved, you'll receive documentation certifying you as a *Servas* traveler. There is a membership fee of $55 for an individual, and there also is a deposit of $25 to receive the host list, refunded on its return. The list gives the name, address, age, occupation, and other particulars of each host, including languages spoken. From then on, it is up to you to write to prospective hosts directly, and *Servas* makes no guarantee that you will be accommodated.

Servas stresses that you should choose only people you really want to meet, and that during your stay (which normally lasts between 2 nights and 2 weeks) you should be interested mainly in your hosts, not in sightseeing. It also suggests that one way to show your appreciation once you've returned home is to become a host yourself. The minimum age of a *Servas* traveler is 18 (however, children under 18 may accompany their parents), and though quite a few are young people who have just finished college, there are travelers (and hosts) in all age ranges and occupations. Contact *Servas* at 11 John St., Room 407, New York, NY 10038-4009 (phone: 212-267-0252).

Another organization offering home stays with French families is *Friends in France.* Travelers can choose from over 40 homes, ranging from simple country homes to stately châteaux. Prices for a double room can range from $55 to $80 (depending on the level of elegance), although breakfast always is included. In this sense these resemble bed and breakfast accommodations rather than the traditional home stay arrangement; however, the host families are from a diverse spectrum of backgrounds and occupations, and their participation in the program generally is indicative of an interest in people and an eagerness to share their own little corner of France with their visitors. Through a detailed questionnaire, plus follow-up contact, *Friends in France* helps select the most suitable home or homes for your stay. There is a minimum stay of 3 nights and a maximum of 2 weeks with any one family; you can visit one or several homes during the course of your stay. About half the host families have an English-speaking member and the visitor's knowledge of French is taken into account when selecting the host family. A free brochure describing the program and a booklet for $7 describing the participating properties are available from *Friends in France* at PO Box 1044, Rocky Hill, CT 06067 (phone: 203-563-0195).

You also might be interested in a publication called *International Meet-the-People Directory,* published by the *International Vistors Information Service.* It lists several agencies in a number of foreign countries (37 worldwide, 18 in Europe) that arrange home visits for Americans, either for dinner or overnight stays. To order a copy, send $5.95 to the *International Visitors Information Service* (1623 Belmont St. NW, Washington, DC 20009; phone: 202-939-5566). For other local organizations and services offering home exchanges, contact the local tourist authority.

Time Zones, Business Hours, and Public Holidays

TIME ZONES: The countries of Europe fall into three time zones. Greenwich Mean Time — the time in Greenwich, England, at longitude 0°0′ — is the base from which all other time zones are measured. Areas in zones west of Greenwich have earlier times and are called Greenwich Minus; those to the east have later times and are called Greenwich Plus. For example, New York City — which falls into the Greenwich Minus 5 time zone — is 5 hours earlier than Greenwich, England.

France and Monaco are both in Greenwich Plus 1 time zone — which means that the time in these countries is 1 hour later than in Greenwich, England, and when it is noon in Paris and Monte Carlo, it is 6 AM in New York and Washington, DC.

Like most Western European nations, France (and Monaco) moves its clocks ahead an hour in the spring and back an hour in the fall. France goes on daylight saving time the last Sunday in March, whereas the US does so on the first Sunday in April. Similarly, France goes off daylight saving time the last Sunday in September, while the US changes its clocks on the last Sunday in October. Therefore, during a bit of April there is a 7-hour time difference between the US East Coast and France, and for most of October there is a 5-hour difference.

French and other European timetables use a 24-hour clock to denote arrival and departure times, which means that hours are expressed sequentially from 1 AM. By this method, 9 AM is recorded as 0900, noon as 1200, 1 PM as 1300, 6 PM as 1800, midnight as 2400, and so on. For example, the departure of a train at 7 AM will be announced as "0700"; one leaving at 7 PM will be noted as "1900."

BUSINESS HOURS: Travelers who are used to the American workday may be surprised to find that the French, like many other Europeans, follow a more eccentric schedule. Business (office) hours are from 9 AM to 6 PM, traditionally with a generous 2½-hour lunch break (although the current trend is toward shorter, closer to 1-hour, breaks) starting at 12:30 or 1 PM. Banks generally are open on weekdays from 9 or 9:30 AM to 4:30 PM; in addition, in the countryside, banks may close between noon and 2 PM for lunch.

Department stores and other large emporia generally are open from about 9:30 AM to 6:30 PM Mondays through Saturdays; they usually have 1 or 2 days when they are open until 9 or 10 PM. Fashion boutiques, perfume shops, and similar retail establishments, usually are open Tuesdays through Saturdays from 10 AM to noon, and from 2 to 6:30 or 7 PM; some also may be open on Mondays (for a full day or just the afternoon). Small food stores such as butcher shops and bakeries may open at 9 AM, close for lunch around 12:30 or 1 PM, reopen at 3:30 or 4 PM, and close between 7 and 8 PM. They and other small shops close for part of Monday and sometimes for the whole day, but if open Sunday, close by 1 or 2PM.

PUBLIC HOLIDAYS: France shuts down even more thoroughly than the US does on public holidays. Banks, offices, stores, museums, and public monuments — even most gas stations — are closed tight, and banks and some offices also close at *noon* the day before a holiday. The French national holidays are as follows:

> *New Year's Day* (January 1)
> *Easter Sunday* (April 11)
> *Easter Monday* (April 12)
> *Labor Day* (May 1)
> *V-E Day* (May 8)
> *Ascension Thursday* (May 20)
> *Whitmonday* (May 31)
> *Bastille Day* (July 14)
> *Feast of the Assumption* (August 15)
> *All Saints Day* (November 1)
> *Armistice Day* (November 11)
> *Christmas Day* (December 25)

Monaco celebrates most of the same holidays and adds a few of its own, including the *Feast Day of* St-*Dévoté,* patron saint of the principality (January 27), and *National Day* (November 19).

Mail, Telephone, and Electricity

MAIL: Post offices in France are indicated by signs with the letters "PTT" (which stands for "Postes, Télécommunications, et Télédiffusion," and is pronounced *Pay-Tay-Tay*) or by a sign with a blue bird (looking something like an arrow) on a white disk. Stamps can be bought both there, at *tabacs* (tobacco shops), or at coin-operated vending machines painted yellow. Letter boxes also are yellow. Note that there no longer is such a thing as a *lettre pneumatique* in Paris. The old system, by which a letter (a *pneu,* for short) could be whooshed through a tube of compressed air from one end of the city to the other in a matter of hours, was shut down in 1984 after more than a century of service.

The French postal code consists of a 5-digit number. The first 2 digits indicate in which of the country's 95 *départements* the address is located and the remaining numbers indicate the town, city, or, more specifically, the district. For instance, all addresses in the city of Paris (a *département* unto itself), begin with 75; a postal code number of 75001 or 75002 means that the address is in the first or second of the city's 20 *arrondissements*. The postal code always should be specified. Sometimes this will merely speed delivery, but sometimes — because many small towns in France have the same name — delivery of a letter may depend on it. (If you do not have the correct postal code, call a French consulate or embassy and ask them to look it up.) Alternatively, you could call the addressee directly — if you have the telephone number — and although this will be costly, it may be worth it to ensure delivery of your correspondence.

Letters sent from France to the US always should be sent via air mail *(Par Avion)* — otherwise they may end up going the *long* way by boat. Although letters have been known to arrive in as short a time as 5 days, it is a good idea to allow at least 10 days for delivery in either direction. If your correspondence is important, you may want to send it via one of the special courier services: *Federal Express, DHL,* and other international services are available in France. The cost is considerably higher than sending something via the postal service — but the assurance of its timely arrival is worth it.

There are several places that will receive and hold mail for travelers in France. Mail sent to you at a hotel and clearly marked "Guest Mail, Hold for Arrival" is one safe approach. Post offices also will extend this service to you if the mail is addressed to the French equivalent of US general delivery — called *Poste Restante*. This probably is the best way for travelers to have mail sent if they do not have a definite address. As there often are several post office locations in major cities, it is important that the address and/or specific name of the office be indicated (not just the name of the city), in addition to the words *Poste Restante*. Be sure to call at the correct office when inquiring about mail.

In Paris, the main post office, open 24 hours a day, is at 52 Rue du Louvre (Paris 75001). If your mail is addressed to you, simply, "Poste Restante, Paris," this is where it will be delivered. But in Paris (and other large cities), mail marked "Poste Restante" can be directed to a post office closer to where you will be staying by having the sender add the correct *arrondissement* number — or full postal code (see below) — in addition to the name of the city. In this case, your mail will go to the main post office in the appropriate district, not to one clear across town. There is a small charge for picking up your mail. And don't forget to take your passport with you when you go to collect it; the post office requires formal identification before it will release anything. The Ministry of Posts, Télécommunications, and Télédiffusion distributes a brochure in several languages (including English) entitled *Bienvenue*. Ask for it at the post office.

If you are an *American Express* customer (a cardholder, a carrier of *American Express* traveler's checks, or traveling on an *American Express Travel Related Services* tour), you can have mail sent to some of its offices in cities along your route. (Of *American Express*'s 24 offices in France, 14 accept client mail; one of these is in Paris at 11 Rue Scribe, Paris 75009; phone: 1-47-77-77-07.) Letters are held free of charge — registered mail and packages are not accepted. You must be able to show an *American Express* card, traveler's checks, or a voucher proving you are on one of the company's tours to qualify for mail privileges. Those who aren't clients cannot use the service. There also is a forwarding fee of $5 (at press time). Mail should be addressed to you, care of *American Express,* and should be marked "Client Mail Service." Additional information on its mail service and the addresses of *American Express* offices in France are listed in the pamphlet *American Express Travelers' Companion,* available from any US branch of *American Express.*

While US embassies and consulates abroad will not under ordinary circumstances accept mail for tourists, they *may* hold mail for US citizens in an emergency situation or if the papers sent are particularly important. It is best to inform them either by separate letter or cable, or by phone (particularly if you are in the country already), that you will be using their address for this purpose.

TELEPHONE: The French telephone system is not too different from our own. The French have direct dialing (within the country, between nations, and overseas), operator-assisted calls, collect calls, and so on.

When to Call – As in the US, phone rates in France vary substantially, depending on the time of day that you place your call. The following reductions were in effect at the time of this writing: For long-distance calls *within* France, a 65% reduction in rates is in effect weekdays from 11:30 PM until 10 AM the next day. On Saturdays, the reduced rate goes into effect from 8 to 10 AM and from 5:30 PM on, and continues all day Sunday until 8 AM Monday. (This reduction also is in effect all day on national holidays.) For calls to the US, the reduction in rates, approximately between 20% and 45%, is not so dramatic, but it is in effect longer. Reduced rates are in effect Mondays through Saturdays from noon to 2 PM and from 8 PM to 2 AM, and effective all day on Sunday. The lowest discount rate is effective everyday from 2 AM until noon.

For the most current information on telephone rates, refer to *France Telecom*'s telephone directory. Also, don't forget the time difference when placing your call (see *Time Zones, Business Hours, and Public Holidays* in this section).

How to Call – All French telephone numbers have 8 digits. The procedure for calling most areas of France from the US is as follows: dial 011 (the international access code) + 33 (the country code) + the local 8-digit number (which includes the city code). For example, to place a call from anywhere in the US to Lyons, dial 011 + 33 + the local 8-digit number. The only exception to this rule is when calling the Paris/Ile-de-France area: You must add a 1 (the city code) before the local 8-digit number. For instance, to make a call from the US to Paris, dial 011 + 33 (the country code) + 1 (the city code) + the local 8-digit number.

The procedure for making a station-to-station call to the US from France is as follows: dial 19 (wait for a dial tone) + 1 (the US country code) + the area code + the local number. For instance, to call directly to New York from anywhere in France, dial 19 + 1 + 212 + the local number. For an operator-assisted call to the US, dial 19, wait for a dial tone, then dial 3311. If you need a French number and can speak a minimum of French, dial 12 for directory assistance.

France is divided into essentially two zones: Paris/Ile-de-France and all the rest, that is, the provinces. The procedure for dialing within France is as follows:

> *To call within Paris and the Ile-de-France area:* Dial the local 8-digit number (beginning with 4, 3, or 6).
>
> *To call from the Paris/Ile-de-France area to the provinces:* Dial 16 (wait for a dial tone) + the local 8-digit number.
>
> *To call from the provinces to the Paris/Ile-de-France area:* Dial 16 (wait for a dial tone) + 1 + the local 8-digit number.
>
> *To call between provinces:* Dial the local 8-digit number.

For emergency assistance throughout France: Dial 17 for the police (who can arrange for other emergency assistance) or dial 18 for the fire department. For further information on what to do in the event of an emergency, see *Staying Healthy,* in this section.

Where to Call From – Public pay phones are found in post offices, cafés, and in booths on the street. Phone booths from which you can direct-dial long-distance calls within France, as well as international calls to most European countries and the United

States, are now found in even the smallest French towns. Instructions on their use usually are in the booth. Simply put, a fistful of coins is dropped into the phone before you begin. When your call is connected, the coins begin to drop automatically and you can continue to feed coins as you talk. Any unused coins are returned after your call is completed.

If you have trouble placing a call from a phone booth or if you cannot gather a sufficient amount of change, remember that long-distance and international calls also can be made at post offices in France. In fact, this may be the simplest way to place such a call. Go to the telephone counter and explain what kind of call you want to make. You may be assigned a *cabine* (booth) from which to direct-dial the call yourself, or the clerk may put the call through for you, telling you which *cabine* to go to when he or she is about to connect the call. In either case, after you have hung up, return to the counter and pay the clerk for the call. There is no extra charge for phone calls made at the post office with or without the assistance of the attendant (surcharges for operator-assisted calls such as collect and person-to-person still apply, naturally); the only drawback to using the post office is that there frequently is a line of people already waiting for an empty booth.

Though many French pay phones still take coins (inserted before dialing), most pay phones in major cities now use plastic phone cards, *télécartes,* which may be purchased at post offices, train stations and other transportation centers, and tobacco shops or newsstands. The *télécarte* may be purchased in three denominations: 40, 50, and 120 units. (Note that 50-unit cards can be purchased in the US from *Marketing Challenges International,* 10 E. 21st St., Suite 600, New York, NY 10010; phone: 212-529-8484.) The units, like message units in US phone parlance, are a combination of time and distance. To use the card, you insert it into a slot in the phone and dial the number you wish to reach. A display gradually will count down the value (in francs) that remains on your card. When you run out of units on your card, you can insert another.

Although you can use a telephone-company credit card number on any phone, pay phones that take major credit cards (*American Express, MasterCard, Visa,* and so on) are increasingly common worldwide, particularly in transportation and tourism centers. Also now available is the "affinity card," a combined telephone calling card/bank credit card that can be used for domestic and international calls. Cards of this type include the following:

> *AT&T/Universal* (phone: 800-662-7759). Cardholders can charge calls to the US from overseas.
>
> *Executive Telecard International* (phone: 800-950-3800). Cardholders can charge calls to the US from overseas, as well as between most European countries.

Similarly, *MCI VisaPhone* (phone: 800-866-0099) can add phone card privileges to the services available through your existing *Visa* card. This service allows you to use your *Visa* account number, plus an additional code, to charge calls on any touch-tone phone in the US and Europe.

Hotel Surcharges – A lot of digits may be involved once a caller starts dialing beyond national borders, but avoiding operator-assisted calls can cut costs considerably and bring rates into a somewhat more reasonable range — except for calls made through hotel switchboards. One of the most unpleasant surprises travelers encounter in many foreign countries is the amount they find tacked onto their hotel bill for telephone calls, because foreign hotels routinely add on astronomical surcharges. (It's not at all uncommon to find 300% or 400% added to the actual telephone charges.)

Until recently, the only recourse against this unconscionable overcharging was to call collect from abroad or to use a telephone credit card — available through a simple procedure from any local US phone company. (Note, however, that even if you use a telephone credit card, some hotels still may charge a fee for line usage.) Now, *American*

Telephone and Telegraph (AT&T) offers *USA Direct,* a service that connects users, via a toll-free number, with an *AT&T* operator in the US, who will then put the call through at the standard international rate. An added feature of this service is that travelers abroad can reach US toll-free (800) numbers by calling a *USA Direct* operator, who will connect them. Charges for all calls made through *USA Direct* appear on the caller's regular US phone bill. To reach *USA Direct* in France, you dial 19, wait for a dial tone, then dial 0011. For a brochure and wallet card listing toll-free numbers by country, contact International Information Service, *AT&T Communications,* 635 Grant St., Pittsburgh, PA 15219 (phone: 800-874-4000).

AT&T also has put together *Teleplan,* an agreement among certain hoteliers that sets a limit on surcharges for calls made by guests from their rooms, and currently is in effect in selected hotels in France. *Teleplan* agreements stipulate a flat, low rate for calling card or collect calls (currently between $1 and $10), and a flat percentage (between 20% and 100%) on calls paid for at the hotel. In addition, guests can make long distance calls from their hotel rooms using *AT&T*'s *USA Direct* service (see above) without incurring any additional hotel surcharges. For further information, contact *AT&T*'s International Information Service (address above).

Until such services become universal, it's wise to ask the surcharge rate *before* calling from a hotel. If the rate is high, it's best to use a telephone credit card, or the direct-dial service listed above; make a collect call; or place the call and ask the party to call right back. If none of these choices are possible, to avoid surcharges make international calls from the local post office or one of the special telephone centers located throughout the country. Another way to keep down the cost of telephoning from France is to leave a copy of your itinerary and telephone numbers with people in'the US so that they can call you instead.

Other Resources – Travelers to France who don't speak fluent French may be interested in *AT&T*'s Language Line Service. By calling 800-628-8486, you will be connected with an interpreter in any one of 143 languages and dialects (including French), who will provide on-line interpretive services for $3.50 a minute. From the US, this service is particularly useful for booking travel services in Europe where English is not spoken or not fluently spoken — such as France. Once in Europe, this number can be reached by using the *USA Direct* toll-free (800) number connection feature described above — it will enable you to make arrangements at foreign establishments or to reach emergency or other vital services with which you would otherwise have trouble communicating due to the language barrier. For frequent business travelers, AT&T offers this service on a membership basis. For further information, contact *AT&T* at the address above or call 800-752-6096.

Particularly useful for planning a trip is *AT&T*'s *Toll-Free 800 Directory,* which lists thousands of companies with 800 numbers, both alphabetically (white pages) and by category (yellow pages), including a wide range of travel services — from travel agents to transportation and accommodations. Issued in a consumer edition for $9.95 and a business edition for $14.95, both are available from *AT&T Phone Centers* or by calling 800-426-8686. Other useful directories for use before you leave and on the road include the *Toll-Free Travel & Vacation Information Directory* ($4.95 postpaid from Pilot Books, 103 Cooper St., Babylon, NY 11702; phone: 516-422-2225) and *The Phone Booklet,* which lists the nationwide, toll-free (800) numbers of travel information sources and suppliers — such as major airlines, hotel and motel chains, car rental companies, and tourist information offices (send $2 to *Scott American Corporation,* Box 88, W. Redding, CT 06896).

 ELECTRICITY: The US runs on 110-volt, 60-cycle alternating current. France runs on 220-volt, 50-cycle alternating current, as does most of the rest of Europe, although 240-volt also may be used. In a few areas of France, 110-volt current still exists and some large tourist hotels also *may* offer

110-volt current for your convenience — but don't count on it. The difference between US and European voltage means that, without a converter, the motor of a US appliance used overseas at 220 or 240 volts would quickly burn out.

Travelers can solve the problem by buying a lightweight converter to transform foreign voltage into the US kind (there are several types of converters, depending on the wattage of the appliance) or by buying dual-voltage appliances, which convert from one to the other at the flick of a switch (hair dryers of this sort are common). The difference between the 50- and 60-cycle currents will cause no problem — the American appliance simply will run more slowly — but it still will be necessary to deal with differing socket configurations before plugging in. To be fully prepared, bring along an extension cord (in older or rural establishments the electrical outlet may be farther from the sink than the cord on your razor or hair dryer can reach), and a wall socket adapter with a full set of plugs to ensure that you'll be able to plug in anywhere.

One good source for sets of plugs and adapters for use worldwide is the *Franzus Company* (PO Box 142, Beacon Falls, CT 06403; phone: 203-723-6664). *Franzus* also publishes a useful brochure, *Foreign Electricity Is No Deep Dark Secret*, which provides information about converters and adapter plugs for electric appliances to be used abroad but manufactured for use in the US. To obtain a free copy, send a self-addressed, stamped envelope to *Franzus* at the above address; a catalogue of other travel accessories is available on request.

Staying Healthy

The surest way to return home in good health is to be prepared for medical problems that might occur on vacation. As is always the case with both diseases and accidents, prevention is the best cure. Below, we've outlined some things you need to think about before your trip.

BEFORE YOU GO: Older travelers or anyone suffering from a chronic medical condition, such as diabetes, high blood pressure, cardiopulmonary disease, asthma, or ear, eye, or sinus trouble should consult a physician before leaving home. Those with conditions requiring special consideration when traveling should consider seeing, in addition to their regular physician, a specialist in travel medicine. For a referral in a particular community, contact the nearest medical school or ask a local doctor to recommend such a specialist.

Also be sure to check with your insurance company ahead of time about the applicability of your hospitalization and major medical policies away from home; many policies do not apply, and others are not accepted in France. Older travelers should know that Medicare does not make payments for medical services provided outside the US and its territories. If your medical policy does not protect you while you're traveling, there are comprehensive combination policies specifically designed to fill the gap. (For a discussion of medical insurance and a list of inclusive combination policies, see *Insurance,* in this section.)

First Aid – Put together a compact, personal medical kit including Band-Aids, first-aid cream, antiseptic, nose drops, insect repellent, aspirin (or non-aspirin tablets), an extra pair of prescription glasses or contact lenses (and a copy of your prescription for glasses or contact lenses), sunglasses, over-the-counter remedies for diarrhea, indigestion, and motion sickness, a thermometer, and a supply of those prescription medicines you take regularly.

In a corner of your kit, keep a list of all the drugs you have brought and their purpose, as well as duplicate copies of your doctor's prescriptions (or a note from your doctor). As brand names may vary in different countries, it's a good idea to ask your doctor for the generic name of any drugs you use so that you can ask for their equivalent should you need a refill. It also is a good idea to ask your doctor to prepare a medical identification card that includes such information as your blood type, your social security number, any allergies or chronic health problems you have, and your medical insurance information. Considering the essential contents of your kit, keep it with you, rather than in your checked luggage.

MINIMIZING THE RISKS: Travelers to France — and to Western Europe in general — do not face the same health risks involved in traveling to many other destinations around the world. Although traveling always entails *some* risks of injury or illness, neither is inevitable, and with some basic precautions, your trip will proceed untroubled by ill health.

Sunburn – The burning power of the sun can quickly cause severe sunburn or sunstroke. To protect yourself against these ills, wear sunglasses, take along a broad-brimmed hat and cover-up, and, most importantly, use a sunscreen lotion.

Water Safety – France is famous for its beaches, but it's important to remember that the sea can be treacherous. A few precautions are necessary. Beware of the undertow, that current of water running back down the beach after a wave has washed ashore; it can knock you off your feet and into the surf. Even more dangerous is the riptide, a strong current of water running against the tide, which can pull you out to sea. If you get caught offshore, don't panic or try to fight the current, because it will only exhaust you; instead, ride it out while waiting for it to subside, which usually happens not too far from shore, or try swimming away parallel to the beach.

Sharks are sometimes sighted, but they usually don't come in close to shore, and they are well fed on fish. Should you meet up with one, just swim away as quietly and smoothly as you can, without shouting or splashing. Although not aggressive, eels can be dangerous when threatened. If snorkeling or diving in coastal waters or freshwater lakes or streams, beware of crevices where these creatures may be lurking. The tentacled Portuguese man-of-war and other jellyfish also may drift in quiet salt waters for food and often wash up onto the beach; the long tentacles of these creatures sting whatever they touch — a paste made of household vinegar and unseasoned meat tenderizer is the recommended treatment.

If complications, allergic reactions (such as breathlessness, fever, or cramps), or signs of serious infection result from any of the above circumstances, *see a doctor.*

Insects and Other Pests – Flies and mosquitoes can be troublesome, so it is a good idea to use some form of topical insect repellent — those containing DEET (N,N-diethyl-m-toluamide) are among the most common and effective. The US Environmental Protection Agency (EPA) stresses that you should not use any pesticide that has not been approved by the EPA (check the label) and that all such preparations should be used in moderation. (Use solutions containing no more than a 15% solution of DEET on children, for example, and apply only to clothing, not directly to the skin.) If picnicking or camping, burn mosquito coils or candles containing allethrin, pyrethrin, or citronella, or use a pyrethrum-containing flying-insect spray. For further information about active ingredients in repellents, call the *National Pesticide Telecommunications Network*'s 24-hour hotline number: 800-858-7378.

If you do get bitten — by mosquitoes, horse or black flies, or other bugs — the itching can be relieved with baking soda, topical first-aid creams, or antihistamine tablets. Should a bite become infected, treat it with a disinfectant or antibiotic cream.

Though rarer, bites from snakes or spiders can be serious. If possible, always try to catch the villain for identification purposes. If bitten by these creatures or *any* wild animal, the best course of action may be to head directly to the nearest emergency ward or outpatient clinic of a hospital. Cockroaches, waterbugs, and termites thrive in warm climates, but pose no serious health threat.

Food and Water – Tap water generally is clean and potable throughout most of France. Ask if the water is meant for drinking — if it isn't, it should be marked *eau* *non potable.* You may want to drink bottled water, as do the French, at least at the beginning of the trip. This is not because there is something wrong with the water as far as the residents are concerned, but new microbes in the digestive tract to which you have not become accustomed may cause mild stomach or intestinal upsets. Particularly in rural areas, the water supply may not be thoroughly purified, and local residents either have developed immunities to the natural bacteria or boil the water for drinking. You also should avoid drinking water from freshwater streams, rivers, or pools. In campgrounds water usually is indicated as drinkable or for washing only — again, if you're not sure, ask.

Milk is pasteurized throughout France, and dairy products are safe to eat, as are fruit, vegetables, meat, poultry, and fish. Because of Mediterranean pollution, however, fish and shellfish should be eaten cooked, and make sure it is *fresh,* particularly in the heat of summer, when inadequate refrigeration is an additional concern.

Following all these precautions will not guarantee an illness-free trip, but should minimize the risk. For more information regarding preventive health care for travelers, contact the *International Association for Medical Assistance to Travelers (IAMAT;* 417 Center St., Lewiston, NY 14092; phone: 716-754-4883). This organization also assists travelers in obtaining emergency medical assistance while abroad (see list of such organizations below).

MEDICAL ASSISTANCE IN FRANCE: Nothing ruins a vacation or business trip more effectively than sudden injury or illness. Fortunately, should you need medical attention, competent medical professionals perfectly equipped to handle any medical problem can be found throughout the country. Most French towns and cities of any size have a public hospital, and even the tiniest of villages has a medical clinic or private physician nearby. All hospitals are prepared for emergency cases, and many hospitals also have walk-in clinics to serve people who do not really need emergency service, but who have no place to go for immediate medical attention. The level of medical care in France generally is excellent, providing the same basic specialities and services that are available in the US.

French hospitals fall into three categories, with the CHRU (Centre Hôpital Régional et Universitaire, or Central Regional University Hospital), a large, full-service hospital associated with a major medical university, at the top of the list. Others are the CHR, which designates a full-service regional hospital, and the CH, which means that the hospital is the central one in its town or city (and probably has 24-hour emergency service).

Emergency Treatment – You will find, in the event of an emergency, that most tourist facilities — transportation companies, hotels, and resorts — are equipped to handle the situation quickly and efficiently. Outside of such facilities, however, if a bona fide emergency occurs, an inability to speak French can pose a serious problem, not in receiving treatment at a large teaching hospital such as a CHRU, where many doctors — *médecins* in France — and other staff members will speak English, but in getting help elsewhere or in getting to the place where help is available. The fastest way to get attention may be to go directly to the emergency room of the nearest hospital.

In every city, an emergency number for *SAMU (service d'aide médicale urgente,* "medical help for serious emergencies") is listed in the front of the telephone directory along with other emergency numbers. *SAMU* sends out well-equipped and well-staffed ambulances, but the ambulance dispatcher probably will not be bilingual, and unless you speak French, he or she will be unable to determine the nature of the emergency, what equipment will be needed, or even where to send the ambulance. Travelers with little or no French language ability should try to get someone else to make the call. If the situation is desperate, an international operator may be able to make the call to the local emergency service and stay on the line as interpreter. To reach an international operator in France, dial 19, wait for a dial tone, then dial 3311.

Another alternative also requiring a basic command of French is to dial 17 for the police (who can connect you to other emergency services) or to dial 18 for the fire department. (These numbers both are valid nationwide.)

Non-Emergency Care – If a doctor is needed for something less than an emergency, there are several ways to find one. If you are staying in a hotel or at a resort, ask for help in reaching a doctor or other emergency services, or for the house physician, who may visit you in your room or ask you to visit an office. Travelers staying at a hotel of any size probably will find that the doctor on call speaks at least a modicum of English — if not, request one who does. When you register at a hotel, it's not a bad idea to include your home address and telephone number; this will facilitate the process of notifying friends, relatives, or your own doctor in case of an emergency.

Dialing the local *SAMU* emergency number also may be of help in locating a doctor in a non-emergency situation (again, if you can speak French). Most likely, you will be given the name of a general practitioner in the area. If you require a specialist, call the appropriate department of a teaching hospital (if one exists nearby) or the nearest US consulate or embassy (see *Legal Aid and Consular Services,* in this section, for addresses), which also maintains a list of English-speaking doctors and dentists. It also usually is possible to obtain a referral through a US consulate (see addresses and phone numbers below) or directly through a hospital, especially if it is an emergency. If you are already at the hospital, you can see a specialist there or make an appointment to be seen at his or her office.

Pharmacies and Prescription Drugs – French drugstores, *pharmacies,* are identified by a green cross out front. There should be no problem finding a 24-hour drugstore in any major French city — for one thing, pharmacists who close often give the addresses of the nearest all-night drugstores in the window. In some areas, night duty may rotate among pharmacies, and, again, closed pharmacies should have a sign in the window telling you the location of the pharmacy staying open on that day. In small towns, where none may be open after normal business hours, you may be able to have one open in an emergency situation — such as for a diabetic needing insulin — although you may be charged a fee for this off-hour service.

Again, bring along a copy of any prescription you may have from your doctor in case you should need a refill. In the case of minor complaints, French pharmacists *may* do some prescribing, and *may* agree to fill a foreign prescription; however, do not count on this. In most cases, you probably will need a local doctor to rewrite the prescription. Even in an emergency, a traveler will more than likely be given only enough of a drug to last until a local prescription can be obtained.

Travelers also will notice that some drugs sold only by prescription in the US are sold over the counter in France (and vice versa). Although this can be quite handy, be aware that common cold medicines and aspirin that contain codeine or other controlled substances will not be allowed back into the US.

ADDITIONAL RESOURCES: Medical assistance also is available from various organizations and programs designed for travelers who have chronic ailments or whose illness requires them to return home:

International Association of Medical Assistance to Travelers (*IAMAT;* 417 Center St., Lewiston, NY 14092; phone: 716-754-4883). Entitles members to the services of participating English-speaking doctors around the world, as well as clinics and hospitals in various locations. Participating physicians agree to adhere to a basic charge of around $50 to see a patient referred by *IAMAT.* To join, simply write to *IAMAT;* in about 3 weeks you will receive a membership card, the booklet of members, and an inoculation chart. A nonprofit organization, *IAMAT* appreciates donations; with a donation of $25 or more, you will receive a set of worldwide climate charts detailing weather and sanitary conditions. (Delivery can take up to 5 weeks, so plan ahead.)

International Health Care Service (New York Hospital–Cornell Medical Center,

525 E. 68th St., Box 210, New York, NY 10021; phone: 212-746-1601). This service provides a variety of travel-related health services, including a complete range of immunizations at moderate per-shot rates. A pre-travel counseling and immunization package costs $255 for the first family member and $195 for each additional member; a post-travel consultation is $175 to $275, plus lab work. Consultations are by appointment only, from 4 to 8 PM Mondays through Thursdays, although 24-hour coverage is available for urgent travel-related problems. In addition, sending $4.50 (with a self-addressed envelope) to the address above will procure the Service's publication, *International Health Care Travelers Guide,* a compendium of facts and advice on health care and diseases around the world.

International SOS Assistance (PO Box 11568, Philadelphia, PA 19116; phone: 800-523-8930 or 215-244-1500). Subscribers are provided with telephone access — 24 hours a day, 365 days a year — to a worldwide, monitored, multilingual network of medical centers. A phone call brings assistance ranging from a telephone consultation to transportation home by ambulance or aircraft, or, in some cases, transportation of a family member to wherever you are hospitalized. Individual rates are $35 for 2 weeks of coverage ($3.50 for each additional day), $70 for 1 month, or $240 for 1 year; couple and family rates also are available.

Medic Alert Foundation (2323 N. Colorado, Turlock, CA 95380; phone: 800-ID-ALERT or 209-668-3333). If you have a health condition that may not be readily perceptible to the casual observer — one that might result in a tragic error in an emergency situation — this organization offers identification emblems specifying such conditions. The foundation also maintains a computerized central file from which your complete medical history is available 24 hours a day by phone (the telephone number is clearly inscribed on the emblem). The onetime membership fee (between $35 and $50) is based on the type of metal from which the emblem is made — the choices range from stainless steel to 10K gold-filled.

TravMed (PO Box 10623, Baltimore, MD 21204; phone: 800-732-5309 or 410-296-5225). For $3 per day, subscribers receive comprehensive medical assistance while abroad. Major medical expenses are covered up to $100,000, and special transportation home or of a family member to wherever you are hospitalized is provided at no additional cost.

■ **Note:** Those who are unable to take a reserved flight due to personal illness or who must fly home unexpectedly due to a family emergency should be aware that airlines may offer a discounted airfare (or arrange a partial refund) if the traveler can demonstrate that his or her situation is indeed a legitimate emergency. Your inability to fly or the illness or death of an immediate family member usually must be substantiated by a doctor's note or the name, relationship, and funeral home from which the deceased will be buried. In such cases, airlines often will waive certain advance purchase restrictions or you may receive a refund check or voucher for future travel at a later date. Be aware, however, that this bereavement fare may not necessarily be the least expensive fare available and, if possible, it is best to have a travel agent check all possible flights through a computer reservations system (CRS).

Helpful Publications – Practically every phase of health care — before, during, and after a trip — is covered in *The New Traveler's Health Guide,* by Drs. Patrick J. Doyle and James E. Banta. It is available for $4.95, plus postage and handling, from Acropolis

Books Ltd., 13950 Park Center Rd., Herndon, VA 22071 (phone: 800-451-7771 or 703-709-0006).

The *Traveling Healthy Newsletter,* which is published six times a year, also is brimming with health-related travel tips. For a year's subscription, which costs $24 (sample issues are available for $4), contact Dr. Karl Neumann (108-48 70th Rd., Forest Hills, NY 11375; phone: 718-268-7290). Dr. Neumann also is the editor of the useful free booklet *Traveling Healthy,* which is available by writing to the *Travel Healthy Program* (Clark O'Neill Inc., Broad Ave., Fairview, NJ 07022; phone: 201-945-3400).

The Centers for Disease Control publishes a comprehensive booklet, *Health Information for International Travel,* which covers numerous destinations worldwide, including France. To order send a check or money order for $5 to the Superintendent of Documents (US Government Printing Office, Washington, DC 20402), or charge it to your credit card by calling 202-783-3238. For information on vaccination requirements, disease outbreaks, and other health information pertaining to traveling abroad, you also can call the Centers for Disease Control's 24-hour International Health Requirements and Recommendations Information Hotline: 404-332-4559.

Legal Aid and Consular Services

There is one crucial place to keep in mind when outside the US, namely, the American Services section of the US Consulate. If you are injured or become seriously ill, the consulate will direct you to medical assistance and notify your relatives. If, while abroad, you become involved in a dispute that could lead to legal action, the consulate, once again, is the place to turn.

It usually is far more alarming to be arrested abroad than at home. Not only are you alone among strangers, but the punishment can be worse. Granted, the US Consulate can advise you of your rights and provide a list of English-speaking lawyers, but it cannot interfere with the local legal process. Except for minor infractions of the local traffic code, there is no reason for any law-abiding traveler to run afoul of immigration, customs, or any other law enforcement authority.

The best advice is to be honest and law-abiding. If you get a traffic ticket, pay it. If you are approached by drug hawkers, ignore them. The penalties for possession of marijuana, cocaine, and other narcotics are even more severe abroad than in the US. (If you are picked up for any drug-related offense, do not expect US foreign service officials to be sympathetic. Chances are, they will notify a lawyer and your family and that's about all. See "Drugs," below.)

In the case of minor traffic accidents (such as a fender bender), it often is most expedient to settle the matter before the police get involved. If, however, you are involved in a serious accident, where an injury or fatality results, the first step is to contact the nearest US consulate (for addresses, see below) and ask the consul to locate an attorney to assist you. If you have a traveling companion, ask him or her to call the consulate (unless either of you has a local contact who can help you quickly). Competent English-speaking lawyers practice throughout Europe and it is possible to obtain good legal counsel on short notice.

The US Department of State in Washington, DC, insists that any US citizen who is arrested abroad has the right to contact the US embassy or consulate "immediately," but it may be a while before you are given permission to use a phone. Do not labor under the illusion, however, that in a scrape with foreign officialdom the consulate can act as an arbitrator or ombudsman on a US citizen's behalf. Nothing could be farther from the truth. Consuls have no power, authorized or otherwise, to subvert, alter, or contravene the legal processes, however unfair, of the foreign country in which they serve. Nor can a consul oil the machinery of a foreign bureaucracy or provide legal advice. The consul's responsibilities do encompass "welfare duties," including providing a list of lawyers and information on local sources of legal aid, informing relatives in the US, and organizing and administrating any defense monies sent from home. If a case is tried unfairly or the punishment seems unusually severe, the consul can make a formal complaint to the authorities. For questions about US citizens arrested abroad, how to get money to them, and other useful information, call the *Citizens' Emergency Center* of the Office of Special Consular Services in Washington, DC, at 202-647-5225. (For further information about this invaluable hotline, see below.)

Other welfare duties, not involving legal hassles, cover cases of both illness and destitution. If you should get sick, the US consul can provide names of English-speaking doctors and dentists, as well as the names of all local hospitals and clinics; the consul also will contact family members in the US and help arrange special ambulance service for a flight home. In a situation involving "legitimate and proven poverty" of an US citizen stranded abroad without funds, the consul will contact sources of money (such as family or friends in the US), apply for aid to agencies in foreign countries, and in a last resort — which is *rarely* — arrange for repatriation at government expense, although this is a loan that must be repaid. And in case of natural disasters or civil unrest, consulates around the world handle the evacuation of US citizens if it becomes necessary.

The consulate is not occupied solely with emergencies and is certainly not there to aid in trivial situations, such as canceled reservations or lost baggage, no matter how important these matters may seem to the victimized tourist. The main duties of any consulate are administrating statutory services, such as the issuance of passports and visas; providing notarial services; distributing VA, social security, and civil service benefits to US citizens; taking depositions; handling extradition cases; and reporting to Washington, DC the births, deaths, and marriages of US citizens living within the consulate's domain.

We hope that none of the information in this section will be necessary during your stay in France. If you can avoid legal hassles altogether, you will have a much more pleasant trip. If you become involved in an imbroglio, the local authorities may spare you legal complications if you make clear your tourist status. And if you run into a confrontation that might lead to legal complications developing with a French citizen or with local authorities, the best tactic is to apologize and try to leave as gracefully as possible. Do not get into fights with residents, no matter how belligerent or provocative they are in a given situation.

Following are the US embassy and consulates in France. If you are not in any of the cities mentioned when a problem arises, contact the nearest office. If you are not a US citizen, contact the consulate of your own nation. Note that mailing addresses may be different — so call before sending anything to these offices.

Bordeaux: US Consulate General (22 Cour du Maréchal Foch, Bordeaux 33080; phone: 56-52-65-95).

Lyons: US Consulate General (7 Quai Sarrail, Lyons 69454; phone: 78-24-68-49).

Marseilles: US Consulate General (12 Bd. Paul Paytral, Marseilles 13286; phone: 91-54-92-00).

Nice: US Consulate General (31 Rue du Maréchal-Joffre, Nice 06000; phone: 93-88-89-55).

Paris: US Embassy (2 Av. Gabriel, Paris 75008; phone: 1-42-96-12-02 or 1-42-61-80-75) and US Consulate (2 Rue St. Florentin, Paris 75001; same phone numbers as Embassy).

Strasbourg: US Consulate General (15 Av. d'Alsace, Strasbourg 67082; phone: 88-35-31-04).

You can obtain a booklet with addresses of most US embassies and consulates around the world by writing to the Superintendent of Documents (US Government Printing Office, Washington, DC 20402; phone: 202-783-3238) and asking for publication #744-006-0000-7, *Key Offices of Foreign Service Posts.*

As mentioned above, the US State Department operates a *Citizens' Emergency Center,* which offers a number of services to US citizens traveling abroad and their families at home. In addition to giving callers up-to-date information on trouble spots, the center will contact authorities abroad in an attempt to locate a traveler or deliver an urgent message. In case of illness, death, arrest, destitution, or repatriation of a US citizen on foreign soil, it will relay information to relatives at home if the consulate is unable to do so. Travel advisory information is available 24 hours a day to people with touch-tone phones (phone: 202-647-5225). Callers with rotary phones can get information at this number from 8:15 AM to 10 PM (eastern standard time) on weekdays; 9 AM to 3 PM on Saturdays. In the event of an emergency, this number also may be called during these hours. For emergency calls only, at all other times, call 202-634-3600 and ask for the Duty Officer.

Drinking and Drugs

DRINKING: The French are well known for their production and enjoyment of fine wines and liqueurs, and many would not contemplate a dinner — or even lunch — unaccompanied by a glass of wine. The consumption of wine, beer, and other alcohol is viewed more casually in France than in the US, and alcoholic beverages can be bought at corner cafés, supermarkets, and small grocery stores, as well as from special shops featuring vintage wines and liqueurs.

There are fewer restrictions on the sale of wine and liquor in France than in the US. The legal drinking age is 16 for purchasing or ordering alcohol, but this is enforced primarily in nightclubs and discotheques, and persons under the age of 16 can be served in a bar, café, or restaurant if accompanied by a parent or guardian. Wine and liquor can be sold 7 days a week, 365 days a year, although on holidays you may have trouble finding a store open for business.

Cafés, the (often) inexpensive streetside establishments that serve liquor in addition to coffee and simple fare, generally open in the morning, sometimes as early as 5 or 6 AM, and close at around 1 to 3 AM. Specific hours are determined by local regulations, but some cafés can and do receive permission to stay open 24 hours. Bars — more expensive establishments — and nightclubs have no mandated closing times: Some may close as early as 11 or 12 PM, while others may stay open through dawn, depending on the proprietor. There is no "last call" in France — if an establishment is open, drinks are served, although the proprietor does reserve the right to refuse service to anyone who appears drunk.

Visitors to France may bring in 2 liters of wine and either 2 liters of alcohol under 38.8 proof or 1 liter above 38.8 proof duty-free. If you are buying any quantity of alcohol (such as a case of wine) in France and traveling through other European countries on your route back to the US, you will have to pass through customs and pay duty at each border crossing, so you might want to arrange to have it shipped home. Whether bringing it with you or shipping, you will have to pay US import duties on any quantity over the allowed 1 liter. And remember that individual US states have the power to impose additional restrictions on the import of liquor across their borders, so check with the appropriate state agency before you travel (see *Customs and Returning to the US,* in this section).

DRUGS: Illegal narcotics are not as prevalent in France as in the US, and the moderate legal penalties and vague social acceptance that marijuana has gained in the US have no equivalents in France. Due to the international war on drugs, enforcement of drug laws is becoming increasingly strict throughout the world. Local European narcotics officers and customs officials are renowned for their absence of understanding and lack of a sense of humor — especially where foreigners are involved.

Opiates and barbiturates, and other increasingly popular drugs — "white powder" substances like heroin, cocaine, and "crack" (the cocaine derivative) — continue to be of major concern to narcotics officials. Most European countries — including France — have toughened laws regarding illegal drugs and narcotics, and it is important to bear in mind that the type or quantity of drugs involved is of minor importance. Particularly for foreigners, the maximum penalties may be imposed for possessing even *traces* of illegal drugs. There is a high conviction rate in these cases, and bail for foreigners is rare. Persons arrested are subject to the laws of the country they are visiting, and there isn't much that the US consulate can do for drug offenders beyond providing a list of lawyers. The best advice we can offer is this: Don't carry, use, buy, or sell illegal drugs.

Those who carry medicines that contain a controlled drug should be sure to have a current doctor's prescription with them. Ironically, travelers can get into almost as much trouble coming through US customs with over-the-counter drugs picked up abroad that contain substances that are controlled in the US. Cold medicines, pain relievers, and the like often have codeine or codeine derivatives that are illegal, except by prescription, in the US. Throw them out before leaving for home.

■ **Be forewarned:** US narcotics agents warn travelers of the increasingly common ploy of drug dealers asking travelers to transport a "gift" or other package back to the US. Don't be fooled into thinking that the protection of US law applies abroad — accused of illegal drug trafficking, you will be considered guilty until you prove your innocence. In other words, do not, under any circumstances, agree to take anything across the border for a stranger.

Tipping

 Throughout France (and in most of the rest of Western Europe), you will find the custom of including some kind of service charge — generally 12% to 15% — in the bill for a meal or accommodations more common than in the US. This can confuse Americans not familiar with the custom. On the one hand, many a traveler, unaware of this policy, has left many a superfluous tip. On the other hand, travelers aware of this policy may make the mistake of assuming that it takes care of everything. It doesn't. While "service included" in theory eliminates any question of how much and whom to tip, in practice there still are occasions when on-the-spot tips are appropriate. Among these are tips to show appreciation for special services, as well as tips meant to say "thank you" for services rendered. So keep a pocketful of 5F coins and hand these out like dollar bills.

In French restaurants, the service charge may appear in one of two ways: If you see *service compris* (s.c.) in the fine print at the bottom of the menu, the service charge already is calculated in the prices listed. If you see *service 12% en sus,* it means that a charge of 12% will be added to the final bill. (If you are at all unsure if the service charge already has been added, you should feel no embarrassment about asking a waiter when the bill is presented.) Unlike a tip in the US, this service charge is rarely optional. What is optional is the decision to do as the French might and leave the waiter several extra coins if you liked the service. In the rare instance where a service charge isn't added, a 15% tip to the waiter — just as in the US — usually is a safe figure, although one should never hesitate to penalize poor service or reward excellent and efficient attention by leaving less or more.

Although it's not necessary to tip the maître d' of most restaurants — unless he has been especially helpful in arranging a special party or providing a table (slipping him something in a crowded restaurant *may* get you seated sooner or procure a preferred table) — when tipping is desirable or appropriate, the least amount should be the current equivalent of $5. In the finest restaurants, where a multiplicity of servers are present, plan to tip 5% to the captain. The sommelier (wine waiter) is entitled to a gratuity of approximately 10% of the price of the bottle. Tipping in bars and cafés is similar to tipping in restaurants: Service usually is included, but you may wish to leave a few extra francs on the table.

In allocating gratuities at a restaurant, pay particular attention to what has become the standard credit card charge form, which now includes separate places for gratuities for waiters and/or captains. If these separate boxes are not on the charge slip, simply ask the waiter or captain how these separate tips should be indicated. Be aware, too, of the increasingly common — and devious — practice of placing the amount of an entire restaurant bill (in which service already has been included) in the top box of a charge slip, leaving the "tip" and "total" boxes ominously empty. Don't be intimidated: Leave the "tip" box blank and just repeat the total amount next to "total" before signing. In some establishments, tips indicated on credit card receipts may not be given to the help, so you may want to leave tips in cash.

As in restaurants, visitors usually will find a service charge of 10% to 15% included in their final bill at most French hotels. No additional gratuities are required — or expected — beyond this billed service charge. It is unlikely, however, that a service charge will be added to bills in small family-run guesthouses, inns, or bed and breakfast establishments. In these cases, guests should let their instincts be their guide; no tipping is expected by members of the family who own the establishment, but it is a nice gesture to leave something for others — such as a dining room waiter or a maid — who may have been helpful. A gratuity of around $1 per night is adequate in most cases.

If a hotel does not automatically add a service charge, it is perfectly proper for guests to ask to have an extra 10% to 15% added to their bill, to be distributed among those who served them. This may be an especially convenient solution in a large hotel, where it's difficult to determine just who out of a horde of attendants actually performed particular services.

For those who prefer to distribute tips themselves, a chambermaid generally is tipped at the rate of $1 per day. Tip the concierge or hall porter for specific services only, with the amount of such gratuities dependent on the level of service provided. (Remember, if he has obtained theater or concert tickets for you, he most likely has included a service charge in the price — if in doubt, ask. You still may want to tip in advance to encourage him to use his influence in obtaining hard-to-get tickets.) For any special service you receive in a hotel, a tip is expected — the current equivalent of $1 being the minimum for a small service.

Bellhops, doormen, and porters at hotels and transportation centers generally are tipped at the rate of $1 per piece of luggage, along with a small additional amount if a doorman helps with a cab or car. Once upon a time, taxi drivers in Europe would give you a rather odd look if presented with a tip for a fare, but times have changed, and 10% to 15% of the amount on the meter is now a standard gratuity.

Miscellaneous tips: Tipping ushers in a movie house, theater, or concert hall used to be the rule, but is becoming less common — the best policy is to check what other patrons are doing and follow suit. Most of the time, the program is not free, and in lieu of a tip it is common practice to purchase a program from the person who seats you. Sightseeing tour guides also should be tipped. If you are traveling in a group, decide together what you want to give the guide and present it from the group at the end of the tour ($1 per person is a reasonable tip). If you have been individually escorted, the amount paid should depend on the degree of your satisfaction, but it should not be less than 10% of the total tour price. Museum and monument guides also usually are tipped, and it is a nice touch to tip a caretaker who unlocks a small church or turns on the lights in a chapel for you in some out-of-the-way town.

In barbershops and beauty salons, tip as you would at home, keeping in mind that the percentages vary according to the type of establishment — 10% in the most expensive salons; 15% to 20% in less expensive establishments. (As a general rule, the person who washes your hair should get a small additional tip.) Washroom attendants should get a small tip — they usually set out a little plate with a coin already on it indicating the suggested denomination. Coat checks are worth about 50¢ to $1 a coat. And don't forget service station attendants, for whom a tip of around 50¢ for cleaning the windshield or other attention is not unusual.

Tipping always is a matter of personal preference. In the situations covered above, as well as in any others that arise where you feel a tip is expected or due, feel free to express your pleasure or displeasure. Again, never hesitate to reward excellent and efficient attention and to penalize poor service. Give an extra gratuity and a word of thanks when someone has gone out of his or her way for you. Either way, the more personal the act of tipping, the more appropriate it seems. And if you didn't like the service — or the attitude — don't tip.

Duty-Free Shopping and Value Added Tax

DUTY-FREE SHOPS: Note that at the time of this writing, because of the newly integrated European economy, there were some questions as to the fate and number of duty-free shops that would be maintained in international airports in European Economic Community (EEC) member countries. Those traveling between EEC countries and any country *not* a member of the Common Market will still be entitled to buy duty-free items. Since the United States is not a Common Market member, duty-free purchases will continue to be available to US travelers for the foreseeable future.

If common sense says that it always is less expensive to buy goods in an airport duty-free shop than to buy them at home or in the streets of a foreign city, travelers should be aware of some basic facts. Duty-free, first of all, does not mean that the goods travelers buy will be free of duty when they return to the US. Rather, it means that the shop has paid no import tax acquiring goods of foreign make because the goods are not to be used in the country where the shop is located. This is why duty-free goods are available only in the restricted, passengers-only area of international airports or are delivered to departing passengers on the plane. In a duty-free store, travelers save money only on goods of foreign make because these are the only items on which an import tax would be charged in any other store. There usually is no saving on locally made items, but in countries such as France that impose Value Added Taxes (see below) that are refundable to foreigners, the prices in airport duty-free shops also are minus this tax, sparing travelers the often cumbersome procedures they otherwise have to follow to obtain a VAT refund.

Beyond this, there is little reason to delay buying locally made merchandise and/or souvenirs until reaching the airport (for information on local specialties, see the individual city chapters in THE CITIES, and *Shopping Spree,* in DIVERSIONS). In fact, because airport duty-free shops usually pay high rents, the locally made goods sold in them may well be more expensive than they would be in downtown stores. The real bargains are foreign goods, but — let the buyer beware — not all foreign goods are automatically less expensive in an airport duty-free shop. You can get a good deal on even small amounts of perfume, costing less than the usually required minimum purchase, tax-free. Other fairly standard bargains include spirits, smoking materials, cameras, clothing, watches, chocolates, and other food and luxury items — but first be sure to know what these items cost elsewhere. Terrific savings do exist (they are the reason for such shops, after all), but so do overpriced items that an unwary shopper might find equally tempting. In addition, if you wait to do your shopping at airport duty-free shops, you will be taking the chance that the desired item is out of stock or unavailable.

Duty-free shops are located in most major international airports throughout Europe. Among the airports with duty-free shops in France are Bordeaux, Lille, Lyons, Marseilles, Montpellier, Nantes, Nice, Paris (both Charles de Gaulle and Orly), and Strasbourg.

In France, there are many shops *not* at the airport that call themselves duty-free shops. This can be confusing, because they are subject to the same rules as other shops but you must show a foreign (not French) passport to shop there. Foreign goods, if any, sold there have not escaped the import tax, and no purchases, French or foreign, become free of value added taxes until you buy enough to fulfill the minimum (see explanation below). You still are required to turn in export forms at the *détaxe* booth on departure in order to receive the refund. A few shops pay the refund on the spot, but they are trusting that you won't forget to turn in the forms. If you do forget or simply don't bother, they are out of pocket: They must pay to the government the tax they already have refunded to you.

What "tax-free" means in the case of shops such as these is something of an advertising strategy. They are announcing loud and clear that they do, indeed, offer the VAT refund service. Because they handle such sales in volume, these shops frequently have streamlined the paperwork. But because they have had to hire extra personnel to do so, they are less likely than other shops to refund the entire amount of the VAT, retaining some of it as reimbursement for their higher overhead. Prices may be no better at these stores and could be even higher due to the addition of this service.

VALUE ADDED TAX: Commonly abbreviated as VAT, this is a tax levied by various European countries, including France, and added to the purchase price of most goods and services. In France, it is known as the *taxe à la valeur ajoutée (TVA),* and it ranges from a low of 5.5% to 7% on food (usually depending on the government rating of the restaurant or hotel: a luxury hotel restaurant can charge a higher tax than a moderate hotel restaurant) to a high of 22% on such luxury items as furs, jewelry, and perfume. Typically, the rate is 18.6%, as on most clothing, for instance. However, travelers do not always get a full refund. As in the case of general merchandise like clothing, shoes, or leather goods, the purchaser can only get 13% refund out of the 18.6% tax. The tax is meant to apply only to residents of France, but visitors are required to pay it, too, unless they have purchases shipped directly to an address abroad by the store. If visitors pay the tax and take purchases with them, however, they generally are entitled to a refund (except on purchases of antiques and works of art worth over 30,000F, gold, food, wine, medicine, and tobacco), provided the total value of purchases in a single store amounts to 2,000F or more and provided the articles in question leave France with them. A further proviso is that the store agrees to participate in the tax-refund scheme — paperwork is involved and no store is obliged to do it. They are not required by law to participate in the scheme; however, most stores in France now offer this service, especially those in major cities. If they post a sign indicating that they do provide the refund, however, they are required to follow through with this policy.

To claim the refund, shoppers must ask the store clerk for an export sales form, a document that will be given to them in triplicate along with a stamped envelope addressed to the store. Proof of eligibility (such as a passport) must be shown, and the form must be signed in the store. At departure time, this same document must be presented with the merchandise (do not pack it in the bottom of your suitcase), with the envelope, and by the same person who signed it in the store, to the French customs *détaxe* (tax refund) booth in the airport (or at the railroad station if departure from France is by train). This must be done before going through passport control, and since there are frequently lines of other travelers waiting to go through the same formalities, early arrival at the airport or station is recommended. The customs official returns one copy of the form, countersigned, to the buyer, to be saved until reimbursement is received. Tax-refund forms for purchases made in Monaco also are handled by French customs.

When and how the refund is received varies. At Paris's Charles De Gaulle and Orly international airports, immediate payment in cash is possible if you are able to present the proper paperwork. Certain of the large department stores in Paris — *Galeries Lafayette* and *Au Printemps,* for example — have an arrangement that allows payment at an airport bank window before travelers proceed through the remaining departure formalities. In most cases, however, customs returns a copy of the export document to the store, which then mails a refund check, in French francs, to your home address. The drawback to this method is that it can take months before you receive the refund, and if the refund is less than a significant amount, charges imposed by US banks for converting foreign currency refund checks — which can run as high as $15 or more — could make the whole exercise hardly worth your while.

Far less costly is sending the foreign currency check (after endorsing it) to *Ruesch International,* which will convert it to a check in US dollars for a $2 fee (deducted from the dollar check). Other services include commission-free traveler's checks and foreign currency which can be ordered by mail. Contact *Ruesch International* at one of the following addresses: 191 Peachtree St., Atlanta, GA 30303 (phone: 404-222-9300); 3 First National Plaza, Suite 2020, Chicago, IL 60602 (phone: 312-332-5900); 1925 Century Park E., Suite 240, Los Angeles, CA 90067 (phone: 213-277-7800); 608 Fifth Ave., "Swiss Center," New York, NY 10020 (phone: 212-977-2700); and 1350 Eye St. NW, 10th Floor and street level, Washington, DC 20005 (phone: 800-424-2923 or 202-408-1200).

Two other methods of reimbursement are possible if the purchases in France are made by credit card. One is that the store will agree to make two credit card charges, one for the price of the goods, the other for the amount of the tax. Then, when the stamped copy of the form arrives from customs, the store simply tears up the charge slip for the sales tax and the amount never appears on your account. The other possibility is that, upon receipt of the stamped form, the store requests the international billing center to credit your account with the amount of the sales tax.

Religion on the Road

 France is predominantly Catholic, and every town, right down to the most isolated village, has its own church. In larger, more heavily populated areas, some amount of religious variety is reflected in the churches of other denominations, synagogues, and the occasional mosque or temple.

The surest source of information on English-language religious services in an unfamiliar country is the desk clerk of the hotel or guesthouse in which you are staying; the local tourist information office, a US consul, or a church of another religious affiliation also may be able to provide this information. If you aren't in an area with services held in your own denomination, you might find it interesting to attend the service of another religion. You also might enjoy attending a service in French — even if you don't understand all the words. Some of the most beautiful cathedrals in the world are found in France, and few things are more inspiring than a high mass set amidst medieval arches and stained glass.

Customs and Returning to the US

 Whether you return to the United States by air or sea, you must declare to the US Customs official at the point of entry everything you have bought or acquired while in Europe. The customs check can go smoothly, lasting only a few minutes, or can take hours, depending on the officer's instinct. To speed up the process, keep all your receipts handy and try to pack your purchases together in an accessible part of your suitcase. It might save you from unpacking all your belongings.

DUTY-FREE ARTICLES: In general, the duty-free allowance for US citizens returning from abroad is $400. This duty-free limit is based on the provision that your purchases accompany you and are for personal use. This limit includes items used or worn while abroad, souvenirs for friends, and gifts received during the trip. A flat 10% duty based on the "fair retail value in country of acquisition" is assessed on the next $1,000 worth of merchandise brought in for personal use or gifts. Amounts over the basic allotment and the 10% dutiable amount are dutiable at a variety of rates. The average rate for typical tourist purchases is about 12%, but you can find out rates on specific items by consulting *Tariff Schedules of the United States* in a library or any US Customs Service office.

Families traveling together may make a joint declaration to customs, which permits one member to exceed his or her duty-free exemption to the extent that another falls short. Families also may pool purchases dutiable under the flat rate. A family of three, for example, would be eligible for up to a total of $3,000 at the 10% flat duty rate (after each member had used up his or her $400 duty-free exemption) rather than three separate $1,000 allowances. This grouping of purchases is extremely useful when considering the duty on a high-tariff item, such as jewelry or a fur coat.

Personal exemptions can be used once every 30 days; in order to be eligible, an individual must have been out of the country for more than 48 continuous hours. If any portion of the exemption has been used once within any 30-day period or if your trip is less than 48 hours long, the duty-free allowance is cut to $25.

There are certain articles, however, that are duty-free only up to certain limits. The $25 allowance includes the following: 10 cigars (not Cuban), 50 cigarettes, and 4 ounces of perfume. Individuals eligible for the full $400 duty-free limit are allowed 1 carton of cigarettes (200), 100 cigars, and 1 liter of liquor or wine if the traveler is over 21. Under federal law, alcohol above this allowance is liable for both duty and an Internal Revenue tax. Note, however, that states are allowed to impose additional restrictions and penalties of their own, including (in Arizona and Utah, for example) confiscation of any quantities of liquor over the statutory limit. Antiques, if they are 100 or more years old and you have proof from the seller of that fact, are duty-free, as are paintings and drawings if done entirely by hand.

To avoid paying duty twice, register the serial numbers of computers, watches, and electronic equipment with the nearest US Customs bureau before departure; receipts of insurance policies also should be carried for other foreign-made items. (Also see the note at the end of *Entry Requirements and Documents,* in this section.)

Gold, gold medals, bullion, and up to $10,000 in currency or negotiable instruments may be brought into the US without being declared. Sums over $10,000 must be declared in writing.

The allotment for individual "unsolicited" gifts mailed from abroad (no more than one per day per recipient) is $50 retail value per gift. These gifts do not have to be declared and are not included in your duty-free exemption (see below). Although you should include a receipt for purchases with each package, the examiner is empowered to impose a duty based on his or her assessment of the value of the goods. The duty owed is collected by the US Postal Service when the package is delivered (also see below). More information on mailing packages home from abroad is contained in the US Customs Service pamphlet *Buyer Beware, International Mail Imports* (see below for where to write for this and other useful brochures).

CLEARING CUSTOMS: This is a simple procedure. Forms are distributed by airline or ship personnel before arrival. (Note that a $5-per-person service charge — called a user fee — is collected by airlines and cruise lines to help cover the cost of customs checks, but this is included in the ticket price.) If your purchases total no more than the $400 duty-free limit, you need only fill out the identification part of the form and make an oral declaration to the customs inspector. If entering with more than $400 worth of goods, you must submit a written declaration.

Customs agents are businesslike, efficient, and not unkind. During the peak season, clearance can take time, but this generally is because of the strain imposed by a number of jumbo jets simultaneously discharging their passengers, not because of unwarranted zealousness on the part of the customs people.

Efforts to streamline procedures used to include the so-called Citizens' Bypass Program, which allowed US citizens whose purchases were within their duty-free allowance to go to the "green line," where they simply showed their passports to the customs inspector. Although at the time of this writing this procedure still is being followed at some international airports in the US, most airports have returned to an earlier system. US citizens arriving from abroad now have to go through a passport check by the Immigration & Naturalization Service (INS) prior to recovering their baggage and proceeding to customs. (US citizens will not be on the same line as foreign visitors, but this additional wait does delay clearance on re-entry into the US.) Although all passengers have to go through this obligatory passport inspection, those entering with purchases within the duty-free limit may be spared a thorough customs inspection; however, inspectors still retain the right to search any luggage they choose — so don't do anything foolish.

It is illegal not to declare dutiable items; not to do so, in fact, constitutes smuggling, and the penalty can be anything from stiff fines and seizure of the goods to prison sentences. It simply isn't worth doing. Nor should you go along with the suggestions of foreign merchants who offer to help you secure a bargain by deceiving customs officials in any way. Such transactions frequently are a setup, using the foreign merchant as an agent of US Customs. Another agent of US Customs is TECS, the Treasury Enforcement Communications System, a computer that stores all kinds of pertinent information on returning citizens. There is a basic rule to buying goods abroad, and it should never be broken: *If you can't afford the duty on something, don't buy it.* Your list or verbal declaration should include all items purchased abroad, as well as gifts received abroad, purchases made at the behest of others, the value of repairs, and anything brought in for resale in the US.

Do not include in the list items that do not accompany you, i.e., purchases that you have mailed or had shipped home. As mentioned above, these are dutiable in any case, even if for your own use and even if the items that accompany your return from the same trip do not exhaust your duty-free exemption. It is a good idea, if you have accumulated too much while abroad, to mail home any personal effects (made and bought in the US) that you no longer need rather than your foreign purchases. These personal effects pass through US Customs as "American goods returned" and are not subject to duty.

If you cannot avoid shipping home your foreign purchases, however, the US Customs Service suggests that the package be clearly marked "Not for Sale" and that a copy of the bill of sale be included. The US Customs examiner usually will accept this as indicative of the article's fair retail value, but if he or she believes it to be falsified or feels the goods have been seriously undervalued, a higher retail value may be assigned.

FORBIDDEN IMPORTS: Narcotics, plants (unless specifically exempt and free of soil), and many types of food are not allowed into the US. Drugs are totally illegal, with the exception of medication prescribed by a physician. It's a good idea not to travel with too large a quantity of any given prescription drug (however, in the event that a pharmacy is not open when you need it, bring along several extra doses) and to have the prescription on hand in case any question arises either abroad or when re-entering the US.

Any sculpture that is part of an architectural structure, any authentic archaeological find, or other artifacts may not be exported from France without the permission of *Safico (Service for Financial and Commercial Authorization);* for information on items that might fall into this category, contact *Safic*o (42 Rue de Clichy, Paris 75436; phone: 1-42-81-91-44) or the French customs information center in Paris (phone: 1-40-01-02-06). If you do not obtain prior permission of the proper regulatory agencies, such items will be confiscated at the border, and you run the risk of being fined or imprisoned.

Tourists have long been forbidden to bring into the US foreign-made US trade-marked articles purchased abroad (if the trademark is recorded with US Customs) without written permission. It's now permissible to enter with one such item in your possession as long as it's for personal use.

The US Customs Service implements the rigorous Department of Agriculture regulations concerning the importation of vegetable matter, seeds, bulbs, and the like. Living vegetable matter may not be imported without a permit, and everything must be inspected, permit or not. Approved items (which do not require a permit) include dried bamboo and woven items made of straw; beads made of most seeds (but not jequirity beans — the poisonous scarlet and black seed of the rosary pea; *some* viable (living) seeds; cones of pine and other trees; roasted coffee beans; most flower bulbs; flowers (without roots); dried or canned fruits, jellies, or jams; polished rice, dried beans and teas; herb plants (not witchweed); nuts (but not acorns, chestnuts, or any nuts with outer husks); dried lichens, mushrooms, truffles, shamrocks, and seaweed; and most dried spices.

Other processed foods and baked goods usually are okay. Regulations on meat products generally depend on the country of origin and manner of processing. As a rule, commercially canned meat, hermetically sealed and cooked in the can so that it can be stored without refrigeration, is permitted, but not all canned meat fulfills this requirement. Be careful when buying European-made pâté, for instance. Goose liver pâté in itself is acceptable, but the pork fat that often is part of it, either as an ingredient or a rind, may not be. Even canned pâtés may not be admitted for this reason. (The imported ones you see in US stores have been prepared and packaged according to US regulations.) So before stocking up on a newfound favorite, it pays to check in advance — otherwise you might have to leave it behind.

The US Customs Service also enforces federal laws that prohibit the entry of articles made from the furs or hides of animals on the endangered species list. Beware of shoes, bags, and belts made of crocodile and certain kinds of lizard, and anything made of tortoiseshell; this also applies to preserved crocodiles, lizards, and turtles sometimes sold in gift shops. Most coral — particularly black coral — also is restricted (although small quantities of coral incorporated into jewelry or other craft items usually are permitted). And if you're shopping for big-ticket items, beware of fur coats made from the skins of spotted cats. They are sold in Europe, but they will be confiscated upon your return to the US, and there will be no refund. For information about other animals on the endangered species list, contact the Department of the Interior, US Fish and Wildlife Service (Publications Unit, 4401 N. Fairfax Dr., Room 130, Arlington, VA 22203; phone: 703-358-1711), and ask for the free publication *Facts About Federal Wildlife Laws.*

Also note that some foreign governments prohibit the export of items made from certain species of wildlife, and the US honors any such restrictions. Before you go shopping in any foreign country, check with the US Department of Agriculture (G110 Federal Bldg., Hyattsville, MD 20782; phone: 301-436-8413) and find out what items are prohibited from the country you will be visiting.

The US Customs Service publishes a series of free pamphlets with customs information. It includes *Know Before You Go,* a basic discussion of customs requirements pertaining to all travelers; *Buyer Beware, International Mail Imports; Travelers' Tips on Bringing Food, Plant, and Animal Products into the United States; Importing a Car; GSP and the Traveler; Pocket Hints; Currency Reporting; Pets, Wildlife, US Customs; Customs Hints for Visitors (Nonresidents);* and *Trademark Information for Travelers.* For the entire series or individual pamphlets, write to the US Customs Service (PO Box 7474, Washington, DC 20044) or contact any of the seven regional offices — in Boston, Chicago, Houston, Long Beach (California), Miami, New Orleans, and New York.

Note that the US Customs Service has a tape-recorded message whereby callers using touch-tone phones can obtain free pamphlets on various travel-related topics; the number is 202-566-8195. These pamphlets provide great briefing material, but if you still have questions when you're in Europe, contact the nearest US Consulate or the US Embassy.

Sources and Resources

Tourist Information

 The French Government Tourist Office has introduced a telephone information service for US travelers. Called "France On Call," it provides details on all of the historical and geographical provinces of France, including schedules of cultural and special events, a variety of travel services (airlines, car rentals, package tours, and so on), current weather conditions, currency exchange rates, and visa and passport requirements. To reach this service, dial 900-990-0040 (there is a 50¢ per minute charge for all calls, which will appear on your telephone bill). When calling this number, you also may want to request a copy of the French Government Tourist Office's 1993 *France Discovery Guide,* which features information on sightseeing, current discount travel offers, and detailed itineraries for planning your trip. Other than the per-minute call cost, there is no charge for this publication. For additional information about designing your own itinerary, see *Package Tours,* earlier in this section.

Another information service for travelers in France is *minitel,* a computerized information system that is available at most French hotels rated two stars or above. Hotel guests will find a computer terminal located in the lobby that will provide a variety of information for a number of regions (there is a "menu" specifying selections). For instance, by entering 3615-BORDEAUX, travelers will be given information on facilities, tourist attractions, and so on in the province of Bordeaux. This service is also available in many post offices.

Below is a list of the French and Monegasque government tourist offices in the US. They offer a wide variety of useful travel information, and most of their publications are free for the asking. For the best results, request general information on specific cities or provinces, as well as publications relating to your particular areas of interest: accommodations (châteaux-hotels, resorts, the type of country rental or guesthouse known as a *gîte,* and so on), restaurants, special events, tourist attractions, guided tours, and facilities for specific sports and other activities. There is no need to send a self-addressed, stamped evelope with your request, unless specified.

French Government Tourist Offices
Chicago: 645 N. Michigan Ave., Suite 630, Chicago, IL 60611-2836 (phone: 312-337-6301).

Dallas: 2305 Cedar Springs Rd., Suite 205, Dallas, TX 75201 (phone: 214-720-4010).

Los Angeles: 9454 Wilshire Blvd., Suite 303, Beverly Hills, CA 90212-2967 (phone: 213-271-6665).

New York City: 610 Fifth Ave., New York, NY 10020-2452 (requests by mail only); walk-in office on street level: 628 Fifth Ave., New York, NY 10020 (phone: 212-757-1125).

Monaco Government Tourist and Convention Bureau
Chicago: 542 S. Dearborn St., Suite 550, Chicago, IL 60605 (phone: 312-939-7863).

New York: 845 Third Ave., 19th Floor, New York, NY 10022 (phone: 212-759-5227).

Information on the major cities of France may be requested from the tourist offices cited (with addresses and phone numbers) in the *Sources and Resources* section of the relevant chapters in THE CITIES section. In addition, nearly every town and village in France has its own Syndicat d'Initiative, which serves as a tourist information center. These are too numerous to mention, but since most Americans arrive in France via Paris, listed below are the Paris offices of the Maisons de Province — the central sources of tourist information for each region. (Note that the telephone numbers listed below include the city code, 1, for Paris; if calling within the city, do not dial the initial 1.)

Alsace-Lorraine: *Maison de l'Alsace,* 39 Av. des Champs-Elysées, Paris 75008 (phone: 1-42-25-93-42 or 1-42-56-15-94).

Brittany: *Maison de Bretagne,* 17 Rue de l'Arrivée, Paris 75015 (phone: 1-45-38-73-15).

Central France: *Maison du Limousin,* 30 Rue Caumartin, Paris 75009 (phone: 1-40-07-04-67).

French Alps (Eastern Region): *Maison des Hautes Alpes,* 4 Av. de l'Opéra, Paris 75001 (phone: 1-42-96-05-08; 1-47-03-91-18 for a recording in French on snow and other weather conditions).

French Alps (Western Region): *Maison des Alpes Dauphiné,* 2 Pl. André-Malraux, Paris 75001 (phone: 1-42-96-08-43 or 1-42-96-08-56).

Garonne River Valley: *Maison du Lot-et-Garonne,* 15-17 Passage Choiseul, Paris 75002 (phone: 1-42-96-51-43 or 1-42-97-51-43).

Gascony: *Maison du Gers et de l'Armagnac,* 16-18 Bd. Haussmann, Paris 75009 (phone: 1-47-70-39-61).

North Atlantic Coast: *Maison de la Région Nord–Pas de Calais,* 18 Bd. Haussmann, Paris 75009 (phone: 1-47-70-59-62).

Pyrénées Mountain Region: *Maison des Pyrénées,* 11 Rue Rameau, Paris 75002 (phone: 1-42-61-58-18).

Rhône River Valley: *Maison de la Drôme,* 14 Bd. Haussmann, Paris 75009 (phone: 1-42-46-66-67).

Savoy: *Maison de la Savoie et de la Haut-Savoie,* 31 Av. de l'Opéra, Paris 75001 (phone: 1-42-61-74-73).

South Central France: *Maison de l'Auvergne,* 194 *bis* Rue de Rivoli, Paris 75001 (phone: 1-42-61-82-38).

Southwest France: *Maison du Périgord,* 30 Rue Louis-le-Grand, Paris 75002 (phone: 1-47-42-09-15).

Western Coastal Region: *Maison du Poitou-Charentes,* 68 Rue de Cherche-Midi, Paris 75006 (phone: 1-42-22-83-74).

Monaco: *Office du Tourisme de la Principauté de Monaco,* 9 Rue de la Paix, Paris 75002 (phone: 1-42-96-12-23).

The French Embassy and Consulates in the US

The French government maintains an embassy and a number of consulates in the US. One of their primary functions is to provide visas for certain resident aliens (depending on their country of origin) and for Americans planning to visit for longer than 3 months, or to study, reside, or work in France. Consulates also are empowered to sign official documents and to notarize copies or translations of US documents, which may be necessary for those papers to be considered legal in France.

The French Embassy is located at 4101 Reservoir Rd. NW, Washington, DC 20007-2176 (phone: 202-944-6000). Listed below are the French consulates in the US. Also listed is the Monegasque consulate, although the French consulates also often handle consular matters for Monaco. In general, these offices are open 9 AM to 1 PM, Mondays through Fridays — call ahead to be sure.

French Consulates in the US
Boston: *For visa applications:* 20 Park Plaza (in the Statler Office Bldg.), Suite 1123, Boston, MA 02116 (phone: 617-482-2864/6). *All other business:* 3 Commonwealth Ave., Boston, MA 02116 (phone: 617-266-9413).

Chicago: Olympia Center, 737 N. Michigan Ave., Suite 2020, Chicago, IL 60611 (phone: 312-787-5359, 312-787-5360, or 312-787-5361; recorded visa information: 312-787-7889).

Houston: 2727 Allen Pkwy., Suite 976, Houston, TX 77019 (phone: 713-528-2181).

Los Angeles: 10990 Wilshire Blvd., Suite 300, Los Angeles, CA 90024 (phone: 213-479-4426).

Miami: 1 Biscayne Tower, Suite 1710, 2 S. Biscayne Blvd., Miami, FL 33131 (phone: 305-372-9798).

New Orleans: The Lykes Bldg., 300 Poydras St., Suite 2105, New Orleans, LA 70130 (phone: 504-523-5772).

New York City: *Main office and to apply by mail for a visa:* 934 Fifth Ave., New York, NY 10021 (phone: 212-606-3688; recorded visa information: 212-606-3680).

San Francisco: 540 Bush St., San Francisco, CA 94108 (phone: 415-397-4330).

Monegasque Consulate in the US
New York City: *Consulat Général de Monaco,* 845 Third Ave., 19th Floor, New York, NY 10022 (phone: 212-759-5227).

Theater and Special Event Tickets

In more than one section of this book you will read about events that spark your interest — everything from music festivals and special theater seasons to sporting championships — along with telephone numbers and addresses to which to write for descriptive brochures, reservations, or tickets. The French Government Tourist Office can supply information on these and other special events and festivals that take place in France, though they cannot in all cases provide the actual program or detailed information on ticket prices.

Since many of these occasions often are fully booked well in advance, you should think about having your reservation in hand before you go. In some cases, tickets may be reserved over the phone and charged to a credit card, or you can send an international money order or foreign draft. If you do write, remember that any request from the US should be accompanied by an International Reply Coupon to ensure a response (send two of them for an airmail response). These international coupons, money orders, and drafts are available at US post offices.

For further information, write for the *European Travel Commission*'s extensive list of events scheduled for the entire year for its 24 member countries (including France). For a free copy, send a self-addressed, stamped, business-size (4 x 9½) envelope, to

"European Events," *European Travel Commission,* PO Box 1754, New York, NY 10185.

Books, Newspapers, Magazines, and Newsletters

BOOKS: Throughout GETTING READY TO GO, numerous books and brochures have been recommended as good sources of further information on a variety of topics.

Suggested Reading – The list below comprises books we have read and think worthwhile; it is by no means complete — but meant merely to start you on your way. These titles include some informative guides to special interests, solid historical acounts, and books that call your attention to things you might not otherwise notice.

General Travel

Birnbaum's Paris 1993, edited by Alexandra Mayes Birnbaum (HarperCollins; $11).

France on the TGV: How to Use the World's Fastest Train to Get the Most Out of France, by Mark Beffart (National Book Network; $9.95).

France: Provence & Côte d'Azur (Visitor's Guide Series; Hunter Publishing; $13.-95).

French Country Welcome: Bed & Breakfast Guide, Official Guidebook (Fédération Nationale des Gîtes de France; $21.50).

The French Way: An Insider's Guide to the Hotels and Restaurants of France, by Roland Escaig and Maurice Beaudoin (Warner Books; $16.95).

The Gateway to France: Flanders, Artois, and Picardy, by James Bentley (Viking; $21.95).

The Literary Map of Paris, by Aaron Blake (SCB Distributors; $4.95).

A Little Tour in France, by Henry James (Weidenfeld & Nicolson; $24.95).

Paris Dreambook: An Unconventional Guide to the Splendor and Squalor of the City, by Lawrence Osborne (Pantheon Books; $21).

The Pyrénées, by Bob Gibbons and Paul Davies (University of Nevada Press; $24.95).

Through the French Canals, by Philip Bristow (A&C Black Publishers Ltd.; $16.95).

Toujours Provence, by Peter Mayle (Knopf; $10).

The Unknown South of France: A History Buff's Guide, by Henry Reuss (Harvard Common; $12.95).

Walks in Hemingway's Paris: A Guide to Paris for the Literary Traveler, by Noel Fitch (St. Martin's Press; $16.95).

Walks in Provence: A Guide to over 300 Kilometers of Footpaths Through the Hills of Provence Down to the Sea, by the French Ramblers Association Staff (Footpaths of Europe Series; $19.95).

A Year in Provence, by Peter Mayle (Knopf; $10).

Poetry and Fiction

Baudelaire, Rimbaud, and Verlaine: Selected Verse and Prose Poems, edited by Joseph M. Bernstein (Carol Publishing; $6.95)

Beauties, Beasts, and Enchantment: Classic French Fairy Tales, translated by Jack Zipes (Meridian; $12.95).

Candide, by Voltaire (Penguin; $3.95).

The Count of Monte Cristo, by Alexandre Dumas (Bantam; $4.95).

A Day in the Country and Other Stories, by Guy de Maupassant (Oxford University Press; $5.95).

Don Juan and Other Plays, by Molière (Oxford University Press; $4.95).

Eugénie Grandet, by Honoré de Balzac (Penguin; $5.95).

Gargantua and Pantagruel, by François Rabelais (Norton; $17.95).

The Hunchback of Notre Dame, by Victor Hugo, (New American Library; Bantam $2.95).

The Lover, by Marguerite Duras (HarperCollins; $10).

Madame Bovary, by Gustave Flaubert (Penguin; $3.50).

The Malady of Death, by Marguerite Duras (Grove Press; $7.95).

Stéphane Mallarmé: Selected Poetry and Prose (New Directions; $8.95).

Les Misérables, by Victor Hugo (Fawcett; $4.95).

Random House Book of Twentieth-Century French Poetry, edited by Paul Auster (Random House; $19.95).

Remembrance of Things Past, by Marcel Proust (Random House; $52.85).

The School for Wives, by Molière (Harcourt Brace Jovanavich; $6.95).

A Tale of Two Cities, by Charles Dickens (Random House; $7.95).

The Three Musketeers, by Alexandre Dumas (Penguin; $5.95).

Tartuffe, by Molière (New American Library; $4.95).

History

Citizens, by Simon Shama (Random House; $29.95).

The Days of the French Revolution, by Christopher Hibbert (Morrow Quill Paperbacks; $12.95).

A Distant Mirror, by Barbara Tuchman (Random House; $45).

France, 1814–1940, by J. P. Bury (Routledge, Chapman, & Hall; $16.95).

France under the German Occupation, 1940–1944: An Annotated Bibliography, by Donna Evleth (Greenwood Publishing Group; $45).

The Middle Ages: A Concise Encyclopedia, edited by H. R. Loyn (Thames & Hudson; $24.95).

A Traveller's History of France, by Robert Cole (Interlink Publishing Group; $10.95).

The United States & the Making of Postwar France, 1945–1954, by Irwin M. Hall (Cambridge University Press; $47.50).

The Vichy Syndrome: History and Memory in France Since 1944, by Henry Rousso (Harvard University Press; $37.50).

Culture

Between Meals: An Appetite for Paris, by A. J. Liebling (North Point Press; $10.95).

France, by Donna Bailey & Anna Sproule (Steck-Vaughn Co.; $16.15).

Literary France: The Making of a Culture, by Priscilla Parkhurst Clark (University of California Press; $12.95).

Theatre de la Mode, by Susan Train (Rizzoli International Press; $45).

Art and Architecture

Art & Architecture in France 1500–1700, by Anthony Blunt (Penguin; $21.95).

The French Château: Life Style Tradition, by Christiane de Nicolay-Mazery and Jean-Bernard Naudin (W.W. Norton; $45).

The Guide to the Architecture of Paris, by Norval White (Macmillan Publishing Co.; $24.95).

Impressionism, by Phoebe Pool (Thames-Hudson; $14.95).

Inside Paris: Discovering the Period Interiors of Paris, photographed by Jerome Darblay (Rizzoli International Publications; $37.50).

Lives of the Artists, by Giorgio Vasari (Penguin Classics; published in two volumes, $5.95 each).

The Lure of Paris: 19th-Century American Painters and Their French Teachers, by H. Barbara Weinberg (Abbeville Press; $95).

Museums of Paris, by Eloise M. Danto (Surrey Books; $8.95).

Paris and the Surrealists, by George Melly (Thames & Hudson; $35).

Paris in Bloom, by Jean-Pierre and Denise Le Dantec (Abbeville; $50).

The Story of Art, by E. H. Gombrich (Prentice Hall; $43).

Undiscovered Museums of Paris, by Eloise M. Danto (Surrey Books; $8.95).

Versailles Gardens: Sculpture & Mythology, photographed by Jacques Girard (Vendome Press; $50).

Autobiography and Biography

The Last Days of Marie Antoinette: An Historical Sketch, by Ronald Charles Sutherland Gower (AMS Press; $22.50).

Matisse, Picasso, Miro as I Knew Them, by Rosamond Bernier (Knopf; $50).

Memories of Madame Vigée Lebrun, translated by Lionel Strachey (George Braziller; $12.95).

Michael Foucault, by Didier Eribon (Harvard University Press; $27.95).

Moveable Feast, by Ernest Hemingway (Macmillan Publishing Co.; $9.95).

Napoleon Bonaparte, by J. M. Thompson (Basil Blackwell; $22.95).

Food & Wine

Bordeaux: A Comprehensive Guide to the Wines Produced from 1961–1990, by Robert Parker (Simon and Schuster; $35).

The Cooking of South West France, by Paula Wolfert (HarperCollins; $10.95).

The Food of France, by Waverly Root (Random House; $10.95).

Food Lover's Guide to Paris, by Patricia Wells (Workman Press; $12.95).

France for the Gourmet Traveler, by Pamela Van Dyke Price (Passport Books; $16.95).

France: The Beautiful Cookbook, by Elisabeth Scotto, Marianne Comolli, and Michele Carles (Collin Publishing; $45).

Lichine's Guide to Wines, by Alexis Lichine (Random House; $18.95).

Long Ago in France: The Years in Dijon, by M. F. K. Fisher (Prentice-Hall; $17.95).

Menu French: The A to Z of French Food, edited by G. de Temmerman and D. Chédorge (Editions Scribo; $16.95).

Michelin Red Guide to France (Michelin; $24.95).

A Taste of Alsace, by Sue Style (William Morrow & Co.; $25).

Two Towns in Provence, by M. F. K. Fisher (Vintage Books; $15).

The Wine Lover's Guide to France, by Michael Busselle (Trafalgar Square; $22.-95).

The Wines of Bordeaux and Western France, by John J. Baxevanis (Rowman & Littlefield; $32.95).

The Wines and Vineyards of France: A Complete Atlas and Guide, by Pascal Ribereau-Gayon (Penguin; $40).

In addition, *Culturgrams* is a handy series of pamphlets that provides a good sampling of information on the people, cultures, sights, and bargains to be found in over 90 countries around the world. Each four-page, newsletter-size leaflet covers one country, and France is included in the series. The topics included range from customs and courtesies to lifestyles and demographics. These fact-filled pamphlets are published by the David M. Kennedy Center for International Studies at Brigham Young University; for an order form contact the group c/o Publication Services (280 HRCB, Provo, UT 84602; phone: 800-528-6279 or 801-378-6528). When ordering from 1 to 5 *Cultur-*

grams, the price is $1 each; 6 to 49 pamphlets cost 50¢ each; and for larger quantities, the price per copy goes down proportionately.

Another source of cultural information is *Do's and Taboos Around the World,* compiled by the Parker Pen Company and edited by Roger E. Axtell. It focuses on protocol, customs, etiquette, hand gestures and body language, gift giving, the dangers of using US jargon, and so on, and can be fun to read even if you're not going anyplace. It's available for $10.95 in bookstores or through John Wiley & Sons, 1 Wiley Dr., Somerset, NJ 08875 (phone: 908-469-4400).

Sources – The books listed above may be ordered directly from the publishers or found in the travel section of any good general bookstore or any sizable public library. If you still can't find something, the following stores and/or mail-order houses also specialize in travel literature. They offer books on the US along with guides to the rest of the world, and in some cases, even an old Baedeker or two.

Book Passage (51 Tamal Vista Blvd., Corte Madera, CA 94925; phone: 415-927-0960 in California; 800-321-9785 elsewhere in the US). Travel guides and maps to all areas of the world. A free catalogue is available.

The Complete Traveller (199 Madison Ave., New York, NY 10016; phone: 212-685-9007). Travel guides and maps. A catalogue is available for $2.

Forsyth Travel Library (PO Box 2975, Shawnee Mission, KS 66201-1375; phone: 800-367-7984 or 913-384-3440). Travel guides and maps, old and new, to all parts of the world, including France. Ask for the "Worldwide Travel Books and Maps" catalogue.

Globe Corner (1 School St., Boston, MA 02180; phone: 617-523-6658). Travel guides, maps, histories, and language aids.

Phileas Fogg's Books and Maps (87 *Stanford Shopping Center,* Palo Alto, CA 94304; phone: 800-533-FOGG or 415-327-1754). Travel guides, maps, and language aids.

Powell's Travel Store (Pioneer Courthouse Sq., 701 SW 6th Ave., Portland, OR 97204; phone: 503-228-1108). A panoply of travel-related books and materials (over 15,000 titles, as well as globes, maps, language aids, and videos), supplies and accessories (luggage, travel irons, electrical converters, etc.), and service (there is even a travel agency on the premises) — essentially "one-stop shopping" for the traveler.

The Reader's Catalog (250 W. 57th St., Suite 1330, New York, NY 10107; phone: 800-733-BOOK or 212-262-7198). This general mail-order catalogue business will make recommendations on travel — and other — books, and ship them anywhere in the world.

Tattered Cover (2955 E. First Ave., Denver, CO 80206; phone: 800-833-9327 or 303-322-7727). The travel department alone of this enormous bookstore carries over 7,000 books, as well as maps and atlases. No catalogue is offered (the list is too extensive), but a newsletter, issued three times a year, is available on request.

Thomas Brothers Maps & Travel Books (603 W. Seventh St., Los Angeles, CA 90017; phone: 213-627-4018). Maps (including road atlases, street guides, and wall maps), guidebooks, and travel accessories.

Traveldays Book Shop (317 Columbus City Center, Columbus, OH 43215; phone: 614-221-0506). Maps, guidebooks, travel videos, and language aids.

Traveller's Bookstore (22 W. 52nd St., New York, NY 10019; phone: 212-664-0995). Travel guides, maps, literature, and accessories. A catalogue is available for $2.

In addition, the *Librairie de France/Librería Hispanica* (French and Spanish Book Corporation), which specializes in language dictionaries and French and Spanish fiction and nonfiction, carries some guidebooks published in France. Of the company's two stores in New York, the one at 610 Fifth Ave., New York, NY 10020 (phone: 212-581-

8810), has the greatest selection of travel material; the other is at 115 Fifth Ave., New York, NY 10003 (212-673-7400).

For yet more sources of reading material, here are some bookstores in Paris with a selection of books in English:

L'Astrolabe (46 Rue de Provence; phone: 1-42-85-42-95).
Brentano's (37 Av. de l'Opéra; phone: 1-42-61-52-50).
Galignani (224 Rue de Rivoli; phone: 1-42-60-76-07).
Itinéraires (60 Rue St-Honoré; phone: 1-42-33-92-00).
W. H. Smith (248 Rue de Rivoli; phone: 1-42-60-37-97).
Ulysse (26 Rue St-Louis-en-l'Ile; phone: 1-43-25-17-35). Specializes in travel books on France, as well as those on international travel.

NEWSPAPERS AND MAGAZINES: A subscription to the *International Herald Tribune* is a good idea for dedicated travelers. This English-language newspaper is written and edited mostly in Paris, and is *the* newspaper read most regularly and avidly by Americans abroad to keep up with world news, US news, sports, the stock market (US and foreign), fluctuations in the exchange rate, and an assortment of help-wanted ads, real estate listings, and personals, global in scope. Published 6 days a week, it is available at newsstands throughout the US and in cities worldwide. In addition to being available on newsstands throughout France, larger hotels may have copies in the lobby for guests — if you don't see a copy, ask the hotel concierge if it is available. A 1-year's subscription in the US costs $369 (believe it or not, it's $20 less in New York City: $20). To subscribe, write or call the Subscription Manager, *International Herald Tribune,* 850 Third Ave., 10th Floor, New York, NY 10022 (phone: 800-882-2884 or 212-752-3890).

Among the major US publications that can be bought (generally a day or two after distribution in the US) in many of the larger cities and resort areas, at hotels, airports, and newsstands, are the *Los Angeles Times, The New York Times, USA Today,* and the *Wall Street Journal.* As with other imports, expect these and other US publications to cost more in France than in the US.

The French are well known for their fine food and sampling the regional fare is likely to be one of the highlights of any visit. You will find reading about local edibles worthwhile before you go or after you return. *Gourmet,* a magazine specializing in food, frequently features mouth-watering articles on the foods of France (particularly Paris), although its scope is much broader. It is available at newsstands throughout the US for $2.50 an issue or for $18 a year from *Gourmet* (PO Box 53780, Boulder, CO 80322-2886; phone: 800-365-2454). There are numerous additional magazines for every special interest available; check at your library information desk for a directory of such publications, or look over the selection offered by a well-stocked newsstand.

NEWSLETTERS: Throughout GETTING READY TO GO we have mentioned specific newsletters which our readers may be interested in consulting for further information. One of the very best sources of detailed travel information is *Consumer Reports Travel Letter.* Published monthly by Consumers Union (PO Box 53629, Boulder, CO 80322-3629; phone: 800-999-7959), it offers comprehensive coverage of the travel scene on a wide variety of fronts. A year's subscription costs $37; 2 years, $57.

The following travel newsletters also provide useful up-to-date information on travel services and bargains:

Entree (PO Box 5148, Santa Barbara, CA 93150; phone: 805-969-5848). This newsletter caters to a sophisticated, discriminating traveler with the means to explore the places mentioned. Subscribers have access to a 24-hour hotline providing information on restaurants and accommodations around the world. Monthly; a year's subscription costs $59.

The Hideaway Report (Harper Associates, Subscription Office: PO Box 300, Whitefish, MO 59937; phone: 406-862-3480; Editorial Office: PO Box 50, Sun

Valley, ID 83353; phone: 208-622-3193). This monthly source highlights retreats — including French idylls — for sophisticated travelers. A year's subscription costs $90.

Romantic Hideaways (217 E. 86th St., Suite 258, New York, NY 10028; phone: 212-969-8682). This monthly newsletter leans toward those special places made for those traveling in twos. A year's subscription costs $65.

Travel Smart (Communications House, 40 Beechdale Rd., Dobbs Ferry, NY 10522; phone: 914-693-8300 in New York; 800-327-3633 elsewhere in the US). This monthly covers a wide variety of trips and travel discounts. A year's subscription costs $44.

In addition, the following two newsletters are devoted exclusively to France:

La Belle France: The Sophisticated Guide to France (Travel Guide, PO Box 3485, Charlottesville, VA 22901; phone: 804-295-1200). This 8-page monthly newsletter contains hotel and restaurant reviews, as well as shopping information for Paris and other cities, and often includes short articles spotlighting a luxury destination. A year's subscription costs $67.

France Today (1051 Divisadero St., San Francisco, CA 94115; phone: 415-921-5100). Focuses on French politics, business, and culture, as well as travel and events. A year's subscription (ten issues) costs $29.

■**Computer Services:** Anyone who owns a personal computer and a modem can subscribe to a database service providing everything from airline schedules and fares to restaurant listings. Two such services of particular use to travelers are *CompuServe* (5000 Arlington Center Blvd., Columbus, OH 43220; phone: 800-848-8199 or 614-457-8600; $39.95 to join, plus usage fees of $6 to $12.50 per hour) and *Prodigy Services* (445 Hamilton Ave., White Plains, NY 10601; phone: 800-822-6922 or 914-993-8000; $12.95 per month's subscription, plus variable usage fees).

Before using any computer bulletin-board services, be sure to take precautions to prevent downloading of a computer "virus." First install one of the programs designed to screen out such nuisances.

APPROXIMATE EQUIVALENTS

Metric Unit	Abbreviation	US Equivalent
LENGTH		
meter	m	39.37 inches
kilometer	km	.62 mile
millimeter	mm	.04 inch
CAPACITY		
liter	l	1.057 quarts
WEIGHT		
gram	g	.035 ounce
kilogram	kg	2.2 pounds
metric ton	MT	1.1 ton
ENERGY		
kilowatt	kw	1.34 horsepower

CONVERSION TABLES METRIC TO US MEASUREMENTS		
Multiply:	**by:**	**to convert to:**
LENGTH		
millimeters	.04	inches
meters	3.3	feet
meters	1.1	yards
kilometers	.6	miles
CAPACITY		
liters	2.11	pints (liquid)
liters	1.06	quarts (liquid)
liters	.26	gallons (liquid)
WEIGHT		
grams	.04	ounces (avoir.)
kilograms	2.2	pounds (avoir.)
US TO METRIC MEASUREMENTS		
LENGTH		
inches	25.	millimeters
feet	.3	meters
yards	.9	meters
miles	1.6	kilometers
CAPACITY		
pints	.47	liters
quarts	.95	liters
gallons	3.8	liters
WEIGHT		
ounces	28.	grams
pounds	.45	kilograms
TEMPERATURE $°F = (°C \times 9/5) + 32$ $°C = (°F - 32) \times 5/9$		

Weights and Measures

When traveling in France, you'll find that just about every quantity, whether it is length, weight, or capacity, will be expressed in unfamiliar terms. In fact, this is true for travel almost everywhere in the world, since the US is one of the last countries to make its way to the metric system. Your trip to France may serve to familiarize you with what one day may be the weights and measures at your grocery store.

There are some specific things to keep in mind during your trip. Fruits and vegetables at a market are recorded in kilos (kilograms), as are your luggage at the airport and your body weight. (This latter is particularly pleasing to people of significant size, who, instead of weighing 220 pounds hit the scales at a mere 100 kilos.) A kilo equals 2.2 pounds and 1 pound is .45 of a kilo. Body temperature is measured in degrees centigrade or Celsius rather than on the Fahrenheit scale, so that a normal body temperature is 37C, not 98.6F, and freezing is 0 degrees C rather than 32F.

Gasoline is sold by the liter (approximately 3.8 liters to 1 gallon). Tire pressure gauges and other equipment measure in kilograms per square centimeter rather than pounds per square inch. Highway signs are written in kilometers rather than miles (1 mile equals 1.6 km; 1 km equals .62 mile). And speed limits are in kilometers per hour, so think twice before hitting the gas when you see a speed limit of 100. That means 62 miles per hour.

The tables and conversion factors listed above should give you all the information you will need to understand any transaction, road sign, or map you encounter during your travels.

Cameras and Equipment

 Vacations are everybody's favorite time for taking pictures and home movies. After all, most of us want to remember the places we visit — and show them off to others. Here are a few suggestions to help you get the best results from your travel photography or videography.

BEFORE THE TRIP

If you're taking your camera or camcorder out after a long period in mothballs, or have just bought a new one, check it thoroughly before you leave to prevent unexpected breakdowns or disappointing pictures.

1. Still cameras should be cleaned carefully and thoroughly, inside and out. If using a camcorder, run a head cleaner through it. You also may want to have your camcorder professionally serviced (opening the casing yourself will violate the manufacturer's warranty). Always use filters to protect your lens while traveling.
2. Check the batteries for your camera's light meter and flash, and take along extras just in case yours wear out during the trip. For camcorders, bring along extra Nickel-Cadmium (Ni-Cad) batteries; if you use rechargeable batteries, a recharger will cut down on the extras.
3. Using all the settings and features, shoot at least one test roll of film or one videocassette, using the type you plan to take along with you.

EQUIPMENT TO TAKE ALONG

Keep your gear light and compact. Items that are too heavy or bulky to be carried comfortably on a full-day excursion will likely remain in your hotel room.

1. Invest in a broad camera or camcorder strap if you now have a thin one. It will make carrying the camera much more comfortable.
2. A sturdy canvas, vinyl, or leather camera or camcorder bag, preferably with padded pockets (not an airline bag), will keep your equipment organized and easy to find. If you will be doing much shooting around the water, a waterproof case is best.
3. For cleaning, bring along a camel's hair brush that retracts into a rubber squeeze

bulb. Also take plenty of lens tissue, soft cloths, and plastic bags to protect equipment from dust and moisture.

■**Note:** If you will be using your camcorder in Europe, note that most European countries (including France) operate on a different electrical current than the US, so you should make sure that the battery charger that comes with your camcorder is compatible with the current in the countries you're visiting. You'll also need a plug adapter kit to cope with the variations in plug configurations found in Europe. And don't expect to be able to play back your tape through a European TV set or VCR. The US and Canada use a different television standard than most European countries; these systems are incompatible with each other and multiple-standard TV sets are rare.

FILM AND TAPES: If you are concerned about airport security X-rays damaging undeveloped film (X-rays do not affect processed film) or tapes, store them in one of the lead-lined bags sold in camera shops. In the US and Canada, incidents of X-ray damage to unprocessed film (exposed or unexposed) are few because low-dosage X-ray equipment is used virtually everywhere. However, when crossing international borders, travelers should know that foreign X-ray equipment used for carry-on baggage may deliver higher levels of radiation and that even more powerful X-ray equipment may be used for checked luggage, so it's best to carry your film on board.

If you're traveling without a protective bag, you may want to ask to have your photo equipment inspected by hand. In the US, Federal Aviation Administration regulations require that if you request a hand inspection, you get it, but overseas the response may depend on the humor of the inspector. One type of film that should never be subjected to X-rays is the very high speed ASA 1000; there are lead-lined bags made especially for it — and, in the event that you are refused a hand inspection, this is the only way to save your film. The walk-through metal detector devices at airports do not affect film, though the film cartridges may set them off. Because cassettes have been favorite carriers for terrorist explosives over the years, airport officials probably will insist that you put these through the X-ray machine as well. If you don't have a choice, put them through and hope for the best.

You should have no problem finding film or tapes throughout Europe. When buying film, tapes, or photo accessories the best rule of thumb is to stick to name brands with which you are familiar. Different countries have their own ways of labeling camcorder tapes, and although the variations in recording and playback standards won't affect your ability to use the tape, they will affect how quickly you record and how much time you actually have to record on the tape. The availability of film processing labs and equipment repair shops will vary from area to area.

■**A note about courtesy and caution:** When photographing individuals in France (and anywhere else in the world), ask first. It's common courtesy. Furthermore, some governments have security regulations regarding the use of cameras and will not permit the photographing of certain subjects, such as particular government and military installations. When in doubt, ask.

Useful Words and Phrases

The French as a nation have a reputation for being snobbish and brusque to tourists, and, unfortunately, many Americans have allowed this stereotype to dissuade them from visiting France. The more experienced traveler, however, knows that on an individual basis, the French people are usually cordial and helpful, especially if you speak a few words of their language. Don't be afraid of misplaced accents or misconjugated verbs — in most cases you will be understood (and possibly corrected) and then advised on the menu or pointed in the right direction. Below is a basic guide to pronunciation, as well as a selection of commonly used words and phrases to speed you on your way.

French words are stressed on the vowel preceding the last consonant in the word, except that a final accented *e* (*é*) is stressed. Final consonants are pronounced only if they precede words beginning with vowels. Vowels preceding nasals (*m, n*) are nasalized (i.e., pronounced with emission of air through the nose) and the *m* or *n* is not pronounced.

French consonants are pronounced almost as in English, with these exceptions:

ch is pronounced like *sh* in *push*
c before *e, i,* or *y* is pronounced *s;* otherwise as *k*
s is pronounced as *z* between vowels
gn is pronounced like *ny* in canyon
g before *e, i,* or *y* is pronounced like *si* in vision; otherwise like *g* in *go*
j is pronounced like *si* in vision
ll following *i* is pronounced like *y* in year
qu is pronounced as *k* (not *kw*)
h is silent

French vowels are different from those in English, but usually can be pronounced intelligibly following these rules:

Final unaccented *e* is silent; it signals that a preceding consonant is pronounced.
é is pronounced like the *a* in *late*
è is pronounced as in *met*
i is pronounced as in *machine*
o is pronounced like *ou* in *ought*
u is pronounced like *ee* in *beet* but with the lips rounded
an and *en* are pronounced like the *a* in *father* but nasalized
in is pronounced with the vowel of *met* but nasalized
ai is pronounced like *e* in *met*
au is pronounced like *o* in *cold*
oi and *oy* are pronounced *wa*
ou is pronounced as in *youth*
eu is pronounced like the *e* of *men* but with the lips rounded
Final *er* is pronounced like the *ay* of *delay*

Greetings and Everyday Expressions

Good morning! (Hello!)	*Bonjour!*
Good afternoon, good evening!	*Bonsoir!*
How are you?	*Comment allez-vous?*
Pleased to meet you!	*Enchanté!*
Good-bye!	*Au revoir!*
See you soon!	*A bientôt!*
Good night!	*Bonne nuit!*
Yes!	*Oui!*
No!	*Non!*
Please!	*S'il vous plaît!*
Thank you!	*Merci!*
You're welcome!	*De rien!*
Excuse me!	*Excusez-moi* or *pardonnez-moi!*
It doesn't matter.	*Ca m'est égal.*
I don't speak French.	*Je ne parle pas français.*

Do you speak English?	*Parlez-vous anglais?*
Please repeat.	*Répétez, s'il vous plaît.*
I don't understand.	*Je ne comprends pas.*
Do you understand?	*Vous comprenez?*
My name is . . .	*Je m'appelle . . .*
What is your name?	*Comment vous appelez-vous?*
miss	*mademoiselle*
madame	*madame*
mister/sir	*monsieur*

open	*ouvert*
closed	*fermé*
entrance	*entrée*
exit	*sortie*
push	*poussez*
pull	*tirez*
today	*aujourd'hui*
tomorrow	*demain*
yesterday	*hier*

Help!	*Au secours!*
ambulance	*l'ambulance*
Get a doctor!	*Appelez le médecin!*

Checking In

I have (don't have) a reservation.	*J'ai une (Je n'ai pas de) réservation.*
I would like . . .	*Je voudrais . . .*
a single room	*une chambre pour une personne*
a double room	*une chambre pour deux*
a quiet room	*une chambre tranquille*
with bath	*avec salle de bain*
with shower	*avec douche*
with a sea view	*avec une vue sur la mer*
with air conditioning	*une chambre climatisée*
with balcony	*avec balcon*
overnight only	*pour une nuit seulement*
a few days	*quelques jours*
a week (at least)	*une semaine (au moins)*
with full board	*avec pension complète*
with half board	*avec demi-pension*
Does that price include breakfast?	*Est-ce que le petit dejeuner est inclus?*
Are taxes included?	*Est-ce que les taxes sont comprises?*
Do you accept traveler's checks?	*Acceptez-vous les travellers-chèques?*
Do you accept credit cards?	*Acceptez-vous les cartes de crédit?*

Eating Out

ashtray	*un cendrier*
bottle	*une bouteille*
(extra) chair	*une chaise (en sus)*
cup	*une tasse*
fork	*une fourchette*

knife	*un couteau*
spoon	*une cuillère*
napkin	*une serviette*
plate	*une assiette*
table	*une table*
beer	*bière*
coffee	*café*
black coffee	*café noir*
coffee with milk	*café au lait*
cream	*crème*
fruit juice	*jus de fruit*
lemonade	*citron pressé*
milk	*lait*
mineral water	
(non-carbonated)	*l'eau minérale*
mineral water (carbonated)	*l'eau gazeuse*
orangeade	*orange pressée*
port	*vin de porto*
sherry	*vin de Xérès*
red wine	*vin rouge*
white wine	*vin blanc*
rosé	*rosé*
tea	*thé*
water	*eau*
cold	*froid*
hot	*chaud*
sweet	*doux*
(very) dry	*(très) sec*
bacon	*bacon*
bread	*pain*
butter	*beurre*
eggs	*oeufs*
soft boiled	*à la coque*
hard boiled	*oeuf dur*
fried	*sur le plat*
scrambled	*brouillé*
poached	*poché*
ham	*jambon*
honey	*miel*
sugar	*sucre*
jam	*confiture*
juice	*jus*
orange	*jus d'orange*
tomato	*jus de tomate*
omelette	*omelette*
pepper	*poivre*
salt	*sel*
Waiter!	*Garçon!*
Waitress!	*Mademoiselle!*

I would like	*Je voudrais*
a glass of	*un verre de*
a bottle of	*une bouteille de*
a half bottle of	*une demie-bouteille de*
a liter of	*un litre de*
a carafe of	*une carafe de*

The check, please.	*L'addition, s'il vous plaît.*
Is the service charge included?	*Le service, est-il compris?*
I think there is a mistake in the bill.	*Je crois qu'il y a une erreur dans l'addition.*

See also the glossary of food terms in *Food and Drink,* PERSPECTIVES.

Shopping

bakery	*boulangerie*
bookstore	*librairie*
butcher store	*boucherie*
camera shop	*magasin de photographie*
clothing store	*magasin de vêtements*
delicatessen	*charcuterie*
department store	*grand magasin*
drugstore (for medicine)	*pharmacie*
grocery	*épicerie*
jewelry store	*bijouterie*
newsstand	*kiosque à journaux*
notions (sewing supplies) shop	*mercerie*
pastry shop	*pâtisserie*
perfume (and cosmetics) store	*parfumerie*
pharmacy/drugstore	*pharmacie*
shoestore	*magasin de chaussures*
supermarket	*supermarché*
tobacconist	*bureau de tabac*

cheap	*bon marché*
expensive	*cher*

large	*grand*
larger	*plus grand*
too large	*trop grand*
small	*petit*
smaller	*plus petit*
too small	*trop petit*

long	*long*
short	*court*
old	*vieux*
new	*nouveau*
used	*d'occasion*
handmade	*fait à la main*

Is it machine washable?	*Est-ce que c'est lavable à la machine?*
How much does this cost?	*Quel est le prix?/Combien?*
What is it made of?	*De quoi est-ce fait?*
camel's hair	*poil de chameau*
cotton	*coton*
corduroy	*velours côtelé*
filigree	*filigrane*
lace	*dentelle*
leather	*cuir*
linen	*lin*
silk	*soie*
suede	*daim*
synthetic	*synthétique*
wool	*laine*
brass	*cuivre jaune*
copper	*cuivre*
gold (plated)	*or (plaqué)*
silver (plated)	*argent (plaqué)*
wood	*bois*
May I have a sales tax rebate form?	*Puis-je avoir la formulaire pour la détaxe?*
May I pay with this credit card?	*Puis-je payer avec cette carte de crédit?*
May I pay with a traveler's check?	*Puis-je payer avec des travellers-chèques?*

Getting around

north	*le nord*
south	*le sud*
east	*l'est*
west	*l'ouest*
right	*droite*
left	*gauche*
Go straight ahead	*tout droit*
far	*loin*
near	*proche; près*
airport	*l'aéroport*
bus stop	*l'arrêt de bus*
gas station	*station service*
train station	*la gare*
subway	*le métro*
map	*carte*
one-way ticket	*aller simple*
round-trip ticket	*un billet aller et retour*
gate	*porte*
track	*voie*
in first class	*en première*

in second class	*en deuxième*
no smoking	*défense de fumer*

Does this subway/bus go to . . . ?	*Est-ce que ce métro/bus va à . . . ?*
What time does it leave?	*A quelle heure part-il?*

gas	*essence*
regular (leaded)	*ordinaire*
super (leaded)	*super*
unleaded	*sans plomb*
diesel	*diesel*
Fill it up, please.	*Le plein, s'il vous plaît.*

the tires	*les pneus*
the oil	*les huile*

Danger	*Danger*
Caution	*Attention*
Detour	*Détour*
Dead End	*Cul-de-sac*
Do Not Enter	*Défense d'entrer*
No Parking	*Défense de stationner*
No Passing	*Défense de doubler*
No U-turn	*Défense de faire demi-tour*
One way	*Sens interdit*
Pay toll	*Péage*
Pedestrian Zone	*Zone piétonnière*
Reduce Speed	*Ralentir*
Speed Limit Reminder	*Rappel*
Steep Incline	*Côte à forte pente*
Stop	*Stop; Arrêt*
Use Headlights	*Allumez les phares*
Yield	*Cédez le passage*
Where is the . . . ?	*Où se trouve . . . ?*
How many kilometers are we from . . . ?	*Combien de kilomètres sommes nous de . . . ?*

Personal Items and Services

aspirin	*aspirine*
Band-Aids	*pansements*
barbershop	*coiffeur pour hommes*
bath	*bain*
bathroom	*salle de bain*
beauty shop	*salon de coiffure*
condom	*préservatif*
dentist	*dentiste*
disposable diapers	*couches*
dry cleaner	*nettoyage à sec* or *teinturerie*
hairdresser	*coiffeur pour dames*
laundromat	*lavomatique* or *blanchisserie automatique*
post office	*bureau de poste*
postage stamps (air mail)	*timbres (par avion)*
razor	*rasoir*

sanitary napkins	*serviettes hygiéniques*
shampoo	*shampooing*
shaving cream	*crème à raser*
shower	*douche*
soap	*savon*
tampons	*tampons*
tissues	*mouchoirs en papier*
toilet	*toilette* or *WC*
toilet paper	*papier hygiénique*
toothbrush	*brosse à dents*
toothpaste	*dentifrice*

Where is the men's/ladies' room?	*Où sont les toilettes?*

Days of the Week

Monday	*lundi*
Tuesday	*mardi*
Wednesday	*mercredi*
Thursday	*jeudi*
Friday	*vendredi*
Saturday	*samedi*
Sunday	*dimanche*

Months

January	*janvier*
February	*février*
March	*mars*
April	*avril*
May	*mai*
June	*juin*
July	*juillet*
August	*août*
September	*septembre*
October	*octobre*
November	*novembre*
December	*décembre*

Numbers

zero	*zéro*
one	*un*
two	*deux*
three	*trois*
four	*quatre*
five	*cinq*
six	*six*
seven	*sept*
eight	*huit*
nine	*neuf*
ten	*dix*
eleven	*onze*
twelve	*douze*
thirteen	*treize*

fourteen	*quatorze*
fifteen	*quinze*
sixteen	*seize*
seventeen	*dix-sept*
eighteen	*dix-huit*
nineteen	*dix-neuf*
twenty	*vingt*
twenty-one	*vingt-et-un*
thirty	*trente*
forty	*quarante*
fifty	*cinquante*
sixty	*soixante*
seventy	*soixante-dix*
eighty	*quatre-vingts*
ninety	*quatre-vingt-dix*
one hundred	*cent*
1993	*mille neuf*
	cent quatre-vingt
	treize

Colors

black	*noir*
blue	*bleu*
brown	*brun*
gray	*gris*
green	*vert*
orange	*orange*
pink	*rose*
purple	*violet*
red	*rouge*
yellow	*jaune*
white	*blanc*

Writing Reservations Letters

Restaurant/Hotel Name
Street Address
Postal Code, City
France

Dear Sir:

I would like to reserve a table for (number of) persons for lunch/dinner on (day and month), 199?, at (hour) o'clock.

or

I would like to reserve a room for (number of) people for (number of) nights.

Would you be so kind as to confirm the reservation as soon as possible?

Monsieur:

Je voudrais réserver une table pour (number) personnes pour le déjeuner/dîner du (day and month) 199?, à (time using the 24-hour clock) heures.

or

Je voudrais réserver une chambre pour (number) personne(s) pour (number) nuits.

Auriez-vous la bonté de bien vouloir me confirmer cette réservation dès que possible?

I am very much looking forward to meeting you. (The French usually include a pleasantry such as this.)

J'attends avec impatience le plaisir de faire votre connaissance.

With my thanks,
(Signature, followed by your typed name and address)

Avec tous remerciements,

PERSPECTIVES

Food and Drink

France is the gastronomic capital of the world; it's no accident that so many food-related words — cuisine, gourmet, menu, sauté — come from the French language. So it's only natural that the French are very serious about food and drink. They fuss over the quality of ingredients, prepare each dish with great care and style, and eat with even greater enthusiasm. As a result, dining in France can be the most memorable aspect of any visit — or the most uncomfortable. French dining customs are just enough like ours to make the differences hard to notice, but those differences count for a lot in a nation preoccupied with gastronomy. Fortunately, it's not hard to pick up the French manner and tempo of eating if you look about you and notice what's going on.

THE FRENCH DINING EXPERIENCE

Start with breakfast, which in France generally consists of coffee and rolls. The coffee is strong, usually mixed half and half with hot milk (*café au lait*), although you also can have it black (*café noir*) or take tea (*thé*) or hot chocolate (*chocolat*) instead. Rolls — plain crusty French bread rolls; flaky, buttery croissants; or somewhat sweeter, doughy *brioches* — are served with butter and jam. The French don't much care for the fruit juice, eggs, bacon, cereal, and pancakes of the staple American or English breakfast. If you insist, you can get them, but in all but the most tourist-oriented hotels they will bear little relationship to what you know. And in any case you'll pay preposterous prices for disappointing examples, since the French think of them as exotic — and charge accordingly.

Lunch has its special customs, too. Most French restaurants traditionally serve a full dinner at midday: at least three courses, accompanied by wine. However, if you can't handle a major meal at noon or if you're saving yourself for a three-star extravaganza at dinner, you may prefer something light. Don't go to an elaborate restaurant for a quick bite; you will almost certainly wind up with more food — and a higher bill — than you intended, and the meal likely will last a couple of hours. Try a bistro or brasserie instead, one which serves simple meals; a pizzeria (now common almost everywhere in France and often quite good); or a snack bar (found in abundance around the universities and other gathering places of the young). At any of these you can find an omelette or a slice of quiche.

Or try a sandwich. In France this usually means a length of crisp French bread covered by a very thin layer of good ham or cheese — period. It's basic, but very satisfying. The *croque-monsieur,* a toasted (French toast, natch) ham and cheese sandwich, (or a *croque-madame;* the feminine form sports a fried egg on top), also is delicious and inexpensive, as is *steak frites.* In the latter, the piece of meat will be small and nearly paper thin, but it will be competently grilled and very tasty — even pink inside if you so request. And it's served with lots of those fine *frites;* after all, this is the home of the original French fry.

Perhaps the very best option at lunchtime is to hunt out the local public market or food shopping street. Every town and neighborhood has one, since the French shop for their food a day (sometimes a meal) at a time, bringing home whatever appeals to them for that afternoon or evening. Tiny butcher stores, fishmongers, greengrocers, pastry shops, and bread bakers form a cluster of tempting sights and scents. Best of all are the *charcuteries* and *traiteurs,* shops that sell everything from simple salads, pâté, ham, cheese, and sausage to whole geese in *galantine,* sparkling with aspic, lapped in creamy *chaud-froid* sauce, and garlanded with cut-vegetable "flowers." You can go from shop to shop and, for remarkably little money, acquire two or three slices of pâté or *saucisson* (salami), a chunk of cheese, a quarter-pound of olives, some vegetables in vinaigrette, a crusty *baguette* of bread, and a small bottle of wine or mineral water — then go sit in a nearby park or by a scenic river for a glorious *picnique* (the French invented that, too). For the more timid traveler, all this can be accomplished, with far less stress, and a minimal knowledge of the language, by going to a local *supermarché* (supermarket). In addition to the conventional variety, you can find them in the *sous sol* (basement) of any major department store. Be prepared to be dazzled — these places bear little resemblance to your neighborhood *A&P.* You also can find a wide choice of wines and spirits, at prices far lower than at formal wine shops.

But there's no reason to pass up a full-course restaurant meal at lunch (traditionally served only between 12 and 2 PM) and another at dinner (served between 7 and 9 PM) if your waistline, appetite, and schedule can stand it. Travelers will find that almost every city or region has too many interesting restaurants to be sampled during the course of the average visit. For the best dining experience, it pays to select both your restaurant and your meal carefully.

First, choose a restaurant based on your budget and the sort of meal you'd most like to sample. In general, there are three basic types of restaurants in France: the temples of haute cuisine, the bistro serving *cuisine bourgeoise,* and the neighborhood brasserie or hangout. The dining experience in each is dramatically different.

The temples of haute cuisine are supremely elegant and quite formal. Their menus are diverse, though they bear a family resemblance to those in the more ambitious French restaurants in major American cities. (Note that without exception, these dining bastions require reservations well in advance. See *Useful Words and Phrases,* GETTING READY TO GO, to help you write for reservations.) The taste of similar dishes will be subtly better in France, however, because the ingredients are more likely to have been raised *sans* additives and also usually are fresher. In this type of restaurant you'll find the perennially aristocratic appetizers — caviar, oysters, smoked salmon, pâté, and terrine; noble meat and game dishes such as venison, wild boar, grouse, and pheasant; severely simple roasts with luscious, complex sauces; exquisite sautés of veal and chicken with cream and wild mushrooms; an enormous spectrum of fish (many with unfamiliar names) prepared in a dazzling variety of ways; perfect vegetables lavishly set forth as courses in themselves; a cheese selection seemingly without end; and dessert carts laden with finely sculptured fantasies executed in pastry, whipped cream, and meringue. These are the makings of magnificent meals, though hardly the sort of feast one would want every day; even the French don't eat this way all the time. Our advice, therefore, is to plan just a few of these glorious dinners and space them out for the most dramatic gastronomical memories.

At the opposite end of the spectrum are the unpretentious neighborhood brasseries, where the food is relatively quick and simple. It's easy to enjoy a full meal at this kind of place as long as you stay within the limits of the kitchen's power. That means that if someone has been so misguided as to put pheasant Souvaroff with truffles and foie gras on the menu at the equivalent of $8 a portion, don't order it. It won't be the dish it should be. Order instead such dependable dishes as onion soup gratinée, grilled or sautéed cutlets, chops, sausages, roast chicken, or the hearty stew or fricassee of the day. For an appetizer, try freshly made vegetable soup or fresh asparagus if they happen to be in season; for dessert, a slice of apple tart, some chocolate mousse, or caramel custard. These are dishes that the humblest restaurants in France can do well. But once again, it would be a pity to eat *only* in places of this kind, because you'll miss most of the truly interesting dishes France has to offer.

Perhaps the most fun of all is the third type of restaurant, the medium-priced establishment that serves *cuisine bourgeoise,* the traditional cooking of a particular region. There are at least half a dozen distinct styles of regional French cooking, ranging from the steamy *choucroutes* of Alsace to the spicy sauces of Provence. The chefs at these little bistros and family-run eateries take classic dishes, add their personal interpretations, and produce food that is both strongly individual and thoroughly representative of their area. They use the best ingredients from the markets — meat, fish, fruits, vegetables, and dairy products. Even the traveler who knows little about either France or food will enjoy the marvelous diversity of most *cuisine bourgeoise.*

So much for the restaurants; the next step is to figure out the menu. At first glance, a French menu can inspire culture shock, for it's often handwritten in indecipherable script. Do not be stampeded into ordering the first items you recognize. Let the waiter help, but don't let him rush you. Take your time; remember, the table is yours for as long as you want it. Also remember that many restaurants post menus outside, so you might combine an afternoon's sightseeing with a little menu reading before dinner.

Most French menus are divided into à la carte offerings and prix fixe (fixed price) meals, called *menus,* which offer good value for the money. There may be several different *menus,* ranging from the economical *menu touristique,* which usually offers the most pedestrian dishes, to the more expensive *menu gastronomique* or *menu de dégustation,* which may run to five or nine or more small courses and feature regional specialties, seasonal delicacies, and the dishes of which the chef is most proud. The latter can be a wonderful way to taste a bit of everything that's best in the local cuisine, wherever in France you may be.

The sequence of courses in France is fairly similar to that in the US, but a few differences are worth noting. For example, appetizers in France are served at almost every lunch and dinner, but are called *entrées*. Also, unless otherwise specified, *salade* means only lettuce — good flavorful greens — tossed with a simple vinaigrette dressing. Salad is never eaten early in a meal — although you can order crudités (an assortment of fresh raw vegetables) as an *entrée* — and it isn't served automatically. Rather, it's presented as an abundant, separate course, after the main dish and before cheese or dessert; the idea is that its astringency clears the palate to prepare for fuller enjoyment of what follows.

Cheese also plays a more prominent role in a French dinner than in the American equivalent. It's customary to drink wine at dinner, and ordering some cheese "with which to finish the wine" is a pleasant part of that custom. The better the restaurant, the more pride it will take in a full and varied cheese tray — offering as many as forty varieties at a time. This can be intimidating if you don't recognize more than one or two of them, but just ask the waiter to name what's unfamiliar and explain whether they are strong, sharp, soft, runny, creamy, or crumbly. You may request small portions of two or three different cheeses or a substantial piece of the one that looks most appealing. Cheese typically is accompanied by bread and sometimes butter, especially if one of the selections is hard or dry.

Finally, there is the matter of drink. The American custom of starting a meal in a restaurant with a cocktail comprised of hard liquor very seldom is duplicated in France. A French "drink" is far more apt to be a house aperitif — perhaps a glass of champagne with a dash of raspberry liqueur — or a glass of wine. You can ask to see the wine list right away or simply request a carafe of the house's red, white, or rosé to sip while reading the menu. (Carafe wine is relatively inexpensive and can be undistinguished, but almost always is potable.) Alternatively, mineral water (with or without gas) is a common initial request, especially since glasses of cold water seldom appear on a French table as a matter of course. Mineral water also is a common beverage (along with wine) during a meal. Coffee never is served during a meal, but rather at the very end, in small cups; it's a strong, dark brew into which the French often stir great quantities of sugar, but no milk. The French also brew first-rate decaffeinated coffee (*décaféinée*) that is far better than the watery equivalent most often served in American restaurants. A beverage called "American coffee" is served in many places, but usually it's awful, so beware.

France also produces some of the world's best wines, and every visitor should try them. Bordeaux, Burgundy, and Champagne are widely known for their fine wines, although almost every corner of France has its own. When ordering wine, remember that the local wine usually marries well with the local cuisine. It's also wise to remember that no one is as familiar with a restaurant's wine list as that restaurant's own staff, especially when the list has a heavy bias of wines from an unfamiliar region, including wines from small producers. So when ordering wine, as with food, don't hesitate to ask questions and take advice. (Don't be looking for the 1991 vintage in years to come, as a severe frost killed grapes from Bordeaux to Champagne during the spring, and at least half of that year's crops were destroyed.) Below is a region-by-region discussion and description of the foods and wines for which France is famous.

REGIONAL SPECIALTIES

BRITTANY: In this seafaring province, concentrate on the seafare: Brittany is renowned for its wonderful variety of Atlantic ocean fish, including bass, cod, herring, mackerel, sardines, sole, tuna, and turbot. Equally good are the crustaceans: clams, lobsters, mussels, oysters, scallops, sea urchins, winkles, and whelks. A tasty mussel dish called *moules marinières* is served everywhere along the coast, and the famous Bélon oysters, known for their delicate and characteristic flavor, are enjoyed throughout the world. Two other popular Breton seafood dishes are *assiette de fruits de mer,* a large platter of mixed shellfish, and *cotriade,* a chowder of fish and mussels, potatoes, cream, and sorrel. Confirmed meat eaters should try the region's famous *pré-salé* lamb, derived from animals grazed in salt marshes so that the flesh acquires an intriguing tang. The bounty of Brittany also extends to myriad fresh fruits and vegetables — strawberries (especially from Plougastel), blueberries, blackberries, artichokes, peas, potatoes, cabbage, cauliflower, and beans. Finally, for dessert or a snack anytime, have a *galette* (the Breton name for crêpe), a paper-thin pancake that can be eaten either dusted with powdered sugar or filled with cheese, fruit, jam, eggs, or ham.

Brittany is one of the very few French provinces without its own vineyards. The nearby Loire Valley, however, provides a ready selection of wines, including muscadet, a popular fruity white wine that goes beautifully with fish and seafood. Although most of the wine drunk in Britanny is white — and drunk young — a chilled beaujolais or light red sometimes is served, especially if the fish is accompanied with a red wine sauce. With oysters, chablis, blanc de blancs, and champagne are time-honored dinner partners.

As an alternative to wine, sparkling or still cider is served in *crêperies* as well as in many other restaurants. Two varieties are offered: one is dry and "hard;" the other is sweet, more like apple juice. You may order a bottle or a *bol* (the bowl usually used in French homes for *café au lait*).

NORMANDY: Another seacoast province, Normandy also is known for many of the same fish and seafoods as Brittany; particularly prized here are turbot and Dover sole. Be sure to try this region's famous *sole normande,* garnished with mussels, shrimp, and mushrooms, *moules à la crème* (mussels in cream sauce), as well as the fish stew called *matelote à la normande,* a tasty mixture of shellfish, fin fish, cream, and cider. These last two ingredients suggest Normandy's other great specialties, dairy products and apples. The area's lush, green pastures and ubiquitous brown and white cattle yield a wonderful, thick, nutty, ivory cream; rich butter; and extraordinary cheeses (for example, camembert, pont-l'évêque, and livarot). The several varieties of apples produced by Normandy's acres of orchards are used widely in local cookery: in main dishes along with fish or meat, as well as in pies, turnovers, fritters, cakes, and jams. Apples also are pressed into a strong, dry cider and a fiery apple brandy called calvados, both of which are used in many dishes.

Since Normandy produces no wine of its own, many wine lists include a good selection of Loire wines: sancerre and muscadet are reliable white wines with fish and seafood; the rosés and soft reds of Chinon and Bourgeuil are versatile. The spectacular cheese trays call for a medium- to full-bodied red bordeaux, burgundy, or côte du rhône. As in Brittany, cider is an alternative to wine, especially with simple meals or in dishes prepared with cider. Calvados can be poured during a pause in the middle of an elaborate meal, known as "Le Trou Normand."

CHAMPAGNE AND THE NORTH: More famous for its wines than for its cuisine, the Champagne region nevertheless offers several specialties worth noting. For example, the *charcuterie* is excellent, particularly the *andouillettes de Troyes* (chitterling sausages) and *pieds de porc Ste-Menehould* (breaded and grilled pigs' feet). Fish from the area's rivers and streams are prepared in a number of ways — sautéed or braised and served with champagne sauce or *à la nage* (in a light, buttery, brothy sauce). Herring from the English Channel is salted, smoked, or marinated. The cornucopia of vegetables harvested from Champagne's broad, fertile fields — artichokes, asparagus, beans, cabbage, carrots, cauliflower, leeks, peas, and potatoes — has inspired several hearty regional dishes: *parmentier,* a leek and potato soup; *flamiche,* a leek quiche; and *potée champenoise,* a pork, cabbage, and potato soup. The verdant northern flatlands also produce many flavorful cheeses, among them brie and coulommiers (soft), boursin (creamy), and maroilles (strong).

Champagne, the sparkling wine that derived its name from the region, makes up 60% to 80% of the region's wine lists. Who could wish for or imagine anything else? Champagne is safe to order since it goes well with almost everything — except spicy dishes — and certainly with the fish and seafood that are most often prepared with a champagne sauce. If you wish to indulge in a few bottles at the source — where prices for the bubbly are as low as they get — start with a light champagne such as a *blanc de blancs* or a *crémant* or even a glass of the white *côteaux champenois* (still wine), and with the main dish move to a fuller type of champagne, which might even be a rare vintage. Champagne will go well with a mild cheese; otherwise, accompany the local cheeses with a red *côteaux champenois* such as bouzy, cumières, or ambonnay, which are similar to beaujolais but have more fragrance. For a final touch, consider a glass of *marc de Champagne,* the local brandy.

ALSACE-LORRAINE: Here, on the border of France and Germany, look for dishes with a German influence, cooked with a French flair, such as dumplings, *spaetzle,* noodles, and that big dish of mixed meats (pork, sausage, goose) and spicy sauerkraut called *choucroute garnie.* Ham, smoked bacon, many kinds of sausages, pâtés, and terrines make up this region's delicious *charcuterie;* particularly famous are the *saucisse de Strasbourg,* a kind of knockwurst, and the *boudin noir* (black pudding) of Nancy. Alsace is perhaps best known for its foie gras, a lush pâté made from the livers of specially fattened geese; geese and duck feature very prominently on menus in both areas and are served in a number of succulent ways — roasted, braised, or preserved in a *confit.* Chefs make skillful use of the salmon, trout, and other freshwater fish caught in the region's icy streams, as well as of the wild mushrooms and game taken from its forests. Several dishes associated solely with Lorraine are *potée lorraine,* a pork, cabbage, and potato soup; *tourte à la lorraine,* a pie containing pork, veal, and egg custard; and that classic, *quiche lorraine,* a tart made with bacon, eggs, and cream. For dessert in Alsace, try the *kugelhopf,* a sweet coffee cake made with almonds and raisins; in Lorraine, macaroons or *madeleines* (finger-size sponge cakes); or in both areas, a tart made from luscious native fruits.

The wine in Alsace, one of France's most abundant wine producing areas, can be outstanding. The spicy, dry, and fragrant area wines are all white and drunk young except for the "reserve" bottlings, which benefit from some bottle age and can be surprisingly long-lived. Alsatian wines are known by the name of the variety of grape from which they are made. Riesling, gewürztraminer, sylvaner, and pinot gris (or tokay d'Alsace) are the best, and they offer a range of tastes to complement the region's diversity of dishes. Sylvaner, the region's most plentiful wine, is a fresh and fruity dry wine of moderate distinction that is served as an aperitif or as an accompaniment to some of the traditional, earthy dishes such as brain salad, pigs' feet, onion pie, or platters of *choucroute.* For fish, seafood, and poultry, Riesling is a fine choice — dry and elegant, crisp and fruity. Tokay d'Alsace is a good alternative for fowl or white meat; it has the fullest body of the wines of Alsace, broader than the others. Gewürztraminer is a dry, fruity, spicy wine with an unmistakable zing that helps it stand up to powerfully flavored dishes. It goes well with the stronger regional cheeses and the renowned foie gras. In Lorraine, the wines of Alsace are preferred, and there is the local *vin gris* of the Côtes de Toul, pale beige and rosé in color and as unpretentious as the food of the region. Both provinces make superb fruit brandies, often served chilled, that are well worth contemplating at the close of a meal. Known as *eaux-de-vie* or *alcools blancs,* they are colorless and made from a broad range of fragrant fruits: *kirsch* (cherry), *framboise* (raspberry), *mirabelle* (small yellow plum), *quetsch* (purple plum), and *poire* Williams (pear).

BURGUNDY AND THE NORTHERN RHÔNE: For the most part, Burgundian cuisine is not subtle or sophisticated but hearty and lusty — the perfect foil for the big, complex red and white wines of the region. Typically very satisfying, several Burgundy dishes will be familiar to many Americans, for example, that classic *escargots à la bourguignonne,* snails in their shells, stuffed with shallot-and-parsley-seasoned garlic butter. Three other fine Burgundian specialties, which are all enhanced by the same rich, red wine sauce made with bacon, tiny white onions, and mushroom caps, are *boeuf bourguignon, coq au vin,* and *oeufs en meurette;* the first is based on beef, the second on chicken, the third on poached eggs. One item that Americans may find disappointing, however, is the much-prized Charolais beef: Those brought up on prime Black Angus often find this French beef unimpressive. Its texture tends to be softer than the American equivalent, though it is quite tasty. Instead, try the chicken from Bresse, renowned for its flavor and distinguished by a numbered tag on each bird (also by its blue feet), or ham from the Morvan hills, particularly when served cold in parsleyed aspic as a first course, called *jambon persillé.* From the Dijon area, two food items not to be missed are the mustard — creamy or whole grain, plain or flavored — and *pain d'épice,* a strong, delicious gingerbread.

The favorite aperitif taken before a meal in Burgundy is kir, dry white wine with black currant liqueur (cassis). During a meal, red wines generally are enjoyed with red meats, game, or cheeses, and white wines with hors d'oeuvres, oysters, fish, shellfish, and white meats. In choosing Burgundies, look for the name of the town rather than a château: Beaune, Chambertin, Clos de Vougeot, Corton, Musigny, Nuits-St-Georges, Pommard, and Vosne Romanée are famous for their red wines; Chablis, Corton, Meursault, and Montrachet for their whites. The name of the producer is an important clue to quality, and restaurateurs should be able to point out local wines produced in very limited quantities that are good values. Complex, quality burgundies need some bottle age to reach their peak. For reds, good recent vintages are 1981, 1978, 1976, 1972, and 1971; for whites, 1982, 1981, 1979, 1978, and 1976.

The most popular red wine in Burgundy is beaujolais, a versatile and reliable wine that comes in four grades of increasing quality: Beaujolais, Beaujolais Supérieur, Beaujolais-Villages, and Cru Beaujolais, the latter bearing the name of one of nine villages. The most popular white wine is chablis, which is dry and flinty (slightly metallic) and which also comes in four categories of increasing quality: Petit Chablis, Chablis, Chablis Premier Cru, and Chablis Grand Cru, the latter bearing one of seven small vineyard names. Delicate pouilly-fuissé and refreshing mâcon are two other white wines widely available and moderately priced.

The wines of the Rhône Valley are mostly red and robust. The southern vineyards produce the area's most celebrated red, the dark, full-bodied châteauneuf-du-pape, as well as gigondas, which goes well with red meat and cheeses. In the northern area, the best wines are the rich, strong côte Rôtie and hermitage and the more delicate St-Joseph. Côtes du rhône and côtes du rhône villages are generally soft, flavorful table wines that are fine values. The Rhône also produces France's best rosé wine, the fruity tavel, which is a possible accompaniment to spicy, Mediterranean dishes.

THE ALPS: The cuisine of these provinces, like the landscape, is remarkable yet basic, drawing upon the many lakes, streams, forests, fields, and pastures for a wide variety of fresh ingredients. Regional menus include many kinds of fish, such as grayling, trout, perch, and pike (the latter is best when formed into dumplings called *quenelles* and served *à la nantua,* with a sauce made of puréed crayfish and cream — a great local favorite). Meat dishes range from wild game — venison, boar, hare — to *charcuterie* — ham, pâté, and sausage. Wild mushrooms often are used in sautés, stews, and fricassees; look especially for the distinctive, wrinkled, black *morilles* (morels) in cream sauce or pastry. Another Alpine specialty is the local dairy produce, and visitors will delight in the wonderful cheeses made from the milk of high-pasture herds (gruyère, comté, reblochon, tomme de Savoie, vacherin, beaumont, morbier) and also enjoy the savory and imaginative use of cheese in fondues and gratins.

In the Alps, most of the local wine is very dry, light, and white. Seyssel, the local sparkling wine, is probably the area's best and makes a good aperitif and accompaniment to fish dishes. The reds of the neighboring Côtes du Rhône are well stocked and marry splendidly with the hearty regional cuisine. For a cordial, try chartreuse, the famous green or yellow liqueur made from assorted herbs and aromatic plants.

PROVENCE: Provençal food epitomizes Mediterranean-style cooking in France. Many dishes are fragrant with such herbs as fennel, thyme, rosemary, and bay leaf; others are composed of tomatoes, garlic, olive oil, and olives. In fact, olives of every conceivable size and color, cured with herbs or salt or flavored oil, feature prominently in the cuisine. For example, *tapenade,* a popular appetizer, is a lively spread of minced black olives, garlic, and anchovies served on crackers, bread, or raw vegetables. Also typically Mediterranean is the extensive use of seafood (clams, cockles, crabs, mussels, sea anemones, sea urchins) and fish (bass, red mullet, sardines), either grilled or combined in chunky, spicy soups. The most famous of the latter is the bouillabaisse of Marseilles, a soup based on Mediterranean rockfish seasoned with saffron, cayenne, garlic, tomatoes, and herbs and served with a fiery mayonnaise known as rouille, made of garlic, red pepper, bread crumbs, olive oil, and fish broth. It is said that only Mediterranean bouillabaisse is authentic, for it is only here that the essential fish ingredient called *rouget* is found. (Elsewhere in the region, similar fish soups usually are called *bourrides* or *soupes de poisson.*) The ties to Italian cuisine are very close in Provence, as seen in the frequent appearance of *pistou,* a paste of basil, cheese, garlic, and olive oil that's stirred into soups or used as a sauce for fish or gnocchi or pasta (like its Italian cousin, pesto). And Nice has its version of the pizza in its *pissaladière niçoise,* a thin base of bread or pastry baked with a topping of succulently braised onions, olive oil, anchovies, and black olives. Nice also is famous for its *salade niçoise* — tuna, tomatoes, black olives, capers, potatoes, string beans, and hard-boiled eggs. Its sandwich form, *pan bagnat,* is available at every local snack bar. A well-kept secret (by the locals) is *socca,* ground chick-peas spread in a pizza pan and baked in a brick oven until it rises to a light, fluffy pancake. Consumed with generous sprinklings of coarse ground pepper, and washed down with numerous glasses of ice-cold rosé, this indulgence is a 4 PM ritual for beachgoers fleeing the hot afternoon sun to go to the cool back alleys of Nice's Vieille Ville (Old City).

The celebrated aperitif along the Mediterranean coast is *pastis* (essence of aniseed), which is high in alcohol and is usually served diluted with ice water. The local wines are uncomplicated but perfect with the well-seasoned food and the ambience: eating outdoors overlooking the sea calls for a nice, refreshing, fruity wine, and Côtes de Provence, mostly dry rosés, are just that. Or try a bottle of bandol rouge (red), blanc de Provence (white), or bellet (red or white).

LANGUEDOC: Although allied with Provence to the east and Gascony to the west, this area has a cuisine all its own. For example, the popular and well-known dish called cassoulet, a rich ragout of white beans, lamb, pork, sausage, and (usually) preserved goose or duck, is a great specialty and source of regional pride; in fact, you'll find slightly different and very personal versions of cassoulet offered by almost every restaurant chef in Toulouse, Carcassonne, and Castelnaudary. Try to sample it late in the week, when it's had a chance to age in the pot for a few days. Also indigenous is *brandade de morue,* a purée of olive oil, milk, garlic, and cod (usually dried salt cod that has been reconstituted by long soaking, an amazingly successful process). Once again, the area's *charcuterie* — ham, pâté, sausage — is superior, and pork and lamb often appear in flavorful *fricassées à la languedocienne;* that is, stewed with tomatoes, eggplant, garlic, and wild mushrooms. Finally, Languedoc is the home of roquefort, the world-famous blue cheese that's ripened in the mountain caves of the Rouergue area.

Languedoc-Roussillon is the largest wine producing area in France, yet most of the wine is only mediocre and is distributed as *vin ordinaire.* The local food requires full-bodied reds, and only the area's best reds — corbières, minervois, and fitou — are worthwhile, as is clairette du Languedoc, a full-bodied white wine. With roquefort, try one of the sweet white wines such as banyuls or muscat de Frontignan or perhaps a sauternes or barsac from not-too-distant Bordeaux.

GASCONY AND THE PYRÉNÉES: The cuisine in this southwestern corner of France is strongly influenced by Basque cookery. An example is the sauce called *pipérade,* a mixture of red and green sweet peppers, onions, and tomatoes, to which eggs or ham may be added. It is particularly tasty when served with the region's fish — sardines, tuna, swordfish, and fresh anchovies. Bayonne ham, uncooked and spicily dry-cured in salt and red pepper, also is typically Basque and is eaten alone or included in a variety of dishes. Geese and duck are widely bred in these provinces and commonly prepared in two ways: *confit,* in which the meat is cooked and preserved in its own fat, and *magret,* in which the boneless breast is sliced into fillets and grilled. Goose livers become foie gras, and goose necks (*cous d'oie*) are stuffed with various ingredients — pork, foie gras, truffles — and served rather like a sausage. The wild mushrooms known as *cèpes* are much prized here; when stewed in goose fat with garlic and shallots, they make a side dish sometimes richer than the main one.

Most wine lists in these areas include a nice selection from neighboring Bordeaux that will stand up to the hearty food. So will the local full-bodied reds from Madiran, which also go well with the various duck and goose preparations. Another possibility is the white wine made in the Jurançon region of the Pyrénées; it's a deep gold, with a flowery bouquet and often a heavy, sweet taste. Not to be missed after a meal is an aged armagnac, the region's fiery brandy that is similar in character and quality to cognac.

BORDEAUX: Perhaps best known for its great vineyards and fine wines, Bordeaux also produces some superb cooking. Two kinds of oysters highly prized in France — *claires* and *portugaises* — are gathered from the estuaries of the Gironde River (although Americans familiar with fresh bluepoints and chincoteagues may not find these so extraordinary). Another delicacy is caviar derived from the sturgeon that swim up the Gironde to spawn. Since this is prime wine country, it's not surprising that many dishes — mussels, crayfish, chicken, *cèpes* — are rendered *à la bordelaise;* that is, with a rich red or white wine sauce. A particular favorite of the town of St-Emilion, *lamproie à la bordelaise,* is lamprey eel (once again, from the Gironde) cooked in a dense, spicy sauce of red wine, leek, garlic, and the eel's own blood. Another specialty, *entrecôte à la bordelaise,* is filet of beef prepared with a sauce of red wine, shallots, and beef marrow. Delicious fruits from neighboring areas — for example, the Charentais melon (similar to a tiny canteloupe) and prunes from Agen — often are used in fine cakes and pastries.

In Bordeaux do as the Bordelais do: drink bordeaux. It is hard to go wrong, and besides, most wine lists will offer very few wines from other regions except champagne. Although good dry white wines are produced in Graves and lighter and fruitier whites in Entre-Deux-Mers, it is the reds for which Bordeaux is famous, and the Bordelais even drink a light red wth their fish. The rich, full-bodied, and long-lived reds of the various Bordeaux *communes* (villages) are perfect with red meats, game, and cheeses.

Hundreds of château-bottled wines are available; thus the choices can be overwhelming, but any waiter in a reliable restaurant should be helpful. Look for some bottle age in quality reds, though there are lesser "Cru Bourgeois" reds that are good and ready to drink young. Recent vintages of merit are 1982, 1981, 1979, 1978, 1976, 1975, and 1970. In 1855, the wines of the Médoc were classified in an attempt to distinguish their relative quality. The so-called first growths — Château Lafite-Rothschild, Château Latour, Château Margaux, Château Mouton-Rothschild (added later), and Château Haut-Brion — are unquestionably the greatest wines of Bordeaux, along with four other Bordeaux wines from outside the classified area: Château Pétrus in Pomerol, Château Ausone and Château Cheval-Blanc in St-Emilion, and Château d'Yquem (a sweet white dessert wine) from Sauternes. These wines of undisputed quality bear a price to prove it. The 1855 classification included second-, third-, fourth-, and fifth-growth wines as well, but with the varying fortunes of the châteaux over the years, the classifications are somewhat unreliable today beyond the first growths. Some wines from the lesser growths have, in fact, risen almost to the quality of the first growths without bringing the corresponding high prices and are often excellent values.

Perhaps the most fitting conclusion to a fine meal in Bordeaux would be the famous *digestif* produced in nearby Cognac.

DORDOGNE, PÉRIGORD, AND QUERCY: These ancient provinces are the home of the black truffle, and the regional cuisine makes liberal use of that exotic underground mushroom. Fresh truffles (incomparably better than canned) enliven omelettes, pâtés, sauces, and sautés. Any dish labeled *périgourdine* or *quercynoise* inevitably will contain an abundance of truffles and often foie gras as well. Walnuts and walnut oil also are regional specialties and are used in many dishes. To accompany the hearty portions of this area, try the full-bodied deep reds from Cahors, the reds from Bergerac (especially from Pécharmant), or those from nearby Bordeaux. A plate of fresh foie gras is complemented nicely by a glass of sweet white wine — for example, a montbazillac, made in Périgord — or perhaps a sauternes or barsac, both truly fine wines from Bordeaux.

LOIRE VALLEY: The cuisine of this region makes extensive use of fish from that great river, the Loire: pike and shad, prepared with *beurre blanc,* a rich white butter sauce; and salmon and mullet, grilled and served with *beurre à la maître d'hôtel* (parsley butter). Another favorite is *petite friture,* a platter of tiny fish (2 to 3 inches long), lightly floured and crisply deep-fried. Sometimes featured as a first course, the *charcuterie* is rich and varied, including pâtés and terrines, a delicate white sausage called *boudin blanc,* pungent *andouillettes* (sausages made from hog chitterlings), and succulent potted pork in the form of *rillettes* (shredded) or *rillons* (chunked). The fertile Loire Valley also yields some very fine fruits and vegetables — apples, apricots, cherries, melons, peaches, pears, plums, and strawberries; the Vineuil asparagus is especially prized. Small, piquant cheeses are also a Loire specialty; look for valençay, pyramide, crottin, and St-Maure. For dessert, don't miss the luscious *gâteau Pithiviers,* buttery puff pastry filled with almond cream.

The wine regions of the Loire produce a wealth of good white wines to go with the wonderful fish. Dry, light, flinty sancerre and pouilly-fumé are interesting and reliable alternatives to muscadet, the dry, soft, inexpensive wine that goes so well with fish. The ever-popular muscadet comes in three designations of increasing quality: Muscadet, Muscadet des Côteaux de la Loire, and Muscadet de Sèvre-et-Maine. This diverse wine region also produces two slightly sweet sparkling white wines, saumur and vouvray, and sweet white and rosé wines from Anjou. The latter sometimes marry well with *charcuterie,* pâtés, and pork dishes, as do the pleasant local reds, especially chinon and bourgeuil. All of the wines of the Loire are best when drunk young.

FOOD TERMINOLOGY

agneau: lamb

aïoli: garlic mayonnaise

américaine, à l': (usually lobster), sautéed in olive oil with garlic and tomatoes

anchois: anchovy

andouillette: chitterling sausage

aneth: dill

anis: aniseed

apéritif: before-dinner drink

asperge: asparagus

assiette de . . . : plate of . . .

aubergine: eggplant

avocat: avocado

baguette: long, thin loaf of bread

ballottine: roll of boned, stuffed meat or fish

bar: sea bass

barbue: brill

basilic: basil

béarnaise, à la: Béarn style, with a rich sauce made of egg yolks, vinegar, shallots, tarragon, white wine, and butter

béchamel: white sauce made with milk, flour, and butter

beignet: fritter

beurre: butter

beurre à la maître d'hôtel: parsley butter

bifteck: steak

bigorneaux: winkles

billy by: cream of mussel soup

blanc de volaille: white meat of chicken

blanquette de veau: veal stew in white cream sauce

boeuf: beef

bordelaise, à la: Bordeaux or bordelaise style, with a sauce of red wine, shallots, and bone marrow

boudin: black pudding

bouillabaisse: fish stew

bourguignonne, à la: Burgundy style, with a red wine sauce of onions, mushrooms, and bacon

bourride: fish stew

brandade de morue: purée of salt cod made with oil, garlic, and cream

brioche: sweet roll

brochet: pike

brochette de . . . . : meat or fish grilled on a skewer

café au lait: coffee mixed with hot milk

café crème: coffee served with cream or warm milk

café noir: black coffee

calvados: apple cider brandy

canard: duck

carbonnade: beef braised in beer and onions

carré d'agneau: rack of lamb

cassoulet: casserole made of white beans and pork

cèpe: wild mushroom

cerise: cherry

champignon: mushroom

chantilly: whipped cream

charcuterie: pork products such as hams, sausages, pâtés, and terrines

chaud: hot

chevreau: kid

chevreuil: venison

chiffonnade: thin strips, usually of vegetables

chou: cabbage

choucroute: sauerkraut

choucroute garnie: platter of mixed meats such as pork, sausage, and goose served with sauerkraut

chou-fleur: cauliflower

ciboulette: chive

cidre: cider

citron: lemon

civet: rich stew

concombre: cucumber

confiture: jam

coq: cock, also used to indicate hen or chicken

coques: cockles

coquillages: shellfish

coquilles St-Jacques: scallops

côte: rib, chop

côtelette: cutlet, usually of lamb or mutton

crème: cream

crème brûlée: custard topped with carmelized brown sugar crust

crème fouettée: whipped cream

crème fraîche: slightly soured cream

crêpe: thin pancake

cresson: watercress

crevette: shrimp, prawn

croque-monsieur: toasted cheese sandwich with ham

croûte, en: in a pastry crust

daurade: sea bream

dijonnaise, à la: Dijon style, with mustard sauce

dinde, dindon, dindonneau: turkey

eau minérale: mineral water

eaux-de-vie: colorless fruit brandies

échalote: shallot

écrevisse: crayfish

entrecôte: rib steak

entrée: appetizers

épices: spices

épinard: spinach

escargots: snails

estragon: tarragon

faisan: pheasant

farci: stuffed

fenouil: fennel

feuilleté: flaky or puff pastry

fines herbes: mixture of herbs, including parsley, chives, tarragon, and chervil

flan: custard tart

foie gras: goose liver, usually cooked, seasoned, and served as a pâté

fondue (de fromage): melted cheese

frais/fraîche: fresh

fraise: strawberry

framboise: raspberry

frappé: iced, frozen

fricassée: stew

frites: French fries

friture: small fried fish

froid: cold

fromage: cheese

fruits de mer: seafood

fumé: smoked

galantine: boned meat, fish, or poultry served in aspic

galette: pancake filled with cheese, jam, ham, or egg

garbure: thick bean and vegetable soup

gâteau: cake

gelée: aspic

gigot: leg, usually of lamb or mutton

glace: ice cream

gratin: dish with toasted cheese on top

grenouille: frog; usually refers to frogs' legs

grillade: food that has been grilled

grive: thrush

haricot: bean

homard: lobster

huile: oil

huître: oyster

jambon: ham

jardinière, à la: garden style, with mixed fresh vegetables

julienne: vegetables cut in thin strips

jus d'orange: orange juice

lait: milk

lamproie: lamprey eel

langouste: spiny lobster

langue: tongue

lapin: rabbit

légumes: vegetables

madeleines: small sponge cakes

magret: filet of duck breast

maître d'hôtel: head waiter

maquereau: mackerel

marron: chestnut

matelote: fish and seafood stew

merlan: whiting

meunière, à la: fish dusted with flour and sautéed in butter, parsley, and lemon

meurette: red wine sauce made with mushrooms, onions, bacon, and carrots

morille: morel

mornay sauce: white sauce made with milk, flour, butter, and cheese

morue: salt cod

moule: mussel

mousse: dessert of sweetened cream that's been flavored (for example, with chocolate) and whipped to a froth

moutarde: mustard

mouton: mutton

myrtille: blueberry

nantua, à la: Nantes style cream sauce made with puréed crayfish

niçoise, à la: in the style of Nice, made with tomatoes, onions, anchovies, and olives

nouilles: noodles

oeuf: egg

oie: goose

oignon: onion

oseille: sorrel

oursin: sea urchin

pain: bread

palourde: clam

pâté: a rich spread of minced meat or fish seasoned with herbs, baked, and usually served cold

pâtisserie: pastry shop

pêche: peach

persil: parsley

persillade: a mixture of parsley and garlic or shallot

petit pain: roll

pied: foot, usually of pig or sheep

pipérade: a mixture of red and green sweet peppers, onions, and tomatoes, often stirred into eggs or an omelette and served with ham

piquant: spicy

pistou: basil, cheese, garlic, and olive oil paste, sometimes stirred into soups

Pithiviers: puff pastry filled with almond cream

plat du jour: specialty of the day

poire: pear

poireau: leek

pois: peas

poisson: fish

poivre: pepper

poivre vert: green peppercorns

pomme: apple

pomme de terre: potato

porc: pork

potage: soup

pot-au-feu: beef boiled with vegetables

potée: pork, cabbage, and potato soup

poularde, poule, poulet: chicken

poussin: very young chicken

provençale, à la: in the style of Provence, with tomatoes, onions, olives, and garlic

prune: plum

pruneau: prune

quenelle: light dumpling made of fish, veal, or chicken

quiche lorraine: tart made with eggs, cream, and bacon

ragoût: stew

raisin: grape

ratatouille: vegetable casserole made of eggplant, tomatoes, onion, pepper, and olives

rillettes: shredded, cooked pork

rillons: chunked, cooked pork
ris: sweetbreads
riz: rice
rognon: kidney
rôti: roast meat
roulade: rolled and stuffed meat or fish
salade verte: green salad
saucisse, saucisson: sausage, salami
saumon: salmon
sauté: fried lightly
sel: salt
serviette: napkin
sorbet: sherbet
sucre: sugar
suprême de . . . : boneless fillet, usually chicken or fish
terrine: baked minced meat or fish seasoned with herbs and served cold

thé: tea
thon: tuna
tournedos: fillet of beef
truffe: truffle
truite: trout
vapeur: steamed
veau: veal
velouté: creamy and smooth
vichyssoise: potato and leek soup, usually served cold
vin: wine
vinaigre: vinegar
vinaigrette: salad dressing made of oil, vinegar, herbs, and mustard
volaille: chicken
vol-au-vent: puff pastry shell

History

The history of France is the history of an ancient, brilliant, powerful, and learned society. It is the history of a country without whose
aid the American Revolution would not have succeeded. It also is
the history of division, for the absence of an internal national con-
sensus has been a constant. Early on, there were fraternal and dynastic battles,
struggles between feudal lords and the central monarchy; later there were
religious wars, then revolution, and still more divisions — monarchists battling republicans, Nazi collaborators battling French *résistants,* and today the
strong ideological right vies with the equally strong ideological left for power.
In so many ways a model for Western civilization, France nonetheless differs
from Anglo-Saxon nations in one critical respect: It remains splintered on the
basic question of precisely which form of government its people desire, a
stubborn legacy of divisiveness handed down through the centuries.

THE GAULS AND THE ROMANS

The history of the region today known as France begins well before the
history of the people known as French. It begins with cavemen in the paleolithic and neolithic eras, first hunters and then farmers. And it begins with
art, for these cavemen left magnificent drawings in the caves of Lascaux. But
the history of a clearly identified, distinctive people begins only around the
5th century BC with the Celts, Germanic tribes who occupied the area in
successive waves. The Celts became known as Gauls; their empire, extending
west to Portugal, rivaled that of Rome in size. Primarily a rural people, with
superior agricultural tools and prodigious metallurgical skills, the Gauls
possessed a common language and a power structure based on warriors,
nobles, and priests. And their character included traits not wholly foreign to
their eventual descendants: a passion for luxurious fashion, pride, and a
distinct dislike for centralized authority. Yet the Gauls implanted a civilization, not a state, and this was the weakness of their empire. Gaul's wealth was
great, its internal power struggles greater still, and the combination inevitably
made it a tempting prize for potential conquerors.

Of these, the Romans were the most powerful. In the 2nd century BC, the
Romans conquered Provence, which lay on the road to Spain. The rest of
Gaul fell in 52 BC, when Julius Caesar defeated the Gallic chief Vercingétorix.
Caesar took all of Gaul, dividing it (as he wrote) into three parts and institut-
ing a Roman rule that brought two crucial innovations, roads and urban
centers, and the development of a Gallo-Roman civilization. The Gauls'
Indo-European language blended with Latin, customs blended, and religions
blended, too, and when the Roman emperor Constantine converted to Christianity in the 4th century AD, Gaul also became Christian.

During 5 centuries of Roman rule, Gaul became again the richest territory in Western Europe; it was once more a most tempting jewel for invaders — whose course was hardly checked by a series of ineffectual emperors and the empire's consequent internal decline. The new invaders — mostly Germanic tribes, but also the Mongolian Huns — came at first to pillage, their continuous incursions further weakening the empire. Then, in the 5th century, one of these Germanic groups, the Franks, came not just to pillage but to stay — men, women, and children crossing the Rhine in a massive migration. By AD 476, the date that traditionally marks the fall of the Roman Empire in the West, they had gained a foothold in Gaul, and in 486, under their chieftain Clovis I, they threw out the last Roman governor.

THE EARLY DYNASTIES

Clovis was the first of the Merovingian dynasty of Frankish kings. He converted to Christianity, enlarged the domain of the Frankish kingdom, made Paris his capital, and achieved the territorial unification of most of the realm. But when he died in 511 he divided the kingdom among his sons in accordance with Frankish tradition, and the result was disastrous. Family quarrels ensued, independent areas and small kingdoms resurfaced. The Merovingian monarchy came to rule only in name, the real power passing to "palace mayors" such as Pepin of Herstal in 687 and then to his son, Charles Martel, celebrated for defending southern France against Arab invaders in 732.

Then, a second dynasty was established. Martel's son, Pepin the Short (Pépin le Bref), imposed himself over the last of the Merovingians and became King of the Franks in 751. The first of the Carolingian dynasty, he left two crucial legacies. The first was the institution of the *sacre* (practiced in 754 by Pope Boniface himself), a religious ritual that proclaimed the divine right of the king to rule. The second was a son, Charles. Crowned king in 768, Charles defended the faith, attacked the Muslims in Spain, conquered the Lombards in Italy and the Bavarians and Saxons to the east, led a cultural and scientific renaissance, and became master of most of the European continent. In 800, he was crowned emperor of the West by Pope Leo III; he was known to the world as Charlemagne.

But in 814 Charlemagne, too, died, and his empire and his dynasty would in time follow. His son Louis the Pious (Louis le Pieux) ruled it all, but *his* sons stopped at nothing, including civil war, in their scramble for territory. In 870, the Treaty of Mersen divided Charlemagne's empire into a "French" West Frankish kingdom, a Germanic East Frankish kingdom, and a kingdom of Italy.

A third dynasty eventually emerged in the West Frankish kingdom that would develop into modern France. Its founder was Hugh Capet, named king in 987. He succeeded, where others before him had failed, in at last establishing the principle of primogeniture — the eldest son would get everything. With the cry "The King is dead, long live the King," the central flaw of all the preceding dynasties was effaced, an orderly succession of power finally assured. But the king did not have a great deal left over which to reign — a small area around Paris, in the case of the first Capetian — because the disorder of the times had, in the meantime, fostered the development of the feudal system, in which royal land was given to a noble class of feudal lords in return for their services — military and other — to the king. Frequently, these vassals became richer and more powerful than the king, as happened with the Dukes of Burgundy, Brittany, and Aquitaine, the Counts of Flanders, Champagne, and Anjou, and, above all, with William the Conqueror, Duke of Normandy, who conquered England in 1066 and sat on its throne.

But the church called the faithful to the Crusades. Powerful lords departed to fight in distant lands, and in their absence the French monarchy had its first real opportunity to regain its lands and consolidate its influence. Well known to readers of Shakespeare, Philip Augustus (Philippe-Auguste; 1180–1223), the Capetian king, was the principal actor in this power play. He ascended the throne to find his rule precarious: a mixture of marriage, acquisition, and annexation had placed the greater part of his realm in the hands of the great-grandson of William the Conqueror, Henry Plantagenet, who was not only King Henry II of England but also the Duke of Normandy and Lord of Brittany, Anjou, and Aquitaine as well. In short, Henry, a vassal of the King of France, presided over French possessions about six times larger than those ruled by the King of France himself.

Philip set about to change this embarrassing state of affairs by plotting with Henry's son, Richard the Lion-Hearted (Coeur de Lion). Henry died in battle in France. Richard became king. Philip plotted against Richard. Richard died in battle in France. Philip fought with Richard's successor, John. Before it was over, Philip had won back almost all of the Plantagenet's French possessions, except for southern France, and annexed his conquests to his kingdom. Philip Augustus died in 1223, but his dynasty continued; among the Capetians who followed him were two other famed kings. One was Louis IX (1226–70). As Louis the Iron-Gloved, he dominated his vassals and further strengthened his central authority, encouraged the terror of the Inquisition, and put yellow badges on the Jewish citizens of his realm; as St. Louis, he was known as a just, generous, charitable man, a patron of the arts and learning. The other renowned Capetian was Philippe le Bel (Philip the Fair; 1285–1314), who provoked the Papal Schism and saw Pope Clement V install his court in Avignon (1305); and it was the complexities of his succession that led to a catastrophe, a war that raged for an entire century.

THE HUNDRED YEARS WAR

From the very first, French history and English history were inextricably intertwined. The Iron Age Celts who had settled France later moved on to settle England, and already Frenchmen had sat, simultaneously and contradictorily, as vassals owing allegiance to the French king and as sovereigns of England. The Hundred Years War was born of the continuing dynastic quarrels between these two sibling peoples: Philip the Fair's sons produced no male heirs; the Capetian dynasty in France thus passed to the Valois family, with Philip VI of Valois named king (1328–50). But King Edward III of England was a Capetian — his mother was a daughter of Philip the Fair — and he claimed the French throne for himself. In 1337, Edward and Philip went to war. France relied on the traditional use of knights; England, in a military innovation, introduced archers, foot soldiers with long bows, for whom the saddled knights became sitting ducks. In 1346, the English decimated the French cavalry at the battle of Crécy; 10 years later, the English won again at Poitiers and took as prisoner King John II of France. All the while the Black Death raged. The first round of the war ended in 1360 with the Treaty of Brétigny, which freed John in exchange for a ransom and granted to the English a significant expanse of French territory.

Another round of the war took place under King Charles V of France (1364–80), who by the time of Edward III's death in 1377 had managed to recapture almost all of the French territory in England's possession. Then Charles VI (1380–1422) became the French king; during his reign the military situation again became dramatic. In 1415 the English attacked France and won the decisive battle of Agincourt, with great slaughter of French knights. By now, the powerful Dukes of Burgundy were allied with the English against the French crown, and in 1420 the three parties concluded the fateful Treaty of Troyes in an attempt to end the hostilities. By its terms, Henry V of England was named "heir to France"; that is, Charles VI would rule until his death and then be succeeded by the English king, thereby disinheriting his own son, the dauphin (later Charles VII).

France was thus about to cease its existence as an independent nation when a small woman stepped in and changed the course of history. Joan of Arc's mission was to see the dauphin crowned king. Though the young Charles repudiated the treaty signed by his father and undertook to rule at his father's death in 1422, he was a weak and vacillating king and his realm was small. The English already controlled most of France north of the Loire at that point, and his attempts to oppose their advance southward were halfhearted. Joan rallied the French troops and led them to a crucial victory over the English at Orléans in 1429. She then accompanied Charles to Reims — where French kings traditionally were crowned — for his coronation as Charles VII (1422–61) in the cathedral. The next year she was captured by the Burgundians, turned over to the English, and delivered to a court of clergymen at Rouen. She was burned as a witch in 1431, but in the meantime she had given Charles the impetus he needed to carry on alone. By 1453 only Calais remained English, and Louis XI (1461–83) finished his father's work. The Hundred Years War was over; France was at last French again.

A SOCIETY IN FLUX

The second half of the 15th century was largely a time of reconstruction and economic development. France became rich and powerful, and Lyons became one of the great financial and trading capitals of Europe. The French kings, free from the English menace, now had powerful dreams. Charles VIII (1483–98) and Louis XII (1498–1515) were "chivalry kings," with knightly visions of adventure and glory. Their object was Italy, to which France held some dynastic claims. Charles invaded, so did Louis; sometimes the French ruled parts of Italy, at other times they were pushed back to their own borders. The next king, Francis I (1515–47), ended the campaign. The enduring result of the Italian wars was not geopolitical but cultural. They brought the French into contact with the art, architecture, and literature of the Italian Renaissance and spread it to and through France. Leonardo da Vinci, Benvenuto Cellini, and Andrea del Sarto worked at the court of Francis I, a patron of the arts and letters, whose reign was marked by the greatest flowering of the French Renaissance.

Society began to change. The period of transition from the Middle Ages to the Renaissance also was a period of transition from the old feudal society to a "modern" bourgeois society. New ideas were propagated by Erasmus, Rabelais, and Montaigne. Church reform was preached by the German Martin Luther and John Calvin, a Frenchman. A good portion of Catholic France converted to Protestantism. Oddly, the monarchy, a beneficiary of the Catholic *sacre*, showed tolerance toward the new Protestants — or Huguenots, as they were known in France — and advocated limited religious freedom for all. But radicals on both sides soon made tolerance impossible, and the two religious movements quickly became political.

A series of civil and religious wars (the Wars of Religion, or the Huguenot Wars) broke out in France in 1562. In 1572, thousands of leading Huguenots were killed in Paris (the St. Bartholomew's Eve Massacre) and thousands more were slaughtered in the provinces; later, fanatical Catholic leaders were killed in a plot orchestrated by the French monarchy itself. Then a new crisis came in 1589, when the last Valois king was killed and the French throne was empty. Religious fervor reached a new peak. The new dynasty was the Bourbon family; the presumed new king, Henri of Navarre. But Henri was a Protestant, and the Catholic factions quickly rejected his claim, supporting a Catholic Bourbon instead. War came again, now with all the European powers taking sides.

Henri of Navarre won the military battle for France, but Paris remained staunchly Catholic. Perched at the gates of the capital and faced with a hostile population, the victorious Henri made a decision summed up by his alleged remark: "Paris is well worth a mass." He ruled as Henri IV, a Catholic king and a great king, who accorded the Protestants limited religious freedoms once again in the Edict of Nantes (1598). Thus, 36 years of civil and religious war came to an end. Agriculture, trade, and commerce prospered under Henri's chief minister, Sully. But his reign ended abruptly when a madman assassinated him in 1610.

Louis XIII was a minor at the time of his father's death. During most of his reign, real power rested with a remarkable, worldly, and very determined churchman, Cardinal Richelieu, whose goal was to establish an absolute monarchy. His plan and his power, however, aroused opposition and provoked numerous conspiracies. Nevertheless, Richelieu went a long way toward realizing his goal before his death in 1642. A year later Louis XIII died, too. Again the heir was a minor, and again power fell to a churchman, Richelieu's disciple, Cardinal Mazarin. This cardinal also survived plots, a revolt (the Fronde), and even exile, but he educated the heir to the French throne in a fashion true to Richelieu's dream. And when Mazarin died in 1661, the young French king personally assumed all power.

ABSOLUTISM: LOUIS XIV

Mazarin's avid pupil was Louis XIV (1643–1715). "L'état c'est moi," he proclaimed ("I am the state"), and this absolutism would be the model, not only for 17th-century France, but for most other European countries throughout the 18th century. Louis XIV in effect created the modern state. He monopolized the administration of justice and the use of armed force. His finance minister, Colbert, put the French economy in order, applying Richelieu's mercantilist philosophy to expand trade, promote industry, create strict quality controls, institute protective tariffs, and to grant subsidies to build a merchant marine. The king took the *sacre,* establishing his domination over the church as well as rule by divine right over his subjects. And Louis XIV dominated the nobility. He brought the nobility to himself and smothered it. He built the enormous palace of Versailles, more magnificent than anything Europe had ever known, and created rituals wherein it was an honor to attend the king's person, to be present at his arising, his meals, his preparation for bed. He patronized the arts, letters, and sciences, attracting the most brilliant of their practitioners to his court. All revolved around Louis, the sun whose light shone on the favored. So Louis XIV was dubbed the Sun King; the country he ruled over was the France of the Illumination. Its population was three times that of England. The French were laying claim to Canada, exploring the Great Lakes and the Mississippi, building plantations in the West Indies, and constructing the most imposing navy in Europe. Nicolas Poussin and Claude Lorrain painted; Corneille, Racine, Molière, Descartes, and Pascal wrote. French culture, architecture, and engineering were emulated everywhere; the French language became the mark of the civilized man. Under Louis XIV, France was the splendor of Europe.

But the Sun King lived too long and would see the eclipse. Influenced by the Counter Reformation, he revoked the Edict of Nantes. The result was not only the end of France's religious tolerance (unique in Europe at the time) but also the costly emigration of skilled and industrious Huguenot merchants and artisans. Louis's extravagant spending finally alienated his subjects. But above all, his grandiose wars undid him. Louis XIV fought the War of Devolution, the Dutch Wars, the War of the League of Augsburg, and the War of the Spanish Succession. Territory was gained — Louis's grandson sat on the throne of Spain — but the wars devastated the French economy and united Louis's foreign enemies against him. Disastrous harvests followed at home, then famine. The nobility grew restless. In 1715, Louis XIV died. As heir to his rule of 7 decades, he left a 5-year-old child.

THE FRENCH REVOLUTION: ITS ADVENT AND PHASES

The new king, Louis XV, would occupy the throne just short of 60 years. A regent was appointed to rule during his minority, which lasted until 1723, and for 2 decades after that his early reign was guided by his chief adviser, Cardinal Fleury. The nobility took heart, and some power. The philosophers of the Enlightenment — Montesquieu, Voltaire, and Rousseau among them — were popularizing ideas of justice quite incompatible with an absolute monarchy. But Louis XV, too, engaged in ruinous wars, first the War of the Austrian Succession and then the Seven Years War, which cost France its Canadian possessions. The country was living through a financial crisis, which was not new, only newly acute. And it was paradoxical, because though France was a wealthy country, most of its rich were exempt from taxes, a holdover of privilege from feudal times. The poor were burdened unjustly and resentful; the government was poor to the verge of bankruptcy. Louis XIV had attempted reform toward the end of his reign, but the effect had been negligible. Louis XV was unable to institute remedies.

The reign of Louis XVI, who came to the throne in 1774, was dominated by the financial crisis. The king's ministers, one after another, sought reforms that would make the privileged classes — clergy and nobles — pay their fair shares of the burden, but the fearful king failed to provide strong support. The crisis deepened, aggravated by the expense of French help in the American Revolution. Further attempts to impose taxation on the privileged were blocked by the Assembly of Notables and the Parlement of Paris, both of them referring to the ancient consultative institution, the Estates-General, as the only body with the power to approve new taxes.

The Estates-General dated from feudal times but, in fact, had not met since 1614. It recognized representation from three social castes: the clergy (First Estate), the nobles (Second Estate), and "everyone else" (Third Estate) — a formula that effectively ignored the emergence of an important new class, the bourgeoisie. Thus, any meeting of the Estates-General in 18th-century France invited an almost inevitable clash between the aristocracy and the new bourgeoisie, the former seeking to recoup power lost to the absolute monarchy, the latter, creditors of the state, making a bid for recognition and influence equal to its economic contribution. Convening the Estates-General posed still another threat. Despite its divisive potential and its obsolescence, it was a national institution. The French monarchy had succeeded in unifying a nation, and now general discontent in France could be expressed on a national level far more easily than in other countries of the era.

As a last resort, the king called a meeting of the Estates-General to discuss fiscal reform. Lists of grievances were ordered to be drawn up in the provinces. Though they were intended merely to stimulate discussion, they raised expectations, and by the time the assembly met at Versailles in May 1789, the Third Estate and the less conservative nobles and clergy saw it as a true embodiment of the will of the people, a forum for initiating sweeping general reforms.

The struggle for control of the Estates-General came to a head immediately in the question of voting procedure. If tradition were respected, voting would be by order, and the first two estates always would outnumber the third; if voting were by head count, the Third Estate, which had more delegates, always would outnumber the first two. Louis wavered, and on June 17, 1789, the Third Estate broke away and declared itself a National Assembly. On June 27, 1789, Louis recognized the fait accompli, but some of his actions gave rise to rumors that he meant to suppress the assembly. On July 14, an angry mob took its first collective steps and stormed a prison in Paris, the

Bastille, a symbol of the *ancien régime.* Then the *grande peur* (great fear) began, fed by alarm over food shortages and economic depression. The peasants revolted in the countryside; labor problems ignited the cities. The French Revolution was under way.

The outbreak of revolution in France had a far greater impact than the earlier outbreak of revolution in America, a distant, new land. At the time of the storming of the Bastille, France, for all its internal problems, was still the power center of Europe, the leader in intellectual thought, the most populous country under a single government, the model for most of the Western world. Against the background of the 18th century, the French Revolution was the most momentous revolutionary movement in history, and its repercussions were not to be equaled until the Bolshevik Revolution of 1917 in Russia.

The National Assembly at Versailles took control and set about changing French society. The nobles and clergy were forced to relinquish their traditional privileges, and the feudal system was swept from the land. Legal equality was established in "The Declaration of the Rights of Man and Citizen." The revolution remade France in a bourgeois and secular mold. Economic controls and restrictive labor unions were abolished; all trades were opened up to all men. Church property was confiscated, religious orders suppressed. All previous administrative structures were erased; a system of departments, similar to states, came into being. And in 1791 a constitution was proclaimed, reducing the absolute monarchy to a constitutional monarchy.

This was the point at which the revolution's moderates would like to have stopped, but once again, the moderate cause was not advanced by the king's actions. Louis and his queen, Marie-Antoinette, attempted to flee to join counter-revolutionary émigré groups abroad. They were arrested at Varennes, brought back to Paris, and forced to accept the constitution. The monarchy thus discredited, the advantage in the National Assembly passed to the republicans. Royalist émigré circles, in the meantime, rallied kings, nobles, and clergy in the rest of Europe to unite in restoring the monarch to his former authority. Austria took the lead, and in April 1792 France responded to the threat by declaring war. The military emergency gave more voice to radical forces. The Jacobins, initially a middle-of-the-road group, gained leadership; then, led by Danton, Marat, and Robespierre, they adopted ever more extreme positions. In August 1792, the royal family was imprisoned. An insurrectionary government, the Commune of Paris, was set up, and there were massacres and general hysteria.

This was the second, or radical, phase of the French Revolution. The Commune forced the National Assembly to order elections for a National Convention, which would draw up a new constitution. At its first meeting, on September 21, 1792, the convention abolished the monarchy and proclaimed the First French Republic (a French revolutionary calendar would later count time from its birth). The republic continued to wage war and for a while was victorious, occupying Savoie and Belgium and crossing the Rhine. But Louis XVI and Marie-Antoinette had been accused of treason for collusion with the Austrian enemy. After Louis was guillotined on January 21,

1793, the enemies of the new republic found allies, and France was soon at war with all of Europe.

This emergency gave rise to the Reign of Terror. The new constitution drawn up by the National Convention finally was finished, but it never was put into effect. Instead, in April 1793, the Committee of Public Safety came into being, essentially a dictatorship to defend the Revolution from enemies within and without, and to pull France back from the edge of anarchy. Robespierre emerged as its leader. Denounced by some as a bloodthirsty fanatic, praised by others as an idealistic patriot, Robespierre was not controversial only in terms of his personal honesty and true revolutionary commitment. He repressed counter-revolutionary strife with a vengeance. Before the Reign of Terror was over, nearly 40,000 had died, many by the guillotine, including Marie-Antoinette ("The people have no bread? Let them eat cake!"), many by mass drowning. Improvement of France's military fortunes allowed public reaction to set in, just as more repressive measures aroused fears in the National Convention that the Reign of Terror would turn on its own members. Robespierre was arrested and sent to the guillotine in July 1794. After a period of White Terror, when many former terrorists lost their lives, the radical phase of the Revolution was over.

Still another new government, the Directory, was formed in 1795. It was reactionary and not a solution. In March 1797, elections were held. The constitutional monarchists won, but the Directory annulled most of the election results. Revolts came, more annulled elections followed, and purges took place on all sides of the political spectrum. The Directory was now in effect a dictatorship. All the classic reasons for a coup d'état again existed; it came on November 9, 1799. Its leader was a popular and victorious young general who proclaimed a new system of government for the republic, a Consulate, and designated himself first consul. His name was Napoleon Bonaparte.

THE EMPIRE

Once more a strong, controversial leader was in charge of France, and also a brilliant one. With Talleyrand as his foreign minister, Bonaparte quickly restored peace, concluding treaties with Austria and Great Britain. A concordat with the papacy recognized Roman Catholicism as the religion of most of the French in return for recognition of the republic by the Vatican and its acceptance of the French principle of religious tolerance. The major advances of the Revolution were institutionalized and the modern state began to take clear form. Bonaparte reorganized the government and the educational system, ended tax privileges, developed a sound currency and public credit, and founded the Bank of France. He reformed the legal system, codifying French laws for the first time in the Napoleonic Code (1804), and made justice in France uniform, assuring all citizens equal civil rights. Commercial and criminal codes followed.

Immensely popular, Bonaparte was elected first consul for life in 1802. Then, 2 years later, he turned the Consulate into an Empire and had himself made Emperor Napoleon I. What had been a welcome stabilization took on more authoritarian tones — it is a common distinction of the French to admire Bonaparte while expressing doubts about Napoleon — and France soon was deeply involved in a resumption of foreign wars. Only a brief peace in 1801 and 1802 had separated what history calls the French Revolutionary Wars from what it calls the Napoleonic Wars. Similarly, there are no clear turning points to mark the transitions from early warfare to protect the Revolution from foreign interference, warfare to extend it to other countries, and wars of pure conquest.

Napoleon had little trouble exporting the Revolution. United at home, the French were unstoppable beyond their borders. The emperor came closer than anyone in history to imposing real political unity on the European Continent, and it was not always by force alone. In the early stages of the Empire, progressives welcomed the ideas of the French Revolution; it was the conservative governments, afraid of the reforms that came with the emperor's armies, that organized alliances against him. By 1810, Napoleon's territorial influence covered the entire European mainland with the exception of the Balkan peninsula. His brothers sat as Kings of Spain, Holland, and Westphalia; his sister as Queen of Naples; he himself as King of Lombardy, Venetia, and the former papal states. Having had his childless marriage with Josephine annulled, he married Marie-Louise, the daughter of the Emperor of Austria. Napoleon was supreme. Historians refer to him as "an enlightened despot." The reforms he carried to all of Europe explain the adjective, his means explain the noun.

But Napoleon's downfall finally came. From 1803, France had been at war with Great Britain. Victorious on land, the emperor was defeated at sea in the Battle of Trafalgar (1805), so he decided to wage economic warfare. In 1806, he launched the Continental System, a boycott that forbade trade with the British by France or any of her European allies. The Continental System, however, ruined continental shippers and exporters, and resentment grew among the merchant classes. In the meantime, the progressives who had hailed Napoleon's reforms now had the reforms and no longer needed Napoleon; strong nationalist movements were beginning to develop. Yet until an ally changed camps, no one could challenge Napoleon's army. The ally who bolted was Alexander I, Czar of Russia. Dissatisfied with the meager fruits of his alliance with the emperor, Alexander withdrew from the Continental System. Napoleon determined to crush him.

The story, a military nightmare, is well known. Intending a short, flash war, Napoleon entered Russia in June 1812 with a huge army and very few supplies. After a battle at Borodino, which resulted in severe loss of life on both sides, the Russian forces changed tactics and refused to fight again, retreating into the heart of Russia and devastating the land as they went. Napoleon pursued them into Moscow in September; the city burst into flames, leaving the emperor and his Grand Army camping in a ruin. Without hope of replenishing supplies from the devastated countryside and far from his own supply line, he attempted to negotiate. The czar refused. Napoleon ordered a retreat in mid-October, not wanting to be in Moscow with his army in the winter. But in 1812, winter came unusually early and with unusual severity. By late November, the Grand Army had been decimated.

The forces against Napoleon now converged; his allies deserted him. Finally, the Quadruple Alliance — Russia, Prussia, Austria, and Great Britain — attacked; their combined armies entered Paris. In April 1814, the emperor abdicated and was sent into exile on Elba. He regained power for 100 days, but after his defeat at Waterloo in June 1815, the Napoleonic Empire was ended definitively. The Congress of Vienna remade the map of Europe, shrinking France to its borders of 1790. The former emperor was exiled to the island of St-Helena, leaving behind him an immense legend and institutional transformations that remain throughout Europe to this day.

THE NINETEENTH CENTURY

The collapse of the Empire was followed by the Restoration, a return to the monarchy. From 1815 to 1830, the Bourbon family — Louis XVIII and Charles X — again ruled, but it ruled over a new France, one that permitted no return to the old, prerevolutionary order. France was a bourgeois country now, with a prosperous middle class. So when an ultra-royalist movement developed and seemed poised to reinstate the *ancien régime,* it was the middle class that reacted, throwing out Charles X in the July revolution of 1830 and bringing to power a king with liberal, bourgeois leanings. The king was Louis-Philippe, of the house of Bourbon-Orléans; his reign is known as the July Monarchy. For nearly 2 decades he ruled over a country primarily concerned with developing industry and modern transportation systems, in the process largely ignoring parliamentary reform and social legislation. Hence he became increasingly unpopular, satisfying neither monarchists nor the lower classes. The result was the fall of the monarchy anew, in 1848.

The July Monarchy immediately was replaced by the Second Republic, destined to last only 4 years. Its president was none other than Louis-Napoleon Bonaparte, the nephew of the deposed emperor, elected both by virtue of his apparent liberalism and the country's nostalgia for Bonapartism. Louis began to consolidate his authority, and the fact that reactionary forces in France still were strong and republicanism still a revolutionary idea did not work against him. When a workers' revolt broke out, followed by social unrest and economic crisis, republicanism became synonymous with disorder. Louis was ready. In December 1851, he pulled off a coup d'état, giving himself dictatorial powers. In November 1852, he made the Second Republic the Second Empire and himself France's second emperor, Napoleon III. Plebiscites approved both moves.

In many respects, his reign was brilliant. The Industrial Revolution advanced, the bourgeoisie grew in strength, a modern infrastructure for the country developed, construction boomed. But Napoleon III was unsuccessful in his attempts to found an empire in Mexico, although he acquired other colonial possessions, and in the end he was brought down by a foreign war, the Franco-Prussian War of 1870–71. Napoleon had underestimated the force of German unity fostered by Otto von Bismarck. The Prussians marched through a Paris magnificently rebuilt by Baron Haussmann; France lost Alsace and Lorraine; and the Second Empire collapsed.

France's Third Republic dates from 1870, when Napoleon III was captured by the Prussians and effectively deposed, but a few years went by before the form of the new government was sure. The Germans needed a properly constituted French government to sign peace terms. An election was held for a National Assembly, its expressed duties to ratify Bismarck's harsh treaty and to write a new constitution. The monarchists came to power in the elections, prepared to bow to Bismarck's humiliating terms. But the republicans of Paris revolted and set up, once again, a revolutionary Commune of Paris. The Commune of 1871 was short-lived: Civil war broke out between it and the National Assembly at Versailles; government troops besieged the city, and the Communards took to the barricades. Before it was crushed, however, the fighting exceeded that of any of the French Revolution.

France might have become a monarchy again had the monarchist camp not soon split between supporters of the Bourbon family and of the Orléans family. This division allowed the adoption, in 1875, of a republican constitution and preserved the Third Republic. Contemporary France began to emerge. The establishment of secular, compulsory public education, the expansion of the railroads, the recognition of labor unions, and the separation of church and state all came in this period. The country's acquisitions abroad developed into a veritable colonial empire. The arts at home glittered spectacularly.

Yet there still was no universal agreement on a form of government. The monarchists still held some power, and much of the Third Republic's energy was spent simply fighting the enemies of the republican system. And there was the Dreyfus Affair, an ugly incident in which a Jewish army officer was falsely accused and convicted of treason. The celebrated author Emile Zola wrote an explosive letter, "J'Accuse," demanding a new trial. The affair shook the country and caused an international furor. Finally, in 1899, Dreyfus was pardoned and in 1906 fully exonerated.

THE WORLD WARS

The Third Republic nonetheless endured. While ministerial instability was chronic, continuity of policy was sustained, and in time republicanism became a credible form of government in France. The country was relatively comfortable. Then, in 1914, the Great War, World War I, broke out.

Much of the war — the battle of the Ardennes, the first battle of the Marne, the battle of Verdun, the battle of the Somme, the second battle of the Marne — was fought on French soil. Joffre, later Nivelle (eventually removed for incompetence), then Pétain (who came out of the war a hero) and Foch (who was made supreme commander of the French, British, and American armies) were the military leaders; Premier Clemenceau maintained morale and led the French delegation to the Paris Peace Conference in 1919. The war was one of attrition, at times of useless carnage in defense of positions more symbolic than strategic, of horrifying trench fighting, of poison gas. Nearly 2 million Frenchmen died; a sixth of the nation's revenue was lost. As one of the victors, France was rewarded with the return of Alsace and Lorraine, but the price had been deadly. Afterward, the French sought only recovery and reconstruction.

In the early postwar years the country was run by a series of conservative coalitions; then, in the mid-1920s, by the Radical Socialists, a center-left party committed to private enterprise but advocating progressive social legislation. In the meantime, politics on both sides was becoming polarized. On the left, the Communists broke off from the more moderate Socialists; on the right, Action Française, an extremist group with royalist tendencies, began to agitate. France's economic recovery, dependent on war reparations from Germany, collapsed when Germany failed to pay. The Great Depression arrived. And France had other problems: While its own government changed hands continually, Adolf Hitler came to power in neighboring Germany.

In 1934, a political and financial scandal, the Stavisky Affair, rocked the country, discrediting the Radical Socialist party and provoking fascist riots. Faced with the threat, the left closed ranks; Radical Socialists, Socialists, and Communists formed the Popular Front. In 1936, the Front won a decisive electoral victory. Premier Léon Blum put through a vast program of social reform, including the 40-hour work week, paid vacations, and collective bargaining laws. Steps were taken to put strategic industries under government control, to curtail private influence over the Bank of France, and to provide price supports for farmers. The Popular Front was a French New Deal, more radical only in its proclamations. Nonetheless, the French right saw it as a revolution and noisily protested that Catholic France had fallen into the hands of a leftist, a Socialist, a Jew.

In truth, the Popular Front was the right government at the wrong time. The 40-hour work week was long overdue in France, but it came into being just as Germany was working day and night to manufacture arms. The German effort obliged the French to do the same, and the simultaneous imposition of emergency rearmament and reform labor laws was an economic impossibility. In 1937, the Blum government fell, brought down by a Senate that refused to grant it emergency financial powers.

The new government was formed by the Radical Socialists. Abandoning its allies on the left, it took a conservative turn. Edouard Daladier became premier. He quickly proved incapable of dominating France's internal problems, weaker still in facing the ever-growing threat from Germany. It was Daladier's France that appeased Nazi Germany at Munich.

But war with Germany came nonetheless. On September 3, 1939, 2 days after the German invasion of Poland, France and Great Britain declared war. In May 1940, Germany entered France. Surprised by the attack route, lacking armored divisions and air force resources, divided as a nation, and governed by a small group of defeatist politicians, France fell. On June 13, 1940, Paris was occupied by Nazi soldiers. On June 16, Premier Paul Reynaud resigned rather than agree to surrender, and an 84-year-old man, Marshal Pétain, the same gentleman who had commanded so nobly in World War I, succeeded him. On June 22, France signed an armistice with Nazi Germany. The world was stunned. The country was divided into two zones: the occupied zone north of the Loire, including Paris; and, south of the Loire, the so-called free zone, meaning only that for a time German soldiers did not physically occupy the soil. In July, Pétain moved the government south from occupied Paris to Vichy, the Third Republic was voted out of existence, and the Government of Unoccupied France came into being, with Pétain as "chief of state." That he was remembered as a war hero was unfortunate, confusing a large portion of the French population, who followed him blindly.

In fact, the Vichy government was a national disgrace. Behind the aged Pétain stood Pierre Laval, a cynical, dishonorable man who openly proclaimed his hopes for a Nazi victory. The slogan "Liberty, Equality, Fraternity," born in France, was banned from official use as Pétain and Laval led their country into its most ignominious period. The Vichy government was not passive; it embraced the Nazis, it collaborated actively, it went beyond even German demands in enthusiastically delivering French Jews to Nazi concentration camps. Later, the French militia under Joseph Darnand would show more viciousness than even the German SS.

There was another France as well: that of Charles de Gaulle, Jean Moulin, Pierre Mendès-France, André Malraux, and men and women of all political colors who refused to collaborate and who together formed the *Résistance*. Some, like de Gaulle, went into exile, establishing a Free French movement in London; others remained on French soil, fighting at enormous risk as an effective anti-Nazi underground. After the German invasion of Russia, French Communists joined en masse. The French Résistance was a genuinely heroic movement, but it included only a shamefully small fraction of the French population. By an overwhelming majority, the French people were collaborators, active or passive. And this division — collaborator versus *résistant* — virtually was a moral civil war, far outlasting the division of French territory by the occupying army.

The territorial division ended in 1942 as a result of the Allied invasion of North Africa, and the Germans occupied all of France. In one act of national courage, the French fleet at Toulon scuttled itself rather than fall into German hands, a sacrifice that destroyed French naval power. Two years later the occupation ended. On June 6, 1944, British and American forces began the liberation of France by invading Europe via the beaches of Normandy. In August, Paris was liberated, and de Gaulle, the symbol of Free France, entered the city as head of a provisional government. (A story sworn to by all Frenchmen is that Paris, which had been mined by the Germans, still was standing because of the man who until the last moment had subjugated it. The Nazi general in Paris was an art lover and he knew the Nazi cause was lost. When headquarters gave the order to blow the city up, he refused.) By the end of 1944, all of France had been liberated. Spontaneous reprisals against collaborators took an ugly turn in many parts of the country. Laval and Pétain both were tried for treason. Laval was shot in 1945. Pétain's death sentence was commuted to life imprisonment by de Gaulle.

POSTWAR FRANCE

The provisional government ruled only until a new republic, the Fourth Republic, was proclaimed in 1946. The new constitution, much like that of the Third Republic, did not provide for as strong an executive as de Gaulle would have liked, and he retired from the scene. The government again became an affair of shaky coalitions, which nevertheless undertook to rebuild the economy with the aid of the US Marshall Plan. The nationalization of the banks and major industries took place. The French statesmen Jean Monnet and Robert Schuman were instrumental in setting Europe on the course of economic and political cooperation that in time resulted in the European Community. But inflation was rising and there were colonial problems. Ho Chi Minh declared Vietnam an independent republic in 1945; French troops arrived to fight the insurgents the following year. Cambodia was granted its independence in 1949, Laos in 1950. In 1954, the fall of Dien Bien Phu effectively brought an end to French power in Indochina. In North Africa, Morocco and Tunisia became independent in 1956. And there was war in Algeria.

The Algerian independence movement violently divided the French people, for administratively Algeria was not a *colonie* but a *département* of France. Ultra-nationalists and major portions of the army considered the independence movement a war of secession and intended to keep Algeria French at all costs. More liberal factions saw the justice of the Algerian National Liberation Front's cause. At the height of the hostilities, there were approximately 500,000 French troops and some 1,000,000 European colonists in Algeria. In 1958, extremists of both groups, fearing that the French government would come to terms with the Algerians, threatened a military and civilian revolt that brought the situation to a head. An appeal was made to the only person thought strong enough to bring France through the emergency.

Charles de Gaulle responded to the appeal and the Fourth Republic was replaced by the Fifth Republic. De Gaulle designed a new constitution that allowed for a bicameral legislature but invested immense power in the presidency, perhaps the unavoidable compromise for a nation traditionally torn between the reign of a king and the democratic process. In January 1959, de Gaulle became president, his urgent task the resolution of the Algerian crisis in the midst of increasing violence. Demonstrations by colonists and the army in Algeria gave way to the terrorist campaign of the violent, dangerous, and deadly efficient OAS (Secret Army Organization), an extreme right-wing group agitating against any accord with the Algerians. There were assassination conspiracies everywhere.

De Gaulle overrode all threats. Courageous, and above all realistic, he accepted the inevitable and granted Algeria's independence. The hostilities ended in 1962, though the loss of Algeria remained for years a bitter issue for the country's right wing and ultra-nationalists. As for the Algerians, not until 1983 — and then only out of consideration for the new French Socialist government — did an Algerian head of state visit France.

After Algeria, de Gaulle devoted himself to realizing his vision of France as the leader of Europe. He saw to the development of nuclear weapons and asserted an independent foreign policy, recognizing the People's Republic of China, withdrawing from the military wing of NATO, blocking Britain's entry into the Common Market, and boycotting meetings while still believing in a Europe strong enough to act as a third force between Russia and the United States. De Gaulle was again, for many Frenchmen, the symbol of a free France, in both physical stature and national legend a figure larger than life. But he had a consistent attitude of arrogant grandeur and, in time, while his personal integrity was unquestioned, some saw him assuming the posture of a monarch more than that of a president.

The nation grew restless once more. Labor unions protested inflation and a lack of housing, students protested government expenditures on arms as well as an obsolete educational system, and opposition leaders protested the government's control over the mass media. In May 1968, these forces came together in an explosion whose force has often been underestimated outside France. Students demonstrated by the hundreds of thousands and 10 million workers went out on strike; the country was paralyzed, the government close to being overthrown. Only by securing the support of the army and by promising reforms was de Gaulle able to survive. Then an equally strong counterreaction set in, and in the next general election the Gaullists won a major victory.

But in April 1969 de Gaulle planted the seeds of his own political demise by proposing a national referendum on a complex series of constitutional reforms, announcing that he would consider the results a vote of confidence on himself. The reforms were defeated by a small margin. August, austere, always a symbol, de Gaulle was true to his word. He retired to his country home, where he died a year later. For most Frenchmen, he remains a figure of sincere admiration.

The Fifth Republic went on. In 1969, Georges Pompidou, a Gaullist, became president and served until his death in 1974. Then Valéry Giscard d'Estaing, a conservative (but not a member of the Gaullist party), was elected president in a close race that had the country split nearly evenly at the polls between right and left. In the next elections, in May 1981, the almost even split went the other way, and François Mitterrand, a Socialist, became president.

To the relief of some and the disappointment of others, socialism has not really changed the face of France very much. Some industries have been nationalized, but other industries and most banks had already been run by the state under previous governments. Civil liberties have been assured in a more typically American fashion than before. The death penalty has been abolished. On questions of foreign policy, such as relations with the Soviets, the Middle East (particularly 1991's Persian Gulf War), cooperation with NATO, and missile deployment, France under the Socialists has moved closer to American positions; only Central America, energy, and international monetary policy remain real differences.

Domestically, however, France has been plagued by severe economic problems — high unemployment, inflation, a heavy burden of social services, a relatively weak currency, and a balance of payments deficit. Insoluble labor problems were avoided only because of the unions' onetime ideological support of the government, though economic reality forced severe (and unpopular) austerity measures.

So unpopular were these Socialist edicts that the Socialists lost control of the French legislature to a coalition of centrists and conservatives in March 1986, and the neo-Gaullist Mayor of Paris, Jacques Chirac, became prime minister. When Mitterrand ran against Chirac in the presidential elections of mid-1988, however, Mitterrand won a second term as president. His victory was by such a decisive margin that he called for early parliamentary elections, hoping to win back a Socialist majority in the 577-seat National Assembly and end 2 years of "cohabitation."

But the predicted landslide did not materialize. Although the Socialists won a bloc of 276 seats, they fell short of a majority, as did the center-right alliance, which emerged from the voting with 271 seats. On the far right, the voters rejected the xenophobic rhetoric of the National Front of Jean-Marie Le Pen, who blamed most of France's problems on its immigrant population, thereby cutting its parliamentary representation from 32 seats to 1 seat. This result was due as much to a recent change in the voting system, which made it difficult for small parties to win seats, as to a defection by supporters. On the left, the Communists salvaged 27 of their 35 seats.

Over the last few years, however, France's Fifth Republic has become more markedly conservative, and the right-left political division has been considerably weakened. Since 1988, French voters have gravitated toward the middle of a winding road, and social and political life seem to have become more reactive than purposeful. Cabinet dissension and strikes among public workers occur regularly; recent incidents such as the shutdown of the métro and railroad systems have paralyzed Paris.

The unification of Germany stirred newly animated concern among those with long memories, while at the same time, overt anti-Semitic acts seem to be on the rise. France, alone among the NATO allies, has been willing to negotiate for the release of French hostages with Middle Eastern terrorists, and France seems to be just about the only Western nation to have created a nuclear energy policy that's still growing with the blessing of the majority of French citizens. In addition, many fear that a new Europe dominated by Germany and the Bundesbank will mean a loss of France's cherished international prestige. There are also serious concerns about the future of the agricultural sector, which traditionally has been the backbone of France. French farmers can no longer produce crops that can effectively compete with those produced in poorer EC countries, and the recent ban on the exportation of unpasteurized products, including camembert, has forced many farmers to sell their land to developers.

Thus the mosaic of French life in the 1990s can be described accurately as varied and often contradictory. President Mitterrand occupies the position of an elderly uncle (his nickname is "Tonton"), yet he is considered a very clever politician by those who admire his unflagging support for the Socialist Party. Mitterrand's current 7-year term is up in 1995, but the president may call a referendum to shorten the presidential term to 5 years, and try to appoint a Socialist successor. Some of his recent decisions have cast a blight on his popularity; his appointment of Edith Cresson as Prime Minister in 1991 (the first woman ever to hold that post in France) proved disastrous. Cresson's overt racial remarks resulted in her resignation less than a year later, and she was replaced by Pierre Bérégovoy, whose main political aim has been to strengthen the value of the franc against the Deutsche mark. In 1992, regional elections showed a greater uncertainty over the fate of the Socialist Party in

France, with many French casting their votes for the controversial National Front candidate Jean-Marie Le Pen and other strongly conservative coalitions.

For the most part, France remains a prosperous place perched on the beginning of a new century, but whether its political complexion will change from socialism to a predominately right-wing government remains to be seen.

Literature

 In France, the life of the mind always has flourished right along with the life of the senses. So the same country that can boast of offering the world's hautest cuisine, greatest wines, and most elegant fashions (not to mention many of Europe's greatest artistic and architectural masterpieces) also can legitimately claim to have produced some of the world's greatest literature.

The early Middle Ages produced a great military epic, the "Chanson de Roland" (Song of Roland; ca. 1100), which made Charlemagne's defeat at Roncevaux, in 778, into a heroic legend. The medieval era also was one of chivalry and courtly love, as reflected in the verse tales of Chrétien de Troyes (ca. 1135–1183), in the poetry of the southern troubadours, and in the 13th-century philosophical allegory *Roman de la Rose* (Romance of the Rose). In 1431, the year Joan of Arc was burned at the stake, France's greatest poet of the Middle Ages was born: François Villon. Though educated at the Sorbonne, he often associated with thieves and criminals and, in 1462 or 1463, was sentenced to be hanged for the murder of a priest. The sentence was commuted, but he left Paris and disappeared without a trace. His poetry reflects a graphic preoccupation with death and a poignant regret for his deeds.

By the 16th century, Pierre de Ronsard (1524–85), the most successful poet of his day, was writing charming love poems in which the transience of youth and the inevitability of death are arguments for enjoying the here and now. He and the six other poets of the Pléiade group used Latin, Greek, and Italian examples to set new formal standards for French verse and to enrich the French language to enable it to develop a literature to rival the models.

François Rabelais (ca. 1494–1553), a monk who gave up the religious life to practice medicine in Lyons (a lively intellectual center at the time), usually is regarded as the first French prose writer to reflect the spirit of Renaissance humanism, and he did it with a bang. With an avid interest in all the forms of learning, he celebrated the pleasures of both the mind and the body, unabashedly mixing scatology and scholarship, erudition and hedonism. His satirical novels about two giants, *Pantagruel* (1532) and *Gargantua* (1534), were lusty, witty, coarse, and irreverent, and they were condemned as sacrilegious and obscene by the theologians at the Sorbonne. Rabelais mocked religious dogma and medieval asceticism. The philosophy that emerges from his writings is progressive and optimistic, rooted in a spirited love of life and faith in the goodness of human nature.

While Rabelais gave his name to a singular style of humor, Michel Eyquem de Montaigne (1533–92), the other towering figure of the age, invented the short form of expository writing known as the essay. He spent years of his life cloistered in the tower library of his château in the Périgord (while the religious wars raged nearby), writing his engaging *Essais,* meaning "attempts"; two books appeared in 1580, a third in 1588. In his loose, casual style, he set out to study in depth a most fascinating subject — himself — and in so doing he entertained his reader by discussing nearly every topic of interest to mankind. Montaigne was a skeptic, and his views are surprisingly modern. He was repelled by dogmatic opinion and constantly stressed the relativity of all customs and beliefs. In addition, he favored the acquisition of judgment and wisdom over bookishness for its own sake, preferring "a well-made head rather than a well-filled one."

Montaigne's outlook paved the way for the 17th-century classical ideal of the *honnête homme* — a cultured and harmonious being, innately refined, elegant, and poised. This paragon of good taste and civilized virtues — measured, thoughtful, discreet, gallant, and brave — probably still lurks as a model of behavior somewhere in the French collective unconscious, lodged there by the insistent drilling of the works of the country's great classical writers into the head of every schoolchild.

Two events traditionally are regarded as having ushered in the golden age of classicism. The first was the founding of the Académie Française by Cardinal Richelieu after writers had begun meeting secretly to discuss literary matters. The Academy was recognized by Louis XIII in 1635 and still is a powerful institution (housed, since 1805, in one of the most beautiful buildings in Paris, the 17th-century Institut de France). From the beginning, its function was to purify the language, establish linguistic standards and grammatical rules, and pass judgment on literary works; the opportunity to exercise this last function came almost immediately, with the appearance in 1636 of the second event to launch the golden age, a fiery play by Pierre Corneille (1606–84).

Corneille's *Le Cid* was an immense popular success ("beautiful as *Le Cid*" became a common catch phrase), but it was criticized by the Academy for its insufficient adherence to the classical rule of the three unities. This rule required that for the sake of verisimilitude (presumably), a play's action had to unfold within 24 hours, in a single setting, and without extraneous subplots or changes in mood (violent events or deaths were not permitted to occur onstage, either). The Academy's criticism of *Le Cid* probably was instigated by Cardinal Richelieu (himself a writer) out of jealousy, yet this extreme concern for fixed rules, correctness, order, and regularity is characteristic of the period. Oddly enough, in spite of these restrictions — or perhaps thanks to them — the classical movement engendered masterpieces of stylized, polished perfection that helped set the tone for the long and absolutist reign of Louis XIV, who ascended to the throne at the age of 5 in 1643 and reigned from 1661 to 1715. Under the Sun King, French letters truly reached their zenith. As Louis's splendid court radiated brilliance from Versailles, as French artists and writers responded to the encouragement of royal patronage, and as aristocratic salons proliferated in Paris, French literature and art came to dominate Europe, and French became the common language of its educated classes.

The degree to which it respected the unities notwithstanding, *Le Cid* was the first masterpiece of French classical tragedy. It dealt inspiringly with the noble conflict between love and honor, a theme Corneille so exploited in all his tragedies that it became known as a *situation cornélienne.* His heroes always are well born, ardent souls who dominate their unruly passions and weaknesses through reason and will power. This optimistic, rational view of human psychology foreshadowed the *Treatise on Passions* (1649) by René Descartes (1596–1650), the great mathematician and creator of analytic geometry, whose *Discours de la Méthode* (Discourse on Method; 1637) — "I think, therefore I am" — laid the foundations of modern philosophy. In contrast, the tragedies of Corneille's younger rival, Jean Racine (1639–99), are emotional and pessimistic in the extreme, bearing the mark of his austere upbringing according to the doctrines of Jansenism, a Roman Catholic reform movement to which a belief in predestination was fundamental.

While some critics feel that the tighter tragedies Corneille wrote after *Le Cid* are his true masterpieces (*Horace* and *Cinna* in 1640, *Polyeuctus* in 1643), others speculate that if he had not been obliged to fetter his baroque genius and conform to the rule of the three unities, he might have been as great as Shakespeare. This issue doesn't arise in the case of Racine; the three unities suited him perfectly. Like the proverbial chef who can whip up an unforgettable meal out of nothing, Racine required few ingredients to create moving, sublime tragedies. A master stylist, his plays *Andromache* (1667) and *Phaedra* (1677) are both "fire under ice," the action hinging entirely on the violent psychological reactions of his characters. His heroes and heroines are the obsessive, helpless victims of their emotions — unrequited love, jealousy, ambition, pride, hatred, and cruelty — a spectrum with which Racine probably was intimately acquainted, for he was a particularly odious man, disloyal and ruthlessly selfish (he even was accused of poisoning his mistress, a celebrated actress).

On the other hand, the man who launched Racine's career (and whom Racine promptly double-crossed) is very fondly remembered. Molière (the pseudonym of Jean-Baptiste Poquelin, 1622–73) was a native Parisian (his parents lived near *Les Halles,* at 96 Rue St-Honoré) who rebelled against his prosperous bourgeois background to found a theatrical company. After touring the provinces for 12 years, the troupe returned to Paris in 1658 and won the Sun King's enduring patronage. An inscription at the corner of Rue de Valois and Rue St-Honoré marks the spot where Molière's *Palais-Royal* used to stand (it burned down in 1781). This was the theater in which he produced most of his own plays and where, just hours before his death, he struggled through his last comic performance, ironically in the title role of the hypochondriac in *La Malade Imaginaire* (The Imaginary Invalid).

Molière used a whole gamut of comic devices, from slapstick farce to refined verbal satire, to expose a wide range of human failings, including pretension, affectation, pedantry, and misguided aspirations. As a result, he created a hilarious but thought-provoking form of comedy based on the portrayal of contemporary mores and universal character types: *Le Bourgeois Gentilhomme* (The Would-Be Gentleman) and *Les Femmes Savantes* (The Learned Women). He was not a social reformer, but the wickedness and hypocrisy that he exposed in his two most heartfelt comedies, *Tartuffe* and *Le Misanthrope,* provide a rather bleak view of mankind and society. Perhaps this was inevitable. In the beginning of his career, Molière obstinately had tried to produce tragedies (the "nobler" genre); by the end of his life, he had succeeded in elevating comedy to the level of tragedy.

There were other important 17th-century literary figures. The posthumously published *Pensées* (Thoughts) of Blaise Pascal (1623–62), a mathematical prodigy and Jansenism's deepest thinker, anticipated modern Existentialism. Jean de La Fontaine (1621–95), a worldly, amused observer of human nature and social behavior, is best remembered for his witty and vivid verse *Fables*. François de La Rochefoucauld (1613–80), on the other hand, produced his *Maximes* (Maxims), the darkest book of observations the world has ever known, pithily demonstrating that all our noblest sentiments really are dictated by self-love and self-interest. Meanwhile, his great friend Madame de La Fayette (1634–92) wrote the first French psychological novel, *La Princesse de Clèves*, a concise analysis of the inner workings of love and jealousy. Finally, Madame de Sévigné (1626–96), their common friend and fellow aristocrat, has gone down in history for her extraordinarily lively letters, mostly to her beloved daughter, describing the literary, political, and cultural events of the capital. From 1677 to her death, she lived in the magnificent mansion in Paris that now is the *Musée Carnavalet.*

The absolute monarchy of Louis XIV left the kingdom bankrupt. In the 18th century, as the monarchy continued to decline under Louis XV and Louis XVI, the court ceased to be the center of cultural and artistic life and became a target of intellectual criticism. In Parisian salons and the new cafés (like *Le Procope,* which still stands on Rue de l'Ancienne-Comédie), the *philosophes* of the Enlightenment (when they weren't in jail or exile for their writings) and other brilliant conversationalists mixed with disciples, artists, scientists, or eminent foreigners to reappraise absolutism and challenge all existing institutions and values. The democratic reforms these thinkers advocated, their belief in progress and the perfectibility of man, eventually cleared the way for momentous events such as the American and French Revolutions. In the meantime, they helped make Paris, which already was Europe's capital of refinement and elegance, into an exciting cosmopolitan center bristling with wit, daring, and intellectual ferment.

Six years after Louis XIV's death, the critical disposition of the new century was made tangible by Charles Louis de Secondat de Montesquieu (1689–1755) in his immensely successful *Lettres Persanes* (Persian Letters; 1721), in which contemporary French customs and institutions were seen through the "naive" eyes of visiting Persians. Anglophilia soon was in the air, as well as a growing admiration for the works of English philosophers and scientists. Montesquieu spent almost 2 years in England and came away commending the democratic features of its constitutional monarchy. The same was true of François-Marie Arouet, known as Voltaire (1694–1778). After 3 years of political exile across the Channel, he presented his observations and praise in a book entitled *Lettres Philosophiques* (Philosophical Letters on the English; 1733), an implicit attack on the bigotry, intolerance, and despotism of the French regime that caused enough of a furor to be banned. He is best known for his much later work, *Candide* (1759), a masterful tale that ironically refutes simplistic optimism and passivity and is written in his characteristically witty, clear, and simple prose style. As a polemicist, playwright, poet, novelist, historian, critic, and letter writer, Voltaire's literary output was staggering; in addition, he was a very clever financier and landowner, a guest at the "enlightened" courts of Europe, and, at the end of his long life, a revered patriarchal figure (Benjamin Franklin, for one, made a point of taking his grandson to visit him). For all these reasons, it is not surprising that the 18th century is sometimes called the Age of Voltaire.

However, it is customary to regard Voltaire as the last representative of the classical era and his younger, even more influential contemporary, the Swiss Jean-Jacques Rousseau (1712–78), as the herald of the new era of Romanticism. Rousseau opposed Voltaire and the other *philosophes* by challenging the values imposed by so-called progress and civilization and by viewing with contempt the conformist ideal of the *honnête homme*. He first drew the spotlight to himself in 1750 by winning an essay contest with his negative response to the question of whether progress in the arts and sciences contributed to the improvement of human nature. His discourse on inequality (1754) was more outspoken, and by the time *The Social Contract* appeared in 1762, opening with the ringing "Man is born free, and is everywhere in chains" — and further denouncing the corrupting influence of society and the evils of property, social inequality, and tyranny — Rousseau was a hero to some, a heretic to others. That same year, in *Emile,* he advocated an educational approach that would allow human potential to develop freely, an approach that formed the basis of all subsequent theories of progressive education. As a philosopher and political thinker, Rousseau directly inspired the French Revolution. At the same time, his nonconformity, his feeling for nature, his concern for sincerity, and his overt *sensibilité* — qualities that permeate such works as the epistolary novel *La Nouvelle Héloise* (The New Heloise; 1761) and the autobiographical *Confessions* (published posthumously) — touched off the Romantic movement.

Rousseau was such a controversial, indeed pivotal, figure that he tends to eclipse that other "emotional" *philosophe,* his sometime friend Denis Diderot (1713–84). Novelist, playwright, essayist, art critic, and protégé of Catherine the Great of Russia, Diderot struggled for many years, in spite of political opposition, to edit the 17 volumes of his monumental *Encyclopédie* (1751–65), one of the great liberal achievements of the period.

By the time Louis XVI came to the throne in 1774, indignation at the abuses and privileges of the hereditary aristocracy was running high. Pierre-Augustin Caron, called Beaumarchais (1732–99), a noble by marriage rather than birth, voiced this pre-Revolutionary discontent in his widely acclaimed comedies *The Barber of Seville* (1775) and *The Marriage of Figaro* (1784), which later inspired the famous operas by Rossini and Mozart.

The years of the French Revolution and of the Napoleonic regime, from 1789 to 1815, were years of upheaval and of limited literary output. The best writer publishing at the time (while many of his fellow aristocrats were being guillotined) was François-René de Chateaubriand (1768–1848), a founder of the Romantic movement in French literature. A 5-month stay in America in 1791–92 inspired him to write lush but inaccurate descriptions of the American wilderness (and of Niagara Falls) in tales that promoted an idealized, drawing room view of the American Indian. He exploited all the future Romantic themes and, above all, elaborated on a new persona, the sensitive genius with uncommon vision, who, ever since Rousseau, had begun to appear in fiction as in life. His restless, introspective hero, René, suffered from the insatiable, melancholic longings that became typical of the Romantic personality.

Even so, Romanticism came into full flower in France only as a result of foreign exposure. As the works of German and English authors became known, a new vitality was injected into the literary climate and young writers began rebelling against the strictures of their classical heritage. The four major Romantic poets were Alphonse de Lamartine (1790–1869), Alfred de Vigny (1797–1863), Victor Hugo (1802–85), and Alfred de Musset (1810–57), who also was an excellent playwright. The dominating figure was Hugo. A poet of great power, scope, and technical virtuosity, he dealt with every possible lyrical theme and also wrote gripping, melodramatic novels, of which the most famous remain *The Hunchback of Notre-Dame* (1831) and *Les Misérables* (1862). In 1830, the first performance of his Romantic drama, *Hernani*, was such a radical departure from the conventional theater that it prompted a riot between the classicists and Hugo's young Romantic supporters, the classicists objecting to Hugo's violation of the rules, the Romantics ultimately prevailing. For Hugo, Romanticism included political liberalism; he actively sympathized with the downtrodden and fought against social injustice, with the result that his opposition to Napoleon III sent him into exile for 20 years in the Channel Islands. He returned to France at the proclamation of the Third Republic in 1870 and was idolized as a leftist and champion of the people. The house he lived in from 1838 to 1843, at 6 Place des Vosges, now is a museum.

The growing influence of science during the 19th century led writers to try to depict people objectively, in their specific social milieus. In fiction, Romanticism gradually gave way to Realism, while at the end of the century, Realism gave way to Symbolism, particularly in poetry.

No writer better portrayed the social changes wrought by industrialization or the transformation of the rich bourgeoisie into the new ruling class than Honoré de Balzac (1799–1850). In close to 100 novels and short stories, grouped under the general title of *La Comédie Humaine* (The Human Comedy), he created a vast fresco of urban and rural France from 1815 to 1848. Despite the breadth of the undertaking, his characters are not simply social types but also highly individual flesh-and-blood human beings, with overriding passions and gripping personal dramas. Money is a major theme in Balzac's work, as it was in his own life. He wrote night and day in order to repay the debts he had incurred from disastrous business ventures. In fact, the coffeepot that provided the necessary stimulant to his effervescent imagination can be seen at the *Musée Balzac,* his home from 1842 to 1848, at 47 Rue Raynouard, a street that also briefly housed Jean-Jacques Rousseau and Benjamin Franklin.

Balzac was one of the rare contemporaries to fully appreciate the genius of Henri Beyle, known as Stendhal (1783–1842). In his own day, Stendhal wrote, as he said, "for the happy few"; today his masterpieces, *Le Rouge et le Noir* (The Red and the Black; 1831) and *La Chartreuse de Parme* (The Charterhouse of Parma; 1839), are widely admired for their psychological insight, political liberalism, and sober, ironic style.

While Stendhal wrote *La Chartreuse de Parme* in a record-breaking 7 weeks, Gustave Flaubert (1821–80) labored for nearly 5 years to produce that cool and scathing indictment of bourgeois provinciality, *Madame Bovary* (1857). The same painstaking care went into his other novels, including *L'Education Sentimentale* (The Sentimental Education; 1869). A meticulous researcher and perfectionist, he read each sentence of his impersonal prose out loud and rewrote paragraphs over and over again until he had found exactly the right words and rhythms.

It would seem that no novelist could have had a clearer or more pessimistic view of the contrast between our exalted romantic illusions and the actual platitude, or uneventfulness, of our lives than Flaubert. Yet his disciple Guy de Maupassant (1850–93), the master of the short story (who also produced some first-rate novels), was even more pessimistic. Though he, too, was a superb craftsman, he did not share Flaubert's religious devotion to the cause of art. For him, no pursuit or conviction could give a larger meaning to human life, which he portrayed in his fiction, with the sparsest means and seeming impartiality, as absurd, brutal, or pitiful.

Emile Zola (1840–1902), a friend and admirer of Flaubert and de Maupassant, went beyond Realism and forsook their economical, selective style to become the leader of the Naturalist School. Sheer weight characterizes his writing. Starting where Balzac left off, he produced the 20 heavily documented "slice of life" novels of the Rougon-Macquart series (1871–93), tracing the "natural and social history of a family under the Second Empire" (1852–70). The series covers almost every possible occupation and shows the grimmest aspects of lower class life, all with the scientist's aim of illustrating how heredity, biology, and the environment determine human behavior. A reformer and a socialist, in 1898 Zola wrote his famous open letter to the president of France, "J'Accuse," in defense of Captain Alfred Dreyfus, the Jewish army officer whom he believed wrongly convicted of treason.

One of Zola's supporters in this courageous stand was the novelist, poet, playwright, and critic Jacques-Anatole Thibault, or Anatole France (1844–1924), whose first full-length novel, *La Crime de Sylvestre Bonnard* (1881), had been a great success. As a result of the Dreyfus Affair, which he made the subject of four novels, France's work became increasingly devoted to political satire. His *Les Dieux Ont Soif* (The Gods Are Thirsty; 1912), a novel about the French Revolution and a searingly ironical indictment of political fanaticism, is considered his masterpiece. After a long career, France was awarded the Nobel Prize for literature in 1921.

Some of the other popular 19th-century writers still are read today. Alexandre Dumas (1802–70), for example, is remembered for *Les Trois Mousquetaires* (The Three Musketeers) and *Le Comte de Monte Cristo* (The Count of Monte Cristo); his son, Alexandre Dumas *fils* (1824–95), wrote the autobiographical novel and stage play *La Dame aux Camélias,* which inspired Verdi's *La Traviata* (not to mention 23 motion pictures, including *Camille* with Greta Garbo). Jules Verne (1828–1905), the author of *Vingt Mille Lieues sous les Mers* (Twenty Thousand Leagues under the Sea) and *La Tour du Monde en Quatre-Vingt Jours* (Around the World in Eighty Days), is regarded as the grandfather of contemporary science fiction.

French poets of the latter half of the 19th century reacted against the vague emotion of Romanticism on the one hand and the Realism of contemporary prose on the other. The Symbolists — Verlaine, Rimbaud, and Mallarmé — sought to go beyond transient, sensory reality to suggest the inner, eternal absolute. Symbolism's precursor was Charles Baudelaire (1821–67), whose *Les Fleurs du Mal* (Flowers of Evil; 1857) influenced not only the French but also English-language poets such as Swinburne, T. S. Eliot, Pound, and Yeats. He himself had found a kindred spirit in Edgar Allan Poe and worked for years on a translation of Poe's tales. Baudelaire was a dandy and a decadent; he drank to excess, he experimented with opium and hashish, and he spent the last years of his life in physical and mental torment. His poems have been described as "suggestive magic," yet they are unflinchingly honest about depravation, misery, and his personal sense of despair.

In contrast, Paul Verlaine (1844–96), who lived just as dissolute a life as Baudelaire, wrote poetry that is gentle and melancholic, candid and poignant. His notorious 2-year relationship with the rebellious, visionary boy genius Arthur Rimbaud (1854–91) ended disastrously. During one of their drunken arguments, Verlaine shot and wounded Rimbaud and, as a result, spent 2 years in prison for attempted murder. Rimbaud, on the other hand, after having completely revolutionized poetry with his hallucinatory imagery, complex rhythms, and free verse, gave up writing at the age of 19. He traveled widely and finally settled into the trade of coffee, arms, and slaves in Abyssinia.

Stéphane Mallarmé (1842–98) led the quiet life of an English teacher ascetically devoted to his art. Only when he began to be known in the mid-1880s did young writers and admirers flock to the Tuesday evening gatherings at his tranquil apartment on Rue de Rome to listen to his theories of poetry. His work is extremely complex and elusive, built on the suggestive music of words, and one of his longer poems, "L'Après-midi d'un Faune" (The Afternoon of a Faun; 1867), inspired Debussy's orchestral "Prélude" (1887).

Paris at the turn of the century was a lively, high-spirited city. The Belle Epoque flourished, with its great expositions, its literary cabarets and cafés (one of the most famous, the *Lapin Agile* in Montmartre, still exists), controversial art exhibitions, theaters, vaudeville shows, music halls, literary reviews, and the first movie projections. There was increasing interaction among the various arts, as painters, writers, musicians, and actors stimulated, supported, and opposed one another. Out of this exchange arose an unprecedented number of schools, cliques, and movements.

The Romantics and some of the Symbolist poets already had rejected tradition, defied convention, and scandalized public opinion. The avant-garde followed boldly in their wake. Today, we almost expect to be bewildered by new trends in art, and the nonconformist writer or artist is practically a cliché. It is hard for us to imagine, for example, the effect produced by Alfred Jarry (1873–1907) when he appeared at Mallarmé's funeral dressed like a bicycle racer, with bright yellow shoes. A forerunner of the Dadaist and Surrealist movements as well as of the later Theater of the Absurd represented by Samuel Beckett (1906–89), Eugène Ionesco (b. 1912), and Jean Genet (1910–86), Jarry's grotesque farce, *Ubu-Roi,* caused a scandal on its opening night in 1896 comparable to the one caused by Victor Hugo's *Hernani* in 1830.

Meanwhile, just as Baudelaire, as an art critic, had shown unerring taste in defending the controversial painters of his time (Delacroix, Corot, Manet, Daumier), the poet Guillaume Apollinaire (1880–1918) promoted the works of the innovative painters of his day: Vlaminck, Derain, Chagall, Duchamp, Modigliani, Rousseau, De Chirico, Picabia, Delaunay, Léger, Picasso, Braque, and Gris. He dominated the avant-garde from 1913 to his death, and his poetic innovations opened the path to Surrealism, a term credited to him. The Surrealist movement, which thrived between the two world wars, drew inspiration from Freud and tried to unleash the forces of the unconscious through automatic writing and free association.

The discovery of the unconscious also dominated the fiction of this period. Many good French novelists turned out excellent sagas in the tradition of Balzac and Zola — notably the Nobel Prize winners Romain Rolland (1866–1944) and Roger Martin du Gard (1881–1958) as well as Georges Duhamel (1884–1966) and Jules Romains (1885–1972). But all these works pale next to the beauty and complexity of Marcel Proust's monumental cycle novel, *Remembrance of Things Past* (the French title is *A la Recherche du Temps Perdu;* In Search of Lost Time, "lost" implying both "gone" and "wasted"). Like Stendhal, Proust (1871–1922) is admired more today than he was by his contemporaries, though he owes part of his fame to the conditions under which he wrote. A social butterfly in his youth, severe asthma and total dedication to his artistic mission turned him into a recluse working in bed in a darkened, cork-lined room. The first volume of this masterpiece was rejected by several publishers so Proust had it printed at his own expense. Yet it now is clear that he wrote one of the greatest novels ever. Living up to Mallarmé's remark that "the world was made to end up in a beautiful book," he put all his energy and experience of life into his work. Thanks to pitiless self-analysis, he reached beyond the traditional, static views of human psychology and created a richly textured social universe activated by the forces of love, jealousy, death, memory, and time.

The only contemporary novelist comparable to Proust in intensity may be James Joyce, who lived from time to time in Paris and serves to recall another important feature of the city before World War II: It was the home of so many Irish, English, and American writers. "Paris was where the 20th century was," said Gertrude Stein, who entertained America's "lost generation" of writers (as well as painters like Cézanne and Picasso) at 27 Rue de Fleurus. Beginning with Oscar Wilde, who spent his last days at *L'Hôtel* on Rue des Beaux-Arts in 1900, the list of expatriates who lived and worked in Paris is impressive: Ernest Hemingway, F. Scott Fitzgerald, Sherwood Anderson, John Dos Passos, Jean Rhys, Ford Madox Ford, D. H. Lawrence, Henry Miller, Anaïs Nin, George Orwell, Samuel Beckett. Others, like Ezra Pound, T. S. Eliot, and Thornton Wilder, often passed through. Though they frequented all the cafés of Montparnasse — *Le Dôme, Le Sélect, La Rotonde, La*

Coupole, La Closerie des Lilas — their great haunt was *Shakespeare & Company,* the bookshop owned by Sylvia Beach, an American, at 12 Rue de l'Odéon (it no longer exists; the bookshop of the same name on the quai is not the original). Sylvia Beach also published Joyce's *Ulysses* (1922), a work that encountered monumental publication and censorship difficulties elsewhere because of charges of obscenity.

At the same time, many important French writers emerged: Colette (1873–1954), for example, who began by ghostwriting for her first husband, Willy, and whose *Gigi* was made into a Hollywood movie; the great poet and essayist Paul Valéry (1871–1945); Catholic novelists and playwright-poets such as Nobel Prize winner François Mauriac (1885–1970), Georges Bernanos (1888–1948), Paul Claudel (1868–1955), and Charles Péguy (1873–1914); novelists of adventure and heroism like André Malraux (1901–76), who became minister of culture under de Gaulle, and Antoine de St-Exupéry (1900–44); the historical novelist Marguerite Yourcenar (1903–1987), the first woman to be elected to the French Academy, in 1982; the Belgian-born detective story writer Georges Simenon (1903–89), famous for his Inspector Maigret series; and André Gide (1869–1951), winner of the Nobel Prize for Literature in 1947. Gide's writings raised moral issues that foreshadowed the philosophical school of Existentialism. He also made formal innovations, such as in his novel *Les Faux-Monnayeurs* (The Counterfeiters; 1926), that prepared the way for the *nouveau roman* (new novel) of the 1950s and 60s.

World War II brought the Existentialists to the forefront. Jean-Paul Sartre (1905–80) and Simone de Beauvoir (1908–86), as well as their friend, the Algerian-born Albert Camus (1913–60), who actually evolved his own philosophy of the absurd, grew increasingly influential in France and abroad, and by now a whole generation has been bred on their philosophy of free will, moral responsibility, and political commitment. In postwar Paris, Sartre and Simone de Beauvoir also helped make the *Café Flore* and *Les Deux Magots,* on Boulevard St-Germain, into fashionable intellectual watering holes. Camus — novelist, playwright, essayist — received the Nobel Prize in 1957, while Sartre — philosopher, novelist, playwright, literary critic, and Marxist — turned it down in 1964.

Parallel to these writers, who used fiction and drama as their vehicles, there arose the technical experiments of the new novelists, or anti-novelists, including Nathalie Sarraute (b. 1902), Claude Simon (b. 1913), Alain Robbe-Grillet (b. 1922), and Michel Butor (b. 1926), all of whom still are writing today; Simon won the Nobel Prize in 1985. In a complete departure from the traditional novel, they proceeded to "decompose" reality by dispensing with chronology, plot, character, and meaning — either by magnifying the ephemeral and contradictory elements of life, by jumbling chronology and plot, or by concentrating on the description of the flat surface of things (leading some readers to feel that human psychology has been unfairly replaced by the legs of chairs).

The late Samuel Beckett (1906–1989) — who wrote in both French and English — and Marguerite Duras (b. 1914) do not properly belong to this school, yet they, too, rejected the conventional novel. Both also have written excellent plays, while Duras and Robbe-Grillet have put their talent into films as well. French cinema always has had a literary bent (as exemplified in the 1940s by the collaboration between the poet Jacques Prévert and the director Marcel Carné, and by the experimental films of Jean Cocteau) and one of the most exciting artistic developments of the 1960s was the New Wave cinema of directors led by Alain Resnais, Claude Chabrol, Eric Rohmer, Jean Eustache, Jean-Luc Godard, and the late François Truffaut.

French intellectual life today is as lively as ever, particularly in the social sciences. The study of linguistics and the work of the anthropologist Claude Lévi-Strauss (b. 1908) engendered a method of analysis called Structuralism, which focuses on the patterns of relationships within systems of communications. A lively school of New Criticism, headed by Roland Barthes (1915–80), attacked the orthodox, academic approach to literary criticism and opened the door to every kind of interpretation — structural, linguistic, psychoanalytic, Marxist. Sociologists, philosophers, and historians also are producing interesting work, while the difficult, pun-filled writings of France's leading psychoanalyst, Jacques Lacan (1901–81), are the subject of heated debate. Because most poets, novelists, and playwrights draw inspiration from these recent trends, cut-and-dried distinctions between imaginative and scholarly writing are hard to make. But one thing is certain: French writers today know they are part of one of the world's oldest, most distinguished literary traditions.

Painting

Compared to the history of Italian or Flemish art, the history of French painting begins relatively late. To be sure, there was painting in France from the earliest times. Witness the cave drawings at Lascaux: mysterious dots, bars, and bison-like images thought to represent hunting scenes or symbolic rituals. But the development of a great and characteristically French school of painting did not really begin until the 17th century. Before that, the creative genius that eventually made French painting dominant in the world of art found expression in other forms, and where painting did appear, its style usually was borrowed, in no way particularly French. The Celts, who settled France before the Christian era, and the Franks, who came in the 5th century, made gold and silver objects and splendid jewelry. Architecture and sculpture were the preeminent arts of the Romanesque period, and the Gothic period added the glorious art of stained glass, which reached its height in the cathedral at Chartres.

Painting in the form of manuscript illumination flourished in various centers throughout the Middle Ages. In the early 15th century, the Duke of Berry employed a distinguished group of miniaturists at his court, including the Franco-Flemish Limbourg brothers, whose *Très Riches Heures du Duc de Berry* (*Book of Hours;* 1415) is a masterpiece of refined elegance in the International Gothic style. Painting in other forms appeared sporadically; one of the earliest examples was a medieval panel portrait of King John the Good (1360–64). During the 14th and 15th centuries, a flowering of the arts took place in the south of France, first around the papal court in Avignon, then at the court of Good King René in Aix-en-Provence. The frescoes on the walls of the Palace of the Popes (the religious cycles were done by an Italian, Matteo Giovanetti, but the secular hunting, fishing, and landscape scenes are thought to be the work of French artists) belong to the mid-14th century. And two panel paintings — the *Pietà* of Villeneuve-les-Avignon, attributed to Enguerrand Charonton, and the *Aix Annonciation,* by the Master of the Annunciation of Aix — are masterpieces of Provençal painting in the mid-15th century.

Nor were other areas of France lacking in painters in the 15th century. Jean Fouquet (ca. 1420–80), a native of Tours and a leading illuminator as well as *peintre du roi* (court painter) to Louis XI, is remembered not only for the illuminations in his *Book of Hours of Etienne Chevalier* (ca. 1450–55) but also for his panel portraits, *Charles VII* and *Guillaume Juvénal des Ursins.* The *Moulins Triptych* (1498–99), by the Master of Moulins, is an outstanding example of late-15th-century portraiture. Nevertheless, painting in France at this time was neither a first art nor, since strongly suggestive of its Flemish and Italian sources, an original one.

Painting did play a notable role in the French Renaissance, but its style still was imported, the result of contact with the Italian Renaissance through the

Italian Wars begun by Charles VIII in 1494. And what was imported was not the High Renaissance but the post-Renaissance, or Mannerism, an exaggerated, self-conscious, luxurious, elitist style. The two most prominent French painters of the early 16th century were Jean Bourdichon (1457–1521) and Jean Perréal (ca. 1455–1530), about whom almost nothing is known. What is known is that when Francis I, whose reign is considered the height of the French Renaissance, became king in 1515, he set about bringing the greatest painters in Italy to his court. Leonardo da Vinci came in 1516; during the 1530s, Il Rosso and Francesco Primaticcio arrived to direct the decoration of the Galerie François I at the Fontainebleau palace. Thus the School of Fontainebleau was born. French artists began working beside the Italian masters, and the new Mannerist style of painting — along with a taste for elaborate stucco work — took hold in the country, to remain in vogue for the rest of the century. But it still was not a French style, and there still was no painting that could legitimately be called French.

THE SEVENTEENTH-CENTURY BEGINNINGS

It was during the baroque period (1600–1750) that the history of French painting really began. The masters of the early French baroque were Georges de La Tour (1593–1652) and the Le Nain brothers, Antoine (1588–1648) and Mathieu (1607–77). Influenced by Caravaggio, La Tour explored *chiaroscuro,* painting nocturnal scenes in the main and mastering the effects of lighting from hidden or revealed sources (*Magdalen with the Night Light*). The Le Nain brothers concentrated instead on the effects of daylight. But the three shared one innovation: Their scenes gave an importance to daily life, not just to historical, allegorical, or religious themes. The Le Nains in particular were the first of the great baroque painters to portray unsentimentalized scenes of peasants, and their work later influenced the 19th-century painters Courbet and Manet.

It was also in the 17th century that there first appeared French painters whose names are readily recognized today. Claude Gellée, known as Claude Lorrain (1600–82), and Nicolas Poussin (1594–1665), both of whom worked in Italy, were masters of baroque landscape painting. They drew their inspiration from the Italian countryside and painted primarily for an Italian elite, but both remained profoundly French as painters. Together they represented the polarity within the baroque movement as a whole. Poussin was a model of classical reason and restraint, using Italian landscapes as a background for monumental figure paintings based on classical texts and exploiting classical references for their narrative value (*Arcadian Shepherds,* 1650). Lorrain was the model of unrestrained romanticism, of the irrational and magical, using the Roman countryside as a nostalgic backdrop for minute, at times inconsequential, figures, and exploiting symbols from the past for their emotive value (*Landscape with a Rustic Dance,* 1639).

While Poussin and Lorrain were working in Italy, Philippe de Champaigne (1602–74) was working in Paris. His stunning portrait of his daughter, a nun, and her prioress in their cell (*Ex-Voto,* 1662) is unusual in its directness and psychological perspective. But the most influential painter working in Paris was Simon Vouet (1590–1649), court painter to Louis XIII. Vouet, too, had been to Rome, and it was Poussin's classicism that prevailed in his work; his style tempered the exuberance of the late Mannerists to the taste of the French monarchy, and he was a master of pictorial decoration. Vouet was the artistic arbiter of the first half of the 17th century, the head of a large *atelier* (studio), yet he is remembered chiefly for one student, Charles Le Brun (1619–90), the man who ruled artistic tastes in the second half of the century.

As court painter to Louis XIV, Le Brun was the interior decorator of Versailles. He decorated the Grands Apartements; he painted the ceiling of the Galerie des Glaces (Hall of Mirrors) in allegories to Louis's glory. He married the classical spirit to the flamboyance of the baroque and dedicated the union to serve the Sun King's visions of grandeur, thereby giving lavish visual form to the ideology behind the absolute monarchy and making its setting the marvel of Europe.

Le Brun, in essence, created the Louis XIV style, an accomplishment made possible also because he was the director of the Gobelins tapestry manufactory and the chancellor of the Académie Royale de Peinture et de Sculpture of Paris. The former had been bought by Louis in the 1660s and had been turned into a workshop of the decorative arts, producing everything from jewelry to furniture. The latter, an association of artists founded in 1648, had grown under royal patronage into a powerful palace school of art, dictating aesthetic rules for painting and sculpture just as the French Academy dictated grammar and style for language and literature.

THE EIGHTEENTH CENTURY

Because Louis XV was only 5 years old when Louis XIV died, a regent ruled France from 1715 to 1723. This period of transition, appropriately known as the Regency, was a time of general relaxation from the rigid ceremonial and public lifestyles imposed by the Sun King. For a while Paris, not Versailles, was the center of society and artistic activity. This change in atmosphere marked art, as did architectural changes. Townhouses became the focus of the artist's attention, architectural proportions were reduced, and smaller, more intimate genre paintings now were required for decoration. Regular salons came into being, offering a showcase for artists not trained at the Academy. Antoine Watteau (1684–1721), who studied with a painter of theatrical scenes and with a decorative painter, was one such artist. He showed his works of fashionable people amusing themselves under the heading of *"fêtes galantes."* These scenes of love and gallantry, influenced by earlier Venetian styles, took place outdoors, where lovers in shimmering silk finery met beneath flesh-like statues in otherworldly parks. They differed in every way from the state portraits and massive allegorical themes that had dominated painting style for more than a century, just as their poignant evocation of mystery, their suggestion of the transitoriness of love and life, set them apart from the *fêtes* of artists still to come. Watteau also introduced characters from the Italian and French comedy into his work, thus beginning a tradition in French painting — the theater as material for pictorial art — that lasted until the end of the 19th century.

But Watteau was the important exception. The mainstream of official French art passed through a lesser artist, François Le Moyne (1688–1737). Le Moyne's classicism, his large scale, and his use of allegory were 17th-century baroque, but his lightness, elegance, and clear colors were of the 18th century, representing the transition to the new style, rococo. And Le Moyne had an important pupil, François Boucher (1703–70), who became court painter to Louis XV and a favorite of the king's favorite, Madame de Pompadour (for whom he created Boucher blue). If Le Brun had captured the spirit of the Sun King's *grand siècle*, Boucher captured the lightheartedness and frivolity of the rococo period. He employed sweet pastel colors, pinks and blues that evoked a fairy-tale tone, and he was versatile. Along with large, mythological schemes, he painted landscapes, portraits, erotic scenes, and "keyhole" paintings, glimpses into the intrigues of a leisure class the painter knew well.

Jean-Honoré Fragonard (1732–1806) carried on in Boucher's tradition during the reigns of both Louis XV and Louis XVI. He was a specialist in small boudoir scenes and airy, graceful *fêtes galantes*, set in Italianate or frankly artificial decors. Paintings such as *The Swing* (1766) or the large *Progress of Love* panels (1771) painted for the house of Madame du Barry captured all the empty gaiety and beauty of the 18th century. Fragonard's use of paint, applied with direct, impromptu strokes (*Inspiration*, 1769), recalls the spontaneity of Rubens from Flanders, while his ease and grace reflect the influence of the Italian Tiepolo.

Fragonard, however, fell out of step with the times, as a reaction to the fashionably meaningless set in. Art critics, including the renowned Diderot, criticized the frivolity at court and the works of Boucher and Fragonard associated with it. They championed simpler paintings, such as still lifes and domestic scenes with humble subjects whose moral overtones were in keeping with the ideas of the Enlightenment philosophers — paintings by the likes of Jean-Baptiste Oudry (1686–1755), Jean-Baptiste-Siméon Chardin (1699–1779), and Jean-Baptiste Greuze (1725–1805).

Of the three, Chardin was the master. In ideological terms, his depictions of the family life of the Parisian middle classes, done in straightforward, muted colors, were seen as the healthy antithesis to court art and the life it reflected. In technical terms, his still lifes are extraordinarily executed (*The Rayfish*, 1727) and show a deep reverence for the everyday objects of the "common man." His genre scenes recall those of the Le Nains, yet rival those of Vermeer as among the finest ever painted (*The Morning Toilet*, 1740). Their technical purity, subtle color harmonies, and quality of composition would be later recognized by, among others, Paul Cézanne.

THE NINETEENTH CENTURY

The 19th century in French art was, quite simply, spectacular. The history of modern Europe often is dated from the French Revolution, and the beginning of modern art often is dated from one French painter, Jacques-Louis David (1748–1825), who was, initially, court painter to Louis XVI. David became the spokesman for the enormous artistic changes that corresponded to the political and philosophical changes taking place in late 18th-century France, and his oeuvre constitutes a bridge to the 19th century. A reaction against the frivolities of rococo and an interest in archaeological excavations came together at this time in a new appreciation for classical standards of excellence. Simultaneously, revolutionary ideas were leading steadily to the conclusion that the moment was heroic.

Joseph-Marie Vien (1716–1809) already had shown a willingness to move toward the neo-classical, and David had been his pupil. Now, having studied in Rome, David began to produce large canvases, based on ancient legends, that visually communicated a libertarian message. His monumental *Oath of the Horatii* (1784), a celebration of the stoic virtues of family and national honor, was shown at the Salon (the official art exhibition held by the Academy since 1737 and at this point open only to Academy members) and won for David dual recognition as the interpreter of the republican spirit and the apostle of neo-classicism. Baroque compositional methods were abandoned. Instead, David strove for the neo-classic ideals of precision and clarity of space and forms, rejecting clutter. Also remarkable is his strong use of sharply focused light, derived from Caravaggio. David became the "official" artist of the Revolution; he even designed festivals and processions as propaganda for the cause. Then, when Napoleon came to power, he became the official recorder of the Napoleonic epic. He was, in addition, a magnificent portrait painter (*Madame Récamier*, 1800), and although he was criticized for his rigid adherence to neo-classical theory in his later years, he dictated standards of academic teaching in France for a generation.

But neo-classicism was short-lived as a school, and for the most part it soon degenerated into mediocre pastiches of antiquity. There were two exceptions, both students of David: Baron Antoine Gros (1771–1835), a painter of battle scenes glorifying Napoleon, and Jean-Auguste-Dominique Ingres (1780–1867), who clearly wanted to break from his teacher. Ingres was both the last great neo-classicist and an experimenter. He distorted nature for dramatic effect, used sensuous color schemes, and frequently chose themes that were more exotic than classical, but, in the tradition of Poussin, his draftsmanship was fastidious, his work the epitome of cool, finished clarity. Ingres was a master of portraiture, attaining an astounding unity of precise observation and psychological perception. He stood on the road between neo-classicism and the movement that followed, Romanticism.

Romanticism had its precursors in the landscape painter Hubert Robert (1733–1808) and the marine painter Claude-Joseph Vernet (1714–89). There were also David's "opponent," Pierre-Paul Prud'hon (1758–1823), who interpreted reality more than reproducing it, and Théodore Géricault (1791–1824), who explored the extremes of human sentiment and experience.

But one man soon came to embody all that was Romanticism in France. Eugène Delacroix (1798–1863) was the Romantic temperament itself; he sought liberty, change, and emotions for their own sake. He visited North Africa and thereafter frequently chose exotic subjects; he filled his work with movement and excitement. He was at the same time the last great decorative painter in the French style (he painted the library of the Palais-Bourbon and the ceiling of the Galerie d'Apollon in the *Louvre,* among other projects) and the man who liberated draftsmanship, composition, and, above all, color, from neo-classical restraint. His influence on the Impressionists, the post-Impressionists, and even on the early Modernist painters who used color to express emotion was substantial.

Meanwhile, other painters worked as well. Honoré Daumier (1808–79), the caricaturist and social satirist, often has been compared to Rembrandt because of the boldness of his acute observation (*Chess Players,* 1863). Théodore Chassériau (1819–56) was renowned for his paintings of Arab subjects; Georges Michel (1763–1843) painted simple landscapes in the environs of Paris. The Barbizon School, an informal group of landscape painters active from roughly the 1830s to the 1870s, was at work in the town of Barbizon, near the Fontainebleau forest, continuing a study of the effects of light on landscape that had begun in the 17th century. Led by Théodore Rousseau (1812–67) and including such painters as Jules Dupré (1812–89) and Charles-François Daubigny (1817–78), they painted sunrises and sunsets that at times verged on the sentimental, but at their best the Barbizon painters showed a perception of natural phenomena that linked them to the later Impressionists.

Both Camille Corot (1796–1875) and Jean-François Millet (1814–75) painted with the Barbizon group, but they evolved in different directions. Corot's early works were strikingly simple and direct, even though he is best known for his Arcadian landscapes — Italian and French countrysides bathed in silvery light and populated with dancing nymphs and shepherds. Millet concentrated on the real people who inhabited the landscapes, producing large-scale figure paintings of peasants that elevated their lives and work to almost spiritual levels (*The Sower,* 1848). While his subject matter again recalled the Le Nains, his treatment marked the transition from Romanticism to Realism.

Realism in France had a standard bearer in Gustave Courbet (1819–77), an admirer of Millet and a professed socialist (he eventually was exiled). Several of his works had already either been banned from the Salon (which in this period was opened to all, not just Academy artists, although the Academy approved the exhibitions) or had scandalized public and critics alike. Then, having been refused admission to the *Paris World Exhibition of 1855,* Courbet held his own "anti-establishment" exhibition, posting at the entrance just one word: "Realism." According to Courbet, art should reflect the customs, ideas, and appearances of its time as perceived by the artist, but his honest portrayal of these elements was not without controversy. Unlike Millet, he did not elevate nature with dignified peasants, and because of both his naturalistic style and his subject matter — everything from scenes of daily life, nudes, and landscapes to a peasant funeral and drunken priests — Courbet's works were at times accused of the most terrible offense: ugliness.

In breaking with what was considered appropriate subject matter, Courbet flouted academic convention, and this was crucial. It led to the work of perhaps the most important figure of the 19th century, Edouard Manet (1832–83). In 1863, Manet's *Luncheon on the Grass* was rejected by the jury of the official Salon and even shocked the audience at the Salon des Refusés, a special show organized to display the works of the by now numerous painters who had incurred Academy disfavor. The painting had an "outrageous" subject, a nude (the artist's model and mistress) sitting with two fully clothed gentlemen while another woman prepared to dip into a shallow pool in the background. That Manet had borrowed the subject from 16th-century Italian masters was lost in the general outcry, which seemed more moral than aesthetic in motivation.

Yet Manet indeed was making an aesthetic statement. The surprising juxtaposition of nude and clothed figures in a landscape — unbelievable subject matter, devoid of any historical or allegorical significance — was his way of declaring his independence from the requirement that a painting have literal, storytelling content. He chose to combine or select any elements for the sake of artistic unity and made color balance and composition the prime pictorial concerns. Emotional and symbolic content is eliminated; technique is emphasized. In Manet's paintings there is no illusion of space, no modeling to create depth. The painting is no longer a "window on the world" but a two-dimensional surface that is given significant form by strictly visual elements. This has been called "pure painting" or "art for art's sake," and it became of fundamental importance to painting in the 20th century.

Manet was a pivotal figure in the course of French painting, the point of departure for the technical and stylistic development of the next half century, when one school of art would become the most celebrated, the most easily accessible, the most coveted internationally, and perhaps the most universally appreciated of any in the history of painting: Impressionism. The Impressionists included Claude Monet (1840–1926), Alfred Sisley (1839–99), Camille Pissarro (1830–1903), Pierre-Auguste Renoir (1841–1919), and others who, after their rejection by the Salon of 1873, organized an independent exhibition in 1874, the first of eight Impressionist exhibitions during the 1870s and 1880s. Direct descendants of the Barbizon painters and their *plein air* studies, the Impressionists also were primarily concerned with landscapes, French landscapes. Of them, Monet was the Impressionist par excellence. It was his painting of 1872, *Impression — Sunrise,* that had given the group its name, and it was his focus on light — its effects on objects and colors as the essence of the painting — that defined the group. He and the other Impressionists translated this sensation of light and color to their canvases in freely applied brushstrokes.

Monet and Renoir are the most famous of this group today, yet they did not follow the same path. Monet sought to carry naturalism to its optical ultimate, to portray the constant changes of the landscape bathed in constantly changing light. Form dissolves into shimmering color; objects seem weightless (as in his series pictures, *Poplars, Haystacks, Rouen Cathedral,* and *Water-Lilies*). Renoir began as an Impressionist, but his fascination with chic, gay society and his sheer delight in the warmth and sensuality of the female figure refused to be limited by the Impressionists' stricter study of the visual effects of light. He is best known for his luminous, porcelain-like portraits of women — shopgirls, laundresses, upper class women and children. He revived the spirit of Boucher and Fragonard, and, in a mix of realism and idealism, he blended Impressionistic color and spontaneity with a recollection of the 18th century.

Another internationally recognized painter also took part in the first Impressionist exhibition but never fully adapted to the Impressionist style. Edgar Degas (1834–1917) adhered more closely than the Impressionists to the 19th-century tradition of figure painting, draftsmanship, and strong composition. Like Manet, Degas was a member of the most social and cultivated Parisian circles. For him, no sunlit landscapes; his interest was less in light than in gesture, and his "landscapes" were of city life, theater, the ballet, cafés, and concert halls. A detached and aloof observer of women, Degas did not portray the "feminine charm" of voluptuous, idealized women as Renoir did; his women are performers, and their beauty is expressive and active.

By the mid-1880s, Impressionism was no longer new. If not unanimously accepted, it certainly was well established, and an assortment of styles grouped under the general heading of post-Impressionism began to emerge. Henri de Toulouse-Lautrec (1864–1901) was indebted to the innovations of the Impressionists, although his main source of inspiration was Degas. Lautrec, too, painted dancers, but of a different sort: cabaret dancers. A member of an ancient noble family, he arrived in Paris in 1881 and began painting posters spotlighting the dancers of the Moulin Rouge. Though his career was relatively brief, Lautrec produced more than 360 lithographs, pastels, and highly animated line drawings of subjects in dance halls, cafés, circuses, and brothels, testimonials to the life he led around his Montmartre studio.

Paul Cézanne (1839–1906), Georges Seurat (1859–91), Paul Gauguin (1848–1903), and Vincent Van Gogh (1853–90) all had their roots in the Impressionist style, yet they all felt the need to go beyond the mere study of light and color and its momentary effects. Cézanne and Seurat explored the architectonic elements of form and color, striving to attain harmony and balance in their compositions. Seurat sought a more scientific method with which to reproduce the special quality of light in nature, and by studying contemporary theories of color and vision and applying them to his work methodically, he arrived at Divisionism, a technique using pigments of pure color systematically applied to the canvas like a mosaic, to be blended by the eye of the viewer and fused by the optical response alone. The technique, also known as Pointillism, distinguished the neo-Impressionists, as Seurat and his followers — including Paul Signac (1863–1935) — were known. Seurat's greatest work, *Sunday Afternoon on the Island of La Grande Jatte* (1886), while Impressionistic in color, is a carefully designed composition of geometrically divided space, and it had a major impact on avant-garde movements in Europe at the end of the century. Nonetheless, it was Cézanne who was the truly revolutionary figure, certainly one of the most important painters of the century.

Cézanne had been one of the original artists at the Impressionist exhibition of 1874, but he was unable to reconcile the transitory quality and lack of clarity of the Impressionist images with his admiration for the old masters, especially Poussin. He felt they had achieved a balance, harmony, and monumentality in their work that had yet to be surpassed, even though their traditional approach now was seen as academic, not the result of direct observation, and thus unfaithful to nature. Cézanne wanted to "make of Impressionism something solid and durable, like the art of the museums," while still respecting the actual appearance of nature. The search for structure and balance led him to simplify forms and to use color to model fundamental shapes. His patches of pigment and parallel and regular brushstrokes explore and define the basic structure of his subjects. If necessary, he was not averse to distortion to enhance their essence. "We must seek the cylinder," he said, "the sphere, and the cone in nature." As a result, his landscapes, while vibrant with color, had a new solidity and strength. This formal discipline and analysis of space and composition became a key source for the 20th-century Cubists.

Gauguin and Van Gogh had different ambitions. For them, nature was only the starting point. They found the extreme objectivity of the Impressionists stifling, and they searched for meaning in subject matter and color. Gauguin wrote that the Impressionists painted what was in front of their eyes, rather than what lay in the "mysterious center of thought." He fostered a Synthetist school of thought based on the use of symbols to convey descriptive or emotive power. Inspired by medieval stained glass and folk art, he sought more primitive sources for his work, and his search for the unspoiled life finally led him to Tahiti, where he settled for the rest of his life. His canvases from the South Seas seemed barbaric, not only in their exotic subjects, but also in their broad areas of brilliant, "unnatural" color, which had nothing of Cézanne's structural modeling. His bold compositions aimed at conveying the simplicity and directness of primitive society; they stood as a powerful rejection of the civilization he had left behind as well as of its art.

The story of Van Gogh's life and the intermittent insanity that caused him to cut off his ear and eventually kill himself is the stuff of legend. He absorbed the lessons of the Impressionists and for a time was Gauguin's painting companion, but he was closest to his brother, Théo, to whom he wrote that he painted to make life "bearable . . . Really, we can speak only through our paintings." Most of the paintings for which he is remembered were done during a period of only 3 years in the South of France. Van Gogh simplified forms, heightened color, applied pigment thickly in vigorous strokes, and often resorted to distortion to express his feelings. The swirling *Starry Night* (1889), with its startling, violent, blazing blue and yellow bands of color, is a prime example; it was painted in an asylum a year before his death. Another example is his dramatic *Portrait of Dr. Gauchet,* painted only months before the artist took his own life. (It is the consummate irony that this canvas was sold several years ago for $82.5 million — the highest price ever paid for a painting — as Van Gogh earned not one centime from his work during his lifetime.) His paintings display a passion and intensity that reflect his torment and go well beyond a naturalistic representation of reality.

While Van Gogh's work influenced the later Fauves in France and the German Expressionists, Gauguin's already had given rise, in the 1890s, to a series of artistic currents referred to as Symbolism. Gustave Moreau (1826–98) and Odilon Redon (1840–1916), both rooted in the Romantic tradition, made use of the works of literary Symbolists (Baudelaire, Mallarmé) to paint often strange, dreamlike visions. Followers of Gauguin — Paul Sérusier (1864–1927), Maurice Denis (1870–1943), Pierre Bonnard (1867–1947), and Edouard Vuillard (1868–1940) — merged in the Nabi group (from the Hebrew word for "prophet"). The latter two often are called Intimists because they later applied Impressionist technique to the painting of domestic interiors rather than landscapes. Their work is abstract and decorative, almost Oriental in feeling, emphasizing the flat painting surface, brushwork, and radiant color. Also working at this time was Henri Rousseau (1844–1910), a folk artist of genius whose magical paintings of enchanted forests and animals achieve the directness and innocence that Gauguin left France to pursue.

THE TWENTIETH CENTURY

The first of the avant-garde "isms" to develop in the 20th century was Fauvism, which carried on the legacy of both Van Gogh and Gauguin. It took its name — *fauves* means "wild beasts" — from critical reaction to the distorted forms and the exuberant, violent colors, used for their expressive qualities, in the paintings exhibited by a group of artists in 1905. Henri Matisse (1869–1954), the foremost of the Fauves, was influenced by North African and Near Eastern art, and their effect can be seen in his transformation of reality into large surfaces of pure color and brilliantly colored decorative patterns. Maurice Vlaminck (1876–1958) and André Derain (1880–1954) were also Fauves, though the group was loosely constituted otherwise. Raoul Dufy (1877–1953) was influenced by them; Georges Rouault (1871–1958), who had exhibited with the group initially, and Georges Braque (1882–1963), who had shown with it subsequently, both went their own ways. By the end of the decade, the group no longer existed, but it had during its brief life announced the definitive end of the 19th-century concept of realism.

And in the meantime another movement, much more cerebral, was making its appearance on the Parisian art scene: Cubism. It was heralded in 1907 by a startling Salon entry, *Les Demoiselles d'Avignon,* by Pablo Picasso (1881–1973). Picasso's inspiration was Cézanne rather than the post-Impressionist strains that were tending to the dissolution of nature into color and light. Cézanne's analysis of space and composition, his emphasis on structure, concurred with Picasso's interest in primitive art and its simplification of form, becoming, together, the source of his abstraction. He began dissecting objects to reveal several views of them simultaneously, fragments of the three-dimensional subject appearing in various shallow, or flat, planes in the two-dimensional picture.

Picasso's collaborator in this novel approach to the problem of depth versus surface was Braque, who simultaneously began emphasizing flat planes, rigid geometric forms, and subdued colors. Taken together, their work constitutes the first, or analytical, phase of Cubism, which gave way, after 1912, to a synthetic phase, in the development of which Juan Gris (1887–1927) played a role. This later phase, characterized by a brighter palette and by the use of collage (which Braque had invented by the inclusion of typographical letters in his pictures), continued into World War I. Collage Cubism, by using cut and pasted scraps of recognizable material such as newspaper, finally totally eliminated the illusion of space and was a revolutionary development in the history of painting. The Cubists were the most significant of all the early-20th-century art movements. Their point of departure — to show an object not as it was, but in its totality as the mind's eye perceived it — both suggested and complemented the abstract movements begun by artists outside France. Cubism was the seminal moment in the evolution of modern abstract and nonobjective art.

Inevitably their experiments were reinterpreted by other artists. Robert Delaunay (1855–1941) led the Orphist group, combining the Cubists' faceting of the object with the Fauvists' color concerns and the Italian Futurists' emphasis on frenetic modern rhythms. Later, Delaunay became clearly abstract. Fernand Léger (1881–1955), meanwhile, used large humanized machine forms, painted with brilliant metallic primary colors, to "mechanize" his interpretations of pre- and postwar Europe. He, in turn, influenced still another group, the Purists, who criticized Cubism as overly decorative and celebrated the machine as a form devoid of unnecessary detail. Amédée Ozenfant (1886–1966) and Le Corbusier (Charles Edouard Jeanneret; 1887–1965) formulated Purism, which, more than in painting, was of consequence in the field of architecture.

Before the 19th century was over, Paris had become the center of the art world, and even before World War I there was a large group of expatriate painters living and working in the French capital. Not only Picasso and Gris, but Amedeo Modigliani (1884–1920) and Chaim Soutine (1894–1943) were here. Marc Chagall (1887–1985), who combined a Cubist influence with personal fantasy, came before the war and returned after it. The School of Paris — those artists based in the city between the two world wars — was thus a fully international company. And during the 1920s, it produced another art movement of spectacular importance: Surrealism.

Surrealism grew out of and was tied closely to Dada, a nihilistic "anti-art" movement that mocked the solemnity of aesthetic doctrines. Dadaism's major French exponents were Marcel Duchamp (1887–1968) and Francis Picabia (1879–1953). While the origin of its name — *dada* means "hobbyhorse" in French — is controversial, it is thought to have been chosen at random, as though to underscore the movement's preoccupation with absurdity and chance. Dada died quickly, but its concerns became part of the premise of Surrealism, which further explored the possibilities of chance, the depth of the unconscious as revealed by Freud, and the Symbolism of painters such as Redon. All came together in the Surrealists' dedication to an expression of thought, or of the imagination, free of the conscious control of reason and free of any aesthetic convention or moral constraint.

Surrealists painting in Paris included Max Ernst (1891–1976), Jean Arp (1887–1966), Yves Tanguy (1900–55), Salvador Dalí (1904–1989), André Masson (1896–1987), Joan Miró (1893–1983), and Roberto Matta (b. 1911). Some, such as Tanguy and Dalí, depicted dream images, distortions of familiar objects, hallucinatory "versions" of reality. Ernst, too, worked in this vein and also invented the technique of *frottage* (in a word, rubbings). Others, such as Miró and Masson, moved toward a personal set of symbols, a kind of calligraphy that was the pictorial response to the "automatic writing" of the literary Surrealists André Breton and Louis Aragon. But even though their work developed in more than one direction, the impact of the Surrealist movement was great. Picasso's *Guernica* (1937) would certainly not have taken the same form without it, and Jackson Pollock's Abstract Expressionism owed its origins to Surrealist automatic writing.

Surrealism marked a decisive moment in the history of French painting. It was the last major international art movement to originate and be centered in Paris. During World War II, Paris was occupied by the Nazis, and many of the leading Surrealists fled to the United States, shifting the center of their activity to New York. Nevertheless, while the war put an end to certain aspects of Parisian artistic life, it was not the end of French painting.

In France, Maurice Estève (b. 1904), Edouard Pignon (b. 1905), and Jean Bazaine (b. 1904) carried on in the mostly nonfigurative style of the School of Paris. A diluted version of American Abstract Expressionism, *art informel,* also grew up, exemplified by Georges Mathieu (b. 1921) and Pierre Soulages (b. 1919). Nicolas de Staël (1914–55) produced works that read either as a representation of reality or as a series of abstract forms and colors. Other painters, such as Balthus (Balthasar Klossowski de Rola; b. 1908) and Alberto Giacometti (1901–66), returned to the figurative tradition. The former created realistic paintings rich in erotic evocations. Giacometti's figures have an elongated, gnawed appearance, as if the images were about to disappear in space. Jean Dubuffet (1901–85), recognized as a master artist with roots in the Dada-Surrealist tradition, became known for his *art brut.* The work of the mentally insane and children were among his sources. Even his working materials, such as sand mixed with paint, were unconventional.

No one cohesive style has emerged in contemporary France. There have been Op and Pop movements. New Realism was practiced by Arman (b. 1928) and especially by the wildly eccentric Yves Klein (1928–62), who used women for paintbrushes and created huge monochromatic blue and gold canvases, enigmatic in their simplicity. Kinetic art was explored by Victor Vasarely (b. 1908), whose geometric optical forms largely erase the boundary between painting and sculpture. And no one movement is any longer exclusively French.

Communication among capitals, among artists through travel, exhibitions, and the media, has to a large extent decentralized art styles in the postwar period; there are no clear-cut textbook divisions, and Paris no longer is the uncontested center of organized art movements. Still, few countries can rival France in the history of painting. And the largest population of artists in Europe still is found in one single shining city: Paris.

Architecture

 The architecture of France — as much as the landscape, the food, and the wine — is to be seen and savored. More than 2,000 years of history remain very much alive here, and almost every building style found in the Western world is present in some form. The French architectural panorama includes the religious — churches, monasteries, and abbeys; military — castles built during the Middle Ages and fortifications such as those of the Marquis de Vauban, a 17th-century military engineer; domestic — châteaux, manor houses, and palaces; and commercial — coaching inns, water mills, town halls, and so on. Some of these buildings were constructed over a period of time — sometimes several centuries — and may reflect several different architectural styles; they also may have been adapted to new tastes and needs over time. The transition from one style to another never is clear-cut, and regional variations of any given style persist.

Most cities, even those with a restored old section, contain this mixture of architecture. Although many people are shocked today at the proximity of the brazenly modern *Centre Georges Pompidou* (often referred to simply as "the Beaubourg") to beautiful old Parisian houses, it actually is quite common throughout France to find ornate 19th-century structures next to simple 16th-century dwellings. Such contrasts are inevitable, and sometimes can be appealing. Unfortunately, I.M. Pei's futuristic glass pyramids, which are set smack in the center of the historic museum's courtyard and serve as the new entrance to the *Louvre,* is not a case in point and is the subject of heated controversy.

The caves of La Madeleine, close to Sarlat in the Dordogne region, contain three different architectural layers, one on top of the other: the first, 10,000 years old, from the Magdalenian (or upper paleolithic) period; the second, a troglodyte village, where primitive cave dwellers lived; and finally, the ruins of a feudal castle. In effect, the caves provide an abbreviated account of history. (The Dordogne, it should be noted, is famous for its prehistoric sites — close to 200 have been discovered — such as Celtic tombstones and graves, from which ornamental collars, bracelets, and helmets have been extracted.)

The Romans, who appeared in France during the 1st century BC, also left striking reminders of their stay. Designers of roads, aqueducts, amphitheaters, and other public places, they extended their civilization to every land they conquered. Nîmes retains some especially outstanding Roman vestiges: the Pont du Gard aqueduct (19 BC); the Maison Carrée, or Square House (1 BC); and the amphitheater (AD 50). The 3rd century marked the beginning of the end of the Roman Empire, and during the next 600 years continual fighting and turmoil reaped much more destruction than construction; the creation of the feudal system in the 9th and 10th centuries brought a semblance of order once again. Although very little remains today from this turbulent time, some interesting monuments and graves from the Merovingian and Carolingian periods (the 6th through the 9th centuries) can be found, often deeply hidden in the crypts of early churches, as in St. Peter's in Vienne and the tomb of St. Martin in Tours.

From the mid-11th to the mid-12th century, Romanesque architecture thrived in France. It derived its inspiration from Rome, not only the source of style for the Holy Roman Empire, but also the seat of papal authority, and it was affected as well by Byzantine and Islamic influences (mosaics and pointed arches, for example). In France, Romanesque buildings were characterized by solidity and massive size, heavy walls, barrel vaults, rounded arches, and flattened columns, or pilasters; structures were imposing and the space within them clearly defined. This was an age of great economic prosperity closely tied to technological development and a strong religious fervor, as seen in the number of Romanesque churches remaining today. Churches, abbeys, and castles had sparse decoration. Outstanding examples of existing Romanesque architecture include St. Front Cathedral in Périgueux in the Dordogne, Autin Cathedral in Burgundy, and the château of La Cité in Carcassonne.

The Gothic period in France began in the middle of the 12th century and lasted until the Renaissance, at the end of the 15th century. It was characterized by the pointed arch, flying buttresses (which reinforced the walls and enabled great stained glass windows to be set in them), rose windows (large, round, stained glass windows that resemble an open rose) over the center portal of the west front of the church or at one or both transept ends, ribbed vaulting, and often heavily decorated portals. This style gave the impression of lightness and soaring spaces.

Early, primitive Gothic architecture in the late 12th and the 13th centuries gave way to a style known as Rayonnant in the 14th century, which moved from solid walls to a skeletal masonry frame interspersed with stained glass unmatched today for its beauty and craftsmanship; Ste-Chapelle in Paris, with walls seemingly made entirely of glass, is the most striking example of this. Late, Flamboyant Gothic architecture, which dominated the 15th century, was ornamented more elaborately. Over 3 centuries the Gothic designs became increasingly more vertical, especially in comparison to the Romanesque box shape; religious sculpture became more realistic, and flowers and plants began to serve as subject matter for reliefs. Notre-Dame of Paris, built between 1163 and 1330, is one of the finest examples of Gothic architecture; others include the cathedrals of Chartres and Strasbourg and the house of Jacques Coeur in Bourges.

The Renaissance period flourished in France in the 16th and 17th centuries, heralding a return to classic (Greek and Roman) architecture. The Roman arch, vault, dome, and the Corinthian column reappeared; stairs were straight; and buildings, which were harmonious and symmetrical with traditional proportions, often had several stories, an upper floor mirroring the ones below it. Renaissance buildings focused inward, with their center — usually under the dome — as their focal point. Francis I, a prolific builder who was impressed with the art and architecture of Italy, encouraged its classical form in his own country; he built Chambord and Fontainebleau as well as a wing of the lovely château at Blois. The château at Chenonceaux also was constructed during this period, as were other magnificent estates along the Loire, Seine, and Marne rivers.

The baroque style was popular in France during the 17th and 18th centuries; though still classical in form, it differed from the Renaissance in that its structures expanded outward instead of inward. Massive, elegant, and theatrical, they employed opulent, sculptured decoration and curving stairs. During this period, grand planning that included the integration of buildings and landscapes became very important, as witnessed by the work of André Lenôtre, a third-generation landscape architect, in the Tuileries Gardens and the gardens of Versailles.

François Mansart built the Château Maisons, now known as Maisons-Lafitte, near Paris; the gardens and park that surrounded the château no longer exist, but the interior remains almost the same as when it was built in the mid-1600s. It was Mansart who designed and popularized the sloping roof that became known as the mansard roof. Other striking examples of the French baroque style include the Place des Vosges, the Colonnade (east front) of the *Louvre,* and the Luxembourg Palace in Paris as well as many of the houses in the old section of Bordeaux. The use of double columns to line the fronts of buildings was seen for the first time during this period; prominent examples include the palace of Versailles and the *Louvre.*

By the end of the 18th century, rococo — a style similar to baroque but lighter in character and execution — had become popular in French architecture, especially in and around Paris. The geometrical forms used in the baroque style became more complex in rococo; buildings were asymmetrical; naves of churches were longer; arches displayed abundant ornamentation; and white interiors with gold gilding were popular. A rococo building appears more sculpture than structure, like a gigantic wedding cake. Shells, scrolls, flowers, and plants monopolize motifs; in fact, the term most likely comes from the French *roc* and *coquille,* "rock" and "shell." At this time, people demanded comfort above showiness, and rococo designs emphasized intimacy rather than grandeur, with rooms that, while still opulent, were also playful. The Petit Trianon at Versailles, built as a retreat from formal palace life for Mme. du Barry and later enjoyed by Marie-Antoinette — exemplifies the rococo style.

The curtain fell on this exuberant period of almost 300 years of power, prestige, and wealth — all reflected in 16th-, 17th-, and 18th-century French architecture — with the beginning of the French Revolution in 1789.

Neo-classicism was highly espoused by the prestigious Ecole des Beaux-Arts (School of Fine Arts) in Paris in the 19th century. Though classical in design, it was looser and more natural in execution. (*Neo* means "in the style of" an earlier period, though usually employing different materials and technology.) Neo-classical buildings often were constructed in the shape of an H or a U, with wings that opened out to their environments rather than closing off from it and directing the focus inward, as was common during the Renaissance. Examples of this style include the Madeleine (Church of St. Mary Magdalen) and the Arc de Triomphe in Paris.

The Industrial Revolution brought inevitable changes after 1830. Architects and engineers, working with iron — and soon steel and reinforced concrete — conceived new designs for bridges, train stations, and other public spaces and structures. Arches and columns of metal became commonplace, and buildings stretched to greater heights; the combination of glass and metal created walls and roofs that were seemingly transparent. A striking symbol of this period is the Eiffel Tower, built for the *Paris Exhibition of 1889*.

Art Nouveau emerged briefly in the late 19th and early 20th centuries. Important because it fostered a complete break with tradition and paved the way for new thinking about architecture, it was characterized by highly decorative, elongated ornamentation — long, sinuous, intertwining curves — based on vegetable images. Façades often were asymmetrical, with a lot of metalwork and glasswork in free-flowing, three-dimensional designs. Hector Guimard's wrought-iron entrances to the Paris métro are outstanding reminders of this brief period in French architectural history.

Modernism followed closely on the heels of Art Nouveau during the early 20th century; it rejected previous styles and emphasized simplicity and purity of line. The destruction during the two world wars forced massive reconstruction, and the growing need for housing led to innovations in technology and architecture, and to more sophisticated and rational structures to fit emerging lifestyles. Le Corbusier, a creative renegade who became the father of modern French architecture, designed *unités d'habitation* ("housing units") in accordance with a communal vision of society. His Unité d'Habitation in Marseilles incorporates shops, services (including a gymnasium, swimming pool, and nursery), a small hotel, and 2-level apartments for 1,600 residents. His Villa Savoye, in Poissy, has a glass-enclosed living area on the ground floor, continuing windows around the second, and a rooftop garden and solarium. In the words of the architect, who died in 1965, these various creations were *machines à habiter* ("machines to live in"), a functionalist's vision of life and a response to the political anarchy that had prevailed for the past century. Le Corbusier also built the concrete Notre-Dame du Haut pilgrimage chapel at Ronchamp, modeled on a nun's pointed headdress, with an outdoor pulpit and altar, a small indoor chapel, irregular, wedge-shape stained glass windows, and a jaunty roof slightly raised to permit a strip of daylight to enter.

French architecture gradually has developed an international style during the 20th century, and numerous French architects have succeeded in building interesting, sometimes controversial structures. Among them: Emile Aillaud, who designed the headquarters of the Communist party in Paris; Paul Chemetov and Henri Cireani, whose reinforced-concrete housing projects (in Illkirsch, in the Bas-Rhin; in the St-Denis suburb of Paris; and in nearby Marne-La-Vallée) are livable and visually appealing; and François Rodier, who uses traditional brick in very modern ways in northern France. The revival of interest in rehabilitating France's city centers has encouraged contemporary French architects to approach urban housing with renewed interest, including restoring existing structures, be they old factories or historic landmarks. The wealth of architectural riches in this one country is enormous. French architecture, whether it attracts, inspires, or intimidates, constantly makes its presence felt. The traveler who appreciates it is bound to come away with a fuller sense of the country, its history, its joie de vivre.

THE CITIES

AIX-EN-PROVENCE

Paris may be a typical American's dream of the best place to live in France, but Parisians frequently dream of living in Aix-en-Provence. Aix is the provincial city that most French admire, according to recent polls, and the reasons are entirely understandable. There's the matter of size, for one thing. With 130,000 residents and a significant university population, the city is large — and sophisticated — enough to have its share of good restaurants, smart shops, art galleries, serious libraries and bookstores, cafés and nightclubs, theater and music, and other urban amenities. Yet it's still small enough that almost everything is within easy walking distance, little of interest is ever more than 20 minutes away, and — miraculous in this age of urban sprawl — the countryside starts at the end of the bus lines (except if you're headed toward Marseilles).

Aix often *feels* small, too. Perhaps because of its Mediterranean character, daily life still proceeds at a comparatively slow, human pace, although this is changing. And despite the construction accompanying its recent rapid growth, most of its buildings still have comfortable proportions that are easily dwarfed by the limestone massif — the Mont-Ste-Victoire — that the talent of native son Paul Cézanne transformed into the most famous monument of the nearby landscape. Sadly, however, almost all of the lush pine trees on the lower slopes of Ste-Victoire have burned during forest fires in the last several years. Ste-Victoire gets its name from a battle that was fought at the bottom of the mountain by Marius, the popular Roman general who defeated the invading Teutonic tribes, killing more than 100,000 Teutons and taking as many prisoners in the process. To this day, many sons of the region still are named Marius.

Even the city's location strikes the perfect balance. It's close to the Mediterranean beaches, but aloof from the noise and the crowds. It's near the hills and valleys of rustic Provence but far enough away to escape the torpor of the backcountry. Once the capital of Provence, it's off the main rail lines today, though still a crossroads. But people don't only pass *through* Aix; they come *to* Aix. And starting in 1994, it will be only a 3-hour trip from Paris on the *TGV*.

Ever since Roman times, people have come for Aix's warm thermal springs, which were well known to the ancient world. Before the arrival of the Romans, the area had been occupied for centuries by a Celto-Ligurian tribe whose capital, Entremont, was on a plateau north of the present Aix and whose faith in the local water extended to a belief that it assured fertility. The Roman consul Caius Sextius destroyed Entremont in 123 BC and the following year established a fortified camp near the springs, calling it Aquae Sextius (Waters of Sextius). The boulevards circling Aix today (its modern name is a contraction of the Latin name) follow the line of the old ramparts, and a huge 18th-century spa, including the recently renovated *Hôtel des Thermes,* stands on the Cours Sextius, near the site of the original Roman baths. Aix's thermal springs continue to be noted for their purity and nearly sodium-free quality, good for circulatory ailments, and people continue to come to drink the water, immerse themselves in it, and otherwise submit to the 3-week "cure."

Others come during the summer for the *International Festival of Lyric Art and Music.* One of Europe's better-known music festivals and possibly France's best, it features first-rate singers, instrumentalists, and ensembles in concerts and fully staged operas in historic settings around town. Hotels are booked months in advance, the tempo of the Provençal lifestyle accelerates in anticipation, and for the 3 weeks of the festival, the city is filled with action.

Aix's cultural traditions predate its festival by some 800 years. In the 12th century, the Counts of Provence made the town their capital, and their court soon became known for its love of music and poetry. This was the age of the troubadors, the poet-musicians who traveled from court to court singing their ballads in the Provençal tongue and spreading ideals of chivalry and romantic love throughout Europe. The town's most civilized era, however, was the 15th century. In 1409, both the university and "Good King René" (1409–80) were born. Called "the last of the troubadors," René held the title of Count of Provence among others (he was also Duke of Anjou and titular King of Naples) and proved to be in all respects a remarkable example of the culture of his time. He was a patron of the arts as well as a poet, musician, and painter himself; he was a student of classical languages, mathematics, and law, yet at the same time an unaffected man of the people who organized popular festivals, tilled the soil, and introduced the muscatel grape to the region. The people were not happy, however, when René levied heavy taxes and printed worthless money to finance his cultural projects.

Provence was added to the kingdom of France a few years after the death of René, though Aix remained important as the seat of the provincial *parlement,* or court of justice, from 1501 to 1790. It flourished during the 17th and 18th centuries in particular, when wealthy and noble magistrates, church officials, and prosperous merchants built many of the elegant *hôtels,* or townhouses, that give the city its characteristic look today. The period also is remembered in Aix's main thoroughfare, named for Count Mirabeau, a prominent resident of the latter part of the 18th century. Before achieving the eminence that brought him immortality in the Cours Mirabeau, the count had achieved some notoriety by tricking a rich heiress of Aix into marriage (as well as many other women into his bedroom) and then running up debts large enough to bring about his imprisonment. Even jail did not teach him a lesson, however, and he continued to pursue women for their money and be sent back to prison for his philanderings. This made him very popular with the masses (if not with his fellow nobles), and when Louis XVI summoned the States-General of 1789 — a meeting that proved to be the first step toward ending the monarchy — Mirabeau was easily elected to represent the third estate (nobility is the first and clergy the second) for Aix-en-Provence. He went on to become the leading statesman of the first years of the French Revolution. A statue of Mirabeau is in St-Cannat, about 20 miles (32 km) north of Aix;

true to life, the skin on the statue is pockmarked, the result of Mirabeau's bout with smallpox.

The Revolution swept away the *ancien régime* and the provincial *parlements* along with it. As Marseilles grew during the 19th century, Aix went into a period of decline from which it began to rise only in the mid-20th century, but with a vengeance. Its recent growth has been astronomical, in fact (the population in 1950 was a mere 50,000, less than half of what it is today), and one reason Aix thrives again — besides its music festival and its thermal springs — is successful light industry: clothing and, notably, candy. Many of the remarkably sweet Provençal almonds go into *calissons d'Aix,* oval-shaped candies that are protected and controlled, like fine wines, as an *appellation d'origine* item. This delicious trademark, a mixture of almonds and melon preserves, has a history to equal its status. In the 17th century, *calissons* were blessed by the bishop and distributed to the faithful in an annual ceremony commemorating the end of the plague of 1630. Only in the mid-19th century, however, did the making of them become an actual industry, and now the rich candies are exported worldwide.

Critics say that after the music festival, Aix goes back to being a sleepy university town. They complain that there's more theater in nearby Avignon, more excitement in even closer Marseilles. But visitors come even when there's no festival, gravitating to the Cours Mirabeau, again the perfect balance. It has something of the old grandeur of the Champs-Elysées, a bit of the chic of the Boulevard St-Germain in the late 1940s, and a touch of the boisterousness of the Boulevard St-Michel in the 1960s — but with its arch of plane trees, it's almost intimate, especially since it can be walked in just a few minutes. It is a meeting place, as well as a place to be seen. Settling in at a sidewalk café, visitors and natives alike linger over a *pastis* or a cool beer — or an ice cream sundae. (Coffee machines tend to be shut off in midafternoon to encourage customers to order more expensive drinks.) Eventually they may stroll over to one of the nearby outdoor markets to breathe the distinctive Provençal scents of rosemary, thyme, and basil and to enjoy the visual barrage of pulpy red tomatoes, dark green *courgettes* (zucchini), luscious melons, bins of variously colored and flavored olives, and tables strewn with garlic tresses and other produce.

Natives and long-term residents complain that these scenes are becoming more and more scarce as the city grows and fast-food establishments mar the landscape along the Cours Mirabeau. They wistfully recall when Aix was just a big village and the major roads that lead out of it today were truly country lanes. Those living in Petit Rocquefavour, at the edge of town, remember hearing the tinkle of sheep bells at night, as flocks were led around the town to their summer pasture in the Alps. Today, they are more likely to hear the blare of traffic as exasperated drivers search in vain for a parking place, or the sound of an automobile alarm going off as someone tries to break into a car.

Even so, when one needs a refuge from modern sounds and pressures, there's always the silence of the charming cloister of the Cathédrale St-Sauveur or the immense cathedral itself. And when one becomes weary after roaming through the inviting maze of Old Aix's pedestrian zones, benches seem to beckon everywhere. And you still can turn down almost any street — on foot — to find one of the city's ever-present fountains, whose sounds quickly soothe the nerves. Massive or tiny, traditional or original, they are pretty places to sit, read, or meet people, and they're among Aix's most endearing features. Along with the festival, the thermal cure, and the diet-smashing *calissons,* they make clear what matters most to this delightful city, which, despite staggering growth, rarely puts progress ahead of *douceur de vivre.*

AIX AT-A-GLANCE

SEEING THE CITY: The town itself is so flat and its skyline, happily, so low, that a panoramic view is hard to find. Outside the city, the best vista is from the excavations of the pre-Roman settlement on the Plateau d'Entremont, 2 miles (3 km) miles north of Aix by the road to Puyricard (open from 9 AM to noon and 2 to 5 PM daily except Tuesdays; a bus leaves every half hour, or every hour on Sundays, from the *Bar Corona,* Bd. de la République). You'll have a striking view of the Montagne Ste-Victoire, too, which dominates Aix to the east. To get to the villages of Le Tholonet or Vauvenargues at the bottom of Ste-Victoire, take a bus from Gare Routière; they run from 9 AM to 8 PM. Also recommended is the tourist bureau's tour of private homes.

SPECIAL PLACES: Most of the sights in Aix are within the circle of boulevards that follow the outline of the city's ancient walls. North of the Cours Mirabeau — the café-filled main thoroughfare, which cuts across the circle in an east-west direction — is Vieil Aix (Old Aix), a zone of old squares and narrow streets, many of them pedestrian islands. South of the Cours is the newer Quartier Mazarin, a neighborhood of 17th- and 18th-century *hôtels* (town-houses), which looks like a grid on the map; it was planned by Michael Mazarin, an Archbishop of Aix and a brother of Cardinal Mazarin. The whole of the area north and south of the Cours can be walked easily, and you probably will be tempted to explore more of it than is required to visit the specific sites listed below. On the way to Place St-Jean-de-Malte in the Quartier Mazarin, for instance, you may want to detour ever so slightly to see the Fontaine des Quatre-Dauphins, whose four delightful dolphins have graced the pretty square of the same name since 1667. On the other side of the Cours, just off Rue Espariat in Vieil Aix, Place d'Albertas is a cobblestone square with a fountain in the middle and no modern intrusion to mar its 18th-century serenity. A bit farther north, around the corner from the Hôtel de Ville, Place des Cardeurs is a long, open space where people come to sit. It's paved with brick and stone, surrounded by old buildings in varying stages of restoration, and outfitted with plenty of benches. An antiques fair takes place here in summer.

Cours Mirabeau – Four rows of shady plane trees distinguish this lovely wide avenue that's been the focal point of Aix since the 17th century (though it takes its name from a statesman and revolutionary of the 18th century). It is one of France's most appealing boulevards, and it's so short it can be walked in barely 10 minutes. The stately 17th- and 18th-century *hôtels* that line it have become, on one side, mostly banks (note the giant male caryatids holding up a wrought-iron balcony at No. 38, now a university building). On the other side are mostly bookshops, restaurants, and lively cafés. At each end is a 19th-century fountain: a large one topped by three female figures in the center of the circular Place de la Libération (popularly called La Rotonde), where the Cours begins, and a smaller one of Good King René holding a bunch of grapes where it runs into the Hôtel de Poët and ends. Two other fountains are along the way: the 17th-century Fontaine des Neuf-Canons and the Fontaine d'Eau-Chaude, the latter no more than a large moss-covered rock from which warm (well, tepid — and non-potable) water still springs, just as it did for the Romans 2,000 years ago. (The pipes transporting the water have rusted, though, and it no longer tastes as good as it once did.) The cafés are the main attraction of the Cours, however, and each has its own personality. Stake out a sidewalk table at aperitif time and, especially when the university is in session and the weather is warm, more people than Aix possibly could hold seem to pass in review, most on foot, but enough aboard cars and motorbikes to set the roadway buzzing.

VIEIL AIX

Cathédrale St-Sauveur – A curious blend of architectural styles, spanning 15 centuries, makes this massive cathedral an unusual sight. The baptistry, off to the far right (southern) side as you enter, is the oldest part, dating to the 4th and 5th centuries; its eight Roman columns are a stark contrast to the gilt 16th-century Renaissance cupola they support. From right to left, then, the church grows progressively younger. The southernmost aisle, Romanesque, was the nave of a 12th-century church. To its left is a Gothic nave, built from the 13th to the 15th centuries, and to the left of that is a newer, baroque aisle from the 17th century. One of the treasures of the church, the 15th-century *Triptyque du Buisson Ardent* (Triptych of the Burning Bush), is on the wall of the Gothic nave and usually is closed, showing only two panels in grisaille depicting the Virgin and a praying angel, but ask the caretaker to open it and you will see the brilliance of its colors (predominantly red) fairly gleam in the interior dimness. Done by Nicolas Froment, court painter to King René, it shows the Virgin and Child in the center, with the king and his wife, Queen Jeanne, kneeling in the side panels. Upon request, the caretaker also will uncover the 16th-century sculptured wooden doors on the exterior of the Gothic nave, another of the church's treasures. Unfortunately, few of the 16th-century Flemish tapestries of the life of the Virgin, originally woven for Canterbury Cathedral and later owned by St-Sauveur, are likely to be on view. Some were sold centuries ago, while others were stolen just a few years back. Concerts are given here in July. Pl. de l'Université (phone: 42-23-45-65). Information about the concerts also can be obtained at the tourist office (2 Pl. du Général-de-Gaulle; phone: 42-26-02-93).

Cloître St-Sauveur – This delightful small Romanesque (12th-century) cloister is reached through a doorway on the right aisle of the cathedral or from the street. It's a favorite spot of Aix residents, who come to sit and chat or read a newspaper under its arches, which rest on pairs of delicate columns, some plain and some carved, with carved capitals. Pl. des Martyrs-de-la-Résistance.

Musée des Tapisseries – In the former archbishop's palace adjoining the cloister and cathedral, this small, now renovated museum contains some very rare Beauvais tapestries, including a series on the life of Don Quixote dating from the 17th and 18th centuries. A few pieces of furniture from the same period also are on display. The interior courtyard is the focal point of Aix's music festival in July and August, when it turns into an elaborate outdoor opera house. Closed Tuesdays and from September to June, from 12:30 to 2:30 PM. Admission charge. Palais de l'Ancien Archevêché (stairway on the left), 28 Pl. des Martyrs-de-la-Résistance (phone: 42-23-09-91).

Musée d'Histoire Naturelle – Don't miss the dinosaur egg exhibit. Also pay particular attention to the painted wood panels from the 17th century. Closed mornings. Admission charge. Hôtel Boyer d'Equilles. 6 Rue Espariat (phone: 42-26-23-67).

Place de l'Hôtel de Ville – The 16th-century clock tower at one corner of this square catches the eye first. On high, it has ornate wrought-iron trim, including an ironwork Provençal bell cage at the very top. Farther down and less prominent is a mechanical statue representing the season, one of four that rotate and make their appearance during the course of the year. The 17th-century building with the Italianate façade next to the clock tower is the Hôtel de Ville (Town Hall). Built by Parisian architect Pierre Pavillon, it is notable for its sculpted wooden doors and a beautiful wrought-iron balcony and archway in the interior courtyard. The building once contained an outstanding 300,000-volume library, the Bibliothèque Méjanes, named for the Marquis de Méjanes, who founded it in the 18th century. The library has since been moved to a former match factory near the Gare Routière on Espace Méjanes (phone: 42-25-98-88). Closed Sundays, Mondays, and Thursdays. Admission charge. On the south side of the square the old grain market, an 18th-century building decorated with carvings by Chastel, an Aix sculptor of the period, now houses a branch of the post office. The square itself, surrounded by plane trees and with another of Aix's many fountains at its center, is the site of a colorful flower market. When the vendors move off, the cafés put out their tables.

Eglise Ste-Marie-Madeleine – Its west front was redone in the mid-19th century, though the church dates from the 17th century. Inside are some interesting artworks, including a very large painting (in the aisle left of the altar) that has alternately been attributed to Rubens and to Rembrandt, and the center panel of a highly original 15th-century triptych of the Annunciation, with inexplicable diabolical figures. There is a marble Virgin by Chastel from the 18th century, who's also credited with the Preacher's Fountain out front. Pl. des Prêcheurs (phone: 42-38-02-81).

Outdoor Produce Market – A Provençal market is a market par excellence, and the one that takes place in Aix on Tuesday, Thursday, and Saturday mornings is the crème de la crème. There's everything here to stock a larder or supply a memorable picnic: ripe fruit, vegetables, cheese, ham, sausage, pâté, herbs and spices, dozens of varieties of olives, huge crusty country bread. The crowded, sprawling marketplace, alas, is a favorite with pickpockets. There also is a flea market here on Tuesday, Thursday, and Saturday mornings. Pl. des Prêcheurs. (A smaller market takes place daily on Pl. Richelme.)

Chapelle du Sacré-Coeur – A replica of the one in the palace at Versailles, this beautiful 17th-century Jesuit chapel was known to the public for 300 years by its ornate façade alone. For the last decade, however, its striking cream-colored architecture — with vaulted ceilings and stone columns — has been an inviting setting for art exhibits. Reopened at the initiative of two art lovers, its restoration is being financed by proceeds from the activities. It's also a pleasant, refreshingly cool place to stroll. Open during exhibitions only; schedules are posted on the door and listed in a brochure available at the tourist office. 20 Rue Lacépède (phone: 42-38-03-74).

QUARTIER MAZARIN

Musée Granet – Aix's museum of fine arts and archaeology was founded in the late 18th century and eventually took its name from the early-19th-century Aixois painter François-Marius Granet, a major donor (many of his own works are displayed, and there is a portrait of him by Ingres). Today, the museum is considered among the finest in Provence. In a 17th-century building, the former priory of the Knights of Malta, it contains three watercolors, two drawings, and eight oil paintings by Cézanne — a recent donation and all that there is in Aix of its native son's work — and a very good collection of Provençal, Flemish, and Italian paintings from the 16th to the 19th century. There also are pieces from 20th-century masters such as Martung, Léger, and Matisse and works of contemporary artists and, in summer, some avant-garde paintings. Also exhibited are archaeological finds from the pre-Roman settlement at Entremont — such things as death masks, warriors' torsos, and other examples of Celto-

Ligurian statuary — and exhibits of Egyptian, Greek, and Roman origin. Closed from noon to 2 PM daily, Tuesdays, and some holidays. Open daily during the summer from 11 AM to 7 PM. Admission charge. Pl. St-Jean-de-Malte and 13 Rue Granet (phone: 42-38-14-70).

Eglise St-Jean-de-Malte – This 13th-century church is next door to the *Musée Granet,* once the chapel of the Knights of Malta priory. The church was the first Gothic building in Provence, and though the tarnished façade has been sorely neglected, its interior is worth a visit. There are lovely stained glass windows to the front and back, and the motif of the Maltese cross is repeated on pillars and windows throughout. Pl. St-Jean-de-Malte (phone: 42-38-25-70).

ELSEWHERE

Pavillon de Vendôme – This elegant 17th-century mansion, just beyond the Old Town, originally was built as the provincial residence of the Cardinal de Vendôme. It has some fine 17th- and 18th-century furnishings and paintings, but its attraction lies particularly in its overall architecture and lovely grounds. These include a rose garden, a playground, and various semiprivate nooks, in addition to the main formal garden of velvety green lawn dotted with boxwood carved into swirling shapes, like the tops of mad ice cream cones. All of this is hidden from the bustle of the town by a high wall, and the Aixois who retreat here to push prams, read, or knit on the park benches seem oblivious to the suffering of the two striking male figures holding up the balcony of the building, visibly groaning from the weight of it on their heads. Closed Tuesdays, and daily from noon to 2 PM; admission charge. 32 Rue Celony (phone: 42-21-05-78).

Atelier de Cézanne (Cézanne's Studio) – The 2-story, brown-shuttered house that the artist built in 1897 (and used until his death in 1906) is a bit of a walk uphill at the edge of the city, but the intimate glimpse of his working conditions that it provides makes the effort worthwhile. Only the actual studio — one high-ceilinged room with a huge northern window and other windows overlooking the treetops to the south — can be visited. The studio has been preserved just as he left it, with his cap and cape on a wall hook, a coal stove, a few pieces of furniture, some sketches, letters, and books, and a profusion of vases, bottles, pitchers, dried flowers, and fresh and dried fruit (they're changed from time to time) — the subjects of numerous still lifes. The garden surrounding the house is quietly pleasant. Closed Tuesdays; admission charge. 9 Av. Paul-Cézanne (phone: 42-21-06-53).

Fondation Vasarely – This huge building decorated with alternating black and white circles is hard to miss in the hilly suburb west of town. Devoted to the oeuvre of the Hungarian geometric artist Victor Vasarely, the largely glass structure consists of eight hexagonal main rooms, pleasantly lit with natural light from skylights. The giant floor-to-ceiling works include the artist's vibrantly colored wall murals, Aubusson tapestries, and multidimensional works, including a revolving sculpture. In an upstairs gallery, you can learn all about Vasarely and get a glimpse from overhead at some of his massive creations. Occasionally, there are shows of other artists. Open from 9:30 AM to 12:30 PM and 2 to 5:30 PM; closed Tuesdays. Admission charge. Take bus No. 12 from La Rotonde. 1 Av. Marcel-Pagnol, Jas-de-Bouffan (phone: 42-20-01-09).

■**EXTRA SPECIAL:** The landscape surrounding Aix, with the stark white Montagne Ste-Victoire jutting dramatically above it, is still much as it appears in so many of Cézanne's canvases. Route D17 leading east toward the village of Le Tholonet was enough of a favorite of the painter to be called now the Route de Cézanne, and to follow in his footsteps, whether by car, bicycle, or with your own footsteps, is a memorable part of a stay in Aix. From the top of the Cours, take Rue Maréchal-Joffre and follow it as it becomes Boulevard des Poilus, then Avenue des Ecoles-Militaires-St-Cyr-et-St-Maixent, and eventually D17. It's 3½ miles

(6 km) to Le Tholonet, where you can sit down for a sip before turning back or proceeding to the mountain, which has paths for hikers (at various levels of proficiency). These paths look deceptively simple, so be careful if you are not fit. Alternatively, go on one of the guided visits (in French) to sites associated with Cézanne organized by the Aix Tourist Office on Fridays, April through November, for a modest fee. During the summer, an English version is offered.

In 1990, the city laid out another route — a footpath called "Sur les Pas de Cézanne" — which goes through Aix and into the suburbs. Brass plates along the pavement guide visitors to 12 sites connected with the life and work of the great Impressionist. An English-language brochure and map are available from the tourist office.

SOURCES AND RESOURCES

TOURIST INFORMATION: The Office du Tourisme (2 Pl. du Général-de-Gaulle; phone: 42-26-02-93) is just off La Rotonde and has an English-speaking staff. Open daily from 8 AM to 10 PM in summer and from 8 AM to 7 PM the rest of the year (hours are shorter on Sundays and holidays), it stocks the usual brochures listing hotels, restaurants, sights, sports facilities, villas and flats for rent, and other pertinent information. It also distributes free, large maps, organizes guided tours of the city and surrounding area (some in English during summer months), exchanges currency (in the summer only), and publishes an inexpensive monthly brochure, *Le Mois à Aix,* listing events.

Local Coverage – *Le Provençal* and *Le Méridional* are two regional dailies with Aix editions. *La Semaine d'Aix* is a free weekly that can be picked up in a number of places; it gives mostly movie schedules and reviews. *Le Mois à Aix* is an exhaustive monthly guide to everything from health food stores and hairdressers to fencing clubs and all-night gas stations. They all are in French. *Paradox* (2 Rue Reine-Jeanne; phone: 42-26-47-99) is a good English-language bookstore with material on the region.

TELEPHONE: The city code for Aix-en-Provence is 42, which is incorporated into all local 8-digit numbers. When calling a number in Aix from the Paris region (including the Ile-de-France), dial 16, wait for a dial tone, then dial the 8-digit number. When calling a number from outside Paris, dial only the 8-digit number. When calling from the US, dial 33 (which is the country code), followed by the 8-digit number.

GETTING AROUND: Incontestably the best way to see Aix is on foot. It's a walker's paradise, manageable in size and brimming with pedestrian islands. Conversely, it's a driver's nightmare, with narrow streets and few parking spots. Illegally parked cars are swiftly towed away, especially if they have out-of-region plates.

Bicycle – Bikes can be rented at *Cycles Nadeo* (Montée d'Avignon; phone: 42-21-06-93) and at *Avis* (11 Cours Gambetta; phone: 42-21-64-16).

Bus – About a dozen main lines serve the city, most of them departing from La Rotonde or the Gare Routière, and there's also a limited minibus system. Tickets are sold individually on the bus or in economical *carnets* (packets) of ten. Most lines stop before 8 PM, and weekend service is skimpy. The tourist office and *Autobus Aixois* (phone: 42-26-37-28) have schedules. The Gare Routière (on Rue Lapierre) is the depot for intercity bus service (phone: 42-27-20-92). There are regular buses to Arles, Avignon, Marseilles, and other points in Provence and along the coast as far as Nice. *Le Comette* buses (phone: 91-98-32-05) run frequently between Gare Routière and Marignane Airport (for schedule information, phone 42-27-17-91 or 42-27-82-50).

Car Rental – *Hertz* has an office (43 Av. Victor-Hugo; phone: 42-27-91-32) as does *Avis* (11 Cours Gambetta; phone: 42-21-64-16). Other major international and European firms also are represented.

Taxi – There are stands at the train and bus stations and around the city, and cabs also can be hailed on the street. To phone for one, call, among others, *Taxi Mirabeau* (phone: 42-21-61-61) or *Les Artisans* (phone: 42-26-29-30 day and night). Radio taxi service is very reliable (phone: 42-27-71-11), as is the cab service at the train station (phone: 42-27-62-12) and at Gare Routière (phone: 42-27-20-92). A taxi to the airport costs about 250F ($42).

Train – The train station (Gare SNCF) is at the end of Avenue Victor-Hugo (phone: 42-27-51-63 or 42-08-50-50), but Aix is not very well connected to its neighbors by rail. In most cases, you'll have to change at Marseilles or take the bus (see above).

SPECIAL EVENTS: Aix's *Festival International d'Art Lyrique et de Musique* (International Festival of Lyric Art and Music), an annual event since 1948, is one of the most famous in Europe. Though almost any kind of classical music can be heard, the emphasis is on vocal music. In fact, three operas are staged each year — anything from Rameau to Britten, but almost always something by Mozart, after whom the festival originally was named — and the singers are internationally known. The *Théâtre de l'Archevêché* — the outdoor courtyard of the archbishop's palace — usually is the setting for the operas, while the settings for the concerts include the Cathédrale St-Sauveur, where symphonies, oratorios, and even solo recitals take place, and the adjoining Cloître St-Sauveur, where more intimate works are presented. The festival goes on for approximately 3 weeks, from mid-July to early August, and tickets sell out fast, even though they're pricey — as high as 450F ($75). Programs are available at French tourist offices abroad and throughout France; you can write for information and reservations directly to the festival office at the Palais de l'Ancien Archevêché (13100 Aix-en-Provence; phone: 42-23-37-81; for reservations, 42-23-11-20 or 42-17-59-00). Bookings by mail should be made 3 months in advance; reservations are advisable, especially for the Mozart operas. Other events in Aix include *Aix en Musique,* 2 weeks of primarily classical — but also jazz and ethnic — music in late June or early July, mostly for free; and *Danse à Aix,* 10 days of modern dance and ballet in early July. For details, see *Le Mois à Aix* or consult the tourist office.

MUSEUMS: In addition to those mentioned in *Special Places,* other museums of interest include the following:

Musée du Vieil Aix – Honors Aix's glorious past with old *Carnival* puppets and *santons,* hand-painted clay figures of religious or Provençal characters. Closed Mondays and lunchtime. Admission charge. 17 Rue Gaston-de-Saporta (phone: 42-21-43-55).

Musée Paul-Arbaud – A large collection of old Provençal ceramics, paintings, and books on Provence. Open afternoons; closed Sundays. Admission charge. 2 Rue du Quatre-Septembre (phone: 42-38-38-95).

SHOPPING: Some of the best-known souvenirs of Aix are ultra-rich sweets (surely not part of the thermal cure): the traditional almond paste *calissons d'Aix,* the hazelnut-flavored nougat *victorines,* and unforgettable fresh chocolates from the nearby Puyricard chocolatiers, among France's best.

Less caloric treats are the Côtes de Provence wines and the fragrant herbs of Provence. Colorful and distinctive Provençal cotton fabrics, antiques, and designer clothes are among other treasures to be found in the lovely shops on pedestrian streets such as the Rue Fabrot, Rue Marius-Reinaud, and Rue des Cordeliers. The Place de Verdun crafts and flea market, on Tuesday, Thursday, and Saturday mornings (it's actually an extension of the Place des Prêcheurs food market), is a good place to browse (since everything is overpriced) for interesting old postcards, maps, jewelry, and furniture. During the summer Place des Cardeurs has a flea market on Saturdays. Note that some shops are open on Sunday mornings, but many are closed on Mondays.

Bacchus – A great wine cellar in which to find out about any kind of alcoholic beverage — and bottled water, too — but the proprietors speak very broken English. Closed 1 week in February. 27 Rue d'Italie (phone: 42-38-07-41).

Béchard – The best pastry shop in Aix. 12 Cours Mirabeau (phone: 42-26-06-78).

Calissons du Roi René – A *calissons d'Aix* maker with very reasonable prices. 7 Rue Papassaudi (phone: 42-20-18-89).

Chocolaterie de Puyricard – An outlet of the nearby factory. 7 Rue Rifle-Rafle (phone: 42-21-13-26).

Confiseririe Nouvelle – Makers of *calissons d'Aix* and other nougat sweetmeats. RN7 La Petite Calade, Puyricard (phone: 42-21-23-38).

Galerie Manuel – Art gallery featuring Aixois painters, with four exhibits each year. 4 Rue Manuel (phone: 42-27-59-40).

Leonard Parli – Established in 1874, it's among the oldest makers of *calissons d'Aix*. 35 Av. Victor-Hugo (phone: 42-26-05-71).

Les Olivades – Provençal prints by the yard and in bags, eyeglass cases, bedspreads, and other articles, plus painted furniture. 5 Rue des Chaundronniers (phone: 42-23-57-47).

Souleiado – Beautiful Provençal prints — yard goods, ready-to-wear, and gift items. Pl. des Chapeliers (phone: 42-26-12-90).

SPORTS AND FITNESS: Golf – There is a course at *Golf Club Aix-Marseille,* Domaine de Riquetti, Les Milles (phone: 42-24-23-01).

Horseback Riding – The tourist office has a list of riding clubs, some of which offer daily rates.

Jogging – A good course stretches along the Arc River at Pont de l'Arc under the trees.

Swimming – The *Piscine Municipale* (Rte. du Tholonet; phone: 42-21-44-37) is not too far from the center and is open daily year-round — covered in winter, uncovered in summer. Another pool, the *Piscine du Jas-de-Bouffan,* is in suburban Jas-de-Bouffan (on Av. Marcel-Pagnol; phone: 42-20-00-78).

Tennis – There are hard-surface public courts at the municipal stadium (on Rte. du Tholonet; phone: 42-26-64-58) and in Jas-de-Bouffan (Av. Marcel-Pagnol; no phone).

THEATER: For mainstream productions, go to the *Théâtre Municipal* (on Rue de l'Opéra; phone: 42-38-07-39). It hosts the French classics and foreign ones in translation and other types of *spectacles,* including dance and numerous musical events from recitals to operettas and opera. Mime, songs, and poetry are the province of *La Fontaine d'Argent,* a popular *café-théâtre* — with a *crêperie* open before the show (5 Rue Fontaine d'Argent; phone: 42-38-43-80). For other French theaters, see *Le Mois à Aix. Ciné Mazarin* (6 Rue Laroque; phone: 42-26-99-85) comprises three theaters that feature films in their original languages — often English — with French subtitles, as well as debates and appearances by guest stars; free movie gazette available. *Le Keaton* (45 Rue Manuel; phone: 42-26-86-11) also shows films in English.

MUSIC: Aix is not completely silent after the summer festival season is over. Its churches and cloisters continue to be the austere settings for concerts of classical music. Several operas and operettas can be heard each year, most of them at the *Théâtre Municipal* (see address above). The former also is the scene of classical concerts, whereas the music heard at the latter is likely to be in a more popular vein — *chansons,* jazz, and rock. A jazz pianist plays at the *Blue Note* restaurant (see *Eating Out*). In December, a *Foire aux Santons* (a figurine fair) is held next to the tourist office. Consult *Le Mois à Aix* and *Le Provençal,* both local papers, then check posters for last-minute events.

NIGHTCLUBS AND NIGHTLIFE: A fashionable (but young) disco-oriented crowd heads slightly out of town to the *Rétro 25* (Rte. N8, Pont de Luynes; phone: 42-24-01-00), an "in" club enlivened with video films and fashion shows; the older crowd goes dancing and sometimes listens to excellent live jazz at *Le Hot Brass* (Rte. d'Equilles, Celony; phone: 42-21-05-57). *Le Richelme* (Rue de la Verrerie; phone: 42-23-49-29) is for the young disco set. A popular nightspot is *Oxydium* (Farm Le Fangas on the road to Les Milles; phone: 42-27-92-16). Most clubs open at 10 PM and are closed Mondays. *Le Cintra* (14 Pl. Jeanne-d'Arc) offers a vast selection of domestic and imported beers (115 in all) and a noisy crowd that seems hell-bent on sampling each brand.

BEST IN TOWN

CHECKING IN: Aix has many hotels, but rooms seem to vanish during the festival, having been spoken for months in advance. Note that most hotel rates do not include breakfast (a pleasant alternative is taking a fresh croissant and *café au lait* at a sidewalk café on the Cours Mirabeau). Expect to pay $100 to $150 for a double room at hotels listed as expensive; from $50 to $100 for those listed as moderate; and less than $50 for hotels we call inexpensive (usually starting at $25).

Les Augustins – Converted from an old convent built in the 12th century, this small place has been beautifully restored. Just off the Cours Mirabeau, it has 32 rooms with vaulted ceilings. Reserve in advance; ask for one of the two rooms (each has a terrace) overlooking the 15th-century Campanile des Augustins. No restaurant, but breakfast is served in the garden. Major credit cards accepted. 3 Rue de la Masse (phone: 42-27-28-59; fax: 42-26-74-87; telex: 441052). Expensive.

Mas d'Entremont – Comfort and charm are appealingly combined in this *mas,* or large, Provençal farmhouse. Its 14 rooms and bungalows (with kitchenette) are beautifully furnished and the pine- and cypress-filled grounds overlooking Aix are an enchanting setting. It has a fine restaurant featuring seafood and other light dishes (closed Sundays for dinner, Mondays for lunch, and from November to *Easter*). Visa accepted. Montée d'Avignon, 2 miles (3 km) north of Aix on N7 (phone: 42-23-45-32; fax: 42-21-15-83). Expensive.

Mercure Paul Cézanne – This delightful hostelry excels not only in its decor — all 44 rooms are done tastefully, usually with fine antiques — but also in its atmosphere and service. Near the train station, it has one drawback: an occasional problem with street noise. Ask for an air conditioned room. No restaurant. Major credit cards accepted. 40 Av. Victor-Hugo (phone: 42-26-34-73; fax: 42-27-20-95; telex: 403158). Expensive.

Le Pigonnet – Tucked amid shady chestnut trees and lovely flowered grounds near the outskirts of the city, this is more a typical Provençal mansion. The 50 carefully decorated rooms, some of which are air conditioned, fulfill the promise of their bucolic setting. There's a pool, too, and a fine restaurant, *Le Patio* (see *Eating Out*). The hotel is closed for the first 2 weeks in February. Major credit cards accepted. 5 Av. du Pigonnet (phone: 42-59-02-90; fax: 42-59-47-77; telex: 410629). Expensive.

Le Domaine de Tournon – Not centrally located, but the countryside here is worth the detour. A luxury hotel, it has comfortable rooms (all with color TV sets), a swimming pool, tennis courts, and a restaurant that serves traditional fare. Major credit cards accepted. On D63C toward Les Pinchinats; take the Périphérique to Place Bellegarde and turn right on the Ancienne Route des Alpes (phone: 42-21-22-05; fax: 42-21-38-61; telex: 441530). Expensive to moderate.

Le Manoir – A converted 14th-century cloister with 43 rooms and period furnishings. The public rooms have exposed beams and French Provincial furniture, and there's a pretty, shaded terrace on a gravel courtyard off the street — an exceedingly quiet street though quite centrally located. No restaurant. Closed mid-January to mid-February. Major credit cards accepted. 8 Rue d'Entrecasteaux (phone: 42-26-27-20; fax: 42-27-17-97; telex: 441489). Moderate.

Le Nègre-Coste – In the oldest 18th-century *hôtel* on the Cours Mirabeau, this is a favorite among traveling theater and journalists. Its 37 renovated and soundproof rooms have retained their period character and furnishings. No restaurant. There's a garage. Major credit cards accepted. 33 Cours Mirabeau (phone: 42-27-74-22; fax: 42-26-80-93; telex: 440184). Moderate.

Quatre-Dauphins – This unpretentious family place primarily has economy and a lovely neighborhood to recommend it. The 13 rooms, all with private bath, have been redecorated. Visa accepted. 54 Rue Roux-Alphéran (phone: 42-38-16-39; fax: 42-38-60-19). Moderate.

Le Moulin – At this hostelry beyond the railroad station, in the vicinity of Parc Joseph-Jourdan and the university (not the most central location) there are 37 simple, white rooms — 12 with kitchenettes and private baths. Parking on the premises. Closed December 15 to January 6. Visa accepted. 1 Av. Robert-Schuman (phone: 42-59-41-68; fax: 42-20-44-28). Moderate to inexpensive.

Cardinal – Small, extremely pleasant, and near the *Musée Granet,* this is perhaps the best buy for the money in Aix. Its 31 simple rooms are comfortable and thoughtfully decorated and nearly all of them have a private bathroom. The two top-floor rooms have a lovely rooftop view. Most of the staff speak English. Visa accepted. 24 Rue Cardinale (phone: 42-38-32-30; fax: 42-26-39-05). Inexpensive.

 EATING OUT: Though Aix has only a handful of truly fine restaurants, it does offer a choice of cuisines — Provençal, traditional, regional, and foreign. Provençal cooking draws inspiration from the celebrated local aromatic herbs and also makes good use of olive oil, garlic, tomatoes, and onions. Since this is the south, the accent is on light dishes, and seafood is common. Pizza parlors abound, serving far better than what passes for the species in Paris. Other types of snack shops — even fast-food outlets on Cours Mirabeau — also can be found. Note that service often is unbearably slow, and most restaurants take their last orders before 9:30 or 10 PM. Expect to pay $100 and up for a three-course dinner à la carte for two including wine and service in restaurants listed as expensive, $50 to $100 in the moderate ones, and less than $30 in the inexpensive ones.

Le Clos de la Violette – By far the best dining room in Aix, and the only one with a Michelin star. Cooking is Provençal, with most of the herbs and some of the vegetables coming from the owner's garden. Reserve well in advance. Closed Sundays, Mondays for lunch, and 3 weeks in March. Reservations necessary. Most major credit cards accepted. 10 Av. Violette (phone: 42-23-30-71; fax: 42-21-93-03). Expensive.

Le Patio – Framed by the varied hues of green on the beautiful grounds of the *Pigonnet* hotel, this terrace restaurant looks like a Renoir painting. Try the *noisette d'agneau au basilic,* one of the delicious specialties, and delight in the refuge from city life provided by the setting. Closed Saturdays, Sundays for lunch, the first 2 weeks in February, and the first 3 weeks in November. Reservations unnecessary. Major credit cards accepted. 5 Av. du Pigonnet (phone: 42-59-02-90; fax: 42-59-47-77). Expensive.

Relais Ste-Victoire – A small (there are 4 rooms and 6 suites) stopover for travelers, located outside town in beautiful Cézanne country. There is also a swimming pool and a tennis court. The menu of sumptuous Provençal specialties changes with the seasons. Closed Sundays and Mondays and during school vacation in November, February, and the first week in January. Reservations necessary. Major credit cards accepted. Beaurecueil (phone: 42-66-94-98). Expensive to moderate.

La Brocherie – Attractively rustic with a pleasant courtyard, it, too, specializes in meat grilled over a wood fire. With good service, this is an excellent buy. Closed Sundays and from August 10 through September 10. Reservations are essential for the courtyard. Most major credit cards accepted. 5 Rue Fernand-Dol (phone: 42-38-33-21). Moderate.

Cay Tam – Good Vietnamese and Chinese cooking. Try the spring rolls and the lacquered pork. Open evenings only; closed Mondays for lunch. No reservations. Visa accepted. 29 Rue Verrerie (phone: 42-27-28-11). Moderate.

Chez Jo (Le Bar des Augustins) – One of Aix's best pizzerias, it also serves traditional Italian dishes. Very informal, with tightly packed tables inside as well as out, it's a late favorite with the fashionable crowd. Closed Sundays. Reservations advised. Major credit cards accepted. 59 Rue Espariat (phone: 42-26-12-47). Moderate.

Le Picotin – This small spot, decorated in a simple country style, specializes in southwestern French and local cooking. Duck dishes are prominent, desserts are excellent, and the friendly owner attentive. Closed Sundays and August. Reservations necessary. Visa accepted. 16 Rue de la Paix (phone: 42-27-95-44). Moderate.

Le Vieux Lyon – Excellent regional food from Lyon and burgundy wines. English is spoken. Closed Sundays. No reservations. Visa accepted. 17 Rue du Petit Saint Esprit (phone: 42-26-49-49). Moderate.

Cactus – Pizza, steaks, and salads are served with fast and friendly service. Open daily. No reservations. Visa accepted. 1 Av. Victor-Hugo (phone: 42-26-05-55). Inexpensive.

Al Dente – Only pasta is served here, but it's fresh, light, and well prepared. Closed Sundays for lunch. No reservations. No credit cards accepted. 14 Rue Constantin (phone: 42-96-41-03). Inexpensive.

Bar à Thé – Besides a half-dozen teas, the fare here consists of excellent vegetable *tartes,* salads, and homemade cakes (expecially the chocolate cake). This is a tiny dollhouse of a place, but the decor is tasteful rather than cute. It's become one of Aix's more fashionable spots, a pleasant place to linger — especially at the tables outside on the quiet square (just off the main *place*) — from noon to 10 PM. Closed Sundays, Mondays, and from early August to early September. No reservations. No credit cards accepted. 66 Pl. Richelme (phone: 42-23-51-99). Inexpensive.

Blue Note – Hidden on a side street, Aix's *restaurant américain* is informal and friendly, with old American posters and a dartboard decorating the exposed brick walls. Its burgers, ribs, corn on the cob (a rarity in France), and especially its cheesecake please many more than homesick Americans. Open till midnight, there's a jazz pianist. Closed in August. No reservations. No credit cards accepted. 10 Rue de la Fonderie (phone: 42-38-06-23). Inexpensive.

Croque-Mitoufle – The specialties of this charming tearoom next to Aix's beautiful music conservatory include spinach and endive *tartes,* homemade ice cream, and 30 kinds of teas. Open daily for lunch and tea only; closed Sundays, 1 week during the spring school break, and the month of August. No reservations. Most major credit cards accepted. Rue Joseph-Cabassol (phone: 42-26-25-42). Inexpensive.

El Patio – Good Spanish and Mexican dishes are offered in a friendly environment. Closed Mondays. No reservations. No credit cards accepted. 7 Rue de la Couronne. (phone: 42-27-90-90). Inexpensive.

 BARS AND CAFÉS: Aix's premier sidewalk café, without any doubt, is *Les Deux Garçons* (55 Cours Mirabeau; phone: 42-26-00-51), so named for the two waiters who bought it. Whether outside in the shade of the plane trees or inside in the midst of its lovely rococo decor, it has been *the* place for people watching since 1793. It's open till 2 AM daily, and it also serves a full menu that is fairly expensive. It also is one of the few places, however, where you still can order only coffee or tea any time of the day or night. Many bars no longer offer customers these drinks after 5 PM because of the low profit margin. *Le Cintra* (14 Pl. Jeanne-d'Arc) has a pleasant terrace and offers a choice of 115 international beers (plus Alsatian specialties such as *choucroute*) with which to while away the hours up to the 3 AM closing time. *Le Petit Verdot* (7 Rue Entrecasteaux; phone: 42-27-30-12) is a wine bar that serves food; it is open for lunch and dinner daily except Sundays and Monday noon. *Le Grimaldier,* a nicely renovated café-restaurant (1 Av. des Belges), attracts a cosmopolitan crowd for drinks or ice cream until 1 AM. The "in" place in Aix for the young university crowd is *Bistro Aixois* (37 Cours Sextius; phone: 42-27-50-10). Live rock music is one of its draws.

AVIGNON

Avignon grew up in a strategic spot just north of the intersection of the Rhône and Durance rivers. On the traditional route from Paris to the Mediterranean, it always has had the vibrant style of a crossroads town. But Avignon also is a monument to one crucial period of glory, and to appreciate the city it's best to get right to the point, which is the history of the papacy in the 14th century.

Very early in that century, a pope was elected who refused — largely because of continuous internecine violence in Italy — to take up residence in Rome. Why he decided to live in a relatively anonymous town in Provence instead was not exactly a quirk of fate. Pope Clement V was a Frenchman by birth and somewhat beholden to Philippe-le-Bel (Philip the Fair), then King of France, for his election. Avignon, though not a part of the French kingdom (it belonged to the Counts of Provence), was close enough to be within the king's sphere of influence. In addition, it had a strategic riverside location and was also next to a papal possession, the Comtat Venaissin. Clement V arrived in Avignon in 1309, and while he preferred to live (for the most part) in the peaceful countryside of the neighboring papal territory, his official presence instantly transformed the relatively unknown town into a capital of the Christian world.

The Avignon Captivity had begun. For almost 70 years thereafter, a total of seven popes, all French, reigned from here. Clement V's successor, John XXII (who had been a bishop in Avignon before becoming pope), was the first to establish his permanent residence in Avignon proper; he moved into the episcopal palace, found it too small, and enlarged it. Pope Benedict XII, who succeeded John XXII in 1334, found it still wanting, and the next year began to demolish it to make way for his own palace, a structure that left no doubt of his intention to remain in Avignon. Nor was there any doubt in the mind of his successor, Clement VI, pope from 1342 to 1352, who bought the city from the Countess of Provence and spent the duration of his papacy completing what Benedict XII had begun, doing it so zealously, in fact, that his additions amounted to an entirely new palace attached to the older one.

By the time Innocent VI succeeded Clement VI in 1352, Avignon's main tourist attraction — the massive and staunch Palace of the Popes — was essentially the same size and shape it is today. Innocent VI added reinforcements to the structure, including two towers, and Urban V, his successor in 1362, added little more than a gallery in the garden, no longer extant. Urban V did, however, make an attempt to restore the papacy to Rome, leaving Avignon in 1367, but returned (after finding the Eternal City still too prone to violence and another French king too vehemently opposed to the move) a few months short of his death in 1370. The next pope, Gregory XI, accomplished the return to Rome in 1377, just before his death in 1378.

The Avignon Captivity also has gone down in history as the "second Babylonian Captivity" because of charges that Avignon was Babylon, a "scarlet whore heralding the world's end." This wasn't entirely exaggeration, for the holy site had become a place of exceeding worldliness, of which the flagrantly luxurious palace was a telling symbol. And across the river in Villeneuve-lès-Avignon, the sumptuous homes of the cardinals almost rivaled that of the popes. Throughout this period, the city also was the banking and commercial center of southern Europe.

With so much money flowing from the church's coffers, the arts flourished — the Sienese painter Simone Martini worked here from 1339 to 1344, painting frescoes on the porch of the cathedral, and he was followed by other Italian artists who worked in the palace. The great Italian poet Petrarch spent many years in Avignon, and it was here that he met Laura, who inspired his famous love lyrics. Petrarch was a regular at the court of Clement VI (and in his later years an active champion of the return of the papacy to Rome). Troubadours and mountebanks came to Avignon, as well as processions of penitents, religious minorities seeking the pope's protection, and every kind of thief and evildoer seeking refuge within the boundaries of the papal enclave. A spirit of tolerance prevailed; crime and prostitution prospered — Petrarch called the city "a sink of vice."

When Gregory XI moved the papacy back to Rome, Avignon's tenure as the capital of Christianity was over, but it did not exactly fade into immediate obscurity. No sooner had a new pope, Urban VI, replaced Gregory XI than his attempt to introduce reforms caused the College of Cardinals to declare his election null and void and choose a second pope, Clement VII, who returned to Avignon. During the resulting Great Schism, the Christian world had two popes reigning simultaneously, one in Rome and one in Avignon — each excommunicated the other one — and there was even a third pope during the later years. All but those of the Roman line were declared antipopes after the healing of the schism by the Council of Constance in 1415, but before that happened, two popes of the Avignon line managed to prolong the city's period of glory past the turn of the century: Clement VII lived in the palace from 1378 to 1394; Benedict XIII, from 1394 to 1409. At the height of the papacy in Avignon, the city had 35 monasteries and 60 churches, whose bells rang so often that the French writer François Rabelais named it "La Ville Sonnant," the bell-ringing city.

When the schism ended, Avignon became merely an important provincial city, with merchants manufacturing silk and smuggling salt and tobacco. The palace housed the papal legates who fought with the French kings until it became part of French territory, along with the Comtat Venaissin, in 1791. For a time the palace served as a prison, a barracks, and an archive before restoration began in the early 20th century. Today, it still dominates the city, just as its reason for being dominates the city's history, but it would be a mistake to think it is the only reminder of the past in Avignon.

In fact, from the moment you step inside the city walls — also built by the popes and still intact — testaments of many other periods of Avignon's past surround you, though they may be less conspicuous than the remnants of the

14th century. Retreat north from the barren stone of the palace to the calm greenery of the Rocher des Doms (Doms' Rock) park and consider that ducks swim, pigeons roost, and children giggle down the slide on the very spot that was the cradle of Avignon, inhabited some 4,000 years before Christ. Go to the lookout point for a breath of cool river air and there beneath you, in splendid incompleteness, is the 12th-century Pont St-Bénézet, the bridge better known everywhere as "le Pont d'Avignon" celebrated in the children's song. Across the Rhône, at what was once the bridge's western end, is the square fortress built by Philip the Fair in the last decade of the 13th century. If you visit the upper class Balance quarter west of the palace to admire its beautiful, restored 17th-century townhouses, be aware that 1st-century pottery and other Gallo-Roman relics were unearthed here during the neighborhood's renewal in the 1960s. This was the site of Roman arcades, or "fusteries," as is evident from street names in the vicinity. Some relics are on display in the neighborhood. Nearby, the central Place de l'Horloge was the site of the Roman forum.

All in all, today's town of nearly 90,000 people (fewer than 20% of whom live within the familiar ramparts) contains nearly 100 national historic monuments. Like the walls, often lined by open-air vegetable markets (or by parked cars when the markets are closed) and encircled by busy, six-lane streets, or the Palace of the Popes, with its modern convention center, most of them are the sites of contemporary cultural events, part of a living, thriving present. In the center of the city is the Place Agricole Perdiguier, the restored 200-year-old botanical garden that offers cool shade just off Cours Jean-Jaurès (the main boulevard). In recent decades, in fact, Avignon, which once answered a religious call, seems to be responding more and more to a clearly cultural vocation. This is evident in the number of artists living on and enlivening the beautiful Rue des Teinturiers, in the number of art cinemas, galleries, and experimental theaters populating the inner city. But it is much more evident in the annual international *Festival d'Avignon,* one of France's liveliest arts gatherings and its most important theater festival.

Each summer, professional and amateur artists and spectators, serious and less serious, descend on the city in droves; café prices soar (though not so high as along the Riviera), and Place de l'Horloge seems taken over by all the flower children who've survived from the 1960s — among other tourists. Between the official festival events and those along its fringes, more than 100 different *spectacles* take place every day for a month. Divine intervention also still seems to be present in Avignon — a few years ago, during a performance of Shakespeare's *The Tempest,* there was a half-minute windstorm, occurring at the precise moment that it came up in the text. While an avant-garde dance performance or a controversial drama enjoys the spotlight in the courtyard of the palace, a mime or a fire-eater holds court out front in the palace square, which always is filled with people looking for a "show." Something of the lust for life of former times is well in evidence then, and 5 centuries after the departure of the popes, Avignon — the capital of Vaucluse, one of the most charming provinces of southern France — once again stands out as one of the remarkable cities of Provence.

AVIGNON AT-A-GLANCE

SEEING THE CITY: On the far bank of the Rhône, directly opposite "le Pont d'Avignon" and at the entrance to the unspoiled medieval town of Villeneuve-lès-Avignon, is the Tour Philippe-le-Bel (Philip the Fair Tower). From the top of this late-13th-century edifice there is a striking 180° view of Avignon, with the vast Palace of the Popes in the foreground, the city's densely packed rooftops beyond, and Mont Ventoux in the distance. The tower is open daily except Tuesdays and the month of February. Admission charge. Montée de la Tour Philippe-le-Bel, Villeneuve-lès-Avignon (phone: 90-27-49-49).

SPECIAL PLACES: The sights of Avignon are arranged conveniently. If you're coming from the station, you'll have a good view of a stretch of city wall as you enter the historic center at Porte de la République. Then it's straight ahead along tree-lined Cours Jean-Jaurès and Rue de la République to Place de l'Horloge, which is not only Avignon's main square but also only a few steps from Place du Palais, where the immense medieval papal palace as well as the city's cathedral, its main museum, and the lovely public park are all located. Across Place du Palais from the palace, signs point down a side street and steps to the famous bridge. Place de l'Horloge also gives access to a pedestrian shopping zone around Rue de la Bonneterie, which eventually leads to Rue des Teinturiers, perhaps the street that best provides a feeling of old Avignon unadorned. All the sights below are within walking distance of each other except Villeneuve-lès-Avignon, which is 2 miles across the Rhône. As in other towns in southern France, museums and churches generally are closed between noon and 2 PM.

CITY CENTER

Palais des Papes (Palace of the Popes) – This imposing fortress-residence was the home of five of the seven popes of the Babylonian Captivity and of two of the antipopes of the Great Schism. If you face it, you will see that it's actually two palaces, with a total area of more than 150,000 square feet, whose differing styles reflect less the passage of time than the differing personalities of the popes who commissioned them. The austere Romanesque "old palace" on the left was built from 1335 to 1342 under the ascetic Benedict XII, while the "new palace" on the right, in the more ornate Flamboyant Gothic style, was built from 1342 to 1352 under the more worldly Clement VI. Unfortunately, both parts of the palace now are mostly bare. A fire in 1413 devastated paintings and ceilings in the two huge halls (Consistory and Grand Tinel, or Banquet Hall), looting and vandalism during the French Revolution destroyed furniture and statuary, and when the palace later served as a barracks and prison, frescoes were literally cut up and removed. In recent years, centuries-old tapestries have been added throughout and wooden ceilings have replaced lost ones in a few rooms (including the Consistory and Grand Tinel), but the highlights of the hour-long tour are the rooms where the original decoration remains. Among these are St. John's Chapel, with frescoes attributed to Matteo Giovanetti, and St. Martial's Chapel, with frescoes definitely by Giovanetti and remarkable for the predominant, vivid lapis lazuli blue. (The quaint graffiti here date from the 15th century.) The walls of the Pope's Bedchamber, covered with a pattern of oak and grape foliage on a dark blue ground, may reflect the taste of either Benedict XII or Clement VI, who both used the room; the colorful glazed tiles of the redone floor are copies of 14th-century designs. The Chambre du Cerf (Deer Room), Clement VI's study, is outstanding. Its painted wooden ceiling, protected by a false one in the 18th century, is in its original state, and the walls are full of surprisingly secular hunting, fishing, and bird trapping frescoes.

The palace is open daily year-round, with guided tours leaving hourly or half-hourly depending on the season. Its imposing courtyard — Cour d'Honneur — is not open to the public in late spring and early summer when it becomes the setting for the *Festival d'Avignon*. In summer, there are two tours a day in English, but unguided visits are permitted; off-season, guided tours are obligatory and in French. Tours are often modified because of continuous restoration work on the palace. Admission charge. Pl. du Palais (phone: 90-86-03-32).

Cathédrale de Notre-Dame des Doms – Next up the hill from the palace is Avignon's cathedral. It dates from the 12th century, was partly rebuilt from the 14th to the 17th century, and was topped by a tall gilded statue of the Virgin — which towers over the area — in the 19th century. Inside are the tombs of Popes John XXII and Benedict XII; outside on the porch are sketches of two frescoes by Simone Martini (the upper layers have been removed and are on display in the palace). Pl. du Palais (phone: 90-82-36-55).

Rocher des Doms – This rocky promontory overlooking the Rhône is a short climb uphill from the cathedral. The highest point in the city, it was inhabited in prehistoric times, but today it is a delightful public park. With sloping lawns, lovely trees and flowerbeds, a duck pond and a grotto for swans, a shaded playground for children and a shaded café for their elders, it is also something of a rarity among French parks, meant to be enjoyed rather than simply admired. There is an immense esplanade from which you'll have a wonderful, broad view across the river to the vast green fields of Villeneuve-lès-Avignon (a viewing table at one corner explains what is what as far as the eye can see) or, looking back, over the red roofs of the city. Follow the esplanade around to the left and you'll look right down upon the Pont St-Bénézet. North of the cathedral; a toylike mini-train leaves regularly in season from Place du Palais, a boon if you're too tired to walk.

Musée du Petit Palais – The "little palace" was built in the 14th century shortly after the arrival of the papacy in Avignon and became the official archbishop's palace when the "big palace" was built across the square for the popes. Remodeling in the 15th century gave the medieval building a Renaissance finish, and today, with its striking white stone and graceful archways, it superbly suits its role as a museum (which it has been since 1976). On display are paintings and sculpture of the Avignon School from the 12th to the 16th century and Italian paintings from the 13th to the 16th century. Some 300 of the paintings are a minuscule part of an enormous hoard put together by a rich 19th-century Roman count and amateur archaeologist, Gian Pietro Campana. Campana's passion for art exhausted his own finances, depleted the coffers of the bank of which he was director, and ended with his imprisonment for misappropriation of funds, but not before he had acquired approximately 15,000 objets d'art, including 1,100 paintings (so many that he ran his own restoration workshops, not always with felicitous results). Napoleon III eventually bought the collection with a view to opening a museum. Instead, it was divided among the *Louvre* and 100 or so provincial museums, and only recently have some of the paintings been reassembled here. Particularly rich in Italian and Provençal painting from the Middle Ages and the Renaisance, the selection is representative, ranging from a Virgin and Child by the Sienese Taddeo di Bartolo to a Holy Conversation by the Venetian Carpaccio, and includes an early Botticelli madonna. In addition to the art, it is impossible to miss the stunning views of the Rhône River and Villeneuve-lès-Avignon. Closed Tuesdays and holidays. Admission charge. Pl. du Palais (phone: 90-86-44-58).

Pont St-Bénézet – According to legend, France's most famous bridge, "le Pont d'Avignon," immortalized in a song known by children everywhere, was built as a result of the divine vision of a young shepherd named Bénézet. When it was completed in 1185, an engineering miracle, it was 1,000 yards long and had 22 arches across the Rhône. Only four remain now, the rest destroyed by the Rhône's high waters in the middle of the 18th century, and the bridge stops tantalizingly short of the Ile de la Barthelasse, which divides the river into two branches at this point. It was actually on the island and *under* the bridge rather than *on* it — *sous le pont* rather than *sur le pont* — that everyone danced in circles. Still standing on the narrow cobblestone span is the 2-story, 13th-century St. Nicholas Chapel, bare but for modern graffiti, in which St. Bénézet is said to be buried. The entrance to the bridge is somewhat obscure: If you're coming from the Porte du Rhône, turn right, pass under the bridge, and go into the postcard shop just beyond it. Open daily in summer; closed December 25 through January 2. Admission charge. Quai de la Ligne (phone: 90-85-60-16).

Place de l'Horloge (Clock Tower Square) – This large bustling 15th-century square is the center of Avignon and you'll undoubtedly pass through it en route to the Palais des Papes. It's brimming with sidewalk cafés and assorted street performers, and in summer the "show" goes on until the wee hours. On your immediate left coming from the train station is the stately Hôtel de Ville (enter to see its massive columns), built in the mid-19th century around the old Gothic belfry that gives the square its name. Next door is the elegant *Théâtre Municipal* from the same decade. The square is on the site of a Roman forum, many of whose assorted 1st-century vestiges have been removed to a nearby street corner (Rues St-Etienne and Racine).

Rue des Teinturiers – A charming cobblestone street, it's lined on one side by a narrow canal — part of the Sorgue River — whose brush-like waterwheels rise above a stone wall. The waters once served the cloth dyers for whom the street is named. On the other side of the street are old-fashioned upholstery, photography, and antiques shops as well as restaurants and café-theaters.

City Walls – The 3 miles of turreted and battlemented stone ramparts encircling the historic center of Avignon were built in the 14th century as the popes' first line of defense against marauders and foreign armies. If today they don't seem high enough for defensive purposes, it's because the moat — through which the Sorgue River used to flow — that originally surrounded them has not been excavated. The area is now a huge parking lot. Originally, also, there were only seven *portes* (gates) leading into the city; the other openings were added in the 19th century when the walls were restored by the architect Viollet-le-Duc.

ENVIRONS

Villeneuve-lès-Avignon – This area first was occupied by Gaul–Romans. After Ste-Cesarie's death in the 6th century, the place became a site of devotion, where Benedictine monks later built a small monastery and started a settlement. Philippe-le-Bel (Philip the Fair), the French king, founded the "new town by Avignon" as a stronghold in the late 13th century, when Avignon belonged to the Counts of Provence and the territory on this side of the river belonged to France. He began by constructing the square keep of the Tour Philippe-le-Bel in 1293, to which an upper story and watchtower were added in the 14th century. Later 14th-century kings built the Fort St-André, whose crenellated walls completely enclose the top of a nearby hill and end in twin round towers defending a massive gateway. But the development of the "new city" really was due to the arrival of the papacy, when it was named Villeneuve (New City). Because 14th-century Avignon was too crowded to accommodate all the papal court, this is where cardinals built their grand residences, thus turning Villeneuve into a wealthy residential suburb that witnessed a brilliant ecclesiastical life until the French Revolution.

Today, besides Tour Philippe-le-Bel (see *Seeing the City*) and Fort St-André, from which there is also a remarkable view, there are several other places to visit in this small and quiet medieval town. The ruined 14th-century Chartreuse du Val-de-Bénédiction

(Val de Bénédiction Charterhouse), on Rue de la République, was once the largest and most important Carthusian monastery in France and a small part is now being restored. It was founded in 1356 by Pope Innocent VI, whose white marble tomb is in a chapel of the church. Open daily (phone: 90-25-05-46). The *Musée Municipal* (phone: 90-27-49-66), in a 17th-century building on Rue de l'Hôpital, contains many items from the charterhouse and a notable 15th-century painting, Enguerrand Charonton's *Coronation of the Virgin*, considered a masterpiece of the Avignon School. The parish Church of Notre-Dame (Pl. J.-Meissonier), founded as the collegiate church in the 14th century, holds another of Villeneuve's treasures: a small ivory Virgin and Child following the curve of the elephant's tusk from which it was carved. A festival of music and dance, held here every summer, is a perfect complement to the *Festival d'Avignon* (see below). Villeneuve-lès-Avignon is 2 miles (3 km) northwest of Avignon and can be reached by bus No. 20 from the Avignon train station. (The bus takes you to, but not *into*, Villeneuve; ask where to get off.) There is a local tourist office (1 Pl. Charles-David; phone: 90-25-61-33).

Roquemaure – Just 10 miles (16 km) north on D980 is this town where the remains of St-Valentine lie in a 14th-century church. They were brought here in 1868 from Italy and, every February 14, lovers come from all over to receive the saint's blessings.

■**EXTRA SPECIAL:** The *Festival d'Avignon*, begun in 1947, is France's foremost theater festival — though to call it that alone is to fail to communicate its scope, because it's also an international festival of dance, film, music, and every other possible manifestation of the performing arts. Still, its core is theater. From early July to early August, almost any French troupe of any note will make an appearance here. Similarly, the audience is full of Parisian playgoers taking their measure and trying to discern which way the French theater is heading, since a good number of the French productions are premieres of plays by living playwrights of international reputation. These are interspersed with performances of Racine and other French classics and with productions by foreign companies of their ancients and moderns, including, occasionally, productions in English. The main stage is the courtyard — Cour d'Honneur — of the Palais des Papes, but the list of parallel "Off Avignon" activities is by now so long that all of the city becomes a stage at this time, with concerts, debates, café-theater, and street theater going on in theaters, churches, cloisters, and squares throughout. For details, contact the tourist office or the *Festival d'Avignon*, 41 Cours Jean-Jaurès (phone: 90-82-65-11).

SOURCES AND RESOURCES

TOURIST INFORMATION: Avignon's Office du Tourisme (41 Cours Jean-Jaurès; phone: 90-82-65-11) is open daily from mid-June to mid-August and closed Sundays the rest of the year. It handles information and currency exchange and — through the *Accueil de France* accommodations service — will book you a room for a fee. Just outside the train station, the hotel-run *VTH* reservation center, which books rooms in and around Avignon and the Vaucluse region, also is open to change money on weekends (phone: 90-82-05-81). The tourist office distributes a free brochure with map, *Avignon Pratique*, listing useful data on hotels, restaurants, and sights. A free monthly brochure on cultural events is published in the off-season only, since the festival calendar dominates the summer months.

Local Coverage – The regional dailies *Le Provençal, Vaucluse Matin, Gazette Provençale*, and *Le Méridional* all have Avignon editions (in French, naturally). The

Maison de la Presse, the stationery store opposite the tourist office, carries books and maps on Avignon and the region in English.

 TELEPHONE: The city code for Avignon is 90, which is incorporated into all local 8-digit numbers. When calling a number in Avignon from the Paris region (including the Ile-de-France), dial 16, wait for a dial tone, then dial the 8-digit number. When calling a number from outside Paris, dial only the 8-digit number. When calling from the US, dial 33 (which is the country code), followed by the 8-digit number.

 GETTING AROUND: The ramparts and one-way streets make driving in Avignon difficult and slow. Almost everything within the walls can be seen easily — and best — on foot. For the rest of the city or across the Rhône, there are alternatives.

Bicycle – Rental bikes are available at *Dopieralski* (80 Rue Guillaume-Puy; phone: 90-86-32-49); and at *Masson* (19 Rue Florence; phone: 90-82-32-19 or 90-86-86-99).

Boat – Cruise boats leave Avignon for 2-day trips to Lyons on Tuesdays and Wednesdays and for a 7-hour trip to Aigues-Mortes, in the Camargue region, on Mondays and Fridays. For more information, contact *SNCM* (3 Rue Président-Carnot, Lyons; phone: 72-41-61-10). For information about other boat trips on the Rhône, contact *Le Cygne* in Beaucaire (phone: 66-59-35-62) and *Grands Bateaux de Provence* in Avignon (phone: 90-85-62-25).

Bus – Tickets can be bought individually on the bus or, before boarding, in economical packets of ten from booths in Place Pie or at Porte de la République (phone: 90-82-68-19). Obtain schedules there, too. There's no evening service, and weekend service is skimpy.

Car Rental – All the major firms are here, plus *SNCF*'s own *Train + Auto* rental plan with *Avis* at the station (phone: 90-82-26-33). *Hertz* is another good option (6 Rte. de Lyon; phone: 90-86-61-69).

Taxi – There are stands at the train station and scattered around Avignon, or call *Radio Taxis* (phone: 90-82-20-20).

Train – The train station (Gare *SNCF*) is just outside Porte de la République at the foot of Cours Jean-Jaurès. Avignon is well served by trains en route between Paris and Nice. The *SNCF* has extended its high-speed *TGV* (*train à grand vitesse*) network southeast from Paris to Marseilles via Avignon. For information, call 90-82-50-50.

 SPECIAL EVENTS: Besides the summer drama festival (see *Extra Special*), there's a month-long dance festival in February. Two secondhand dealers' fairs take place yearly by the river on Les Allées des Oulles, one in spring during *Pentecost* weekend and one in early September; there is an artisans' fair also by the river each July. The flea market is held every Sunday at Place des Charmes. On July 14, *Bastille Day,* there are extraordinary fireworks off the Pont St-Bénézet, with dancing on the bridge into the night. In mid-November, young côtes du rhône wine is baptized during the *Wine Festival.*

 MUSEUMS: In addition to those mentioned in *Special Places,* the following museums are of interest:

Musée Calvet – A diverse art collection (including David, Daumier, Delacroix, Soutine, Vlaminck, Dufy, and the 18th-century Avignon painter Joseph Vernet), archaeological artifacts, and a collection of wrought-iron hardware from the 15th to the 19th century are housed in a classic 18th-century mansion with exceptional grounds. Long closed for restoration, the museum is due to reopen in 1993. 65 Rue Joseph-Vernet (phone: 90-86-33-84).

Musée Lapidaire – Gallo-Roman objects displayed in a former Jesuit chapel. Some of the major works from the *Musée Calvet* (above) are on display here while that museum is closed. Closed Tuesdays. No admission charge. 27 Rue de la République (phone: 90-86-33-84).

SHOPPING: The side streets off Rue de la République — notably the pedestrian zone dominated by Rue de la Bonneterie — are filled with quality shops, particularly for clothing and Provençal antiques. The parallel Rue Joseph-Vernet is another elegant shopping street, featuring well-known Parisian names. Local specialties include excellent eaux de vie and liqueurs made from peaches and pears by the Manguin family on the Ile de la Barthelasse and the tasty, liquor-filled chocolate candies called (naturally enough in this city of the popes) *papalines*. Also available are regional items such as the colorful Provençal cottons and aromatic *herbes de Provence*–scented products.

Cristallerie des Papes – Unique hand-crafted and hand-blown glass. At Fontaine de Vaucluse, 15 miles (25 km) south of Avignon (phone: 90-20-32-52; fax: 90-20-20-16).

Librairie Roumanille – A publishing house and bookstore selling rare books and manuscripts about Provence and also old prints. 19 Rue St-Agricol (phone: 90-86-12-40).

Olivades – Fabric and gifts of Provence. 28 Rue des Marchands (phone: 90-86-13-42).

Salle d'Exposition, Espace St-Bénézet – A group of artisans sell items ranging from almond cookies to herbal products to hand-painted scarves. Closed October to mid-March. Entrance on Rue Ferruce or on Quai de la Ligne, next to the bridge.

Souleiado – Marvelous Provençal fabric, fashions, and gift items. 3 Rue Joseph-Vernet.

La Taste – Provençal goods — wine, soap, honey, and more. 5 Rue de la Balance (phone: 90-86-13-14).

SPORTS AND FITNESS: Basketball – Avignon boasts a basketball team, *Entente Sportif Avignonese* (*ESA*), in the national league. The caliber of play is equal to the better American college squads, and the season runs from September to May. *ESA* plays at *Cosec St. Chaman's*, Av. Elsa Trilet (phone: 90-87-13-00).

Mountain Climbing – Scale the slopes at Les Dentelles de Montmirail and around Fontaine de Vaucluse. For information, contact *Club Alpin Français* (7 Rue St-Michel, Avignon 84000; phone: 90-38-14-77). The club is open only on Thursday afternoons for visits and Tuesday afternoons for phone information.

Swimming – One Olympic-size pool (phone: 90-82-54-25) is on the Ile de la Barthelasse, open June 1 to early September; another, the *Piscine Municipale* (phone: 90-87-00-90), is on Av. Pierre de Coubertin, part of the Route de Marseille.

Tennis – Reserve in advance for the municipal courts at the *Tennis Club d'Avignon* (Av. Pierre de Coubertin; phone: 90-87-45-51), next to the municipal swimming pool on the Route de Marseille. Among the private courts are those at the *Tennis Club de la Duplessis* (Ile de la Barthelasse; phone: 90-86-17-56) which has both indoor and outdoor courts.

THEATER: Drama is alive and well year-round, but except when it's absolutely kicking during the *Festival d'Avignon,* it is rarely in English. The *Amis du Théâtre Populaire* (17 Pl. du Palais; phone: 90-82-59-24) would know of any productions in English in the area. The *Théâtre Municipal* (Pl. de l'Horloge; phone: 90-82-23-44) stages a wide range of established theatrical works as well as opera, operettas, and ballet, whereas important new works often originate at the *Théâtre du Chêne Noir* (8 *bis* Rue Ste-Catherine; phone: 90-86-58-11; fax: 90-85-82-05). The *Théâtre des Halles* (4 Rue Noël-Biret; phone: 90-85-52-57) is a company that stages the works of contemporary playwrights. There's amateur theater at *La Tarasque* (14 Pl. d'Etudes; phone: 90-85-43-91). There's also much exciting café-theater, notably at the *Théâtre du Chien Qui Fume* (75 Rue des Teinturiers; phone: 90-85-25-87), with various performances daily from morning till night (closed Mondays), and at *La Tache d'Encre* (22 Rue des Teinturiers; phone: 90-85-46-03), a pleasant restaurant with weekend performances in its tiny back room.

The *Utopia* cinema complex (Rue Figuiére and Rue République; phone: 90-82-65-36) features films in original languages, many in English. It also has a cafeteria, a bulletin board, and its own free French newspaper.

 MUSIC: For classical, contemporary, or jazz, the eclectic *Théâtre Municipal* (see above) is still the place, as is the *Chapelle des Pénitents Blancs* (Pl. Principale; phone: 90-86-49-27), which often has art exhibits as well. There's frequently jazz, folk, or rock at *La Tache d'Encre* (address above). Major rock acts perform at the *Palais des Expositions* (on the Rte. de Marseilles). For information on jazz concerts, contact the *A.J.M.* — part of the *Théâtre du Chêne Noir* (8 *bis* Ste-Catherine; phone: 90-86-58-11; fax: 90-85-82-05).

 NIGHTCLUBS AND NIGHTLIFE: Seven miles (11 km) out of town, is *Sholmes* (at Rochefort-du-Gard, phone: 90-31-73-43), a splashy, upper class nightclub complete with pool, restaurant with Moroccan specialties, and dance floor (no jeans or sneakers here). Other places include the *Ambassy Club* (27 Rue Bancasse; phone: 90-86-31-55) and *Club 5.5* (Porte St-Roch; phone: 90-85-46-76).

BEST IN TOWN

CHECKING IN: Avignon has a large inventory of hotels, particularly when you include the 20 or so just across the river in Villeneuve-lès-Avignon, but there are never enough during the peak festival period. If you're driving, consider the numerous two-star (for example, *Ibis* and *Climat*) and three-star (*Mercure* and *Novotel*) chain hotels on the roads leading into town, none more than a 10-minute ride away. There also are many country hotels in villages on both sides of the Rhône, all the way to Arles. Note that most hotel rates don't include breakfast. Expect to pay $175 and up for a double room at hotels listed as very expensive, from $125 to $175 for those listed as expensive, $90 to $125 for those listed as moderate, and less than $90 for the inexpensive ones.

Le Prieuré – This distinguished *hostellerie* was built in the 14th century as a residence for a cardinal, then became a priory. Now renovated (with no sacrifice of its period charm) and supplemented by a modern wing, it's *the* luxury hotel of the area — a Relais & Châteaux member — and reason enough to cross the Rhône. It's removed from the sounds of the city, yet has a fine view, and it's set in shady grounds that have room for a large swimming pool and tennis courts. The modern annex, by the pool, has larger rooms (with better views) than those in the original building, but both sections are equally refined and all 35 rooms are exquisitely furnished. Another plus is a restaurant where diners can eat indoors or on the outdoor terrace amidst lavender and roses. Closed from early November to mid-March. Major credit cards accepted. 7 Pl. du Chapitre, Villeneuve-lès-Avignon (phone: 90-25-18-20; fax: 90-25-45-39; telex: 431042). Very expensive.

Europe – This former 16th-century palace, the best hotel in the city, has a graceful elegance. Aubusson tapestries decorate the high walls in the antiques-furnished public rooms, and the 47 bedrooms, with beamed ceilings of dark wood, are richly appointed. In summer its pleasant, recently renovated restaurant (one Michelin star), *La Vieille Fontaine,* serves meals in the lovely courtyard amid huge plants, a stone sundial over the doorway, and, of course, the old fountain. The restaurant is closed Saturday lunch and Sundays. Major credit cards accepted. 12 Pl. Crillon (phone: 90-82-66-92; fax: 90-84-43-66; telex: 431965). Expensive.

Les Frênes – Three miles (5 km) from Avignon, it has an imposing garden with roses and century-old trees, antiques-filled guestrooms, and a swimming pool. Its restaurant boasts a Michelin star. The *hostellerie* is a member of the presitigious Relais & Châteaux group. Closed November 15 to March 15 (restaurant opens April 1). Major credit cards accepted. Av. Vertes Rives, Montfavet (phone: 90-31-17-93; fax: 90-23-95-03; telex: 431164). Expensive.

La Magnaneraie – A 15th-century residence with 19th-century furniture and 20th-century comforts, offering peace and quiet in a pine forest setting. The restaurant serves traditional French and Provençal fare and has a very good selection of wines. Major credit cards accepted. 37 Rue Camp de Bataille, Villeneuve-lès-Avignon (phone: 90-25-11-11; fax: 90-25-46-37; telex: 432640). Expensive.

Mercure Palais des Papes – Although in the heart of the city — midway between the Pont St-Bénézet and the Palace of the Popes — this was designed around a courtyard and is a remarkably quiet enclave. The building is tastefully modern, its sandstone color blending harmoniously with the restored townhouses in the surrounding La Balance quarter. The 85 soundproof rooms have all the amenities of a classic luxury hotel. Rue Ferruce (phone: 90-85-91-23; fax: 90-85-32-40; telex: 431215). Expensive.

Angleterre – Modest, but very clean and pleasant, and just a short walk from the train station in a quiet neighborhood. All rooms have direct-dial phones and some look out onto a large terrace. The majority have a private bathroom, making it an exceptionally good buy. Closed from mid-December to February 1. Major credit cards accepted. 29 Bd. Raspail (phone: 90-86-34-31; fax: 90-86-86-74). Moderate.

Auberge de Cassagne – All 19 guestrooms at this tranquil inn are simply yet tastefully furnished *à la Provençal,* and many overlook a beautiful garden. Philippe Boucher, a onetime apprentice in the three-star kitchens of Georges Blanc and Paul Bocuse, has recently been awarded a Michelin star for his masterful meals served in the dining room (see *Eating Out*). Open year-round. Major credit cards accepted. Rte. de Vedene (phone: 90-31-04-18). Moderate.

Cité des Papes – Literally down the street from the papal palace and just off Place de l'Horloge, this shiny modern hotel has an unbeatable, if noisy, location. Fortunately, its 63 pretty rooms are soundproofed and well furnished, though occasionally quite small. Closed from December 18 to January 23. Major credit cards accepted. 1 Rue Jean-Vilar (phone: 90-86-22-45; fax: 90-27-39-29; telex: 432734). Moderate.

Danieli – This centrally located 19th-century hostelry with 29 rooms is not as luxurious as its Venice namesake (it once was a brothel), but it is a pleasant and comfortable place to stay. Open year-round. Major credit cards accepted. 17 Rue de la République (phone: 90-86-46-82; fax: 90-27-09-24). Moderate.

La Ferme – In a tranquil setting outside the city this old farmhouse that became a 20-room hotel. It has a restaurant that serves traditional dishes and a swimming pool. Closed in January. Most major credit cards accepted. About 3 miles (5 km) from Avignon on Chemin des Bois, Ile de la Barthelasse (phone: 90-82-57-53; fax: 90-27-15-47). Moderate.

La Ferme Jamet – A true 16th-century Provençal farm, with 4 bedrooms, 3 bungalows, and 4 apartments with kitchenette and living room. There's also a private garden, tennis court, and swimming pool; honey, jams, and wine are for sale. Closed November through February. Visa accepted. Ile de la Barthelasse (phone: 90-86-16-74; fax: 90-86-17-72). Moderate.

Mignon – Translated it means cute, and it really is. Set 200 yards from the Palais de Papes, it has 15 rooms tastefully decorated and soundproofed. Visa accepted. 12 Rue J.-Vernet (phone: 90-82-17-30; fax: 90-85-78-46). Moderate.

Le Rocher Pointu – In the hamlet of Aramon, 7½ miles (12 km) outside Avignon, this bed and breakfast establishment in a farmhouse on 7 isolated acres has 4 guestrooms, each with private bath. Swimming pool, kitchen, barbecue, and a lounge are at patrons' disposal. Closed from mid-November to mid-March. Visa accepted. Plan-de-Dève, Aramon (phone: 66-57-41-87; fax: 90-14-02-18). Moderate.

Régina – A very conveniently situated budget hotel just off Place de l'Horloge on the main street leading from the train station. Ask for a quieter room in the back during the festival. Nothing fancy here (only the lobby is air conditioned), but it's clean and comfortable and almost all rooms have a toilet. Closed in November and December. No credit cards accepted. 6 Rue de la République (phone: 90-86-49-45). Inexpensive.

EATING OUT: Ever since the popes arrived, there's been a tradition of good eating in Avignon. Besides the dining "palaces," there are many topnotch restaurants charging moderate prices and serving a wide range of foods from Provençal (heavy on olive oil, tomatoes, and local herbs) to Oriental. Pizzerias are particularly plentiful and frequently quite good. Note that many restaurants take their last orders as early as 9 PM. Expect to pay $125 and up for a meal for two without wine in restaurants listed as expensive, from $90 to $125 in those listed as moderate, and from $75 to $90 in the inexpensive ones. A service charge usually is included in the price.

Brunel – The two young Brunel cousins have a solid reputation for inventive cooking and perfectly fresh products, and have earned themselves one Michelin star. Their specialties include hot oysters with curry, a warm pâté of duck and gigondas wine, and a luscious strawberry mousse. The prix fixe menu, available at lunch only, is an excellent bargain. Closed Sundays, Mondays (except in June and July), 2 weeks in late February, and August 1–15. Reservations necessary. Most major credit cards accepted. 46 Rue de la Balance (phone: 90-85-24-83; fax: 90-86-26-67). Expensive.

Hiély-Lucullus – From its simple façade and unprepossessing location upstairs on a commercial street, you wouldn't suspect the exquisite dining reigning at one of Avignon's best restaurants (one Michelin star). There is only a prix fixe menu here (no à la carte), but the choice for each course is wide, cheese and dessert are included, and the value is extraordinary (the best for the money in Avignon). The emphasis is regional, with such specialties as *pieds et paquets provençale* (mutton, tripe, and feet in a stew) and grilled Alpilles lamb. There are fine local wines from the Côtes du Rhône, including good carafes, and the service is gracious and professional. Closed Sunday evenings, Mondays (except in summer), Tuesdays for lunch, and 2 weeks in January and June. Reservations necessary. Visa accepted. 5 Rue de la République (phone: 90-86-17-07; fax: 90-86-32-38). Expensive to moderate.

Auberge de la Cassagne – A former pupil of three-star masters Georges Blanc and

Paul Bocuse, Philippe Boucher pays homage to their teachings in this cheerful dining room. Among the more tempting dishes served here are *terrine provençale* accompanied by foie gras, *filets des rouget poêlés au citron vert* (fried mullet filets in lime juice), and *emincé d'agneau de lapereau panées* (thinly sliced lamb and rabbit coated with breadcrumbs). Monsieur Boucher's efforts have recently won him his first Michelin star. Open daily. Reservations necessary. Major credit cards accepted. Rte. de Vendene (phone: 90-31-04-18). Moderate.

Le Cintra – This brasserie-type dining spot offers traditional French fare such as steak *au poivre,* and stays open late. The service is very friendly, particularly in the early morning hours. Open daily. No reservations. Visa accepted. 44 Cours Jean-Jaurès (phone: 90-82-29-80). Moderate.

La Fourchette II – Long a popular favorite for quality dining at low prices and for its decor. The menu includes delicious terrines, grilled sea bass with ratatouille, and homemade sherbets. Closed Saturdays, Sundays, and the last 2 weeks in June. Reservations necessary. Visa accepted. 17 Rue Racine (phone: 90-85-20-93). Moderate.

L'Isle Sonnante – After working in many restaurants throughout France, Mr. and Mrs. Gradassi chose to open their own place in what used to be *La Fourchette I.* They have adapted their background in preparing traditional French fare to Provençal dishes. All wines come from nearby vineyards. Closed Sundays, Mondays, January 1 to February 27, and 2 weeks in August. Reservations necessary. Visa accepted. 7 Rue Racine (phone: 90-82-56-01). Moderate.

Les Trois Clefs – This small, pretty place has a young chef with big ideas and the menu reflects his very personal style. Specialties include delicious veal kidneys with a honey sauce and eggs poached *à la cantadine.* The warm decor is highlighted by mounted photos of old Avignon, ca. 1900; service is similarly warm. Closed Sundays and during school vacation in November and February. Reservations necessary. Most major credit cards accepted. 26 Rue des Trois Faucons (phone: 90-86-51-53). Moderate.

Le Vernet – Nice touches such as tasty hors d'oeuvres brought before you order and chewy sweets brought with your coffee add to the atmosphere here, which is equally pleasurable whether you dine inside the stately 18th-century building or amid the statuary behind a high wall in the courtyard. Also pleasurable is the food; try the deliciously light asparagus flan and the roast young rabbit with garlic (available only during the autumn hunting season). Closed Saturday dinner, Sundays (except from May 1 to October 1), and February. Reservations unnecessary. Visa accepted. 58 Rue Joseph-Vernet (phone: 90-86-64-53; fax: 90-85-98-14). Moderate.

Au Pied de Boeuf – The orange awning and large potted plants of this friendly and informal place stand out on a dreary stretch of storefronts beyond the ramparts but within walking distance of the center. The couple who run it serve a meal of top value made up of such things as a variety of filling salads, grilled *magret* (breast of duck) with mustard, and good strawberry *tartes.* Closed Sundays and the first 2 weeks of August. Reservations unnecessary. Major credit cards accepted. 49 Av. Pierre-Sémard (phone: 90-82-16-52). Moderate to inexpensive.

Le Taste-Vin – Simple French fare, but the draw here is the 100 different wines that are served. The specialty is châteauneuf-du-pape (it can cost at least $50 a bottle). Closed Sundays except in the summer. No reservations. Visa accepted. 37 Rue St-Michel (phone: 90-86-86-45). Moderate to inexpensive.

Cafeteria Flunch – For delicious ice cream sundaes (though the salads and hot dishes merely are acceptable), try this simple place. Open daily except *Christmas* and *New Year's* eve. No reservations. Visa accepted. 11 Bd. Raspail (phone: 90-86-06-23). Inexpensive.

Crêperie du Cloître – Open for lunch and dinner, it has a large choice of crêpes and salads, as well as live entertainment on Friday nights during the summer. Closed Sundays in off-season. No reservations. Most major credit cards accepted. 9 Pl. du Cloître, St. Pierre (phone: 90-85-34-63). Inexpensive.

Pain Bis – At this vegetarian eatery, even the wine is organic. The food is well prepared, tasty, and varied, with daily menu changes, and the atmosphere is warm and friendly. Closed Sundays and Monday evenings. No reservations. Visa accepted. 6 Rue Armand de Pontmartin (phone: 90-86-46-77). Inexpensive.

Simple Simon's – For meat loaf Indian-style or just tea and scones, this authentic English restaurant and tearoom can't be beat. The decor and service are charming. Open till 2 AM during the summer (orders taken only until 7 PM the rest of the year); closed Sundays and Mondays except during festivals, and all of August. No reservations. No credit cards accepted. 26 Rue Petite-Fusterie (phone: 90-86-62-70). Inexpensive.

 BARS AND CAFÉS: For a late drink, the lively Place de l'Horloge is always a good bet, though prices often are higher here. One of the picks on this street is *Bar la Civette,* seedy and cool, where the artists meet after the show. Elsewhere, there's *Le Pezet* (Cours Jean-Jaurès), a comfortable bar.

BIARRITZ

The premier resort city on France's Atlantic coast is well down in the south-west corner of the country on the Bay of Biscay, at the edge of Basque country, about 20 miles (32 km) from the Spanish border. It is modern in comparison to many French cities, for most of its fanciful pastel structures were built in the last 100 years or so. Not too much before that — before the Second Empire (1852–70) of Napoleon III — it was little more than a fishing village, but when a stroke of luck caused Napoleon and Empress Eugénie to spend their summers here, Biarritz quickly became not only a notable French resort town, but one of the most fashionable seaside watering spots in the world. Until well into the 20th century it was "the Beach of Kings and the Queen of Beaches," and today it remains a very popular and busy summer place, though its days of glory are long gone.

Once before in its history Biarritz experienced a similar change of fortune. As markings on the cliffs around Pointe St-Martin seem to attest, the site is believed to have been inhabited during various prehistoric periods. However, it wasn't until approximately the 12th century that it gradually began to be known as a fishing village and small whaling port. Whaling was lucrative and the village grew prosperous, thanks in large part to nearby Bayonne, the major market for its catch and by-products. A church — Eglise St-Martin — was built, one of the few vestiges today of this early prosperity. Then the whales left the Bay of Biscay and a grave crisis hit the city. From the beginning of the 16th century to the beginning of the 19th, Biarritz was a fairly sleepy place, though not without some notable activity, such as the restoration of the church in 1541 and the construction of the first lighthouse.

Gradually, the inhabitants of Bayonne began to come here to enjoy the beauty of the coast and to bathe in the sea, a new activity that caught on quickly. They were followed by the Spanish nobility, especially many exiles from the Carlist wars who were unable to set foot in nearby San Sebastián, in their native Spain. Most fateful for Biarritz was the arrival of the Countess de Montijo, who came here regularly after 1838 with her two beautiful daughters, one of whom, Eugénie, was destined to marry Napoleon III in 1853. Remembering her summers in Biarritz, Eugénie persuaded Napoleon to accompany her in 1854 and he was charmed enough by the sight to begin immediately to build an extravagant villa-palace, the Villa Eugénie, in which the couple spent their summers until 1868. Forthwith, Biarritz became the summer capital of France.

By the fall of the empire, the cachet of the city was well established, so that even after Eugénie sold the villa from her exile in England (it became the Palais-Biarritz, then the *Hôtel du Palais*), royalty came to call. The Avenues Reine-Victoria, Edouard-VII, and Alphonse-XIII are named after only a few of the European kings and queens who wintered or summered here. So many

Grand Dukes and Princes of Russia regularly vacationed here that they even built their own church. Through the Belle Epoque and the Roaring Twenties — until the Great Depression — Spanish and French aristocracy, English gentry, and American millionaires mixed at the gaming tables and at the balls, played golf, tennis, and water polo, strolled the promenades, and tooled about town in their Bugattis, Hispano-Suizas, and Rolls-Royces. Shortly, they were sharing their playground with the masses.

The city's star began to fade a bit during the 1950s, when the spotlight turned to the Mediterranean's Côte d'Azur and chic spots such as St-Tropez, which was unknown before Brigitte Bardot. For a time, Biarritz seemed like a fading dowager, obliged to content itself with the memory of a glorious past. Of late, though, as the Côte d'Azur becomes more and more crowded and expensive and less and less friendly, a gradual shift back to the Atlantic coast seems to have begun. Visitors who've sampled life on both coasts find the residents of Biarritz approachable and sincere, even humble, in comparison. Often, a fruit seller or a waiter or a woman in a butcher shop is happy just to chat, to talk about the region. Their patience may be thinner during July and August — high tourist season — but they have not yet become so bored with their returning popularity that they are offhand and condescending.

In recent decades, Biarritz also has gained a reputation among the international surfing set as the scene of some of the world's best waves. In addition, almost every imaginable sport can be pursued here, from golf — at the *Centre International d'Entraînement au Golf,* Europe's most extensive golf training center (see *Sports and Fitness*) — to horseback riding to people watching. The grand promenade takes place nightly on Place Clemenceau, Place Ste-Eugénie, and on the pathways that wind above the shore from one end of town to the other, laid out to take advantage of the city's splendid natural beauty. Otherwise, Biarritz, with a population of approximately 30,000 people, is refreshingly free of obligatory tourist sights. The main ones still are the wide sandy beaches, framed by rocky cliffs and green hills blooming with blue and mauve hydrangeas. In this setting, the pale Victorian buildings — tawdry turn-of-the-century marvels that look like giant bits of confectionery — add a touch of fantasy that gives the city a special appeal.

BIARRITZ AT-A-GLANCE

SEEING THE CITY: The most outstanding of a number of panoramic vistas in Biarritz is the one from Pointe St-Martin, a high plateau at the northern tip of the city. It can be reached by taking the narrow paths that twist precariously through the Pointe St-Martin gardens along the tops of cliffs dropping straight down to the shore. From the point, even without climbing the lighthouse, the eye can take in most of the Biarritz waterfront: wide sweeps of sandy beach, sharply rising cliffs that serve as dramatic pedestals for frivolous Victorian villas, a blue and white casino, rocks, and a tiny port in the distance. The St-Martin headland marks the dividing line between the Landes region north of Biarritz, characterized by sand dunes and forests, and the wild, rugged terrain of the Côte Basque south of it, and the contrast between the two is visible. While you're here, note the lighthouse. It was built in 1834, is 240 feet high, and can be climbed in summer. It also is possible to climb down a few steps below the lighthouse to a cave, La Grotte de la Chambre d'Amour. According to legend, this was the secret meeting place of the son of a wealthy landowner and the daughter of a poor peasant family, forbidden by their parents to marry. One night the couple met in the cave as the tide was rising, and a sudden swell swept them to their deaths — whether accident or suicide is not known.

 SPECIAL PLACES: Biarritz's seafront and the promenade — *promenade du bord de mer* — that accompanies much of it are the resort's primary attractions. The promenade consists of sinuous paths that have been carved by man along the plateaus and into the cliffsides, turning the fern- and flower-carpeted rocks into a magnificent public park. From the Pointe St-Martin gardens, instead of following the sidewalks of Avenue de l'Impératrice, go down the staircase marked "Descente de l'Océan," which takes you to Allée Winston-Churchill, a paved walkway running along the Plage Miramar. After passing the stately *Palais* hotel, the path widens into the Quai de la Grande Plage. This is the main promenade, which continues to the opposite end of the city and a final viewpoint overlooking the southernmost stretch of beach. At a leisurely pace, the walk requires about 3 hours; it takes you past most of the points of interest listed below and several magnificent seascapes.

SEAFRONT

Hôtel du Palais – Unquestionably the most arresting manmade sight in Biarritz is this large red brick building with white trim and a gray roof, fronted by ample green lawn and set in a commanding spot on the Grande Plage, the resort's most popular beach. Napoleon III built it in the 1850s as a summer palace for himself and Empress Eugénie, who had summered in Biarritz as a girl. Known then as the Villa Eugénie (and dubbed by some "Eugénie's Basque folly"), it saw its share of eminent personages when Eugénie was in residence; today, as a luxury hotel, it maintains its regal bearing. Even if you're not a guest, you can glimpse some of the palatial trappings in the public rooms or dine in style in one of its restaurants. 1 Av. de l'Impératrice (phone: 59-24-09-40).

Eglise Orthodoxe Russe – A Byzantine Russian church across Avenue de l'Impératrice from the hotel, built in 1892 by the colony of Russian notables who wintered here. It has a striking, sky blue dome. 1 Rue de Russie.

Grande Plage – One of the town's four main beaches. In the city's heyday around the turn of the century, it was the site of leisurely promenades by ladies with long, billowing skirts, wide-brimmed hats, and lacy parasols to protect them from the sun. Today, the scene is a lot less *habillé* — few of the female bathers bother to wear bathing-suit tops — and the beach is one of the two most favored by surfers, though the surf here is not as rough as that of the Plage de la Côte des Basques. Sprawled along the Grande Plage like an albino whale is the *Casino Municipal,* now a theater and concert hall. The resort's casino, the *Casino Bellevue,* the giant blue and white wedding cake on the hill above the southern end of the beach, offers glamorous gaming and a nightclub (phone: 59-24-11-22). The Grande Plage is extended north to Pointe St-Martin by the Plage Miramar.

Place Ste-Eugénie – From the southern edge of the Grande Plage, steps and a path lead past the Rocher du Basta to this gracious open *place* lined with hotels and their terraced restaurants, one of the gathering places of the resort. The Eglise Ste-Eugénie, at one end of the square, is relatively modern. From the Place Ste-Eugénie, Rue Mazagran — full of pedestrians browsing through charming shops — climbs gradually to the Place Clemenceau, the city's main shopping area.

Port des Pêcheurs – This small fishing port below Place Ste-Eugénie is one of the most picturesque places in Biarritz. It is crowded with boats, slight wooden houses and shacks backed up against a small cliff, huge piles of lobster traps, driftwood, rope, and other scattered fishing paraphernalia. There's also a collection of small harborside restaurants and cafés from which to choose. The little harbor is protected from the surf by a system of manmade breakwaters and concrete walls; in order to reach open water, the boats pass through several canals and compartments and then navigate between dangerous-looking rocks that jut out beyond the walls.

Rocher de la Vierge – The rocky Plateau de l'Atalaye forms one side of the Port des Pêcheurs. Walk through the tunnel Napoleon III had carved through the plateau to reach an esplanade from which a metal footbridge leads several hundred feet out into the sea to a magnificent rock islet. This, the Virgin's Rock, is named for the statue of the Virgin crowning it, whose duty it has been since 1865 to protect the sailors and fishermen of the Bay of Biscay. The metal footbridge, built during the 1880s by craftsmen of the famous engineer Eiffel, replaces an earlier wooden one that was meant to be part of a large port Napoleon intended to build. The bridge allows visitors to walk all the way out to the terraced edge of the rock, a dramatic spot high above the crashing surf, for classic views of the sea, the coastline, or, simply, down. Esplanade de la Vierge.

Musée de la Mer – The same esplanade that gives access to the Rocher de la Vierge also holds a simple but touching monument to the city's casualties during the two World Wars as well as this museum, dedicated to the sea and its inhabitants. It is scheduled to undergo a much-needed renovation next year which will include building a new aquarium. Founded in 1933, it has 3 floors of marine exhibits, maps of the ocean floor, and remnants of Biarritz's past whaling culture, including the impressive skull of a colossal whale. The museum's roof tank, home of three species of seals, also is being expanded and modernized. If you can, catch the seals at feeding time — 10:30 AM and at 5 PM each day. Open daily from 9 AM to noon and 2 to 6 PM; open from 9 AM to 7 PM in July and August. Admission charge. Esplanade de la Vierge, 14 Plateau Atalaye (phone: 59-24-02-59).

Plage du Port-Vieux – This small horseshoe beach is along the pathway on the other side of the Atalaye plateau. It's well protected by rocks, and the shallow, calm waters are favored by families with children. The *Port Vieux Club* is tucked into the rocks at the back of the beach.

La Perspective – From Port Vieux, the path leads up to yet another plateau, where the flower-lined promenade offers tremendous views north over the distance already covered and south over the vast and rocky Plage de la Côte des Basques as far as the mountains of Spain. Paved, switchback paths lined with benches and stone balustrades crisscross the steep incline that drops from La Perspective to the beach, which is the wildest and most exposed in Biarritz and the one most highly regarded by surfers. At high tide, however, the entire stretch of the Plage de la Côte des Basques is forbidding, with breakers crashing at the base of the cliffs and splashing onto Boulevard du Prince-de-Galles only feet away from the seawall. In the cliff face over the boulevard are the remains of bunkers from World War II.

Musée de l'Automobile Miniature – One of the newest additions to Biarritz's museums, this one houses a collection of over 6,000 miniature models of cars, fire trucks, and other vehicles. There's an audiovisual presentation of the history of the automobile. Open daily from 10 AM to 7 PM (until 9 PM on Fridays) during the summer; daily from 2 to 6 PM weekdays, and from 10 AM to 12:30 PM and 2 to 6 PM on weekends from mid-September through mid-June. Admission charge. 13 Plateau Atalaye (phone: 59-24-56-88).

ELSEWHERE

Eglise St-Martin – Biarritz's only old religious monument is up the hill and away from the beaches and the town center. Probably begun in the 12th century, it was restored in 1541 and has a Flamboyant Gothic chancel. Rue St-Martin.

Musée du Vieux Biarritz – Housed in a former church, this museum displays paintings, costumes, objets d'art, and documents that illustrate the two principal activities of this port — fishing and agriculture. There also are exhibits showing life during

Biarritz's golden era, when it was known as the "Beach of Kings," during and after the reign of Napoleon III. Closed Thursdays and Sundays. Open 3 to 6 PM. Salle Saint Andrew's, Rue Broquedis (phone: 59-24-86-28).

ENVIRONS

Musée Basque – An excellent museum of Basque culture, one of the best regional museums in France, is 5 miles (8 km) away in Bayonne. It has everything from traditional costumes, furniture, typical Basque interiors, and the tools of various local trades to theater, dance, and local history. A museum within the museum is devoted to the Basque game of *pelote,* with examples of the balls, gloves, rackets, bats, and baskets used, plus models of frontons. At press time, the museum was closed for renovations and no reopening date had been set. Corner of Rue Marengo and Quai des Corsaires, Bayonne (phone: 59-59-08-98).

Musée Bonnat – This stately museum, also in Bayonne, was built at the end of the 19th century to house the works of art bequeathed to the city by a native son, the 19th-century painter and collector Léon Bonnat. Certainly one of the country's outstanding art galleries, its collection includes works from the 13th century to the Impressionists. Among them are — in addition to Bonnat's own paintings — some lovely Aragonese primitives, paintings by such Old Masters as Rubens and Rembrandt as well as such later masters as Goya, Ingres, Delacroix, and Degas, an archaeological collection, and a huge lode of drawings by Flemish, Dutch, Italian, French, and German artists from the Renaissance to the 19th century, which are displayed in changing exhibitions. Closed Tuesdays and holidays; admission charge. 5 Rue Jacques-Laffitte, Bayonne (phone: 59-59-08-52).

■**EXTRA SPECIAL:** One of the main reasons to make a day trip south along the Côte Basque is to visit St-Jean-de-Luz, 9 miles (14 km) away. If Biarritz is "the Queen of Beaches," then this delightful resort, about half its size but with a broad scallop of safe and sandy beach on a well-protected bay, is at least a crown prince or princess. Like Biarritz, St-Jean is a former whaling port turned fishing village, but in the process of becoming a resort, it has retained more of its Basque character than its neighbor and has not put its seafaring past entirely behind it. It remains an important fishing port, though the catch these days is largely tuna — in fact, an annual tuna festival is one of the town's summer celebrations (others are the weekly bullfights and a festival in honor of the Basque fish soup *ttoro*). The picturesque port and the maze of streets behind it are among the sightseeing attractions, as is the house in which Louis XIV lived in 1660 when he came here to marry Marie-Thérèse, the Infanta of Spain, as well as the interesting, typically Basque church where the ceremony took place. After a stop in St-Jean-de-Luz (for restaurants or hotels, see the *Pyrénées* tour, DIRECTIONS), you can continue along the coastal road — Corniche Basque — to Hendaye, another popular resort, about 9 miles (14 km) away at the Spanish border. The views are magnificent en route, and some people consider the beaches of Hendaye the best on the coast.

SOURCES AND RESOURCES

 TOURIST INFORMATION: Biarritz's Tourist Information Office, the Comité du Tourisme et des Fêtes (phone: 59-24-20-24), has its administrative headquarters centrally located in a suitably grand edifice (its public information office is next door) — the Javalquinto Palace, former residence of the Dukes of Osuna — on Square d'Ixelles, near the corner of Avenue Joseph-Petit and

Rue Louis-Barthou. It is open daily except Sundays year-round and on Sunday mornings in season. The friendly, efficient staff, most of whom speak fluent English, will provide maps, hotel and restaurant listings, and any other information you might need, at no charge, and will assist in choosing a hotel or making reservations. A small pamphlet listing pertinent information about the city's amenities and essential services is available for a few francs. The tourist office operates regular sightseeing tours, furnishes guides for larger groups, and supplies information about a number of local companies operating excursion buses to the Pays Basque and other neighboring regions.

Local Coverage – The daily newspaper is *Sud-Ouest.* Many bookstores and other shops in the heart of town carry newspapers and magazines in English.

 TELEPHONE: The city code for the Biarritz area (including Anglet, Bayonne, and St-Jean-de-Luz) is 59, which is incorporated into all local 8-digit numbers. When calling a number in the Biarritz area from the Paris region (including the Ile-de-France), dial 16, wait for a dial tone, then dial the 8-digit number. When calling a number from outside Paris, dial only the 8-digit number. When calling from the US, dial 33 (which is the country code), followed by the 8-digit number.

 GETTING AROUND: The most practical way to get around the center of town is to walk.

    Bicycle – *Capdeboscq* (16 Av. Jaulerry; phone: 59-24-13-64) and *Sobilo* (24 Rue Peyreloubith; phone: 59-24-94-47) rent bikes.

Bus – Public buses do not operate within Biarritz, but there is service (every half hour) between the center and the train station, and there are regular connections between Biarritz and neighboring communities. Call *STAB* (phone: 59-24-26-53) for information on buses to Anglet and Bayonne, *ATCRB* for information on buses to St-Jean-de-Luz (phone: 59-24-36-72), and *TPR* (phone: 59-27-45-98) for information on buses to Pau.

Car Rentals – The major companies represented here include *Avis* (25 Av. Edouard-VII; phone: 59-24-33-44); *Budget* (32 Av. de Bayonne; phone: 59-63-11-77); and *Europcar* (Rte. de Cazalis, near the airport; phone: 59-23-82-82).

Taxi – Though taxis don't generally cruise the winding streets in the heart of town, there's a station on Avenue de Verdun (phone: 59-24-16-13) and there are radio taxi services, including *B.A.B. Radio Taxi* (phone: 59-63-17-17).

Train – The Biarritz–La Négresse train station is almost 2 miles (3 km) southeast of the center of town, about 10 minutes by bus. Along with Bayonne and St-Jean-de-Luz, the resort is a regular stop for trains en route from Paris and Bordeaux to points in Spain. The *TGV* (*Trains à grande vitesse*) has cut the rail time from Paris to 4¾ hours instead of the nearly 8 hours the trip used to take. The trip from Biarritz to Bayonne takes approximately 10 minutes by train; to St-Jean-de-Luz, about 15 minutes. For train information, call 59-55-50-50. For reservations on the *TGV,* call 59-55-11-88.

 SPECIAL EVENTS: Biarritz's ambitious tourist authorities have worked hard over the past few years to enhance the city's appeal with creative and lively events, such as the city's *Fêtes Musicales* in May. Concerts are heard at various locations including the *Hôtel du Palais,* the Eglise Ste-Eugénie, and the sparkling *Palais des Festivals,* formerly a train station and transformed into a multipurpose cultural center. Other events include the annual *Salon des Antiquaires* (an antiques show) at the Palais Bellevue in late April or early May, the *Festival de l'Image de l'Entreprise* (Industrial Film Festival) in June, as well as the *International Bridge Festival,* also in June, and yearly golf tournaments during the summer. The city's *Bastille Day* fireworks, July 14, are stunning. The *Concours Hippique International,* a jumping championship in which equestrians from a dozen or more nations compete, falls in August. On August 15, *Nuit Féerique* (roughly translated, "magic" or "fairy" night), a grand fireworks display lights up the Grande Plage and the cliffs along the seafront. The following Sunday, for the traditional *Fête de la Mer* (Sea Festival), a helicopter drops flowers on the Rocher de la Vierge in memory of Biarritz's sailors, and there is a naval parade in late August, followed by the *Imperial Ball,* a relatively recent Biarritz tradition with much sparkle and magic. There are French-style bullfights in August and September at the *Arènes Bayonne/Biarritz.* Also in September are the *Biarritz Arena Surf Masters* (the world championship of professional surfing) and the *Festival du Film Ibérique et Latino Américain,* a Spanish- and Portuguese-language film and television festival. A music festival, predominantly classical, is held every fall. Two golf tournaments also take place in the fall: The *Pro-Am de Bulles Laurent Perrier,* which draws as many as 800 participants annually, takes place the last week of September or the first week of October; the annual *AGF Biarritz Ladies Open* is in late October.

SHOPPING: The best shopping streets are Avenue Victor-Hugo, Rue Mazagran, Avenue Edouard VII, and Avenue Maréchal-Foch, all of which converge on Place Clemenceau, the heart of town. Such well-known names as *Cartier, Hermès, Cacharel,* and *Kenzo* are represented here by boutiques, even though, for the most part, the activity on the beaches is more important than that in the shops. Particularly noteworthy are a handful of shops specializing in household linen and other articles made of the colorful cotton and wool of the nearby Pays Basque. (You may pay more for them here than you would in the small towns in the Pyrénées, but the shops in Biarritz offer a wider selection and many will accept credit cards.) There also are several shops selling the gastronomic delicacies of the neighboring Landes and Gers regions — foie gras (goose liver), *confit d'oie* and *confit de canard* (flavorful preserved goose and duck), and armagnac, to name just a few.

Arostéguy Maison – An *épicerie* carrying everything from Petrossian caviar to canned cassoulet. 5 Av. Victor-Hugo (phone: 59-24-00-52).

Bakara – Interesting antiques, old dolls, curiosities. 23 Rue Mazagran (phone: 59-22-08-95).

Boutique Fancy – A small ladies' specialty shop with a lovely, albeit expensive, selection of casual wear. 20 Pl. Clemenceau (phone: 59-24-22-75). A second shop, specializing in shoes, is at 2 Av. Maréchal-Foch.

Cannelle – Another women's boutique, with *prêt-à-porter* for summer and winter. 12 Rue Mazagran (phone: 59-24-51-47).

Christine C – Chantal Thomass's line is the main drawing card of this boutique across from the *Palais* hotel. 1 Av. Reine Victoria (phone: 59-24-73-59).

Daranatz – One of the best chocolate shops in Biarritz. 12 Av. Maréchal-Foch (phone: 59-24-21-91).

Dodin – The chocolate sold here is devastatingly tempting. 9 Pl. Clemenceau (phone: 59-24-16-37) and 7 Rue Gambetta (phone: 59-24-16-37).

Filippini – Sleek and trendy women's ready-to-wear in a stark boutique in the heart of Biarritz's best shopping area. 8 Av. Edouard-VII (phone: 59-24-62-74).

Galérie des Arceaux – One of several local antiques shops, this one specializes in 19th-century furniture and porcelain. 14 Av. Edouard-VII (phone: 59-22-08-00).

Henriet – Chocolates, made with oranges, pistachios, and almonds. The *"rocher de Biarritz"* is a specialty. Pl. Clemenceau (phone: 59-24-24-15).

Hermès – For those who didn't have time to visit the Paris shop, this one offers much the same merchandise, with an emphasis on beachwear. Av. Edouard-VII (phone: 59-24-00-64).

Maud Frizon – A tiny outlet displaying the best of this designer's fancy (and sporty) footwear. 5 Av. Edouard-VII (phone: 59-24-04-03).

Mille et Un Fromages – Cheese, wine, and other fixings for a picnic or a snack. 8 Av. Victor-Hugo (phone: 59-24-67-88).

Natacha – Actually three boutiques next door to each other (same address) that stock merchandise from such famous names as Stéphane Kélian and Sonia Rykiel. 3 Av. Edouard-VII (phone: 59-24-55-44).

Nouvelles Galeries-Biarritz Bonheur – The town's major department store, with everything from bikinis to bicycles and a supermarket in the basement. 17 Pl. Clemenceau (phone: 59-24-45-25).

Parfumerie Royale – The best names in perfume: Yves Saint Laurent, Guerlain, Shiseido, and many others. 1 Rue Mazagran (phone: 59-24-00-17).

Paries – A place for chocoholics. 27 Pl. Clemenceau (phone: 59-22-07-52).

Saint Léon – One of the most extensive collections of Basque linen. 18 Av. Victor-Hugo (phone: 59-24-19-81).

 SPORTS AND FITNESS: Not surprisingly, one of the city's strongest points is the wide range of sporting activities possible — on the water, on land, and at the well-equipped *Parc des Sports d'Aguiléra* complex east of town (Rue Henri-Haget; phone: 59-23-93-42). The most popular spectator sport is the exceedingly fast *cesta punta,* one of the many varieties of the Basque ball game known as *pelote* (and very similar to the form of the game known in the United States as jai alai). Frequent *cesta punta* games are played at the *Euskal-Jaï* fronton (phone: 59-23-91-09) at the *Aguiléra* sports complex. Other forms of *pelote* are played at the open-air fronton at *Parc Mazon* (Av. Maréchal-Joffre); at the fronton at *Plazi-Berri* (Av. Maréchal-Foch; phone: 59-23-06-86); and at the *Trinquet St-Martin* (Av. Pasteur; phone: 59-23-11-23).

Bowling – *Silver Bowling* is at the *Casino Municipal* and is open every day year-round from 3 PM to 2 AM. Enter from the Grande Plage (phone: 59-24-12-12).

Fishing – Surf casting and fishing from the rocks are popular. Contact the tourist office for information.

Golf – The city is justifiably proud of its elaborate *Centre International d'Entraînement au Golf* (Golf Training Center; Av. Reine-Nathalie, Bidart; phone: 59-23-74-65). And for practicing newly acquired skills, there are four topnotch golf courses within 15 miles (24 km) of the city. The two closest are *Golf du Biarritz* (Av. Edith-Cavell; phone: 59-03-71-80) and *Chiberta* (104 Bd. des Plages, in Anglet; phone: 59-63-83-20). Visitors are welcome. For information on other courses, contact the tourist office.

Horseback Riding – To hire a horse, go to *Centre Equestre* (Allée Gabrielle-Dorziat; phone: 59-41-27-32), which also organizes group rides along the beach and offers instruction.

Sailing – *Monsieur Hontebeyrie,* at Port des Pêcheurs, rents Hobie Cats. The *International Sailing School* (phone: 59-47-06-32 or 59-02-38-06), in operation from mid-June to mid-September in nearby Socoa, next to St-Jean-de-Luz, offers courses for all age groups at reasonable prices. *Haizean* (phone: 59-23-34-07) organizes day or week-end cruises.

Scuba Diving – The ocean floor, at depths of 15 feet and more, can be very beautiful when the weather is good. For information about equipment, lessons, and clubs, contact the tourist office.

Spas – Biarritz is a saltwater spa town: The *Centre de Thalassothérapie Louison Bobet* (Av. de l'Impératrice; phone: 59-24-20-80) and *Thermes Marins* (80 Rue de Madrid; phone: 59-23-01-22) both offer a variety of spa therapies. In 1989, the latter moved into modern, sun-flooded quarters overlooking the sea, with state-of-the-art equipment and facilities.

Squash – *Milady Squash* (phone: 59-23-27-29) is at 86 Rue de Simonnet.

Surfing – Introduced in 1958 and one of Biarritz's big draws. The most intrepid surfers head for the Plage de la Côte des Basques; the Grande Plage is somewhat less exposed. *Ecole de Surf Plums* (5 Pl. Clemenceau; phone: 59-24-08-04) offers group and individual lessons. *Moraiz Surf Shop* (25 Rue Mazagran; phone: 59-24-22-09) offers classes, and sells and rents boards, as does the *Freedom Surf Shop* (2 Av. Reine-Victoria; phone: 59-24-38-40). *Biarritz Surf Training* (Av. Edouard-VII; phone: 59-23-34-13) also offers lessons.

Swimming – The safest beach is the *Plage du Port-Vieux*. In addition to that and all the other beaches, there are swimming pools. The *Piscine Municipale* (phone: 59-24-05-83), an indoor pool of heated seawater at the *Casino Municipal*, and the outdoor pool at the *Palais* hotel (phone: 59-24-09-40), also heated sea-water, can both be used for a fee.

Tennis – *Biarritz Olympique Tennis* (phone: 59-41-20-80) has 14 courts (4 are covered), and professionals are available for lessons. Or reserve a court at the *Côte Basque Country Club* (phone: 59-52-22-55), just outside Biarritz along N10.

Windsurfing – Lessons and boards are available at *Yacht Club Basque* in Ciboure (phone: 59-47-18-31) or at *Point Glisse Océan* in Guethary (phone: 59-26-56-60).

THEATER AND MUSIC: Performances of Basque music and dancing take place frequently during the summer season. Two or three times a week, at either Parc Mazon or Plaza Berri, you'll be able to see a *pelote* match and a folklore exhibition. Much less frequently, the highly respected *Groupe Oldarra* presents its own Basque song and dance *spectacle*, also usually at Parc Mazon. In addition to the annual fall music festival and the *Fêtes Musicales* in May, concerts by visiting and local artists and ensembles take place year-round in venues such as the Eglise Ste-Eugénie, the *Palais* hotel, the *Casino Bellevue*, and the *Palais des Festivals*.

NIGHTCLUBS AND NIGHTLIFE: About a dozen establishments in Biarritz call themselves nightclubs. Among the more sophisticated and popular of the lot are the chic *Copacabana* (22 Av. Edouard-VII; phone: 59-24-65-39); the *Play Boy* (Rue Monhau; phone: 59-24-38-46), an old if now slightly fading favorite where the music is recorded and shifts in mood with the mood of the disk jockey; *Caveau* (4 Av. Gambetta; phone: 59-24-16-17), where a chic mixed crowd gathers; and the *Brasilia* (Av. Edouard-VII; phone: 59-24-65-30) for Brazilian cocktails and salsa music. For piano music, try *Le Piano Bar* (*Hôtel du Palais;* phone: 59-24-09-04) and *Carlos* (Côte des Basques; phone: 59-24-95-51), with a terrace overlooking the sea. The *Blue Note* (21 Av. Edouard-VII; phone: 59-24-78-10) features jazz nightly. Dress is casual in all. The *Casino Bellevue* (Pl. Bellevue; phone: 59-24-11-22) is open daily in season from about 4 PM. General entry is free, but you pay a small sum to enter the room where baccarat, roulette, and blackjack are played. It has a nightclub, *La Plantation*.

BEST IN TOWN

CHECKING IN: At last count, Biarritz's hotel inventory numbered nearly 1,000 rooms, their comforts ranging from the super luxe of the *Palais* to the simplicity of various small budget hotels that are nevertheless near the beaches and in the path of refreshing sea breezes. A healthy number of rooms in all categories have ocean views, and about 60% of the hotels are open year-round. During high season — July through September — some of the hotels operate on a full-pension system, charging a flat rate per person for room and board, including

continental breakfast, lunch, and dinner. Reserving in advance is recommended highly
if you want a room during July or August, but the tourist office will try to assist
travelers who need help finding rooms. There also are a number of hotels in the
neighboring beach communities of Bidart and Anglet, both rapidly becoming important
resorts in their own right. In the hotels listed below, expect to pay $100 and up for a
double room in high season (without full pension) in the expensive category, from $60
to $100 in the moderate category, and under $60 in the inexpensive category.

Château de Brindos – A charming Italianate villa hidden in a thick grove of trees
at the edge of a lake filled with water lilies and some swans. The lovely surroundings, the grand interiors, the highly rated restaurant (see *Eating Out*), and the
availability of only 12 rooms make it a perfect choice for those who prefer tranquillity to proximity to the beach (though the hotel does have a heated swimming pool
as well as a tennis court). Major credit cards accepted. Lac de Brindos, approximately 3 miles (5 km) southeast of Biarritz, off N10 (phone: 59-23-17-68; fax:
59-23-48-47). Expensive.

Miramar – Although the building itself looks like a nuclear-age command center,
the 126 rooms and suites are undeniably comfortable, the service is excellent, and
the restaurant has earned a Michelin star. It also has a lobby bar, boutiques, gym,
sauna, heated seawater swimming pool (outdoor), and the *Centre de Thalassothérapie Louison Bobet* (a saltwater spa). Major credit cards accepted. 11 Av. de
l'Impératrice (phone: 59-41-30-00; fax: 59-24-77-20). Expensive.

Palais – This imposing imperial villa dominating the Grande Plage still looks much
as it did when Eugénie and Napoleon spent their summers here in the 19th
century. In its reincarnation as a hotel with more than 160 rooms, it offers a
renovated version of the Old World grandeur to which its original owners were
accustomed: public rooms still rife with marble floors, columns, chandeliers, and
draperies; guestrooms done with period furnishings; attentive service. The heated
seawater swimming pool on a terrace by the beach has cabañas and a casual
poolside restaurant that draws the lunch crowd, and there are two more formal
restaurants, *La Rotonde* and *Le Grand Siècle* (see *Eating Out* for both). Closed
from February through March. Major credit cards accepted. 1 Av. de l'Impératrice (phone: 59-24-09-40; fax: 59-24-36-84). Expensive.

Régina et Golf – A luxury hostelry that offers old-fashioned grandeur on a small
scale. It's set majestically above the city on a plateau near the lighthouse, public
gardens, and golf course, and many of its 71 rooms, have breathtaking views.
There also is a restaurant specializing in seafood. Closed from November 18
through December 22. Major credit cards accepted. 52 Av. de l'Impératrice
(phone: 59-41-33-00; fax: 59-41-33-99). Expensive.

Plaza – Fairly modern and unpretentious, this 60-room place has a gracious air and
a prime location overlooking the beaches and the center of Biarritz. The rooms
are spacious and well furnished, and most have balconies commanding an ocean
view. The bar is a rich, elegant room; the staff understands some English; there
are parking facilities. Actually, you get more than you pay for here. Open year-
round. Major credit cards accepted. Av. Edouard-VII (phone: 59-24-74-00; fax:
59-22-22-01). Expensive to moderate.

Président – A typical "French modern" property that might seem more at home
in a business center than a resort. Nonetheless, its 64 rooms are comfortable, and
it's handy for the beach, restaurants, and shopping. No restaurant. Open year-
round. Major credit cards accepted. Pl. Clemenceau (phone: 59-24-66-40). Expensive to moderate.

Le Château du Clair de Lune – Just 10 minutes from Biarritz, this is an exquisite
miniature château set well back from the road and surrounded by gardens and
woods. A treasure of simple refinement, it has 7 individually decorated rooms and

the ambience of a private home. Major credit cards accepted. 48 Av. Alan Seeger, Rte. d'Arbonne (phone: 59-23-45-96). Moderate.

Windsor – The oceanside door of this 53-room hostelry is just a frog's leap from the Grande Plage. The welcome is friendly, and the rooms, many with views, were redecorated in a comfortable modern style, and a restaurant has been added. Closed from mid-January to mid-February. Major credit cards accepted. 11 Av. Edouard-VII, Grande Plage (phone: 59-24-08-52). Moderate.

Le Petit Hôtel – One of the best bargains in town, on a tiny street in the heart of Biarritz. It has a fresh, pretty lobby and 12 cheerful rooms. The owners, Mme. and M. Puig, are charming people. Major credit cards accepted. 11 Rue Garderes (phone: 59-24-87-00). Moderate to inexpensive.

Edouard-VII – Simple, with 15 rooms and up the hill from the beaches and town center. The jovial proprietor is a gem, and his rooms are clean (though not fancy). Closed from October through February. No credit cards accepted. 21 Av. Carnot (phone: 59-24-07-20). Inexpensive.

Palacito – Though the welcome here can be curt, this 26-room hotel is conveniently located, clean, reasonably priced, and open all year except for the month of January. No restaurant. Major credit cards accepted. Sq. Gambetta (phone: 59-24-04-89; fax: 59-24-33-43). Inexpensive.

 EATING OUT: From a gastronomic point of view, Biarritz is ideally situated. A rich fishing center with all manner of fresh fish and seafood, it also benefits from its proximity to the Landes and Gers regions, rich in foie gras, and to the Basque country, famous for air-dried ham, fish soups (such as the peppery *ttoro*), and Basque cakes. The resort's restaurants, therefore, are impressive in their number and variety, and the quality is, for the most part, high, while the prices remain reasonable. (A definite trend is the proliferation of ample, inexpensive fixed-price menus in places that would otherwise be considered very pricey.) Dinner for two in an expensive restaurant will cost $85 and up, not including wine (service usually is included); in a restaurant listed as moderate, between $60 and $85; and in an inexpensive eatery, less than $50. With your meal, try the madiran and jurançon wines of the region.

Café de Paris – An airy, garden-like spot in the shadow of the *Casino Bellevue,* considered by some to be the best dining establishment on France's Atlantic coast, although it lost its Michelin star in 1991. Pierre Laporte, son of the founder of this Biarritz landmark, opened in 1927, directs the kitchen and is undertaking an expansion that will include guestrooms. Reservations advised. Major credit cards accepted. 5 Pl. Bellevue (phone: 59-24-19-53; fax: 59-24-18-20). Expensive.

Château de Brindos – It's worth a visit to this tranquil villa-hotel if only to enjoy a meal in its beautifully appointed dining room overlooking the lake. The food won't let you down, however; Basque specialties and dishes include a *mousseline* of turbot encased in puff pastry. Open daily. Reservations advised. Major credit cards accepted. About 3 miles (5 km) southeast of Biarritz, just off N10 (phone: 59-23-17-68; fax: 59-23-48-47). Expensive.

Le Grand Siècle – The *Palais* hotel's "gastronomic" restaurant brims with Belle Epoque charm and pomp. Its kitchen has won accolades for dishes such as langoustine on a bed of Basque-style *pipérade* (a mixture of green and red sweet peppers, onions, and tomatoes), and veal wrapped in celery root. Open daily from 8 AM to 10 PM. Reservations necessary. Major credit cards accepted. *Hôtel du Palais,* 1 Av. de l'Impératrice (phone: 59-24-09-40). Expensive.

La Rotonde – Though the ornate chandeliers, marble columns, and other Belle Epoque touches of the *Palais*'s panoramic round dining room set you up for the rather dusty old clichés of hotel food, there have been some well-received shifts to lighter, more modern specialties lately. Closed from mid-October to May. Reservations advised. Major credit cards accepted. *Hôtel du Palais,* 1 Av. de l'Impératrice (phone: 59-24-09-40). Expensive.

Galion – Ocean views, a marine motif, and nouvelle cuisine featuring fresh seafood are the attractions of this local favorite. Closed Sunday dinners, Mondays (except during July and August), and during February. Reservations advised. Major credit cards accepted. 17 Av. Général-de-Gaulle (phone: 59-24-20-32). Expensive to moderate.

La Gascogne – A staid, conservative, yet comfortable sort of place, where people talk in whispers above their china dinner plates. Its fixed-price menus are a comparative bargain. For lunch, they feature such things as *salade basquaise* and *poulet basquaise;* at dinnertime, one of the recommended combinations includes fresh, giant oysters followed by a three-layered fish pâté and a chicken dish served with a delicious tarragon and cream sauce. Closed Wednesdays, Sunday evenings, and November to March. Reservations advised. Major credit cards accepted. 11 Av. du Maréchal-Foch (phone: 59-24-20-12). Expensive to moderate.

Les Platanes – An inviting Basque-style house not far from town where Arnaud and Véronique Daguin have opened an original and personal style of restaurant — nothing here is a cliché, from the Plexiglass-encased menu that changes every few days to the food to the decor (there's a huge tableau of nudes behind the bar). Closed Mondays and Tuesday lunch. Reservations advised. Visa accepted. 32 Av. Beausoleil (phone: 59-23-13-68). Expensive to moderate.

La Belle Epoque – The entrance to this genteel dining room is through a crystal and silver boutique. The decor is true to the name, with handsome wood and a central dining court with palm trees. The food, however, is up to date and creative. The *ragoût du pêcheur* (fish stew) contains everything that swims. Closed Mondays off-season. Reservations advised. Major credit cards accepted. 10 Av. Victor-Hugo (phone: 59-24-66-06). Moderate.

Chez Albert – The largest and best known of a handful of delightful, casual seafood eateries tucked away in the old Port des Pêcheurs, below Place Eugénie. Dinner comes with entertainment in the form of Albert, your flamboyant host. Closed Wednesdays and from December to April. Reservations advised. Major credit cards accepted. Port des Pêcheurs (phone: 59-24-43-84). Moderate.

Le Comptoir – Sleek and rather high-tech, this brasserie near the center of town looks onto a garden and offers good quality at a resonable price. Open daily for lunch and dinner. Reservations advised on weekends. Major credit cards accepted. On the corner of Rue Monhaut (phone: 59-24-46-46). Moderate.

Tantina de Bourgos – One of a wave of Spanish restaurants and *tapas* bars to open here in recent years, this place is notable for its grilled fresh fish and meat. Open daily except Sundays for dinner. Reservations advised. Major credit cards accepted. 2 Pl. Beaurivage (phone: 59-23-24-47). Moderate.

Les 3 Salsas – For those homesick for south-of-the-border fare, this casual, popular spot specializes in Mexican dishes. Closed off-season. Reservations unnecessary. No credit cards accepted. 5 Rue Harispe (phone: 59-23-04-53). Moderate.

Le Vaudeville – A trendy spot, where residents and well-informed visitors enjoy fine food at reasonable prices. Closed Monday and Tuesday for lunch. Reservations advised. Major credit cards accepted. 5 Rue du Centre (phone: 59-24-34-66). Moderate.

Auberge de la Négresse – Bright, active, and near the train station, it's off the beaten beach track, a bit tricky to find but worth the search. The simple, traditional specialties that keep it crowded include foie gras, grilled *louvine* (sea bass, or *loup,* in local parlance), and roast milk-fed lamb. The head cook also is a butcher and does wonders with meat dishes. Closed Mondays and October. Reservations unnecessary. Visa accepted. 10 Av. de l'Aérodrome, under the viaduct (phone: 59-23-15-83). Moderate to inexpensive.

Les Flots Bleus – Perched on the cliffs overlooking Plage de la Côte des Basques, this wonderful family place is far from the commotion of the town center. You can order anything from Italian food to Moroccan couscous to *crêpes à la provençale,* though the specialties are seafood dishes of the region, including a fresh fish soup that could feed a boatload of people. If you're lucky, you'll be served by Madame Casagrande, originally from Venice, who has customers returning from as near as Bordeaux and as far as the Jersey shore and San Diego. When you meet her, you'll understand why. Open year-round. Reservations unnecessary. Major credit cards accepted. 41 Perspective Côte Basques (phone: 59-24-10-03). Moderate to inexpensive.

 BARS AND CAFÉS: A popular spot with locals and visitors alike is *Les Colonnes* (4 Av. Edouard-VII). It has a perfectly coordinated wood, leather, brass, and bamboo interior, a terrace in front with tables and chairs set under a portico, and a view of the ocean. *Le Choucas,* a lively, sleek, but not overbearing café on Place Clemenceau, is perfect for people watching. Also on Place Clemenceau is *La Coupole* (phone: 59-24-09-96) and the café/bar *Le Royalty* (phone: 59-24-01-34). Recorded pop/rock plays continually and a live band performs several nights a week and on weekends (from 10 PM until customers feel like going home). Snacks are served at any hour. *Le Corsaire,* on the tiny waterfront of Port des Pêcheurs, used to be a highly regarded seafood restaurant. Now it is an intimate bar, small and cozy inside, with stucco walls, brass lamps, and popdisco playing softly from the speakers. Other alternatives: Tea at the *Miremont* (1 Pl. Georges Clemenceau; phone: 59-24-01-38) where there's a spectacular view of the sea, or *tapas* at *El Callejon* (Rue Monhau; phone: 59-24-99-15), a popular spot on a tiny street in the center of town.

BORDEAUX

The people of Bordeaux pronounce the name of their city slowly, with great import. They roll the syllables on their tongues as if each vowel were a fine wine to be savored and appreciated. Bordeaux, originally the Latin *Burdigala,* was founded on the bank of the Garonne River where it suddenly diverts from its meandering path to take the shape of a gigantic crescent moon. A quick glance at a map will show how the city also has taken this shape, as have the two major roads that loop around it. It's only fitting that the symbol of Bordeaux, then, is a crescent moon.

Originally a village of Gallic tribes, Bordeaux prospered as a military headquarters for the colonizing Romans, who introduced grape growing to the region. The town withstood assaults by successive waves of Visigoths, Arabs, and Normans, and first began to achieve mercantile fame as an English city. It was part of the dowry of the colorful Eleanor (Alienor), daughter of the ruling Duke of Aquitaine and Count of Poitiers, on her marriage, at age 15, to the future Louis VII of France. In 1152, after 15 years and two daughters, Louis sued for annulment and, in his eagerness to be rid of his high-spirited wife, tossed back the riches she had brought to the ill-fated union. Eleanor, then 30 years old, packed up and left "the monk in a crown," as her circle contemptuously referred to him, and to the amazement of all married the teenage Henry Plantagenet, Duke of Normandy and Count of Anjou, 2 months later. The gilded couple's combined territories in France equaled those of the French sovereign, and when Henry inherited the crown of England in 1154, a long struggle for the possession of the Aquitaine began between the English and French.

Throughout the Anglo-French wars of the next 3 centuries, the Bordelais considered themselves more English than French and were content to remain under the rule of England. The laissez-faire policies of the English crown granted a privileged independence to the shippers and traders of the city, and the English taste for claret, as the English alone called the red wines of Bordeaux, allowed the wine growers to increase their production many times over. By the middle of the 14th century, the equivalent of a million modern cases of wine was leaving the port of Bordeaux yearly, much of it for the thirsty market across the English Channel.

Bordeaux, along with the rest of the province of Aquitaine, reverted to France at the conclusion of the Hundred Years War in 1453. Although the English influence then waned, the long arm of the Parisian government did not make itself felt in any consistent way until the 18th century, when Louis XV ascended the throne. An economic boom, begun during the reign of Louis XIV, was well under way in Bordeaux. The city was shipping wine, foodstuffs, and textiles as far away as the expanding colonial markets in America and the West Indies, and wine, armaments, hardware, and manufactured goods to Africa. Foreign ships brought fine wood, tobacco, rum, sugar, coffee, and raw materials into its port.

This enormously profitable mercantile operation enriched both private and public purses, and provided a steady flow of cash for the vast program of public works that transformed Bordeaux into one of the most handsome provincial cities in France. The king, aware of Bordeaux's commercial and strategic importance, appointed governors (*intendants*) to oversee the city during this period, and it is to them that it owes its modern face. Each *intendant* in turn tried to outdo his predecessor in clearing away slums, crowded alleyways, and swampy marshland to create broad quays, public parks, and boulevards lined with splendid *hôtels particuliers*. Many of these mansions still stand today as townhouses for the wealthiest shippers and wine growers. Public buildings dating from this era include the 18th-century architectural ensemble of Place de la Bourse, with the Hôtel des Douanes (Customs House) and the Hôtel de la Bourse (Stock Exchange), the Hôtel de Ville (originally the Palais Rohan) with its beautifully landscaped mayoral garden, and the *Grand Théâtre*. Other striking samples of this heritage can be seen around Place de la Comédie, Place Gambetta, and Place Tourny and the streets connecting them — Cours Clemenceau, Cours de l'Intendance, and Allées de Tourny.

During the late 19th century, Bordeaux suffered a disastrous and bewildering upheaval brought about by the invasion of the American vine louse *Phylloxera vastatrix,* which ate the roots of the source of "red gold" in the surrounding vineyards. The cost to France was incalculable, but one estimate puts it at more than that of the Franco-Prussian War of 1870–71. Finally, the roots of native American species, which were immune to the parasite, were grafted onto the French vine stocks, and eventually business resumed and Bordeaux recovered its economic balance. Even with the foreign roots, the growers assert that the vineyards reach deep into French soil and the wine produced is purely French.

The life, livelihood, and lure of Bordeaux do not rest solely on the reputation of the wine produced almost in its backyard, as the Bordelais are the first to tell you. The city also is well known for its interest in architectural revival, particularly of buildings dating from the 18th century. Everywhere in the city, restoration and rehabilitation are in progress, but nowhere is this resurgence more obvious and exciting than in the old part of town by the river, Vieux Bordeaux. Restoration work has extended into the adjacent St-Michel quarter. Along many of the cobbled streets of these old quarters, workers are busily scraping away dingy façades and exposing amber stone, drawing deserved attention to ancient doorways, window trims, and gracefully curving stairways. Everywhere, too, the eye is entertained by fine examples of the ornamental ironwork and hardware — lacy balcony railings, handsome door knockers and hinges — with which Bordeaux's buildings, particularly those of the 18th century, are so admirably adorned.

Bordeaux is also a cultural and trade center, holding important industrial conferences at a complex called Le Lac. And it is a vacation spot as well, because in every direction, and in each case no more than an hour away, lie places to go for a day, a weekend, or a week or more of relaxation, exercise, or cultural diversion. Due east lies the picturesque medieval village and wine producing area of St-Emilion; due south, the serene forests of Les Landes, with tiny villages and extensive bicycle and horse trails; to the southwest, the Arcachon Basin and the old resort town from which it takes its name; and west and northwest lie miles of beaches backed by forest and two large lakes perfect for swimming, fishing, and boating. And almost due north lies the Médoc, acres of the most noble vineyards in France. Nestled in a bend of the Garonne River, Bordeaux beckons travelers not only to a vital urban center, the home of almost 600,000 people and filled with attractions to look at, stroll through, buy, and admire, but also to an entire region of abiding richness and beauty.

BORDEAUX AT-A-GLANCE

SEEING THE CITY: Bordeaux is a flat city that boasts no skyscraper or revolving rooftop restaurant from which to view the pleasing network of wide boulevards, smaller streets, and winding passageways. The tower of Eglise St-Michel, the tallest structure in the city, unfortunately is not open to the public. Visitors can, however, go up to the Porte Cailhau for a view of the Pont de Pierre and the river. It is open Tuesdays and Saturdays from 2 to 6 PM and there is a guided visit every 45 minutes (phone: 56-79-05-39). Call in advance to arrange for an English-speaking guide. For a view of the city and the cathedral, climb the Tour Pey-Berland (Pl. Pey-Berland; phone: 56-81-26-25); open daily from 10 AM to 12:30 PM and 2 to 6 PM. You can get a marvelous view, especially in the evening, by crossing over to the east bank of the Garonne on the Pont de Pierre and heading north until you are opposite the Place de la Bourse and Porte Cailhau; from here you see the impressive buildings along the quays and the entry to the Old City. In the center, marvelous squares — Place de la Comédie, Place Gambetta, Place du Parlement, Place Tourny, for instance — with streets branching off them in every direction open up to give the effect of looking at different parts of the city through a wide-angle lens.

SPECIAL PLACES: Bordeaux is best seen on foot. The downtown area, for example, is traversed easily beginning at the Place de la Comédie, the heart of town. Wander up Cours de l'Intendance as far as Place Gambetta, stopping at Eglise Notre-Dame on Place du Chapelet (Rue Martignac leads there). At Place Gambetta, you can sip coffee at the outdoor café, *Le Dijeaux,* study a map, and people watch. From Porte Dijeaux — an early corruption of Porte des Juifs — follow Rue Bouffard to its end, where you will find Cathédrale St-André on your left and the Hôtel de Ville (Town Hall), backed by the *Musée des Beaux-Arts,* on your right; flip a coin to decide which to visit first. Then follow the pedestrian Rue des Trois Conils along the modern St-Christoly commercial center toward the river as far as Place St-Projet, the oldest town square in the city and once a source of fresh water from underground springs for the community. Turn left onto Rue Ste-Catherine, another pedestrian street (but don't be surprised when motorcycles, even cars, whiz by) that will take you back to the Place de la Comédie. If you have a little energy left, stroll along Allées de Tourny, surely one of the loveliest thoroughfares in Bordeaux, named after the governor who perhaps did the most to beautify the city. Another area, the most exciting these days because of the continuing restoration movement and the proliferation of small restaurants, shops, and galleries, is Vieux Bordeaux (Old Bordeaux). This section twists and turns from the river at Porte Cailhau, and almost every street leads to a pleasant discovery of one kind or another. It's the kind of place that encourages you to get happily and irrevocably lost, though in your meanderings be sure to find Rue des Argentiers and Rue des Bahutiers — silversmiths' and chestmakers' streets — named for the merchants who used to work along them. Finally, there are the special places that require a bit of a hike, a drive, a bus ride, or perhaps a boat ride, but are their own reward for the effort it takes to get there.

DOWNTOWN

Grand Théâtre – Designed by the architect Victor Louis (who also designed the famous arcades of the Palais-Royal in Paris) and completed in 1780, this theater, with its 12 Corinthian pillars, has been the inspiration for theaters around the world, including *L'Opéra* in Paris. The 12 statues of muses and goddess-patrons of the arts, posed regally on the front balcony, extend an open invitation to enjoy a theatrical, operatic, or philharmonic event. The interior is richly decorated and the acoustics are practically perfect. Pl. de la Comédie (phone: 57-79-01-66; for reservations, 56-48-58-54).

Maison du Vin – This striking, flatiron-shaped building is a source of information about wine, wine making, and châteaux in the region that are open for tours and tastings. Changing exhibits, as well as tastings (Mondays through Fridays beginning at 10 AM and 2:30 PM) in the handsome, remodeled ground-floor center, make it all the more interesting. Open weekdays from 8:30 AM to 6 PM, and on Saturdays from 8:30 AM to 6 PM in summer. 1 Cours du 30-Juillet (phone: 56-00-22-66).

Eglise Notre-Dame – An Italian Revival church of the late 17th and early 18th century, completely restored inside and out. Tucked away on Place du Chapelet at the end of Rue Martignac, just off Cours de l'Intendance.

Musée des Beaux-Arts (Fine Arts Museum) – In existence since the early 19th century, this small museum was created at the behest of Napoleon Bonaparte when he was premier consul of France. It houses an important collection of paintings and sculpture, with the emphasis on French works (Delacroix, Redon, Corot, Matisse, Seurat, Renoir, and Rodin), although Italian and Flemish painters also are well represented. Open 10 AM to noon and 2 to 6 PM; closed Tuesdays. Guided visits by appointment. Entrance in the garden of the Hôtel de Ville, Cours d'Albret. The *Galerie des Beaux-Arts,* cater-cornered to the museum and entered from Pl. du Colonel-Raynal, is open only for special exhibitions (phone: 56-10-17-49).

Musée d'Aquitaine – Bordeaux's oldest museum (1781) is in a restored and modernized 1885 building. It houses permanent collections and temporary exhibitions covering the Bordeaux area from prehistoric times to the present. The history, agriculture, aquaculture, viticulture, commerce, art, and daily life of the province are well illustrated, in almost an acre of rooms (many of them have been renovated), through artworks, tools, documents, and more. Also displayed are some of the books of Nobel Prize winner François Mauriac, one of France's most famous contemporary writers (d. 1970). A Bordeaux native, Mauriac drew much inspiration for his work from the area. The museum is open from 10 AM to 6 PM; closed Mondays; no admission charge on Wednesdays. 20 Cours Pasteur at the corner of Cours Victor-Hugo (phone: 56-10-17-58).

Hôtel de Ville (Town Hall) – Formerly the Palais Rohan, it was built in the 18th century for the prince-archbishop, later cardinal, de Rohan, who declared, when he insisted on the lavish dwelling, "I am not a king, I wouldn't consider being a prince, I am a Rohan!" Features of the original decoration include finely carved wainscoting, the grand staircase, and the monotone mural paintings (grisailles) by the Bordelais painter Lacour in the grand dining room. The interior now consists mainly of offices and state rooms, which are closed to all except groups (ask at the tourist office or the

Town Hall), but the exterior is worth a look for its simple, striking lines. The lintels of the windows in the side sections are decorated with garlands of fruit; the interior wainscoting is the work of the Bordeaux sculptor Cabirol. Guided visits on Wednesdays at 2:30 PM are open to the public. The garden, flanked on one side by the *Musée des Beaux-Arts*, closes at 6:30 PM, except 8:30 or 9 PM in summer. Pl. Pey-Berland (phone: 56-90-91-60).

Cathédrale St-André – The original cathedral was built during the 11th and 12th centuries and portions were added during the boom period of British rule; when the funds ran out, the building-in-progress stopped. To an amateur's eye, at least, the existing hodgepodge, complete with flying buttresses, appears all of a piece, if not downright winsome, in its gracefully landscaped setting. Inside, the cathedral is surprisingly light and airy, and a magnificent organ fills the back of it. Through its impressive 13th-century Porte Royale have passed the lowly and the great. Viollet-le-Duc made moldings of some of the statues of the door to use in his restoration of Notre-Dame in Paris. The representations of the Apostles, Last Judgment, Resurrection, and Divine Court are particularly beautiful. Pl. Pey-Berland.

Centre National Jean Moulin – The center is named for the writer, artist, and Résistance hero who was murdered by Klaus Barbie's Gestapo headquartered at Lyons. Only a few years old, it houses an extensive collection related to the events of World War II, including important documents and photographs detailing the history and achievements of the Resistance. Don't overlook the powerful paintings by Jean-Jacques Morvan on the second floor and the re-creation of Moulin's clandestine office on the third floor. Open weekdays from 2 to 6 PM; closed weekends and holidays. Pl. Jean-Moulin (phone: 56-10-15-80).

VIEUX BORDEAUX (OLD BORDEAUX)

Porte Cailhau – This is one of the entries to the Old City, dating from 1495. Although it now stands alone, it's possible to see where the ramparts once were attached. It can be visited on Wednesdays and Saturdays from 2 to 6 PM. There are guided tours every 45 minutes. Just north of Pont de Pierre at Quai de la Douane.

Eglise St-Pierre – A small Romanesque church built from the 15th to the 19th century. On Thursday mornings, the food market in the square facing the church is a good place for lunch. Pl. St-Pierre.

Place du Parlement – Constructed primarily around 1760, this is one of the quietest, sunniest, and most tranquil of Bordeaux's lovely *places*. Any of the small streets branching from it inevitably lead to a restaurant or a tiny shop full of treasures. Due east is the Place de la Bourse.

Place de la Bourse (former Stock Exchange) – This square was laid out and built from 1730 to 1755. The beautiful grouping of warm, gold-tinged stone laced with elegant wrought iron is a fitting symbol of the wealth and taste of the age. Quai de la Douane, north of Pont de Pierre.

Les Quais – Walk along the quays from St. Michael's Church to Place de la Bourse — braving the noise and car fumes — to appreciate the backdrop of 18th-century buildings. Most notable are the faces carved over doorways and in walls; called *mascarons,* they represent the people of Bordeaux at that time, from shipper to slave, as well as mythology and fantasy. Supposedly there are a couple of hundred *mascarons,* no two of them alike. Quais des Salinières, Quai Richelieu, Quai de la Douane.

Pont de Pierre – It's impossible not to notice this graceful, low-slung, bridge with its 17 arches looping the Garonne. Remarkably, it was Bordeaux's only bridge from the time it was built, in 1822, until the completion of Pont St-Jean in 1965. It's most beautiful at dusk. Opposite Pl. de Bir-Hakeim.

Eglise St-Michel – The basilica of St. Michael's was badly damaged during World War II, but the modern stained glass windows over the high altar work well in their

15th-century setting. Two original windows from the 16th century remain in the transept. The bell tower, built separately, at 375 feet is the tallest in the south of France. Pl. St-Michel at Rue des Faures.

La Grosse Cloche (The Great Bell) – Along busy Cours Victor-Hugo, lined with 18th- and 19th-century buildings, this 13th- to 16th-century clock tower looks oddly out of place. The bell used to signal the beginning of the grape harvest but now chimes only on days of national rejoicing. Beside the tower is the tiny Eglise St-Eloi, which was built into the wall of the Old City. There is a movement afoot to restore this church, named after the patron saint of ironworkers; it is not now open to the public. Rue St-James, just off Cours Victor-Hugo.

Maison des Montaigne – Built in the 16th century, the family home of the philosopher Michel de Montaigne still stands, though it is privately owned and not open to the public. (The Château de Montaigne, where he was born and died, is about 30 miles/48 km east of Bordeaux.) 23-25 Rue de la Rousselle.

Cité Internationale des Vins – This ambitious project, which was scheduled to open at press time, is a 5-acre trade and cultural center dedicated to the wine industry. It is in the Chartrons district, where for centuries the majority of the wine activity of the region was carried on. The area includes restored *chais,* an international *maison des vins* and market, a wine museum, a research center, shops, pedestrian walks, and restaurants. Bordered by Cours Xavier-Arnozan (where many of the elite of Bordeaux have their mansions), Cours de Verdun, and Quai des Chartrons.

Casa de Goya and Espace Goya – Two institutions in the house where the painter lived and died in exile. They include a permanent exhibition of Goya's life in Bordeaux and replicas of his rooms, and a Spanish cultural center offering occasional movies, concerts, lectures, and exhibitions. Open weekdays from 1:30 to 6 PM and also Wednesday mornings from 9 to noon; closed on weekends. There are guided tours the first Friday of the month at 2:30 PM for a small fee. 57 Cours de l'Intendance (phone: 56-52-79-37).

ELSEWHERE

Musée d'Art Contemporain/L'Entrepôt Lainé – During the 1800s and early 1900s this was the storehouse for the coffee, rum, wood, and spices shipped to Bordeaux from its colonies. Today it is a storehouse for talent, the up-and-coming modern arts center in southwest France. In 1973 the city saved the building from demolition and completely remodeled it inside to accommodate art exhibits and to house the *Musée d'Art Contemporain,* incorporating the *Centre d'Art Plastique Contemporain (CAPC).* From its beginning as a center with temporary exhibits, the *CAPC* has blossomed into an increasingly important museum. Closed Mondays. Admission charge. The museum café is pleasant and inexpensive. Near Quai des Chartrons and the Esplanade des Quinconces. 7 Rue Ferrère at Rue Foy (phone: 56-44-16-35).

Jardin Public – A 5-minute walk from the Place Tourny or Esplanade des Quinconces, this idyllic spot, surrounded by 19th-century townhouses, is the place to see the Bordelais at rest and at play — young children, with a parent or two in tow, and retired friends knitting, reading, or chatting on park benches. The tiny pond is put to good use by swans, ducks, and by children going for a joy ride in a small boat called *Le Petit Mousse.* Also here is an old and charming botanical garden and a bust by the sculptor Zadkine of 20th-century writer François Mauriac, a native son of Bordeaux and a Nobel Prize winner. Open until 8 PM, and an hour later in summer. Cours de Verdun.

Palais Gallien (Roman Palace) – A relic of Bordeaux's distant past, this 3rd-century Roman amphitheater could accommodate 15,000 spectators. The ruins are blocked from public access, but it is possible to get a couple of worthwhile views of them. Just follow Rue du Palais Gallien to its end, in the direction of the traffic.

Eglise St-Seurin – In the middle of a busy commercial and residential neighborhood, this appears to be an edifice that time forgot. Residents walk their dogs and chat in the church grounds, while 100 feet away lies an 11th-century crypt with 6th-century tombs, discovered only in the 1960s. Guided tours of the crypt are offered by the tourist office, and an audiovisual show about the archaeological findings is presented from April through October on Tuesday and Saturday afternoons at 2 and 6 PM. Painters often congregate in the garden here the first Saturday afternoon of each month. Pl. des Martyrs-de-la-Résistance (phone: 56-79-05-39).

Quartier Mériadeck – Although this modern complex of chrome, concrete, and steel buildings is almost right across the street from the *Fine Arts Museum,* it's easy to miss if you don't know it's here. Not only interesting as a modern center for living, working, and shopping in what is essentially an 18th-century city, its plaza and the varied styles of its buildings deserve a look. While you're here, drop by the 5-story *Centre Commercial de Mériadeck* with 100 boutiques. Between Rues Jean-Fleuret and Claude-Bonnier, opposite the garden of the Hôtel de Ville.

Cimetière de la Chartreuse – Graveyard lovers should wend their way a few blocks west of Mériadeck to this very old cemetery, with its interesting tombs, at St. Bruno's Church; both church and cemetery date from the 18th century. The church has a painting by Philippe de Champaigne and a statue by Bernini; the cemetery has a monument marking the spot where Goya was temporarily buried. Open 8 AM to 5:30 PM. Corner of Rue François-de-Sourdis and Rue Georges-Bonnac (phone: 56-93-17-20).

Le Lac – North of downtown Bordeaux — and a car, bus, or taxi ride away — this is a conference and exposition center with a lake for sailing, a golf course, as well as a stadium and a rose garden. In June, Le Lac is the site of a well-known wine exposition. It also is the site of several comfortable hotels (see *Checking In*). The drawbacks of Bordeaux-le-Lac are that it is out of the way in a not very attractive area, and as one Bordelais summed it up, "The lake is artificial, but the mosquitoes are real." West of the Pont d'Aquitaine.

ENVIRONS

Blaye – This small walled city, built in 1688–89, is on the right bank of the Gironde about 30 miles (48 km) north of Bordeaux. It can be reached by boat, and of the several boat trips possible from Bordeaux, this one is most highly recommended. Excursion days — which begin at 9:30 AM and end at 6 PM — are posted in the tourist office, where tickets can be purchased. Pack a picnic or eat at *La Citadelle* (phone: 57-42-10-34), in the citadel in Blaye; it's good if expensive. To reach Blaye by land, drive to Lamarque and take the ferry across the Gironde or go by way of St-André-de-Cubzac, following the scenic route along the Dordogne and stopping to admire the view from the terrace of the Château de Bourg. From May to mid-October, the tourist office (phone: 57-42-12-09) offers bus excursions to different vineyards in the area. Buses leave the tourist office daily at 1:30 PM for the 1½-hour trip.

Château de la Brède – The birthplace and home of Montesquieu from 1689 to 1775, this castle-like château was built from the 13th to the 15th century. Surrounded by a large moat, the impressive dwelling is open daily, except Tuesdays, from 2 to 6 PM from July through September, and weekdays from 2 to 5:30 PM from *Easter* through June. Admission charge. About 12 miles (19 km) south of Bordeaux via N113 and D108 (phone: 56-20-20-49). The Bordeaux Tourist Office has the best information (phone: 56-44-28-41).

Château Haut-Brion – In 1855, the wines of 60 or so of the 100 châteaux in the Médoc were classified according to excellence. The famous red wine produced here, only a few miles southwest of the center of Bordeaux, was the only one outside the Médoc to be included in the classification, and this is the perfect place for visitors who want to visit a vineyard but have no time, or perhaps transportation, to go to the Médoc. The château is now owned by the US Ambassador to France under Dwight D. Eisenhower, Douglas Dillon, and most of its wine is sold to the United States. Tours take place mornings and afternoons, but reservations are necessary. Closed weekends and in August. No admission charge. In Pessac, via N650, or take a bus from Quai Richelieu in Bordeaux (phone: 56-00-29-30).

■**EXTRA SPECIAL:** St-Emilion is one of the most picturesque wine villages of France, and it is only a 45-minute drive east from Bordeaux. Follow N89 and signs to Libourne/Périgueux, and from Libourne those toward La Réole and Bergerac on D17E until you come to the steep hills, narrow, winding cobblestone streets, small ocher stone houses with red tile roofs, and the bustling square of this minuscule town. During the 12th century, this was the stopping place for pilgrims on their way to Santiago de Compostela in Spain, and pilgrims of one sort or other have been passing through ever since.

Park at the top of the hill (and the town) near the Eglise Collégiale or behind the museum and walk to the Place du Clocher for a sweeping view of the Dordogne Valley and the town. The tourist office (at Pl. de Créneaux; phone 57-24-72-03) has maps of St-Emilion (sometimes) and a list of the châteaux and vineyards open to the public (English is spoken at châteaux Ausone, Figeac, Cheval-Blanc, Beauséjour, and at Haut-Sarpe, where there also is a village). The Maison du Vin de St-Emilion is at Place Pierre-Meyrat (phone: 57-74-42-42); open daily from 9:30 AM to 12:30 PM and 2 to 6 PM (7 PM in summer) except *Christmas* and *New Year's.*

The Eglise Monolithe is almost unique in Europe — a subterranean church hewn into the side of a limestone cliff. Begun in the 9th century and consistently enlarged through the 12th century, probably by chipping away at existing grottoes, cracks, and crevices, it stands on top of catacombs dating from the 8th or 9th century, discovered when a citizen tried to enlarge his wine cellar. The eerie, cobweb-strewn church is used only twice a year, once for the celebration of the beginning of the grape harvest, famous throughout Europe. Wine producers, called the *jurade* and garbed in bright red robes and caps and white capes, parade through the town, hold a torchlit initiation ceremony in the church, and, at day's end, climb the steep steps to the top of the early-13th-century Tour du Roi to proclaim the *ban des vendanges,* sending the people of St-Emilion into the vineyards according to a tradition that dates back to Richard the Lion-Hearted. If you plan to attend — it's always on the Sunday closest to September 20 — arrive by midmorning and stand near the door of the church to ensure a good view. There also are exhibitions, lectures, and very good concerts in St-Emilion, especially during the *Grandes Heures de St-Emilion,* when music is performed in an ancient church or perhaps a private castle.

Be sure to visit the Cordelier Cloisters, on Rue des Cordeliers, a 14th-to-15th-century convent and cloister that is now an arresting, overgrown shell of stone walls, stairways, and columns. Of the town's two hotels, the better is the *Hostellerie de Plaisance,* which has 12 large, comfortable, expensive bedrooms, and a moderately priced restaurant (Pl. du Clocher; phone: 57-24-72-32; fax: 57-74-41-11). Of the town's ten restaurants, the rustic, moderately priced *Logis de la Cadène* (Pl. de Marche au Bois; phone: 57-24-71-40) is open for lunch and dinner in season, except on Mondays and Sunday nights, lunch only in the off-season, and closed in December. And don't leave town without sampling the *truffes au vin,* chocolate truffles filled with St-Emilion wine.

Just south of St-Emilion lies the charming region known as Entre-Deux-Mers, a patchwork of green hills, windmills, water mills, small vineyards, abbeys, castles, and villages nestled between the Garonne and the Dordogne rivers. Visit the picturesque village of La Réole, the medieval towns of St-Macaire and Castelmo-ron-d'Albret, the *bastides* (medieval fortified cities) of Créon and Sauveterre-de-Guyenne, and the nearby Labarthe mill on the Gamage River. St-Ferme, the beautiful ruins of Blasimon with its carved doorway, and La Sauve-Majeure are ancient abbeys. Among the castles to be explored are La Benauge, Cadillac, Duras, and Rauzan. Just a bit farther south lies the renowned Sauternes region and châteaux Yquem, Filhot, and de Malle. Only a little farther still is Bazas, with its 17th-to-19th-century houses and 13th-to-14th-century cathedral. Nearby are Roquetaillade Castle and the villages of Villandraut and Uzeste. A music festival is held in Uzeste every summer. Discovering and exploring these special, tucked-away parts of the region is one of the greatest pleasures of a visit to the area.

SOURCES AND RESOURCES

TOURIST INFORMATION: The Office du Tourisme de Bordeaux (12 Cours du 30-Juillet; phone: 56-44-28-41) can provide maps and information as well as set up tours in and around the city and, through its *Accueil de France* accommodations service, reserve hotel rooms. There also are branch tourist offices at the Gare Saint-Jean (phone: 56-91-64-70) and at the airport (phone: 56-34-39-39). They also sell a ticket permitting entry to ten Bordeaux museums. The office often is crowded, and you may feel pressured to ask your questions in a hurry and move along; sometimes it's simpler to ask to see the book of information about museums and activities. Perhaps more useful, especially for sports and cultural activities, is the Centre d'Information Jeunesse Aquitaine, a block south of Cathédrale St-André (5 Rue Duffour-Dubergier; phone: 56-48-55-50). Officially an information center for cultural and sports events, the center, which with its bright red exterior looks like an arcade from outside, has a helpful staff that offers maps and information to anyone who enters. Check the bulletin boards for announcements of concerts, movies, and lectures. A recording of tourist information in English is available by calling 56-48-04-61. For information which châteaux are open for tours and tastings, visit the Maison du Vin (phone: 56-00-22-66), across from the tourist office.

Local Coverage – The French daily *Sud-Ouest* is published in Bordeaux and distributed all over the southwest. *Bordeaux Journal Municipal d'Information,* published monthly by the mayor's office, is packed with news about sports, expositions, and cultural events. It is available free at the office of l'Entrepôt Lainé (3 Rue Ferrère; phone: 56-90-91-60), or at the Town Hall (Hôtel de Ville). The tourist office publishes a free quarterly newsletter, *Euro-Tourist,* which lists upcoming performances, cultural and sports events, expositions, and so on. Tourist information also is obtainable through *Minitel,* France's computerized information system that is available at some hotels. To access the information, dial 3615-BORDEAUX. The annual, student-produced *Le Bordeluche* is a guide to restaurants, entertainment, sports facilities, city services, and such things as baby-sitters, private detectives, and 24-hour gas stations. All of these are in French.

Bradley's Bookshop, Bordeaux's only English-language bookstore (32 Pl. Gambetta; phone: 56-52-10-57), stocks phrase books, maps, guidebooks, and dictionaries, as well as best sellers and classics. Even if you don't read French, drop by *Mollat* (9-15 Rue Vital-Carles; phone: 56-44-84-87), a revered and lovely bookstore in an early-19th-century building on the spot where Montesquieu's last home once stood. The selection of books on Bordeaux is outstanding. Closed Monday mornings.

English newspapers and other international publications are sold at the newsstand in front of the *Grand Théâtre* (2 Pl. de la Comédie), *Maison de la Presse* (68 Rue St-Rémi, just below Rue Ste-Catherine), and *Le Temps de Vivre* (63-65 Rue Ste-Catherine).

TELEPHONE: The city code for Bordeaux is 56, which is incorporated into all local 8-digit numbers. When calling a number in Bordeaux from the Paris region (including the Ile-de-France), dial 16, wait for a dial tone, then dial the 8-digit number. When calling a number from outside Paris, dial only the 8-digit number. When calling from the US, dial 33 (which is the country code), followed by the 8-digit number.

GETTING AROUND: Airport – The Airport International de Bordeaux-Mérignac is France's fifth-largest airport, routing over 2 million passengers a year. To reach the center of Bordeaux from the airport, take bus No. 73 (about a 30-minute ride), the *CCI* shuttle, or a taxi. For airport information, call 56-34-50-50.

Boat – Guided boat tours are given of the Bordeaux harbor. Information and tickets are available on Wharf des Quinconces (or Wharf des Queyries on the other side of the river) as well as at the tourist office.

Bus – The city bus system, *CGTFE,* serves Bordeaux and some of the suburbs. A single ticket, which must be stamped when you enter the bus, is good for only one ride. Buy a *carnet* of 10 tickets; they not only are less expensive, but each one can be used for four rides within an hour. Free maps and schedules can be obtained from major terminals such as those at Gare St-Jean or Place Gambetta, near Place Tourny, at 10 Cours de Verdun, or easily located Place Jean-Jaurès, near the quais. Long-distance buses to the coast, the Arcachon Basin, and other points outside Bordeaux are provided by *CITRAM,* 14 Rue Fondaudège (phone: 56-43-68-67).

Car Rental – Major companies, including *Avis* (phone: 56-91-65-60), *Budget* (phone: 56-39-40-40), *Europcar* (phone: 56-92-01-74), and *Hertz* (phone: 59-91-01-71), are represented, as are a number of local firms. They are all within a block or two of the train station (*Budget* also has an office at the airport; phone: 56-47-84-22) and are easy to spot. Ask about special rates; the weekend rate — from midnight Friday until midnight Monday — is often the best buy.

Taxi – Cabs come in all shapes, sizes, and colors, and can be distinguished by a small sign on top of the vehicle. Taxi stands are designated by a triangular sign with a "T". Two centrally located ones are at the Place Gambetta end of Cours Clemenceau and at the corner of Rue Esprit-des-Lois and the *Grand Théâtre;* there's also one at the train station. To call a cab day or night, dial 56-96-00-34, 56-80-70-37, or 56-31-61-07.

Train – Gare St-Jean, Bordeaux's main train station, is south of the center, just inland from the river and Pont St-Jean. For information, call 56-92-50-50; for reservations, call 56-92-76-56.

SPECIAL EVENTS: Bordeaux is charged with creative energy, and calendars fill up quicker than usual in May and November. The *Festival International de Bordeaux* (better known as the *Mai Musicale*) is a month-long music extravaganza, when performers from solo pianists to massed choirs to jazz groups take up residence at the *Grand Théâtre* (Pl. de la Comédie; phone: 56-48-58-54), the cathedral, and at various châteaux within easy reach of the city. Information about performers, dates, and locations may be obtained from the tourist office. In November, the spotlight is on dance, as well as contemporary arts, when the annual *SIGMA* festival lures well-known international soloists and groups to Bordeaux for 2 weeks. For information, contact the tourist office (phone: 56-44-28-41). In the summer, and sometimes in September, the *Nuit du Vieux Bordeaux* fills the streets of the St-Pierre quarter with music, crowds, and a holiday atmosphere. To give inanimate objects their share of attention, the city holds a *foire à la brocante,* or flea market, in May and November at Place des Quinconces. Antiques fairs, *foires aux antiquaires,* are held annually in January at Le Lac and in February at Hanger 5 (on the river). The *Semaine Mondiale de Vins,* one of Europe's most important wine fairs, will be held this year from June 21 to 25.

MUSEUMS: Noteworthy museums not mentioned in *Special Places* include the following:

Maison des Métiers de l'Imprimerie – Dedicated to the art of printing, this small museum includes a dozen or so old presses displayed in an old factory. Open from 2 to 6 PM Mondays and Wednesdays, and from 9 AM to 1 PM Saturdays. Admission charge. 10 Rue Ft.-Louis (phone: 56-92-61-17).

Musée des Arts Décoratifs – In the former Hôtel Lalande, this museum — one of Bordeaux's loveliest — displays ceramics, glassware, ironwork, furniture, and other *objets,* much of it from 18th-century Bordeaux. There also are changing exhibitions. Open daily except Tuesdays from 10 AM to 6 PM; no admission charge Wednesdays. 39 Rue Bouffard (phone: 56-90-91-60).

Musée des Douanes – A well-restored floor of one of the 18th-century Place de la Bourse buildings is dedicated to customs' history. Open daily except Mondays from 10 AM to noon and 1 to 5 PM (6 PM in summer). Admission charge. 1 Pl. de la Bourse (phone: 56-52-45-47).

Musée d'Histoire Naturelle – Tucked away in the back of the Jardin Public, this small, well-maintained museum in the late-18th-century Hôtel de Lisleferme has simple but well-executed exhibitions. Be sure to see the butterflies on the third floor and the photographs that show how the museum's stuffed elephant was mounted and carried through the streets of Bordeaux to its present home in the lobby. Open daily except Tuesdays from 2 to 5:50 PM. Admission charge. 5 Pl. Bardineau; enter through the gate of the garden or Rue Emile-Zola (phone: 56-48-29-86).

Musée des Chartons – Devoted to wine making, this semiprivate museum exhibits collections of old bottles, labels, tools. Open Tuesdays through Fridays from 10 AM to 12:30 PM and 2 to 5:30 PM; open from 10 AM to 5 PM on Saturdays. Admission charge. 41 Rue Borie (phone: 56-44-27-77).

SHOPPING: When it comes to buying gifts and souvenirs, Bordeaux is a gold mine for the unique to the utilitarian. If it's clothes you want, traverse the "golden triangle," whose angles are Place Gambetta, Place Tourny, and Place de la Comédie and whose sides are Cours de l'Intendance, Cours Clemenceau, and Allées de Tourny, where the well-heeled citizens of Bordeaux shop. The *Galeries des Grands Hommes,* located at the Place des Grands Hommes in the center of the "golden triangle," is one of the city's newest additions to chic shopping. It is a sparkling glass and brass rotunda of boutiques — including *Pierre Cardin, Charles Jourdan, Habitat,* and *Laure Japy.* Place du Parlement has become popular for clothing, shoes, and accessories for a young clientele. If you prefer riding escalators to walking, head to the shopping center at Mériadeck and its 100 boutiques. If it's antiques you're after, the best bets are Rue Bouffard, Rue des Remparts, and Rue Notre-Dame, but you also can snoop along the small streets around St. Michael's Church. Don't overlook *Village Notre-Dame,* an old covered market filled with shops, near the church on the outskirts of Les Chartrons. Occasionally, an object of real interest and value (although usually in need of restoration) turns up among the run-of-the-mill wares at the flea market in front of the church on Sunday mornings. The Bordelais swear that the best cheese comes from *Jean d'Alos* (4 Rue Montesquieu; phone: 56-44-29-66); they also swear by the fresh, homemade products at *Cerruti* (21 Rue Voltaire; phone: 56-44-24-51), a deluxe grocery with a certain snob appeal. By contrast, the Thursday-morning market in front of St. Peter's Church, bright tents and umbrellas and all, looks like an encampment of Gypsies. In fact, they are farmers and vendors of organically grown produce, homemade bread, quiches, tarts, and pies, and homemade wines made from organically grown grapes. Get here early to buy the best produce or go for an informal lunch (wine can be purchased by the glass). If you find yourself reconnoitering Rue Ste-Catherine at lunchtime, you might want to pick up a sandwich of *jambon de Bayonne,* a ham similar to the famous Parma ham, from the stand called *Laurent Petricorena* (33 Rue Ste-Catherine, near Rue Porte-Dijeaux).

Wine connoisseurs have many choices for browsing, gleaning information, and buying (1985 and 1986 vintages are very good and still reasonably priced, but will benefit from additional years before being opened). The best-known, and purportedly the best, wine stores in Bordeaux are *Badie* (Place Tourny; phone: 56-52-23-72), and *La Vinothèque,* near the tourist office (Cours du 30-Juillet; phone: 56-52-32-05). Also near the tourist office are two other excellent wine shops: *Bordeaux Magnum* (3 Rue Gobineau; phone: 56-48-00-06) and *L'Intendant* (2 Allées de Tourny; 56-48-01-29), a striking shop with a dramatic spiral staircase leading to 4 levels of wine. For a more intimate experience, visit a *cave* (cellar), generally a fresh, dark, somewhat old shop where Bordelais buy simple wines (but good and very good wines also can be found here). Another interesting alternative is to buy from a local wine maker, such as Pierre Roubin, who sells on Thursdays at the organic market at St. Peter's or on the weekends from his home in Bellefond, near Rauzan (phone: 56-23-93-71).

Cadiot Badie – Excellent bonbons in pretty tin boxes. 26 Allées de Tourny (phone: 56-44-24-22).

La Comtesse du Barry – A wide choice of regional and national food specialties, some made from the recipes of well-known French chefs. They will send goods by mail. 2 Pl. Tourny (phone: 56-44-81-15).

Galerie Présidence – The work of up-and-coming French artists, displayed in impressively restored gallery space. 20 Rue du Parlement St-Pierre (phone: 56-52-29-57).

Jacqueline Dourthe – Original creations by the well-known Bordeaux dress designer. 18 Rue Lafaurie de Monbadon (phone: 56-52-35-78).

Interchasse – Men's and women's fashion, hats, jewelry, and gift items in an interesting atmosphere. 19 Rue des Remparts (phone: 56-44-56-83).

M. Mazuque – A small gift shop in Vieux Bordeaux that specializes in engraving glass and crystal. Items are for sale at reasonable prices and can be mailed home. 6 Rue de Parlement Ste-Catherine (phone: 56-52-94-14).

Pictures – Movie posters of French, English, and American films. In front of the *Musée d'Aquitaine,* at 25 Cours Pasteur (phone: 56-44-50-88).

La Soierie – Silk and leatherware for *les dames.* Closed at lunchtime and Mondays in winter. 27 Rue du Parlement St-Pierre (phone: 56-51-23-75).

 SPORTS AND FITNESS: If you're inclined to get lots of exercise on vacation — or to watch professionals do so — Bordeaux has ample opportunities. It is within an hour of the Arcachon Basin and the Côte d'Argent, where golf, tennis, swimming, biking, and horseback riding can be enjoyed. Information of particular interest to handicapped sports enthusiasts is available from Mr. Dachary at the *Amicale Sportive des Handicapés Physiques d'Aquitaine* (phone: 56-50-31-12).

Bowling – A 24-lane bowling alley has been added to the Mériadeck sports complex. Terrace Général-Koenig, Rue Corps Franc de Pommiers (phone: 56-93-05-85).

Golf – Two 18-hole municipal courses are just north of Le Lac (Av. de Pernon; phone: 56-50-92-42); clubs can be rented; closed Tuesdays. There also is an 18-hole course at *Golf Bordelais* (Av. d'Eysines; phone: 56-28-56-04); closed Mondays. Just 20 miles (32 km) northwest of the city on D211 is the *Golf du Médoc* (Le Pian-Médoc, Blanquefort; phone: 56-72-01-10), a course that vies for honors as one of France's most deluxe golfing facilities. Each of its 18 holes is sponsored by a different wine château.

Horse Racing – Every Sunday in spring and summer races are run at the *Hippodrome,* northwest of the downtown area, and the "Derby of the South" is held here each year (phone: 56-28-34-19).

Ice Skating – A large *patinoire* (rink) is at Mériadeck (100 Cours du Maréchal-Juin; phone: 56-93-11-11). The space also is used for concerts, hockey competitions, boxing matches, and even the circus. Closed in summer. Call ahead for exact days and hours. For diehards who like to ice skate in summer, there's a rink open in nearby Arcachon (Allée de Mimosa; phone: 56-83-24-56).

Rugby – For information about upcoming games, call 56-85-94-01 or check the newspapers.

Soccer – The popular local team, *Les Girondins de Bordeaux,* plays at the *Stade Municipal.* Pl. Johnston (phone: 56-08-63-63).

Squash – For a refreshing break from sightseeing, stop by *Squash de Bordeaux,* where exercise combines readily with lunch, dinner, or a drink at the bar. You bring your own athletic shoes and clothes; they provide rackets, 3 courts, saunas — and a pleasant restaurant for *après* sport. Sometimes closed 1 month in summer. 369 Av. de Verdun, Mérignac (phone: 56-97-51-12).

Swimming – A municipal pool (covered) is in the Grand Parc (6 Av. Généraux-Duché; phone: 56-98-77-34); it is accessible to handicapped swimmers.

Tennis – Several clubs in the area have courts available to visitors. For information, contact the *Ligue de Guyenne* (53 Rue de Colonel-Moll, 33400 Talence; phone: 56-37-02-90). The indoor courts at Mériadeck are open daily and can be rented by the hour. Terrace Général-Koenig, Rue Corps Franc de Pommiers (phone: 56-96-21-39).

 THEATER: The major theaters in town are the *Grand Théâtre* (Pl. de la Comédie; phone: 56-48-58-54), where operas and ballets are performed; a few blocks away, at *Théâtre Fémina* — not a feminist theater as its name might imply (Rue de Grassi; phone: 56-52-45-19) — classical and contemporary plays are performed regularly. The *Théâtre du Port de la Lune* (Pl. Renaudel; phone: 56-91-98-00), opened in 1987, hosts classic and modern plays. An additional room has doubled the theater's seating capacity. The *Théâtre de Poche de Saint-Michel* (48 Rue Carpenteyre; phone: 56-92-25-06) is a small café-theater mounting a wide variety of pieces.

To find out what's happening at these and other theaters, pick up the latest free copy of the *Bordeaux Journal Municipal d'Information* (phone: 56-90-91-60), or even better the free *BordeauxScope,* available at the tourist office.

 MUSIC: The Bordelais love music and have numerous opportunities to listen to it. The *Orchestre National Bordeaux-Aquitaine,* the *Orchestre de la Musique Municipale,* the *Jeunesses Musicales de France,* and chamber music groups perform, most often at the *Grand Théâtre* (Pl. de la Comédie), the *Théâtre Fémina* (Rue de Grassi), the modern *Centre André-Malraux–Conservatoire National de Region* (22 Quai St-Croix), the *Palais des Sports* (Rue Ravez, off Cours d'Alsace et Lorraine), in the *patinoire* at Mériadeck (be forewarned that the acoustics are bad at the highest, and least expensive, tier of seating), and in the cathedral or various churches in the city. Churches, most notably Notre-Dame and St-Seurin, also sponsor musical events.

NIGHTCLUBS AND NIGHTLIFE: Bordeaux is much livelier during the day than in the evening, and a big night out for residents appears to be dinner and a movie. If you decide to follow suit, see *Eating Out* and take in a classic or second-run avant-garde film at *Cinema Trianon–Jean Vigo* (6 Rue Franklin; phone: 56-44-35-17); first-run films, primarily French and American, are shown at the *Gaumont, Marivaux, Ariel,* and *Français* cinemas, all near Place Gambetta.

The following discos are popular, though most are off the beaten track: the equally chic *Studio 21* (21 Rue Mably; phone: 56-44-35-22) and *Sénéchal* (57 Quai de Paludate; phone: 56-85-54-80); *Performance* (at the corner of Rue Ramonet and Quai des Chartrons; phone: 56-48-50-44), with video screens, electronic games, and a young crowd; phone: 56-36-66-30); *Macumba* (Rte. du Cap-Ferret, Mérignac; phone: 56-34-05-48); and *Pacha* (Rte. d'Arcachon, toward Pessac l'Alouette; phone: 56-36-66-30). For cocktails, go to *L'Orchidée Noire* (2 Pl. Pey-Berland; phone: 56-44-40-04); for cocktails plus rock 'n' roll and video entertainment, to *Babylone* (67 Rue de la Rousselle; phone: 56-44-35-78). An increasingly good place to try is *Le Salon Jaune* (32 Rue Cornac; phone: 56-44-47-67), a bar-restaurant with videos and cinema. For jazz, drop in at *Black Jack,* a piano bar (35 Pl. Gambetta; phone: 56-81-71-38). Café-theaters include *L'Onyx* (11 Rue Fernand-Philippart; phone: 56-44-26-12), *Théâtre Boîte Jouer* (50 Rue des Lombards; phone: 56-50-08-24), and the *Théâtre de Poche de Saint-Michel* (49 Rue Carpenteyre; phone: 56-92-25-06). For rock and jazz, go to *Le Café Carabosse* (Rue de Bègles between the railway station and the *Capucins Market;* phone: 56-91-43-27); the *White Spirit* (15 Rue Notre-Dame; phone 56-52-37-82); and *Le Comptoir des Iles,* an exotic place, perfect for the last drink of the evening (Pl. du Gen.-Sarrail, at Rue Ste-Catherine near Pl. de la Victoire; phone: 56-94-50-71). For music with a Latin beat, try *Le Chaski,* in a 12th-century room (at 8 Rue de Mérignac; phone: 56-44-78-12). Whenever possible, call ahead to verify days and times that clubs are open.

BEST IN TOWN

 CHECKING IN: Bordeaux is full of hotels within walking distance of almost anything a visitor might want to do or see. Expect to pay more than $120 for a double room at a very expensive hotel; $75 to $120 at an expensive one; between $50 and $75 for moderate lodging; and under $50 in the inexpensive range.

Sofitel – If you plan to spend a lot of time in Le Lac (for, perhaps, a conference or an exposition), this is a comfortable, freshly modernized place to which to return at the end of the day. It has 212 rooms and a swimming pool. Major credit cards accepted. Bordeaux-le-Lac (phone: 56-50-83-80; fax: 56-39-73-75). Very expensive.

Pullman-Mériadeck – Modern and bustling, this hotel in the Quartier Mériadeck has 196 rooms, the elegant, highly touted *Le Mériadeck* restaurant, and a bar. Major credit cards accepted. 5 Rue Robert-Lateulade (phone: 56-56-43-43; fax: 56-96-50-59). Very expensive to expensive.

Burdigala – This classic old edifice in the Mériadeck section has been transformed into an elegant establishment. Its 71 rooms and 7 duplex suites offer modern comforts. Major credit cards accepted. 115 Rue Georges-Bonnac (phone: 56-90-16-16; fax: 56-93-15-06). Expensive.

Château Chartrons – Recently reopened, this deluxe property in the heart of Bordeaux's historic Chartrons quarter and near the Cité Internationale des Vins (see *Special Places*) was built by a major Bordeaux wine company. The decoration of its 119 rooms and 32 suites was inspired by the area's wine trade, its traditions, history, and famous individuals in the wine industry. There is a restaurant (*Nova Magus*), wine bar, and private parking. Major credit cards accepted. 81 Cours St-Louis (phone: 56-43-15-00; fax: 56-69-15-21). Expensive.

Mercure Pont d'Aquitaine – A 100-room property near the *Sofitel,* with a heated swimming pool and a tennis court. Major credit cards accepted. Rue Grand Barrail, Bordeaux-le-Lac (phone: 56-50-90-14; fax: 56-50-23-95). Expensive.

Grand Hôtel Français – Totally renovated in 1990, this old standby has risen to new heights of comfort and elegance. A grand stairway and gracious sitting rooms recall Vieux Bordeaux. There's an excellent room service menu with food provided by a well-respected local caterer. Major credit cards accepted. 12 Rue du Temple (phone: 56-48-10-35; fax: 56-81-76-18). Expensive to moderate.

Sainte-Catherine – Warm golden stones and wrought iron give this deluxe hostelry in the heart of Old Bordeaux a special charm. The 91 rooms are large and comfortable. There's a restaurant and piano bar. Major credit cards accepted. 27 Rue du Parlement Ste-Catherine (phone: 56-81-95-12; fax: 56-44-50-51). Expensive to moderate.

Arcade – Across from the railroad station and a short bus ride from the center of town, this modern, efficient 140-room hotel is a good value, though not in the classiest part of town. Major credit cards accepted. 60 Rue Eugène-Le-Roy (phone: 56-91-40-40; fax: 56-31-92-33). Moderate.

Gambetta – An old hotel on a pedestrian street that has been renovated inside (not out); its 33 rooms, though small, are comfortable, with TV sets, private bath, and mini-bar. There's also a lounge, elevator, and friendly management. Breakfast is available. Dogs welcome, too. Major credit cards accepted. 66 Rue Porte-Dijeaux (phone: 56-51-21-83; fax: 56-81-00-40). Moderate.

Hôtel du Théâtre – The welcome is warm and the rooms pleasant at this 18th-century structure in the heart of Bordeaux. There's also a bar, a small meeting room, a sauna, and solarium. Major credit cards accepted. 10 Rue Maison-Daurade (phone: 56-79-05-26; fax: 56-81-15-64). Moderate.

Normandie – A classic hotel with a refurbished stone façade, it has 98 rooms and a bar. Major credit cards accepted. In front of the tourist office, at 7 Cours du 30-Juillet (phone: 56-52-16-80; fax: 56-51-68-91). Moderate.

Royal Médoc – Charming and just a few blocks from the Place de la Comédie, this place offers 45 modern, tastefully decorated rooms and also has a bar. Major credit cards accepted. 3-5 Rue de Sèze (phone: 56-81-72-42; fax: 56-51-74-98). Moderate.

Bayonne – Quiet and comfortable, it's conveniently near the *Grand Théâtre.* Major credit cards accepted. 15 Cours de l'Intendance (phone: 56-48-00-88; fax: 56-44-59-58). Moderate to inexpensive.

Continental – This old hotel with its floor-to-ceiling windows and stately armoires retains its share of elegance. Just off Place Gambetta, it has 50 rooms. Major credit cards accepted. 10 Rue Montesquieu (phone: 56-52-66-00; fax: 56-52-77-97). Moderate to inexpensive.

Saint Clair – Though not classy, it's pleasant and just a block from the *Grand Théâtre.* The hallways are a little dreary, but the spiral staircase that leads to the 14 rooms is light and airy. Major credit cards accepted. Near Rue Ste-Catherine, at 18 Rue des Piliers de Tutelle (phone: 56-48-51-03). Moderate to inexpensive.

Vieux Bordeaux – Mme. Ortenzi gives guests a warm welcome in this neat 18th-century house in Quartier St-Pierre, then sends them up to one of the 11 simple, clean rooms — ask for one on the street side. Major credit cards accepted. A couple of blocks from both Place du Parlement and Place St-Pierre. 22 Rue du Cancéra (phone: 56-48-07-27). Inexpensive.

EATING OUT: The food of southwest France has come into its own as a distinct cuisine to be appreciated and enjoyed, and Bordeaux's vast array of restaurants gives ample opportunities to do so. Regional delights include foie gras (fattened goose or duck liver), *confit* (preserved fattened goose or duck), *cèpes* (dark wild mushrooms, usually sautéed in oil with garlic), entrecôte (steak grilled over the coals of dried grapevine prunings and garnished with shallots), and seafood such as *lamproie* (eel), *huîtres* (oysters, served with whole wheat bread in these parts), and *alose,* a fish that usually is grilled, then presented in elegant and exciting ways. The fact that many restaurants are in beautifully restored buildings only enhances the pleasures of eating out here. Expect to pay $130 or more for a meal for two at restaurants listed as very expensive; between $90 and $130 at restaurants listed as expensive; between $75 and $90 in the moderate range; and under $75 at those listed as inexpensive. A service charge usually is included. These prices do not include wine, which can cost as little as $10 or $15 a bottle or as much as you're willing to pay. In a few restaurants you can buy regional wines by the glass, which provides an opportunity to try different varieties and vintages with each course. Although it's easy to think of Bordeaux wines as primarily red, like those of the Médoc and St-Emilion, don't overlook the whites of Graves and Sauternes (a classic with foie gras).

St-James – Despite their regal interpretations of local delicacies, as well as an exhaustive wine list, this establishment has lost one of its two Michelin stars, probably the result of recent echoes of disappointment that there has been a slight dip in quality (hopefully temporary). An addition of a controversial new wing with 18 starkly modern guestrooms caused a stir, too. Nonetheless, the setting, high on a ridge with a commanding view of vineyards and the Garonne River, still is sublime. The house's second restaurant, *Le Bistroy,* is highly recommended for its casual atmosphere and reasonably priced bistro fare. Open daily. Reservations necessary. Major credit cards accepted. Across the Garonne and well away from the center, in suburban Bouliac at 3 Pl. Camille-Hostein (phone: 56-20-52-19; fax: 56-20-92-58). Very expensive to expensive.

Le Clavel Barnabet – Tasty variations on regional specialties, such as *lapereau à la royale* (rabbit stuffed with foie gras) and *lamproie à la bordelaise* (eel in red wine sauce), are served in a historic 19th-century structure with rock-work decorations. There also is a 5,000-bottle wine cellar. Closed Sundays and Monday lunch. Reservations advised. Major credit cards accepted. 44 Rue Charles Domercq (phone: 56-92-91-52). Expensive.

Jean Ramet – This simple, well-loved place has friendly service, an intimate atmosphere, and well-prepared food that has earned a star from Michelin. Popular entrées include *salade tiede de homard* (lobster salad), and *pigeonneau de Madame Raymonde* (squab). Try the *délice glacé au pralin* for dessert. Prices on the lunch menu (weekdays only) are agreeably lower. Open Mondays through Fridays for lunch and dinner. Reservations advised. Major credit cards accepted. Near Pl. de la Bourse, at 7 Pl. Jean-Jaurès (phone: 56-44-12-51). Expensive.

Le Cailhau – From the cheery awning and cobblestone sidewalk in front to the beamed ceilings and dozens of tables with candelabra and fresh flowers inside, this is an inviting, romantic place. Linger over your meal, then stroll along the streets of Vieux Bordeaux. Especially tasty is the *homard au citron* (lobster in lemon). Closed Saturdays at lunch, Sundays, and August. Reservations advised. Major credit cards accepted. Beside Porte Cailhau, at 3 Pl. du Palais (phone: 56-81-79-91). Expensive to moderate.

La Tupina – The classic and very good cooking of southwest France is the strength of this friendly restaurant. It is becoming more and more known, yet it's still the sort of place where if you ask to see the kitchen, they'll show it to you. Lunch and dinner daily except holidays and Sundays. Reservations unnecessary. Major credit cards accepted. 6 Rue Porte-de-la-Monnaie (phone: 56-91-56-37). Expensive to moderate.

Le Bistrot de Bordeaux – Cozy and busy, this place serves up tasty bistro fare; skate salad and *filet mignon de canard au cidre et aux pommes* (duck filet with cider and apples), a well-known house specialty, get top billing. Local wine is sold by the glass, and there is a wine boutique on the second floor for heftier purchases. Closed Saturday lunch and Sundays. Reservations necessary for large groups. Major credit cards accepted. 10 Rue des Piliers-de-Tutelle (phone: 56-01-27-96). Moderate.

Le Mousquetaire – In a charming 2-story house near the *Grand Théâtre*, this place serves seafood, salads, and regional specialties. With its cheerful black and white tile floor, wooden stairs, and lace-curtained windows that look out onto the busy street, it has the feel of country in the city. Closed Sundays. Reservations unnecessary. Major credit cards accepted. 4 Rue des Piliers-de-Tutelle (phone: 56-48-00-39). Moderate.

La Ténarèze – On one of Bordeaux's loveliest, quietest squares, sit outdoors in summer and enjoy some of the tasty dishes of southwest France, especially from Armagnac and Gers. Closed Sundays in summer and Wednesdays in winter. Reservations necessary for dinner. Major credit cards accepted. 18 Pl. du Parlement (phone: 56-44-43-29). Moderate.

Le Vieux Bordeaux – You'll appreciate the refined cooking — it has been awarded one Michelin star — and the elegant surroundings. Highlights on the menu include *saumon frais à la pipérade* (fresh salmon with vegetables), *pigeon rôti aux gousses d'ail et ses pommes croustillantes* (roast squab with garlic and crisp potatoes), and creative desserts, such as *nougat glacé au coulis de framboises* (iced nougat with raspberry relish). Closed Saturday lunch, Sundays, and August. Reservations necessary for dinner. Visa accepted. 27 Rue Buhan (phone: 56-52-94-36). Moderate.

Le Chalut – Well-prepared seafood dishes at reasonable prices. Treat yourself to the fish *rillettes* and the fish soup. Closed Sundays and Monday lunch. Reservations advised for dinner. Major credit cards accepted. 59 Rue du Palais-Gallien (phone: 56-81-43-51). Moderate to inexpensive.

Dominique – A bustling bistro filled with loquacious customers, who spend just as much time commenting on the fine fare served here as they do consuming it. Simple yet artfully prepared specialties such as char-grilled salmon accompanied by pasta drizzled with olive oil win high praise. Closed Sundays and Mondays. Reservations advised. Major credit cards accepted. 2 Cours de l'Intendance (phone: 56-52-59-79). Moderate to inexpensive.

L'Ombrière – A typical brasserie that's a local favorite for good, simple food and its open terrace on the Place du Parlement. Closed Sundays and Mondays. Reservations unnecessary. Major credit cards accepted. 14 Pl. du Parlement (phone: 56-44-82-69). Moderate to inexpensive.

Darricau – The crème de la crème of *pâtisseries/salons de thé*. Sit in the upstairs salon if it's open (it has windows that look out onto the pleasant little square), and take a minute to admire the mirrored Art Deco doors (leading to *les toilettes*) on the landing. Open daily. Reservations unnecessary. Major credit cards accepted. 7 Pl. Gambetta (phone: 56-44-21-49). Inexpensive.

Jegher – Dating from 1856, it offers out-of-this-world pastries, chocolates, and ice cream in an Old World setting across from the Jardin Public. Closed Sundays in summer. Reservations unnecessary. No credit cards accepted. 36 Cours de Verdun (phone: 56-52-15-28). Inexpensive.

Le Morne Rouge – A cozy, semi-exotic spot where the Bordelais go when they are tired of French cooking. The menu features specialties from the French island of Martinique in the West Indies. Open for dinner only; closed Sundays, Mondays, and August. Reservations advised for weekends. No credit cards accepted. 48 Rue du Hâ (phone: 56-81-39-26). Inexpensive.

BARS AND CAFÉS: Step through the door at *Le Lug* (5 Rue des Faussets; phone: 56-81-04-87), and you suddenly go from Vieux Bordeaux to Greenwich Village — at least that's the way it feels in this little coffeehouse filled with parsons tables and benches, original works by local artists, and a sideboard laden with cheeses, breads, and desserts. Coffee beans are ground right on the premises and exotic teas are sold as well. Come here for lunch or an evening snack; and when the weather chills, sit on the couch in front of the fire and sip your coffee. It's open daily except Sundays until 1 AM. A good place to sample Bordeaux's famous wines is *Le Bistro du Sommelier* (167 Rue Georges Bonnac; phone: 56-96-71-78). It's open daily except Saturdays for lunch, Sundays, and holidays. For beer, the widest selection is at *A l'Entracte* bar, also an inexpensive snack bar, near Place Gambetta (17 Rue du Palais Gallien; phone: 56-44-92-14). A popular coffee bar is *Brûlerie Gama* (just off Pl. Gambetta; 109-111 Rue Porte-Dijeaux), where you can rub elbows with the Bordelais as you stand at the counter and have a quick cup of coffee or cappuccino. It's open during business hours only.

CANNES

Some towns are important as centers of political power, commerce, or industry, others as focuses of artistic creativity or religious pilgrimage. Cannes is nothing more and never anything less than a playground — its raison d'être is pleasure. Over the past decade, the growth of convention business has brought professionals from all over the world, particularly in the spheres of film, television, music, and advertising. They arrive, pale and earnest, with impressive-looking attaché cases. But in each one, under the files and computer printouts, is a swimsuit. When they leave Cannes, tanned and relaxed, whatever business has been done has for the most part been done over a shrimp salad at a beachside restaurant or an aperitif on the terrace of one of the great seafront hotels. The majority of the 70,000 people who live in Cannes work in the service industry, and even they manage to make their labors their pleasures. In fact, work in Cannes is a delightful joke and there's no attempt to hide it — they call the conventions here "festivals."

It would be difficult to have it otherwise along La Croisette, the splendid promenade of palms and plane trees that curves gently around the bay from the Vieux Port to the *Palm Beach Casino*. On one side of the street are the dazzling white hotels — "palaces," the French call them — and condominiums; on the other, the tempting gravelly sands of the well-kept beaches. The whole is framed by the Esterel plateau, its deep red, even purple, rocky soil thickly overgrown with pines, cork oaks, and lavender. The air is sweet with the roses, mimosa (brought from Australia in 1880), and begonias of the town's gardens. In the old port, only a few diligent fishing boats bob up and down among the hundreds of motor launches and yachts of the idle rich.

For centuries even the French didn't realize the pleasurable possibilities of that exquisite bay. Since the 10th century, Cannes — named after the cane reeds of its old marshlands — had been nothing but a fishing port with a tower and fortifications, built by abbots from the nearby Iles de Lérins to protect the villagers against Saracen pirates. In 1834, an English lord led a benevolent invasion. Turned back at the Italian frontier because of the fear of a cholera epidemic spreading from Provence, Lord Brougham (pronounced *Broom*) was obliged to spend the night in Cannes. The bouillabaisse he was served for dinner that evening and his walk along the seafront the next morning persuaded him that here was a place where a man might comfortably escape the winter chills of the north. After a distinguished political career, during which he spearheaded the movement to abolish slavery in England, Lord Brougham built a home in Cannes and was followed, not only by the fashionable aristocracy of England, but also by their cousins and fellow nobles from Russia, Germany, and Switzerland. They built grandiose villas, a yacht club, and a casino, and the French gradually tumbled to the idea that in Cannes they might have a gold mine.

The French contingent was led by the writer Prosper Mérimée, best known for the story of *Carmen* that inspired Bizet's opera. He had come on an official inspection of historic monuments in the region and stayed to cure his asthma; he died here in 1870. Other notables included Guy de Maupassant, who sailed in Cannes Bay for many years, and Frédéric Mistral, who wrote poems about the city. In those days, many rheumatics believed that to lie on the beach mummified in the Cannes sand (rather than the nastier pebbles of Nice) was enough to cure what ailed them. Europe's upper crust was soon convinced that Cannes was a good place to live and a good place to die.

During the fabled years of the Belle Epoque at the turn of the century, Cannes was clearly established as one of the major poles of attraction for a sparkling society of princes, archdukes, successful artists, and their plethora of mistresses. Before he became King Edward VII, the Prince of Wales liked to sail his yacht *Britannia* into the harbor and dally with one of his ladies at the old *Gray d'Albion* hotel. (His not so clandestine visits are commemorated on the port's Albert Edouard Jetty, and his bronze bust stands in the gardens of La Croisette.) It was in a Cannes restaurant that the prince first tasted some flambéed crêpes, which he named after his dinner companion, Suzette. One of his favorite ladies was the actress "the Belle Otéro," whose breasts are said to have been the model for the domes at either end of the great *Carlton* hotel.

This preposterous, glorious wedding cake of an edifice, one of those legendary places that people visit whether they're staying there or not, was built just before World War I. It served first as a hospital for the wounded, but came into its own as the very symbol of Cannes's hedonism in the 1920s. In other towns, the monuments are cathedrals and castles. In Cannes, the monuments are the great hotels. People will argue forever over the relative merits of the *Majestic-Croisette,* the *Grand,* the *Martinez,* the *Gray d'Albion* — or the *Carlton* — and though their budgets may not be able to afford the price of a room, they'll at least check out the bar on the terrace and, for a half hour or so, join the Cannes elite.

This "elite" doesn't actually live in Cannes — it's a transient group of shooting stars that flash through from season to season. They come as long as the sun shines, often expense-accounted on one of those convention junkets, but their most glittering moment is the *International Film Festival.* This glamorous institution has placed Cannes second only to Hollywood as a focus for the world's movie industry, though it certainly got off to a false start when its opening took place on the day Hitler invaded Poland, September 1, 1939. It then was launched with proper honors in 1946, when Ray Milland won the Best Actor award for *Lost Weekend.* Each merry month of May since, the festival cleverly has combined the tinsel of cavorting topless starlets with nobler claims to cinematic art in the person of a Fellini, a Bergman, a Coppola, or a Scorsese, each evening ending in a gala made glittering by an ocean of stunning dresses and dinner jackets. This spicy mixture of the gaudy and the sophisticated has come to epitomize the very spirit of Cannes. The locals love to complain about the flashy interlopers, but they also love to gather at the *Palais des Festivals* to watch the stars arrive for the evening film debuts. In Cannes, glamour and luxury have always been condemned and indulged with equal enthusiasm.

Whereas the population of other towns along the coast is solidly Provençal, the Cannois are a colorful mixture of retired Parisians, affluent onetime refugees from Eastern Europe and North Africa, and since the 1970s, a considerable contingent of wealthy transplants from the oil kingdoms of the Persian Gulf and war-torn Lebanon (you'll notice that the signs in many banks and jewelry shops are posted in French, English, and Arabic). Close to 100 newspapers, in almost as many languages, are sold on Cannes newsstands. Much of the cosmopolitan populace lives in seafront condominiums and in the grand villas on the eastern heights of town, La Californie. But the true natives are by no means submerged. Their domain is north and west of the Vieux Port, and in the cool of the day you'll see the men lobbing their *boules* in the sandy gravel among the plane trees of the Allées de la Liberté. In the Old Harbor itself, the seamen putter about in their boats with ropes and sails and paint and varnish, as in any other Mediterranean port, just a few yards — but a whole world — away from the gaudy glitter of La Croisette.

CANNES AT-A-GLANCE

SEEING THE CITY: Cannes is very proud of the panorama of its bay and the surrounding countryside, and to show it off to best advantage it has built an observatory, unashamedly called Super-Cannes, high on a hill above the eastern edge of town, about 2½ miles (4 km) from the center. An elevator takes you up to a deck some 1,000 feet above sea level, from which the view really is spectacular on a clear day — all the way over to the Côte d'Azur, including Nice and Monte Carlo, to the Italian Riviera, and, on the many clear days, south to Corsica and northeast to the snow-capped Alps. By car, drive north on Boulevard de la République, east on Avenue de Vallauris, and turn right onto Boulevard Beausoleil. Also recommended is the romantic nighttime view of the city lights from the tower and ramparts up on Le Suquet at the western edge of town. When it comes to sensational views, Cannes offers something for everyone. Those who spend nights on the town can enjoy glorious sunrises, while those who retire early can admire the spectacular sunsets.

SPECIAL PLACES: Roughly speaking, there are two sides to Cannes, with the Vieux Port as the dividing line. West (and north) of it is the "old town," topped by the hill of Le Suquet. East of it is the more modern resort, strung along the tree-lined promenade that traces the curve of the bay. Both of these areas can and should be seen on foot, but to visit La Californie, the hill north of Pointe de la Croisette and east of the center, and Super-Cannes at its top, a car or taxi or the bus is desirable.

La Croisette – Rarely has a town been so dominated by one street as Cannes is by the Boulevard de la Croisette. Named after a little cross that once adorned the point at its eastern end, this seafront promenade provides an indispensable introduction to the town's glossy elegance. A walk of a mile and a half along the palm trees will take you from the Old Harbor (Vieux Port) at its western end past cafés, antiques shops, art galleries, boutiques, and the great hotels — beware of Rolls-Royces gliding silently from the driveways — to the quieter residential neighborhood of the condominiums. The best time for people watching — Cannes's main sightseeing activity — is between

11 AM and noon, when the late risers are looking for a salad-brunch on the beach, and at the end of the afternoon, when the beautiful people are out admiring each other's suntan and new casual wear (nighttime brings out male and female prostitutes). In the gardens of the more sedate condominium stretch of La Croisette, take a look at the marvelous profusion (according to season) of primroses, cyclamens, snapdragons, and begonias amid the pink and white blossoming tamarisks, and red and purple bougainvillea hanging from balconies or climbing walls. The best public displays are the 14,000 roses of the Parc de la Roseraie, just north of the Port Pierre-Canto. Like La Croisette itself, this riot of flowers owes its beginnings to the English, who, in a perennially mild climate, were finally able to realize their green-thumbed dreams outside the hothouse.

Pointe de la Croisette – This promontory at the far eastern end of Boulevard de la Croisette closes the bay of Cannes and embraces the town's second harbor, the Port Pierre-Canto, which has become the favorite mooring for some of the Mediterranean's most luxurious yachts. Conveniently nearby is the gleaming white *Palm Beach Casino,* founded with typical Cannes insouciance in 1929, the year of the great Wall Street crash. The *Palm Beach*'s own little harbor is the home of the ultra-swank *Yacht Club.*

Beaches – These spotless golden strands are the town's pride and joy, swept and sifted daily and reinforced with new sand at the slightest hint of erosion. They are divided into three areas: two stretches of mainly public beach — the Plages du Midi beyond the Old Harbor on the west side of town and the Plage Gazagnaire around Pointe de la Croisette on the east side of town — plus the mainly private beaches along La Croisette, attached to the big hotels or beachfront restaurant concessions. You can picnic and bathe for free on the public beaches — Gazagnaire is good for morning sun, the Plages du Midi better for the afternoon. But the more chic Croisette beaches are the heart of Cannes's resort life and, even though private, are open to anybody willing to rent a beach mattress and/or umbrella (about $10 each for a half day). Waiters will serve you drinks, snacks, and desserts right there by your mattress. Pedal boats can be rented on beaches, too.

Palais des Festivals – At the western end of La Croisette, overlooking the Old Harbor, this sprawling 5-tiered beige and white convention hall is the home of the *International Film Festival* and other shows throughout the year. (Though it's been open since 1982, many still refer to it as the "new" *Palais* to distinguish it from the still-standing "old" *Palais.*) Many find its north front — the film crowd calls it the "bunker" — a little forbidding, but the formal gardens at the rear with a small amphitheater, fountains, and reflecting pools offer a pleasant refuge from the madding crowd. If you have business inside the *Palais* — equipped with every imaginable audiovisual device — the idea is to make it as quickly as you can to one of the upper terraces for a lovely view of the bay. Its Grand Hall can accommodate 2,400 people and its screen, 73 feet long and 35 feet high, is one of the largest in the world. There is also the *Salle Claude Debussy,* with 1,000 seats, as well as 10 smaller halls with seating capacities from 40 to 300, a small nightclub (open all year), a gaming room (open from November 1 to May 31), and a room filled with slot machines, which is open year-round. Since 1985, the walkway around the *Palais* and adjoining the Georges Pompidou Gardens has become a "starwalk," where film actors (mostly French) imprint their hands in wet cement. A handful of Americans, Anthony Quinn and Meryl Streep among them, have left their mark as well.

Vieux Port – The Old Harbor is a great place to browse in the early morning, when the town's last 100 or so fishermen and few remaining "old salts" are fixing up their boats. They pick up their tackle and equipment at the ship chandlers tucked in among the restaurants and pizzerias on the Quai St-Pierre, which forms the western arm of the port. Opposite, on the Jetée Albert-Edouard, which forms the eastern arm, is the Gare Maritime, from which you can take bay cruises to the Iles de Lérins just offshore (see *The Côte d'Azur,* DIRECTIONS). Moored at the far end of the Quai Laubeuf in the

Vieux Port is a three-masted galleon. The *Neptune,* built for a phenomenal $8.2 million, was featured in Roman Polanski's 1986 *Cannes Film Festival* entry, *Pirates* (a phenomenal flop!). Note the figurehead and abundant woodcarvings. It's open to the public daily from 10 AM to sunset; there is a nominal admission charge.

Rue Meynadier – Before Cannes became a resort town, this was Main Street (it links the old and new parts of the city) — its original name was Rue Grande. You can still see some splendid carved doors on the 18th-century houses of the town's wealthier merchants (a particularly fine specimen is No. 18). Today, it's a lively pedestrian zone, with boutiques and excellent cheese and specialty food shops leading to the covered market, *Marché Forville,* on the site of the old *Halles* at the western end of the street. The market is closed on Mondays.

Allées de la Liberté – Running east of the Mairie (City Hall) in front of the harbor, these delightful avenues of plane trees shelter a flower market every morning except Monday, *boules* players in the afternoon, and a flea market all day Saturday. Just north of the Allées, in the little Square Brougham, is a statue of the English lord who "created" modern Cannes.

Le Suquet – This is the little fortified hill, also known as Mont-Chevalier or La Castre (The Fortress), to which old Cannes clung in medieval days under the very nominal protection of the abbots of the Iles de Lérins. Narrow streets, some of them just a series of spiraling steps, wind their way up around the hill to leave the modern resort far below. Rue Louis-Perrissol takes you to the ramparts and square tower, Tour de Mont-Chevalier, erected at the top between 1070 and 1385 as a lookout against invading pirates. The late Gothic church nearby, Notre-Dame-d'Espérance, was completed in the 17th century and has a madonna to which miraculous powers were attributed. Just south of the church and built from rock carved out of the hillside is the 12th-century Romanesque Chapelle Ste-Anne with its 15th-century woodcarvings, which is part of the *Musée de la Castre.* Many shops and restaurants are under the medieval arches of Suquet, and a market is held here every morning except Sundays.

Musée de la Castre – In the remains of the abbots' old fortress, also at the top of Le Suquet, the museum draws on the wide-ranging archaeological collections donated to the town in the 19th century by the Dutch Baron Lycklama. Pride of place is given to sculpture, ceramics, and artifacts of the Mediterranean (Egyptian, Greek, Roman, Etruscan, and North African) and the Middle East (Babylonian and Persian). But there also are some fine pre-Columbian sculpture and weavings from Mexico, some important Oriental exhibits — Chinese porcelain and sculpture, Japanese military uniforms, and sculpture from Thailand and Laos — and last but not least, a fine collection of regional paintings. Closed Tuesdays and holidays; admission charge (phone: 93-38-55-26).

La Californie – This luxury residential area rises on the northeast side of town with its pinnacle at Super-Cannes. If it's at all reminiscent of California, it's because of the rugged terrain and wild vegetation, which recall the Hollywood Hills overlooking Los Angeles. A half-hour's drive around its winding roads — Avenue Fiesole, Boulevard des Pins, Boulevard Alexandre-Lacour — will give you a glimpse of the grand villas built by the old European aristocracy and the new Persian Gulf plutocracy who underwrite the city's tax base.

■ **EXTRA SPECIAL:** The terrace of the *Carlton* hotel bar is perhaps the best-known spot in Cannes, yet many people steer clear of it, motivated either by a process of inverted snobbery (by which they refuse to be seen in such a place) or by fear of the price of a drink. They are wrong, for the terrace is without a doubt the absolute quintessence of Cannes's mystique, a stage for whatever is magic or merely gloriously vulgar about the town. Think of the exorbitant cocktail as the price of a ticket to one of the great shows of European razzmatazz. Curtain time is around 9 PM, and the show goes on, on balmy nights, into the wee small hours of the morning. 58 La Croisette.

SOURCES AND RESOURCES

TOURIST INFORMATION: The Cannes Office du Tourisme (*Palais des Festivals,* 1 La Croisette; phone: 93-39-24-53 or 93-39-01-01), is open daily in the summer from 9 AM to 8 PM; daily except Sundays in the winter from 9 AM to 7 PM. It provides brochures, maps, assistance with guided tours of the surrounding countryside, and an *Accueil de France* service, which books hotel rooms in the vicinity for a fee. Be sure to pick up the indispensable, free booklet *Mois à Cannes,* which is packed with information on what's happening and useful addresses as well as *7 Jours et 7 Nuits,* a free weekly guide (in French) of the Côte d'Azur. There's a branch of the tourist office at the train station (phone: 93-99-19-77). It is open daily except Sundays in the summer and Monday through Friday in the winter.

Local Coverage – The principal daily newspaper of the Côte d'Azur, *Nice-Matin,* has a regional edition for Cannes and Grasse worth consulting for information about movies, concerts, and other events. *Paris–Côte d'Azur* is a bimonthly magazine covering cultural and social events in Cannes. The monthly *Gault Millau* magazine publishes a detailed Cannes restaurant guide in its May issue to coincide with the film festival. (Both magazines are in French.) Bookstores often stock back numbers if you're here later in the summer. *Semaine des Spectacles de la Côte d'Azur,* in French, is a weekly guide on sale at bookstores. The *Cannes English Bookstore* (11 Rue Bivouac Napoléon; phone: 93-99-40-08) has English-language books, but no newspapers, which are found on newsstands along La Croisette.

TELEPHONE: The city code for Cannes is 93, which is incorporated into all local 8-digit numbers. When calling a number in Cannes from the Paris region (including the Ile-de-France), dial 16, wait for a dial tone, then dial the 8-digit number. When calling a number from outside Paris, dial only the 8-digit number. When calling from the US, dial 33 (which is the country code), followed by the 8-digit number.

GETTING AROUND: Bicycle – The best way to see the surrounding countryside. Bicycles (and motorcycles) can be rented at *Fam Corot* (54 Rue Georges Clemenceau; phone: 93-39-22-82), *Cannes Location Rent* (5 Rue Allieis; phone: 93-39-46-15), or the Gare SNCF (phone: 93-47-01-01).

Boat – Boats leave daily from the port, at Jetée Albert-Edouard, for day trips to the Lérin Islands. At St-Honorat, monks guide visitors through the monastery where Lerina liquor is made. Call Gare Maritime des Iles (phone: 93-99-62-01).

Bus – The terminus of the *Société des Transports Urbains de Cannes* (*STUC*) is at Place de l'Hôtel-de-Ville (phone: 93-39-18-71). Seven main routes operate in town and minibus No. 8 runs along La Croisette to Palm Beach. Buses for the Nice airport also leave every hour from 9 AM to 7 PM from the Hôtel de Ville terminus (phone: 93-39-11-39).

Car Rental – All the major international companies are represented: *Avis* (69 La Croisette; phone: 93-94-15-86); *Budget* (1 Rue André-Chaude; phone: 93-99-44-04);

Europcar (3 Rue du Commandant-Vidal; phone: 93-39-75-20); *Hertz* (147 Rue d'Antibes; phone: 93-99-04-20).

Taxi – Meter rates operate inside town; set rates are used for excursions beyond the city limits. Besides the Place de l'Hôtel-de-Ville (phone: 93-39-60-80) and the train station (phone: 93-38-30-79), cabstands are outside the main hotels, most conveniently at the *Majestic* (phone: 93-99-52-10) and the *Carlton* (phone: 93-38-09-76). A taxi to the airport costs about 350F ($58).

Train – Most trains running along the coast between Marseilles and Nice also stop in Cannes. Gare *SNCF* is on Rue Jean-Jaurès, a few blocks back from La Croisette. Call 93-99-50-50 or 93-99-19-77 for information.

SPECIAL EVENTS: The old tradition of folkloric flower battles and mimosa festivals has given way to stylish conventions and sporting events. In January, *MIDEM* (*Marché International du Disque et de l'Edition Musicale*) draws professionals of the classical and popular music recording and publishing industry. *Carnaval de Cannes* takes place on the last Sunday of March. The prestigious *International Film Festival* runs for 2 weeks in May. (If you're not assured of accreditation as a professional, it's unlikely you'll get a hotel room. You probably won't get tickets for the main festival screenings, either, though screenings of many, many films that are not part of the competition take place at the same time and you will be able to see a movie or two.) Also in May, there's an international horse show, *Concours Hippique,* at the *Stade des Hespérides.* On *Bastille Day* (July 14), *St-Mery* (August 15), and *August 24,* the anniversary of the 1944 liberation of Cannes, fireworks light up the bay. Also in July, there is a music festival at Le Suquet (on the western edge of town), along with jazz and theater festivals. The *Yacht Club* stages a *Regatta* in September, and in October, *Vidcom* brings the video industry to town (the tourist office can tell you how to get in to see the latest gadgetry).

SHOPPING: Many of the most fashionable boutiques of Paris have well-stocked branches down here, particularly those that specialize in casual and beach wear. Those who, like Holly Golightly, can afford only "breakfast" at *Tiffany's* might like at least to munch a croissant outside the eye-boggling windows of the jewelry shops along La Croisette. La Croisette is the prime focus of the town's most elegant shops, but many also are found inside the great hotels. The shopping center of the *Gray d'Albion* (17 La Croisette) is perhaps the most opulent on the Côte d'Azur.

The second main shopping street, running parallel to the seafront, is the Rue d'Antibes, with a more democratic mix of prices from the expensive down to the moderate. There seems to be nothing really inexpensive in Cannes, and the best bet for a bargain is at the *Marché aux Puces* (Flea Market), held on the Allées de la Liberté on Saturdays from 9 AM to about 7 PM. The Rue Meynadier pedestrian zone is devoted mainly to high class food shops, but these provide excellent gifts — the better shops package wines and food delicacies for shipment abroad. This area is also popular among the attractive young Cannois for the great bargains to be had in the trendy, open-air boutiques that overflow into the street. If you're buying food for a picnic or other immediate consumption, don't forget the *Marché Forville* (closed Mondays), the covered market for vegetables, fruit, and fish. This is *not* a good town for buying art and antiques, though there are plenty of both.

Alexandra – High class women's wear — carrying the major younger French and Italian labels — Chloé, Jean-Louis Scherrer, Giorgio Armani, and Christian Lacroix. Rond-Point Duboys-d'Angers (phone: 93-38-41-29).

Cannolive – Over 100 years old, this shop features olive oil, Provençal liqueurs, and orange wine (a local aperitif). 16 Rue Vénizelos (phone: 93-39-08-19).

Cartier – Home of the ultimate in jewelry and leather goods. 57 La Croisette (phone: 93-99-58-73).

Ernest – A first class delicatessen — ham, sausage, but especially exquisite pâté in cans, earthenware, or airtight glass containers. Its pastry shop is across the street. 52 Rue Meynadier (phone: 93-39-25-96; pastries, 93-39-19-07).

La Ferme Savoyarde – Great for cheese. 22 Rue Meynadier (phone: 93-39-63-68).

Gérard – Jewelry designs with a touch of fantasy. In the *Hotel Majestic,* 14 La Croisette (phone: 93-99-10-12).

Hermès – Quite apart from the classic leathers and silks, they make the world's greatest beach towels. *Gray d'Albion,* 17 La Croisette (phone: 93-39-08-90).

Maiffret – The venerable manufacturer of sinfully good chocolates and candy, particularly the local specialty, candied figs, apricots, strawberries, pears, plums, and melon. Watch them being made in the mezzanine "lab." 31 Rue d'Antibes (phone: 93-39-08-29).

Putterflam – Classic and modern chinaware and silver. 109 Rue d'Antibes (phone: 93-38-54-06).

Sadya – The sexiest lingerie in town. 19 Rue du Commandant André (phone: 93-39-09-58).

Van Cleef & Arpels – Exquisite gold jewelry and gems. 61 La Croisette (phone: 93-94-15-08).

 SPORTS AND FITNESS: For any information about sports, call the Office Municipal de la Jeunesse (2 Quai St-Pierre; phone: 93-38-21-16 or 93-99-20-96). The most relaxing spectator sport in town — and free — is *boules* at the *Boulodrome de la Pantiero* on Allées de la Liberté.

Fishing – Deep-sea fishing is organized by the *Club de Pêche Sportive de Cannes* at the *Sofitel-Méditerranée* hotel (Bd. Jean-Hibert; phone: 93-63-73-67), and the *Fishing Club de Cannes-Mandelieu* (phone: 93-49-83-94). Fishing equipment is available at *La Cible 06* (13 Bd. Carnot; phone: 93-99-24-02) and at *Atrizzi Serge* (5 Rue Félix-Faure; phone: 93-39-10-41).

Golf – Your hotel can advise you about access to the *Golf Club de Cannes-Mandelieu* (phone: 93-49-55-39), the *Golf Country Club de Cannes-Mougins* (phone: 93-75-79-13), or *Golf de Valbonne* (phone: 93-42-05-30).

Sailing and Windsurfing – As with scuba diving (see below), these sports are organized by the *Centre Nautique Municipal* (2 Quai St-Pierre; phone: 93-38-21-16). Equipment can be rented at the *Base du Mouré Rouge* (9 Rue Esprit-Violet; phone: 93-43-83-48). Sailboats (and motorboats) are also for rent at *New Boat* (Port de la Napoule; phone: 93-93-12-34).

Scuba Diving – Contact the *Centre Nautique Municipal* (address and phone above).

Swimming – The public beaches are the Plage du Midi and Plage Gazagnaire; private beaches are along La Croisette. Pool fanciers can try *Piscine Municipale* (Av. Pierre de Coubertin; phone: 93-47-12-94), or the swimming pools at the *Palm Beach Casino* (phone: 93-43-91-12), or — if you're a guest — at the *Pullman Beach, Majestic, Martinez, Montfleury, Sofitel-Méditerranée, Beau Séjour,* or *Cannes Palace* hotels.

Tennis – Your hotel can help you get one of the many courts at the *Complexe Sportif Montfleury* (Av. Beauséjour; phone: 93-38-75-78); *Gallia Tennis Club* (Bd. de Strasbourg; phone: 93-38-75-78); or *Tennis-Club* (Municipal de l'Aérodrome, 220 Av. Francis-Tonner; phone: 93-47-29-33). Lessons are available at the *Cannes Tennis Club* (1 Rue Lacour; phone: 93-43-58-85).

Volleyball – Cannes is home to one of the best French volleyball teams. They usually play their home matches in winter and spring on Saturdays and Sundays at the *Palais des Sports,* Av. du Docteur Picaud (phone: 93-39-60-47).

MUSIC: The *Orchestre Cannes–Provence–Côte d'Azur* gives classical music concerts in the *Salle Claude Debussy* of the *Palais des Festivals.* Chamber music recitals can be heard at Notre-Dame-d'Espérance on Le Suquet.

NIGHTCLUBS AND NIGHTLIFE: The smartest discos — don't go before midnight — are the *Jackpot* (at the *Palm Beach Casino;* phone: 93-43-91-12) and *Jane's* (in the *Gray d'Albion;* phone: 93-68-54-54). Gays and celebrities dance under laser beams at *Whiskey-à-Gogo* (115 Av. de Lérins; phone: 93-43-20-63). For jazz, try *Le Duke* (at the casino of the *Palais des Festivals;* phone: 93-38-12-11) or *Le Ragtime* (opposite the *Palais des Festivals,* La Croisette; phone: 93-48-47-10); and for an English pub atmosphere, complete with dart games — as well as *Rolling Stones* music — join the young clientele at *The Swan* (4 Rue Clemenceau; phone: 93-39-05-57). *Jimmy's,* at the *Palais de Festival,* is currently in vogue (1 Bd. de la Croisette; phone: 93-68-00-07), as is the *Studio Circus Cannes Disco and Nightclub* (48 Bd. de la République; phone: 93-38-59-78).

The other action in town is gambling — from 5 PM daily November through May at the *Casino Croisette* of the *Palais des Festivals* (phone: 93-38-12-11); from 7 PM daily June through October at the much more elegant *Palm Beach Casino* on Pointe de la Croisette (phone: 93-43-91-12). There's an entrance fee and you'll need your passport; jackets, but not formal wear, are required for men. The games include roulette, baccarat, and blackjack (no craps). At the tables of the *Casino Club* at the *Carlton Inter-Continental* (58 Bd. de la Croisette; phone: 93-68-00-33), you can win or loose at roulette, baccarat, or chemin-de-fer all year-round. The *boule* room at the *Palais des Festivals* offers a proletarian form of low-stakes roulette in which a golf-size ball teeters around a tableful of numbers. It won't break you or make you rich, but you get a nice high watching the ball.

BEST IN TOWN

CHECKING IN: Before even thinking of checking into a Cannes hostelry, consider that it's neither possible nor desirable to do this town on the cheap. It's not like one of the major European capitals, where there's so much going on in the theaters, museums, and concert halls that it doesn't really matter what kind of hotel you choose — or where it's situated. This is an expensive resort town where the Mediterranean is the whole story, and it's just no fun being in a third-rate hotel far from the sea. Even if they're not on La Croisette, the hotels near the water are hardly inexpensive. You'll find a few that are conveniently located and reasonably priced, but nothing under $90 for double occupancy — and you'll have to book several months in advance to get those prices. Prices go up in May during the film festival and hotels always are booked; be prepared to reserve possibly years in advance. Hotels in the expensive category — the so-called palaces — run from $200 and way up for a double room with continental breakfast. Moderate hotels range from $100 to $150, and inexpensive ones, for the most part out in the boondocks, under $100.

Carlton Inter-Continental – Numero uno in terms of old-fashioned prestige and glamour, the decor has retained its Belle Epoque charm, and renovations — by Japanese owners — of the 325 rooms and 30 suites have modernized the traditional comforts. The bathrooms alone are monumental enough to justify a good part of the price, and the view of La Croisette and the sea is magnificent. Its 13-room penthouse Imperial Suite offers all the comforts at $6,000 a day. The service (outside film festival time) is efficient without being obsequious. In addition to the famous big bar and terrace, there's a delightful, intimate, smaller bar off the lobby. There is also a gym/health center on the seventh floor. The food at *La Côté* (see *Eating Out*) and *La Belle Otéro* restaurants has won them each a Michelin star. No swimming pool, but a private beach. Major credit cards accepted. 58 Bd. de la Croisette (phone: 93-68-91-68; fax: 93-38-20-90; telex: 470720). Expensive.

Grand – The most discreet of the "palaces," set back at the end of an avenue of palms winding among tailored lawns and flowerbeds, this is the place to get away from the mob in perfect modern comfort. Service and amenities in the 76 rooms and 2 apartments have an appropriate refinement. Swingers may find the bar *too* quiet. Major credit cards accepted. 45 La Croisette (phone: 93-38-15-45; fax: 93-68-97-65; telex: 470727). Expensive.

Martinez – Located along Cannes Bay, this luxurious establishment offers elegance *and* pluperfect service. All 417 rooms are tastefully appointed with Art Deco furnishings; no less magnificent are the restaurants — one of which, *La Palme d'Or* (see *Eating Out*) — has won two coveted Michelin stars for its fare. Other amenities include a pool and a private beach. Major credit cards accepted. 73 Bd. Croisette (phone: 93-94-30-30 or 92-98-30-18; fax: 93-39-67-82; telex: 470 706). Expensive.

Gray d'Albion – The most modern of Cannes's properties is part of a huge luxury shopping and apartment complex. The 186 rooms and 14 suites boast all the most up-to-date comforts, including phones in the bathrooms and VCRs in the suites. Set away from the sea, the eighth and ninth floors have a Mediterranean view. The hotel has its own discotheque, *Jane*, a piano bar, a private beach, and a great restaurant, *Royal Gray* (see *Eating Out*). Major credit cards accepted. 38 Rue des Serbes (phone: 93-68-54-54; fax: 93-99-26-10; telex: 470744). Expensive.

Majestic – Many connoisseurs insist this is really the best of the "palaces," more sophisticated than its more celebrated rival, the *Carlton*. Certainly the 248 rooms and 13 suites and their amenities are impeccable, and the service is very good, if sometimes a little overconfident. Its great asset is the lovely seawater swimming pool in tree-shaded grounds that set the hotel quietly back from the bustling Croisette. Its restaurant, *Le Sunset,* is slowly gaining a reputation as one of Cannes's better eating places. The bar and terrace are a joy. Open year-round. Major credit cards accepted. 6 La Croisette (phone: 93-68-91-00; fax: 93-38-97-90; telex: 470475). Expensive.

Novotel Montfleury – In the middle of a park looking down a hill to the sea, this is the luxury spot for the sporting crowd. The *Complexe Sportif Montfleury* shares the location, and hotel guests can avail themselves of heated swimming pools, tennis courts, a volleyball court, and other facilities, including a skating rink in winter. It's perhaps the one place in Cannes where you won't mind not being near La Croisette. The 180 rooms, many with spacious balconies, and Presidential Suite are very modern and superbly furnished. Ask for a room above the fourth floor to get a good view of the sea. Major credit cards accepted. 25 Av. Beauséjour (phone: 93-68-91-50; fax: 93-38-37-08; telex: 470039). Expensive.

Sofitel-Méditerranée – Located at the western end of the Old Port, this lovely hostelry has 150 rooms and 5 suites. It might have the best view not only in Cannes, but on the Côte d'Azur. There is a good restaurant, *Le Palmyre,* and a swimming pool on the seventh floor. Major credit cards accepted. 2 Bd. Jean-Hibert (Plage du Midi; phone: 93-99-22-75; fax: 93-39-68-36; telex: 470728). Expensive.

Splendid – By a stroke of luck, this modest but well-run and comfortable place near the Old Harbor hit the jackpot when the *Palais des Festivals* was built just across the street. This, combined with a ringside view of the *boules* games on the Allées de la Liberté, gives it one of the best locations in town. There is no restaurant, but breakfast service is fine, and 40 out of the 64 rooms come with a kitchenette for those who want to take advantage of the nearby food market. Major credit cards accepted. 4-6 Rue Félix-Faure (phone: 93-99-53-11; fax: 93-99-55-02; telex: 470990). Expensive.

Palma – By the rose garden at the east end of La Croisette, this hostelry has 52 small, bright, cozy rooms, most with ocean views. Those that don't face the sea, however, offer the best summer rates in town. The service is without a doubt the friendliest on La Croisette. Major credit cards accepted. 77 La Croisette (phone: 93-94-22-16; fax: 93-94-02-45; telex: 470826). Expensive to moderate.

Beau Séjour – Very well equipped, with 46 rooms, it is 300 yards from the beach and has its own swimming pool and garden. The service is efficient and the restaurant, less pretentious than those of the "palaces," is a pleasant surprise. Closed from mid-October to mid-December. Major credit cards accepted. 5 Rue des Fauvettes (phone: 93-39-63-00; fax: 92-98-64-66; telex: 470975). Moderate.

Canberra – The 42 rooms are simply but nicely done, with air conditioning and television sets. There is a small bar and a quiet little garden, and it's in the shopping district or just a few steps away from the beach. if you walk in the opposite direction. Major credit cards accepted. 120 Rue d'Antibes (phone: 93-38-20-70; fax: 92-98-03-47; telex: 470817). Moderate.

Century – This modern hotel has only 35 rooms, but they're big and have air conditioning, TV sets, and — important in this busy shopping area — good sound-proofing. Closed December 1 to January 7. Major credit cards accepted. 133 Rue d'Antibes (phone: 93-99-37-64; fax: 93-68-26-03; telex: 470090). Moderate.

Corona – Modest, clean rooms, air conditioned and soundproof, and only a short walk from La Croisette and the railroad station. What you save on the hotel bill you can spend at the *Gray d'Albion Shopping Center* across the street. Closed in November. Major credit cards accepted. 55 Rue d'Antibes (phone: 93-39-69-85). Moderate.

EATING OUT: Cannes's fancy touch has been more successful in creating great hotels than great cuisine, though things are getting better, particularly at the upper end of the price scale, and only a few miles away in Mougins, one of the most famous restaurants in France continues to satisfy (and satiate) the most stringent of critics. In the more modest bistros, however, it's best to choose simpler fare — straightforward seafood dishes, for instance — rather than the attempts at something more elaborate. Note that the local cooking is not especially Provençal, no more so than the resident population. But the fruit and vegetables season is longer than in other parts of France, and fresh fish is in abundance; therefore, you can be assured of eating light and quickly prepared dishes. For ice cream lovers, however, Cannes is a paradise. Beside the traditional chocolate, coffee, and nut flavors, there are licorice, ginger, and honey ices, cream cheese sherbets, and even *croque-monsieur* ice cream, a type of ice cream sandwich. As with hotel prices, restaurant prices must be seen in a specifically Cannes context: At the very expensive restaurant listed, expect to pay $200 and up for a meal for two; in the ones in the expensive range, $150 to $200; moderate means $70 to $150; while $70 or as little as $25 for two is considered inexpensive. Prices do not include drinks or wine; usually a service charge is included.

Le Moulin de Mougins – One of the best dining rooms in all of France is just outside the charming market town of Mougins, a 15-minute drive from Cannes. Roger Vergé, the owner and master chef, offers a warm welcome to the converted 16th-century mill where he won the coveted three Michelin stars only 5 years after opening. Among his specialties are *salade Mikado,* a creation of mushrooms, avocado, tomato, and truffles; violet asparagus with truffles; artichokes, scallops, and smoked salmon in lime sauce; *aiguillettes de canard de Challons au sang,* strips of duck breast followed by the grilled legs; and, for dessert, *soufflé glacé aux fraises des bois,* cold wild strawberry soufflé. Reservations are essential, as are coat and tie. Organic products, made by the master chef himself, are sold in the adjacent boutique. Closed Mondays off-season, Thursdays at lunchtime, and from January 29 to *Easter.* Major credit cards accepted. On D3 at Notre-Dame-de-Vie, about 4 miles (6 km) north of Cannes (phone: 93-75-78-24; fax: 93-90-18-55; telex: 970732). Very expensive.

Le Festival – One of the best of the swank spots on La Croisette, though for those who come here to be seen, a good meal is quite secondary. Best bet is the fish, especially salmon *à la menthe* (mint), and nearly everything on the pastry trolley is lethally good. Closed Sundays for dinner, Mondays from January to *Easter,* and November 19 to December 27. Reservations necessary. Major credit cards accepted. 52 La Croisette (phone: 93-94-00-61). Expensive.

La Palme d'Or – Provençal fare par excellence, served in an Art Deco room hung with photos of Hollywood stars. It won its second Michelin star in 1991, most likely for its delectable, delicate entrées. A meal here must end with the beautiful cheese selection or a superb dessert — or both! Closed Mondays and Tuesday afternoons, and mid-November to mid-January. Reservations necessary. Major credit cards accepted. 73 La Croisette (phone: 92-98-30-18 or 93-94-30-30). Expensive.

Royal Gray – On the first floor of the *Gray d'Albion,* this is a marvelously imaginative exception to the disappointments that the restaurants of many large hotels can be (not just in Cannes), and it has justifiably been given two Michelin stars. Conceding nothing in the elegance of its pink and violet decor, it manages to give courteous, efficient, and unpompous service, for one thing. For another, the cooking of Chef Jacques Chiboisit is inventive rather than flashy (a salad of fresh salmon marinated in ginger on a bed of green vegetables), or straightforward without being dull (sea perch with truffles and squash, or sliced duck *aiguillettes* in burgundy with spring turnips). The sweet-toothed would die rather than miss the apple *mille-feuille* pastry in caramel sauce or the hot walnut cake. And the terrace is famous in its own right. The restaurant will move to the second floor this year, overlooking the garden. Closed Sundays (except in summer), Mondays, and February 1 through March 6. Reservations necessary. Major credit cards accepted. 38 Rue des Serbes (phone: 93-99-04-59 or 93-68-54-54). Expensive.

La Côté – One of the most beautiful dining rooms in the south of France, offering fine, light food (it was awarded a Michelin star in 1991). Try the fresh pasta with seafood or any fish dish. Closed Tuesdays, Wednesdays, and mid-February through March. Reservations necessary. Major credit cards accepted. 58 Bd. de la Croisette (phone: 93-68-91-68). Expensive to moderate.

Villa Dionysos – A small, Italian-style palace, where a woman chef makes some of the simplest and purest food on the entire Riviera. Two excellent fixed-price menus make this restaurant irresistible. Those who disdain the odor of tobacco smoke can request a table in the nonsmoking area. Open year-round. Reservations necessary. Major credit cards accepted. 7 Rue Marceau (phone: 93-38-79-73). Expensive to moderate.

Chez Astoux – Great trays of oysters, clams, mussels, sea urchins, winkles, crabs, and shrimp that will keep you busy all evening are one reason not to overlook this seafood bistro close to the Old Harbor. The scrumptious chocolate profiteroles are another. The atmosphere is noisy, lively, and very friendly. Open daily. Reservations advised. Visa accepted. 43 Rue Félix-Faure (phone: 93-39-06-22). Moderate.

Gaston et Gastounette – This comfortable place facing the Old Port offers a variety of fish and Provençal dishes. Closed 2 weeks in mid-January. Reservations advised in summer. Major credit cards accepted. 6 Quai St-Pierre (phone: 93-39-49-44 or 93-39-47-92). Moderate.

Au Mal Assis – Nicely situated on the Old Harbor, and you're much better seated than the name implies (the name actually derives from the family — Malassis — who ran the establishment over a century ago). The fish is first class, the service amiable. Closed mid-October to late December. Reservations advised in season. Visa accepted. 15 Quai St-Pierre (phone: 93-39-05-35 or 93-39-13-38). Moderate.

Le Maschou – This place stands out for its good charcoal-grilled steaks and its candlelit setting, where the plain look pretty and the pretty stunning. It's a favorite with the *jeunesse dorée.* Dinner only. Closed November to mid-December. Reservations necessary. Visa accepted. 17 Rue St-Antoine (phone: 93-39-62-21). Moderate.

La Mère Besson – A rarity in Cannes: an authentic Provençal restaurant. It's very fashionable, always crowded, and everybody table-hops. Try the fragrant beef stew, *daube provençale.* Closed Sundays except off-season, and 1 week in February. Reservations necessary. Major credit cards accepted. 13 Rue des Frères-Pradignac (phone: 93-39-59-24 or 93-38-94-01). Moderate.

Au Bec Fin – Fine, straightforward cooking prevails here. The excellent steaks are served thick, the plain grilled fish — local *daurade* (sea bream), *rascasse* (hogfish), or sea bass — graced with perhaps a touch of fennel, and the salads are among the best in town. Closed Saturdays for dinner, Sundays, and mid-December to mid-January. Reservations necessary. No credit cards accepted. Near the railroad station; 12 Rue du 24-Août (phone: 93-38-35-86). Inexpensive.

Beach Restaurants – These establishments defy classification. Strung along La Croisette, some of them are connected to the big hotels, all of them are relatively expensive, but they're still a delightful way to enjoy the beach at lunchtime. Your best bet is to have the prix fixe menu of the day or one of the very good salads — *niçoise,* shrimp, or crabmeat — plus a small carafe of wine or mineral water, and maybe some strawberries. Service is slow, but nobody's in a hurry on the beach. The best people watching locations — make a reservation — are the *Maschou Beach* (phone: 93-39-37-37), *Hawaii Beach* (phone: 93-38-17-47), *Lido Plage* (phone: 93-38-25-44), *Plage Club des Sports,* where volleyballers go (phone: 93-38-59-72), and the *Plage de Sport* (phone: 93-47-49-62). Also excellent are *L'Ondine,* with some of the best cooking on the beach at the best prices (phone: 93-94-23-15), and *Le Goéland* (phone: 93-38-22-05), where the mattress comes with the beach's admission price, and lots of fresh vegetables garnish the fish dishes. For good salads, try *Volier* (phone: 93-94-25-46), open year-round.

 BARS AND CAFÉS: The *Petit Carlton* — no relation (93 Rue d'Antibes; phone: 99-39-27-25) — is a rather scruffy tavern staked out at festival time by movie buffs who can't or don't want to afford the "grand" *Carlton.* It serves merely edible meals and retains its counterculture ambience the rest of the year. *Le Ragtime* is a fashionable piano bar decked out in smart 1920s decor (phone: 93-68-47-10). Strategically opposite the "new" *Palais des Festivals* at La Croisette, it functions as a tearoom in the afternoon, an expensive restaurant at night, and as a bar all day. (At night, the restaurant musicians are piped down to the bar on a video screen.) At the risk of tiresome repetition, the best hotel bars remain the *Carlton* terrace and the *Majestic,* the latter with superior potato chips.

CHARTRES

There are places in the world where the center seems to hold, and Chartres is one of them. An enduring gift of the Middle Ages, the town wraps itself around the treasure casket of an incomparable cathedral and its unrivaled collection of stained glass and sculpture. To the traveler scaling the steep, winding streets and wandering along the banks of the river Eure, with its reedy waters and stone bridges, there are no jarring notes.

Since 1963, the municipality has been carefully restoring the town, shoring up timbers and gables and respecting the integrity of the original houses, but this city is not a museum. Though Chartres no longer is the bustling cross-roads that supported the extravagant building projects of the 13th century, it still is a prosperous market town, sitting at the center of some of France's richest arable land. On Saturdays, when the gardeners of the Beauce region are out in force for the *Marché des Fleurs* and farmers stack their produce under the arches of the covered market, crowds of shoppers mill around well-kept stores in the pedestrian zones. In the back streets, matronly neighbors in blue aprons gossip from their windows, and inviting courtyards offer glimpses of ancient iron pumps and greenery within. And on the feast days that draw pilgrims with their backpacks to special services at the cathedral, there may be a lean and tousle-headed ascetic pacing the cobbles and wrangling with himself, a shade of the many pilgrims who have passed this way.

Recent excavations have shown that a settlement flourished here under the Romans, who first called it Autricum and then "the town of the Carnutes" — after the Gallic tribe of the area — and built a forum, an amphitheater, and a temple on the banks of the Eure. Until the Romans and Christianity took hold, Chartres was an important center of the druid religion in Gaul; in fact, the Roman temple and, in the 4th century, the first Christian church seem to have risen on the same spot already hallowed by the druids. Then, after 876, when Charles the Bald, the French king, gave the city the Sancta Camisia (the robe Mary is said to have worn when she gave birth to Christ), Chartres became an important center of the cult of the Virgin Mary.

By the end of the 10th century, under the leadership of counts such as Thibaut the Cheat, whose domain extended as far as Blois in the Loire Valley, Chartres had become one of medieval Europe's most exciting cities. It was a center of learning, the home of scholars such as its Bishop Fulbert, who set about building a predecessor of Chartres's cathedral after an earlier church had been destroyed by fire in 1020; of Bernard of Chartres, who preached the Crusades here in the 12th century; and John of Salisbury, the secretary of Thomas à Becket. All the while, pilgrims flocked in, bringing offerings to Mary's shrine.

In 1194, a fire razed the flourishing town, leaving only the crypt, parts of the façade, and a steeple of the cathedral. But the holy relic miraculously escaped damage, fueling enthusiasm for the construction of a new building on the old foundations. The main body of the cathedral that stands today was completed between 1194 and 1225, financed by gifts from the crowned heads of Europe and the well-heeled merchants of the city. Chartres's status as a spiritual center persisted into the 14th century, when the county became a dependency of the Kings of France, many of whom became its benefactors, and in 1594 Henri IV of Navarre had himself crowned here, one of the few exceptions to the rule that French kings be crowned in Reims Cathedral.

Some residents of Chartres complain that interest focuses so heavily on the medieval city that history here seems to stop in the 18th century. In fact, Chartres contributed several important figures to the French Revolution, including the revolutionary theorist Abbé Sieyès, who lived in Chartres and wrote his treatise on the third estate here. When the Revolution broke out, the cathedral was declared a Temple of Reason; there was talk of pulling the place to the ground and its treasure was plundered, but its statuary and stained glass escaped the excesses of vandalism.

By the 19th century, although Chartres had lost its political importance, the beauty of the town attracted writers and artists (the musical tradition surrounding the cathedral had always been strong). The writer Théophile Gautier frequently stayed in the area, as did Anatole France and Alfred de Musset, who wrote a novella here. Corot painted a fine canvas of the cathedral, now in the *Louvre,* showing its former dark lead roof, which was replaced with today's blue-green copper one after a fire in 1836. Much later, the Lithuanian painter Chaim Soutine translated the landscapes of the Eure Valley into swirling canvases during the Nazi occupation, which he spent in hiding nearby because he was a Jew. The town's World War II hero and one of the architects of the French Resistance was Jean Moulin, who was prefect of the Eure-et-Loir *département* at the beginning of the war.

More recent town leaders have worked to ensure the city's continued evolution. Ambitious projects such as the multipurpose exhibition hall, *Chartrexpo* (capacity 7,000), should help this medieval city ease into the 21st century.

Yet, despite all the evidence of its continuing vitality through the centuries, Chartres *is* its cathedral. It is in its picture of medieval life that Chartres lives most intensely: in the clear gaze of its statues and the intense colors of its stained glass, undimmed by time.

CHARTRES AT-A-GLANCE

SEEING THE CITY: Nobody forgets seeing Chartres cathedral for the first time across the Beauce plain, its two spires like the masts of a sailing ship afloat on a sea of grain. Because it sits on a spur of elevated ground, it looms onto the horizon whether you arrive by road, on the A10 past Versailles from Paris or on N154 from Rouen and Normandy, or by rail (there are trains roughly every hour from the Gare Montparnasse in Paris). As you approach, the layers of the city peel off: sprawling 20th century, sturdy bourgeois 19th century, then the unspoiled medieval core. It all can be seen from the highly decorated turrets of the cathedral's North Tower, a winding walk up narrow stairs (entrance inside the North Door); from May through September, 9:30 to 11:30 AM and 2 to 5:30 PM (shorter hours in low season); closed Sunday mornings and the month of January. Admission charge.

The stone bridges on the river Eure along the Rue de la Foulerie-Frou and the Rue de la Tannerie in the Basse Ville (Lower Town) also give an unforgettable view of the city. Flanked by sober medieval buildings, the narrow stream flows past tree-lined banks, carrying the eye up to the cathedral, and low walls provide a comfortable resting place for contemplation. Two other good views: a profile of the town's major churches from the Pont de la Courtille at the extreme southeast of the Old Town, and from the well-mown terraced lawns of the Bishop's Garden, immediately behind the cathedral, a panorama over to the rich countryside on which Chartres's prosperity was based.

For easy sightseeing of the charming old quarters along the banks of the river Eure, take a ride on *Le Petit Train de Chartres.* This open-air trolley, run by the local tourist office, travels a 35-minute route, with commentary in English. Hourly departures from 10 AM to 7 PM *Easter* to November; admission charge. For information, inquire at the tourist office, Pl. de la Cathédrale (phone: 37-21-50-00).

 SPECIAL PLACES: All the sights below, with the exception of the last one, Eglise St-Martin-au-Val, are in the Old Town, the hub of which is the cathedral and which has upper and lower levels. The Haute Ville (Upper Town) takes in the cathedral as well as the area south and west of it, including the commercial center around Place des Epars and such streets as Rue Noël-Ballay and Rue du Cygne. The Basse Ville (Lower Town) is east of the cathedral, running along the river. All of this is easily walked; even St-Martin-au-Val, which actually is beyond the limits of the Old Town, is no more than a 15-minute walk from Notre-Dame. On your way back, be sure to wander along Rue aux Herbes, Rue de la Petite Cordonnerie, and the Place de la Poissonnerie, where curious old houses give one a sense of the medieval city come alive.

CHARTRES CATHEDRAL

If the Parthenon sums up Greek civilization and St. Peter's in Rome stands for the Renaissance, Notre-Dame de Chartres is the last word in Gothic architecture. The cathedral of today is probably the fifth church to be built on the spot — fires and sword destroyed its previous incarnations — and because most of it was constructed within a period of 30 years (1194–1225), it has an unusual architectural homogeneity. Its two spires, which do not match and give it a lopsided look, are from completely different eras. The South Tower to the right (called the Clocher Vieux, or Old Tower) is in the Romanesque style, elegantly sober and unadorned to the tip of its steeple; it was finished in about 1160 for the previous cathedral and survived the fire of 1194. The North Tower to the left (the Clocher Neuf, or New Tower) is, at least at its base, which also survived the fire of 1194, older than the Old Tower, but its steeple in the convoluted Flamboyant style of the early 16th century was built by Jean Texier, or Jehan de Beauce, to replace a wooden one that burned in 1506. The 12th- and 13th-century statuary surrounding the cathedral's three main doorways — the Royal Portal in the western façade and the porches of the northern and southern transepts — is a gold mine of information on the life and thought of the people of the Middle Ages, and its stained glass windows are considered the most beautiful in France, a country where exquisite stained glass has been preserved in remarkable quantity.

Excavations are still in progress in the square in front of the cathedral. Archaeologists already have uncovered traces from the *maisons canoniales,* where church canons were stored during the 13th century. Although there has been talk of someday transforming the site into a museum, the excavations are expected to continue for several years.

■**Note:** Tourists are restricted from entering the cathedral during its most important masses. Therefore, visitors not attending mass will not be permitted to go into the nave from Saturday at 7:45 PM until Sunday at noon.

Nave – The size of the building staggers even the blasé modern observer; there can be few structures, one feels, that enclose as much space. The nave is broader than any other in France. The ogival arches rise to 122 feet; and the walls, opened up by flying buttresses that carry the weight of the vaults, are studded with 27,000 square feet of mostly medieval stained glass, the most complete collection anywhere in the world. Brilliant reds, yellows, and greens puncture the deep aquamarine background that has come to be known as Chartres blue, telling the familiar Bible stories over and over again. It's best to come armed with binoculars (available at the *Optique des Changes,* 9 Rue des Changes; phone: 37-21-51-390; and at *La Crypt,* 18 Cloître Notre-Dame; phone: 37-21-56-33) to appreciate, frame by frame, the detail of these luminous texts. Most prized are the three 12th-century lancet windows under the spire of the west front, retrieved, like the famous Blue Virgin window by the choir (Notre-Dame de la Belle Verrière), from the earlier Romanesque cathedral. They show the Tree of Jesse (on the right), scenes from the life of Christ (middle) and the Passion (left). It's well worth unraveling it all with the help of the detailed brochures available in English.

Choir – Like the massive baroque altarpiece, which is a little out of place here but striking in its sweep and movement, the ornate stone tableaux of the choir screen were an afterthought, embellishments on the Gothic. Begun by Jehan de Beauce in 1516 and finally completed in 1716, they show scenes in the lives of Christ and the Virgin, but are more eloquent about the courtiers and seamstresses of the Renaissance.

Chapelle de St-Piat – The cathedral's treasure house, behind the choir, displays the famous relic of the Virgin's robe as well as embroidered vestments and other precious objects given to the church. Closed during lunch, Sunday mornings, and January.

Crypt – The third-largest in the world (after those at Canterbury Cathedral in England and St. Peter's in Rome), the U-shaped crypt houses some interesting 12th-century murals, statues rescued from the Royal Portal, and a carved Madonna that is a replica of one burned during the French Revolution. The crypt is the oldest part of the cathedral, most of it dating back to Fulbert's time in the 11th century, but it contains an even earlier crypt (that of a 9th-century church) and parts of Gallo-Roman origin. Guided tours (the only way the crypt can be visited and for which there is a charge) leave several times daily from the *La Crypt* (18 Cloître Notre-Dame; phone: 37-21-56-33), a café located just across from the cathedral.

Royal Portal – The sculpted triple doors that make up the entrance in the western façade survive from the earlier cathedral and are considered among the finest examples of French Romanesque art. They present the stern and ethereal mid-12th-century vision of Christ in majesty, the figures elongated, the lines pure.

North Porch – The three arches here, carved in the 13th century, concentrate on the Old Testament and the prophecies of Christ's coming, with, in parentheses, the story of the Creation and a fascinating series showing the months, the arts, and the virtues as seen through medieval eyes.

South Porch – Also 13th century, the sculpture of the southern doorway (Portail du Midi) focuses on Christ, who is seen presiding at a vividly depicted Last Judgment, complete with sinners and demons, and surrounded by phalanxes of martyrs and confessors of the church. The grisly end awaiting martyrs and sinners makes compulsive viewing, and there are some exquisite visions of the ideal courtly knight (watch for St. George and St. Maurice, outermost figures flanking the entrance).

AROUND THE TOWN

Musée des Beaux-Arts – Behind the cathedral are the former Bishop's Palace, built during the 17th and 18th centuries, and the Bishop's Garden, which falls in terraces toward the river and provides a view over the Lower Town and beyond. The palace, now a fine arts museum, contains tapestries, furniture, and enamels as well as an exceptional collection of ten paintings by the Fauvist Maurice Vlaminck, together with part of his collection of African sculpture. Closed Sunday mornings in winter and Tuesdays year-round; admission charge. 29 Cloître Notre-Dame (phone: 37-36-41-39).

Enclos de Loëns/Centre International du Vitrail – The fine ogival arches of this 13th-century cellar, down a small side street north of the cathedral, were built, unusually, for a secular purpose: Wine was stored here by the priests. The spacious beamed attic houses the *Centre International du Vitrail* (International Stained Glass Center), which features displays of ancient and contemporary stained glass and permanent exhibitions that detail the history and techniques of stained glass making. The art continues to flourish in workshops around town. There also are frequent temporary exhibitions. Open daily from 10 AM to 12:30 PM and from 1:30 to 6 PM. Admission charge. 5 Rue Cardenal-Pie (phone: 37-21-65-72).

Tertre St-Nicolas – These stone steps — built during the 14th century — descend precipitously from the *Musée des Beaux-Arts* to Place St-André and the river and afford a lovely view of the city.

Eglise St-André – This 12th-century Romanesque church, deconsecrated since the Revolution, gave its name to Chartres's *St. Andrew's Fair,* held in November (see *Special Events*). The back wall carries the stump of a bridge, now covered with greenery, that used to reach over the river Eure. Rue de la Brèche, just beyond Pl. St-André.

Porte Guillaume – From the ruins of the city's last remaining 14th-century gate, fortified in the Hundred Years War and bombed by the Nazis, there are some bucolic views of the river. On the banks of the Eure, at Rue du Bourg–Porte Guillaume.

Eglise St-Pierre – If Chartres ever lost its cathedral, it would still be remembered for this late-13th-century church, once the church of a Benedictine abbey. The graceful ribs of its flying buttresses, each finished with a fearsome gargoyle, leave room inside for wall-to-wall stained glass (13th to 16th century) and a unique impression of light and air. Pl. St-Pierre.

Eglise St-Aignan – Less elegant, and balanced on a single flying buttress, this 16th-century structure has an interesting sculpted doorway and exquisite Renaissance stained glass windows, including one that shows the life of the Virgin (the fourth along from the entry). The highly decorative and colorful polychrome interior is a change from Gothic sobriety. Pl. St-Aignan, off Rue des Grenets.

Escalier de la Reine Berthe – At the junction of Rue du Bourg and Rue des Ecuyers, is a house with an unusual timbered spiral staircase from the 16th century decorated with weatherbeaten wooden sculptures. The name recalls the wife of a 10th-century Count of Chartres who went on to marry a King of France. 35 Rue des Ecuyers.

Eglise St-Martin-au-Val – This church includes a fine crypt, some of whose pillars date from just before Charlemagne, and the tombs of 6th-century bishops. Pl. St-Martin-au-Val, off Rue St-Brice.

■**EXTRA SPECIAL:** Malcolm Miller, the well-tailored Englishman who conducts tours of the cathedral, has become something of an institution among English-speaking visitors here. Miller has made the cathedral his life's work, and his descriptions of the stained glass and sculpture have set audiences alight from Chartres to Kalamazoo. If he's not off lecturing somewhere else, try to catch him holding court during his noon and 2:45 PM tours, held daily except Sundays from January through *Easter,* — imaginatively explaining the principles of medieval architecture by getting his audience to impersonate flying buttresses. Miller has been training a young man to take over when he's away, so even if you land here in February or March, a good English tour should be available through the tourist office. Private tours can be arranged in advance by contacting Miller in his superb medieval home at 26 Rue des Ecuyers (phone: 37-28-15-58).

SOURCES AND RESOURCES

 TOURIST INFORMATION: Chartres's Tourist Office, or Syndicat d'Initiative is just to the left of the square in front of the cathedral (Pl. de la Cathédrale; phone: 37-21-50-00). Maps, pamphlets, and information are dispensed from 9:30 AM to 6:30 PM daily from May to October; closed Sundays and holidays off-season. In season, from May through September, a currency exchange booth stays open from 9:30 AM to 6 PM daily, including Sundays and holidays, on the square in front of the cathedral. The tourist office also keeps tabs on Malcolm Miller's whereabouts. Off-season, call the tourist office ahead of time to be absolutely certain of an English-speaking guide. There are, alternatively, French tours at 10:30 AM and 3 PM from *Easter* to October except on Sunday and Monday mornings, and at 2:30 PM from November through *Easter.* For self-guided tours of the Old Town, the tourist office also rents an hour-long cassette tape (in English, French, or German); it comes complete with a tape player and a map.

Local Coverage – Two daily newspapers, *L'Echo Républicain* and *La République du Centre,* are published in Chartres and carry movie listings. Books about Chartres and its cathedral can be purchased in the cathedral shop and at local bookstores. Malcolm Miller's books, in English, are excellent. *Le Guide de Chartres* by Jean Villette is good for those who read French. A pamphlet on Chartres and its main attractions, in English, is available for a small charge at the tourist office.

 TELEPHONE: The city code for Chartres is 37, which is incorporated into all local 8-digit numbers. When calling a number in Chartres from the Paris region (including the Ile-de-France), dial 16, wait for a dial tone, then dial the 8-digit number. When calling a number from outside Paris, dial only the 8-digit number. When calling from the US, dial 33 (which is the country code), followed by the 8-digit number.

 GETTING AROUND: Like any medieval city, Chartres is best appreciated on foot. A good pair of legs is the best vehicle to negotiate the steep and winding streets of the Old Town, and pedestrian zones have been instituted in the commercial center. The town's area is easily manageable, and all the major sights can be fit into a day, though the fare is rich and is worth a longer visit.

Bicycle – These can be rented by the half-day, the day, or longer at the train station (phone: 37-36-18-56).

Bus – A good network of local buses serves the immediate neighborhood; information can be obtained from the Gare Routière, adjacent to the train station (phone: 37-21-30-35).

Car Rental – Major companies represented include *Avis* (36 Av. du Maréchal-Leclerc in Lucé; phone: 37-28-37-37); *Europcar* (16 Av. Jehan-de-Beauce; phone: 37-21-49-39); and *Hertz* (3 Rue du Grand Faubourg; phone: 37-21-90-90).

Taxi – Taxis congregate outside the train station, or call 37-36-00-00. For a lightning visit of a few hours, and with a couple of other people, it would be feasible to rent a cab for the 55-mile (88-km) ride from Paris.

Train – The train station, at Place Pierre-Sémard, is west of the cathedral and within walking distance (the cathedral is plainly visible from the station). For train information, call 37-28-50-50 or 37-18-60-60. The trip between Chartres and Paris's Gare Montparnasse takes about an hour, and service is frequent.

SPECIAL EVENTS: On Sundays in late April and May, student pilgrims crowd into Chartres after their 25-mile hike through the forest of Rambouillet. The pilgrimages are a tradition started early in this century by the Catholic poet Charles Péguy, who originally made the trip on foot from Paris when his son fell dangerously ill (the child survived). Contact l'Abbé Legaux (phone: 37-21-32-33). The *Chartres Organ Festival,* attracting performers from all over the world, takes place in July and August in the cathedral; and the *Concours International d'Orgue,* one of the world's most important organ competitions, takes place in Chartres in mid-September of even-numbered years. The *Samedis Musicaux* (Musical Saturdays) series, featuring chamber and choral music, takes place periodically during the year in a variety of historic buildings. An antiques fair takes place every October at the Collegiate Church of St. Andrew, and a flea market on the fourth Sunday of each month at the Place St-Pierre. *St. Andrew's Fair* — a lot of bumper cars and candy apples with little trace of its historic origins — comes in late November or early December.

MUSEUMS: The *Musée des Beaux-Arts* is described in *Special Places.* Prehistoric remains found locally are in the *Museum of Natural Sciences* (Square Noël-Ballay, Bd. de la Courtille; phone: 37-28-36-09). *La Maison Picassiette* (22 Rue du Repos; phone: 37-34-10-78), east of town, features an unorthodox naïf art form: murals made from pieces of broken plates. It is open from *Easter* through September. There's also the *Musée de l'Ecole* (1 Rue du 14 Juillet; phone: 37-34-46-97 or 37-35-46-85), with a classroom from the days of the Third Republic and a remarkable collection of authentic furniture and equipment; open Wednesdays during the school year and by appointment. *Le COMPA (Conservatoire du Machinisme et des Pratiques Agricoles),* one of Chartres's newest museums, is devoted to the history and future of agrarian societies. The emphasis is on agricultural techniques and the equipment of "La Planète Agricole" (Agricultural Planet). Closed Mondays. Open 10 AM to 12:30 PM and 1:30 to 6 PM (7 PM on weekends). 1 Rue de la République (phone: 37-36-11-30).

SHOPPING: For a town of its size, Chartres's shopping facilities are impressive. There is a branch of the *Au Printemps* department store (Rue Marceau) and a *Monoprix* supermarket (Rue Noël-Ballay), together with a healthy overspill of Paris fashions. *Galerie de France* is a horseshoe-shaped minimall in the main shopping area just off Place des Epars on Rue Noël-Ballay. Its dozen or so shops include *Rodier, Maison de la Presse,* and more.

The town's good burghers evidently are fond of their food, to judge by the appetizing terrines (Chartres's pâtés are a specialty) sold at local charcuteries. Another local specialty, the attractive, glazed pottery, *poterie du marais,* can be purchased at *Deco Faïence* (15 Pl. du Cygne; phone: 37-36-05-53). Other shops of note include the following:

Ariane – Original hand-knit sweaters, antique lace, linen, and children's wear, some made by the friendly proprietress Annich Laillet. 39 Rue des Changes (phone: 37-21-20-68).

Le Collectionneur – Beautiful old leatherbound books, as well as prints and a variety of gift items. 3C Cloître Notre-Dame (phone: 37-21-90-89).

Darreau Charcuterie des Epars – A variety of sausage, salami, and pâté. 6 Rue Delacroix.

Ferme Sainte-Suzanne – More than 150 farm-fresh cheeses. 7 Rue de la Pie (phone: 37-21-88-24).

La Galerie du Cloître – Located in a beamed stone loft, it features a wide variety of art forms — painting, sculpture, glasswork, tapestry — made mainly by local artists. 8 Cloître Notre-Dame (phone: 37-36-30-37).

Le Prieuré – Displays and sells the work of contemporary artists, in the dramatic setting of an old priory. 12 Rue Porte Cendreuse (phone: 37-30-99-22).

La Galerie du Vitrail – Old and new stained glass pieces are on exhibit and for sale. There also are audiovisual presentations on the subject. 17 Cloître Notre-Dame (near the cathedral; phone: 37-36-10-03).

Tartine & Trottinette – Charmingly cluttered toy and crafts shop with some very unusual items. 38 Rue des Changes (phone: 37-36-03-38).

SPORTS AND FITNESS: Chartres has public swimming pools and tennis courts, and there are several riding schools in the area (ask at the tourist office for information). In the leafy setting of the Eure at the Pont de la Courtille, the friendly man at *La Petite Venise* rents flat blue rowboats that seat four or five, from *Easter* to the end of October. During less temperate seasons, *sportifs* can try *Chartres Bowling* (Barjouville-Rocade; phone: 37-35-82-82), or enjoy a game of squash at *Horizon de Beaulieu* (8 Rue des Petits Clos; phone: 37-35-90-25). There are also frequent horse races at the *Hippodrome* (Av. Jean Mermoz; phone: 37-34-93-73).

THEATER: Fast trains and Chartres's proximity to the capital haven't done much for the performing arts; however, artists occasionally give pre-premiere performances before opening in Paris. The *Forum de la Madeleine* (1 Mail Jean-de-Dunois; phone: 37-35-08-83) puts on frequent performances, predominantly *chanson française* and comedies, while the *Théâtre Municipal* (Bd. Chasles; phone: 37-21-57-29), with its Italianate interior, presents plays as well as regular programs of music and modern dance from September to June.

MUSIC: Fine organ music adds another dimension to the beauty of Notre-Dame de Chartres, and though concerts are held throughout the year, the height of musical activity comes in July and August with the free Sunday concerts of the *Chartres Organ Festival,* a chance to hear internationally known musicians play one of France's great organs in this magnificently resonant space. The classical concerts of the *Samedis Musicaux* (Musical Saturdays) take place periodically in a variety of historic buildings. Programs of jazz and rock are part of the fare at the *Théâtre Municipal* (see above); opera fans follow the playgoers to Paris.

NIGHTCLUBS AND NIGHTLIFE: Hardly a Chartres specialty, but the fearless may like to try the *Lido-Club* (Av. Marcel-Proust; phone: 37-34-41-41). There's even a roller disco, called *Roller Star System,* off the RN10 at *Le Bois Paris* (phone: 37-31-62-54). Another popular nightspot is *Le Privilège* (1 Rue St-Pierre; phone: 37-35-52-02). For just hanging out, there are some comfortable piano bars: *L'Escalier* (1 Rue du Bourg; phone: 37-28-11-25) is open late and frequently features live music, guitar or piano.

BEST IN TOWN

 CHECKING IN: Chartres is a cosmopolitan rendezvous from mid-April through mid-November, and since there are few hotels, it's important to book ahead for this period. Perhaps because most of the 2 million or so annual visitors come only for the day, Chartres's hotels are disappointing for a tourism center of this importance and, with one or two exceptions, are only for the most intrepid. None is in the heart of the medieval town. *Chartrexpo*, a vast exhibition center on the eastern outskirts of town, has stimulated the development of new hotels: most of them of characterless modern chains, however. The tourist office can supply names of a few friendly families in the Old Town who offer bed and breakfast in their homes. It is said that the best view of the cathedral is from the youth hostel. A double room listed here as very expensive will cost $110 and up; an expensive one from $75 to $110; the moderate category ranges from roughly $40 to $75; and inexpensive, less than $40.

Château d'Esclimont – One of France's most elegant château hostelries, this 50-room Renaissance palace is flanked by four round towers and surrounded by a tranquil park; only a few miles from Chartres. A member of the prestigious Relais & Châteaux group, it boasts both *grand* comfort and luxury, and offers golf, a pool, and tennis. There also is a restaurant. Major credit cards accepted. Saint Symphoriem le Château (phone: 37-31-15-15; fax: 37-31-57-91). Very expensive.

Grand Monarque – The town's most imposing establishment has an impressive façade on the central Place des Epars, a good (if expensive) restaurant offering a mix of classic and nouvelle cuisine, and a popular bar with its own attempt at stained glass. In the 19th century, the building was composed of two grand townhouses, with room for a coach and horses to pass in the space now occupied by the *réception*. Renovations have spiffed up the lobby and restaurant and added a conference room, a winter garden, and 15 additional rooms with wood-beamed ceilings and modern marble baths. The 42 older rooms are individually decorated, and most look onto the courtyard where horses once were stabled. Major credit cards accepted. 22 Pl. des Epars (phone: 37-21-00-72; fax: 37-36-34-18). Expensive.

Le Manoir du Palomino – This elegant hostelry, only 4 miles (6 km) from Chartres, offers not only good food but golf as well. Some rooms are more deluxe (and more expensive) than others; ask for the best and book well in advance. Closed mid-January to mid-February. The restaurant is closed Mondays. Major credit cards accepted. 28300 St-Prèst (phone: 37-22-27-27; fax: 37-22-24-92). Expensive.

Mercure Chartres-Châtelet – Part of the nationwide chain, this 48-room hotel opened a decade ago with a mock medieval lobby and a modern wing that the architect cleverly angled toward the cathedral. A majority of the functional, well-equipped rooms look over an uncluttered space to the great landmark, making up for the lack of inspiration within. It is on the leafy avenue leading down to the train station and is associated with a nearby restaurant, *L'Arlequin*. Major credit cards accepted. 6-8 Av. Jehan-de-Beauce (phone: 37-21-78-00; fax: 37-36-23-01). Expensive.

Boeuf Couronné – Half of the 26 spotless rooms here, at the top of the avenue leading to the train station, look out to the cathedral. There are a bar and outside terraces, and a restaurant that serves local specialties with a reasonably priced menu. Restaurant closed Mondays in off-season. Major credit cards accepted. 15 Pl. du Châtelet (phone: 37-21-11-26). Moderate.

De la Poste – Few of the 60 rooms look onto the cathedral, but most do overlook a courtyard. A relatively peaceful night is guaranteed. The restaurant has three copious, reasonably priced menus. Major credit cards accepted. 3 Rue du Général-Koenig (phone: 37-21-04-27; fax: 37-36-42-17). Moderate.

Ibis – A member of the nationwide chain, what this motel lacks in Old World charm it makes up for in such practicalities as meeting rooms, easy parking, and an inexpensive restaurant with fast service. Set beside the river, with about 15 of the 79 rooms overlooking the cathedral. Major credit cards accepted. Pl. de la Porte-Drouaise (phone: 37-36-06-36; fax: 37-36-17-20). Moderate.

Saint-Jean – One of Chartres's better bargains, this 19th-century bourgeois house near the train station offers simple, clean rooms and renovated baths (with or without WC). Major credit cards accepted. 6 Rue de Faubourg Saint-Jean (phone: 37-21-35-69). Inexpensive.

 EATING OUT: Chartres's restaurants, all in all, don't live up to the promise of the shopfronts of its butchers and bakers, but one or two illustrious names have come to nest here. At the lower end of the market is a cosmopolitan selection of Vietnamese and Algerian restaurants and pizza parlors, but variety may not make up for an absence of overall quality. Don't miss the local specialty, *marsauceux,* a soft-crusted cheese wrapped in chestnut leaves. Meals at the established and expensive restaurants cost $75 to $100 (and up) for two, with service usually included; at restaurants in the moderate range, $50 to $75; and in inexpensive restaurants, $25 to $50.

La Vieille Maison – Elegant dining in an old house near the cathedral. Bernard Roger, the unassuming chef, uses the freshest produce to create a varied menu; his favorites are poultry from nearby Brou, game, and a sweetbread dish cooked with foie gras and homemade noodles. Closed Sunday evenings and Mondays. Reservations advised. Major credit cards accepted. 5 Rue au Lait (phone: 37-34-10-67). Expensive.

Le Bistrot de la Cathédrale – This restaurant–wine bar has a fine location facing the cathedral. Comfortably rustic decor, a tile floor, and an open, uncluttered atmosphere supply the backdrop for some imaginative country food and some good Loire wines. Closed Sunday evenings and Mondays in winter. Reservations advised in summer. Major credit cards accepted. 1 Cloître Notre-Dame (phone: 37-36-59-60). Moderate.

Le Buisson Ardent – One of those fancy places that are a bit too heavy on the decor for comfort, it offers two good prix fixe menus. There's also a cocktail bar and a tearoom. Closed Sunday and Tuesday evenings and Wednesdays. Reservations advised. Major credit cards accepted. 10 Rue au Lait (phone: 37-34-04-66). Moderate.

Café Serpente – The proprietor has his hands on a prime location: the former post office building, classified as a monument and facing the cathedral. The place is done up as a turn-of-the-century bistro, with a moderately priced fixed menu. It also caters to the tourist in a hurry with a selection of fast food. Closed the first 2 weeks of January. Reservations unnecessary. Major credit cards accepted. 2 Cloître Notre-Dame (phone: 37-21-68-81). Moderate to inexpensive.

Le Tripot – The chic local crowd eats here. Bunches of dried flowers hang from the rafters, an open fire burns in the winter, and the attempt to make rustic elegant succeeds. Straightforward country food is appetizingly presented, with multicolored pickle jars and lots of salad greens, and there is a pleasing selection of good Loire Valley wines. Closed Sundays. Reservations advised. Major credit cards accepted. 11 Pl. Jean-Moulin (phone: 37-36-60-11). Moderate to inexpensive.

Le Biniou – An unpretentious Breton *crêperie* that serves everything on a pancake, using such ingredients as fried onions, scrambled eggs, and fresh cream for the savory versions, and calvados and apple compote for dessert. Bowls of Breton cider help wash it all down. Cassette tapes alternate with an occasional group that plays live music, showing off the sounds of the Breton bagpipe that gives the restaurant its name. Closed Sundays and Mondays. Reservations unnecessary. No credit cards accepted. 7 Rue Serpente (phone: 37-21-53-12). Inexpensive.

Le Trois Lys – Another *crêperie*, this one nestled cozily in a crooked old half-timbered house by the river, in one of the oldest parts of Chartres. Pleasant atmosphere, affordable prices, and scenic surroundings make it worth the short walk down to the river and the Basse Ville. Closed Sundays and Monday evenings in off-season. Reservations unnecessary. Major credit cards accepted. 3 Rue Porte Guillaume (phone: 37-28-42-02). Inexpensive.

 BARS AND CAFÉS: The river Eure flows slowly by at *Le Moulin de Ponceau* (21 Rue de la Tannerie; phone: 37-35-87-87), an idyllic spot for a long cocktail. In winter, there is a log fire and comfort; in summer, a wooden patio over the water. Drinks (including an exotic punch) do not come cheap, but the setting is impeccable. Closed Sunday evenings and Mondays.

DIJON

Arriving at the Dijon train station, a traveler has little sense of the enchanting medieval city just a few blocks away. The streets on the outskirts of town are very much a part of the 20th century: Dijon's skyline is mostly marked by high-rises and industrial plants. But walk into the center of town and you're immediately transported into an earlier time and place, where the routines of the 20th century fit unobtrusively into the older fabric of the city. Here is Dijon's most dazzling architectural sight, the Palace of the Dukes of Burgundy, and around it are narrow cobblestone streets, one leading into the next, lined with old houses, mansions, and cathedrals.

Dijon dates back to Roman times. But it was relatively unknown until 1015, when Robert I, the first Duke of Burgundy of the Capetian line, chose it as the capital of his duchy. It still was nothing more than that in 1364, when Philip the Bold became the first Duke of Burgundy of the Valois line. Then, in slightly more than 100 years, the four Valois dukes — Philip the Bold, John the Fearless, Philip the Good, and Charles the Bold — transformed Dijon into a fit setting for their increasingly princely reign. The borders of the duchy quickly expanded to include other parts of France and even parts of today's Belgium, the Netherlands, and Luxembourg, and the power of the dukes came to equal that of the French king — or of any other ruler of Christendom, for that matter. So rich and splendid was the court at Dijon that the Valois Dukes of Burgundy shortly became known as the Grand Dukes of the Occident.

As patrons of the arts, the dukes, especially the two Philips, attracted the greatest masters of the time to Dijon and left the city with an outstanding architectural and artistic heritage. Philip the Bold, who ruled for 40 years, embarked on the construction of the ducal palace and of a mausoleum in the 14th century; Philip the Good, who ruled for 48 years, greatly enlarged the palace in the 15th century (adding, among other things, the kitchen seen today; it was at the legendary banquets of the dukes that many of the city's great culinary traditions began).

All along, the dukes were a powerful force in European politics. Both John the Fearless and Philip the Good allied themselves with the English against the French during the Hundred Years War; it was Philip the Good, in fact, who captured and sold Joan of Arc to her English enemies after her string of victories for Charles VII, the French king. But Charles the Bold's conniving with the English against Louis XI led to the end of the duchy of Burgundy. In 1477, after a reign of only 10 years, Charles was defeated and killed in battle, and Louis XI seized the duchy for the French crown.

Dijon's most glorious age was over, though the city did not fade completely into obscurity. It remained the capital of the province of Burgundy, and substantial townhouses continued to be built. At the end of the 17th century, the States-General of Burgundy, a regional assembly of nobles, clergy, and the third estate that met once every 3 years, voted to add to the palace in order to accommodate their gatherings and their permanent bureaucracy. The man chosen for the project was Jules Hardouin-Mansart, the architect and town planner of Louis XIV. Mansart was responsible not only for the design of the new section but also for the redesign of older sections and of the square in front of the palace — a much larger conception that, when finished in the 18th century, unified these disparate elements into a classical whole.

The 18th century also brought Dijon its university and the Canal de Bourgogne, a romantic body of water that weaves its way through the city and eventually flows into the river Saône (pronounced *Sown*). The 19th century was marked by the coming of the railroad, an event of definite consequence in Dijon's fortunes. The city became one of France's major transportation crossroads, and its population grew from 20,000 in 1850 to approximately 150,000 today (250,000 including the surrounding areas). Dijon also developed as an important industrial and commercial center known especially for its gastronomic specialties — above all, mustard.

Although mustard seeds date back to prehistoric times, local legend has it that it was the great Dukes of Burgundy who first gave mustard its name during their lengthy and elaborate banquets. In the early 1500s it was difficult to preserve meat, so the dukes had their chefs create a sauce that would disguise the meat's often rancid smell and taste. *Moult ma tarde,* meaning "a long time I delay my meal," was the term given to this spicy condiment; later, the phrase was shortened to *moutarde* ("mustard").

But mustard is hardly Dijon's only gastronomic contribution. Classic Burgundian dishes such as escargots (snails) in garlic butter, coq au vin, and the famed *boeuf bourguignon* are featured in the city's bistros, cafés, and fine restaurants, many of them housed in historic buildings with huge stone fireplaces and decorated with period furniture. The best are the old family-run restaurants, where third- and in some cases fourth-generation sons and daughters are maintaining the culinary traditions created by their fathers, grandfathers, and great-grandfathers. These are places to linger in, for it is here that the Dijonnais are truly in their element.

Because Dijon is the capital of Burgundy, set at the northern tip of the Côte d'Or, the region's "golden slope" (or its gold coast) wine area, it is not surprising that its restaurants offer some of the finest wines in France, if not the world. Within an hour's drive are the vineyards that produce beaujolais, pouilly-fuissé, romanée-conti, and a wide variety of other, equally exquisite red and white burgundies. Dijon also is the home of cassis, a sweet, burgundy-colored liqueur made from fresh black currants. (The trendy drink *kir,* a combination of *aligoté* — a dry white wine — and cassis, is named for a much beloved Dijon mayor, Canon Kir.)

Travelers often use Dijon as a starting point for a tour of the vineyards of Burgundy, traveling by waterway or taking the famed Route des Grands Crus (the national highway that links the major wine producing communes of the Côte d'Or). While it's certainly true that the landscape around Dijon is quite lovely, don't make the mistake that many do and head directly out of town. The Dijonnais have spent a lot of time and energy preserving their heritage.

Many of the old streets and buildings have been restored with loving care, and a walking tour through the center of the city takes you past some of the most impressive medieval mansions and Gothic cathedrals in France. Dijon is a beautiful city that deserves attention.

DIJON AT-A-GLANCE

SEEING THE CITY: Toward the middle of the 15th century, Philip the Good, the reigning Duke of Burgundy, added a tall tower to his palace so that he would always be able to keep watch against invaders. Today that tower, Tour Philippe-le-Bon, offers the city's most spectacular views. There are 316 steps to the top; spread out below is the beauty of Dijon's colorful rooftops, its dramatic church steeples, and the tranquil surrounding valleys. From this vantage point, the late afternoon light gives Dijon a magical glow.

SPECIAL PLACES: The Palais des Ducs et des Etats de Bourgogne (known as the Palais des Ducs for the sake of brevity) is the focal point of Dijon. Except for two of them, all the sights listed below are within walking distance of this monument. The Chartreuse de Champmol and Lake Kir are farther out, beyond the railroad station to the west of central Dijon.

Palais des Ducs et des Etats de Bourgogne (Palace of the Dukes and of the States-General of Burgundy) – This huge, highly ornate set of buildings gives a good sense of the power of the Dukes of Burgundy and of the continuing importance of the city even after the duchy had been annexed to the French crown. Its construction spanned 5 centuries. Begun by Philip the Bold in the 14th century, it grew substantially under Philip the Good in the 15th century, continued to expand despite the dukes' downfall, and was completed in the 19th century. A great transformation came during the 17th and 18th centuries, when additions were built for the Etats de Bourgogne, a regional assembly, and the medieval ducal quarters gained a classic veneer designed by Jules Hardouin-Mansart, the architect of Versailles.

Today, part of the palace houses Dijon's Hôtel de Ville (Town Hall) and as such is open to the public (you may have to ask to see specific rooms, however), and part of it houses the *Musée des Beaux-Arts* (see below). Throughout, there are impressive architectural details such as grand marble staircases and giant banquet halls — ask to see the extravagantly decorated fireplace in the Salon de la Renommée in the Hôtel de Ville section — though one of the most interesting rooms, the kitchen built by Philip the Good, requires some imagination to make it come alive. What was once the finest kitchen in all of Burgundy is bare today, but its six fireplaces, each with its own chimney, are enormous. The huge glass window, made from the bottoms of wine bottles, is noteworthy, too; the well directly outside the kitchen in the courtyard was once the site of the palace bakery. The most famous room in the palace, also dating back to Philip the Good, is the Salle des Gardes (Guard Room), entered through the museum. It contains the marble and alabaster tombs of Philip the Bold and John the Fearless, both originally in the Chartreuse de Champmol, the Carthusian monastery founded by Philip toward the end of the 14th century to use as a ducal mausoleum. His tomb, built between 1385 and 1410, is one of the masterpieces of the Flemish sculptor Claus Sluter, who was assisted by his nephew and student, Claus de Werve. Pl. de la Libération.

Musée des Beaux-Arts – This museum's eclectic collection is considered one of the most impressive in France, surpassed only by the *Louvre* in Paris. Installed largely in one of the newer sections of the palace, it contains an assortment of paintings and sculptures ranging from early French and Flemish masters to more contemporary artists such as Picasso, Matisse, and Rodin. The museum has a variety of other art objects including Byzantine enamelwork, Renaissance furniture, and primitive masks and sculptures from Africa. Some of the palace's original furnishings, dating back to the 1500s, also are on view. Be sure to visit the wing housing the modern art collection, too. Particularly interesting here is the way in which the art is displayed — thematically rather than by period or artist. Closed Tuesdays. Admission charge. Pl. de la Ste-Chapelle (phone: 80-74-52-70).

Place de la Libération – Across the street from the palace, this late-17th-century square and the Louis XIV houses that line it also came off the drawing board of Hardouin-Mansart. The palace façade, the square (actually a semicircle), and the houses create one harmonious classical ensemble.

Eglise Notre-Dame – Built in the 13th century, this church is considered the finest surviving example of Gothic architecture in Burgundy. For the most dramatic view of its unusual exterior, walk around the corner from the Rue de la Chouette and look directly up at the gargoyles that sit in three rows on the upper half of the façade and seem to take on a life of their own. One of the church towers houses the famous Flemish mechanical clock, Jacquemart, which Philip the Bold brought back from Courtrai as a war trophy in 1383. At that time, there was only the little iron blacksmith, who hit the bell every hour on the hour. At the beginning of the 17th century the people of Dijon, thinking the blacksmith might be lonely, gave him a wife, Jacqueline. In the early 18th century, they produced a son, Jacquelinet, and a daughter, Jacquelinette, followed in 1881. Along the Rue de la Chouette (Owl Street), you'll see a small stone owl set into the church's exterior. It is said that if you place your left hand on the owl, it will bring good luck. Inside the church, the 11th-century Vierge Noire (Black Virgin), in a chapel to the right of the choir, is one of the oldest wooden statues in France and an object of veneration. Pl. Notre-Dame.

Eglise St-Michel – A second major church in Dijon, St. Michael's is a fascinating mixture of styles. It was begun at the end of the 15th century in the Gothic style (note the Flamboyant Gothic side doors) and all but finished in the 16th century with a full Renaissance façade. The towers came later. Pl. St-Michel.

Cathédrale St-Bénigne – This Gothic cathedral has been rebuilt four times since the 6th century. The most interesting part of the present structure, which rose between 1280 and 1314 on the site of a Romanesque basilica, is what remains of the basilica: the 10th-century crypt with the tomb of St. Bénigne. The cathedral's 18th-century organ is outstanding. Frequent recitals take place here; check with the tourist office for further information. Pl. St-Bénigne.

Historic Homes – Dijon has a wealth of beautifully preserved townhouses and other buildings dating back to the 15th to 18th century. The historical society has designated many of these as landmarks and provided each one with a plaque giving its date, original use, and outstanding architectural feature. Be sure to see the buildings along Rue de la Chouette, Rue des Forges, and Rue Berbisey and note the Hôtel Chambellan at 34 Rue des Forges and the Hôtel de Vogüé at 8 Rue de la Chouette. The 15th-century Hôtel Chambellan, with its beautifully carved staircase and balcony in the courtyard, is considered a very fine example of Flamboyant Gothic architecture, and the Hôtel de Vogüé, built in the early 17th century, sports an eye-catching patterned tile roof typical of Burgundian architecture.

Les Halles Centrales (Central Market) – Every Tuesday, Friday, and Saturday, the streets surrounding *Les Halles* fill with vendors and merchants selling everything from fresh braids of garlic from the south of France to antique kitchenware and books. The market itself — a huge, open building — is a wonderful place to gather picnic makings or simply to gaze at the glories of French food. There also are little coffee counters where you can grab an espresso and a croissant. Rue Quentin.

Jardin de l'Arquebuse et Jardin Botanique – Described in the brochure as "an island of calm, green, and flowers in the heart of the city," these idyllic gardens are precisely that. There are virtually acres to explore, scattered with elaborate flower beds and herb gardens. The unusual name comes from the Compagnie de l'Arquebuse, which installed itself here in the 16th century and used the area for archery and *harquebus* (a gun of the times) practice. The *harquebusiers* barracks now houses the *Musée de l'Histoire Naturelle* (see *Museums*) and a large flower, herb, and botany library. Rue de l'Arquebuse.

Chartreuse de Champmol (Champmol Charterhouse) – In 1383, Philip the Bold founded a Carthusian monastery and set about establishing a necropolis for the dukes within its confines. Though the monastery was destroyed in 1793 and the site is now occupied by a psychiatric hospital, two important works of sculpture by Claus Sluter can still be seen: a chapel doorway and the Puits de Moïse (Well of Moses), actually the hexagonal pedestal of a former calvary group. Sluter was the greatest of the artists in service to Philip the Bold, and the six powerful figures of prophets on the well are notable as milestones in the development of realism in medieval sculpture. They rank as one of the Flemish artist's two masterpieces, along with the tomb of Philip made for Champmol and now in the *Museum of Fine Arts*. Open to visitors during office hours, despite the current renovation. About a 30-minute walk west of the center; entrance from Bd. Chanoine-Kir.

Lac Kir – Named for Dijon's popular mayor, the late Canon Kir, this manmade lake is about a 15-minute drive from downtown. Though it is surrounded by some of Dijon's more modern buildings and can get crowded in the summer, it is a pleasant spot for water sports and an afternoon picnic. A nighttime addition to the area is *Le Cygne* (Lac Kir, Plombières-lès-Dijon; phone: 80-41-02-40), a terraced lakeside restaurant that offers a variety of *Soirs de Spectacle* (dinner shows). The repertoire ranges from contemporary theatrical comedies to evenings of jazz and French song. Reachable by bus No. 18 or via the N5 toward Paris.

■**EXTRA SPECIAL:** A good mustard should be hot enough to "tweak" your nose, but not so hot that it's unenjoyable. That's how the people of Dijon describe their legendary condiment. One of the best places to visit to get a "taste" of the pungent spread is the *Grey Poupon* shop (32 Rue de la Liberté; phone: 80-30-41-02). It has been selling mustard since 1777, and residents still bring in empty crocks and jars to be filled with the golden paste. Be sure to see the collection of antique mustard jars belonging to the Grey and Poupon families; they are unusually beautiful. Assorted mustards, vinegars, and other condiments produced by Maille, one of the better Dijon brands, are on sale, as are replicas of the old china crocks; they'll even fill them with mustard and pack them for traveling.

SOURCES AND RESOURCES

TOURIST INFORMATION: The Dijon Office du Tourisme is in the center of town (Pl. Darcy; phone: 80-43-42-12). Open daily from 9 AM to 9 PM in July and August; 9 AM to 7 PM the rest of the year (closed during lunchtime). They stock a wide variety of maps, brochures, and guidebooks on all aspects of the city, many of them in English, and are well supplied with information about touring the surrounding wine country of Burgundy. The offices also distribute lists of hotels and restaurants in the city and its environs, and will try to help book rooms locally. (For those late arrivals without accommodations, there is a lighted bulletin board outside the main tourist office that lists room availability in Dijon.) The tourist office's *Accueil de France* accommodations service can book rooms anywhere in France for a small fee. It also has a currency exchange. Another bulletin board announces concerts, university events, sporting events, and festivals. Guided walking tours of the city (in French) leave here at 3 PM daily during the summer, from early July through September. There is a small charge. Ask at the tourist office for information about tours in English.

If you are still in the early planning stages of a tour of Burgundy and are interested in wine (and in purchasing local wine), contact the tourist office in Beaune or the *Bureau Interprofessionnel de la Côte d'Or et de l'Yonne pour les Vins d'Appellation Contrôlée de Bourgogne* (Rue Henri-Dunant, 21200 Beaune; phone: 80-22-21-35), which puts out pamphlets on the wine growers. If you only have a day to explore Dijon and Burgundy's great vineyards, a guided tour (in English and French) in a luxury bus of Dijon, Beaune, and the celebrated Clos de Vougeot is a practical solution. Tours take place every Thursday and Saturday from late April to late October; they depart from Dijon in the morning and return at 6:30 PM. The itinerary includes the "Route des Grands Crus" past various vineyards, a tour of the caves at the Château du Clos de Vougeot, a visit at the 18th-century *Demeure St-Martin* in Beaune, with a wine tasting included, an optional lunch featuring regional cuisine, and a guided walking tour through Dijon's Old Quarter. For information and reservations, contact the Dijon Tourist Office (phone: 80-43-42-12) or the tour's organizers, *Bourgogne Tour Incoming* (14 Rue du Châpeau-Rouge; phone: 80-39-49-49; fax: 80-30-69-87).

Local Coverage – Consult *Le Bien Public* or *Les Dépêches*. The *Maison de la Presse* (26 Rue de la Liberté; phone: 80-30-45-62) is a good place to buy French magazines and newspapers as well as English and American newspapers and stationery items.

TELEPHONE: The city code for Dijon is 80, which is incorporated into all local 8-digit numbers. When calling a number in Dijon from the Paris region (including the Ile-de-France), dial 16, wait for a dial tone, then dial the 8-digit number. When calling a number from outside Paris, dial only the 8-digit number. When calling from the US, dial 33 (which is the country code), followed by the 8-digit number.

GETTING AROUND: Central Dijon is compact. By far, the easiest and most pleasant way to see the city is on foot.

Bus – City bus service is provided by *STRD* (*Société des Transports Routiers Dijonnais*), which operates an easily used network throughout Dijon and its environs. Bus maps are available from the tourist office or from the central bus station (Pl. Grangier; phone: 80-30-60-90). In addition to individual tickets, there are unlimited-travel tickets, sold on a weekly basis for a very good price. Buses stop running at 8:30 PM, and there is no bus service on Sunday morning.

Car Rental – All the major firms are represented. Near the train station are *Avis* (5 Av. Foch; phone: 80-43-60-76) and *Hertz* (18 Av. Foch; phone: 80-43-55-22). *Europcar* also has an office (47 Rue Guillaume Tell; phone: 80-43-28-44). There are underground parking facilities at several locations, including Rue du Bourg, Place Grangier, and a garage under Place Darcy.

Taxi – Taxis are available 24 hours a day at the train station and at the post office on Place Grangier. You also can call *Taxi Radio* (phone: 80-41-41-12) directly. Prices are reasonable, but fares double after 8 PM. Dijon taxis also offer city tours, narrated in English on cassette, and various itineraries for excursions outside of town — to the vineyards of Burgundy, for example. For reservations or additional information, call *Central Radio Taxi Dijon* (phone: 80-41-41-12), or ask the tourist office for a brochure about this service.

Train – The Gare de Dijon-Ville is at the opposite end of Avenue du Maréchal-Foch from Place Darcy (phone: 80-41-50-50 for information, 80-43-52-56 for reservations). The renovated train station has a sleek Salon d'Affaires, a business lounge equipped with a fax machine, telephones, small conference rooms, video equipment, and other amenities for the business visitor to Dijon. For information and membership details, call 80-40-12-49.

SPECIAL EVENTS: *Florissimo,* a major floral exhibition held every 3 or 4 years showcasing the exotic blooms of five continents, will take place this year in mid-March (at the *Palais des Congrès,* just outside the center of town at 3 Bd. de Champagne; phone: 80-71-44-34). The huge *Antiques Fair* in mid-May and the *Puces Dijonnaises* (Dijon Flea Market) in early September both take place in the *Forum* (Rue Général-Delaborde). The *Eté Musical,* when local artists present classical and jazz concerts at many of Dijon's most beautiful monuments, occurs during the month of June. *Estivade,* a festival of theater and music, is held from mid-June through mid-August. Late August is the time for the traditional *Folkloriade Internationale* (International Folk Dance and Song Festival). For true food and wine lovers, and for those whose business it is, however, the above is simply an appetizer for the *Foire Internationale et Gastronomique* (International Food and Wines Fair), held the first 2 weeks of November. This is one of the country's major trade fairs, a showcase for the very finest edibles and potables from all over France and the world, and an opportunity for some magnificent tasting. It takes place at the *Palais des Congrès* (phone: 80-71-44-34). A *Salon de l'Artisanat d'Art et du Cadeau* (Crafts and Gifts Fair) is usually organized in December; contact the tourist office for details.

MUSEUMS: The city offers a special entry card, good for a year, that allows visitors to enter all of its museums (except the *Espace Grévin*) for one very reasonable fee. In addition to those mentioned in *Special Places,* museums of interest (all are closed on Tuesdays except where noted) include the following:

Espace Grévin – One of the newest of Dijon's museums is a franchise of Paris's well-known wax museum. It houses an exhibit portraying the history of the Burgundy region through Grévin's famous wax figures (M. Grévin was considered the Mme. Toussaud of Paris). There's a wine tasting facility next door (see *Eating Out*). Open daily. Admission charge. 13 *bis* Av. Albert-1er (phone: 80-41-76-37).

Musée Archéologique – In the dormitory of the former Benedictine Abbey of St. Bénigne, this small museum has an impressive collection of Gallo-Roman and medieval artifacts and a famous bust of Christ by Claus Sluter. Admission charge. Next to the Cathédrale St-Bénigne, at 5 Rue Dr.-Maret (phone: 80-30-88-54 or 80-30-86-23).

Musée d'Art Sacré – Ever-changing exhibits of religious art from churches of the region. Many works currently are being housed here while the churches they belong to undergo repair or restoration. Open 9 AM to noon and from 2 to 6 PM; closed holidays. Admission charge. 15 Rue Ste-Anne (phone: 80-30-06-44).

Musée d'Histoire Naturelle – Geological and zoological specimens of the Dijon region are displayed in the old barracks of the *harquebusiers* (see *Special Places*). Admission charge. 1 Av. Albert-1er, Jardin de l'Arquebuse (phone: 80-41-61-08).

Musée Magnin – Housed in the Hôtel Lantin, a gorgeous 17th-century mansion — renovated last year — bequeathed to the city by Maurice Magnin, this collection documents elegant 17th-century life with period furniture and paintings. Open afternoons only. Admission charge. 4 Rue des Bons-Enfants, off Pl. de la Libération (phone: 80-67-11-10).

Musée Rude – A local favorite dedicated to the works of the 19th-century sculptor François Rude, set up in the transept of a deconsecrated church. Formerly open by appointment only, in season, it now is open to the public from 10 AM to noon and from

2 to 7:30 PM.. In winter, contact the *Musée des Beaux Arts* (phone: 80-74-52-70) for an appointment to visit here. No admission charge. 8 Rue Vaillant (phone: 80-66-87-95).

Musée de la Vie Bourguignonne (Museum of Burgundian Life) – This museum occupies two rooms of a 15th-century building. One room is filled with heraldry and authentically costumed models of medieval Burgundian knights and the other is devoted to wine — antique wine presses, corkscrews, bottles, labels, tools, and other wine making equipment. 17 Rue Ste-Anne (phone: 80-30-65-91).

 SHOPPING: The city's best shopping is along the Rue de la Liberté, and food and wine are among the best buys. Look for such regional specialties as mustard, cassis (black currant liqueur), *pain d'épice* (gingerbread), and burgundy wines. On the last Sunday of every month, there is a flea market at the *Forum* (Rue Général-Delaborde). At the edge of town on the road to Langres is *Centre Commercial de la Toison d'Or,* a modern shopping center next to the *Toison d'Or* amusement park that uses Burgundian history as a springboard for its diverse recreational attractions. Dijon is also a good place to hunt for antiques, especially 18th- and 19th-century Burgundian furniture. Several stores are found on or near the Rue Verrerie near Nôtre Dame. Other antiques shops well worth a visit are *Michel Guillemard* (22 Rue Verrerie; phone: 80-31-89-11), *Au Vieux Dijon* (8 Rue Verrerie; phone: 80-31-89-08), and *Atelier de la Tour Saint Nicolas* (61 Rue J.J. Rousseau; phone: 80-73-41-69).

Auger – Although not as well-known as *Mulot et Petitjean* (below), this shop offers delicious *pain d'épices* (gingerbread). 21 Pl. Darcy (phone: 80-41-45-74).

La Boucherie Nouvelle – This butcher shop and *charcuterie* is a good place to get a sample of *jambon persillé,* a Burgundian specialty, perfect for a picnic lunch. Closed Thursday afternoon, Sundays, and August. 27 Rue Pasteur (phone: 80-66-37-10).

Dubard – Fine antiques are bought and sold by this prestigious company, which also offers decorating advice. 25 *bis* Rue Verrerie (phone: 80-30-50-81).

Escargots de Bourgogne – Fresh, canned, or in sealed glass jars — nothing but escargots in this crowded little shop operated by savvy, friendly Mme. Verdier. 14 Rue Bannelier (phone: 80-30-22-15).

Galerie 6 – Fine 17th- to 19th-century paintings are restored and sold here; there also are occasional art exhibitions. 6 Rue Auguste Comte (phone: 80-71-68-46).

Golmard – This shop specializes in 17th- and 18th-century furniture and objets d'art. 5 Rue Chaudronnerie (phone: 80-67-14-15).

Laura Ashley – Her standard designs by the yard, in ready-to-wear clothing, and home decorating items. 18-20 Rue Piron (phone: 80-30-04-44).

Monique Buisson – An antiques dealer specializing in 18th-century Burgundian furniture. 21 Rue Verrerie (phone: 80-30-31-19).

Mulot et Petitjean – A good place for gifts: regional foods and wines including *pain d'épice* in a variety of shapes (a wine bottle or a snail) and tastes, some plain, some filled with *cassis* cream. 1 Pl. Notre-Dame; also at 16 Rue de la Liberté and 13 Pl. Bossuet (phone: 80-30-07-10).

Nouvelles Galeries – Everything from clothing and cosmetics to sewing equipment and fabrics at a moderately priced department store. The food and wine department downstairs is an ideal place for preparing a picnic. 41-49 Rue de la Liberté (phone: 80-44-82-12).

Occasions – French, English, and Chinese furniture, as well as antique carpets. 29 Rue Auguste Comte (phone: 80-73-55-13).

Oudebert – Dijon's most established women's specialty shop. Everything from accessories to undergarments. 62-68 Rue de la Liberté. (phone: 80-30-44-56).

Au Pain d'Autrefois – Behind a fancified façade hides the heart and soul of this bread maker — an old bread oven. Pick up some interesting breads to accompany your wine and cheese purchases. 47 Rue du Bourg (phone: 80-37-47-92).

Rafael – Chic boutique near the Palais des Ducs, with elegant women's clothing by Armani, Celine, and others. 10 Rue Piron (phone: 80-30-97-07).

Simone Porcheret – A dream of a cheese shop with some of the most wonderful and aged cheeses likely to be found anywhere. Ask for *citeaux* made by local monks. 18 Rue Bannerlier (phone: 80-30-21-05).

 SPORTS AND FITNESS: Ballooning – Hardly the do-it-yourself version of the sport, and expensive. Nevertheless, a trip over the Burgundy vineyards in a hot-air balloon can be thrilling on a clear day. You'll be picked up at a major Dijon hotel; all flights end with a bottle of burgundy wine. Contact *Air Escargot* (Remigny, 71150 Chagny; phone: 85-87-08-84) or *Bourgogne Tour Incoming* (14 Rue du Chapeau Rouge; phone: 80-30-49-49; fax: 80-30-69-87).

Boating – For a day of cruising through the canals, motorboats can be rented from *Locadif* (Gissey-sur-Ouche, Pont de Pany; phone: 80-49-04-76). Various companies offer week-long cruises on luxury hotel barges departing from Dijon; well-equipped self-piloted boats may also be rented for cruises of a weekend or week, or more. Contact the tourist office for information (phone: 80-43-42-12).

Golf – The 18-hole *Golf de Bourgogne* course (Norges-la-Ville; phone: 80-35-71-10) is 6 miles (10 km) from Dijon, but there is no equipment for rent. *Golf de Beaune à Levernois,* a public course (in Levernois, 1½ miles/2 km from Beaune toward Verdun-sur-le-Doubs; phone: 80-24-10-29), is another option. One of the most recent additions to the Dijon golf scene and the closest to the city is *Golf de Quetigny,* an 18-hole course, 4 miles (6 km) away (Quetigny; phone: 80-46-69-00).

Jogging – A number of parks throughout town are ideal for jogging. The most accessible is probably Place Darcy, a small park in the center. The Parc de la Colombière (dating from Louis XIV) has 80 acres to roam somewhat south of the center. In addition, there is Lake Kir, the artificial lake west of the center, and the beautiful Parc de la Combe à la Serpent, also west of town.

Sailing and Windsurfing – Equipment for these can be rented at Lake Kir. Take N5 out of Dijon toward Paris.

Swimming – Swimming is forbidden at Lake Kir because of pollution, but indoor pools open to the public are *Piscine du Carrousel* (Cours du Parc; phone: 80-67-20-12); *Piscine de la Fontaine d'Ouche* (Fontaine d'Ouche, Av. du Lac; phone: 80-43-38-19); and *Piscine des Grésilles* (Bd. Champollion; phone: 80-71-37-35).

Tennis – The *Parc des Sports* (Pl. Gaston-Gérard; phone: 80-71-29-43) has 17 outdoor courts open to the public, and there also are courts at Lake Kir (phone: 80-41-69-66).

 THEATER AND MUSIC: The very elegant *Théâtre Municipal,* set off to one side of the ducal palace at Place du Théâtre (phone: 80-67-23-23), is Dijon's oldest theater and its main site for a full range of theatrical activity including plays, operettas, opera, ballet, and classical concerts. The city's avant-garde theater, *Théâtre du Parvis St-Jean* (Rue Danton; phone: 80-30-12-12), puts on a wide variety of experimental productions as well as music and dance. Dijon University also holds a number of noteworthy theater, dance, and musical events (call 80-66-64-13 for information), while various churches — especially St-Michel and St-Bénigne — are used for organ recitals and choral and orchestral concerts. The *Eldorado* (21 Rue Alfred-de-Musset; phone: 80-66-12-34 or 80-66-51-89) is an old movie house specializing in "art films," frequently in English. The *Bistro de la Scène* (203 Rue d'Auxonne; phone: 80-67-87-39), a café-theater, presents plays, jazz, and concerts. Occasional concerts are given in the *Palais des Sports* (17 Rue Léon Mauris; phone: 80-71-13-89).

A pamphlet listing cultural events, called "Dijon Culture," is published monthly by the city and is available at the tourist office.

 NIGHTCLUBS AND NIGHTLIFE: Dijon is not noted for a wild nightlife. What most people do for an evening's entertainment is eat and drink, often stretching dinner out to 10 or 11 PM and then lingering at the bar with a snifter of cognac or Burgundian *marc* (grape brandy). But because this is a university town, nightclubs and discos do exist, such as *La Jamaïque* (14 Pl. de la République; phone: 80-73-52-19), a popular meeting spot serving exotic cocktails and playing a West Indian beat. For a more tranquil setting beside Lac Kir, go to *Le Cygne* (Plombières-lès-Dijon; phone: 80-41-02-40), a restaurant that has dinner shows offering theater and jazz.

BEST IN TOWN

 CHECKING IN: Compared to those in Paris, the prices in Dijon are extremely reasonable. Accommodations here in a very plush first class hotel can cost as little as $100 — less than a third of the tariff for similar digs in the capital. A double room below in the expensive category will cost from $70 to $100, $50 to $70 in moderate, and under $50 in inexpensive — where you may end up sharing a toilet down the hall. Breakfast, unless otherwise noted, is not included.

Altéa – About a 15-minute walk from the center of town and convenient to the *Palais des Congrès,* this sleek, modern hotel is part of the national chain. The 114 rooms and 7 suites are very comfortable, with extremely large bathrooms. Rear rooms all have views of the center. There's a restaurant, *Le Château-Bourgogne* (see *Eating Out*), plus conference rooms, bar, and swimming pool. Major credit cards accepted. 22 Bd. de la Marne (phone: 80-72-31-13; fax: 80-73-61-45). Expensive.

Le Chapeau Rouge – A small, well-respected place next to the St. Bénigne cathedral. A few of the 29 rooms and 2 suites have beautiful 18th-century furniture; the rest are tastefully decorated with a good balance of old and new. The front rooms have double-paned windows for protection from noise in this central location, and a few of the side rooms have dramatic views of the cathedral. Over half of its rooms have been renovated and some now include a saltwater Jacuzzi. There is a restaurant (see *Eating Out*) and a bar. Major credit cards accepted. 5 Rue Michelet (phone: 80-30-28-10; fax: 80-30-33-89). Expensive.

La Cloche – The building dates back to 1424, but all that remains of the original structure are the exterior walls, including the façade. Following a complete renovation and takeover in 1990 by the Pullman chain, it now ranks as Dijon's most elegant hostelry, with 76 attractively furnished rooms and suites enhanced by wonderful views of the Place Darcy park and the hotel's own peaceful little garden. The rooms *en duplex* (with mezzanines) are especially charming. A tea and coffee shop overlooks the garden; there's an excellent restaurant, *Jean-Pierre Billoux* (see *Eating Out*), a bar, and a boutique. Phones are in the rooms, and in many of the bathrooms as well. Major credit cards accepted. 14 Pl. Darcy (phone: 80-30-12-32; fax: 80-30-04-15). Expensive.

Garden Court Holiday Inn – This branch (104 rooms) of the American chain offers a good value for families. It also is close to the city's *Toison d'Or* theme park. The hotel has a restaurant. Major credit cards accepted. Parc de la Toison d'Or, 1 Pl. Marie-de-Bourgogne (phone: 80-72-20-72; fax: 80-72-32-72). Moderate.

Jura – A friendly place with a lovely private garden. The rooms are comfortable with modern decorations, and those that face the street — the main thoroughfare between Place Darcy and the railroad station — have soundproof windows. Bar; no restaurant. Closed *Christmas* to mid-January. Major credit cards accepted. 14 Av. du Maréchal-Foch (phone: 80-41-61-12; fax: 80-41-51-13). Moderate.

Nord – Run by the same family for four generations, this charmer feels more like a country inn than a city hotel. The 26 rooms are clean and quiet with large baths and fluffy down comforters on every bed, and there's a wine bar in the cellar where you can try out the tastes of Burgundy. There is also a good restaurant, *La Porte Guillaume* (see *Eating Out*). Closed *Christmas* through mid-January. 2 Rue de la Liberté (phone: 80-30-58-58; fax: 80-30-61-26). Moderate.

Wilson – Ceiling beams, warm stone hearths, and a central courtyard, all relics of the 17th-century coaching inn, within whose frame this hotel was constructed, make this a charming place to stay. The *Thibert* restaurant (see *Eating Out*) has won considerable praise for its innovative menu. Major credit cards accepted. 10 Pl. Président-Wilson (phone: 80-66-82-50). Moderate.

Jacquemart – The choice of visiting actors and artists, this 30-room, 2-suite hotel is beautifully furnished. It is particularly well-located for antiques hunters, since it's located on Dijon's main drag for antiques shops. Major credit cards accepted. 32 Rue Verrerie (phone: 80-73-39-74; fax: 80-73-20-99). Moderate to inexpensive.

Du Palais – In the heart of the city's historic quarter, this fine old building is just down the street from the Palais de Justice. Many of the 17 recently renovated rooms have antique furnishings and often are frequented by visiting lawyers. Major credit cards accepted. 23 Rue du Palais (phone: 80-67-16-26). Moderate to inexpensive.

Terminus et Grande Taverne – Small and family-run, it has been in business for more than a century. The rooms are quiet, with simple, old-fashioned decor. Convenient to the train station. There's a bar and a brasserie. Major credit cards accepted. 24 Av. du Maréchal-Foch (phone: 80-43-53-78; fax: 80-42-84-17). Moderate to inexpensive.

Thurot – Down a quiet side street just a few minutes' walk from the train station, this place is a bit like a motel, though the rooms are clean and comfortable, and while there is no restaurant, the little bar downstairs dispenses drinks and coffee. Major credit cards accepted. 4 Passage Thurot (phone: 80-43-57-46; fax: 80-42-86-57). Inexpensive.

 EATING OUT: Dijon is considered one of the capitals of French haute cuisine and is a wonderful place to sample traditional Burgundian food and wine at very reasonable prices. Specialties to look for include *kir* and *kir royal* (aperitifs made of cassis — black currant liqueur — mixed with *aligoté*, a dry white wine or champagne), served at virtually every bar and restaurant in town; *escargots à la bourguignonne* (snails in garlic butter); *jambon persillé* (ham in parsleyed aspic); *oeufs pochés en meurette* (eggs poached in red wine with mushrooms and ham); *rognon de veau à la dijonnaise* (veal kidney in a Dijon mustard sauce); coq au vin (chicken in wine); and the famed *boeuf bourguignon* (beef stewed in wine). Burgundian food tends to be hearty and satisfying, though a number of chefs in town are producing lighter food, in the nouvelle style, with good results. Burgundy's vineyards also yield some of the best wines of France, if not the world, and Dijon's restaurants and bistros offer these, too, at extremely reasonable prices. Beaujolais nouveau often goes for as little as $10 a bottle. Expect to pay from $100 and up for dinner for two at restaurants listed below as expensive; between $50 and $90 at those listed as moderate; and under $50 at the inexpensive ones. Prices do not include wine; usually a service charge is included.

Le Chapeau Rouge – In the *hostellerie* of the same name, this recently renovated candlelit dining room serves excellent regional and nouvelle cuisine that has won it a Michelin star. Start with *croustade d'escargots à la crème de basilic,* and then move on to the *rognon de veau à la dijonnaise* (veal kidney in mustard sauce), or *filet de sandre au cidre* (pickerel in a cider-based sauce). We're forced to note recent complaints about the uneven quality of the dishes. The pastry cart, however, is impressive, as is the plate of petits fours served at the end of every meal. Excellent wine list. Open daily. Reservations necessary. Major credit cards accepted. 5 Rue Michelet (phone: 80-30-28-10). Expensive.

Le Château-Bourgogne – Not the old-fashioned setting its name suggests, but a spare, contemporary dining room in the *Altéa* hotel. The Burgundian chef who runs the well-respected kitchen received his training from the famed Troisgros brothers. The menu is primarily nouvelle, although you'll also find classic dishes such as fresh duck foie gras and *ris et rognons de veau à la moutarde* (veal sweetbreads and kidneys in mustard sauce). Quite a good wine list. Open daily. Reservations necessary. Major credit cards accepted. 22 Bd. de la Marne (phone: 80-72-31-13; fax: 80-73-61-45). Expensive.

La Chouette – This small, medieval dining room down the street from the Eglise Notre-Dame serves some of the best food in town, although it recently lost its one Michelin star. Try the delicate (and very fresh) *lotte aux raisins* (monkfish with raisins in a mercurey wine sauce), the *petits escargots à la crème aux herbes et champignons* (snails in cream sauce with herbs and mushrooms), the *pigeon de Bresse rôti aux morilles farci au foie gras* (pigeon stuffed with goose liver and roasted with wild mushrooms), and any of the first-rate desserts. Closed Monday evenings and Tuesdays, and late June to mid-July. Reservations necessary. Major credit cards accepted. 1 Rue de la Chouette (phone: 80-30-18-10). Expensive.

Jean-Pierre Billoux – Considered by many to be Dijon's best chef, Monsieur Billoux has a Michelin star (admittedly a comedown from his original two-star rating) for refined and original fare that includes dishes such as *suprême de pintade au foie de canard et aux câpres* (guinea hen with duck liver and capers), *canette rosée en cocotte* (casserole-roasted duck served rare), and *poireaux frits* (fried leeks). An elegant room, it is in the old *caves* (wine cellars) of the renovated 15th-century *Hôtel de la Cloche.* Closed January. Reservations necessary. Major credit cards accepted. 14 Pl. Darcy (phone: 80-30-11-00). Expensive.

CBDO La Toison d'Or (Restaurant de la Compagnie Bourguignonne des Oenophiles) – Dining here is an experience that should not be missed. It's a 17th-century mansion, where the original beams, huge stone fireplaces, and a decoration of tapestries, period furniture, and a view onto a small garden give it the feel of an elegant country inn. The food is a mixture of hearty Burgundian specialties — rabbit *en gelée* and coq au vin — and lighter, nouvelle dishes such as salmon, turbot, and spinach terrine and thinly sliced breast of duck with grapes. A good wine list, though not an outstanding one considering the restaurant's affiliation; the *compagnie* also stocks its own wine for sale direct from growers. Before dinner, be sure to visit the adjoining 15th-century courtyard and museum (see *Museums*). Open daily. Reservations necessary. Major credit cards accepted. 18 Rue Ste-Anne (phone: 80-30-73-52; fax: 80-30-95-51). Expensive to moderate.

Thibert – Sophisticated decor with baroque chamber music playing in the background and refined cooking have won Jean-Paul Thibert a Michelin star. Savory dishes include *foie de canard et salade d'oseille crue* (duck liver with sorrel salad) and *pieds de porc avec huîtres chaudes et endives grillés* (pigs' feet served with warm oysters and grilled Belgian endive). A favorite with locals, this place also is situated on one of Dijon's most beautiful squares. Closed Sunday dinner, Monday lunch, 3 weeks in January, and 2 weeks in August. Reservations necessary. Major credit cards accepted. 10 Pl. Wilson (phone: 80-67-74-64). Expensive to moderate.

Le Chabrot – Christian Bouy, the jovial, mustachioed owner, supplies a warm welcome and a menu prepared by his young chef, Joel Guillaud, who is particularly talented with fish — the salmon menu has 15 versions of that *poisson* alone. In addition to the main dining room, there's a wine bar and a 12th-century *cave*. Closed Sundays and Monday mornings. Reservations advised. Visa and Carte Bleue accepted. 36 Rue Monge (phone: 80-30-69-61). Moderate.

Le Petit Vatel – Solid traditional French cuisine, with an old-fashioned decor and good prices. A long-standing favorite, although it no longer has its one Michelin star. Try the *pâté d'escargots à la bourguignonne*. Closed Saturday lunch, Sundays, and mid-July to late August. Reservations advised. Major credit cards accepted. 73 Rue d'Auxonne (phone: 80-65-80-64). Moderate.

La Porte Guillaume – This fourth-generation establishment in the *Nord* hotel is one of the most charming — and moderately priced — dining rooms in town. Don't be surprised by the abundance of mustachioed waiters here; it's a tradition that's been observed for more than a century (take a look at the old family photo on the wall above the fireplace and you'll see). The food, too, is traditional, and it is delicious. The escargots are loaded with garlic, the coq au vin and *boeuf bourguignon* can't be beat, and there are about 25 varieties of cheese on the cheese tray. Both the *menu dégustation* and the *menu bourguignon* are worth the price. Open daily. Reservations advised. Major credit cards accepted. 2 Rue de la Liberté, at Pl. Darcy (phone: 80-30-58-58). Moderate.

Hostellerie de l'Etoile – An ancient façade and a warm, wood-paneled dining room on one side contrast with a modern exterior and eating area on the other side of this restaurant, which occupies an entire block (there's an entrance on each side). Despite the large number of diners served daily, the quality is high and prices reasonable. Try *oeufs pochés en meurette* (poached eggs in red wine with mushrooms and ham), the Dijon specialty that is prepared perfectly here. Ask for a table in the old room when you reserve if you're partial to "La Vieille France." Closed Sundays and Monday lunch. Reservations advised. Major credit cards accepted. 1 Rue Marceau (phone: 80-73-20-72). Moderate to inexpensive.

Brasserie du Théâtre – A popular university hangout known for its good, inexpensive food. In the summer, there is outdoor dining on the terrace. Open daily. Reservations unnecessary. Major credit cards accepted. 1 *bis* Pl. du Théâtre (phone: 80-67-13-59). Inexpensive.

Le Bouchon du Palais – A small, friendly eating spot that features traditional dishes, with customers seated *coude à coude* (elbow to elbow). Regulars often lunch on big platters of *charcuterie* and a glass of wine at the bar. Closed Sundays. Reservations advised. Major credit cards accepted. 4 Rue Bouhier (phone: 80-30-19-98). Inexpensive.

Le Dôme – A favorite gathering spot after the Saturday market at *Les Halles*. Good home cooking, with an accent on classic recipes from southwest France, such as foie gras and *confit de canard* (salted duck slowly cooked in its own fat). Closed Monday and Saturday evenings, and Sundays. Reservations unnecessary. Major credit cards accepted. 16 *bis* Rue Quentin (phone: 80-30-58-92). Inexpensive.

 BARS AND CAFÉS: The *Concorde* (2 Pl. Darcy) is a turn-of-the-century brasserie and a favorite local hangout. People congregate here for a carafe of wine, a cold mug of imported or Alsatian beer, or a demitasse of excellent coffee. Another place to people watch on Place Darcy is the redecorated *Le Glacier,* a popular brasserie and café with a nice selection of wine and beer and a limited menu. Sit by the window and you'll be mesmerized for hours. The *Brighton* (33 Rue Auguste-Comte) is an agreeable "English-style" pub, and *Messire* (3 Rue Jules-Mercier) is another popular bar with a good selection of wine and beer.

■ **Note:** There are a growing number of wine bars and tasting rooms offering visitors the opportunity to sample some of Burgundy's fine wines by the glass. *Le Caveau de la Porte Guillaume* (Pl. Darcy; phone: 80-30-59-59) has tastings from noon to 3 AM. Choose from among some 20 wines — cost of sampling is about $7. *La Cave du Clos* (3 Rue Jeannin; phone: 80-67-64-62) has a renovated wine bar/tasting boutique where a glass of Santenay Premier Cru, for example, can be tasted for $7 or less. *Les Caves de l'Espace Grévin* (13 Av. Albert-1er; phone: 80-42-03-03) opened in June 1990. This tasting center next to the *Espace Grévin* has three vaulted ceiling *caves* where tasters can choose from among 150 burgundy wines. Admission charge is about $7 per person; a *tastevin* (a souvenir tasting cup) is included.

LYONS

Lyons is something of an enigma, a city of contradictions, which may have something to do with its geography. It's essentially a northern city that faces south, so that a whiff of the Mediterranean coming up from Marseilles is often mixed with a chilly blast from the Alps. It has been a border city, at various times in its history the Roman headquarters of Gaul, part of the Holy Roman Empire, and for a long time only tenuously under the French crown, as well as a crossroads, where foreign traffic and trade have always been heavy. A city in the midst of plenty, it has a magnificent site at the confluence of the Rhône and Saône rivers, within easy reach of the Bresse, Charolais, Beaujolais, Burgundy, Forez, Jura, Dauphiné, and other regions, all producers of good things to eat and drink. "Lyons is washed by three rivers," goes one saying, "the Rhône, the Saône, and the Beaujolais," and it certainly is true that the best beaujolais gets only as far as Lyons, and stops there.

Until Michel Noir was elected Mayor of Lyons in 1989, only three people had held that office since 1905 — solid evidence, one would think, of conservatism — if not outright passivity. Yet the city's mayor from 1905 to 1957 was Edouard Herriot, a stormy, anti-clerical Radical Socialist who was Premier of France more than once during those many years. And during the German occupation of France in World War II — while Herriot was a Nazi prisoner — Lyons was the capital of the French Résistance; its *traboules,* the secret passages in the old sections that connect street to street by cutting through the buildings, served as passageways for daring patriots. Today, Lyons probably is the most dynamic and forward-looking city in France. It already has decided that the Lyons of the 21st century will be across the Rhône, east of the peninsula that has been its center for more than 2 centuries, and it already has built a new center to match.

Today, Lyons has a population of more than 400,000 in the city proper and 1.12 million in the greater urban area, making it France's third-largest city. At least twice in its history, it outstripped Paris in importance. It celebrated its 2,000th anniversary more than a quarter of a century ago, taking the date from October 10, 43 BC, when a former lieutenant of Julius Caesar, Lucius Munatius Plancus, founded a colony named Lugdunum on one of the hills of Lyons — Fourvière. There are various versions of the origin of the name; *dunum* means "hill," and *Lug* seems to have referred to an early deity of the Celts, who were established at the confluence of the two rivers at least 6 centuries before the Romans.

Lugdunum became the capital from which the Romans administered the three provinces of Gaul, and their emperors made it into a substantial city. Between 16 and 14 BC, Augustus built a 4,500-seat theater on Fourvière, which was enlarged in Hadrian's time to hold 10,000 people. Nearby, a smaller theater was built for music and speeches. The town also had a circus for chariot races, since gone, and in a settlement called Condate across the Saône on the slope of another hill, the Croix-Rousse, the Amphithéâtre des Trois-Gaules, discovered in 1958. This appears to have been the periodic gathering place of delegates of the 60 Gallic tribes into which the Romans had further divided the three provinces, and the site, in the 2nd century, of the martyrdom of early Christians. Another area, on what was then an island in the Rhône (but is now the peninsula that holds the heart of the city), was a commercial zone of warehouses and workshops and a wealthy residential district.

As the Roman Empire declined, so, too, did the influence of Lyons, though it remained a city of religious consequence, gaining in churches and abbeys and ruled by its archbishops until the 14th century, when it was added to the French kingdom. Then, with the Renaissance, came its second great period of history. Already a crossroads of trade and commerce, Lyons now became the center of banking, printing, and the silk trade in France. Charles VII virtually secured the city's economic future by authorizing its first trade fairs in 1420, two per year at first (later extended to four), events that continue today after occasional interruptions over the centuries. Merchants flocked from all over Europe, bankers arrived from Italy in the late 15th century, and, when François I granted the Lyonnais the privilege of manufacturing silk free of taxes (just as they had earlier been granted a monopoly in the sale of silk), silk weavers arrived from Genoa in the first part of the 16th century.

Lyons soon was the foremost silk producer of Europe, richer and more populous during this period than Paris. Merchants and bankers built impressive *hôtels,* or townhouses, in the new center of the city, the area between Fourvière and the Saône, now known as Vieux Lyon. But the city also was a renowned intellectual center. German printers had come in the late 15th century and printing shops flourished, attracting scholars and writers, among them Rabelais, who practiced medicine in Lyons and published two volumes of his *Gargantua and Pantagruel* here on the occasion of trade fairs in 1532 and 1534.

Lyons was then and still is a working city. Strikes by journeyman printers around 1540 were among the first real labor disputes in history. The silk industry was subject to repeated boom-and-bust cycles, and the brutally repressed uprisings of the silk workers, called *canuts,* of the Croix-Rousse in the 1830s are landmarks in the history of the labor movement. Eventually, the introduction of the power loom during the 1870s put an end to the clacking of tens of thousands of hand looms in the *ateliers* of Lyonnais *canuts,* and though today the city is the center of a vast industrial agglomeration in which the manufacture of textiles (silk and synthetics) is still important, the metallurgical and petrochemical industries are no less vital.

Lyons and the Lyonnais have something of a reputation for secrecy, so it is perhaps the city's place in the history of printing that explains why such an ostensibly reticent place should produce so many books about itself — its cooking, its history and geography, its dialect and argot (a rich subject going back to Greco-Roman origins), its humor (self-deprecatory, except where food is concerned). And if these days Lyons is making an effort to be more open toward visitors, it hardly can be described as ready to surrender itself on first acquaintance. As in many similar mercantile cities, you are welcome but left pretty much on your own. "The outsider who disembarks at Lyons immediately feels more of an outsider than anywhere else," the writer Frédéric Dard, a Lyonnais himself, has written. "Everyone understands that he has just arrived in a forbidden city having nothing to offer but its work and its cooking."

Even discounting the exaggeration, that is not a bad start, because Lyons is, more or less by common consent, the gastronomic capital of France. For many a traveler, food is just about the *only* reason to stop here en route to the Côte d'Azur, the Alps, or Italy. For many a Frenchman, that — besides business — may be the reason, too, but enough of one to make a special trip. Indeed, the institution of the 2-hour high-speed *TGV* train between Paris and Lyons has made it possible — and by no means unheard of — for a Parisian to visit Lyons for lunch and be back home in time for dinner.

The Lyonnais pride themselves as connoisseurs of the art of *bien manger,* and their patronage of the art supports a reported 700 to 800 restaurants, with presumably not a bad one in the lot. In fact, cooks who open a new restaurant in Lyons need nerves of steel and good financial backing to tide them over the initial period of skepticism, but there is ample potential reward. A restaurant that does good business in Lyons is the closest thing to a sinecure that life can offer.

One reason for the city's high culinary standards is its location in the midst of a region of agricultural abundance, producing the finest of raw ingredients. Another may be something in the genes or the genealogy of the Lyonnais that has by now set a precedent for producing the finest of cooks. Superchefs of such worldwide fame as Paul Bocuse, Georges Blanc, Pierre Troisgros (along with the late Jean, one of the two legendary Troisgros *frères*), and the late Alain Chapel, though not working in Lyons, all are local boys, descendants of local chefs, practicing their trade in the Lyonnais region, 7, 12, 41, and 53 miles (11, 19, 66, 85 km) away, respectively. The restaurant of Fernand Point, *La Pyramide* (sold in 1987 to a Parisian real estate company following the death of M. Point's widow), where they all studied, is now reopened and is only 18 miles (29 km) away. But behind the great male chefs is a tradition of female restaurateurs, the great *mères* or *cuisinières lyonnaises,* whose interpretations of home cooking gave rise to some of the classic specialties of Lyons. That tradition goes back at least to the 18th century, when Mère Guy de la Mulatière opened a restaurant that still exists in Lyons (under the name *Roger Roucou;* see *Eating Out*), and was brought into the 20th century by Mère Filloux, long since gone, who taught Mère Brazier, now also gone. One of the last of the line, Léa Bidault of *Chez Léa,* now is retired.

It's safe to say, then, that the average Lyonnais takes cooking very seriously, as seriously as the average Frenchman takes love, and that in the heart of the Lyonnais love and food are equally sacrosanct. Among food fanciers in the know, one fable that combines the two has become the stuff of legend in Lyons. It's said that in 1847, Mme. Célestine Blanchard opened the *Restaurant du Cercle.* One day her chef, Jacques Rousselot, feeling especially inventive, whipped up a new chicken dish for her that he dubbed *poulet Célestine.* The dish was so marvelous that Célestine fell in love with Jacques — and consummated the affair by marriage. Only in Lyons could it have happened — or would people believe it might have happened — that cuisine would be the catalyst for *amour*.

LYONS AT-A-GLANCE

SEEING THE CITY: There are two natural vantage points for a panoramic view. One is from the slopes or the top of Fourvière, on the right bank of the Saône, and more particularly from the *observatoire* of the basilica at the top of the hill, open daily from March through October and on Saturdays and Sundays the rest of the year. Pending payment of the admission charge and a climb of almost 300 steps (or you can take the funicular), you'll have a splendid view of the city and the surrounding countryside. The other is from the height of Croix-Rousse, between the two rivers a bit north of the center. From here you can descend toward the flat ground of the peninsula by several routes that offer excellent, sometimes unexpected views. (Head down via Rue des Pierres-Plantées and the Montée de la Grande-Côte, for instance, or via Place Bellevue and Rue des Fantasques. On the west, Place Rouville has a view of Fourvière and the bend in the Saône.) A manmade height is the Crédit Lyonnais tower in the Part-Dieu quarter on the flat left bank of the Rhône. The *Pullman Part-Dieu* hotel, its restaurant, and *Panache Bar* occupy the 31st to 41st floors of the tower, with views toward the city or the Alps, depending on which side of the cylindrical building you find yourself.

SPECIAL PLACES: Overall, Lyons covers a large area, but for sightseeing purposes it can be broken down into distinct, compact areas defined by the two rivers that meet in the city. The Saône flows into the city from the north, curving first around Croix-Rousse and then Fourvière. The Rhône flows in from the northeast, and the two run nearly parallel for a short distance, creating between them a narrow peninsula of a few miles before they meet and flow south as one. The heart of the city is on the peninsula, or *presqu'île*. To the west, on the right bank of the Saône, is the old quarter, Vieux Lyon, at the foot of Fourvière. To the east is the left bank of the Rhône, where the main attractions for visitors are a park and the urban complex, La Part-Dieu. Sightseeing can be managed by foot, with an occasional shortcut by public transport.

FOURVIÈRE AND VIEUX LYON

Vieux Lyon – Stretched out for about half a mile and squeezed between the slope of Fourvière and the Saône River, this is the most extensive and homogeneous urban Renaissance ensemble in France. Its three *quartiers* of St-Paul, St-Jean, and St-Georges include some 200 buildings dating from the end of the Gothic period to the 17th century when this was the center of town. In poor condition at the end of World War II, the area has been extensively renovated (under the auspices of the Comité pour la Renaissance du Vieux-Lyon, 5 Pl. de la Baleine; phone: 78-37-16-04), and it now is a lively and animated quarter day and night. To explore it, walk along such streets as Rue St-Jean (the main street), Rue Lainerie, Rue Juiverie, and Rue du Boeuf, and if possible, poke into courtyards and cut through the *traboules* (see *Extra Special*) that lead through buildings from one street to another. If you are interested in a detailed visit and read a minimum of French, a booklet called *Miniguide du Vieux-Lyon,* available at most bookstores and some newsstands, will greatly enhance a walking tour.

Cathédrale St-Jean – One of the prime reference points of Vieux Lyon. Begun in the 12th century with an apse in the Romanesque style, it was completed in 1420 in Flamboyant Gothic. Despite the mixture of styles, it forms a harmonious mass whose four relatively short towers give it a powerful, rather low-slung look. It is richly decorated and has interesting stained glass windows, the earliest of which are from the 13th century. The cathedral was the site of two church councils in the 13th century, of the consecration of Pope John XXII in the 14th century, of the marriage of Henri IV and Marie de Médicis in 1600, and of Richelieu's receiving his cardinal's hat in 1622. A curiosity is the astronomical clock in the transept, which strikes the hours from noon to 3 PM accompanied by the crowing of a mechanical rooster and a procession of figures representing the Annunciation. Pl. St-Jean.

Hôtel de Gadagne – The most imposing Renaissance mansion in Vieux Lyon was built in the early 16th century for two brothers, each of whom had a wing; it then was purchased by a rich Italian banking family, from which it gets its name. Two museums are housed behind its façade: the city's historical museum and one devoted to marionettes (see *Museums*). Open 10:45 AM to 6 PM, Fridays until 8:30 PM. Closed Tuesdays. No admission charge. Pl. de Petit-Collège (phone: 78-42-03-61).

Place du Change – This square is framed principally by two buildings. The Loge du Change (on the uphill side), now a church, formerly housed money changers. It owes its present aspect to the 18th-century architect Jacques Soufflot (he designed the Panthéon in Paris), but it incorporates parts of an older commercial exchange building. Opposite, at No. 2, is the Maison Thomassin, from the 14th and 15th centuries. Its Gothic façade and courtyard make it probably the finest pre-Renaissance house in Vieux Lyon.

La Tour Rose – This building with the splendid Florentine façade takes its name from the circular stair tower in the courtyard. Typical of many buildings in this quarter, the hill behind is so steep that every floor was in effect a ground floor, with terraces and a hanging garden. It was said not jokingly of such houses that the people lived downstairs and stabled their horses on the fourth floor. 16 Rue du Boeuf.

Nouveau Guignol de Lyon – At the end of the 18th century, an unemployed silkworker, Laurent Mourguet, invented the puppet named Guignol, the principal character — along with his wife, Madelon, and his friend, Gnafron (whose nose is the color of beaujolais) — in countless comedies. There are Guignol theaters all over France and several in Lyons, and until they were purchased by the Christian Capezzone company 2 years ago, a Mourguet descendant had always been involved in the Lyons theater. The theater is now in the basement of the Palais du Conservatoire. The characters are spiritual ancestors of every Lyonnais, and their language is full of the almost forgotten local argot. Even Guignol's costume, with its pigtail and tight black hat, is that of a Lyons silkworker of the period. Performance times vary, so check ahead. Entrance on Rue Louis-Carrand (phone: 78-28-92-57 or 78-37-31-79). Note to Guignol fans: Related addresses in the neighborhood are 2 Pl. St-Paul, the house where Mourguet lived and first gave performances; 53 Rue St-Georges, the home of *Le Petit Bouif* (the Cercle Laurent Mourguet), which also gives performances and can claim direct descent — call 78-37-31-79 for information; and 2 Montée du Gourguillon, the *Maison de Guignol,* a kind of museum of original Guignol sets and costumes.

Théâtres Romains de Fourvière (Roman Theaters) – Uncovered by archaeological digs in the 1930s, the two theaters, halfway up Fourvière from Vieux Lyon, are the most important visible remnants of Gallo-Roman Lugdunum. The large theater, the oldest in France and the same size as the more famous ones in Orange and Arles, once held as many as 10,000 spectators. A smaller theater, or *odéon,* similar in layout to the large theater but seating only 3,000, is nearby, as are the ruins of a Temple of Cybèle and ongoing archaeological explorations. Open daily 9 AM to sundown. No admission charge. You can reach the site from Vieux Lyon by walking up the Montée de Gourguillon or by taking the funicular. 6 Rue de l'Antiquaille (phone: 78-25-94-68).

Musée Gallo-Romain – Adjacent to the two Roman theaters, this splendid museum, laid out in an assembly of spiral ramps, is a comprehensive presentation of the history of Lugdunum from prehistoric through Roman times. Two inscriptions on bronze — the Gallic calendar from Coligny and the Claudian table — are among the most interesting exhibits: The text of the former is the longest inscription in the Gallic language still extant, and that of the latter is a speech delivered before the Roman Senate by the Emperor Claudius in AD 48. Also interesting are several mosaic floors, including the beautiful mosaic of *Cupid and Pan Fighting,* as well as the huge one with a recurring swastika motif, in which some versions of the motif are clearly defined and others somewhat deformed and harder to find. The museum also has models of the two Roman theaters as they were in ancient times set up near floor-to-ceiling windows looking out onto the ruins as they are now. Admission charge. Open Wednesdays through Sundays from 9:30 AM to noon and 2 to 6 PM. 17 Rue Cléberg (phone: 78-25-94-68).

Basilique Notre-Dame de Fourvière – The top of Fourvière had already been a place of pilgrimage for centuries when, in 1870, the Archbishop of Lyons invoked the aid of the Virgin in keeping Prussian troops out of Lyons during the Franco-Prussian War and vowed, in return, to build a church worthy of the miracle. The resulting edifice, built during the last 3 decades of the 19th century, is a curious mixture of all possible styles, visible from almost everywhere, and, with its four ungainly towers, it has been likened to an elephant on its back. Inside are mosaic murals and stained glass windows; the rest of the church, inside and out, is elaborately carved stone. The 12th-to-18th-century chapel to the right of the church, the place of pilgrimage proper, contains the miracle working statue of the Virgin. The esplanade to the left affords a view of the city stretching to and beyond the Rhône, with the façade of St-Jean directly below and Place Bellecour behind it. The observatory (admission charge) in one of the towers affords a more circular view. Pl. de Fourvière.

PRESQU'ÎLE (PENINSULA)

Basilique St-Martin-d'Ainay – All that remains of an important ensemble of religious buildings belonging to a Benedictine abbey on what used to be an island in the Rhône. Consecrated by Pope Pascal II in 1107, it is, despite later additions, considered a fine illustration of the Carolingian style. 5 Rue de l'Abbaye-d'Ainay.

Place Bellecour – This square was laid out in the last years of the reign of Louis XIV (1710–14) on what was then open land belonging to the Ainay abbey. The buildings that originally surrounded it were torn down during the Revolution; these, in Louis XVI style, were put up when Napoleon came to power. The vast rectangular open space measures more than 200 by 300 yards and includes an equestrian statue of the Sun King, also a replacement of one torn down during the Revolution, and the pavilion of the Lyons Tourist Office, in the southeast corner by the florists' kiosks.

Musée Historique des Tissus (Museum of Textile History) – In the former Hôtel de Villeroy (1730), this is perhaps the finest fabric museum anywhere and a reminder of Lyons's past importance as a silk center. Its 28 rooms house a collection of European, Near Eastern, and Far Eastern fabrics ranging from ancient ones made before Christ to modern ones designed by Raoul Dufy and Sonia Delaunay. The French collection is dominated by the work of the 18th-century designer of Lyonnais silks, Philippe de Lasalle, including creations made for Marie-Antoinette and Catherine the Great of Russia. Open 10 AM to 5:30 PM. Guided tours are given Tuesdays through Sundays at 2:30 PM. Closed Mondays and holidays; admission charge includes entrance to the adjoining *Musée des Arts Décoratifs.* 34 Rue de la Charité (phone: 78-37-15-05).

Musée des Arts Décoratifs – Next door to and a logical extension of the textile museum, its collection covers furniture, *boiserie* (woodwork), tapestries, silver, porcelain, clocks, and the like, all installed in the former Hôtel de Lacroix-Laval. Hours are the same as those above; tickets for one are valid for the other. 30 Rue de la Charité (phone: 78-37-15-05).

Rue Mercière – The Via Mercatoria (Merchants' Street) of Roman times was an outright slum about a decade ago, but, along with the parallel Quai St-Antoine, it has undergone a dramatic revival and now is a center of small restaurants and boutiques and Lyonnais nightlife. In the morning, the Quai St-Antoine is the scene of one of France's most abundant and colorful street markets for food and flowers, worth a visit even if you're not buying.

Eglise St-Nizier – This church stands on the presumed site of an early Christian sanctuary that may have been Lyons's cathedral until the 6th century. The present church is largely from the 15th century, as is one of its towers; the contrasting one is from the 19th century. The interior is Flamboyant Gothic. The church gained a certain notoriety some years ago when it was occupied by the city's prostitutes protesting police harassment. Rue de Brest at Pl. St-Nizier.

Place des Terreaux – Roughly speaking, this is where, in the city's early history, the Rhône and Saône met — *terreaux* refers to the alluvial soil carried by the Rhône that made this area into terra firma. It lies at the foot of Croix-Rousse and is bordered on the south by the Palais St-Pierre and on the east by the Hôtel de Ville. At the western end is a monumental fountain by Bartholdi (of Statue of Liberty fame) of a team of galloping horses representing "the rivers flowing to the sea." The city of Bordeaux, for which it was made, refused it, and the city fathers of Lyons apparently decided it could just as well represent Lyons's Rhône and Saône as Bordeaux's Garonne and Dordogne.

Hôtel de Ville – One of the handsomest Town Halls in France, according to some. It was built in the mid-17th century by the Lyonnais architect Simon Maupin, partly destroyed by fire in 1674, and restored by the noted architects Jules Hardouin-Mansart and Robert de Cotte. It consists of an imposing rectangle of buildings around a central courtyard on two levels, separated by a peristyle, and includes several magnificently decorated ceremonial rooms. Pl. des Terreaux.

Musée des Beaux-Arts – The Palais St-Pierre, built in the 17th century as an abbey for the Benedictine Dames de St-Pierre, now serves as a museum, and one of the principal pleasures of a visit is entering the arcaded cloister with its statues, among them works by Rodin and Bourdelle. The comprehensive collection includes ancient and more modern sculpture and paintings by Veronese, Tintoretto, Rubens, El Greco, Cranach, Lyonnais artists of various periods, Impressionists, and other 19th-century artists. Admission charge. Open Wednesdays through Sundays from 10:30 AM to 6 PM. Closed holidays. Pl. des Terreaux (phone: 78-28-07-66).

Amphithéâtre des Trois-Gaules – The ruins of this amphitheater on the slope of the Croix-Rousse came to light in 1958. It apparently was the site of combats between animals and gladiators, public executions, and the martyrdom of early Christians as well as the site of annual meetings of delegates from the 60 Gallic nations into which the Romans had subdivided the three provinces of Gaul. Entrance from 1 Rue Lucien-Sportisse.

THE LEFT BANK OF THE RHÔNE

Parc de la Tête d'Or – Covering more than 250 acres, this park was created at a bend of the Rhône in 1856 and it contains a large lake, a zoo, botanical gardens, and a Guignol theater. The 100,000-plant rose garden is heaven in June. The main entrance is at Place du Général-Leclerc.

La Part-Dieu – The name of this modern urban complex derives from the earlier *quartier* where, during the early 1960s, the city decided to create a new city center before the fact, anticipating and encouraging Lyons's push to the east. It lies on the flat plain on the left bank of the Rhône, unhemmed by nature as are the peninsula (by the Rhône and Saône) and Vieux Lyon (by Fourvière and the Saône). One of the first buildings to open was the central food market, *Les Halles* (1971), at 102 Cours Lafayette on the northern edge of the complex; another was the Maison de la Radio-Télévision (1972). Now this administrative, commercial, and cultural city of concrete, steel, plastic, and glass includes a railroad station (where the high-speed *TGV* trains stop 2 hours after leaving Paris), the 41-story Crédit Lyonnais–*Pullman Part-Dieu* hotel tower, the 2,000-seat *Auditorium Maurice Ravel* (mainly for concerts, but also for opera and ballet), a municipal library of more than 2 million volumes, numerous government buildings, and the *Centre Commercial,* billed as the largest shopping center in Europe. There is parking for 10,000 cars and the city's métro (which is still growing) also provides easy access.

■ **EXTRA SPECIAL:** Unique to Lyons are its *traboules,* corridors that link one street to another by passing through two or more buildings. The word comes from the Latin *trans ambulare,* "to walk through"; there is even a verb, *trabouler.* They are found in two neighborhoods — Vieux Lyon and the Croix-Rousse slope — both once centers of the silk industry. In Vieux Lyon they are of architectural interest, with vaulted Gothic ceilings; in Croix-Rousse, where they were the scene of bloody uprisings of the silkworkers in 1831 and 1834, they are part of a partly abandoned working class area, filthy but evocative. The *traboules* probably were created originally to conserve land in cramped areas, but they lend themselves easily to the Lyonnais penchant for secrecy and privacy. In Croix-Rousse, a businessman could always appear to be going to or coming from some business appointment while in fact ducking through to an adjacent street of ill repute. They were practical ways, too, of moving a roll of silk from one place to another in the rain without getting it wet. It is possible to go from the top of Croix-Rousse to Place des Terreaux at the bottom by using *traboules* and their interior staircases for the descent, emerging into each street only long enough to cross it. And you cannot really explore Vieux Lyon without going into its *traboules.* Neither can be done without extraordinary patience and determination, however, unless you have a map such as the ones in the Michelin *Vallée du Rhône* guide, the *Miniguide du Vieux-Lyon,* and other guidebooks. Go into any substantial-looking bookstore and make your desire to *trabouler* known.

SOURCES AND RESOURCES

TOURIST INFORMATION: The city and regional tourist office (Office du Tourisme de Lyon/Communauté–Syndicat d'Initiative) has two locations. The Pavillon du Tourisme (Pl. Bellecour; phone: 78-42-25-75) is the more central. It dispenses general information, maps, and brochures, and houses an *Accueil de France* accommodations service, which can book rooms anywhere in France (for a nominal fee). Open daily 10 AM to 6 PM from June 15 to September 15; closed Sundays the rest of the year. The other location is the Centre d'Echanges de Perrache (at the Perrache railroad station; phone: 78-42-22-07), also closed Sundays. During the summer, there also is an information center on the Esplanade de Fourvière. Walking tours to various parts of the city — Vieux Lyon by day or night, *Musée Gallo-Romain* and the Roman theaters, the Croix-Rousse *traboules* — and a general city tour by bus also are organized by the tourist office, with varying frequency in varying languages depending on the season.

Local Coverage – A little rudimentary French will come in handy in Lyons, where foreign-language tourist guides hardly exist. The principal daily newspaper is *Le Progrès,* which carries information on entertainment and other events. There also is *Lyon Matin,* and Lyons editions of two Paris dailies, *Liberation* and *Le Figaro,* are available. The most useful guide to entertainment, theater, music, and the like, is the weekly *Lyon Poche,* available at all newsstands. A virtually indispensable guide to restaurants in Lyons and environs is *Lyon Gourmand,* a booklet published annually and available (until it sells out) at bookstores and newsstands; its commentary is in French, but a system of symbols makes it easy to tell what to expect. (*Lyon Gourmand* is, in fact, one of a series of miniguides issued by the same publisher — to different aspects of Lyons history, to surrounding regions, and so on — that readers of French will find useful. Each costs only a few dollars.) Another guide, *Le Petit Futé,* is for long-term visitors; it lists such things as beauty shops, dance schools, and libraries as well as restaurants, bars, and nightclubs. The Lyons map and street guide of the *Plan Guide Blay* series (there is one for every French city of any size) is useful for finding out-of-the-way *rues;* it also contains a map of the métro system. Lyons is prolific in books about itself, anything from coffee table picture volumes to obscure histories and multi-volume works on the Lyonnais dialect and slang. Some large bookstores, such as *Flammarion* (19 Pl. Bellecour, across from the Pavillon du Tourisme), group them all in one section for easy perusal. The Lyons Tourist Office also publishes a monthly listing of local cultural events; it is available free at their offices.

 TELEPHONE: The city code for Lyons is 78, which is incorporated into all local 8-digit numbers. When calling a number in Lyons from the Paris region (including the Ile-de-France), dial 16, wait for a dial tone, then dial the 8-digit number. When calling a number from outside Paris, dial only the 8-digit number. When calling from the US, dial 33 (which is the country code), followed by the 8-digit number.

 GETTING AROUND: Air – Lyons's Satolas International Airport is served by direct *Air France* flights twice a week from New York's JFK Airport, as well as by daily flights from Paris and other European cities. A major expansion of the airport was started in late 1990. When completed, it will increase the facility's annual passenger capacity from 4 to 8 million people. The first step — the construction of a second runway — was completed last year.

Bicycle – Bicycles can be rented at *Loca Sport* (62 Rue Colombier; phone: 78-61-11-01).

Boat – For information on daily sightseeing boat rides on Lyons's two rivers, contact *Navig'Inter* (13 *bis* Quai Rambaud; phone: 78-42-96-81). Boats leave every afternoon from April to November from the left bank of the Quai des Célestins. Lunch and dinner cruises aboard *L'Hermès* depart from Quai Claude-Bernard (phone: 78-42-96-81).

Bus – Lyons's public transport system, *TCL,* operates 90 bus lines in the city and suburbs; 4 métro, or subway, lines; and 2 funiculars. The same tickets are good for all three modes of transport (and combinations thereof) and can be used for 1 hour after validation, but not for return trips. Tickets may be purchased singly or in books of six (for a 20% discount) from bus drivers and at *TCL* kiosks around the city, but the simplest method is to use the automatic coin machines in métro stations. The tickets must be validated in the ticket-stamping machines on the buses and at the gates to métro trains and funiculars before boarding. Of particular interest to the short-term visitor is the *ticket liberté,* 2- or 3-day unlimited-travel tickets costing, respectively, seven and ten times the price of a single ticket — the 48 (and 72) hours begin from the time the ticket is first validated. These tickets can be purchased at the Perrache bus-métro station, at the *TCL* office (43 Rue de la République) and at *TCL* kiosks. Maps of the system are available in the same places. The métro and most bus lines run from 5 AM to midnight. For information, call *TCL* at 78-71-70-00.

Car Rental – All the major firms are represented at Satolas Airport and in the city, and *SNCF*'s *Train + Auto* plan is available at Lyons's railroad stations. But while a car can be useful for excursions in the region or for the greater distances on the left bank of the Rhône, Vieux Lyon and the center of the city between the two rivers are much better negotiated on foot and by public transportation.

Funicular – Known locally as the *ficelle.* The two lines both leave from Gare St-Jean, at the end of Avenue Adolphe-Max near the Cathédrale St-Jean. One goes to the top of Fourvière, depositing passengers in front of Notre-Dame de Fourvière; the other climbs the St-Just hill, making an intermediate stop at the Minimes station, near the Théâtres Romains de Fourvière. Bus-métro tickets are valid for the *ficelle,* but you also can buy a discounted round-trip ticket valid for a day. Service on the *St-Just* line stops at 9 PM and on the *Fourvière* line at 9:30 PM.

Métro – The 4-line subway system is very easy to use provided you have a map showing where to transfer from one line to another. *Line A,* the backbone of the system, runs north from Gare de Perrache to, among others, Place Bellecour and the Hôtel de Ville (switch here to *Line C* for Place de la Croix-Rousse), then goes to the left bank of the Rhône and runs to the eastern fringes of the city. Switch to *Line B* at the Charpennes station for Gare des Brotteaux and Part-Dieu. *Line D,* goes from Gorge de Loup to Parc de Parilly. (See the discussion of bus lines above.)

Taxi – Lyons is amply served by taxis. They generally can be flagged on principal thoroughfares, and there are cab stands at main squares and intersections. In general, it does not take long for a hotel concièrge or a restaurant employee to call one by phone.

Train – Lyons has two train stations, the Gare de Perrache on the central peninsula at Cours de Verdun and Place Carnot, and the newer Gare de la Part-Dieu, in the Part-Dieu urban complex on the left bank of the Rhône. Trains to and through Lyons, including *TGV* trains, usually stop at both stations; trains originating in Lyons leave from Perrache. For train information, call 78-92-50-50; to reserve a seat on the *TGV,* call 78-92-50-70).

SPECIAL EVENTS: Of increasing popularity is the *Salon des Métiers de Bouche,* a food trade fair that displays the culinary talent and gastronomic riches of the region, held in January or February of odd-numbered years. (In alternate years, it takes place in Paris.) For information about next year's fair, call 72-22-33-44. The *Foire Internationale de Lyon,* held for 2 weeks in late March or early April, is an event that traces its origins back to 1420. Lyons's marathon, *25 Kilometres de Lyon,* is run in April. Held for the first time in 1987, the colorful *Les Pennons* enlivens the Lyons scene in mid-June. In the style of Siena's famous *Palio,* horsemen garbed in the colors and arms of the quarters of Old Lyons compete in a race around Tête d'Or Park. The *Brocante du Vieux Lyon,* a flea market (phone: 78-37-00-68), is also held annually in June, usually on the third weekend of the month. The *Biennale de la Musique Française,* strictly a music festival, is held every 2 years (odd-numbered) and devotes 10 days in September to the music of Hector Berlioz and other French composers, including Ravel, Franck, and Debussy. Contact the festival office (Pl. Bellecour; phone: 72-40-26-26) for details. In even-numbered years, the *Festival International Biennal de la Danse* replaces the *Biennale de la Musique Française.* Held during the same 10-day period in mid-September, this festival welcomes classical as well as contemporary artists and dance groups from around the world. This year, the music of Girot and Le Loi will be featured. The *Grand Prix de Tennis de Lyon* takes place in October. For information, call 78-23-45-45. Every November and December, there are classical concerts at the *Festival de la Musique du Vieux Lyon,* some of which are held in churches throughout the city. Two dates on the church calendar celebrated in a decidedly lay fashion are the long weekend of *Pentecost,* when a national *boules* tournament is held in the *Stade Municipal de Gerland,* and December 8, the *Feast of the Immaculate Conception,* when candles are lighted in the windows of the city, the streets are illuminated, and the *Christmas* season is semi-officially ushered in to general merriment, Lyonnais style.

MUSEUMS: Give or take a few, there are 2 dozen museums in Lyons, of which the most important are listed in *Special Places*. Some others of interest include the following:

Musée de l'Automobile Henri Malartre – One hundred and fifty vehicles, including Hitler's Mercedes, housed in an imposing château high on the left bank of the Saône. Open daily 9 AM to 6 PM. Admission charge. Rochetaillée-sur-Saône, 7 miles north of Lyons (phone: 78-22-18-80).

Maison des Canuts – An ensemble that includes a museum of silk weaving — looms set up with work in progress — and a shop with a limited selection of items, mostly silk ties, for sale. Open 8:30 AM to noon and 2 to 6 PM. Closed Sundays and holidays. Admission charge. 10-12 Rue d'Ivry (phone: 78-28-62-04).

Musée Guimet d'Histoire Naturelle – Collections of Far Eastern art and Egyptology as well as natural history. Open Wednesdays through Sundays from 2 to 6 PM. No admission charge. 28 Bd. des Belges (phone: 78-93-22-44).

Musée Historique de Lyon – In the Renaissance Hôtel de Gadagne, a survey of the city's history from Roman times. Open 10:45 AM to 6 PM. Closed Tuesdays. Admission charge. Pl. du Petit-Collège (phone: 78-42-03-61).

Musée de l'Imprimerie et de la Banque (Museum of Printing and Banking) – In the 15th-century Hôtel de la Couronne, it commemorates the city's importance as the birthplace of French printing and banking. Open Wednesdays through Sundays from 9 AM to noon and 2 to 6 PM. Admission charge. 13 Rue de la Poulaillerie (phone: 78-37-65-98).

Musée International de la Marionnette – In the Hôtel de Gadagne along with the *Musée Historique*. The heart of this museum is a history of Lyons's own marionette, Guignol, along with a collection ranging from European puppets to Indochinese shadow theater. Open 10:45 AM to 6 PM. Closed Tuesdays. No admission charge. Pl. du Petit-Collège (phone: 78-42-03-61).

Musée de la Résistance – Through documents and photographs, this museum commemorates Lyons's role as the center of the French Resistance during World War II. Open Wednesdays through Sundays from 10:30 AM to noon and 1 to 6 PM. No admission charge. 5 Rue Boileau (phone: 78-93-27-83).

Musée St-Pierre d'Art Contemporain – Installed 8 years ago in the same former monastery that houses the *Musée des Beaux-Arts,* but with a separate entrance, this addition presents temporary exhibitions of the works of contemporary artists as well as its own collection of works dating from 1960. Open from noon to 6 PM. Closed Tuesdays. Admission charge. 16 Rue Edouard-Herriot (phone: 78-30-50-66).

Musée de Train Miniature des Brotteaux – One of Lyons's newest museums, with its collection of miniature trains, actually is an old favorite. Open from 9 AM to 6 PM. Admission charge. 4 Pl. Jules-Ferry (phone: 78-34-31-17).

SHOPPING: Two pedestrian streets on the central peninsula form the main shopping axis: Rue Victor-Hugo, which runs from the Gare de Perrache to Place Bellecour, and Rue de la République, which continues from Place Bellecour to the Hôtel de Ville. These streets, and the nearby parallel and cross streets (including the particularly chic Rue Emile-Zola), include most of Lyons's fashionable shops, many of them outposts of famous Paris or even London shops. In addition, the restoration of Vieux Lyon and the ongoing urban renewal centered on Rue Mercière and Quai St-Antoine have attracted a wide variety of specialty boutiques and crafts to these quarters, and the ultramodern *Part-Dieu* complex, on the left bank of the Rhône, has the *Centre Commercial,* a shopping center of department stores and some 200 boutiques, and *Les Halles,* the central food market at 102 Cours Lafayette. The city is rich in fine charcuteries (delicatessens), bakeries, pastry shops, cheese, wine, and other specialty food stores. Silk, historically a Lyons specialty, is another matter.

A walk around the old silkworkers' quarter on the slope of Croix-Rousse is evocative of the past, but no longer a place to find small silk *ateliers.* The leading department store on the peninsula is *Au Printemps* (42 Pl. de la République); *Galeries Lafayette* and *Jelmoli,* a Swiss department store, are in the *Centre Commercial Part-Dieu.* For antiques, browse along the Rue Auguste-Comte just south of the Place Bellecour or take a short taxi ride to the Boulevard Stalingrad behind the Parc de la Tête d'Or, where in 1988 an old market was transformed into an antiques forum containing nearly 100 stores. Stores generally are open from 9 AM to 7 PM, with a midday closing for smaller establishments. They all are closed on Sundays, except for food stores, many of which are open on Sunday morning and then closed until Tuesday morning.

Atelier d'Art – Typical Vieux Lyon handicrafts: painted silk, clothing, woven lampshades. 1 Pl. de la Baleine (phone: 78-37-72-76).

Ateyer de Guignol – Hand-crafted marionettes: Guignol and others with heads made to order. 4 Pl. du Change (phone: 78-29-33-37).

Bernachon – A superb pastry shop and justly celebrated *chocolatier;* all the chocolates are made from scratch on the premises and sold here only. Among the mouth-watering morsels are praline chocolate and bitter chocolate candies. 42 Cours Franklin-Roosevelt (phone: 78-24-37-98).

Boîte à Soie – Silk accessories, including scarves, sashes, ties, and handkerchiefs, for men and women. 3 Quai Gl.-Sarrail (phone: 78-52-06-08).

Cavon de Lyon – A fine wine shop. 6 Rue de la Charité (phone: 78-42-86-87).

Chorliet – Perhaps the most Lyonnais of charcuteries, as well as a leading caterer. 12 Rue du Plat (phone: 78-37-31-95).

Clementine – Headquarters of Lyons's most successful contemporary designer, whose updated classics for women also are featured in shops in Paris and other European cities. 18 Rue Emile-Zola (phone: 78-37-03-10).

Hermès – For elegant, susurrous scarves from the Paris purveyors of things silk and leather (the factory is in town; alas, not open to the public). 95 Rue du Président-Herriot (phone: 78-42-25-14).

Maréchal – Cheeses of enormous variety and superb quality. One of the two cheese merchants in *Les Halles* supplying the city's leading restaurants. 102 Cours Lafayette (phone: 78-62-36-77).

Au Petit Paris – For silk and other textiles by the meter. 9 Pl. des Jacobins (phone: 78-37-08-21).

Le Petit Train Bleu – Toys, in particular toy soldiers, model trains, and chess sets. 7 Rue de la Charité (phone: 78-37-61-81).

Pignol et Vital – For pastry, quiche, and the like, which can also be consumed at tables for a snack or lunch. 17 Rue Emile-Zola (phone: 78-37-39-61).

Renée Richard – More superb cheeses. The other *Les Halles* cheese merchant catering to the city's leading chefs. 102 Cours Lafayette (phone: 78-62-30-78).

Sibilia – Colette Sibilia's sausages and other Lyonnais meats are among the best and most famous in town. Stop by her stand in the *Halles* to stock up for a picnic. 102 Cours Lafayette (phone: 78-62-36-28).

Souvenirs Saint-Jean – Everything from pencils with Guignol heads, T-shirts, and key rings, to watercolors and *cocons,* Lyonnais sweets made with almond paste and covered with chocolate. 8 Pl. St-Jean (phone: 78-92-94-36).

Tourtiller – Less renowned than *Bernachon,* this is an excellent place for exquisite chocolates. 4 Cours F.-Roosevelt (phone: 78-52-20-69).

 SPORTS AND FITNESS: Lyons has a wide range of facilities for spectator sports, including the *Stade Municipal de Gerland* (Allée de Coubertin; phone: 78-72-66-06), home field of the city's *Olympique* soccer team, and the *Palais des Sports* (350 Av. Jean-Jaurès; phone: 78-72-62-02), as much a site for large-scale music events (pop, rock, classical) as for basketball and boxing. Facilities for active sports are not lacking either, even though the real Lyonnais sport is *boules,* of which Lyons claims to be the birthplace. Its version differs somewhat from that practiced in Provence, but, as elsewhere in France, impromptu games take place almost anywhere there is flat dirt ground. A national tournament is held in the *Stade Municipal de Gerland* each year during the 4 days of *Pentecost* weekend.

Ice Skating – There are two *patinoires municipales* — municipal skating rinks (100 Cours Charlemagne; phone: 78-42-64-56; and 52 Rue Baraban; phone: 78-54-20-33). Both are open September to May.

Swimming – The *Centre Nautique* (Quai Claude-Bernard; phone: 78-72-04-50) has outdoor pools on the Rhône, very centrally located (open June to September). *Piscine Garibaldi* (221 Rue Garibaldi; phone: 78-60-89-66) is open September to May; closed Tuesdays.

Tennis – Public courts can be found at the *Stade Municipal de Gerland* (89 Av. Tony Garnier; phone: 78-72-63-93).

 THEATER: Lyons is a lively theater town, and if you understand French, you'll have no trouble finding something worth seeing. As the country's second largest city, it has many resident theaters, ranging from the well known and well established to flocks of fly-by-nights, and it is on the circuit for touring French and foreign productions. Among the foremost theaters is the *Théâtre National Populaire (TNP)* (8 Pl. Dr.-Lazare-Goujon; phone: 78-03-30-30), run by the actor, author, and stage director Roger Planchon in the working class suburb of Villeurbanne. The *TNP* is one of France's leading state-subsidized theaters (one of its most talked-about theaters, too), a very official establishment yet at the same time avant-garde in its stagings and leftist in its political orientation — which used to mean a lot of Brecht, new leftist works, and daring productions of the classics, but the boundaries are getting fuzzy. At the opposite pole is the *Théâtre des Célestins* (Pl. des Célestins; phone: 78-42-17-67), a handsome 19th-century building where the repertory is quite eclectic (Molière, Wilde, Pinter, Feydeau, Balzac, Shakespeare) but quite traditional in style, appealing to a bourgeois audience — it's known familiarly as Lyons's *Comédie-Française.* Other leading theaters, appealing to a younger, rather serious public, are the *Carrefour Européen du Théâtre du Huitième* (8 Av. Jean-Mermoz; phone: 78-74-32-08), which may do Dario Fo, Sartre, or Shakespeare — it tends toward modern plays, but not exclusively — or book a guest dance group; and the *Théâtre de Lyon* (7 Rue des Aqueducs; phone: 78-36-67-67), which stages both traditional and contemporary works, from Maupassant to Mrozek. On the lighter side, don't forget that Lyons is the birthplace of Guignol. One of several places to catch the puppet in action is the *Nouveau Théâtre du Guignol* (Rue Louis-Carrand; phone: 78-28-92-57). It gives matinee performances of the classic Guignol repertory, mainly for kids, and evening performances of new pieces intended for adults ("adult" in the sense of political satire, not X-rated). *Maison de la Danse* (Pl. J.-Ambre; phone: 78-29-43-44), a converted 1930s movie house, exists exclusively for dance, and books French and foreign companies from fall through spring. Ballet occasionally is presented at the *Auditorium Maurice Ravel* (see above).

 MUSIC: The *Orchestre de Lyon,* under musical director Emmanuel Krivine, generally plays in the *Auditorium Maurice Ravel* (see above). Some opera productions take place here, too, along with some of the *Biennale de la Musique Française* concerts, other classical concerts (including those of the annual *Festival de la Musique du Vieux Lyon,* which takes place in November and December; phone: 78-30-00-86). As the main auditorium of the music conservatory, the *Salle Molière* (18 Quai de Bondy) used to be the primary concert hall, but as much of this activity has been transferred to the *Auditorium Maurice Ravel,* the *Salle* is being used more and more for other purposes (for information, call the Lyons Tourist Office at 78-42-25-75). Visiting pop and rock groups that draw crowds usually check into the *Palais des Sports* (350 Av. Jean-Jaurès; phone: 78-72-62-02).

NIGHTCLUBS AND NIGHTLIFE: Two parts of town to explore are the Rue Mercière–Quai St-Antoine neighborhood on the peninsula and Vieux Lyon, across the Saône, both of them endowed with a rich choice of bars and clubs, some of which stay open all night. If you feel like a pub crawl in the first area, try the *Saint-Louis,* a piano bar (61 Rue Mercière; phone: 78-92-99-83); *Colonial Café* (1 Quai des Célestins; phone: 78-37-41-80); or the *Bar du Bistrot* (64 Rue Mercière; phone: 78-37-18-44), an annex to the *Bistrot de Lyon* restaurant, and certainly one of the most popular in a busy street. Nearby are *Le Saint-Antoine* (37 Quai St-Antoine; phone: 78-37-01-35), a nightclub/disco frequented by a sophisticated, well-dressed crowd. In Vieux Lyon is the *Vieille Rhumerie* (12 Quai R.-Rolland; phone: 78-37-03-62) and *Chantaco* (21 Quai R.-Rolland; phone: 78-37-67-77). *Eddie et Domino* (6 Quai Gailleton; phone: 78-37-20-29) has a stunning collection of old and straight malt whiskies, and Eddie, who is practically an adopted Scot, always is ready to discuss or instruct; it's open from 5 PM until everyone goes, except on Sundays and holidays. Nearby on the lively pedestrians-only Rue des Marronniers is *Empika* (7 Rue des Marronniers; phone: 78-37-13-90), worth a visit for its blue lights, frescoes, and exotic cocktails. A fashionable young crowd gathers at *Le Bar du Passage* (Rue du Plâtre; phone: 78-37-81-54) to sit in red-plush seats amid the trompe l'oeil and velvet-covered walls, and eat the acclaimed cooking of the neighboring *Le Passage* restaurant, which is served until 11 PM. Among the more active jazz clubs are the *Hot Club* (26 Rue Lanterne; phone: 78-39-54-74) and the *Fregoli* in the *Sofitel* hotel (20 Quai Gailleton; phone: 72-41-20-20). For dancing to an orchestra, go to the *Caveau* (50 Rue de la République; phone: 78-37-46-90), which is open every night. For gambling, there's the sparkling, remodeled *Casino le Lyon Vert,* a short drive west of Lyons in Charbonnières (200 Av. du Casino, La Tour de Salvagny; phone: 78-87-02-70). Open daily 3 PM to 2 AM (3 AM on Fridays and Saturdays).

BEST IN TOWN

CHECKING IN: It must be said that Lyons is not a great hotel town. Most of the city's hotels are aimed at the commercial traveler (apropos of which, expect the *complet* — sorry, full up — sign to go up early in the day during the week, even during the off-season when there are few tourists around). Most hotels in the central peninsula date from early in the century or were built between the wars and have subsequently been modernized (to a greater or lesser degree) or are still in the process of being brought up to date. While there are some very modern ones, there is a paucity of cozy, small, or quaint hostelries of the kind that one might find, say, on the Left Bank in Paris. In general, accommodations also are on the expensive side. For purposes of classification here, expensive means paying more, sometimes *much* more, than $95 for a double room with bath or shower, between $70 and $95 for moderate, while inexpensive means paying less than $70. Remember that here, as elsewhere in France, single occupancy of a double room will not mean much of a saving.

Concorde – Though traditional, modernized, and soundproof, this establishment (143 rooms) hardly is deluxe. Major credit cards accepted. 11 Rue Grolée (phone: 72-40-45-45; fax: 78-37-52-55). Expensive.

Cour des Loges – A luxurious property on a winding street in Vieux Lyon that combines the best of the old and the new. Creatively installed in three graceful, renovated Renaissance mansions, it features a spacious interior courtyard, 63 unusual rooms and suites (many of them duplexes), a restaurant, hanging gardens, a swimming pool, sauna, meeting rooms, and a garage. One of the city's most charming, unique, and priciest hotels. Major credit cards accepted. 2-4-6-8 Rue du Boeuf (phone: 78-42-75-75; fax: 72-40-93-61). Expensive.

Holiday Inn Crowne Plaza – With 159 comfortable rooms, it offers all the comforts and services typically found in the top of Holiday Inn's line. Near the Part-Dieu station, it features a New Orleans–style restaurant. Major credit cards accepted. 29 Rue de Bonnel (phone: 72-61-90-90; fax: 72-61-17-54). Expensive.

Pullman Part-Dieu – Its 245 rooms are stacked on the top 10 floors of the city's only real skyscraper, the 41-story, cylindrical Crédit Lyonnais tower in the *Part-Dieu* center on the left bank of the Rhône. The view is unlimited, and the style is functional luxury. It also has one of the city's better restaurants, *L'Arc en Ciel* (see *Eating Out*). Major credit cards accepted. 129 Rue Servient (phone: 78-62-94-12; fax: 78-60-41-77). Expensive.

Pullman Perrache – A turn-of-the-century grand railroad hotel, renovated, but still with period charm. Its 120 rooms, many quite spacious, are only a few steps from the Perrache railroad station. Major credit cards accepted. 12 Cours de Verdun (phone: 78-37-58-11; fax: 78-37-06-56). Expensive.

Sofitel – Modern and well equipped; indeed, it has all the services one would find in a major hotel in an American city: shops, hairdresser, bank, florist, an outstanding restaurant, *Les Trois Dômes* (see *Eating Out*), a snack bar open until 2 AM, and a jazz club. Not far from Place Bellecour, there are 183 rooms and suites, some looking directly onto the Rhône. Major credit cards accepted. 20 Quai Gailleton (phone: 72-41-20-20; fax: 72-40-05-50). Expensive.

La Tour Rose – When Philippe Chavent moved his highly rated restaurant of the same name (see *Eating Out*) into new quarters, he decided to crown it with this deluxe 12-room hotel. The rooms have a warm, personal style, richly decorated with the textiles and silks for which this city is famous. Major credit cards accepted. 22 Rue du Boeuf (phone: 78-37-25-90; fax: 78-42-26-02). Expensive.

Metropole – With 119 rooms, this is slightly out of the center of town on the left bank of the Saône, but as compensation for any inconvenience, it has a swimming pool and tennis and squash courts as well as a restaurant, a grill, and a bar. Major credit cards accepted. 85 Quai Joseph-Gillet (phone: 78-29-20-20; fax: 78-39-99-20). Expensive to moderate.

Royal – Another traditional grande dame that has been modernized, and now is part of the Best Western chain. Its 90 rooms are a few steps from the pedestrian shopping streets. Major credit cards accepted. 20 Pl. Bellecour (phone: 78-37-57-31; fax: 78-37-01-36). Expensive to moderate.

Altéa Park – Completely updated, this traditional place has 72 rooms, a garden, and a patio restaurant (in good weather). It is on the eastern side of the city. Major credit cards accepted. 4 Rue du Professeur-Calmette (phone: 78-74-11-20; fax: 78-01-43-38). Moderate.

Des Artistes – Plain and quiet, with 46 modern rooms, it is centrally situated on a peaceful square dominated by the *Théâtre des Célestins* (and a favorite of the actors playing there). No restaurant. Major credit cards accepted. 8 Rue Gaspard-André (phone: 78-42-04-88; fax: 78-42-93-76). Moderate.

Carlton – This gem of a hotel is a link in the Best Western chain. All 83 rooms are meticulously appointed with antique furnishings, and are soundproofed for privacy. Traces of the old Belle Epoque decor linger, especially in the elegant coffered lobby ceiling, and the beautiful old elevator. There is no restaurant on the premises. Major credit cards accepted. 4 Rue Jussieu, near the Place de la République (phone: 78-42-56-51; fax: 78-42-10-71). Moderate.

Charlemagne – A good bet, this 116-room hotel near the Parrache station is simple, clean, and comfortable. Major credit cards accepted. 23 Cours Charlemagne (phone: 78-92-81-61; fax: 78-42-94-84). Moderate.

Créqui – This is a small, modern spot in the vicinity of the *Part-Dieu* center. It has 28 rooms, some opening onto an interior garden. No restaurant. Major credit cards accepted. 158 Rue de Créqui (phone: 78-60-20-47; fax: 78-62-21-12). Moderate.

Grand Hôtel de Bordeaux – A traditional establishment, next to the Perrache railroad station, it has a simple, pleasant style. Some of the 79 rooms are furnished with antiques. Major credit cards accepted. 1 Rue du Belier (phone: 78-37-58-73; fax: 78-37-48-02). Moderate.

Roosevelt – Quiet, modern, and attractive, with 87 rooms, in the Brotteaux quarter, the commercial neighborhood on the left bank of the Rhône. No restaurant, but there is a bar. Major credit cards accepted. 25 Rue Bossuet (phone: 78-52-35-67; fax: 78-52-39-82). Moderate.

Bellcordière – A small, 35-room hotel with brightly decorated, comfortable accommodations near the Place Bellecour, where the Office du Tourisme is located. No restaurant. Major credit cards accepted. 18 Rue Bellcordière (phone: 78-42-27-78). Moderate to inexpensive.

Berlioz – Bright and cheerful, this remodeled hostelry, directly behind Lyons's Perrache station, has 40 small but functional rooms. Major credit cards accepted. 12 Cours Charlemagne (phone: 78-42-30-31; fax: 72-40-97-58). Moderate to inexpensive.

La Résidence – Centrally located on the pedestrian shopping street between Place Bellecour and the Perrache station. It has a somewhat sterile style, but it's clean, convenient, and reasonably priced. Major credit cards accepted. 18 Rue Victor-Hugo (phone: 78-42-63-48; fax: 78-42-85-76). Moderate to inexpensive.

Bayard – Not only is this the best situated of the city's less pricey hotels, but charm lurks behind the modern entrance. The 15 rooms are quite nicely outfitted. No restaurant. Major credit cards accepted. 23 Pl. Bellecour (phone: 78-37-39-64). Inexpensive.

Moderne – A functional establishment about halfway between Place Bellecour and Place des Terreaux. About half of the 31 rooms have private baths; and a few have lovely old fireplaces. No restaurant. Major credit cards accepted. 15 Rue Dubois (phone: 78-42-21-83; fax: 78-83-84-51). Inexpensive.

Morand – Timeworn stone stairwells, Renaissance courtyards, and funky floral carpeting on walls and doors make this hotel a quaint mix of ancient and modern. During summer, the proprietress plants flowers in the courtyards, and guests breakfast leisurely amid the blooms. Major credit cards accepted. 99 Rue de Créqui (phone: 78-52-29-96; fax: 78-24-87-88). Inexpensive.

 EATING OUT: Foremost among the solid reasons for Lyons's eminence in cuisine is geography. Wine flows in from the Beaujolais and Burgundy regions just to the north, from the Côtes du Rhône to the south, and from the Jura to the northeast. The chicken of Bresse, the beef of Charolais, the freshwater fish of countless nearby rivers, and the robust cheeses of surrounding dairy regions all funnel into the city's markets and restaurants. Nothing has to be imported any great distance. Thus Lyons (along with its surrounding region) has more than its share of great and near-great restaurants, but the distinctive and astonishing thing is that while the cooking in the great restaurants may be more complex, the standards are often as high in the least expensive places as in the most. At all economic levels the Lyonnais are very demanding, and although it may be possible to eat a bad meal in this city, there is no excuse for it.

Most of the world's (and Lyons's) great chefs may be men, but the cuisine of Lyons is basically a *cuisine des femmes,* home cooking raised to the *n*th degree. Many of the famous *mères de Lyon* have passed on now, but their names live on in the enduring influence of their hearty, straightforward style of preparing food, in the legacy of certain Lyonnais specialties — *volaille demi-deuil, fonds d'artichauts au foie gras, quenelles au gratin* — forever associated with them and, sometimes, in the names of restaurants (*Mère Brazier, Roger Roucou/Mère Guy*) descended from them and still operating. A corollary to this, perhaps, is that restaurants in the Lyons area seem to stay in the family for a long time, and even when (as in the case of the celebrated Bocuse) an establishment develops from a riverside inn into one of the world's most formidable restaurants, the contact with the past still seems to be there.

A small lexicon might be helpful. The simplest kind of Lyonnais restaurant is a *bouchon,* often an unpretentious mom-and-pop enterprise with marvelous beaujolais or Côtes du Rhône served in a *pot lyonnais* (a heavy bottle of 46 centiliters — about a pint) and simple cooking in which pork products weigh heavily. A *mâchon* used to be a hearty midmorning snack for the working stiff, but the word tends now to be used for the least expensive prix fixe menus, which might start with a *saladier lyonnais,* usually a rolling table with a dozen or so cold dishes such as potato salad, cold lentils, herring and onion in oil, pig's (or sheep's) feet *rémoulade,* and the like. Lyonnais gastronomic humor is reflected in the *tablier de sapeur* (literally, a fireman's or engineer's apron, referring to the thick leather apron of a Napoleonic army engineer), which is a slab of beef tripe breaded and grilled or sautéed, and *cervelle de canut* (literally, silkworker's brains), a soft white cheese into which a variety of herbs has been mixed. This does not mean that such places will not also have such familiar offerings as *boeuf bourguignon* or coq au vin. *Quenelles,* a traditional Lyonnais dish, are light, mousse-like dumplings made of pike, veal, or poultry (although pike is by far the preferred ingredient), and are usually served with a rich sauce.

In Lyons and its immediate region, the rough rule of thumb is that expensive means it is difficult (or impossible) to hold the bill to less than $160 for two people, and $200 is not uncommon; inexpensive means that it should not take too much effort to keep the bill to $65 for two; the price of a moderate meal lies somewhere in between. These prices usually include a service charge; wine, however, is not included. Reservations are always a good idea — and for the three-star establishments should be made in advance *in writing* — but if you are headed toward a popular *bouchon* on the spur of the moment for lunch, don't be much later than midday and don't be surprised to be turned away, for there may be only one sitting. Even in places noted as expensive, one can usually limit the financial damage by ordering from the more moderate prix fixe menu, while moderate places can rapidly become expensive if the temptation to sample fine wine takes over. In the case of month-long summer closings, exact dates can vary, so check carefully before visiting.

Alain Chapel – Among France's greatest restaurants, this gem still sparkles in a tiny village 12 miles (19 km) north of Lyons, where Chapel's parents ran a restaurant known as *Chez la Mère Charles* (his mother was Mère Charles). Although it lost one of its three Michelin stars 2 years ago following the death of its owner and namesake, M. Chapel's legacy continues. The chefs he trained produce the same inspired cuisine, including a fabulous lobster salad, lobster with noodles, stuffed calf's ear, *gâteau de foies blonds* (a pie of chicken livers and foie gras), and other specialties that vary with the season and were the master's stock in trade. In warm weather, tables placed outdoors on a lovely patio overlooking gorgeous gardens make it hard to conceive of a nicer place to enjoy a midsummer lunch. There also are 13 small yet pleasing rooms with bath. Closed Mondays, Tuesday lunch, holidays, and January. Reservations necessary. Major credit cards accepted. On N83 in Mionnay (phone: 78-91-82-02). Expensive.

Les Frères Troisgros – Pierre and Jean studied under the late Fernand Point at *La Pyramide,* then returned in the 1950s to take over their father's 25-room hostelry, right across from the train station on Place de la Gare. The brothers became three-star chefs in 1968. The restaurant flies on one wing now, following the death of Jean Troisgros, although Pierre's son, Michel, second in command, now fills the gap. Pierre rejoices in the natural flavor of foods delicately enhanced and underscored. The menu changes with the season to use the area's fresh vegetables, poultry, shrimp, and snails to best advantage. Recent renovations include a dramatic glass and brass façade. Closed Tuesdays, Wednesday lunch, most of January, and most of August. Reservations necessary. Major credit cards accepted. *Hôtel des Frères Troisgros,* Pl. de la Gare, Roanne, 53 miles (85 km) northwest of Lyons (phone: 77-71-66-97). Expensive.

Georges Blanc – An institution, on the bank of the River Veyle in the picturesque village of Vonnas, where it has occupied the same premises since the great-grandmother of the present chef opened it in 1872. M. Blanc's award-winning menu — a combination of traditional regional and nouvelle cuisine — won him three stars in 1981. Outstanding features include braised sweetbreads in spinach, lamb tenderloin with fresh wild mushrooms, and a dessert cart brimming with 15 to 20 pastry selections. Closed Wednesdays, Thursday lunch, and January. Reservations necessary. Major credit cards accepted. 41 miles (66 km) north of Lyons in Vonnas (phone: 74-50-00-10; fax: 74-50-08-80). Expensive.

Léon de Lyon – Jean-Paul Lacombe continues to serve the traditional Lyonnais specialties his father served (*gras double* — finely chopped tripe sautéed with onion, parsley, garlic, and white wine — as done here would convert anyone to tripe), but he also has expanded his repertoire with nouvelle cuisine creations. It is a member of the Relais Gourmand, and has one Michelin star. It also has a nonsmoking dining room. Closed Sundays, Monday lunch, and 2 weeks in August. Reservations necessary. Major credit cards accepted. 1 Rue Pléney (phone: 78-28-11-33). Expensive.

Nandron – Gérard Nandron's one-star restaurant on a quay overlooking the Rhône is another place with a family tradition behind it and a menu midway between classic Lyonnais and innovative. Closed Saturdays and August. Reservations necessary. Major credit cards accepted. 26 Quai Jean-Moulin (phone: 78-42-10-26). Expensive.

Paul Bocuse – One of France's best-known dining rooms, it earned its reputation after generations in the Bocuse family. This three-star institution is about 7 miles (11 km) north of Lyons on the right bank of the Saône. The quality of the food can suffer from M. Bocuse's frequent international journeys; still, there are those who'd cross continents to try the *soupe aux truffes noires* (truffle soup) and the *loup en croûte* (sea bass in a crust), two of the chef-host's most famous creations. Service can be indifferent to first-timers, but for some the hauteur is part of the appeal. Closed most of August. Reservations necessary. Major credit cards accepted. Pont de Collonges, Collonges-au-Mont-d'Or (phone: 78-22-01-40). Expensive.

Pierre Orsi – M. Orsi is an already well-established but still rising star (whose inspired and imaginative cooking won him two Michelin stars in past glory days, although he recently has been downgraded to only one). The already elegant dining room has been renovated. Closed Sunday evenings and weekends in August. Reservations necessary. Major credit cards accepted. 3 Pl. Kléber (phone: 78-89-57-68). Expensive.

La Pyramide – A French gastronomic shrine that was closed following the death of Mado Point, widow of renowned chef Fernand Point, it is beginning to shine again. Now owned by a Parisian real estate company, it reopened in July 1989 after extensive remodeling; its 60-seat dining room (recently awarded two Michelin stars) has a 1920s graciousness with a garden and terrace; 28 guestrooms were added, making this a fitting monument to what some consider this century's greatest French chef. Closed Wednesdays and Thursday lunch and most of February. Reservations necessary. Major credit cards accepted. 14 Bd. de la Pyramide, Vienne (phone: 74-53-01-96). Expensive.

Roger Roucou (La Mère Guy) – On the right bank of the Saône, south of the center, it was a river fishermen's eatery in the 18th century, but now is one of the city's most elegant establishments, although relatively little known. Closed Sunday evenings, Mondays, and August. Reservations necessary. Major credit cards accepted. 35 Quai Jean-Jacques-Rousseau, La Mulatière (phone: 78-51-65-37). Expensive.

La Tour Rose – Philippe Chavent, one of Lyons's ambitious young chefs, has one Michelin star to his credit. He has established himself grandly on Vieux Lyon's winding, cobblestone Rue du Boeuf. Noted for very nouvelle cuisine and for a moderate prix fixe menu that makes it accessible to many, Chavent also runs a shuttle service with a London taxi between the restaurant and the parking lot on Quai Romain-Rolland. Closed Sundays and the last 2 weeks of August. Reservations necessary. Major credit cards accepted. 22 Rue du Boeuf (phone: 78-37-25-90). Expensive.

Le Vivarais – Onetime pupil of the late (and truly great) chef Alain Chapel, Robert Duffaud displays his culinary panache in this upscale establishment. His artistic efforts give new meaning to the phrase "fashion plate," for each dish is imaginatively and exquisitely presented. Sausage poached in beaujolais with succulent lentils or veal cutlets with chanterelles will make you sigh with pleasure. Closed Sundays. Reservations advised. Major credit cards accepted. 1 Place Gailleton (phone: 78-37-85-15).

Le Gourmandin – Lyons's long-abandoned Brotteaux train station was the inspiration for the relocation of this long-established local favorite serving traditional fare. Owner Daniel Abattu has successfully combined existing turn-of-the-century murals with Italian high-tech and French modern art to create what is certainly the city's most avant-garde dining atmosphere. Closed Sundays. Reservations advised. Major credit cards accepted. Gare des Brotteaux, 14 Pl. Jules-Ferry (phone: 78-52-02-52). Expensive to moderate.

Les Quatre Saisons – A traditional bourgeois decor belies the nouvelle recipes produced here; everything from duck with ratatouille and ginger to warm lobster with caper sauce is absolutely delicious. The simply grilled fish and bouillabaisse are excellent, and the wine list offers more than its share of consistently good vintages. Closed Saturdays for lunch, Sundays, and 2 weeks in August. Reservations advised. Major credit cards accepted. 15 Rue Sully (phone: 78-93-76-07). Expensive to moderate.

L'Alexandrin – This cozy, family-run restaurant near the central market features generous portions of light dishes with a southern French accent, such as an omelette with red peppers, salmon, and leek purée. Excellent wine list. Closed Sundays, Mondays, 3 weeks in December, and most of August. Major credit cards accepted. 83 Rue Moncey (phone: 72-61-15-69). Moderate.

L'Arc en Ciel – A very fine hotel restaurant, not to mention the fact that from the 32nd floor of the Crédit Lyonnais tower on the left bank of the Rhône, it has the best view in town. Closed Sunday and Monday evenings, and from mid-July to mid-August. Reservations necessary. Major credit cards accepted. *Pullman Hotel*, 129 Rue Servient (phone: 78-62-94-12). Moderate.

Bistrot de Lyon – Jean-Paul Lacombe of *Léon de Lyon* (see above) is a partner in this booming enterprise. Open until 3 AM and full of all sorts of night people, including actors and their audiences after the theaters have rung down the curtain. The food is unpretentious, with a Lyonnais accent, and the wines are good. Closed 10 days at *Christmas.* Reservations advised. Major credit cards accepted. 64 Rue Mercière (phone: 78-37-00-62). Moderate.

Le Bouchon aux Vins – Located on Rue Mercière, the Champs-Elysées of Lyons *bouchons,* this pleasant place serves the usual fare as well as more refined dishes, such as duck breast with pears. Thirty wines are offered by the glass — from a rare white beaujolais to an old graves to the standard house red beaujolais. Closed Sundays. Reservations advised. Major credit cards accepted. 62 Rue Mercière (phone: 78-42-88-90). Moderate.

Bourillot – Chef Christian Bourillot is known for his classic cooking and for maintaining a consistently high standard of excellence in this one-star restaurant on an attractive square. The *quenelles* in lobster sauce are fabulous. Closed Sundays and holidays, July, and for 10 days at *Christmas.* Reservations necessary. Major credit cards accepted. 8 Pl. des Célestins (phone: 78-37-38-64). Moderate.

Chez Raymond – Open only for lunch, when this prosaic-looking café is transformed into a trencherman's paradise of only about 20 seats. A *plat du jour* is preceded by a gigantic *saladier lyonnais* and followed by excellent cheeses and an immense choice of desserts set out buffet style. The *patron* is a former maître d'hôtel for *Bocuse,* and his wife presides in the large, well-equipped kitchen. Closed weekends. Reservations advised. Major credit cards accepted. 21 Rue des Rancy (phone: 78-60-58-67). Moderate.

Chez Rose – The ambience, food, and wines are those of a classic Lyonnais bistro. Closed Sundays and holidays year-round; Saturdays in July and August. Reservations advised. Major credit cards accepted. 4 Rue Rabelais (phone: 78-60-57-25). Moderate.

Les Fantasques – This is doubtless the outstanding seafood spot in Lyons. It serves a bouillabaisse that would hold its own in Marseilles. Closed Sundays and 2 weeks in mid-August. Reservations advised. Major credit cards accepted. 47-51 Rue de la Bourse (phone: 78-37-36-58). Moderate.

Henry – Among Lyonnais in the know, this is considered a sure bet for traditional food — particularly fish and game — prepared with finesse and served with style. Closed Mondays. Just off Place des Terreaux. Reservations advised. Major credit cards accepted. 27 Rue de la Martinière (phone: 78-28-26-08). Moderate.

La Mère Brazier – The *mère* has gone (and so has her erstwhile Michelin three-star restaurant outside town), but her one-star place, which has recently celebrated its 75th anniversary, remains in family hands and adheres to the purest Lyonnais traditions. *Volaille demi-deuil* (chicken in half-mourning, in which the bird is poached with truffles under its skin, the black color of which gives the dish its name) is sacrosanct here, as are the artichoke bottoms with foie gras and *quenelles* made with *béchamel* or lobster sauce. Closed Saturday lunch, Sundays, and August. Reservations advised. Major credit cards accepted. 12 Rue Royale (phone: 78-28-15-49). Moderate.

La Mère Vittet, Brasserie Lyonnaise – The best reason for keeping this spot in mind is that it closes only on May 1 (Europe's *Labor Day*) and always is ready to serve a meal, a rarity in France. It also is a well-run establishment with decent food and good wines. Reservations advised. Major credit cards accepted. Near the Perrache railroad station. 26 Cours de Verdun (phone: 78-37-20-17). Moderate.

Le Passage – Long a favorite with Lyonnais in the know, this lace-curtained Belle Epoque–style restaurant, hidden away in a passage near the Place des Terreaux, has earned a star from Michelin for its traditional fare. Chef Daniel Ancel is becoming well-known for revolutionizing classic dishes with foreign seasonings, such as vegetable terrine and oxtail pâté. Closed Saturday lunch, Sundays, and holidays. Reservations advised. Major credit cards accepted. 8 Rue Plâtre (phone: 78-28-11-16). Moderate.

Le St-Alban – Nouvelle interpretations of classic bourgeois recipes such as *pot-au-feu* made with duck instead of beef, and a rabbit terrine garnished with parsley. Very reasonable prices make it a winner. Reservations essential. Closed Saturdays for lunch, Sundays, 2 weeks in February, and 3 weeks in August. Major credit cards accepted. 2 Quai Jean Moulin (phone: 78-30-14-89). Moderate.

La Tassée – The Borgeot family runs this marvelously classic Lyonnais bistro, an appealing place with amusing murals. The menu ranges from a *mâchon lyonnais* to solid bourgeois fare — served to about 10 PM — and there is a wide range of excellent regional wines. Closed Saturdays from July to September, Sundays, and for 10 days at *Christmas*. Reservations advised. Major credit cards accepted. 20 Rue de la Charité (phone: 78-37-02-35). Moderate.

Les Trois Dômes – Another of the few hotel dining rooms to compete seriously in this city. This one, too, has a panoramic view, though only from the eighth floor, but it does take in three churches as well as the banks of the Rhône. Open daily. Reservations advised. Major credit cards accepted. *Hôtel Sofitel,* 20 Quai Gailleton (phone: 78-42-72-50). Moderate.

La Voûte (Chez Léa) – Léa, probably the last of the great *mères lyonnaises,* has retired, but her successors are keeping the same down-to-earth Lyonnais tradition, and at last report Léa was still coming around from time to time to check on things. The reasonably priced prix fixe menu usually includes *tablier de sapeur* and the typically Lyonnais *salade de mesclun* (a mixture of wild greens). Closed Sundays and July. Reservations advised. Major credit cards accepted. 11 Pl. Antonin-Gourju (phone: 78-42-01-33). Moderate.

Chez Georges – The truculent Georges Drebet, who made this place, is long gone, but it is still in the genuine *bouchon* tradition. Closed Saturdays at midday and Sundays. Reservations advised. Major credit cards accepted. 8 Rue du Garet (phone: 78-28-30-46). Moderate to inexpensive.

Chez Hugon – Classic Lyonnais *bouchon,* complete with red-checkered tablecloths, tightly packed tables, rustic woods, and a motherly *cuisinière* at the stove serving up copious portions of simple, soul-satisfying local specialties. Closed evenings and weekends. Reservations advised. Major credit cards accepted. 12 Rue Pizay (phone: 78-28-10-94). Moderate to inexpensive.

Le Garet – A long-established *bouchon.* The menu is classic Lyonnais, the service, agreeable, and the beaujolais, excellent. Closed weekends, holidays, August, and a week at *Christmas.* Reservations advised. Major credit cards accepted. 7 Rue du Garet (phone: 78-28-16-94). Moderate to inexpensive.

La Meunière – A 1930s *bouchon* with all the predictable trappings — worn tables and tiles, smoke-stained walls and ceiling — and above all, some of the most generous and best offerings in town. Go with an appetite, and if you haven't already tried the local *poulet au vinaigre* (chicken in a tomato and vinegar sauce), do so here — it's exemplary. Closed Sundays, Mondays, and mid-July to mid-August. Reservations advised. Major credit cards accepted. 11 Rue Neuve (phone: 78-28-62-91). Moderate to inexpensive.

Le Petit Léon – The newest venture of superchef Jean-Paul Lacombe, this modest, lunch-only *bouchon* is tiny and reasonably priced. Its menu changes daily and features dishes such as *boudin* and lentil salad and *poulet au vinaigre.* Open for lunch only. Closed Sundays. Reservations unnecessary. Major credit cards accepted. 3 Rue Pléney (phone: 72-00-08-10). Moderate to inexpensive.

Les Adrets "Le Tire-Cul" – Delightful atmosphere, good quality, and reasonable prices make this place on a winding street in Vieux Lyon a local favorite. Closed weekends. Reservations advised. No credit cards accepted. 38 Rue du Boeuf (phone: 78-38-24-30). Inexpensive.

Bar de l'Entracte (Chez Marcelle) – This popular *bouchon* on the left bank of the Rhône has relatively late service for the type of place it is — orders are taken until about 9:30 PM. Closed weekends and August. Reservations unnecessary. Visa accepted. 71 Cours Vitton (phone: 78-89-51-07). Inexpensive.

Brasserie Georges – Since 1836, this huge, bustling dining room has been serving wonderful bistro classics. Try the lentil salad with *chèvre* (goat cheese), and the pears laced with red wine. Open daily. Major credit cards accepted. 30 Cours de Verdun (phone: 78-37-15-78; fax: 78-42-51-65). Inexpensive.

Café-Comptoire de Lyon (Chez Sylvain) – Keep this spot in mind when the weather is fine — it is one of the few in town with outdoor dining. The food is prepared by a trained chef who traded haute-cuisine pretentions for honest *bouchon* fare. His classic offerings, however, often include a touch of originality — he adds *rillettes* (a spread made from goose fat and meat) to the potatoes au gratin, and makes the *quenelles* with red-, rather than white-wine sauce. Closed Saturdays and Sundays in August. Reservations advised. No credit cards accepted. 4 Rue Tupin (phone: 78-42-11-98). Inexpensive.

Café des Fédérations – More typical Lyonnais *bouchon* fare, an excellent *pot de Morgon,* and a decor of sausages hanging from the ceiling and photos and old newspaper clippings on the wall. Closed weekends and August. Reservations unnecessary. Major credit cards accepted. 8 Rue du Major-Martin (phone: 78-28-26-00). Inexpensive.

Le Comptoir du Boeuf – Philippe Chavent has a successful low-budget alternative to *La Tour Rose* in this colorful little café-restaurant in Vieux Lyon. You can snack on oysters or terrines or order a *plat du jour* until midnight or later. Closed Sundays. Reservations unnecessary. Visa accepted. 3 Pl. Neuve-St-Jean (phone: 78-92-82-35). Inexpensive.

La Mère Jean – The reason this place always seems noisy and crowded, full of students, journalists, soccer players, and whatnot, with loud debates going on between tables, is that hearty Lyonnais home cooking has been served here for over a half century at minuscule prices. Closed Saturdays and Sundays. Reservations advised. Visa accepted. 5 Rue des Marronniers (phone: 78-37-81-27). Inexpensive.

Le Tavernier de Saint Paul – A lively new eating spot that offers good *moules-frites* (steamed mussels with French fries), as well as regional specialties. Closed May 1. Major credit cards accepted. 2 Rue Octavio Mey (phone: 78-39-48-48). Inexpensive.

 BARS AND CAFÉS: Most Lyonnais are likely to feel that the best thing to do with the late afternoon–early evening happy hour is to split a *pot* of beaujolais with a friend, perhaps in the same place they had lunch. Other possibilities include most of the bars listed under *Nightclubs and Nightlife* or two hotel bars with a view: *Le Melhor* in the *Sofitel* hotel and the *Panache Bar* in the *Pullman Perrache* hotel. The *Grand Café des Négociants* (1 Pl. Francisque-Regaud) is just about the last example of an old-fashioned grand café of the turn of the century, while the *Cintra* (43 Rue de la Bourse) is a haven of anglophilic understatement.

MARSEILLES

Some cities pass through a chrysalis stage as important ports before they emerge into greatness as commercial centers or industrial powers. Not so Marseilles. As it has been for 25 centuries, since before the Greeks controlled the wine-dark seas of the Mediterranean, modern Marseilles is above all else a port city. In 600 BC, Phocaean Greeks from Asia Minor founded the city, calling it Massalia, and then, as now, it acted as port of entry for goods, people, ideas, and most of all, history. (A commemorative block near Marseilles's thriving Vieux Port proclaims with perfect accuracy and stunning lack of modesty: "They founded Marseilles, from which civilization reached the West.")

With a population just brushing 900,000, Marseilles is France's second-largest city. But that may say more about the importance of the Mediterranean to France than of France's influence on Marseilles. Landlocked Paris, so gay in springtime and so gray in winter, is another country, 500 miles away, every mile of which must be traveled on land. It is a journey that traditional Marseillais, otherwise so effusive and warm, are reluctant to make. Marseilles and its people face steadfastly toward the sea, from which they have always drawn such strength.

When the city provisioned the Crusaders and welcomed back their booty, it was trading with Africa, the Near East, and the Far East. Today the names have changed, but France's major port does business with the same countries, and a lot more besides. Marseillais have as much in common with Italians and Greeks — fellow Mediterraneans — as they do with Parisians.

Unlike Paris, which has become predictable and bourgeois by comparison, Marseilles is France's connection to the sensuous, boisterous world of the Mediterranean. Sailors from all over the world roam the Canebière, the famous street leading up from the Vieux Port (Old Port), in search of women, excitement, or perhaps a little bit of smuggling on the side on their next tour of duty. And frequently violence still erupts, as it did in the gangland murder at the *Bar du Téléphone* not too many years ago. The milieu of the French underworld endures as a presence, for Marseilles remains, as both Interpol and Hollywood would have it, "the French connection." Even though many of the drug middlemen have moved on to Amsterdam or Berlin, Gene Hackman still would recognize the place. But an odd question lingers: Do we consider port cities wicked because of Marseilles, or do we feel such thrilling wickedness in Marseilles because it is so much the port city of our dreams?

As in all great port cities, numerous foreigners and immigrants have settled in Marseilles — particularly industrial workers from the island of Corsica and a large number of North Africans. Often poor, many Algerians, Tunisians, and Moroccans live in slums around the Porte d'Aix and the Rue Ste-Barbe, where shops sell inexpensive North African items, but where few people feel comfortable wandering after dark. The area is perfectly safe in the daytime, however, and it's worth a visit for the colors and smells alone.

Life is lived boisterously in the Marseilles streets, particularly in the area around the Vieux Port, which now is a harbor for pleasure boats and for sidewalk restaurants offering bouillabaisse. Although the Germans dynamited much of the picturesque but seedy Old Quarter during World War II (because it was a center for the Résistance), some reminders of Marseilles's tradition still survive.

From the beginning, the city prospered at the hands of the Greek traders, declined under Roman rule, and was revived by the Crusaders, whom Marseilles supplied with food and weapons. Devastated by the great plague in 1720, in which 50,000 of its citizens perished, Marseilles rose again to support the French Revolution with enthusiasm. In 1792, 500 volunteers marched to Paris, singing a new war song composed at Strasbourg by a young officer named Rouget de Lisle. All the way to Paris, the Marseillais sang the new song with Mediterranean exuberance. Practice improved their performance, so that when the troops reached Paris, their expert chorus electrified all listeners. The song caught on and became France's stirring national anthem, named not for the city but for those staunch choristers, "La Marseillaise." A recent ground swell of public opinion that the original lyrics of "La Marseillaise" have become obsolete has prompted the French government to consider rewriting the words.

One hundred years later, the opening of the Suez Canal virtually assured the continued maritime success of Marseilles, and commercial traffic abandoned the small Vieux Port for a new one directly to the north. The new port was also destroyed during World War II, but it was rebuilt and expanded. Flat, nondescript, and soulless buildings have risen on the once vibrant site of the Old Quarter. Ironically, every new groundbreaking brings the possibility of unearthing still more traces of earlier civilizations, like the Roman docks discovered in the 1940s or the Greek ramparts found in 1967. Medieval churches now stand side by side with steel and glass apartment buildings. The excavations at the Centre Bourse are open to visitors.

Many visitors to Marseilles are heading off to the Côte d'Azur and are in the city only to change trains at the rebuilt Gare St-Charles or planes at the modern Aéroport de Marignane. But there's sufficient reason to linger. Step into a café on the Vieux Port as the burning Mediterranean sun starts to sink in the sky and order a milky white *pastis,* an anise-flavored aperitif. (Or duck into the less seedy *La Samaritaine* on Bd. de la République.) Around you are spectacular white limestone hills and in front, a harbor filled with the cries and accents of far-off lands. Drink it all in, along with your *pastis.* Who knows? You may, like the late American writer M.F.K. Fisher, fall in love with Marseilles and stay longer, soaking in its rich Mediterranean atmosphere and exploring its abundant historic remains.

MARSEILLES AT-A-GLANCE

SEEING THE CITY: Take the No. 60 bus up to this hilly city's most imposing height, a 531-foot limestone bluff crowned by the Basilica of Notre-Dame-de-la-Garde, known to the Provençal as La Bonne Mère. There's an extraordinary view — particularly at sunset — from the terrace: The boats on the Vieux Port, the white rocky islands, and the densely built city stretch out below. The half-Roman, half-Byzantine basilica itself, topped by a huge gilded statue of the Virgin, is far less of a draw than its view, but inside it does have interesting hand-painted offerings to the Virgin as thanks for curing various ailments. Pl. du Colonel Eden.

SPECIAL PLACES: If you walk down the Gare St-Charles's monumental staircase and continue on the Boulevard d'Athènes, you'll come to a busy central shopping street, the Canebière. Visitors are sometimes disappointed at the modern, occasionally tacky appearance of this celebrated boulevard that runs into the Vieux Port. During the Middle Ages there were hemp fields here, or *chénevières* (hence the name Canebière); the broad plane-tree-lined concourse is still the key artery — and essential reference point — of Marseilles. During December, it becomes the backdrop for the colorful *santons* fair, where folk art takes center stage in the form of clay figures, some 2 to 3 feet tall, representing both the *Christmas* story and Provençal life in centuries past.

IN THE CITY

Vieux Port – Follow the Canebière down to the Quai des Belges and you'll arrive at the Vieux Port. Today a harbor for small fishing boats and yachts, it's far more picturesque than the burgeoning new port to the north. Its entrance is framed by the 17th-century forts of St-Jean and St-Nicolas (a Foreign Legion base). Terraced restaurants featuring bouillabaisse (at staggering prices) overlook the animated marina. A fresh-fish market does a lively business every morning. This is the heart of Marseilles. It still is possible to ferry from one side of the Vieux Port to the other, as in Marcel Pagnol's films. Ferries make the trip every 10 minutes from 7 AM to 6:30 PM daily. There also is a sightseeing train — *Le Petit Train de la Bonne Mère* — that leaves frequently from the Vieux Port to the Basilica of Notre-Dame-de-la-Garde from 2:15 to 6:15 PM; from 2:15 to 4:15 PM from January through March; and from 2:15 to 5:15 PM in November and December.

Musée des Beaux-Arts (Fine Arts Museum) – In the 19th-century Palais de Longchamp — noteworthy in its own right for impressive fountains and gardens (and even a zoo) — the museum offers a considerable display of art. Paintings from the Italian, Flemish, Dutch, and French (David, Courbet, Ingres) schools share the palace's left wing with works by Marseilles natives Honoré Daumier and Pierre Puget and by other Provençal artists. On the ground floor is a charming children's museum. The right wing of the palace contains a natural history museum. The *Beaux-Arts* is open daily from 10 AM to 5 PM (until 6 PM in summer); the natural history museum is open daily except Tuesdays and Wednesday mornings from 10 AM to noon and 2 to 6 PM. Separate admission charge for each museum. Pl. Bernex (phone: *Beaux-Arts,* 91-62-21-17; natural history museum, 91-62-30-78).

Musée Grobet-Labadié – Near the Longchamp Palace, this 19th-century showplace is furnished opulently, exactly as it was when the musician Louis Grobet lived there. Stop by before or after visiting the *Fine Arts Museum.* Open daily from 10 AM to 5

PM in winter, and 11 AM to 6 PM in summer. Admission charge. 140 Bd. Longchamp (phone: 91-62-21-82 or 91-08-96-04).

Outdoor Markets – Wander through the city's raucous market areas and take in their vivid sights and smells. They're particularly alive in the mornings on the Quai des Belges, where the fishermen and their wives sell their catch directly. Also, note the food market on Rue Longue des Capucins (at Rue Vacon, near the Canebière); the flea markets near the Porte d'Aix (that is, the triumphal arch in Pl. Jules-Guesde at the end of Rue d'Aix); the daily book market on Le Cours Julien; and Rue St-Barbe in the Algerian quarter (but avoid this racially troubled area after dark).

Le Cours Julien – This unique public square has splashing fountains, interesting boutiques, bookstores, restaurants, and an innovative art gallery (see *Shopping*). It will take an hour to explore the whole plaza, but allow yourself the pleasure of real contact with the youth, vigor, and creativity of Marseilles. To get here, walk north from the Old Port, up the Canebière, then East onto Bd. Garibaldi, which crosses Le Cours Julien.

Musée des Docks Romains – An unexpected benefit came from the Germans' 1943 bombing of the Old Quarter. Fascinating remains of long-buried Roman docks and statuary were unearthed in the course of rebuilding the area, and the museum incorporates the original setting plus objects retrieved offshore. Open daily from 10 AM to 5 PM in winter; from 11 AM to 6 PM in summer. Admission charge. 28 Pl. Vivaux (phone: 91-91-24-62).

Musée d'Histoire de Marseille – The excavations of the ancient Greek port and ramparts are now a museum. The open-air archaeological dig features the remains of a boat excavated on the site. Open daily from noon to 7 PM. Closed Sundays. Admission charge. Pl. Belsunce (phone: 91-90-42-22).

Le Panier – From the Quai du Port, the narrow streets climb toward what little remains of Old Marseilles. Reminiscent of Paris's Montmartre (and likewise beginning to suffer the same "renewal" fate), the Panier quarter is a maze of tiny streets reverberating with the exuberant sounds of daily life in a Provençal neighborhood. It is not lacking for art galleries or interesting bistros. Behind the Hôtel de Ville, climb the steps to the left of Notre-Dame-des-Accoules's bell tower, the remains of a 12th-century church.

La Vieille Charité – Located in the Panier district, this baroque building of rose stone with an egg-shaped cupola was designed as a prison hospital by Pierre Puget and took 75 years to build — from 1640 to 1715. Abandoned in the early part of this century, it was taken over by squatters until 1986, when a vast renovation restored the building to its original state. It currently is home to several research institutes and houses temporary exhibitions of predominantly contemporary art as well as Egyptian and Greek artifacts. Open Mondays through Fridays from 10 AM to 5 PM in winter, and from 11 AM to 6 PM in summer. Admission charge. 2 Rue de la Charité (phone: 91-56-28-38).

Cathédrales de la Major – Reminiscent of Moslem mosques, the cathedrals' domes and cupolas dominate the Quai de la Tourette. The sadly battered Ancienne (Ancient) Major was built in the 12th century in pure Romanesque style on the ruins of the Roman Temple of Diana. The huge, ostentatious cathedral next to it was built in the 19th century in a Romanesque-Byzantine style. Pl. de la Major.

Abbaye St-Victor – The present fortified Gothic church dates from the 11th to the 14th century, but the real interest lies below, in its crypt, which actually is an ancient basilica founded in the 5th century in honor of the 3rd-century martyr St. Victor. This abbey contains a chapel and the tomb of two 3rd-century martyrs in addition to pagan and early Christian catacombs. The church also hosts concerts; call for the program. The abbey is open daily from 8 AM to noon and from 2 to 6 PM. Crypt closed Sundays. Admission charge. At the end of Rue Sainte (phone: 91-33-25-86).

Cité Radieuse – Designed by the renowned Le Corbusier, the 17-story housing development — or *unité d'habitation* — was avant-garde for its time (1947–52) and is still a landmark in modern functional architecture. There is a moderately priced hotel with a number of shops on the premises. 280 Bd. Michelet.

Parc Borély – This is a lovely stretch of greenery where you can take some sun by the lake or rent a bicycle. There's also a quaint racetrack on the same site. The park itself closes after dark. Promenade de la Plage and Av. Clot-Bey.

Château Gombert – This neighborhood just inside the city limits claims the *Musée des Arts et Traditions Populaires du Terroir Marseillais* (Museum of Popular Art and Traditions), 5 Pl. des Héros (phone: 91-68-14-38). Among its exhibitions are pottery, pewter, and glass displays. Open daily from 2:30 to 6:30 PM. Admission charge. In summer the town holds a festival of Provençal folklore. Follow the autoroute north toward Lyons and exit at La Rose.

OUT OF TOWN

Promenade de la Corniche – This scenic coast road that winds for some 3 miles (5 km) south of the Vieux Port passes in its course Marseilles's most spectacular homes and a breathtaking view of the sea and the islands, including the Château d'If and the Frioul Islands (see below). Also known as the Corniche Président-J.-F.-Kennedy, it passes a picture-postcard fishing port, Vallon des Auffes, and lovely rocky coves before it becomes the Promenade de la Plage (with Parc Borély) and continues toward Cassis, a beautiful fishing town, now also a summer resort, that was celebrated by Derain, Vlaminck, Matisse, and Dufy. Cassis is 14 miles (22 km) from Marseilles. Beautiful, sandy Prado Beach is also along the Corniche road; watch for signs. Pick up Corniche Président-J.-F.-Kennedy at Rue des Catalans.

Château d'If – Set on a rocky island, this beautiful castle was built in the 16th century for defense, and then turned into a state prison whose most famous "guest" was Alexandre Dumas's Count of Monte Cristo. Inside some cells are carvings by Huguenot prisoners. Open daily; admission charge. The château can be reached by boats that leave about every hour for a 20-minute ride from the Quai des Belges (phone: 91-55-50-09).

Allauch – On a cliff with a church on top and windmills all around, the town offers a good view of Marseilles and the harbor and is known for *suce-miel,* a type of lollipop made of honey, and *croquants aux amandes,* almond biscuits. To get here, take Boulevard de la Libération out of Marseilles and follow signs north to St-Barnabé/Allauch.

Frioul Islands – These islands southwest of Marseilles have sparkling creeks that provide an idyllic retreat from the city's sometimes torrid atmosphere. Boats leave for the islands from the Quai des Belges every hour year-round. Les Armateurs Côtiers (phone: 91-55-50-09).

■ **EXTRA SPECIAL:** For unsurpassed and unspoiled natural beauty, don't leave the region without seeing its spectacular *calanques* along the coast between Marseilles and Cassis. The *calanques* are crystal-clear narrow creeks running between stark white limestone cliffs that soar up to 650 feet, much like small fjords. They can be approached only by foot (about 1½ hours each way) or by boat, thereby ensuring a minimum number of tourists. The closest *calanques* — Sormiou and Morgiou — lie at the terminus of bus No. 20. A free map of the *calanques* is available at the tourist office. For information on organized hiking ventures, visit *Les Excursionnistes Marseillais* (16 Rue de la Rotonde; phone: 91-84-75-52), Tuesdays through Saturdays from 6 to 8 PM. Otherwise, boats leave from Quai des Belges Wednesdays, Saturdays, and Sundays at 2 PM and return at 6 PM from June 15 through September 15 (phone: 91-55-50-09).

SOURCES AND RESOURCES

 TOURIST INFORMATION: The English-speaking staff of the Office du Tourisme (4 La Canebière; phone: 91-54-91-11) provides hotel reservations, maps, guides, and advice; also ask for *La Charte de la Bouillabaisse,* which gives the real recipe for this much maligned and poorly imitated fish soup and provides a list of those restaurants serving the authentic concoction. A second tourist office is at Gare St-Charles (phone: 91-50-59-18).

For a closer look at Marseilles, read *A Considerable Town,* by the American M.F.K. Fisher; it's a charming and personal account of a city she loves.

A good index-indexed map is the *Carte et Plan Frézet,* available at major bookstores along the Canebière. They also carry general English-language guidebooks, but no local English publications exist. Also, pick up a copy of *A Tout Marseille,* a bimonthly magazine in French of what's happening, put out by the tourist office and distributed free of charge.

From late May to October, 3-hour guided bus tours of Marseilles are available in English from *Protour* (4 Bd. Baille; phone: 91-94-00-44), for about $18.

Local Coverage – The local newspapers, *Le Méridional* and *Le Provençal,* are available at any newsstand.

 TELEPHONE: The city code for Marseilles is 91, which is incorporated into all local 8-digit numbers. (*Note:* The area code for the airport is 42.) When calling a number in Marseilles from the Paris region (including the Ile-de-France), dial 16, wait for the dial tone, then dial the 8-digit number. When calling a number from outside Paris, dial only the 8-digit number. When calling from the US, dial 33 (which is the country code), followed by the 8-digit number.

 GETTING AROUND: Airport – Marseilles-Marignane Airport is about 18 miles (29 km) northwest of the city (phone: 42-78-21-00). International and domestic terminals are adjacent in the main airport concourse. For a taxi into town, 24 hours a day, call 42-78-24-44; the 20- to 30-minute ride will cost about 200F ($33). There are buses every 20 minutes in both directions from 6 AM to 9:50 PM and according to flight schedules; the approximate time to Gare St-Charles, the main train station, is 30 minutes, and the fare is about 36F ($6). For information on regular bus service to the airport from Marseilles, call 91-50-59-34.

Boat – Boats leave for the Frioul Islands (see *Special Places*) from the Quai des Belges approximately every hour. Les Armateurs Côtiers (phone: 91-55-50-09).

Bus and Métro – Marseilles's attractive subway system is coordinated with the buses, allowing easy — and free — transfers between systems. The métro goes in only two directions, so it's difficult to get lost. Buy a *carnet* (packet) of six tickets instead of the single ticket. The métro shuts down each night at 9 PM, though there are many buses that run later, some offering service throughout the night. For information, call 91-91-92-10. For information about regular bus service to Marseilles-Marignane Airport, call 91-50-59-34.

Car Rental – Major international firms are represented.

Ferry – For ferries to Corsica, inquire at *SNCM,* 61 Bd. des Dames (phone: 91-56-62-05 or 91-56-32-00).

Taxi – There are cabstands around the city, or call *Taxi Tupp* (phone: 91-05-80-80),

Marseille Taxi (phone: 91-02-20-20), *Maison du Taxi* (phone: 91-95-92-50), or *Taxi Radio France* (phone: 91-49-91-00).

Train – Marseilles's train station is Gare St-Charles (phone: 91-08-50-50 for information, 91-08-84-12 for reservations). The extension of the Paris-Lyons high-speed *TGV* line to Valence, which has experienced considerable resistence from locals who want to preserve the environment, will (if and when completed) cut travel time between Paris and Marseilles to just over 3 hours; until then, it takes about 4½ hours.

 LOCAL SERVICES: In town, the *Centre Méditerranéen de Commerce International,* known as *CMCI* (Rue Henri-Barbusse; phone: 91-08-60-00), is a one-stop center for the visiting businessperson operated by the Chamber of Commerce. Available under one roof are individual offices for rent; meeting and conference rooms; telex, photocopying, and word processing services; multilingual secretarial help; translation services; ultramodern teleconference and telecommunications facilities; and professional business advice and information on the Marseilles region. It is within walking distance of the Stock Exchange (Bourse) and the Old Port in the heart of the business and commercial center of the city.

Dentist (English-Speaking) – *Dr. Simon,* 14 Av. de Toulon (phone: 91-78-34-63).

Dry Cleaner/Tailor – *Pressing,* open from 8 AM to 5:15 PM. 22 Av. du Prado (phone: 91-37-40-02).

Limousine Service – *René Dissaux,* 20 Rue Mazenod (phone: 91-91-36-10 or 91-32-75-92).

Medical Emergency – *SAMU* (*Service d'Aide Médicale Urgente;* phone: 91-49-91-91), an emergency medical service with a specially equipped ambulance, is for serious emergencies only and is available 24 hours a day. Two other services are *SOS Médicins* (phone: 91-52-91-52) and *SOS Dentistes* (phone: 91-25-77-77).

Messenger Service – *Marseille Courses,* 147 Rue Paradis (phone: 91-37-57-82).

National/International Courier – *DHL International,* Cil la Bastide Blanche, Quartier du Griffon, Vitrolles (phone: 78-90-80-80).

Office Equipment Rental – *Bureaux & Machines,* 33 Bd. Vauban (phone: 91-81-78-60).

Pharmacy – *Grande Pharmacie Castellane,* open from 8 AM to 9 PM (11 Pl. Castellane; phone: 91-48-70-20). Open all night is the *Pharmacie de Garde* — the drugstore on duty — the location of which is posted on the window of all pharmacies.

Photocopies – At most photographic stores in the city, as well as most supermarkets. Also at *Service 2A* (at the airport), and at *CMCI* (Rue Henri-Barbusse; phone: 91-08-60-00).

Post Office – The main post office is open Mondays through Fridays from 9 AM to 7 PM, and on Saturdays from 9 AM to noon. 13 Rue Henri-Barbusse (phone: 91-95-40-00).

Secretary/Stenographer (English-Speaking) – *Manpower* (96 Rue de la République; phone: 91-91-09-22) and *RMO* (31 Cours Julien; phone: 91-48-05-74).

Teleconference Facilities – At *CMCI* (Rue Henri-Barbusse; phone: 91-08-60-00).

Telex – At the post office (1 Rue Henri-Barbusse; phone: 91-08-60-11, and at *CMCI* (Rue Henri-Barbusse; phone: 91-08-60-00).

Translators/Interpreters – Contact the Chamber of Commerce (Palais de la Bourse; phone: 91-39-33-33) or the *CMCI* (Rue Henri-Barbusse; phone: 91-08-60-00).

 SPECIAL EVENTS: There's an *International Folklore Festival* in early July at the Château Gombert (Pl. des Héros) as well as a live crèche at *Christmas.* The best events during the rest of the year are the *Santons Fair,* during which the traditional hand-painted clay statuettes fill *Christmas* crèches all over the city (December 26 to February 2); the *Garlic Fair,* when mounds of garlic cover the sidewalks of Cour Belsunce (June 15 to July 15); and the *L'Eté Marseillais* (inaugurated in 1990) which is an extension of the traditional *Islands Festival* (July and August). The fete runs from mid-June to mid-September and includes a wide range of performances — from classical music and dance to jazz and theater — that take place in the city's parks, churches, monuments, and on the islands off the port of Marseilles.

 MUSEUMS: Besides those described in *Special Places,* there are three other notable Marseilles museums:

Musée Cantini – Provençal ceramics and often outstanding contemporary art exhibitions. Open daily from 10 AM to 5 PM in winter, and 11 AM to 7 PM in summer. Admission charge. 19 Rue Grignan (phone: 91-54-77-75).

Musée de la Moto – Opened in 1990, the collection of motorcycles here includes a De Dion Bouton (1898), a Moto Guzzi (1947), a Motosacoche 215cc (1904), and many more. Open daily except Sundays from 8 AM to noon and 1 to 6:30 PM; open from 10 AM to 6 PM on Tuesdays. Admission charge. Traverse St-Paul, Quartier le Merlan (phone: 91-02-29-55).

Musée du Vieux Marseille – A folklore museum set up in a 16th-century house, the Maison Diamantée (Diamond House), so called for the shape of its stone facing and best known for its *santon* collection (see *Shopping*). Open daily from 10 AM to 5 PM in winter and 11 AM to 7 PM in summer. Admission charge. Rue de la Prison (phone: 91-55-10-19).

 SHOPPING: Major department stores, elegant couturier and gift shops, and enough shoe shops to make a centipede happy are clustered in the frenetic area around the Canebière (Rue de Rome, Rue Paradis, and the pedestrian-only Rue St-Ferréol, where some of the trendiest shops are found). The flashy and trendy *Centre Bourse* is a shopping center north of the Canebière. Less expensive shops, usually selling North African items, are in the vicinity of the Porte d'Aix (Arc de Triomphe).

Typical Marseillais souvenirs include clay *santons,* which can be found in tourist shops or at numerous booths set up for the *Christmas Santons Fair* on the Canebière. The word *santon* is derived from the Italian *santibelli,* "the beautiful saints." These small, naively modeled and brightly colored figurines represent both biblical figures and traditional characters of Provence life such as the Gypsy, the shepherd, and the milkmaid.

Les Arcenaux – A bookstore and publishing house that sells new and old editions. It also has a tearoom, a restaurant, and an antiques shop. 25 Cours Estienne d'Orves (phone: 91-54-77-06).

Le Four des Navettes – Try some *navettes* (half bread, half cake loaves, which stay fresh for months) from this remarkable 200-year-old bakery. 136 Rue Sainte (phone: 91-33-32-12).

Galerie Roger Pailhas – An art gallery that promotes the work of international artists, including some of Marseilles's most original ones. 61 Cours Julien (phone: 91-42-18-01).

Hermès – Among the best-known names in elegant and expensive French accessories, including their famous *carré* silk scarves, ties, and handbags. 93 Rue Paradis (phone: 91-53-24-57).

Parenthèses – Jazz bookstore and publisher, it's a storehouse of books on music, the arts, and architecture. 72 Cours Julien (phone: 91-48-74-44).

Soleiado – A bright boutique featuring the gay, Provençal print fabrics of its namesake, as well as skirts, quilted bags and accessories, placemats, and tablecloths. 101-103 Rue Paradis (phone: 91-37-83-16).

Au Tastevin – A slightly cluttered, old-fashioned shop where wines of the nearby

384 MARSEILLES / Sources and Resources

Cassis and Bandol regions can be bought, as well as foie gras, truffles, and a limited selection of Fauchon food products. 8 Rue Edmond-Rostand (phone: 91-37-10-62).

SPORTS AND FITNESS: Professional sports include auto racing, basketball, horse racing, ice hockey, rugby, and soccer. Inquire at the tourist office.

Fishing – Notably for gilt-head and mackerel: off the Corniche, in the *calanques,* the Frioul Islands, and in nearby fishing villages.

Golf – Tee off at *Golf de la Salette,* an 18-hole course less than 5 miles (8 km) from central Marseilles (phone: 91-27-12-16). To get there, take the autoroute east and exit at La Valentine. About 14 miles (22 km) from the city is the *Golf Club Aix-Marseille* (Domaine de Riquetti, Les Milles, Aix-en-Provence; phone: 42-24-20-41).

Horseback Riding – Inquire at the *Centre Equestre de la Ville de Marseille,* 33 Carthage (phone: 91-73-72-94).

Jogging – Take bus No.21 to Domaine de Luminy, about 4 miles (6 km) from the city center. Or try Parc Borély, 3 miles (5 km) south of the city by the Promenade de la Corniche.

Sailing – Contact *Centre Municipal de Voile* (Plage due Roucas-Blanc; phone: 91-76-31-60) or *Centre Nautique Roucas-Blanc* (Plage du Roucas-Blanc; phone: 91-22-72-49).

Swimming – *Piscine Luminy,* Rte. Léon Lachamp (phone: 91-41-26-59).

Tennis and Squash – Try the courts at *Tennis Municipaux* (Allée Ray-Grassi; phone: 91-77-83-89) or *Tennis Didier* (81 *bis* François-Mauriac; phone: 91-26-16-05). Both *Set-Squash Marseille* (265 Av. de Mazargues; phone: 91-71-94-71) and *Prado Squash* (26 *bis* Bd. Michelet; phone: 91-22-83-90) provide facilities for tennis as well as squash.

Water Sports – For information, call or visit the *Fédération des Sociétés Nautiques des Bouches du Rhône,* 10 Av. de la Corse (phone: 91-54-34-88).

THEATER: Theater is booming in Marseilles, with more than 10 new stages opening in the past few years. There's a surprisingly good choice of theater activity year-round. The choices range from the intimate *Centre Culturel* for theater and music (33 Cours Julien; phone: 91-92-02-16) to the *Café-Théâtre du Vieux Panier* (52 Rue Ste-Françoise; phone: 91-91-00-74) and the *Théâtre de Poche* (see above) to the more ambitious national theater, *La Criée* (30 Quai de Rive-Neuve; phone: 91-54-74-54 or 91-54-70-54), where reservations are necessary. An especially interesting program is offered by the *Théâtre du Gyptis* (136 Rue Loubon; phone: 91-08-10-18). The *Théâtre Toursky* (16 Passage du Théâtre; phone: 91-02-58-35) reopened in 1990 and features a wide variety of contemporary and classic performances. The *Théâtre Massalia* (60 Rue Grignan; phone: 91-55-66-06) has been converted into a unique marionette theater featuring performances by marionette companies from all over Europe. For experimental theater, visit *Théâtre de Poche* (see above), *Théâtre de Lenche* (4 Pl. de Lenche; phone: 91-91-55-56 or 91-91-52-22), *Théâtre Chocolat* (59 Cours Julien; phone: 91-42-19-29), and *Espace Julien* (33 Cours Julien; phone: 91-47-09-64). (*Note:* Those who don't speak French will endure no handicap while enjoying operettas or mime performances, which are presented frequently.) In addition, the *Opéra de Marseille* is the home of the *Compagnie Roland Petit,* France's well-known ballet company. For theater information and tickets, visit the office of the *FNAC* at *Centre Bourse,* north of the Canebière.

MUSIC: The Marseillais know good opera and ballet as well as they know bouillabaisse. The sometimes outstanding *Opéra de Marseille* (Pl. de l'Opéra; phone: 91-55-00-70 or 91-55-14-99) and the *Théâtre de Recherche de Marseille* (*TRM;* Espace Massalia, 60 Rue Grignan; phone: 91-55-66-06)

both have devoted followings. Chamber music and organ recitals are frequent at major churches and occasionally outdoors on the Vieux Port. Popular music doesn't fare nearly as well. Concerts are occasionally held at the *Palais des Sports* (phone: 91-75-50-50).

NIGHTCLUBS AND NIGHTLIFE: Marseilles does not suffer from inactivity after dark, with action ranging from the sedate to the frenetic. In the former category, visitors will find soothing piano bars such as *Le Beauvau* in the *Pullman Beauvau* hotel (9 Rue Beauvau; phone: 91-54-91-00), whose barman really knows his trade. The most "in" nightspots include *Bunny's Club* (2 Rue Corneille; phone: 91-54-09-02), with a packed dance floor and an excellent sound system; *Abbaye de la Commanderie* (20 Rue Corneille; phone: 91-33-45-56), a cabaret that draws its neighbor's overflow with a *sympathique* evening of nonstop songs; and *London Club* (73 Corniche Président-J.-F.-Kennedy; phone: 91-52-64-64), a friendly nightclub/disco. At the moment, the young set favors *Le Rock A Billy* (5 Rue Molière; phone: 91-54-70-36). Other current popular nightspots include *L'Ascenseur* (22 Pl. Thiars; phone: 91-33-13-27); *Roll's Club* (76 Corniche Président-J.-F.-Kennedy; phone: 81-52-21-21), *Le Club* (116 Rue du Chantier; phone: 91-33-77-22), *Le Trolley Bus* (Quai de la Rive Neuve; phone: 91-54-30-45), and *La Maison Hantée* (Quai de la Rive Neuve; phone: 91-92-09-40). Unique *Espace Julien* (33 Cours Julien; phone: 91-47-09-64) offers jazz occasionally and an open cabaret where anyone can perform; it's also a learning center for everything from musical instruments to dance to gymnastics.

BEST IN TOWN

CHECKING IN: Marseilles traditionally has had a meager selection of good hotels. With a recent spurt of hotel construction there's now an overabundance of higher priced, ultramodern rooms, but not much improvement in the lower price ranges. Expect to pay $130 and up for a double room (not including breakfast) in a very expensive hotel; $90 to $120 in an expensive one; $60 to $90 for moderate; and under $60 for an inexpensive one.

Le Petit Nice – Small (18 rooms and suites in 2 buildings) and gracious, this member of the Relais & Châteaux group was built in the 19th century as a private villa. There's a shaded garden and a superb two-Michelin-star restaurant (see *Eating Out*), all looking out over the Mediterranean from a magnificent position on the Corniche. The restaurant is closed Mondays, and Tuesdays during the winter; the hotel is closed during January and the first week in February. Business facilities include foreign currency exchange, secretarial services in English, and express checkout. Major credit cards accepted. 160 Corniche Président-J.-F.-Kennedy (phone: 91-59-25-92; fax: 91-59-28-08; telex: 401565). Very expensive.

Concorde Palm Beach – A supermodern spot by the sea, with an outdoor pool and a good restaurant, *La Réserve*. Business facilities include meeting rooms for up to 500, an English-speaking concierge, foreign currency exchange, secretarial services in English, audiovisual equipment, photocopiers, translation services, and express checkout. Major credit cards accepted. 2 Promenade de la Plage (phone: 91-76-20-00; fax: 91-77-37-83; telex: 401894). Expensive.

Mercure – Just a 5-minute walk from the Old Port, the former *Altéa* hotel, has been taken over by the Mercure chain. It distinguishes itself by its taste, pleasant piano bar, and an outstanding restaurant, *L'Oursinade* (see *Eating Out*). Its 200 rooms have all the expected luxury hotel amenities. Business facilities include 24-hour room service, meeting rooms for up to 450, foreign currency exchange, audiovisual equipment, and photocopiers. Major credit cards accepted. Rue Neuve-St-Martin (phone: 91-39-20-00; fax: 91-56-24-57; telex: 401886). Expensive.

Pullman Beauvau – Next to the tourist office and just down the street from the *Opéra,* this is one of Marseilles's best properties. Most of its 72 rooms face the Vieux Port. Business facilities include meeting rooms for up to 30, English-speaking concierge, foreign currency exchange, audiovisual equipment, and photocopiers. Major credit cards accepted. 4 Rue Beauvau (phone: 91-54-91-00; fax: 91-54-15-76; telex: 401778). Expensive.

Sofitel Vieux Port – Magnificent and modern, with a splendid view from its perch above the entrance to the Old Port, near the *Palais du Pharo.* It has some 200 rooms, air conditioning, a heated outdoor pool, a cozy bar, and a fine restaurant, *Les Trois Forts* (see *Eating Out*). Business facilities include 24-hour room service, meeting rooms for up to 150, an English-speaking concierge, audiovisual equipment, photocopiers, translation services, and express checkout. Major credit cards accepted. 36 Bd. Charles-Livon (phone: 91-52-90-19; fax: 91-59-28-08; telex: 401270). Expensive.

Astoria – One of a number of small, old, Marseilles hostelries that have been renovated, this turn-of-the-century relic now has a bright, skylit lobby filled with plants, and contemporary furnishings in the guestrooms. Major credit cards accepted. 10 Bd. Garibaldi (phone: 91-33-33-50; fax: 91-54-80-75; telex: 402175). Moderate.

Bompard – In a quiet park on a hill not far from the sea, only a 5-minute drive (on the coastal road) from the bustle of the Vieux Port. Some of its 40-plus rooms — in the main building or surrounding bungalows — have kitchenettes. No restaurant. Business facilities include 24-hour room service, meeting rooms for up to 40, an English-speaking concierge, foreign currency exchange, audiovisual equipment, photocopiers, and express checkout. Major credit cards accepted. 2 Rue des Flots-Bleus (phone: 91-52-10-93; fax: 91-31-02-14). Moderate.

St-Ferréol – Located just off the main pedestrian shopping street near the Canebière and the Old Port. This renovated 19-room hotel is stylish and comfortable with extras such as a Jacuzzi in some rooms, marble baths, elegant fabrics, and a cozy little bar for breakfast and drinks. An excellent value. Major credit cards accepted. 19 Rue Pisançon (phone: 91-33-12-21; fax: 91-54-29-97). Moderate.

Hermès – Renovated with a neo-Greek theme, the main attractions of this 30-room hostelry are its location just off the quai, its reasonable prices, and its fifth-floor rooms with terraces that overlook the Old Port. Major credit cards accepted. 2 Rue Bonneterie (phone: 91-90-34-51; fax: 91-91-14-44). Moderate to inexpensive.

Alizé – This renovated 35-room portside hotel with a yellow stone façade is a welcome addition to the lower-price hostelries. Ask for a room with a view of the Old Port. Major credit cards accepted. 7 Quai des Belges (phone: 91-33-66-97; fax: 91-54-80-06). Inexpensive.

Capitainerie des Galères – Formerly the *Urbis,* this modern hotel has 148 rooms, a restaurant, a bar, and conference facilities. Close to the Vieux Port and 1 block above the Cours d'Estienne d'Orves. Business facilities include meeting rooms for up to 60, foreign currency exchange, audiovisual equipment, and photocopiers. Major credit cards accepted. 46 Rue Sainte (phone: 91-54-73-73; fax: 91-54-77-77). Inexpensive.

Grand Hôtel de Genève – Old, but now modernized, it is in a quiet pedestrian precinct just behind the Old Port. No restaurant. Major credit cards accepted. 3 *bis* Rue Reine-Elizabeth (phone: 91-90-51-42; fax: 91-90-76-24). Inexpensive.

EATING OUT: What it has traditionally lacked in hotels, Marseilles always has made up for in restaurants; they are among France's finest, and that is saying a lot. Besides classic French cuisine, be sure to try Provençal (from Provence — the southern region of France that straddles the Rhône River) specialties. The city virtually is synonymous with bouillabaisse, a dish not to be missed. In its classical form, this soup is based on Mediterranean rockfish (called *rouget*), but other fish and shellfish usually are added, particularly lobster and crab. The seasoning (cayenne, garlic, tomatoes, herbs) is very special, but the star ingredient is saffron, which gives bouillabaisse its golden color. It often is served with rouille, a relish made of red pepper, garlic, and fish broth, as well as with aioli, a delicious olive-oil-based garlic mayonnaise. Another dish common on menus in Marseilles is bourride, a fish stew that some prefer to bouillabaisse.

Other regional specialties include *anchoïade,* anchovies and olive oil mashed into a paste that accompanies raw vegetables; *poutargue,* fish eggs grated in oil, then pressed and dried to become a sort of white caviar; *navettes,* flat biscuits flavored with orange-flower water; and *fougasses,* flat, salty breads in leaf designs, flavored with walnuts, olives, bacon, or cheese.

You also may wish to sample *pastis,* the anise-flavored aperitif that tastes something like licorice. Usually colorless, *pastis* is served diluted with ice water, which turns it cloudy white. Also try wines from Provence, particularly the dry, pleasant rosé.

Expect to pay $80 and considerably higher in the expensive category (for two without wine); from $50 to $80 in the moderate range; and under $50 in the inexpensive category. Prices include a service charge.

Le Petit Nice – A two-star Michelin establishment that deserves a third rosette. Our favorite dining spot in Marseilles; the view alone is worth the price of admission. The tomato tart appetizer is the most beautiful single menu item we've ever had on our *plats,* and the lobster ragout is equally impressive. Closed Mondays, and Tuesdays during the winter. Reservations necessary. Major credit cards accepted. 160 Corniche Président-J.-F.-Kennedy (phone: 91-59-25-92). Very expensive.

Calypso – This outstanding dining room offers a classic sea view and, some still swear, Marseilles's best bouillabaisse — although it lost its Michelin star in 1991). No meat or vegetables here, just impeccably served seafood. But the quality and quantity leave nothing to be desired. Its twin and peer — *Michel* — is across the street. Open daily. Reservations necessary. Major credit cards accepted. 3 Rue des Catalans (phone: 91-52-64-00).

Chaudron Provençal – Copper cauldrons hang from wide ceiling beams in this rustic little fish restaurant located in the Panier district. Diners choose from the day's fresh fish displayed in baskets next to the tiny open kitchen; you pay by weight. The quality is high, with prices to match. Closed Saturday lunch and Sundays. Reservations advised. Major credit cards accepted. 48 Rue Caisserie (phone: 91-91-02-37). Expensive.

Chez Brun (Aux Mets de Provence) – At this venerable family-run place, you'll eat in the *ancienne* style. Up to 20 dishes of the true Provençal cuisine, which means fish and olive-spiced specialties. Closed Sundays, Mondays, and holidays. Reservations necessary. Major credit cards accepted. 18 Quai du Rive-Neuve, on the 2nd Floor; the entrance is hard to find, so watch closely (phone: 91-33-35-38). Expensive.

Chez Fonfon – In an old fishing club, it's heavy on local color and boat scenes, real bouillabaisse, and other fish dishes. Closed Saturdays, Sundays, and 2 weeks at *Christmastime.* Reservations unnecessary. Major credit cards accepted. 140 Vallen des Auffes (phone: 91-52-14-38). Expensive.

Michel (Les Catalans) – Across the street from the *Calypso.* The menu is short and the seafood is succulent, even though its Michelin star was taken away in 1991. Don't miss the bouillabaisse. Closed Tuesdays and Wednesdays. Reservations unnecessary. Major credit cards accepted. 6 Rue des Catalans (phone: 91-52-30-63). Expensive.

Miramar – Touted by locals as one of the best sources on the quai of the Old Port for authentic bouillabaisse, this modern dining place also serves a wide variety of other fish dishes and regional specialties. Closed Sundays, Saturday lunch, and during August. Reservations unnecessary. Major credit cards accepted. 12 Quai du Port (phone: 91-91-10-40). Expensive.

New York – For seafood again, try this restaurant in the old harbor area. Especially good are the fish terrine and the bourride. The owner fell in love with New York when he was a sailor — thus the name. Open daily. Reservations unnecessary. Major credit cards accepted. 7 Quai des Belges (phone: 91-33-60-98 or 91-33-91-79). Expensive to moderate.

L'Oursinade – In the *Mercure* hotel, this place serves very fine Provençal dishes in an atmosphere of understated elegance. Closed Sundays and late July through August. Reservations unnecessary. Major credit cards accepted. Rue Neuve-St-Martin (phone: 91-39-20-00). Expensive to moderate.

Les Trois Forts – You'll find a panoramic view of the Old Port here, and such inventive dishes as lamb's liver braised with melon and honey. Open daily. Reservations unnecessary. Major credit cards accepted. *Sofitel Vieux Port*, 36 Bd. Charles-Livon (phone: 91-52-90-19). Expensive to moderate.

L'Avant-Scène – The food here runs to fairly light French, and the place actually is a café/art gallery/theater/magazine shop all rolled into one. The theater is downstairs, and there's a fashion designer's atelier upstairs. Open Tuesdays through Saturdays from 8 PM to 2 AM. Reservations unnecessary. Major credit cards accepted. 59 Cours Julien (phone: 91-42-19-29). Moderate.

Chez Caruso – Where the locals go when they crave some delicious Italian food. Closed Sunday nights, Mondays, and from mid-October through mid-November. Reservations unnecessary. Major credit cards accepted. 158 Quai du Port (phone: 91-90-94-04). Moderate.

Cousin, Cousine – Interesting nouvelle cuisine is served here, along with good local wines. Try the hot oysters with broccoli and pheasant in wine sauce. Closed Sundays and Mondays. Reservations unnecessary. Major credit cards accepted. 102 Cours Julien (phone: 91-48-14-50). Moderate.

Au Pescadou – On entering, you'll be dazzled immediately by the spectacular array of fresh oysters, clams, mussels, and other seafood delicacies. With ingredients like these, only the simplest preparation is needed. Closed Sunday nights and July and August. Reservations advised. Major credit cards accepted. 19 Pl. Castellane (phone: 91-78-36-01). Moderate.

Les Platanes (Restaurant des Abattoirs) – By the slaughterhouse, at the city's northern extreme, this immense old café is where the butchers themselves eat. Choose from beef, pork, veal, and a great selection of sausages. Closed Saturdays and Sundays. Reservations advised. Major credit cards accepted. 7 Av. Journet (phone: 91-60-93-17). Moderate.

Texas Fiesta – Run by a Frenchman who used to live in Houston, this lively spot serves up Tex-Mex food, margaritas, American beer, and, on Tuesday nights, country music. Open daily. Reservations unnecessary. Major credit cards accepted. 70 Cours Julien (phone: 91-48-49-24). Moderate.

Aux Baguettes d'Or – Located just behind the *Opéra*, it offers authentic Vietnamese food and friendly service, and sometimes is frequented by singers after performances. Closed Sundays. Reservations advised. Major credit cards accepted. 65 Rue Francis-Davso (phone: 91-54-20-39). Moderate to inexpensive.

Dimitri – Hungarian and Russian specialties are the order of the day. Closed Sundays and Mondays. Reservations advised. Major credit cards accepted. 6 Rue Meolan (phone: 91-54-09-68). Inexpensive.

La Kahenas – This Tunisian eatery offers daily specials, mint tea, pastries, and is crowded at lunch. Closed Sundays. No reservations. No credit cards accepted. 2 Rue de la République (phone: 91-90-61-93). Inexpensive.

Tarte Julie – Every pie imaginable, sweet or salty, is here, along with pizza and salads. Closed Sundays. No reservations. Major credit cards accepted. 14 Av. du Prado (phone: 91-37-23-45). Inexpensive.

 BARS AND CAFÉS: At 5 PM the old Marseillais (barely a woman in sight) gather for *pastis* and tall tales at *Au Vieux Panier,* a café just outside Marseilles (52 Rue Ste-Françoise). Facing the Vieux Port is *Le Petit Pernod* (30 Rue des Trois Mages) where the bourgeoise congregate. *Le Bistrot Thiars* (38A Pl. Thiars) is an artists' haunt that becomes even more popular in the summer, when it attracts tourists and theater people to its alfresco dining. The barman really knows his stuff at *Le Beauvau* (9 Rue Beauvau).

MONACO
(and Monte Carlo)

The independent principality of Monaco is one of the smallest states in Europe, but because of its wealth and glamor, it is also one of the most famous. Visually, it is a mixture of old and new, with sleek modern buildings next to the pastel stucco and blue tile of traditional 19th-century French Mediterranean architecture and the extravagant silhouettes of the Belle Epoque. Everywhere the emphasis is on sumptuous elegance. Yachts of the rich and famous fill the port; the shops display vintage wine, rare jade and ivory, costly jewels, couturier clothes and furs. Tourists, dazzled by the spectacle, may sometimes forget that Monaco is more than just a stage for conspicuous consumption and that with its rare climate, its turbulent history, and the diversity of activities that take place within its borders, it has other resources besides manmade, tangible riches.

The location of this picturesque country, in something of a natural amphitheater between the Mediterranean and the foothills of the French Maritime Alps, gives it a climate much like that of Southern California. Winters are mild (in January and February, the average low temperature is 46F and the average high is 55); summers are warm (July and August have an average low of 72F and an average high of 79); and there is little rain. The vegetation, too, is like Southern California's, with orange and lemon trees, palms, and live oaks. The water temperature is ideal for swimming. In fact, the only shortfall in this natural endowment was an adequate supply of beach. Monaco's most exclusive stretch of beach is actually just over the border, in France, and its own beach is all manmade. The principality is divided into two parts: Monaco is its proper overall name and also designates the older neighborhood where the palace and the *Oceanographic Museum* are located; Monte Carlo is the center of tourism, with the classiest hotels, ritziest clubs, trendiest boutiques, restaurants, and casinos, which perpetuate the reputation of this unique enclave.

What Monaco had from the very beginning was a natural harbor next to a high, rocky promontory jutting into the sea — a natural fortress. The rock itself first was colonized in the 6th century BC by the Monoikos Ligurian tribe (the probable origin of the name Monaco). Later, it was inhabited by Romans, and Julius Caesar allegedly sailed from the port to do battle in Greece.

At the end of the 12th century, this strategic configuration belonged to the Genoese, who, in 1215, sent men and material to begin the process of fortifying the Rocher, or the Rock of Monaco, as it is called. In the 13th century, the Republic of Genoa (along with the rest of Italy) was torn by strife between the Guelphs and the Ghibellines, opposing political parties favoring the pope and the emperor respectively. When the Ghibellines came to power in Genoa in 1295, they threw out the Guelphs, including the noble Ligurian Grimaldi family and one Francesco Grimaldi, immortalized as Malizia (the Cunning One). Not intending to suffer insult for very long, Malizia, disguised as a monk and accompanied by a band of partisans, went to the Rock one night early in 1297 to ask for shelter. The guard agreed, opened the gates, and Malizia and his companions stormed the fortress and took it.

The two monks brandishing swords on the Grimaldi coat of arms commemorate this event. They can be seen above the main door of the palace that evolved from the fortress on the Rock and in which the Grimaldi rulers of Monaco still live, though the ensuing centuries were not without incident. For more than 100 years, the family fought Genoa to maintain — or regain — control of its conquest, and once the matter with Genoa was settled, the tiny state still had to contend with other foreign influences. In 1419, Jean Grimaldi officially founded the state, incorporating Menton and Roquebrune into Monaco. From 1524 to 1641, it was a protectorate of Spain; from 1641 to 1793, a protectorate of France. Came the French Revolution, and in 1793 it was annexed to France as part of the Alpes-Maritimes *département,* under the name Port Hercules — because the legendary Greek figure allegedly stopped here on his way to the Strait of Gibraltar. The Treaty of Paris (1814) restored it to sovereignty, but from 1815 to 1861 it was again a protectorate, this time of the kingdom of Sardinia. The period was not a prosperous one for Monaco, given the economic deprivation of the revolutionary years and the constant threat of annexation by Sardinia. When the cities of Menton and Roquebrune, which separate the principality from the Italian border and which had been part of it for centuries, declared themselves free cities in 1848, Monaco was virtually beginning to come apart.

The turning point came with Prince Charles III, who ruled from 1856 to 1889. In 1861, he negotiated a treaty with France establishing Monégasque sovereignty without any doubt and without any protectors and then underscored that sovereignty by minting gold coins and issuing postage stamps. Because the loss of Menton and Roquebrune had reduced the revenues as well as the size of the principality, he took up his father's idea of opening a gambling casino to replenish the treasury. The Société des Bains de Mer (Sea Bathing Society), which was to run the enterprise and organize resort facilities, was formed, and a gaming house of sorts began to operate, but it wasn't until the prince put François Blanc — the "wizard" who had run the casino at Bad Homburg — in charge of the project that Monaco was on its way to solvency. In 1864 a luxury hotel, the *Hôtel de Paris,* opened on the Spélugues plateau across the harbor from the Rocher, and in 1865 the casino next door began to function. Through Blanc's efforts — he even hired boats and carriages to bring well-heeled tourists to Monaco from up and down the coast — the casino became so fashionable and successful that by 1869 the prince was able to abolish direct taxes for his citizens. Monte Carlo, or Mount Charles, as the development on the plateau was renamed in the prince's honor, had been born.

Charles's son, Prince Albert I (on the throne from 1889 to 1922), was another Grimaldi who proved critical in the development of the principality.

Known as "the scholar prince" because of his passionate interest in oceanography, he was anything but a dilettante in his field. He undertook numerous scientific expeditions to study the seas and built the prestigious *Oceanographic Museum* to house the results and promote further research (he also founded the Oceanographic Institute in Paris in 1906). In addition, Monaco is indebted to him for the Exotic Garden and the *Museum of Prehistoric Anthropology*, for the construction of the port, for the establishment of numerous schools and a hospital, for its first constitution, and for the automobile rally.

Prince Rainier III, the present ruler (and great-grandson of Albert I), came to the throne in 1949 and has changed the face of Monaco no less than his ancestors. His marriage to the late American actress Grace Kelly in 1956 turned the international spotlight on the principality as never before, making it a household word that was all but synonymous with fairy-tale romance. The great charm and beauty of Princess Grace (who died in an automobile accident in 1982), and the caliber of the international clientele she attracted to the social and cultural events of her new home, in no small way complemented the prince's efforts to bring about a major overhaul of the principality in the postwar period, especially of its tourist industry. (In 1990, fate again struck Monaco when the husband of Princess Caroline — daughter of Prince Rainier and Princess Grace — died in a boating accident.) Modern high-rise apartment buildings (which block the sunshine in some streets), roads and tunnels, underground parking lots, public elevators, a new port, new hotels, new parks, and new beaches have all been built and, indeed, some of the development has taken place on land that itself was built up, or reclaimed, from the sea (77 acres), enlarging Monaco's area to a total of 482 acres. Monaco also is becoming something of a banking center (there are no taxes), and after work, many an international deal is made at one of the city's luxury spots. Unfortunately for its banking business, money-laundering operations have infiltrated Monaco and the financial authorities are trying very hard to weed out the less-than-legal deals from the legitimate ones.

The modern *Monte Carlo Convention Center and Auditorium,* built in 1974, is part of an ongoing effort to attract the business traveler and the convention trade, while the gaming tables, nightclubs, fashionable galas, and arts and sporting events that traditionally have drawn visitors — gamblers, jet setters, the international *beau monde* — to this most chic of Riviera resorts continue to do so. The Société des Bains de Mer, the company with which François Blanc created the Monte Carlo scene and in which the principality today has a controlling interest, continues to be responsible for most of the luxurious resort installations and much of the resort activity. At latest count, SBM owned four of the most deluxe hotels, 18 restaurants, the *Monte Carlo Country Club,* the *Monte Carlo Golf Club,* the *Monte Carlo Sporting Club,* the *Monte Carlo Casino,* and more.

The Monégasques enjoy a limited democracy. Since 1962, the principality has been administered by a national council, while the Monte Carlo City Hall is ruled by a community council whose members are elected every 4 years. Although Monaco is a sovereign state, with its own postage stamps (favorites with collectors) and license plates, it exhibits a few peculiarities. It has had a customs union with France since 1865 and thus there are no formalities crossing the border — you may not even realize when you've done it. And French money is the medium of exchange, though Monégasque coins bearing Prince Rainier's likeness are circulated and are fully convertible in France. The principality's security is assured by French *gendarmes* and colorful local police. French, too, is the primary language spoken, though Italian also is common and English is spoken in hotels, restaurants, and at the casinos. Less frequently will you hear the singular Monégasque dialect, a mixture of Italian and Niçois, though it is officially encouraged and is taught in the schools. Finally, the majority of Monaco's population of 28,000 are foreign residents, largely of French (12,700), but also of Italian, Swiss, British, and American origin. Only approximately 4,500 are Monégasques — that is, citizens of Monaco. Citizenship is not easy to come by, is expensive, and is not necessarily granted even to those born here. Those who have it are excluded from the gaming tables, but in return do no military service and pay no income tax, privileges somehow fitting for the nationals of a country just about the right size for the pages of a storybook.

MONACO AT-A-GLANCE

SEEING THE CITY: Because the "old" city of Monaco is built on top of a promontory of rock and everywhere else the principality climbs from the coast toward the rocky mountain peaks behind it, panoramic places are not in short supply. The Place du Palais in Old Monaco is one. It offers a breathtaking view of the harbor and Monte Carlo, a view that should be seen again at night when the lights of this tiny enclave glitter against the mountainous backdrop. The Exotic Garden, set even higher on a steep slope behind the Rock, is another. From here (a sign points the way to the lookout point), the view takes in the whole of the principality and beyond to the Italian coast, including a grand expanse of blue Mediterranean. Some of the most spectacular views of Monaco are found about 1 mile (1.6 km) from the city, on the Cannes–Nice highway.

SPECIAL PLACES: Monaco's 468 acres are divided into four parts: Monaco-Ville, containing Old Monaco on top of the Rock; Monte Carlo, the "new" city with the casino, most of the hotels, shops, and beaches; La Condamine, the more commercial harbor area between Monaco-Ville and Monte Carlo (you'll often hear La Condamine referred to simply as Monaco); and Fontvieille, 20 acres of reclaimed land on the west side of the Rock, now developed into commercial, residential, and industrial areas. Most of what visitors want to see is in Monaco-Ville and Monte Carlo, two districts in marked contrast to each other. One is a traffic-free maze of narrow cobblestone streets and 3-story, tile-roofed houses tightly contained within a girdle of fortifications. The other is a seaside sprawl of modern luxury high-rises, broad avenues, and highways, with the respite of palm trees and gardens and several particularly opulent examples of the architecture of the last century.

OLD MONACO (LE ROCHER)

Palais Princier (Prince's Palace) – The first foundation stone of the manmade fortress on top of the natural fortress of the Rock was laid in 1215, and for a few hundred years thereafter the structure remained largely defensive. Its transformation into something more fit for habitation by a prince is largely the work of two of the 17th-century Grimaldis, Prince Honoré II and Prince Louis I. What they and their successors accomplished was then almost destroyed by the French Revolution, when the palace was looted and used for a time as a military hospital, its treasures dispersed. Nineteenth-century restoration, continued modification, and the return of much lost furniture and artwork brings us the palace of today. With its crenelated tower sporting a rather anachronistic clock and its cannons (a gift of Louis XIV) complete with neat piles of cannonballs, it looks like a castle from an operetta set, perfect for a miniature monarchy. The changing of the guard at the candy-striped sentry boxes takes place each day precisely at 11:55 AM (go early for a good view). From July through September, you also can go inside the palace. You'll see the Cour d'Honneur surrounded by mainly 17th-century frescoes, the sumptuously decorated State Apartments, and the Throne Room. Guided tours last about 35 minutes. Open daily from June to October; admission charge. Pl. du Palais (phone: 93-25-18-31).

Musée du Palais Princier – This museum in the south wing of the palace also is called the *Napoleonic Museum*. It houses souvenirs of Napoleon and his family — such as his field glasses, watch, and decorations — gathered by Prince Louis II, the grandfather of Prince Rainier. Documents relating to the history of the principality also are on display, along with a collection of rare 19th-century Monégasque postage stamps, a series of coins minted by the princes since 1640, and uniforms of the prince's guards. Closed lunchtime and Mondays, and from October 23 to December 5; admission charge. Palais Princier (phone: 93-25-18-31).

Jardins St-Martin – The old fortifications surrounding the Rock have been turned into garden walks, a peaceful place to stroll amid Mediterranean flowers and shady trees. The gardens run roughly from the palace around to the point of the Rock at Fort Antoine.

Cathédrale – Near the St. Martin Gardens, Monaco's cathedral is an 1875 edifice built on the site of a 13th-century church (St. Nicholas), which was demolished to make way for the new one. The white stone exterior is Romanesque in style; the interior, which contains two 16th-century altarpieces by Louis Bréa preserved from the original church, shows a Byzantine influence. The burial chapel is in the west part of the transept and the tombs of the Princes of Monaco — among whom Princess Grace was laid to rest — are in the crypt. Av. St-Martin at Rue de l'Eglise (phone: 93-30-88-13).

Musée Océanographique et Aquarium – Not only a museum, but a working scientific research institute, this was the brainchild of "the scholar prince," Albert I. Prince Albert wanted a museum to promote the science of oceanography and to house the results of his expeditions around the world, and this building on the Rock, at the edge of a sheer drop, was a bold construction for its day. Pillars had to be built from sea level to support it, and the rocks below had to be hollowed out to let in sea water for the aquarium. Though the work began in 1899, the inauguration did not take place until 1910.

Start your visit on the lowest level, with the aquarium. It's one of the finest in the world — not surprising when you learn that the director of the museum is Jacques-Yves Cousteau. His films are shown in the conference hall. On the ground floor are zoological exhibits, skeletons of large marine mammals, and specimens that Prince Albert brought back from his travels. The top floor is perhaps the most interesting, with the prince's whaleboat, 19th-century brass navigational instruments, and, in complete contrast, ultramodern diving equipment. Open daily 9:30 AM to 7 PM; admission charge. Av. St-Martin (phone: 93-15-36-00).

MONTE CARLO

Casino de Monte Carlo – Even if you're not a gambler, this landmark is a must, but don't dress too casually or you won't get in. The original casino of 1865 quickly became too small, and in 1878 Charles Garnier, the architect of the Paris *Opéra,* was commissioned to design the casino seen today. Stop for a moment in front to appreciate the drama of the setting, the immaculate gardens with sculpture exhibitions, the coming and going of glamorous patrons in elegant limousines and sports cars, and the building itself, with its copper roof enhanced by a green patina. Then enter the Atrium, a grand foyer lined with brown marble columns supporting an elaborate second-story gallery and a stained glass ceiling. To the left are the gaming rooms, beginning with the American Room, a rococo splendor in gold with gambling by American rules and some 140 incongruous slot machines; the adjoining Pink Salon, now a bar but previously used as a smoking room (witness the cigar-puffing nudes painted overhead); and the red-carpeted and -curtained White Salon, also with American games. Next come the European gaming rooms: the Touzet Rooms, swathed in paintings; the large and regal Salon Privé (Private Room), reserved for high rollers; and, finally, a Salon Super-Privé, which caters to visiting royalty, celebrities, and the super-rich, and is open by appointment only.

To the right of the Atrium, past glass cases holding memorabilia and costumes from famous performances, is the obscure entrance to the *Salle Garnier,* Monte Carlo's opera house. In 6 months, Garnier transformed what was once a small concert room into a jewel of a theater lavish with gold-leaf medallions, garlands, and scrolls, allegorical statues, a Romantic painted ceiling, and an 18-ton gilt bronze chandelier. Sarah Bernhardt starred on opening night in 1879 and the acts that followed were no less illustrious: Diaghilev created the *Ballets Russes de Monte Carlo* on this stage, Nijinsky danced here, and Caruso, Lily Pons, and other legends have sung here.

The casino is open daily (except May 1); the American Room and Touzet Rooms at 10 AM, other rooms later. You can go as far as the American Room and White Salon without restriction, though you may be asked to show a passport to prove you're over 21. A passport and an admission charge are required for the European gaming rooms. The *Salle Garnier* can be seen only by attending a performance. Pl. du Casino (phone: 93-50-69-31; for the opera house, 93-50-76-54).

Musée National – This is billed as perhaps the most complete collection of dolls and "automata" (mechanical dolls) in the world, objects that may seem unusual for a national museum unless the size of the nation and its penchant for play are taken into account. The 2,000-plus objects here, mostly from the 18th and 19th centuries and donated to the principality by the descendants of Mme. de Galéa, their collector, include not only the 400 exquisitely dressed dolls but also the delicately crafted miniature furniture and accessories that surround them in their elegantly composed settings; e.g., a quaint attic full of old treasures, a tearoom, and a wedding hall. The centerpiece of the collection is a remarkable 18th-century Neapolitan crèche. All of this is housed in another Garnier design, the beautiful Villa Sauber, the grounds of which are rampant with roses and scattered with sculptures by Rodin, Maillol, and others. Open daily, mornings and afternoons (except holidays and during the *Grand Prix*), but be sure to go between 3:30 and 5:30 PM, when the automata come to life. Admission charge. 17 Av. Princesse-Grace (phone: 93-30-91-26).

ELSEWHERE

Jardin Exotique – Another of the projects of Prince Albert I, this is a cactus garden, but no ordinary cactus garden. It clings to the side of a rocky cliff at the western approach to Monaco, more than 300 feet above the sea, and at one time was called "the suspended garden." The inclination of the cliff provides protection from northern winds and maximum exposure to the winter sun, and thus the 7,000 species of cacti and succulents, weird and wonderful examples from semi-arid climes around the world (particularly from Africa and Latin America), thrive as well here as they would in their native habitats. Equally impressive is the view from the garden, a sweeping one that embraces the whole of the principality.

Within the garden, actually at the base of the cliff, are the Grottes de l'Observatoire (Observatory Caves). Although today you're most likely to notice the stalagmites and stalactites, at one time the caves housed prehistoric man, whose bones have been found as a record of his stay. You can take a guided tour of the caves, but note that the climb up and down totals 558 steps. Open daily; a single admission charge covers the garden, caves, and the nearby *Museum of Prehistoric Anthropology,* Bd. du Jardin-Exotique (phone: 93-30-33-65).

Musée d'Anthropologie Préhistorique – This museum safeguards what archaeologists have found on the site and elsewhere in the principality and its environs. Fossils of animals now extinct, primitive tools, the remains of Cro-Magnon man, skeletons and fauna from 5000 to 500 BC, with some Roman jewelry, and other relics discovered during excavations at the harbor in 1879 are on display. Open May to September. The admission charge includes the Jardin Exotique and Observatory Caves (see above). Bd. du Jardin-Exotique (phone: 93-30-33-65).

Centre d'Acclimatation Zoologique – A tiny zoo at the foot of the Rock that has various monkeys and apes, lions and other large cats, wild birds, an elephant, and many specimens of tropical (mainly African) fauna. It opened in 1955, a creation of Prince Rainier. Open daily; admission charge. Pl. du Canton (phone: 93-25-18-31).

■**EXTRA SPECIAL:** The south of France is noted for its colorful produce markets, and Monaco is no exception. To take the measure of one and meet some real Monégasques, go to Place d'Armes, a small square not far from the port, at the base of the Rock, in the Condamine district. Under the arches of the square stands a beautiful open-air market selling fruits and vegetables, flowers, pasta, bread, fresh fish, and more. You might have a bite to eat while savoring all this Mediterranean abundance. A typical snack consists of a glass of red wine with hot *socca* (a thin pancake made with chick-pea flour) or a slice of *pissaladière* (a type of thick pizza with onions, a specialty of Nice). In addition to Monaco's market, there's the one at the totally renovated *Beausoleil,* open mornings only; it's just above Monte Carlo's Eglise St-Charles, on Rue du Marché. There are both indoor and outdoor markets and many specialty food shops in the surrounding streets.

SOURCES AND RESOURCES

TOURIST INFORMATION: Monaco's Direction du Tourisme et des Congrès, or tourist and convention bureau, is in Monte Carlo (2a Bd. des Moulins, just above the gardens of the casino; phone: 93-50-60-88; for weekly programs in English, 93-30-87-01). It is open daily (half days on Sunday) to provide maps, detailed brochures on the principality's sights, restaurants, and hotels, and, if necessary, to make hotel reservations. The free monthly brochure *Bienvenue à Monte Carlo* lists events and much other pertinent information in four languages: English, French, German, and Italian.

Local Coverage – The daily French newspaper *Nice Matin* covers the southeast of France, including Monaco. *La Gazette,* an attractive bimonthly newsmagazine that covers Monaco, the Riviera, and Europe, is more society-oriented (the magazine is printed in Monaco, in French and English), as is the slick *Riviera,* which is available in English. French and other international newspapers and magazines can be found at the *Café de Paris* (on Pl. du Casino) or at the *Loews Monte Carlo* hotel (on Av.

Spélugues). The bookstore *Scruples* (9 Rue Princesse-Caroline; phone: 93-50-43-52) sells English-language books, maps, travel guides, and posters.

TELEPHONE: The city code for Monaco is 93, which is incorporated into all local 8-digit numbers. When calling a number in Monaco from the Paris region (including the Ile-de-France), dial 16, wait for a dial tone, then dial the 8-digit number. When calling a number from outside Paris, dial only the 8-digit number. When calling from the US, dial 33 (which is the country code), followed by the 8-digit number.

GETTING AROUND: Monaco is one of the few countries visitors can see from border to border by foot (though strictly speaking there is no border and you can suddenly find yourself in France by just crossing the street). Transportation is simple and well organized, but driving is often tricky because the streets are narrow and steep.

Bus – Of the four main bus lines, two depart from Place de la Visitation in Monaco-Ville (which is now closed to all traffic except local buses, taxis, and cars with Monégasque plates) and go as far as the casino, and two depart from the station at Avenue Prince-Pierre. Route 1 goes to the east border (Monte Carlo, the *National Museum,* the beaches, the *Monte Carlo Country Club*); Route 2 goes to the west border (the Exotic Garden); Route 4 goes east to the Larvotto beaches; and Route 5 does a sort of figure eight, one loop encompassing Fontvieille, the other the Princess Grace Hospital Center. (A fifth route, No. 3, is in operation at *Easter* and during the summer season only.) There are frequent stops; buses run every 11 minutes during the week; every 20 minutes on Sundays and holidays. A bus service also runs to and from Nice airport. For more information, contact the tourist office.

Car Rental – Given Monaco's modest size, a car is hardly a necessity, but if you intend to roam the surrounding region, rentals are available, with or without chauffeur, from a number of agencies. *Avis* (9 Av. d'Ostende; phone: 93-30-17-53), *Europcar* (47 Av. de Grande-Bretagne; phone: 93-50-74-95), and *Hertz* (27 Bd. Albert-Ier; phone: 93-50-79-60) are all represented, and the tourist office has a list of local firms.

Elevator – Public underground elevators have been installed to facilitate pedestrian traffic between the various sections of the principality and to eliminate some hill-climbing. They connect the Exotic Garden to the port (near the Pl. Ste-Dévote end of Bd. Albert-Ier) and the center of Monte Carlo (Pl. des Moulins) to Av. Princesse-Grace and the Larvotto beach area.

Helicopter – *Héli-Air Monaco* (Héliport de Fontvieille; phone: 93-05-00-50; fax: 93-30-37-89) offers an aerial tour of the principality as well as 6-minute transfers to and from Nice–Côte d'Azur International Airport, 14 miles/22 km away (about $50 one-way). It also links Monaco to Italy. Reservations are necessary.

Taxi – Phone for a cab or walk to the nearest cab stand. The three major stands are at the train station, at the casino end of Avenue des Beaux-Arts (phone: 93-50-56-28), and on Avenue Princesse-Grace (phone: 93-50-47-26). Also try *Radio Taxi* (phone: 93-15-01-01). Taxis are expensive but worth it, since the fleets are composed mainly of comfortable Mercedes-Benzes, BMWs, and Peugeots.

Train – The Gare de Monaco–Monte Carlo, on Avenue Prince-Pierre in the Condamine district, is a regular stop for French trains running along the Riviera, and several international trains stop here, too. In summer, the *Métrazur,* a special *SNCF* service shuttling along the Côte d'Azur between Menton and Cannes, stops here every half hour. For train information, call 93-87-50-50 or 93-25-54-54; from Nice Airport call 93-21-34-62. For reservations, call 93-30-74-00. Currency exchange at the station is from from 8 AM to noon and 2 to 5 PM (phone: 93-30-74-00).

SPECIAL EVENTS: In January, specially made cars are in abundance for the *Monte Carlo Rallye,* a particularly prestigious motor rally because it's been on the calendar since 1911, almost as long as cars have been in existence. The *Festival of Ste-Dévote,* on January 26 and 27, is a public holiday honoring the patron saint of the principality and its ruling family. February heralds the *International Circus Festival* and *International Festival of Television,* and March, the *Rose Ball.* The *International Tennis Championships* at the *Monte Carlo Country Club* are the highlight of April along with the *International Dog Show,* and May brings an event that's been run almost uninterruptedly since 1929: Monaco's *Grand Prix,* when the best drivers in the world take state-of-the-art Formula 1 cars onto the Belle Epoque streets to compete on one of the most hazardous circuits in motor racing. In July, the *Open Golf Tournament* takes place. In July and August, the *Festival International de Feux d'Artifice de Monte Carlo* (International Fireworks Festival) gives specialists of various nations a chance to fill the skies over the port of Monaco with color and excitement; a different country presents each of the several nights of pyrotechnics. November 19 is the *Fête Nationale* (National Day), an excuse for a small parade in Old Monaco, fireworks, and other merriment. In February, the Big Top is set up on the Fontvieille Esplanade and the *International Circus Festival* — 5 nights of competition to choose the best acts from the world's circuses — gets under way. Finally, though high-caliber musical performances, including an occasional opera, can be seen throughout the year, they are concentrated during the 3 weeks at *Easter* known as the *Printemps des Arts de Monte Carlo.*

 MUSEUMS: Monaco's major museums are described in *Special Places.* Other museums or exhibitions open to the public include the following:

Musée des Cires (Wax Museum) – This small museum, on one of Monaco's most picturesque streets, re-creates the history of the principality and of the Grimaldi dynasty in 24 life-size scenes. Open daily. Admission charge. 27 Rue Basse (phone: 93-30-39-05).

Porcelaines d'Art de Monaco et Monte Carlo – Locally hand-crafted porcelain and small souvenirs bearing Monaco's national colors (red and white) are on display and for sale. Closed Sundays. No admission charge. 16 Rue des Géraniums (phone: 93-50-59-24).

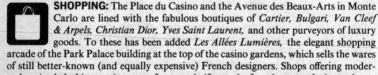 **SHOPPING:** The Place du Casino and the Avenue des Beaux-Arts in Monte Carlo are lined with the fabulous boutiques of *Cartier, Bulgari, Van Cleef & Arpels, Christian Dior, Yves Saint Laurent,* and other purveyors of luxury goods. To these has been added *Les Allées Lumières,* the elegant shopping arcade of the Park Palace building at the top of the casino gardens, which sells the wares of still better-known (and equally expensive) French designers. Shops offering moderately priced clothing, antiques, perfume, and gifts can be found among the immoderate ones on the Boulevard des Moulins and the Boulevard Princesse-Charlotte, Monte Carlo's major shopping streets. In the Condamine district, the two main commercial streets are Rue Princesse-Caroline and Rue Grimaldi. Another shopping arcade, the *Galerie du Sporting d'Hiver,* is across the street from the *Hôtel de Paris.* The *Metropole* hotel houses *Les Galeries du Metropole,* with more than 100 elegant boutiques.

Atmosphère – Particularly outstanding leatherwear. *Les Allées Lumières,* 27 Av. de la Costa (phone: 93-25-00-03).

Benetton – The popular international chain has inexpensive cardigans, turtlenecks, and shirts for each season, in many colors. 37 Bd. des Moulins (phone: 93-50-50-42 or 93-50-63-84).

Cassio International Mode – The best copies of designer jewels money can buy. 10 Bd. des Moulins (phone: 93-25-55-10).

Christofle Pavillon – A glistening array of crystal, silverware, and china. 42 Bd. des Moulins (phone: 93-25-20-20).

Façonnable – Preppy pullovers, socks, shirts, and pants, supposedly for men only, but women like them, too. 23 Bd. des Moulins (phone: 93-50-50-66).

Godiva – An immovable feast for chocolate lovers. *Galerie du Metropole* (phone: 93-25-75-47).

Jaguy – Good menswear — a wide range of attractive suits, pants, and sweaters — at affordable prices. 17 Bd. Princesse-Charlotte (phone: 93-30-84-56).

Katy – Christian Dior lingerie, but mainly an especially wide selection of women's bathing suits. 10 Bd. des Moulins (phone: 93-50-66-22).

Old River – Exclusive men's fashions at competitive prices. 17 Bd. des Moulins (phone: 93-50-33-85) and 17 Av. de Spélugues (phone: 93-50-06-01).

■ **Note:** The lovely *Boutique du Rocher,* created by Princess Grace to support local artisans, offers ceramics, embroidery, stuffed dolls, items made of Provençal fabrics, and other things suitable as souvenirs or gifts — all handmade. There are two locations: 1 Av. de la Madone (phone: 93-30-91-17) in Monte Carlo, and 11 Rue Emile-de-Loth (phone: 93-30-33-99) on the Rock.

SPORTS AND FITNESS: Archery – There's a stand at *Rainier III* (Terre-Plein de Fontvieille; phone: 93-30-32-80).

Golf – The 18 holes of the *Monte Carlo Golf Club* are actually in France, some 2,600 feet above sea level on top of Mont-Agel, a spot from which the view of the principality and the surrounding Riviera is particularly enchanting. The club, about 20 minutes from the center of Monte Carlo by car, is open all year (closed Mondays October through June), with numerous tournaments held throughout the year. For details, write to the *Monte Carlo Golf Club,* La Turbie 06320, France (phone: 93-41-09-11).

Sailing – The *Yacht Club de Monaco* (16 Quai Antoine-Ier; phone: 93-50-58-39) sometimes gives sailing lessons during July and August.

Swimming – A favorite year-round activity in Monaco, which has not only built numerous pools but has also given Mother Nature a hand by importing sand for its beaches. The *Plage du Larvotto,* the large, popular public beach off Avenue Princesse-Grace (phone: 93-15-28-76), is an example, an entirely artificial stretch of sand deposited along the shoreline between two strips of land that once upon a time did not exist. It's open from May to October (the rest of the year it's barricaded to hold the sand in place) and there's no charge. Next door, the *Monte Carlo Sea Club* (20 Av. Princesse-Grace; phone: 93-30-82-36), a private bathing complex with a double pool of heated sea-water and a private beach, is open to season members only, but it also is open (free) to guests of the *Beach Plaza* hotel. Another, even more exclusive club, the *Monte Carlo Beach* (Av. Princesse-Grace, St-Roman; phone: 93-78-21-40), is *the* place to be seen and to see the "who's who" of Monte Carlo. In addition to its cachet, it offers an Olympic-size, heated seawater pool, a snack bar, two restaurants, and a pebble beach lined with pretty striped cabañas, all of which are just beyond the eastern border of Monaco on French territory (perhaps the reason this is the only Monégasque establishment allowing topless sunbathing). The club is open from April to about mid-October and is free to guests of all SBM hotels (see *Checking In*). Others pay a daily admission charge.

Among the pools of Monaco are the Olympic-size heated seawater pool at the *Stade Nautique Rainier III* (Quai Albert-Ier; phone: 90-15-28-75), open to the public from April through October for a small admission charge, and the indoor heated freshwater pool at the *Stade Louis II* (3-7 Av. Castelans; phone: 92-05-00-00), closed in August. The stadium is part of a complex with facilities for just about every sport imaginable.

Tours are conducted daily between 3 and 4 PM. The luxurious health spa *California Terrace* (2 Av. de Monte Carlo; phone: 92-16-40-02) has an indoor heated seawater pool and a restaurant besides its spa facilities, and it stays open year-round from 9 AM to 8 PM.

Tennis and Squash – The *Monte Carlo Country Club* has 23 tennis courts (4 lighted), 2 squash courts, and beautiful clubhouse facilities. The courts are laid out on terraces overlooking the Mediterranean above the private *Monte Carlo Beach,* just beyond the eastern edge of Monaco, and are open year-round. For details, contact the *Monte Carlo Country Club* (St-Roman; phone: 93-78-20-45). The *Tennis Club de Monaco* (29 Bd. de Belgique; phone: 93-30-01-02) has 13 courts (5 lighted), a sauna, and a clubhouse that's open all year. The *Monte Carlo Squash Racquets Club* (*Stade Louis II;* phone: 93-15-42-22 or 92-05-40-00) has 4 courts and is open year-round.

Windsurfing – Skim the water's surface at the *Monte Carlo Beach* (Av. Princesse-Grace, St-Roman; phone: 93-78-21-40), from April to October; or the *Monte Carlo Sea Club* (22 Av. Princesse-Grace; phone: 93-30-98-30), May to September.

 THEATER AND MUSIC: The *Théâtre du Fort-Antoine,* an open-air theater in the old fortifications of the Rock, has a short season of plays, folkloric dance, and concerts from June through August. Tickets are sold at the theater 45 minutes before each performance; if you need details, call the Direction des Affaires Culturelles (phone: 93-15-80-00). The lovely *Théâtre Princesse Grace* (12 Av. d'Ostende; phone: 93-25-32-27), designed by the late princess, presents a season of comedy and drama (anything from the French classics to the latest foreign plays in translation), variety acts, and concerts from October through May.

The *Orchestre Philharmonique de Monte Carlo,* with internationally known guest artists, can be heard from October through April in the *Convention Center*'s 1,100-seat *Auditorium Rainier III* (Bd. Louis II; phone: 93-50-93-00), the largest theater in Monaco. Then, in July and August, it presents a series of gala summer concerts in the *Cour d'Honneur* of the Prince's Palace. The box office for information and advance tickets for both series is in the atrium of the casino (phone: 93-50-93-00); closed Mondays. The orchestra also participates in the *Printemps des Arts de Monte Carlo,* 2 weeks of concerts by visiting chamber groups, singers, instrumentalists, and dance companies that take place around *Easter* in the convention center auditorium, the *Théâtre Princesse Grace,* or in the casino's *Salle Garnier,* also known as the *Monte Carlo Opera House,* a jewel of a theater where such legends as Diaghilev's *Ballet Russes de Monte Carlo,* Nijinsky, Caruso, Gigli, and Lily Pons all performed. Today, Monte Carlo has an opera company whose season runs from December or January through March; a resident ballet company, created in 1985, and visiting troupes dance during the *National Day* (November 19), *Christmas,* and *New Year's* holidays, as well as at *Easter* as part of the *Printemps* program.

 NIGHTCLUBS AND NIGHTLIFE: Quite a bit of the excitement after dark takes place in the *Casino de Monte Carlo* (phone: 93-50-69-31), even though gamblers have been at it in some rooms since 10 AM (the slot machines in the American Room open at 10 AM, the tables and the White Salon open at 4 PM; the Salon Privé opens at 3 PM; the Salon Super-Privé by appointment). Dress is casual for gambling American style (women in slacks and men without ties are welcome), but if you penetrate as far as the European gaming rooms, coats and ties for men are required (and you won't feel ill at ease in black tie or chiffon). Monte Carlo also has two other casinos. There's an all-American casino in the *Loews Monte Carlo* hotel (12 Av. des Spélugues; phone: 93-50-65-00), and a "summer" casino is part of the lure of the *Monte Carlo Sporting Club* (Av. Princesse-Grace; phone: 93-30-71-71 or 93-50-80-80). This lavish, modern pleasure complex, built on a spit of land reclaimed from the sea at the far end of Avenue Princesse-Grace, opens at 10 PM in July and August. Its focal point is the large Salle des Etoiles, so called because of a roof that rolls back to reveal the stars. The room is the site of Monte Carlo's famous Friday night galas — grand dinner dances topped off with fireworks held to herald a new show or an international star's opening night and, not incidentally, to allow those in attendance to dress up (*tenue de soirée* is de rigueur for galas). On other nights, the dinner and show continue without the fireworks and without the formal dress requirement. The price of an evening at the Salle des Etoiles varies with the occasion. For information and reservations, call 93-50-80-80; after 6 PM, dial 93-30-71-71.

Also at the sporting club are *Jimmy'z de la Mer* (phone: 93-25-14-14), the most attractive (it overlooks a Japanese garden), most chic (sartorial slouches are not likely to be admitted), and most expensive (including a tip to the bouncer to get in) disco in Monte Carlo, open from 11 PM to dawn every night in July and August; *Parady'z* (also open July and August; 16 Av. Princesse-Grace; phone: 92-16-22-66), a second, less formidable disco formerly run by Régine; and the *Maona* restaurant (phone as for the Salle des Etoiles above), a dinner-dance spot with a tropical theme.

From September through June, *Jimmy'z* moves to winter quarters (Pl. du Casino; phone: 93-50-80-80). *The Living Room,* a popular bar and disco (7 Av. des Spélugues; phone: 93-50-80-31) is open year-round. *Loews Monte Carlo* has the *Folie Russe* supper club (phone: 93-50-65-00), where an elaborate Las Vegas–type show goes on every night but Mondays. A sophisticated evening in a more formal, old-fashioned setting is possible at the *Casino Cabaret* (phone: 93-50-69-31 or 93-50-80-80), in what was formerly a concert room of the casino, open from September through June, but closed Tuesdays. An elevator in the Salon Privé takes you down or you can enter from Place du Casino.

BEST IN TOWN

 CHECKING IN: Choosing a hotel in Monaco is not easy, because the selection is wide and each hotel has its own charm or a special view. Note that the four *Société des Bains de Mer* (*SBM*) hotels (the *Hôtel de Paris, Hermitage, Mirabeau,* and *Monte Carlo Beach*) issue guests a Carte d'Or (Gold Card) at registration. The card provides free entrance to the European gaming rooms at the casino, to the indoor pool at the *California Terrace,* and to the *Monte Carlo Beach Club;* discounts of 50% on greens fees and court fees at the *Monte Carlo Golf Club* and the *Monte Carlo Country Club;* and the privilege of charging meals at any SBM establishment directly to your room. Note also that should you arrive in Monaco during the summer without a reservation, it will be practically impossible to find a room, though the tourist and convention bureau is ready to provide assistance.

For a luxurious double room in hotels listed in the very expensive category, expect to pay $250 and up; $130 to $250 in a hotel listed as expensive; a nice room in a moderate hotel will cost between $75 and $100; and a very adequate double room in a small, inexpensive hotel will cost $75 or less.

Hermitage – Like its sister, the *Hôtel de Paris,* though somewhat lower key, this is Belle Epoque splendor, the sort of Riviera "palace" where even the least creative imagination can easily picture a cat burglar dropping from balustrade to balcony to loggia en route to some dowager's emeralds. Opened in 1899, it has, besides its exquisite façade, two public rooms that are among the showplaces of the principality: the *Belle Epoque* dining room, where pink marble columns hold up an extravagant gilt and frescoed ceiling, and the Art Nouveau winter garden, a simpler, airier space encircled by a wrought-iron balcony and topped with a stained glass dome.

The hotel is built on a rock that faces the harbor and Le Rocher de Monaco, and thus many of its 240 luxurious rooms have enchanting views. All of them have period touches, such as brass beds, though the fixtures and fittings are mostly modern. There is also has a swimming pool and a gym. Major credit cards accepted. Sq. Beaumarchais (phone: 93-50-67-31 or 93-50-67-38; fax: 93-50-47-12; telex: 479432). Very expensive.

Hôtel de Paris – This opulent Beaux Arts confection has been on the scene longer than the *Hermitage*. It opened in 1864, just before the casino, and still looks every bit the setting for the reigning royalty, deposed royalty, prima donnas, and plutocrats it has welcomed in its lifetime. The architectural tours de force here are the appropriately named *Salle Empire* dining room, a thoroughly imperial composition in cream and gold, with marble columns, classical statuary, and crystal chandeliers; and the glass-domed rotunda lobby (where a statue of Louis XIV on horseback has been rubbed to a luster by guests in need of luck at the casino, a roll of the dice away). *Le Grill* offers dining under the stars, and the three-star *Louis XV* offers spectacular Provençal cuisine by Alain Ducasse in an elegant setting (for both, see *Eating Out*). The 255 spacious rooms and 39 suites have modern comforts and beautiful views, and guests have access to the indoor pool of the *California Terrace,* via an underground passageway. There is also a spa and the well-known *Le Bar Américain*. Major credit cards accepted. Pl. du Casino (phone: 93-50-80-80; fax: 93-25-59-17; telex: 469925). Very expensive.

Beach Plaza – Besides the *Monte Carlo Beach,* this is the only other hotel in Monaco with a beachfront location, and it's a great favorite with families. It has its own heated freshwater pool and private beach in addition to the facilities (2 more pools, more beach, and a mini-club for children) of the adjoining *Monte Carlo Sea Club.* The hotel is modern; its 320 rooms are nicely decorated, and many have a water view. In the summer, an open-air grill restaurant is set up by the pool. Major credit cards accepted. 22 Av. Princesse-Grace (phone: 93-30-98-80; fax: 93-50-23-14; telex: 479617). Expensive.

Loews Monte Carlo – Huge and thoroughly modern, this American-managed hotel expresses a spirit entirely different from that of Monte Carlo's two landmark palaces — some would call it the spirit of Las Vegas. Set on pilings driven into the sea, it sprawls along the water at the foot of the casino. All the rooms (and suites) — there are 650 — have terraces, many with direct water views. The hotel has 5 restaurants (see *Eating Out* for *Le Pistou*), its own gambling casino, a nightclub, a lavish marble promenade level with attractive boutiques, an open-air heated pool on the roof garden, and a health and fitness club. Major credit cards accepted. Av. des Spélugues (phone: 93-50-65-00; fax: 93-30-01-57; telex: 479435). Expensive.

Metropole Palace – One of the city's newer additions, which opened in the spring of 1990, this establishment is a member of Conrad International (a division of Hilton Hotels of the US). In keeping with Monte Carlo's Belle Epoque architecture, $120 million was spent to restore this neo-classical–style hotel, located just a few blocks away from the casino. It features 170 rooms, plus an indoor-outdoor pool, 3 restaurants, and over 130 boutiques. Major credit cards accepted. 4 Av. de la Madone (phone: 93-15-15-15; fax: 93-25-24-44; telex: 489836). Expensive.

Mirabeau – Small and elegant, it occupies several floors of a modern high-rise, centrally located not far from the casino. It has 113 comfortable rooms (all with terraces, some with a view of the water), 2 restaurants (see *Eating Out*), and its own heated seawater pool. Comfortable, if not particularly rich in character. Major credit cards accepted. 1 Av. Princesse-Grace (phone: 93-25-45-45; fax: 93-50-84-85; telex: 479413). Expensive.

Monte Carlo Beach – A compromise between the sumptuously baroque and the brashly up-to-date look of the other deluxe properties. Built in 1928, this terra cotta–roofed structure in the shape of a crescent is on the edge of the sea just beyond the eastern border of the principality, about 1½ miles (2 km) from the casino. There are 46 small, elegant rooms, each with a balcony over the ocean; the ambience is quiet and private, a bit less formal than the "palaces," remote from the nightlife of Monte Carlo, but full of charm. The hotel shares the beach, 2 pools, cabañas, and restaurants of the exclusive *Monte Carlo Beach Club,* literally at its front door. Open from mid-April to October. The restaurant is closed from September 12 to June 6. Major credit cards accepted. Av. Princesse-Grace, St-Roman, Roquebrune-Cap-Martin (phone: 93-78-21-40; fax: 93-78-14-18; telex: 462010). Expensive.

Abela – This property overlooks the sea and has more than 200 rooms and suites with French windows and private terraces, plus 3 restaurants and a lobby bar. One floor is reserved for nonsmokers. Conveniently situated in Fontvieille, 2 minutes from the heliport and 5 minutes from the train station. Major credit cards accepted. 23 Av. des Papalins (phone: 92-05-90-00; fax: 93-05-91-67; telex: 489307). Expensive to moderate.

Alexandra – A modest hostelry at the intersection of two major shopping streets near the casino in the center of Monte Carlo, it has 55 comfortable rooms, many with bath or shower. Major credit cards accepted. 35 Bd. Princesse-Charlotte (phone: 93-50-63-13; telex: 489286). Moderate.

Balmoral – Conveniently located, this traditional ·hostelry has 70 rooms, some overlooking the harbor, all with either bath or shower. A restaurant is on the premises. Closed Sundays, Mondays, November, and *Christmas.* Major credit cards accepted. 12 Av. de la Costa (phone: 93-50-62-37; fax: 93-15-08-69; telex: 479436). Moderate.

Louvre – A small hotel that is on the main shopping street of Monte Carlo. The 32 cozy and comfortable rooms all have a private bath and some have a view of the water. Major credit cards accepted. 16 Bd. des Moulins (phone: 93-50-65-25; fax: 93-30-23-68; telex: 479645). Moderate.

Helvetia – Another small, clean hotel, this one has 28 rooms (18 with bath or shower), and its attractive restaurant, favored by locals, is a bargain for Monaco. It's in the Condamine district near the Place d'Armes market. Visa accepted. 1 *bis* Rue Grimaldi (phone: 93-30-21-71). Inexpensive.

Terminus – Also in the Condamine district, adjacent to the train station; there's no view, but each of the 54 comfortable, air conditioned rooms comes with bath or shower, a television set, and radio. There is a restaurant, but it's closed in October and November. Visa accepted. 9 Av. Prince-Pierre (phone: 93-30-20-70). Inexpensive.

■**Note:** Beaulieu, the French commune bordering Monaco several blocks to the north of the casino, has several hotels that are more down-to-earth and more modestly priced than those in the principality, and as conveniently located as any in Monte Carlo. Among them is the *Olympia* (Bd. Général Leclerc — just east of the Crédit Lyonnais building; phone: 93-78-12-70). Only 5 minutes from the casino, its 24 rooms are still affordable. Two traditional two-star hotels are nearby: the *Cosmopolite* (phone: 93-78-36-00), next door; and the recently renovated *Boeri* (29 Av. Général Leclerc; phone: 93-78-38-10). All are moderate.

EATING OUT: The choice of restaurants in Monaco ranges from haute cuisine to typical corner bistros, and includes several Italian restaurants and pizzerias serving very good, inexpensive food. Traditional Monégasque cooking — reminiscent of the cooking of Nice — can be sampled at bistros near the marketplace or on the Rock. Among the specialties are *barbagiuan,* a fried pocket of dough with a rich filling of zucchini, garlic, eggs, cheese, and rice; *pan bagnat,* a round bun of country bread that is "bathed" in olive oil, vinegar, garlic, and basil, then stuffed with a *salade niçoise;* and stockfish, a type of dried codfish stewed in a succulent wine and tomato sauce, with garlic, onions, and olive oil. Generally speaking, however, the quality of the cuisine in Monaco is a cut below the level of the food found in surrounding France.

Dinner for two (excluding wine) will cost at least $200 and up in the restaurant listed below as very expensive; $100 to $200 in the expensive places; $50 to $100 in ones listed as moderate; and less than $50 in the inexpensive places. Despite its ritzy reputation, Monte Carlo offers a wide variety of inexpensive restaurants. Service usually is included.

Le Louis XV – The only hotel restaurant in the history of the *Michelin Guides* to be awarded three stars. The chef, Alain Ducasse, learned his trade in France's best restaurants before coming to work in Monaco. Sea scallops with black truffles, risotto with white truffles, and wild strawberries are his masterpieces. Dine in heaven. Closed Tuesdays and Wednesdays off-season, November 20 to December 19 and February 26 to March 13. Only 50 people can eat here at any one time, so be sure to reserve far ahead. Major credit cards accepted. *Hôtel de Paris,* Pl. du Casino (phone: 93-50-80-80 or 93-30-23-11; 93-25-43-46). Very expensive.

La Coupole – The atmosphere is contemporary, soft, and elegant; the food refined nouvelle cuisine. One Michelin star. Closed for lunch during July and August. Reservations necessary. Major credit cards accepted. *Mirabeau Hotel,* 1-3 Av. Princesse-Grace (phone: 93-25-45-45). Expensive.

Le Grill – The rooftop restaurant of the *Hôtel de Paris* is swank and the view is delightfully romantic (it overlooks the turrets of the casino on one side and the harbor and Old Monaco on the other). In summer, the ceiling opens up to the sky and stars. Among the *grillades* are succulent lamb noisettes, *côte de boeuf,* and veal paillard; there is a lobster tank; and, for dessert, there are delicate tangerine and raspberry soufflés. The hotel's wine cellar, carved out of the rock about a decade after the hotel was built, holds some 200,000 bottles. One Michelin star. Closed first 3 weeks of December. Reservations necessary. Major credit cards accepted. *Hôtel de Paris,* Pl. du Casino (phone: 93-50-80-80; fax: 93-25-59-17). Expensive.

Rampoldi – Pleasant and very fashionable, this chic brasserie serves good French and Italian food in a 1930s setting of polished wood paneling and mirrors. Closed November. Reservations necessary. Major credit cards accepted. 3 Av. des Spélugues (phone: 93-30-70-65). Expensive.

Saint Charles – This small and very fine, though unpretentious, eatery specializes in seafood. Menu favorites include the flavorful Mediterranean snapper, sea bass (*loup*), fresh clams and mussels, and wonderful Bélon oysters. Closed Saturdays for lunch and Sundays. Reservations necessary. Major credit cards accepted. 33 Av. St-Charles (phone: 93-50-63-19). Expensive.

Café de Paris – A true French brasserie, with two terraces for outdoor dining and people watching, it's in a shopping-and-casino complex restored to turn-of-the-century grandeur. Note the stained glass windows representing the four seasons and the zodiac signs, designed by Charles Garnier of opera house fame. Open daily. Reservations unnecessary. Pl. du Casino (phone: 93-50-57-75). Moderate.

Le Pinocchio – Not one of the pasta dishes is likely to disappoint in this very small, cozy spot with a vaulted ceiling in Old Monaco. Closed Wednesdays from September to April and from December 1 through January. Reservations advised. Visa accepted. Rue Comte-Félix-Gastaldi (phone: 93-30-96-20). Moderate.

Le Pistou – Good Monégasque and Provençal cooking at reasonable prices is the draw of this rooftop hotel restaurant. Try the *pissaladière* (Nice's version of onion pizza) or the *tian d'aubergines* (eggplant gratin). Closed from mid-November to mid-December. Reservations unnecessary. Major credit cards accepted. *Loews Monte Carlo,* 12 Av. des Spélugues (phone: 93-50-65-00). Moderate.

Polpetta – Delicious food and a warm Italian atmosphere make this lovely dining room very popular. Closed Tuesdays, Saturday lunch, 3 weeks in February, and 2 weeks in October. Reservations necessary. Visa accepted. 2 Rue Paradis (phone: 93-50-67-84). Moderate.

Port – A charming place near the port, as its name suggests, with outdoor tables in summer. The menu leans to local fish, meat, and pasta. Closed Mondays, and from November 11 to December 5. Reservations unnecessary. Visa accepted. Quai Albert-Ier (phone: 93-50-77-21). Moderate.

Santa Lucia – This upstairs place is recommended for its pizza, risotto, and grilled meat. A pianist performing Italian songs and, on request, old American tunes animates the quaint Italian setting. Open every evening. Reservations unnecessary. Visa accepted. 11 Av. des Spélugues (phone: 93-50-96-77). Moderate.

Castleroc – From the outside tables of this informal eating place there's a view of the Prince's Palace and the water. It's one place to try stockfish or other Monégasque specialties. Lunch only; closed Saturdays and December and January. No reservations. Major credit cards accepted. Pl. du Palais (phone: 93-30-36-68). Inexpensive.

Le Périgordin – A small eatery near the railroad station serving good fare of southwest France. Closed Saturdays for lunch, Sundays, and August. No reservations. Major credit cards accepted. 4 Rue Turbie (phone: 93-30-06-02). Inexpensive.

Saint Nicolas – The food is very good in this small place just behind the cathedral, and the price tag on a three-course meal makes it one of Monaco's better values. Closed Wednesdays, the first 3 weeks in December, and the last 3 weeks in January. No reservations. Visa accepted. 6 Rue de l'Eglise (phone: 93-30-30-41). Inexpensive.

Vin sur Zinc – Along with a fine selection of classic French wines, this wine bar offers a menu of salads and light fare as well as full meals. Closed Saturday lunch and Sundays. Reservations advised at lunchtime. No credit cards accepted. 24 Bd. Princesse-Charlotte (phone: 93-25-61-11). Inexpensive.

 BARS AND CAFÉS: Part outdoor café (with indoor tables, too), part drugstore (with a newsstand, cigarettes, stamps, and even slot machines), and part restaurant, the *Café de Paris* is open daily until 4 AM, but it's the perfect place to sip a Campari after 5 o'clock while watching the comings and goings on Place du Casino. *Le Bar Américain* in the *très* glittering *Hôtel de Paris* is a very posh place, definitely a spot where the elite gather to see and be seen as well as to find out the latest — the experience is fun but expensive, and reservations are necessary (phone: 93-50-80-80) if you want a good table, especially in summer. *Tip-top,* a comparatively plain, small snack bar with sidewalk tables (11 Av. de Spélugues; phone: 93-50-69-13), nevertheless becomes very popular with Monaco's jet set after midnight in the summer, and it stays open all night. Another unassuming place, the *Bar de la Crémaillère* (31 Bd. Princesse-Charlotte; phone: 93-50-66-24), is a simple bistro with small outside tables (closed Sundays and mid-December to mid-January). *Flashman's,* in the Sun Tower Building (7 Av. Princesse-Alice; phone: 93-30-09-03), and *The Living Room* (7 Av. des Spélugues; phone: 93-50-80-31), are both piano bars, among other things: *Flashman's,* which is also a restaurant, is fancy, good for late snacking on English food to easy-listening music until 4 AM; *The Living Room* has a dance floor, an Irish manager, and a pleasantly old-fashioned atmosphere.

NICE

Those who remember the halcyon days of ornate villas, swaying palms, and languid luxury under an azure sky may shake their heads sadly at the Côte d'Azur of today: a symphony in cement, a real estate speculator's orgy of high-rise apartment blocks, pillbox hotels, honky-tonk pizza parlors, and shiny fast-food factories. Its once-quaint little marinas are linked by a permanent shoreline traffic jam, and some of its renowned beaches now look more like a horde of people dangling their feet from the edge of a freeway.

Although Nice has managed to keep its head above the concrete and retain its special flavor — a mixture of Marseilles, the *Mardi Gras,* and the Mediterranean, it slowly is becoming a place where tourism is more of a burden than a cultural exchange between visitors and natives. But at the first shine of sun, the café tables come out, the awnings unfurl, and strollers in sandals are back clacking along the Promenade des Anglais and, until the hordes of tourists invade its beach in July and August, you can enjoy the undeniable charms of the city. In the summer, the population of 340,000 burgeons with holiday makers from Paris, Piccadilly, Peoria — and once again from St-Petersburg — and an empty or moderately priced hotel room is harder to find than a winning lottery ticket. And a lot more scarce than a movie star. All the streets — particularly the Promenade des Anglais — are mobbed with traffic and the deafening noise competes with the burning sun, making summer in Nice a less than desirable experience. But in mid-autumn, when the locals and a few visitors take advantage of the last hot days to dip into the still-warm sea, you can again begin to feel that Nice is nice.

The Greeks from nearby Massalia (today's Marseilles) founded the city in the 5th century BC as a little market town and auxiliary port, and named it Nikaia. Continuous lootings by pirates from the Ligurian coast caused Nikaia's citizens to ask for military help from the Romans. They made their military camp on the side of Cimiez Hill, protected the city, and discovered the pleasures of the Riviera. The remains of their lavish colonization are evident today in the Arena and the Baths on the hill at Cimiez — the city's elegant residential section. During the fall of the Roman Empire, barbarians from the north and pirates from North Africa invaded Nice and brought about its decline. In 1388, the House of Savoy wrested the growing city from the Counts of Provence (who had brought the city back to its former state in the 10th century) and retained almost unbroken possession of it for close to 500 years. Napoleon lived for a time at No. 6 on what is today the Rue Bonaparte, later on Rue St-François-de-Paule by the opera house. In 1860, the head of the House of Savoy and King of newly unified Italy, Victor Emmanuel II, ceded the region to France in return for military support against an Austrian invasion (he did this after the citizens of Nice voted in favor of being under French control). Giuseppe Garibaldi, the Italian patriot, was born here, as was Masséna, the general Wellington admired most after Napoleon. In modern times, the beauty and climate of Nice have made it the amusement park of the European aristocracy, an off-season refuge from harsh northern climes and irritating revolutions. Today, a good portion of the city's income comes from various high-tech industries (e.g., electronics) rather than tourism.

The city, between Cannes and Monte Carlo, is one big easy-to-scan color postcard: the lapis lazuli of the Bay of Angels (Baie des Anges), the activity of the Vieux Port, and the timelessness of the towering Castle (Château) — the name given to the hill with the ruins of an old fortress that looms over the harbor. Along the bay runs the fabled Promenade des Anglais, a broad seafront avenue that resembles a mile-long outdoor café. At one end of the promenade is the city's pulse, Place Masséna: semitropical Albert Ier gardens set against crimson buildings and cool graceful arcades. Avenue Jean-Médecin (named after a former Mayor of Nice for 38 years, whose son — also a Mayor of Nice for 24 years — not long ago fled to South America to escape being arrested for tax evasion and fraud and was tried in absentia) is Main Street, bisecting the city in a straight line from the Place Masséna to the railroad station. The Old City, La Vieille Ville, is a little piano-shaped quarter — all narrow and cobbled and noisy, and pungently southern — that huddles in the shadow of the Château. La Vieille Ville's boundaries are the Quai des Etats-Unis and the Boulevard Jean-Jaurès beside the Paillon River, which is covered in parts by esplanades and divides the Old City from modern Nice to the west. In the past few years, Nice has spread farther to the west, past the airport that was expanded onto land reclaimed from the Baie des Anges.

Nice's heritage is culturally rich. Rodin, Modigliani, and Toulouse-Lautrec were among the numerous artists to have converged on the city starting in the 19th century. Matisse spent the last years of his life close to Nice, and for many years Chagall lived nearby; their works can be seen in the city's *Musée Matisse* and *Musée National Marc Chagall.* Music lovers flock to the renowned *Opéra de Nice,* and a variety of concerts are performed all year long throughout the city. And if you prefer fun and frolicking to art and music, Nice offers that too — not just with its usual festivities, but with a big bang during *Carnival.*

NICE AT-A-GLANCE

SEEING THE CITY: The long azure sweep of the bay, the compact jumble of red tile roofs in La Vieille Ville, the foothills of Provence, and the Maritime Alps rising sharply just outside the city are best seen from a viewing platform at the summit of the 300-foot Château. It can be reached by an elevator — or a 300-step climb — at the end of the Quai des Etats-Unis, where the quay joins the Rue des Ponchettes. Now there is a daily train from the Esplanade Albert Ier at the beginning of the Promenade des Anglais that goes through La Vieille Ville en route to the hills of the Château; from there, an exceptional panorama of Nice's port and the Bay of Angels unfolds before you. For information and reservations, call *Les Trains Touristiques* (phone: 93-18-81-58).

 SPECIAL PLACES: Nice is a city to be seen casually, to be ambled through under a morning or late-afternoon sun, especially in and around the Old City and the renowned flower market, *Le Marché aux Fleurs* at Cours Saleya. Let your discoveries be guided by casual occurrences: the purchase of a peach in an open market, a cold glass of Corsican white wine at a portside café, the scent of thyme wafting from the flower market.

IN THE CITY

Promenade des Anglais – If you only have an hour in Nice, spend it strolling along this promenade from the Place Masséna to the *Négresco* hotel (see *Checking In*). Ornate hotels grace one side, and a narrow, crowded strip of pebbled beach separates you from the brilliant blue of the bay. The promenade takes its name from the city's English colony, which constructed the path (in the middle of the last century) that was the predecessor of this one. You can lunch in your bathing suit on several excellent private beaches along the Promenade des Anglais. Prices are moderate and carafe wines are good.

La Vieille Ville (Old City) – Old Nice is a tight labyrinth of winding streets and alleys, steep ascents between medieval buildings, and balconies festooned with rainbows of drying laundry. The character of the city as it grew down the slopes of the Château from the 14th to the 18th century is in striking contrast to the city of expansive patrician promenades that developed in more modern times. Of late, La Vieille Ville has shown indications of evolving into Nice's artists' quarter. Explore the Rue Rossetti, the Rue de la Boucherie, or the Rue du Collet. Crowd your way through the teeming street markets. Stop in at the 17th-century religious edifices, Cathedral of Ste-Réparate, and churches of St-Martin-St-Augustin and that of St-James. Also worth visiting is the Old City cemetery.

Le Marché aux Fleurs (Flower Market) – On the edge of the Old City, just behind the Quai des Etats-Unis, you'll find the wholesale flower market that offers one of Nice's most colorful spectacles. The varieties of blossoms are dazzling, the aromas heady, and there are a few well-placed cafés, where you can see, sniff, and sip, all at the same time. Closed Mondays and Sunday afternoons. Cours Saleya.

Le Marché de la Brocante (Antiques Market) – On Monday mornings, the huge square where the flower market is held becomes an antiques and bric-a-brac market of unusual allure. In the late afternoon on Wednesdays, local artisans and painters display their often-expensive works. Cours Saleya.

Palais Lascaris (Lascaris Palace) – A splendid private palace of the 17th century in Genoese style, this is the former residence of the Count Lascaris-Ventimiglia. It is noted for its ceilings with frescoes, its decorative woodwork, and its regal staircase. Closed Mondays in summer; Mondays, Tuesdays in off-season, some public holidays; and November. 15 Rue Droite (phone: 93-62-05-54).

Vieux Port (Old Port) – To the east of the Château, the harbor of Nice is an artful array of multicolored boats, from one-man dinghies and kayaks to the white steamers that make the crossing to Corsica. Excursion boats leave from the port and putter along to nearby Riviera towns. To reach the port, go out around the base of the Château at the far end of Quai des Etats-Unis or take Rue Cassini southeast from Place Garibaldi.

Cathédrale Orthodoxe Russe – A reminder of the days when the royal Romanovs roamed the Riviera and the promenade bustled with grand dukes, ballerinas, and an occasional Bolshevik, the cathedral was built in the Belle Epoque of the 19th century, under the auspices of Czar Nicholas II himself. Built from 1903 to 1912, it is considered one of the most beautiful churches of its style outside of Russia. The church supports a bouquet of ornate onion domes in the ancient Russian style, and its exterior is a mixture of pink brick, grey marble, and colored ceramic tiles. Inside are a rich collection of icons and an impressive, carved iconostasis — the traditional screen that separates the altar from the nave in an Orthodox church. No visitors are permitted during the Sunday morning service. Admission charge. Bd. du Tzarewitch (phone: 93-96-88-02).

Musée National Marc Chagall – Built on a wooded hill in Cimiez in 1972, this modern museum houses works donated by Chagall, including the 17 canvases, painted over a 13-year-period, that make up his *Biblical Message*. In addition to the many fine paintings, the museum has sculptures, mosaics, sketches, and lithographs, all by Chagall. In summer, a tearoom is set up in the garden. Closed Tuesdays. Admission charge. Av. du Dr.-Ménard and Bd. de Cimiez (phone: 93-81-75-75).

Musée Matisse et d'Archéologie – Henri Matisse had his studio in the Cimiez section of Nice, and a representative collection of his work — canvases, drawings, and sculpture done at various stages of his career — along with some of the artist's personal effects and his private art collection, are in the village here. A separate building houses the collection of archaeological objects found at the Roman site of Cimiez. Matisse's tomb is at the north end of a nearby cemetery, where Raoul Dufy also is buried. Closed for renovations until the summer, when it will be open from 10 AM to noon and from 2 to 6 PM; closed Mondays and Sunday mornings. No admission charge. 164 Av. des Arènes de Cimiez (phone: 93-53-17-70).

Musée d'Art Moderne et d'Art Contemporain – The largest modern art complex in southern France, this museum offers not only excellent canvases, but good views of the city from the top of its four towers. Opened in 1990, it displays works from such world-renowned artists as César, Klein, Christo, Warhol, Lichtenstein, Morris, and Louis. Closed Tuesdays. No admission charge. Promenade des Arts (phone: 93-62-61-62).

ENVIRONS

Eze Village – Perched on a rock spike 1,550 feet above the sea, this unusual village — once a medieval fortress — offers a splendid panorama of the Riviera. It also has a tropical garden (Jardin Exotique) and a church with a beautiful 15th-century font. Nietzsche is supposed to have first worked out his masterpiece, *Thus Spake Zarathustra,* here. The walk from the Lower (Inferieure) Corniche up the Nietzsche Pass (Sentier Nietzsche) is picturesque and well worth the effort, and ends at Eze-Bord-de-Mer, by the water. Eze is less than 7 miles (11 km) from Nice, along the Middle (Moyenne) Corniche, on the way to Monte Carlo.

■**EXTRA SPECIAL:** The Chapelle du Rosaire (Rosary Chapel), designed and decorated by Matisse (who thought it his masterpiece) between 1947 and 1951, is the main reason so many people have rediscovered Vence, a picturesque old market town some 13½ miles (22 km) northwest of Nice (also see *The Côte d'Azur,* DIRECTIONS). The stunning stained glass windows (which Matisse executed to express his gratitude to the Dominican monks who protected him during World War II), the murals, and the church vestments created by Matisse may bring you here, but you'll also enjoy the setting — on a rock promontory, sheltered by the last foothills of the Alps — and the charm of the old town, enclosed in elliptical walls and entered through five arched gateways. Restricted access and the small dimensions of the chapel can result in its being crowded, however, especially when a tour bus unloads its contents. The chapel (on Av. Henri-Matisse) is open Tuesdays and Thursdays from 10 to 11:30 AM and 2:30 to 5:30 PM; other days by appointment made at least a day in advance (phone: 93-58-03-26). For those who are interested in exploring the town of Vence itself, a stop at the tourist office in the central plaza (Pl. du Grand-Jardin; phone: 93-58-06-38) will provide ample ideas about what to see and how to get there.

SOURCES AND RESOURCES

 TOURIST INFORMATION: The Nice Office du Tourisme–Syndicat d'Initiative, whose hostesses speak English, has three branches: next to the railway station on Avenue Thiers (phone: 93-87-07-07), 5 Avenue Gustave (phone: 93-87-60-60). There's also a welcome desk near the airport.

Local Coverage – The daily newspaper of the area is *Nice-Matin.* A free weekly directory of activities on the Riviera, *Sept Jours–Sept Nuits,* is distributed in the lobbies of most hotels. Also pick up the weekly *Semaine des Spectacles* for 5F. All are in French, but they're easy to decipher.

 TELEPHONE: The city code for Nice is 93, which is incorporated into all local 8-digit numbers. When calling a number in Nice from the Paris region (including the Ile-de-France), dial 16, wait for a dial tone, then dial the 8-digit number. When calling a number from outside Paris, dial only the 8-digit number. When calling from the US, dial 33 (which is the country code), followed by the 8-digit number.

 GETTING AROUND: It's a good thing that central Nice is compact and easily accessible by foot, because traffic becomes ludicrous during the tourist seasons. Many areas have become pedestrian zones, such as Rue Masséna and some of its cross streets, as well as numerous streets in La Vieille Ville. If you want to move faster, rent a motorbike, moped, scooter, or bicycle from *Nicea Location Rent,* 29 Rue Paganini (phone: 93-16-10-30).

Airport – Nice–Côte d'Azur Airport (phone: 93-21-30-30), about 4 miles (6 km) west of the city, handles both domestic and international traffic. The approximately 10-minute taxi ride into town costs about 100F–150F (about $17–$25). The airport shuttle is part of the municipal bus network, *Transports Urbains de Nice* (24 Rue Hôtel des Postes; phone: 93-62-08-08). Leaving about every 20 minutes, it makes runs to the airport from 6 AM to 8 PM and continues to bring passengers into town (to Bd. Jean-Jaurès) from the airport until 11 PM. The shuttle leaves Nice from Avenue Félix-Faure next to the information office at the Gare Routière; some of the buses (such as the No. 23) into Nice go directly to the train station. The fare is 8F.

There also is a shuttle service from the Nice airport to Menton, which stops at the coastal resorts along the way — Villefranche, Beaulieu, Eze, Cap d'Ail, Monaco, Monte Carlo, and Roquebrune. Leaving approximately every hour from 7 AM to 8 PM, depending on the season, the trip takes about 1½ hours each way and costs 57F ($10) one way, 100F ($18) round trip (phone: 93-21-30-83). In addition, helicopter service to Monaco is available. For details, call *Héli-Air Monaco* (phone: 93-21-34-62 at the airport, 93-30-80-88 at the Héliport de Fontvieille in Monaco).

Boats – In summer, *Gallus* boats cruise along the Riviera. Apply to *SATAM* (Quai Lunel; phone: 93-55-33-33). For ferries to Corsica, inquire at *SNCM* (Quai du Commerce; phone: 93-13-66-60).

Bus – You can hop on a bus for outlying districts, such as Cimiez, at the Place Masséna. The central station for the urban bus network is at 10 Avenue Félix-Faure (Traverse Flandres Dunkerque; phone: 93-62-08-08). Nearby, the main station for regional buses is the Gare Routière (Bd. Jean-Jaurès and Promenade Paillon; phone: 93-85-61-81).

Car Rental – Major international firms represented, both downtown and at the airport, are *Avis* (phone: 93-80-63-52 and 93-87-90-11); *Budget* (phone: 93-87-63-87 and 93-21-36-50); *Europcar* (phone: 93-88-64-04 and 93-21-36-44); and *Hertz* (phone: 93-21-36-72).

Taxi – Cabs are expensive, so watch the meter and remember streets often are clogged with traffic at certain hours. There usually are plenty of cabs at designated stands, and they also can be hailed in the streets; or call 93-80-70-70.

Train – The Gare *SNCF* is on Avenue Thiers (phone: 93-87-50-50). Another station, Gare de Provence (33 Av. Malausséna; phone: 93-82-10-17), belongs to the *Chemins de Fer de Provence* (Provence Railways), a narrow-gauge railway that operates daily on a scenic route between Nice and Digne, approximately 100 miles (160 km) to the northwest. The one-way trip takes about 3½ hours.

 LOCAL SERVICES: *Service 2A* (phone: 93-21-30-73; fax: 93-21-31-81), at Nice–Côte d'Azur Airport, is a general business service operated by the Nice Chamber of Commerce and linked to similar services at airports in Marseilles, Lyons, Paris, London, and Frankfurt. The staff can coordinate practically any kind of business need, including catering, secretarial assistance, telecommunications, and conference arrangements. Private offices and conference rooms (for up to 10 people) are for rent by the hour or day, and customized VIP services are available for individuals and groups.

Dentist (English-Speaking) – *Mme. Favot* (49 Rue Pastorelli; phone: 93-62-30-54 or 93-80-76-36); *Syndicat des Chirurgiens Dentistes des Alpes-Maritimes* (28 Bd. Raimbaldi; phone: 93-80-36-66 or 93-80-38-40).

Dry Cleaner – *Express Nettoyage,* 22 Av. Buénos Ayres.

Limousine Service – *Garage Plaza,* 12 Av. de Verdun (phone: 93-87-82-34 or 93-87-97-23).

Medical Emergency – *Hôpital St-Roch,* 24-hour service (5 Rue Pierre-Devoluy; phone: 92-03-33-33) or *S.A.M.U.* for emergency ambulance service (phone: 93-92-55-55).

National/International Courier – *DHL International* is in Lyons, but serves Nice and surrounding municipalities (phone: toll-free in France, 05-20-25-25); *Chrono Post* is located in all branches of the post office.

Office Equipment Rental – *Service 2A* (phone: 93-21-30-73); *Bureco,* for photocopiers and typewriters only (53 Rue Rossini; phone: 93-87-20-80).

Pharmacy – *De Nuit,* open 24 hours. 7 Rue Masséna (phone: 93-87-78-94).

Photocopies – *Service 2A* at the airport (phone: 93-21-30-73); also at most photographic stores and hotels in the city, at all post offices, department stores and large supermarkets.

Post Office – There are two main post offices (23 Av. Thiers, near the train station; phone: 93-16-06-45; and at Rue de l'Hôtel des Postes and Pl. Wilson; phone: 93-85-94-20). Both are open weekdays from 7:30 AM to 8 PM and Saturday mornings.

Secretary/Stenographer (English-Speaking) – *Service 2A* at the airport (phone: 93-21-30-73) or through your hotel.

Teleconference Facilities – *L'Acropolis* is the best equipped (Esplanade Kennedy; phone: 93-92-83-00); *Palais des Congrès* (Av. Gallieni; phone: 93-92-83-00); *Nice Congrès at Palais des Expositions* (Esplanade de Lattre de Tassigny; phone: 93-92-83-00).

Telex/Telefax – At the post office (Rue de l'Hôtel des Postes and Pl. Wilson); also at major hotels.

Translator – *Denise Chabert,* 10 Av. Général Leclerc, Villefranche-Sur-Mer (phone: 93-01-80-25; fax: 93-76-73-18).

SPECIAL EVENTS: The Nice event par excellence is *Carnival,* which begins 3 weekends before *Lent* and ends when His Majesty, King Carnival, is burned in effigy on *Shrove Tuesday.* The festivities include myriad parades and floats, marching bands and majorettes, fireworks and flowers, giant papier-mâché heads and masked balls. The *Fête des Mais* is a month of Sundays in May, with special merriment in the gardens of the *Roman Arena* at Cimiez. In July, the 10-day *Grande Parade du Jazz,* also in the Cimiez gardens, is the biggest jazz festival in Europe. In September, the *Triathlon de Nice* draws some of the world's best athletes who swim across the Baie des Anges for 3 miles (5 km), run in a 27-mile (42 km) marathon, and bicycle for 62 miles (100 km). To find out more about special events in Nice, contact *Comité des Fêtes* (5 Promenade des Anglais; phone: 93-87-16-28).

MUSEUMS: The *Chagall, Matisse,* and *Modern Art* museums described in *Special Places* are the most impressive in Nice, but there are several others of interest.

Musée des Beaux-Arts Jules Chéret – Nice's municipal art museum, with works by Fragonard, Renoir, Degas, Picasso. This is one of the few authentic buildings remaining from *La Belle Epoque.* Closed Mondays. No admission charge. 33 Av. des Baumettes (phone: 93-44-50-72).

Musée d'Histoire Naturelle or Musée Barla (Natural History Museum) – Exhibitions on marine life, paleontology, and mineralogy. Closed Tuesdays. No admission charge. 60 *bis* Bd. Risso (phone: 93-55-15-24).

Musée International d'Art Naïf Anatole Jakovsky (Anatole Jakovsky International Museum of Naive Art) – Jakovsky's collection of almost 600 paintings documenting naive art from the 18th century to the present, representing some 27 countries. Closed Tuesdays. No admission charge. Château Ste-Hélène, Av. Val-Marie (phone: 93-71-78-33).

Musée Masséna – Memorabilia of Napoleon's trusted marshal and exhibitions on the history of Nice. Closed Mondays. No admission charge. 65 Rue de France (phone: 93-88-11-34).

Musée Naval – From its perch atop the Tour Bellanda (a former residence of Berlioz), this museum overlooks spectacular grounds. It houses the expected — ship models, arms, navigation instruments — and the not so expected, such as models of the port at various times in its history. Closed Tuesdays. No admission charge. Tour Bellanda, Parc du Château (phone: 93-80-47-61).

Musée de Terra Amata – Artifacts from this excavated prehistoric site that is about 400,000 years old. Closed Mondays and 2 weeks in September. No admission charge. 25 Bd. Carnot (phone: 93-55-59-93).

SHOPPING: Street market shopping in La Vieille Ville is the least expensive and the most fun. Rue Masséna, Place Magenta, and Rue Paradis are the pedestrian zone of shops and cafés, with Rue Paradis noted for its elegant shops. There's also a flea market on Quai Infernet, Tuesdays through Saturdays.

Alziari – Oils, spices, rustic wooden kitchenware, and olive oil soap. 14 Rue St-François-de-Paule (phone: 93-85-76-92).

Auer – A fine selection of handmade chocolates; so tempting that you'll be hard-pressed not to purchase a year's supply. 7 Rue St-François-de-Paule (phone: 83-85-77-98).

Cat Whiskers – A charming English bookshop that carries an impressive selection of both new and old titles. 26 Rue Lamartine (phone: 93-80-02-66).

Comtesse du Barry – Toulouse food delicacies of every description; 57 varieties of foie gras. 5 Rue Halévy (phone: 93-88-49-16).

Confiserie du Vieux Nice – A sweets factory with Provence specialties such as candied fruits and flowers. Watch the stuff being made downstairs, then buy it upstairs. 14 Quai Papacino and Rue Robilante (phone: 93-55-43-50).

Galeries Lafayettes – Part of the nationwide chain of department stores that has a VAT rebate for tourists and an English-speaking staff. 6 Av. Jean-Médecin (phone: 93-85-40-21).

Louis Vuitton – Handbags, luggage, and other items with the status LVs. English is spoken, and prices are high. Check erratic seasonal opening hours. 2 Av. de Suède (phone: 93-87-87-47).

Nice-Etoile – A shopping mall with clothing, shoe, and perfume shops, plus an art gallery on the second floor. 24 Av. Jean-Médecin.

Promenade des Antiquaires – Houses a complex of 22 antiques galleries. 7 Promenade des Anglais.

Riviera Bookshop – A wide choice of new and secondhand books in English. 10 Rue Chauvain (phone: 93-85-84-61).

Vogade – For chocolate lovers. 1 Pl. Masséna (phone: 93-87-89-41).

SPORTS AND FITNESS: Boating – Various kinds of small boats are available for hire in the Vieux Port. Windsurfing craft, *planches à voile,* can be rented at bathing establishments along the promenade.

Bowling – At 5 Esplanade Kennedy (phone: 93-55-33-11); open from 11 AM to 2 AM.

Fitness Center – The *Centre Profil* at the *Meridien* hotel (1 Promenade des Anglais; phone: 93-87-73-57) has English-speaking instructors and is open to the public.

Golf – The most spectacular course is at Mont-Agel in the hills above Monte Carlo (phone: 93-41-09-11). There also are two good 18-hole courses near Nice — *Golf de Biot* (Ave. Jules-Grec, Biot 06410; phone: 93-65-08-48) and *Golf du Valbonne* (Château de la Begude, Valbonne 06160; phone: 93-42-05-30).

Horse Racing – Thoroughbred racing takes place at the *Hippodrome de Côte d'Azur* in nearby Cagnes-sur-Mer (phone: 93-20-30-30).

Horseback Riding – Horses can be rented at *Club Hippique de Nice* (368 Rte. de Grenoble; phone: 93-13-13-16); *Centre Regional de Randonnées et de Tourisme Equestre* (Rte. de St-Vallier-de-Thiey 06460; phone: 93-42-62-98); and *Relais Equestre de la Ferme* (Rte. Nationale 98, Hyères 83400; phone: 94-66-41-78).

Jogging – The wide sidewalk on the sea side of the Promenade des Anglais is good for early morning jogging. The Parc de Vaugrenier, 5 miles (8 km) west of Nice on N7, has a jogging track equipped with exercise stations.

Skiing – From November to April, you can ski on the slopes at Valberg, Isola, Esteng d'Entraunes, Auron, and Gréolières-les-Neiges in the Alps, only an hour or two away. For information, contact the *French Ski Federation* (phone: 93-80-65-77).

Swimming – The Ruhl Plage is the most central of Nice bathing beaches. Castel Plage is set right into the rock of Pointe de Rauba Capeu below the Château. In winter, you can swim at *Piscine Municipale J. Médecin* (178 Rue de France; phone: 93-86-24-01) or try *Piscine Jean Bouin* in the *Palais des Sports* (next to the Acropolis, near the Palais de l'Exposition; phone: 93-13-13-13).

Tennis and Squash – Contact the *Nice Lawn Tennis Club* (Parc Imperial, 5 Av. Suzanne Lenglen: phone: 93-96-17-70). Squash is played at *Club Vauban* (18 Rue Mal-Vauban; phone: 93-29-09-78).

THEATER: In summer, all of Nice's best theatrical experiences take place outdoors: cabarets, concerts, theater, and folkloric shows at *Théâtre de Verdure,* in the Albert Ier Garden (just off Place Masséna; phone: 93-87-77-39 or 93-82-38-68) and at the *Roman Arena* in Cimiez. Check with the tourist office or the *FNAC* record store (30 Av. Jean-Médecin; phone: 93-92-09-09) for more information. *Théâtre Francis Gag* (4 Rue St-Joseph; phone: 93-62-00-03) is a music hall with operettas and dancing. The *Nouveau Théâtre de Nice* (Esplanade des Victoires; phone: 93-80-52-60) presents a season of plays in French from October through April. For modern theater, try the *Théâtre de l'Alphabet* (10 Bd. Carabacel; phone: 93-13-08-88).

MUSIC: In addition to musical performances outdoors in summer, there is an opera season at the *Théâtre de l'Opéra* (Quai des Etats-Unis) from November through April. The box office is at 4 Rue St-François-de-Paule (phone: 93-80-59-83 for information; 93-85-67-31 for reservations). The *Nice Philharmonic Orchestra* offers a musical spring and a musical autumn at the opera house. Jazz can be heard from October to June at Cimiez's *Centre de Diffusion et d'Action Culturelle de Cimiez* (49 Av. de la Marne; phone: 93-81-09-09).

NIGHTCLUBS AND NIGHTLIFE: Probably the best-known nightspot in Nice is the *Casino Ruhl,* on the ground floor of the *Meridien* hotel (1 Promenade des Anglais; phone: 93-82-25-25 or 93-87-95-87). Smaller than its counterparts in Monte Carlo, its only *jeux* are slot machines, but it does have a Las Vegas–style cabaret and a disco called the *Jok' Club. Sphynx* (29 Rue de Préfecture; phone: 93-62-28-62) hosts a cool crowd, features video clips, and serves breakfast from 5 AM on weekends. Gambling enthusiasts can also go to Cannes, 20 miles (32 km) southwest, or Monte Carlo, 13 miles (21 km) northeast.

BEST IN TOWN

CHECKING IN: Nice hotels can be divided into those along the Promenade des Anglais, with a view of the bay — and the traffic — and those set back on quieter streets. At an expensive hotel expect to pay above $200 per night for a double (although rates can be much higher for suites at hotels such as the *Négresco*); $150 to $200 at a moderately priced hotel; less than $100 is inexpensive. However, expect prices to leap upward by one-half in summer, and perhaps even double on the most expensive end. Do not show up in the summer high season without a reservation unless you want to become an expert in Riviera hotel lobbies. Be aware, though, that Nice has a good supply of furnished rooms for visitors who plan to stay a week or more; a brochure is available upon request from the Tourisme-Syndicat d'Initiative.

Beach Regency – A deluxe, modern, and fully air conditioned 332-room hotel. The management has established a very fine restaurant, *Le Regency* (closed in July and August, when meals are served on the roof terrace), and such lively activities as *thés dansants* (tea dances) and festive buffet lunches on Sundays. And there's still a swimming pool on the roof as well as a good terrace restaurant, featuring Lebanese specialties, overlooking the bay. The location is a bit away from the center, toward the airport, but the street address still is right. Business facilities include meeting rooms for up to 400, English-speaking concierge, foreign currency exchange, secretarial services in English, audiovisual equipment, photocopiers, cable television news, translation services, and express checkout. Major credit cards accepted. 223 Promenade des Anglais (phone: 93-37-17-17; fax: 93-71-21-71; telex: 461635). Expensive.

Elysée Palace – This elegant hostelry boasts all the amenities desired by travelers on holiday or business. It's set 100 feet from the sea, yet is near the center of town, with 150 rooms and suites. Facilities include a rooftop swimming pool with a bar, a fitness room and sauna, a garage, 3 conference rooms, and an excellent restaurant. Outside, the hotel's signature is a 250-ton, 80-foot-high bronze statue of a woman by Sacha Sosno. Business facilities include meeting rooms for up to 120, an English-speaking concierge, foreign currency exchange, secretarial services in English, audiovisual equipment, photocopiers, cable television news, translation services, and express checkout. Major credit cards accepted. 33 Rue François-Ier (phone: 93-86-06-06; fax: 93-44-50-40; telex: 970336). Expensive.

Grand Hôtel Aston – Recommended not only because it is in the center of town, but also because it faces the fountains in the Place Masséna and its restaurant, *Le Champagne,* offers creditable fare. Business facilities include meeting rooms for up to 180, an English-speaking concierge, foreign currency exchange, secretarial services in English, audiovisual equipment, photocopiers, cable television news, translation services, and express checkout. Major credit cards accepted. 12 Av. Félix-Faure (phone: 93-80-62-52; fax: 93-80-40-02; telex: 470290). Expensive.

Holiday Inn – Opposite the airport, this place provides a regular free shuttle. Air conditioned throughout, it has modern luxury appointments, a pool, sauna, and solarium. Business facilities include meeting rooms for up to 200, an English-speaking concierge, foreign currency exchange, secretarial services in English, audiovisual equipment, photocopiers, cable television news, translation services, and express checkout. Major credit cards accepted. Nice Airport, 179 Bd. René-Cassin (phone: 93-83-91-92; fax: 93-21-69-57; telex: 970202). Expensive.

Meridien – Above the *Ruhl Casino* near the Albert I Garden, this shiny, modern, somewhat impersonal hotel has lots of glass and escalators, and is luxurious in a more streamlined way than the Victorian dowager hotels that gave the Riviera its reputation. There's a good restaurant, piano bar, health club, a roof terrace, and a swimming pool, as well as an underground parking lot that offers access to the pedestrian zone. Business facilities include meeting rooms for up to 400, an English-speaking concierge, foreign currency exchange, secretarial services in English, audiovisual equipment, photocopiers, cable television news, translation services, and express checkout. Major credit cards accepted. 1 Promenade des Anglais (phone: 93-82-25-25; fax: 93-16-08-90; telex: 470361). Expensive.

Négresco – One of those Côte d'Azur landmarks where everyone should stay at least once before doomsday. A great wedding cake hotel overlooking the promenade, with elaborately appointed rooms, a fine restaurant called *Chantecler* (see *Eating Out*), and staff in 18th-century rainment. In the central atrium, a ton of Baccarat crystal is suspended over what is allegedly the largest Aubusson carpet in the world (a similar chandelier is in the Kremlin). The 1913 building itself has been designated a national monument. Major credit cards accepted. Business facilities include meeting rooms for up to 400, an English-speaking concierge, foreign currency exchange, secretarial services in English, audiovisual equipment, photocopiers, cable television news, translation services, and express checkout. 37 Promenade des Anglais (phone: 93-88-39-51; fax: 93-88-35-68; telex: 460 040). Expensive.

Plaza Concorde – A traditional palace, it is beautifully restored and in the center of town facing Albert I Garden and the sea. The view from the rooftop terrace is magnificent. Business facilities include meeting rooms for up to 550, an English-speaking concierge, foreign currency exchange, secretarial services in English, audiovisual equipment, photocopiers, cable television news, translation services, and express checkout. Major credit cards accepted. 12 Av. de Verdun (phone: 93-87-80-41; fax: 93-88-61-11; telex: 460979). Expensive.

Pullman – In the center of town, this deluxe hotel is a 5-minute walk from Place

Masséna. The rooms are air conditioned and soundproof. Among the hotel's attractions are a Polynesian bar, pool and sauna, exotic interior gardens, and a great view from the rooftop terrace. Business facilities include meeting rooms for up to 80, an English-speaking concierge, foreign currency exchange, secretarial services in English, audiovisual equipment, photocopiers, cable television news, translation services, and express checkout. Major credit cards accepted. 28 Av. Notre-Dame (phone: 93-13-36-36; fax: 93-62-61-69; telex: 470662). Expensive.

Splendid-Sofitel – This 100-year-old dowager has been run by the same family for three generations, though it's been modernized, with television sets and air conditioning. One floor is reserved for nonsmoking guests. Only 500 yards from the sea, but it, too, has a pool as well as a sauna on the premises. Business facilities include meeting rooms for up to 100, an English-speaking concierge, foreign currency exchange, secretarial services in English, audiovisual equipment, photocopiers, cable television news, translation services, and express checkout. Major credit cards accepted. 50 Bd. Victor-Hugo (phone: 93-88-69-54; fax: 93-87-02-46; telex: 460938). Expensive.

Westminster Concorde – This lovely 19th-century establishment is in the grand tradition, facing the sea. All the air conditioned rooms have been soundproofed, and there's a good restaurant, bar, and disco. Business facilities include meeting rooms for up to 350, an English-speaking concierge, foreign currency exchange, secretarial services in English, audiovisual equipment, photocopiers, cable television news, translation services, and express checkout. Major credit cards accepted. 27 Promenade des Anglais (phone: 93-88-29-44; fax: 93-82-45-35; telex: 460 872). Expensive.

Albert I – One of the best situated properties in Nice, it is 50 yards from the beach and Place Masséna and a 2-minute walk from the pedestrian zone. Good views of the sea and the gardens. Business facilities include an English-speaking concierge and a meeting room that holds up to 50. Visa accepted. 4 Av. des Phocéens (phone: 93-85-74-01; fax: 93-80-36-09; telex: 970 575). Expensive to moderate.

La Pérouse – A charming small hostelry at the far end of the Quai des Etats-Unis, with a view of the entire bay, particularly spectacular at sunset. It offers gardens, pool, sauna. One drawback: traffic noise on an uphill curve outside; however, since the rooms are now air conditioned, the summertime noise level has been considerably reduced. No restaurant. Business facilities include meeting rooms for up to 25, an English-speaking concierge, foreign currency exchange, secretarial services in English, audiovisual equipment, photocopiers, translation services, and express checkout. Major credit cards accepted. 11 Quai Rauba-Capeu (phone: 93-62-34-63; fax: 93-62-59-41; telex: 461411). Expensive to moderate.

West End – Here is traditional elegance of a somewhat British flavor. A faithful clientele seems to have been coming back each year since the Crimean War. There are 130 rooms in this seafront location, but no restaurant. Business facilities include meeting rooms for up to 120, an English-speaking concierge, foreign currency exchange, secretarial services in English, audiovisual equipment, photocopiers, translation services, and express checkout. Major credit cards accepted. 31 Promenade des Anglais (phone: 93-88-79-91; fax: 93-88-85-07; telex: 460879). Expensive to moderate.

Brice – This old hotel is 4 blocks from the Promenade des Anglais, in a delightful flower garden with orange and palm trees. Business facilities include meeting rooms for up to 30, secretarial services in English, audiovisual equipment, photocopiers, translation services, and express checkout. Major credit cards accepted. 44 Rue Maréchal-Joffre (phone: 93-88-14-44; fax: 93-87-38-54; telex: 470658). Moderate.

Frantour-Napoléon – This typical, gracious, Niçois building is on a quiet corner a few streets back from the beachfront, near the pedestrian zone. The atmosphere is warm and welcoming. Bar, but no restaurant. Business facilities include meeting rooms for up to 40, audiovisual equipment, and photocopiers. Major credit cards accepted. 6 Rue Grimaldi (phone: 93-87-70-07; fax: 93-16-17-80; telex: 460 949). Moderate.

Georges – Only 18 rooms, but each is comfortable, clean, well cared for, and looks as if it's been decorated with surplus *Négresco* furnishings. Rooms are understandably hard to come by in the summer, but it's well worth the necessary advance planning. Major credit cards accepted. 3 Rue Henri-Cordier (phone: 93-86-23-41). Moderate.

Grand Hôtel de Florence – Small, centrally located yet quiet, and the 53 rooms are air conditioned. There is no restaurant. 3 Rue Paul-Déroulède (phone: 93-88-46-87; fax: 93-88-43-65; telex: 470652). Moderate.

Primotel Suisse – A small modern hotel in the traditional style, close to the Old City. Its restaurant offers a panoramic view of the Bay of Angels. Major credit cards accepted. 15 Quai Rauba-Cape (phone: 93-62-33-00; fax: 93-85-30-70; telex: 461 646). Moderate.

New York – An old white building with tropical flora in its entrance court, on a side street off the busy Avenue Jean-Médecin. Centrally located and remodeled despite its elderly-looking exterior. Major credit cards accepted. 44 Av. Maréchal-Foch (phone: 93-92-04-19; fax: 93-92-04-19; telex: 470 215). Moderate to inexpensive.

Résidencehôtel Ulys – Among the finest and most economical choices of Nice's many apartment hotels. The 88 studio and 1-bedroom apartments are clean, modern, and fully equipped with kitchens, and many have balconies overlooking the sea. Maid service by the day or week. Remember to reserve well in advance, since the rates are unusually reasonable. Major credit cards accepted. 179 Promenade des Anglais (phone: 93-96-26-30; fax: 93-86-61-62). Moderate to inexpensive.

Berne – Small, comfortable, and completely renovated, it is directly opposite the train station. No restaurant, but there's a pleasant cafeteria decorated in a rustic style. Visa accepted. 1 Av. Thiers (phone: 93-88-25-08). Inexpensive.

Impérial – In a garden with palm trees and exotic plants, this quiet hostelry is a bit out of town but close to the Exhibition Center and Congress Hall. Restaurant on the premises. Closed November through January. Visa accepted. 8 Bd. Carabacel (phone: 93-62-21-40). Inexpensive.

EATING OUT: The food found in Nice is a curious mixture of Parisian, native Provençal, and neighboring Italian. However, the city can claim specialties of its own, and some are described in the popular *Cuisine of Nice* (Penguin) by the city's flamboyant former mayor, Jean Médecin, who is married to an American. Specialties include *pissaladière,* a kind of pizza topped with black olives, onions, and anchovies; *stocaficada,* a ragout of stockfish, served with potatoes, tomatoes, peppers, and zucchini; *gnocchi à la niçoise,* a kind of potato dumpling,; and *pain bagnat,* a loaf of French bread split down the middle, soaked in olive oil, and garnished with tomatoes, radishes, peppers, onion, hard-boiled egg, black olives, and parsley. *Soupe au pistou* is a vegetable bean soup with garlic, basil, and herbs. *Socca,* a popular dish in bars of the Old Town and port, is an enormous pancake made from chickpea flour and olive oil, baked like pizza or fried in oil. It is usually washed down with a solid red wine or a little glass of *pointu* (chilled rosé). And the eponymous *salade niçoise* involves tuna fish, hard-boiled eggs, potatoes, string beans, tomatoes, and black olives. Fast food also has come to Nice; there are signs posted throughout the city giving directions to various quick eats.

Nice has the distinction of being the only major city in France, apart from Bordeaux, which grows its own Appellation Contrôlée wines within the city limits. These are the

Bellet reds, whites, and rosés, which must be tried during your stay here. At a very expensive restaurant, expect to pay $200 or more for two for dinner; $100 to $150 at expensive restaurants; $50 to $100 at moderately priced restaurants; and less than $50 at inexpensive restaurants. Prices don't include drinks or wine; usually a service charge is included.

Chantecler – Since 1990, chef Dominique le Stanc has been whipping up such specialties as *gourmandise de foie gras* (a luxurious pâté), a fish fantasy called *charlotte de St-Pierre,* and inventive dishes like lobster ravioli, which rate one Michelin star. The *menu dégustation* features tiny, elegant portions of a dozen different dishes. Closed mid-November to mid-December. Reservations necessary. Major credit cards accepted. 37 Promenade des Anglais (phone: 93-88-39-51; fax: 93-88-35-68). Very expensive.

Le Moulin de Mougins – One of the most extraordinary dining experiences on the Côte d'Azur thrives in Roger Vergé's converted 16th-century mill in the charming market town of Mougins. The cuisine justifiably has earned three Michelin stars, and among the specialties to be enjoyed are braised slivers of Provençal duck in honey and lemon sauce, escalope of fresh salmon, lobster fricassee pâté of sole, and for dessert, cold wild strawberry soufflé. There also are 5 guestrooms. Closed Mondays off-season, Thursday afternoons, and from January 29 to *Easter.* Reservations necessary. Major credit cards accepted. About 20 miles (32 km) west of Nice in Mougins (phone: 93-75-78-24). Very expensive.

L'Ane Rouge – Fine seafood specialties at this fancy restaurant in the old fort include oysters in champagne, lobster, and bourride (fish stew) — or try the sweetbreads. Closed mid-July to September, Saturdays, and Sundays. Reservations necessary. Major credit cards accepted. 7 Quai des Deux-Emmanuels (phone: 93-89-49-63). Expensive.

Château de la Chèvre d'Or – For a special treat — one Michelin star — drive east out of Nice on the Moyenne Corniche to the perched village of Eze (see *Special Places*), where you will find this excellent restaurant in a restored medieval manor house with a garden. (It's also a hotel, and a member of the Relais & Châteaux group.) Dine on lobster mousse or rack of lamb, while enjoying a spectacular panorama of the sea. Closed from December 2 to March 2 and Wednesdays during off-season. Reservations necessary. Major credit cards accepted. Moyenne Corniche, Eze (phone: 93-41-12-12; fax: 93-41-06-72; telex: 970839). Expensive.

Coco Beach – A large fish restaurant a few yards from the sea that is popular with residents who appreciate good food. Renowned for its bouillabaisse, lobster, and grilled fish of all kinds. *Very* crowded during summer months. Closed Mondays and Sunday evenings and 2 weeks in March and December. No reservations. Visa accepted. 2 Av. Jean-Lorrain (phone: 93-89-39-26). Expensive.

Colombe d'Or – This gallery–dining room in a small hotel (with a pool) just outside the gates of the old town in St-Paul-de-Vence is most noted for its collection of post-Impressionist art. (It was here that the late Simone Signoret met Yves Montand, and later married him in the presence of the hotel owner.) Matisse and other artists sometimes paid their bills during the 1920s and 1930s with the paintings that now decorate the walls. The restaurant specializes in grills and roasts, and there is a lovely view from its terrace in summer. Closed early November to mid-December. Reservations advised. Major credit cards accepted. About 14 miles (22 km) northwest of Nice in St-Paul-de-Vence (phone: 93-32-80-02; fax: 93-32-77-78; telex: 970607). Expensive.

Chez Don Camillo – A tranquil, intimate place that offers an appetizing taste of Italy (in case you're not going to make it across the border), but with a Niçois accent. Closed Sundays, Mondays, the second half of August, and school holidays in November and February. Reservations necessary. Visa accepted. 5 Rue des Ponchettes (phone: 93-85-67-95). Expensive to moderate.

Rôtisserie de St-Pancrace – Dine on prawn stew, quenelles of salmon, roast squab, or ravioli stuffed with foie gras, among other dishes. A lovely view from the garden terrace. Closed Sunday evenings, Mondays except in July and August and from early January to early February. Reservations necessary. Visa accepted. In the village of St-Pancrace, about 5 miles (8 km) north of Nice on D914 (phone: 92-09-94-94). Expensive to moderate.

La Toque Blanche – This 10-table spot offers magnificent fish dishes and has a fixed-price lunch weekdays. Closed Sunday evenings, Mondays, and mid-July through August 1. Reservations necessary. Visa accepted. 10 Rue de la Buffa (phone: 93-88-38-18). Expensive to moderate.

Auberge de Bellet – Beautifully decorated, it is the ideal place to sample the range of local Bellet wines. Accompany them with braised chicken with mint or the fricassee of fish with herb butter. In summer dine outdoors in the shaded garden. Closed Tuesdays and the first 2 weeks in February. Reservations unnecessary. Major credit cards accepted. A mile (1.6 km) to the west of St-Pancrace in the village of St-Roman-de-Bellet (phone: 93-37-83-84). Moderate.

Bông Laï – For a change of pace, this Vietnamese-Chinese restaurant is quite good, especially the lacquered duck and the fish in ginger — even the chop suey. Closed Mondays, Tuesdays, and 2 weeks in mid-December. Reservations unnecessary. Major credit cards accepted. 14 Rue Alsace-Lorraine (phone: 93-88-75-36). Moderate.

Le Champagne – The emphasis is on fish, delicately prepared with fine sauces and served in a comfortable setting. Closed Sundays. Reservations unnecessary. Visa accepted. 12 Av. Félix-Faure (phone: 93-80-62-52). Moderate.

Au Chapon Fin – This charming place in the old quarter has a limited menu of delicious regional food. Closed Sundays, Monday lunch, holidays, mid-June to July 8, and 2 weeks at *Christmas*. Reservations unnecessary. Visa accepted. 1 Rue du Moulin (phone: 93-80-56-92). Moderate.

Chez Michel – Also called *Le Grand Pavois,* this place has very good seafood dishes, especially the fish soup, stuffed mussels, and the sole meunière. Closed Mondays. Reservations unnecessary. Visa accepted. 11 Rue Meyerbeer (phone: 93-88-77-42). Moderate.

Chez les Pêcheurs – The specialties of this seafood spot in the Old Port include fish pâté and grilled deep sea bass (*loup de mer*). Closed Tuesday evenings in season, Wednesdays, Thursday for lunch in season, and November. Reservations unnecessary. Major credit cards accepted. 18 Quai Docks (phone: 93-89-59-61). Moderate.

Au Ciel d'Azur – Elegant dining where you'd least expect it — on the second floor of the airport. Very good fish, especially the sole, and luscious desserts. (There's a nonsmoking section.) And if you find yourself at the airport with time to kill but little appetite, the restaurant's adjoining bar is a comfortable refuge from the crowded self-service restaurant-bar on the third floor. Open daily. Reservations unnecessary. Major credit cards accepted. Aéroport de Nice (phone: 93-21-36-36). Moderate.

Au Passage – A Vietnamese eatery with French cooking, too. Excellent sauces; simple atmosphere. Closed Sundays and the last 2 weeks of August. No reservations. Visa accepted. 11 *bis* Bd. Raimbaldi (phone: 93-80-23-15). Moderate.

A la Ribote – The crazy-quilt menu lists oysters, fish, paella, and couscous, along with a daily special. Closed Saturdays, and the last week in August. No reservations. Most major credit cards accepted. 5 Av. de Bellet, Pl. de Caserne des Pompiers Magnan (phone: 93-86-56-26). Moderate.

Ruhl Plage – The best of the beach restaurants along the Promenade des Anglais serves good grilled fish, salads, and carafe wines. A pool for children and all kinds of water sports facilities make it a popular summer lunch spot with the Niçois.

Open from March through November, or as long as the weather stays warm. No reservations. Major credit cards accepted. Opposite the *Casino Ruhl,* which is at 1 Promenade des Anglais (phone: 93-87-09-70). Moderate.

L'Univers "César" – A great place for pasta, which is served in all shapes and styles. *Loup de mer* (sea bass) with *cèpes* (mushrooms) and artichokes is another specialty of the house. Open daily until 2 AM. Reservations necessary. Visa accepted. 54 Bd. Jean-Jaurès (phone: 93-62-32-22). Moderate.

La Belle Niçoise – A popular, unpretentious seafood restaurant that displays its wares on the street and also prepares food to take out. Good for oysters. Closed Mondays. No reservations. Major credit cards accepted. 32 Cours Saleya (phone: 93-80-12-63). Moderate to inexpensive.

Rendez-Vous des Sportifs – A cheery family-run place specializing in Niçois cooking. Here you can sample the whole range of regional specialties, including *pissaladière,* stockfish, and *aubergine* (eggplant) fried in olive oil. Closed Sundays. No reservations. No credit cards accepted. 120 Bd. de la Madeleine (phone: 93-86-21-39). Moderate to inexpensive.

Bièrerie Chez Nino – You may find yourself the only out-of-towner in this small old bistro tucked away in a tiny street near the train station. The place features a hundred different beers (both bottled and draft) from 22 countries, and its friendly owner will help you choose the right one to accompany your meal. Good grills and stockfish. The pictures on display are painted by local artists, and there are *chansonniers.* The clientele is a democratic mix of business suits and leather jackets. Closed Sundays and August. No reservations. Visa and Carte Bleue accepted. 50 Rue Trachel (phone: 93-88-07-71). Inexpensive.

La Méranda – Simple and plain but highly recommended by the Niçois, this tiny, crowded place near the flower market is run by a husband and wife team. Service is a bit slow, as each dish is prepared to order. Tripes *niçoises* and pâtés *au pistou* are splendid choices. Closed February, August, Saturday evenings, Sundays, and Mondays. No reservations. Visa accepted. 4 Rue de la Terrasse (no phone). Inexpensive.

La Nissarda – In an attractive setting just a 10-minute walk from Place Masséna, serving many local specialties. Closed Sundays and August. No reservations. No credit cards accepted. 17 Rue Gubernatis (phone: 93-85-26-29). Inexpensive.

La Pizza – The best pizza this side of Ventimiglia (and possibly Milan), and good pasta, too. Young folks congregate en masse here until 1 AM. Open daily from 11:30 AM. No reservations. Visa accepted. In the heart of the pedestrian zone, at 34 Rue Masséna (phone: 93-87-70-29). Inexpensive.

Rive Gauche – A small, friendly bistro with an Art Deco interior. Good food, like calves' liver and duck, and an excellent value. Closed Sundays. No reservations. Most major credit cards accepted. 27 Rue Ribotti (phone: 93-89-16-82). Inexpensive.

Taverne du Château – Good Niçois cooking in a lively family place in Old Nice. Open daily. No reservations. No credit cards accepted. 42 Rue Droite (phone: 93-62-37-73). Inexpensive.

 BARS AND CAFÉS: The *Scotch Tea House* (4 Av. de Suède; phone: 93-16-03-55) is very British and proper. *Chez Wayne* (15 Rue de Préfecture; phone: 93-13-46-99) is also British (from London), and caters to a young crowd who likes beer and rock 'n' roll. *Café de France* (12 Bd. Gambetta; phone: 93-88-50-81) is a landmark where old and young Niçois alike, as well as out-of-towners, drink coffee or beer or dine from a light menu. An older crowd frequents *Le Mississippi* (5 Promenade des Anglais; phone: 93-82-06-61). At water's edge is *Le Queenie* (19 Promenade des Anglais; phone: 93-88-52-50), a café with a bamboo and glass decor.

Bar L'Hermitage — also called *Bar des Oiseaux* (5 Rue St-Vincent; phone: 93-80-27-33) — is a colorful place where, legend has it, the owner carries a bird on her shoulder; ask for a *piconbière,* the house specialty. *Le Valentino* (3 Promenade des Anglais; phone: 93-87-09-27) features live music in decor centered on black lacquered wood. There's also live music at *Le Pam-Pam Masséna* (1 Rue Desboutin; phone: 93-80-21-60). *L'Isle au Zebre* is a *cave* restaurant with French Caribbean music, a dance floor, and a billiard table (19 Rue Droite; phone: 93-80-56-27). Late-night places include *Bar-Tabac des Fleurs* (13 Cours Saleya), a bar near the *Marché aux Fleurs* that *opens* at 4 AM; and *Le Frog,* where you can drink, eat Tex-Mex food, and listen to live music after the restaurant closes (closed Sundays; Rue Milton Robbins; phone: 93-85-85-65). *Le Cheap* features spare ribs, some French food, and good cocktails, and a great lineup of sounds from rock to jazz and soul (closed Sundays; 4 Rue de la Barillerie; phone: 93-80-46-76).

PARIS

It was Victor Hugo, the great French poet and novelist, who captured the true spirit of his native city when he called it "the heir of Rome, the mundane pilgrim's home away from home." If Rome, for all its earthly exuberance, never lets a visitor forget that it is the spiritual home of the West, Paris — with its supreme joie de vivre and its passion for eating, drinking, and dressing well — belongs unabashedly to the material world.

Like a magnet, Paris always has attracted visitors and exiles from all corners of the earth. At the same time, it remains not so much an international city as a very French one, and a provincial one at that. Paris has its own argot, and each neighborhood retains its peculiar character, so that the great capital is still very much a city of 20 villages.

But parochialism aside — and forgetting about the consummate haughtiness of Parisians (someone once remarked that Parisians don't even like themselves) — the main attraction of the City of Light is its beauty. When you speak of the ultimate European city, it must be Paris, if only for the view fro the Place de la Concorde or the Tuileries up the Champs-Elysées toward the Arc de Triomphe, or similarly striking sights beside the Seine. Here is the fashion capital of the world and the center of gastronomic invention and execution. Here the men all seem to swagger with the insouciance of privilege, and even the humblest shopgirl dresses with the care of a haute couture mannequin. Paris is the reason "foreign" means "French" to so many travelers.

Paris is in the north-central part of France, in the rich agricultural area of the Seine River Valley. With a population of over 2 million people, it is France's largest city, an industrial and commercial hub, an important river port, as well as an undisputed center for arts and culture. Roughly elliptical in shape, the city has more than doubled in size in the last century, although the population has decreased in the past decade as residential buildings are converted to offices and the city becomes increasingly too expensive for large families. Its limits now are the ring of mid-19th-century fortifications that once were well beyond its boundaries. At its western edge is the vast Bois de Boulogne and to the east the Bois de Vincennes — two enormous parks. Curving through Paris, the Seine divides the city into its northern Right Bank (La Rive Droite) and southern Left Bank (La Rive Gauche). The Right Bank extends from the Bois de Boulogne on the far west, through Place Charles-de-Gaulle (l'Etoile), which surrounds the Arc de Triomphe, and farther east to the Tuileries Gardens and the fabulous *Louvre*. North of the *Louvre* is the area of the Grands Boulevards, centers of business and fashion; farther north is the district of Montmartre, built on a hill and crowned by the domed Basilica of Sacré-Coeur, an area that has attracted great artists (and many of markedly less greatness) since the days of Monet and Renoir.

The Left Bank sweeps from the Eiffel Tower on the west through the Latin Quarter, with its university and bohemian and intellectual community. Southwest of the Latin Quarter is Montparnasse, once inhabited jointly by artists and intellectuals and laborers, now a large urban renewal project that includes a suburban-style shopping center around the Tour Montparnasse. To the south of Montparnasse are charming, turn-of-the-century, middle class residential districts.

In the middle of the Seine are two islands, the Ile de la Cité and the Ile St-Louis, the oldest parts of Paris. It was on the Ile de la Cité (in the 3rd century BC) that Celtic fishermen known as Parisii first built a settlement they named Lutetia, "place surrounded by water." Caesar conquered the city for Rome in 52 BC, and in about AD 300, Paris was invaded by Germanic tribes, the strongest of which were the Franks. In 451, when Attila the Hun threatened to overrun Paris, a holy woman named Geneviève promised to defend the city by praying. She succeeded — the enemy decided to spare the capital — and Geneviève became the patron saint of Paris. Clovis I, the first Christian King of the Franks, made Paris his capital in the 6th century. Relentless Norman sieges, famine, and plague curtailed the city's development, but at the end of the 10th century peace and prosperity came with the triumph of Hugh Capet over the Carolingians. Capet ascended the throne, the first of a long line of Capetian kings, and Paris became the "central jewel of the French crown," a great cultural center and seat of learning.

The Capetian monarchs contributed much to the growth of the city over the next few centuries. A defensive wall was begun in 1180 by Philip Augustus to protect the expanding Right Bank business and trading center, as well as the intellectual quarter around the newly formed university on the Left Bank. He then built a new royal palace, the *Louvre,* just outside these ramparts, but he never lived there. Medieval Paris was a splendid city, a leader in the arts and in the intellectual life of Europe. The Sorbonne attracted such outstanding scholars as Alexander of Hales, Giovanni di Fidanza (St. Bonaventure), Albertus Magnus, and Thomas Aquinas.

The Ile de la Cité remained a warren of narrow streets and wood and plaster houses, but the banks of the Seine continued to be built up in both directions. Renaissance kings, patrons of the arts, added their own architectural and aesthetic embellishments to the flourishing city. Major streets were laid out; some of Paris's most charming squares were constructed; the Pont-Neuf, the first stone bridge spanning the Seine, was completed; and Lenôtre, the royal gardener, introduced proportion, harmony, and beauty with his extraordinary Tuileries.

Louis XIV, who was responsible for many of the most notable Parisian landmarks, including Les Invalides, moved the court to Versailles in the late 17th century. Paris nevertheless continued to blossom, and it was under the Sun King's rule that France and Paris first won international prestige. Visitors were drawn to the city, luxury trades were begun, and the Panthéon, Champ-de-Mars parade ground, and Ecole Militaire were built. In 1785, at age 16, Napoleon Bonaparte graduated from this military school with the notation in his report: "Will go far if circumstances permit!"

French history reflects the conflict between the two extremes of the French character, both equally strong: a tradition of aristocracy and a penchant for revolution. To the French aristocracy we owe magnificent palaces like the *Louvre,* the Luxembourg Palace, and Versailles, with their formal gardens. At the same time, the people of Paris have always been noisily rebellious and independent: from 1358, when the mob rebelled against the dauphin, to the Fronde in 1648–49, the great French Revolution of 1789, the 1830 and 1848 revolutions that reverberated throughout Europe, the Paris Commune of 1870–71, and finally the student rebellion of 1968, which nearly overthrew the Fifth Republic. The most profound one of all was the French Revolution at the close of the 18th century, the bicentennial of which was celebrated in grand style in 1989.

The excesses of the French court, the consummate luxury of the Versailles of Louis XIV, cost the French people dearly in taxes and oppression. The Parisians, fiercely independent, forced the French king to his knees with their dramatic storming of the Bastille in 1789. Inspired by the ideas of the French and English philosophers of the Enlightenment, just like the American founding fathers in 1776, the French subsequently overthrew their monarchy.

During the Revolution, unruly mobs damaged many of the city's buildings, including Ste-Chapelle and Notre-Dame, which were not restored until the mid-19th century. Napoleon, who came to power in 1799, was too busy being a conqueror to complete all he planned, though he did manage to restore the *Louvre,* construct the Carrousel Arch and Place Vendôme victory column, and begin work on the Arc de Triomphe and the Madeleine. Though he was something of a tyrant, Napoleon's conquests spread the new ideas of the Revolution — including the Code Napoléon, a system of laws embodying the ideals of "Liberty, Equality, Fraternity" — to places as far away as Canada and Moscow.

Later in the 19th century, Paris was reorganized and modernized by a great urban planner, Baron Haussmann. He instituted the brilliant system of squares as focal points for marvelous, wide boulevards and roads; he planned the Place de l'Opéra, the Bois de Boulogne and Bois de Vincennes, the railway stations, the boulevards, and the system of 20 *arrondissements* (districts) that make up Paris today. He also destroyed most of the center of the old Cité, displacing 25,000 people.

During the peaceful lull between the Franco-Prussian War and World War I, the city of Paris thrived as never before. These were the days of the Belle Epoque, the heyday of *Maxim's,* the *Folies-Bergère,* and the cancan, whose spirit is captured so well in Offenbach's heady music for *Gaieté Parisienne.* Montmartre, immortalized by Toulouse-Lautrec, was so uninhibited that the foreign press dubbed Paris the "City of Sin."

In the 2 decades before World War II, this free-spirited city attracted politically and socially exiled artists by the dozens: Picasso, Hemingway, Fitzgerald, and Gertrude Stein were just a few. Only in Paris could such avant-garde writers as James Joyce and D. H. Lawrence, and later, Henry Miller, find publishers. And Paris, which witnessed the first Impressionist exhibition in 1874 — introducing Monet, Renoir, Pissarro, and Seurat — heard the first performance of Stravinsky's revolutionary "Sacre du Printemps" (Rite of Spring) in 1913, even though the baffled audience jeered loudly.

As the quintessentially beautiful center of intellectual life and home of the arts, Paris can claim to have earned its City of Light title. Even though it, like other modern cities, is troubled by a rise in crime — at *Maxim's,* for instance, a precautionary bulletproof window has been installed — its beauty and libertarian atmosphere remain. Its supreme talent for civilized living has made the city beloved by the French and foreigners alike. After all, these are the people who made food preparation a fine art, and despite the unfortunate presence of fast-food vendors on the Champs-Elysées, the French passion for haute cuisine remains unrivaled. And as the undisputed capital of fashion, male and female, Paris continues to be the best-dressed city in the world, and the Rue du Faubourg-St-Honoré remains the standard by which all other shopping streets are measured.

However avant-garde in dress, Parisians are a conservative lot when it comes to any changes in the appearance of their beloved city. When the Eiffel Tower was built in 1889, Guy de Maupassant commented, "I spend all my afternoons on the Eiffel Tower; it's the only place in Paris from which I can't see it." Not long ago, Parisians grumbled about the ultramodern *Centre Georges-Pompidou,* now a focus for every type of modern art: theater, music, dance, circus, painting, sculpture, photography, and film, and about *Le Forum des Halles,* a sunken glass structure filled with boutiques in what was once *Les Halles,* the bawdy produce market. Today these are popular tourist attractions, and the symbols of the new, modern Paris. More recent issues that have sparked criticism and controversy include the I.M. Pei glass pyramids that form the new entrance to the *Louvre,* and a project to replace the Bibliothèque Nationale with a giant, glass library.

Parisians accept innovations reluctantly because they want their city to remain as it has always been. They love their remarkable heritage inordinately, and perhaps it is this love, together with the irrepressible sense of good living, that has made Paris so eternally attractive to others.

PARIS AT-A-GLANCE

SEEING THE CITY: It's impossible to single out just one perfect Paris panorama; they exist in profusion. The most popular is the bird's-eye view from the top of the Eiffel Tower on the Left Bank; there are several places to have snacks and drinks and enjoy a view (on a clear day) of more than 50 miles. (There also are three restaurants where you can enjoy fine dining.) The tower is open daily, 10 AM to 11 PM; admission charge (Champ-de-Mars, 7e; phone: 45-55-91-11). From the top of the towers of Notre-Dame, eager spectators enjoy close-ups of the cathedral's Gothic spires and flying buttresses, along with a magnificent view of the Ile de la Cité and the rest of Paris. Start climbing the steps at the foot of the north tower. Open daily from 10 AM to 12:30 PM and 1:45 to 5 PM; admission charge (Rue du Cloître Notre-Dame, 4e; phone: 43-29-50-40). On the Right Bank there's a stunning view from the terrace of Sacré-Coeur. The observatory on Tour Montparnasse also offers a striking panorama, as does the landing at the top of the escalator at the *Centre Georges-Pompidou,* and the observation deck of *Samaritaine,* the 10-floor department store at the foot of the Pont-Neuf.

The most satisfying view, if not the highest, is from the top of the Arc de Triomphe.

The arch is the center of Place Charles-de-Gaulle, once Place de l'Etoile (Square of the Star), so called because it is the center of a "star" whose radiating points are the 12 broad avenues, including the Champs-Elysées, planned and built by Baron Haussmann in the mid-19th century. Open daily, 10 AM to 5:30 PM; admission charge (phone: 43-80-31-31). Another spectacular cityscape can be seen from the Grande Arche de la Défense. Located just to the west of the city, the Grande Arche completes the axis that starts at the *Louvre* and runs through the Champs-Elysées and the Arc de Triomphe. Open Mondays through Fridays, 9 AM to 5 PM, and Saturdays and Sundays from 10 AM to 7 PM. Admission charge. 1 Cour de la Défense, Puteaux (phone: 49-07-27-57).

SPECIAL PLACES: Getting around this sprawling metropolis isn't difficult once you understand the layout of the 20 *arrondissements*. We suggest that visitors orient themselves by taking one of the many excellent sightseeing tours offered by *Cityrama* (4 Pl. des Pyramides, 1er; phone: 42-60-30-14) or *Paris Vision* (214 Rue de Rivoli, 1er; phone: 42-60-31-25). Their bubble-top, double-decker buses are equipped with earphones for simultaneous commentary in English and several other languages. Reserve through any travel agent or your hotel's concierge.

Once you have a better idea of the basic layout of the city, buy a copy of *Paris Indispensable* or *Plan de Paris par Arrondissement* at any bookshop or newsstand. These little lifesavers list streets alphabetically and indicate the nearest métro station on individual maps and an overall plan. Now you're ready to set out by foot (the most rewarding) or by métro (the fastest and surest) to discover Paris for yourself.

Street addresses of the places mentioned throughout the chapter are followed by their *arrondissement* number.

LA RIVE DROITE (THE RIGHT BANK)

Arc de Triomphe and Place Charles-de-Gaulle – This monumental arch (165 feet high, 148 feet wide) was built between 1806 and 1836 to commemorate Napoleon's victories. It underwent a major cleanup and restoration for the bicentennial of the French Revolution. Note the frieze and its 6-foot-high figures, the ten impressive sculptures (especially Rude's *La Marseillaise* on the right as you face the Champs-Elysées), and the arches inscribed with the names of Bonaparte's victories, as well as those of Empire heroes. Beneath the arch is the French Tomb of the Unknown Soldier and its Eternal Flame, which is rekindled each day at 6:30 PM. An elevator (or 284 steps) carries visitors to the top for a magnificent view of the city and the 12 avenues radiating from l'Etoile. Admission charge. Pl. Charles-de-Gaulle, 8e (phone: 43-80-31-31).

Champs-Elysées – Paris's legendary promenade, the "Elysian Fields," was swampland until 1616. It once was synonymous with everything glamorous in the city, but the "Golden Arches" and shlocky shops recently have replaced much of the old glamour (a commission was formed in 1990 to try to restore some of the old elegance). The Champs-Elysées stretches for more than 2 miles between the Place de la Concorde and the Place Charles-de-Gaulle (l'Etoile). The very broad avenue, lined with rows of plane and horse chestnut trees, shops, cafés, and cinemas, still is perfect for strolling, window shopping, and people watching.

The area from the Place de la Concorde to the Rond-Point des Champs-Elysées is a charming park, where Parisians often bring their children. On the north side of the gardens is the Palais de l'Elysée, the official home of the President of the French Republic. Ceremonial events, such as the *Bastille Day Parade* (July 14), frequently take place along the Champs-Elysées.

Grand Palais – Off the Champs-Elysées, on opposite sides of Avenue Winston-Churchill, are the elaborate turn-of-the-century *Grand Palais* and *Petit Palais* (Large Palace and Small Palace), built of glass and stone for the *1900 World Exposition*. With its stone columns, mosaic frieze, and flat glass dome, the *Grand Palais* contains a large area devoted to temporary exhibits, as well as the *Palais de la Découverte* (the Paris science museum and the planetarium). Open daily from 10 AM until 6 PM; 7 PM on Sundays. Closed Mondays. Admission charge. Av. Franklin-Roosevelt, 8e (phone: 40-59-18-21; 40-74-80-00).

Petit Palais – Built contemporaneously with the *Grand Palais,* it has exhibits of the city's history, as well as a variety of fine and applied arts and special shows. Open 10 AM to 5:40 PM. Closed Mondays. Admission charge. Av. Winston-Churchill, 8e (phone: 42-65-12-73).

Place de la Concorde – This square, surely one of the most magnificent in the world, is grandly situated in the midst of equally grand landmarks: the *Louvre* and the Tuileries on one side, the Champs-Elysées and the Arc de Triomphe on another, the Seine and the Napoleonic Palais Bourbon on a third, and the pillared façade of the Madeleine on the fourth. Designed by Gabriel for Louis XV, the elegant square was where his unfortunate successor, Louis XVI, lost his head to the guillotine, as did Marie-Antoinette, Danton, Robespierre, Charlotte Corday, and others. It was first named for Louis XV, then called Place de la Révolution by the triumphant revolutionaries. Ornamenting the square, the eight colossal statues representing important French provincial capitals were polished and blasted clean for the bicentennial celebration in 1989. The 3,300-year-old, 75-foot-high obelisk was a gift from Egypt in 1829.

Jardin des Tuileries – Carefully laid out in patterned geometric shapes, with clipped shrubbery and formal flower beds, statues, and fountains, this is one of the finest examples of French garden design (in contrast to an informal English garden, exemplified by the Bois de Boulogne). It is currently undergoing extensive renovations which will be completed in 1997. Along the Seine, between the Place de la Concorde and the *Louvre.*

Orangerie – A museum on the edge of the Tuileries gardens, it displays a series of large paintings of water lilies by Monet called the *Nymphéas* and the collection of Jean Walter and Paul Guillaume, with works by Cézanne, Renoir, Matisse, Picasso, and others. Open 10 AM to 5:15 PM; closed Tuesdays. Admission charge. Pl. de la Concorde and Quai des Tuileries, 1er (phone: 42-97-48-16).

Rue de Rivoli – This charming old street has perfume shops, souvenir stores, boutiques, bookstores, cafés, and such hotels as the *Meurice* and the *Inter-Continental* under its 19th-century arcades. The section facing the Tuileries, from the Place de la Concorde to the *Louvre,* is an especially good place to explore on rainy days.

Louvre – Built on the site of a medieval fortress on the banks of the Seine, this palace was the home of the French kings during the 16th and 17th centuries, until Louis XIV moved the court to Versailles in 1682. In 1793 it became a museum, and now is one of the world's greatest art repositories. It's easy to spend a couple of days here, savoring treasures like the *Venus de Milo, Winged Victory,* the *Mona Lisa,* and the French crown jewels — just a few of the 297,000 pieces in six different collections.

Nor is the outside of this huge edifice to be overlooked. Note especially the Cour Carrée (the courtyard of the old *Louvre*), the southwest corner of which, dating from the mid-1550s, is the oldest part of the palace and a beautiful example of the Renaissance style that François I had so recently introduced from Italy. Note, too, the Colonnade, which forms the eastern front of the Cour Carrée, facing the Place du Louvre; fully classical in style, it dates from the late 1660s, not too long before the Sun King left for Versailles. Newer wings of the *Louvre* embrace the palace gardens, in the midst of which stands the Arc de Triomphe du Carrousel, erected by Napoleon. From here, the vista across the Tuileries and the Place de la Concorde and on up the Champs-Elysées to the Arc de Triomphe is one of the most beautiful in Paris — which says a lot. The glass pyramids — designed by I. M. Pei and opened in 1989 — sit center stage in the *Louvre*'s grand interior courtyard, and the largest of the intrusive trio now is the museum's main entrance. The controversial structure now houses the *Louvre's* underground galleries and shops, along with an exhibit space that connects the North and South wings, increasing museum exposition space by almost 80%.

Good guided tours in English, covering the highlights of the *Louvre,* are frequently available, although not every day, so be sure to check in advance. Open from 9 AM to 6 PM; Mondays and Wednesdays from 9:45 AM to 9:45 PM; closed Tuesdays. Admission charge. Pl. du Louvre, 1er (phone: 40-20-51-51 for recorded information in French and English, or 40-20-50-50 for more detailed information).

Place Vendôme – Just north of the Tuileries is an aristocrat of a square, one of the loveliest in Paris, the octagonal Place Vendôme, designed by Mansart in the 17th century. Its arcades contain world-famous jewelers, perfumers, and banks, the *Ritz* hotel, and the Ministry of Justice. The 144-foot column in the center is covered with bronze from the 1,200 cannon captured at Austerlitz by Napoleon in 1805. Just off Place Vendôme is the famous Rue du Faubourg-St-Honoré, one of the oldest streets in Paris, which now holds elegant shops selling the world's most expensive made-to-order items. To the north is the Rue de la Paix, noted for its jewelers.

Opéra – Charles Garnier's imposing rococo edifice stands in its own busy square, its façade decorated with sculpture, including a copy of Carpeaux's *The Dance* (the original is now in the *Musée d'Orsay*). The ornate interior has an impressive grand staircase, a beautiful foyer, lavish marble from every quarry in France, and Chagall's controversially decorated dome. These days, the opera house is home to the *National Ballet,* while almost all operatic performances have been relocated to the *Opéra de la Bastille.* Visitors may explore its magnificent interior and enjoy its special exhibitions daily from 11 AM to 4:30 PM, except on the days when there are special performances. Admission charge. Pl. de l'Opéra, 9e (phone: 47-42-57-50).

Opéra de La Bastille – In sharp contrast to Garnier's *Opéra* is the curved glass façade of 20th-century architect Carlos Ott's new Paris opera house. Set against the historic landscape of the Bastille quarter, this austere, futuristic structure houses over 30 acres of multipurpose theaters, shops, and urban promenade. Inaugurated for the bicentennial of the revolution on July 14, 1989, the opera house opened in March 1990 with a production of Berlioz's *Les Troyens.* It looks a lot like the prison-fortress that started the French Revolution. Pl. de la Bastille, 11e (phone: 40-01-17-89).

La Madeleine – Starting in 1764, the Church of St. Mary Magdalene was built and razed twice before the present structure was commissioned by Napoleon in 1806 to honor his armies. The church is based on a Greek temple design, with 65-foot-high Corinthian columns supporting the sculptured frieze. From its portals, the view extends down Rue Royale to Place de la Concorde and over to the dome of Les Invalides. Nearby are some of Paris's most tantalizing food shops. Open from 7:30 AM to 7 PM as well as during concerts (held 4 PM Sundays) and other frequent musical events. Pl. de la Madeleine, 8e (phone: 42-65-52-17).

Sacré-Coeur and Montmartre – Built on the highest of Paris's seven hills, the white-domed Basilica of Sacré-Coeur provides an extraordinary view from its steps, especially at dawn or sunset. The area around the church was the artists' quarter of late-19th- and early-20th-century Paris. The more garish aspects of Montmartre's notoriously frivolous 1890s nightlife, particularly the dancers and personalities at the *Moulin Rouge,* were immortalized by the paintings of Henri de Toulouse-Lautrec. And if the streets look familiar, chances are you've seen them in the paintings of Utrillo; they still look the same. The Place du Tertre is still charming, though often filled with tourists and overly eager, mostly undertalented artists. Go early in the day to see it as it was when Braque, Dufy, Modigliani, Picasso, Rousseau, and Utrillo lived here. Montmartre has the last of Paris's vineyards — and still contains old houses, narrow alleys, steep stairways, and carefree cafés enough to provide a full day's entertainment; at night, this is one of the centers of Paris life. Spare yourself most of the climb to

Sacré-Coeur by taking the funicular (it has been replaced by a more modern, glass contraption — bringing the *Louvre's* main pyramid to mind) or the Montmartre bus (marked with an icon of Sacré-Coeur on the front instead of the usual number) from Place St-Pierre. Butte Montmartre, 18e.

Les Halles – Just northeast of the *Louvre,* this 80-acre area, formerly the *Central Market,* "the Belly of Paris," was razed in 1969. Gone are most of the picturesque early-morning fruit-and-vegetable vendors, butchers in blood-spattered aprons, and truckers bringing the freshest produce from all over France. Their places have been usurped by trendy shops and galleries of youthful entrepreneurs and artisans, small restaurants with lots of charm, the world's largest subway station, acres of trellised gardens and playgrounds, and *Le Forum des Halles,* a vast complex of boutiques, ranging from the superchic designer ready-to-wear to more ordinary shops, as well as concert space and movie theaters. Touch-sensitive locator devices, which help visitors find products and services, are placed strategically. A few echoes of the earthy past remain, however, and you can still dine at *Au Pied de Cochon, Le Pharamond,* and *L'Escargot Montorgueil,* or have a drink with the few remaining workmen (before noon) at one of the old brasseries.

Le Centre National d'Art et de Culture Georges-Pompidou (Le Centre Georges-Pompidou) – Better known as "the Beaubourg," after the plateau on which it is built, this stark, 6-level creation of steel and glass, with its exterior escalators and blue, white, and red pipes, created a stir the moment its construction began. Outside, a computerized digital clock ticks off the seconds remaining until the 21st century. This wildly popular museum brings together all the contemporary art forms — painting, sculpture, the plastic arts, industrial design, music, literature, cinema, and theater — under one roof, and that roof offers one of the most exciting views of Paris. The old houses and cobbled, tree-shaded streets and squares vie for attention with galleries, boutiques, and the spectacle provided by jugglers, mimes, acrobats, and magicians in the plaza out front. The scene in the courtyard often rivals the exhibits inside. Open weekdays from noon to 10 PM; 10 AM to 10 PM weekends. Closed Tuesdays; no admission charge on Sundays except for special exhibitions. Rue Rambuteau, at the corner of Rue St-Martin, 4e (phone: 42-77-12-33).

Le Marais – Northeast of the *Louvre,* a marshland until the 16th century, this district became the height of residential fashion during the 17th century. But as the aristocracy moved on, it fell into disrepair. Recently, after a long period of neglect, the Marais has been enjoying a complete face-lift. Spurred on by the opening of the *Picasso Museum* in the Hôtel du Salé, preservationists have lovingly restored more than a hundred of the magnificent old mansions to their former grandeur. They now are museums of exquisite beauty, with muraled walls and ceilings, and their courtyards are the sites of dramatic and musical presentations during the summer *Festival du Marais.* Among the houses to note are the Palais de Soubise, now the National Archives, and the Hôtels d'Aumont, de Clisson, de Rohan, de Sens, and de Sully (*hôtel* in this sense means private residence or townhouse). The Caisse Nationale des Monuments, housed in the last one, can provide maps of the area, as well as fascinating and detailed tours. It also offers lectures on Saturdays and Sundays. 62 Rue St-Antoine, 4e (phone: 42-74-22-22).

Place des Vosges – In the Marais district, the oldest square in Paris — and also one of the most beautiful — was completed in 1612 by order of Henri IV, with its houses elegantly "built to a like symmetry." Though many of the houses have been rebuilt inside, their original façades remain, and the restored square is one of Paris's enduring delights. Corneille, Racine, and Mme. de Sévigné lived here. At No. 6 is the *Maison de Victor-Hugo,* once the writer's home and now a museum. Closed Mondays; admission charge (4e; phone: 42-72-10-16).

Musée Carnavalet (Carnavalet Museum) – Also in the Marais, this once was the home of Mme. de Sévigné, a noted 17th-century letter writer, and now its beautifully arranged exhibits cover the history of the city of Paris from the days of Henri IV to the present. Its recent expansion through the *lycée* next door and into the neighboring *Le Peletier* hotel doubled the exhibition space, making it the largest museum in the world devoted to the history of a single capital city. The expansion, done primarily to house a permanent major exhibit on the French Revolution, was part of Paris's celebration of the Revolution's bicentennial. Watch for special exhibitions here. The museum also rents out its concert hall to various music groups. Closed Mondays; no admission charge on Sundays. 23 Rue de Sévigné, 3e (phone: 42-72-21-13).

Musée Picasso (Picasso Museum) – This long-awaited museum, which contains a large part of the artist's private collection, is at the Hôtel du Salé. To tell the truth, the building is at least as interesting as the artwork it houses — too many recent works, too few early ones — but a visit is worthwhile just to see Picasso's collection of works by other artists (the Cézannes are best). Open Mondays and Thursdays through Saturdays from 9:15 AM to 5 PM, Wednesdays from 9:15 AM to 10 PM. Admission charge. 5 Rue de Thorigny, 3e (phone: 42-71-25-21).

Cimetière Père-Lachaise (Père-Lachaise Cemetery) – For those who like cemeteries, this one is a beauty. In a wooded park, it's the final resting place of many illustrious personalities. A map is available at the gate to help you find the tombs of Balzac, Sarah Bernhardt, Chopin, Colette, Corot, Delacroix, Héloise and Abélard, La Fontaine, Modigliani, Musset, Edith Piaf, Rossini, Oscar Wilde, Yves Montand, and even Jim Morrison (of the *Doors* rock group), among others. Note, too, the legions of resident cats. Open daily from 8 AM to 5:30 PM. Bd. de Ménilmontant at Rue de la Roquette, 20e (phone: 43-70-70-33).

La Villette – The City of Sciences and Industry, a celebration of technology, stands in its own park on the northeastern edge of the capital and houses a planetarium, the spherical *Géode* cinema, lots of hands-on displays, and a half-dozen exhibitions at any given time. The newest feature is the *Cinaxe,* a movie theater that simulates a rocket launch. Viewers are strapped into their seats, and watch a film while the theater shakes and vibrates. A must for children. Restaurants and snack bars. Open 10 AM to 6 PM. Closed Mondays. Admission charge. 30 Av. Cotentin-Cariou, 20e (phone: 40-05-70-00 or 40-05-80-00).

Bois de Boulogne – Originally part of the Forest of Rouvre, on the western edge of Paris, this 2,140-acre park was planned along English lines by Napoleon. Ride a horse or a bike, row a boat, shoot skeet, go bowling, smell roses, picnic on the grass, see horse races at *Auteuil* and *Longchamp,* visit a children's amusement park (*Jardin d'Acclimatation*) and a zoo, see a play, walk to a waterfall — and there's lots more. A particularly lovely spot is the Bagatelle château and park; a former residence of Marie-Antoinette, it boasts a magnificent rose garden (on the Rte. de Sevres in Neuilly, 16e; phone: 40-71-75-23). Closed Mondays. Admission charge. Try to avoid the park after dark, when it becomes a playground for prostitutes and transvestites who actively solicit passersby. Recent attempts by the French government to stop the nighttime activity by banning cars from the park have begun to alleviate the situation (métro: Port d'Auteuil).

Bois de Vincennes – As a counterpart to the Bois de Boulogne, a park, a palace, and a zoological garden were laid out on 2,300 acres during Napoleon III's time. Visit the 14th-century château and its lovely chapel; the large and lovely floral garden; and the zoo, with animals in their natural habitat. It's at the southeast edge of Paris (métro: Château de Vincennes).

Located on the eastern edge of the Bois de Vincennes is another fascinating spot, the *Musée National des Arts Africains et Océaniens* (Museum of African and Polynesian Art); it houses an extensive collection of art from France's former colonies. Open weekdays except Tuesdays from 10 AM to noon, and from 1:30 to 5:30 PM; Saturdays and Sundays from 12:30 to 6 PM. 293 Av. Daumesnil, 12e (phone: 43-43-13-54).

Palais de Chaillot – Built just off the Seine, near the Arc de Triomphe, for the *Paris Exposition of 1937* — on the site of the old Palais du Trocadéro left over from the *Exposition of 1878* — its terraces have excellent views across gardens and fountains to the Eiffel Tower on the Left Bank. Two wings house a theater, a *Cinémathèque,* and four museums — *du Cinéma* (phone: 45-53-74-39), *de l'Homme* (anthropology; phone: 45-53-70-60), *de la Marine* (maritime; phone: 45-53-31-70), and *des Monuments Français* (monument reproductions; phone: 47-27-35-74). Closed Tuesdays and major holidays. Pl. du Trocadéro, 16e.

LA RIVE GAUCHE (THE LEFT BANK)

Tour Eiffel (Eiffel Tower) – It is impossible to imagine the Paris skyline without this mighty symbol, yet what has been called Gustave Eiffel's folly was never meant to be permanent. Originally built for the *Universal Exposition of 1889,* it was due to be torn down in 1909, but it was saved because of the development of the wireless — the first transatlantic wireless telephones were operated from the tower in 1916. Its centennial was celebrated with great fanfare in 1989. Extensive renovations have taken place, and a post office, three restaurants (*Jules Verne* is the best), and a few boutiques have opened up on the first-floor landing. On a really clear day, it's possible to see for 50 miles. Open daily from 10 AM to 11 PM; in the summer from 9:30 AM to midnight. Admission charge. Champ-de-Mars, 7e (phone: 45-55-91-11).

Chaillot to UNESCO – From the Eiffel Tower, it is possible to look out over a group of Paris's 20th-century buildings and gardens on both sides of the Seine, including the Palais de Chaillot, the Trocadéro and Champ-de-Mars gardens, and the UNESCO buildings. Also part of the area (but not of the same century) is the huge Ecole Militaire, an impressive example of 18th-century French architecture on Avenue de la Motte-Picquet. The Y-shaped building just beyond it, facing Place de Fontenoy, is the main UNESCO building, dating from 1958. It has frescoes by Picasso, Henry Moore's *Reclining Silhouette,* a mobile by Calder, murals by Miró, and Japanese gardens by Noguchi.

Les Invalides – Built by Louis XIV as a refuge for disabled soldiers, this vast classical building has more than 10 miles of corridors and a golden dome by Mansart. For yet another splendid Parisian view, approach the building from the Alexandre III bridge. Besides being a masterpiece of the age of Louis XIV (17th century), the royal Church of the Dôme, part of the complex, contains the impressive red-and-green granite Tomb of Napoleon (admission charge). Also at Les Invalides is the *Musée de l'Armée,* one of the world's richest museums, displaying arms and armor together with mementos of French military history. Open daily from 10 AM to 5 PM. Admission charge. Av. de Tourville, Pl. Vauban, 7e (phone: 45-55-37-67).

Musée d'Orsay (Orsay Museum) – This imposing former railway station has been transformed (by the Milanese architect Gae Aulenti, among others) into one of the shining examples of modern museum curating. Its eclectic collection includes not only the Impressionist paintings decanted from the once-cramped quarters in the *Jeu de Paume,* but also less consecrated academic work and a panorama of the 19th century's achievements in sculpture, photography, and the applied arts. Open Tuesdays through Saturdays from 10 AM to 6 PM; Thursdays until 9:45 PM; and Sundays from 9 AM to 6 PM. Admission charge; reduced on Sundays. 1 Rue de Bellechasse, 7e (phone: 40-49-48-14).

Musée Rodin (Rodin Museum) – The famous statue *The Thinker* is in the garden of this splendid 18th-century residence. The chapel and the mansion also contain Rodin sculpture. Open from 10 AM to 5 PM. Closed Mondays. Admission charge. 77 Rue de Varenne, 7e (phone: 47-05-01-34).

Montparnasse – Just south of the Luxembourg Gardens, in the early 20th century there arose an artists' colony of avant-garde painters, writers, and Russian political exiles. Here Hemingway, Picasso, and Scott and Zelda sipped and supped in places like

La Closerie des Lilas, La Coupole, Le Dôme, Le Select, and *La Rotonde.* The cafés, small restaurants, and winding streets still exist in the shadow of a new shopping center.

Tour Montparnasse – This giant complex dominates Montparnasse. The fastest elevator in Europe whisks Parisians and tourists alike (for a fee) up 59 stories for a view *down* at the Eiffel Tower, from 9:30 AM to 9:30 PM daily; Fridays and Saturdays until 10:30 PM. The shopping center here boasts all the famous names, and the surrounding office buildings are the headquarters of some of France's largest companies. 33 Av. du Maine, 15e, and Bd. de Vaugirard, 14e (phone: 45-38-52-56).

Palais et Jardin du Luxembourg (Luxembourg Palace and Garden) – In what once were the southern suburbs, the Luxembourg Palace and Garden were built for Marie de Médici in 1612. A prison during the Revolution, the Renaissance palace now houses the French Senate. The classic, formal gardens, with lovely statues and the famous Médicis fountain, are popular with students meeting under the chestnut trees and with neighborhood children playing around the artificial lake. 15 Rue de Vaugirard, 6e.

Mosquée de Paris (Paris Mosque) – One of the most beautiful structures of its kind in the non-Muslim — or even in the Muslim — world, it is dominated by a 130-foot-high minaret in gleaming white marble. Shoes are taken off before entering the pebble-lined gardens full of flowers and dwarf trees. Inside, the Hall of Prayer, with its lush Oriental carpets, may be visited daily, except Fridays (the weekly prayer day for Muslims), from 9 AM to noon and 2 to 6 PM. Admission charge. Next door is a restaurant and a patio for sipping Turkish coffee and tasting Oriental sweets. Pl. du Puits-de-l'Ermite, 5e (phone: 45-35-97-33).

Panthéon – This 18th-century "nonreligious Temple of Fame dedicated to all the gods" has an impressive interior, with murals depicting the life of Ste-Geneviève, patron saint of Paris. It contains the tombs of Victor Hugo, the Résistance leader Jean Moulin, Rousseau, Voltaire, and Emile Zola. Open daily from 10 AM to noon and 2 to 5 PM. Admission charge. Pl. du Panthéon, 5e (phone: 43-54-34-51).

Quartier Latin (Latin Quarter) – Extending from the Luxembourg Gardens and the Panthéon to the Seine, this famous neighborhood still maintains its unique atmosphere. A focal point for Sorbonne students since the Middle Ages, it's a mad jumble of narrow streets, old churches, and academic buildings. Boulevard St-Michel and Boulevard St-Germain are its main arteries, both lined with cafés, bookstores, and boutiques of every imaginable kind. There are also some charming old side streets, such as the Rue de la Huchette, near Place St-Michel. And don't miss the famous *bouquinistes* (bookstalls) along the Seine, around the Place St-Michel on the Quai des Grands-Augustins and the Quai St-Michel.

Eglise St-Germain-des-Prés (Church of St-Germain-des-Prés) – Probably the oldest church in Paris, it once belonged to an abbey of the same name. The original basilica (AD 558) was destroyed and rebuilt many times. The Romanesque steeple and its massive tower date from 1014. Inside, the choir and sanctuary are as they were in the 12th century, and the marble shafts used in the slender columns are 14 centuries old. Pl. St-Germain-des-Prés, 6e (phone: 43-25-41-71).

Surrounding the church is the *quartier* of Paris's "fashionable" intellectuals and artists, with art galleries, boutiques, and renowned cafés for people watching such as the *Flore* (Sartre's favorite) and *Les Deux Magots* (once a Hemingway haunt).

Musée de Cluny (Cluny Museum) – One of the last remaining examples of medieval domestic architecture in Paris. The 15th-century residence of the abbots of Cluny later became the home of Mary Tudor and now is a museum of medieval arts and crafts, including the celebrated *Lady and the Unicorn* tapestry. Open daily, except Tuesdays, from 9:30 AM to 5:15 PM. Admission charge. 6 Pl. Paul-Painlevé, 5e (phone: 43-25-62-00).

Eglise St-Séverin (Church of St. Séverin) – This church still retains its beautiful

Flamboyant Gothic ambulatory, considered a masterpiece of its kind, and lovely old stained glass windows dating from the 15th and 16th centuries. The small garden and the restored charnel house also are of interest. 3 Rue des Prêtres, 5e (phone: 43-25-96-63).

Eglise St-Julien-le-Pauvre (Church of St. Julian the Poor) – One of the smallest and oldest churches (12th to 13th century) in Paris offers a superb view of Notre-Dame from its charming Place René-Viviani. 1 Rue St-Julien-le-Pauvre, 5e (no phone).

THE ISLANDS

Ile de la Cité – The birthplace of Paris, settled by Gallic fishermen about 250 BC, this island in the Seine is so rich in historical monuments that an entire day could be spent here and on the neighboring Ile St-Louis. A walk all around the islands, along the lovely, tree-shaded quays on both banks of the Seine, opens up one breathtaking view of Notre-Dame Cathedral after another.

Cathédrale de Notre-Dame de Paris (Cathedral of Our Lady) – It is said that the Druids once worshiped on this consecrated ground. The Romans built their temple, and many Christian churches followed. In 1163, the foundations were laid for the present cathedral, one of the world's finest examples of Gothic architecture, grand in size and proportion. Henri VI and Napoleon were crowned here. Take a guided tour (offered in English at noon Tuesdays and Wednesdays and in French at noon other weekdays, 2:30 PM Saturdays, and 2 PM Sundays) or quietly explore on your own, but be sure to climb the 225-foot towers for a marvelous view of the city and try to see the splendid stained glass rose windows at sunset. Pl. du Parvis, 4e (phone: 43-26-07-39).

Palais de Justice and Sainte-Chapelle – This complex recalls centuries of history; it was the first seat of the Roman military government, then the headquarters of the early kings, and finally the law courts. In the 13th century, St-Louis (Louis IX) built a new palace and added Sainte-Chapelle to house the Sacred Crown of Thorns and other holy relics. Built in less than 3 years, the chapel, with its 8 splendid stained glass windows and 247-foot spire, is one of the jewels of Paris. Open daily from 10 AM to 5 PM. Admission charge. 4 Bd. du Palais, 1er (phone: 43-54-30-09).

Conciergerie – This remnant of the Old Royal Palace was used as a prison during the Revolution. Here Marie-Antoinette, the Duke of Orléans, Mme. du Barry, and many others of lesser fame awaited the guillotine. It was restored extensively for the celebration of the bicentennial of the French Revolution, and the great arch-filled hall is especially striking. Open daily from 10 AM to 5 PM. Admission charge. 4 Bd. du Palais, 1er (phone: 43-54-30-06).

Ile St-Louis – Walk across the footbridge at the back of Notre-Dame and you're in a charming, tranquil village. This "enchanted isle" has managed to keep its provincial charm despite its central location. Follow the main street, Rue St-Louis-en-l'Ile, down the middle of the island, past courtyards, balconies, old doors, curious stairways, the Eglise St-Louis, and discreet plaques bearing the names of illustrious former residents (Mme. Curie, Voltaire, Baudelaire, Gautier, and Daumier, for example); then take the quay back along the edge.

■**EXTRA SPECIAL:** Versailles, by far the most magnificent of all the French châteaux, is 13 miles (21 km) southwest of Paris, accessible by train or bus. Louis XIV, called the Sun King because of the splendor of his court, took a small château used by Louis III, enlarged it, and really outdid himself. The vast, intricate, formal gardens, designed by the great Lenôtre, cover 250 acres and include 600 fountains, for which a river had to be diverted. At one time, the palace itself housed 6,000 people, and the court numbered 20,000. Louis kept his nobles in constant competition over his favors, hoping to distract them from any opposition to his rule. It's impossible to see all of Versailles in one day, but don't miss the Hall of Mirrors, the Royal Apartments, and the Chapel. Also on the grounds are the Grand Trianon, a smaller palace often visited by Louis XIV, and the Petit Trianon, a favorite of Marie-Antoinette, who also liked Le Hameau (the hamlet), a model farm where she and her companions played at being peasants. More than 20 additional rooms — the apartments of the dauphin and dauphine — are open to visitors Thursdays through Sundays. The gardens are open daily from 9 AM to 5 PM; the château and Trianons are closed Mondays and holidays. Guided tours in English are available from 10 AM to 3:30 PM. Admission charge (phone: 30-84-74-00). A spectacular illumination and display of the great fountains takes place on Sunday afternoons during the summer. For more information, contact the Versailles Tourist Office, 7 Rue des Réservoirs (phone: 39-50-36-22).

SOURCES AND RESOURCES

 TOURIST INFORMATION: For information in the US, contact the French Government Tourist Office (610 Fifth Ave., New York, NY 10020; phone: 212-757-1125). In Paris, the Office du Tourisme de Paris (127 Champs-Elysées, 8e; phone: 47-23-61-72), open daily from 9 AM to 8 PM, is the place to go for information, brochures, maps, or hotel reservations. If you call the office, be prepared for a 4- to 5-minute wait before someone answers. Other offices are found at major train stations, such as the Gare du Nord (phone: 45-26-94-82) and the Gare de Lyon (phone: 43-43-33-24).

Local Coverage – *Paris Selection* is the official tourist office magazine in French and English. It lists events, sights, "Paris by Night" tours, places to hear jazz, some hotels, restaurants, shopping, and other information. Far more complete are three weekly guides, *L'Officiel des Spectacles, Paris 7,* and *Pariscope.* All are in simple French and are available at newsstands.

For insights on eating out and finding the best of French food and wine, consult *The Food Lover's Guide to Paris* (Workman, $12.95) by American-in-Paris Patricia Wells. She also contributes a weekly column on restaurants to the *International Herald Tribune.*

 TELEPHONE: All phone numbers in Paris begin with the prefix 4 (incorporated into the numbers given here); in the area surrounding Paris, they are preceded by either 3 or 6. When calling a number in the Paris region (including the Ile-de-France) from Paris, dial only the 8-digit number. When calling a number from outside the Paris region, dial 1, then the 8-digit number. When calling from the US, dial 33 (which is the country code), followed by 1, and the 8-digit number.

Many pay phones on Paris street corners accept only phone cards. They are available in 40- and 120-franc denominations at post offices and tobacco shops. Before dialing from a pay phone, put the card into the slot on the phone and close the hood. When the franc value remaining on the card is displayed, you can dial your call.

GETTING AROUND: Airports – Charles de Gaulle Airport (Roissy, 16 miles — 25 km — northeast of Paris; phone: 48-62-12-12) has two terminals: Aérogare 1, for foreign airlines, and Aérogare 2, predominantly for *Air France* flights. The two terminals are connected by a free shuttle bus.

Air France airport buses (phone: 42-99-20-18), open to passengers of all airlines for 40F (about $7), leave for the Palais des Congrès (métro station: Porte Maillot) every 12 minutes from 5:40 AM to 11 PM and take between 30 and 50 minutes, depending on traffic. City bus No. 350 between the airport and the Gare du Nord train station also is available, but generally is slow, taking up to an hour. *Roissy-Rail* runs between the airport and the Gare du Nord every 15 minutes and takes about 35 minutes. (A shuttle bus connects the airport to Roissy station, and from there to the Gare du Nord is by train.) Taxis into town cost 160F (about $27) or more for most destinations.

Orly Airport (10 miles — 16 km — south of Paris; phone: 49-75-52-52) has two terminals: Orly Ouest, mainly for domestic flights and flights to Geneva, and Orly Sud, for international flights. The two terminals are connected by a free shuttle bus. *Air France* buses (phone: 43-23-97-10) leave for a terminus on the Esplanade des Invalides (métro station: Invalides) every 12 minutes and take from 30 to 45 minutes, depending on traffic. You can purchase tickets ($10 one way, $20 round trip) in the US from *Marketing Challengers International* (10 E. 21st St., New York, NY 10010; phone: 212-529-8484). City bus No. 215, which links the airport to Denfert-Rochereau, in southern Paris, takes about a half hour. *Orly-Rail,* a combination shuttle bus to Orly station and train to various stops in the city such as Luxembourg, St-Michel, and Invalides, runs every 15 or 30 minutes depending on the time of day and takes 35 to 50 minutes, according to the stop. A taxi into town costs 100F (about $17) and up.

Buses linking Charles de Gaulle and Orly airports run roughly every half hour and take from 50 to 75 minutes.

Boat – See Paris from the Seine by day and by night for about 30–35 francs (about $5–$6). Modern, glass-enclosed river ramblers provide a constantly changing picture of the city. Contact *Bateaux-Mouches* (Pont d'Alma, 7e; phone: 42-25-96-10), *Les Bateaux Parisiens* (Pont d'Iéna, 7e; phone: 47-05-50-00), or *Vedettes Pont-Neuf* (Square Vert-Galant, 1er; phone: 46-33-98-38). For 90F ($15), *Paris Canal* (phone: 42-40-96-97) and *Canauxrama* (13 Quai de la Loire; phone: 42-39-15-00) offer 3-hour barge trips starting on the Seine, then navigating through some of the city's old canals, locks, and a subterranean water route under the Bastille. An interesting commmentary is given in both English and French. *Paris Canal* also has two trips daily between the *Musée d'Orsay* and the Parc de la Villette — one leaves from the *Musée d'Orsay* at 9:30 AM and the other departs from the Parc de la Villette at 2:30 PM. *Canauxrama* boats leave from the Bassin de la Villette at 9:15 AM and 2:45 PM, and also from the Port de l'Arsenal at 9:45 AM and 2:30 PM.

Bus – They generally operate from 6:30 AM to 9:30 PM, although some run later. Slow, but good for sightseeing. Métro tickets are valid on all city-run buses. Lines are numbered, and both stops and buses have signs indicating routes. One or two tickets may be required, depending on the distance traveled. The *RATP,* which operates both the métro and bus system, also has designated certain lines as being of particular interest to tourists. A panel on the front of the bus indicates in English and German "This bus is good for sightseeing." *RATP* has a tourist office at Place de la Madeleine, next to the flower market (phone: 43-46-14-14), which organizes bus trips in Paris and the region.

Car Rental – Book when making your plane reservation, or contact *Avis* (phone: 45-50-32-31), *Budget* (phone: 46-86-65-65), *Europcar* (phone: 45-00-08-06), *Hertz* (phone: 47-88-51-51), or *Rent-A-Car* (phone: 43-45-98-99).

Métro – Operating from 5:30 AM to about 1 AM, it is safe, clean, quiet, easy to use, and since the Paris regional rapid transit authority (*RATP*) began to sponsor cultural events and art exhibits in some subway stops in an effort to cut down on crime and make commuting more enjoyable, entertaining as well. The events have been so popular that so far they've been offered in about 200 of Paris's 368 métro stations.

The different lines are identified by the names of their terminals at either end.

Every station has clear directional maps, some with push-button devices that light up the proper route after a destination button is pushed. Keep your ticket (you may need to show it to one of the controllers who regularly patrol the métro) and don't cheat; there are spot checks. The Paris Regional Transit Authority recently abolished the métro's long-standing first and second class system. There is now only one class of ticket.

A 10-ticket book (*carnet*) is available at a reduced rate. The Paris-Visite card, a tourist ticket that entitles the bearer to 1, 3, or 5 consecutive days of unlimited travel on the métro and on city-run buses, may be purchased in France upon presentation of your passport at 44 subway stations and 4 regional express stations, or at any of the 6 *French National Railroad* stations. In the US, the card is available by money order from *Marketing Challengers International* (10 E. 21st St., New York, NY 10010; phone: 212-529-8484) — $7.50 for a 1-day ticket, $20 for a 3-day ticket, and $30 for a 5-day ticket, plus $3 for postage and handling.

Motorcycle – For those traveling with less than the requisite four suitcases, this is the fastest (and most unusual) method of getting to Orly airport. *Omega Transport* (phone: 42-42-11-11) offers a 30-minute ride on BMW motorcycles from the center of Paris out to the airport ($76).

SITU – Handy streetside bus and subway directions are now available in some métro stations from *SITU* (*Système d'Information des Trajets Urbains*), a computer that prints out the fastest routing onto a wallet-size piece of paper, complete with the estimated length of the trip. The *RATP* service is free and augments the lighted wall maps that guide métro riders. High-traffic spots such as the Châtelet métro station, outside the Gare Montparnasse, and on the Boulevard St-Germain, now sport *SITU* machines.

Taxi – Taxis can be found at stands at main intersections, outside railway stations and official buildings, and in the streets. A taxi is available if the entire "TAXI" sign is illuminated (with a white light); the small light *beside* the roof light signifies availability after dark. But be aware that Parisian cab drivers are notoriously selective about whom they will pick up, and how many passengers they will allow in their cab — a foursome inevitably has trouble. (Good news for those who don't appreciate being snubbed by cabbies: The Paris taxi drivers' association has instituted a new program to teach potential drivers good manners, along with a soupçon of English.) You also can call *Taxi Bleu* (phone: 49-36-10-10) or *Radio Taxi* (phone: 47-39-33-33). The meter starts running from the time the cab is dispatched, and a tip of about 15% is customary. Fares increase at night and on Sundays and holidays.

Train – Paris has six main train stations, each one serving a different area of the country. The general information number is 45-82-50-50; for telephone reservations, 45-65-60-60. North: Gare du Nord (18 Rue de Dunkerque; phone: 42-80-63-63); East: Gare de l'Est (Pl. du 11-Novembre; phone: 42-03-96-31); Southeast: Gare de Lyon (20 Bd. Diderot; phone: 40-19-60-00); Southwest: Gare d'Austerlitz (51 Quai d'Austerlitz; phone: 45-84-14-19); West: Gare Montparnasse (17 Bd. de Vaugirard; phone: 40-48-10-00); West and Northwest: Gare St-Lazare (20 Rue de Rome; phone: 42-85-88-00). The *TGV* (*train à grande vitesse*), the world's fastest train, has cut 2 hours off the usual 4-hour ride between Paris and Lyons; it similarly shortens traveling time to Marseilles, the Côte d'Azur, the Atlantic Coast, and Switzerland. It leaves from the Gare de Lyon, except for the Atlantic Coast run, which departs from the Gare Montparnasse; reservations are necessary. A new *TGV* station has opened in Massy, 16 miles (25 km) south of Paris. Located right near Orly, a 15-minute ride on the *RER* (suburban train), it is ideal for those who are traveling to other parts of France and want to avoid going into Paris. There also is a new train (called the *Orlyval*) that travels between Orly Airport and Paris in less than half an hour.

LOCAL SERVICES: Baby-Sitting – One of the many agencies in Paris is *Kid's Service* (17 Rue Molière, 1er; phone: 42-96-04-16). Whether the sitter is hired directly or through an agency, ask for and check references.

Dentist (English-Speaking) – Dr. Edward Cohen, 20 Rue de la Paix, 2e (phone: 42-61-65-64 or 42-61-78-71).

Dry Cleaner/Tailor – Dry cleaners are available throughout the city. Note that many have two different price schedules, one for "economic" service, another for faster, more expensive service. The less expensive prices may be posted outside, but unless you specify, your clothes will be given the expensive treatment. *John Baillie, Real Scotch Tailor* (1 Rue Auber at Pl. de l'Opéra, 2e; phone: 47-42-49-24 or 47-42-49-17) is a reputable firm that does tailoring French-style, despite its name.

Limousine Service – *Compagnie des Limousines* (37 Rue Acacias, 17e; phone: 43-80-79-41); *Executive Car/Carey Limousine* (25 Rue d'Astorg, 8e; phone: 42-65-54-20; fax: 42-65-25-93).

Medical Emergency – The *American Hospital* has 24-hour emergency service. The hospital also has a dental service and maintains an extensive network of English-speaking specialists. 63 Bd. Victor-Hugo, Neuilly (phone: 46-41-25-25).

Messenger Service – *Neuilly Courses,* 6 Villa des Sablons, Neuilly (phone: 47-45-54-00; fax: 46-24-70-71).

National/International Courier – *Federal Express Copyshop* (44 Rue du Colisée, 8e; phone: 45-33-33-55); *DHL International* (59 Av. d'Iéna, 16e; phone: 45-01-91-00 or 48-63-70-00).

Office Equipment Rental – *Chapchool Distribution,* for typewriters with English keyboards (minimum 2-week rental). 11 Rue Etienne-Marcel, Pantin (phone: 48-45-05-25).

Pharmacy – *Pharmacie Derhy* is open 24 hours a day, including holidays. Located in the *Galerie Les Champs,* 84 Av. des Champs-Elysées, 8e (phone: 45-62-02-41).

Photocopies – In addition to the numerous small outlets specializing in photocopies, facilities are available in many stationery stores and post offices.

Post Office – The main post office (52 Rue du Louvre, 1er; phone: 40-28-20-00) is open 24 hours a day; night hours are restricted to simpler operations such as posting a registered letter. Other branches are open from 8 AM to 7 PM on weekdays and until noon on Saturdays.

Secretary/Stenographer (English-Speaking) – *Multiburo* also rents office space. 17 Rue Galilée, 16e (phone: 47-23-47-47).

Teleconference Facilities – *Hôtel Méridien,* 81 Bd. Gouvion-St-Cyr, 17e (phone: 40-68-34-34).

Telex – *PTT* (Postes et Télécommunications), open daily, including Sundays, from 8 AM to 7:30 PM, at 7 Rue Feydeau, 2e (phone: 42-33-20-12), and from 8 to 10:30 PM at 5 Rue Feydeau, just next door.

Translator – *Bilis Traduction,* 24 Rue Lafitte, 9e (phone: 47-70-50-80).

Tuxedo Rental – *Au Cor de Chasse,* 40 Rue de Buci, 6e (phone: 43-26-51-89).

SPECIAL EVENTS: After the *Christmas* season, Paris prepares for the January fashion shows, when press and buyers come to town to pass judgment on the spring and summer haute couture collections. (The general public can see what the designers have wrought after the professionals leave.) More buyers come to town in February and March for the ready-to-wear shows (fall and winter clothes), open to the trade only. March is the month of the first *Foire Nationale à la Brocante et aux Jambons* of the year. This fair of regional food products held concurrently with an antiques flea market (not items of the best quality, but not junk, either) is repeated in September. The running of the *Prix du Président de la*

République, the first big horse race of the year, takes place at *Auteuil* in April. From late April to early May is the *Foire de Paris,* the capital's big international trade fair. In late April or May there's the *Paris Marathon;* in late May (through early June), the *French Open Tennis Championships.* Odd years only, the *Paris International Air Show* is an early June attraction at Le Bourget Airport. Horse races crowd the calendar in June — there's not only the *Prix de Diane* at *Chantilly,* but also the *Grande Semaine* at *Longchamp, Auteuil,* and *St-Cloud.* And in the middle of June, the *Festival du Marais* begins a month's worth of music and dance performances in the courtyards of the Marais district's old townhouses. *Bastille Day,* July 14, is celebrated with music and fireworks, parades, and dancing till dawn in every neighborhood. Meanwhile, the *Tour de France* is under way; the cyclists arrive in Paris for the finish of the 3-week race later in July. Also in July, press and buyers arrive to view the fall and winter haute couture collections, but the ready-to-wear shows (spring and summer clothes) wait until September and October, because August for Parisians is vacation time. Practically the whole country takes a holiday then, and in the capital the classical concerts of the *Festival Estival* (in July and August) are among the few distractions. When they finish, the *Festival d'Automne,* a celebration of the contemporary in music, dance, and theater, takes over (from mid-September through December). The *Foire Nationale à la Brocante et aux Jambons* returns in September, but in even-numbered years it's eclipsed by the *Biennale des Antiquaires,* a major antiques event from late September to early October. Also in even years, usually in November, is the *Paris Motor Show.* Every year on the first Sunday of October, the last big horse race of the season, the *Prix de l'Arc de Triomphe,* is run at *Longchamp;* and every year in early October, Paris holds the *Fête des Vendanges à Montmartre* to celebrate the harvest of the city's last remaining vineyard. On November 11, ceremonies at the Arc de Triomphe and a parade mark *Armistice Day.* An *International Cat Show* and a *Horse and Pony Show* come in early December; then comes *Christmas,* which is celebrated most movingly with a *Christmas Eve* midnight mass at Notre-Dame. At midnight a week later, the *New Year* bows in to spontaneous street revelry in the Latin Quarter and along the Champs-Elysées.

MUSEUMS: Many museums (*musées*) in Paris charge an admission fee, unless otherwise indicated below. Many museums are free or offer reduced admission fees on Sundays, so call ahead before you go. "La Carte," a pass that can be used at over 60 museums and monuments in the city, is available at métro stations and at major museums (or in the US from *Marketing Challengers International,* 10 E. 21st St., New York, NY 10010; phone: 212-529-8484). Prices are the equivalent of $12 for a 1-day pass, $24 for a 3-day pass, and $32 for a 5-day pass. Note that "La Carte" is not valid for certain special exhibits. Museums of interest not described in *Special Places* include the following:

   Archaeological Crypt of Notre-Dame – Under the square in front of walls and floor plans from later periods. Open daily from 10 AM to 4:30 PM. Parvis de Notre-Dame, 4e (phone: 43-29-83-51).

   Catacombs – Dating from the Gallo-Roman era and also containing the remains of Danton, Robespierre, and many others. Bring a flashlight. Closed Mondays. 1 Pl. Denfert-Rochereau, 14e (phone: 43-22-47-63).

   Egouts (Sewers of Paris) – Underground city of tunnels, a very popular afternoon tour, daily except Thursdays and Fridays, and on holidays and the days preceding and following them. Pl. de la Résistance, in front of 93 Quai d'Orsay, 7e (phone: 47-05-10-29).

   Galerie Nationale de Jeu de Paume – Inaugurated in June 1991, this museum (which originally was built as a tennis court for Napoleon III's son) is devoted to contemporary art from 1960 on and includes paintings, sculpture, photographs, and videos, all installed in what was formerly the temple of Impressionism — the *Jeu de Paume,* at one end of the Tuileries. The interior has been redone to provide more and better exhibition space. Open Wednesdays, Thursdays, and Fridays from noon to 7 PM; Tuesdays from noon to 9:30 PM; and Saturdays and Sundays from 10 AM to 7 PM. Corner of the Tuileries gardens at the Place de la Concorde.

Maison de Balzac – The house where the writer lived, with a garden leading to one of the prettiest little alleys in Paris. Closed Mondays. 47 Rue Raynouard, 16e (phone: 42-24-56-38).

Manufacture des Gobelins – The famous tapestry factory, in operation since the 15th century. Guided tours of the workshops take place Tuesdays, Wednesdays, and Thursdays from 2:15 to 3:15 PM. 42 Av. des Gobelins, 13e (phone: 43-37-12-60).

Mémorial de la Déportation – Set in a tranquil garden in the shadow of Notre-Dame at the tip of Ile de la Cité, this monument is dedicated to 200,000 French women and men of all religions and races who died in Nazi concentration camps during World War II. Sq. de l'Ile-de-France, 4e.

Mémorial du Martyr Juif Inconnu – A moving tribute to Jews killed during the Holocaust, this 37-year-old, renovated memorial includes World War II documents and photographs. Open daily, except Friday afternoons and Saturdays, from 10 AM to noon and 2 to 5:30 PM. 17 Rue Geoffroy L'Asniers, 4e (phone: 42-77-44-72). The French Government Tourist Office has published a booklet, *France for the Jewish Traveler,* that describes these two memorials, as well as other places of interest to Jews visiting France.

Musée des Antiquités Nationales – Archaeological specimens from prehistoric through Merovingian times, including an impressive Gallo-Roman collection. Open daily, except Tuesdays, from 9:30 AM to noon and 1:30 to 5:15 PM. Pl. du Château, St-Germain-en-Laye (phone: 34-51-53-65).

Musée des Arts Africains et Océaniens – One of the world's finest collections of African and Oceanic art. Closed Tuesdays. 293 Av. Daumesnil, 12e (phone: 43-43-14-54).

Musée National des Arts Décoratifs – Furniture and applied arts from the Middle Ages to the present, Oriental carpets, and Dubuffet paintings and drawings. Galerie Art Nouveau–Art Deco features Jeanne Lanvin's bedroom and bath. It also houses 3 centuries of French posters formerly displayed in the now-closed *Musée de l'Affiche et de la Publicité.* Closed Mondays and Tuesdays. 107 Rue de Rivoli, 1er (phone: 42-60-32-14).

Musée des Arts et Traditions Populaires – Traditional arts and crafts from rural France. Open daily from 9:45 AM to 5:15 PM. Closed Tuesdays. 6 Av. du Mahatma-Gandhi, 16e (phone: 40-67-90-00).

Musée Cernuschi – Art of China. Closed Mondays and holidays. 7 Av. Vélasquez, 8e (phone: 45-63-50-75).

Musée de la Chasse et de la Nature – Art, weapons, and tapestries relating to the hunt. Of particular interest is the courtyard where horses once were kept — it is decorated with sculpture. Open daily except Tuesdays from 10 AM to 12:30 PM and 1:30 to 5:30 PM. 60 Rue des Archives, 3e (phone: 42-72-86-43).

Musée Cognacq-Jay – Art, snuffboxes, and watches from the 17th and 18th centuries. Located in a stunningly beautiful mansion in the Marais. Closed Mondays. 8 Rue Elzévir, 3e (phone: 40-27-07-21).

Musée des Collections Historiques de la Préfecture de Police – On the second floor of the modern police precinct, in the 5th *arrondissement,* are historic arrest orders (for Charlotte Corday, among others), collections of contemporary engravings, and guillotine blades. Open Mondays through Saturdays from 9 AM to 5 PM. 1 *bis* Rue des Carmes, 5e (phone: 43-29-21-57).

Musée Eugène-Delacroix – Studio and garden of the great painter; exhibits change yearly. Closed Tuesdays. 6 Rue de Furstenberg, 6e (phone: 43-54-04-87).

Musée Grévin – Waxworks of French history from Charlemagne to the present day. 10 Bd. Montmartre, 9e (phone: 47-70-85-05). A branch devoted to La Belle Epoque is in the *Forum des Halles* shopping complex. Open daily. Pl. Carrée, 1er (phone: 40-26-28-50).

Musée Guimet – The *Louvre*'s Far East collection. Closed Tuesdays. 6 Pl. d'Iéna, 16e (phone: 47-23-61-65).

Musée Gustave-Moreau – A collection of the works of the early symbolist. Closed Mondays and Tuesdays. 14 Rue de la Rochefoucauld, 9e (phone: 48-74-38-50).

Musée de l'Institut du Monde Arabe – Arab and Islamic arts from the 9th to the 19th centuries. Open from 1 to 8 PM. Closed Mondays. 23 Quai St-Bernard, 5e (phone: 40-51-38-38).

Musée Jacquemart-André – Eighteenth-century French decorative art and European Renaissance treasures, as well as frequent special exhibitions. Closed Mondays and Tuesdays. 158 Bd. Haussmann, 8e (phone: 42-89-04-91).

Musée Marmottan – Superb Monets, including the nine masterpieces that were stolen in a daring 1985 robbery. Happily, however, all were recovered in a villa in Corsica and have been cleaned — some for the first time — before being rehung. Closed Mondays. 2 Rue Louis-Boilly, 16e (phone: 42-24-07-02).

Musée de la Mode et du Costume – A panorama of French contributions to fashion in the elegant Palais Calliéra. Closed Mondays. 10 Av. Pierre-I de Serbie, 16e (phone: 47-20-85-23).

Musée de la Monnaie – More than 2,000 coins and 450 medallions, plus historic coinage machines. Open daily, except Mondays, from 1 to 6 PM. 11 Quai de Conti, 6e (phone: 40-46-55-35).

Musée Montmartre – A rich collection of paintings, drawings, and documents depicting life in this quarter. Open Mondays through Saturdays from 2:30 to 6 PM, Sundays from 11 AM to 6 PM. 12 Rue Cortot, 18e (phone: 46-06-61-11).

Musée Nissim de Camondo – A former manor house filled with beautiful furnishings and art objects from the 18th century. Closed Mondays, Tuesdays, and holidays. 63 Rue de Monceau, 8e (phone: 45-63-26-32).

Musée de Sèvres – Just outside Paris, next door to the Sèvres factory, is one of the world's finest collections of porcelain. Closed Tuesdays. 4 Grand-Rue, Sèvres (phone: 45-34-99-05).

Musée du Vin – Housed in a 13th-century abbey that was destroyed during the revolution, the museum was restored in 1981. The history and making of wine is traced through displays, artifacts, and a series of wax figure tableaux. Open daily, except Mondays, from noon to 6 PM; Saturdays and Sundays to 5:30 PM. Admission charge includes a glass of wine. 5-7 Sq. Charles-Dickens, 16e (phone: 45-25-63-26).

Parc Océanique Cousteau – Based on the work of the French oceanographer, this museum houses ocean exhibits and interactive displays. Open Mondays, Tuesdays, and Thursdays from noon to 7 PM; Wednesdays, Saturdays, Sundays, and holidays from 10 AM to 7:30 PM. *Forum des Halles,* Pl. Carrée, 1er (phone: 40-28-98-98).

Pavillon des Arts – An exhibition space in the mushroom-shaped buildings overlooking the *Forum des Halles* complex. Presentations range from ancient to modern, paintings to sculpture. Closed Mondays and holidays. 101 Rue Rambuteau, 1er (phone: 42-33-82-50).

Vidéothèque de Paris – A veritable treasure trove of information about the City of Light, this extensive computerized video archive contains thousands of films, documentaries, and videos on Paris dating from the turn of the century to today. Open Tuesdays through Sundays from 12:30 to 8:30 PM. 2 Grand Galerie, 1er (phone: 40-26-34-30 or 40-26-30-60).

GALLERIES: Few artists live in Montparnasse nowadays, as the center of the Paris art scene has shifted from the narrow streets of the Latin Quarter, which set the pace in the 1950s, to the Right Bank around the *Centre Georges-Pompidou.* Here are some galleries of note:

Agathe Gaillard – Contemporary photography, including Cartier-Bresson and the like. 3 Rue du Pont-Louis-Philippe, 4e (phone: 42-77-38-24).

Artcurial – Early moderns, such as Braque and Sonia Delaunay, as well as sculpture and prints, with an extensive, multilingual collection of art books in its bookshop. 9 Av. Matignon, 8e (phone: 42-99-16-16).

Beaubourg – Well-known names in the Paris art scene, including Niki de Saint-Phalle, César, Tinguely, Klossowski. 23 Rue du Renard, 4e (phone: 42-71-20-50).

Caroline Corre – Exhibitions by contemporary artists, specializing in unique artists' books. 14 Rue Guénégaud, 6e (phone: 43-54-57-67).

Claude Bernard – Francis Bacon, David Hockney, and Raymond Mason are among the artists exhibited here. 5 Rue des Beaux-Arts, 6e (phone: 43-26-97-07).

Daniel Malingue – Works by the Impressionists, as well as notable Parisian artists from the 1930s to the 1950s — Foujita, Fautrier, and so forth. 26 Av. Matignon, 8e (phone: 42-66-60-33).

Daniel Templon – Major contemporary American and Italian artists are featured. 30 Rue Beaubourg, 3e (phone: 42-72-14-10).

Darthea Speyer – Run by a former American embassy attaché, now an art dealer. Contemporary painting. 6 Rue Jacques-Callot, 6e (phone: 43-54-78-41).

Galerie de France – A prestigious gallery located in a majestic space features the works of historical avant-garde artists such as Brancusi and Gabo, as well as contemporary artists such as Matta, Aillaud, and Arroyo. 52 Rue de la Verrerie, 4e (phone: 42-74-38-00).

Hervé Odermatt Cazeau – Early moderns — among them Picasso, Léger, Pissarro — and antiques. 85 *bis* Rue du Faubourg-St-Honoré, 8e (phone: 42-66-92-58).

Isy Brachot – Master surrealists, American hyper-realists, and new realists. 35 Rue Guénégaud, 6e (phone: 43-54-22-40).

Jean Fournier – This dealer defended abstract expressionism in 1955 and remains faithful to the cause in his main gallery, where he also exhibits the works of promising young artists. 44 Rue Quincampoix, 4e (phone: 42-77-32-31).

Maeght-Lelong – The great moderns on display include Chagall, Tàpies, Bacon, Moore, Miró. 13-14 Rue de Téhéran, 8e (phone: 45-63-13-19).

Nikki Diana Marquardt – Spacious gallery of contemporary work opened by an enterprising dealer from the Bronx. 9 Pl. des Vosges, 4e (phone: 42-78-21-00).

Virginia Zabriskie – Early and contemporary photography by Atget, Brassaï, Diane Arbus. Also painting and, occasionally, sculpture. 37 Rue Quincampoix, 4e (phone: 42-72-35-47).

Yvon Lambert – A dealer with an eye for the avant-avant-garde, he also exhibits the works of major artists from the 1970s and 1980s, including Jammes, Lewitt, and Schnabel. 108 Rue Vielle-du-Temple, 3e (phone: 42-71-09-33).

SHOPPING: From new-wave fashions to classic haute couture, Paris starts the trends and sets the styles the world copies. Prices are generally high, but more than a few people are willing to pay for the quality of the products, not to mention the cachet of a Paris label, which enhances the appeal of many things besides clothing. Perfume, cosmetics, jewelry, leather goods and accessories, wine and liqueurs, porcelain, and art are among the many other things for which Paris is famous.

The big department stores are excellent places to get an idea of what's available. They include *Galeries Lafayette* (40 Bd. Haussmann, 9e; phone: 42-82-34-56; and other locations); *Au Printemps* (64 Bd. Haussmann, 9e; phone: 42-82-50-00); *Aux Trois Quartiers-Madelios* (21 Bd. de la Madeleine, 1er; phone: 42-60-39-30); *La Samaritaine* (19 Rue de la Monnaie, 1er; phone: 40-41-20-20); *Le Bazar de l'Hôtel de Ville* (52 Rue de Rivoli, 4e; phone: 42-74-90-00); and *Au Bon Marché* (22 Rue de Sèvres, 7e; phone: 45-49-21-22). Two major shopping centers — *Porte Maillot* (Pl. de la Porte Maillot) and *Maine Montparnasse* (at the intersection of Bd. Montparnasse and Rue de Rennes) — also are worth a visit, as is the lovely *Galerie Vivienne,* one of Paris's glass-roofed *galeries,* the 19th-century precursors of the modern-day shopping mall (main entrance at 4 Rue du Petits-Champs, 2e). *Les Trois Quartiers,* the old department store on the Boulevard de la Madeleine (21 Bd. de la Madeleine, 8e), has re-opened as a luxury mall with more than 50 shops, including *Kenzo* and *Emmanuelle Khanh* designer boutiques.

There are several shopping neighborhoods, and they tend to be specialized. Haute couture can be found in the streets around the Champs-Elysées: Av. George-V, Av. Montaigne, Rue François Ier, and Rue du Faubourg-St-Honoré; famous designers are also represented in department stores. Boutiques are especially numerous on Avenue Victor-Hugo, Rue de Passy, Bd. des Capucines, in the St-Germain-des-Prés area, in the neighborhood of the *Opéra,* in the *Forum des Halles* shopping center, around the Place des Victoires, and on or near the Rue des Rosiers in the Marais district. The Rue d'Alésia has several blocks devoted solely to discount fashion shops.

The Rue de Paradis is lined with crystal and china shops, and St-Germain-des-Prés has more than its share of art galleries. The best and most expensive antiques dealers are along the Faubourg-St-Honoré on the Right Bank. On the Left Bank there's *Le Carré Rive Gauche,* an association of more than 100 antiques shops in the area bordered by Quai Voltaire, Rue de l'Université, Rue des Sts-Pères, and Rue du Bac. Antiques and curio collectors should explore Paris's several flea markets, which include the *Montreuil,* near the Porte de Montreuil, especially good for secondhand clothing; *Vanves,* near the Porte de Vanves, for furniture and fine bric-a-brac that is often snapped up by antiques dealers (it's best to arrive early on Saturday morning); and the largest and best-known, *Puces de St-Ouen,* near the Porte de Clignancourt, which offers an admirable array of antiques.

A few more tips: Sales take place during the first weeks in January and in late June and July. Any shop labeled *dégriffé* (the word means, literally, "without the label") offers year-round discounts on brand-name clothing, often last season's styles. Discount shops also are known as "stock" shops. The French value added tax (VAT; typically 18.6% and as high as 33.33% on luxury articles) can be refunded on most purchases made by foreigners, provided a minimum of 2,000F (about $400 at press time) is spent in one store. Forms must be filled out and the refund usually is mailed to your home. Large department stores and the so-called duty-free shops have facilitated the procedure, but refunds can be obtained from any store willing to cooperate. If the refund is not exactly equal to the tax — 15% to 25% refunds are common — it's because stores may retain some of it as reimbursement for their extra expense in handling the paperwork.

Here is a sampling of the wealth of shops in Paris, many of which have more than one location in the city:

Absinthe – Chic is the word here — everything from one-of-a-kind silk hats to satin-covered settees — in this elegant little shop near the Place des Victoires.

Accessoire – Very feminine footwear, often seen on the pages of *Elle* magazine. 6 Rue du Cherche-Midi, 6e, and other locations around the city (phone: 45-48-36-08).

Agnès B – Supremely wearable, trendy, casual clothes. Four stores — one for men, one for women, one for little girls, and one for young children and infants — on the block-long Rue du Jour, 1er (phone: 40-26-36-87); 13 Rue Michelet, 6e (phone: 46-33-70-20); 17 Av. Pierre-I-de-Serbie, 16e (phone: 47-20-27-35); and 81 Rue d'Assas, 6e (phone: 43-54-69-21).

Alfred Dunhill – Menswear, toiletries, and luggage articles from the celebrated English tobacconist. 15 Rue de la Paix, 2e (phone: 42-67-57-58).

Après-Midi de Chien – Women's and children's formfitting togs in what the French dub "Anglo-Saxon"-style — tweedy jackets, jodhpurs, and print skirts. 10 Rue du Jour, 1er (phone: 40-26-92-78) and other locations.

Arnys – Conservative and elegant men's clothing. 14 Rue de Sèvres, 7e (phone: 45-48-76-99).

Azzedine Alaïa – The Tunisian designer who brought the body back. 18 Rue de la Verrerie, 4e (phone: 42-72-19-19).

Baccarat – High-quality porcelain and crystal. 30 *bis* Rue du Paradis, 10e (phone: 47-70-64-30); and 11 Pl. de la Madeleine, 8e (phone: 42-65-36-26).

La Bagagerie – Perhaps the best bag and belt boutique in the world. 12 Rue Tronchet, 8e (phone: 42-65-03-40), and other locations.

Au Bain Marie – The most beautiful kitchenware and tabletop accessories, with an emphasis on Art Deco designs. 8 Rue Boissy-d'Anglas, 8e (phone: 42-66-59-74).

Balenciaga – Ready-to-wear and designer haute couture. 10 Av. George-V, 8e (phone: 47-20-21-11).

Bazar de Hôtel de Ville – Perhaps the world's most celebrated hardware store — with everything from nuts and bolts to a French bistro sign or a washing machine. Some people travel to Paris just to visit *BHV*'s grim, cavernous expanse. 52 Rue de Rivoli, 3e (phone: 42-74-90-00).

Beauté Divine – Antique perfume bottles, Art Deco bathroom accessories, glove stretchers, nail buffers, and mustache cups. 40 Rue St-Sulpice, 6e (phone: 43-26-25-31).

Boucheron – One of several fine jewelers clustered around the elegant Place Vendôme. 26 Pl. Vendôme, 1er (phone: 42-61-58-16).

Brentano's – British and American novels, critiques on the American arts, and a variety of books on technical and business subjects — in English. 37 Av. de l'Opéra, 2e (phone: 42-61-52-50).

Cacharel – Fashionable ready-to-wear in great prints. 34 Rue Tronchet, 8e (phone: 47-42-12-61), and other locations.

Cadolle – Founded in 1889 by the woman credited with inventing the brassiere, it still sells corsets as well as other items of frilly, pretty lingerie. 14 Rue Cambon, 1er (phone: 42-60-94-94).

Carel – Beautiful shoes. 12 Rond-Point des Champs-Elysées, 8e (phone: 45-62-30-62), and other locations.

Carita – Paris's most extensive — and friendliest — beauty/hair salon. 11 Rue du Faubourg-St-Honoré, 8e (phone: 42-68-13-40).

Cartier – Fabulous jewelry. 11-13 Rue de la Paix, 2e (phone: 42-61-58-56), and other locations.

Castelbajac – Trendy designer togs for men and women. 5 Rue des Petits-Champs, 1er (phone: 42-60-37-83), and other locations.

Castorama – One of 86 stores throughout France, this department store sells 45,000 European-designed housewares — from flowerpots to home security systems. 1-3 Rue Caulaincourt, 18e (phone: 45-22-07-11).

Caves Taillevent – One of Paris's best and most fairly priced wine shops, run by the owners of the three-star restaurant of the same name. 199 Rue du Faubourg-St-Honoré, 8e (phone: 45-61-14-09).

Cedre Rouge – Sophisticated, trendy souvenirs that range from brightly colored porcelain to beautiful gardening tools to whimsical doormat designs. 22 Av. Victoria, 1er (phone: 42-33-71-05).

Céline – A popular women's boutique for clothing and accessories. 24 Rue François-1er, 8e (phone: 47-20-22-83); 3 Av. Victor-Hugo, 16e (phone: 45-01-70-48).

Cerruti – For women's clothing, 15 Pl. de la Madeleine, 8e (phone: 47-42-10-78); for men's, 27 Rue Royale, 8e (phone: 42-65-68-72).

Chanel – Classic women's fashions, inspired by the late, legendary Coco Chanel, now under the direction of Karl Lagerfeld. 42 Av. Montaigne, 8e (phone: 47-20-84-45) — this address covers three individual buildings: one for shoes, another for clothing and cosmetics, and the third for watches; and 29-31 Rue Cambon, 1er (phone: 42-86-28-00), headquarters for haute couture as well as ready-to-wear and accessories. The newest branch at 5 Pl. Vendôme, 1er (phone: 42-86-28-00) sells nothing but Chanel-designed watches.

Chantal Thomass – Ultra-feminine fashions, 5 Rue du Vieux-Colombier, 6e (phone: 45-44-60-11); sexy lingerie, 12-14 Galerie du Rond-Point, 8e (phone: 43-59-87-34), and other locations.

Charles Jourdan – Sleek, high-fashion shoes. 86 Av. des Champs-Elysées, 8e (phone: 45-62-29-28); 5 Bd. de la Madeleine, 1er (phone: 42-61-50-07); and other locations.

Charley – Excellent selection of lingerie at fairly low prices. 14 Rue du Faubourg-St-Honoré, 8e (phone: 47-42-17-70).

Charvet – Paris's answer to Savile Row. An all-in-one men's shop, where shirts are the house specialty — they stock more than 4,000. Ties, too. 28 Pl. Vendôme, 1er (phone: 42-60-30-70).

La Châtelaine – Where all of Paris shops for exquisite (and costly) toys and clothing for children and grandchildren. 170 Ave. Victor-Hugo, 16e (phone: 47-27-44-07).

Chaumet – Crownmakers for most of Europe's royalty. Expensive jewels, including antique watches covered with semi-precious stones. 12 Pl. Vendôme, 1er (phone: 42-60-32-82); and 46 Av. George-V, 8e (phone: 49-52-08-25).

Chloé – Designs for women. 3 Rue de Gribeauval and 60 Rue du Faubourg-St-Honoré, 8e (phone: 42-66-01-39).

Christian Dior – One of the most famous couture names in the world. 28-30 Av. Montaigne, 8e; *Miss Dior* and *Baby Dior* for children also are at this location (phone: 40-73-54-44).

Christian Lacroix – The first major new fashion house to open in Paris in 2 decades. Offers the "hautest" of haute couture. 73 Rue du Faubourg-St-Honoré, 8e (phone: 42-65-79-08).

Christofle – The internationally famous silversmith. 9 Rue Royale, 8e (phone: 49-33-43-00).

Claude Montana – Ready-to-wear and haute couture from this au courant designer. 31 Rue de Grenelle, 7e (phone: 42-22-69-56).

Coesnon – Arguably one of Paris's finest *charcuteries,* in spite of its diminutive size. The terrines, pâtés, *boudin blanc aux truffles,* and other temptations are the best of their kind. 30 Rue Dauphine, 6e (phone: 43-54-35-80).

Commes des Garçons – Asymmetrical-style clothing for *des filles* and *des garçons.* 40-42 Rue Etienne-Marcel, 1er (phone: 42-33-05-21).

Au Comptoir du Chineur – The home of 1950s memorabilia, its collection includes everything from Coca Cola wall thermometers to Elvis records. 49 Rue St-Paul, 4e (phone: 42-72-47-39).

Comptoirs de la Tour d'Argent – Glassware, napkins, silver items, and other objects bearing the celebrated restaurant's logo. 2 Rue de Cardinal-Lemoine, 5e (phone: 46-33-45-58).

Courrèges – Another bastion of haute couture, with its own boutique. 40 Rue François-Ier, 8e (phone: 47-20-70-44) and 46 Rue du Faubourg-St-Honoré, 8e (phone: 42-65-37-75).

Dalloyau – Fine purveyor of pastries and inventor of the sinful (and incredibly delicious) *gâteau opéra,* a confection of coffee and chocolate cream frosted with the darkest of chocolate and topped with an edible gold leaf. 99-101 Rue du Faubourg-St-Honoré, 8e (phone: 43-59-18-10), 2 Pl. Edmond-Rostand, 6e (phone: 43-29-31-10), and other locations.

Daniel Hechter – Sportswear and casual clothing for men and women. 146 Bd. St-Germain, 6e (phone: 43-26-96-36), and other locations.

Destination Paris – Glittering selection of knickknacks, hand-painted T-shirts, scarves, picture frames, and souvenirs. 9 Rue du 29 Juillet, 1er (phone: 49-27-98-90).

Diners En Ville – Irresistible antique glassware, dishes, and tablecloths. 27 Rue de Varenne, 7e (phone: 42-22-78-33).

Dorothée Bis – Colorful women's knit sportswear. 33 Rue de Sèvres, 6e (phone: 42-22-02-90).

Les Drugstores Publicis – A uniquely French version of the American drugstore, with an amazing variety of goods — perfume, books, records, foreign newspapers, magazines, film, cigarettes, food, and more, all wildly overpriced. 149 Bd. St-Germain, 6e (phone: 42-22-92-50); 133 Av. des Champs-Elysées, 8e (phone: 47-23-54-34); and 1 Av. Matignon, 8e (phone: 43-59-38-70).

E. Dehillerin – An enormous selection of professional cookware. 18-20 Rue Coquillière, 1er (phone: 42-36-53-13).

Emanuel Ungaro – Couturier boutique for women. 2 Av. Montaigne, 8e (phone: 47-23-61-94).

Emiliana Zapata – An eclectic collection of women's fashions in brightly colored fabrics and stylish cuts. 35 Rue de Sèvres, 6e (phone: 45-48-92-71).

Emmanuelle Khanh – Feminine clothes in lovely fabrics, including embroidered linen. 2 Rue de Tournon, 6e (phone: 46-33-41-07).

Erès – Avant-garde sportswear for men and women. 2 Rue Tronchet, 8e (phone: 47-42-24-55).

Fabrice – Trendy, fine costume jewelry. 33 and 54 Rue Bonaparte, 6e (phone: 43-26-57-95).

Fauchon – *The* place to buy fine food and wine of every variety, from *oeufs en gelée* to condiments and candy. At shops across from one another at 26 and 30 Pl. de la Madeleine, 8e (phone: 47-42-60-11 and 47-42-66-68 respectively). *Fauchon* has reopened its *pâtisserie/boulangerie* across the street. 28 Pl. de la Madeleine, 8e (phone: 47-42-60-11).

Fer 7 – Stylish men's fashions at reasonable prices. 19 Rue de Sèvres, 6e (phone: 45-44-97-16).

FNAC Internationale – A stunning new bookstore in the Latin Quarter featuring English and other "international" books. Worth a visit just to see the interior design. 71 Bd. St-Germain, 5e (phone: 44-41-31-50).

Fouquet – Beautiful displays of chocolates, fresh fruit candies, herbs, condiments, and jams. 22 Rue François-Ier, 8e (phone: 47-23-30-36), and other locations.

France Faver – Top-quality beautiful and comfortable shoes for women. 79 Rue des Sts-Pères, 6e (phone: 42-22-04-29).

Fratelli Rossetti – All kinds of shoes, made from buttery-soft leather, for men and women. 54 Rue du Faubourg-St-Honoré, 8e (phone: 42-65-26-60).

Freddy – A popular shop for gifts, perfume, gloves, ties, scarves, and other items at good prices. 10 Rue Auber, 9e (phone: 47-42-63-41).

Galignani – This shop sells books in English and French. It has been run by the same family since the beginning of the 19th century. 224 Rue de Rivoli, 1er (phone: 42-60-76-07).

La Gaminerie – Reasonably priced, good sportswear; outstanding window displays. 137 Bd. St-Germain, 6e (phone: 43-26-27-98).

Georges Rech – Currently one of the most popular makers of classy, very Parisian styles, and at more affordable prices than other manufacturers of similarly styled goods. 273 Rue St-Honoré, 1er (phone: 42-61-41-14); and 23 Av. Victor-Hugo, 16e (phone: 45-00-83-19).

Gianni Versace – Women's clothing. 11 Rue du Faubourg-St-Honoré, 8e (phone: 42-65-27-04); and 67 Rue des Sts.-Pères, 7e (phone: 42-84-00-40). The renowned Italian designer has opened a mega-store across from the Elysée Palace at 62 Rue du Faubourg-St-Honoré, 8e (phone: 42-65-27-04). On 3 levels, and adorned with Empire antiques, it sells Versace men's, women's, and children's lines. A smaller Left Bank outlet featuring only women's clothing is at 67 Rue des Sts-Pères, 6e (phone: 42-84-00-40).

Givenchy – Beautifully tailored clothing by the master couturier. 3 Av. George-V, 8e (phone: 47-23-81-36).

Le Gourmet – The *Galeries Lafayette*'s chic, recently opened grocery featuring exotic and high-priced food, wine, and confections from around the world. 40 Bd. Haussmann, 9e (phone: 48-74-37-13).

Guerlain – For fine perfume and cosmetics. 2 Pl. Vendôme, 1er; 68 Champs-Elysées, 8e (phone: 45-62-52-57); 29 Rue de Sèvres, 6e (phone: 42-22-46-60); and 93 Rue de Passy, 16e (phone: 42-91-60-02).

Guy Laroche – Classic and conservative couture. 30 Rue du Faubourg-St-Honoré, 8e (phone: 42-65-62-74); and 29 Av. Montaigne, 8e (phone: 40-69-69-50).

Hanae Mori – The grande dame of Japanese designers in Paris. 17 Av. Montaigne, 8e (phone: 47-23-52-03); and 9 Rue du Faubourg-St-Honoré, 8e (phone: 47-42-78-78).

Hédiard – Pricey but choice food shop, notable for its assortment of coffees and teas. Chic tearoom upstairs. 21 Pl. de la Madeleine, 8e (phone: 42-66-44-36).

Hermès – For very high quality ties, scarves, classic clothes, handbags, shoes, saddles, and accessories, though the prices may send you into cardiac arrest. 24 Rue du Faubourg-St-Honoré, 8e (phone: 40-17-47-17).

Hôtel Drouot – Paris's huge auction house operates daily except Sundays. Good buys. 9 Rue Drouot, 9e (phone: 48-00-20-20).

IGN (French National Geographic Institute) – All manner of maps — ancient and modern, foreign and domestic, esoteric and mundane — are sold here. 136 *bis* Rue Grenelle, 7e (phone: 42-25-87-90); and 107 Rue La Boëtie, 8e.

Inès de la Fressange – The former Chanel model recently opened this shop, which sells everything from classic white silk shirts to furniture gilded with her signature oak leaf. 14 Av. de Montaigne, 8e (phone: 47-23-08-94).

Issey Miyake – "In" shop, selling women's clothing made by the Japanese artist-designer. Classic, more expensive line at 201 Bd. St-Germain, 7e (phone: 45-44-60-88); latest collections at 3 Pl. des Vosges, 4e (phone: 48-87-01-86).

Jacadi – Classic designs for children from 3 months to 12 years. Excellent quality for a relatively affordable price. 7 Rue Gustave-Courbet, 16e (phone: 45-53-33-73); 51 Rue de Passy, 16e (phone: 45-27-03-01); and other locations.

Jean-Louis Scherrer – A top designer, whose clothes are favored by the Parisian chic. 51-53 Av. Montaigne, 8e (phone: 45-59-55-39).

Jean-Paul Gaultier – Designer clothes for men and women. 6 Rue Vivienne, 2e (phone: 42-86-05-05).

Jule des Prés – Bouquets of dried flowers and herbs, as well as dried aromatic plants made into potpourri. 8 and 19 Rue du Cherche-Midi, 6e (phone: 45-48-26-84); 46 Rue du Roi-de-Sicile, 4e (phone: 45-48-26-84).

Karl Lagerfeld – Women's clothing. 17 Rue du Faubourg-St-Honoré, 8e (phone: 42-66-64-64).

Kenzo – Avant-garde fashions by the Japanese designer. A *Kenzo* children's shop is located in the passageway next to the store. 3 Pl. des Victoires, 1er (phone: 40-39-72-02).

Lachaume – Stem for stem, the most beautiful flower shop in Paris. Buy a bouquet for an *ami(e)* or for *vous-même*. 10 Rue Royale, 8e (phone: 42-60-57-26).

Lalique – The famous crystal. 11 Rue Royale, 8e (phone: 42-65-33-70).

Lancôme – Cosmetics. 29 Rue du Faubourg-St-Honoré, 8e (phone: 42-65-30-74).

Lanvin – Another fabulous designer, with several spacious, colorful boutiques under one roof. 15 and 22 Rue du Faubourg-St-Honoré, 8e (phone: 42-65-14-40); and 2 Rue Cambon, 1er (phone: 42-60-38-83).

Laura Ashley – The English designer's familiar and not-as-fresh-as-they-once-were Victorian styles. 94 Rue des Rennes, 6e (phone: 44-48-43-81); and 261 Rue St-Honoré, 1er (phone: 42-86-84-13).

Legrand Filles et Fils – Fine wines and spirits and articles for the *cave* and table, such as *rattes* (wrought-iron candle holders used in real wine cellars), plus excellent maps of French wine regions. 1 Rue Banque, 2e (phone: 42-60-07-12).

Light – Top designer fashions from the studios of St. Laurent, Montana, and Ungaro are the attractions at this Champs-Elysees boutique.

Loewe – Classic leather goods in elegant quarters. One of Spain's oldest and highest-quality names in leather, and owned since 1985 by Louis Vuitton. 57 Av. Montaigne, 8e (phone: 45-63-73-38).

Lolita Lempicka – Iconoclastic, formfitting women's wear. 3 *bis* Rue de Rosiers, 4e (phone: 42-74-42-94), and other locations.

Louis Féraud – Couturier fashions for women at 88 Rue du Faubourg-St-Honoré, 8e, and for men at No. 62 (phone: 40-07-01-16), and other locations.

Louis Vuitton – High-quality luggage and handbags. The agreeable, efficient, and well-mannered staff at the modern Avenue Montaigne branch are a pleasure after the chilly reception at the original Avenue Marceau shop. 54 Av. Montaigne, 8e (phone: 45-62-47-00) and 78 *bis* Av. Marceau, 8e (phone: 47-20-47-00).

Maison de la Truffe – The world's largest truffles retailer. (They're fresh, not preserved, from November to March.) 19 Pl. de la Madeleine, 8e (phone: 42-65-53-22).

Marché aux Puces – Paris's famous *Flea Market*, with 3,000 dealers in antiques and secondhand items, who are clustered in various smaller markets. The *Marché Biron* for fine bric-a-brac is one of the best. Open Saturdays, Sundays, and Mondays. Bargaining is a must. Porte de Clignancourt, 18e.

Maria Luisa – The hautest of haute couture and daring new looks from Paris's top designers are the stock in trade at this Rue Cambon boutique.

Marie Papier – Handsome marbled stationery and writing accessories. 26 Rue Vavin, 6e (phone: 43-26-46-44).

Marithé & François Girbaud – Not just jeans at this shop for men and women. 38 Rue Etienne-Marcel, 2e (phone: 42-33-54-69).

Maud Frizon – Sophisticated, imaginative shoes and handbags. 83 Rue des Sts-Pères, 6e (phone: 45-49-20-59).

Miss Maud – Shoes aimed at a young market, but classy and fashionable enough for all ages. No longer connected with *Maud Frizon,* above. Several locations, including 90 Rue du Faubourg-St-Honoré, 8e (phone: 42-65-27-96).

Missoni – Innovative, original Italian knitwear. 43 Rue du Bac, 7e (phone: 45-48-38-02).

Monique Germain – Unique hand-painted silk clothing at affordable prices: cocktail dresses, bridal wear, padded patchwork jackets. 59 Bd. Raspail, 6e (phone: 45-48-22-63).

M.O.R.A. – One of Paris's "professional" cookware shops, though it sells to individuals as well. Just about any piece of equipment you can imagine, and an interesting selection of cookbooks — in French. 13 Rue Montmartre, 1er (phone: 45-08-19-24).

Morabito – Magnificent handbags and luggage at steep prices. 1 Pl. Vendôme, 1er (phone: 42-60-30-76).

Muriel Gâteau – An eclectic shop, with silk blouses and fine table linen. Jardin du Palais-Royal, under the arcade, 1er (phone: 42-20-90-30).

Le Must de Cartier – Actually two boutiques, on either side of the *Ritz* hotel, offering such Cartier items as lighters and watches at prices that, though not low, are almost bearable when you deduct the 25% VAT tax. 7-23 Pl. Vendôme, 1er (phone: 42-61-55-55).

Au Nain Bleu – The city's greatest toy store. 408 Rue St-Honoré, 8e (phone: 42-60-39-01).

Nina Ricci – Women's fashions, as well as the famous perfume. 17 Rue François Ier, 8e (phone: 47-23-78-88); and 39 Av. Montaigne, 8e (phone: 47-23-78-88).

Les Olivades – Provençal printed yard goods, a little less pricey than *Souleiado* (see below). Shops throughout France, including 25 Rue de l'Annonciation, 16e (phone: 45-27-07-76).

L'Olivier – The finest cooking oils, from several varieties of olive oil to walnut, hazelnut, and more. 23 Rue de Rivoli, 4e (phone: 48-04-56-59).

Paloma Picasso – Perfume, clothing, and jewelry from one of France's preeminent designers and you-know-who's daughter. 5 Rue de la Paix, 2e (phone: 42-86-02-21).

Per Spook – One of Paris's best young designers. 18 Av. George-V, 8e (phone: 47-23-00-19), and elsewhere.

Petit Bateau – Extremely well made children's togs in pure cotton. 81 Rue de Sèvres, 6e (phone: 45-49-48-38), and other locations.

Le Petit Faune – A marvelous place to buy children's things. 33 Rue Jacob, 6e (phone: 42-60-80-72), and other locations.

Au Petit Matelot – Classic sportswear, outdoor togs, and nautical accessories for men, women, and children. Especially terrific are their Tyrolean-style olive or navy loden coats. 27 Av. de la Grande-Armée, 16e (phone: 45-00-15-51).

Phist – Stylish men's clothing at reasonable prices. 23 Bd. Madeleine, 8e (phone: 49-27-07-55) and 19 Rue Vieux-Colombie, 6e (phone: 45-48-57-84).

Pierre Balmain – Couturier boutique for women's fashions. 44 Rue François-Ier, 8e (phone: 47-20-98-79), and other locations.

Pierre Cardin – A famous designer's own boutique. 83 Rue du Faubourg-St-Honoré, 8e (phone: 42-66-62-94); 27 Av. Victor-Hugo, 16e (phone: 45-01-88-13); 14 Pl. François-Ier, 8e (phone: 45-63-29-13); and other locations.

Pixi & Cie. – Terrific collection of dolls, toy soldiers, and antique windup cars. 95 Rue de Seine, 6e (phone: 43-25-10-12).

Popy Moreni – Unusually designed unisex clothes inspired by the commedia dell'arte, located in one of the loveliest squares in the city. 13 Pl. des Vosges, 4e (phone: 42-77-09-96).

Porthault – Terribly expensive, but elegantly exquisite bed and table linen. 18 Av. Montaigne, 8e (phone: 47-20-75-25).

Puiforcat – Art Deco tableware in a beautiful setting. 22 Rue François-Ier, 8e (phone: 47-20-74-27).

Raymond – Charming and fairly inexpensive Porcelaine de Paris items. 100 Rue du Faubourg-St-Honoré, 8e (phone: 42-66-69-49).

Robert Clergerie – Among Paris's finest footwear, these slightly chunky, thick-soled shoes and boots will actually stand up to the perils of cobblestone streets. 5 Rue Cherche-Midi, 6e (phone: 45-48-75-47), and other locations.

Romeo Gigli – Men's and women's arty ready-to-wear and haute couture. 46 Rue de Sévigné, 3e (phone: 42-71-08-40).

Sabbia Rosa – Simple, chic, and sexy lingerie is sold in this tiny shop on the Left Bank. 73 Rue des Sts-Pères, 6e (phone: 45-48-88-37).

Shakespeare and Company – This legendary English-language bookstore, opposite Notre-Dame, is something of a tourist attraction in itself. 37 Rue de la Bûcherie, 5e (no phone).

Simon – A wide range of professional cookware, and a dazzling, but confusing, array of bistroware, flatware, cheese trays, snail holders, and tiny terrines. 36 Rue Etienne-Marcel, 2e (phone: 42-33-71-65).

Sonia Rykiel – Stunning sportswear and knits. 6 Rue de Grenelle, 15e; and 70 Rue du Faubourg-St-Honoré, 8e (phone: 42-65-20-81).

Souleiado – Vibrant, traditional Provençal fabrics made into scarves, shawls, totes, and tableware. 78 Rue de Seine, 6e (phone: 43-54-62-25); and 83 Av. Paul-Doumer, 16e (phone: 42-24-99-34).

Stéphane Kélian – High-fashion, high-quality, and high-priced (but not completely unreasonable) men's and women's shoes, in several locations, including 4 Pl. des Victoires, 1er (phone: 42-61-60-74).

Tartine et Chocolat – Clothing for children, from infancy to 12 years old, and dresses for moms-to-be. Their trademark item: striped unisex overalls (about $90). 90 Rue de Rennes, 6e (phone: 42-22-67-34).

Ted Lapidus – A compromise between haute couture and excellent ready-to-wear. 23 Rue du Faubourg-St-Honoré, 8e (phone: 44-60-89-91); 35 Rue François-Ier, 8e (phone: 47-20-56-14); and other locations.

Thierry Mugler – Dramatic ready-to-wear for women. 49 Av. Montaigne, 8e (phone: 47-23-37-62).

Torrente – Women's fashions. 60 Av. Montaigne, 8e (phone: 42-56-14-14).

Trussardi – Italian ready-to-wear from a designer whose leather goods and canvas carryalls are much appreciated by the French and Japanese. 21 Rue du Faubourg-St-Honoré, 8e (phone: 42-65-11-40).

La Tuile à Loup – Crafts from France's provinces, including Burgundy pottery and Normandy lace. 35 Rue Daubenton, 3e (phone: 47-07-28-90).

Upla – Sporty handbags, scarves, shoes, and casual clothing. 17 Rue des Halles, 1er (phone: 40-26-49-96).

Valentino – Ready-to-wear and haute couture fashions for men and women from the Italian designer. 17-19 Av. Montaigne, 8e (phone: 47-23-64-61).

Van Cleef & Arpels – One of the world's great jewelers. 22 Pl. Vendôme, 1er (phone: 42-61-58-58).

Vicky Tiel – Strapless evening gowns decorated with beads and bows, as well as contemporary sweaters and baseball-style jackets. 21 Rue Bonaparte, 6e (phone: 46-33-53-58).

Victoire – Ready-to-wear from up-and-coming designers such as André Walker, with attractive accessories. 12 Pl. des Victoires, 2e (phone: 42-61-09-02), and other locations.

Virgin Megastore – The British have taken over the Parisian market in CDs, records, and video cassettes. Though the selection is staggering, the store is usually so crowded that browsing is impossible. 56-60 Champs-Elysées, 8e (phone: 40-74-06-48).

Walter Steiger – Some of the capital's most expensive and exclusive footwear for men and women. The flagship shop displays satin slippers like precious jewels — and with prices to match. 83 Rue du Faubourg-St-Honoré, 8e (phone: 42-66-65-08).

W. H. Smith and Sons – The largest bookstore in Paris (with more space now that the upstairs tearoom has been converted into additional book displays) for reading material in English. It sells the Sunday *New York Times,* in addition to many British and American magazines and books. 248 Rue de Rivoli, 1er (phone: 42-60-37-97).

Yohji Yamamoto – This designer presents highly unusual outerwear, which may make timid souls think twice before donning an outfit. 25 Rue du Louvre, 1e (phone: 42-21-42-93) and 69 Rue des Sts-Pères, 6e (phone: 45-48-22-56).

Yves Saint Laurent – The world-renowned designer, considered one of the most famous names in high fashion. The Right Bank location on the Faubourg-St-Honoré has been redesigned and serves as the prototype for the remodeling of all the couturier's shops around the world. 38 Rue du Faubourg-St-Honoré, 8e (phone: 42-65-01-15); 5 Av. Marceau, 8e (phone: 47-23-72-71); 6 Pl. St-Sulpice, 6e (phone: 43-29-43-00); and other locations.

BEST DISCOUNT SHOPS

If you're one of those — like us — who believes that the eighth deadly sin is buying retail, you'll treasure these inexpensive outlets.

Anna Lowe – Saint Laurent's styling, among others, at a discount. 35 Av. Matignon, 8e (phone: 43-59-96-61).

Anne Parée – Great buys on French perfume, Dior scarves, men's ties, Limoges china, and Vuarnet sunglasses. A 40% discount (including VAT) is given on purchases totaling 1,500F (about $250) or more. Mail order, too. 10 Rue Duphot, 1er (phone: 42-60-03-25; fax: 42-60-14-29).

Bab's – High fashion at low — or at least reasonable — prices. 29 Av. Marceau, 16e (phone: 47-20-84-74) and 89 *bis* Av. des Ternes, 17e (phone: 45-74-02-74).

Biderman – Menswear from Yves Saint Laurent, Kenzo, and Courrèges, in a warehouse of a store in the Marais. 114 Rue de Turenne, 3e (phone: 44-61-17-00).

Boëtie 104 – Good buys on men's and women's shoes. 104 Rue La Boëtie, 8e (phone: 43-59-72-38).

Boutique Stock – A vast selection of big-name knits at less than wholesale. 2 Rue Cadet, 9e (phone: 48-24-26-87).

Cacharel Stock – Surprisingly current Cacharel fashions at about a 40% discount. 114 Rue d'Alésia, 14e (phone: 45-42-53-04).

Catherine Baril – Women's ready-to-wear by designers such as Yves Saint Laurent and Jean-Louis Scherrer. 14-15 Rue de la Tour, 16e (phone: 45-20-95-21).

Chercheminippes – One of the biggest Parisian *dépôt-vente* shops for high-quality children's clothes. The adult clothing *dépôt-vente* collections just down the street are also worth a visit. 160 Rue du Cherche-Midi, 6e (phone: 92-22-33-89).

Dépôt des Grandes Marques – A third-floor shop near the stock market, featuring up to 50% markdowns on Louis Féraud, Cerruti, Renoma, and similar labels. 15 Rue de la Banque, 2e (phone: 42-96-99-04).

Didier Ludot – Designer fashions at down-to-earth prices at this thrift shop across from the Jardin du Palais Royal. 23-24 Galerie Montpensier (phone: 42-96-06-56).

Dorothée Bis Stock – Ms. Bis's well-known designs at about 40% off. 76 Rue d'Alésia, 14e (phone: 45-42-40-68).

Drôles des Choses pour Drôles de Gens – Half-price clothes by Marithé and François Girbaud. 33 Rue Etienne-Marcel, 1er (phone: 43-72-15-23).

Emmanuelle Khanh – The designer's clothes at a substantial discount. 6 Rue Pierre-Lescot, 1er (42-37-12-24).

Griff 'Mod – Names like Laroche and Lapidus at sale prices. 20 Rue des Petits-Champs, 2e (phone: 42-97-47-45).

Halle Bys – High fashions at discount prices. 60 Rue de Richelieu, 2e (phone: 42-96-65-42).

Jean-Louis Scherrer – Haute couture labels by Scherrer and others at about half their original prices. 29 Av. Ledru-Rollin, 12e (phone: 46-28-39-27).

Lady Soldes – Prime fashion labels at less than normal prices. 221 Rue du Faubourg-St-Honoré, 8e (phone: 45-61-09-14).

Lanvin Soldes Trois – Lanvin fashions at about half their normal retail cost. 3 Rue de Vienne, 8e (no phone).

La Marette – Clothes that are too elegant to be called merely "used" (even though they are); there are many designer items here, including a large selection of stylish children's outfits and accessories. 21-25 Galerie Vivienne, 2e (phone: 42-60-08-19).

Mendès – Less-than-wholesale prices on haute couture, especially Saint Laurent and Lanvin. 65 Rue Montmartre, 2e (phone: 45-08-52-62 or 42-36-83-32).

Michel Swiss – Huge selection of perfume, cheerful service, and discounts of almost 44% to American visitors who pay with cash or traveler's checks, and who buy more than 1,200F ($200) of scents. 16 Rue de la Paix, 2e (phone: 42-61-71-71).

Miss Griffes – The very best of haute couture in small sizes (up to size 10) at small prices. Alterations, too. Open Mondays through Fridays from 11 AM to 6 PM. 19 Rue de Penthièvre, 8e (phone: 42-65-10-00).

Mouton à Cinq Pattes – Ready-to-wear clothing for men, women, and children at 50% off original prices. 8 and 18 Rue St-Placide, 6e (phone: 45-48-86-26).

Pierre Cardin Stock – Terrific buys on the famed designer's men's clothing. 2 Rue Vauvilliers, 1er (phone: 40-26-74-73).

Réciproque – Billed as the largest *"dépôt-vente"* in Paris, this outlet features names like Chanel, Alaia, Lanvin, and Scherrer. Several hundred square yards of display area are arranged by designer and by size. 95 Rue de la Pompe, 16e (phone: 47-04-30-28); men's clothing and accessories next door at No. 101. New boutiques are at Nos. 89, 91, and 123 Rue de la Pompe.

Stéphane – Men's designer suits by Pierre Balmain, Ted Lapidus, and André Courrèges at 25% to 45% discount. 130 Bd. St-Germain, 6e (phone: 46-33-94-55).

Stock Coupons – Features discounted Daniel Hechter for men, women, and children. 92 Rue d'Alésia, 14e (phone: 45-42-82-66).

Stock Griffes – Women's ready-to-wear apparel at 40% off their original prices. 7 Rue St-Merri, 4e (phone: 48-04-93-89).

Stock System – Prêt-à-porter clothing for men and women at a 30% discount. 112 Rue d'Alésia, 14e (phone: 45-43-80-86).

Also, Rue du Paradis (10e) is the best area to shop for crystal and porcelain — Baccarat, Saint-Louis, Haviland, Bernardaud, and Villeroy & Boch — at amazing prices. Try *Cristalerie de Paris* at No. 7; *Boutique Paradis,* No. 1 *bis; L'Art et La Table,* No. 3; *Limoges-Unic,* Nos. 8 and 12; *Porcelain Savary,* No. 9; *Arts Céramiques,* No. 15; and *Cristallerie Paradis,* at No. 17.

■ *Note:* For a modest price ($15 and up), you can also take home a bit of the *Louvre.* The museum's 200-year-old Department of Calcography houses a collection of 16,000 engraved copper plates — renderings of monuments, battles, coronations, Egyptian pyramids, and portraits — dating from the 17th century. Prints made from these engravings come reproduced on thick vellum, embossed with the *Louvre's* imprint. The Calcography Department (open daily, except Tuesdays, from 2 to 5 PM) is 1 flight up from the Porte Barbet de Jouy entrance on the Seine side of the *Louvre.*

 SPORTS AND FITNESS: Biking – Rentals are available in the Bois de Boulogne and the Bois de Vincennes, or contact the *Fédération Française de Cyclo-tourisme* (8 Rue Jean-Marie-Jégo, 13e; phone: 45-80-30-21); *Bicyclub* (8 Pl. de la Porte-Champerrat, 17e; phone: 47-66-55-92); or *Paris-Vélo* (2 Rue du Fer-à-Moulin, 5e; phone: 43-37-59-22). In addition to renting bicycles, *Paris by Cycle* (99 Rue de la Jonquière, 17e; phone: 42-63-36-63) arranges guided group tours of the city, Versailles, and bike trips alternating with horseback rides. The world-famous *Tour de France* bicycle race takes place in July and ends in Paris.

Fitness Centers – The *Garden Gym* (65 Av. des Champs-Elysées, 16e; phone: 42-25-87-20 and 123 Av. Charles-de-Gaulle, Neuilly; phone: 47-47-62-62) is open daily to non-members for a fee.

Golf – For general information, contact the *Fédération Française de Golf* (69 Av. Victor-Hugo, 16e; phone: 45-02-13-55). It usually is possible to play on any course during the week by simply paying a greens fee. Weekends may be more difficult. *Ozoir-la-Ferrière* (Château des Agneaux, 15 miles/24 km away; closed Tuesdays; phone: 60-28-20-79) welcomes Americans; and *St-Germain-en-Laye* (12 miles/19 km away; phone: 34-51-75-90) accepts non-members on weekdays only (closed Mondays). The *Racing Club de France* (La Boulie, Versailles; phone: 39-50-59-41) and *St-Nom-la-Bretèche* (in the suburb of the same name; phone: 34-62-54-00) accept only guests of members. It's best to call at least 2 days in advance to schedule a time.

Horse Racing – Of the eight tracks in and around Paris, two major ones are in the Bois de Boulogne: *Longchamp* (phone: 42-24-13-29) for flat races and *Auteuil* (phone: 45-27-12-24) for steeplechase. *St-Cloud* (phone: 43-59-20-70), a few miles west of Paris, and *Chantilly* (phone: 42-66-92-02), about 25 miles (40 km) north of the city, are both for flat racing. *Vincennes* (Bois de Vincennes; phone: 47-42-07-70) is the trotting track. Important races take place from spring through fall, but the *Grande Semaine* (Big Week) comes in mid-June, when nine major races — beginning with the *Grand Steeplechase de Paris* at *Auteuil* and including the *Grand Prix de Paris* at *Longchamp* — are scheduled.

Ice Skating – Last year's winter *Olympics* in Albertville inspired city planners to give Paris a new outdoor ice skating rink, *Le Patinoire du Vieux Montmartre,* near Sacré-Coeur in Montmartre. The rink is open daily to would-be *Olympic* contenders and other lovers of the sport on Mondays, Tuesdays, Thursdays, and Fridays from 1 to 10 PM, and Wednesdays, Saturdays, and Sundays from 9 AM to 10 PM. Admission charge (phone: 42-62-21-21).

Jogging – The streets and sidewalks of Paris may be ideal for lovers, but they're not meant for runners. There are, however, a number of places where you can jog happily; one of the most pleasant is the 2,500-acre Bois de Boulogne. Four more central parks are the Jardin du Luxembourg (reachable by métro: Luxembourg), the Champ-de-Mars gardens (just behind the Eiffel Tower; métro: Iéna), Parc Monceau (métro: Monceau), and the Jardin des Tuileries (métro: Tuileries, Louvre, or Concorde).

Soccer – There are matches from early August to mid-June at Parc des Princes (Av. du Parc-des-Princes, 16e; phone: 42-88-02-76).

Swimming – At the heart of Paris, rather unsuitably near the National Assembly, lies the *Piscine Deligny,* notorious in the summer for its acres of topless women bathers and, on the top deck, nude sunbathers of both sexes. The pool is set in a floating barge on the Seine beside the Concorde bridge; it is, says the sign, filled with fresh water. Open May to September (25 Quai Anatole-France, 7e; phone: 45-51-72-15). Other pools include *Piscine des Halles* (10 Pl. de la Rotonde, 4e; phone: 42-36-98-44), *Piscine du Quartier Latin* (19 Rue de Pontoise, 5e; phone: 43-54-82-45), *Butte-aux-Cailles* (5 Pl. Paul-Verlaine, 13e; phone: 45-89-60-05), *Keller* (14 Rue de l'Ingénieur-Robert-Keller, 15e; phone: 45-77-12-12), *Jean-Taris* (16 Rue Thouin, 5e; phone: 43-25-54-03), *Tour Montparnasse* (beneath the tower at 66 Bd. de Montparnasse, 15e; phone: 45-38-65-19), *Piscine Georges-Vallerey* (148 Av. Gambetta, 20e; phone: 40-31-15-20); *Aquaboulevard* (5 Rue Louis-Armand, 15e; phone: 40-60-15-15), *Roger La Gall* (34 Bd. Carnot, 12e; phone: 46-28-77-03), and *Neuilly* (50 Rue Pauline-Borghèse, Neuilly; phone: 47-22-69-59).

Tennis – For general information, call *Ligue Régionale de Paris* (74 Rue de Rome, 17e; phone: 45-22-22-08), or the *Fédération Française de Tennis* (*Roland Garros Stadium,* 16e; phone: 47-43-48-00). Americans who wish to attend the annual *French Open Tennis Tournament* may write in advance to the *Fédération Française de Tennis Billetterie* (Service Reservation, BP 33316, Paris 75767; phone: 47-43-48-00). Courts are available in the Jardins du Luxembourg for a nominal fee. Be certain to arrive early, as this is a popular spot.

THEATER: The most complete listings of theaters, operas, concerts, and movies are found in *L'Officiel des Spectacles* and *Pariscope* (see *Tourist Information,* above). The season generally is from September to June. Tickets are less expensive than in New York and are obtained at each box office, through brokers (*American Express* and *Thomas Cook* act in that capacity and are good), via your hotel's trusty concierge, or with the high-tech Billetels at the *Galeries Lafayette,* the *Centre Georges-Pompidou,* and other locations. Insert a credit card into a slot in the Billetel and choose from over 100 upcoming theater events and concerts. The device will spew out a display of dates, seats, and prices, from which you can order your tickets — they will be printed on the spot and charged to your account. Half-price, day-of-performance theater tickets are available at the kiosks at the Châtelet-les Halles, 1er (Tuesdays through Saturdays from 12:45 to 7 PM), and at 15 Place de la Madeleine, 8e (Tuesdays through Saturdays from 12:30 to 8 PM, Sundays from 12:30 to 4 PM). The curtain usually goes up at 8:30 PM.

For those who speak French: Performances of classical plays by Molière, Racine, and Corneille take place at the *Comédie-Française* (2 Rue de Richelieu, 2e; phone: 40-15-00-15). Two other national theaters are *L'Odéon–Théâtre de l'Europe* (1 Pl. Paul-Claudel, 6e; phone: 43-25-70-32) and *Théâtre National de Chaillot* (Pl. du Trocadéro, 16e; phone: 47-27-81-15). Last, but not least, the *Théâtre du Soleil,* in an old cartridge factory, La Cartoucherie de Vincennes (on the outskirts of Paris in the Bois de Vincennes, 12e; phone: 43-74-24-08 or 43-74-87-63), offers colorful productions ranging from contemporary political works to Shakespeare.

It's not really necessary to speak the language to enjoy the opera, dance, or musical comedy at *L'Opéra* (Pl. de l'Opéra, 9e; phone: 47-42-55-71), the *Opéra de La Bastille* (120 Rue de Lyon, Pl. de la Bastille, 11e; phone: 44-73-13-00), *Salle Favart–Opéra Comique* (5 Rue Favart, 2e; phone: 42-86-88-83), or *Théâtre Musical de Paris* (1 Pl. du Châtelet, 1er; phone: 40-28-28-40). Theater tickets can be reserved through *SOS-Théâtre* (73 Champs-Elysées, 8e; phone: 42-25-67-07).

For those who consider French their second language, Paris's many café-theaters offer amusing songs, sketches, satires, and takeoffs on topical trends and events. Among them are *Café de la Gare* (41 Rue du Temple, 4e; phone: 42-78-52-51) and *Café d'Edgar* (58 Bd. Edgar-Quinet, 14e; phone: 42-79-97-97).

 CINEMA: With no fewer than 200 movie houses, Paris is a real treat for film buffs. No other metropolis offers such a cinematographic feast — current French chic, recent imports from across the Atlantic, grainy 1930s classics, and the latest and most select of Third World and Eastern European offerings. In any given week, there are up to 200 different movies shown, the foreign films generally in their original versions with French subtitles.

Film distribution is erratic, to say the least, so the French often get their *JFK* and *Prince of Tides* flicks up to 6 months late. But the system works both ways: Many of the front-runners at Cannes first hit the screens here, which gives you a jump on friends back home.

Both *Pariscope* and *L'Officiel de Spectacles,* which come out on Wednesday, the day the programs change, contain the full selection each week. *Pariscope* has thought of almost every possible way to classify films, sorting them into new releases and revivals, broad categories (for instance, the *drame psychologique* label means it will be heavier than a *comédie dramatique*), location by *arrondissement,* late-night showings, and so on.

Films shown with their original-language soundtracks are called VO (*version originale*); it's worth watching out for that crucial "VO" tag, or you may find yourself wincing at a French-dubbed version, called VF (*version française*). Broadly speaking, the undubbed variety of film flourishes on the Champs-Elysées and on the Left Bank, and it's also a safe bet to avoid the mostly French-patronized houses of les Grands Boulevards.

The timetables aren't always reliable, so it's worth checking by telephone — if you can decipher the recorded messages that spell out exactly when the five or so showings a day begin. A *séance* (sitting) generally begins with advertisements, and the movie proper begins 15 to 20 minutes later.

There's more room in the big movie houses on the Champs-Elysées, but the cozier Latin Quarter establishments tend to specialize in the unusual and avant-garde — often the only showing such films will ever get. The ultimate in high-tech, the *Géode,* offers a B-Max hemispherical screen, cupped inside a reflecting geodesic dome, at La Villette Sciences and Industry complex. The program is, however, limited to a single scientifically oriented film at any given time, whereas the *Forum Horizon,* in the underground section of the *Forum des Halles,* offers a choice of four first-run movies and claims to have one of the city's best sound systems. Some more out-of-the-way venues like the *Olympique Entrepôt* and the *Lucernaire* in Montparnasse are social centers in themselves, incorporating restaurants and/or other theaters.

Paris's *Cinémathèque* — at the Palais de Chaillot, which also has an interesting *Cinema Museum* — runs a packed schedule of reruns at rates lower than those of the commercial cinemas. Daily afternoon and evening programs from the museum's eclectic archives of over 20,000 films often include several running concurrently, so that a James Cagney gangster epic can share billing with a 1950s British comedy and a Brazilian thriller (phone: 47-04-24-24). The *Cinémathèque* also operates theaters in the *Centre Georges-Pompidou*'s Salle Garance (phone: 42-78-37-29) and in the *Palais de Tokyo* (13 Av. President-Wilson, 16e; phone: 47-04-24-24). The *Vidéothèque de Paris,* in the *Forum des Halles,* is the world's first public video library. Visitors can select individual showings or attend regularly scheduled theater screenings of films and television programs chronicling Paris's history (phone: 40-26-34-30).

Then there are two period pieces almost worth a visit in themselves. *Le Ranelagh* (5 Rue des Vignes, 16e; phone: 42-88-64-44) has an exquisite 19th-century interior where films are screened and live theater performed. *La Pagode* (57 *bis* Rue de Babylone, 7e; phone: 47-05-12-15), with flying cranes, cherry blossoms, and a tearoom, is built around a Japanese temple that was shipped over to Paris by the proprietor of a department store in the 1920s.

MUSIC: The *Orchestre de Paris,* under the direction of Semyon Bychkov, is based at the *Salle Pleyel* — the *Carnegie Hall* of Paris (252 Rue du Faubourg-St-Honoré, 8e; phone: 45-61-06-30). Other classical recitals are held at the *Salle Gaveau* (45 Rue La Boëtie, 8e; phone: 49-53-05-07), at the *Théâtre des Champs-Elysées* (15 Av. Montaigne, 8e; phone: 47-20-36-37), and at the *Palais des Congrès* (Porte Maillot, 17e; phone: 40-68-00-72). The *Nouvelle Orchestre Philharmonic* performs at a variety of places, including the *Grand Auditorium* at *Maison de Radio France* (116 Av. du Président-Kennedy, 16e; phone: 42-30-15-16 or 42-30-18-18). Special concerts frequently are held in Paris's many places of worship, with moving music at high mass on Sundays. The *Palais des Congrès* and the *Olympia* (28 Bd. des Capucines, 9e; phone: 47-42-25-49) are the places to see well-known international pop and rock artists. Innovative contemporary music — much of it created by computer — is the province of the *Institut de Recherche et de Coopération Acoustique Musique* (*IRCAM*), whose musicians can be heard in various auditoriums of the *Centre Georges-Pompidou* (31 Rue St-Merri, 4e; phone: 42-77-12-33).

NIGHTCLUBS AND NIGHTLIFE: Organized "Paris by Night" group tours (*Cityrama, Paris Vision,* and other operators offer them; see *Special Places*) include at least one *"Spectacle"* — beautiful women in minimal, yet elaborate, costumes, with lavish sets and effects and sophisticated striptease. Most music halls offer a package (starting as high as $120 per person), with dinner, dancing, and a half bottle of champagne. It is possible to go to these places on your own, save money by skipping dinner and the champagne (both usually way below par), and take a seat at the bar to see the show. The most famous extravaganzas occur nightly at *Crazy Horse* (12 Av. George-V, 8e; phone: 47-23-32-32), *Folies-Bergère* (32 Rue Richer, 9e; phone: 42-46-77-11), *Lido* (116 *bis* Champs-Elysées, 8e; phone: 40-76-56-10), *Moulin Rouge* (Pl. Blanche, 18e; phone: 46-06-00-19), and *Paradis Latin* (28 Rue du Cardinal-Lemoine, 5e; phone: 43-29-07-07). An amusing evening can also be spent at such smaller cabarets as *René Cousinier* (*La Branlette;* 4 Impasse Marie-Blanche, 18e; phone: 46-06-49-46), *Au Lapin Agile* (22 Rue des Saules, 18e; phone: 46-06-85-87), and *Michou* (80 Rue des Martyrs, 18e; phone: 46-06-16-04). Reserve all a few days in advance.

There's one big difference between discotheques and private clubs. Fashionable "in" spots like *Le Palace* (8 Rue Faubourg-Montmartre, 9e; phone: 42-46-10-87), *Régine's* (49 Rue de Ponthieu, 8e; phone: 43-59-21-60), *Chez Castel* (15 Rue Princesse, 6e, members only; phone: 43-26-90-22), *Olivia Valère* (40 Rue de Colisée, 8e, members only; phone: 42-25-11-68), *Les Bains* (7 Rue du Bourg-l'Abbé, 3e; phone: 48-87-01-80), and *Elysées Matignon* (48 Av. Gabriel, 8e; phone: 42-25-73-13) superscreen potential guests. No reason is given for accepting some and turning others away; go here with a regular or look as if you'd fit in with the crowd. Go early and on a weeknight — when your chances of getting past the gatekeeper are at least 50-50. Don't despair if you're refused; the following places are just as much fun and usually more hospitable: *La Scala* (188 *bis* Rue de Rivoli, 1er; phone: 42-61-64-00), *L'Aventure* (122 Rue d'Assas, 6e; phone: 46-34-22-60), and *L'Ecume des Nuits* (*Hôtel Méridien,* 81 Bd. Gouvion-St-Cyr, 17e; phone: 40-68-34-34). A newcomer on the cultural scene is the *American Center in Paris,* located in Bercy Park near the new Ministry of Finance building. Designed by Frank Gehry, this unusual, modern structure contains theaters for live performances, rehearsal space, housing accommodations for visiting artists, exhibition galleries, and classrooms.

Some pleasant, popular bars for a nightcap include *Bar de la Closerie des Lilas* (171 Bd. Montparnasse, 6e; phone: 43-26-70-50), *Harry's New York Bar* (5 Rue Daunou, 2e; phone: 42-61-71-14), *Fouquet's* (99 Champs-Elysées, 8e; phone: 47-23-70-60), *Ascot Bar* (66 Rue Pierre-Charron, 8e; phone: 43-59-28-15), *Bar Anglais* (*Plaza-Athénée Hôtel,* 25 Av. Montaigne, 8e; phone: 47-23-92-36), and *Pub Winston Churchill* (5 Rue de Presbourg, 16e; phone: 40-67-17-37).

Jazz buffs have a large choice including *Caveau de la Huchette* (5 Rue de la Huchette, 5e; phone: 43-26-65-05), *Le Bilboquet* (13 Rue St-Benoît, 6e; phone: 45-48-81-84), *New Morning* (7-9 Rue des Petites-Ecuries, 10e; phone: 45-23-51-41), *La Villa* (29 Rue Jacob, 6e; phone: 43-26-60-00), and *Le Petit Journal* (71 Bd. St-Michel, 6e; phone: 43-26-28-59).

Enghien-les-Bains, 8 miles (13 km) away, is the only casino in the Paris vicinity (3 Av. de Ceinture, Enghien-les-Bains; phone: 34-12-90-00). Open 3 PM to about 4 AM, it easily can be reached by train from the Gare du Nord.

BEST IN TOWN

CHECKING IN: Paris offers a broad choice of accommodations, from luxurious palaces with every service to more humble budget hotels. However, they all are strictly controlled by the government and must post their rates, so you can be sure that the price you are being charged is correct.

Below is our selection from all categories; in general, expect to spend (gulp!) at least $600 and way up per night for a double room in the "palace" hotels, which we've listed as very expensive; from $300 to $600 in the expensive range; $200 to $300 is considered moderate; $100 to $200 is inexpensive; and $100 or less is very inexpensive (a miracle!).

Except for July, August, and December, the least crowded months, hotel rooms usually are at a premium in Paris. To reserve your first choice, we advise making reservations at least a month in advance, even farther ahead for the smaller, less expensive places listed. Watch for the dates of special events, when hotels are even more crowded than usual. The apartment rentals offered by *Paris Accueil/Paris Séjour* are an alternative to the hotel options listed here. For further information see CITY ACCOMMODATIONS.

Street addresses of the hotels below are followed by the number of their *arrondissement* (neighborhood).

Bristol – A palace with a special, almost intimate cachet. Service is impeccable, as are the 200 spacious, quiet rooms and huge baths. Every *centime* and iota of work that has gone into the renovation of this establishment has been expended with consummate taste and effectiveness. It is hard to think of a hostelry in the City of Light that equals, much less surpasses, it. (The beautiful glass, wrought-iron, and brass elevator is worth numerous trips up and down.) The wood-paneled, one-Michelin-star restaurant and lobby cocktail lounge are both sumptuous. The hotel service is only perfect, and the enlargement of the new marble bathrooms makes for an especially comfortable stay. There also is another wing with a heated swimming pool and a sauna on the sixth-floor terrace. Business facilities include 24-hour room service, meeting rooms for up to 100, an English-speaking concierge, foreign currency exchange, secretarial services in English, audiovisual equipment, photocopiers, computers, cable television news service, and translation services. Major credit cards accepted. 112 Rue du Faubourg-St-Honoré, 8e (phone: 42-66-91-45; fax: 42-66-68-68; telex: 280961). Very expensive.

Crillon – No sign out front, just discreet gold "C's" on the doors, it is currently the only "palace" hotel in Paris still owned by a Frenchman. The rooms on the Place de la Concorde side, though rather noisy, have the view of views; rooms facing the courtyards are just as nice and much more tranquil. Many of the 163 elegant guestrooms and suites have recently been renovated. The Leonard Bernstein suite, renamed in the late composer's honor (these were his favorite Paris digs), has been discreetly and delightfully redecorated by fashion designer Sonia Rykiel. The popular bar and 2 elegant restaurants, *L'Obélisque* and *Les Ambassadeurs* (which for good reason rates two Michelin stars; see *Eating Out*), often are frequented by journalists and US and British embassy personnel. Business facilities include 24-hour room service, meeting rooms for up to 150, an English-speaking concierge, foreign currency exchange, secretarial services in English, audiovisual equipment, photocopiers, computers, cable television news, translation services, and express checkout. Major credit cards accepted. 10 Pl. de la Concorde, 8e (phone: 42-65-24-24; fax: 47-42-72-10; telex: 290204). Very expensive.

George V – This nonpareil pick of movie moguls and international tycoons has 298 elegantly traditional or handsome contemporary rooms and 61 suites: some, facing the lovely courtyard, have their own balconies; those on the upper floors, a nice view. And there are 2 restaurants, *Les Princes* and a grill, as well as a tearoom. One of the liveliest and chicest bars in the city is here, with a bartender who mixes a mean martini. The patio is a summer delight. Business facilities include 24-hour room service, meeting rooms for up to 20, an English-speaking concierge, foreign currency exchange, secretarial services in English, audiovisual equipment, photocopiers, computers, cable television news, and express checkout. Major credit cards accepted. 31 Av. George-V, 8e (phone: 47-23-54-00; fax: 47-20-40-00; telex: 650082). Very expensive.

Meurice – Refined Louis XV and XVI elegance and a wide range of services are offered at prices slightly below those of the other "palaces." The hotel, a member of the CIGA chain, has 179 rooms and especially nice suites, a popular bar, *Le Meurice* (a restaurant overlooking the Rue de Rivoli), and the chandeliered *Pompadour* tearoom. The location and hospitality couldn't be better, and the first-floor public room has been restored. Business facilities include 24-hour room service, meeting rooms for up to 150, an English-speaking concierge, foreign currency exchange, secretarial services in English, audiovisual equipment, photocopiers, computers, cable television news, and translation services. Major credit cards accepted. 228 Rue de Rivoli, 1er (phone: 42-60-38-60; fax: 49-27-94-91; telex: 2306737). Very expensive.

Plaza-Athénée – One of the legendary hotels, this favorite of the sophisticated seeking serene surroundings and superior service has 217 rooms, some which have been recently refurbished. This is an haute bastion that takes its dignity very seriously (a discreet note in each bathroom offers an unobtrusive route in and out of the hotel for those in jogging togs). The *Relais* tables are much in demand at lunch and late supper, and the two-star *Régence,* summer patio, tea tables, and downstairs English bar are places to see and be seen. Business facilities include 24-hour room service, meeting rooms for up to 120, an English-speaking concierge, foreign currency exchange, secretarial services in English, audiovisual equipment, photocopiers, computers, translation services, and express checkout. Major credit cards accepted. 25 Av. Montaigne, 8e (phone: 47-23-78-33; fax: 47-20-20-70; telex: 650092). Very expensive.

Pont Royal – Understated elegance and privacy are the watchwords likely to be uttered when describing this luxurious 78-room establishment. Right in the midst of Paris's most exclusive antiques and shopping district, this former 18th-century *hôtel particulier* (private home) has been a well-kept secret. Each of the spacious rooms is tastefully appointed with fine French antiques and sumptuous fabrics. The formal dining room, *Les Antiquaires,* serves fine fare — perfect after a day of browsing and buying. Business facilities include an English-speaking concierge, foreign currency exchange, secretarial services in English, and computers. Restaurant closed Sundays. Major credit cards accepted. 7 Rue Montalembert, 7e (phone: 45-44-38-27; fax: 45-47-92-07). Very expensive.

Relais Carré d'Or – For those visitors who are in Paris for a long stay, this hostelry (with all the amenities of a luxury hotel) provides a variety of accommodations — from studios to multi-room apartments — all with modern kitchens, marble bathrooms, and lovely, understated furnishings. Most have a balcony overlooking the hotel's garden or Avenue George-V. Business facilities include 24-hour room service, meeting rooms for up to 30, an English-speaking concierge, foreign currency exchange, secretarial services in English, audiovisual equipment, photocopiers, computers, cable television, translation services, and express checkout. Major credit cards accepted. 46 Av. George-V, 8e (phone: 40-70-05-05; fax: 47-23-30-90; telex: 640561). Very expensive.

Résidence Maxim's – Pierre Cardin's luxurious venture is located near the Elysée Palace. No expense has been spared here to create sybaritic splendor. The 40 suites range in style from sleek modern to Belle Epoque, with original Art Nouveau pieces from Cardin's own collections, and every bathroom has been individually designed. *Atmosphere,* its restaurant, has made a name in the city, and has a pleasant terrace in summer; *La Tonnelle* serves breakfast, and doubles as a tea salon; and the bar, *Le Maximin,* is open late. Business facilities include 24-hour room service, meeting rooms for up to 70, an English-speaking concierge, foreign currency exchange, secretarial services in English, audiovisual equipment, photocopiers, cable television news, translation services, and express checkout. Major credit cards accepted. 42 Av. Gabriel, 8e (phone: 45-61-96-33; fax: 42-89-06-07; telex: 642794F). Very expensive.

Ritz – Optimum comfort, privacy, and personal service are offered here, in one of the world's most gracious and distinguished hotels. There is an extraordinary underground health club (with pool, sauna, squash courts, ozone baths, Jacuzzi, and massages), an extensive business center, and the Ritz Escoffier Ecole de Cuisine. The latest addition is the *Ritz Club,* a nightclub and discotheque on the hotel's lower level that is open to hotel guests and club members only. The 187 recently redecorated rooms still preserve their antique treasures. This turn-of-the-century monument is *the* place to splurge, and even its sale to Egyptian interests (some say the Sultan of Brunei is the real financial force) has not diminished the glow one iota. The bars are fashionable meeting places, and the two-star *Ritz-Espadon* restaurant carries on the tradition of the legendary Escoffier. Business facilities include 24-hour room service, meeting rooms for up to 150, an English-speaking concierge, foreign currency exchange, secretarial services in English, audiovisual equipment, photocopiers, computers, cable television news, translation services, and express checkout. Major credit cards accepted. 15 Pl. Vendôme, 1er (phone: 42-60-38-30; fax: 42-86-00-91; telex: 220262). Very expensive.

Royal Monceau – This elegant, impeccably decorated property, not far from the Arc de Triomphe, has 3 restaurants — including one with an attractive garden setting — as well as 2 bars, a fitness center, pool, Jacuzzi, and beauty salon. The Sunday brunch, with classical and jazz music providing a soothing accompaniment, is a delight. Business facilities include 24-hour room service, meeting rooms for up to 250, an English-speaking concierge, foreign currency exchange, secretarial services in English, audiovisual equipment, photocopiers, computers, translation services, and express checkout. Major credit cards accepted. 37 Av. Hoche, 8e (phone: 45-61-98-00; fax: 45-63-28-93; telex: 650361). Very expensive.

St. James's Club – Located in a château in a residential section of the city, this hotel is really a private club (there are others in this group: one in London, one in Antigua, another in Los Angeles). For an additional 55F ($10), non-members can stay here for a few nights and feel as if they are living in an elegant home. The penthouse suites have a winter roof garden. There's a health center (which includes a sauna, Jacuzzi, a billiard room, a tanning salon, and massage), a 10,000-volume library, and 2 restaurants. Business facilities include 24-hour room service, meeting rooms for up to 35, an English-speaking concierge, foreign currency exchange, secretarial services in English, audiovisual equipment, photocopiers, computers, translation services, and express checkout. Major credit cards accepted. 5 Pl. Chancelier-Adenauer, Av. Bugeaud, 16e (phone: 47-04-29-29; in the US, 800-641-0300; fax: 45-53-00-61). Very expensive.

San Régis – This is an elegant place to feel at home in comfortable surroundings. There are 44 beautifully appointed guestrooms, as well as a restaurant. Business facilities include an English-speaking concierge, foreign currency exchange, photocopiers, computers, and cable television news. Major credit cards accepted. 12 Rue Jean-Goujon, 8e (phone: 43-59-41-90; fax: 45-61-05-48; telex: 643637). Very expensive to expensive.

La Trémoille – Built in 1886, this former *hôtel particulier* (private home) is a true gem. Each of the 110 spacious rooms in this charming building, which has recently been declared a historical landmark, is beautifully appointed. The atmosphere here is one of understated elegance, and the location, just off Avenue Montaigne, a winner. Business facilities include a meeting room for up to 10, an English-speaking concierge, secretarial services in English, and audiovisual equipment. Major credit cards accepted. 14 Rue de la Tremoille, 8e (phone: 47-23-34-20). Very expensive to expensive.

Westminster – Between the *Opéra* and the *Ritz,* this establishment has regained some of its lost luster. The paneling, marble fireplaces, and parquet floors of its traditional decor remain; air conditioning has been installed in most rooms; and a new restaurant, *Le Céladon*, and cocktail lounge replace the old grill and bar. Some of the 101 rooms and apartments overlook the street, some an inner courtyard. Business facilities include 24-hour room service, meeting rooms for up to 70, an English-speaking concierge, foreign currency exchange, secretarial services in English, audiovisual equipment, photocopiers, and translation services. Major credit cards accepted. 13 Rue de la Paix, 2e (phone: 42-61-57-46; fax: 42-60-30-66; telex: 680035). Very expensive to expensive.

Balzac – Very private, this luxurious, charming hotel with 70 rooms and suites is ideally located off the Champs-Elysées. Another plus is that the Paris branch of the *Bice* restaurant is right there. Those who enjoy nocturnal pleasures can dance until dawn in the new discotheque. Business facilities include 24-hour room service, an English-speaking concierge, foreign currency exchange, and photocopiers. Major credit cards accepted. 6 Rue Balzac, 8e (phone: 45-61-97-22; fax: 45-25-24-82; telex: 290298). Expensive.

Colbert – Each of the 40 rooms in this Left Bank hostelry has a glass door leading onto a balcony. Decorated in pastel tones, there is a mini-bar and television set in each one. No restaurant, but breakfast included. Major credit cards accepted. 7 Rue de l'Hôtel-Colbert, 5e (phone: 43-25-85-65; in the US, 800-366-1510). Expensive.

Grand – This recently renovated property, part of the Inter-Continental chain, has long been a favorite of Americans abroad, with its "meeting place of the world," the *Café de la Paix*. It has 514 rooms and 10 luxurious suites, plus cheerful bars and restaurants — and a prime location (next to the *Opéra*). For exercise enthusiasts, there is a health spa on the fifth floor, which offers free weights, a sauna, and massage. Other improvements include the sumptuous, glass-ceilinged marble lobby, which houses a restaurant and lounge. Business facilities include 24-hour room service, meeting rooms for up to 1,200, an English-speaking concierge, foreign currency exchange, secretarial services in English, audiovisual equipment, photocopiers, cable television news, and express checkout. Major credit cards accepted. 2 Rue Scribe, 9e (phone: 40-07-32-32; 800-327-0200; fax: 42-66-12-51; telex: 220875). Expensive.

Holiday Inn Place de la République – In the heart of town, in a 120-year-old edifice that evokes the grandeur of the Second Empire — its façade is unlike any *Holiday Inn* you've seen before. Of the 318 pleasantly decorated rooms, those facing the courtyard are preferable to those facing the square. Restaurant, piano bar, and air conditioning. Major credit cards accepted. 10 Pl. de la République, 11e (phone: 43-55-44-34; fax: 47-00-32-34; telex: 210651). Expensive.

L'Hôtel – Small, but chic, this Left Bank hostelry is favored by experienced international travelers (Oscar Wilde died here). The 27 rooms are tiny, but beautifully appointed (antiques, fresh flowers, marble baths). The attractive restaurant, complete with waterfall, serves first-rate fare. Business facilities include meeting rooms for up to 50, an English-speaking concierge, foreign currency exchange, secretarial services in English, photocopiers, translation services, and express checkout. Major credit cards accepted. 13 Rue des Beaux-Arts, 6e (phone: 43-25-27-22; fax: 43-25-64-81; telex: 270870). Expensive.

Hôtel des Saints-Pères – In a great location in the heart of the Left Bank, its 40 attractively decorated guestrooms, courtyard garden, and a charming bar make this one of Paris's best little hotels. Book far in advance — it's often difficult to get a room. Business facilities include an English-speaking concierge, foreign currency exchange, and photocopiers. Major credit cards accepted. 65 Rue des Sts-Pères, 6e (phone: 45-44-50-00; fax: 45-44-90-83; telex: 205424). Expensive.

Inter-Continental – The 452 rooms and suites have been meticulously restored to re-create turn-of-the-century elegance with modern conveniences. The top-floor Louis XVI "garret" rooms are cozy and look out over the Tuileries. There's an American-style coffee shop, a grill, and a popular bar. Business facilities include 24-hour room service, meeting rooms for up to 1,000, an English-speaking concierge, foreign currency exchange, secretarial services in English, audiovisual equipment, photocopiers, translation services, and express checkout. Major credit cards accepted. 3 Rue de Castiglione, 1er (phone: 44-77-11-11; fax: 44-77-14-60; telex: 220114). Expensive.

Lancaster – Small and still smart (it's where chic and savvy visitors — both American *and* French — return again and again), this 66-room (no more than 10 on each of its 6 floors) townhouse has quiet, comfortable accommodations. Many of the double rooms and suites have a balcony or terrace. Ask for a suite on the top floor, where some of the views offer a glimpse of the Eiffel Tower or Sacré-Coeur. There are flowers everywhere, a cozy bar, a topnotch restaurant with courtyard service in summer, and underground parking. Run by London's Savoy group, the bar-cum-lounge is warm and welcoming. Business facilities include 24-hour room service, meeting rooms for up to 20, an English-speaking concierge, foreign currency exchange, secretarial services in English, audiovisual equipment, photocopiers, and cable television news. Major credit cards accepted. 7 Rue de Berri, 8e (phone: 43-59-90-43; fax: 42-89-22-71; telex: 640991). Expensive.

Lutétia – This recently renovated Belle Epoque hostelry is centrally located between Montparnasse and Odéon. Almost all of its 270 spacious and stylishly decorated rooms have air conditioning. Its *Le Paris* restaurant has been awarded one Michelin star. Business facilities include 24-hour room service, meeting rooms for up to 450, an English-speaking concierge, foreign currency exchange, secretarial services in English, audiovisual equipment, photocopiers, translation services, and express checkout. Major credit cards accepted. 45 Bd. Raspail, 6e (phone: 45-44-38-10; fax: 45-48-98-28; telex: 270424). Expensive.

Méridien – *Air France*'s well-run, 1,025-room, modern American-style property has all the expected French flair. Rooms are on the small side, but tastefully decorated, quiet, and with good views. There are 4 attractive restaurants (one of which serves Japanese fare), a shopping arcade, lively bars, and a chic nightclub, *L'Ecume des Nuits*. Business facilities include 24-hour room service, meeting rooms for up to 2,000, an English-speaking concierge, foreign currency exchange, secretarial services in English, audiovisual equipment, photocopiers, translation services, and express checkout. Major credit cards accepted. 81 Bd. Gouvion-St-Cyr, 17e (phone: 40-68-34-34; fax: 40-68-31-31; telex: 651952). Expensive.

Méridien Montparnasse – With 952 rooms, this ultramodern giant is in the heart of Montparnasse. It has a futuristic lobby, efficient service, a coffee shop, bars, and the *Montparnasse 25* restaurant, with a view, and in summer, a garden restaurant. There is also an ample brunch served in the restaurant on Sunday mornings. Business facilities include 24-hour room service, meeting rooms for up to 2,000, an English-speaking concierge, foreign currency exchange, secretarial services in English, audiovisual equipment, photocopiers, computers, translation services, and express checkout. Major credit cards accepted. 19 Rue du Commandant-René-Mouchotte, 14e (phone: 43-20-15-51; fax: 43-20-61-03). Expensive.

Montalembert – Completely renovated inside (its lovely façade remains), this small and exquisite hotel is known for its privacy. The 56 rooms, suites, and public areas are decorated in Art Deco style. A favorite spot for the literary and artistic crowd. The menu at its restaurant emphasizes simplicity and freshness. Business facilities include 24-hour room service, meeting rooms for up to 30, an English-speaking concierge, foreign currency exchange, secretarial services in English, audiovisual equipment, photocopiers, and express checkout. Major credit cards accepted. 3

Rue Montalembert, 7e (phone: 45-48-68-11; in the US, 800-628-8929; fax: 42-22-58-19; telex: 200132). Expensive.

Paris Hilton International – Its 455 modern rooms are only a few steps from the Eiffel Tower. Those facing the river have the best view. *Le Western* serves T-bone steaks, apple pie à la mode, and brownies (mostly to French diners). The coffee shop is a magnet for homesick Americans. Business facilities include 24-hour room service, meeting rooms for up to 1,000, an English-speaking concierge, foreign currency exchange, secretarial services in English, audiovisual equipment, photocopiers, translation services, and express checkout. Major credit cards accepted. 18 Av. de Suffren, 15e (phone: 42-73-92-00; fax: 47-83-62-66; telex: 200955). Expensive.

Pavillon de la Reine – Supreme location for the Marais's only luxury hotel, owned by the management of the *Relais Christine* (see below) and similarly appointed. Its 55 spacious rooms look out on a garden or courtyard. The setting on the Place des Vosges is regal, and the *Picasso Museum* is only a couple of minutes away on foot. Business facilities include 24-hour room service, foreign currency exchange, and photocopiers. Major credit cards accepted. 28 Pl. des Vosges, 3e (phone: 42-77-96-40; fax: 42-77-63-06; telex: 216160). Expensive.

Prince de Galles – An excellent location (a next-door neighbor of the pricier *George V*) and impeccable style make this hostelry a good choice. All 173 rooms and suites are individually decorated. This Marriott member offers a restaurant and an oak-paneled bar; parking is available. Business facilities include 24-hour room service, meeting rooms for up to 150, English-speaking concierge, foreign currency exchange, secretarial services in English, audiovisual equipment, photocopiers, computers, translation services, and express checkout. Major credit cards accepted. 33 Av. George-V, 8e (phone: 47-23-55-11; fax: 47-20-96-92; telex: 280627). Expensive.

Pullman St-Jacques – This four-star hotel has 797 up-to-date rooms, a nice shopping arcade, 4 restaurants (one Japanese, one Chinese, one French, and an informal coffee shop), and the lively *Bar Tahonga*. A bit out of the way, but the métro is close by. Business facilities include 24-hour room service, meeting rooms for up to 3,000, an English-speaking concierge, foreign currency exchange, secretarial services in English, audiovisual equipment, photocopiers, computers, translation services, and express checkout. Major credit cards accepted. 17 Bd. St-Jacques, 14e (phone: 40-78-79-80; fax: 45-88-43-93; telex: 270740). Expensive.

Raphaël – A very spacious, stately place, with a Turner in the lobby downstairs and paneling painted with sphinxes in the generous rooms. Other elegant touches are red velvet upholstered furniture and Oriental rugs. Less well known among the top Paris hotels, but favored by film folk and the like. And for those who savor strolling down the Champs-Elysées, it's only a short walk away. Business facilities include 24-hour room service, meeting rooms for up to 150, an English-speaking concierge, foreign currency exchange, secretarial services in English, audiovisual equipment, photocopiers, computers, translation services, and express checkout. Major credit cards accepted. 17 Av. Kléber, 16e (phone: 44-28-00-28; fax: 45-01-21-50; telex: 610356). Expensive.

Relais Christine – This lovely small hotel, with modern fixtures, 31 rooms, and lots of old-fashioned charm, formerly was a 16th-century cloister. Ask for a room with a courtyard or garden view (we especially like No. 31; other rooms tend to be small and noisy). Business facilities include meeting rooms for up to 20, foreign currency exchange, and photocopiers. Major credit cards accepted. 3 Rue Christine, 6e (phone: 43-26-71-80; fax: 43-26-89-38; telex: 202606). Expensive.

Le Relais Saint-Germain – In a 17th-century building, this hostelry with 10 guestrooms and 1 suite is ideally situated on the Left Bank just steps from the Boulevard

St-Germain and the area's best shops, eateries, and galleries. It is attractively decorated, and charming down to its massive ceiling beams and huge flower bouquets. A rare find. Major credit cards accepted. 9 Carrefour de l'Odéon, 6e (phone: 43-29-12-05; fax: 46-33-45-30; telex: 201889). Expensive.

Résidence du Roy – Within easy reach of the Champs-Elysées, this establishment offers self-contained studios, suites, and duplexes, complete with kitchen facilities. No restaurant. Business facilities include meeting rooms for up to 20, English-speaking concierge, audiovisual equipment, photocopiers, and express checkout. Major credit cards accepted. 8 Rue François-Ier, 8e (phone: 42-89-59-59; fax: 40-74-07-92; telex: 648452). Expensive.

Le Vernet – This sister hotel to the elegant *Royal Monceau* has 57 modern rooms and suites and is located just a few steps from the Arc de Triomphe. Guests have complimentary access to the health club at the *Royal Monceau*. Business facilities include 24-hour room service, meeting rooms for up to 15, an English-speaking concierge, foreign currency exchange, audiovisual equipment, photocopiers, computers, translation services, and express checkout. Major credit cards accepted. 25 Rue Vernet, 8e (phone: 47-23-43-10; fax: 40-70-10-14; telex: 290347). Expensive.

Abbaye St-Germain – On a quiet street, this small, delightful place once was a convent. The lobby has exposed stone arches, and the elegant public and private rooms are furnished with antiques, tastefully selected fabrics, and marble baths. There's a lovely garden and a bar, but there continue to be some complaints about the service. Recent renovations have resulted in more ample accommodations; we especially admire Nos. 3 and 4 on the ground floor, whose doors open out onto the charming courtyard garden. Business facilities include an English-speaking concierge, foreign currency exchange, and photocopiers. Major credit cards accepted. 10 Rue Cassette, 6e (phone: 45-44-38-11; fax: 45-48-07-86). Expensive to moderate.

Angleterre – Its 29 classic, clean, unpretentious rooms are in what once was the British Embassy, now a national monument. Business facilities include an English-speaking concierge, foreign currency exchange, and photocopiers. Major credit cards accepted. 44 Rue Jacob, 6e (phone: 42-60-34-72; fax: 42-60-16-93). Moderate.

Britannique – Within minutes of the *Louvre* and Notre-Dame, this hotel was a Quaker mission house during World War I. All 40 rooms are equipped with mini-bars, hair dryers, and satellite television. Major credit cards accepted. 20 Av. Victoria, 1er (phone: 42-33-74-59; in the US, 800-366-1510). Moderate.

Danube St-Germain – The 45 rooms, with their four-poster bamboo beds, are comfortable, and some of them overlook an attractive courtyard typical of the Left Bank. American Express accepted. Business facilities include foreign currency exchange and photocopiers. 58 Rue Jacob, 6e (phone: 42-60-34-70; fax: 42-60-81-18; telex: 211062). Moderate.

Deux Continents – A cozy red sitting room looks invitingly onto the street here, in this 40-room establishment on the Left Bank. Major credit cards accepted. 25 Rue Jacob, 6e (phone: 43-26-72-46). Moderate.

Deux Iles – This beautifully redecorated 17th-century house is on the historic Ile St-Louis. It has a garden with a Portuguese fountain and the decor is in bamboo, rattan, and braided rope. The 17 rooms have French provincial fabrics and Louis XIV ceramic tiles in the bathrooms. But there's one drawback: The rooms aren't very large. Business facilities include foreign currency exchange. No credit cards accepted. 59 Rue St-Louis-en-l'Ile, 4e (phone: 43-26-13-35; fax: 43-29-60-25). Moderate.

Duc de St-Simon – If you're in search of things past, this may be one of the best places in town, despite the rather small rooms. In two big townhouses in a beautiful, quiet backwater off the Boulevard St-Germain, this elegant little spot veritably reeks of Proust. Just a 5-minute walk from the spectacular *Musée d'Orsay*. Business facilities include a foreign currency exchange and photocopiers. No credit cards accepted. 14 Rue de St-Simon, 7e (phone: 45-48-35-66; fax: 45-48-68-25; telex: 203277). Moderate.

Grand Hôtel Taranne – Anybody anxious to get into the Left Bank scene should love it here, for the 35 rooms are literally on top of the *Brasserie Lipp*. Each room is unique: No. 4 has exposed beams, a TV set, and a mini-bar; No. 3 has a Louis XIII–style bed; No. 17, the oddest, has lights and a disco ball. At press time, the hotel was undergoing major renovations, so guests may bid farewell to the disco ball forever. Business facilities include foreign currency exchange and photocopiers. Major credit cards accepted. 153 Bd. St-Germain, 6e (phone: 42-22-21-65; fax: 45-48-22-25; telex: 205340). Moderate.

Grand Hôtel de l'Univers – Modern and tucked away on a quiet street, it's also only 2 steps away from St-Germain-des-Prés and the Latin Quarter. No restaurant. Major credit cards accepted. 6 Rue Grégoire-de-Tours, 6e (phone: 43-29-37-00; fax: 40-51-06-45; telex: 204150). Moderate.

Jeu de Paume – The architect-owner of this former *jeu de paume* (tennis court) has artfully married old and new in this addition to the exclusive Ile St-Louis hotels. High-tech lighting, modern artwork, and a sleek glass elevator are set against ancient ceiling beams and limestone brick hearths. There's a country feeling here. Rooms are comfortable and reasonably priced, and each one overlooks the lovely garden. There is also a music salon with a piano. Business facilities include 24-hour room service, meeting rooms for up to 30, foreign currency exchange, secretarial services in English, and photocopiers. Major credit cards accepted. 54 Rue St-Louis-en-l'Ile, 4e (phone: 43-26-14-18; telex: 205160). Moderate.

Lord Byron – On a quiet street off the Champs-Elysées, it has a pleasant courtyard and 30 comfortable, homey rooms. The staff is friendly and speaks good English, and a family atmosphere prevails. Major credit cards accepted. 5 Rue de Chateaubriand, 8e (phone: 43-59-89-98; fax: 42-89-46-04; telex: 649662). Moderate.

Lutèce – Here are 23 luxurious rooms (one split-level) on the charming Ile St-Louis. Positively ravishing, with exquisite toile fabric and wallpaper and raw wood beams. 65 Rue St-Louis-en-l'Ile, 4e (phone: 43-26-23-52; fax: 43-29-60-25). Moderate.

Madison – Offers 55 large, bright rooms, some recently renovated, some with balconies, and all with air conditioning. Major credit cards accepted. 143 Bd. St-Germain, 6e (phone: 43-29-72-50; fax: 43-29-72-50; telex: 201628). Moderate.

Montaigne – One of Paris's newest additions, this unpretentious establishment is a true find. Each of its 29 rooms is comfortable, clean, and chicly decorated. There's a bar and a breakfast room, but no restaurant. Major credit cards accepted. 6 Ave. Montaigne, 8e (phone: 47-20-30-50; fax: 47-20-94-12). Moderate.

Odéon – Small, modernized, and charming, it's in the heart of the St-Germain area on the Left Bank. No restaurant. Major credit cards accepted. 3 Rue de l'Odéon, 6e (phone: 43-25-90-67; fax: 43-25-55-98; telex: 202943). Moderate.

Parc St-Séverin – An interesting property in the heart of the 5th *arrondissement* on the Left Bank, it has a total of 27 rooms, including a top-floor penthouse with a wraparound balcony. The decor is modern but understated, and the overall ambience is appealing even though the neighborhood is less than the quietest in Paris. Major credit cards accepted. 22 Rue de la Parcheminerie, 5e (phone: 43-54-32-17; fax: 43-54-70-71). Moderate.

Pavillon Bastille – A small 19th-century *hôtel particulier* with a 17th-century fountain in its courtyard, conveniently located near the Place de la Bastille. All 24 tiny rooms and 1 suite are cheerfully decorated in blues and yellows, and are equipped with mini-bars. No restaurant. Major credit cards accepted. 65 Rue de Lyon, 11e (phone: 43-43-65-65; fax: 43-43-96-52). Moderate.

Regent's Garden – On a quiet street near l'Etoile, it has 39 spacious rooms, some with large marble fireplaces. The property is run by young hoteliers who make you feel as if you are in your own home. A country atmosphere pervades. There's also a garden and parking. Major credit cards accepted. 6 Rue Pierre-Demours, 17e (phone: 45-74-07-30; fax: 40-55-01-42; telex: 640127). Moderate.

Résidence Charles-Dullin – In a sleepy corner of Montmartre, near the leafy square of the *Théâtre de l'Atelier*, this residential hotel charges nightly, weekly, and monthly rates. The recently renovated apartments have kitchens, and some over-look a peaceful garden. Major credit cards accepted. 10 Pl. Charles-Dullin, 18e (phone: 42-57-14-55; fax: 42-54-48-87). Moderate.

Ste-Beuve – A stylish place in Montparnasse with rooms and lobby designed by David Hicks. Major credit cards accepted. 9 Rue Ste-Beuve, 6e (phone: 45-48-20-07; fax: 45-48-67-52). Moderate.

Le St-Grégoire – A small 18th-century mansion on the Left Bank, this hostelry has an intimate cozy atmosphere, a warm fire in the hearth, and 20 tastefully furnished rooms, 2 with terraces overlooking a garden. Major credit cards accepted. 43 Rue de l'Abbé-Grégoire, 6e (phone: 45-48-23-23; fax: 45-48-33-95). Moderate.

St-Louis – On magical Ile St-Louis, practically in the shadow of Notre-Dame, this small hotel will make the first-time visitor fall in love with the city forever. The 21 rooms aren't large, but they're pretty, and the 3 fifth-floor rooms under the eaves are enchanting, with tiny balconies overlooking Parisian rooftops. No TV sets, but baths are clean and modern, and there's a charming breakfast room and a warm welcome. No credit cards accepted. 75 Rue St-Louis-en-l'Ile, 4e (phone: 46-34-04-80; fax: 46-34-02-13). Moderate.

St-Louis Marais – On a quiet residential street on the edge of the newly chic Marais (Paris's oldest neighborhood), this tiny hotel is a short walk from the Place des Vosges, the *Louvre,* the quays along the Seine, and the Bastille nightclubs. Dating from the 18th century, when it belonged to the Celestins Convent, it has 15 small but recently remodeled rooms. Historical status has barred the installation of an elevator, however. No credit cards accepted. 1 Rue Charles-V, 4e (phone: 48-87-87-04; fax: 46-34-02-13). Moderate.

St-Merri – A stone's throw from the *Centre Georges-Pompidou* arts complex, this mock-medieval establishment may be the most bizarre hotel in Paris. It not only backs onto the Eglise St-Merri, but it has a communion rail as a banister and ancient oaken confessionals as broom closets. The rooms, hung with dark, de-monic oil portraits, have church pews for benches, and some rooms are even spliced by a flying buttress. In dubious taste, perhaps, but there's nothing else like it. No credit cards accepted. 78 Rue de la Verrerie, 4e (phone: 42-78-14-15; fax: 40-29-06-82). Moderate.

Suède – A delightful hotel situated in the quiet seventh *arrondissement,* just around the corner from the prime minister's residence. All 41 rooms are beautifully appointed. Breakfast is served in a simple salon or, in good weather, in a beautiful courtyard. Major credit cards accepted. 31 Rue Vaneau, 7e (phone: 47-05-00-08). Moderate.

Tuileries – With a good location in a "real" neighborhood in the heart of the city, it has a well-tended look and attractive carved wood bedsteads. Major credit cards accepted. 10 Rue St-Hyacinthe, 1er (phone: 42-61-04-17 or 42-61-06-94; fax: 49-27-91-56). Moderate.

L'Université – Its 28 charming rooms of all shapes and sizes are in a former 18th-century mansion. No credit cards accepted. 22 Rue de l'Université, 7e (phone: 42-61-09-39). Moderate.

Vendôme – This older "house" has 36 immaculate high-ceilinged rooms with brass beds, and the location couldn't be better. There is a small restaurant with a limited menu, and a bar. Major credit cards accepted. 1 Pl. Vendôme, 1er (phone: 42-60-32-84; fax: 49-27-97-89). Moderate.

La Villa – Popular with American fashion writers, this 35-room hostelry in the St-Germain area was completely renovated in post-modern decor. Although the rooms are incredibly small, the luxurious bathrooms alone are worth a stay here. Jazz concerts add a lively note (or two) to weekend evenings. Major credit cards accepted. Business facilities include an English-speaking concierge and foreign currency exchange. 29 Rue Jacob, 6e (phone: 43-26-60-00; fax: 45-44-89-97; telex: 202437). Moderate.

West End – Friendly, with 60 rooms, it's on the Right Bank. The front desk keeps a close, concerned watch on comings and goings, which some may find reassuring. Major credit cards accepted. 7 Rue Clément-Marot, 8e (phone: 47-20-30-78; fax: 47-20-34-42). Moderate.

Chomel – Sprucely decorated, this establishment is near the *Au Bon Marché* department store. Major credit cards accepted. 15 Rue Chomel, 7e (phone: 45-48-55-52; fax: 45-48-89-76). Moderate to inexpensive.

Ferrandi – Popular with international businessmen, this recently renovated, no-frills hostelry is done up in browns and blues, with a winding wood staircase and a quiet lounge. Major credit cards accepted. 92 Rue du Cherche-Midi, 6e (phone: 42-22-97-40). Moderate to inexpensive.

Des Marroniers – Good rates and an excellent location, in the heart of the Left Bank, makes this 37-room hotel a real bargain. It has a courtyard and pretty breakfast room. No credit cards accepted. 21 Rue Jacob, 6e (phone: 43-25-30-60). Moderate to inexpensive.

St-Thomas-d'Aquin – Built in the 1880s, this unpretentious hotel is a simple, functional base from which to explore a shopper's paradise of new wave designer boutiques and tiny restaurants. The 21 rooms are clean and neat, and baths are modern (though tubs are half-size). Breakfast is included. Major credit cards accepted. 3 Rue d'Pré-aux-Clercs, 7e (phone: 42-61-01-22; fax: 42-61-41-43). Moderate to inexpensive.

Amélie – Centrally located, this comfortable spot has 15 rooms, each with color TV set, direct-dial telephone, and mini-bar. Breakfast is included in the rate, which makes this one of Paris's better bargains. Major credit cards accepted. 5 Rue Amélie, 7e (phone: 45-51-74-75; fax: 45-56-93-55). Inexpensive.

D'Argenson – The upper middle class residential district in which this hotel is located is off the typical tourist track but convenient to major department stores on the Boulevard Haussmann and a 15-minute walk from the *Opéra*. The showplace rooms — Nos. 23, 33, 43, and 53 — feature fireplaces and up-to-date bathrooms. Room rate includes breakfast. Some major credit cards accepted. 15 Rue d'Argenson, 8e (phone: 42-65-16-87). Inexpensive.

De Bellevue et du Chariot d'Or – Slightly eccentric, but friendly, this is the best of more than a score of tiny hotels in the wholesale garment district. Although the hallway carpets and wallpaper are in dire need of replacement, the rooms are clean and comfortable, and most of the baths have been redone. Room No. 110 is on the courtyard (which means it's quiet) and has twin beds, a pink bathroom, and a marble fireplace. Some rooms are large enough to sleep four. Breakfast included. Major credit cards accepted. 39 Rue de Turbigo, 3e (phone: 48-87-45-60; fax: 48-87-95-04). Inexpensive.

Bretonnerie – This restored 17th-century townhouse takes itself seriously, with petit point, dark wood furnishings, and several attic rooms with beams that overlook the narrow streets of the newly fashionable Marais area. Major credit cards accepted. 22 Rue Ste-Croix-de-la-Bretonnerie, 4e (phone: 48-87-77-63; fax: 42-77-26-78). Inexpensive.

Ceramic – Close to the Champs-Elysées, the Faubourg St-Honoré, and the métro, this 53-room establishment with an Art Nouveau façade has been designated a national historic treasure. Request a room facing the street, particularly No. 412 — enormous, with a crystal chandelier and wide bay windows. Major credit cards accepted. 34 Av. de Wagram, 8e (phone: 42-27-20-30; fax: 46-22-95-83). Inexpensive.

Delavigne – Good value and location (just down the street from the *Odéon* theater), it has an enlightened manager who says he isn't interested in simply handing out keys, but enjoys introducing foreigners to Paris. Major credit cards accepted. 1 Rue Casimir-Delavigne, 6e (phone: 43-29-31-50; fax: 43-29-78-56). Inexpensive.

Esmeralda – Some of the rooms look directly at Notre-Dame over the gardens of St-Julien-le-Pauvre, one of Paris's most ancient churches. The oak beams and furniture round out the medieval atmosphere. Small and friendly, especially popular with the theatrical crowd. No credit cards accepted. 4 Rue St-Julien-le-Pauvre, 5e (phone: 43-54-19-20). Inexpensive.

Family – A longtime favorite with Americans — you're treated just like part of the family. There are 25 small but comfortable rooms, which have been recently renovated. Major credit cards accepted. 35 Rue Cambon, 1er (phone: 42-61-54-84). Inexpensive.

Grandes Ecoles – Just the sort of place that shouldn't appear in a guidebook (even the proprietress says so) and that people recommend only to the right friends. Insulated from the street by a delightful courtyard and its garden, it is a simple 19th-century private house with plain comforts, but it's long on atmosphere. There aren't many like it in Paris, but beware that booking is difficult and the owner has been known to give away reserved rooms. Major credit cards accepted. 75 Rue Cardinal-Lemoine, 5e (phone: 43-26-79-23; fax: 43-25-28-15). Inexpensive.

Le Jardin des Plantes – In addition to a magnificent setting across from the Parisian Botanical Gardens, near the Sorbonne, there are 33 airy, spotless rooms and baths, each with its own floral motif. The owner, a psychologist, has anticipated the traveler's every need: All rooms have mini-bars, TV sets, and hair dryers; some have alcoves large enough for extra beds for children; a sauna is available in the basement. Breakfast can be enjoyed in the sunny ground-floor coffee bar or on the fifth-floor terrace and rose garden. Art exhibits and classical music concerts are held on Sundays in the vaulted cellar. Major credit cards accepted. 5 Rue Linné, 5e (phone: 47-07-06-20). Inexpensive.

Jeanne d'Arc – This little place on a quiet street in the Marais doesn't get top marks for decor and its facilities are simple, but somehow its appeal has spread from Minnesota to Melbourne. It's well placed at the colorful end of the Rue de Rivoli, and the management is friendly and speaks English. Major credit cards accepted. 3 Rue Jarente, 4e (phone: 48-87-62-11). Inexpensive.

Lenox – Between the busy St-Germain area and the boutiques nearby, it's small and very tastefully done, with a small bar. Popular with the fashion crowd. Major credit cards accepted. 9 Rue de l'Université, 7e (phone: 42-96-10-95; fax: 42-61-52-82). Inexpensive.

London – In the heart of the business district, this recently renovated, comfortable hotel has 50 rooms, each with color TV set and direct-dial telephone. Major credit cards accepted. 32 Bd. des Italiens, 9e (phone: 48-24-54-64; fax: 48-00-08-83). Inexpensive.

Prima Lepic – A 38-room hotel in Montmartre, a busy neighborhood of winding little streets that evoke the romance of *la vie bohème,* Utrillo, Picasso, Toulouse-Lautrec and the *Moulin Rouge.* Decorated by cheerful young owners, rooms sport pretty floral wallpapers and one-of-a-kind furnishings — a wicker chair, a mirrored armoire, a 1930s lamp. No. 56, on the top floor, looks out over Paris, and travelers with a child should make special note of room No. 2, which connects to another room. There's an elevator, and the public spaces are charming. Major credit cards accepted. 29 Rue Lepic, 18e (phone: 46-06-44-64). Inexpensive.

Prince Albert – Despite its unprepossessing aura of faded glory, this has its site to recommend it: just off the quiet and unspoiled Marché St-Honoré and a hop, skip, and jump from the Tuileries. Major credit cards accepted. 5 Rue St-Hyacinthe, 1er (phone: 42-61-58-36; fax: 42-60-04-06). Inexpensive.

St-André-des-Arts – A rambling old favorite among the chic and hip whose purses are slim but whose tastes are discerning. No credit cards accepted. 66 Rue St-André-des-Arts, 6e (phone: 43-26-96-16). Inexpensive.

Sévigné – If it's a little noisy (right on the Rue de Rivoli), the warm welcome (although the owner professes not to be very fond of Americans) and handy location make up for it. Major credit cards accepted. 2 Rue Mahler, 4e (phone: 42-72-76-17). Inexpensive.

Solférino – A cozy place with Oriental rugs scattered about. The 34 tiny rooms have floral wallpaper, and there's a plant-filled breakfast and sitting room. Major credit cards accepted. 91 Rue de Lille, 7e (phone: 47-05-85-54). Inexpensive.

Le Vieux Marais – Near the *Centre Georges-Pompidou,* this is one of the few agreeable hostelries in the Marais area, with brightly sprigged walls in the cheerful, if not very large, rooms. The breakfast room has an impressive wall-size engraving of the Place des Vosges, not far away. Major credit cards accepted. 8 Rue du Plâtre, 4e (phone: 42-78-47-22; fax: 42-78-34-32). Inexpensive.

Welcome – Overlooking the Boulevard St-Germain, it's simple but comfortable. No credit cards accepted. 66 Rue de Seine, 6e (phone: 46-34-24-80; fax: 40-46-81-59). Inexpensive.

Boucherat – A plain, friendly establishment with no airs and with a clientele that returns. Near the Place de la République. Room rates include breakfast. Major credit cards accepted. 110 Rue de Turenne, 3e (phone: 42-72-86-83). Very inexpensive.

Du Globe – Tiny and charming, it's on a quiet street in the heart of the St-Germain area. No credit cards accepted. 15 Rue des Quatre-Vents, 6e (phone: 43-26-35-50). Very inexpensive.

Henri IV – No one could call this modern — the fittings obviously haven't been changed for decades, and there's only a bidet and basin in the room, since the bathrooms are down the hall. But it has a reputation and a history, not least because it is the only hotel on the Place Dauphine on the Ile de la Cité — the real core of Paris. Prices are breathtakingly low. No credit cards accepted. 25 Pl. Dauphine, 1er (phone: 43-54-44-53). Very inexpensive.

EATING OUT: Paris considers itself the culinary capital of the world, and you will never forget food for long here. Whether you grab just a freshly baked croissant and café au lait for breakfast or splurge on an epicurean fantasy for dinner, this is the city in which to indulge all your gastronomic dreams. Remember, too, that there is no such thing as "French" food; rather, Paris provides the perfect mosaic in which to try regional delights from Provence, Alsace, Normandy, Brittany, and many other delicious places.

Restaurants classed as very expensive charge $250 and way up for two; expensive is $150 to $200; moderate, $100 to $150; inexpensive, less than $100; and very inexpensive, $50 or less. A service charge of 15% is added to the bill, but most people leave a small additional tip for good service; wine is not included in the price. Street addresses of the restaurants below are followed by their *arrondissement* number.

Note: To save frustration and embarrassment, always *reconfirm* dinner reservations before noon on the appointed day. (For information about making written dinner reservations, see USEFUL WORDS AND PHRASES.) Also remember that some of the better restaurants do not accept credit cards; it's a good idea to check when making your reservations. It may come as a surprise to discover that many of the elite Paris restaurants close over the weekend; also note that many Paris restaurants are closed for part or all of July or August. It's best to check ahead in order to avoid disappointment at the restaurant of your choice, and it's also worth remembering that many offer special lunch menus at considerably lower prices. Here is a sampling of the best restaurants that Paris has to offer:

Les Ambassadeurs – A two-Michelin-star dining establishment that reaffirms one's faith in a soul-satisfying meal gracefully presented in surroundings only surpassed by Versailles's Hall of Mirrors. The atmosphere is the epitome of elegance — from the 20-foot-high ceilings to the massive crystal chandeliers to the stunning views of the Place de la Concorde. Delicious dishes such as *gratin dauphinois de homard avec crème au caviar* (potato gratin with lobster in caviar sauce) and veal sweetbreads in a light wine sauce are perfectly complemented by one of the exceptional wines from the *cave.* Open daily. Major credit cards accepted. 10 Pl. de la Concorde, in the *Crillon,* 8e (phone: 44-71-16-16; fax: 44-71-15-02). Very expensive.

L'Ambroisie – Quietly elegant, beneath the arcade of historic Place des Vosges, this is the showcase for chef Bernard Pacaud's equally elegant cuisine, which features unusual combinations of herbs and spices. The menu is limited to a few sublime dishes, such as turbot braised with tiny purple artichokes or rack of lamb with basil butter sauce. The quality has earned the place three Michelin stars, though a few fussy gastronomes say the stars have dimmed just a bit. Closed Sundays, Monday lunch, August, and holidays. Reservations necessary. Major credit cards accepted. 9 Pl. des Vosges, 4e (phone: 42-78-51-45). Very expensive.

Beauvilliers – Deliciously flirtatious and festive, this restaurant on the northern slope of the Butte of Montmartre is one of the most romantic spots in Paris. Proust or Balzac might have felt at home in its intimate dining rooms or on hydrangea-rimmed summer terraces in the shadow of a white-stone cathedral. The food — a rich, generous cuisine prepared in the best bourgeois tradition — complements the surroundings. Try the aspic of sweetbreads with tiny quail eggs, *turbot au jus de jarret,* and a remarkable praline chocolate cake. Closed the first 2 weeks in September, Monday lunch, and Sundays. Reservations necessary. Major credit cards accepted. 52 Rue Lamarck, 18e (phone: 42-54-54-42). Very expensive.

Le Grand Véfour – Founded in 1760, this sedately elegant Empire-style establishment near the Palais Royale — with paintings on the mirrors — is known for refined menus (two Michelin stars) and perfect service. Although plagued by the frequent changing of chefs in the past 2 years, the dining room remains one of the most beautiful and historic in Paris, maintaining its culinary reputation with such delectable dishes as *lapereau en cocotte* (stewed young rabbit). Closed Saturdays at lunch, Sundays, and August. Reservations necessary. Major credit cards accepted. 17 Rue Beaujolais, 1er (phone: 42-96-56-27). Very expensive.

Jamin – Due to the culinary talents of owner-chef Joël Robuchon, this is one of the city's finest restaurants — with a three-star ranking by Michelin — and one of the most difficult to get into. Robuchon calls his cuisine "moderne," similar to but not always as light as nouvelle. The restaurateur believes that "one can never eat too many truffles" — we're inclined to agree — and uses the pungent edible to enhance many of the dishes in his ever-changing menu. If available, we recommend the sea scallops with a truffle salad. The dining room is *very* small, so reserve far in advance. Waiting time is almost 8 weeks. Closed weekends and July. Reservations necessary. Major credit cards accepted. 32 Rue de Longchamp, 16e (phone: 47-27-12-27). Very expensive.

Lasserre – The ultimate in luxury, with a magical ceiling that opens periodically during dinner to reveal the nighttime sky. Equally sublime is the food, served in the *style Lasserre* — that is, vermeil dessert settings, plates rimmed in gold, and extravagant garnishes with each dish. The classic menu is heavy on foie gras, caviar, truffles, and rich sauces. Michelin downgraded the food to two stars a few years ago, and the atmosphere can be a bit overwhelming and formal, but the extravagance makes it memorable. Closed Sundays, Monday lunch, and August. Reservations necessary. Major credit cards accepted. 17 Av. Franklin-D.-Roosevelt, 8e (phone: 43-59-53-43). Very expensive.

Lucas-Carton – Once proprietor of the Michelin three-star restaurant called *L'Archestrate,* chef Alain Senderens dropped that name (but not his triple-star rating) in 1985 when he moved to larger, more elegant quarters in a historic building that boasts a gorgeous Belle Epoque interior. Senderens enjoys the reputation of being one of France's most innovative culinary talents, combining many tenets of nouvelle cuisine with Oriental influences. Try the sea scallops with *crème de cèpes* (mushroom sauce). Closed Saturdays, Sundays, and most of August. Reservations necessary. Major credit cards accepted. 9 Pl. de la Madeleine, 8e (phone: 42-65-22-90). Very expensive.

Maxim's – A legend for its Belle Epoque decor and atmosphere. It's good for celebrations, but though the service is impeccable, it's hard to feel comfortable if you aren't known here. Owned by fashion designer Pierre Cardin, this is one of the few places in Paris where you are expected to dress formally — on Friday evenings. There's an orchestra for dancing from 9:30 PM until 2 AM. Closed Sundays in July and August. Reservations necessary. Major credit cards accepted. 3 Rue Royale, 8e (phone: 42-65-27-94). Very expensive.

Régine's – The food actually is good in this beautifully decorated nightclub, which is frequented by Parisians as well as the chic international set. Ask your hotel manager to get you in, because it's nominally a private club. Try the foie gras (made on the premises) and the goose. Closed Sundays. Reservations advised. Major credit cards accepted. 49 Rue de Ponthieu, 8e (phone: 43-59-21-60). Very expensive.

Taillevent – Full of tradition, Louis XVI furnishings, 18th-century porcelain dinner service — all in a 19th-century mansion — this epicurean haven offers no-nonsense *cuisine classique:* subtle, even simple, but always sublime. Try the terrine of truffled sweetbreads, seafood sausage, duck, game in any form, a spectacular chocolate cake with pistachio sauce, and especially chef Claude Deligne's soufflés in original flavors like Alsatian pear. Three stars in the *Guide Michelin.* Closed weekends, part of February, and most of August. Reservations necessary. Americans often have difficulty reserving here (although it's a bit easier if there are four in your party), and it's best to try at least 60 days ahead. Major credit cards accepted. 15 Rue Lamennais, 8e (phone: 45-61-12-90). Very expensive.

La Tour d'Argent – Another of the five Parisian restaurants to be awarded three stars by the *Guide Michelin* and probably the best known — though recent visits have not been up to the standards of years past. The spectacular view of Notre-Dame and the Ile St-Louis competes with the food for the attention of a very touristy clientele. Pressed duck — prepared before you — is the specialty, but the 15 other varieties of duck are equally interesting. A single main dish here can cost $100, and to be quite frank, it just ain't worth it. Closed Mondays. Reservations necessary. Major credit cards accepted. 15 Quai de la Tournelle, 5e (phone: 43-54-23-31). Very expensive.

Vivarois – Claude Peyrot is one of France's finest chefs. Specialties in his small, elegant eating place feature *la cuisine du marché,* so offerings may vary according to what is available when the chef goes to market, but a splendid grilled turbot with capers is usually on the menu. Michelin has awarded it two stars. Closed weekends and August. Reservations necessary. Major credit cards accepted. 192 Av. Victor-Hugo, 16e (phone: 45-04-04-31). Very expensive.

L'Ami Louis – This is the archetypal Parisian bistro, unattractive physically but with huge portions of food that we rate as marvelous. Though the original Louis is gone, his heirs have maintained the rough welcome and informal ambience. Specialties include formidable servings of foie gras, roast chicken, spring lamb, ham, and burgundy wines. A favorite among Americans, this is the place to sample authentic French fries. Closed Mondays, Tuesdays, and most of July and August. Reservations necessary. Major credit cards accepted. 32 Rue de Vertbois, 3e (phone: 48-87-77-48). Expensive.

Amphyclés – Since it opened in May 1989, Philippe Groult's tiny restaurant near the Arc de Triomphe has won praise and two Michelin stars. A former student of star-chef Joël Robuchon, this Norman chef prefers using natural meat juices, and adds fresh herbs and truffles to his native cream and butter sauces; many of his recipes — such as a *salade de homard aux poivrons doux* (lobster salad with sweet red peppers) reveal a southern influence. Closed Saturday lunch and Sundays. Reservations necessary. Major credit cards accepted. 78 Av. des Ternes, 17e (phone: 40-68-01-01). Expensive.

Apicius – Jean-Pierre Vigato's highly original recipes have won him a reputation as one of Paris's finest chefs (and earned him two Michelin stars). Favorites include a *tourte de canard* (duck in pastry), potato purée with truffles, and *turbot rôti aux lardons* (roast turbot with smoked bacon). Closed weekends and August. Reservations necessary. Major credit cards accepted. 122 Av. de Villiers, 17e (phone: 43-80-19-66). Expensive.

L'Arpège – Paris's current rage is two-star chef Alain Passard, who prepares specialties such as *terrine de gibier au foie gras* (game terrine with foie gras) and *homard et navets à la vinaigrette aigre-douce* (lobster and turnips in a sweet-and-sour vinaigrette sauce). The prix fixe lunch at this eatery near the *Musée Rodin* is easily the best bargain around. Closed Saturdays and Sunday lunch and August. Reservations necessary. Major credit cards accepted. 84 Rue de Varenne, 7e (phone: 45-51-47-33). Expensive.

Le Carré des Feuillants – Alain Dutournier of *Le Trou Gascon* has set up shop right in midtown. The cuisine is still Gascon-inspired, but Dutournier is allowing his imagination more license with, for example, such creations as *perdreau sauvage* (wild partridge) with cumin, apricots, and fresh coriander. Michelin has awarded him two stars. Closed Saturdays for lunch and Sundays. Reservations necessary. Major credit cards accepted. 14 Rue de Castiglione, 1er (phone: 42-86-82-82). Expensive.

Castel – You might be able to get a reservation at this, one of the few private clubs in Paris, if you ask for help from the concierge at one of the town's grand hotels. The Belle Epoque interior is breathtaking, the cooking fine, and there's a disco in the basement. Specialties include lobster and chicken with cucumbers. Closed Sundays. Reservations necessary. Major credit cards accepted. 15 Rue Princesse, 6e (phone: 43-26-90-22). Expensive.

Chiberta – Elegant and modern, and boasting the acclaimed (two Michelin stars) nouvelle cuisine of Jean-Michel Bédier. Try *salade de pigeonneau et d'homard à l'arome de truffe* (salad of young squab and lobster flavored with truffles) and *filets de rouget à la crème d'olives* (mullet filets with olive purée). Closed weekends and August. Reservations necessary. Major credit cards accepted. 3 Rue Arsène-Houssaye, 8e (phone: 45-63-77-90). Expensive.

Le Divellec – This bright and airy place serves some exquisitely fresh seafood. Try the sea bass, the *rouget,* and the sautéed turbot. The latter is served with "black pasta" — thick strips of pasta flavored with squid ink — an unusual and delicious concoction. It has been awarded two Michelin stars. Closed Sundays, Mondays, and August. Reservations necessary. Major credit cards accepted. 107 Rue de l'Université, 7e (phone: 45-51-91-96). Expensive.

Dodin-Bouffant – Popular because it was set up by the gifted, imaginative, and long-gone Jacques Manière, it still offers excellent seafood, game in season, such as a spectacular roasted *col vert* (wild duck), and other inventive dishes (it has been awarded one Michelin star). Open late. Closed Sundays, 2 weeks at *Christmastime,* and August. Reservations necessary. Major credit cards accepted. 25 Rue Fréd-éric-Sauton, 5e (phone: 43-25-25-14). Expensive.

Drouant – Founded in 1880, this classic favorite reopened after an extensive face-lift, with an ambitious chef who favors classic French recipes. Michelin has awarded it one star. Open daily. Reservations necessary. Major credit cards accepted. 18 Rue Gaillon, 2e (phone: 42-65-15-16). Expensive.

Duquesnoy – Jean-Paul Duquesnoy, one of Paris's most promising young chefs, is in his element in nifty quarters. Warm carved woods and tasteful decor set the stage for specialties that include grilled sardines with *tapenade* (olive purée) lasagna as well as more classic concoctions; the crème brûlée with walnuts is a delight. Two Michelin stars. Closed Saturday lunch and Sundays. Reservations necessary. Major credit cards accepted. 6 Av. Bosquet, 7e (phone: 47-05-96-78). Expensive.

Faugeron – Among the finest nouvelle restaurants, awarded two stars by Michelin, its menu includes simple but exquisitely prepared dishes such as soft-boiled eggs with truffle purée. Lovely service, and one of Paris's prettiest table settings in what once was an old school. Closed weekends and August. Reservations necessary. Major credit cards accepted. 52 Rue de Longchamp, 16e (phone: 47-04-24-53). Expensive.

Fouquet's Bastille – Sister restaurant to the Champs-Elysées institution (see *Wine Bars and Cafés*), this post-modern location next to Paris's new *Opéra Bastille* offers traditional fare with a modern touch. Closed Saturday lunch and Sundays. Reservations advised. Major credit cards accepted. 130 Rue de Lyon, 12e (phone: 43-42-18-18). Expensive.

Gérard Besson – Michelin has given this small and formal eatery two stars. The service is impeccable and the classic menu includes specialties such as a savory *poulet de Bresse en cocotte* (casserole-roasted free-range chicken). Closed Saturdays and Sundays July 13 to 30, and from December 22 to January 7. Reservations necessary. Major credit cards accepted. 5 Rue Coq-Héron, 1er (phone: 42-33-14-74). Expensive.

Jacques Cagna – This establishment has a quintessential Left Bank look and a mix of nouvelle and classic dishes. The talented eponymous chef always provides an interesting menu at these charming premises on the Left Bank, very near the Seine. *Guide Michelin* has awarded it two stars. Closed August, *Christmas* week, Saturdays, and Sundays. Reservations necessary. Major credit cards accepted. 14 Rue des Grands-Augustins, 6e (phone: 43-26-49-39). Expensive.

Lamazère – Truffle heaven. The menu is a triumph of rich products from the southwest of France. The owner is a magician in the real sense of the word, as well as with food. The elegant bar and salons are open late. Closed Sundays and August. Reservations necessary. Major credit cards accepted. 23 Rue de Ponthieu, 8e (phone: 43-59-66-66). Expensive.

Ledoyen – This grand dowager of Paris dining places received a major face-lift in 1988 when Régine, the capital's nightlife queen, took it over. She recently sold the restaurant, and her head chef has also gone. This place will probably remain popular with high-powered businesspeople regardless of the quality of the food (which is tolerably good), but it is not the spot for a cozy tête-à-tête. Michelin has awarded it one star. Closed Sundays. Reservations necessary. Major credit cards accepted. Carré des Champs-Elysées, 8e (phone: 47-42-23-23). Expensive.

Miravile – Gilles Epié, one of Paris's promising young chefs, recently moved across the river into larger quarters. He brought with him his customers, his Michelin star, and memorable dishes such as *lapin aux olives* (rabbit with olives) and other recipes with a Provençal flavor. Closed Saturday lunch and Sundays. Reservations necessary. Major credit cards accepted. 72 Quai de l'Hôtel-de-Ville, 4e (phone: 42-74-72-22). Expensive.

Olympe – Dominique Nahimias, one of France's most highly lauded chefs (and the first female chef to be awarded three toques — very high honors — by Gault Millau) is no longer here, but the standard of excellence she established is being painstakingly maintained by her ex-husband Albert. The nouvelle cuisine continues to be simply glorious; an excellent wine list adds to the meal's enjoyment. Closed Saturday and Sunday lunch, Mondays, and August. Reservations necessary. Major credit cards accepted. 8 Rue Nicolas-Charlet, 15e (phone: 47-34-86-08). Expensive.

Le Petit Montmorency – In his location near the Champs-Elysées, chef Daniel Bouché presents one of the most consistent menus in Paris, offering such specialties as a fresh truffle roasted in pastry (in winter) and a *soufflé aux noisettes* (hazelnut soufflé). Very, very popular. Closed weekends and August. Reservations necessary. Major credit cards accepted. 5 Rue Rabelais, 8e (phone: 45-61-01-26). Expensive.

Pré Catelan – It's the large restaurant right in the middle of the Bois de Boulogne, and believe it or not, the food here is very good. Ingredients are fresh and sauces are light. Specialties include four or five new dishes daily. In the summertime, dining on the flower-decked terrace is a sheer delight. Michelin has awarded it one star. Closed Sunday evenings, Mondays, and 2 weeks in February. Reservations necessary. Major credit cards accepted. Rte. de Suresnes, Bois de Boulogne, 16e (phone: 45-24-55-58). Expensive.

Relais Louis XIII – Old-style decor and new cuisine in one of Paris's prettiest houses. The *Guide Michelin* has demoted it to one star. Closed Sundays, Monday lunch, and August. Reservations advised. Major credit cards accepted. 1 Rue Pont de Lodi, 6e (phone: 43-26-75-96). Expensive.

Tan-Dinh – The perfect pause from a constant diet of French specialties. Despite the loss of its Michelin star, its Vietnamese specialties are simply superb. Shrimp rolls, Vietnamese ravioli, and minced filet of beef are only three examples of the marvelous menu (ask for the version in English), although the main draw here is the extensive wine list — boasting, among other vintages, a rare bordeaux. Closed Sundays and August. Reservations advised. Major credit cards accepted. 60 Rue de Verneuil, 7e (phone: 45-44-04-84). Expensive.

Le Toit de Passy – Not only is the food here good (Michelin has awarded chef Yann Jacquot one star), but the rooftop view in one of Paris's more exclusive districts is spectacular. Try specialties such as *pigeonneau en croûte de sel* (squab in a salt crust) while dining outdoors. Closed Saturdays (except for September through mid-December), Sundays, holidays, 1 week in May, 1 week in September and *Christmas* week. Reservations necessary. Major credit cards accepted. 94 Av. Paul-Doumer, 16e (phone: 45-24-55-37). Expensive.

Auberge des Deux Signes – This place was once the cellars of the priory of St-Julien-le-Pauvre; try to get an upstairs table overlooking the gardens. Auvergnat cooking à la nouvelle cuisine. Closed Sundays. Reservations necessary. Major credit cards accepted. 46 Rue Galande, 5e (phone: 43-25-46-56). Expensive to moderate.

Bistro 121 – A hearty menu and excellent wines are offered in a modern setting that's always chic and crowded. Try the *canard au fruit de la passion* (duck with passion fruit) or one of the many first-rate fish dishes. One Michelin star. Closed Sundays, Mondays, and mid-July to mid-August. Reservations advised. Major credit cards accepted. 121 Rue de la Convention, 15e (phone: 45-57-52-90). Expensive to moderate.

Le Bistrot d'à Côté Flaubert – Chef Michel Rostang offers *cuisine de terroir* (uncomplicated, back-to-basics regional fare) in a turn-of-the-century bistro. Closed Saturday lunch, Sundays, and holidays. Reservations advised. Major credit cards accepted. 10 Rue Gustave-Flaubert, 17e (phone: 42-67-05-81). Expensive to moderate.

Le Bistrot de Paris – Michel Oliver offers informality, original and classic bistro fare, and a good wine list, which attract a crowd. Closed Saturdays for lunch and Sundays. Reservations advised. Major credit cards accepted. 33 Rue de Lille, 7e (phone: 42-61-15-84). Expensive to moderate.

Brasserie Lorraine – Bustling and convivial until late at night, this place pulls in the neighborhood's bourgeoisie for animated evenings over the foie gras salads. Open daily from noon to 2 AM. Reservations unnecessary. Major credit cards accepted. Pl. des Ternes, 8e (phone: 42-27-80-04). Expensive to moderate.

La Cantine des Gourmets – This restaurant specializes in light, inventive creations of high quality (one Michelin star). Closed Sundays. Reservations advised. Major credit cards accepted. 113 Av. Bourdonnais, 7e (phone: 47-05-47-96). Expensive to moderate.

Chez Benoît – A pretty but unpretentious bistro with wonderful old-fashioned Lyonnaise cooking and exquisite wines. Just about at the top of the bistro list, it's rated one Michelin star. Closed weekends and August. Reservations necessary. No credit cards accepted. 20 Rue St-Martin, 4e (phone: 42-72-25-76). Expensive to moderate.

La Coquille – A classic bistro, where the service is unpretentious and warm, and the food consistent, although the seafood (except the scallops) is usually overcooked. From October to May, the house specialty is *coquilles St-Jacques,* a version that consists of scallops roasted with butter, shallots, and parsley. Closed Sundays, Mondays, holidays, and August. Reservations advised. Major credit cards accepted. 6 Rue du Débarcadère, 17e (phone: 45-74-25-95). Expensive to moderate.

Le Duc – The atmosphere is warm and comfortable, and Paul Minchelli is incomparably inventive with fish and shellfish (cooked and raw). Quality and variety are the rule here, with such specialties as curried oysters, scallop and sea bass tartare (*coquilles St-Jacques cru*), and an extraordinary seafood platter. Closed Saturdays, Sundays, and Mondays. Reservations necessary. No credit cards accepted. 243 Bd. Raspail, 14e (phone: 43-22-59-59 or 43-20-96-30). Expensive to moderate.

Faucher – Rising star Gerard Faucher opened this elegant restaurant 3 years ago and has drawn praise for his light touch with fish dishes and desserts ever since. Michelin awarded him a star last year. Closed Saturday lunch and Sundays. Reservations necessary. Major credit cards accepted. 123 Av. Wagram, 17e (phone: 42-27-61-50). Expensive to moderate.

La Ferme St-Simon – Among our favorites for wholesome *cuisine d'autrefois* (old-fashioned cooking). Nothing very chichi here, just well-prepared, authentic dishes — the kinds you'd expect from a traditional Left Bank restaurant. Leave room for dessert; the owner once was a top assistant to Gaston Lenôtre. A perfect place for lunch. Michelin has awarded it one star. Closed Saturday lunch, Sundays, and August. Reservations advised. Major credit cards accepted. 6 Rue de St-Simon, 7e (phone: 45-48-35-74). Expensive to moderate.

Morot-Gaudry – On the top floor of a 1920s building with a great view of the Eiffel Tower, especially from the flowered terrace. Among the inventive dishes, all very fairly priced, is *pigeon en papillote* (squab steamed in its own juices); many dishes have a Mediterranean accent. One Michelin star. Closed weekends. Reservations necessary. Major credit cards accepted. 6 Rue de la Cavalerie, 15e (phone: 45-67-06-85). Expensive to moderate.

Pavillon des Princes – Under the direction of Pascal Bonichon, it serves produces delicious duck sausage salad with avocado, *coquilles St-Jacques* with fresh pasta, and lamb nuggets with cabbage and tomatoes. On the edge of the Bois de Boulogne. Open daily. Reservations advised. Major credit cards accepted. 69 Av. de la Porte d'Auteuil, 16e (phone: 47-43-15-15). Expensive to moderate.

Au Quai d'Orsay – Fashionable, sophisticated, very French, and very intimate. Traditional copious bourgeois cooking and good beaujolais. Closed Sundays. Reservations advised. Major credit cards accepted. 49 Quai d'Orsay, 7e (phone: 45-51-58-58). Expensive to moderate.

Le Récamier – The so-called garden is actually a courtyard between a couple of high-rise buildings, but as the sun goes down, it's a very congenial place to dine in good weather. Martin Cantegrit is a perfect host, and the menu features first-rate (and one-Michelin-star) fish dishes (try the turbot, if possible). The apple tart for dessert is special (order it warm), and the wine list is one of the most fairly priced on the Left Bank. Closed Sundays. Reservations necessary. Major credit cards accepted. 4 Rue Récamier, 7e (phone: 45-48-86-58). Expensive to moderate.

Timonerie – Be sure to reserve 3 or 4 days in advance in order to dine at this one-Michelin-star restaurant. Specialties include *sandre rôti au chou et pommes de terre* (pickerel with cabbage and potatoes) and the chocolate tart. Especially recommended is the very affordable prix fixe lunch. Closed Mondays from March to August, Saturdays from September to February, Sundays, and mid-February to mid-March. Visa and MasterCard accepted. 35 Quai de la Tournelle, 5e (phone: 43-25-44-42). Expensive to moderate.

Le Train Bleu – Fine food, good wine, and baroque decor so gorgeous it's been made a national monument. And it's in a train station. Open daily for lunch and dinner. Reservations advised. Major credit cards accepted. Gare de Lyon, 20 Bd. Diderot, 12e (phone: 43-43-38-39). Expensive to moderate.

Le Trou Gascon – Alain Dutournier created the inspired and unusual cooking that features southwestern French specialties and a vast choice of regional wines and armagnacs. He has moved on to a more elegant neighborhood, but his wife holds down the fort at this one-Michelin-star restaurant. Closed weekends. Reservations advised. Major credit cards accepted. 40 Rue Taine, 12e (phone: 43-44-34-26). Expensive to moderate.

Allard – A very popular bistro with huge helpings of hearty country cooking and excellent burgundy wines. Snails, turbot, and beef bourguignon are the prime lures, though the quality of the fare can sometimes be uneven. Spring, when white asparagus and the new turnips arrive, is a special time here. Don't miss the chocolate charlotte for dessert. Closed weekends and August and for 10 days at *Christmas*. Reservations advised. Major credit cards accepted. 41 Rue St-André-des-Arts, 6e (phone: 43-26-48-23). Moderate.

L'Amanguier – This series of garden restaurants serves an appetizing brand of nouvelle cuisine. Stick to a main course, which comes with a choice of appetizers, and the price is surprisingly low. The desserts are tempting. Open daily for lunch and dinner. Reservations advised. Major credit cards accepted. 51 Rue du Théâtre, 15e (phone: 45-77-04-01); 110 Rue de Richelieu, 2e (phone: 42-96-37-79); 43 Av. des Ternes, 17e (phone: 43-80-19-28); and 12 Av. de Madrid, Neuilly (phone: 47-45-79-73). Moderate.

Ambassade d'Auvergne – Its young chef creates delicious, unusual, classic Auvergnat dishes with a modern touch (try the lentil salad and the sliced ham), as well as *aligot*, a purée of potatoes and young cantal cheese. Also known for seasonal specialties and wonderful cakes. Open daily for lunch and dinner. Reservations advised. Major credit cards accepted. 22 Rue du Grenier-St-Lazare, 3e (phone: 42-72-31-22). Moderate.

Astier – An honest-to-goodness neighborhood hangout that always is packed, because the clientele knows they can rely on it for the staples of bourgeois cooking, lovingly prepared and remarkably inexpensive. Closed Saturdays, Sundays, and August. Reservations advised. Major credit cards accepted. 44 Rue Jean-Pierre-Timbaud, 11e (phone: 43-57-16-35). Moderate.

Balzar – Perhaps because of its location right next to the Sorbonne, this mirrored brasserie has always attracted well-heeled intellectuals. The steaks and *pommes frites* also are worth a visit. Open daily for lunch and dinner; closed *Christmas* week and August. Reservations necessary. Major credit cards accepted. 49 Rue des Ecoles, 5e (phone: 43-54-13-67). Moderate.

La Barrière Poquelin – The excellent cooking à la nouvelle cuisine includes a splendid foie gras salad. Closed Saturdays for lunch, Sundays, and 3 weeks in August. Reservations advised. Major credit cards accepted. 17 Rue Molière, 1er (phone: 42-96-22-19). Moderate.

Le Boeuf sur le Toit – In the building that once housed a restaurant of the same name, a haunt of Jean Cocteau and other Paris artists in the 1940s, this eatery off the Champs-Elysées is managed by the Flo group, well known for good value in atmospheric surroundings. Piano bar until 2 AM. Open daily. Reservations advised. Major credit cards accepted. 34 Rue du Colisée, 8e (phone: 43-59-83-80). Moderate.

Bofinger – For magnificent Belle Epoque decor, this is the place; it's one of Paris's oldest brasseries and it is beautiful, even if the food is occasionally disappointing. Order onion soup and *choucroute* and you won't be unhappy. Open daily. Reservations advised. Major credit cards accepted. 15 Rue de la Bastille, 4e (phone: 42-72-87-82). Moderate.

Café de la Jatte – Only those in the know venture this far down the Seine for dinner. This leafy island, l'Ile de la Jatte, was ripe for a smart renovation, and this huge, high-ceilinged dining room, with half-moon-shaped windows and a pink floor, is now full of the chicest local clientele. The fare is healthy and simple: generous salads and roast chicken along with more nouvelle items. Open daily for lunch and dinner. Reservations advised. Major credit cards accepted. 60 Av. Vital Bouhot, Neuilly, 15 minutes by car from central Paris (phone: 47-45-04-20). Moderate.

Le Caroubier – A family-run couscous restaurant with some of the best hand-rolled couscous grains in town, accompanied by good vegetables (a rarity in such restaurants), grilled meat, and a delicious *pastilla,* a flaky pastry with a spicy meat filling. Pour the vegetable broth on the delicate couscous, add a little hot pepper sauce, and you'll feel as if you've been transported to North Africa. Closed Sunday nights and Mondays. Reservations advised. Visa accepted. 122 Av. du Maine, 15e (phone: 43-20-41-49). Moderate.

Charly de Bab-ed-Oued – This is a quintessential Parisian North African eatery, with mosaics on the walls, palm trees, and even a fountain. The food is luscious, a great introduction to couscous and other Moroccan specialties such as *tajinas* (spicy meat dishes simmered in covered ceramic pots) and pistachio-filled pastries. Open daily. Reservations advised. Major credit cards accepted. 95 Bd. Gouvion-St-Cyr, 17e (phone: 45-74-34-62). Moderate.

Chez André – A classic, bustling bistro near the chic shopping of Avenue Montaigne. Although a bit too noisy and crowded, it is quite popular with the well-heeled crowd, perhaps because it offers impeccably prepared sole meunière, *blanquette de veau, gigôt d'agneau,* and other traditional dishes. Open daily. Reservations advised. Major credit cards accepted. 12 Rue Marbeuf, 8e (phone: 47-20-59-57). Moderate.

Chez Georges – This narrow, old-fashioned bistro — with a whole platoon of matronly waitresses in starched aprons — is a bastion of traditional French cooking. Closed Sundays and holidays. Reservations advised. Major credit cards accepted. 1 Rue du Mail, 2e (phone: 42-60-07-11). Moderate.

Chez Josephine and La Rôtisserie Chez Dumonet – Two restaurants share the same building and the same management. *Josephine* is an old-time bistro with traditional cuisine and an excellent wine cellar; the *Rôtisserie* is lively and more modern, with steaks and grills over an open fire. *Josephine* is closed weekends and July; the *Rôtisserie,* Mondays, Tuesdays, and August. Reservations advised. Major credit cards accepted. 117 Rue du Cherche-Midi, 6e (phone: 45-48-52-40). Moderate.

Chez Maître Paul – The cooking of the Franche-Comté region is the specialty of this recently expanded restaurant with an *auberge* ambience. Try the *saucisse Montbéliard* (smoked garlic sausage), the *poulet au vin jaune* (chicken cooked in Jura wine), and the *gâteau aux noix* (nut cake). The prix fixe menu is a good value. Closed Saturday lunch and Sundays. Reservations advised. Major credit cards accepted. 12 Rue Monsieur-le-Prince, 6e (phone: 43-54-74-59). Moderate.

Chez Pauline – The perfect bistro. The tiny, wood-paneled downstairs room (ask to be seated there) is brightened by large mirrors and fresh flowers; the place settings look like Florentine marbling. Try the oysters in a watercress sauce or the assortment of seafood with a saffron sauce, and save room for dessert — *mille-feuille* of orange with raspberry sauce is sublime. Closed Saturdays, Sundays, July, and from December 24 to January 2. Reservations advised (and should be made well in advance). Major credit cards accepted. 5 Rue Villedo, 1er (phone: 42-96-20-70). Moderate.

Chez Pierre Vedel – Truly original cuisine with garlic-rich Mediterranean specialties. Closed weekends, from mid-July to mid-August, and at *Christmastime*. Reservations advised. Major credit cards accepted. 19 Rue Duranton, 15e (phone: 45-58-43-17). Moderate.

Chez René – This neighborhood bistro in the heart of the Left Bank offers hearty helpings of regional fare. Charcuterie and an earthy *gratin de blettes* (chard) are among the specialties, and the selection of cheese is not to be missed. There is even (gasp!) a room for nonsmokers. Closed Saturdays, Sundays, August, and *Christmas* week. Reservations advised. Major credit cards accepted. 14 Bd. St-Germain, 5e (phone: 43-54-30-23). Moderate.

Chez Toutoune – This modest place specializing in Provençal dishes has become very popular for two good reasons: The food is tasty and the prices are fairly reasonable. The five-course, prix fixe menu features a rather short but very interesting selection of appetizers, entrées, and desserts. Closed Sundays, Monday lunch, and mid-August to mid-September. Reservations advised. Major credit cards accepted. 5 Rue de Pontoise, 5e (phone: 43-26-56-81). Moderate.

La Coupole – A big, brassy brasserie, once the haunt of Hemingway, Josephine Baker, and Picasso, it is owned by the Flo group. The atmosphere is still great, the food improving. Open daily until 2 AM. Closed August. Reservations advised. Major credit cards accepted. 102 Bd. du Montparnasse, 14e (phone: 43-20-14-20). Moderate.

Aux Crus de Bourgogne – An old-fashioned, slightly scruffy-looking bistro near the lively Rue du Montorgueil market. It attracts a chic crowd of regulars who appreciate the bourgeois meat dishes and especially the wonderful *langouste* (rock lobster) served cold with homemade mayonnaise. Don't be surprised if the well-behaved house cat pays you a visit. Open for lunch and dinner Mondays through Fridays. Reservations advised. Visa accepted. 3 Rue Bachaumont (phone: 42-33-48-24). Moderate.

Le Dômarais – This used to be the Crédit Municipal, or state pawnshop, and its elegant cupola now houses a sophisticated restaurant (albeit with a restrained atmosphere) serving such inventions as camembert fondue, grilled Bayonne ham, and a *petit salé* of duck. Closed Saturdays for lunch and Mondays. Reservations advised. Major credit cards accepted. 53 *bis* Rue des Francs-Bourgeois, 4e (phone: 42-74-54-17). Moderate.

L'Escargot Montorgueil – The polished wood paneling, the brass fittings, and the spiral staircase at this beautiful place, which dates from 1830, only add to the pleasure of a meal that might include snails in any of half a dozen styles or duck with orange sauce. Closed Monday lunch. Reservations advised. Major credit cards accepted. 38 Rue Montorgueil, 1er (phone: 42-36-83-51). Moderate.

Au Gamin de Paris – Combines the coziness of a classic bistro with the chic of a historic Marais building and serves well-prepared, imaginative food. Open daily. No reservations after 8 PM. Major credit cards accepted. 51 Rue Vieille-du-Temple, 4e (phone: 42-78-97-24). Moderate.

Le Grand Colbert – Bright and brassy, with delightful polychrome, Belle Epoque motifs, and traditional offerings such as *boeuf gros sel* (boiled beef with coarse salt) and *merlan Colbert* (lightly breaded, pan-fried whiting), this renovated 19th-century brasserie is next to the Bibliothèque Nationale and the lovely *Galerie Vivienne.* Open daily. Reservations advised. Major credit cards accepted. In the *Galerie Colbert,* 2 Rue Vivienne, 2e (phone: 42-86-87-88). Moderate.

Jo Goldenberg – The best-known eating house in the Marais's quaint Jewish quarter, with good, albeit a tad overpriced, chopped liver and cheesecake and a range of Eastern European Jewish specialties. It's also a fine place to sip mint tea at the counter in the middle of a busy day. Open daily. Reservations unnecessary. Major credit cards accepted. 7 Rue des Rosiers, 4e (phone: 42-77-67-74). Moderate.

Julien – Belle Epoque decor with all the flourishes. Reliable, if uninspired, meals are served in a bustling atmosphere until 1:30 AM. Open daily. Reservations advised. Major credit cards accepted. 16 Rue du Faubourg-St-Denis, 10e (phone: 47-70-12-06). Moderate.

La Manufacture – The second eatery of two-star chef Jean-Pierre Vigato (of *Apicius*), this starkly modern place in an old cigar factory at the southern edge of Paris offers an excellent quality/price ratio. Closed Saturday afternoons and Sundays. Reservations advised. Visa accepted. 30 Rue Ernest-Renan, Issy-les-Moulineaux, 15e (phone: 40-93-08-98). Moderate.

La Marée – Unobtrusive on the outside, there is great comfort within — also the freshest of fish, the best restaurant wine values in Paris, and fabulous desserts. Michelin has awarded it one star. Closed weekends, holidays, and August. Reservations advised. Major credit cards accepted. 1 Rue Daru, 8e (phone: 43-80-20-00). Moderate.

Moissonier – Little has changed for the past 30 years on the menu of this Lyonnais restaurant across the street from what was once Paris's wine depot district (now a branch of the University of Paris) — except the prices. A cart of mostly meaty hors d'oeuvres is wheeled to your table for a choice of appetizers, and the seafood, tripe dishes, and beaujolais are bourgeois cuisine at its best. Closed Sunday nights and Mondays. Reservations advised. Visa accepted. 28 Rue Fossés-St-Bernard, 5e (phone: 43-29-87-65). Moderate.

Le Moulin du Village – Light and airy, especially in summer, when tables are put out on the cobbles of Cité Berryer, a tiny pedestrian alley very near the Madeleine, just off the Rue Royale. Cuisine is nouvelle and wines good. Closed Sundays. Reservations advised. Visa accepted. 25 Rue Royale, 8e (phone: 42-65-08-47). Moderate.

Le Muniche – St-Germain's best brasserie is a bustling place with a rather extensive menu, and it's popular until 3 AM. Open daily. Reservations advised. Major credit cards accepted. 22 Rue Guillaume-Apollinaire, 6e (phone: 46-33-62-09). Moderate.

La Petite Chaise – Founded in 1680, it occupies 2 stories of a 17th-century stone house on the Left Bank. The intimate (and slightly run-down) atmosphere of the home of an ancient aunt characterizes this place, with brocaded walls, brass chandeliers, and antique oils contributing to the period decor. The trout you see swimming in a tank also are on the menu, as are specialties like shellfish crêpes and veal Pojarsky, in which the meat is combined with minced chicken. Always open. Reservations advised. Major credit cards accepted. 36 Rue de Grenelle, 7e (phone: 42-22-13-35). Moderate.

Aux Petits Pères – Truly the least expensive one-Michelin-star restaurant in Paris. Although the atmosphere can be a bit staid, the food is wonderful. Run by a husband-wife team, this is traditional French cooking at its best. Closed Saturdays and Sundays. Reservations advised. Major credit cards accepted. 8 Rue Notre-Dames-des-Victoires, 1e (phone: 42-60-91-73). Moderate.

Au Pied de Cochon – No more *choucroute* on the menu (sob!). Crowded and colorful 24 hours a day, and its customers enjoy shellfish, pigs' feet, and great crocks of onion soup, all in the old *Les Halles* area. Unfortunately, the food and service aren't what they used to be, and a garish redecoration has mangled most of the old atmosphere. But it still has atmosphere. Reservations advised. Major credit cards accepted. 6 Rue Coquillière, 1er (phone: 42-36-11-75). Moderate.

Pierre au Palais Royal – A delightful place with admirable bourgeois cooking (one Michelin star) from a variety of French provinces, made from the freshest ingredients, and lovely chinon and saumur wines. Always open. Reservations necessary. Major credit cards accepted. 10 Rue de Richelieu, 1er (phone: 42-96-09-17). Moderate.

Le Pharamond – Serves only the best Norman food in a beautiful Belle Epoque, timbered townhouse that has been declared a historic monument by the French government. Famous for *tripes à la mode de Caen* and *pommes soufflés* since 1862. Closed Sundays, Monday lunch, and July. Reservations advised. Major credit cards accepted. 24 Rue de la Grande-Truanderie, 1er (phone: 42-33-06-72). Moderate.

Pile ou Face – The name means "heads or tails," but you won't take chances on quality here; super-fresh ingredients come from the owners' own farm. Try the *lapin en marmelade de romarin* (rabbit in a rich rosemary-flavored sauce). Closed weekends, *Christmas* to January, and 3 weeks in August. Reservations advised. Major credit cards accepted. 52 *bis* Rue Notre-Dame-des-Victoires, 2e (phone: 42-33-64-33). Moderate.

Restaurant du Marché – Cuisine Landaise, which means solid, country-style cooking — foie gras, *confits d'oie,* and fine wines from the Landes region in the southwest of France, near Bordeaux. An amazing choice of herb teas, and a pretty terrace for summer dining. Open daily for lunch and dinner. Reservations advised. Major credit cards accepted. 59 Rue de Dantzig, 15e (phone: 48-28-31-55 or 45-33-23-72). Moderate.

La Rôtisserie du Beaujolais – A de rigueur spot for Paris's "in set" is Claude Terrail's casual canteen on the quay in the shadow of his three-star gastronomic temple, *La Tour d'Argent.* Most of the meat, produce, and cheese served come from Lyons; the Georges Duboeuf beaujolais is superb. Closed Monday and Tuesday afternoons. No reservations. Major credit cards accepted. 19 Quai de la Tournelle, 5e (phone: 43-54-17-47). Moderate.

La Rôtisserie d'en Face – Comfortably low-key decor, tiled floors, and an open, uncluttered atmosphere provide the backdrop for simple, sustaining fare such as grilled chicken, roast leg of lamb, and thick steaks. Closed Saturday for lunch and

Sundays. Reservations advised. Visa accepted. 2 Rue Christine, 6e (phone: 43-26-40-98). Moderate.

Le Soufflé – On the street just behind the Rue Rivoli, not far from Place Vendôme, this is the place to enjoy an orgy of soufflés. We suggest crayfish soufflé for an appetizer, cheese soufflé as a main course, and chocolate soufflé for dessert — then head directly to your cardiologist! Closed Sundays. Reservations advised. Major credit cards accepted. 36 Rue du Mont-Thabor, 1er (phone: 42-60-27-19). Moderate.

Le Télégraphe – This former dormitory for female employees of the French post office attracts a trendy crowd, including Princess Stephanie of Monaco. The food is simple — *saumon unilatéral* (salmon filet cooked on one side with olive oil and herbs) — and not great. You pay for the ambience. Good *crème brûlée*. Open daily. Reservations advised. Major credit cards accepted. 41 Rue de Lille, 7e (phone: 40-15-06-65). Moderate.

Terminus Nord – Another lively member of the Flo group, this brightly lit, bustling brasserie is a great place late at night for seafood platters. The Gare du Nord is just across the street, but don't try to dine before catching your train; even if you reserve, you may have to wait for a table at peak times. Open daily. Reservations advised. Major credit cards accepted. 2723 Rue Dunkerque, 10e (phone: 42-85-05-15). Moderate.

Ty-Coz – Breton cuisine features fish, cider, and crêpes; no meat, no cheese. Closed Sundays and Mondays. Reservations advised. Major credit cards accepted. 35 Rue St-Georges, 9e (phone: 48-78-34-61). Moderate.

Yvan – Bistro cooking such as *ris de veau aux cèpes* (sweetbreads with boletus mushrooms) and some nouvelle dishes, along with a wonderful cheese selection. Stylish atmosphere and very reasonable prices. Closed Saturday lunch and Sundays. Reservations essential. Major credit cards accepted. 1 *bis* Rue Jean-Mermoz, 8e (phone: 43-59-18-40). Moderate.

Le Zeyer – After a hard morning discount shopping on the nearby Rue d'Alésia, here's a good neighborhood place for mussels *marinière*, grilled *lotte* with sorrel, or platters of shellfish. Open daily. Reservations unnecessary. Major credit cards accepted. 234 Av. du Maine, 14e (phone: 45-40-64-51). Moderate.

Androuët – There's a great cheese emporium on the main floor and, upstairs, a unique restaurant where cheese is the base of every dish. In recent years the quality has slipped somewhat, but it still is a unique experience. Closed Sundays. Reservations advised. Major credit cards accepted. 41 Rue Amsterdam, 8e (phone: 48-74-26-93). Moderate to inexpensive.

Brasserie Lipp – This famous café is fashionable for a late supper of *choucroute* and Alsatian beer and for people watching inside and out, although guests not known to the staff sometimes receive less than welcoming treatment. The food's just as good there, however. Closed 15 days at *Christmas*. Reservations advised. Major credit cards accepted. 151 Bd. St-Germain, 6e (phone: 45-48-53-91). Moderate to inexpensive.

Chez Marius – A real find. The rotund chef really loves his work and the three-dish prix fixe dinner is a great deal. The atmosphere is Old World cozy and the service comes with a smile. Specialties are bouillabaisse and grilled fish. Closed Saturday lunch and Sundays from October to June, 1 week at *Christmas*, and August. Reservations advised. Major credit cards accepted. 5 Rue Bourgogne, 7e (phone: 47-05-96-19). Moderate to inexpensive.

Chez La Vieille – Adrienne's cooking is simple, savory, and very popular. For lunch only. Closed weekends. Reservations necessary — and are hard to come by if you are not known here. No credit cards accepted. 37 Rue de l'Arbre-Sec, 1er (phone: 42-60-15-78). Moderate to inexpensive.

Coup de Coeur – The once stark Philippe Starck decor has been modified a bit, and the inventive cooking, eager waiters, and an interesting wine list attract a stylish young crowd. Closed Saturday lunch and Sundays. Reservations advised. Major credit cards accepted. 19 Rue St-Augustin, 2e (phone: 47-03-45-70). Moderate to inexpensive.

Aux Délices de Szechuen – Admittedly the Chinese fare here won't compare with New York's Chinatown, but the terrace for summer dining is splendid. For those evenings when you want a change of pace from French food. Closed Mondays. Reservations advised. Major credit cards accepted. 40 Av. Duquesne, 7e (phone: 43-06-22-55). Moderate to inexpensive.

La Gitaine – A pleasant bistro serving moderately priced dishes. Closed Sundays. Reservations advised. Major credit cards accepted. 53 *bis* Av. La Motte-Piquet, 15e (phone: 47-34-62-92). Moderate to inexpensive.

Les Grandes Marches – Formerly the *Tour d'Argent Bastille,* though never related to Claude Terrail's 3-star temple overlooking the Seine, it is a bustling, turn-of-the-century-style brasserie serving oysters and shellfish platters, fish, and grilled meat. Located next to the new *Opéra de La Bastille.* Open daily. Reservations advised. Major credit cards accepted. 6 Pl. de la Bastille, 11e (phone: 43-42-90-32). Moderate to inexpensive.

Joe Allen's – Just like the original on West 46th Street in New York City, it has good T-bone steaks, hamburgers, chili, and apple pie. Open daily until 1 AM. Reservations advised after 8 PM. Major credit cards accepted. 30 Rue Pierre-Lescot, 1er (phone: 42-36-70-13). Moderate to inexpensive.

Les Noces de Jeannette – Under new management, this place now offers inventive cuisine at reasonable prices. Closed Sunday evenings. Reservations advised. Major credit cards accepted. 14 Rue Favart, 2e (phone: 42-96-36-89). Moderate to inexpensive.

Le Petit Niçois – This tiny bistro, serving delicious bouillabaisse, is a favorite of French TV news crews who broadcast from a nearby building. A few good specials vary from night to night. Closed Sundays and Monday lunch. Reservations advised. Major credit cards accepted. 10 Rue Amélie, 7e (phone: 45-51-83-65). Moderate to inexpensive.

Au Petit Riche – Genuine 1900s decor, subtle Touraine cooking, and inexpensive vouvray, chinon, and bourgueil wines. Closed Sundays and August. Reservations advised. Major credit cards accepted. 25 Rue Le Peletier, 9e (phone: 47-70-68-68). Moderate to inexpensive.

Quercy – Traditional Gallic cooking at reasonable prices. Closed Sundays. Reservations advised. Major credit cards accepted. 36 Rue Condorcet, 9e (phone: 48-78-30-61). Moderate to inexpensive.

L'Ami Jean – Good Basque cooking at a good price. Closed Saturday evenings and Sundays. No reservations. No credit cards accepted. 27 Rue Malar, 7e (phone: 43-36-34-13). Inexpensive.

Atelier Maître Albert – Unlike most other eateries on the Left Bank, this one is pleasantly roomy, with a log fire in winter and an honest prix fixe menu year-round. Notre-Dame looms up in front of you as you walk out the door and onto the quay. Open daily except Sundays for dinner. Reservations advised. Major credit cards accepted. 1 Rue Maître-Albert, 5e (phone: 46-33-13-78). Inexpensive.

Aux Bigorneaux – A souvenir of the old *Les Halles,* this place is frequented by arty types and journalists. Especially recommended are the *foie gras frais maison,* the chicory salad, the steak *au poivre,* the Réserve Maison wine, and the sumptuous desserts. Closed Sundays, Mondays, and for dinner in winter. Reservations advised. Major credit cards accepted. 12 Rue Mondétour, 1er (phone: 45-08-49-33). Inexpensive.

Le Bistro Mazarin – Basic, solid food, grilled steaks, and a *plat du jour,* in the heart of St-Germain des Prés. Open daily. Reservations advised. Most major credit cards accepted. 42 Rue Mazarine, 6e (phone: 43-29-99-01). Inexpensive.

Brasserie Fernand – A nondescript hole in the wall that produces surprisingly tasty dishes. *Pot-au-feu,* steaks with shallots, and fish pâté all are first-rate, but the real lure is the huge tub of chocolate mousse served for dessert — a chocoholic's fantasy come true. Open evenings only. Reservations advised. Visa accepted. 13 Rue Guisarde, 6e (phone: 43-54-61-47). Inexpensive.

Brasserie Flo – One of the last of the brasseries of the 1900s, owned by the enterprising Flo group. Hidden in a hard-to-find courtyard, it's excellent for oysters, foie gras, wild boar, and Alsatian specialties. Open daily and late. Reservations advised. Major credit cards accepted. 7 Cour des Petites-Ecuries, 10e (phone: 47-70-13-59). Inexpensive.

Brissemoret – Popular with Parisians, this eatery serves basic quality food at bargain prices. The tasteful ambience is a perfect setting for excellent foie gras, raw salmon marinated in fresh herbs, and great sauces (try the breast of duck in wine sauce). Closed Saturdays and Sundays. Reservations necessary. Major credit cards accepted. 5 Rue St-Marc, 2e (phone: 42-36-91-72). Inexpensive.

Chez Jenny – A roisterous Alsatian brasserie, where the waitresses still wear white lace collars and dirndls. There are oysters year-round, though perhaps more in keeping with the place's character are the huge platters of *choucroute* (sauerkraut and assorted pork meat) accompanied by good riesling wine. Open daily. No reservations. Major credit cards accepted. 39 Bd. du Temple, 3e (phone: 42-74-75-75). Inexpensive.

Chez Marianne – A friendly Jewish delicatessen and restaurant; the falafels make nourishing fuel for any exploration of the Marais. Closed Fridays. Reservations unnecessary. Major credit cards accepted. 2 Rue des Hospitalières-St-Gervais, 4e (phone: 42-72-18-86). Inexpensive.

Chez Yvette – This excellent, small, bourgeois restaurant has good home cooking, lots of choices, and great desserts. Closed weekends and August. Reservations advised. Major credit cards accepted. 1 Rue Alençon, 15e (phone: 42-22-45-54). Inexpensive.

Chicago Meatpackers – If homesickness strikes, head here for hamburgers or chili; finish your American food fix with apple pie or chocolate chip cheesecake. Children are very welcome here. Open daily. Reservations unnecessary. Major credit cards accepted. 8 Rue Coquillière, 1er (phone: 40-28-02-33). Inexpensive.

Dilan – Paris's only Kurdish restaurant, with a remarkable hors d'oeuvres platter of mostly Middle Eastern delicacies, and grilled meat entrées. Open daily. Reservations advised. Visa accepted. 13 Rue Mandar, 2e (phone: 42-21-46-38). Inexpensive.

Gérard – A hearty *pot-au-feu* and other country favorites are served at this bistro. Closed Saturday lunch and Sundays. Reservations unnecessary. No credit cards accepted. 4 Rue du Mail, 2e (phone: 42-96-24-36). Inexpensive.

Hard Rock Café – Die-hard fans of rock 'n' roll gather here religiously to savor their favorite music along with a bite to eat. This is the first Parisian branch of the Hard Rock Café dynasty, which has already established eateries from Acapulco to Singapore. A treasure trove of rock memorabilia hangs on the walls, including a black evening gown once sported by chanteuse Edith Piaf, Jim Morrison's leather jacket, French rock star Johnny Hallyday's shirt, and Buddy Holly's tuxedo. Always open. Reservations advised. Major credit cards accepted. 14 Bd. Montmartre (phone: 42-46-10-00; fax: 42-46-49-700). Inexpensive.

Le Jardin de la Mouffe – A choice of hors d'oeuvres, entrées, and desserts, plus a cheese course, half a carafe of wine, and a pretty garden view. Closed Mondays. Reservations unnecessary. Visa accepted. 75 Rue Mouffetard, 5e (phone: 47-07-19-29). Inexpensive.

La Lozère – Some authentic country cooking from the Lozère region in the south of France, which specializes in charcuterie and cassoulet. Closed Sundays. Reservations advised. No credit cards accepted. 4 Rue Hautefeuille, 6e (phone: 43-54-26-64). Inexpensive.

Lunchtime – One of the few eateries in Paris that satisfies the desire for a light lunch, serving crispy mixed salads made with the freshest greens and a wide range of sandwiches, including blue cheese with cream, curried chicken with currants, and American standbys such as roast beef. The desserts are homemade and delicious. Lunch only. Closed Saturdays, Sundays, holidays, and August. Reservations unnecessary. No credit cards accepted. Two locations: 156 *bis* Av. Charles-de-Gaulle, Neuilly (phone: 46-24-08-99), and 255 Rue St-Honoré, 1er (phone: 42-60-80-40). Inexpensive.

Moulin à Vent (Chez Henri) – Located across the street from what was once Paris's wine market, this bistro's decor has remained intact for over 40 years. The bar is adorned with half barrels and small lights that are inscribed with the names of different wines and growers. The menu of meat (especially sausages from the Ardèche) and salads also has stayed the same. Try the frogs' legs and the steaks with shallots. Closed Sundays, Mondays, and August. Reservations necessary. Major credit cards accepted. 20 Rue des Fossés-St-Bernard, 5e (phone: 43-54-99-37). Inexpensive.

Parraudin – A typical student hangout in the middle of the Latin Quarter with classic regional fare such as *blanquette de veau,* coq au vin, and *boeuf bourguignon* — and to mention brusque service. But no one ever went away hungry. Open daily. No reservations. No credit cards accepted. 157 Rue St-Jacques, 5e (phone: 46-33-15-75). Inexpensive.

Paul – Once a secret bistro, it is now known by the whole world. There's good solid fare here, and the premises always are packed. Closed Mondays, Tuesdays, and August. Reservations advised. No credit cards accepted. 15 Pl. Dauphine, 1er (phone: 43-54-21-48). Inexpensive.

Petit Zinc – A popular late (3 AM) spot for fish, oysters, foie gras, and an ample, reasonably priced wine list. Open daily. Reservations advised. Major credit cards accepted. 11 Rue St-Benoît, 6e (phone: 46-33-51-66). Inexpensive.

Polidor – Regulars here keep their napkins in numbered pigeonholes, and the place's history includes frequent patronage by such starving artists as Paul Verlaine, James Joyce, Ernest Hemingway, and, more recently, Jean-Paul Belmondo. The *College de Pataphysique,* founded by Raymond Queneau and Ionesco, still meets here regularly for the good family-style food. Ask to see the house scrapbook. Closed in August. Reservations unnecessary. No credit cards accepted. 41 Rue Monsieur-le-Prince, 6e (phone: 43-26-95-34). Inexpensive.

Le Procope – One of Paris's oldest restaurants, where the food is reasonably good and the atmosphere couldn't be more Parisian; the service, however, leaves a lot to be desired. Open daily. Reservations advised. Major credit cards accepted. 13 Rue de l'Ancienne-Comédie, 6e (phone: 43-26-99-20). Inexpensive.

Relais de Venise – There's always a crowd waiting outside this place near the Porte Maillot, better known as "L'Entrecôte." The prix fixe menu includes free second helpings of steaks with pepper sauce and French fries. Fancy strawberry desserts cost extra. Open daily. No reservations. Major credit cards accepted. 271 Bd. Péreire, 17e (phone: 45-74-27-97). Inexpensive.

Robert et Louise – Family bistro, with warm paneled decor and a very high standard for ingredients and cooking. Try the *boeuf bourguignon* or the open-fire–grilled *côte de boeuf.* Also good are the *fromage blanc* and the *vin en pichet.* Closed Sundays, holidays, and August. Reservations unnecessary. No credit cards accepted. 64 Rue Vieille-du-Temple, 3e (phone: 42-78-55-89). Inexpensive.

Le Roi du Pot-au-Feu – A very good place to sample this delicious peasant dish. Closed Sundays. Reservations advised. Major credit cards accepted. 34 Rue Vignon, 9e (phone: 47-42-37-10). Inexpensive.

La Route du Beaujolais – It's a barn-like workers' bistro on the Left Bank, serving Lyonnaise specialties and beaujolais wines. Don't miss the charcuterie and the fresh bread here, and try the *tarte tatin* (caramelized apple tart) for dessert. Closed Saturday lunch and Sundays. Reservations unnecessary. Visa accepted. 17 Rue de Lourmel, 15e (phone: 45-79-31-63). Inexpensive.

Le Trumilou – The formidable proprietress sets the tone of this robust establishment, which serves huge, steaming portions of game in season, *truite aux amandes* (trout with almonds), and chicken under a frieze of some excruciatingly bad rustic oils. Amazingly cheerful service. Closed Mondays. Reservations unnecessary. Major credit cards accepted. 84 Quai de l'Hôtel-de-Ville, 5e (phone: 42-77-63-98). Inexpensive.

Vagenende – An Art Nouveau spot with fantasy decor that has changed little since it opened in 1898. It features adequate, filling meals at low prices. Open daily until 1 AM. Reservations unnecessary. Major credit cards accepted. 142 Bd. St-Germain, 5e (phone: 43-26-68-18). Inexpensive.

Assiette au Boeuf – Steaks, salad, and *pommes frites,* with music in the evening. Open daily until 1 AM. No reservations. Major credit cards accepted. 123 Champs-Elysées, 8e (phone: 47-20-01-13). Very inexpensive.

Bistro de la Gare – Michel Oliver offers a choice of three appetizers and three main courses with *pommes frites.* Excellent for a quick lunch. Open daily. No reservations. Major credit cards accepted. Ten locations, including 1 Rue du Four, 6e (phone: 43-25-87-76); 59 Bd. Montparnasse, 6e (phone: 45-48-38-01); 30 Rue St-Denis, 1er (phone: 40-26-82-80). Very inexpensive.

Chartier – Huge, turn-of-the-century place with lots of down-to-earth food for the money. The famous *pot-au-feu* is still served on Mondays. Open daily. No reservations. No credit cards accepted. 7 Rue du Faubourg-Montmartre, 9e (phone: 47-70-86-29). Very inexpensive.

Chez Germaine – Around the corner from *Au Pied de Fouet* (see below), the service here is even faster and friendlier. The homemade *clafouti avec crème anglaise* is particularly recommended for dessert. Just stroll up and join the queue. Open daily. No reservations. No credit cards accepted. Rue Rousselet, 7e. Very inexpensive.

Drouot – The younger member of the Chartier family, but less known, and with more berets and fewer tourists. The waiters and waitresses, clad in black and white, look as if they emerged from a Renoir painting, although the decor is 1920s, with brass hat stands. The simple food is a bargain. To avoid a long wait for a table, arrive before 9 PM. Open daily. No reservations. No credit cards accepted. 103 Rue de Richelieu, 2e (phone: 42-96-68-23). Very inexpensive.

L'Etoile Verte – Not much to look at, but always full, it serves fresh and generous helpings of standard French classics — quenelles, seafood timbales, and so forth — at rock-bottom prices. Open daily. Reservations unnecessary. Major credit cards accepted. 13 Rue Brey, 17e (phone: 43-80-69-34). Very inexpensive.

Fontaine de Mars – A simple, family-style restaurant with traditional French cooking, with specialties such as *quenelles de brochet* (pike dumplings) and chocolate cake. In summer, diners can sup outdoors on the patio. Open daily. No reservations. Major credit cards accepted. 129 Rue St-Dominique, 7e (phone: 47-05-46-44). Very inexpensive.

Minim's de Paris – The younger but no less elegant sibling of *Maxim's,* this intimate dining room serves traditional fare, such as *salade niçoise,* at very reasonable prices. Closed Saturdays for lunch and Sundays. Reservations advised. Most major credit cards accepted. 76 Rue du Faubourg-St-Honoré, 7e (phone: 42-66-10-09). Very inexpensive.

L'Olympic Bar – Crowded at all hours, this popular hangout is open for meals at lunch only. Blue-collar workers, students, executives, fashionable women, and others eat and drink with pinball noise as a background. The decor is nothing to speak of, but the food is good, the portions are huge, and the price is right. Closed Sundays and sometimes for Saturday lunch. Reservations unnecessary. No credit cards accepted. 77 Rue St-Dominique, 7e (phone: 45-51-75-87). Very inexpensive.

Le Petit Gavroche – A hole-in-the-wall bistro-cum-restaurant with a lively clientele, an inexpensive and classic menu, and the feeling that nothing has changed in years. Closed Sundays. Reservations unnecessary. No credit cards accepted. 15 Rue Ste-Croix-de-la-Bretonnerie, 4e (phone: 48-87-74-26). Very inexpensive.

Le Petit St-Benoît – French cooking at its simplest, in a plain little place with tiled floors and curlicued hat stands. Open weekdays. Reservations unnecessary. No credit cards accepted. 4 Rue St-Benoît, 6e (phone: 42-60-27-92). Very inexpensive.

Au Pied de Fouet – This former coach house has had its habitués, including celebrities as diverse as Graham Greene, Le Corbusier, and Georges Pompidou. Service is fast and friendly, and it's a place to order the daily special. Desserts, such as *charlotte au chocolat,* are marvelous. Arrive early; it closes at 9 PM. Closed Saturday evenings, Sundays, 2 weeks at *Christmas* and *Easter,* and August. No reservations. No credit cards accepted. 45 Rue de Babylone, 7e (phone: 47-05-12-27). Very inexpensive.

Thomieux – A large neighborhood bistro, not far from the Eiffel Tower, it offers one of the heartiest cassoulets in Paris. For such as simple place, it attracts a stylish crowd. Open daily. No reservations. No credit cards accepted. 79 Rue St-Dominique, 7e (phone: 47-05-49-75). Very inexpensive.

■ **EXTRA SPECIAL:** Although we've noted the existence of *Fauchon* in *Shopping,* we would be remiss in omitting it from the restaurant listings. Actually three spectacular stores stocking elegant edibles (at 26, 28, and 30 Pl. de la Madeleine, 8e), *Fauchon* is considered so much a bastion of the privileged that one of its stores was bombed by radicals back in 1978. But the shops thankfully have long been back in full working order, which is a blessing for every abdomen in town.

One *Fauchon* shop specializes in the most beautiful fruits and vegetables available anywhere, plus pâtés, terrines, and as many other incomparable culinary items as even the most jaded gourmet's palate could conceive. If you're planning any sort of picnic, and are looking for something out of the ordinary, this is the place to pack your hamper. There also is a new trattoria on the first floor (remember, that we'd call this the second floor) that offers a variety of pasta dishes, salads, and other light luncheon food that can be eaten at tables or on stools at chic counters.

Catercorner to this shop (at Rue de Séze), another member of the *Fauchon* food trilogy carries breads, pastries, and candies. The newest of the three, is where all of Paris congregates for a variety of delicious reasons: The main floor of this shop is stocked with house brand vinegars, olive oils, teas, and coffees; the first floor houses *Le 30,* a charming garden-style restaurant which serves first-rate seafood and veal dishes, along with some spectacular desserts. But for nonpareil pastries, coffee, and a wide variety of light lunches or snacks, folks in the know head for the basement. Chocolate *opéra* cakes and macaroons in many hues, as well as *mille-feuilles* and other custardy concoctions, are sold by the slice and can be sampled at this downstairs spot, Paris's "in" place for standup snacking; there also are casual communal tables. Breakfasts, lunches, snacks, and coffee are served downstairs throughout the day, while the restaurant upstairs is open for lunch and dinner. If you need a sugar surge during the course of your Paris meanderings, these are the places to take your high-caloric breaks.

For chocoholics: The very best hot chocolate in Paris (if not the universe) is served at *Angelina's* on the Rue de Rivoli, 1er, and at its other location in the Palais de Congrès, near the Porte Maillot métro. The best chocolate ice cream in the City of Light is at *Berthillon* on the Ile St-Louis (31 Rue St-Louis-en-l'Ile, 4e). The best (and most generous) servings of chocolate mousse are offered at *Chez Fernand* (13 Rue Guirsade, 6e, on the Left Bank).

The crusty sourdough loaf — *pain Poilâne* — so beloved by the French comes from the tiny bakery *Poilâne* (8 Rue du Cherche-Midi, 6e; phone: 45-48-42-59). Also be sure not to miss their flaky apple tarts, flan, or the hearty walnut bread, and take a peek at the chandelier made of bread dough that lights up Monsieur Lionel Poilâne's office. Open daily, except Sundays, from 7:15 AM to 8:15 PM.

 WINE BARS AND CAFÉS: Choosing a place to drink is not a pressing problem in Paris. Following is a selection of watering holes to suit a variety of tastes and thirsts. Prices tend to be higher than in the United States, with a *café crème* or a glass of red wine costing $3 or more in the more expensive establishments. The moderate ones charge $2 to $3 for the same, and you pay less than $2 in the inexpensive spots.

Café Costes – Paris's post-post-modernism, designed by Philippe Starck, and something of a pioneer on the scene. It has an impressive marble stairway, a clock inspired by Fritz Lang's film *Metropolis,* some wild high-tech restrooms, and a fashionable complement of lounge lizards. Open daily. Reservations unnecessary. Major credit cards accepted. 4 Rue Berger, 1er (phone: 45-08-54-38 or 45-08-54-39). Expensive.

Fouquet's – All the cafés on the Champs-Elysées are overpriced and most are nasty, so it may be worth paying the inflated tab for a coffee at this one (also a full-blown and overblown restaurant), which at least has more style than all the rest — as well as a large corner for outdoor tables in summer. Always open. Reservations advised for dinner; unnecessary for the café. Major credit cards accepted. 99 Champs-Elysées, 8e (phone: 47-23-70-60). Expensive.

Harry's Bar – The son of the original Harry, who opened this celebrated establishment in 1911, is still at the helm here. And the memories of past patrons like Ernest Hemingway, Gertrude Stein, and George Gershwin are almost as tangible as the university flags and banners that hang from the paneled walls. Open 10:30 AM to 4 AM every day but *Christmas.* Reservations unnecessary. Major credit cards accepted. 5 Rue Daunou, 2e (phone: 42-61-71-14). Expensive.

Willi's – An enterprising Englishman set up this smart little wine bar, a pleasant walk through the Palais Royal gardens and only minutes from the *Louvre.* The wine selection — a list of 150 — is one of the best in Paris, with an emphasis on Côtes du Rhône. The chef creates some appetizing salads as well as a *plat du jour.* Closed Sundays. Reservations unnecessary. Major credit cards accepted. 13 Rue des Petits-Champs, 1er (phone: 42-61-05-09). Expensive to moderate.

Blue Fox – On a cobbled market street behind the Madeleine, this wine bar has a list of about 20 reasonably priced wines by the glass that changes every 2 weeks. And there's good charcuterie to go with them. Closed Saturday evenings and Sundays. Reservations unnecessary. Major credit cards accepted. Cité Berryer, 25 Rue Royale, 8e (phone: 42-65-08-47 or 42-65-10-72). Moderate.

L'Ecluse – This unassuming wine bar looking onto the Seine has fathered five others, more sophisticated, in the Rue François Ier, at the Madeleine, at the *Opéra,* in

Le Forum des Halles, and in Neuilly. Its red velvet benches and wooden tables — not to mention its bordeaux and its fresh, homemade foie gras and spectacular chocolate cake — remain unchanged. Open daily. Reservations unnecessary. Major credit cards accepted. 15 Quai des Grands-Augustins, 6e (phone: 46-33-58-74), and several other locations in Paris. Moderate.

Au Franc Pinot – A restaurant has operated on this spot for 350 years, making this Paris's oldest "wine bar." In a lovely setting on the Ile St-Louis, the bar offers regional wines, many from the Loire, and delicious snacks. Closed Sundays and Mondays from 2 to 7 PM. Reservations unnecessary. Major credit cards accepted. 1 Quai Bourbon, 4e (phone: 43-29-46-98). Moderate.

Le Pain et Le Vin – An imaginative wine bar with daily hot luncheon specials. It's operated by four Parisian chefs, including Alain Dutournier of *Le Carré des Feuilliants* and *Le Trou Gascon.* Closed Wednesday evenings. Reservations unnecessary. Major credit cards accepted. Several locations, including 1 Rue d'Armaille, 17e (phone: 47-63-88-29). Moderate.

Le Repaire de Bacchus – A wine bar specializing in unusual regional wines, displayed in crowded rows. You can buy wine by the bottle to take home or on a picnic, or sample them at the counter with cheese and charcuterie. Closed Sundays and Mondays. Reservations unnecessary. Major credit cards accepted. 13 Rue du Cherche-Midi, 6e (phone: 45-44-01-07). Moderate.

Taverne Henri IV – A selection of nearly 20 wines are offered by the glass in this bar, which is located at the foot of the Pont Neuf, along with generous servings of simple food such as open sandwiches of ham, cheese, sausage, or a terrine of wild boar. You also can order cold food combinations by the platter. Closed weekends and August. Reservations unnecessary. No credit cards accepted. 13 Pl. du Pont-Neuf, 1er (phone: 43-54-27-90). Moderate.

Zimmer – Centrally located and with new moldings and chandeliers, this is the place to stop off for a drink before or after a show at one of the nearby theaters. Open daily. Reservations unnecessary. Major credit cards accepted. 1 Pl. du Châtelet, 4e (phone: 42-36-74-04). Moderate.

La Cloche des Halles – The dim lighting and dark wood paneling at this cozy establishment only add to the pleasure of sampling the wine here. Those with a hunger pang can sample the generous cheese platter or try a plate of charcuterie. 28 Rue Coquillière, 1er (phone: 42-36-93-89). Inexpensive.

Au Duc de Richelieu – Specializes in the wines of Beaujolais, Chiroubles, Juliénas, St-Amour, and so on. A cozy atmosphere and lots of wine tasting certificates on the walls. Closed Sundays and August. Reservations unnecessary. No credit cards accepted. 110 Rue de Richelieu, 2e (phone: 42-96-38-38). Inexpensive.

Grenache – A new wine bar near the Boulevard St-Michel that features wines from France's Languedoc region, accompanied by simple dishes from the same area. Bar open Monday through Friday and Saturday nights; restaurant open Monday through Friday. Reservations unnecessary. Visa accepted. 8 Rue de La Harpe, 5e (phone: 43-29-86-51). Inexpensive.

Jacques Melac – An old-fashioned wine bar run by a young, extravagantly mustachioed man from the Auvergne, who bottles and sells his own rustic wines and even stages a harvest celebration in honor of the restaurant's vineyard. Note the sign above the bar that asserts that water should only be used for cooking potatoes. Closed Sundays and Mondays. Open until 6:30 PM, except Tuesdays and Thursdays when a set dinner is served. Open Tuesday through Friday. No reservations. No credit cards accepted. 42 Rue Léon-Frot, 11e (phone: 43-70-59-27). Inexpensive.

La Palette – This Left Bank hideaway on a quiet square, with outdoor tables during the summer, stays lively with a young crowd until 2 AM every day except in

August. Perhaps the monocled gentlemen on the 1930s tiles and the oils hung on the walls paid the bills of never-to-be-successful painters. Closed Sundays, holidays, and August. Reservations unnecessary. No credit cards accepted. 43 Rue de Seine, 6e (phone: 43-26-68-15). Inexpensive.

Relais Chablisien – As the name implies, this wine bar, with its wood-beamed ceilings and warm atmosphere, specializes in chablis. Sandwiches and snacks also are available. Closed Sundays and 2 weeks in August. Open daily. Reservations advised. Major credit cards accepted. 4 Rue Bertrand-Poirée, 1e (phone: 45-08-53-73). Inexpensive.

Le Rubis – A tiny corner bar with an old-fashioned atmosphere and a big selection of wines — about 30 in all. With your glass of wine try the pork *rillettes,* a savory meat paste made on the premises. Closed on weekends and 2 weeks in August. No reservations. No credit cards accepted. 10 Rue du Marché-St-Honoré, 1er (phone: 42-61-03-34). Inexpensive.

Le Sancerre – This hospitable spot features sancerre and nothing but sancerre. Simple lunches of omelettes, charcuterie, apple tarts, and *petits goutés* (snacks) such as goat cheese marinated in olive oil, are the perfect accompaniment for bottles of excellent red, white, and rosé. Closed Saturday lunch and Sundays. Major credit cards accepted. 22 Av. Rapp, 7e (phone: 45-51-75-91). Inexpensive.

Au Sauvignon – The no-nonsense couple in blue overalls who run this tiny corner bar look as if they just stepped in from the country. They seem to be in perpetual motion, pouring the sauvignon (or the white quincy and beaujolais nouveau in November and January) and carving up chunky sandwiches with bread from the famous *Poilâne* bakery not far away. Closed Sundays, 2 weeks in January, *Easter,* and August. Reservations unnecessary. No credit cards accepted. 80 Rue des Sts-Pères, 7e (phone: 45-48-49-02). Inexpensive.

La Tartine – One of the old, authentic bistros, where Trotsky was once known to sip a glass or two of wine, with a colorful local clientele and a good selection of wine by the glass. Closed Tuesdays and Wednesday mornings. Reservations unnecessary. No credit cards accepted. 24 Rue de Rivoli, 4e (phone: 42-72-76-85). Inexpensive.

La Tour de Monthlery – Hidden away on a small street near *Le Forum des Halles,* this animated bistro with sawdust on the floor and hams hanging from the rafters serves hearty, simple fare at bargain prices. Reservations unnecessary. Major credit cards accepted. 5 Rue de Prouvaires, 1er (phone: 42-36-21-82). Inexpensive.

TEAROOMS: Yes, you have crossed the Channel, but even in Paris, taking tea is a revitalizing mid-afternoon break from frantic sightseeing and window shopping. The *salon de thé* originally was the refuge of patrician Parisian ladies, who lingered over ambrosial pastries and fragrant, steaming cups of *cerise* (cherry) tea between social calls. Today, tearooms still lure many a Parisian and visitor alike to partake of their caloric delights. Here is a sampling of some of the best in town: *L'Arbre à Canelle* (57 Passage des Panoramas, 2e; phone: 45-08-55-87), a relative newcomer to the scene, offers a scrumptious chocolate-pear and apple tart in a stylish setting. *Angelina* (226 Rue de Rivoli, 1er; phone: 42-60-82-00, and 10 Pl. de Mexico, 16e; phone: 47-04-89-42) deserves the highest praise for its *chocolat l'Africain* (merely the greatest hot chocolate in the world), which will astonish even the most jaded chocoholic with its rich flavor. Those with discriminating tea tastes frequent *A La Cour de Rohan* (59-61 St-André-des-Arts, 6e; phone: 43-25-79-67), which offers over 20 varieties — described in almost religious detail. Hot apple tarts and cozy surroundings are among the finer points at *Fanny Tea* (20 Pl. Dauphine, 4e; phone: 43-25-83-67) — quite a contrast to the *plus raffiné* Belle Epoque atmosphere at *Ladurée* (16 Rue Royale, 8e; phone: 42-60-21-79). It would be a shame to ignore the masterfully decorated petits fours, marrons glacés, and macaroons; besides, what could be more appropriate to nibble in this elegant establishment? Nowhere in Paris is tea taken more seriously than at *Mariage Frères* (30-32 Rue du Bourg-Tibourg, 4e; phone: 42-72-28-11); with a supply of 450 different kinds of tea, it's perhaps wisest to close your eyes and choose a blend at whim. Neo-classical art, tranquil ambience, and classical music all contribute to the success of *A Priori Thé* (35-37 *Galerie Vivienne*, 2e; phone: 42-97-48-75), conveniently located across the street from the Bibliothèque Nationale in the *Galerie Vivienne*.

REIMS

This busy provincial center is in many ways more French than Paris. For one thing, it is far more representative of the majority of French cities. For another, it offers a little of everything that the mind's eye tends to include in a mental image of France. It has a glorious cathedral, impressive medieval churches, and elegant châteaux, sidewalk cafés and eminent restaurants, stylish shops, the headquarters of famous wine firms — even barges floating downriver and a canal through the center of town. And just outside the city are the celebrated vineyards of Champagne, as well as the not-so-celebrated battlefields of World Wars I and II, and many a place to linger for a lovely pastoral view.

The first settlement on the Vesle River had been for centuries the capital of a Gallic tribe, the Remi, before Caesar conquered Gaul from 58 to 51 BC. During the Roman occupation it became one of the main and most beautiful cities of Gaul, a crossroads rich in commerce and monuments, far outstripping the village of Paris in importance. The Romans called their city of more than 80,000 inhabitants Durocortorum. Later the name became Rheims, and in the 18th century the "h" was dropped, leaving today's Reims (pronounced *Rance* — it rhymes with France). It is still common in English to use the antiquated spelling, but in French and in France all signs and references are to Reims.

Four dates stand out in the exceptional history of this city: 496, 1429, 1914, and 1945. The history of France may be said to have begun in Reims in 496 when St. Remi, the Bishop of Reims, baptized and crowned Clovis I King of all the Franks in a church that preceded Reims Cathedral. Though Clovis (a name that in time evolved into "Louis") chose Paris as his capital, it was in memory of this ceremony that Reims later became the city of coronations. From Louis VII, who ascended the throne in 1137, to Charles X, who was crowned in 1825, it was customary for the Kings of France to be crowned in Reims Cathedral, and the extent to which this setting became a prerequisite to royal legitimacy is illustrated by the most famous of the coronations, that of Charles VII in 1429.

In an attempt to end the Hundred Years War with England, Charles's father had agreed to a treaty appointing the King of England heir to France. Though the disinherited Charles repudiated the treaty and undertook to rule, his authority was limited to a small realm and contested by both the English and their French allies. It was at this point that Joan of Arc, driven by visions and voices, appeared in aid of her beleaguered king. After rallying his forces and leading them to an important victory at Orléans, she insisted that he go to Reims, advising him that "there lies the salvation of France." "But I was crowned at Poitiers!" he is reported to have replied. "Poitiers can only crown the Kings of Bourges" was her response. "Kings of France are made at Reims."

In all, 37 Kings and 11 Queens and Regents of France went to Reims to be "made," and the city, which already enjoyed a reputation for the making of saints (13 came from Reims between the 3rd and 8th centuries), came to be regarded somewhat as hallowed ground.

Unfortunately, as far as geography is concerned, the ground on which Reims stands is in a rather fateful position. Its region — Champagne — is largely an expanse of open, level land that has been a route of invasion and a battlefield throughout European history. As a consequence, numerous wars, well before and well after the Hundred Years War, have raged in and around the city. In fact, between the 5th and 10th centuries, Reims was flattened to the ground seven times. In the modern age, however, no war left its mark on the body and spirit of the city more than World War I. The Germans occupied Reims for 10 days in 1914, but for almost 3 years they controlled the surrounding heights, from which they unceasingly bombarded it for 1,051 days. Reims was virtually leveled. Some 80% of its homes were destroyed, and most public buildings were severely damaged, including the cathedral.

In World War II, the German occupation lasted much longer, for 4 years, and war damage once again was not minimal. After Allied soldiers liberated Reims in 1944, General Eisenhower established his headquarters in a large technical high school here, and it was in one of its schoolrooms that the unconditional surrender of the Third Reich was signed on May 7, 1945.

Today, although quite a few things in Reims are of historical or artistic note, most visitors include the city in their itinerary for one of two reasons if not for both: the soaring Gothic Cathedral of Notre-Dame and the ancient, labyrinthine cellars of the great champagne houses, full of millions of bottles of truly sparkling wine. These two tourist "musts" rank with the best France has to offer. Notre-Dame de Reims is commonly ranked with Notre-Dame de Paris and Notre-Dame de Chartres as the most sublime of France's cathedrals and among the most magnificent in the world. Champagne is, considering its nearly universal connotation of joy and celebration, doubtless the most famous wine in the world, and it comes only from this area.

Reims also is a center of the textile industry, known especially for woolens as far back as the 12th century. It also has long been recognized for its university, which Pope Paul III founded in 1547. The destruction and rebuilding of this century have left it with extensive suburbs and its share of high-rise buildings, and it must be said that Reims today is not the most stunning of cities. However, its center is particularly lively, especially on the Rue de Vesle and on the long Place Drouet-d'Erlon, and enough of it has survived the wars and invasions to tell a fascinating tale of French history.

REIMS AT-A-GLANCE

SEEING THE CITY: The vine- and tree-covered hills that surround Reims provide more than one place for a panoramic view, and if you have a car, you no doubt will find your own spot, probably en route to the grape-growing region of the Montagne de Reims to the south. Be aware that the modern buildings on the outskirts of Reims sometimes block out the city's most impressive structure, the Cathedral of Notre-Dame, and that the ancient church you see may be the Basilique St-Remi rather than the cathedral itself. In the center of the city, you can survey the area from the cathedral towers.

For leisurely ground-level viewing, try a 45-minute jaunt on the sightseeing train called *Petit Train de Reims* or a horse-drawn carriage ride. The train operates on weekends in May and June, and every day in July and August. Departures every half hour, beginning at 2 PM, from in front of the cathedral. Horse-drawn carriage rides are offered in July and August daily except Tuesdays and on rainy days. Departures are at 2 PM in front of the cathedral, where tickets for both excursions are available. Two bus tours, *Reims à Travers Les Ages* (Reims Through the Centuries) and *Au Coeur du Vignoble Champenois* (The Heart of Champagne's Vineyards), are given on weekends in June and every day in July and August; a glass of champagne is offered at the end of each tour. Tickets are available at the tourist office near the cathedral; request information about tours in English (phone: 26-47-25-69).

SPECIAL PLACES: Long, wide Place Drouet-d'Erlon, lined with hotels, cafés, and arcaded houses, is a good place to begin a tour of the city. Near one end of it is the Rue de Vesle, from which you can easily walk to the cathedral and surrounding sights. At the other end it runs into Boulevard Foch–Boulevard Général-Leclerc across from the railroad station and at the midpoint of a huge mall. The Place de la République, with the Porte Mars, is at the northern extreme of the mall, and from here it is the Rue de Mars that will set you toward the cathedral, while the Rue du Champ-de-Mars heads toward the Chapelle Foujita and the cellars of several of the major champagne firms. Other champagne firms are on the other side of town, clustered in the vicinity of the Basilique St-Remi and Parc Pommery.

THE CITY

Cathédrale Notre-Dame de Reims – This magnificent cathedral is one of the most historic structures to be seen in France today. The first church on the spot was the Cathédrale St-Nicaise, in which Remi baptized Clovis I and crowned him King of the Franks in 496. The event became the basis of a later precedent, and from the coronation of Louis VII in the second church on the spot in 1137 to the coronation of Charles X in the third and present church in 1825, the Kings of France, with few exceptions, were crowned here. The cathedral is also one of the most important monuments of the French artistic heritage. After the second church was destroyed by fire in 1210, construction of the edifice seen today began in 1211 and was all but complete a mere century later (the towers were added in the 15th century). Consequently, the style of Notre-Dame de Reims, conceived by master builder Jean d'Orbais and largely respected by his successors, is pure 13th century, representative — along with the cathedrals of Chartres, Paris, and Amiens — of the classic period, or the golden age, of French Gothic architecture. This unity endures, even though the cathedral suffered heavy shelling during World War I, which burned the roof, damaged the apse, and caused a section of the arches to fall down, requiring a long restoration. Also in this century, some of the statuary — either damaged or weatherworn — has been removed from the exterior and replaced by copies.

The cathedral's western façade is one of the most splendid conceptions of the 13th century. Its three deep doorways constitute a Bible in sculptured stone, with the central doorway dedicated to the Virgin, the left door to the saints and martyrs, and the right door to Christ and the prophets. Among the glorious statues, note the groups representing the Visitation and the Presentation to the Temple in the central door and the two angels flanking the scalped St. Nicaise in the left door. One of these, the *ange au sourire* (the smiling angel), is the most famous of the cathedral's many angels and also is known as the *sourire de Reims* (the smile of Reims). The upper part of the façade is ornamented with a gallery of colossal statues of kings.

Inside, the tall windows, the clerestory, and the spectacular stained glass windows provide superb lighting for the nave. Much of the 13th-century glass, including the awe-inspiring rose window of the western façade and the rose window in the northern transept, was restored after World War I. Other windows are completely modern, including the six windows in the axial chapel drawn by Marc Chagall and executed in 1974. Not to be overlooked is the interior sculpture, as in the remarkable ensemble of masterly statues in niches surrounding the smaller rose window of the façade and in the very beautiful capitals of the columns.

No matter when you visit the cathedral, try to come back to see the façade and the stained glass–lit nave in the early morning or at twilight. Then, too, is when the face of the *ange au sourire* is most beguiling. For a lovely view of the spectacular flying buttresses, stand in the garden of the adjacent *Palais du Tau.* There's also an interesting view of the cathedral, and of surrounding Reims, from atop its towers (entry possible at 11 AM and 3, 4, and 5 PM). Sonetlumière (sound-and-light) shows are presented at the cathedral and at the Palais du Tau (see below) on Thursdays, Fridays, and Saturdays from June through September. Son-et-lumière presentations of the coronations also take place. They are shown on Saturdays evenings at 9:30 PM from late June to mid-August. For information, call the tourist office at 26-47-25-69. Enter the cathedral from Pl. du Cardinal-Luçon.

Palais du Tau – Next door to the cathedral, this rebuilt archbishop's palace takes its name from the shape of the original plan of the building (the Greek letter "T," or "tau"). It was the residence of the king at the time of the coronations, and the site of post-coronation banquets. Now a museum, it contains monumental sculptures from the exterior of the cathedral, magnificent 16th-century tapestries of the life of the Virgin, and the cathedral treasury, including a 9th-century pendant said to have been the talisman of Charlemagne, a 12th-century chalice used in numerous coronations, and mementos of the coronation of Charles X. Open daily, except holidays, from 10 AM to noon and 2 to 5 PM in winter, and from 9:30 AM to 6:30 PM in summer. Admission charge. Pl. du Cardinal-Luçon (phone: 26-47-74-39).

Basilique St-Remi – In almost any other city, the glories of this ancient abbey church of the Benedictines would be legend. It is the oldest of Reims's churches and, like the cathedral whose fame overshadows it, it has been beautifully restored following the damage of World War I. Most impressive are its Romanesque nave and transept, which date from the middle of the 11th century, and its immense choir, an example of the primitive Gothic style of the end of the 12th century. The Flamboyant Gothic façade of the southern transept dates from the 16th century. The church also contains the tomb of St-Remi (actually a 19th-century reconstruction of a previous tomb). Open daily. Next door, the old abbey, which was begun at the end of the 12th century, now serves as the city's archaeological museum (see *Museums*). A sound and light show is presented free of charge Saturdays at 9:30 PM in July, August, and September. Rue Simon (phone: 26-85-35-22).

Musée des Beaux-Arts – This fine arts museum houses a rich collection of tapestries and ceramics, 13 sketches of German princes by both the elder and younger Cranach, and French paintings from the 17th century to the present. With 27 canvases on display, Corot is the most heavily represented of the French painters, but there are also paintings by pre-Impressionists, Impressionists, and post-Impressionists, including Boudin, Pissarro, Monet, Sisley, Renoir, Dufy, Matisse, and Picasso. The gardens also may be visited. Open daily, except Tuesdays, from 10 AM to noon and 2 to 6 PM. Admission charge. 8 Rue Chanzy (phone: 26-47-28-44).

Place Royale – The main square of the city is a beautiful example of 18th-century architecture, a legacy of the reign of Louis XV, whose statue stands in the middle. The original statue by Pigalle was destroyed during the French Revolution, though this one, by Cartellier, is still set off by Pigalle's pedestal statues.

Porte Mars – A remnant of Gallo-Roman times when Reims was known as Durocortorum, this imposing 3rd-century triumphal arch is a memorial to Augustus Caesar. During the Middle Ages, it became a gate in the city's ramparts. Pl. de la République.

Chapelle Foujita – This striking chapel in the Romanesque style was designed and decorated by the famous Japanese painter of the School of Paris, Léonard Foujita, who converted to Catholicism late in his life. The color, freshness, and individuality of the stained glass windows and frescoes are stunning. A gift of Mumm Champagne to the city, the chapel, also known as Notre-Dame de la Paix, was opened in 1966. Closed Wednesdays and in very cold weather. Admission charge. 33 Rue du Champs-de-Mars.

Salle de Reddition – General Eisenhower's headquarters during the final days of World War II were in a high school behind the railroad station. The Germans signed an unconditional surrender in a simple schoolroom here on May 7, 1945 — *VE Day* — and the room has been preserved as it was that day, with operational maps on the wall. Open daily, except Tuesdays and holidays from 10 AM to noon and 2 to 6 PM. Admission charge. 12 Rue Franklin-Roosevelt (phone: 26-47-84-19).

CHAMPAGNE CELLARS

After a visit to the cathedral, a tour of one or more champagne cellars is a second "must" for visitors to Reims — especially for those who are not going on to the much smaller city of Epernay, which rivals Reims as the capital of the champagne industry. Reims is the home of a greater number of champagne houses, and some of its cellars are the oldest in the region, dating back to ancient times when the Romans excavated huge chalk pits (*crayères*) in the limestone base of the city, creating inverted funnels that they undoubtedly used as cool pantries. These gigantic cones often were connected underground, and in recent centuries, it was discovered that conditions in this netherworld were perfect for the aging of champagne. (For an introduction to the history of champagne and how it is made, see the beginning of the *Champagne* tour route in DIRECTIONS.) Today, the underground tunnels have been expanded so that there are miles and miles of them, some with the bare chalk walls still exposed, some covered by brick, tile, and other materials. Of the more than a dozen champagne houses in Reims that open their cellars to visitors, a number are beyond the Place de la République in the Champ-de-Mars section of the city; others are beyond the Basilique St-Remi around Place des Droits-de-l'Homme and nearby streets including Avenue du Général-Giraud, Boulevard Henri-Vasnier, and Rue des Crayères.

Before descending into any of the caves, be sure to have a sweater or jacket handy; a constant temperature of 45F to 50F is one reason the cellars are ideal for making champagne. Also be reasonably well shod, because in most cases you'll be doing a fair amount of walking in a damp and dimly lit environment. All the champagne houses listed below offer guided tours; unless otherwise indicated, visits are weekdays, except holidays and the month of August, and by appointment only (9 AM to noon and 2 to 5 PM are accepted hours). Champagne houses can be divided into those that court large tour groups and those that prefer individuals or small groups with a sincere interest in learning about champagne production. Most offer tours in English but travelers should verify that an English-speaking guide will be available when setting up an appointment. With the exception of Taittinger, which has a minimal charge of 15F (under $3), the tours are free, and usually end with a complimentary champagne tasting.

Charles Heidsieck – Fifty rooms of pure chalk linked by galleries. The Gallo-Roman *crayères,* shaped like a bottle end, were rediscovered in the 18th century. Tours are not always available; call ahead for reservations and information. 3 Pl. des Droits-de-l'Homme (phone: 26-36-46-07; fax: 26-36-23-40).

Krug – Madame Catherine Seydoux, a Krug family member, gives tours (in English upon request) of this serious champagne house, which still has the venerable oak barrels used for the first fermentation. Write or call well in advance for appointments. Visits can be arranged Mondays through Fridays through the year, except for a period in the summer when Madame Seydoux is on vacation. 5 Rue Coquebert (phone: 26-88-24-24; fax: 26-40-60-18).

Lanson – Beautiful wine presses are among the things that make this an interesting visit. Tours by appointment only. 12 Bd. Lundy (phone: 26-78-50-50).

Louis Roederer – The enormous oak tuns (casks) here are extraordinary. Make reservations to see them well in advance of a visit. Closed Friday afternoons, weekends, and July. 21 Bd. Lundy (phone: 26-40-42-11; fax: 26-47-66-51).

Mumm – No appointment required to tour the 11 miles of gigantic cellars, open weekdays from 9 to 11 AM and 2 to 5 PM from *Easter* through October 31; closed weekends and holidays in winter. The tour is very informative — one of the best. 34 Rue du Champ-de-Mars (phone: 26-49-59-70).

Piper-Heidsieck – No appointment is required here, either, where part of the visit is aboard an electric train. Open daily from 9 AM to 6 PM March through November 30; 9 to 11:45 AM and 2 to 5:15 PM October through March; open weekdays only December through March. 51 Bd. Henry-Vasnier (phone: 26-85-01-94).

Pommery – Fascinating cellars: Down 116 steps are 11 miles of avenues with their crossroads, statues (including a 14th-century Virgin), bas-reliefs, and extraordinary *crayères* that form pyramidal wells reaching through smooth white walls to daylight. The caves can be visited year-round from 9 AM to noon and 2 to 6 PM March through November. Open Mondays through Fridays, afternoon only, from November through March. Appointments necessary. 5 Pl. Général-Gouraud (phone: 26-61-62-63).

Ruinart Père & Fils – This dedicated champagne house prefers to give tours to groups of ten or fewer. The pyramidal *crayères* date from the 2nd century BC and are the only ones in the region classified as a historic landmark. Appointments necessary. Closed weekends and holidays. 4 Rue des Crayères (phone: 26-85-40-29).

Taittinger – An interesting historical slide show precedes the tour of cellars set up in the crypt of the former abbey of St. Nicaise and remarkable for their pointed arches. Other cellars are in beautiful triangular *crayères* of the 3rd and 4th centuries. Open daily from March through November; closed weekends in winter. No appointment necessary. Admission charge. 9 Pl. St-Nicaise (phone: 26-85-45-35).

Veuve Clicquot – These extraordinary funnel-shaped *crayères*, which date from Gallo-Roman times, include 15 miles of underground galleries with splendid bas-reliefs carved into the walls. Open every day except Sunday from April to October. Visits by appointment only. 1 Pl. des Droits-de-l'Homme (phone: 26-40-25-42).

ENVIRONS

Fort de la Pompelle – This 1880-vintage fort, which stood in defense of Reims during World War I, contains a museum of war mementos — decorations, uniforms, arms, and an exceptional collection of German helmets — of interest to military history buffs. Open daily, 8:30 AM to 7 PM from mid-March to mid-November; 10 AM to 5 PM the rest of the year. Admission charge. About 3 miles (5 km) east of Reims via N3 and then N44 (phone: 26-49-11-85).

■**EXTRA SPECIAL:** If you have a car, don't miss a drive through the undulating hills and valleys of the Montagne de Reims, the Valley of the Marne (site of *Euro Disney,* which opened last year), and the Côte des Blancs — nearby areas where the grapes that go into champagne are grown. Not only will you glimpse some of the finest, most famous, and most expensive vineyards in the world, but you will glimpse the quintessential French provincial life, passing through tiny villages with fascinating churches, frequently of the 12th or 13th century, and through lovely pastoral settings. For a suggested itinerary, see *Champagne,* in DIRECTIONS. Better still is a breathtaking balloon flight, with licensed pilots, over Champagne vineyards and villages. Their balloons soar from April through October. Contact *Air Show* (15 *bis* Pl. St-Nicaise; phone: 26-82-59-60; fax: 26-82-48-62).

SOURCES AND RESOURCES

 TOURIST INFORMATION: The Reims Office du Tourisme is at the Square du Trésor, just to the left of the cathedral (2 Rue Guillaume de Machault; phone: 26-47-25-69). Besides some useful free brochures, it provides a walking tour of the cathedral and central city on an audiocassette, which can be rented for about $5. It also houses the Champagne branch of *Accueil de France,* which will book accommodations in or out of the city for a fee.

Local Coverage – Consult Reims's daily newspaper, *L'Union,* published in French.

 TELEPHONE: The city code for Reims is 26, which is incorporated into all local 8-digit numbers. When calling a number from the Paris region (including the Ile-de-France), dial 16, wait for the dial tone, then dial the 8-digit number. When calling a number from outside Paris, dial only the 8-digit number. When calling from the US, dial 33 (which is the country code), followed by the 8-digit number.

 GETTING AROUND: For much of your visit, probably the best means of transportation will be your own two feet. Many of the shops, restaurants, hotels, churches, and other monuments you will want to see are in the center of the city, within walking distance of the cathedral. It's a hike, though, from there to the Basilique St-Remi and to many of the champagne cellars, so you'll probably want an alternative mode, especially if you plan to cover the surrounding area.

Airport – Aéroport Reims accommodates a limited number of regional flights (Reims-Lyons is one) and special charters. Betheny (phone: 26-07-18-85) and the Aérodrome Reims-Prunay (phone: 26-49-10-92) both have landing facilities for private planes.

Bus – There's a local bus company (phone: 26-88-25-38) and a long-distance bus company (phone: 26-65-17-07).

Car Rental – Among the firms with offices in Reims are *Avis* (Cour de la Gare; phone: 26-47-10-08), *Budget* (Garage Moine, Zone Industrial Moulin de l'Ecaille Tinqueux; phone: 26-40-01-02); *Europcar* (25 Rue du Temple; phone: 26-88-38-38), and *Hertz* (26 Bd. Joffre; phone: 26-47-98-78).

Taxi – Short of renting a car, a taxi is probably the most expedient way to see the city and its environs. Find one at a designated stand — at the station, for instance, and in plenty of other spots — or telephone for one (phone: 26-47-05-05).

Train – The station is on Boulevard Joffre, across the mall from the north end of Place Drouet-d'Erlon (phone: 26-88-50-50). There are several trains daily to Paris (1½ hours) and to Epernay (25 minutes).

 SPECIAL EVENTS: If you plan to be in Reims during January and February and have children with you, don't miss a series of annual special performances given by *Centre des Formations des Art du Cirque* (1 Rue du Cirque, Chalons sur Marne 51000; phone: 26-21-12-43). Or contact the *Comité Central des Fêtes,* France's national circus school (phone: 26-82-45-66). An international horse show takes place in May, as does an annual canoe-kayak regatta. The second weekend in June, processions, historical parades, and secular and religious plays and songs are all part of the *Fêtes de Jeanne d'Arc,* celebrating her return to Reims with the dauphin for his coronation as Charles VII. Coinciding with these events is *Les Sacres du Folklore,* a weekend-long festival during which folkloric groups from around the world, dressed in native costume, parade through the streets, and a *Foire Médiévale* (Medieval Fair), featuring artisans showing and selling crafts in the ancient streets in the center of the city. From late June through August, the city sponsors *Flâneries Musicales* (Musical Strolls), a series of public concerts (most of them free) featuring such international artists as Yehudi Menuhin. In the center of the city on July 13, the eve of *Bastille Day,* which is celebrated by a fireworks display in Parc Léo Lagrange, a *bal populaire* (dancing in the streets) takes place. In early fall (usually the third weekend in September), the city's *Automnales* (Autumn Festival) annually draws 100,000 visitors for fairs and fireworks at the Place de la République. During the same weekend, there's a harvest car rally for vintage autos. St. Remi, the holy bishop who inspired the tradition of royal coronations in Reims, is usually honored in October with a religious festival that includes fine concerts. The *Reims Marathon,* one of France's most important, takes place in late October or early November, and attracts 7,000 to 8,000 runners.

MUSEUMS: *The Palais du Tau* and the *Musée des Beaux-Arts* are described in *Special Places.* There are three other noteworthy museums:

Centre de l'Automobile Française – This museum houses the private collection of engineer/inventor Philippe Charbonneaux, and includes 130 automobiles dating from 1897 to today. In addition, there is a remarkable collection of toy and model cars, and old posters. Open daily April through October from 10 AM to noon and 2 to 5 PM; open weekends only or by appointment in winter. Admission charge. 84 Av. Georges-Clemenceau (phone: 26-82-83-84).

Musée-Abbaye St-Remi – An ancient abbey next door to the Basilique St-Remi, this is now an archaeological museum, also known as the *Musée d'Histoire et d'Archéologie,* with items from prehistoric times to the Middle Ages, including some interesting Gallo-Roman mosaics and tombs. Ranked among France's 50 most beautiful museums, *St-Remi* also has an exhibit on regional military history that was recently enlarged. There are free sound-and-light shows on Saturday evenings at 9:30 PM from July through September. Open weekdays from 2 to 6:30 PM, Saturdays and Sundays from 2 to 7 PM; closed some holidays. Admission charge to the museum. 53 Rue Simon (phone: 26-85-23-36).

Musée-Hôtel le Vergeur – Also known as the *Musée du Vieux Reims* (Museum of Old Reims), it contains sculptures, paintings, drawings, and plans relating to the history of Reims and to the splendors of the coronations; two rooms of Flemish and Dutch artists, including a collection of Dürer engravings; and attractive apartments with 19th-century furnishings. Open daily, except Mondays and holidays, from 2 to 6 PM. Admission charge. 36 Pl. du Forum (phone: 26-47-20-75).

SHOPPING: Much of the best shopping in Reims can be found on the streets and malls near the cathedral. Local specialties are champagne and biscuits, and if you wish to stock up on the former, the prices in the wine shops in the vicinity of the cathedral are slightly lower than those found in Paris. Better shops for men and women line the Cours Langlet and the Rue de Vesle.

Fossier – The best place to buy Reims's delicious *croquignolles* (dry biscuits). 25 Cours Langlet (phone: 26-47-59-84).

Galerie des Sacres – A small shopping mall, with a variety of stores, including clothing boutiques, an ice cream parlor, and art galleries. On Rue Libergier, near the cathedral.

La Garinie – For arts and crafts. 6 Rue de l'Université (phone: 26-88-43-91).

Maison Coeuriot/Au Cochon Sans Rancune – This shop stocks the finest of *charcuterie* — perfect for an impromptu picnic. 47 Rue de Vesle (phone: 26-47-33-35).

La Petite Friande – A good chocolate shop — it specializes in chocolate champagne corks. 15 Cours Langlet (phone: 26-47-50-44).

Aux Spécialités Remoises – Savory *biscuits de Reims* to accompany champagne and wonderful *pain d'épices* (gingerbread) are just two of the wonderful edibles found here. Place du Cardinal-Luçon (phone: 26-47-64-32).

 SPORTS: The huge *Parc Pommery* offers plenty of opportunity for outdoor recreation.

Golf – A private course, the 18-hole *Golf Club of Reims* (Château des Dames de France, in nearby Gueux; phone: 26-03-60-14), often admits non-members for a fee. From Reims take exit Reims-Tinqueux, turn onto N31 toward Soissons, but quickly turn off it onto D27 toward Gueux. Farther away on Route Monmirail (18 miles/29 km from Epernay; 31 miles/50 km south of Reims) is a public golf course with 18 holes, *La Vitarderie* (phone: 26-58-25-09).

Swimming – Among the public pools is the *Piscine Olympique,* 41 Chaussée Bocquaine (phone: 26-82-60-00).

Tennis and Squash – Tennis courts at *Parc Pommery* (10 Av. du Général-Giraud; phone: 26-85-23-29); squash courts (10 Rue Gabriel-Voisin; phone: 26-85-40-80).

 THEATER: *La Comédie de Reims/Centre Dramatique National* (3 Chaussée Bocquaine; phone: 26-48-49-00) has a varied repertory. For ballet, the *Grand Théâtre* (9 Rue Chanzy; phone: 26-47-43-41). A multipurpose cultural center, *Le Manège* (2 Bd. du Général-Leclerc; phone: 26-47-30-40), hosts a wide variety of live performances including concerts, dance, and theater as well as housing historical and art exhibitions. Located across from the train station, this graceful red brick building formerly was a site for traveling circuses and equestrian training until it was restored and reopened in 1990.

 MUSIC: The *Grand Théâtre* (9 Rue Chanzy; phone: 26-47-43-41) is the place for opera and concerts. The ticket office is open from 10 AM to noon and from 2:30 to 5:30 PM except Mondays. Popular music can be heard in some of the bars and cabarets (see below).

 NIGHTCLUBS AND NIGHTLIFE: Though the people of Reims are reputed to be serious, family-oriented stay-at-homes who do their champagne drinking over dinner with friends and relatives, somebody is keeping the bars, cafés, and cabarets open at night. The champagne bar at *Boyer "Les Crayères"* (64 Bd. Henri-Vasnier; phone: 26-82-80-80) is open Tuesdays through Sundays from 11 AM to 1 PM. *L'Aquarium* (93 Bd. du Général-Leclerc; phone: 26-47-34-29) offers danceable, albeit retro, disco music. Outside town, in the middle of a woods in Cernay-les-Reims, there's *La Bergerie* or the *Discothèque de l'Ermitage* (Rte. de Luxembourg; phone: 26-89-01-16) also open after 10 PM, except Mondays. Other bars and cafés with music are *La Boîte à Cocktails* (6 Pl. du Forum; phone: 26-47-56-58), with a pianist nightly except Sundays and mid-July to mid-August, when it's closed; *Le Duke,* in the *Altéa* (phone: 26-88-53-54), an "American bar" where the live music includes some mild jazz that can be accompanied by three or four dozen brands of champagne.

BEST IN TOWN

 CHECKING IN: With a few exceptions, hotels are not among Reims's major assets. There are plenty of beds, but if you have a car you might consider staying in one of the lovely country inns nearby (see the "Checking In" sections in *Champagne,* in DIRECTIONS) before settling for an undistinguished hostelry. However, there are plenty of two-star chain hotels on the periphery, and future plans include the construction of new three- and four-star hotels. Due to the generally lower prices found outside Paris, rates are reasonable. Expect to pay $130 or more for a double room in hotels classified as expensive; $60 to $130 for those in the moderate range; and less than $60 for those listed as inexpensive.

Boyer "Les Crayères" – If you want the best — and are willing to pay for it — this is the place to stay. Though the château was built early in this century, it imitates the grand style of the past, and its setting, in a lovely private park, gives it an approach through elegant gates and a long driveway. All 16 rooms and 3 suites at this member of the prestigious Relais & Châteaux group are large, individually (and beautifully) decorated in Provençal prints, and are complete with an entry hall, a dressing room, and a sizable bathroom. All have views of the majestic trees and green lawns of the park and some have views of the Basilique St-Remi, which is nearby, and of the cathedral. The hotel's three-Michelin-star restaurant is one of the greats in France (see *Eating Out*). Major credit cards accepted. 64 Bd. Henri-Vasnier (phone: 26-82-80-80; fax: 26-82-65-52). Very expensive.

Grand Hôtel des Templiers – This renovated 19th-century bourgeois mansion with 17 rooms and 2 suites on a quiet street a bit removed from the city center is one of the latest additions to Reims's slim complement of luxury hotels. It has large, individually decorated rooms, sleek marble baths, a winter garden, and an indoor pool as well as a sauna, steambath, and tanning room. Major credit cards accepted. 22 Rue des Templiers (phone: 26-88-55-08; fax: 26-47-80-60). Expensive.

Altéa – If need be, you should be able to find a vacancy here; it's one of the largest hotels in the region (124 rooms). It's expensive for what's delivered, however, though the rooms are modern and reasonably comfortable (40 have color TV sets and air conditioning). Service is problematic; there's a bar and a restaurant, *Les Ombrages,* without much to recommend it. Major credit cards accepted. 31 Bd. Paul-Doumer (phone: 26-88-53-54; fax: 26-40-35-51). Expensive to moderate.

Château de la Muire – An ambitious expansion has doubled the size of this hotel in Tinqueux, near the city limits, with the addition of 32 rooms, bringing the total to 62. There also is a quick-service eatery, a one-star restaurant, *L'Assiette Champenoise* (see *Eating Out*), swimming pool, and conference rooms. Modern and comfortable, it occupies a niche between the deluxe *Boyer* and the simple chain hotels. Major credit cards accepted. 40 Av. Paul-Vaillant-Couturier, Tinqueux (phone: 26-04-15-56; fax: 26-04-15-69). Moderate.

Novotel – Just outside Reims, this modern hotel-motel (part of the popular chain), with 125 rooms, is well run and convenient. Its bar and grill are open until midnight, and the amenities include a swimming pool. Major credit cards accepted. Rte. de Soissons (phone: 26-08-11-61; fax: 26-08-72-05). Moderate.

La Paix – The best bet in the city — a friendly, efficiently run property with 105 comfortable and well-equipped rooms. *La Taverne de Maître Kanter* restaurant, which is linked to the hotel but has a separate entrance is not very exciting, perhaps, but getting better. Major credit cards accepted. 9 Rue Buirette (phone: 26-40-04-08; fax: 26-47-75-04). Moderate.

Continental – A vintage hotel from the 1860s whose lobby has a tawdry charm, with wood-trimmed, print armchairs, frayed Oriental rugs, and a monumental ceiling lamp of brass and glass. Rooms are simple and comfortable. There are breakfast and meeting rooms and a somewhat overpriced restaurant. Major credit cards accepted. 93 Pl. Drouet d'Erlon (phone: 26-40-39-35; fax: 26-47-51-12). Inexpensive.

Du Nord – An old-fashioned hostelry in the heart of Reims, it was renovated to include comforts and charm that come as a surprise after passing through its drab lobby. Offers excellent value (and clean rooms) for a very reasonable price. Major credit cards accepted. 75 Pl. Drouet d'Erlon (phone: 26-47-39-03; fax: 26-40-92-26). Inexpensive.

 EATING OUT: There's no reason for not eating well in Reims or in the Champagne region in general. A similar statement surely could be made about any major French city or region, but in the case of Reims and its surrounding area it is particularly applicable. The regional cuisine includes anything cooked *au champagne* (with champagne), *potée champenoise* (a hearty meat stew), and *matelote,* (a fish stew). Spectacular local cheeses include brie de meaux (the king of bries), vhaource (a creamy, delicately flavored white cheese), and tangy, richly scented maroilles. Reims and its environs have a number of excellent restaurants, in and of themselves worth a visit. According to the tourist office, Reims now boasts more Michelin stars than any other French city of its size. At the better restaurants, expect dishes that marry particularly well with champagne — fish, seafood, poultry, and veal dishes.

For a full lunch or dinner for two, excluding beverages (service often is included in the price, but check because this is becoming less common), expect to pay $150 or more at places we list as expensive; $80 to $150 for those in the moderate range; and less than $80 for those listed as inexpensive.

Boyer "Les Crayères" – Nary a pilgrim leaves this temple of haute cuisine in less than a state of bliss. It isn't just the best restaurant in the region, it is one of the best in France (which to some gastronomes means the world). And even after Gérard Boyer and his wife, Elayne, have earned innumerable accolades, including a three-star rating from Michelin, they keep getting better. The greeting here is sunshine — some say the best welcome this side of heaven — and there is a warmth and glow in the restaurant that quickly converts to the comfort and contentment of its diners. The menu is seasonal, brilliantly inspired, and loaded with foods that have an affinity to Champagne. Try the *escalope de foie gras,* the delicate and elegant fish dishes, the cabbage stuffed with langoustines, Boyer's famous truffle in puff pastry, the no less famous *salade du Père Maurice,* and the local cheeses. Save room for the riches of the dessert cart, which might include *soupe au chocolat* (chocolate soup) served with a slice of *pain d'épices,* and a *glace au pain d'épices* (gingerbread topped with ice cream). The *cave* is a wine lover's dream, and also is stocked with rare champagnes. Closed Mondays, Tuesdays at lunch, and mid-December to mid-January. Reservations essential. Major credit cards accepted. 64 Bd. Henri-Vasnier (phone: 26-82-80-80). Very expensive.

L'Assiette Champenoise – Still one of the best in town. The fish preparations are exquisite, the daily specials are a sure bet, but the desserts are forgettable — except for the bittersweet chocolate cake. Michelin has awarded it one star. Open year-round. Reservations necessary. Major credit cards accepted. 40 Av. Paul-Vaillant-Couturier, Tinqueux (phone: 26-04-15-56). Expensive.

Le Florence – This luxurious restaurant offers refined cooking characterized by delicate sauces, and some locals feel it offers the best food for the money in town. It's especially strong on fish dishes (crayfish, lobster, turbot, oysters), offal (which tastes better than the word suggests), and a *filet de boeuf au bouzy* (beef filet in a bouzy wine sauce). Tantalizing desserts and a remarkable selection of champagne also are offered. One Michelin star. Closed Sunday evenings from November to *Easter* and from July 20 to August 11; terrace dining in summer. Reservations advised. Major credit cards accepted. 43 Bd. Foch (phone: 26-47-12-70). Expensive.

Le Chardonnay – This was the site of Boyer's original restaurant. When they moved to new quarters across town, they left behind Dominique Giraudeau, a young chef with impeccable training, who continues to offer fine fare here. This restaurant earned its first Michelin star in its first year and now unfailingly serves meals that are the equal of (or superior to) many two-star operations. Try the steamed shrimp in a champagne-vinegar sauce, duck breasts with sesame seeds, and exquisite desserts, especially the sherbet and the orange flan. Closed Saturdays at lunch, Sundays, most of August, and from December 22 to mid-January. Reservations advised. Major credit cards accepted. 184 Av. d'Epernay (phone: 26-06-08-60). Expensive to moderate.

La Garenne – Chef Laurent LaPlaige was awarded his first Michelin star in 1990 at this restaurant in Champigny, just 4 miles (6 km) outside of Reims. His specialties include *filet de veau aux gambas* (veal with prawns) and *ragoût de rognons de veau au bouzy* (ragout of veal kidneys in a sauce made from the Champagne region's little-known but excellent red wine, bouzy). Closed Sunday evenings, Mondays, a week in February, and 3 weeks in August. Reservations necessary. Major credit cards accepted. On the RN31 to Soissons (phone: 26-08-26-62). Expensive to moderate.

La Côte 108 – A bit out of town, and the first impression here can be disappointing — the dining room is large and seems to lack ambience — but the food will make you forget the decor. In the fall, there are wonderful *feuilletés* with wild mushrooms. Fish always is cooked to perfection, and dishes of wild duck *magrets* (slices of boneless breast) or lamb medallions with garlic cloves are superb. The balanced *menu dégustation* is a feast. Closed Sunday evenings, Mondays, and from December 20 through January. Reservations advised. Major credit cards accepted. In Berry-au-Bac, 7½ miles (12 km) from Reims via N44 (phone: 23-79-95-04). Moderate.

Au Petit Bacchus – Old and new mix harmoniously in this wine bar/lunch spot located on a small street behind the cathedral. Ceiling beams, wood-paneled walls, and rose marble tables add warmth to an otherwise modern motif. Daily specials chalked on blackboards announce light lunchtime platters, including cheese trays, smoked salmon, and such extravagances as caviar. As the name hints, wines take priority; the cave is excellent. Open from 11 AM to 9:30 PM daily. Reservations advised. Major credit cards accepted. 11 Rue de l'Université (phone: 26-47-10-05). Moderate.

Au Petit Comptoir – The bistro trend continues, and like many of France's starred chefs, Gérard Boyer (see "*Les Crayères*"above) has opened his version. A cozy, casual spot in the heart of Reims's old market area, it has all the requisite elements — a frosted glass façade, marble tables, zinc bar, and well-prepared, refined fare that can be had for an extremely fair price. Closed Saturday lunch, Sundays, from late December to mid-January, and 2 weeks in August. Reservations advised. Visa accepted. 17 Rue de Mars (phone: 26-40-58-58). Moderate.

Le Vigneron – Local cuisine par excellence is the stock in trade of the two small dining rooms in this 17th-century house. The rooms are decorated with old posters and a collection of rare wine labels; the atmosphere is friendly and very French.

Among the menu choices are Reims ham with grapes, pike in a champagne sauce, and *potée champenoise* (a stew of smoked ham, bacon, sausages, and cabbage). The wine list is reasonably priced and features an extensive selection of champagne and local still wines. Closed Saturday lunch, Sundays, from *Christmas* to mid-January, and 2 weeks in August. Reservations unnecessary. Visa accepted. Pl. Jamot (phone: 26-47-00-71). Moderate to inexpensive.

Waida – A popular pastry shop with a classic 1930s tearoom, complete with ceiling fans, inlaid woods, and an Art Deco–stained glass backdrop. Open daily from 7 AM to 8 PM; closed Sundays from 1 to 3:30 PM. Reservations unnecessary. Major credit cards accepted. 3-5 Pl. d'Erlon (phone: 26-47-44-49). Inexpensive.

ROUEN

"Oh, Rouen, art thou then my final resting place . . . ?" With this plaintive cry, Joan of Arc was led off to her execution and to a destiny that bound her to this city forever. Indeed, so strong is this association, fueled by writers from Schiller to Shaw, that for the visitor it tends to obscure other aspects of Rouen's history, not to mention its current stature as a port and manufacturing center. Given its location, in Normandy on the Seine — near the mouth of the river at the English Channel — it is the country's fourth-largest port, the port of Paris, in fact. The rich agricultural lands and forests surrounding Rouen and the chemical, petroleum, paper, metallurgical, and textile industries operating in Greater Rouen all profit by the port's proximity, fueling an economy that supports more than half a million people.

The Gauls had a settlement here called Ratuma, but it was the ever-efficient Romans who established this as the first point upstream from the Channel where a bridge could be built. The Romans settled on the right bank of the great loop in the river, in the natural amphitheater created by the steep surrounding hills that remains the heart of the city, and were still there when the earliest bishops arrived to convert the citizens and countryfolk to Christianity in the 4th century. Then both the Romans and their city disappeared into the shadows of the Dark Ages, when invading barbarians swept away nearly all of the physical and spiritual manifestations of the Pax Romana and plunged Europe into disorder.

That something of Rouen must have endured, or been rebuilt, seems likely, for when the city's recorded history resumed almost 5 centuries later, with the creation of the duchy of Normandy in 911, the new duke chose it as his capital. From the time of this Duke of Normandy — Rollo — until another Duke of Normandy — William — crossed the Channel, conquered England, and made himself its king in 1066, Rouen thrived as an independent capital. Even after the Conquest it was second only to London in importance among the possessions of the Norman-English kings, and it maintained that standing until 1204, when the luckless King John of England lost his Norman possessions to Philippe-Auguste of France, who annexed them to the French crown. From then on it became one of the most sought-after prizes in the on-again, off-again tug-of-war between France and England that reached its climax in the Hundred Years War (1337–1453). In 1418 and 1419, Rouen endured a 6-month siege that ended with its capitulation to the English, whom the Normans dubbed "Goddons" because of their noticeable addiction to the oath "Goddamn!" Under John of Lancaster, Duke of Bedford and brother of Henry V (the duke is buried in the cathedral), the Goddons controlled Rouen for the next 30 years.

It was during this time that Joan of Arc walked into the pages of history and the popular imagination. Born in Domrémy (Lorraine) in approximately

1412, she began at an early age to hear voices and see visions urging her to go to the aid of the feeble heir to the French throne, the future King Charles VII. In an attempt to end the Hundred Years War, Charles's father had agreed in 1420 to a treaty naming Henry V, King of England, his successor as King of France. Though the young Charles repudiated the treaty when his father died in 1422, he ruled over a small realm confined south of the Loire while the English, with the help of their French allies, the Dukes of Burgundy, extended their rule over an increasingly larger part of France north of the Loire. The important town of Orléans — on the Loire and thus considered the gateway to southern France — probably would have fallen to the English, too, had not the young peasant girl convinced the fainthearted Charles of her divine inspiration and led his troops to raise the months-long siege in 1429. Forever after known as the Maid of Orléans, she then led her king to be crowned in Reims Cathedral, adding legitimacy to his royal title, and went on to other battles. The next spring, however, she was captured by the Burgundians during the defense of Compiègne.

Joan had been captured after an astonishing series of victories in which her role seems to have been talismanic rather than tactical. Nevertheless, her influence was powerful even as a mascot, and the English commanders were anxious to see her destroyed. Having paid her Burgundian captors the requisite 30 pieces of silver at the inflationary rate of 10,000 ducats, Richard de Beauchamp, Earl of Warwick, handed her over to the ecclesiastical court of Rouen to be tried for heresy and witchcraft. Joan's prison was in a tower of the castle that Philippe-Auguste had built 200 years before. The keep, now called Tour Jeanne-d'Arc, is all that remains of the castle, and it was here that she was shown some convincing instruments of torture for the first time. Her trial, before Pierre Cauchon, the Bishop of Beauvois, lasted 3 months. Then, on May 24, 1431, she was taken to the cemetery of the Abbey of St. Ouen (now the garden of the Hôtel de Ville) where she publicly renounced the "voices" she had heard. In return for recanting, her inquisitors condemned her not to death but to life imprisonment, though one condition of their leniency was that she wear only women's clothes.

Not satisfied, the English pressed for more definitive measures until, by a trick, the Maid was forced to dress once more in the male garb she had worn while fighting, and she was accused of breaking her oath. On May 29, in a room of the Archbishop's Palace (only an outer wall of the room now remains on Rue St-Romain), Warwick and Winchester and the other villains who have since enlivened stages around the world condemned her to death. The next day, on Place du Vieux-Marché, she was burned at the stake. Still the English feared her. Already she was being talked of as a martyr, and lest any of her mortal remains become a rallying point for the French, they were thrown into the Seine in what must rank as one of history's more spiteful moments. Twenty-five years later, at the instigation of the spineless Charles VII, she was rehabilitated by Cardinal d'Estouteville in the same room where she had been condemned.

The English finally left Rouen in 1449, and during the 100 years that followed, building flourished in the city on an unprecedented scale. One of the most perfect examples of the Flamboyant Gothic style in all Europe, the

Eglise St-Maclou, belongs to this period, as do the Cathédrale de Notre-Dame's Butter Tower and those superb Renaissance mansions, the Hôtel de Bourgtheroulde and the Palais de Justice. All of these, along with the famous Gros-Horloge, still form part of the city's backdrop. They seem even more spectacular set against the simple *maisons de pans de bois,* those exquisite examples of domestic architecture with exposed beams, gables, *colombages,* and leaded windows that survive in profusion in Rouen. During World War II, Rouen suffered the brunt of aerial and tank bombardments from the advancing German forces, then from Allied (mainly British) air attacks aimed at the entrenched invaders.

As an integral final stop en route to the capture of Paris, the city was taken by Rommel's 5th Panzer Division on June 10, 1940, and occupied for the next 4 years, experiencing near-total destruction. The area between the cathedral and the river was obliterated. It is estimated that during 1 night in 1944, 345 bombs were dropped on Rouen. But all the town's treasures — many of the oldest stained glass windows, paintings, ceramics, antiques, and book collections — had been stowed away for protection. The city was liberated by Canadian forces on August 30, 1944. The war had ravaged hundreds of acres of land, destroyed 9,500 houses and 14 monuments, and buried 1,600 people in debris. Ninety political prisoners and Résistance members, and 250 of the city's Jews, had been arrested, never to return.

Rouen is a survivor, though. Except for the destroyed Church of St- Vincent, the major architectural wonders remain — those damaged were repaired; those demolished have been rebuilt. Despite the losses of war, Rouen has maintained the profound spirit of its past with the continuing rush of its present, such that the ancient building at 31 Place du Vieux-Marché exists still as a restaurant, *La Couronne* (it claims to be the oldest restaurant in France), as it has for hundreds of years, serving the dishes — duck, ham, sheep's feet, cheeses — and the cider that are part of the Norman gastronomic heritage. So, too, the school that Pierre Corneille attended and that is now named for him still drums Latin, Greek, and logic into the heads of tomorrow's leaders, just as the city's hundreds of bells still call the faithful to mass and remind them twice a day of the Angelus, and as scenes depicted in the masterpiece *Madame Bovary* attract fans of native son Gustave Flaubert.

ROUEN AT-A-GLANCE

SEEING THE CITY: The best view of the city is from the viewing table on the Côte Ste-Catherine (St. Catherine's Hill), southeast of the center. It takes in the towers and belfries of the city and the serpentine Seine and is especially attractive in the glow of early evening. From the summit of N182 in Canteleu, on the other side of town, there is a view eastward down the valley, over the docks to the city. Another fine view — across the roofs and over the gables of the Old Town — is from the Beffroi (Belfry) of the Gros-Horloge. Or you could explore the *quais* of the Seine on foot or by bicycle, which are humming with industrial activity. Although they are not conventionally picturesque like those of Paris, they show an important facet of contemporary Rouen. Rue Grand Pont leads down to the Seine from in front of the cathedral.

SPECIAL PLACES: In addition to one of France's major cathedrals, Rouen has other important churches as well as a number of secular monuments, museums, and picturesque streets. All of the sights below are within walking distance of each other in the Old Town, on the right bank of the Seine. On the left bank is the modern St-Sever quarter.

Cathédrale de Notre-Dame – The best way to approach this famous cathedral, whose architecture can best be described as *dentelle en pierre* (lacy stone), for the first time is from Rue du Gros-Horloge. As you walk along that narrow street into Place de la Cathédrale, the extraordinary contours of the great west façade beloved of Monet gradually appear, a mesmerizing spectacle of statues, pinnacles, and mismatched towers that amounts to an object lesson in 400 years of ecclesiastical architecture. Included, apart from the Romanesque base of the Tour St-Romain (St. Romanus Tower), to the left as you face the church, are styles from four different Gothic periods: primitive Gothic, in the middle tiers of the Tour St-Romain; pure Gothic in the portals of St-Jean-Baptiste and St-Etienne flanking the main door; Rayonnant in the windows above St. Stephen's door and the four major pinnacles of the façade; and Flamboyant in the famous Tour de Beurre (Butter Tower), so named because it was paid for by local gourmands who preferred to buy indulgences to eat butter during *Lent* rather than do without it for 40 days. The detail of the west portals, as well as that of the north door, the Portail des Libraires, and the south door, the Portail de la Calende, is absorbing, always full of narrative, often of humor. The sculptures surrounding the Portail des Libraires (Booksellers' Door), for instance, show beasts of fact, fable, and fantasy, among them a philosopher with the head of a pig and a pig playing a violin. In the Cour des Libraires leading to the door, there is a workshop where 20th-century sculptors chisel away at reproductions of the medieval saints that will replace those disfigured beyond repair. It is an intriguing sight, suggesting that the cathedral is a living work of art.

Though the exterior embraces several epochs and styles, beginning with vestiges of the ancient Romanesque church, which burned down in 1200, through to the finishing touches of the 16th century (the cast-iron spire of the central lantern tower was a final 19th-century flourish, replacing a wooden one), the interior speaks basically of only the pure Gothic style of the 13th century, when the nave with its 4 great stories of arches, false tribunes, triforia, and high windows was completed. The choir, also from the 13th century, was lovingly restored after extensive damage in World War II; the 15th-century misericords survived the bombing, and their carvings still provide a colorful illustration of the costumes, customs, trades, and work implements of the period. Some 13th-century stained glass survives in the ambulatory, most notably in the windows of St. Julian l'Hospitalier; here, too, are several 13th-century tombs, including that of Richard Coeur de Lion, whose lion heart alone is buried below his effigy, his other earthly remains resting elsewhere. (The heart of Charles V is entombed in the crypt, another of the few parts of the ancient Romanesque church still extant.)

In the north arm of the transept, the Escalier des Libraires (Booksellers' Staircase) dates from the 15th century and is famous for its lacelike banister. The Chapelle de la Vierge (Chapel of the Virgin) in the apse contains 14th-century stained glass windows depicting 24 of Rouen's bishops and archbishops, but it is dominated by two 16th-century tombs. On the right facing the altar, the two cardinals d'Amboise, Georges I and his nephew Georges II, kneel in prayer above their sumptuously decorated burial place. Constructed between 1515 and 1525 in the overlush style of the early Renaissance, the tomb is an ornate monument of arabesque and Italianate details at once gorgeous and grotesque. That of Louis de Brézé (he was the husband of Diane de

Poitiers, mistress of Henri II of France), on the left facing the altar, reflects the more sober taste of the Renaissance not too many years later (1535); its simple Corinthian columns and graceful caryatids provide a marked contrast to the tomb of the cardinals. A wonderful 17th-century Spanish-style reredos adds confusion to the styles in the chapel. Painted in gold and crowned by a statue of the Virgin with Child standing in a high niche, it has a charming painting, *The Adoration of the Shepherds* by Philippe de Champaigne, at its center.

Guided tours of the cathedral (in French) take place several times daily during the summer (with a shortened schedule on Sundays and religious holidays), and on Saturday and Sunday afternoons the rest of the year; participants gather in the nave. Except for guided tours (check with the tourist office for times), the Chapelle de la Vierge is closed Mondays through Fridays. It is best seen early on Sunday mornings when, in preparation for the first mass at 7 AM, it is the only illuminated spot in the vast, gray gloom of the church. The Portail de la Calende on the Rue des Bonnetiers side of the cathedral is open at that hour to admit worshipers. The cathedral takes on a magical quality at night, when the spire is illuminated. Pl. de la Cathédrale.

Place de la Cathédrale – The cobbled square where Monet sat to paint is overwhelmed by the cathedral that inspired him. There is, in addition, the beautiful early-16th-century building that houses the tourist office, the former Bureau des Finances. Before checking out the brochures, look inside the marvelous courtyard. There are some largish brasseries on the south side of the *place* for beer swilling and people watching.

Gros-Horloge (Great Clock) – Rouen's best-known secular monument used to be in the Beffroi (Belfry) next to it, but in 1527 the town's proud burghers decided to show it off to greater advantage and built the present gatehouse-like clock tower that spans the street. The extraordinary conglomeration abutting, adjacent to, overshadowed by, and looming down upon the clock is best seen from the west side of the gatehouse, where the eye takes in all at once a collage of buildings and styles spreading across 4 centuries. The two lower stories of the Belfry are Rayonnant Gothic of the 13th century; the top story is Flamboyant; the clock tower itself is in the Renaissance style of the late 1520s and 1530s; the half-timbered houses nearby are in the simpler domestic style of the same epoch; the gatekeeper's house nestling against the clock tower and the Belfry is 17th-century classical; and the vaguely baroque fountain next to it dates from the reign of Louis XV in the 18th century. The gilded and painted clock face marks the hour with only one hand, and the clock also tells the days of the week and the phases of the moon. The clockwork mechanism inside the cupola is among the oldest still functioning in Europe. One of the clock's two bells, named the Cache-Rimbaud, has been in service since 1260; the other, Rouvel, cracked in 1904. The Belfry offers an interesting view of the roofs and gables of the old quarter and of the cathedral; it is open daily except Tuesdays and Wednesday mornings from *Easter* to October. Entrance to the *Musée des Beaux-Arts* and the *Musée Le-Secq-des-Tournelles* is included in the admission charge. Rue du Gros-Horloge.

Rue du Gros-Horloge – For close to 2 centuries, this, Rouen's most famous street, has been the city's main commercial strip. But in spite of the boutiques, burger joints, and bars, several old houses give just the faintest hint of what it was once like. The house at No. 161 dates from the early 1500s, No. 146 from a little later. The corner house next to the Belfry on the Rue Thouret side was the city's original town hall (1608).

Archevêché – The Archbishop's Palace behind the cathedral is a great Gothic mansion that can be visited only by special arrangement (ask at the tourist office). The outstanding reward is the Great Hall, called the Hall of the States of Normandy, with four 18th-century pictures by Hubert Robert of Dieppe, Le Havre, Gaillon, and Rouen itself. Entrance on Rue des Bonnetiers.

Rue St-Romain – This picturesque street is famous for its half-timbered houses of the Middle Ages and late Renaissance. Some of these have overhanging upper stories, which meant that slops thrown from the top floors did not soil people passing close to the house or leaning from windows below. Two such are those at Nos. 11 and 13, which date from the early 1400s and were the only houses in the city never covered by plaster. The Cour des Libraires leading into the cathedral from the street is named for the booksellers that used to congregate here. Adjacent is the wall of the Archbishop's Palace with a plaque marking the spot below the room, no longer extant, where Joan of Arc was sentenced to death and where 25 years later Cardinal d'Estouteville proclaimed her innocence. Standing underneath the overhanging housefront, opposite the plaque, you peer through the moss-covered stonework of the walls of the archbishopric to view the cathedral's massive central spire. The old house at No. 56 almost certainly was standing in Joan's day. Leading off Rue St-Romain into Rue St-Nicolas is the narrow alley known as the Rue des Chanoines (Street of the Canons). Thoroughfares in Old Rouen had to be wide enough to permit the passage of a horse's hindquarters. This one qualifies — just.

Eglise St-Maclou – Behind the cathedral across Rue de la République is this striking church built in the 15th and 16th centuries and dedicated to St. Maclou, the Welsh saint who turns up in Brittany as St. Malo. Connoisseurs agree that the west façade, with its fan-shaped porch of five pinnacled arches, is one of the most perfect examples of Flamboyant Gothic in France. Inside, the visitor is immediately struck by the soaring vertical lines of the nave, which give an impression of dynamic upward surge — in fact, when the organ swells during the recessional after 10 o'clock mass, it seems that the church might take off like a rocket. The decorative carvings on the door panels are splendid examples of wooden sculpture of the late 16th century. The famous one showing the baptism of Christ (left door of the two-door main entrance) is in a framed medallion supported by St. John, St. Luke, St. Mark, and St. Matthew. Recently, centuries of grime were scoured off the church's exterior, returning it to a gleaming white. Organ recitals are held here in July and August. Pl. St-Maclou.

Place Barthélémy – This square in front of the Eglise St-Maclou was once several narrow streets and tiny blocks. Some years ago, the central buildings were torn down, producing a view of the church's façade that was so stunning, no one dared to replace the buildings. It was not only the church that profited; the half-timbered houses on either side also were seen in a new perspective that showed off their gables and fine exterior (but walled-in) staircases to excellent advantage. The lower floors of these handsome houses, which were restored after massive damage during World War II bombardments, are almost all antiques shops.

Rue Martainville – A street of 17th-to-18th-century houses once occupied by prosperous merchants and professional men. Today some of them are bookshops and galleries. In the corner by the Eglise St-Maclou is a *"manneken-pis"* fountain. Hidden behind No. 186 is the Aître St-Maclou (see *Extra Special,* below).

Rue Damiette – Another street of ancient houses, many turned into antiques shops. Especially worth a glance is the 17th-century Hôtel de Senneville at the end of an alley at No. 30. Damiette leads into the colorful, small Place Lieutenant-Aubert, where there is an outstanding 15th-century house with a sculpted porch at No. 6. The view of the tower of St-Ouen from Rue Damiette is splendid. The tower often is called the Ducal Crown of Normandy, and from this perspective it is clear why.

Rue Eau-de-Robec – Now lined with antiques shops, this is the street Flaubert described in *Madame Bovary.* The houses at the western end have overhanging eaves built so that their medieval residents, mostly dyers, could hang wool out to dry.

Eglise St-Ouen – The abbey church of St. Ouen is longer and higher than the cathedrals of Rouen and Notre-Dame in Paris. It also is cool to look at, almost to the point of austerity. Although it took 300 years to build, beginning in 1318, the pure

Gothic lines of the original plan were rigidly followed. Thus, the arches, triforium, and clerestory add up to a textbook example of how a Gothic church of the Middle Ages should look. Because of the lack of decoration, the visitor tends to focus on the windows. Most of the glass in these, from the 14th to the 16th century, was removed at the beginning of World War II and has now been returned. Especially remarkable are the rose windows in the north and south transepts, the latter a treatment of the tree of Jesse in blue and gold designed by Colin de Berneval, the son of the cathedral's architect. Note, too, the organ, built in 1630 and famous enough for its tone to draw organists from all over Europe. Outside on the north flank of the church are the one remaining gallery of the old abbey cloister and 18th-century abbey buildings now serving as the Hôtel de Ville (Town Hall). The gardens behind the Hôtel de Ville and the church were once the abbey cemetery, where Joan of Arc was brought to renounce her voices publicly. The view of the church from here includes its central tower, the *tour couronnée* referred to as the Ducal Crown of Normandy. Pl. du Général-de-Gaulle.

Musée des Beaux-Arts – One of France's greatest provincial collections. The emphasis is on European paintings, from the Flemish primitives (Gerard David's somber *Virgin and the Saints*) to the Impressionists and post-Impressionists (among them, Dufy's *Beach at Ste-Adresse*). One room is devoted to Delacroix's *Justice of Trajan,* another to works by Géricault, a native of Rouen, including his *Slaves Stopping a Horse* and *Portrait of Delacroix.* There are views of Rouen by Van Ruisdael and Van Goyen in rooms devoted to Dutch and Flemish masters, and among the Monets there is one of the series of paintings he executed of the cathedral. A first-floor room contains portraits by Jacques-Emile Blanche of his contemporaries (Claudel, Cocteau, Stravinsky, Montherlant, Giraudoux, Maeterlinck) in the heady years before and after World War I. There also is a celebrated ceramics collection showing the development and decline of Rouen faïence (a type of ceramic) from 1550 to 1800. Closed Tuesdays, Wednesday mornings, and holidays. Admission charge. Square Verdrel (phone: 35-71-28-40).

Musée Le-Secq-des-Tournelles – Here are thousands of pieces of *ferronnerie* (ironwork), from the Dark Ages to the 19th century. It is a feast of intricately wrought lamps, gates, balconies, grilles, keys, weapons, kitchen utensils, candelabra, and religious and secular ornaments beautifully hung or mounted in what was formerly the Eglise St-Laurent, a Flamboyant Gothic edifice built in the 15th and 16th centuries. Closed Tuesdays, Wednesday mornings, and holidays. Admission charge, but the entry ticket for the Musée des Beaux Arts may be used here as well. Rue Jacques-Villon (phone: 35-71-28-40).

Musée des Antiquités – A Gallo-Roman mosaic from nearby Lillebonne is one of the outstanding sights of this museum, which is in a former convent (Cloître Ste-Marie) dating from the 17th century. Although there are items from the Middle East and farther afield, the emphasis is on holdings with a Norman connection. A 13th-century Virgin and Child in ivory and a famous 15th-century tapestry, *Les Cerfs Ailés* (Winged Stags), are especially appealing. Furniture, corbels, cornices, statues, ornaments, and household items from medieval Rouen throw a fascinating light on what some of the wonderful houses a few blocks from the museum originally contained. Closed Thursdays and holidays. Admission charge. 198 Rue Beauvoisine (phone: 35-98-55-10).

Tour Jeanne-d'Arc – A round tower — the keep — is all that remains of the castle built by Philippe-Auguste in the first decade of the 13th century. The part of the castle in which the Maid was imprisoned is no longer standing, but the starkly simple round room in which she was interrogated and threatened with torture is open to the public. Closed Thursdays, holidays, and during November. Admission charge. Rue du Donjon (phone: 35-98-16-21).

Eglise St-Patrice – This was the parish church of what was once upon a time

Rouen's "Irishtown," the quarter where Irish merchants and traders lived. Flamboyant Gothic in style, though comparatively subdued inside, the church is famous chiefly for its 16th- and 17th-century stained glass windows, especially those illustrating the Passion and Resurrection of Christ and one based on a Dürer engraving of the legend of St. Eustachius. The church also contains a collection of religious paintings. 22 Rue St-Patrice, entrance on Rue de l'Abbé-Cochet.

Palais de Justice – Students of architecture consider this an exquisite example of a municipal building in the Flamboyant Gothic style. Note, as you look at the famous façade, that the decoration becomes increasingly richer the higher it goes, so that the pinnacles atop the buttresses on the roof look like upended, intricately carved icicles. The main part of the building was built in 1508 and 1509; the left wing was begun slightly before that, from 1493 to 1508; and the right wing is a 19th-century reconstruction. Ironically, the newest part was spared the ravages of World War II, which particularly damaged the oldest part, including the Salle des Procureurs, where Pierre Corneille appeared as king's counsel and which is today a magnificent restoration. The Procurer's Room (take the staircase on the left) is open to visitors on weekdays only. Pl. Foch, Rue aux Juifs.

Monument Juif (Jewish Monument) – During excavations in 1976, the remains of a 12th-century Romanesque building were unearthed in the courtyard of the Palais de Justice. Certain graffiti and Hebrew inscriptions indicated that it had been a center of some importance to the Jews of Rouen, who lived in the adjacent ghetto until they were expelled by Philip the Fair in the early 14th century. Since there already was one synagogue serving the community, it has been suggested that the building housed a yeshiva, or school, making it one of the oldest universities in Europe. It can be visited at 11 AM Sundays from April to September, and at 2 PM Saturdays in winter months, by applying at least 2 days in advance at the tourist office. Admission charge. Rue aux Juifs.

Eglise Ste-Jeanne-d'Arc – One of the most modern churches in France, it was built on the site where Joan of Arc was burned and is part of the revamping of Place du Vieux-Marché. It is worth visiting only for the stained glass windows it incorporates, which date from the 16th and 17th centuries; they were originally in the chancel of the old Eglise St-Vincent, which stood here until it was destroyed in World War II. The windows are devoted to traditional religious themes such as the Passion, Crucifixion, and Resurrection of Christ, and Adam and Eve. In addition, many of them show typically garbed figures from the various trades and guilds that paid for them. In the background, bottom right, of the window devoted to St. Peter, the churches of St. Maclou and St. Ouen are clearly depicted in stained glass. The irregularly crested roof of Eglise Ste-Jeanne-d'Arc has been intrepreted by some as a representation of tongues of flame; others see it as a stylized version of a ship. Both views seem reasonable. Pl. du Vieux-Marché.

Place du Vieux-Marché – Besides the Eglise Ste-Jeanne d'Arc, the other modern building in the not quite square square is the covered marketplace, where flowers, produce, and fish are sold Tuesdays through Saturdays. On the west side of the square are the remains of the Eglise St-Sauveur, from which a cross was brought to comfort the Maid at the stake. The south and east sides of the square are taken up largely by restaurants, among them the famous *La Couronne* (see *Eating Out*), which is near a waxworks museum, the *Musée Jeanne-d'Arc*.

■**EXTRA SPECIAL:** Walk under the arch at 186 Rue Martainville, through an ancient courtyard and under a gatehouse, and suddenly you are in a tree-lined quadrangle enclosed by low, 2-story timbered buildings. This is the Aître St-Maclou (St. Maclou Cloister), one of the few remaining charnel houses in France, used for the burial of plague victims. It was founded in 1348 when 100,000 people in Rouen succumbed to the Black Death. During the various plagues that raged from the 14th to the 17th century, the cemetery became overcrowded, and it was necessary to dig up the bones and place them in specially built gallery-like cloisters that served as ossuaries. Two were built in 1526, one in 1533, and a final one in 1640. On the supporting timbers carpenters carved macabre skulls, crossbones, spades, hoes, and crosses — all the iconography of death that still can be seen quite clearly today. It has not been used as a cemetery since the French Revolution. The grounds and building were restored in 1851, and the entire complex became a girls' school. Since October 1940 it has housed the Ecole des Beaux-Arts. In a corner by the entrance to the courtyard, a glass case embedded in the wall contains the mummified remains of a cat, supposedly a witches' familiar. This is the only grisly feature in what is otherwise, oddly enough, a very serene retreat in this ancient city. Open daily for visits.

■ **A Very Special Village:** Only 8 miles (13 km) south outside Rouen (on the N138 and then the D64), at the first big curve the Seine makes after Rouen on its way to the sea, is a bit of medieval France remarkably well preserved: the village of La Bouille. Every street seems to have its own special example of medieval architecture, from half-timbered houses to tiny alleyways where one would not be surprised to meet a roving minstral. The Camelot atmosphere is especially evident in summer, when the whole town seems to be decked out in flowers. Notice the house decorated with an archangel on the Place St-Michel.

SOURCES AND RESOURCES

TOURIST INFORMATION: For brochures, maps, and lists of hotels and restaurants, go to the Office du Tourisme, where English is spoken (25 Pl. de la Cathédrale; phone: 35-71-41-77). The beautiful Renaissance mansion, erected between 1505 and 1510, used to be the Treasury of Normandy. Go to the same address to take advantage of the *Accueil de France* accommodations service (for a small fee) if you need help finding a hotel. The tourist office provides daily guided walking tours in French (although you can request an English-speaking guide) of Rouen's historical neighborhoods from mid-June to late September, and on weekends and holidays from *Easter* to mid-June. Visitors also can take a 40-minute guided tour of the city by miniature train. The train goes along the city's principal streets and crosses the river to the left bank. From April through November, the train leaves regularly starting at 10 AM from the Place de la Cathédrale. The tourist office's *Guide Officiel de Rouen,* in both French and English, is very good. The exhaustive *Le P'tit Normand,* in French, is available in bookshops all over Normandy and in Paris. A sort of yellow-pages-cum-encyclopedia of the city, it is an indispensable guide to Rouen and the region. *The City of Rouen,* published in English by Editions Ouest France, is a useful, illustrated guide to the city's most famous historical points. It is available for a few dollars in all bookshops and in most places where postcards are sold. There are no monthly or weekly guides to Rouen in English.

Local Coverage – The regional newspaper *Paris-Normandie* is published daily in Rouen. You'll find English-language books — mainly literature, cookbooks, and guidebooks — at the *ABC Book Shop,* 11 Rue des Faulx (phone: 35-71-08-67).

TELEPHONE: The city code for Rouen is 35, which is incorporated into all local 8-digit numbers. When calling a number in Rouen from the Paris region (including the Ile-de-France), dial 16, wait for a dial tone, then dial the 8-digit number. When calling a number from outside Paris, dial only the

8-digit number. When calling from the US, dial 33 (which is the country code), followed by the 8-digit number.

GETTING AROUND: Bus – The best way to penetrate the suburbs and the hills above the Seine. The Station du Théâtre des Arts, at the foot of Rue Jeanne-d'Arc (phone: 35-52-52-52), is the main terminal for city and suburban buses, which are operated by two companies: *SATAR* (Rue des Charrettes; phone: 35-71-81-71) and *TCAR* (79 Rue Thiers; phone: 35-98-02-43). Monthly and weekly tickets and tickets for 20 journeys can be purchased at the main terminal at reduced rates, and 1- to 3-day Sympabus Tourism passes, allowing unlimited rides on local buses, also can be purchased at the tourist office or the bus station. The station also has timetables and maps of the 26 lines served. Long-distance buses (*autocars*) to cities such as Dieppe, Le Havre, and Fécamp are operated by *CNA* and leave from the Gare Routière (on Rue des Charrettes, close to the Station du Théâtre des Arts; phone: 35-71-81-71). Another line, *Bus Verts* (phone: 31-44-74-44), goes to Le Havre, Deauville, Honfleur, and Caen.

Bicycle Rental – *Rouen Cycles et Motos* (45 Rue St-Eloi; phone: 35-71-34-30) rents bicycles.

Car Rental – *Avis* (24 Rue Malouet; phone: 35-72-77-50) rents campers as well as cars. Also try *Avis* (14 Rue de Lisbonne; phone: 35-98-64-38 and Gare *SNCF;* phone: 35-70-95-12) and *Europcar* (17 Quai Pierre-Corneille; phone: 35-70-18-30). *Hertz* (38 Quai Gaston Boulet; phone: 35-98-16-57) has special rates for trips from Rouen to Orly or Charles de Gaulle airports in Paris. *SNCF*'s Train + Auto rental plan also is available with *Avis*.

Taxi – Cabs are relatively inexpensive. They don't cruise, but they congregate outside the Gare *SNCF* and in Place Foch, and they can be flagged down when passing. The best way to get one is to telephone *Radio Taxis* (67 Rue Thiers; phone: 35-88-50-50), or the group of independent drivers operating out of 18 Rue Wagner (phone: 35-61-20-50).

Train – The Gare *SNCF* (Gare Rive-Droite), at the top of Rue Jeanne-d'Arc, underwent a vast renovation in recent years. For information, call 35-98-50-50. The trip to Paris takes about an hour and 10 minutes, and there are frequent round trips daily.

SPECIAL EVENTS: Secondhand furniture is the order of the day at the *Puces Rouennaises,* a large flea market held at *Parc des Expositions* in mid-February. The *Salon des Antiquaires,* an annual antiques fair at the *Halle aux Toiles,* is held in April or early May. The *Fêtes Jeanne d'Arc* (Joan of Arc Commemoration), on the weekend nearest May 30, the day of her death in 1431, is a time for pageants and plays about the saint in the Place du Vieux-Marché and the Aître St-Maclou. A *Randonnée Pédestre* (Walking Tour) is organized each year in mid-June; contact the tourist office for details. The *Salon des Artistes Indépendents Normands* (Independent Normandy Artists' Show) is held in late June; contact the tourist office for times and location. And the second half of October brings Rouen's major antiques event, the *Salon National des Antiquaires.* From mid-October to mid-November is the *Tapis de Fleurs,* a beautiful display of chrysanthemums, with patterns of vibrant colors that virtually carpet the square in front of the cathedral.

MUSEUMS: Apart from those discussed in *Special Places,* Rouen's museums tend to concentrate on some famous people.

Manoir Pierre-Corneille – A delightfully timbered, many-gabled house containing books, manuscripts, prints, and pictures relating to the playwright, whose country place this once was. Rue Pierre-Corneille, in the suburb of Petit-Couronne, 5 miles (8 km) southwest of the city's center. Closed Thursdays and holidays. Admission charge. For information, ask at the tourist office (phone: 35-68-13-89).

Musée Céramique – Collections of the highly decorative faïence de Rouen, famous since the 17th century, are exhibited here. The museum also houses rare pottery and porcelain from the 16th to the 18th century and from other regions in France, as well as China, Japan, England, and Italy. Closed Tuesdays, Wednesday mornings, and holidays. Admission charge. Hôtel d'Hocqueville, 1 Rue Fauçon (phone: 35-07-31-74).

Musée Corneille – A fine old Rouennais townhouse, where Corneille was born, that gives a wonderful idea of how a well-to-do professional man — in this case, a lawyer — lived in the 17th century. Since the lawyer was also one of France's greatest dramatists, there is the added charm of seeing his birth certificate and a library full of finely bound first editions and translations of his works and related tomes. Closed Tuesdays, Wednesday mornings, and holidays. Admission charge. 4 Rue de la Pie (phone: 35-71-63-92).

Musée Flaubert et d'Histoire de la Médecine – The writer's birthplace is full of 17th- and 18th-century medical equipment in wood, metal, and faïence de Rouen as well as of statues of saints famed for curing incurable ailments. (Flaubert's father and brother were surgeons.) There is also a room where manuscripts, books, photographs, and other Flaubert memorabilia are displayed. Closed Sundays, Mondays, and holidays. Admission charge. 51 Rue de Lecat (phone: 35-08-81-81, ext. 52467).

Musée Jeanne-d'Arc – Essentially a super-kitsch wax museum with life-size tableaux showing the saint's progress from her home in Domrémy to the spot in Rouen, a few steps away, where she was burned. The few contemporary seals and charters and intricately built cardboard models of the events in her life are more interesting than the grisly dioramas. Closed Mondays in winter. Admission charge. 33 Pl. du Vieux-Marché (phone: 35-88-02-70).

Musée d'Histoire Naturelle – Dioramas of animals *chez eux* — at home, that is. Local prehistoric finds and pre-Norman ethnography are well illustrated. Closed Sunday mornings, Mondays, Tuesdays, and holidays. Next to the *Musée des Antiquités* at 198 Rue Beauvoisine (phone: 35-71-41-50).

Pavillon Flaubert – All that remains of the riverside house where Flaubert wrote *Madame Bovary.* It contains furniture, bibelots, and other mementos of the author not found downtown. Closed Tuesdays, Wednesday mornings, and holidays. Croisset, 3 miles (5 km) west of Rouen by D51 (phone: 35-36-43-91).

 SHOPPING: Not surprisingly, antiques are the shopping specialty in Rouen. Streets noted for this trade are Rue Eau-de-Robec, Place Barthélémy, Rue Damiette, and Rue St-Romain, all in the heart of the Old Town. Prices can be up to 50% less than those asked in the United States, and though many stores sell country armoires, chests, tables, and other pieces too large for the average traveler to transport, most also have more portable items. In addition to the shops, antiques auctions are scheduled throughout the year at the *Salles des Ventes* (25 Rue du Général-Giraud; phone: 35-71-13-50; and 20 Rue de la Croix-de-Fer; phone: 35-70-32-89). Faïence de Rouen — ceramicware once made locally in traditional patterns — is easily obtained. Beautifully bound books, some with delicate tooling, and old prints also are abundant and comparatively inexpensive, though to find the latter one occasionally has to sift through considerable quantities of dross to get to the real thing. There is a flea market in Place St-Marc each Saturday and Sunday and in Place des Emmurées on Thursdays, although both spots are heavier on blue jeans than antique christening mugs. The first Saturday of each month, bric-a-brac and antiques are sold at the market set up along the stream on Rue Eau-de-Robec. Ask at the tourist office for the leaflet *Rouen Ville d'Art,* which lists antiques shops, galleries, painters, stained glass, and so on. Smaller *foires à la brocante* (antiques fairs) are organized throughout the year in various locations; check with the tourist office or watch for posters advertising the event.

Large French and European chains are represented among the many other types of stores in Rouen, though on a modest scale compared to Paris, whose proximity diverts a lot of shoppers from Rouen. Most privately owned stores are closed Sundays and Mondays.

Antic St-Maclou – Antique silver jewelry, ivory bibelots, and books with fine bindings are among the bargains. 178 Rue Martainville (phone: 35-89-52-61 or 35-98-36-31).

L'Armitière – A large, modern bookstore near the *Musée des Beaux-Arts,* with a wide selection of books on Normandy (in French) and a small group of English and American works in paperback. 5 Rue des Basnages (phone: 35-70-57-42).

Atelier St-Romain – Old French and English prints plus a wide variety of antique objets d'art. 28 Rue St-Romain (phone: 35-88-76-17).

Burton's – Basically British, though not exclusively, for men. English-cut jackets made from fine, sturdy tweeds are good bargains. 54 Rue du Général-Leclerc (phone: 35-71-58-80).

Aux Ducs de Gascogne – Specialties from the southwest of France, one of the country's most famous gastronomic regions: pâtés, foie gras, *confits,* and esoteric soups in aristocratic-looking cans. 7 Rue de l'Epicerie (phone: 35-88-06-04).

E. Bertram – Carved wooden furniture from the 18th and 19th centuries, as well as rare books from the 15th century to modern times. 108 Rue Molière (phone: 35-70-79-96).

Echec et Mat – Jigsaw puzzles, building blocks, chess sets, and other games, with the emphasis on good design. 115 Rue St-Sever (phone: 35-73-38-88) and 9 Rue Rollon.

Herboristerie St-Romain – Time-worn domain of a local herbalist, worth a visit — if only to admire the half-timbered structure built in 1480 as the private residence of the director of Rouen's fine arts school. 74 Rue St-Romain (phone: 35-71-28-23).

Laura Ashley – Multilevel boutique featuring the usual selection of flowered frocks. 19 Rue du Gros-Horloge (phone: 35-70-20-02).

M. Bertram – Owned by the brother of *E. Bertram,* this shop specializes in French paintings from every era. 100 Rue Molière (phone: 35-98-24-06).

Médiane – An art gallery specializing in works by contemporary Norman painters. 74 Rue d'Amiens (phone: 35-88-85-71).

Du Mesnil Gaillard – Antique decorative items and 18th- and 19th-century furniture are among the intriguing items found here. 54 Rue des Bons Enfants (phone: 35-71-05-97).

Michel Carpentier – Discriminatingly crowded with reproductions of engravings of Rouen's street scenes and churches. Carpentier also owns the faïence shop next door. Both are very reasonable. 26 Rue St-Romain (phone: 35-88-77-47).

Michel Garnier – Antique lamps in faïence, ceramics, glass, and brass; Tiffany lamps and lamps from the Far East; lamps from the Belle Epoque, the Edwardian era, and Victoria's England. 11 Rue Damiette (phone: 35-88-66-85).

Minitrain – Model trains, reproductions, miniatures in wood and metal. 28 Rue Jeanne-d'Arc (phone: 35-70-70-58).

Monique – Ladies' hats that are soigné, outré, *raffiné,* and just plain passé, all at prices that Paris cannot cap. 58 Rue St-Romain (phone: 35-98-07-03).

M. et Mme. Ester – A colorful variety of eggcups, decanters, fluted champagne glasses, and other bibelots jam this beautiful, attic-like antiques store. 190 Rue Eau-de-Robec (phone: 35-98-04-26).

P. Chasset – Old glasses and bottles, fascinating antique playing cards, Tarot cards, and children's games in beautifully decorated boxes. 12 Rue de la Croix-de-Fer (phone: 35-70-59-97).

Paillard – Chocolates, nougats, pastries . . . ecstasy. 32 Rue du Gros-Horloge (phone: 35-71-10-15).

Poulingue – Nineteenth-century Norman furniture for those who'd like to own a bit of French history. 4 Place Barthélémy (phone: 35-98-09-56).

Au Printemps – One of France's major department stores, it is inclined toward the trendy rather than the traditional. 4-14 Rue du Gros-Horloge (phone: 35-71-74-75).

Vieux Rouen – A good source (with a large choice) for faïence de Rouen, the decorative tableware and accessories once made here. The items in this small shop near the cathedral are hand-painted, modern reproductions now made in the east of France. 44 Rue de la Tour-de-Beurre (phone: 35-70-54-36).

Wenley – The newest in a wave of British-style boutiques (opened by French, not British retailers) sprouting up around France, this one has pretty tableware, decorative items, jams, sachets, scented soaps, whiskeys, and even English fudge. 15 Rue Rollon (phone: 35-98-11-00).

 SPORTS: Facilities are better in the suburbs than they are in the city.

Ballooning – *Paul Fleury* (1453 Rue de l'Eglise, Bois-Guillaume; phone: 35-60-59-59) will pilot your maiden — or umpteenth — flight over the Norman countryside for an hour or a day from nearby Bois-Guillaume.

Golf – There are 18 holes overlooking the city at *Golf de Rouen* (Rte. Maromme in Mont-St-Aignan; phone: 35-74-10-91 or 35-75-38-65). It's more bracing at *Golf d'Etretat* (outside Etretat, a 40-minute drive from Rouen; phone: 35-27-04-89), and more posh at the *New-Golf Club de Deauville* (outside Deauville, an hour's drive away; phone: 31-88-20-53).

Hiking – Contact the *Association Rouennaise de Randonnée Pédestre* (58 Rue du Général-Giraud; phone: 35-62-02-49).

Horseback Riding – You can mount a steed at the *Centre Hippique des Cateliers* (Houppeville; phone: 35-59-14-06), for riding through the Forêt Verte, or at the *Centre Hippique de Génétey* (St-Martin de Boscherville; phone: 35-32-00-44), for riding through the Forêt de Roumare.

Ice Skating – Glide away at *Patinoire Municipale de Rouen* (Rue Ste-Amélie; phone: 35-71-05-69), on the Ile Lacroix in the Seine.

Rugby – This is the number one sport in the southwest of France, but since Rouen is in the north, the *Racing Rugby Club de Rouen* (phone: 35-34-45-69) might be considered bush. See them play at *Stade Jean-Mermoz* (Rue de la Motte; phone: 35-62-09-15).

Soccer – Rouen's soccer team, *FCR,* plays at the *Stade Robert-Diochon,* 48 Av. des Canadiens, Petit-Quevilly (phone: 35-72-16-25).

Squash – Squeeze into *Rouen Squash* (1 Quai Gaston-Boulet; phone: 35-89-47-80), if you've brought your racket.

Tennis – There are three outdoor courts across the river at the *Centre St-Sever La Maison* (10 Rue St-Julien; phone: 35-72-10-32). For indoor courts, try the *Tennis Club de l'Ile Lacroix* (Rue Stendhal; phone: 35-88-85-36).

 THEATER: The *Théâtre des Arts* (Rue du Docteur Rambert; phone: 35-71-41-36) is the place to see touring hits from Paris, variety shows, and plays put on by famous provincial troupes, besides opera, operetta, and ballet. Experimental theater and dance companies use the *Théâtre Maxime Gorki* (Rue Paul Doumer, in nearby Petit-Quevilly; phone: 35-72-67-55), though you are just as likely to catch a mime, an art exhibit, or a foreign film here. Similarly broad in scope is *L'Espace Duchamp-Villon* (Centre St-Sever; phone: 35-62-31-31), the home of theater, dance, music, and film. The *Théâtre des Deux Rives* (48 Rue Louis-Ricard; phone: 35-70-22-82) is a local company that mounts experimental and avant-garde productions, and occasionally produces some unconventional versions of French classics. One of Rouen's newest performing spaces, *Théâtre de L'Echarde* (16 Rue Flahaut; phone: 35-89-42-13), presents both classic and contemporary works.

 MUSIC: Rouen is a regional opera center; a season of, usually, eight operas plus six operettas is presented at the *Théâtre des Arts* (Rue du Docteur Rambert; phone: 35-98-50-98). *L'Espace Duchamp-Villon* (Centre St-Sever; phone: 35-62-31-31) has an annual program of concerts in which such international artists as Jean-Pierre Rampal perform with the *Orchestre de Chambre de Haute Normandie* and other local groups. A summer program of organ recitals, along with chamber music, takes place on the organ of the Eglise St-Maclou each July and August (for information, call 35-70-84-90). The *Salle Ste-Croix des Pelletiers* (Rue Ste-Croix des Pelletiers; phone: 35-71-59-90 or 35-08-69-00) is used for classical concerts, including performances by young prize winners of international competitions appearing under the auspices of the *Rencontres Internationales de Musique en Normandie* (phone: 35-71-43-61). The best jazz in Rouen is organized by *Rouen Jazz Action* (for information, call 35-98-15-91), which arranges appearances by well-known artists.

 NIGHTCLUBS and NIGHTLIFE: Paris it ain't, nor, for that matter, Nice, Lyons, or Marseilles. Still, the disco habit has hit Rouen. At *La Bohème* (12 Pl. St-Amand; phone: 35-71-53-99), expect an older crowd and the music to be mellower than that of *Crazy Boy* (16 Av. de Bretagne; phone: 35-03-29-36). *Sunset Boulevard* (66 Rte. de Bonsecours; phone: 35-71-12-18) boasts distorted mirrors as part of its idiosyncratic decor, making one question the rather strict dress code. The couples at the *Green Onions Café* (29 Bd. des Belges; phone: 35-70-00-75) are generally over 30. There is a restaurant here, too.

BEST IN TOWN

 CHECKING IN: Because Rouen is only an hour from the hundreds of hotels in Paris and less than an hour from the scores of fine hostelries along the Normandy coast, it has become a city that people visit rather than stay in overnight. The result is a dearth of first-rate hotels, especially in the expensive and moderate categories. Only a very few of the 40-some hotels have toilets and a bath or shower in every room. Others may have both in some rooms, a toilet and bidet in some, a shower and bidet in others, and some have rooms with just a washbasin. Many rooms have no facilities at all, though usually they are just "down the hall." Expensive means more than $85 for a double room with toilet and bath or shower. Moderate means $60 to $85; inexpensive, less than $60. In the moderate and inexpensive categories, accommodations are available at lower prices for anyone prepared to share some or all facilities.

Pullman Albane – In the heart of all that is interesting in Rouen, it is astounding how well this hotel fits into the old quarter. With 121 rooms, it has almost every amenity — mini-bars, TV sets, telex service — expected in an up-to-the-minute hostelry, yet you can sit on your burgundy bedspread and look out into streets redolent of the Middle Ages. Service at the front desk is sometimes distracted, though never quite rude, and all staff members who meet the public speak English. Major credit cards accepted. Rue de la Croix-de-Fer (phone: 35-52-69-52; fax: 35-89-41-46). Expensive.

Carmes – This centrally located property retains the cozy, intimate feel of an old family hotel while offering the comforts of 15 modern rooms with baths. Major credit cards accepted. 33 Pl. des Carmes (phone: 35-71-92-31). Moderate.

Colin's – A contemporary 48-room hostelry, tucked into a medieval courtyard, that offers the most modern comforts in Rouen's charming Old Town. There's a bar, a garden court, and a garage. Ask for a room with a view of the city's rooftops. Major credit cards accepted. 15 Rue de la Pie (phone: 35-71-00-88; fax: 35-70-75-94). Moderate.

Dieppe – Close to the station and 10 minutes by foot from Old Rouen, this establishment has two wings. The older has the atmosphere of a far from sumptuous pre-war place. The newer wing is spare, clean-cut, and functional, with prints and the odd antique to alleviate what might otherwise be a rather spartan atmosphere. All 41 rooms have toilets and baths or showers. The hotel's *Le Quatre Saisons* (see *Eating Out*) is one of the city's better eating places. Major credit cards accepted. Pl. Bernard-Tissot (phone: 35-71-96-00; fax: 35-89-65-21). Moderate.

Le Manoir de St-Adrien – A few miles outside of Rouen, this turn-of-the-century, Anglo-Normande–style manor house with 18 tastefully appointed guestrooms is located in a wooded setting overlooking the Seine. It is half-timbered and quaint outside, with a cozy charm inside. The restaurant serves traditional regional dishes. Major credit cards accepted. 6 Chemin de la Source, St-Adrien (phone: 35-23-32-00; telex: 771649). Moderate.

La Cathédrale – The most famous and colorful hotel in old Rouen is near the cathedral in a quiet, narrow street known for its old houses. There's nothing uniform about any of the 24 rooms: some are Norman rustic, some vaguely Mediterranean, some Directoire. Repeat visitors ask for the ones looking into the flower-filled courtyard. Unfortunately, you cannot dine in this picturesque setting, as there is no restaurant. Major credit cards accepted. 12 Rue St-Romain (phone: 35-71-57-95; telex: 180224F). Moderate to inexpensive.

Gros-Horloge – The elegance has faded somewhat from the Louis XVI furnishings, and the hotel's arcade entrance is cluttered with pinball machines, but its 62 rooms are comfortable and clean. Rooms on the Rue du Gros-Horloge offer a unique closeup of the famous clock. Major credit cards accepted. 91 Rue du Gros-Horloge (phone: 35-70-41-41; fax: 35-88-44-45). Moderate to inexpensive.

Paris – On a nondescript street running down from the Seine, this place is comfortable; breakfast — served either in bed or in the large, salon-style front room — doesn't skimp on coffee. The beds are big, and most of the 22 rooms have a private bath and shower. Parking available. 12-14 Rue de la Champmeslé (phone: 35-70-09-26). Moderate to inexpensive.

La Cache-Ribaud – If it's character you're after, this is it. The 9 bedrooms are wallpapered in the autumnal colors — lots of russets, oranges, and dun browns — found all over Normandy, and they are generally rather cramped, dominated by huge armoires and double beds. Some have washbasins, but for most the facilities are down the hall, which is not too much of an imposition considering that this is like a large family house. The restaurant of the same name downstairs (see *Eating Out*) is beautiful to look at. Major credit cards accepted. 10 Rue du Tambour (phone: 35-71-04-82; fax: 35-07-77-00). Inexpensive.

Lisieux – Five minutes from the cathedral in the postwar complex close to the Seine, here is another hotel of little interior character compensated by a very pleasant management. The 30 rooms are clean and comfortable. Major credit cards accepted. 4 Rue de la Savonnerie (phone: 35-71-87-73; fax: 35-89-31-52). Inexpensive.

Normandie – This small, attractive property with 23 rooms in the heart of the Old Town is much favored by nostalgic alumni of the University of Rouen. Some of the plumbing is picturesque, but it usually is efficient. Major credit cards accepted. 19 Rue du Bec (phone: 35-71-55-77; fax: 35-88-92-36). Inexpensive.

■ **Note:** Most of the major modern French hotel chains such as Ibis are represented in Rouen, many of them located around the periphery of the city at sites accessible to motorists and with parking. One of the newer ones is the *Altéa Champs de Mars* (Av. Aristide-Briand on Pl. Champ du Mars; phone: 35-52-42-32; fax: 35-08-15-06). It is in the expensive to moderate price category and accepts major credit cards.

EATING OUT: Rouen is not the ideal place for dieting. This is, after all, Normandy, synonymous with cream and butter. Duck, ham, rabbit, or hare poached in cider, and desserts laced with calvados, are ubiquitous. Norman cheeses, such as camembert, livarot, and pont-l'evêque, turn up in crêpes and sauces in addition to being served with fresh apples and pears at the end of a meal. Some of the great fishing grounds of the Channel are less than an hour away, so the city has a way with seafood. An *assiette de fruits de mer* — a platter of fresh seafood that includes crayfish, crabs, oysters, clams, mussels, winkles, and two kinds of shrimp — frequently is offered as a first course. Try it at least once. Turbot, sole, and brill, in cream sauces and occasionally, once again, in cider, are favorite dishes. Though Normandy is not a prime wine region, it is nonetheless France, and Rouen's wine cellars can be spectacular. But cider, the local brew, often displaces the *grands crus* of Bordeaux and Burgundy in the hearts of the Rouennais. This is not apple juice but hard cider, harder than most Americans have ever experienced, and it can be bought in bottles in most restaurants. The bottled cider is *doux* (sweet) and slightly carbonated; and real aficionados will tolerate only cider served in *pichets* (stone jugs), which is still and very dry and sometimes quite potent. For those who prefer cider on the dry side, be sure to request *brut.*

At restaurants below rated expensive, dinner for two excluding wine and drinks will come to more than $90. Moderate means $55 to $90; inexpensive, less than $55. Service usually is included.

Le Beffroy – Very Norman in atmosphere and one of the top dining spots in town (one Michelin star). The fish dishes are superb, as are the classic *canette à la rouennaise* and the apple desserts. Closed Sundays, Mondays, and August. Reservations necessary. Major credit cards accepted. 15 Rue Beffroy (phone: 35-71-55-27). Expensive.

Les Capucines – This suburban place is in a modern building of little character, and the dining room is decorated in the autumnal tones that are common in Normandy. It's the duck pâté, apple sherbet, and braised sweetbreads with celery (and much besides) that make the 15-minute ride worthwhile. Closed Sunday evenings. Reservations necessary. Major credit cards accepted. 16 Rue Jean-Macé, Le Petit-Quevilly, southwest of central Rouen (phone: 35-72-62-34; fax: 35-03-23-84). Expensive.

La Couronne – The most famous restaurant in Rouen and reputedly the oldest in France. Don't be deceived by the timber and corbels of the exterior; the façade is barely 50 years old. But the interior is ancient and lovely, with exposed beams, carved woodwork, medieval porcelain in glass cases, and — in fall and winter — a fire that casts a warm glow over the pink napery and sienna ceilings. Duck *à la rouennaise* is the famous dish here, but many regulars prefer other local classics such as *pieds de mouton* (sheep's feet) and *cassolette d'homard* (lobster casserole with fresh vegetables). Open daily. Reservations advised. Major credit cards accepted. 31 Pl. du Vieux-Marché (phone: 35-71-40-90; fax: 35-71-05-78). Expensive.

Dufour – A huge stone fireplace, exposed beams, antique statues of saints in wall niches, and a vast display of fresh seafood in one corner; this is the sort of place where you expect to see the three musketeers drop by any minute to sample huge *assiette de fruits de mer,* oysters, *coquilles, paupiette de saumon fumé aux huîtres* (smoked salmon with oysters), the duck pâté, or duck *rouennais.* It's all worth fighting over. Closed Sunday nights, Mondays, and August. Reservations advised. Major credit cards accepted. 67 *bis* Rue St-Nicolas (phone: 35-71-90-62). Expensive.

Gill – Gilles Tournadre, the young chef, has cultivated the culinary art of subtlety, making even simple dishes like *raviolis de langoustines* or duck liver with leeks seem special. The *ragoût de homard* (lobster stew) and *panaché de poissons* (mixture of fish) both come highly praised. The stark white decor in its quarters on Quai de la Bourse is an anomaly in Rouen. Two Michelin stars. Closed Sundays, Mondays at noon, the first 2 weeks of January, and the last week of August through mid-September. Reservations necessary. Major credit cards accepted. 9 Quai de la Bourse (phone: 35-71-16-14; fax: 35-71-96-91). Expensive.

Le Quatre Saisons – A classic example of the truism that in France, unprepossessing-looking buildings close to railways can house exceptional restaurants. A favorite with discerning business types, its kitchen turns out a wonderful salad of smoked fish in sour cream, a splendid duck pâté, and a much-admired pressed duck. Open daily. Reservations advised. Major credit cards accepted. *Hôtel de Dieppe,* Pl. Bernard-Tissot (phone: 35-71-96-00). Expensive.

La Butte – In Bonsecours, 2 miles (3 km) outside of Rouen, this enchanting country inn of brick and beams, with traditional Norman furnishings, merits a Michelin star for specialties such as *salade tiède de homard frais* (warm, fresh lobster salad) and *andouillette de Vire aux chou rouge* (tripe sausage from Vire with red cabbage). Chef Pierre Hervé manages to wed the traditional and the modern. Closed Sunday and Wednesday evenings, Thursdays, during *Christmas* holidays, and August. Reservations necessary. Major credit cards accepted. 69 Rte. Paris (phone: 35-80-43-11). Expensive to moderate.

L'Episode – One of Rouen's newest dining establishments, conveniently located between the cathedral and the Gros-Horloge. The surroundings may be a bit cramped, but the portions are ample, and if delicacies such as *pommes de terre tièdes aux aiguillettes de canard* (warm potatoes with thin slices of duck breast) don't warm the cockles of your heart, then the engaging staff probably will. Closed Sundays. Reservations essential. Major credit cards accepted. 37 Rue aux Ours (phone: 35-89-01-91). Expensive to moderate.

Les Nymphais – This dining spot features seafood and duck dishes, such as *canard à la rouennaise.* The setting is the former home of one of Normandy's best-known restaurants, the late *Bertrand Warin.* Closed Sunday evenings. Reservations advised. Major credit cards accepted. 7-9 Rue de la Pie (phone: 35-89-26-69). Expensive to moderate.

Les P'tits Parapluies – The Belle Epoque interior of this small, charming restaurant once housed an umbrella shop (*boutique de parapluies*). Hot oysters with salmon roe and *pigeon rôti* (roast squab) will make you forget the rain. Closed Sundays, Monday lunch, and the first 3 weeks of August. Reservations unnecessary. Major credit cards accepted. 46 Rue Bourg-l'Abbé (phone: 35-88-55-26). Expensive to moderate.

La Toque d'Or – A warren of rooms with whitewashed walls, beams going every which way, and flagstone corridors make this the most rustic restaurant in Old Rouen. It's possible to eat here for as little as $15 a head, but dining well on a brioche of salmon with herbs, sweetbreads in port, salad, cream cheese, and *crème caramel* costs more. Open daily. Reservations necessary. Major credit cards accepted. 11 Pl. du Vieux-Marché (phone: 35-71-46-29; fax: 35-71-79-82). Expensive to moderate.

Le Bistrot d'Adrian – A pleasant spot to eat outdoors looking across to the modern Eglise Ste-Jeanne-d'Arc. Although the service can be a little nervous when it's busy, the fish soup, calf's head, and many other items are fine. The menu changes weekly. Open daily. Reservations advised. Major credit cards accepted. 37 Pl. du Vieux-Marché (phone: 35-71-57-73). Moderate.

Le Boeuf Couronné – Terrine of snails and salmon (combined, that is) and oysters cooked in cream make dining here an unusual pleasure. As befits the name, there are also better than average beef dishes. Closed Saturday dinner and Sundays. Reservations advised. Major credit cards accepted. 151 Rue Beauvoisine (phone: 35-88-68-28). Moderate.

La Cache-Ribaud – Atmosphere has run riot in this beguiling old hotel dining place. Beams are exposed, like skeletons, on all sides, the intervening plaster and brick having generally been removed to add light and space to the dining rooms. Try the parsleyed ham, the duck in cider vinegar, or the *fricassée de poulet au citron* (stewed chicken with lemon). Closed Sunday dinner. Reservations unnecessary. No credit cards accepted. 10 Rue du Tambour (phone: 35-71-04-82). Moderate.

Au Chat Bleu – It's hard to miss this busy, popular, and sometimes claustrophobic eatery: The blue lights outside gleam across Place Beauvoisine. Seafood is basically the thing, especially the English Channel version of bouillabaisse served on Fridays. Closed Sundays. Reservations advised. Major credit cards accepted. 113 Pl. Beauvoisine (phone: 35-71-22-76). Moderate.

La Marmite – Dining by candlelight until 2 AM at this small, comfortable spot is very relaxing. Specialties include duck in cider, lamb with white beans, and a casserole of sweetbreads with *cèpes,* a particularly tasty variety of mushroom. Closed Sundays. Reservations advised. Major credit cards accepted. 3 Rue Florence (phone: 35-71-75-55). Moderate.

Mirabelle – Another favorite for dining under the stars on a summer night. The accent is Alsatian, the *choucroute* of various kinds served in generous portions. Open daily. Reservations advised. Major credit cards accepted. 3 Pl. du Vieux-Marché (phone: 35-71-58-21). Moderate.

La Poule au Pot – The place to go is the rotisserie — the grillroom of this bar-hotel-restaurant. The fare consists of fine examples of regional specialties such as rabbit, duck, lamb, or veal served in cream or calvados. Seafood dishes also are plentiful. Closed Mondays. Reservations unnecessary. Major credit cards accepted. 13-15 Rue du Père-Adam (phone: 35-71-09-53). Moderate.

La Rose des Sables – The queen of the couscous houses, the name means the rose of the sands (whatever *that* means) and the restaurant is appropriately decorated in a sandy pink. In addition to couscous, it will produce a complete sheep on request. Open daily. Reservations unnecessary. Major credit cards accepted. 93 Rue Bouvreuil (phone: 35-07-00-39). Moderate.

Charles – An old café transformed into a trendy bistro by one of Rouen's most successful restaurateurs. There is a simple menu of cold items, including smoked salmon, carpaccio, and foie gras, as well as a daily hot special. Whiskey, exotic drink concoctions, and wines by the glass are served at the wooden bar and at classic café tables in the front. Open daily. Reservations unnecessary. Major credit cards accepted. 6 Rue du Général-Giraud (phone: 35-70-73-39). Moderate to inexpensive.

Pain, Amour et Fantaisie – A funky little tea salon–cum–boutique, offering a variety of English cakes, scones, tarts — savory and sweet — and salads. Shelves are cluttered with teas, Crabtree & Evelyn jams, dried flowers, and other items for purchase. Open daily, except Sundays and Mondays, from 11 AM to 6:30 PM. Reservations unnecessary. No credit cards accepted. 25 Rue Cauchoise (phone: 35-07-52-74). Moderate to inexpensive.

La Petite Auberge – An undiscovered pearl worthy of attention. The tipoff is how shy the waiters are with foreigners, meaning they don't often cater to the tourist trade. Seafood is the specialty, and the fish soup and mussels in cream are recommended, though the chicken with lemon and curry also is excellent. The size of the portions is breathtaking, and if you didn't see similar quantities of food all around you, you'd think the chef wished you abdominal harm. Closed Monday dinner. Reservations unnecessary. Major credit cards accepted. 164 Rue Martainville (phone: 35-70-80-18). Moderate to inexpensive.

Les Flandres – Another ideal spot for those in a hurry, although the generous helping of *moules* (mussels) does take time to consume. Entrecôte steaks and super French fries are typical of the menu. Closed Saturday nights, Sundays, and August. Reservations unnecessary. In the *Hôtel des Flandres,* 5 Rue des Bons-Enfants (phone: 35-98-45-16). Inexpensive.

Grande Poste – A local institution, with waiters à l'ancienne and a café-brasserie style that caters to patrons of all ages, at all hours, every day of the year. Reservations unnecessary. Major credit cards accepted. 43 Rue Jeanne-D'Arc (phone: 35-70-08-70). Inexpensive.

Le Grutli – This popular brasserie serves chops, *coquilles,* salads, and a much-praised steak tartare. Open daily. Reservations unnecessary. Major credit cards accepted. 38 Rue de la République (phone: 35-71-09-34). Inexpensive.

Le Long-Van – One of the more elegant Vietnamese eateries in town, with a sleek, wooden latticework ceiling and wall-to-wall bamboo screens. Traditional Vietnamese and Thai dishes are served, though the menu leans toward the ocean. Portions are generous — more than you'd ever be served in a Vietnamese restaurant in Paris. Dinner only; closed Sundays. Reservations unnecessary. Major credit cards accepted. 51 Rue de la République (phone: 35-98-09-65). Inexpensive.

La Tarte Tatin – A *crêperie,* though a rather smart one. Camembert, ham, creamed mushrooms, and crab are among the many fillings available in the beautifully prepared crêpes. It is also a *salon de thé.* Closed Sundays. Reservations unnecessary. Major credit cards accepted. 99 Rue de la Vicomté (phone: 35-89-35-73). Inexpensive.

La Tour de Beurre – This small restaurant is, basically, another *crêperie.* There is a pleasant terrace for sunny days. Closed Sundays. Reservations unnecessary. Major credit cards accepted. 20 Quai Pierre-Corneille (phone: 35-71-95-17). Inexpensive.

Ty Breiz – An ancient, crooked house in the winding old quarter harbors this cozy crêperie, where bowls of cider and variety of simple crêpes are served for a simple price. Closed Sundays and Mondays. Reservations unnecessary. No reservations. No credit cards accepted. 5 Rue du Père-Adam (phone: 35-71-07-67). Inexpensive.

 BARS AND CAFÉS: Two favorites with young Rouennais and visitors are *Le Big Ben Pub,* in the shadow of the Gros-Horloge (30 Rue des Vergetiers; phone: 35-88-44-50), and *La Taverne* (11 Rue St-Amand; phone: 35-88-51-38), a Rouen landmark that counted Sartre among its patrons in the 1930s. At *Le Bateau Ivre* (17 Rue des Sapins; phone: 35-70-09-05), there occasionally are visiting singers and jazz groups. For softer music in a Louis XV atmosphere, try *Le Club XV* (81 Rue Ecuyère; phone: 35-98-60-41). For a nightcap in an intimate ambience (with fellow countrymen usually on hand), there is the *Bar Pullman,* the cocktail bar of the *Pullman Albane* (Rue de la Croix-de-Fer) and the *Altéa Champs de Mars* hotel (Av. Aristide-Briand; phone: 35-08-09-08) has a pleasant piano bar. Many of Rouen's bars stay open until 2 AM most nights of the week. Some close at least 1 day a week.

ST-TROPEZ

Rivaling Cannes as a favorite of the international set, St-Tropez first became famous when Brigitte Bardot made it her home during the 1950s. Her arrival turned a fishing port that had for centuries been a target for pirates and then for painters (such as Bonnard and Matisse) into the headquarters for a whole coterie of starlets, swingers, and spectators, including those ready to give anything to be part of the action. When topless sunbathing appeared — it is said to have originated here at Tahiti Plage — it certainly did nothing to downplay the town's already considerable notoriety; rather, this curious folkway, as reported in newpapers, magazines, and TV programs around the globe, pinpointed St-Tropez on the map for would-be hedonists everywhere. The miracle of St-Tropez is how well it has survived its success. The charm of its setting remains, its marvelous climate — give or take a *mistral* bluster or two around August 15 — endures, and its mystique always seems to triumph over the formidable menace of the annual high summer invasion.

In May and early June, and again in September and October, St-Tropez is at half pace and a joy. Not so in July and August, when people who do not like crowds of any kind should give the St-Tropez mob scene a very wide berth. But those who do brave the traffic jam into town will find the multitudes at the portside cafés and boutiques magically endowed, if only for the short season of their stay, with a style and high spirit many of them knew they possessed. The St-Tropez look, whatever its ingredients, mixes them with a certain aesthetic flair and delightfully meretricious chic that are seductive to even the most blasé visitors. For years, for instance, the town set trends in summer fashions, with no apparent end to their colorful craziness, and while this heavy responsibility is now more evenly shared with other resorts, the clothes still manage to look their sexiest when worn in St-Tropez at six in the evening at *Sénéquier,* the perennially "in" café on the waterfront.

Like many another Mediterranean port, St-Tropez has seen the destruction of pillage and war, but it has resisted the equally devastating assaults of modern real estate development much better than some other coastal towns. The reconstruction after World War II was carried out by a municipality always sensitive to the enchanting allure of old buildings, especially such old buildings as the pink and ocher facades that used to line the main harbor and, in copy, do so once again. Elsewhere, the narrow streets of cream stone houses and the broad main square shaded by plane trees for the market and for the *boules* players are unmistakably Provençal. Considering the kind of commercial exploitation that St-Tropez's fame had every reason to attract, the new architects have kept splendid faith with the old; and fast-food protrusions and condominial blockhouses have been kept to an inconspicuous minimum.

One very good reason that the original appearance of the town escaped wholesale distortion is St-Tropez's sheer inaccessibility at the end of a rocky, hilly peninsula. No train nor airport serves it, and people who come have to really want to; there's no simply passing by. It's a tribute to its charm that all those thousands are still prepared to struggle along the winding mountain route across the Massif des Maures or along the recently widened coastal route to the one road in — and out. The only other way in, and certainly the most romantic way in for first-timers or for sentimental regulars, is by sea just before sunset; even if you don't have a yacht, there are boats from Port Grimaud or Ste-Maxime. You'll be eternally grateful if you can make your first glimpse of town that view of the port from the Gulf of St-Tropez rather than from the traffic jam on N98 (although the road's expansion has eased up the car congestion).

In the old days, everyone came by sea. First, the Greeks. The town that Bardot made famous in the 20th century originally was settled, so the story goes, by another sex goddess, Phrynea, a model and mistress of the great Athenian sculptor Praxiteles. That first Greek settlement, Athenopolis, under the Romans became Heraclea, a natural port of call for ships riding the current from Italy to Spain. On May 17 in the year AD 68 (like all really good legends, there's a precise date for it), the current brought in a boat with a weird trio of passengers — a headless Roman centurion accompanied by a dog and a cockerel. The Roman was Torpes, a converted Christian beheaded by the Emperor Nero. The dog and cockerel were sent along, as was the custom, to devour his body. But they left the martyr — St. Torpes — intact, prompting pious fishermen to make a shrine that became St-Tropez. Torpes is still venerated in Pisa, which claims to have the martyr's head, and the anniversary of his arrival is celebrated annually during *Les Bravades* — May 16 through 18 — in St-Tropez by taking the statue of him (with the dog and the cockerel) out of the parish church and parading with it around the town. The city elects a captain to lead the parade. A similar festival takes place on June 15; this time to celebrate the city's victory over a Spanish fleet that tried to capture St-Tropez back in 1637.

In the Middle Ages, St-Tropez was prey to Saracen pirates from North Africa and the eastern Mediterranean and underwent continuous destruction and reconstruction until Raffaele Garezzio arrived with 60 families from Genoa in 1470, authorized by the rulers of Provence to guarantee its defense in exchange for tax exemption. St-Tropez thus became an independent republic, governed by a council made up of the heads of all families and two elected consuls, until Louis XIV incorporated it into France in 1672. For a few centuries thereafter it remained a quiet little fishing village, then Guy de Maupassant wrote about "this charming and simple daughter of the sea," which he visited on a Mediterranean cruise in 1888. His description attracted the attention of the painter Paul Signac, who made it his home, followed by Pierre Bonnard, Charles Camoin, Henri Matisse for a short while, and later André Dunoyer de Segonzac, all drawn by the bewitching light of this isolated port. The painters in turn attracted Colette to make her summer home here in the 1920s. Decades before it was to delight the paparazzi with its topless, even bottomless customs, St-Tropez shocked the outside world because this emancipated novelist went around with *bare legs*. The influx of celebrity-hungry tourists drove her away in 1938, and, not for the last time, people lamented that St-Tropez wasn't what it used to be.

In August 1944, the Germans nearly destroyed it completely. Faced with American landings along the Mediterranean coast, they blew up the whole port, leaving only a few of the old houses standing behind the Hôtel de Ville (Town Hall). The possibility that St-Tropez would never be the same again was indeed real. Instead, it was lovingly restored, and the returning artists, this time joined by film stars and pop singers, discovered the added pleasures of the nearby, hitherto deserted beaches. Jean Cocteau and the St-Germain-des-Prés crowd flocked here in the early 1950s. In 1953, the director Roger Vadim filmed *And God Created Woman,* starring a (for that time) shockingly nubile Brigitte Bardot, on location on the white sands of Pampelonne Beach. Bardot made her home in a secluded beachfront villa, La Madrague, and she and her succession of playboy lovers created another St-Tropez legend. (She still lives there and has turned her estate into an animal refuge, in keeping with her interest in animal rights.) The town soon was swarming with blond, pouty-lipped, long-legged lookalikes trailed — with poodle-like devotion — by bronzed Nordic gods.

And ever since, hordes of superbly narcissistic Scandinavians, Germans, Britons, Italians, Americans, and not a few French have come to look for each other at sunset on the quay, to dance and make love till dawn, sleep in the sun, and return to the quay the next evening to do it all over again. The 5,700 Tropezians, who've known other invasions, watch it all with a bemused eye — some fishermen, a lot of hotel, restaurant, and shop owners and artists, who are by no means all Signacs and Matisses but who do like painting in the sun. They know the place is infuriatingly irresistible.

ST-TROPEZ AT-A-GLANCE

SEEING THE CITY: If you can't come into St-Tropez by sea, be sure to make your way as quickly as possible to the Môle Jean-Réveille, the pier that runs along the north side of the harbor. Glance back frequently at the unfolding panorama of portside houses embracing yachts and fishing boats. At the lighthouse on the end of the pier, you can take in the Old Town at the foot of the Citadelle on the eastern heights and, to the west across the Golfe de St-Tropez, the castle ruins of Grimaud set against a mountain plateau, the Massif des Maures. The play of light at daybreak is dramatically different from that at sunset, so catch both. For a rear view of the town and gulf, walk up to the ramparts of the Citadelle above the very pretty cemetery. The ultimate pleasure here is to combine the view with one of the concerts held in the summer.

SPECIAL PLACES: St-Tropez is a fishing village turned resort, so it's short on monuments. If you're not staying here — that is, if you're popping in only for a quick visit — you'll find it won't take long to see it all. Except for the beaches, everything is within easy walking distance of everything else, and even the Citadelle requires only the slightest extra effort to make it up the hill. Those staying longer can see what there is to see in a series of walks — or rambles — before and after beach time. Never forget, however, that in St-Tropez people are a very important part of the scene nor that wherever you go (and on the beach in particular), *you* are part of the scenery.

The Port – Fishing is secondary now with only about 20 fisherfolk left, but the port is still the soul of the town. Most of the social and much of the commercial life takes place along the quays, and the spectacle around the cafés, boutiques, and the boats themselves is the essential sight of St-Tropez. Smaller boats — fishing vessels and such — anchor around Quai Frédéric-Mistral, protected by the Môle Jean-Réveille. Luxury yachts, with the captains and their ladies drinking champagne at sundown, have choice moorings around the junction of Quai Jean-Jaurès and Quai Suffren. Farther along, a bronze statue pays tribute to Vice-Admiral Pierre André de Suffren, who grew up in St-Tropez to become one of the great sailors of 18th-century France. Along the west side of the harbor, artists display their works on the Quai de l'Epi.

Musée de l'Annonciade – It comes as a surprise to some people consumed with the material hedonism of the place to discover that St-Tropez has one of France's most exquisite little museums of modern art. Set back on the west side of the harbor, the *Annonciade* is a deconsecrated 16th-century chapel of the White Penitent friars, beautifully converted to a bright 2-story museum to display the collection of the connoisseur Georges Grammont: French paintings and sculpture spanning the half-century from 1890 to 1940. Around Maillol's sensual bronzes hang some fines canvases of Signac, Matisse, Bonnard, Seurat, Derain, Braque, Van Dongen, and Vlaminck. Some of the best pieces are studies of St-Tropez itself. Closed Tuesdays and November; admission charge. Pl. Georges-Grammont, Quai l'Epi (phone: 94-97-04-01).

Old Town – One of the most ancient parts of town, La Glaye was spared the dynamite of the German army in 1944 and offers a delightful alternative to the quayside bustle. Start at the Tour du Portalet, where old men sit on their *banc des mensonges* ("bench of lies") spinning yarns of fish and other wild creatures that got away. The tower is part of the old fortifications in which the houses themselves, built right out of the rock on the little bay of La Glaye, still present a formidable barrier on the seaward side. A couple of blocks inland, the Place de la Mairie is graced by a remarkably unbombastic Hôtel de Ville (Town Hall) and, opposite, by a house with a huge, splendidly ornate carved wooden door brought back by a local sailor from the Arab colony in Zanzibar. Northeast of the harbor.

Eglise Paroissiale (Parish Church) – This dignified, neo-classical 19th-century building with its simple bell tower dating from 1634 is most notable for housing in the chapel left of the entrance the bizarre bust of the city's patron saint. The gaily colored wooden sculpture of the mustachioed St. Torpes (or Tropez, if you prefer) wears a helmet and bejeweled crown, a bemedaled sash, and a slightly dazed look — perhaps because beneath this bust is another version of him *without* his head, watched over by the dog and cockerel in the boat that brought him to town. He's also surrounded by ex-voto gifts, including some smashed blunderbusses and a bosun's whistle. At *Christmas*, a beautiful 19th-century nativity scene with Provençal figures called *santons* is set up in the church. Rue du Clocher, in the Old Town.

Place des Lices – The town's main square is the traditional gathering place of true Tropezians — both year-round residents and seasonal regulars — who appreciate that moment at the end of the afternoon when the shade of the plane trees and the click of the *petanques* provide the perfect setting for a good cool *pastis*. There's a morning market Tuesdays and Saturdays for fruit, vegetables, old clothes, and older furniture. It's also the occasional site of the itinerant amusement park and the place that reminds you that St-Tropez is as much a village as an international playground. Inland from Quai Suffren and identified on some maps by its little-used newer name, Pl. Carnot.

Musée de la Citadelle – On the eastern edge of town, the fortress that France's Henri IV ordered built at the end of the 16th century was the unpopular symbol of

St-Tropez's transformation from an independent republic into just another French town, an assertion of military authority over the region that was a constant bone of contention between Provençal nobles and the French monarchy. Its most recent military function was as the Germans' last bastion of resistance to the American invasion of 1944; Tropezians participated in its recapture on August 15. The hexagonal 16th-century dungeon now houses the *Musée Navale,* full of St-Tropez's history and of Mediterranean shipping, illustrated by an attractive collection of sailor's paraphernalia, ship models, engravings, paintings, and documents. They include a graphic account of the Tropezians' heroic routing of a Spanish fleet in 1637. Closed Thursdays and mid-November through mid-December; admission charge. On the eastern edge of town, in the Citadelle St-Tropez (phone: 94-97-06-53).

Beaches – The dazzling stretches of white sand and umbrella pines are just outside town but absolutely inseparable from the total idea of St-Tropez. *This* is where Vadim created Bardot. The elite arrive at the beach by boat. For ordinary people who walk, the easiest to get to is the Bouillabaisse, a popular family beach a quick 10 minutes southwest of the harbor. Almost as close, going east, is Les Graniers, favored by Tropezians during their lunch break. More fashionable are the Tahiti, around the southern side of the peninsula, and its glorious extension, the 3-mile-long Pampelonne, long enough to dilute the mob scene. These are a short car or taxi ride, or a more leisurely bike ride, 2½ miles (4 km) along the road toward Ramatuelle and are served by some good and a few terrible beach restaurants. The beach mattress rentals may seem a little high at Tahiti and Pampelonne, but the people are more beautiful. For the too mature or exhausted, gin rummy under the umbrella pines is strongly recommended.

■**EXTRA SPECIAL:** In St-Tropez, all is vanity and it is most properly indulged at the café *Sénéquier* (phone: 94-97-00-90). What counts here is not just the place, but the time. If this town is the ultimate in street theater, the play must be seen from the beginning. So between 8 and 9:30 in the morning (at any rate, no later than 10), have breakfast in one of *Sénéquier*'s scarlet canvas chairs at the scarlet tables at the hub of the port. With a newspaper from the nearby *Maison de la Presse* and coffee and a fresh croissant or brioche from the café's own bakery, watch the performers, eccentric and otherwise, as this craziest of resorts comes to life (and a few of last night's owls head for bed). By 10:30 to 11 the mob is up and you'll no longer see the wonderful wood for the trees. Beach time. Act Two begins around 6 PM. Return to *Sénéquier* for the ritual *café glacé* (iced coffee) and watch the same crowd, a little more tanned than at breakfast, parade their stuff and prepare for their nights.

SOURCES AND RESOURCES

TOURIST INFORMATION: St-Tropez's portside Office du Tourisme (Quai Jean-Jaurès; phone: 94-97-45-21) also covers the nearby towns of Ramatuelle and Gassin. Open daily, except on Sundays from mid-October through March. It provides maps and brochures, details of hotel and camping accommodations, and programs of local events, and it is open year round. Inquire here for information about hotels and restaurants, museums, concerts, shopping, and sports for St-Tropez and surrounding villages. Another tourist office is at the Gare Routière (Av. du 8 Mai 1945; phone: 94-97-41-21).

Local Coverage – *Nice Matin* and *Var Matin,* competing regional daily newspapers, both have a special St-Tropez and Ste-Maxime edition, good for gossip.

TELEPHONE: The city code for St-Tropez is 94, which is incorporated into all local 8-digit numbers. When calling a number in St-Tropez from the Paris region (including the Ile-de-France), dial 16, wait for a dial tone, then dial the 8-digit number. When calling a number from outside Paris, dial only the 8-digit number. When calling from the US, dial 33 (which is the country code), followed by the 8-digit number.

GETTING AROUND: Bicycle – A bicycle or a motorcycle is the best way to beat the traffic jams. Rent from *Mas* (Rue Josef Quaranta; phone: 94-97-00-60).

Boat – For transport by boat contact *Messageries Maritimes du Golfe,* known as *MMG* (Quai Jean-Jaurès; phone: 94-96-51-00). Or rent your own, with or without captain, from *Suncap Company* (Passage du Port; phone: 94-97-11-23). For those who like living in style, *Sportmer* (8 Pl. Blanqui; phone: 94-97-32-33) rents houseboats.

Bus – Buses serve the surrounding villages of Grimaud, Gassin, Cogolin, Ramatuelle, La Garde-Freinet, and Croix-Valmer, as well as the railroad station in St-Raphaël. For information, contact the tourist office at Gare Routière (Av. du 8 Mai 1945; phone: 94-97-45-21).

Car Rental – During the summer months, it's advisable to make a reservation well ahead of arrival, as demand is heavy. Among the major companies are *Avis* (Av. de 8 Mai 1945; phone: 94-97-03-10); *Europcar* (Résidence du Port; phone: 94-97-15-41 or 94-97-21-59); and *Hertz* (Rue Nouvelle Poste; phone: 94-97-22-01).

Taxi – Pick one up by the Quai de l'Epi or call 94-97-05-27.

Train – There is no train service to St-Tropez. St-Raphaël (see *Bus* above) is the closest station on the rail line. For information, call *SNCF (Société Nationale des Chemins de Fer Français* (phone: 93-99-50-50 in Cannes; 94-95-13-89 for reservations in St-Raphaël).

SPECIAL EVENTS: Amid all the cosmopolitan frolic and the undeniably lucrative business of catering to tourists, the Tropezians celebrate a few annual events strictly for themselves. Visitors may watch, but there's no attempt to jazz up the folklore for the foreigners — which is what makes *Les Bravades* (May 16 through 18) all the more attractive. The first and most important of these uniquely Tropezian commemorations, the *Grande Bravade,* begins on May 16, the eve of the legendary arrival of St. Torpes. Following a tradition dating back to 1558, the polychrome wooden bust of the martyr is taken out of the parish church and paraded through the streets for 2½ days by gaily uniformed men firing off blunderbusses behind a band of fifes, bugles, and drums. Starting at the Place de la Mairie, it's a raucous celebration of civic pride punctuated by an occasional solemn blessing of the *bravadeurs'* antique arms and by the less solemn tippling of *pastis* or vermouth. A slightly less boisterous *Bravade des Espagnols,* on June 15, celebrates the Tropezians' victory over the hostile Spanish fleet in 1637.

On June 29, *St. Peter's Day,* fishermen celebrate at the old Port des Pêcheurs at the end of Rue de la Ponche. On August 14 and 15, Americans are particularly welcome for the anniversary of the 1944 landings and *Libération,* with fireworks and a midnight mass in the Chapelle Ste-Anne. There also are music-filled evenings scheduled throughout July, August, and September, as well as Provençal dancing, *boules* tournaments, and medieval jousting matches. At the end of September and beginning of October is a series of sailboat races called *La Nioulargue*.

SHOPPING: Resortwear, from sailor suits to monokinis, is the thing to buy here and, like fashion itself, an amazing number of shops in St-Tropez change from season to season — name, management, location. This often is not because of failure or success but, just like the fads, because of a whim. Many big Paris names are currently taking over in town, and though St-Tropez no longer dictates to other resorts what will or won't be worn on the beach or in the nightclubs each year, the flair remains, and the port provides the right ambience for the more outrageous clothes you might not risk back home.

Don't forget the Tuesday and Saturday morning markets at Place des Lices, good for clothing and antiques as well as for food and flowers. If you're around in late August or early September (it varies from year to year), don't miss the *Foire aux Antiquaires* (Antiques Fair) that also takes place at Place des Lices. Paintings can be bought from artists along the harbor.

There are three main shopping areas — the port, the galleries or *passages* between Quai Suffren and Place des Lices, and the Old Town around the Hôtel de Ville. As the "overnight successes" come and go, here are some of the mainstays.

Choses – Caters to the passing port trade — dresses, bathing suits, shirts, jeans, and T-shirts with this year's "look"; many of the fashions are unisex. Quai Jean Jaurès.

Daniel Crémieux – Great for men's shirts and classic casual wear. Passage du Port and Rue Gambetta.

Façonnable – For beachwear and sandals. Passage Gambetta.

Josiane Abrial – Specializes in silk, not only in slinky clothes, but also in grandly ornate bed linen. Rue Sibilli.

Les Petites Canailles – For children who follow their parents' fashion footsteps. 27 and 34 Rue Clémenceau.

Royal Navy – Offers somewhat classic clothes. 9 Rue de la Ponche.

SPORTS AND FITNESS: Other than people watching, the only serious spectator sport in town is *boules,* the court for which is Place des Lices.

Horseback Riding – The *Centre Hippique des Maures* is just outside town at Beauvallon (phone: 94-56-16-55).

Sailing and Windsurfing – The sailing school (*Ecole de Voile*) operates in July and August at the Baie des Canoubiers (phone: 94-97-12-58), and there is good windsurfing along the Pampelonne and Tahiti beaches. Learn to sail or windsurf at *La Moune* (phone: 94-97-71-05), and rent windsurfers at *Windsports* (Rue Paul-Roussel; phone: 94-97-43-25). Make sure not to go out when the mistral is blowing, you might have trouble getting back.

Scuba Diving – This is organized by *Les Plongeurs du Golfe,* whose boat is anchored off the Môle Jean-Réveille from June through September. Inquire at the *nouveau port* (new port) or call (phone: 94-97-08-39; at night, 94-79-27-77).

Tennis – Red clay courts, just like those at the *French Open.* Play and swim at *Tennis Club des Marres* (Rte. des Plages; phone: 94-97-26-68); *Tennis-Club de St-Tropez* (Rte. des Salins; phone: 94-97-80-76); or *US Tennis* (*UST;* Route des Plages; phone: 94-54-82-40).

MUSIC: Recitals and chamber music concerts are held at the Château de la Moutte, at the east end of the peninsula. The Office du Tourisme has details.

NIGHTCLUBS AND NIGHTLIFE: Most of the boîtes are super discos, distinguished from each other mainly by the people they let in or keep out, all with a sweet smile that leaves the banished with the surprisingly comfortable feeling that they wouldn't have been happy there anyway. The two smartest are both in the *Byblos* hotel: *Les Caves du Roy* (entrance off Place des Lices) offers a good live band in season for your gladdest rags; *Le Krak des Chevaliers* is a little more subdued (phone for both: 94-97-00-04). *La Spirale* (3 Rue du Four; phone: 94-97-07-56) prides itself on its exclusive taste and makes an interesting challenge for the not easily daunted — if they're pretty or amusing to look at. The *Papagayo* (Quai de l'Epi; phone: 94-97-07-56) has the most pleasingly insane atmosphere, Chinese exotica, and local eccentrics. *Le Bal* at the *Résidence du Nouveau Port* restaurant (Nouveau Port; phone: 94-97-14-70) is fun for all.

BEST IN TOWN

CHECKING IN: Considering the enduring appeal and celebrity of the resort, hotels in St-Tropez compare in price more than favorably with the rest of France. There is a good selection of expensive hotels, in the $125 and up range for a double room, but a majority are moderate, around $60 to $125, and a fair number are inexpensive at $25 to $60. For anything less expensive, inquire well in advance through the Office du Tourisme (phone: 94-97-45-21) about renting a furnished flat, available during the summer, or about camping and holiday villages (*villages de vacances*), available only around nearby Grimaud, Gassin, Ramatuelle, and La Garde-Freinet. The advice about booking far in advance for *all* accommodations applies here from June through mid-September.

Byblos – This manages to be a truly luxurious hotel without looking or feeling anything like the traditional "palaces" elsewhere along the Côte d'Azur. Built at the beginning of the 1970s and constantly modernizing its amenities to include Jacuzzis, a sauna, and air conditioning, it nevertheless retains the atmosphere of a self-contained Provençal village. The 107 rooms are beautifully, cheerfully furnished, and the youthful spirit of St-Tropez is superbly captured with a personal, unpretentious touch to the service so often sacrificed at these prices. Lunch at the (heated) swimming pool is *the* great midday rendezvous away from the beaches (see *Les Arcades* in *Eating Out*). Closed mid-October to mid-March. Major credit cards accepted. Av. Paul-Signac (phone: 94-97-00-04; fax: 94-97-40-52; telex: 470235). Expensive.

La Mandarine – Designed like a small village with pink-washed walls, it has 42 brightly furnished rooms and apartments separated by hedges, vines, and graveled walks around a quiet courtyard. There is a terrace restaurant. In addition to its own swimming pool, the hotel maintains a private beach out at Pampelonne about half a mile from town. Closed from mid-October to mid-April. Major credit cards accepted. Rte. de Tahiti (phone: 94-97-21-00; fax: 94-97-33-67; telex: 970461). Expensive.

La Ponche – One of the oldest and most charming of the in-town hotels, in the heart of the Vieille Ville (Old City) by the Port des Pêcheurs. The 21 rooms are small but nicely done, several with private terraces providing a splendid view of the Golfe de St-Tropez, a delight at breakfast time. The service is exceptionally friendly. Closed from mid-October to April 1. Major credit cards accepted. 1 Pl. du Révelin (phone: 94-97-02-53; fax: 94-97-78-61; telex: 461516). Expensive.

Résidence de la Pinède – This comfortable hotel, with 34 rooms and 5 suites right on Bouillabaisse Beach, caters very much to the sporting crowd. For those not content with the kidney-shaped pool in the shade of the pine trees, the saunas, or solarium, the private beach offers windsurfing and water skiing. The rooms in this Relais & Châteaux member are spacious and prettily furnished in traditional Provençal style. The restaurant has earned a star from Michelin. Closed from mid-October to mid-March. Most major credit cards accepted. Plage de la Bouillabaisse (phone: 94-97-04-21; fax: 94-97-73-64; telex: 470489). Expensive.

Yaca – An intimate, shady, 22-room hostelry at the edge of the Old Town. It's quiet here — no mean claim in this noisy town. There is a restaurant that is open during the summer months. The cocktail bar has a nice jazz piano. Closed from mid-October to mid-April; open 2 weeks for *Christmas* and *New Year's*. Major credit cards accepted. 1-3 Bd. d'Aumale (phone: 94-97-11-79; fax: 94-97-58-50; telex: 462140). Expensive.

Ermitage – Up on the road leading past the Citadelle, this is one of the few hotels with a panoramic view of the town. There are 29 rooms, and the service is excellent and very friendly. Open all year. Major credit cards accepted. Av. Paul-Signac (phone: 94-97-52-33; fax: 94-97-10-43). Expensive to moderate.

Le Levant – On the road where Colette used to live, it is tranquilly set in a lovely garden by the sea. It has a huge heated pool, beside which the restaurant serves a lunchtime barbecue. 26 modern rooms. The hotel is closed from mid-October to mid-April; restaurant closed from mid-September to mid-June. Major credit cards accepted. Rte. des Salins (phone: 94-97-33-33; fax: 94-97-76-13). Expensive to moderate.

Sube – Set right on the harbor behind the statue of Vice-Admiral Suffren, this famous place has 28 totally renovated rooms, with ringside views of the most amusing resort show on the Côte d'Azur, and a popular restaurant. Make room reservations well in advance. Open year-round; 35% discount on room rates in winter. Major credit cards accepted. 15 Quai Suffren (phone: 94-97-30-04; fax: 94-54-89-08). Expensive to moderate.

Lou Troupelen – Built in the style of Provence are these two pink-washed houses with 44 rooms. Set in a delightful garden surrounded by vineyards, this hostelry is only a short walk from the center of town and an easy ride to the beaches. Closed early November to *Easter*. Major credit cards accepted. Chemin des Vendanges (phone: 94-97-44-88). Moderate.

Le Pré de la Mer – This 12-room, modern motel offers comfort and good value. Closed from October to *Easter*. Visa accepted. Route des Salins (phone: 94-97-12-23). Moderate.

Résidence des Lices – Modern and by the Place des Lices, its 41 rooms are nonetheless peaceful, and it's more attractive from its bougainvillea-festooned inner patio and swimming pool than the rather nondescript street façade suggests. The staff, however, has become surly and downright unhelpful at times. Closed from mid-November to April 1; open for *Christmas*. Visa accepted. Av. Augustin-Grangeon (phone: 94-97-28-28). Moderate.

Les Chimères – Right on the water, this charming guesthouse is nicely situated outside the hustle and bustle of town. Breakfast is served in the garden under cool palms and bougainvillea. No credit cards accepted. Port du Pilon (phone: 94-97-02-90). Inexpensive.

Lou Cagnard – Not far from Place des Lices, it has 19 rooms, a garden, friendly service, and it's quiet. Consider it a great bargain, particularly for the off-season. Closed November 15 to January 3. Visa accepted. Av. Paul-Roussel (phone: 94-97-04-24). Inexpensive.

EATING OUT: With a few noble exceptions, St-Tropez is not a temple of gastronomy. Ambience, table hopping, and general people watching take precedence over sophisticated cuisine, but it's still possible to eat well if you choose the excellent local fish, cooked simply — grilled or baked in Proven-çal herbs. And the local wines (côtes de Provence), which are less impressive transported back home, will taste perfectly good, especially the rosé. While you're sampling, try the local nougat and the *tarte tropézienne,* a pineapple-filled cream sandwich. A meal for two, without wine, in a restaurant listed as expensive will cost around $80 and up; in a moderate one, $40 to $70; and in an inexpensive one, $20 to $40. Service charge is usually included. Closing periods vary from year to year, but most places are open from *Easter* on through the winter onslaught.

Les Arcades – Fish and inventive dishes are the order of the day at this restaurant, poolside at the posh *Byblos* hotel. Open daily. Closed mid-October to March 1. Reservations unnecessary. Major credit cards accepted. Av. Paul-Signac (phone: 94-97-00-04; fax: 94-97-40-52). Expensive.

Bistro des Lices – A popular dining place in St-Tropez, it features traditional cooking and a piano bar. Open daily for dinner in the summer. Closed Tuesdays and early January to April 1. Reservations advised. Major credit cards accepted. Pl. des Lices (phone: 94-97-29-00; fax: 94-97-76-39). Expensive.

Le Chabichou – Considered by many the best in town for decor, service, and exciting food preparation; it's also a good place to spot celebrities. Dinner at this one-star establishment is worth the price, and weekday lunch is a bargain. Open for dinner only in the summer. Closed mid-October to May 1. Reservations necessary. Visa accepted. Av. Foch (phone: 94-54-80-00; fax: 94-97-11-28). Expensive.

Leï Mouscardins – Old-fashioned Provençal cooking in the antique setting of the Old City fortifications leading to the Tour du Portalet, with a superb view of the Golfe de St-Tropez. (Ask for one of the prized tables on the terrace.) The restaurant's habitués swear that the bouillabaisse cannot be beaten in Marseilles. The grilled sea bass is pretty good, too. Count on the best of the local wines. Open daily for lunch and dinner. Closed from mid-October to March 1. Reservations advised. Most major credit cards accepted. Rue Portalet (phone: 94-97-01-53). Expensive.

L'Olivier – A charming place just outside town. The chef hails from the southwest of France and experiments with Mediterranean flavors. Try his classic duck with honey. Open daily for lunch and dinner. Closed January to February, and mid-October to mid-December. Reservations advised. Major credit cards accepted. Rte. des Carles (phone: 94-97-58-16; fax: 94-97-71-21). Expensive.

La Romana – The most fashionable of the town's several Italian trattorie. Fresh pasta and very good pizza in a lovely garden; dinners only. There also are 12 moderately priced rooms. Open daily. Closed from end of September through March. Reservations unnecessary. Major credit cards accepted. Chemin des Conquettes (phone: 94-97-15-50; fax: 94-97-73-49). Expensive.

Club 55 – Like all the beach eateries, this is in a category by itself, one where ambience is everything and cuisine most definitely secondary (however, the fish is very fresh). But the sheer lazy delight of a simple meal at tables set among the umbrella pines a few yards away from the white sands of Pampelonne epitomizes hedonistic St-Tropez more than any other eating place. It grew out of a canteen set up for the film crew of the Vadim-Bardot movie that launched postwar St-Tropez in 1953. Lunch only from mid-November to April 1. Closed Mondays. Reservations unnecessary. No credit cards accepted. Plage de Pampelonne (phone: 94-79-80-14). Expensive to moderate.

La Ponche – This pleasantly calm terrace spot by the Port des Pêcheurs serves a marvelous saffron mussel soup and giant *gambas* (shrimp) in tarragon sauce, but there's also a bargain menu with such things as a fine lamb stew (*navarin*) and a definitive lemon pie. Closed Mondays, and from mid-October to April 1. Reservations unnecesary. No credit cards accepted. Pl. du Révelin (phone: 94-97-02-53). Expensive to moderate.

Café des Arts – A back room behind the bar and through the kitchen serves as one of the perennially fashionable hangouts that does not cold-shoulder newcomers, but welcomes a nice mixture of Tropezians and transients. The food is less brilliant than the clientele. (But try the cold lentil salad. It's only a bistro, so keep it simple and you'll have a good time.) Open daily for dinner only. Closed from January 1 to *Easter*. Reservations unnecessary. Visa accepted. Pl. des Lices (phone: 94-97-02-25). Moderate.

Le Girelier – A good place to enjoy fish salads, views of the yachting harbor, and people watching. Closed January to mid-March. Reservations advised on Saturdays. Major credit cards accepted. Quai Jean-Jaurès (phone: 94-97-03-87 or 94-97-04-47). Moderate.

Le Gorille – For the unserious eater. Open all night (see *Bars and Cafés*), all year — steaks and French fries in one of the town's great institutions, on the port, beside the newspaper shop. No reservations. No credit cards accepted. 1 Quai Suffren (phone: 94-97-03-93). Inexpensive.

Lou Revelen – For the serious eater. Try the *tapenade* (an appetizer of anchovy paste, minced olives, and garlic), the great grilled sardines, and the bourride (a whitefish version of bouillabaisse with cream or milk). The restaurant has its own very honorable wines. Open daily for lunch and dinner; except from January 1 to *Easter,* when it is open only on weekends. Reservations unnecessary. Visa accepted. 4 Rue des Remparts (phone: 94-97-06-34). Inexpensive.

 BARS AND CAFÉS: Hardened Tropezians spend nights at the *Café des Arts* on Place des Lices; they share elbow room with the *boules* players at the great zinc bar. *Le Gorille,* the classic French provincial bar on the port, is rich in sailors and those who went out for a pack of cigarettes and never came back (open all night, all year, on Quai Suffren). The most beautiful people on the port can be found at sundown in the bar at the back of *L'Escale* (Quai Jean-Jaurès). For quieter conviviality, try the bar of *La Ponche* (Pl. du Révelin). The "in" place for young locals is the *Bar à Vins* (13 Rue des Fénier) where you can play billiards squeezed between the tile-covered walls and the small bistro tables where you can get a quick bite to eat.

STRASBOURG

Since 1949, the headquarters of the Council of Europe and, since 1979, the meeting place of the European Community's directly elected European Parliament, Strasbourg is the newest capital on the Continent. Given its international scope, it potentially could be the most imposing of capitals, too, except that the Strasbourgeois don't think of things that way. They seldom mention their newfound prominence and concentrate instead on being perhaps the most amiable and agreeable of capitals. The city fathers welcomed all the multinational activity and concomitant publicity and economic advantages that began with the arrival of the Council of Europe. But they quietly planted the first building to house it — now supplanted by the massively modern Palais de l'Europe — in the suburbs, where it wouldn't interfere with the daily comings and goings and almost casual meanderings of the citizenry.

Strasbourg is a warm, cozy kind of city, tiny, in fact, and very homey. Not every building dates from the 15th, 16th, or 17th century, although in certain sections it may seem that way. Some belong to the 18th and 19th centuries, and some are as recent as the postwar period, since the city suffered considerable damage during World War II. But the overall effect is that of a live-in museum, where the high, narrow half-timbered houses, the steep, massive tile roofs punctured by strange, birdhouse-like dormer windows, and the maze of winding walking streets in Strasbourg — throughout Alsace, in fact — are immensely photogenic. "Restorations" in Strasbourg — throughout Alsace, in fact — have established the practice of removing the plaster covering the wooden structures of traditional houses. The result may appeal to tourists, but the fact is that the houses originally were covered with plaster, except for carved wood decoration around the doors and windows.

The city is rich in art, music, and the intellectual excitement that comes from having a renowned, 4-century-old university, now with some 27,000 students, and major schools of medicine and both Catholic and Protestant seminaries. It is France's main Rhine River port and a major commercial center, but it is also a city on a human scale. Despite the bustle and frequent congestion (which remind you of its modern importance) on Rue des Francs-Bourgeois, the Grand'Rue, the Rue des Grandes-Arcades, and along the quays that circle the central city, around nearly every corner is a street set aside for pedestrians, an escape for the wanderer. Even some of the main streets are less than two cars wide, so traffic tends to roll at about the same speed as the pedestrians.

The Germans have a word — *gemütlich,* meaning comfortable and pleasant — for such a place, and as it happens, German is understood easily here. Strasbourg, the ancient capital of the province of Alsace, is at the very eastern edge of France. The center of the city is on the River Ill, but its port is on the Rhine and the city's neighbors across the water have occasionally considered it to be on the western edge of Germany, most recently in the Franco-Prussian War of 1870–71 and both world wars. As a consequence, and possibly out of a sense of resignation, most Strasbourgeois speak both French and German and sometimes their own Alsatian dialect, a sort of smoothed-out German. They have a strong sense of regionalism, a certain isolation from the rest of France, and especially from Paris. They listen, for example, to German radio for the weather forecast, because, they say, the French national radio spends too much time talking about Normandy and Brittany. It also is said that the Strasbourgeois have the discipline of the Germans and the grace of the French. Add their Alsatian individuality, and a visit to this part of the country is something like seeing three countries at once.

Only in the late 17th century did Strasbourg become French. Settled in 12 BC by Roman legions, who called it Argentoratum and later Strateburgum, or the City of the Roads, Strasbourg became in the 10th century a part of the Germanic kings' revival of the Roman state, the Holy Roman Empire. In the 13th century, it achieved a measure of independence as a free imperial city and as such carried on a flourishing trade, bringing about, in the 14th century, the first of its annual fairs, the first bridge across the Rhine, and its first customs house, which stands today. Prosperity, in turn, attracted artisans, artists, and intellectuals, including a German from Mainz, Johann Gutenberg, who may well have invented printing from movable type during the 14 years he lived here in the mid-15th century.

When the Reformation swept in from the east in the 16th century, Strasbourg became an important center of Protestantism. One result was the founding of the university (which in a later century would have alumni as distinguished as Goethe and Metternich). Another was that mass ceased being said in the cathedral in 1529 and was not said here again until Louis XIV, taking advantage of the effective undoing of the Holy Roman Empire by the Thirty Years War, surrounded the city with his army in 1681 and annexed it to France. Even so, he did not insist on immediate integration. While taking over the city's defense and diplomacy, he allowed it the free exercise of the Protestant faith and a measure of autonomy in political, economic, and social institutions, which endured until the French Revolution.

By then, the Strasbourgeois felt French enough to embrace the principles of "Liberty, Equality, Fraternity" and to defend them from enemies within and without. In fact, in 1792, with invasion by Austrian and Prussian forces imminent and in response to a request by the mayor of Strasbourg, Rouget de Lisle, a poet, musician, and soldier, wrote a rousing marching song for an elite Strasbourg volunteer battalion. The song, called the "Chant de Guerre pour l'Armée du Rhin," became instead the theme of a volunteer battalion from Marseilles and thus acquired its more familiar name, "La Marseillaise," and went on to become the French national anthem. A plaque on the Bank of France building at 4 Place Broglie commemorates the day — April 26, 1792 — when de Lisle first sang it as the mayor's guest.

In 1870, during the course of the Franco-Prussian War, the Germans laid siege to Strasbourg and captured it after 50 days and the loss of 600 French soldiers and about 1,500 civilians. Along with the rest of Alsace and part of

Lorraine, it remained German for 44 years, returning to French rule only as a result of Germany's defeat in World War I. From 1940 to 1944, it again was occupied by the Germans and suffered two aerial bombardments before French forces recaptured it as Allied armies moved into Germany. Thus today, with about 250,000 inhabitants and another 230,000 in the neighboring communities and villages making up the metropolitan area, it ranks as France's sixth-largest city, although many of its older citizens were born German.

Perhaps because of its location, Strasbourg remains virtually undiscovered by Americans, who tend to visit Paris and points north, south, or west. (Most of the tourists here are Germans or Belgians, who seem to resemble the natives, and so the city is unselfconsciously itself.)

Yet there is plenty to see, beginning with one of France's most important cathedrals. Before the New World was even discovered, this was complete, the tallest building in the Old World, and it still towers over everything for miles around, a reassuring beacon that can be glimpsed from virtually everywhere in the city. A few yards away is what might inelegantly be called Museum Row — an 18th-century palace housing three museums, three more in neighboring, still older buildings, and a seventh just over the bridge across the Ill. A 10-minute walk from the cathedral, where the Ill breaks into several small canals, is an old half-timbered neighborhood, La Petite France, once a tradesmen's quarter, now a tangle of shops and artisans' *ateliers* (studios), restaurants, cafés, a tearoom or two, and even a few discos, wrapped in crooked streets and tiny bridges, odd angles, and picturesque corners. Nor elsewhere in Strasbourg are you ever very far from a café, a brasserie, or a pastry shop. Find a suitable one, sit down between sights, order a cold Alsatian beer or some rich *pâtisserie,* and relax as you savor France from a different perspective.

STRASBOURG AT-A-GLANCE

SEEING THE CITY: For a spectacular overview, climb the 330 steps up to the platform of the cathedral tower (there's an admission charge). During his student days in the city, Goethe did this frequently, not only to survey the scene, but also to conquer his fear of heights. The restaurant and tearoom atop the *Printemps* department store and the luxury 14th-floor *Valentin-Sorg* restaurant, both on Place de l'Homme de Fer, are other spots from which to contemplate the rooftops of Strasbourg, while the Barrage Vauban offers a view of the Ponts Couverts (Covered Bridges) and Petite France area such as a bird might have coming in for a landing — broad and explanatory, yet reasonably close to the ground.

SPECIAL PLACES: Central Strasbourg is a flat little island shaped more or less like a ham with the shank chopped short, an image that, as it happens, also symbolizes one of the staples of the Strasbourg diet. The River Ill bounds the south side of the island, and a narrow canal that once served as a moat — the Fossé du Faux-Rempart — lies like a strip of bacon over the north side. Most of Strasbourg's sightseeing attractions are on this central island, as are its main squares: Place Gutenberg, Place Kléber, and Place Broglie — in addition to Place de la Cathédrale. One of the main charms is that at an easy pace you can cross the island east to west in 25 minutes or so, north to south in about 15 minutes. But you wouldn't want to, because Strasbourg is for strollers, with history to be rediscovered at almost every corner. The natural starting point is the cathedral; after that, hardly anything else listed below is more than a 10-minute walk, except for the Palais de l'Europe, the park, and the Brasserie de Kronenbourg.

Cathédrale Notre-Dame – This is the physical and emotional heart of Strasbourg and one of Europe's most striking examples of Gothic architecture. Built of pink sandstone from the nearby Vosges mountains, the so-called *grés des Vosges,* the cathedral is bathed in a rosy hue, as though it were blushing at its own fanciful beauty. Work began in 1015 in the Romanesque style, the church burned several times in the 12th century, and work began again, this time in pure Gothic. When finally complete in 1439, the lacy openwork spire made it the tallest building in Christendom (466 feet), and so it remained for some 400 years. The building has witnessed much of the turbulent history of Alsace and even served the Protestant faith during the Reformation. Louis XIV and Louis XV both worshiped here, and in 1770, Marie-Antoinette was greeted formally here on the way to her wedding to Louis XVI. During the Revolution, many of the cathedral's statues were torn down (a good number of them have since been restored or replaced by copies, with the originals remaining in the *Musée de l'Oeuvre Notre-Dame*). The spire also was threatened (its height offended the principle of *égalité*), but was saved by being crowned with a huge red Phrygian cap. The wars of the 19th and 20th centuries also damaged the structure, which nevertheless survives to present the splendid sight we see today.

Before going inside, note the rich sculptural decoration of the west façade, especially that of the middle of the three doorways, which almost in itself sums up medieval religious belief. Then go around to the double doorway of the south transept, known as the Portail de l'Horloge (Clock Portal). The two female figures to the right and left of the doors, allegories for the Synagogue (the blindfolded figure) and the Church (the one with the Cross), are counted among the masterpieces of the cathedral's sculpture (though these are copies of originals kept in the *Musée de l'Oeuvre Notre-Dame*), as is the moving Death of the Virgin in the left tympanum, a 13th-century original.

Stained glass is the marvel of the cathedral's interior. The large rose window (ca. 1316) in the west front gleams like a jeweled eye, a star-flecked pupil of black surrounded by an iris of white, then rings of deep blue, amber, and muted greens. The windows of the Chapelle Ste-Catherine (ca. 1340), showing the Apostles and two female saints surmounted by tall, thin, shimmering spires in gray-green grisaille are stunning. The oldest windows (late 12th and early 13th century) are in the north transept. The pale green of the robe of the Virgin in the topmost of four medallions in one window and the similar green of the robes of the two saints John in the window next to it is a rare, prized color. Also to be seen inside are an exquisitely intricate late Gothic pulpit in the nave and two other attractions in the south transept. If it is dark, put a franc in the box to light up the Pilier des Anges (Angels' or Doomsday Pillar) or you may miss this masterpiece of 13th-century sculpture. The other attraction, hard to miss, is the wonderful 16th-century astronomical clock, an ingenious device that tells so much to those who know it — the day of the week, sunrise and sunset, saints' days, eclipses of the sun and moon — that it's hard to remember it also, simply, tells the time. Set according to the meridian of Strasbourg, it strikes noon at precisely 12:31 PM each day, and this is the time to see it in action. Toward noon, visitors are asked to leave the south transept and to reenter by the Clock Portal (after paying a small admission charge). A taped recitation in French, German, and English begins at 12:15. When the small cherub on the left (look carefully) strikes the time, the cherub on the right turns over an hourglass, an old man (the last of the four ages of man) passes before Death, the

Twelve Apostles parade before Christ, and the cock above flaps its wings, crowing three times. Guided tours of the cathedral are offered at 10:15 AM, 2:30, and 3:30 PM in French and German during July and August. Admission charge. There is a sound and light show from April through October nightly at 8:15 PM (commentary in German) and at 9:15 PM (commentary in French). Pl. de la Cathédrale.

Place de la Cathédrale – The half-timbered house to one side of the square, wonderfully carved with signs of the zodiac, biblical figures, and ancient and medieval heroes, is the *Maison Kammerzell*. It was built by a rich fabric merchant in the late 16th century (over a ground floor dated 1465) and must have been even then the finest house in the city as well as a prime business location. It takes its name from a grocer who owned it in the 19th century and is today a restaurant (see *Eating Out*). The less ornate timbered building facing the cathedral at the corner of Rue Mercière is the *Pharmacie du Cerf,* the oldest pharmacy in France. It dates from 1268, though it has undergone various transformations since then.

Château des Rohan – This episcopal palace off the south side of the cathedral was commissioned by Cardinal Armand-Gaston de Rohan-Soubise, one of several members of the famous French family to be Archbishop of Strasbourg in the 18th century. It was built from 1730 to 1742 according to the plans of Robert de Cotte and during the course of its history welcomed such illustrious guests as Louis XV, Marie-Antoinette, and Napoleon. Various rooms of the bishops' apartments can be seen — including a dazzling black and white marble salon with two giant faïence (ceramic) stoves, an inviting library, and a chapel — in addition to three museums. The *Musée des Arts Décoratifs* is especially notable for its collection of ceramics, in particular for that produced by the Hannong family of Strasbourg in the 18th century. The *Musée des Beaux-Arts* contains paintings by Italian (Botticelli, Tintoretto, Veronese, Tiepolo), Spanish (El Greco, Zurbarán, Murillo), Flemish and Dutch (Memling, Rubens, Van Dyck, De Hooch), and French (Lorrain, Watteau, Boucher, Fragonard) masters from the 14th to the 19th century. The *Musée Archéologique,* in the basement of the château (recently reopened after extensive renovation), traces civilization in Alsace from Paleolithic to Celtic, Gallo-Roman, and Merovingian times and is regarded as one of the most significant of its kind in France. All are open daily except Tuesdays from 10 AM to noon and 2 to 6 PM. Half of the *Musée des Beaux-Arts* always is closed, with alternate halves of the collection visible on alternate days. Admission charge. 2 Pl. du Château (phone: 88-32-48-95).

Musée de l'Oeuvre Notre-Dame (Our Lady's Work Museum) – The Maison de l'Oeuvre Notre-Dame was built in various stages from the 14th through the 16th century to house the Oeuvre Notre-Dame, the medieval institution founded to collect money for and oversee the construction of the cathedral and then its maintenance. Now the *maison* houses part of this museum, the rest of which rambles through the adjoining 14th-century Hôtellerie du Cerf building and a 17th-century house that once stood on Rue d'Ors but was reconstructed here. Similarly, only part of the museum is devoted to the Cathédrale Notre-Dame. Its broader scope is the art of Alsace of the Middle Ages and Renaissance. Original working drawings of the raising of the cathedral from the 13th to the 15th century are on display, as well as originals of many of the cathedral statues replaced by copies, but so, too, are paintings, sculpture, stained glass, examples of the goldsmith's art, and rooms full of furniture and disparate objects not associated with the cathedral — everything from a head of Christ, made about 1070 for a church in Wissembourg (and considered to be the oldest piece of figurative stained glass in France), to a 17th-century dollhouse. Before leaving, you'll also have seen a courtyard sided with the carved wood balconies of a building demolished on the Grand'Rue. Open 10 AM to noon and 2 to 6 PM. Admission charge. 3 Pl. du Château (phone: 88-32-06-39 or 88-32-48-95).

Musée Historique – The emphasis of this collection, which occupies a former

16th-century slaughterhouse (the Grande Boucherie), is on the military. There are arms, uniforms worn by the Strasbourgeois and Bas-Rhinois from the 18th through the 20th century, and regiment after regiment of antique *petits soldats de Strasbourg,* or toy soldiers — actually much like paper dolls. A highlight is a unique 1:600 scale model of the city made in 1727 by the military engineers of the king. Closed Tuesdays. Admission charge. 3 Pl. de la Grande Boucherie (phone: 88-32-25-63 or 88-32-48-95).

L'Ancienne Douane – This 14th-century customs building, renovated after World War II and formerly the home of the *Musée d'Art Moderne,* now houses special revolving exhibitions only. Open daily except Tuesdays from 11 AM to 6 PM. 1 Rue du Vieux Marché aux Poissons (phone: 88-32-46-07).

Musée d'Art Moderne – The city's impressive permanent collection of modern paintings, sculpture, and stained glass is temporarily housed in a municipal building just behind the post office at the Place de la Cathédrale. It previously was located in the *L'Ancienne Douane,* but the number of pieces increased to a point where the customs building wasn't large enough. Plans for a new modern home for the collection have been approved and the structure currently is scheduled for completion in 1996. In the meantime, only a small portion of the works, including pieces by Monet, Degas, Gauguin, Braque, Chagall, Rodin, Renoir, Klee, and Jean Arp (a native of Strasbourg), as well as *The Kiss* by Gustav Klimt, is displayed in its temporary quarters. Open daily except Tuesdays from 10 AM to noon and 2 to 6 PM. Admission charge. 5 Pl. du Château (phone: 88-32-48-05).

Musée Alsacien – The exhibits of this charming museum document the folk arts, traditions, and everyday activities of the past in rural Alsace. One room, for instance, is given over to a reconstructed early-19th-century *chambre paysanne* fitted out with a large iron stove, table and chairs, rocking horse, swinging cradle, and a plump alcove bed complete with bedside slippers and a chamberpot. The rest of the exhibitions — taking up 3 floors in a characteristic 17th-century house and spilling over into a courtyard and adjacent buildings — include other reconstructed rooms, furniture, ceramics, kitchenware, clothing, work tools and agricultural implements, and Protestant, Catholic, and Jewish religious items from baptismal certificates to *Passover* plates. Closed Tuesdays. Admission charge. 23-25 Quai St-Nicolas (phone: 88-35-55-36).

Eglise St-Thomas – Built in the 13th and 14th centuries, this has been an important Protestant church — called the cathedral of Lutheran Protestantism — since the 16th century. Architecturally, it is a hall church, a style common in Germany and the Netherlands but fairly rare in France. Inside, note the mausoleum of the Maréchal de Saxe, by the 18th-century sculptor Jean-Baptiste Pigalle, and the 18th-century Silbermann organ, on which Albert Schweitzer played concerts commemorating the death of Johann Sebastian Bach. Rue St-Thomas.

Petite France – This most picturesque quarter of Strasbourg, extending roughly from the Eglise St-Thomas to and including the Ponts Couverts (see below), used to be the home of the city's fishermen, millers, and tanners. It is full of postcard-perfect scenes of 16th- and 17th-century houses mirrored in the waters of the River Ill and small canals, of gliding swans, and of small boats and barges nudging through the locks — though explanations of the origin of its name conjure up less sublime images. (The French soldiers of François I used to frequent the area in search of amorous adventures, according to one version; there was once a hospital here to treat the "French" (venereal) disease brought to Alsace by the soldiers of Charles VIII, according to another.) Walk along Rue de la Monnaie and Rue des Dentelles to Place Benjamin-Zix, and the huge, balconied and flower-bedecked *Maison des Tanneurs,* dating from 1572 and now a restaurant, will be at the edge of the water to the left. Other buildings that formerly housed tanners are beyond the *place* in Rue du Bain-aux-Plantes (Plant Bath Street, so called because a bathhouse existed here as early as the 14th century). Be sure also to walk along Rue des Moulins, Quai Woerthel, and Quai de la Petite France. Both of the quays lead to the Ponts Couverts, but the latter, lined on one side with old houses, trees, and a willow or two dipping into the water, is especially appealing.

Ponts Couverts (Covered Bridges) – The three bridges and four towers at the dividing point of the Ill are vestiges of the city's 14th-century fortifications. Originally, the bridges were of wood and uncovered; from the 16th to the 18th century they had roofs; in the 19th century, they were rebuilt in stone. Today they are a promenade, uniquely scenic, and via the Quai de l'Ill, they give access to the Barrage Vauban.

Barrage Vauban (Vauban Dam) – When Strasbourg was annexed to France in the late 17th century, its fortifications were modernized and extended by the French military engineer Sébastien Vauban, who built this dam across the Ill near the Ponts Couverts. You'll find it identified on maps also as L'Ecluse (floodgate), because it allowed the flooding of the southern part of the city if necessary, and as the Terrasse Panoramique, because that is its function today. From here the view includes all the bridges and towers of the Ponts Couverts, the Petite France quarter, and the cathedral in the background. Opening hours vary with the time of year. Admission charge. Quai de l'Ill (phone: 88-36-16-98).

Eglise St-Pierre-le-Vieux – Unusual because Catholic and Protestant churches are joined together in one structure, with rather different architectural design. Among its treasures are the 16th-century carved wall panels. Pl. St-Pierre-le-Vieux.

Eglise St-Pierre-le-Jeune – The most recent of three churches built on the same site since the 7th century, transformed from Catholic to Protestant along the way. The present church dates from the 13th century, though parts of its predecessors remain and the church has been much restored. Pl. St-Pierre-le-Jeune.

Palais de l'Europe – This 1977 building is noteworthy for its striking modern architecture — in the design of its semicircular interior chamber (the hemicycle), in particular — and for its symbolism as the cornerstone of European cooperation. It is the seat of the 26-nation Council of Europe and the meeting place, for a week each month, of some 518 directly elected members of the 12-nation European Parliament (whose secretariat is in Luxembourg). The building is open to the public, guided tours in English are offered weekdays from April to October (when Parliament is not in session) at 10 AM and 4 PM, and if you wish to attend a session, it can be arranged by calling the Council (phone: 88-61-49-61) or the Parliament (phone: 88-17-40-01). A new visitors' center was added last year in an annex of the building. No admission charge. Av. de l'Europe.

Parc de l'Orangerie – Across the road from the Palais, this park was created by Le Nôtre in 1692, although it was transformed in the 19th century. Besides a lake and a zoo, it contains a pavilion built for Empress Josephine in 1805, rebuilt after damage by fire, and now used for exhibitions.

Brasserie de Kronenbourg – This brewery in a northwestern suburb is the home of Strasbourg's most famous beer. Guided tours take place on weekdays (except holidays) at 9 and 10 AM and 2 and 3 PM from April to October, and at 10 AM and 2:30 PM from October to April. No admission charge. 68 Rte. d'Oberhausbergen (phone: 88-27-41-59).

■**EXTRA SPECIAL:** Simply wandering among the old streets and passages under restoration (or still untouched) provides special pleasures in this romantic city. For instance, just off Place du Corbeau is a large, pink-sand-colored building with an old-fashioned roof that is otherwise nondescript. Walk inside the cobblestone courtyard, however, and you will see the kind of high, angled wooden balconies, weathered by age, that musketeers used to leap from. This is the *Hôtellerie du Corbeau,* a coaching inn whose existence at least back to 1538 is documented and whose last guest was received in 1854. Notable travelers included Frederick the

Great, King of Prussia, who stayed here incognito in 1740. The Quai St-Nicolas is an architectural history book, offering side by side buildings from the 15th through the 19th century and best seen the first time from across the river. The Pont du Corbeau used to be the site of executions by drowning. Stroll up the narrow Rue de l'Ecurie, which begins at the Ancienne Douane, becomes Rue de l'Epine, and crosses Rue des Serruriers and Rue Gutenberg. En route, you will see 16th-to 18th-century homes and courtyards encrusted with sculptured lions and ugly faces to scare away the devil, pierced with oval *oeil-de-boeuf* (ox-eye) windows — also known as concierges' windows — and affixed with oriel windows, a form of bay window attached to the corners of the buildings. The rooflines have their own characters, and the steeply sloped tiled roofs of the buildings are pierced with myriad dormer windows. Such windows on each side of the roof provided air circulation and a kind of refrigeration for the Strasbourgeois, who used their attics for food storage. Look, too, for the occasional stork's nest on the roofs. The stork, now rare in Alsace (though efforts are being made to lure them back to the Centre de Réintroduction des Cigognes near Sélestat), has long been considered a lucky bird and a symbol of the city.

SOURCES AND RESOURCES

TOURIST INFORMATION: The Office du Tourisme of Strasbourg and its region has a central branch (10 Pl. Gutenberg; phone: 88-32-57-07) open daily from April through October, closed Sundays the rest of the year. Other locations are the Pavillon du Tourisme across from the train station (Pl. de la Gare; phone: 88-32-51-49) and one near the German border (Pont de l'Europe; phone: 88-61-39-23). Among the literature available is a booklet discussing facilities for the handicapped and access to museums, theaters, and other public buildings. The tourist office has an *Accueil de France* accommodations service, which will make hotel reservations for a fee, and it runs its own tours (in French) for a small charge, including 2-hour guided walking tours departing from 10 Place Gutenberg daily in July and August at 10 AM (check locally for other hours). The tourist office also offers a series of theme tours (in French), including "Strasbourg in the Middle Ages, Renaissance Strasbourg, and The Alsacienne House," for groups of 15 or more.

Other tours include the mini-trains that leave from the south side of the cathedral (Pl. du Château) from *Easter* through October and roll on a 45-minute route among the scenic sections of the Old City or on a slightly longer route that takes in the Parc de l'Orangerie and the Palais de l'Europe. For information and reservations, contact *C.T.S.* (phone: 88-28-90-80). Boat tours of the Ill are offered from March through December. Contact the *Port Autonome de Strasbourg* (25 Rue de la Nuée-Bleue; phone: 88-84-13-13). Cruises on the Rhine also are available from *Alsace Croisières* (12 Rue de la Division-Leclerc; phone: 88-32-44-55) and *Strasbourg Croisières* (5 Rue Deserte; phone: 88-32-67-95). *Alligator* (11 Bd. d'Anvers; phone: 88-61-10-00; fax: 88-60-39-42), a boat restaurant, offers *promenades gastronautiques* (cruises on the city's waterways) that include meals.

Local Coverage – The Strasbourgeois keep up with local news by reading *Les Dernières Nouvelles d'Alsace,* in French, daily, and refer to the monthly booklet *Strasbourg Actualités,* available at all newsstands, for listings of current activities such as theater and sporting events. A billboard in front of the *Marks & Spencer* department store (Pl. Kléber) also gives all the movie and theater timetables, and kiosks along the city streets have posters on the latest cultural happenings. The *Librairie Kléber* (1 Rue des Francs-Bourgeois; phone: 88-32-03-88) is a good source of books in English on various local topics including French and Alsatian history, the cuisine of both cultures, and other lore.

TELEPHONE: The city code for Strasbourg is 88, which is incorporated into all local 8-digit numbers. When calling a number in Strasbourg from the Paris region (including the Ile-de-France), dial 16, wait for the dial tone, then dial the 8-digit number. When calling a number from outside Paris, dial only the 8-digit number. When calling from the US, dial 33 (which is the country code), followed by the 8-digit number.

GETTING AROUND: Walking is the best and easiest way, because the city is small and many streets in the vicinity of the main points of interest are pedestrian zones.

Air – The Aéroport International de Strasbourg-Entzheim connects cities throughout Europe and is about a 15- or 20-minute taxi ride from the heart of town (phone: 88-64-67-67). A taxi from the airport to the city should cost between 150 and 200 francs (about $30 to $40) during the day, and slightly higher at night. Shuttle buses leave for the airport from Place Kléber and Place de la Gare about an hour before the departure of major flights and cost about 30 francs ($5). The *Air France* office is at 15 Rue Francs Bourgeois (phone: 88-32-99-74).

Bicycles – Besides being small, Strasbourg is flat, ideal for cycling. Rentals are available at the train station, 3 Bd. du Président-Wilson (phone: 88-75-41-63).

Bus – Service is good, although on Sundays it can be infrequent. *Carnets* of five tickets (representing a discount of about 30% off the price of singles) can be bought in *tabacs* near the bus stops — the nearest location is marked at the stop — or in the tourist office. Single tickets can be bought on the bus. Once punched, tickets are good for an hour.

Car Rental – Various firms at the airport and in town rent cars, and *SNCF*'s Train + Auto service is available at the train station. But a car is not required or even recommended for city touring because of the narrow streets and pedestrian zones. If you do have one, park it in an underground garage and leave it.

Taxi – Taxis are not inexpensive, but given the city's size, the longest ride to any likely tourist spot should be less than $5. They generally are plentiful, except on weekends. Call *Radio Taxis Strasbourg* at 88-36-13-11 or 88-36-13-13, day or night.

Train – The Gare Centrale *SNCF* is to the west of the Old City, across Pont Kuss at the end of Rue du Maire-Kuss. For train information, call 88-22-50-50; for reservations, call 88-32-07-51. Strasbourg is a rail hub of northeastern France, with good connections to such European cities as Basel, Zurich, Stuttgart, Frankfurt, and Brussels. Paris is less than 4 hours away; when completed, the *TGV* East line will cut travel time down to 2 hours (although at press time, work on it still had not started).

SPECIAL EVENTS: Two events of international scope held annually in Strasbourg are the *Foire Européene,* held for 1 week at the end of April or beginning of May and 12 days in September, and the *Festival International de Musique,* for 2 weeks in June. The latter, a long-standing event, features classical concerts by first-rate guests and ensembles performing in the *Palais de la Musique et des Congrès,* largely but not exclusively; the cathedral and various other churches are other venues. Information and reservations are available from the festival office (24 Rue de la Mésange, 67081 Strasbourg; phone: 88-35-64-00) and bookings by mail can be made about 3 months in advance. A more recent tradition, the *Strasbourg Jazz Festival,* featuring performers such as Herbie Hancock, Art Blakey, and Dizzy Gillespie, takes place the first 2 weeks of July. *Musica,* a festival of contemporary music, takes place here from mid-September to the beginning of October, drawing more than 30,000 people each year. For information call 88-35-32-34. Other events include the *Schilig Sing Immer Noch*, an Alsatian song festival in several parts of Strasbourg and Alsace, but principally in the suburb of Schiltigheim (phone: 88-83-90-00 for information) in April; the *Marathon de Strasbourg*, held in mid-May; and *Christkindelmarik, Christmas* trees and decorations displayed from the first Saturday in December until December 24 at Place Broglie.

MUSEUMS: Most of the museums of greatest interest to visitors are in notable old buildings not far from the cathedral and are discussed in *Special Places*. Elsewhere, Strasbourg also has the following:

Musée Zoologique de l'Université – A small but interesting natural history museum, with special attention paid to endangered species and to Alsace's bird of good fortune, the stork. Open daily except Tuesday; Wednesdays and Sundays from 10 AM to noon and 2 to 6 PM. No admission charge. 29 Bd. de la Victoire (phone: 88-35-85-35).

Planetarium – One of the best in France; lectures on Wednesdays, Thursdays, Fridays, and Saturdays, and guided tours of the dome on the first Tuesday of the month. Admission charge. Rue de l'Observatoire (phone: 88-36-12-50).

SHOPPING: Strasbourg is not particularly a shoppers' paradise. In range and variety of goods, it does not compare to Paris or Lyons, although there's an ample selection of the designer clothes, shoes, furniture, jewelry, tableware, and kitchen equipment for which France is well known. Most of the handicrafts and special products of the region are sold in the smaller towns outside Strasbourg where they originate: pottery and ceramics in Soufflenheim and Betschdorf, embroidery and needlework in Eckbolsheim, and weaving and table linen at Muttersholtz, all within 25 miles (40 km) of the city. In Strasbourg itself, the best shopping buys tend to be food and drink, including such things as the Alsatian white alcohols, or eaux-de-vie — the "waters of life" — distilled from local fruits, and *kugelhopf*, the sweet yeast cake baked in a characteristic fluted pan. The block-long Rue des Orfèvres, besides having some excellent clothing and jewelry boutiques, including *Laura Ashley* and *Céline*, also is the perfect place to shop for the ingredients of an Alsatian picnic. Among the establishments conveniently located along the street are *Au Vieux Gourmet* (No. 3), specializing in cheese; *Naegel* (No. 9), in *pâtisserie; Frick Lutz* (No. 16), in *charcuterie* (delicatessen); *Nicolas* (No. 18), in wine; and *Bretzels Burgard* (No. 22), in pretzels. Nearby, on Rue Chaudron, at No. 9, is *Winckelsass*, Strasbourg's oldest baker, and at No. 5, *Albert Henry*, producing foie gras. Dart through the small alley on Rue des Orfevres to *Ziegler* for fresh fruits and vegetables.

Strasbourg has more than one shopping center and more than one department store. The *Centre Commercial* (Pl. Kléber) has a score or so of stores featuring clothing, records, appliances, and plenty of noise and bustle. The *Centre Halles* complex (at Quai Kléber) has dozens of shops, fast-food restaurants, crowds, and chaos, but it does dispense a large stock of medium-priced merchandise. The *Galeries Arcadia* is on Rue des Grandes Arcades. *Magmod* (34 Rue du 22-Novembre) is an economical, functional department store that also repairs heels in a minute, develops photos in an hour, fixes watches, and has a food market on the third floor. There is a branch of *Au Printemps*, one of France's major department stores (on Pl. de l'Homme de Fer) and *Marks & Spencer*, a branch of the British chain specializing in wearable clothing at moderate prices (on Pl. Kléber). On Wednesday and Saturday mornings, a flea market takes place in Place du Marché-aux-Cochons-de-Lait and Rue du Vieil-Hôpital. It's not very big but worth picking through for books, prints, glassware, and the odd piece collected and discarded more than a few times during the course of the century.

Belles Choses – An interesting assortment of local and regional faïence. 30 Av. de la Marseillaise (phone: 88-35-35-94).

Boulangerie au Vieux Strasbourg (Charles Woerlé) – Cookies, sweets, bread in all shapes and sizes, a 2-pound *kugelhopf* of pure butter, and a smaller one with almonds and walnuts. 10 Rue de la Division-Leclerc (phone: 88-32-00-88).

Boutique des Tanneurs – Rather *touristique*, except for a good selection of small bottles of eau-de-vie packaged for easy shipment and a variety of small cake molds, copies of antique figures from Alsace, that make simple, unusual gifts. 29 Rue du Bain-aux-Plantes (phone: 88-32-93-05).

La Brocanterie – An eclectic collection of dolls, old glassware, lamps, vases, miniatures. Open afternoons only; all day Wednesdays and Saturdays. 18 Rue du Vieil-Hôpital (phone: 88-32-52-79).

A la Civette – A tobacco shop selling pricey but unusual faïence canisters handpainted in old-fashioned designs and flower patterns, plus copies of antiques. 21 Rue des Grandes-Arcades (phone: 88-32-12-85).

Faïencerie à la Petite France – This quaint shop, in a half-timbered building in the Petite France quarter of the city, is chock-full of pottery and porcelain — new and old — from all over France. Prices are fair, and the gentleman who owns the shop is friendly and very informative. 33 Rue du Bain-aux-Plantes (phone: 88-32-33-69).

Fruhauf – For admirers of original jewelry made by a passionate artist. Rue du Chaudron (phone: 88-32-52-27).

La Sommelière – Local wines, Alsatian eaux-de-vie made from raspberries, plums, pears, and nearly every other available fruit of the region, and foie gras and caviar packed in handsome porcelain jars. 1 Rue du Fossé-des-Tailleurs (phone: 88-32-78-59).

 SPORTS AND FITNESS: Besides the tourist office, the *Office Municipal des Sports* (2 Rue Baldung-Grien; phone: 88-36-61-29) has information on sports facilities in the city.

Bowling – There are lanes at the *Bowling de l'Orangerie*, Parc de l'Orangerie (phone: 88-61-36-24).

Fishing – Licenses are obtainable from the *Fédération de la Pêche*, 1 Rue de Nomeny (phone: 88-34-51-86).

Golf – There is an 18-hole course on the Route du Rhin, Illkirch-Graffenstaden (phone: 88-66-17-22). There are two other golf courses in the Strasbourg area — *Golfy*, with 6 holes and a training center (Rte. du Fort-Uhrich, Illkirch-Graffenstaden; phone: 88-67-39-31); and the new 18-hole *Le Kempferhof Golf-Club* (Rue du Moulin, Plobsheim; phone: 88-98-72-72).

Horse Racing – Racing, with pari-mutuel betting, takes place at Hoerdt, 10 miles (16 km) north of Strasbourg, from March through October except in July and August (phone: 88-51-32-44), or call the Horse Federation (phone: 88-36-08-82) for more information.

Ice Skating – *Patinoire du Wacken* (Allée du Printemps; phone: 88-36-60-45) is open from December to March and rents skates.

Swimming – There's an indoor municipal pool (10 Bd. de la Victoire; phone: 88-35-51-56). Open-air pools are on Rue Pierre-de-Coubertin (phone: 88-31-49-10), in the suburb of Wacken, not far from the exhibition ground, and at the Parc du Rhin is the *Oceade Nautique* amusement park and club (phone: 88-61-92-30).

Tennis and Squash – You can rent both tennis and squash courts by the hour at *Tennis Loisirs*, 31 Rte. du Rhin (phone: 88-34-58-79).

 THEATER: The *Théâtre National de Strasbourg* (Pl. de la République; phone: 88-35-44-52; administrative offices: 1 Rue André-Malraux) is probably the institution of major interest among the city's resident theater companies. The *Théâtre Alsacien* performs at the *Théâtre Municipal* (19 Pl. Broglie; phone: 88-75-48-00). The *Maillon* presents contemporary works, as well as music and dance performances, and film (13 Pl. André-Maurois; phone: 88-27-61-71). *Le Choucrouterie* (20 Rue St-Louis; phone: 88-36-07-28), is a lively, popular dinner theater featuring song and·dance, comedies, and satirical pieces. General information on theater in Strasbourg is available from the *Maison des Arts et Loisirs (MAL;* 1 Rue du Pont-St-Martin; phone: 88-32-74-04), and from the *Théâtre Jeune Public* (7 Rue des Balayeurs; phone: 88-35-70-10).

 MUSIC: The *Palais de la Musique et des Congrès* (Av. Schutzenberger; phone: 88-37-67-97) is Strasbourg's main classical music hall. The *Orchestre Philharmonique de Strasbourg,* a leading European orchestra, plays here from October to June (phone: 88-22-15-60), most of the concerts of the *Festival International de Musique* take place here, and so do many concerts by visiting groups and soloists. The *Opéra du Rhin* performs, from November through June, at the 19th-century opera house, *Théâtre Municipal* (19 Pl. Broglie; phone: 88-75-48-23); besides subscription seats, a certain number of seats are set aside for drop-ins and can be reserved up to 6 days before each performance; remaining tickets go on sale 30 minutes before curtain time. Another local group, the widely known *Percussions de Strasbourg,* made up of approximately 150 percussion instruments from around the world, plays at the *Conservatoire de Musique* (7 Pl. de la République; phone: 88-36-55-02). Folk music and dancing are plentiful in summer. Check with the tourist office for information about Alsatian folk dances that are performed frequently during summer months in the courtyard of the *Château des Rohan.* Troops from other nations also occasionally give international folk music and dance shows. For popular music, check the weekly publications to find out who is in Strasbourg and where.

 NIGHTCLUBS AND NIGHTLIFE: Although Strasbourg is an international capital with plenty of international tourism, it is still in many ways a provincial town offering provincial entertainment. On the whole, it becomes extraordinarily quiet right·after dinner. Discos do come and go: *Bogart's* (17 Rue des Moulins; phone: 88-32-05-11), which operates until about 4 AM (except Sundays), seems to flourish. Popular dance spots are *Le Charlie's* (24 Pl. de Halles; phone: 88-22-32-22), with a *Star Wars* motif, and *Rock's* (56 Rue de Jeu-des-Enfants; phone: 88-32-31-22). The largest and most famous of Strasbourg's discos, also on the edge of town, is *Le Chalet* (376 Rte. de la Wantzenau; phone: 88-31-18-31). It is open Tuesdays through Sundays from 7 PM on. *Le Rétro* (43a Rte. de Bischwiller; phone: 88-81-05-43) is another relative newcomer to Strasbourg's dancing spots. Just outside of town, this club is true to its name, offering old-time ballroom dancing in elegant surroundings.

BEST IN TOWN

 CHECKING IN: The *Accueil de France* service at the Office du Tourisme can help find you a place to stay if you arrive in Strasbourg unannounced. But this is not wise, because, while there are a good number of hotels for the size of the city, there are relatively few in the top class, and these are often taken by European bureaucrats and business travelers who visit frequently. On the other hand, since in many ways Strasbourg is still undiscovered by American tourists, prices are quite reasonable. The top hotels in town, listed as expensive, charge about $100 and up for a double room. Moderate means about $70 to $100, and inexpensive can be about $70 or less.

Baumann Kammerzell – The magnificent landmark building *Maison Kammerzell,*

home of chef Guy Baumann's restaurant of the same name (see *Eating Out*), has expanded to a neighboring edifice, where there are 9 ultramodern guestrooms, as well as conference and banquet rooms. Major credit cards accepted. 16 Pl. de la Cathédrale (phone: 88-32-42-14; fax: 88-23-03-92). Expensive.

Hilton International – The chain's first French hotel outside Paris is large (246 rooms), modern, comfortable, and equipped with all the amenities, such as a health club with a sauna, good bars (including one named and decorated in honor of the classic Bugatti automobile, which was built nearby), a fine restaurant, the *Maison du Boeuf*, and another, less formal, eatery. Rooms are equally well equipped (with mini-bars, color TV sets, direct-dial telephones, and, in some cases, with king- or queen-size beds) and there are rooms for the handicapped and nonsmokers. The hotel is in a quiet area across from the park surrounding the Palais de la Musique et des Congrès — a bus ride or a 10-minute walk from downtown. Major credit cards accepted. Av. Herrenschmidt (phone: 88-37-10-10; fax: 88-36-83-27). Expensive.

Holiday Inn – For those who seek a bit of home away from home, this modern 170-room hotel near the Palais de Congrès offers familiar comforts, including a health club with pool, sauna, steambaths, and tennis courts. Major credit cards accepted. 20 Pl. du Bordeaux (phone: 88-37-80-00; fax: 88-37-07-04). Expensive.

Novotel Centre Halles – This member of a major French chain sits atop a bustling commercial center (with shops, restaurants, banks, and a post office) overlooking central Strasbourg. With 97 rooms, it's modern and straightforward, catering to businesspeople with all the necessary amenities. Major credit cards accepted. Quai Kléber (phone: 88-22-10-99; fax: 88-22-20-92). Expensive.

Le Régent Contades – Forty five well-appointed rooms and suites, a gym, sauna, bar, and 24-hour room service. Major credit cards accepted. 8 Av. de la Liberté (phone: 88-36-26-26; fax: 88-37-13-70). Expensive.

Sofitel – Also modern, this member of the reliable chain has an excellent location on a relatively quiet corner in the center of town — the bells of St-Pierre-le-Jeune across the street provide a Sunday wake-up call. Among the amenities are a quiet bar (*Le Thomann*), a good dining room (*Alsace Gourmand*), boutiques, and a pleasant patio and garden, and the 158 rooms have all the comforts expected of a first class hotel. Major credit cards accepted. Pl. St-Pierre-le-Jeune (phone: 88-32-99-30; fax: 88-32-60-67). Expensive.

Cathédrale-Dauphin – An old building, in front of the cathedral, houses this 32-room hostelry, with its crisply modern lobby and tastefully decorated rooms, many with fantastic views of the cathedral and square. Guests have access to a nearby health and fitness club. 12 Place de la Cathédrale (phone: 88-22-12-12; fax: 88-23-51-88). Expensive to moderate.

Dragon – An appealing hostelry located in a calm corner of town just slightly off the beaten track, it is 17th-century outside and Bauhaus modern inside. Its 32 rooms are in shades of gray with reproduction Mallet Stevens chairs; some rooms have views of the cathedral. It's already a favorite of members of the European Parliament. 2 Rue de l'Ecarlate (phone: 88-35-79-80; fax: 88-25-78-95). Expensive to moderate.

Des Rohan – Though it looks like a historic landmark, this small place on a pedestrian street near the cathedral has been completely modernized. The 36 rooms are all decorated differently in 17th- and 18th-century styles, but each has a private bathroom (tub or shower). The front rooms are the quietest because from the back you overlook, and overhear, the flea market in Rue du Vieil-Hôpital on Wednesdays and Saturdays. No restaurant. Major credit cards accepted. 17-19 Rue du Maroquin (phone: 88-32-85-11; fax: 88-75-65-37). Expensive to moderate.

Terminus Grüber – The best among the eight hotels facing the train station on Place de la Gare. It features lots of marble and crystal — an agglomeration of decor throughout — and includes a large country-inn kind of dining room, the *Cour de Rosemont,* with a fireplace, as well as a brasserie and a cozy bar. Many of the 78 rooms are decorated in grand style. Rooms and suites are soundproofed, but not air conditioned (a design quirk in many medium-priced Strasbourg hotels). Major credit cards accepted. 10 Pl. de la Gare (phone: 88-32-87-00; fax: 88-32-16-46). Expensive to moderate.

L'Europe – Old and slightly worn but entirely functional and clean, it is furnished in heavy antiques and reproductions. It's well located for touring the Petite France quarter, with buildings under restoration on all sides. Not all of the 60 rooms have a private bath and there is no restaurant. Major credit cards accepted. 38 Rue du Fossé-des-Tanneurs (phone: 88-32-17-88; fax: 88-75-65-45). Moderate.

Nouvel Hôtel Maison Rouge – Recently renovated with Art Deco reproductions, this centrally situated, 142-room hotel is more original than most — each guest-room has different furnishings and a distinct color scheme. It has a wide range of conference rooms and an efficient, cooperative staff. Major credit cards accepted. 4 Rue Francs-Bourgeois (phone: 88-32-08-60; fax: 88-22-43-73). Moderate.

Le Relais de Strasbourg – An elegant façade and a high-ceiling lobby hint at the former grandeur of this relic, where the 72 rooms have been renovated in modern, minimalist style. Located between the train station and Strasbourg's center, it is clean and affordable. Major credit cards accepted. 4 Rue du Vieux Marché aux Vins (phone: 88-32-80-00; fax: 88-23-08-85). Moderate.

Royal – A pleasant little 52-room hotel on the street leading from the train station to the business center. It offers modern amenities such as meeting rooms and Jacuzzi, but is brimming with Alsatian touches — hand-painted furniture, prints by local artists, and hand-crafted door plates — which add warmth and charm. Major credit cards accepted. 3 Rue du Maire-Kuss (phone: 88-32-28-71; fax: 88-23-05-39). Moderate.

Gutenberg – Small and simple and in an old château just a few steps off Place Gutenberg; is clean if rather spare. About a third of the 50 rooms come with private bathrooms, and many of the rooms already have an extra bed for a third person or a child. Major credit cards accepted. 31 Rue des Serruriers (phone: 88-32-17-15; fax: 88-75-76-67). Inexpensive.

Ibis – A modern, austere hotel that is less expensive than its neighbor, the *Novotel,* atop the *Centre Halles* commercial center. There are 97 functional rooms with private bathrooms. Children under 12 can stay in their parents' room for free. Major credit cards accepted. 1 Rue de Sébastopol and Quai Kléber (phone: 88-22-14-99; fax: 88-23-02-89). Inexpensive.

 EATING OUT: If French nouvelle cuisine attracts the eye, Alsatian cooking attracts the nose. It is fragrant, and the aromas travel through the streets from early morning. Everything is heavy, rich, and has at least some acquaintance with either pork or cabbage or both. There is virtually no limit to the things Alsatians can do with pork, and cabbage may be Strasbourg's "national" flower — the fields around the city are filled with it. (Those that aren't are filled with hops — *houblon* — because when the Strasbourgeois aren't eating, they are drinking — beer or wine or eau-de-vie.) The city is jammed with restaurants, enough to fill several pages of the phone book in very small type. This includes the ones that remember they are, after all, in France and bring to the table some fine French fare. In the rest, emphasized here, where the food is neither French nor German but Alsatian, the terms may be uncommon even to practiced menu readers, requiring some translations. Almost every Alsatian restaurant has one or two versions of *choucroute garnie,* a mound of warm sauerkraut, often flavored with juniper berries, heaped with boiled potatoes and varying combinations of ham, slab bacon, smoked and fresh pork loin or shoulder or similar meat, and smoked and fresh sausage, at least three kinds. The lone diner may greet the arrival of such a monumental platter at once both daunted and drooling to dig in, which brings to mind another characteristic of Alsatian restaurants. Portions are usually large — often huge — and can easily be shared by two and sometimes three people, which restaurant staffs seem willing to accept. Other translations: *Baeckeoffe,* or "baker's oven," is a stew of pork, beef, lamb (sometimes without the latter), potatoes, onions, and spices served in its earthenware cooking pot (again, of generous proportion). *Jambon en croûte* is ham baked in a pastry crust. *Tarte à l'oignon* is a light onion pie; *tarte flambée* is a sort of Alsatian pizza, a thin crust covered with onions, cheese, cream, bacon chunks, and nutmeg, baked crisp enough to be slightly charred ("licked by flames") and served on a flat board. Desserts include *kugelhopf* (a yeast cake) and *tarte alsacienne* (a fruit tart with vanilla cream). The white Alsatian wines flow easily — riesling (try the *coq au riesling,* the local version of coq au vin, served with tiny dumplings called *spaetzle*), gewürztraminer, sylvaner, and tokay d'alsace (pinot gris) — and so does the beer, notably Kronenbourg 1664 and Meteor. The Alsatians eat heartily, with great gusto, and, as a rule, early. Restaurants that are essentially wine bars with food are called *winstubs;* they are generally less formal than the classic restaurant and many are closed at lunchtime. In the list below, expensive means about $100 or more for a meal for two without wine and is reserved for the elegant French dining rooms. Moderate means about $50 to $100 for two, and inexpensive means under $50 for two. A service charge is usually included.

Le Crocodile – With its three Michelin stars, this is unquestionably among the city's — and the region's — leading eating places. The cuisine is French, often with an Alsatian touch; the fish and game specialties, including eel and frogs, are outstanding; and the atmosphere is elegant — definitely a good choice for that special, well-dressed French evening. Closed Sundays, Mondays, from early July to early August, and for 1 week at *Christmas.* Reservations necessary. Major credit cards accepted. 10 Rue de l'Outre (phone: 88-32-13-02). Very expensive.

Buerehiesel – The Alsatian equivalent of a big old château in a lovely park houses this beautifully appointed dining room where the ambience is softly personal, the service extraordinarily attentive, and the food rated worthy of its two Michelin stars. It's favored by many of the visiting European parliamentarians, but that seems to make no difference to the gracious management: Everyone is greeted and treated with equal and unfailing courtesy. Excellent fish and, in season, game birds are on the basically French menu and there is a large selection of fine wines. Open daily. Reservations necessary. Major credit cards accepted. 4 Parc de l'Orangerie (phone: 88-61-62-24). Expensive.

Valentin-Sorg – On the 14th floor of an undistinguished-looking office building in the middle of town, it offers a fine French menu served in a pretty, surprisingly small dining room with a beautiful view of the quaint rooftops of Strasbourg and the towering cathedral above them. The overall tone may be slightly stiff, as though accustomed to looking down at the neighbors, but this is still another good choice for a romantic and elegant dinner. Closed Sunday evenings, Tuesdays, 2 weeks in February, and 2 weeks in August. Reservations necessary. Major credit cards accepted. 6 Pl. de l'Homme-de-Fer (phone: 88-32-12-16). Expensive.

Maison Kammerzell – A 16th-century architectural monument in its own right, it holds down the best corner in town. The elaborate woodcarving continues in the restaurant inside, which has a comfortable dining room downstairs and a more formal room upstairs overlooking Place de la Cathédrale. The sale of this local institution — to Guy Baumann, an Alsatian chef who made it big in Paris with a chain of quality *choucroute* restaurants — doesn't seem to have diminished its popularity or quality. Some claim his classic *choucroute alsacienne* is the city's best. For the adventurous there's the less conventional *choucroute au poisson*. The menu offers a variety of "formulas," including some very reasonably priced offerings, service included. English-speaking waiters. Open daily. Reservations advised. Major credit cards accepted. 16 Pl. de la Cathédrale (phone: 88-32-42-14). Expensive to moderate.

Maison des Tanneurs – This beautiful, giant half-timbered building bedecked with balconies and flowers at the edge of a canal is a restaurant justly reputed to produce one of the best *choucroutes* in Strasbourg. In fact, it bills itself as "La Maison de la Choucroute," but it offers fine dining on other traditional dishes as well in lovely paneled surroundings in the heart of Petite France. Share the *choucroute*. English-speaking waiters. Closed Sundays, Mondays, the first 2 weeks in July, and from the end of December to mid-January. Reservations advised. Major credit cards accepted. 42 Rue du Bain-aux-Plantes (phone: 88-32-79-70). Expensive to moderate.

La Vieille Enseigne – Once a mere *winstub,* this cozy restaurant has a club-like atmosphere that makes it popular with politicians. The food and service have improved over the years, ultimately reaching a very high level in both. Closed Saturday lunch and Sundays. Reservations necessary. Major credit cards accepted. 9 Rue des Tonneliers (phone: 88-32-58-50). Expensive to moderate.

L'Ami Fritz – This is a small, neat, friendly place for Alsatian food in the midst of Petite France. It doesn't have the view that its bigger neighbors have, but it's less pretentious. Closed Sunday evenings and Mondays. Reservations advised. Major credit cards accepted. 8 Rue des Dentelles (phone: 88-32-80-53). Moderate.

Bierstub l'Ami Schutz – A favorite of young businessmen getting away from downtown. It has a good location along the Ponts Couverts with a terrace overlooking the water and the Petite France quarter, and it's a pretty place, albeit slightly stuffy. The setting counts more than the cuisine, even though an effort is made to re-create traditional dishes. The hand-painted dishware can be purchased. Open daily. Reservations unnecessary. Major credit cards accepted. 1 Ponts-Couverts (phone: 88-32-76-98). Moderate.

Au Clou – A straightforward *winstub,* and one of the best in town for rubbing elbows with the gusty Strasbourgeois. Businesspeople, professionals, plain folks, and students (with their allowances from home still fresh) jam together at shared tables with a sense of jovial well-being. The service is gracious and bustling, with portions easily, and willingly, divided for two. This is a good spot to be introduced to *baeckeoffe,* the savory stew of beef, pork, onions, and potatoes layered so the flavors mingle. Good local wines come by the pitcher. Dinner only; closed Sundays and holidays and the last 2 weeks in August. Reservations accepted only for four persons or more. Major credit cards accepted. 3 Rue du Chaudron (phone: 88-32-11-67). Moderate.

Jean dit Carolis – The air in the tiny rooms of this lively regional eatery is fragrant with such Alsatian specialties as *choucroute garnie* and *tarte à l'oignon.* Closed Saturday for lunch. Reservations advised. Major credit cards accepted. 5 Rue de Zurich (phone: 88-37-04-44). Moderate.

La Maison du Boeuf – Those with an irresistible desire for T-bone steaks (imported from the US) or for some local beef specialties will feel at home here. Closed Saturdays and Sundays. Reservations unnecessary. Major credit cards accepted. In the *Hilton,* Av. Herrenschmidt (phone: 88-37-10-10; fax: 88-36-83-27). Moderate.

La Petite Alsace – Rustic wood beams, white lace tablecloths, and a typical Alsatian menu characterize this pleasant spot in the heart of Petite France. Closed Sundays, Mondays, and February. Reservations advised. Major credit cards accepted. 23 Rue du Bain-aux-Plantes (phone: 88-22-04-05). Moderate.

Au Pont du Corbeau – A modern little restaurant catering to businesspeople, only a few steps from the *Musée Alsacien*. It serves French rather than strictly Alsatian food, a half-dozen specialties each day, and you can finish your meal with a *tarte au fromage blanc*, a moist cheesecake about 3 inches high that should not be missed. Open daily. Reservations unnecessary. Major credit cards accepted. 21 Quai St-Nicolas (phone: 88-35-60-68). Moderate.

Au Pont St-Martin – Another beautiful, giant half-timbered building in Petite France. The *winstub*-style restaurant has many tables overlooking the water and the locks, it stays open late at night, and it has a piano. When somebody plays, anybody sings, anything from anywhere. The mood is better than the food, but the view is fine. Open daily. Reservations advised. Major credit cards accepted. 13-15 Rue des Moulins (phone: 88-32-45-13). Moderate.

Le Pied dans le Plat – A small spot in pastel pink with lace tablecloths and paintings on the walls. Meats are tender here, desserts delicious. Closed Saturday lunch and Sundays. Reservations unnecessary. Major credit cards accepted. 8 Rue du Renard-Prêchant (phone: 88-36-00-84). Moderate to inexpensive.

St-Sépulcre (Hailich Graab) – Small, noisy, crowded, and fun. Strangers share long tables for eight, the menu is postcard-size, the food good, the service fast. You'll see children of all ages, because the management splits dishes. Closed Sundays, Mondays, and mid-July to early August. Reservations unnecessary; it's best to arrive before 1 PM to get served. Major credit cards accepted. 15 Rue des Orfèvres (phone: 88-32-39-97). Moderate to inexpensive.

S'Burjerstuewel (Chez Yvonne) – This tiny place is a true *winstub*, chockablock with Strasbourgeois working from a light menu of heavy fare on crowded checkered tablecloths. The specialties include the onion pie and the baked ham that comes with cornichons and horseradish. Or you can perch at the small bar, drink the local wine, and watch the modish, noisy crowd. Serves to 12:30 AM. Closed Sundays, Mondays at lunch, holidays, and mid-July to mid-August. Reservations unnecessary. Major credit cards accepted. 10 Rue du Sanglier (phone: 88-32-84-15). Moderate to inexpensive.

Aux Armes de Strasbourg – The large, crowded room here has a dark wooden ceiling and walls yellowed by numberless winters of warmth. There's a good menu of solid food and the waitress tots up the bill on the paper tablecloth. Closed Tuesdays and Wednesdays. Reservations unnecessary. Major credit cards accepted. 9 Pl. Gutenberg (phone: 88-32-85-62). Inexpensive.

Chez Tante Liesel – If Norman Rockwell had had an Aunt Liesel, this would have been her kitchen. Friendly and cheerful, the tiny room has only nine wooden tables that are quickly crammed with traditional dishes from family recipes and unexpected treats such as a slab of muenster cheese with a little pot of caraway seeds to dip it in or an apple pie topped with a crust filled with walnuts and cinnamon. Closed Tuesdays, Wednesday lunch, *Christmas*, and *New Year's Day*. Reservations advised. Major credit cards accepted. 4 Rue des Dentelles (phone: 88-23-02-16). Inexpensive.

Au Gutenberg – Small and friendly, with a stack of pretzels on each table and service from 10 AM to 1 AM every day of the year. Reservations unnecessary. Major credit cards accepted. 8 Pl. Gutenberg (phone: 88-32-82-48). Inexpensive.

Au Petit Bois Vert – A simple spot serving regional dishes, it has a pretty terrace under a giant canalside plane tree. Closed Wednesdays in winter. Reservations unnecessary. Major credit cards accepted. 3 Quai de la Bruche (phone: 88-32-66-32). Inexpensive.

Pfifferbrieder – This is in a little corner house that looks like something Disney would have drawn for Gepetto. The food is Alsatian — solid, plentiful, and reminiscent of home cooking — and it's served without frills or fanfare. Indeed, if the service is a little harried, you can fill the lapses by contemplating the hearty citizenry. Closed Sundays and August. Reservations unnecessary. Major credit cards accepted. 9 Pl. de la Grande Boucherie (phone: 88-32-15-43). Inexpensive.

S'Marikstuewele – A standard, no-nonsense brasserie, with plenty of children in evidence. The *tarte flambée* served downstairs on Friday and Saturday nights — on a board about a foot long — makes an outstanding meal for two. Closed Sundays. Reservations unnecessary. No credit cards accepted. 6 Rue du Marché (phone: 88-23-24-10). Inexpensive.

Zum Striessel – Reliable Alsatian food, a good selection of Alsatian wines, traditional rustic decor, and quintessential Alsatian atmosphere have made this one of the more popular places among the Strasbourgeois. Its location in the midst of the pedestrian traffic pattern between the museums and the cathedral helps, too. Closed Sundays, Mondays, the last week in February, and the last 3 weeks in July. Reservations advised. Major credit cards accepted. 5 Pl. de la Grande Boucherie (phone: 88-32-14-73). Inexpensive.

 TAKING TEA: If something sweet suffices as a meal, Strasbourg has any number of tearooms. *Christian Meyer* (10 Rue Mercière; phone: 88-22-12-70) has a chocolate and pastry shop downstairs and a tearoom serving coffee, tea, and fine, rich pastries upstairs. The *Salon de Thé Suzel* (at the corner of Rue du Bain-aux-Plantes and Rue des Moulins; phone: 88-23-10-46) is a tiny, welcoming place to drop in for tea and homemade pastries after trooping through Petite France. It's open from noon to 6:30 PM; closed Sundays and Mondays. And if you're an early jogger looking for coffee and a croissant or a slice of *kugelhopf* after a sprint along the quays, try the *Espresso* (17 Rue du Maire-Kuss; phone: 88-32-02-19), between the canal and the train station. It opens at 5 AM every day except *Christmas* and the day after.

 BARS AND CAFÉS: Local watering holes include the *Bugatti Bar* at the *Hilton International* and *Le Thomann* at the *Sofitel*. Two popular bars located across the street from each other on Rue des Soeurs, behind the cathedral, are *Les Aviateurs* (12 Rue des Soeurs; phone: 88-36-52-65) and *Le Nid d'Espion* (3 Rue des Soeurs; phone: 88-37-02-83). A little off the beaten path is *L'Abreuvoir* (3 Pl. de l'Abreuvoir; phone: 88-36-09-36), a good, middle class drinkingman's bar. *Bar Jean et Jacques* (4 Rue des Païens; phone: 88-32-33-44) is a gritty sports hangout for the regulars, the old-timers, and the visitor in search of local color, the sort of place where they'll be knocking them back to open their eyes in the morning. You might try a Picon *bière* — orange bitters and beer — listen to the jukebox, and wait for Belmondo to come in. He probably won't, but if he were around, this is where he'd be.

DIVERSIONS

For the Experience

Quintessential France

 Modern France is much more than baguettes, bicycles, and berets, and there is a terrible temptation to describe the once-treasured glory of this now polyglot nation as gone forever. It's not hard to dismiss any real national identity in a country that sprawls from the shores of the Rhine to the far-flung *départements* of Guadeloupe and Martinique in the Caribbean, for France encompasses the Teutonic types of Alsace, the fractious faction of Basque separatists, the dour Celts of Brittany, and the topless Lolitas of St-Tropez. All this while the smoky bistros fill with North African and eastern European Jews in the Marais and the *Burger King* of the Champs-Elysées have become just as Parisian as the *Café de la Paix*. Still, it would be wrong to despair that the flavor of France had been boiled out of the new French melting pot. Rejoice that authentic bouillabaisse still requires *rouget* scooped fresh from the Mediteranean, that *vin ordinaire* sipped in a crowded café is somehow elevated far above pure plonk, and that the stubborn Gauls still smooch by the Seine, argue using every available limb for emphasis, and happily dance in the streets on *Bastille Day*. Here are some quintessential French experiences to prove the point.

BOULEVARD ST-MICHEL, Paris: In the glitter of street lamps, and the evening glow from floodlit Notre-Dame, there is a simmering mix of arguing students, drumming youths and strumming guitars, roasting chestnuts, and sizzling streetcorner crêpes — a feast that hasn't moved since Hemingway's day. Latin no longer is the *lingua franca* of this quarter, but you'll hear plenty of Greek, Arabic, Farsi, and Wolof, and sharing billboard space in front of the multilingual movie theaters are posters for the latest films from Jakarta to *JFK*. The bookstalls along the Seine hold anything from a first edition of Proust to a paperback mystery from 1962 — or a single, illuminated page from a medieval manuscript.

MEGALITHS OF BRITTANY, Pérros-Guirec and Carnac: The Celts settled along the western rim of the liveable world, where the earth juts out into water and fog. And on this gray-green tongue of Europe they still speak a language closer to Gaelic and Galician than to French. On the northern coast of Brittany, between Pérros-Guirec and Ploumanac'h, the sea has chiseled and the wind has polished huge sculptures of rose-colored granite, challenging humans to match them. Across the Breton peninsula is the competition — thousands of great stone *menhirs* of Carnac, aligned since prehistoric times like petrified cheerleaders in some cosmic half-time show. Long after the Eiffel Tower has collapsed into a twisted heap of scrap metal, this druidic trail marker for the gods will remain a symbol of France. Luckily, there is no quick way to cross Brittany from north to south. So after lying on the sun-warmed, smooth pink boulders perched delicately on a cliffside with nothing below, wander from Carnac to St-Malo, with plenty of stops for fish soups, cider, and seafood crêpes.

BUBBLES AND TRUFFLES AND STAINED GLASS, Reims, Champagne: The ll miles of catacombs under the Pommery vineyards hold that celebratory essence of

France first brought to life by a 17th-century monk, Dom Perignon. Since then, conditions in Champagne have been honed to fastidious perfection, from the grapes grown close to the ground to absorb heat from the chalky soil, to the cellars' naturally constant temperature, to the patient *remueurs* who give each of millions of bottles the requisite fraction of a turn. At the restaurant *Boyer "Les Crayères,"* you will be treated as lovingly as a magnum of Roederer Cristal 1979. If one of the great stars of chefdom, Gérard Boyer, comes to your table in the mansion's lavish dining room to ask if everything is to your liking, the *ris de veau aux graines de sésamé* (sweetbreads with sesame seeds) should give you reason enough to be sincerely ecstatic. The only possible disturbance to dessert on the terrace overlooking the bucolic estate might be the whirr of a helicopter as it deposits a guest from Paris on the restaurant's private landing pad. After dinner, floodlights give a pale yellow tinge to the spikes, spires, and statues that bubble up the fluted façade of Reims's Gothic cathedral, made of the same chalky stone that gives champagne its fizz. But do try to get here during the day, when the principal ornament of the stark interior is a jeweled glimmer thrown by the stained glass windows on the gray stone floor.

ON HORSEBACK THROUGH CORSICA: Take a deep breath when you get to Corsica — in the late spring, the mingled scents from the undergrowth of honeysuckle, lavender, thyme, and mint mix with the salty froth of the Mediterranean and the last snow still clinging to the mountains. Avoid the resorts and the worn roads, and canter through the chestnut forests, the glacial streams, the olive groves, and terraced gardens carved out of steep granite and dense brush. Spend an evening listening to throaty *lamenti,* a kind of Corsican blues sung in the wine bars and cafés of miniscule port towns. This is an island created with a postcard palette — the *maquis* flowering white in May, the electric-colored houses on Cap Corse, the red rock of the Calanques dropping into a sapphire sea at Piana. This banished bit of France, with its Genoese watchtowers and its dialect akin to Sardinian, is so close to Italy that Napoleon could almost see his native Corsica from the Tuscan island of Elba where he was in exile.

LOIRE VALLEY BY BOAT, BALLOON, OR BICYCLE: Ever since the Middle Ages, aristocrats, with a love of rural living but no taste for roughing it, have made the Loire Valley into the ultimate exurb. Go in the fall, when the traffic thins on the rivers, gravel paths, and marble stairways, and when, from the basket of a balloon, you can see the châteaux ensconced in the auburn parkland of their thousand-acre backyards. Don't visit too many, and concentrate on the outside. Better to remember the fairy-tale turrets of Chambord or the graceful arches of Chenonceaux spanning the Cher River than to have it all meld into a sumptuous haze of polished wood and tarnished mirrors and the very chair where Louis the Something sat. Whether you float, fly, or pedal from the catapult-proof towers of Loches to the flower beds of Villandry, the point is to take it slow. Stop during the hottest part of the day for some goat cheese and a glass of dry vouvray, and bask for a while in the delightful sounds of silence.

D-DAY BEACHES, Normandy: Save a gray day for this blowy, empty coast. Roll up your pants' legs and wade along these silent, sandy flats, and listen in a sea shell for the sputter of field radios and the crackle of machine guns and the long-ago crunch of boots on the beach. Or scan the coastline and see the scars from one of the greatest operations in military history — the vast American cemetery, the German pillboxes on the murderous cliff at Pointe du Hoc, the landing craft and giant bulkheads sunk in the sand at Arromanches. You cannot help but be moved, whether you're 20 and read about Omaha Beach in a book, or 70 and have a buddy buried under one of the white marble crosses or Stars of David at St-Laurent-sur-Mer. June 6, 1944, the date of the Normandy landings (like the date the Normans landed in England in 1066) divides European history into before and after.

TURQUOISE, EMERALD, AND GOLD — THE CÔTE D'AZUR: Squeezed between mountains and the Mediterranean, the Côte d'Azur is a glittering strip of low-slung bathing suits and Alps-high prices, the meeting spot of Europe's wealthy worshipers of sun and self. With a croissant and *café crème* on the Promenade des Anglais in Nice comes a ringside seat for people watching — in July and August it's hard to see the beaches for the suntanned bodies. After a long day of windsurfing and body-burnishing, take a sunset convertible ride on the Grande Corniche to the castle town of Roque-brune-Cap Martin, to look down on the sea trails left by waterskiers eking out the last drops of twilight. Look west over the pines and the cactus-covered cliffside of the Riviera toward Monte Carlo, where most of what glistens really is gold, and where suitable attire should include an extra shirt, in case you lose the one you're wearing. From a table in the *Grill Room* atop Monte Carlo's *Hôtel de Paris,* survey the yacht harbor, watering hole of the world's jet set. After dinner, take a deep breath of flower-scented air and walk across the Place du Casino for an evening of serious play among the mirthful rococo motifs and poker-face croupiers in the casino's Salon-Privé.

HARVEST TIME IN BURGUNDY, Beaune: The well-being of Beaune is safeguarded by the phalanx of vines laid out in disciplined rows on the hills outside the city's high medieval walls. The town's veneration of *vin* is such that there is no marked separation between church and grape — the brothers of the Order of the Chevaliers du Tastevin dress in priestly raiments for their tastings in the nearby Château du Clos de Vougeot, whose fabled vineyards were planted by Cistercian monks. Once the local seat of power, the Palace of the Dukes of Burgundy now houses the *Musée du Vin,* virtually a museum of Burgundian civilization. At harvest time, the ripening grapes and turning leaves give the vineyard-patterned hills the same hues as the wine-colored tile designs that adorn Burgundian roofs. Thousands of pickers, armed with shears and giant baskets, fan out among the vines and round up the fruit to be pressed, stomped, aged, and bottled in a Nuits-St-Georges or a pouilly-fuissé. Visit the cellars for a tour and a taste, even if you decide not to bring home a case — you're sure to learn something, whether you've never touched the stuff or already know the difference between an impudent little rosé and a flirtatious, full-bodied red.

RUE DU FAUBOURG-ST-HONORÉ AND RUE ST-HONORÉ, Paris: Like the *Grand Bazaar* of Istanbul, the souk of Marrakesh, and the agora of ancient Athens, the designer sidewalks of the mile-long stretch between the president's palace and the Palais Royal is one of the world's great shopping experiences. It has the finest names in everything, and an unsurpassed array of specialized retailers of chocolate, leather, and lingerie. Try *Au Nain Bleu* for a miniature tea set in Limoges porcelain, *Hermès* for an equestrian-print umbrella, or *Raymond* for gold-plated faucets. Nearby on Place Madeleine, go to *Fauchon* for plum mustard or a salmon mousse sprinkled with caviar, and if you can't live without something nobody else could have, tour the galleries and antiques dealers, and stop in at that ultimate purveyor of the unique — *Louvre des Antiquaires* on the Place du Palais-Royal.

THE BORDER BLEND, Alsace: Alsace often has been the rope in a Franco-German tug-of-war, and now is the French capital of both foie gras and *choucroute.* Although the air is tinged with riesling and the curvy Route des Vins defines the greatest distance between two nearby points, the people here do not live by wine alone — Alsace also produces France's best, most German beer. It is the birthplace of the anthem that got named for Marseilles and of the German invention of movable type. Over the years, the same Strasbourg artery has been named for Napoleon, Kaiser Wilhelm II, the French Republic, Adolf Hitler, and Charles de Gaulle. The city even has a French quarter — La Petite France. The town of Riquewihr, with its gables, cobbles, old wells, storks' nests, and ancient walls, has the Hansel-and-Gretel look of 16th-century Germany. In the fairly large medieval city of Colmar, the *Musée Unterlinden* houses the glowing *Issenheim Altarpiece* by Matthias Grünewald. A bedraggled, tortured Christ hangs from twisted limbs covered in crimson rivulets of blood and then is resurrected in a radiant aura, able-bodied and blond.

PAINTERS' PROVENCE, Arles and Aix-en-Provence: A brooding Dutchman came to Arles and saw the light that soaks the earth, and it gave him the luminous brushstroke that the world associates with Vincent Van Gogh. That same Provençal sun shines through the big picture windows of a studio in Aix, lighting up a canvas that still waits patiently on an easel for Cézanne to finish it. The painter came from this sleepy city cooled by fountains and shaded by the trees on the Cours Mirabeau. A walk out of town along the Route de Cézanne leads to the Montagne Ste-Victoire, still dressed in ocher and pine-tree green, still posing for a post-Impressionist landscape. Arles, too, looks like a canvas come to life, with its brightly painted shutters, its rich surrounding fields of sunflowers and wheat, its sunbaked Arlésiens tossing *boules* on a dusty pitch. Paul Gaugin lived here for a while with Van Gogh, and Picasso loved the town so much that he gave it 57 drawings that are now housed in the *Musée Réattu.*

Romantic French Hostelries

 In an increasingly homogeneous and anonymous world, the fine French hotel remains one of the last bastions of charm and luxury. From the first warm, flaky croissant to the last turned-down eiderdown, a stay in one of them is a study in perpetual pampering which makes for an experience that is not to be missed on any account.

But France also boasts another unique species of hostelry, the wonderful establishment with a certain quality of romance that goes beyond mere splendor. Such a hotel may have a sleek, urbane lobby throbbing with the pulse of Paris. Or a languid arbor overlooking the Mediterranean in a garden full of flowers. It may be a château in the country with a dozen or so crackling fireplaces. These hostelries exist in a certain harmony with their settings; they seem to be a part of the local life rather than something aside from it. They also have a special warmth. And the staff has an ability to make you feel that you count and that they care. Excellent cuisine often is a feature, though not always.

The descriptive list of hotels that follows, a selection of some of the best rather than a comprehensive report, suggests the quantity of such accommodations that the adventurous traveler in France can discover.

HÔTEL DU CAP–EDEN ROC, Antibes, Alpes-Maritimes: A bastion of luxury in a miniature wilderness, this 100-room and 10-suite Riviera landmark and its piney 20-acre park — believed to be the setting for F. Scott Fitzgerald's *Tender Is the Night* — is set above the rocks at the tip of the promontory at the Cap d'Antibes, one of the most exclusive spots on the entire Côte d'Azur. It's *the* place to stay during the *Cannes Film Festival* — if you can get a room. From the edge of the turquoise swimming pool, it's possible to dive right into the aquamarine sea; whole afternoons can be spent simply inhaling the fragrance of wisteria between serves on the 5 private tennis courts. Sea-view dining on the patios of the *Pavillon Eden Roc,* one of the Côte d'Azur's most lordly restaurants, is another none too inconsequential feature here. And all for only pennies more than the price of a few Renoirs. Information: *Hôtel du Cap–Eden Roc,* Bd. Kennedy, Antibes 06602 (phone: 93-61-39-01; fax: 93-67-766-04; telex: 470763).

CHÂTEAU D'AUDRIEU, Audrieu, Calvados: One of the stately homes of France, this historic monument has been lovingly preserved by the family that built it some 2 centuries ago. Now, their castle is your home — complete with exquisite formal gardens, a heated swimming pool, a full complement of antique furniture, 2 splendid and serene dining rooms (see *Haute Gastronomie*), more than 60 acres of verdant parkland,

and a location just a few miles away from the beaches of Normandy — so close, in fact, that the castle narrowly escaped destruction during the *D-Day* invasion. Many of the ancient trees still bear shell scars. A member of the Relais & Châteaux group. Closed in February. Information: *Château d'Audrieu,* Audrieu 14250 (phone: 31-80-21-52; fax: 31-80-24-73).

HÔTELLERIE DU BAS-BRÉAU, Barbizon, Seine-et-Marne: This charming inn is in the midst of a setting that inspired artists like Corot and Rousseau and writers like Robert Louis Stevenson. Indeed, Stevenson wrote *Forest Notes* here, and the inn served as an exhibition hall for Barbizon school painters in the early 20th century. Jean-Pierre Fava is now the proprietor, and he continues a family tradition of charm and comfort outdoors and in. The 12 rooms, 7 apartments, and villa are furnished with antique furniture and fine linen. Outside, the lawns are exquisitely manicured, the flowers meticulously tended. An airy restaurant offers a superb, sophisticated menu. A member of the Relais & Châteaux group. Information: *Hôtellerie du Bas-Bréau,* 22 Rue Grande, Barbizon 77630 (phone: 60-66-40-05; fax: 60-69-22-89).

OUSTAU DE BAUMANIÈRE, Les Baux-de-Provence, Bouches-du-Rhône: Eleven miles (18 km) east of Arles and tucked deftly into the rocky crags of the gleaming limestone Alpilles foothills, this gracious and lushly green oasis has as its centerpiece a venerable old manor house fitted out with accommodations that are no less than princely. Fireplaces crackle under vaulted ceilings. Tapestries surround diners in the two-star restaurant (see *Haute Gastronomie*). Wines are selected from the 35,000 bottles in the famous Baumanière cellars. Four-poster beds cradle bodies wearied from swimming or horseback riding. And no one goes away without sampling the dining room of the nearby one-star *Cabro d'Or,* the management's alternative pleasure dome. Both are members of the Relais & Châteaux group. Information: *Oustau de Baumanière,* Les Baux-de-Provence, Maussane 13520 (phone: 90-54-33-07; fax: 90-54-40-46; telex: 420203).

LA RÉSERVE, Beaulieu-sur-Mer, Alpes-Maritimes: Dining in the sleek salon of *La Réserve* feels a little like sitting at the captain's table on one of the old luxury liners, with the blue sea and bluer-than-blue sky stretching away just beyond the chandeliers. Here, one level down, there's a handsome pool, and a notch below that a stony beach and an amply stocked yacht basin. The grounds are enthralling; those who manage to drag themselves away will find charming Beaulieu to be well worth their effort. And the whole of the Riviera is just a corniche away. A member of the Relais & Châteaux group. Information: *Hôtel La Réserve,* 5 Bd. Général-Leclerc, Beaulieu-sur-Mer 06310 (phone: 93-01-00-01; fax: 93-01-28-99; telex: 470301).

HÔTEL DU PALAIS, Biarritz, Basses-Pyrénées: When this establishment's brochures describe the premises as "a hotel of dramatic extravagance," they demonstrate a commendable degree of self-knowledge. This most patrician of lodging places, in perhaps the most patrician of all French resorts, once was the imperial residence of Napoleon III's Empress Eugénie. There are stunning views of the whole coastline, an elegantly groomed private beach, a gently warmed seawater pool for those who prefer to admire the Atlantic at a distance, and, just down the street, a casino. None of this comes cheap, of course; the empress herself probably couldn't afford to stay here today. Open from March to December. Information: *Hôtel du Palais,* 1 Av. de l'Impératrice, Biarritz 64200 (phone: 59-24-09-40; fax: 59-24-86-84).

CARLTON, Cannes, Alpes-Maritimes: This great white-turreted doyenne presides over La Croisette — the Riviera's principal main drag — like some permanent sand castle for seaside royalty, complete with swaying green palm trees and blue and white umbrellas to shade some of the most beautiful bodies in Europe. Its 2 one-Michelin-star restaurants offer feasts for the palate as well as for the eyes. In this city, May is an especially merry month because of the film festival, but if you plan to see just how merry, count on reserving a decade or two in advance lest you find yourself in a sleeping bag on the beach. Information: *Hôtel Carlton,* 58 Bd. de La Croisette, Cannes 06400 (phone: 93-68-91-68; fax: 93-38-20-90; telex: 470720).

MOULIN DE LA GORCE, La Roche-L'Abeille, Haute-Vienne: A mill has existed at this spot in the countryside near Limoges from the time of the Valois, but the *moulin* here today serves a different sort of client. Jean Bertranet, a former chef at the Elysée Palace, the official residence of the President of France, fell in love with the beauty of the mill's *limousin* surroundings and promptly built this lovely 9-room establishment that recalls a more pristine era. Meals are served on the terrace overlooking a park and a small pond, or, in cooler weather, in the beautiful Louis XVI dining room with a massive brick fireplace. Specialties are richly traditional, such as *oeufs brouillés aux truffes* (scrambled eggs with truffles) and *mélange gourmand de homard et foie gras* (foie gras and lobster). Sumptuously endowed with wines of the Périgord and Bordeaux regions, the *cave* is nothing less than superlative. Accommodations at this member of the Relais & Châteaux group are exceptionally comfortable and tastefully furnished; we'd recommend one of the 6 luxurious rooms located in a separate building between the pond and a rushing trout stream. Closed early January to early February and Sunday evenings and Monday except in summer. Information: *Moulin de la Gorce,* La Roche-L'Abeille, Haute-Vienne 87800 (phone: 55-00-70-66; fax: 55-00-76-57).

NORMANDY, Deauville, Calvados: At its proudest during the city's August racing season, when the casino is wall-to-wall tuxedos and all of Paris has come down for a stroll on the boardwalk, this imposing Norman mansion of a hotel by the sea has a special, more solitary romance during the winter, when wind and rain froth the ocean and lash the Norman coast. Neither discourages the roulette players or the lobster-eaters at *Ciro's,* the hotel's boardwalk restaurant. Information: *Hôtel Normandy,* 38 Rue Jean-Mermoz, Deauville l4800 (phone: 31-98-66-22; fax: 31-98-66-23).

LES GRANDS HÔTELS, Divonne-les-Bains, Ain: In a peaceful arboretum in a placid border village in the quiet foothills of the Jura mountain range. Golfers can test their skills on one of France's finest courses (see also *Great French Golf*); sailors can sample the winds on an extensive artificial lake; hedonists can experience a soak in each of 57 varieties of thermal baths. Anyone else may want to thumb his nose at such sedate pastimes and enjoy lavish predawn dining in the wheelside restaurant of France's busiest and most profitable casino. Geneva is only a quarter of an hour away, so at any given moment the town's demographics will strike a pleasant balance between farmers' daughters and international traveling salesmen. Information: *Les Grands Hôtels,* Divonne-les-Bains 01220 (phone: 50-20-06-63; fax: 50-40-43-24).

ROYAL CLUB EVIAN, Evian-les-Bains, Haute-Savoie: At this Belle Epoque beauty set in 28 acres of woodland high above Lake Geneva, nearly every room has a sunny balcony that faces across the lake to Switzerland or looks south toward the Mont-Blanc range. The modern management — gone pleasantly health and sports mad — has added to this formerly staid center for sylvan pastimes a bristling lot of athletic facilities and programs: a half-dozen Greenset tennis courts (3 lighted for night play) and a tennis academy; a regular shuttle service to the *Royal Golf Club;* an archery range and daily instruction; saunas, hydrotherapy facilities and hydrotherapists; calisthenic sessions; and a jogging circuit with obstacles. The 5 restaurants, including *La Rotonde,* which specializes in dietetic cuisine, provide something to look forward to while sweating. An evening shuttle to the renowned casino is available gratis to hotel guests. Information: *Royal Club Evian,* Av. des Mateirons, Evian-les-Bains 74500 (phone: 50-26-85-00; fax: 50-75-38-40).

CHÂTEAU DE LA CHÈVRE D'OR, Eze-Village, Alpes-Maritimes: This small hotel in a medieval village is perched so splendidly high (1,300 feet) above the Côte D'Azur that it is quiet and calm even on the most intense summer days on the Riviera. Its 12 rooms and 3 suites all look out over the sea, and have the rustic appeal that stone walls and down comforters offer. The one-Michelin-star restaurant is excellent countrifiedchic; try the wild strawberry soufflé. Monte Carlo and Nice are only a few miles away, but you just may decide to save them for another trip. Though it's a bit of a climb from the parking lot *up* to the hotel's front door, it's worth every step. A member of the Relais & Châteaux group. Information: *Château de la Chèvre d'Or,* Eze-Village 06360 (phone: 93-41-12-12; fax: 93-41-06-72; telex: 970839).

CHÂTEAU DE LOCGUÉNOLÉ, Hennebont, Morbihan: A woodland park (250 acres) surrounds this family mansion, now a fine hotel, cushioning guests from the busy beaches of the Breton coast and any other brush with real life. Owned by the same family for more than 500 years, the antiques, paintings, and museum-quality tapestries in this courtly castle grace the stately, yet welcoming lounges. If your mood is correspondingly regal, choose a large velvety room with French doors on the second floor. If your tastes run to the rustic, the exposed beams and flowery prints of the attic floor will charm you. The views over Le Blavet Sound are dazzling from all the rooms. Leave time for sampling local seafood in the renowned restaurant. Swimming, tennis, and fishing are possible without ever stepping out into the rude world. A member of the Relais & Châteaux group. Information: *Château de Locguénolé,* Rte. de Port-Louis (Km. 5), Hennebont 56700 (phone: 97-76-29-04; fax: 97-76-39-47).

FERME SAINT-SIMÉON, Honfleur, Calvados: The Impressionist light of Monet, Renoir, and Corot brightened here at Honfleur. After a day of painting outdoors, the artists played dominoes and drank cider with the local farmers at this member of the Relais & Châteaux group, formerly a 17th-century inn. Today, a modern 19-room annex is cozy and bright, but the original 19 rooms are the most romantic. Ask for one with a view of the Atlantic, and then watch the clouds move against a brilliant blue sky. Dine on lobster stew on the terrace under the trees. Set the morning aside to explore the port of Honfleur and the evening to click chips at the *Deauville* casino. Information: *Ferme Saint-Siméon,* Rue Adolphe-Marais, Honfleur 14600 (phone: 31-89-23-61; fax: 31-89-48-48).

LA CÔTE SAINT-JACQUES, Joigny, Yonne: Before self-indulgence goes out of style, explore its true meaning at this luxurious hotel-restaurant complex on the shore of the Yonne River, bordering Burgundy wine country. The superbly managed family-owned and run restaurant (see *Haute Gastronomie*) is housed in a traditional 18th-century country home, but the newer and more elegant accommodations are in the nearby *Résidence.* Many rooms have soothing river views. You can stagger from your three-star foie gras and truffles to a flower-bedecked bed by going through the glamorously lit vaulted tunnel. There are Parisians who make the 2-hour drive simply to dine here. The hotel and restaurant are closed from early January to early February. A member of the Relais & Châteaux group. Information: *Résidence de la Côte Saint-Jacques,* 14 Faubourg de Paris, Joigny 89300 (phone: 86-62-09-70; fax: 86-91-49-70).

HÔTEL LES LOGES DU MONT-BLANC and CHALET-DU-MONT-D'ARBOIS, Megève, Haute-Savoie: Film buffs will never forget the suave actor Gérard Philippe on the slopes of sophisticated Megève in Roger Vadim's wicked 1959 picture *Les Liaisons Dangereuses.* In the French Alps, these establishments represent the ultimate in jet set chic now as they did then. Still *the* spots where the beautiful people brush the snow from their pastel stretch pants and sip mulled wine by the fire. Or enjoy a cocktail at the bar of *Les Enfants Terribles,* famous for its Jean Cocteau frescoes. The hotel is large and bustling, right in the center of the village; the 20-room chalet (a member of the Relais & Châteaux group), at 4,000 feet, lies on a country road above the town. Information: *Les Loges du Hôtel Mont-Blanc,* Pl. de l'Eglise, Megève 74120 (phone: 50-21-20-02; fax: 50-93-09-52); *Chalet-du-Mont-d'Arbois,* Rte. du Mont-D'Arbois, Megève 74120 (phone: 50-21-25-03; fax: 50-21-24-79).

CHÂTEAU D'ARTIGNY, Montbazon, Indre-et-Loire: Many travelers who have spent the day visiting the châteaux of the Loire Valley experience an unquenchable desire to spend the night sleeping in one — and this is the spot. Built by François Coty (of perfume fame and fortune) on the site of an 18th-century château, this structure has a decorous mansarded exterior that cloaks an interior as ornate and resplendent as anyone could desire. A heated swimming pool and a pair of private tennis courts represent just a couple of the improvements that have been made since the establishment's construction; musical weekends enliven the fall and winter seasons. A member of the Relais & Châteaux group. Information: *Château d'Artigny,* Rte. d'Azay-le-Rideau, Veigné, Montbazon 37250 (phone: 47-26-24-24; fax: 47-65-92-79).

HÔTEL DE PARIS, Monte Carlo, Monaco: That this establishment, opened on *New Year's Day* in 1864, is the dowager queen of the Côte d'Azur is evident in nearly every bit of ornamentation in its nooks and crannies — from the fulsome frescoes in the Empire dining room to the bare-breasted caryatids that gaze across the rows of parked vintage Rolls-Royces to the grand *Casino* across the square (see *Monaco,* THE CITIES). The guestbook reads like a *Who's Who* of the century; Winston Churchill stayed here so often that the management named one of its 30 palatial suites after him. The celebrated wine cellars, carved out of the rock on which the principality sits, are accessible to visitors. And it's possible to pick up a quick Dior in the lobby. The elegantly decorated *Louis XV* restaurant, the only hotel restaurant ever awarded three Michelin stars, is one of the very best on the Côte d'Azur (see *Haute Gastronomie*), while its one-star grill restaurant on the top floor offers the most incredible view in Monaco. Whatever you do, don't forget that caviar and smoked salmon are available 24 hours a day, in case of emergency. Information: *Hôtel de Paris,* Pl. du Casino, Monte Carlo 98000 (phone: 93-50-80-80; fax: 93-25-59-17; telex: 469925).

NÉGRESCO, Nice, Alpes-Maritimes: Though traffic whizzes along the Promenade des Anglais and cement-slab apartment buildings litter the coastline, this grande dame presides over Nice as serenely as ever, as if to remind us that there was once an era when every new building worth mentioning looked like a wedding cake. The whole edifice — from the gilded, inlaid ceilings and the canopied beds to the fluted columns — has been designated a National Historical Monument. Information: *Hôtel Négresco,* 37 Promenade des Anglais, Nice 06000 (phone: 93-88-39-51; fax: 93-88-35-68; telex: 460040).

DOMAINE DES HAUTS-DE-LOIRE, Onzain, Loir-et-Cher: Less overwhelming than some of its fellow castles in the Loire Valley, this erstwhile hunting lodge of some forgotten count comes across as a family-size château; and with its rough oaken beams and gleaming copper cauldrons, it has a pleasant, residential feel that is mirrored in the friendly, thoughtful service. Spring, when flowers bloom in profusion around the velvety lawns and swans glide on the placid pond, is a particularly entrancing time to visit this member of the Relais & Châteaux group. Information: *Domaine des Hauts-de-Loire,* Rte. de Herbault, Onzain 41150 (phone: 54-20-72-57; fax: 54-20-77-32).

LE BRISTOL, Paris: Headquarters to dignitaries visiting the Elysée Palace (the French White House), located just a few steps down the street, this elegant establishment boasts 188 beautifully decorated rooms and 2 restaurants — one for summer and another for winter; the first is a light and airy glassed-in room overlooking the garden; the second is richly wood-paneled, a reassuring reminder of Old World craftsmanship. It's the retention and enhancement of the historic *Bristol* taste and hotel-keeping talent that make it a standout. The open and exquisite elevator — glass wrought-iron and brass — bespeaks an earlier age, the enlargement of the marvelously designed marble bathrooms have transformed them into veritable oases of comfort, and the hotel service is merely superb. An elegant and comfortable lobby and cocktail lounge add to the charm. A wing built in 1985 includes a heated swimming pool on the sixth-floor terrace, an amenity seldom found in Paris hotels. Information: *Hôtel le Bristol,* 112 Rue du Faubourg-St-Honoré, Paris 75008 (phone: 42-66-91-45).

CRILLON, Paris: An apparent proving ground for the entire French automotive industry, the Place de la Concorde has a frenetic atmosphere today far at odds with its spirit in the 18th century. But within its Sienese marble foyers, guests here are insulated from all the brouhaha. Diplomats from nearby Embassy Row buy and sell countries in the bar, and journalists seem always on hand trying to overhear the parameters of the deals. The view from the suites facing the *place* are *sans pareil;* its two-star restaurant, *Les Ambassadeurs* — the only one in Paris — is merely marvelous. This is perhaps Paris's most expertly managed hotel; it is a member of the Relais & Châteaux group. Information: *Hôtel Crillon,* 10 Pl. de la Concorde, Paris 75008 (phone: 42-65-24-24; fax: 47-42-72-10).

GEORGE V, Paris: The lobby is a League of Nations of private enterprise, where wheelers and dealers of every nationality seem to be settling matters of planetary importance. It also seems to be where the *Cannes Film Festival* crowd spends the other 11 months of the year, so numerous are the stars and starlets, directors, producers, and other movie folk who pilgrim here. The Eiffel Tower is just across the river, the Champs-Elysées just down the block, and the Arc de Triomphe around the corner; most of the rest of Paris can be seen from the panoramic windows of rooms higher up in the hotel. Even those who can't afford one of them — or the tranquil chambers facing the gracious courtyard — should be sure to stop for one of the establishment's utterly lyrical croissants. Information: *Hôtel George V,* 31 Av. George-V, Paris 75008 (phone: 47-23-54-00; fax: 47-20-40-00).

LANCASTER, Paris: If location is almost everything, this 19th-century townhouse qualifies: steps from the Champs Elysées (almost at its midpoint) and 2 blocks from the Faubourg St-Honoré. Favored by literati, dignitaries, and Americans in the know, this Savoy Group establishment exudes an air of gentility and calm, and above all, coziness. Each one of its 66 rooms and suites (and there are no more than 10 on each floor) offers its own charm. Try to book accommodations on the sixth — the top — floor, where a view of the Eiffel Tower, of Sacré-Coeur, or the hotel's garden is sure to be had from either a balcony or a terrace. Off the just-renovated lobby is an old-fashioned bar, a delightful spot for coffee, afternoon tea, or a late-night liqueur. The restaurant, with alfresco dining when the weather permits, is relaxed and refined. In sum, personal service and gracious surroundings with nary a glimmer of glitz. Information: *Hôtel Lancaster,* 7 Rue de Berri, Paris 75008 (phone: 43-59-90-43; fax: 42-89-22-71).

PLAZA-ATHÉNÉE, Paris: Careful renovations to preserve the charm of this most charming of European hotels have just been completed — from the guest quarters done in Louis XV and XVI to the *Relais* grill, where *tout Paris* seems to be eternally lunching, and the idyllic *Garden Court* restaurant, which is like a set for some Parisian *Mikado,* with its cheeping birds, pools, and a bridge. On the elegant Avenue Montaigne, this hotel is a little more sedate and a little more French than the *George V* (above). Information: *Hôtel Plaza-Athénée,* 25 Av. Montaigne, Paris 75008 (phone: 47-23-78-33; fax: 47-20-20-70).

RITZ, Paris: The Right Bank establishment that César Ritz created and made synonymous with all the finer things in life is so much a part of French tradition and literature that every year an occasional perambulator, coming upon it suddenly, is startled to find that it still exists, much less reigns as majestically as ever over the Place Vendôme. Marcel Proust wrote most of *Remembrance of Things Past* in a cork-lined room here; Georges-Auguste Escoffier put France at the top of the culinary Olympus from its kitchen. The *Ritz Club,* a nightclub and discotheque built about the same time as its super spa, is open to guests and club members only. Like bagging a tiger under Kilimanjaro or owning a palazzo on the Grand Canal, this is one of those experiences that the truly discriminating owe themselves. And even if you can't afford to stay here, have a glass of champagne in the elegant bar. Information: *Hôtel Ritz,* 15 Pl. Vendôme, Paris 75001 (phone: 42-60-38-30; fax: 42-60-23-71).

BOYER "LES CRAYÈRES," Reims, Marne: With its move to a stunning 19th-century château, this three-star restaurant added lodgings that match its menu. Set on

19 beautifully landscaped acres, just a stone's throw from the twin Gothic towers of Reims cathedral, it has 16 sumptuous rooms and 3 suites, some of which open onto terraces overlooking the gardens, and all of which are decorated differently, mainly in the styles of the Louis Philippe era. A member of the distinguished Relais et Châteaux group, its main attraction is, however, food. The menu's offerings reflect a finely tuned balance between nouvelle and traditional cuisine, and service is helpful rather than overbearing (see *Haute Gastronomie*). In support of the main local industry, the wine list includes more than 60 champagnes. Closed mid-December to mid-January. Information: *Boyer "Les Crayères,"* 64 Bd. Henri-Vasnier, Reims 51100 (phone: 26-82-80-80; fax: 26-82-65-52).

BEL AIR DU CAP-FERRAT, St-Jean-Cap-Ferrat, Alpes-Maritimes: This jewel of a hotel (formerly called the *Hôtel du Cap Ferrat*) is on an isolated peninsula on the Côte d'Azur and has been a winter haven for royalty since the beginning of the century. It is now open year-round, and summertime activities abound. The Club Dauphin, set by the sea, has a lovely, heated saltwater pool, a sauna, sunbathing areas, cabañas, and alfresco restaurant — perfect for lunch. A funicular (what else?) takes guests back up to the hotel where there is a one-star restaurant and a piano bar that was designed to look like the bottom of the ocean. Completely renovated by its Japanese owners, this elegant 59-room oasis is set in a 14-acre park filled with tropical flora. There are those who whisper that its elegance rivals a certain competitor at Cap d'Antibes. A member of the Relais & Châteaux group. Information: *Bel'Air du Cap-Ferrat,* Bd. du Général-de-Gaulle, St-Jean-Cap-Ferrat 02690 (phone: 93-76-00-21; fax: 93-01-62-49).

MAS D'ARTIGNY, St-Paul-de-Vence, Alpes-Maritimes: How can a hotel with 25 small swimming pools be ignored? This ultramodern, ultra-luxurious bastion of the 20th century (and another member of the Relais & Châteaux group) is a complex of suites, each graced by its own private garden and pool, arranged in an emerald and sapphire horseshoe around a main building, which itself boasts a more than adequate pool. Its restaurant has one Michelin star. And Nice and the sea are only a short drive away. Information: *Mas d'Artigny,* Route de la Colle, St-Paul-de-Vence 06570 (phone: 93-32-84-54; fax: 93-32-95-36; telex: 470601).

L'ESPÉRANCE, St-Père-sous-Vézelay, Yonne: The best rooms in this serene country manor house overlook the beautiful garden and the Cure River. The principal indoor activity is dinner in the glass-enclosed dining room, where three-star food is served with just the right degree of unfussy concern for your comfort. The medieval town of Vézelay and the glowing Romanesque church of St. Madeleine are nearby. The hotel and restaurant are closed from early January to early February; restaurant closed on Tuesdays and for lunch on Wednesdays. A member of the Relais & Châteaux group. Information: *L'Espérance,* Saint-Père-sous-Vézelay, Vézelay 89450 (phone: 86-33-20-45; fax: 86-33-26-15).

AUBERGE DU PÈRE BISE, Talloires, Haute-Savoie: Lakes, a principal drawing card for European vacationers in prewar days, are, like spas, coming back into fashion. Lake Annecy and its picturebook environs make a persuasive case for choosing a tranquil lake over a teeming seaside. The village of Talloires, elegant and serene, is the backdrop for the family-owned, recently renovated, two-star restaurant of the same name on the lakefront. Mountains to the left, water to the right, there's no choice but to concede to the temptation of lunching outdoors on duck, lobster tails, and wicked chestnut pastry. Spend the night in a deliciously plush room with a balcony, and start again the next morning. Closed from mid-November to mid-January. The restaurant is closed Wednesdays for lunch and Tuesdays off-season. A member of the Relais & Châteaux group. Information: *Auberge du Père Bise,* Rte. du Port, Talloires 74290 (phone: 50-60-72-01; fax: 50-60-73-05).

LE VIEUX LOGIS, Trémolat, Dordogne: In one of the prettiest and least traveled regions of France, this old dwelling is one of the most picturesque and little-known of French stopping places. Installed in a typical old Périgord house with rustic furnishings, ivied walls, and flowered bowers, it offers fine regional fare, all the truffles the fastidious could fancy, and lots of hunting and fishing nearby for those who want to procure some victuals on their own. An enchanting member of the Relais & Châteaux group. Closed early January to early February; the restaurant is also closed Wednesdays at lunch and Tuesdays in the off-season. Information: *Le Vieux Logis,* Trémolat 24510 (phone: 53-22-80-06; fax: 53-22-84-89).

CHÂTEAU DU DOMAINE SAINT-MARTIN, Vence, Alpes-Maritimes: Set in a 35-acre park overlooking the blue waters of the Mediterranean, this 40-room country estate and castle has a magnificent view of the surrounding area and plenty of pure air (its site is 1,700 feet up). Although this Relais & Châteaux member is incredibly tranquil, it is just minutes away from the bustling activities of Nice, Cannes, and Monte Carlo. Also on the property is a heart-shaped swimming pool set among the olive trees, tennis courts, a one-star restaurant that serves Provençal food — much of which is made with the château's own products. Information: *Château du Domaine Saint-Martin,* Rte. de Coursegoules, Vence 06140 (phone: 93-58-02-02; fax: 93-24-08-91; telex: 470282).

TRIANON PALACE, Versailles: Attached by private gardens to Versailles, this renovated palace is one of France's most historic hotels. Its vaulted-ceilinged marble dining room, resembling a great mirrored ballroom, has played host to the likes of Wilson, Proust, Colette, and Marlene Dietrich. Romantic legends abound here. Sarah Bernhardt used to arrive in a horse-drawn carriage, wrapped from head to wooden leg in tulle and feathers. And when King Edward VIII abdicated the throne of England for the woman he loved, he and the former Wallis Simpson honeymooned here. Michelin-starred chef Gérard Vié presides over the kitchens of *Les Trois Marches;* the beauty salon and spa (described as "a beauty kingdom") are an exclusive Givenchy operation stocked with his signature cosmetics and perfumes; and a hotel conference center, shops, tennis courts, and underground parking are among the amenities. Information: *Trianon Palace,* 1 Bd. de la Reine, Versailles 78000 (phone: 30-84-38-00; fax: 39-49-00-77).

HOSTELLERIE LE PRIEURÉ, Villeneuve-lès-Avignon, Gard: A country inn par excellence (and another member of the Relais & Châteaux group), this ancient priory in the middle of a deep and shady wood now offers such modern pleasures as a swimming pool, tennis courts, and a friendly, highly reputed restaurant, where, when the weather is fine, meals are served in a delightful garden. The *gigot* (leg of lamb) in aromatic herbs, the betruffled tournedos, or lobster lasagna will turn the steadiest head; the homemade *tapenade* is so popular that the kitchen packs it in jars to sell to departing guests. Note that as lovely as the hotel's modern section is, the ancient section is even more appealing. Information: *Hostellerie le Prieuré,* 7 Pl. du Chapitre, Villeneuve-lès-Avignon 30400 (phone: 90-25-18-20; fax: 90-25-45-39; telex: 431042).

Haute Gastronomie

Inspiring the same fierce passions and loyalties that soccer does in Brazil, eating is the French national sport. The French talk about food instead of the weather, reminisce about one meal while downing another, and select restaurants as if they were putting together an investment portfolio. The light, sauce-free fashion of the nouvelle cuisine brought a few mouthfuls of moderation to the nationwide gourmandizing — until the country's superchefs began to recant, labeling it "big plates with small ingredients and nothing in between."

So we're happy to report that France is once again awash in béchamel and ablaze with cognac, and the turbot once again reigns *suprême.*

Before you take to the field, a few morsels of advice. Once you're seated, don't be intimidated by the ritual or its priesthood. Remember that you are quite literally the consumer. While it is customary to conceive of the meal as a whole, insist on ordering one course at a time if you can't think about *moules* and *mousse* at once. In addition, consider that many restaurants are happy and even proud to present their guests with small portions of dishes they'd simply like to sample. And some restaurants also offer *dégustation* menus, which include a sampling of the chef's noblest creations. Ask the wine waiter for advice, but unless you're a true oenophile, don't spend unnecessarily for sought-after châteaux or venerable vintages. Local wines, many of which don't ever find their way out of the immediate neighborhood but are well known to a resident restaurateur, are likely to be the best tasting and least expensive choices. And if a dish is unsatisfactory, by all means send it back to the kitchen. Restaurateurs hold their reputation in deadly earnest (to such an extent that one eminent chef did away with himself on learning he'd been stripped of one of his three Michelin stars). And, above all, be sure to make reservations — if only a few days in advance. Far better, write for reservations months in advance of your anticipated arrival at one of France's authentic temples of gastronomy. There is very little impulse dining in France, and tables at restaurants that are among the most favored are sometimes booked months ahead. This also assures that you won't show up hungry — only to find that the chef has gone off on his annual holiday. In the list of some of the best restaurants in France that follows, we note the *fermetures annuelles* (yearly closings), but do bear in mind that last-minute changes can and frequently do occur. What's more, don't forget to *reconfirm* reservations once you arrive on French soil — even if no request for reconfirmation has been made formally. Reservations at the top restaurants in France are routinely (and automatically) canceled without timely reconfirmation. When making your reservations, check to determine if credit cards are accepted.

Finally, *bon appétit!*

CHÂTEAU D'AUDRIEU, Audrieu, Calvados: According to local legend, the first lord of the 60-acre park that surrounds this beautiful 18th-century castle was the personal chef to no less than William the Conqueror. Today's cuisine, presented in a pair of tasteful and intimate dining rooms, is consummately majestic. The crown jewels are the *soupe de homard et d'escargots* (lobster and snail bisque) and the *aiguillettes de canard aux pêches* (duck in peach sauce). A very fine *dégustation* menu also may be ordered. Closed Wednesdays, Thursday lunch, and from early December to March. Information: *Château d'Audrieu,* Audrieu 14250 (phone: 31-80-21-52).

OUSTAU DE BAUMANIÈRE and LA CABRO D'OR, Les Baux-de-Provence, Bouches-du-Rhône: These two restaurants, a snail's throw from each other and under the same management, are in charming old Provençal manor houses in richly verdant settings. Seated under vaulted ceilings and wooden beams or on a terrace overlooking a fairy tale duck pond, guests are graciously presented with some of the most highly reputed food in France. At the former, a recipient of two Michelin stars (true, it long had three), *filets de rougets au vinaigre* (fish fillets with a vinegar sauce), *pigeon farci au foie gras* (squab stuffed with goose liver), and *gigot d'agneau en croûte* (leg of lamb in a pastry crust) are among the specialties; the latter, which has once again been awarded one Michelin star, offers a fine *terrine de légumes au confit de tomates* (vegetable terrine with a tomato sauce). *Oustau* is closed Wednesdays, Thursday lunch from November through March, and from January 20 to March 4; *La Cabro* shuts down the kitchen on Mondays and Tuesday lunch from November through March, and mid-November to mid-December. Information: *Oustau de Baumanière,* Les Baux-de-Provence, Maussane-les-Alpilles 13520 (phone: 90-54-33-07); *La Cabro d'Or* at the same address (phone: 90-54-33-21).

AUBERGE DES TEMPLIERS, Les Bézards, Loiret: Named for the austere order of religious warriors once headquartered here, this elegant eatery nestles langorously in a quiet oak grove. Guests can enjoy their drinks and relax in front of the immense brick fireplace before moving on to one of the dining rooms where 18th-century tapestries drape from the timbered ceilings to the Oriental carpeted floor. In summer, lunch is served under the rose-studded trellises on the terrace, where the sweet scents of flowers and soufflés stir even the drowsiest palate. Michelin has awarded its kitchen, which specializes in fish — including a variety fresh from the nearby Loire — two stars, and the extensive wine list boasts a 1947 Château Lafite-Rothschild. Closed end of January through mid-March. Information: *Auberge des Templiers,* Les Bézards, Boismorand 45290 (phone: 38-31-80-01).

LE ST-JAMES, Bordeaux, Gironde: Lavishly elegant, this one-star establishment in a large, garden-rimmed stone villa pioneered the nouvelle cuisine revolution in Bordeaux. But still, amid all the watercress mousse, a bounty of sinful savories — most notably the duck liver terrine, the garlic-studded roast lamb, the thyme-perfumed rabbit, and the caramel-lined roast wild duck — can also be found. Meals are served inside the manor and, when the weather is fine, on a pleasantly shady terrace. Information: *Le St-James,* Pl. Camille-Hosteins, Bordeaux-Bouliac 33270 (phone: 56-20-52-19).

CIRO'S, Deauville, Calvados: If you eat one lobster in all of France, eat it here. Crowded but cozy, especially on a weathery Sunday when the Norman rains empty the beach, this bastion of the very rich on Deauville's celebrated boardwalk is under the management of the *Casino* and the *Hôtel Normandy,* which handles its guests with velvet gloves. The fine view of the ocean from which the maritime specialties on the menu have just been hauled is a bonus. Information: *Ciro's,* Promenade des Planches, Deauville 14800 (phone: 31-88-18-10).

LES PRÉS D'EUGÉNIE, Eugénie-les-Bains, Landes: Chef Michel Guérard is to French gastronomy what Joe DiMaggio was to baseball, and this little thermal resort in the southwestern corner of France is where he cooks his home runs. Guérard's three-star *cuisine minceur* (slimming cuisine), the subject of his best-selling cookbook, is notable for allowing diners to make a *cochon* of themselves and stay trim and slender at the same time. The natural products of the region, the bases of this miracle, are selected by Guérard and his staff with the meticulous care of an art dealer shopping for a kilo of Renoirs. And the roster of refined delights seems to get longer, and more bewitching, by the year. Closed from early December to February. Information: *Les Prés d'Eugénie,* Eugénie-les-Bains 40320 (phone: 58-51-19-01).

LES BORIES, Gordes, Vaucluse: This tiny and utterly delightful stone-walled inn with 18 rooms in the heart of Provence has an outdoor terrace with a view that allows for languid lunching in the shade of olive trees while stray shafts of sunlight glow pinkly through a bottle of rosé. Try the feather-light *salade folle* (crazy salad) with duck and crayfish as well as the lamb grilled on an open wood fire. Closed December through mid-January. Information: *Les Bories,* Rte. de Sénanque, Gordes 84220 (phone: 90-72-00-51; fax: 90-72-01-22).

AUBERGE DE L'ILL, Illhaeusern, Haut-Rhin: Serene and exceptionally elegant, this three-star establishment on the willow-feathered shores of the River Ill, surrounded by lovely gardens, serves Alsatian food at its pungent and aromatic best — a creative and elegant mix of the delicacy of the best French haute cuisine and the vigor of the German. This is the place to sample a wild hare salad (if you're in the mood for something light and gamey) or frog soup and pike mousse (if you're feeling adventurous) or simply to dip into one of the almost uncountable number of pâtés. Flan of frogs' legs with watercress, venison in a light pepper sauce, and salmon soufflé are among the other delights. Whatever the selection, let the fruity local riesling flow like the nearby Rhine. Closed Mondays, Tuesdays, most of February, and the first week in July. Information: *Auberge de l'Ill,* Rue de Collonges, Illhaeusern, Ribeauvillé 68150 (phone: 89-71-83-23).

LA CÔTE ST-JACQUES, Joigny, Yonne: Housed in an 18th-century villa overlooking the sleepy river Yonne, this three-star establishment is a Lorain family affair: Michel is chef, Jean-Michel his lieutenant in the kitchen, and Jacqueline is mistress of the wine cellar. Inside, fabric-covered walls, fresh flowers, porcelain, and silver tableware, all aglow in candlelight, set an elegant stage for the main event. The menu offers *cuisine traditionelle,* which includes three courses of lobster, and *cuisine créative,* which features such novel preparations as a *galette de pommes de terre et de pigeon à la muscade* (a "pancake" of potatoes and squab, seasoned with nutmeg). Closed early January to early February. Information: *La Côte St-Jacques,* 14 Fg. Paris, Joigny 89300 (phone: 86-62-09-70).

PAUL BOCUSE, Collonges-au-Mont-d'Or, Lyons, Rhône: The chef whose name this much-publicized culinary magnet (awarded three Michelin stars) bears is a member of the French Légion d'Honneur, and there are those who consider his truffle soup Valéry-Giscard-d'Estaing one of the most important achievements of the nation's previous government. Regrettably, M. Bocuse is often away from his restaurant, tending to gastronomic affairs from Tokyo to *Walt Disney World.* Still, even the supporting kitchen staff can create awesome comestibles well worth a visit. Information: *Paul Bocuse,* Pont de Collonges, Collonges-au-Mont-d'Or, Lyons, Rhône 69660 (phone: 78-22-01-40).

MICHEL (LES CATALANS) and CALYPSO, Marseilles, Bouches-du-Rhône: The seaport of Marseilles brought the world bouillabaisse, the fish stew which thou shalt not leave France without tasting; and these neighboring restaurants serve the best cauldron of it in town. Peek in, sniff, and take your choice. The Mediterranean fish stew called bourride and grilled fish also are available. The old and very traditional *Michel* is closed Tuesdays and Wednesdays; elegant, sea-view *Calypso* is open daily. Information: *Michel (Les Catalans),* 6 Rue des Catalans, Marseilles 13007 (phone: 91-52-30-63); *Calypso,* 3 Rue du Catalans, Marseilles 13007 (phone: 91-52-64-00).

ALAIN CHAPEL, Mionnay, Ain: About 12 miles (19 km) north of Lyons, this lovely little inn, with a whitewashed cloister and a manicured garden, was the base of operations of the late philosopher-chef Alain Chapel, another member of the "All Stars" of French cuisine. Sadly, M. Chapel has passed away. Nonetheless, his legacy remains and although the restaurant lost one of its three Michelin stars after his death, every morsel is still first class, whether a simple omelette or a complex lobster assemblage; a certain well-known pair of French food writers once admitted to having shed real tears over one of Chapel's confections. Lodge in one of the 13 tasteful rooms and you can start all over again the following day. Closed Mondays, Tuesdays for lunch, and the month of January. Information: *Alain Chapel,* RN 83, Mionnay 01390 (phone: 78-91-82-02).

LE LOUIS XV, Monte Carlo, Monaco: Prince Rainier decided to bring culinary greatness to his principality and to spare no expense in doing so. He hired Alain Ducasse, who trained at some of France's best restaurants, to be head chef, and gave him unlimited funds. The result is this wonderful restaurant in the *Hôtel de Paris* that earned three Michelin stars more quickly than any other dining spot in the history of that gastronomic bible. The Belle Epoque setting is perfect for specialties such as *homard thermidor* (lobster in a rich wine sauce), *pigeonneau cuit sur la braise* (braised squab), and *fraises des bois et sorbet au mascarpone* (mascarpone sorbet with wild strawberries). The wines from one of Monaco's (and France's) best cellars help to make this an unforgettable dining experience. Reserve well in advance. Closed Tuesday and Wednesday lunch in off-season, from February 19 to March 6 and November 26 to *Christmas.* Information: *Le Louis XV,* Pl. de Casino, Monte Carlo, Monaco 98000 (phone: 93-50-80-80).

LE MOULIN DE MOUGINS, Mougins, Alpes-Maritimes: In the hills above Cannes, this 16th-century olive oil mill houses one of the Riviera's most gorgeous and glamorous restaurants — with a clientele to match. Dark wood beams stand out against the rustic white walls, and the exotic garden is the "beaker full of the warm south" for which an old French poet once pined. Chef Roger Vergé's braised slivers of Provençal duck in honey and lemon sauce stand out as one of the plainer selections on an entrancing three-star menu, which to the food lover reads like the *Thousand and One Nights* and then some. Don't miss the cold wild strawberry soufflé, the escalope of fresh salmon, the lobster fricassee, and the pâté of sole. Closed Mondays in off-season, Thursday lunch, and late January to *Easter*. In the same town, Vergé also operates the simpler, one-Michelin-star *L'Amandier de Mougins* (phone: 93-90-00-91. Information: *Le Moulin de Mougins,* 424 Chemin du Moulin, Mougins, Alpes-Maritimes 06250 (phone: 93-75-78-24; fax: 93-90-18-55; telex: 970732).

L'ANE ROUGE, Nice, Alpes-Maritimes: *Moules farcies* (stuffed mussels), *oursins* (sea urchins), *loup de mer au fenouille* (sea bass grilled in fennel), *huîtres plates aux champagne* (oysters with champagne), bourride, and just about anything else from the sea can be ordered either in the pretty, flowered dining room of this establishment in Nice's old port or outdoors on the terrace. Closed Saturdays, Sundays, holidays, and from July 20 to September 1. Information: *L'Ane Rouge,* 7 Quai des Deux-Emmanuels, Nice 06300 (phone: 93-89-49-63).

L'AMBROISIE, Paris: Promoted to three-star status by Michelin in 1988, this tiny, quietly elegant establishment on the Place des Vosges is the showcase for chef Bernard Pacaud's equally elegant cuisine. Matched in scale, the menu is limited to only a few entrées, many with a southern French accent, such as *escargots aux herbes niçoises* (snails in a Nice-style herb sauce), and grilled mullet with tiny purple artichokes. But the quality (for most fans) more than compensates for the limited number of choices. Closed Sundays, Monday lunch, August, and holidays. Information: *L'Ambroisie,* 9 Pl. des Vosges, Paris 75004 (phone: 42-78-51-45).

L'AMI LOUIS, Paris: This is the archetypal Parisian bistro, unattractive physically but with huge portions of marvelous food. Specialties include foie gras, spectacular roast chicken, spring lamb, ham, and burgundy wines. It's a particular favorite among Americans, and *the* place to sample authentic and expensive French fries. Though its fabled owner has died, the current regime carries on gallantly. Closed Mondays, Tuesdays, and most of August. Information: *L'Ami Louis,* 32 Rue du Vertbois, Paris 75003 (phone: 48-87-77-48).

CHEZ ALLARD, Paris: *Allard* still has the zinc bar, the smoky windows, and the terra cotta floor sprinkled with sawdust of the traditional Paris bistro of old. It also has some of the finest Burgundy country cooking this side of the Côte d'Or — including garlicky escargots, buttery scallops, turbot in *beurre blanc,* coq au vin, guinea hen, cassoulet, leg of lamb, and a chocolate charlotte that is one of the legends of the Left Bank. Closed Saturdays, Sundays, holidays, August, and 10 days at *Christmas.* Information: *Chez Allard,* 41 Rue St-André-des-Arts, Paris 75006 (phone: 43-26-48-23).

L'ESCARGOT MONTORGUEIL, Paris: The polished wood paneling, the brass fittings, and the stunning spiral staircase at this beautiful restaurant dating from 1830 — the Second Empire period — only add to the pleasure of a meal, which might include snails in any of half a dozen styles or duck with orange sauce. Perhaps less *haute* than some, it has that intangible *je ne sais quoi.* Closed Mondays. Information: *L'Escargot Montorgueil,* 38 Rue Montorgueil, Paris 75002 (phone: 42-36-83-51).

LE GRAND VÉFOUR, Paris: In the stately courtyard of the Palais Royal, this 233-year-old corner of Paris at its most patrician is a place of thick carpets and frescoed mirrors, where the choice dishes (two Michelin stars) have been named for dignitaries who have discussed affairs of state here since the time of Robespierre. The house specialties are every bit as enthralling as the history. In honor of both, gentlemen still are required to wear jacket and tie. Closed Saturday lunch, Sundays, and all of August. Information: *Le Grand Véfour,* 17 Rue Beaujolais, Paris 75001 (phone: 42-96-56-27; fax: 42-86-80-71).

JAMIN, Paris: Due to the culinary talents of owner-chef Joël Robuchon, this is one of Paris's finest restaurants (its *very* formal name *Jamin/Joël Robuchon*), meriting a three-star ranking by Michelin. Robuchon calls his cuisine "moderne," similar to but not always as light as nouvelle. And since the master chef is a firm believer in the divine properties of truffles, it is a rare dish that comes unadorned by the fabulous fungus. The homey dining room is very small, so reserve well in advance. Closed Saturdays, Sundays, and the month of July. Information: *Jamin,* 32 Rue de Longchamp, Paris 75016 (phone: 47-27-12-27).

LASSERRE, Paris: The waiters are in tails, the ceiling glides open to reveal the stars, the decanted burgundy is passed over the flame of a candle to detect sediment, and the impeccable service makes diners feel that somehow they deserve all this. The cuisine is traditional French at its most heavenly (two Michelin stars), and the wine cellar is a virtual museum of French oenology. Not surprisingly, making dinner reservations is akin to booking seats for a sold-out Broadway musical, so think ahead. Way ahead. Closed Sundays, Monday lunch, and August. Information: *Lasserre,* 17 Av. Franklin-Roosevelt, Paris 75008 (phone: 43-59-53-43).

LUCAS CARTON, Paris: The splendid Belle Epoque premises were taken over several years back by the near-legend Alain Senderens, who made his reputation as owner-chef of *L'Archestrate,* once the capital's three-star temple of nouvelle cuisine. The change of surroundings took the chill off the old hauteur somewhat, and the lush, plush premises are the perfect place to sample a few bites of truffle salad or lobster with vanilla. This is innovative cuisine at its quirkiest best, and Michelin lost no time in awarding it three stars. The utensils and serving pieces are almost as alluring as the food. Be sure to reconfirm all reservations. Closed Saturdays and Sundays, most of August, and the last 10 days of December. Information: *Lucas Carton,* 9 Pl. de la Madeleine, Paris 75008 (phone: 42-65-22-90).

TAILLEVENT, Paris: The culinary classic that continues to rise to ever greater heights is arguably the very best in the City of Light. This three-star dining room, named after the famed medieval chef Taillevent (whose real name was Guillaume Tirel), occupies a distinguished 19th-century mansion complete with fine paintings, porcelain dinnerware, and aristocratic decor that make it look as if the French Revolution was really just a bad dream. The salad of warm sweetbreads, the succulent duck dishes, and the rainbow assortment of soufflés are among the pillars of the Parisian gastronomic community. One of the most difficult restaurant reservations in France. A tip: Booking a table for three or more sometimes is easier than trying to book a table for two. Closed Saturdays, Sundays, holidays, part of February, and most of August. Information: *Taillevent,* 15 Rue Lamennais, Paris 75008 (phone: 45-61-12-90).

BOYER "LES CRAYÈRES," Reims, Marne: This three-star establishment is housed in a stunning 19th-century château, set on 19 beautifully landscaped acres, just a stone's throw from the twin Gothic towers of Reims cathedral. The offerings, which include dishes such as mussel soup with saffron and orange, standards such as fois gras, bass with artichokes, or roast pigeon with garlic and parsley, and new creations such as *morue fraîche aux champignons de bois* (fresh cod with wild mushrooms), reflect a finely tuned balance between nouvelle and traditional cuisine. Service is helpful without being overbearing. In support of the main local industry, the wine list includes over 60 champagnes. Closed Mondays, lunch Tuesdays, and mid-December through mid-January. Information: *Boyer "Les Crayères",* 64 Bd. Henri-Vasnier, Reims 51100 (phone: 26-82-80-80).

HÔTEL DES FRÈRES TROISGROS, Roanne, Loire: Just a ramble across the street from the railroad station, this magnet for pilgrims of the plate would warrant the effort to cross the Loire in a colander. From the vegetable terrines and the sorrel-sauced escalopes of salmon to the chicken breasts served in vinegar-spiked and walnut oil–flavored bouillon and the warm honey soufflé, the three-star menu is a tribute to the kaleidoscopic richness of the French countryside, and dinners are composed with all the delicacy of an Impressionist painting. Closed Tuesdays, Wednesdays, and from mid-February to mid-March. Information: *Hôtel des Frères Troisgros,* Pl. Gare, Roanne 42300 (phone: 77-71-66-97).

L'ABBAYE ST-MICHEL, Tonnerre, Yonne: In the middle of the idyllic Burgundy countryside, this 13th-century Benedictine abbey has a cool, stone-vaulted dining room, a gently blossoming garden, a selection of almost lyrical wines from the surrounding vineyards, and a superbly refined two-star cuisine that steals the thunder of even the celestial setting; the *carré d'agneau aux petites fèves* (rack of lamb with young fava beans) is only one example. Closed from January to mid-February, Mondays from September to May, and Tuesday lunch. Information: *L'Abbaye St-Michel,* Montée St-Michel, Tonnerre 89700 (phone: 86-55-05-99).

Shopping Spree

For centuries, France has been producing some of the world's most fashionable clothing, its most delicious food and wine, and its most bewitching perfumes. And all of these items benefit from that same pinch of Gallic flair and good taste that characterize just about everything else to which the French put their hearts and hands. So it's no wonder that shopping in this country is such a delight.

In the provinces, regional specialties are among the best buys — calvados in Normandy, sausage in Toulouse, perfume in Grasse, and wine almost everywhere but especially in the Bordeaux, Burgundy, and Loire Valley growing areas. And all over France — particularly near the Côte d'Azur — there are little *ateliers,* studios, whose potters, weavers, wood carvers, and even glassblowers sell their wares either from tiny shops, in the sunny open-air markets of Nice and Cannes, or in the picturesque roving crafts fairs that periodically visit neighboring towns.

Elsewhere, buy a local newspaper or an information booklet, which may advertise crafts exhibits. Gift shop owners also may know how to contact artisans in their areas. And the official tourist information office (the Office du Tourisme or the Syndicat d'Initiative) almost always can answer specific questions. Shopping in the French provinces offers its own pleasures, mostly related to the leisurely pace that affords time for personal contact between buyer and seller.

However, there seldom is any savings in buying a name-brand cast-iron skillet in the south of France and lugging it back to Paris. French storekeepers nationwide seem to adhere much more closely than their American counterparts to manufacturers' list prices, and if there is any price difference, it may well be that the skillet actually will cost *more* in that isolated shop than it would in a department store in Paris. By the same token, the French capital also boasts the widest selection available of practically every type of merchandise. And since most visitors to France pass through Paris at some point, the city rates as the most convenient place to shop as well.

Long considered the international capital of fashion, Paris excels in the area of stylish, high-quality clothing and accessories. Prices range from the wildly extravagant to the fairly reasonable; but in any case they are far lower than for the same merchandise sold outside France. Perfume, first-rate leather goods, food, wine, and cooking equipment and related items are good buys here.

PARIS SHOPPING STREETS: Stores selling similar merchandise tend to cluster along a certain one of the capital's celebrated boulevards and avenues, and for visitors who want to browse rather than go out of their way to find a specific shop, these are prime destinations:

Boulevard Haussmann – The *Galeries Lafayette* and *Au Printemps,* the city's two leading department stores, and the Paris branch of London's *Marks & Spencer* are here.

Place de la Madeleine – Several emporia purveying fine foods and wine — including *Hédiard,* specializing in exotic fruit and spices at No. 21, and the famous, fabulous *Fauchon* at Nos. 28-30 — can be found here.

Rue d'Alésia – Several blocks of discount shops.

Rue de Rivoli – This is not only the best place to find souvenir scarves decorated with Eiffel Towers and handkerchiefs imprinted with maps of the Paris métro system, but it also abounds in shops selling perfume and other gifts. Two of the city's more famous bookstores with an English-language stock are *W. H. Smith* at No. 248 and *Galignani* at No. 224.

Les Halles – Trendy and often inexpensive clothing boutiques are concentrated in this area.

St-Germain-des-Prés – Sprinkled among the boulevard's famous cafés are not-so-inexpensive shops selling au courant clothing.

Rue du Faubourg-St-Honoré – *The* shopping street for elegant fashions, chic shoes, and leather goods, including *Christian Lacroix, Courrèges, Hermès, Lanvin, Guy Laroche, Yves Saint Laurent,* and others.

Rue des Sts-Pères – Terrific shoes, off Boulevard St-Germain.

Place Vendôme – The *haute joaillerie* of France — the jewelry with the most splendid designs and the highest prices — is sold on this square adjoining the Rue de la Paix at shops such as *Boucheron, Cartier,* and *Van Cleef & Arpels.*

Place des Victoires – Stylish boutiques for women are the specialty, but there are some for men as well.

Rue des Rosiers – Many young designers have opened clothing boutiques (for men and women) on or near this colorful shopping street.

DEPARTMENT STORES NATIONWIDE: The *grands magasins,* as these emporiums are called, stock at least a little bit of everything, so it's hardly necessary to go from shop to shop for many types of items. In addition, these stores offer the opportunity to purchase several small gifts under one roof and thereby qualify to receive a refund of France's value-added tax (VAT).

Galeries Lafayette **and** *Au Printemps* – Of the nation's large stores, these two are deservedly the most popular with visitors. In addition to carrying an extensive and fashionable stock of men's, women's, and children's clothing, housewares, perfume, shoes, gifts, and all the miscellaneous merchandise ordinarily sold by such emporiums, they also provide tourists with special shopping information, translations, and instructions on how to obtain tax refunds on goods purchased here. In Paris, their main stores are next to each other near the *Opéra.*

Note: The Paris flagship of both stores holds excellent fashion shows that are open to the public at no charge. *Galeries Lafayette* has shows on Wednesdays at 11 AM; from April through October, there also are shows on Fridays. Reservations are necessary and you should make them as early as possible by contacting the store (40 Bd. Haussman, 9e; phone: 48-74-02-30 or 42-82-30-25; fax: 40-16-09-15). *Printemps* (64 Bd. Haussman, 9e) holds shows every Tuesday at 10 AM. They also take place on Fridays from March through October, and on Mondays from May through September. Admittance to these shows can be arranged through the store's US representative, *Printemps* (10 E. 21st St., Suite 600, New York, NY 10010; phone: 529-8484). In addition to receiving an invitation card that will get you into fashion shows for a full calendar year, you will receive a discount card that's good for 10% off any *Printemps* purchase over $20.

Galeries Lafayette's main store in Paris is at 40 Bd. Haussmann (phone: 42-82-34-56); it has a branch in the *Maine Montparnasse Shopping Center* (22 Rue du Départ, 14e; phone: 45-38-52-87). There also are stores in several other cities, including Lyons (*La Part-Dieu Shopping Center;* phone: 78-42-53-61), Montpellier (the *Polygone Shopping Center;* phone: 67-64-83-00), Nice (6 Av. Jean-Médecin; phone: 93-85-40-21), and Nantes (18 Rue du Calvaire; phone: 40-48-62-55).

Au Printemps stores include the main one in Paris (64 Bd. Haussmann; phone: 42-85-80-00) as well as three others around Paris and more than 2 dozen in the French provinces, including branches in Auxerre (2 Rue de la Draperie; phone: 86-51-67-77), in Deauville (104 Rue Eugène-Colas; phone: 31-88-21-83), in Dieppe (7 Grand Rue; phone: 35-84-11-35), in Le Havre (32 Av. du René-Coty; phone: 35-42-45-05), in Lille (39-45 Rue Nationale; phone: 20-30-85-33), in Lyons (42 Pl. de la République; phone: 78-42-51-77), in Marseilles (*La Valentine Shopping Center* in the Chemin de la Sablière; phone: 91-44-00-66), in Metz (8-16 Rue Serpenoise; phone: 87-76-03-33), in Poitiers (Pl. du Maréchal-Leclerc; phone: 49-01-82-34), in Strasbourg (1-5 Rue de la Haute-Montée; phone: 88-75-88-75), and in La Valette near Toulon (in the *Grand Var Shopping Center* on the Av. de l'Université; phone: 94-61-96-00).

Monoprix and *Prisunic* – These low-priced stores are good to remember for attractive, inexpensive children's clothing and toys. The fashion accessories, housewares, and stationery departments also can yield treasures.

OPEN-AIR FOOD MARKETS NATIONWIDE: A visit to one of these colorful markets anywhere in France will provide an intimate, surprising, and usually delightful look at not only what the French eat but also how they live their daily lives. They're far too much fun to miss. So wherever you are, find out when the market is held and where, then plunge into the action with camera and shopping bag. Even if you buy no more than a bag of cherries — probably the sweetest you've ever tasted — you'll be glad you saw it all.

Dieppe – The market here reaches inland behind the port. Pots of jam made on nearby farms by the women who sell them are among the more alluring wares.

Lyons – It's at this city's outdoor market, which stretches along the Saône River, that great chefs like Paul Bocuse do their shopping; it's not necessary to be a three-star culinary wizard to do the same.

Mont-de-Marsan – Farm women pedal to the charming and memorable market held each Saturday morning under a high roof in the center of this small town in the Landes region of southwestern France, famed for good eating. Their bicycles are laden with cartons of just-gathered eggs and freshly pulled carrots and the like. Children will love the live chickens, ducks, and rabbits.

Nice – Markets in this area are especially colorful because of their settings — often within a pebble's throw of the brilliant Mediterranean.

Paris – The best and most enjoyable market here is probably the one set up on Wednesday and Saturday mornings on the Avenue du Président-Wilson between Place d'Iéna and Place de l'Alma, both of which have métro stops. Butchers, bakers, and cheese and flower sellers abound here, along with all types of fresh fish, lettuce and herbs just pulled from the ground and trucked in from farms outside the city, and wonderful fruits and other vegetables. Other good roving markets appear in the Place Monge on Wednesdays, Fridays, and Sundays; on the Boulevard Raspail on Tuesdays, Fridays, and Sunday mornings (when the produce is restricted to *biologique,* or organic fruits, vegetables, breads, and other edibles; and on the Boulevard Edgar-Quinet on Wednesdays and Saturdays. Every neighborhood has one, and everyone has his or her favorite.

St-Pol-de-Léon – This small town on Brittany's north coast near Morlaix has one of the liveliest wholesale produce markets in France. Every morning between January and September, farmers gather in the Kérisnel *quartier* to sell their produce by public auction to wholesalers and dealers. Why here, on Brittany's windy, carved-granite coastline? It's because the nearby Gulf Stream keeps Brittany's climate mild so that the bristling artichokes and tender, baby vegetables that grace Paris's temples of gastronomy flourish in this unlikely place.

Sarlat-La-Canéda – This small Dordogne town full of ocher buildings, an irresistible destination for tourists, has a lively market every Saturday morning in the Pl. des Oies.

It's also fun to buy foie gras, walnut oils, *cèpes,* and other Limousin food specialties in any of a handful of shops in the old town.

Thiviers – Another Dordogne town with a wonderful market, ancient Thiviers (once a stronghold of the Gauls and later a Roman camp) is now known for its Saturday morning *marché au gras* (fat market), which is famed for its foie gras, fattened ducks and geese, and truffles (held in Place Foch from November to March). For those who appreciate a bit of history between bites of foie gras, the local *Musée du Foie Gras, Maison de l'Oie et du Canard* (Foie Gras, Goose, and Duck Museum, Place Foch; phone: 53-55-12-50) is open all year except Sundays and Mondays.

CRYSTAL AND CHINA NATIONWIDE: France has crystal and china to make the humblest table gleam like that in a royal banquet hall, and there are two good ways to get an overview of the nation's best: a visit to a porcelain producing center like the town of Limoges, in the Limousin region of southwestern France, and a stroll the length of the somewhat run-down Rue de Paradis in Paris.

Limoges – Do not expect to save money when buying porcelain in this porcelain manufacturing city 250 miles (400 km) southwest of Paris; shopping in France simply does not work that way. In fact, most major firms in Limoges sell no china at their factories, but simply refer purchasers to nearby retail stores, which follow the same price lists as the shops in Paris and other cities.

However, each July through September, Limoges holds a large free exhibition of Limoges porcelain in the *Pavillon du Verdurier* (Pl. St-Pierre), where 4 or 5 dozen small round tables each are set attractively with a sampling of place settings of the patterns currently produced by the principal firms; lists of stores selling the porcelain are available at the door. In addition, the *Musée National Adrien-Dubouché,* described in *Memorable Museums and Monuments,* shows off the city's creations of the past and puts its porcelain history in perspective.

Finally, Limoges does offer the visitor a chance to view the manufacture of porcelain in all of its stages, from the blending of the porcelain paste from feldspar, quartz, and kaolin through its molding into a multitude of forms and its elaborate decoration, much of it still done by hand.

Le Pavillon de la Porcelaine offers the city's most complete exhibition and reserves a special welcome for Americans, both because the firm was founded by the American David Haviland in 1842 and because it always has had a large proportion of Americans among its clients. Demonstrations are free and continuous, and are conducted daily year-round, except Sundays from November to *Easter,* from 8:30 AM to 7:30 PM. Information: *Le Pavillon de la Porcelaine, Z.I. Magré,* Rte. de Toulouse, Limoges 87000 (phone: 55-30-21-86).

La Maison de la Porcelaine, though less prestigious than *Le Pavillon de la Porcelaine,* also provides visitors with a complete view of the manufacturing process — from the raw and biscuit-fired stages to the hand decoration of the pieces with decals and fine brushes through the final firing in large gas kilns. In Aixe-sur-Vienne, 6 miles (10 km) southwest of Limoges on N21 toward Périgueux, the factory (14 Av. du Président-Wilson) offers its free guided tours weekdays at 10 AM and 3 PM. From July through September, there are tours every hour from 10 AM to 5 PM except at lunchtime. Additional tours are organized whenever the demand warrants. And there is an outlet on the premises for both first- and second-quality merchandise (phone: 55-70-14-68).

Pastaud, a small company at (36 Rue Jules-Noriac) in Limoges proper, offers a very close look at its workers embellishing the porcelain that is produced away from a visitor's view — carefully applying intricate decals and painting the finished pieces with amazingly precise brushstrokes. The 19th-century kilns, which have been replaced by modern electric kilns, and some of Pastaud's past work, including a gold-decorated dinner plate made in 1938 for Franklin D. Roosevelt, are also displayed. Appointments are required (phone: 55-77-44-18).

Rue de Paradis, 10e, Paris – The entire street is lined with stores specializing in objects related to what merchants here call "the arts of the table."

Baccarat, a dazzling museum as much as a store at No. 30, is worth a visit even for those with no intention of purchasing an elegantly proportioned champagne flute or a multifaceted crystal champagne bucket (phone: 47-70-64-30 or 40-22-11-00). *Limoges-Unic* has a branch at No. 58, which carries many different types of Limoges china as well as a good supply of typically French Porcelaine de Paris patterns (phone: 47-70-61-49), and another at No. 12, which offers more expensive items, including china decorated with 18-karat gold (phone: 47-70-54-49).

Other Paris Locations – A couple of other places in Paris are worth a detour for those seeking French expertise in matters breakable:

Raymond (100 Rue du Faubourg-St-Honoré, 8e; phone: 42-66-69-49) is noteworthy for its charming and relatively inexpensive Porcelaine de Paris items, including coffee and tea sets, plates, soufflé dishes, mustard pots, and jam jars, all bedecked with wild strawberries, herbs, and garlands of French flowers.

Lalique, famed for its large pieces of sculptured, decorative crystal, has a shop at 11 Rue Royale, 8e (phone: 42-65-33-70).

WOMEN'S CLOTHING: The haute couture designers who put Paris on the map as the center of the fashion world still are flourishing in the French capital, and still welcoming those able to afford their distinctive and luxurious made-to-order clothing. However, they often sell much less expensive clothing of very high quality in couturier boutiques, usually at the same address:

Azzedine Alaïa, 18 Rue de la Verrerie, 4e (phone: 42-72-19-19)

Balenciaga, 10 Av. George-V, 8e (phone: 47-20-21-11)

Chanel, 29-31 Rue Cambon, 1er (phone: 42-86-28-00) and 42 Av. Montaigne, 8e (phone: 47-20-84-45). There are actually three buildings at this latter location — the first stocks shoes, the second has clothing and cosmetics, and the third sells watches.

Christian Dior, 30 Av. Montaigne, 8e (phone: 40-73-54-44)

Christian Lacroix, 73 Rue Faubourg-St-Honoré, 8e (phone: 42-65-79-08)

Claude Montana, 31 Rue de Grenelle, 7e (phone: 42-22-69-56)

Courrèges, 46 Rue du Faubourg-St-Honoré, 8e (phone: 42-65-37-75)

Emanuel Ungaro, 2 Av. Montaigne, 8e (phone: 47-23-61-94)

Gianni Versace, 11 Rue du Faubourg-St-Honoré, 8e (phone: 42-65-27-04); 67 Rue des Sts-Pères, 7e (phone: 42-84-00-40).

Givenchy, 3 Av. George-V, 8e (phone: 47-23-81-36)

Guy Laroche, 29 Av. Montaigne, 8e (phone: 40-69-69-50)

Hanae Mori, 17 Av. Montaigne, 8e (phone: 47-23-52-03)

Jean-Louis Scherrer, 51 Av. Montaigne, 8e (phone: 43-59-55-39). This is the bigger outlet (see below).

Karl Lagerfeld, 17 Rue du Faubourg-St-Honoré, 8e (phone: 42-66-64-64).

Lanvin, 15 and 22 Rue du Faubourg-St-Honoré, 8e (phone: 42-65-14-40); 2 Rue Cambon, 1er (phone: 42-60-38-83)

Louis Féraud, 88 Rue du Faubourg-St-Honoré, 8e (phone: 40-07-01-16)

Nina Ricci, 39 Av. Montaigne, 8e (phone: 47-23-78-88)

Per Spook, 18 Av. George-V, 8e (phone: 47-23-00-19)

Pierre Balmain, 44 Rue François-I, 8e (phone: 47-20-98-79)

Pierre Cardin, 14 Pl. François-I, 8e (phone: 45-63-29-13)

Romeo Gigli, 46 Rue de Sévigné, 3e (phone: 42-71-08-40)

Ted Lapidus, 35 Rue François-I, 8e (phone: 47-20-56-14)

Torrente, 60 Av. Montaigne, 8e (phone: 42-56-14-14)

Valentino, 17-19 Av. Montaigne, 8e (phone: 47-23-64-61)

Yves Saint Laurent, 5 Av. Marceau, 8e (phone: 47-23-72-71); 38 Rue du Faubourg St-Honoré, 8e (phone: 42-65-01-15); and 6 Pl. St-Sulpice, 6e (phone: 43-29-43-00)

For those interested in attending Paris's haute-couture fashion shows (usually limited to buyers and very good customers), *The Anne-Marie Victory Organization* (136 E. 64th St., New York, NY 10021; phone: 212-486-0353) sponsors trips that include viewing collections from fashion designers such as Nina Ricci, Givenchy, Ungaro, Chanel, and Vicky Tiel.

High-Fashion Bargains – The concept of selling at a discount is gradually catching on in France, and new designs from the top couturiers are available a season (sometimes only a few months) later at many outlets.

Anne Lowe carries Chanel, Ungaro, Valentino, and others at savings of up to 50%. 35 Av. Matignon, 8e (phone: 43-59-96-61).

Bab's is one of a trio with an especially devoted following. Most couturiers are represented, and the selection of evening gowns at reasonable prices is exceptional. Several locations include one at 29 Av. Marceau, 16e (phone: 47-20-84-74).

Mendès, another shop particularly well loved by knowledgeable French women, specializes in the creations of Yves Saint Laurent; the winter season's designs are available beginning in mid-January and his summer collection from July 1 — all at substantial markdowns. There are mirrors everywhere, but no dressing rooms; it's the kind of place that inspires a lady to wear her best underwear. 65 Rue Montmartre, 2e (phone: 42-36-83-32 or 45-08-52-62).

Jean-Louis Scherrer is a bit out of the way, but it's possible to make its very inconvenience part of the pleasure of shopping and exploring. Prices for very fancy couturier labels run about 50% less than original retail. 29 Av. Ledru-Rollin, 12e (phone: 46-28-39-27).

Other shops selling high-fashion clothing at discounted prices include the following: *Boutique Stock* (2 Rue Cadet, 9e); *Cacharel Stock* (114 Rue d'Alésia, 14e); *Catherine Baril* (14-15 Rue de la Tour, 16e); *Dorothée Bis Stock* (76 Rue d'Alésia, 14e); *Drôles de Choses Pour Drôles de Gens* (14 Rue Colonnes-du-Trône, 12e); *Halle Bys* (60 Rue Richelieu, 2e); *Le Mouton à Cinq Pattes* (8 and 18 Rue St-Placide, 6e); *Miss Griffes* (19 Rue de Penthièvre, 8e); *Pierre Cardin Stock* (2 Rue Vauvilliers, 1er); *Stéphane* (130 Bd. St-Germain, 6e); *Stock Griffes* (17 Rue Vielle du Temple, 5e); and *Stock System* (112 Rue d'Alésia, 14e).

Boutiques – The attractive and innovative clothing that the French so nicely call *votre bonheur,* "your happiness," is stocked at thousands of small boutiques all over the country. But nowhere are these so abundant as they are in Paris, most notably at the following shops:

Agnès B offers colorful and chic yet wearable fashions from its namesake designer, who has committed herself publicly to holding her prices down. 3 and 6 Rue du Jour, 1er (phone: 45-08-56-56 or 40-26-36-87), and other locations.

Dorothée Bis, long established though still avant garde, specializes in sportswear with a young look. 33 Rue de Sèvres, 6e (phone: 42-22-02-90).

Chantal Thomass is known for her romantic lingerie, her currently de rigueur shiny black opaque stockings, as well as her ready-to-wear, including evening clothes. If you're a fan of bustiers, a visit to one of Thomass's boutiques is essential. 5 Rue du Vieux-Colombier, 6e (phone: 45-44-60-11) and 12-14 Galerie du Rond-Point, 8e (phone: 43-59-87-34).

Georges Rech, with at least three Paris locations, is currently one of the most popular makers of classy, very Parisian styles, and at more affordable prices than other manufacturers of similarly styled goods. 273 Rue St-Honoré, 1er (phone: 42-61-41-14) and 23 Av. Victor-Hugo, 16e (phone: 45-00-83-19).

Kenzo, with its flashy colors and whimsical shapes, is especially fun for young shoppers. 3 Pl. des Victoires, 1er (phone: 40-39-72-03).

Lolita Lempicka designs colorful clothes with sleek silhouettes for the trendy set. 3 *bis* Rue des Rosiers, 4e (phone: 42-74-42-94).

Victoire is slightly crowded but congenial and packed with all types of attractive clothing from top ready-to-wear designers — and coordinated accessories to add extra dash. 12 Pl. des Victoires, 2e (phone: 47-04-49-87).

Lingerie – It's true that many Americans living in France buy their own lingerie in the US, swearing that American products are not only better made and better fitting but even less expensive and prettier than their French counterparts. But the lacy, frilly, silk undergarments sold in France, often covered with polka dots or dripping with ribbons, are the stuff of which fantasies are made, and lingerie makes a delightful souvenir.

Department stores carry a wide selection of brands, styles, and sizes and display their wares clearly, making choices simpler than in small shops, where much of the stock may be tucked in boxes behind the counter.

Cadolle was founded in 1889 by the woman widely credited with inventing the brassiere and is still run by her great-great and great-great-great-granddaughters. They sell charming, ribbon-bedecked garters and lacy bras as well as sturdy, made-to-measure corsets. 14 Rue Cambon, 1er (phone: 42-60-94-94).

Charley, just a few doors away from *Hermès,* offers an excellent selection, personal attention, and relatively low prices. 14 Rue du Faubourg-St-Honoré, 8e (phone: 47-42-17-70).

Christian Dior, while sold all over the world and in many stores in France, makes a few exceptionally lovely articles, including ensembles of gowns and robes, which are sold only in the exclusive collection one flight up from the main Dior saleroom. 28-30 Av. Montaigne, 8e (phone: 40-73-54-44).

Sabbia Rosa specializes in luxurious, chic, and sexy lingerie; there's plenty from which to choose in the pret-à-porter line, but you can also specially order custom-made items for a price. 73 Rue des Sts-Pères, 6e (phone: 45-48-88-37).

MEN'S CLOTHING: Men's clothing is not generally considered to be a good buy, and many a male has gone into shock after looking at a price tag. But for some, the blend of classic styling and French flair is irresistible.

Arnys offers Anglo-French conservatism and elegance in suits, jackets, and the other components of a gentleman's wardrobe. 14 Rue de Sèvres, 6e (phone: 45-48-76-99).

Charvet specializes in shirts, ties, and everything else for the complete — and very affluent — *gentilhomme.* 28 Pl. Vendôme, 1er (phone: 42-60-30-70).

Daniel Hechter has clothing for a sporty lifestyle; it all has a touch of class. 146 Bd. St-Germain, 6e (phone: 43-26-96-36).

Saint Laurent Rive Gauche is well known for its classic designs in suits, shoes, socks, and accessories. 32 Rue du Faubourg St-Honoré, 8e (phone: 42-65-01-16).

CHILDREN'S CLOTHING: Gorgeous hand-smocked and hand-decorated clothing for babies and older children can still be found in France but at prices that are painfully high. For all but the most indulgent grandparents, the best idea is to head for department stores, which generally display a wide selection of charming clothing for youngsters, often decorated with motifs that make them look very French.

Jacadi carries classic designs for children from 3 months to 12 years; their pale blue and white boutiques scattered around Paris offer excellent quality for a relatively affordable price. Two addresses, among many others, are 7 Rue Gustave-Coubert, 16e (phone: 45-53-33-73) and 51 Rue de Passy, 15e (phone: 45-27-03-01).

Tartine et Chocolat opened over a decade ago on the Left Bank's super shopping street (Rue de Rennes). Clothing for newborns to 12-year-olds is sold here. Their trademark item: striped unisex overalls for about $90. They also sell dresses for moms-to-be. 90 Rue de Rennes, 6e (phone: 42-22-67-34).

FOOD AND WINE: At any given point in France, it's possible to put together a sumptuous picnic by making exactly four stops: the closest charcuterie, or butcher shop, often much like a deli; the *fromagerie,* or cheese store; the *marchand de vin,* or wine merchant; and the *boulangerie,* or bakery. Usually, these shops will be within a block or two of one another, sometimes right next door.

Bordeaux – In this city, a shop known as *Cadiot Badie* sells excellent bonbons in pretty tin boxes. 26 Allées de Tourny (phone: 56-44-24-22).

Lyons – Some people take the *TGV* all the way from Paris just to indulge in the chocolates sold at *Bernachon.* 42 Cours Franklin-Roosevelt (phone: 78-24-37-98).

Paris – There are dozens of specialty shops in the capital.

Androuët is devoted to cheese, and many varieties are available either to eat in the restaurant upstairs or to take out. 41 Rue d'Amsterdam, 8e (phone: 48-74-26-90).

Berthillon sells such delicious ice cream that Parisians often line up outside for a small carton for a special party. Flavors, which change with the season, include wild strawberry, calvados crunch, and candied chestnut. 31 Rue St-Louis-en-l'Ile, 4e (phone: 43-54-31-61). Several cafés on the Ile St-Louis also serve scoops of Berthillon.

Dalloyau has been serving Parisians (and anyone else fortunate enough to venture through its doors) the finest of pastries since 1802. Their *pièce de résistance* is the *gâteau opéra,* a confection of coffee and chocolate cream sandwiched between a flaky almond biscuit and dark chocolate frosting, and crowned by an edible gold leaf. Another meltingly good choice is the *régal,* a vanilla biscuit topped with semisweet chocolate mousse and chocolate crème Chantilly. Need we say more? Yes: Indulge in a variety of macaroons. 99-101 Rue du Faubourg-St-Honoré, 8e (phone: 43-59-18-10) and 2 Pl. Edmond-Rostand, 6e (phone: 43-29-31-10), and other locations.

Fauchon is one of the world's great purveyors of food, and every day there's a new exhibition of fresh food from all corners of France and around the world, lavishly laid out with taste and style found nowhere else. Fine wine also is available, along with delicacies prepared in the shop's own charcuterie. Lotus tea (*tchando*) makes a special souvenir. The store is very experienced in shipping gift packages. The two original shops are at 26 and 28 Pl. de la Madeleine, 8e (phone: 47-42-60-11); a grand grocery shop (plus a cafeteria and restaurant) has been added to *Fauchon,* a few doors away at 30 Pl. de la Madeleine, 8e.

Le Gourmet is *Galeries Lafayette*'s chic grocery, featuring exotic and often quite reasonably priced foods, wines, and confections from around the world. 40 Bd. Hauss-mann, 9e (phone: 48-74-37-13).

Hédiard, in business since 1854, sells an array of products similar to Fauchon's, but specializes in exotic fruit and spices. 21 Pl. de la Madeleine, 8e (phone: 42-66-44-36).

Legrand Fille et Fils offers an excellent selection of wine, including bottles that are both good and inexpensive, in a charming old wine shop near the city's stock market. 1 Rue de la Banque, 2e (phone: 42-60-07-12).

Lenôtre specializes in pastries and other desserts, and everything is exquisite, from the simplest éclair to the fruit mousses, charlottes, and chocolates. 44 Rue d'Auteuil, 16e (phone: 45-24-52-52) and several other locations.

La Maison du Chocolat is the place where Robert Linxe, perhaps the most talented chocolate maker in the French capital, produces delicate, meltingly delicious creations such as his raspberry chocolate truffles. He also offers a selection of champagnes and an excellent array of armagnacs. 225 Rue de Faubourg-St-Honoré, 8e (phone: 42-27-39-44) and 6 Rue Pierre Charron, 8e (phone: 47-23-38-25).

La Maison de l'Escargot prepares and sells more than 10 tons of snails annually following a secret recipe that is 75 years old. 79 Rue Fondary, 15e (phone: 45-75-31-09).

Poilâne is considered by many French to sell the best bread in the country, and the large and crusty round country-style loaves dubbed *pain Poilâne,* baked in wood-burning ovens, taste delicious with soup, pâté, cheese, or cassoulet. 8 Rue du Cherche-Midi, 6e (phone: 45-48-42-59).

HOUSEWARES: *Castorama,* a chain with about 100 branches throughout the country, carries 45,000 different European designed basics for the home — from a simple flowerpot to a sophisticated security system. Although you may not want to cart home a bidet or a set of wrought-iron andirons (*Castorama* does not arrange shipping), you will find dozens of moderately priced and stylish smaller items — doorknobs, soap dishes, coat hooks, decorative door plaques — that will travel well and add European panache to your home. Forget about electrical wall switches and anything else you have to connect to existing wiring; the two systems are not compatible.

Antibes – Péage d'Antibes, Rte. de Grasse (phone: 93-33-53-30).

Paris – At Place Clichy, near the St-Lazare railway station, in the basement of a shopping complex, 1-3 Rue Caulaincourt, 18e (phone: 45-22-07-11).

JEWELRY: Several of the world's greatest jewelers are clustered around the elegant Pl. Vendôme in Paris — a dazzling place to window shop if not to pick up an heirloom or two.

Boucheron, 26 Pl. Vendôme, 1er (phone: 42-61-58-16)

Cartier, 13 Rue de la Paix, 2e (phone: 42-61-58-56)

Van Cleef & Arpels, 22 Pl. Vendôme, 1er (phone: 42-61-58-58)

KITCHENWARE: In a country that reveres cooking among the highest of the arts, it is not surprising to find an abundance of kitchen items at nearly every turn.

Paris – Pots and pans that are almost sculptural in their classic beauty are everywhere, as are odd-looking gadgets that perform tasks that most cooks never even imagined. Department stores provide an overview of both the most traditonal and the latest utensils in the world of French cookery. But for real fun, a cook simply cannot beat a store devoted solely to kitchen supplies:

E. Dehillerin is where some of the finest chefs in France have gone to supply their kitchens for the last 150 years. The 2 stories are stacked from nearly floor to ceiling with pots and pans in copper, cast iron, and tin plate in an array that ranges from tiny saucepans to enormous stockpots; with fine carbon steel knives; and with all kinds of casseroles. A number of fascinating little bins contain just about every kind of kitchen accessory conceivable. 18 Rue Coquillière, 1er (phone: 42-36-53-13).

Simon carries a wide range of professional cookware and a dazzling, though confusing, array of bistroware, restaurant flatware, cheese trays, menu slates, snail holders, and tiny terrines. You'll feel like a kid in a candy store here if your interests run to culinary paraphernalia. 36 Rue Etienne-Marcel, 2e (phone: 42-33-71-65).

Villedieu-les-Poëles – This small, rural Norman town takes its name from the *poëles,* frying pans, that have been made here in copper for 300 years, and from one end of the main street to the other, copper gleams through the glass shop windows. Pots come in all different gauges and sizes, and the prices vary accordingly. It is possible to save money over stateside prices for comparable merchandise, but the variety is such that it's necessary to come armed with the exact specifications of the pots you want. About 200 miles (320 km) west of Paris, 14 miles (22 km) northeast of Avranches, and 21 miles (33.5 km) south of St-Lô.

LEATHER GOODS: It is a pleasure to shop for leather goods in France, especially in the best establishments, where every piece of merchandise from the key cases to the steamer trunks is impeccably designed and perfectly crafted. Bear in mind, however, that lower-quality leather goods are probably more expensive and not as well made as comparable items in the US.

Americans should be aware that some exotic skins that are sold legally in France — including certain species of alligator, crocodile, ostrich, and lizard — could be seized on arrival back home, since these animals are on the Endangered Species List in the United States. The best French stores will steer American shoppers to merchandise that meets US import laws, but it's still wise to check the latest regulations with the US Fish and Wildlife Service before leaving home.

Nice – In all of France, the seemingly ubiquitous Louis Vuitton handbags, capacious satchels, suitcases, and dozens of other items (most marked with LVs) — many for traveling — are sold at only a dozen stores in France, one here (2 Av. de Suède; phone: 93-87-87-47) and two others in Paris (78 *bis* Av. Marceau, 8e; phone: 47-20-47-00; and 54 Av. Montaigne, 8e; phone: 45-62-47-00).

Paris – The capital abounds in shops purveying the finest of leather goods.

Céline, whose subdued setting is as classy as its merchandise, offers especially nice small shoulder bags in a great variety of colors and skins. 24 Rue François-Ier, 8e (phone: 47-20-22-83).

Hermès, generally considered *the* place to find leather objects of quality and beauty (at extremely high prices), stocks classics such as the popular Constance and Kelly bags in a wealth of sizes, skins, and colors. And there are attaché cases, suitcases, saddles, and small address books and coin purses that make useful and eminently packable gifts of great cachet. 24 Rue du Faubourg-St-Honoré, 8e (phone: 40-17-47-17).

Louis Vuitton is the first stop in Paris for many affluent shoppers after matched sets of the status LV luggage and leather goods — from billfolds to dog carriers. *Vuitton* has elegant (and friendly) quarters at 54 Av. Montaigne, 8e (phone: 45-62-47-00), as well as many other points of sale in the capital. Its original (and haughtier) headquarters is at 78 *bis* Av. Marceau, 8e (phone: 47-20-47-00).

PERFUME: For centuries, the French have been making enticing scents that are synonymous with luxury and romance, and around the world, in all languages, the adjective that springs most quickly to mind to modify the word "perfume" is "French." Consequently, it's not surprising that perfume heads the shopping lists of more visitors to France than any other item. And department stores around the country, which generally carry the best selections of all the well-known brands (except Guerlain, which sells only from its own shops), do a booming business among tourists.

But today, with virtually all names and sizes of French perfume available in US stores, is there any reason beyond this mystique to buy French perfume in France?

The answer is yes. By shopping in the right places and following the rules for getting tax refunds as described below, it's possible to save some money — and to pay as little as 25–30% less than the price of some of France's most expensive and sought-after perfumes. Even without the additional reduction afforded by the tax refund, in fact, the cost of French perfume in a department store is roughly 90% of what you would pay stateside.

Do not be taken in by the flashy Tax Free signs sported by perfume stores all over the country. Most shops, the major department stores included, sell basically the same brands and sizes at rates set by the manufacturers. Regardless of where you shop, the perfume becomes tax free only after you have purchased enough of it at a single store to qualify for the tax refund set up by the government. The exception, airport duty-free shops, sell without tax even on small bottles of inexpensive perfumes; the selection is more limited than in city stores, however.

Grasse – Visitors to this town, which is perched in the hills 11 miles (18 km) from Cannes and 26 miles (42 km) from Nice and has been an international perfume making center since the 16th century, probably will want to visit a perfume works to see for themselves how the floral essences that go into almost all of their favorite French perfume are extracted from tons of locally grown and imported flowers. They also can view the small plots where neighborhood farmers cultivate jasmine and roses (half a dozen tons of whose petals are required to produce just a quart of essence) or, about 20 minutes into the rocky heights above the town, gather their own fragrant bouquets of wild lavender that grow in beautiful violet patches by the roadside.

The large factories that produce vast quantities of perfume, soap, and cosmetics are closed to the public because of the volatile chemicals they use. However, the laboratories of three manufacturing concerns are open for free tours, during which guides explain in English, French, and other languages how the essences are extracted and distilled and show off magnificent old copper machinery full of curves and spirals:

Fragonard also has an attractive museum of objects associated with perfume since antiquity. 20 Bd. Fragonard (phone: 93-36-44-65).

Galimard is at Esplanade du Cours (phone: 93-09-20-00).

Molinard can be found about a mile from the heart of town. 60 Bd. Victor-Hugo (phone: 93-36-01-62).

The salesrooms in which the tours end are full of pretty souvenirs and small gifts to take home, such as scented candles, soaps, and sachets of lavender and potpourri as well as dozens of bottles of fragrance in all sizes and forms. Each *parfumerie* sells just its own creations — which include not only the brands that are associated with their houses but also many with unfamiliar names that are imitations of the popular scents of other houses (such as YSL's Opium). Discounts of about 5% are available here, and many of the virtually unknown scents are so inexpensive that no one has to think twice about taking a chance on a new perfume. For those who would like to know more about the science of perfume making, the newly opened *Musée International de la Parfumerie* (8 Pl. du Cours; phone: 93-36-80-80) offers a fascinating look into the production of the aromatic liquid.

Paris – In the capital, there are two good addresses for buying perfume. *Michel Swiss* (16 Rue de la Paix, 2e; phone: 42-61-71-71) offers a voluminous selection, cheerful service, discounts of 25% for payment with cash or traveler's checks (20% for credit cards), and, in addition, a 25% tax refund on the balance to American visitors who spend more than 1,200F (about $200). That brings the total discount to almost 44%. *Anne Paree* gives a 40% discount — including VAT — on purchases totaling 1,500F (about $250) or more (6 Rue Castiglione, 1er; phone: 42-60-81-49).

SHOES: France is a country for shoe fiends, and it is full of places to buy footwear that is not only stylish but also — probably because the French walk a good deal themselves and refuse to clump around in ugly shoes — comfortable.

Nationwide, look for the *André* and *Raoul* chains, which stock surprisingly inexpensive shoes in the latest styles and colors — and are consquently the source for the shoe wardrobe of many a fashion-crazy French high school girl.

Paris – This city offers an additional supply of exceptional shoe stores that have few equals in the rest of the country:

Carel sells classy shoes in the latest shapes and colors — sometimes, but not always, suited to the American foot. At several locations, including 12 Rond-Point des Champs-Elysées, 8e (phone: 45-62-30-62).

Charles Jourdan sells high-fashion shoes of good quality. 86 Av. des Champs-Elysées, 8e and other locations (phone: 45-62-29-28).

France Faver offers stylish beauty and welcome comfort in its shoes. They are moderately expensive, but the quality makes them worth the price. 79 Rue des Sts-Pères, 6e (phone: 42-22-04-29).

Maud Frizon offers some of the most sophisticated shoes in Paris. The designs are often lovely and usually costly, especially the boots. 83 Rue des Sts-Pères, 6e (phone: 42-22-06-93).

Stéphane Kélian has several points of sale in the capital for high-fashion men's and women's shoes. Quality is high, as are prices, but the latter are not completely unreasonable. 4 Pl. des Victoires, 1er (phone: 42-61-60-74).

Walter Steiger carries some of the capital's most expensive and exclusive footwear for men and women in his flagship shop on Faubourg-St-Honoré, which displays satin slippers like precious jewels — and with prices to match. 83 Rue du Faubourg-St-Honoré, 8e (phone: 42-66-65-08).

FABRIC: The colorful and distinctive cotton fabrics of the south of France make a delightful souvenir. In Aix-en-Provence, bags, bedspreads, eyeglass cases, and other articles made of this cloth — as well as the cloth by the yard — are available at *Les Olivades*, 5 Rue des Chaudronniers (phone: 42-23-57-47) and 25 Rue Annonciation (phone: 45-27-07-76).

HOW TO GET A TAX REFUND

The values available to visitors in France on certain merchandise become even more compelling when the refund offered by the French government of its special value-added tax (VAT) is added to existing bargains. (See *Shopping* in GETTING READY TO GO for a detailed discussion of the VAT system and tax-free stores.)

To qualify, visitors must be at least 15 years of age, must reside outside France, and must have visited in the country for less than 6 months. No refunds are offered for purchases of food, wine, or tobacco.

To receive a refund, a visitor must spend at least 2,000F (at press time about $360) in a single shop and must show a passport to prove eligibility. The clerk will then give the buyer an export sales document in triplicate, which must be signed and saved, and an envelope addressed to the store. When leaving France, both the forms and the purchased goods must be taken to the French Customs *détaxe* (tax refund) booth. Note that tax formalities must be taken care of *before* checking baggage and *before* going through passport control at an airport or *before* boarding a train at a station.

The same person who signed the refund forms in the store must present the envelope and the three sheets to the customs officials (who will return one, countersigned, to the buyer in case of later difficulties). The traveler will receive a check for the tax refund mailed from the store. Sometimes, if the buyer pays by credit card, the store makes out a credit slip for the amount of the tax and processes the credit after receiving the validated refund forms from French customs. Or the store may simply make up a separate charge slip for the tax and tear it up when the forms arrive.

It is now possible to receive an immediate refund at Paris's Charles de Gaulle and Orly airports if you bring the appropriate paperwork with you. Large department stores such as *Galeries Lafayette* and *Au Printemps* have an arrangement so that visitors can receive a VAT refund at any airport bank window before they depart France.

Casinos Royal

 To anyone who has been brought up on the high-rolling, honky-tonk gambling supermarkets of Las Vegas and Atlantic City, the hushed elegance of France's 153 casinos, Europe's most elaborate gaming network, will require some adjustment — and perhaps some classier clothes. But even for those who only toss an occasional chip onto those lush meadows of felt, the spectacle at the great pleasure domes of Monte Carlo and Deauville is well worth the modest price of admission. Set in some of France's major resort towns (but forbidden within 60 miles — 96 km — of Paris by Napoleonic decree), they draw a crowd that is a heady mixture of Parisian chic and Arab sheik. The scenario is pure Hollywood. In fact, behind all the glitter is a system of tight surveillance by the Brigade des Jeux, France's special branch of gaming police, and a gambling code that regulates everything from the odds on the slot machines to the dinner jacket on the croupier — which has (by law) no pockets. The result is an almost totally aboveboard industry, though internecine squabbles among operators have occasionally evoked memories of Chicago in the 1920s. Players are nonetheless fairly certain to lose their money according to the inexorable laws of mathematics.

Passports are required for admission. Though marathon games of chemin-de-fer are allowed to continue until the players drop, most French casinos open in mid-afternoon and close at 3 or 4 AM day in and day out. Dress has become far more casual in recent years, but there still are many casinos where jacket and tie are de rigueur for gentlemen; in any case, it's always better to err on the side of decorum. A number of the larger casinos have glamorous, first-rate restaurants right on the gaming room floor; their waiters discreetly reheat the food of those kept away from their meal by a winning streak.

The staples of the French casino diet are roulette, baccarat, and *boule;* craps and blackjack increasingly are in evidence, the result of creeping Americanization. If you're not familiar with the rules or the vocabulary, many casinos will provide an explanatory booklet. And still others have roving *chefs de partie* (game chiefs), who will be more than happy to help a player who doesn't mind looking the greenhorn in the midst of all that savoir-faire.

AIX-LES-BAINS, Savoie: At this ancient thermal resort where the Romans once frolicked, titled matrons fresh from the sulfurous mudbaths hoard their chips in silver mesh purses. Hotels bear names like *Iles-Britanniques* and *Angleterre.* And streets are called Victoria and Pierpont Morgan. There is a faintly fin-de-siècle feeling to it all — from the gaming tables in the *Palais de Savoie,* one of France's most distinguished and stately casinos, to the more contemporary *Nouveau Casino* only a chip's throw away. The town lolls at the foot of the Alps on the east bank of lovely Lac du Bourget. When the chips are up, try the half-day boat tour of the lake, which includes the Royal Abbey of Hautecombe. Information: *Casino Grand Cercle,* Rue du Casino (phone: 79-35-16-16); and *Nouveau Casino,* 36 Av. Victoria, Aix-les-Bains 73100 (phone: 79-35-10-00).

ANNECY, Haute-Savoie: Annecy's newly opened *Casino Impérial* is part of the complex of the Impérial Palace, a sumptuous Belle Epoque palace located on a peninsula jutting out into the lake of Annecy. Both modern and traditional slot games are offered at the casino. The crowd here tends to become intensely involved in play, and conversations practically cease after the initial cry of "*Les jeux sont faits!*" And if the roll of the dice proves dicey after a fistful of lost francs, you can take one of the hotel's shuttles to the picturesque historic quarter of Annecy, or a taxi-boat to the town center, or cruise the magnificent shores of the lake. Information: *Le Casino Impérial,* 32 Av. d'Albigny, 74000 Annecy (phone: 50-09-30-00; fax: 50-09-33-33).

LA BAULE, Loire-Atlantique: Gambling is so deeply ingrained in the spirit of this busy, pleasure-mad resort in southern Brittany that the main waterfront promenade, the Esplanade François-André, is reverently named after the founder of a great chain of French casinos. In a manicured park opposite the regal *Royal* hotel is the town's casino. The original building was demolished and replaced 2 years ago. Its restaurant, *La Brasserie du Casino* (phone: 40-60-30-33), is open until 1 AM, and its nightspot, *Le Paradise* (phone: 40-60-80-23) has dining and dancing until dawn in season. Anyone who should happen to rise before the next evening's gaming can shine for a few hours on the resort's splendid 3-mile sweep of beach or on the couple of dozen perfectly maintained clay tennis courts; yacht basins, equestrian centers, and all manner of other facilities effectively banish boredom at La Baule. A new addition to La Baule is *Thalgo* (phone: 40-24-44-88), a state-of-the-art saltwater spa located next to the *Royal.* Information: *Le Casino,* Esplanade François-André, La Baule 44500 (phone: 40-60-20-23).

BIARRITZ, Pyrénées-Atlantiques: The two casinos in this most aristocratic resort attracted kings and princesses to the Atlantic coast long before the reign of the Riviera. Queen Victoria vacationed here, and it was here that King Farouk, a regular, once flipped his solid gold lighter across the roulette table to a lady in need of a light — and then watched while she promptly handed it to the croupier as a tip. The *Bellevue,* set on the cliffs and guarding the beach below like a sentry, still operates as a casino. The *Municipal Casino,* on the sand of the Grande Plage, now is a theater and concert hall. Just beyond the Grande Plage, great gilt-edged hotels like the *Palais, Miramar,* and *Régina et Golf,* which line the Avenue Impératrice, gaze out to sea on a cluster of tiny islands scattered like dice on the blue table of the ocean. Information: *Casino Bellevue,* Pl. Bellevue, Biarritz 64200 (phone: 59-24-11-22).

CANNES, Alpes-Maritimes: The classy *Palm Beach,* whose receipts always are among the highest in France despite its short summer season, now has been joined by the *Casino Croisette* opposite the old harbor. As a result, it's now possible to go broke gracefully all year in this chic resort town. At the other tip of the fashionable Boulevard de la Croisette, the *Palm Beach* sports a swimming pool at the edge of the sea and outdoor dining and dancing by the water with the orchestra in full lilt. "*Le Winter,*" as the *Casino Croisette* is known, has a theater that brings top talent from Paris — everything from *West Side Story* to Nureyev. Information: *Palm Beach Casino,* Bd. de la Croisette, Cannes 06406 (phone: 93-43-91-12); and the *Casino Croisette,* Palais des Festivals, Jetée Albert-Edouard, Cannes 06406 (phone: 93-38-12-11).

DEAUVILLE, Calvados: A gleaming vanilla villa by the sea, the *Deauville* casino and environs have often been called "the 21st Arrondissement of Paris." A playground of the 19th-century jet set, Deauville is in its patrician prime during the July-August horse racing season, when formal dress may still be de rigueur in certain of the casino's sanctums. Trouville, Deauville's neighbor across the River Touques, offers comparable sport, not to mention horseback riding from one end of the beach to the other. The *Deauville* casino also owns two of the town's other delights — the Norman, wooden-gabled *Hôtel Normandy* and a deluxe lobster joint named *Ciro's,* both on the eminently strollable boardwalk and both described at greater length in *Romantic French Hostelries* and *Haute Gastronomie* in this section. Information: *Casino de Deauville,* 1 Rue Edmond-Blanc, Deauville 14800 (phone: 31-98-66-66).

DIVONNE-LES-BAINS, Ain: Open year-round, Divonne is France's top moneymaking casino. In a sleepy border village at the foot of the Juras, it is only about 10 miles (16 km) from vice-free Switzerland and a quarter of an hour from the Geneva Airport. Consequently, the clientele is both prosperous and varied and includes a number of people staying in Geneva for reasons of foreign commerce or private finance. The local thermal baths specialize in dunking "the fatigued, the anguished, and the insomniac"; the lush golf course ranks among France's finest; and there is tranquil sailing on the artificial lake. The centerpiece of a luxurious park and hotel complex, the casino sponsors most of the town's cultural events — most notably the highly reputed summer chamber music festival. Everything from Jura farmyard specialties to Persian caviar is available in the casino's excellent restaurant, right on the gaming room floor. Free champagne is offered with dinner on Mondays and Wednesdays. The dress code is strict — men are required to wear ties and no jeans are allowed. Information: *Le Casino,* Av. de la Divonne, Divonne-les-Bains 01220 (phone: 50-40-34-34).

EVIAN-LES-BAINS, Haute-Savoie: Divonne's competitor for the Swiss connection, the town of Evian is about 25 miles (40 km) by road from Geneva or 40 minutes by boat across Lake Geneva; its casino — a late-19th-century gaming palace that complements that other Evian pleasure dome, the Thermal Baths — is just a few yards from the boat dock. The oldest casino in France, it was immortalized by Ian Fleming in one of his James Bond books, *Casino Royal.* Men need a jacket and tie to get into the first-floor salon; however, casual wear is permitted on the ground floor where the slot machines are found. A large, strobe-lit disco adjoins the casino. The more nostalgic will enjoy strolling past the Baths along the animated, flower-decked Quai de Blonay, where the high born and the high rollers alike contemplate the lake at cocktail hour, and savor the vestiges of the world of wealth and idleness enjoyed by Marcel Proust, who stayed here at the turn of the century. Take a a room at the *Royal,* the most sumptuous hotel in the region — it's a good place to spend any winnings. Information: *Casino Municipal,* Evian-les-Bains 74500 (phone: 50-75-03-78).

FORGES-LES-EAUX, Seine-Maritime: Just outside the 60-mile (96-km) roulette-free zone that Napoleon decreed must surround Paris, Forges attracts all the capital's players who don't want to risk the wheels at the city's various *clandés,* as its clandestine gaming dives are called. Those who can't face the predawn drive back to Paris can stay at the *Continental* hotel, right in the casino complex — and those who lose enough in the course of the evening are guests of the management. Information: *Casino de Forges,* Av. des Sources, Forges-les-Eaux 76440 (phone: 35-09-80-12).

JUAN-LES-PINS, Alpes-Maritimes: The *Eden Beach,* the casino in Juan-les-Pins, actually was founded in 1928 by a Riviera regular, the American railroad tycoon Frank Jay Gould. Nestled between those two specialties of Juan-les-Pins, the emerald pines and the royal blue sea, it became shortly thereafter — and remains today — a principal center for all that is sleekest on the Côte d'Azur nightlife scene. The restaurant is right on the beach, and those who go out for a breath of air between rounds of chemin-de-fer can hear the rhythmic throb of the all-night jazz clubs that animate the town. Nearby, in Antibes, there's the huge *Siesta* casino entertainment complex, which resembles nothing so much as a Mexican village for plutocrats, with 3 restaurants and 5 dance floors — a trio of which are under the stars. Information: *Eden Beach Casino,* Chemin des Sables, Juan-les-Pins 06160 (phone: 92-93-71-71).

MONTE CARLO, Principauté de Monaco: When the brash and brassy Las Vegas-style *Loews Casino* (see *Monaco,* THE CITIES) began to cut into the receipts of Monte Carlo's own staid dowager of a casino, the most legendary in Europe, the latter — designed by Charles Garnier, the architect of *L'Opéra* in Paris — pulled on a pair of jeans over its ball gown and turned its rococo and splendidly gilt Salon de l'Europe into the American Room, all a-clatter with slot machines, fitted out with craps and black-jack tables, staffed by Las Vegas-trained managers and bartenders adept at making screwdrivers and Bloody Marys — and imposing no entrance fee or dress regulations. Still, there are paintings, murals full of nudes, and other Belle Epoque touches throughout, and the old and elegant Salon Privé (Private Room) is as decorous as ever; a passport and admission fee must be presented at the door. The cloistered sanctum known as the Salon Super-Privé, equipped with one table for *banque-à-tout-va,* is available by appointment only; the very knowledge that you have played there should forever banish the need to wear Gucci loafers or drive a Ferrari to prove your worth. Try to get a glimpse of the casino's ornate and fabled theater, a lavish study in gold leaf, scrolls, and garlands, where Lily Pons, Nijinsky, Caruso, and Sarah Bernhardt all performed, the last on opening night in 1879. And to vary the summer gaming diet, stop in at the water's-edge *Monte Carlo Sporting Club,* built on a sea-rimmed, manmade promontory a few miles out of town; there is discreet lighting, a Starlight Room with a 3,300-square-foot roof that opens to the sky, and a Polynesian restaurant nestled amid tropical gardens. Information: *Société des Bains de Mer,* Pl. du Casino, Monte Carlo, Principauté de Monaco 98000 (phone: 93-50-69-31).

Most Visitable Vineyards

It's hard to know just what to expect at a vineyard in France. Arrive when the wine maker is in a chatty, outgoing mood and you may end up staying for hours, sharing recent vintages and discussing French politics and the state of French wine. Another day, you may find yourself in the hands of an ambitious young peasant farmer just getting started in the business, and the next you'll be visiting a château where a wealthy wine maker follows family rules and techniques that go back centuries. In almost every case, a vineyard visit includes a wander through the château's tasting room, normally attached to the cellars, where guests settle down and the most recent vintages are uncorked. Usually, these tastings are free; the wine also is available for purchase. Though almost every vineyard in France welcomes visitors, it always is a good idea to call ahead. Spring and summer visitors are more welcome than those who come in fall, when the harvest keeps the vineyard's entire staff occupied nearly around the clock. Note that although many do not keep official hours — wine makers are farmers, after all — it's most polite to arrive between 10 AM and noon or between 2 and 5 PM.

Consider taking a summer course in wine wisdom with the *CIDD (Centre d'Information, de Documentation, et de Dégustation)*, which includes in its program visits to vineyards and wine cellars. The center has a wide range of activities in English, and occasionally holds an open house to introduce little-known wines to the public. Open Monday through Friday from 1 to 7 PM. Information: *CIDD,* 45 Rue Liancourt, Paris 75014 (phone: 43-27-67-21).

The following is a sampling of France's vineyards; they offer a variety of styles of wine made by a wide assortment of wine makers, who espouse not only different methods of wine making but also varying merchandising programs.

ALSACE: The wines of this area are fragrant, fruity, and white, ordinarily drunk while still young. And they are named for the variety of grape that went into them. Gewürztraminer is dry and spicy, with a certain zing. Pinot gris, also known as tokay d'Alsace, is broad and full-bodied. Riesling is at once dry and fruity, crisp and elegant. And sylvaner, the most plentiful of all, has a distinctive freshness that makes it a fine apéritif.

Léon Beyer, Eguisheim, Haut-Rhin – The Beyer family, tending its vineyards since 1850, makes one of the best and best-known wines of the Alsace wine making region, which is in the foothills of the Vosges mountains facing the Rhine River — a region that, incidentally, offers some of the most charming and lovable villages in all of France. Beyer's riesling shows up on the wine lists of such famous three-star restaurants as *Taillevent* in Paris and *Auberge de l'Ill* in Illhaeusern. The firm's tasting room is in Eguisheim, a most historic and attractive Alsace town full of tidy stone and timber houses with geranium-filled windowboxes. The town, which is centered around a main square with a handsome Renaissance fountain, is on the Wine Road, which takes in several other wineries in the area. See also the tour route *Alsace,* DIRECTIONS. Information: *Léon Beyer,* Eguisheim 68420 (phone: 89-41-41-05).

Hugel et Fils, Riquewihr, Haut-Rhin – Visitors to these *caves* — in a pair of 16th-century houses that have been gutted to make room for the winery — see what's believed to be the oldest cask in the world still in constant use. It was made in 1715 and holds more than 8,800 quarts. Hugel is respected for its elegant, round, supple, well-balanced wines, particularly the dry riesling, with its round bouquet, and its rich, spicy, full-bodied gewürztraminer. The entire town is a historical monument, and the main street is so packed with remarkably well preserved houses that it would warrant a visit in its own right. Information: *Hugel et Fils,* Riquewihr 68340 (phone: 89-47-92-15).

BORDEAUX: From the flat terrain with its precise rows of vines punctuated by red roses near the roadsides to the attractive villages where the wine business occupies everyone — from the joiners who knock together the cases for the bottles to the printers who make up the labels — this region is the home of some of the richest wine country in the world. The vines of the Médoc, the region that stretches along the bank of the Gironde River between Bordeaux and the Bay of Biscay, set the standard. Margaux, Pauillac, St-Estèphe, and St-Julien are among the principal towns, and the area around them has road signs for nearly every château. The *Maison du Vin* in Bordeaux (1 Cours du 30-Juillet, Bordeaux 33075; phone: 56-00-22-66) can provide a list of those open to the public. See also *Bordeaux and the Médoc,* DIRECTIONS.

Château Palmer, Margaux, Gironde – Although the famous 10th-century turreted château that's featured on the elegant and distinctive label of this vineyard's wine can be visited much of the year, it is most popular as a tourist attraction at vintage time, usually in September, since it is one of the few vineyards where visitors can see the old-fashioned destalking of grapes by hand on a wooden tray. The Dutch, French, and British flags fluttering outside honor its successful (if rather unusual) tri-national ownership. Visits are generally available weekdays from 9 to 11:30 AM and from 2 to 5:30 PM, but call ahead. See also *Bordeaux and the Médoc,* DIRECTIONS. Information: *Château Palmer,* Margaux 33460 (phone: 56-88-72-72).

Château Prieuré-Lichine, Margaux, Gironde – The late Alexis Lichine, the best known and most respected American wine maker in France, worked to make the wines of the Château Prieuré-Lichine — in a former Benedictine priory — among the finest and most fragrant produced on the 2,500 vineyard acres cultivated around Margaux. Visitors might find Alexis's son, who took over after his father's death, overseeing the vineyards. The old cloister remains are decked out with fanciful antique cast-iron firebacks that Lichine has collected from all over Europe, and the vat room with its craggy beams was built by the monks who tended the vines long before Lichine was a gleam in his father's eye. Visits are possible from 9 AM to 6 PM daily in winter, to 7 PM in spring and autumn, and to 8 PM in summer. Call for an appointment. See also *Bordeaux and the Médoc,* DIRECTIONS. Information: *Château Prieuré-Lichine,* Margaux 33460 (phone: 56-88-36-28).

Château Beauséjour-Becot, St-Emilion, Gironde – A visitor who comes to this friendly wine maker's château with a few hours on his hands almost certainly will hear, if not Baudelaire, at least the story of how the small but now prosperous 16-acre property was rescued from decline some years ago. M. Becot loves to quote Baudelaire, to sing the well-deserved praise of St-Emilion (both the wine and the charming hilltop village), and to receive visitors — and when the spirit moves him, he sometimes passes out "before" and "after" samples to document the big changes that have occurred since his arrival. See also *Bordeaux,* THE CITIES. Information: *Château Beauséjour-Becot,* St-Emilion 33330 (phone: 57-74-46-87).

BURGUNDY: Burgundian wines include the dry and flinty white made in Chablis; the aromatic, full-bodied reds and whites made south of Dijon in the Côte d'Or; and the light and fruity reds made in Beaujolais. Great wine producing villages are as common as corn in Kansas: Chambertin, Chassagne-Montrachet, Gevrey-Chambertin, Meursault, Mâcon, Morey-St-Denis, Nuits St-Georges, Pommard, Puligny-Montrachet, Pommard, and others. A *Musée du Vin de Bourgogne* in Beaune documents the cultivation of the grape and wine making down through history; there are tours on the hour. Rue d'Enfer (phone: 80-22-08-19).

Domaine de la Romanée-Conti, Auxey-Duresses, Côte d'Or – The main gate of one of the world's most famous vineyards is hidden in the back streets of Vosne-Romanée and visitors are received by appointment only — but then the wines of the Domaine, including the fabulously expensive Romanée-Conti (of which only 6,000 bottles are produced each year) and the equally well-known La Tache — are among the most expensive and revered in the world. Even the likes of Nikita Khrushchev have signed their names in the crimson and gold guestbook. For appointments, contact the *Négociant Leroy,* Auxey-Duresses, Meursault 21120 (phone: 80-21-21-10) or contact *Romanée Conti* directly in Vosne-Romanée (phone: 80-61-04-04).

Domaine Henri Gouges, Nuits St-Georges, Côte d'Or – The village of Nuits St-Georges produces some admirable reds known for their characteristic earthy flavor (*gout de terroir*), and some of Burgundy's best known of these wines come from Domaine Henri Gouges, which supplies Paris's *Taillevent* with the remarkable and rare white wine of the region as well as full-bodied reds. M. Gouges, an amiable man, receives visitors by appointment only. Information: *Domaine Henri Gouges,* 28 Rue du Moulin, Nuits St-Georges 21700 (phone: 80-61-04-40).

Georges Duboeuf, Romanèche-Thorins, Saône-et-Loire – Beaujolais, once a cheap bar wine, is now enjoyed the world over for its fresh, fruity flavor. The area in which it is produced is unquestionably one of France's most picturesque wine regions, and M. Duboeuf is highly respected by his neighbors and colleagues. When visiting him, take the time to drive at least a portion of Beaujolais's Route du Vin, beginning at Juliénas, passing through Chenas, Pontanevaux, then on to Romanèche-Thorins. Open to wine professionals only with an appointment. Information: *Georges Duboeuf,* Romanèche-Thorins 71570 (phone: 85-35-51-13).

CAHORS: This tranquil village, one of the principal gateways to the south of France, is most famous for the hearty red wine made from the grapes grown on the hills along the Lot to the west of town.

Clos de Gamot, Prayssac, Lot – This establishment is a good place to sample some of the "black wine of Cahors." Jean Jouffreau, an excellent and remarkably gregarious grower, tends his vines without chemical sprays and ages his wine in oak casks. The result is a liquid that is dark and weighty, with overtones of cassis, some say; others love it for its vigor and its ability to stand up to the robust food of the region — cassoulet, truffles, *confit,* and hearty breads. Information: *Clos de Gamot,* Prayssac 46220 (phone: 65-22-40-26).

CHAMPAGNE: It was the Romans who planted the first vines in this region an hour and a half from Paris, the northernmost vine growing area in the country; and despite a succession of wars, from the Hundred Years War to World War II, the Champenois have been tending their vines, harvesting their grapes, and bottling their vintages nearly ever since. The sparkling beverage known as champagne, made according to a process developed at the end of the 17th century, is still the lifeblood of the region. Tourist information offices throughout the area publish standard Champagne itineraries and maintain signs along the routes. And a colorful museum full of regional maps, agricultural tools, winepresses, and labels has been set up in the 19th-century Château Perrier. See also *Champagne,* DIRECTIONS.

Ricciuti-Révolte, Avenay-Val-d'Or, Marne – That this bubbly is often described as the champagne with the Baltimore flavor is because the wine maker, Albert Ricciuti, is a Baltimorean who married a Frenchwoman whose family also happened to produce champagne. It all started in 1944, when Mr. Ricciuti, then an American soldier, helped liberate the village of Avenay-Val-d'Or. He met a young Frenchwoman, corresponded with her for 18 years, then returned for a visit. Marriage followed, and since 1963 he's been part of the family champagne business. Mr. Ricciuti is an outgoing, jovial man who loves showing visitors around his vineyards and cellars. Information: *Ricciuti-Révolte,* Avenay-Val-d'Or, Ay 51160 (phone: 26-52-30-27).

Moët & Chandon, Epernay, Marne – The best way to learn about champagne is to watch the painstaking care with which it is made. And one of the best-organized spots to do this is at Moët & Chandon, whose vast and impressive cellars — if not the most beautiful in the area, then certainly the biggest, with their 17 miles of galleries — can be seen on entertaining guided tours daily from April through October, weekdays only the rest of the year. Most impressive is the sight of the *rémueurs,* the men who carefully, and rapidly, turn each bottle precisely one quarter turn (a process called "riddling"). Afterward, guides offer each visitor a drink of the famous white-and-bubbly. Open from 9:30 AM to noon or 12:30 PM and from 2 to 4:30 or 5:30 PM, depending on the day and the season. A museum devoted to the wine as well as several other cellars are along the Avenue de Champagne, and the Syndicat d'Initiative on the same street distributes a pamphlet listing their hours. Information: *Moët & Chandon,* 20 Av. de Champagne, Epernay 51205 (phone: 26-54-71-11). See also *Champagne,* DIRECTIONS.

CÔTES DU RHÔNE: The wines of this area usually are red and ordinarily robust; châteauneuf-du-pape, the most famous wine of the southern vineyards of this area, and the flavorful gigondas, a close second, are just two examples. Those specifically labeled côtes du rhône and côtes du rhône villages are particularly soft and flavorful.

Caves des Vignerons, Beaumes-de-Venise, Vaucluse – The sweet white wine from Beaumes-de-Venise and a fresh melon from nearby Cavaillon, in the south of France, make one of the finest food combinations in the world. The cooperative at Beaumes-de-Venise sells one of the better-known versions of the naturally sweet local dessert wines as well as a variety of other wines, including côtes du rhône villages and côtes du ventoux. Information: *Caves des Vignerons,* Beaumes-de-Venise 84190 (phone: 90-62-94-45).

Domaine de Mont-Redon, Châteauneuf-du-Pape, Vaucluse – In the spotless tasting rooms at this largest, best known, and most respected of the Châteauneuf-du-Pape estates, visitors may sample various recent vintages of Châteauneuf-du-Pape red, a hearty blend of 13 different grape varieties, as well as a lesser-known white that rarely finds its way out of the region. The estate also is proud of its small production of eau-de-vie, a clear liquor made from grape pressings; only about 2,000 bottles are produced each year and most are sold at the château. Information: *Domaine de Mont-Redon,* Châteauneuf-du-Pape 84230 (phone: 90-83-72-75).

Gigondas, Vaucluse – Right in the center of this sleepy little village, visitors will find a tasting room where more than 20 different versions of the heady local red, gigondas, may be sampled. One of the finest comes from Georges Faraud, whose farmhouse is at the edge of the village; his classic, long-lived red received praise from French as well as American critics, and visitors receive a most cordial welcome. Information: *Syndicat d'Initiative,* Gigondas 84190 (phone: 90-65-85-46).

Domaine de la Gautière, La Penne sur Ouvèze, Drôme – Deep in the heart of French lavender country, the Tardieus run a small organic farm where they raise bees for honey, tend ancient olive trees that yield exquisite black olives and fruity, golden olive oil, and produce a delicious red country wine that seems to taste even better when sipped on the family patio. The honey, the olives, the oil, and the wine are all for sale here, and there's a campground attached to the property. Information: *Domaine de la Gautière,* La Penne sur Ouvèze, Buis-les-Barronies 26170 (phone: 75-28-09-58).

Cooperative Vinicole Vinsobraise, Vinsobres, Drôme – The French of this region usually buy their wine in bulk, and usually from a cooperative such as that at Vinsobraise, a large, active group just outside the village of Vinsobres, which makes a strong, substantial wine that ages well and also some lesser-known whites and rosés. All can be sampled at the *Cooperative*'s bar, where visitors also will see local wine makers bringing in their wines and buyers coming in with huge plastic containers for refilling. Information: *Cooperative Vinicole Vinsobraise,* Vinsobres 26110 (phone: 75-27-64-22).

Learning the Culinary Arts: Cooking Schools

The cooking schools of France are as varied as the nation's landscape and regional cuisine. Visitors can study with famous chefs such as Gaston Lenôtre and Roger Vergé. They can gain hands-on experience at the most classic of all cooking schools — Paris's Le Cordon Bleu. And they can take courses with farm wives in the rustic kitchens of the Quercy and the Dordogne in the southwest. Travelers who want to look behind the scenes at restaurant kitchens or to visit the wholesale markets where the chefs themselves shop can go on tour with Robert Noah in Paris. Many schools will tailor special courses for groups of ten or more. The choice is limited only by one's vision and by one's command of French, a knowledge of which goes a long way toward making the experience meaningful, even though translators are usually available. Programs tend to be casual and are geared to novices and experts alike. The point is to go with an open mind and a willing spirit, ready to acquire a few additional culinary skills and authentic French experiences — and have a good time besides. ·

A few words of advice on planning a trip. Don't be afraid to go alone. Many lifelong international friendships have been struck over magnificent soufflés. Most schools operate year-round, and courses in Paris are good anytime; those offered in the southwest and in Provence are probably better in late spring and early fall, when the countryside is at its most beautiful and the pace is a bit less hectic. In any case, be sure to send away for brochures and read them carefully before booking so that you know exactly what to expect.

PROVENÇAL COOKING SCHOOL, Gordes, Provence: Sylvie Lallemand — who speaks English — learned to cook at her Provençal mother's knee, and she passes on the best of the region's dishes and the skills necessary to prepare them as well as an appreciation of Provençal wines to guests who stay in her pine-rimmed country house with a swimming pool. Each morning they investigate the local food markets, afternoons are spent practicing and polishing the skills learned, and evenings are given over to gastronomic indulgence and critique. Week-long courses begin on Saturday afternoons. Also offered is a week-long painting session during which different themes and techniques are explored. In Gordes, 30 miles (48 km) east of Avignon. Closed in July and August. Information: *Provençal Cooking School,* Sylvie Lallemand, Les Mégalithes, Gordes 84220 (phone: 90-72-23-41).

ECOLE DE CUISINE LA VARENNE, Joigny, Burgundy: This well-known cooking school run by the English cookbook author, journalist, and food historian Anne Willan — with Simone Beck and Julia Child as advisers — recently moved all its operations from Paris to its château in Burgundy. Devoted to French cuisine, with classes taught by a staff of French chefs, the school remains particularly popular with Americans. Students may sign up for week-long demonstration and participation courses in the summer and fall in regional cooking, bistro cooking, pastry, and contemporary and classic French cuisine. In addition, intensive 5-week professional diploma courses are offered in May and October. To qualify for these courses, students must have previous culinary training or experience in the field and an understanding of traditional French cooking. Classes are in French, and though English translations are provided, an understanding of the language is most helpful. Reserve a few days in advance for daily demonstrations (limited to about 50 students), several months in advance for longer courses. Students are responsible for their own lodging. Information: *Ecole de Cuisine La Varenne,* PO Box 25574, Washington, DC 20007 (phone: 800-537-6486 or 800-337-0073).

FARM COOKING WEEKENDS, Ladornac, Dordogne: Dany and Guy Dubois work a farm in the lush and hilly Dordogne in France's southwest. But they also conduct informal weekend cooking classes that may include a visit to the town bakery or to an antique but still working walnut oil mill. Students may choose either a weekend *du cochon,* which covers the preparation of pork products such as blood sausage and the curing of a ham, or a weekend devoted to that specialty made of fattened goose livers, foie gras, during which Dany Dubois helps students prepare their own, as well as *confit* and *rillettes,* using the force-fed geese raised on the family farm. Courses, which are taught in French, are limited to six students, and reservations must be made several months in advance. Meals and lodging are included, and the Dubois family will pick up students at the train station in nearby Brive. Courses are offered from September to May. Information: *Dany and Guy Dubois,* Peyrenègre Ladornac 24120 (phone: 53-51-04-24).

INITIATION A LA CUISINE PROVENÇAL, Marseilles, Bouches-du-Rhône: A movable feast combining travel and kitchen wizardry has been cooked up by *La*

Conquête in Marseilles. Guests shop for ingredients and prepare dishes under a chef's guidance in the morning, have lunch, and then tour the region in the afternoon. Based in the small Provençal town of Salon, the course runs 4 days (3 nights). You can form your own group (they recommend 8–15 people) and select your own itinerary. Information: *La Conquête,* 12 Rue de la Bibliotèque, Marseilles 13001 (phone: 91-42-35-66).

ROGER VERGÉ'S L'ECOLE DU MOULIN, Mougins, Provence: As the only Michelin three-star chef to offer regular cooking classes, Roger Vergé runs a school designed for home cooks, and touring American couples come by the dozen for the week-long course taught by various chefs from Vergé's celebrated restaurants, the three-star *Le Moulin de Mougins,* just outside the charming village of Mougins, and the one-star *L'Amandier,* in the heart of it. The participation-demonstration classes take place above the latter; each weekday students prepare a different menu featuring the varied cuisine of Provence. Classes are available in English, French, German, and Japanese, and include lunch but not lodging. There are also classes in flower arranging and table setting. Information: *Le Moulin de Mougins,* 424 Chemin du Moulin, Mougins, Alpes-Maritimes 06250 (phone: 93-75-35-70).

LE CORDON BLEU, Paris: This famous school has been instructing an international group of students in French cooking and pastry making since 1895. During the summer, special 5-week courses are offered in cooking and pastry, while 11-week sessions that give credits toward certificates and diplomas are available during the year. Visitors may reserve a few days ahead for single afternoon demonstrations, with menus available about 30 days in advance for each month's program. There also are intensive 4- or 5-day sessions during holiday periods — *Christmas, Easter,* and throughout the summer. Both the demonstration and intensive courses often are translated into English. Students are responsible for their own lodging. Information: *Le Cordon Bleu,* 8 *bis* Rue Léon-Delhomme, Paris 75015 (phone: 48-56-06-06; in the US, 800-457-2433).

ECOLE FERRANDI: The only Paris cooking school to offer professionally motivated foreigners preparatory courses for a C.A.P., the French government's culinary certification. Though its basic course runs for 9 months (5 days a week) and is recommended only for the most serious students, shorter programs also are offered. They include twice-annual week-long pastry and cuisine courses. Though it is a private school (owned by the Paris Chamber of Commerce), *Ferrandi* courses have been endorsed by such famous French chefs as Joël Robuchon and Pierre Troisgros. Information: *Ecole Ferrandi,* 49 Rue de Richelieu, Paris 75001 (phone: 42-61-35-23; fax: 42-60-39-96).

ECOLE DE GASTRONOMIE FRANÇAISE RITZ-ESCOFFIER, Paris: Escoffier was to food what Daimler was to automobiles. Today, the *Ritz* hotel, where the legendary chef Escoffier made his debut in the last century, houses the ultimate cooking school. Courses last 1 to 6 weeks and involve 25 hours of instruction weekly. There also is a course in *pâtisserie* — the art of cake, ice cream, chocolate, and candy making — and a 12-week program for professionals. Instruction is in French and English. Information: *Ecole de Gastronomie Française Ritz-Escoffier,* 38 Rue Cambon, Paris 75001 (phone: 42-60-38-30).

ECOLE LENÔTRE, Paris: Working in groups of up to a dozen under France's best known and most respected pastry chef, Gaston Lenôtre, professionals and serious amateurs study French pastry, chocolate, bread, ice cream, charcuterie, and catering in the huge, modern, spotless Lenôtre laboratory in the suburb of Plaisir, about 17 miles (28 km) outside Paris. Courses, which are conducted in French, generally last 5 days and include breakfast and lunch (though students are responsible for their own lodging and transportation). Reserve several months in advance. Information: *Ecole Lenôtre,* Rue Pierre-Curie, Plaisir 78370 (phone: 30-55-81-12).

PRINCESS ERE 2001, Paris: A well-appointed apartment in Paris and a château in Normandy are the sites for the programs offered by the outgoing, enthusiastic Princess Marie-Blanche de Broglie. In the capital, these include demonstration courses that deal with cooking professionally, the harmony of wines and foods, pastry, the art of entertaining, and French regional cooking. In Normandy, a month-long session in August — primarily for professionals — includes preparation of meals for visiting tourists. Courses may be arranged in English, French, and Spanish, with translations supplied as necessary. In Paris, the programs run year-round, and students are responsible for their own lodging. In Normandy, lodging is available in an 18th-century house on the estate. Reserve several months in advance. Information: *Marie-Blanche de Broglie, Princess Ere 2001,* 18 Av. de la Motte-Picquet, Paris 75007 (phone: 45-51-36-34).

PARIS EN CUISINE, Paris: Travelers who want to visit the wholesale market in the outskirts at Rungis, tour the kitchens of such well-known Paris restaurants as *Taillevent* or *Chiberta,* attend cooking classes with top chefs like Michel and Pierre Troisgros or Michel Guérard, or get an inside view of a chocolate shop, a *boulangerie,* a *pâtisserie,* or a charcuterie can arrange individual or group visits led by Robert Noah, an American based in Paris with excellent contacts in the French food world. The tours are excellent for those who do not speak French, for Noah is a careful translator and groups are small (usually about ten students, depending on the program). Reserve several months in advance. Students are responsible for their own lodging. Information: *Paris en Cuisine,* 49 Rue de Richelieu, Paris 75001 (phone: 42-61-35-23). Noah also publishes a lively, informative newsletter about food and wine in France. Information: *Paris en Cuisine,* PO Box 50099, St. Louis, MO 63105.

For the Body

Sensational French Skiing

 Unsophisticated skiers initially may think of Switzerland when they daydream about the Alps, but savvier downhill devotees know that the Alps claimed by France boast ski slopes equal to any in the world. French ski resorts, isolated centers of pleasure concentrated in the Haute-Savoie, are scenic and relaxing — not to mention socially enjoyable — and nightlife amid the French mountains is such that France has given the rest of the world the term après-ski, the all-inclusive phrase that describes all that's fun at the end of a hard day on the slopes.

Most major French ski resorts offer economical packages that include room, board, equipment, and lift passes, and these can be irresistible for those looking for the highest quality of European ski experience at the lowest possible cost. It is best to insist on half board — only breakfast and dinner — since returning to a lodging place for lunch almost always is inconvenient, although some hotels include lunch at a designated mountain restaurant for their full-board guests. Prices fluctuate according to the season. Late November and early December are considered low season, and *Christmastime* and February are high season. January, when conditions often areas good as they are a month later, usually falls somewhere in between. During the ski season, you can call "France on Call" (phone: 900-990-0040) to find out about snow conditions in the French Alps. This line also provides information about special package fares and bonuses for US skiers. More information can be obtained at the French Alps Tourism and Trade Commission in New York City (phone: 212-307-8854).

In addition to traditional downhill skiing, most resorts are equipped for the "new" snow sports — monoskiing, surfboarding, free-style skiing, speed skiing — as well as hang gliding and parasailing. Because of several almost snowless seasons, resorts in the French Alps have been forced to develop equipment to attract enthusiasts — snow guns have been installed and new lifts were built to bring skiers to higher elevations where year-round glacier skiing is available. And some resorts have indoor fitness and sports centers that offer a wide range of activities and give children special attention (through schools and nurseries).

All sites described below have a branch of the national ski school, *Ecole du Ski Français,* which provides instructors (most have English-speaking teachers) for skiers at every level — from beginners to those interested in the challenge of *off-piste* (off the marked trails) skiing to snow safaris or helicopter skiing. Ski accident insurance — *La Carte Neige* — also is available for purchase at the *Ecoles.*

Each town, no matter how small, has a tourist office that can provide up-to-date information about hotel availability, unusual tours, ski schools, equipment rental, and so on. For each ski center, we have included a few favorite hotels in each price range: Expensive (E), Moderate (M), Inexpensive (I) — or, at least, more moderate.

CHAMONIX, Haute-Savoie: Ever since the first *Winter Olympics* were held here in 1924, this valley town (sandwiched between the Mont-Blanc range and the Aiguilles-

Rouges) has had a reputation as an important center for mountain pursuits, and it unquestionably is one of the best ski resorts in the French Alps. Since most of the more than 50 trails on the mountains above the busy, small town are within sight of Mont-Blanc, whose 15,771-foot summit makes it the highest peak in the Alps, the scenery is as good as the skiing. Experts can join a guided tour down the challenging Vallée Blanche, a 14-mile-long glacier run. The swimming pool, gym, tennis court, saunas, and ice skating rinks in the sports center round out the offerings. Information: *Office du Tourisme,* Pl. du Triangle de l'Amitié, Chamonix 74400 (phone: 50-53-00-24; fax: 50-53-58-90). Hotels: *Aiglons* (E), *Richemond* (M), *Roma* (I). See also *The Alps* tour route, DIRECTIONS.

COURCHEVEL, Savoie: With 92 trails and some 380 miles of skiing, this resort, which actually is a collection of skiing centers named according to their altitude in meters (1850, 1650, 1550, and 1300), offers some of the finest and certainly the most extensive skiing in France — lending credence to its sobriquet, "The Star." It is part of Europe's largest ski area — "Les Trois Vallées." A network of 200 lifts and 311 miles of marked trails links Courchevel with the resorts of Méribel, Les Menuires, and Val Thorens, making it possible to ski to all of them in 1 day. And there's a huge assortment of other activities to fill the time spent off the slopes: skating, swimming, hang gliding, concerts, language courses, and more, some of which can be found at the resort's sports complex, the *Forum.* Courchevel was the host to the jumping and nordic combined ski events at last year's *Winter Olympics;* Méribel was the site of the women's Alpine ski races and skating events; and Les Menuires played host to the men's slalom. Courchevel is very popular with celebrities and skiers with money and its prices are a reflection of its clientele; it is more expensive than other Alps resorts. See also *The Alps,* DIRECTIONS. Information: *Office du Tourisme,* La Croisette, Courchevel 73120 (phone: 79-08-00-29; fax: 79-08-20-02). Hotels: *Byblos des Neiges* (E), *La Sivolière* (M), *Tournier* (I).

FLAINE, Haute-Savoie: With an altitude of 5,250 feet at the base and 8,860 at the summit, this small but appealingly modern ski station is the highest resort in the Grand Massif of the Haute-Savoie, and with more than 150 miles of slopes and trails served by 80 lifts, it offers skiing of a quality that vindicates the vision of its developers. The recently opened *Grandes Platières* cable lift whisks skiers rapidly up to a breathtaking view of Mont-Blanc. Information: *Office du Tourisme,* Flaine 74300 (phone: 50-90-80-01; fax: 50-90-86-26). Hotels: *Totem* (E), *Gradins Gris* (M), *Aujon* (I).

MEGÈVE, Haute-Savoie: Built around a lovely little 13th-century Savoyard village, with Mont-Blanc as its backdrop and a burbling little stream as its backbone, Megève is one of the country's most fashionable ski resorts. And while the magnitude and quality of the slopes and trails do not quite measure up to those at Val-d'Isère or Chamonix, Megève does attract a contingent of *World Cup* ski racers each winter. Recently built chair lifts and a gondola have brought the number of trails to over 120. The sight of movie stars and other international personalities mingling in its expensive boutiques, pretty cafés, casino, and nightspots also makes this resort very special. Cross-country skiing is good, too. Since snow conditions are reliable only from January to March, the vacation season starts late and ends early here. Information: *Office du Tourisme de Megève,* Megève 74120 (phone: 50-21-27-28; fax: 50-93-03-09). See also *The Alps,* DIRECTIONS. Hotels: *Les Loges du Mont-Blanc* (E), *La Prairie* (M), *Sapins* (I).

MORZINE-AVORIAZ, Haute-Savoie: This resort actually is two towns — traditional Morzine, a sunny, spread-out valley village at an altitude of only 3,000 feet, and modern Avoriaz, perched on a high-altitude (5,400 feet) plain. Their ski trails interlock and there's plenty to challenge an adventurous skier. Together they are part of the huge Franco-Swiss ski system called "Les Portes du Soleil," and are only a chair lift away from Switzerland. Off-slope hours can be spent at Morzine's beautiful indoor skating rink and evenings at one of its fine restaurants. Avoriaz is a friendly resort and its ambience attracts many families. It hosts a yearly *Festival du Film Fantastique* in early January. Information: *Office du Tourisme,* Morzine-Avoriaz 74110 (phone: 50-79-03-45). Hotels: *Les Dromonts* (E), *Le Dahu* (M), *La Musardière* (I).

LA PLAGNE, Savoie: In describing this large and bustling ski destination in the heart of the vast Tarentaise region, the numbers speak for themselves: 27,400 beds, mainly in chalets and private residences since there are only 12 hotels; close to a half-dozen independent ski villages, each with its own eating and drinking spots; and 100 lifts serving 100 trails that take in wide valleys, massive glaciers (skiable even in summer), exceptional powder snow, and picturesque forests alike. Because of the variety of activities, this is an ideal ski station for the skier who wants to mix some serious instruction — in English — with some relaxed enjoyment off the slopes. La Plagne was the host of the bobsled and luge events of the 1992 *Winter Olympics.* Information: *Office du Tourisme,* Le Chalet, 73210 (phone: 79-09-79-79; fax: 79-09-70-10). Hotels: *Christina* (M), *France* (M), *Graciosa* (M).

TIGNES, Savoie: One of the largest French ski resorts, this town — largely built during the 1960s after a new hydroelectric dam and its resultant lake forced the removal of the old village to a site 1,000 feet up the mountain — takes the spillover from neighboring Val d'Isère during busy seasons. And since it is so easy to travel from one to the other on skis, there is even more skiing than suggested by the number of slopes and trails, 61, with 90 miles of runs in all and 2,100 acres of skiing off the main trails. This huge ski area is called "L'Espace Killy," after the *1968 Olympics* star Jean-Claude Killy. It boasts 100 ski lifts, with the capacity to carry 110,000 skiers an hour, and nearly 200 miles of slopes. Tignes offers skiing 365 days a year at the Grande Motte glacier; a new funicular can carry people to the top in just 6 minutes. The possibility of traveling between Tignes and La Plagne with a mountain guide or ski instructor increases the downhill possibilities still further. Tignes is actually three towns — full of boutiques, apartment blocks, and restaurants verging on the futuristic — is intimidatingly modern. Yet oddly enough, it all works with the setting, a treeless and almost lunar sort of landscape. Tignes was the site for the ballet and aerial events for the *1992 Winter Olympics,* as well as moguls and free-style skiing which became *Olympic* events for the first time. Information: *Office du Tourisme,* BP 51, Tignes 73320 (phone: 79-06-15-55; fax: 79-06-45-54). See also *The Alps,* DIRECTIONS. Hotels: *Ski d'Or* (E), *Curling* (M), *Gentiana* (I).

VAL-D'ISÈRE, Savoie: One of the highest resorts in the Savoie, Val-d'Isère is neither as impressive as Chamonix nor as attractive as Megève, but it has been attracting serious Alpine enthusiasts since the turn of the century. It has produced no less an international champion than Jean-Claude Killy, and its world-famous downhill course traditionally is a regular stop on the *World Cup* ski racing tour. As a result, Val-d'Isère draws big spenders who ensure an atmosphere of high fashion. From morning, when the streets are clogged with skiers clumping to the lift base and village buses shuttling less energetic souls to the same destination, until late at night, when the little avenue rings with the cries of merrymakers making their way from one bar or disco to the next, Val-d'Isère is a glamorous, busy place. Summer skiing is available on the 10,000-foot Grand Pissaillas glacier. Val-d'Isère was the site for the men's downhill, giant slalom, and Super G events for last year's *Winter Olympics.* Information: *Office du Tourisme,* Val-d'Isère 73150 (phone: 79-06-10-83; fax: 79-06-26-11). See also *The Alps,* DIRECTIONS. Hotels: *Christiania* (E), *Altitude* (M), *Kern* (I).

VAL-THORENS, Savoie: High and barren, this Alpine resort is a place for the true sports enthusiast. From Val-Thorens, it's possible to ski virtually without interruption for half a day before arriving at Mottaret. Val-Thorens is one of the resorts of Les Trois Vallées, making it possible for an "average" skier to go from Val-Thorens to Les Menuires to Méribel to Courchevel and back (or vice versa) in the same day, using only

12 lifts. For those interested in exploring Les Trois Vallées by ski, as well as the resorts of La Plagne, Les Arcs, Tignes, and Val-d'Isère, *Skiez 12 Vallées* (phone: 79-00-00-95) offers week-long excursions through the Tarentaise Valley on both marked and unmarked trails. Val-Thorens is very popular for *off-piste* skiing, and summer skiing on the glacier (it is the highest resort in Western Europe). The resort has expanded recently with the construction of several new runs and a cable car that can transport up to 3,000 skiers an hour. The altitude — 7,545 feet at the base and 11,155 feet at its highest point — assures good conditions throughout the season. Although most people go to Val-Thorens in winter for the skiing, for those interested in other athletic activities — either at night or on "bad weather" days — Val-Thorens has a huge sports center (phone: 79-00-00-76). Open daily from 9 AM to 10 PM, it offers tennis, squash, golf simulators, badminton, Ping-Pong, volleyball, pool, sauna, whirlpool, weight training, gym, and aerobics and dance classes. Information: *Office du Tourisme,* Maison de Val-Thorens 73440 (phone: 79-00-08-08; fax: 79-00-00-04). Hotels: *Fitz Roy* (E), *Bel Horizon* (M), *La Marmotte* (I).

ALPE D'HUEZ, Isère: Built after World War II, this is one of France's most up-to-date and well-cared-for ski resorts. With a dozen trails for experts (including the 10-mile Sarenne run, ranking as the longest in Europe), it has particular appeal for accomplished skiers. But among its 100 trails there is plenty for everyone, and the network of lifts connecting the three main sections of the skiing terrain is effective enough to keep waiting time down. Tennis, swimming, horseback riding, skating, and glacier skiing allow the resort to remain open year-round. Information: *Office du Tourisme,* L'Alpe d'Huez 38750 (phone: 76-80-35-41; fax: 76-80-69-54). Hotels: *Royal Ours Blanc* (E), *Les Bruyères* (M), *L'Eclose* (I).

LES DEUX-ALPES, Isère: This resort, incongruously modern in a mountain-crowded valley that cries out for quaint chalets, offers an abundance of slopes and trails and vast mountainsides that are spectacular for skiers of all abilities. The *Dôme Express,* France's highest funicular, takes skiers 11,707 feet up to one of Europe's best summer skiing areas. Information: *Office du Tourisme,* Maison des Deux Alpes, Les Deux-Alpes 38860 (phone: 76-79-22-00; fax: 76-79-01-38). Hotels: *Farandole* (E), *Edelweiss* (M), *Brunerie* (I).

Great French Golf

Food, wine, castles, and cathedrals are what first come to mind when thinking about France — not golf. But golf has been a tradition in Gaul since 1856, when the first course was laid out in Pau (in the Pyrénées). Since that time, it has grown enormously in popularity. By the end of 1991 there were 430 courses around the country, and 40 more are expected to be completed by the end of this year. In fact, except for England and Scotland, France has more courses than any other country in Europe (and by 1995, there will be *more* here than in Scotland!).

Until recently, Gallic golf was considered a sport for the rich and the old. But with the construction of 90 municipal courses since 1980, golf has become accessible to a far broader group of people — including foreign visitors. The *Fédération Française de Golf* and the French Ministry of Tourism set up a system whereby travelers and others who are not members of a local golf club can play. Greens fees vary greatly according to the day and season, but average about $45, except during weekends, when prices rise. Call ahead to reserve. Information: *France Golf International,* c/o Maison de la France, 8 Av. de l'Opéra, 75001 Paris (phone: 42-96-10-23) or *Fédération Française de Golf,* 69 Av. Victor-Hugo, 75783 Paris (phone: 45-02-13-55).

France is filled with spots where you can tee off while taking in some of the country's most beautiful sights — layouts by the sea, in valleys, and near cities. Below is a list of courses that are among the best in the country. But be forewarned: golf is considered more sport than leisure in France. Carts are forbidden on most courses, and generally only the courses designed specifically for tourists allow them.

BIARRITZ: Wonderful weather year-round (similar to Monterey, California) makes this region perfect for tee-time anytime. The oldest golf area in the country is the site of Europe's most extensive golf training center, *Centre International d'Entrainement au Golf,* located in a valley right outside Biarritz. Information: *Centre d'Entrainement au Golf,* 10 Rte. National, Biarritz 64200 (phone: 59-23-74-65).

Chiberta – Built in 1927, it is one of the most famous layouts in France. The course (18 holes, 6,400 yards, par 72) varies widely, from 7 holes in a pine forest to wonderful holes at water's edge. Greens fees range from $40 to $50. Information: *Golf de Chiberta,* 104 Bl. des Plages, Anglet 64000 (phone: 59-63-83-20).

Golf Club d'Hossegor – Fifteen miles (24 km) north of Biarritz, this course (18 holes, 6,400 yards, par 72) is set in a pine forest typical of the Basque region. It is challenging, and high scores are solved somewhat by the excellent lunch at the clubhouse. Greens fees range from $40 to $50. Information: *Golf Club d'Hossegor,* Av. du Golf, Hossegor 40150 (phone: 58-43-56-99).

Golf Municipal de Biarritz-Le Phare – In its 100-year history, this lovely, short (5,900 yards) course has attracted some of the world's best players. It is a short walk from the *Hôtel du Palais* (see "Checking In" in *Biarritz,* THE CITIES). Greens fees range from $40 to $50, depending on the season and day of the week. Information: *Golf de Biarritz,* Le Phare, Av. Edith-Cavell, Biarritz 64200 (phone: 59-03-71-80).

Golf de Seignosse – Completed in 1989 by designer Robert Von Hagge, this 18-hole track (6,800 yards, par 72) is considered one of the most spectacular courses in France. Beautifully set in the midst of the Landes pine forest, it is demanding and hilly (luckily carts are available here). Greens fees range from $40 to $50. Information: *Golf de Seignosse,* Seignosse 40510 (phone: 58-43-17-32).

Barbaroux – The first Pete Dye layout to be built in France, its best features include long tees and a splendid setting against a backdrop of pine forests. A private course (18 holes, 7,000 yards, par 72) which has been open since 1987 (its original ownership was somewhat shady), it is cleverly designed to provide many challenges, and at times is quite difficult to read. Carts available. Green fees range between $55 and $70. Information: *Barbaroux,* Domaine de Barbaroux 83170 Brignoles (phone: 94-59-07-63).

CÔTE D'AZUR: Famous for its beaches and casinos, the French Riviera is tops with tourists. Until recently, however, it was lacking in very many good golf courses. In addition to those listed, several more have just been completed.

Cannes Mandelieu – One of France's oldest clubs, it is run by Lucien Barrière Hotels and Casinos (golf packages are available through the *Majestic* hotel in Cannes). This 6,300-yard course, set among beautiful pine trees, hosts 60,000 players each year. Electric carts available. Closed on Tuesdays, the greens fees range between $45 and $55. Information: *Golf Club de Cannes,* Mandelieu 06120 (phone: 93-49-55-39).

Cannes Mougins – Home to 500 members from 28 countries, every year this club hosts the *Cannes Mougins Open* tournament (a stop on the PGA European Tour). The 18-hole course is 6,700 yards, par 72; the clubhouse is in a restored old olive mill. It is closed on Mondays; greens fees range from $50 to $60. Information: *Golf de Cannes Mougins,* 175 Rte. d'Antibes, Mougins 06250 (phone: 93-75-79-13).

Golf de l'Estérel – This very pleasant course (18 holes, 6,500 yards, par 72), designed by Robert Trent Jones, Sr., is set in the middle of the *Latitudes* hotel and resort. Its spectacular 15th hole (par 3) is set in water. There also is a 9-hole course. Greens fees range from $40 to $50; free for hotel guests. Information: *Golf de l'Estérel,* Av. du Golf, St-Raphaël 83700 (phone: 94-82-47-88).

Monte-Carlo – On a clear day, this hilly 6,200-yard course has splendid views of Monaco and the coast from St-Tropez to Italy. It hosts the annual *Monte-Carlo Open* (on the PGA European Tour) in June. A private club, visitors should call in advance to make arrangements. Greens fees range from $55 to $70. Information: *Monte-Carlo Golf Club*, La Turbie 06320 (phone: 93-41-09-11).

LANGUEDOC-ROUSSILON: Running along the Mediterranean Sea to the Spanish border, this part of southern France is one of the fastest growing golf areas in the country. The weather here is ideal almost year-round. Most of the courses here are new and in excellent condition.

Golf du Cap d'Agde – Built in 1989, and already something of a French hot spot, this course is a full 7,000 yards long, and very difficult. Better to play off-season than in the summer when it is jammed toe to tee. Greens fees range from $40 to $50. Information: *Golf du Cap d'Agde*, Cap D'Agde 34300 (phone: 67-26-54-40).

Golf de Nîmes Campagne – Built in 1968, these 6,800 yards are particularly challenging when the wind is blowing (which is quite often). In fact, the club suggests that only those with handicaps under 30 play at all. The 18th hole is next to a beautiful pond surrounded by weeping willows. The clubhouse is called the "White House," and is lined by a splendid alley of sycamore trees. Greens fees range from $40 to $65, depending on the time of year. Information: *Golf de Nîmes Campagne*, Rte. de St-Gilles, Nîmes 30000 (phone: 66-70-17-37).

La Grande Motte – Designed by Robert Trent Jones, Sr. and built in 1987, this resort has both a 9-hole and an 18-hole course. The warm climate, flat land, ponds, flamingos, and the US southern-style architecture of the club will make folks from Florida feel right at home. As with the *Nîmes* course (above), the wind can be a real challenge. Greens fees range from $35 to $50. It is the qualifying site of the PGA European tour. Information: *Golf Club de la Grande-Motte*, La Grande Motte 34280 (phone: 67-56-05-00).

NORMANDY: Because of its relative proximity to the capital, Normandy has become a popular weekend haven for Parisians. Not only are its beaches steeped in history, they are gorgeous as well. That also goes for its golf clubs.

New Golf de Deauville – Designed in 1920, it is one of the oldest golf clubs in France. Its 6,600 yard, 18-hole course, plus another 9-hole layout, make this a golfer's "don't miss." The views of the Norman houses and the surrounding coast are spectacular from the back 9 of the championship course. Greens fees range from $50 to $60. Information: *New Golf de Deauville*, St. Arnoult 14800 (phone: 31-88-20-53).

Omaha Beach – There are three 9-hole courses near the historic *D-Day* beaches, ranging from 3,200 to 3,460 yards. Each has an entirely different design — the *Hedges*, quite flat and running along the Norman countryside; the *Pond*, which offers water hazards on three of its holes; and the *Sea*, with a superb view of the cliffs nearby. Greens fees run from $35 to $45. Information: *Omaha Beach Golf Club*, Port en Bessin 14520 (phone: 31-21-72-94).

BRITTANY: This region, similar to parts of Ireland and northern California and home to small fishing villages and wild moors, is becoming a growing golf center as well. Among some of the more interesting courses are the following three.

Golf de Dinard – Another of the country's old courses, and one of the shortest. But be forewarned: If the wind is blowing, the 5,700 yards will seem far longer very quickly. Greens fees range from $45 to $50. Information: *Golf de Dinard*, St. Briac sur Mer 35800 (phone: 99-88-32-07).

Golf des Ormes – This inland course (18 holes, 6,750 yards, par 72) is part of the estate of the La Chesnais family. A few guestrooms are available in the 18th-century manor house set in the middle of the course. Electric carts are available. Greens fees range from $35 to $45. Information: *Golf des Ormes*, Dol-de-Bretagne 35120 (phone: 99-48-10-19).

Golf Public de Baden – This public 18-hole, 6,700-yard forest layout was completed in 1989. A stone's throw from St-Laurent, it could make a great golf weekend in Brittany. Greens fees range from $30 to $45. Information: *Golf Public de Baden,* Kernic, Baden 56870 (phone: 97-57-18-96).

Golf de St-Laurent Ploermel – Another 18 holes set in a forest, this 6,800-yarder has been the site of the *French PGA Championship* for the past 2 years, and is very popular during the summer. It is located near Carnac, known for its 500 giant prehistoric stone formations. Greens fees range from $30 to $40. Information: *Golf de St-Laurent Ploermel,* Auray 56400 (phone: 97-56-85-18).

LOIRE VALLEY: Set among the famous châteaux of this region (many of which have been converted into luxury hotels) are many golf courses, with several more under construction. The mildness of the area's climate (except in winter) makes it ideal to play a few rounds after visiting the castles.

Golf d'Ardrée – Opened in 1988, this is the first of several courses scheduled to be built over the next few years by a group of French businesses. Located 8 miles (13 km) north of Tours, it is laid out on land that once was a private hunting preserve. The club still has a small château on the property and a modern clubhouse. Electric carts are available to get around the 6,500-yard course. Greens fees are $40 to $50. Information: *Golf d'Ardrée,* St-Antoine du Rocher 37360 (phone: 47-56-77-38).

Golf des Bordes – Texas architect Robert Von Hagge was asked to design a championship course that would respect the landscape. The result is this beautiful 7,100-yard layout, set 10 miles (16 km) southwest of Orléans. There is water on 12 of its 18 holes; perhaps that's why so few come here to tee off. Greens fees range from $70 to $130; electric cars are available. Information: *Golf des Bordes,* St-Laurent Nouan 41220 (phone: 54-87-72-13).

Golf de Cély – This perfectly manicured and landscaped course (18 holes, 6,500 yards, par 72) has a beautiful clubhouse which resembles a medieval castle. Very close to Fontainebleau, Barbizon, and Milly-la-Forêt. Electric carts are available. Greens fees range from $80 to $130. Information: *Golf de Cély,* Le Château, Rte. de St-Germain, Cély-en-Bière 77930 (phone: 64-38-03-07).

NEAR PARIS: Not only is the countryside around Paris enticing for an afternoon excursion (see *The Ile-de-France,* DIRECTIONS), but also for a round of golf. The two courses listed below are open to visitors.

Golf Club de Chantilly – Known for food and lace, Chantilly is also famous for the Château de Chantilly, the home of French kings, and this elegant club, only 5 minutes from the historic castle. With its Old World charm and aristocratic ambience, this British-designed course winds through an impressive forest just 25 miles (40 km) north of Paris. Non-members may play for a fee on weekends. Closed Thursdays. Information: *Golf Club de Chantilly,* 60500 Vineuil-Saint Firmin, Chantilly, France (phone: 44-57-04-43).

Golf National – Owned and operated by the *Fédération Française de Golf,* this huge public golf complex is in St-Quentin-en-Yvelines. The first of its three courses, the 18-hole, 7,400-yard *Albatros* (designed by Hubert Chesneau and Bob Von Hagge), opened in October 1990. This stadium course is host to the *French Open.* Water hazards abound. Greens fees range from $40 to $50. Information: *Golf National,* 2 Av. du Golf, Guyancourt 78280 (phone: 30-43-36-00).

Golf des Yvelines – Set in a protected park, this 18-holer is a par 72 forest course 28 miles (45 km) from Paris. Its clubhouse is in a château. Greens fees are $40 during the week, $60 on weekends. Information: *Golf des Yvelines,* La Queue les Yvelines 78940 (phone: 34-86-48-89).

GOLF AND GOBLETS

Though great golf can be found through much of Europe, leave it to the French to make it even more attractive. With beautiful courses found in Bordeaux, Burgundy, and the

Loire Valley, now it is possible to spend the mornings on the fairway and the afternoons at some of the world's finest vineyards. *Travelinks* (1015 18th St. NW, Suite 805, Washington DC 20036; phone: 202-659-5657) and *Golf International Inc.* (275 Madison Ave., NY, NY 10016; phone: 212-986-9176 or 800-833-1389; fax: 212-986-3720) are a couple of the US tour operators that offer wine and golf packages. Accommodations (often in châteaux), greens fees, tours of the area, and wine tastings at one of the local vineyards are included in the cost. The following two courses, though included in the packages, also are open to non-teetotalers on their own.

Golf du Cognac – The Martell cognac vineyards are the setting for this 6,950-yard, par 72 course. During harvest time, players are treated to the aroma of fermenting grapes. It is an easy 18-holer, but well worth playing for the ambience. Information: *Golf Club du Cognac,* Rue St-Brice, Cognac 16100 (phone: 45-32-18-17).

Le Golf du Médoc – Just 20 minutes from Bordeaux, each of the 18 holes here is named for one of the area's vineyards — the 18th, for example, is Mouton Rothschild. If you make a hole-in-one at the par 3, 155-yard Pontet Canet (the 5th), you get a magnum of the wine. Regional wines also are served at the clubhouse's restaurant with a minimal markup. Information: *Le Golf du Médoc,* Chemin de Courmateau, Louens, Blanquefort 33290 (phone: 56-72-01-10).

Game, Set, and Match: Tennis in France

 Like the United States, France has seen an enormous increase in the interest in tennis over the past 20 years — as a sport for spectators and participants alike. The number of tennis courts and camps in France continues to increase, and there are hundreds of tennis clubs — both private and public. The prime surface of choice is red clay, although there are a fair number of all-weather and hard courts scattered around the countryside. Though it can be hard to get court time in Paris, conditions are far less crowded outside the capital. Attendance at the country's leading international tournament, the *French Open,* has soared to the point where a major expansion of *Roland Garros Stadium* (in Paris) was necessary.

TENNIS CLUBS: The many tennis clubs in France — of which by far the most famous is Paris's *Racing Club,* unquestionably one of the greats among the world's athletic clubs — are organized by *département* or league. Most require annual membership, and virtually all are closed to outsiders who aren't personally acquainted with a member. However, some are less exclusive than others, and occasionally it's possible for business associates to provide an entrée. Also, in resort areas, the best clubs are open to any player willing to pay the sometimes substantial, but by no means prohibitive, admission fee. And many offer *stages,* or instruction sessions, to the general public on a weekend or weekly basis. Instruction usually is in French.

Aix-en-Provence, Bouches-du-Rhône – In this leafy southern town, the *Aixois Country Club* offers 5-day *stages* during school holidays and summer, with instruction from 2½ to 5 hours a day. Information: *Country Club Aixois,* Bastide des Solliers, Puyricard 13540 (phone: 42-92-10-41).

Arcachon, Gironde – This breezy beach town has just the right climate for summer tennis. There are 22 courts at the *Tennis-Club* (*Stade André Dupin*) and 5 more at the *Abatilles Tennis Courts* (165 Bd. de la Côte-d'Argent). Information: *Office du Tourisme,* BP 42, Pl. Roosevelt, Arcachon 33311 (phone: 56-83-01-69).

La Baule, Loire-Atlantique – The *Tennis Country Club* has decidedly the best tennis opportunities in a town that is full of them — 83 courts in all. An establishment worth crossing the Atlantic to experience, it boasts a half-timbered clubhouse with martially squared hedges, an active tournament schedule, 4 all-weather courts, and 25 superbly tended red clay courts. Suzanne Lenglen reigned here for many years, and Ellsworth Vines bowed to Bill Tilden in the men's final in 1933. Now owned by a hotel chain, it offers a wide variety of tennis packages that include lodgings. Information: *Tennis Country Club,* 113 Av. du Maréchal-de-Lattre-de-Tassigny, La Baule 44500 (phone: 40-60-23-44).

Biarritz, Pyrénées-Atlantiques – The tennis club at *Biarritz Olympique Tennis* in this prosperous resort on the southern Atlantic coast is open year-round, and lessons are available by the day or by the week. Of the 14 courts, 11 are clay, and 3 are lighted. Information: *Office du Tourisme,* Square d'Ixelles, Biarritz 64200 (phone: 59-24-20-24).

Deauville, Calvados – The town itself owns 23 courts by the sea and sponsors numerous tennis tournaments, but should you strike it rich at the casino, consider one of the two classic Deauville hotels — the *Normandy* and the *Royal.* The *Normandy,* an oversize Norman cottage in the heart of town, faces its own 21 tennis courts, as well as the Atlantic Ocean. Should the weather disappoint you, jog the underground passage to the casino or swim in the covered heated Olympic-size saltwater pool. Down the street is the *Royal,* with 23 courts. Information: *Hôtel Normandy,* 38 Rue Jean-Mermoz, Deauville 14800 (phone: 31-98-66-22). *Hôtel Royal,* Bd. Cornuché, Deauville 14800 (phone: 31-98-66-33).

Evian-les-Bains, Haute-Savoie – World famous for its casino (see "Casinos Royal" in *For the Experience*), Evian first developed as a spa. Today its water is a household word. A tennis club with 13 courts is another one of its many charms. If money is no object, the *Royal Club* hotel (phone: 50-26-85-00) — see "Romantic French Hostelries" in *For the Experience* — offers an intensive 6-day tennis program combining exercise and 2 hours of daily court play on its own 6 courts. Information: *Office du Tourisme,* BP 988, Evian 74502 (phone: 50-75-04-26).

Hendaye, Pyrénées-Atlantiques – The club in this beach town on the Spanish border has 11 clay courts, 2 of them outdoors. It is most active in July and August but is open year-round. Information: *Tennis Club Parc des Sports,* Rue Elissacilio, Hendaye 64700 (phone: 59-20-02-73).

Nice, Alpes-Maritimes – The *Nice Lawn Tennis Club,* delightfully away from the noisy beach and business districts in a residential section of the city, seems to attract a substantial number of better than average players. Suzanne Lenglen, who grew up just across the street (now renamed to honor her), developed her distinctive balletic playing style on its courts. There now are 19 in all, 13 of them clay. Information: *Nice Lawn Tennis Club,* Parc Impérial, Nice 06000 (phone: 93-96-17-70).

La Plagne, Savoie – The *stages* on the 16 hard courts at this popular ski and summer resort, which include full room and board, are available in July and August. Information: *Eric Loliée Résidence de Plagne Belle-Côte,* Aime 73210 (phone: 79-09-29-00) or *Office du Tourisme,* BP 36, Plagne-Centre, 73210 Aime (phone: 79-09-02-01).

Roquebrune-Cap-Martin, Alpes-Maritime – The *Monte Carlo Country Club* (see *Monaco,* THE CITIES) actually is across the border (in France) from Monaco proper, but don't let that stop you from experiencing one of the most sublime tennis layouts in the country — 23 courts arranged on terraces on a hillside with spectacular Mediterranean views framed by cypress trees, like columns. The clubhouse, with its sunny restaurant embellished with murals and its well-kept, old-fashioned locker rooms (complete with their original wooden lockers), is simply an extra delight. The fact that no less than Prince Rainier III and his son, Crown Prince Albert, still play doubles here is some indication of the quality of the crowd. The best times for playing, as on the rest of the Riviera, are fall and spring. Information: *Monte Carlo Country Club,* Av.

de Monte-Carlo, Quartier St-Roman, Roquebrune-Cap-Martin 06190 (phone: 93-78-20-45).

Tignes, Savoie – The instruction program at this ski and summer resort is rather intensive, with more than 4 hours of instruction a day for 6 days. But after a day of tennis on the 15 hard courts, it's possible to go sailing in the mountain lake, golf, or even ski. Hotels, apartments, and studio lodgings are abundant. Information: *Stage Caujolle, Club Omni-Sports,* Tignes-le-Lac 73320 (phone: 79-06-53-87) or *Club des Sports,* Tignes-le-Lac 73320 (phone: 79-06-53-87; fax: 79-06-46-56).

Trouville-sur-Mer, Calvados – Besides the 7 clay courts, the 2 hard courts, and the single indoor court, the tennis club in this Atlantic-pounded Normandy resort town offers golf, horseback riding, swimming, and windsurfing. Tennis instruction is offered on a weekly basis. Open from April to October. Information: *Trouville Tennis Club,* Trouville-sur-Mer 14360 (phone: 31-88-91-62).

TENNIS CLUBS NEAR PARIS: The following clubs are located close to the capital:

Aubervilliers, Seine-St-Denis – Open year-round (except August), the *Tennis Forest Hill* offers lessons for an hour and a half each day in blocks of 4 days on 18 indoor courts. Information: *Tennis Forest Hill,* 111 Av. Victor-Hugo, Aubervilliers 93300 (phone: 48-34-75-10).

Bois-le-Roi, Seine-et-Marne – With 9 hard courts outdoors and 2 indoors, the *UCPA* offers a 7-hour weekend instruction program year-round. Information: *UCPA,* Rue de Tournezy, Bois-le-Roi 77590 (phone: 64-87-83-00).

Boulogne, Hauts-de-Seine – At the *Tennis Club de Longchamp,* just down the road from *Roland Garros Stadium* in the Bois de Boulogne on the outskirts of Paris, it is possible to enroll for weekly instruction sessions on the 3 hard courts. There is a golf course nearby. Information: *Tennis Club de Longchamp,* 19 Bd. Anatole-France, Boulogne 92100 (phone: 46-03-84-49).

Nanterre, Hauts-de-Seine – Weekend lessons are possible here year-round at the *Tennis Club Défense.* Various periods of instruction and weekend lessons are available on the 8 hard courts. Information: *Tennis Club Défense,* 45 Bd. des Bouvets, Nanterre 92000 (phone: 47-73-04-40).

Villepinte, Seine St. Denis – The *Villepinte Tennis Club* has 7 clay and 6 hard courts, with possibilities for indoor and outdoor play year-round. Weekend and extended courses are offered. Information: *Tennis de Villepinte,* Rue du Manège, Villepinte 93420 (phone: 43-83-23-31).

TENNIS CAMPS: French tennis camps, with highly qualified instructors, offer more intense tutoring than the clubs, usually by the week rather than for a shorter period of time.

Alpe d'Huez, Isère – A popular skiing center in the winter, this most up-to-date and well-cared-for of French resorts offers organized tennis instruction from mid-July to mid-August. Lessons are given on a weekly basis, with lodging in local hotels. Information: *Office du Tourisme,* Alpe d'Huez 38750 (phone: 76-80-35-41) or *Palais des Sports et de Congrès,* Alpe d'Huez (phone: 76-80-30-12; fax: 76-80-69-54).

Les Arcs, Savoie – *Arc 1600* and *Arc 1800,* a pair of ski resorts whose numbers refer to their altitude in meters, offer 6-day tennis camps in July and August at both locations with 3 to 4 hours of instruction per day. There are a total of 40 hard courts and, at *Arc 1800,* a swimming pool and a golf course as well. Lodging is abundant. Information: *Maison des Arcs,* 94 Bd. du Montparnasse, Paris 75014 (phone: 43-22-22-22).

Arles, Bouches-du-Rhône – The camp at *Les Villages du Soleil* offers 4½-hour sessions for 5 days on either the 7 indoor courts or the 23 outdoor hard courts, depending on the season. Lodging with half board is available at the camp, which also has a swimming pool, a sauna, and a squash and volleyball facilities. Information: *Les Villages du Soleil,* Mas de Véran, Arles 13200 (phone: 90-96-50-68 or 90-49-66-27).

Bandol, Var – Open year-round, the relatively inexpensive *Tennis Club Buding* offers 6-day sessions with 2-hour lessons daily on the 30 hard courts. The club is about a mile (1.6 km) from the Mediterranean coast. Accommodations are available on the premises. Information: *Tennis Club Buding,* Quartier du Pont-d'Aran, Bandol 83150 (phone: 94-29-43-36).

Cap d'Agde, Hérault – This famous camp in the Languedoc consumes the life of the village where the former tennis star Pierre Barthès founded it in 1973. From training films to specialty boutiques, tennis rules the day. The instruction programs last for 6 days, 4 hours a day; most of the instructors speak English. There are 64 courts with about as many surfaces as a tennis player can name. Students can lodge at the camp hotel or at any of numerous hotels and bungalows in the area. Information: *Club Pierre Barthès,* Cap d'Agde 34305 (phone: 67-26-00-06).

Flaine, Haute-Savoie – The tennis camp in this modern mountain ski and summer resort may have as many as 10 students per instructor, but there is ample room for practice on the 26 hard courts. *Stages* are offered in July and August. Students lodge in ski chalets or hotels in the area. Information: *Stages Georges-Deniau,* Sepad Loisirs, 23 Rue Cambon, Paris 75001 (phone: 42-61-55-17).

Les Hauts-de-Nîmes, Gard – Run by the same people who stage the camp at Flaine, the one here in the south of France offers sessions of either 2 or 4 hours for each of 6 days on 33 courts (4 indoors). Some instructors speak English. Lodging is available at the camp or in town. Information: *Stages Georges-Deniau,* Sepad Loisirs, Les Hauts-de-Nîmes, Rte. d'Anduze, Nîmes 30900 (phone: 66-23-14-67).

Opio, Alpes-Maritimes – Some of the very best spots for playing tennis in Europe are at the "vacation villages" of *Club Méditerranée,* which consistently offer extensive facilities, first-rate instruction, and settings maintained with ecological fervor. The *Club Med* not far from the Côte d'Azur at Opio spreads out over 125 acres and has 15 tennis courts, 7 of which are lighted. Other *Club Med* sites that are tops for tennis include Cargèse, Pompadour, and Vittel. All offer a variety of other sports as well and are fine for family holidays. Information: *Club Med,* 40 W. 57th St., New York, NY 10019 (phone: 212-750-1670; 800-CLUB MED).

TOURNAMENT TENNIS

There are two major international tournaments in France each year. The *French Open,* which takes place during the last week in May and the first week in June in Paris, is the world's premier red clay court tournament and one of the four *Grand Slam* events (the other three being *Wimbledon,* the *US Open,* and the *Australian Open*), and most of the top international men and women players participate. Tickets for matches early in the tournament generally are easy to obtain at the box office in early May or by mail through the *Fédération Française de Tennis (FFT;* address below). However, seats for the semifinal and final matches go fast and must be requested well in advance.

The *Monte Carlo Open,* France's other big clay court event, also draws most of the world's best. The men's tournament takes place in early April. Information: *Monte Carlo Country Club,* Quartier St-Roman, Roquebrune-Cap-Martin 06190 (phone: 93-78-20-45).

In addition, there are the handful of other French tournaments on the intermediate circuit of the *Grand Prix* professional schedule — that is, the *Challenge Series* tournaments — which, despite the absence of the most famous players, always attract competitors recognizable to anyone who follows tennis regularly. The event that takes place annually in Nice is one of the most popular; there are others in Nancy (March), Aix-en-Provence (April), Bordeaux (September), Toulouse (October), and Paris (November). The *FFT* can supply specifics.

FOR MORE INFORMATION: A complete list of addresses for tennis clubs in France, as well as a roster of club tournaments open to visiting players and competitive events of interest to spectators, may be obtained from the *Fédération Française de Tennis* (*FFT; Roland Garros Stadium,* 2 Av. Gordon-Bennett, Paris 75016; phone: 47-43-48-00).

Sun, Sea, and Sand: France's Best Beaches

 The Riviera is almost everything it is touted to be. The water is clear and tame, the sun reliable, the celebrities abundant. It is a paradise of cool drinks by day and casinos by night; topless tanning very definitely is the rule rather than the exception. And to those who are seeking this kind of getaway, the Riviera will not disappoint.

But most of the beaches are pebbled rather than sandy, and in August, when all of France shuts down so that workers can take the month of vacation that is guaranteed by law, it seldom is possible to find an open patch on which to spread a towel, let alone an empty hotel room.

France does boast some 1,200 miles of beachfront in all, and most of them have a lot more natural scenery to offer than the Côte d'Azur, however glamorous it may be. From the rugged cliffs of Normandy and Brittany down the expansive Atlantic coast to the Mediterranean hideaways of the Languedoc, there are scores of old fishing villages steeped in history, places where a beach vacation can be mixed with the pleasure of exploring a country and its culture.

Note that some beaches are specially designated *naturiste,* connoting nude bathing. However, sunning and swimming in the buff is common enough in other places as well — usually on the fringes of the greatest concentration of swimmers. And topless bathing is the norm for women.

Below is a sampling of the most interesting seaside resorts, following the French coastline counterclockwise from Normandy.

NORMANDY: Best known to the world nowadays as the site of the Allied invasion in 1944, the Normandy coastline is a rugged stretch of sandy beaches and craggy cliffs. Omaha Beach, Utah Beach, and other spots are legend (though they're not swimming beaches); others, among them the western side of the Cotentin Peninsula, are less well known and, therefore, more interesting for the visitor who wants to beat his own pathway. For information about any of these, contact the *Comité Régional du Tourisme de Normandie* (46 Av. Foch, Evreux 27000; phone: 32-33-79-00).

Deauville, Calvados – This town and neighboring Trouville-sur-Mer, both affluent former fishing villages with sandy beaches and seaside restaurants, have drawn the rich and famous over the decades for their casinos, racetracks, chic hotels, and other attractions.

Plages du Débarquement, Calvados – The landing beaches, as this stretch of coastline is known, bore the brunt of the Allied invasion. Luc-sur-Mer, with its museum of seashells, and Bernières-sur-Mer, whose 219-foot belfry is the highest on the Normandy coast, are especially pleasant.

Les Côtes des Grandes Marées, Manche – Before reaching Mont-St-Michel, a motorist arrives at a stretch of magnificent beaches — Carolles, medieval Granville, Jullouville, and St-Pair-sur-Mer. The cliffs just beyond Carolles give a fine view of the northern Brittany coast, while Vauville, farther up the Cotentin Peninsula, is noted for its sand dunes.

BRITTANY: The coastline of this especially scenic province, a picturesque mélange of rocky cliffs, small fishing ports, and sandy coves, has many faces. The northern area offers well-developed beach towns, some as glitteringly sophisticated as the Riviera and some very low-key and family-oriented. The south tends to be a little wilder, particularly around Quiberon.

St-Cast-le-Guildo, Côtes-du-Nord – To avoid the confusion of the Riviera, many families prefer to spend the month of August at this resort known as the pride of the Côte d'Emeraude (Emerald Coast), one of Brittany's largest resorts. There are a dozen public tennis courts and a 9-hole golf course, among other diversions. Information: *Office du Tourisme,* Pl. Général-de-Gaulle, St-Cast-le-Guildo 22380 (phone: 96-41-81-52).

Bénodet, Finistère – It is not always as warm on the pebbled beaches of Bénodet as it is on the sandy beaches farther south, and the water is often chilly. But this district at the mouth of the River Odet in folklore-rich Finistère is renowned for its beautiful camping areas and its fine sailing school. A few miles down the coast is the beautiful, piney Beg Meil. The boat ride along the Odet to Quimper is a popular diversion. Information: *Syndicat d'Initiative,* 51 Av. de la Plage, Bénodet 29118 (phone: 98-57-00-14).

La Baule, Loire-Atlantique – Many believe that the 5 miles of sandy beach at this busy and fashionable resort, farther east along the stretch of Brittany coastline known as the Côte d'Amour, are the loveliest in the country; and the area — so built up as to be almost urban — draws what some French call the "bourgeoisie of the west" to its casino and discotheques, its 70 tennis courts, its pair of equestrian centers (with more than 200 horses), its 18-hole golf course, and its flying club. Information: *Office du Tourisme,* 8 Pl. de la Victoire, La Baule 44500 (phone: 40-24-34-44).

Baie de Quiberon, Morbihan – The most widely heralded beaches in the area around the Morbihan Bay, in the south of Brittany, are at Carnac, which is as famous for its prehistoric megaliths as it is for its resort facilities, at nearby La Trinité, and at Quiberon, which is at the end of a long, rockbound peninsula. While the nights can be cool, the scenery is rugged — just what most visitors travel to Brittany to find. Quiberon is the departure point for trips to Belle-Ile, the largest island in the province and a beach lover's destination in its own right; the terrain rises sharply from the sands that border it and allows for some spectacular coastal views. Information: *Office de Tourisme,* 74 Av. des Druides, Carnac 56340 (phone: 97-52-13-52).

UPPER ATLANTIC COAST: Les Sables-d'Olonne, Vendée – The 7 miles of beach here make these strands of sand among the most popular of all the Atlantic resorts. Many visitors like to go horseback riding through the dunes or visit the aquarium or zoo. La Tranche-sur-Mer, a few miles farther down the coast, is famous for its tulip fields in April and May and popular for its vast sandy beaches all summer long. Information: *Office du Tourisme,* Rue de Maréchal-Leclerc, Les Sables-d'Olonne 85100 (phone: 51-32-03-28).

L'Ile d'Oléron, Charente-Maritime – France's second-largest island, linked to land by a bridge, has lost some of its charm to popularity. But it does have an abundance of marvelous sandy beaches that draw French youth by the thousands. At night, the island bustles; by day, you can visit oyster farms, take sailing lessons, and explore medieval ruins. Information: *Syndicat d'Initiative,* Le Château, L'Ile d'Oléron 17480 (phone: 46-47-60-51).

L'Ile de Ré, Charente-Maritime – Aptly named "the Bright Island" because of the plenitude of sunlight that graces it, this island is a 48-mile-long treasure of tiny villages, whitewashed cottages, and undeveloped land. There's a bird sanctuary, a bicycle livery, a satisfying number of well-marked beaches, and a handful of comfortable hotels. Access is provided by ferry from La Pallice. Information: *Office du Tourisme,* Quai Sénac, La Flotte, Ile de Ré 17630 (phone: 46-09-60-38).

La Rochelle, Charente-Maritime – A thriving port in medieval times, this city boasts the largest pleasure boat basin in all of Europe and a charming fortified old city that was English from the middle of the 12th until the 17th century, when it was besieged by Louis XIII. Now it is closed to traffic on summer weekend evenings. With a population of 85,000, it is no quaint small town; but the city is a dazzler, night or day, and there are bicycles to ride and an antique carousel, and the white sand beaches in its environs — including those at Ile de Ré (above) — are lovely. Information: *Office du Tourisme,* 10 Rue Fleuriau, La Rochelle 17025 (phone: 46-41-14-68).

Royan, Charente-Maritime – Largely rebuilt after World War II, this resort town just north of Bordeaux lacks the charm of many others in a region that has been called the Côte de Beauté (the Beautiful Coast) for its stretch of more than a dozen miles of beaches and rocky coves. The water is relatively chilly, but there are plenty of facilities for golf, tennis, horseback riding, sailing, and water skiing. And near Marennes are huge oyster beds where some of the finest oysters in France are cultivated. Information: *Office Municipal du Tourisme,* Palais des Congrès, Royan 17200 (phone: 46-38-65-11).

L'Ile d'Yeu, Vendée – About 1¼ hours by ferry from Fromentine, this island is so notched by rocky promontories on the south side that the coastline is known as the Côte Sauvage. But elsewhere there are lovely beaches and simple port towns. Marshal Pétain, head of the Vichy government during World War II, was imprisoned here from 1945 to 1951. It is possible to tour the island in a day on foot or by bicycle. Information: *Office du Tourisme,* 1 Pl. du Marché, L'Ile d'Yeu 85350 (phone: 51-58-32-58).

St-Jean-de-Monts, Vendée – The vast beach of St-Jean-de-Monts, back along the coast, has been described as the perfect beach for families because of its exceptionally calm waters. The fact that there are only a handful of hotels suggests just how quiet the place can be. Information: *Office du Tourisme,* Palais des Congrès, St-Jean-de-Monts 85160 (phone: 51-58-00-48).

LOWER ATLANTIC COAST: With almost 150 miles of sand, this stretch of beach backed by the Landes forest and running from the mouth of the Gironde to the Basque country is one of the longest in the world. Environmental regulations have left some sections of the coast delightfully undeveloped; other sections have been allowed to grow so that there are comfortable hotels and restaurants aplenty. Note that the waters often are rough and dangerous, so it is advisable to swim only in designated areas and when there's a green flag flying — meaning that a lifeguard is on duty and swimming is safe.

Arcachon, Gironde – Along the 50-mile perimeter of the Arcachon Basin, where Celts were living around 500 BC, there are about 30 beaches and oyster farms, pine trees by the thousands, and, near Pilat Plage, an immense sand dune (380 feet and still growing) — taller than any other in France. Thousands of sailboats moor here, and in the town of Arcachon proper, the old beachfront hotels, the handsome 19th-century villas, and the promenade edged with feathery tamarisk trees still recall the town's Belle Epoque heyday, when English gentry came here to socialize and French artists like Manet and Toulouse-Lautrec visited to paint. Nearby, at La Hume, the restored medieval village is full of craftspeople costumed as basket makers, bell makers, candle makers, cane makers, clog makers, leaded glass workers, and other artisans of the period. Information: *Office du Tourisme,* BP 42, Pl. Franklin-Roosevelt, Arcachon 33120 (phone: 56-83-01-69).

Lacanau-Océan, Gironde – Visitors to this clean, modern, and quickly developing resort can enjoy not only the sprawling beaches along the coast but also the forest immediately inland and a freshwater lake of almost 5,000 acres. There is an 18-hole golf course, a group of 23 tennis courts, and a sailing school on nearby Lacanau Lake, not to mention excellent cycling and windsurfing. Information: *Office du Tourisme,* Pl. de l'Europe, Lacanau 33680 (phone: 56-03-21-01).

Soulac-sur-Mer, Gironde – A thriving port even before the Middle Ages, Soulac was also one of the stops along the pilgrimage to Santiago de Compostela in Spain. Just south of the Pointe de Grave, this tidy little town full of colorfully trimmed brick houses welcomes about 70,000 holidaymakers each summer. There are tennis courts, a gym, a cinema, a casino, and horses for hire. But most visitors prefer to spend at least some of their time away from the strand to explore the old town with its 12th-century Romanesque church and other relics. Information: *Syndicat d'Initiative,* 95 Rue de la Plage, Soulac-sur-Mer 33780 (phone: 56-09-86-61).

Hossegor and Capbreton, Landes – Hossegor, a modern oyster center, and Capbreton, an ancient fishing village, combine to make one of the loveliest resorts on the south Atlantic coast. The beach is sandy, safe, and vast, and the lake between the two towns tends to be a few degrees warmer than the ocean. A little farther down the coast are other popular beaches as well, most notably Ondres and Labenne-Plage. Information: *Syndicat d'Initiative,* Pl. Louis-Pasteur, Hossegor 40150 (phone: 58-43-72-35) and *Office du Tourisme,* Av. Georges-Pompidou, Capbreton 40130 (phone: 58-72-12-11).

BASQUE COUNTRY: Biarritz, Pyrénées-Atlantiques – Once a favorite residence of Napoleon III, this fashionable resort now is popular with the casino crowd. British sun worshipers congregate here in great numbers. Offshore reefs protect the long sandy beaches under the spectacular rocky cliffs from the force of the surf, so the strands are as fine for bathing as they are for strolls. Information: *Comité du Tourisme et des Fêtes,* Pl. d'Ixelles, Biarritz 64200 (phone: 59-24-20-24).

St-Jean-de-Luz, Pyrénées-Atlantiques – Louis XIV was married to Maria Theresa of Spain in 1660 in the Eglise St-Jean-Baptiste, and the old town has not changed much since. The harbor still bustles with fishermen bringing in their tuna and sardines. The vast and well-patrolled beach has a reputation for being one of the country's safest. Information: *Syndicat d'Initiative,* Pl. du Maréchal-Foch, St-Jean-de-Luz 64500 (phone: 59-26-03-16).

LANGUEDOC-ROUSSILLON: There are more than 100 miles of good sandy beaches backed by the Pyrénées along the Mediterranean coast from the Spanish border — and resorts of all types: ancient fishing villages, modern pleasure grounds, and huge campsites. And in this part of the country, the sunshine is practically guaranteed.

Le Cap d'Agde, Hérault – More than 7 miles of white sand at the foot of an extinct volcano and some 41 tennis courts with various surfaces only begin to suggest why this is one of the Languedoc's most outstanding modern summer resorts. The handful of hotels are expensive; it's better to rent a studio apartment by the week. Information: *Office du Tourisme,* Palais des Congrès, BP 544, Le Cap d'Agde 34300 (phone: 67-26-38-58).

Collioure, Pyrénées-Orientales – This ancient port, a favorite of the 19th-century painters Matisse and Braque, boasts a 15th-century dungeon which Philip II of Spain transformed into a citadel and a medieval château royal with a view of the beaches that constitute one of the area's other charms. Information: *Syndicat d'Initiative,* Pl. 18 Juin, Collioure 66190 (phone: 68-82-15-47).

Argèles-Plage, Pyrénées-Orientales – The population of this massive modern seaside resort swells from its normal level of 5,000 to 300,000 in summer, and together with its neighboring communities, there are literally dozens of places to lodge or camp. A casino is open in Argèles-sur-Mer, a mile or so inland, in the summer. Information: *Office du Tourisme,* Pl. de l'Europe, Argèles-sur-Mer 66700 (phone: 68-81-15-85).

Leucate and Le Barcarès, Pyrénées-Orientales – Between these two ports is a 6-mile stretch of beach that has developed rapidly in the course of the last decade and offers everything from sailing and tennis to water skiing. And the beach is large enough not to seem overcrowded, even when it's teeming with tourists. Information: *Syndicat d'Initiative,* Pl. du Village, BP 16, Port-Barcarès 66420 (phone: 68-86-16-56 or 68-86-18-23).

St-Cyprien Plage, Pyrénées-Orientales – This futuristic resort is one of a handful in France designed to give the impression of paradise. There's a lake inhabited by flamingos and surrounded by sweet-smelling trees, a pair of golf courses, a thousand acres of lovely landscaping, and miles and miles of sandy beach. Information: *Syndicat d'Initiative St-Cyprien,* Quai Rimbaud, St-Cyprien Plage 66750 (phone: 68-21-01-33).

CÔTE D'AZUR: Many of the beaches are more stony than sandy, but the Côte d'Azur has a multitude of them, and they attract thousands of tourists. While hardly the place to get away from it all, the Côte offers spectacular scenery: gracefully curved bays and wildly beautiful coves, often backed by blindingly white cliffs and mountains fuzzed by silvery olive and cypress trees and dark green pines. The water is a dazzling shade of turquoise that almost matches the brilliant, flawless blue of the sky, and the light still possesses the exquisite brightness that lured many of the nation's most distinguished painters to work here at one time or another. There are hotels in all price ranges all along the coast; for people watching, the famous resorts such as Bandol, Cannes, Nice, and St-Tropez hardly can be beat, and for peace and quiet, there are scores of smaller resorts.

Juan-les-Pins, Alpes-Maritimes – About halfway between Cannes and Nice, Juan-les-Pins is as chic and as night-crazed as St-Tropez, with activity focused on the casino, which occupies a cool garden set just away from the sea. During the annual *World Jazz Festival,* things are even more active. The diving and sailing schools have a good reputation, and some 3 dozen hotels rise along the white sandy beach. Information: *Office du Tourisme,* 51 Bd. Charles-Guillaumont, Juan-les-Pins 06160 (phone: 93-61-04-98).

Mandelieu and La Napoule, Alpes-Maritimes – Just west of Cannes, the ancient village of Mandelieu and nearby La Napoule, with its superb sandy beach, make up a spectacular resort with tennis courts, golf courses, and camping facilities. Anyone who scrambles down the stony cliffs from the Corniche de l'Esterel between Cannes and St-Raphaël might claim some picturesque little crescent of sand for the afternoon — to enjoy completely alone. Information: *Syndicat d'Initiative,* Av. de Cannes, Mandelieu-La Napoule 06210 (phone: 93-49-14-39).

Ste-Maxime, Var – While this resort lies just across the bay from St-Tropez, its lifestyle is light-years apart. Some female sunbathers wear tops as well as bottoms, and disco takes second place to quiet dinners and daytime strolls through the many boutiques. Young families are the primary clientele. There also are more than a dozen tennis courts, a 9-hole golf course, a sailing school, a marina full of pleasure craft — and, most delightful of all, a sensational view of mountains and coast just a mile north at the Sémaphore. Information: *Syndicat d'Initiative,* Promenade Simon-Lorière, Ste-Maxime 83120 (phone: 94-96-19-24).

Sanary-sur-Mer, Var – Not far from the famous beaches at Bandol and La Ciotat, Sanary is a quiet place with a beach, an old town, and an open-air theater. And together with the islands of Bendor and Embiez, it is also a fabulous center for water sports. Hotel facilities are limited, so inquire well in advance. Information: *Syndicat d'Initiative,* Jardins de la Ville, Sanary-sur-Mer 83110 (phone: 94-74-01-04).

■**Tide Watching:** The difference between low and high tide in the bay of the Mont-St-Michel is the greatest in Europe — an astonishing 40 feet during the spring and fall equinoxes. At any time of the year, the tide rushes in with the speed of a galloping horse, as the locals will tell you, without exaggeration. Swimming in the bay and hiking across the bed of the bay at low tide to Mont-St-Michel can be very dangerous for the uninformed; high and low tides change fairly drastically from day to day, and there are treacherous currents and a strong undertow in the seemingly placid bay's waters.(If you want to go swimming, try beaches in protected areas with lifeguards, mainly noth of Cancale on the Brittany side and north of Carolles on the Normandy side. Crossing the bay at low tide, a traditional pilgrimage, can be done on foot or horseback, but should *always* be done with a guide. There are several based near the Bed d'Andaine near the Normandy village of Genêts. For a listing of the times and dates of high and low tides, ask for the pamphlet *L'Annuaire des Marées 1993,* available at any Maison de Presse in the area). A perfectly safe and nonetheless dramatic way of experiencing the tides is to watch them from three popular vantage points: Mont-St-Michel itself, Pointe du Grouin north of Cancale (Brittany) and Grouin du Sud, the tip of a small peninsula on the Normandy side of the bay west of Avranches. During the highest equinox tides, finding a good viewing spot on the Mont can be difficult, since every tourist in France seems to be watching along with you. From the two Grouins, however, you will get a good view of the low-tide mudflats transforming into an expanse of shimmering water, and the bonus of Mont-St-Michel itself in the background. One of France's timeless, mystical visions is that of the Mont rising out of the mist above its encircling bay, seemingly unattainable and bound to heaven rather than earth, just as it has appeared to pilgrims for centuries. Winter is the best time to come here; it can be very cold and the tides are not their highest, but as you walk at dawn on a frosty, deserted beach somewhere on the bay, far from the tourist traps that have infiltrated the Mont itself, watching the sun turn the miraculous monument pink and gold, you will understand why Le Mont-St-Michel is truly one of the world's most majestic sites.

Gone Fishing

 One of the most relaxing ways to enjoy the French countryside is to spend a few lazy hours angling in one of its many streams, lakes, and coastal waters. It also offers a fine opportunity to get to know a particular locale in depth by day and to sample regional food and wine by night. It's not surprising that the sport is so popular among the French and visitors alike, from the calm inland waterways of the Auvergne to the turbulent mountain streams of the Pyrénées.

SEA ANGLING: France's 2,550 miles of shoreline are open to ocean and sea anglers year-round, and even amateurs can fish freely for albacore, bass, bonito, conger eel, dogfish, gar, goby, mackerel, mullet, black and yellow pollack, ray, sea bream, sole, and tuna — the fish found off the French coast — as long as they observe the rules relating to military ports, sewage facilities, and bag limits. Amateur sea anglers do not need permits, as a rule, to fish with hand-held rods or lines or to gather shellfish. However, to fish with most nets, a permit must be obtained from the local maritime authority.

It is also possible to fish underwater off the Atlantic and Mediterranean coasts using a harpoon gun, a mask, a breathing tube, and rubber fins. But the most common quarry — moray, mullet, sea perch, ray, rock bass, and turbot — are beginning to get wise and are drawing fishermen increasingly deeper, so that 50 to 65 feet currently is about normal. (The *Conseil Supérieur de la Pêche* in Paris describes this underwater fishing as "a test of endurance and coolness requiring a strong heart, strong lungs, a normal blood pressure, and perfect self-control.")

Instruction centers can be found in resorts such as Aix-en-Provence, Biarritz, Marseilles, Nice, Paris, and Toulon.

For further information, contact local fishing clubs or the *Fédération Française d'Etudes et de Sports Sous-Marins,* 24 Quai de la Rive Neuve, Marseilles 13007 (phone: 91-33-99-31).

FRESHWATER FISHING: All freshwater fishing enthusiasts must belong to a French angling and fisheries association and must pay an annual fisheries tax. This can sometimes be done at tackle shops, but any town Syndicat d'Initiative can provide details about obtaining the necessary documents. General information is available from the *Conseil Supérieur de la Pêche* (134 Av. de Malakoff, Paris 75016; phone: 45-01-20-20). Inland waters are divided into two categories, each with different seasons and regulations. The first category includes waters stocked mainly with trout and salmon, which water pollution has made increasingly rare in France. The trout season normally runs from mid-March to mid-September; the best fishing is usually in June. The second category includes all other waters and a wide variety of fish, including the following:

Barbel (barbeau). Sometimes stretching a yard long and weighing 20 pounds, barbel is among the largest of France's river fish and will fight fiercely. Cheese is normally an excellent bait.

Bleak (ablette). A smallish fish that measures about 8 inches long and weighs about 2 ounces, bleak is abundant in a number of rivers with slow currents and in a few lakes. It is relatively easy to catch with a floating line.

Bream (brème). This fish fills most of the waters in the second category. They can weigh as much as 20 pounds and are known to be attracted by the smell of garlic.

Carp (carpe). An extremely prolific fish, the carp is found most frequently in rivers and pools. It is intelligent and therefore among the most difficult freshwater fish to catch, but it has been seen to bite at worms, potatoes, corn and beans.

Chub (chevesne). Almost every fast-running river in France is loaded with these, which can weigh up to 7 or 8 pounds. A chub eats just about everything it finds and can be caught with a flyrod, a floating line, or by trolling.

Grayling (ombre commun). Now becoming rare in France, it is found primarily in the fast-running cold rivers of the east and central regions. It normally takes skilled fly-fishing to have success with grayling, which spoils easily and therefore must be eaten promptly.

Gudgeon (goujon). Small, like the bleak, the gudgeon often is used as a bait for larger fish such as pike. Generally found near sandbanks, the gudgeon is most frequently caught with earthworms.

Perch (perche). Found in many rivers and lakes, the carnivorous perch is considered by many gourmands to be the tastiest of the freshwater fish. It is also among the most fun for the sports person because it can be caught by dapping, casting, or with ground bait.

Pike (brochet). The pike, which rarely weighs more than 20 pounds and normally grows to about a yard long in France, usually clusters at a particular place and waits for prey. Found in most of the second-category waters in France, pike is most easily caught by trolling with live bait.

Pike perch (sandre). As the name implies, this is a kind of cross between a pike and a perch. It is found in pools, lakes, and temperate rivers throughout France. Like the pike, it eats mainly smaller fish, which are recommended as bait. It is much more prolific than other carnivorous fish and can grow to be 3 feet long and weigh up to 25 pounds.

Roach (gardon). The national fish of France, sometimes carnivorous and sometimes vegetarian, usually weighs in at about a pound or so and is found in most waters of the second category. Worms and corn are the recommended baits.

Salmon (saumon). Born in rivers, salmon swim out to live in the sea for about 3 years and then head back upstream to spawn. They can grow to a length of 4 feet or more and can weigh up to 70 pounds. While becoming rarer in France as a result of pollution, heavy sea fishing, and other factors, salmon are still abundant in the rivers of Brittany, the rushing streams of the Pyrénées, and the Loire and Allier rivers. They are most commonly caught by fly-fishing from a large birch rod, minnow spinning, or by casting with worms; it is illegal to keep fish less than 20 inches in length.

Trout (truite). They can be found in the mountain torrents of the Pyrénées, the Alps, and the Massif Central, as well as in the smaller streams of the plains. Two types are common in France: the indigenous *fario* and the rainbow trout, which was introduced to Europe in the 19th century. There is also a subspecies called the sea trout, which, like the salmon, go to live in the sea before returning to the river to spawn. The *fario*, with its distinctive red spots, usually grows to 5 or 6 pounds. Most trout are caught by artificial-fly-fishing or by casting with worms or natural insects. Experts say that the chances are best at sunrise and immediately before or after a storm.

Some of the outstanding freshwater fishing regions in France include the following:

Auvergne – From the summits of the Massif Central to the plains of the *département* of Allier, the fishing in Auvergne is renowned. Both *fario* and rainbow trout are abundant in the *départements* of Cantal, Haute-Loire, and Puy-de-Dôme. In Allier, most of the water is of the second category, but there is good trout fishing in the streams running from Bourbonnaise Mountain and in those west of Vichy. Salmon of 10 to 20 pounds are abundant in more than 600 miles of stream from their spawning grounds in the Haut-Allier. The streams in Puy-de-Dôme and Haute-Loire are particularly scenic. Barbel, carp, eel, grayling, perch, pike, and roach also are abundant in Auvergne. For more information, contact the *Fédération de Pêche* in each *département:*

Allier: Fédération de Pêche de l'Allier, 25 Bd. du Général-de-Gaulle Cusset 03300 (phone: 70-97-90-42)

Cantal: Fédération de Pêche du Cantal, 14 Allée du Vialenc, Aurillac 15000 (phone: 71-48-19-25)

Haute-Loire: Fédération de Pêche de la Haute-Loire, 32 Rue Henri-Chas, Le Puy en Velay 43000 (phone: 71-09-09-44)

Puy-de-Dôme: Fédération de Pêche du Puy-de-Dôme, 65 Rue de l'Oradou, Clermont-Ferrand 63000 (phone: 73-91-42-33)

For a list of hotels in the area that are ideally situated for fishing, contact the *Comité Régional du Tourisme d'Auvergne,* 43 Av. Julien, BP 395, Clermont-Ferrand 63011 (phone: 73-93-04-03).

Aveyron – The French call the region stretching from the foothills of the Massif Central to the Causses dominating the Languedoc the "Green Country of the Midi," and with good reason. Serene, beautiful, and known for its many castles, cathedrals, and Roman chapels, it offers the angler 4,000 miles of rivers and 8,800 acres of lakes. From the large lakes of Le Lévézou to the valleys of Aveyron, Lot, and Tarn, the region is one of unspoiled natural scenery. The four best rivers for fishing are the Lot, the Aveyron, the Viaur, and the Tarn, which, together with their numerous tributaries, are loaded with barbel, chub, gudgeon, perch, and trout. Of the many lakes, the Castelnau-Lassouts and Golinhac are especially attractive and offer unusually extensive varieties of fishing. Hotels, camping spots, holiday farms, and country lodgings abound. Information: *Fédération de la Pêche,* 52 Rue de l'Embergue, Rodez 12003 (phone: 65-68-41-52).

Brittany – The small country city of Châteaulin on the Nantes–Brest Canal is a pleasant and practical starting point for the fisherman in Brittany. About a tenth of all the salmon caught in France each year, the best of them weighing 24 pounds, come from this waterway. But since some parts of the canal are much better than others, it's a good idea to get some advice first. Sea trout also are abundant here, especially in the section between Guilly-Glas and Châteaulin. The best time is from the end of February to the first of April, while summer salmon can be caught from mid-May to mid-June. The Aulne and Hyères rivers are excellent for other varieties of trout. June and October are the months for pike and whitefish, which normally weigh 5 or 6 pounds. The estuaries abound in bass, eel, mullet, smelt, and sole. Information: *Fédération de la Pêche,* 1 Rue Poher, Quimper 29000 (phone: 98-53-16-61).

Dauphiné – The mountainous Dauphiné region southeast of Lyons may be renowned for its winter sports, but it is popular in summer for its fine rivers, streams, and mountain lakes. The Isère, a first-category water upstream of Grenoble, for instance, has plenty of grayling and trout; the resorts of Brignoud, La Terrace, and Le Versoud make good headquarters for fishing there. Downstream of Grenoble, the stream is second-category water, primarily stocked with pike and roach; the nearest resorts are St-Marcellin and Tullins. South of Grenoble is yet another stream, which splits to become the Drac and Romanche; grayling and trout prevail before the fork, second-category fish afterward. The region also has its lakes — most notably the Monteynard-Avignonet at Avignonet, filled with bream, gudgeon, perch, roach, and trout; the Paladru at Charavines-les-Bains and Paladru, stocked with bream, perch, pike, and trout; and the several lakes around Laffrey, where the fishing is quite varied. Information: *Fédération de la Pêche de l'Isère,* Rue du Palais, Grenoble 38000 (phone: 76-44-28-39).

Hautes-Alpes – Trout fishing is excellent in the torrential mountain streams southeast of Isère, both in the first- and second-category waters and in the mountain lakes. The second-category waters in the area are also rich with chub and barbel, and perch can be found in the Serre-Ponçon lake. A particularly invigorating area for the outdoorsman, this region near the Italian border also has many camping areas and navigable waterways. Information: *Maison des Hautes-Alpes,* 4 Av. de l'Opéra, Paris 75001 (phone: 42-96-05-08) or *Fédération de la Pêche de l'Isère,* 1 Rue Cujas, 38000 Grenoble (phone: 76-44-28-39).

Normandy – After tracing the path of the Allied invasion and tossing back a few drams of the special apple brandy of Calvados, many anglers from abroad seek out the spectacular trout fishing of the heart of Normandy. The *département* of Orne, in particular, boasts of its rivers Huisne, Mayenne, Orne, and Sarthe and of smaller streams like the Egrenne, Noireau, Risle, Rouvre, and Varenne. For pike, try the Sarthe around Mêle-sur-Sarthe and Alençon. Information: *Fédération des Pêcheurs de l'Orne,* 59 Rue Jullien, Alençon 61003 (phone: 33-26-10-66).

Pyrénées – For trout and salmon fishing, it is hard to improve on the Pyrénées, both inside and outside the boundaries of the Pyrénées National Park, a scenic reserve created in 1967 along the Spanish border. About half of the 250 Pyrénées mountain lakes are stocked with various kinds of trout, and there is at least one good fishing stream in each valley; the Gave d'Ossau is particularly fine. Outside the park, the lakes of Barèges and Campan are excellent for a wide variety of fishing. In fact, one of the only problems with the angling in this area is that some of the waters are hard to find or are accessible only by foot. Anglers interested in this area should be sure to investigate the Gave d'Oloron, which is probably the most famous salmon torrent in the western section. One expert recommends following the salmon upstream in February and March from Peyrehorade to Sauveterre, from there in April and May to Navarrenx, and continuing upstream during the summer months to Orlon-Ste-Marie. Information: *Le Parc National des Pyrénées,* Tarbes 65000 (phone: 62-93-30-60); and *La Maison des Pyrénées,* 15 Rue St-Augustin, Paris 75002 (phone: 42-61-58-18).

Var – In the extreme southeastern section of France, where the climate almost always is pleasant and the air has the smell of the sea, this area has plenty of freshwater streams to keep the inland angler happy. The Argens River, with its scenic falls, begins near Seillons and is first-category water until Carces — fast, cold, and full of good trout; though the banks sometimes are steep, the stream always is accessible. In addition, there are a number of tributary brooks with their own population of trout — the Cauron, the Meironne, and the Rigoirds, for instance. Other good fishing waters include the Caramy, teeming with bream, perch, pike, roach, and, at least downstream of Vins, some large trout. Then there's the Issole, a pretty river with a rocky sand bed that draws fishermen from Besse, Cabasse, Flassans, Garéoult, and St-Anasthasie, not to mention the Verdon, the clear green river that flows down from the Hautes-Alpes. The 232-acre Lake Carces, which stretches for 2½ miles from the dam at Caramy, is another favorite fishing hole; famous for pike perch, it also is rich in black bass, bream, carp, chub, pike, and roach. The artificial 1,384-acre St-Cassien Lake, which reaches 28 miles behind Montauroux, is also popular. Information: *Fédération Départemental des Associations de Pêche et de Pisciculture du Var,* BP 104, Brignoles 83170 (phone: 94-69-05-56).

■ **The Rural Angle:** For fisherfolk who want to experience rural life in France, *gîtes de pêche* are an inexpensive choice for lodgings. These *gîtes* (simple guesthouses) are close to good fishing spots, many with a trout stream or river running through their back yards. Contact the *Maison des Gîtes de France* (35 Rue Godot-de-Mauroy, Paris 75009; phone: 47-42-25-43), and ask for the *Gîtes et Logis de Pêche* booklet (about $10), which lists such properties through France and gives detailed descriptions of each one. Rentals are handled either through regional reservations services or directly with the owners of the *gîtes.*

Horsing Around

Holidays on horseback in France unquestionably are among the country's best-kept secrets. That's too bad, because seeing the countryside astride a spirited steed can be pure delight. But whether the animal hauls your belongings while you walk alongside, pulls your wagon, or carries you from farm to village through deep woods, you will travel through stretches of France that few visitors ever see, a countryside whose rugged beauty is only enhanced by the creaking of saddle leather and the steady thud of hooves.

Equestrian holidays come in a variety of breeds. There are centers with riding instruction, multi-day horseback excursions, and week-long expeditions in horse-drawn gypsy carts. Highly organized centers provide expert instruction for every level of rider, including the beginner, while guest farms specialize in horseback *randonées* (rambles) along their area's wooded paths and country roads, with accommodations that can vary from tent to straw-littered barn to cozy hotel. Some programs are designed for teenagers as well. In any case, pastoral-pure air, authentic country food, a relaxed pace, and an almost total absence of tourist hordes (and sometimes even passing vehicles) are the chief allures. Each center can provide specific details on the *randonées* it offers. Reserve in advance since horse farms and riding hotels always are small, family-run affairs with a loyal clientele. And allow plenty of time for exchanges of correspondence.

For those who would rather limit their relationship with horses to admiration from afar, one possibility is a visit to the Ecole Nationale d'Equitation (National Riding School) in St-Hilaire-St-Florent near Saumur in the Loire Valley. Tours of the school are available, and practice sessions and performances of the *Cadre Noir,* France's elite equestrian team, performs the *croupade* and other expert equine feats made famous by Vienna's Spanish Riding School here. France also offers a number of famous racecourses — nine around Paris alone. Deauville, Vichy, and Cagnes-sur-Mer also attract everybody who is anybody during the summer racing season. Chantilly has a most unusual horse museum that is well worth a visit. The *haras nationaux* (national stud farms) are equally fascinating.

For more information about riding in France, contact the *Association Nationale pour le Tourisme Equestre et l'Equitation de Loisirs,* Ile Saint-Germain, 170 Quai de Stalingrad, Issy les Moulineaux 92130 (phone: 45-54-29-54).

CENTRE EQUESTRE DE ZANIÈRES, Ardes-sur-Couze, Puy-de-Dôme: A friendly atmosphere prevails at this family-oriented center specializing in week-long *randonées* around the volcanoes, valleys, and lakes of this varied region. Accommodations are simple, both at the center and on trips into the surrounding area. The horses are knowledgeable. And the riders, who travel up to ten in a group, generally are highly accomplished. *Randonées* are scheduled from May through September. It's also possible to leave a teenager behind in a specially designed riding program for young people. Information: *Centre Equestre de Zanières,* Ardes-sur-Couze 63420 (phone: 73-71-84-30).

LA CHEVAUCHÉE DES DEUX MERS, Aubiet, Gers: Twice each summer, a dozen or so experienced riders cross southeastern France from the Atlantic to the Mediterranean, caravan style. The 300-mile trip is a wonderful fortnight's exploration of a seldom visited slice of the country and includes a stop in glowing Carcassonne. Information: *Le Cheval Vert,* Lussan, Aubiet 32270 (phone: 62-65-93-47).

FERME EQUESTRE DU VAL D'ADOUR, Bazillac, Hautes-Pyrénées: In the high valley of the Adour River, this farm offers hour- and week-long, and weekend riding experiences throughout the year in the lush farmland of a little-known corner of France not far from the national stud farm, the Haras de Tarbes, the home of some magnificent examples of Anglo-Arabian stallions. Run by a family of horse breeders, this is a serious professional center that can guide a visitor from his first time in the saddle to the highest level of horsemanship. Mornings are usually spent on the trail; afternoons are customarily devoted to group instruction. Every sort of accommodation is available, from camping on the farm itself to luxurious quarters at nearby hotels. The atmosphere is intimate, with no more than ten riders accepted at any given time. Information: *Ferme Equestre du Val d'Adour,* Bazillac, Rabastens de Bigorre 65140 (phone: 62-96-59-44).

CERCLE HIPPIQUE DU CHATEAU LA DOUVE, Le Bourge d'Ire, Maine-et-Loire: This handsome hotel is a Loire château recently renovated and transformed with riders in mind. Riding facilities in the park around the hotel are open all year. Accommodations are more luxurious here than the often rustic lodgings found where riding is the star attraction. Information: *Cercle Hippique du Château La Douve,* Le Bourge d'Ire 49780 (phone: 41-61-54-54).

CHANTILLY, Oise, Picardie: Known as "La Ville du Cheval," the city of the horse, Chantilly has an equestrian museum, a racetrack and training center, and a population of more than 3,000 thoroughbreds. The lordly 18th-century stables, which furnished mounts to the royal court in nearby Paris, are open to the public as the *Musée Vivant du Cheval* (the Living Museum of the Horse); they house stallions from all the country's national stud farms, as well as a unique collection of equestrian art. Less than an hour from the Champs-Elysées. Information: *Musée Vivant du Cheval,* Chantilly 60500 (phone: 44-57-13-13).

LES RANDONNÉES SAUVAGE DE L'HABITARELLE, Châteauneuf-de-Randon, Lozère: For the hardy and adventurous, there are 5-to-8-day riding odysseys here in the Cévennes National Park, of Robert Louis Stevenson and *Travels with a Donkey* fame. Other routes go around the volcanoes of the Haut Vivarais area, through the Gorges of the Tarn, or even across Corsica. This is for experienced riders only, those unfazed by tentless, sleeping bag, starlit nights. Information: *Les Randonnées Sauvage de l'Habitarelle,* Châteauneuf-de-Randon, Lozère 48170 (phone: 66-47-90-10).

CORSICA: More than 500 miles of riding trails crisscross this mountainous Mediterranean island, and many of them still are used by shepherds and forest rangers. Picturesque villages along the way offer accommodations ranging from the primitive to the comfortable, and dozens of equestrian centers will organize expeditions that run from a few days to a couple of weeks. Information: *Comité Regional du Tourisme de Corse,* 17 Bd. Roi Jérôme, BP 19, Ajaccio, Corsica 20176 (phone: 95-21-56-56).

DEAUVILLE, Calvados: A sunset gallop along the beach here still ranks among France's prime existential delights, and this is one of the equestrian capitals of Europe. Summer witnesses an orgy of polo and racing, but excellent riding programs and facilities are available year-round. The wonderful seafront mansion known as the *Hôtel*

Normandy, for instance, offers vacation weeks that include free access to the *Club Hippique d'Oxer* (the Oxer Horse Club) and lessons in manège, dressage, and jumping. The food is sensational, the rooms princely, and the location just a canter from France's classiest gambling casino. Information: *Hôtel Normandy,* 38 Rue Jean-Mermoz, Deauville 14800 (phone: 31-98-66-22).

LES BEIGES, La Roche-l'Abeille, Haute-Vienne: Set in a lush forest-bordered valley in a verdant and undisturbed region, this farm offers something for everyone — from 3 hours of daily instruction at the farm itself for the inexperienced to overnight excursions in the surrounding area with stops in neighboring farmhouses for the more expert. Non-riders can join the latter group each evening — arriving in style in horse-drawn carriages. Teenagers who ride well can join week-long excursions especially designed for them or stay on their own at the farm for daily instruction. Information: *Les Beiges,* La Roche-l'Abeille 87800 (phone: 55-00-70-92).

CLUB MÉDITERRANÉE, Pompadour, Limousin: The efficient *Club Med* operation virtually guarantees a successful vacation, and the green paradise at Pompadour is no exception. While riders wander around chestnut-shaded paths or take lessons in the covered riding school, others can use the 22 tennis courts, a 9-hole pitch and putt golf course, and a heated swimming pool. The regal facilities include a pony club for children. A glorious place for riders and non-riders alike. Information: *Club Med,* Domaine de Noailles, Arnac Pompadour 19230 (phone: 55-73-31-33).

CLUB EQUESTRE LOISIRS "LA GRANDE VIGNOBLE," St-Julien-de-Crempse, Dordogne: Surrounded by acres of woods and meadows deep in the countryside, this converted 17th-century manor house built in the days of Louis XIV offers luxurious accommodations, gleaming stirrups, and saddles that look as if they were purveyed by Gucci. Aside from the outstanding riding facilities and instruction that completes the picture, there are tennis courts, a heated swimming pool, bikes to rent, and a sauna to soothe away sore muscles after an active day. Information: *Club Equestre Loisirs "La Grande Vignoble,"* St. Julien-de-Crempse 24140 (phone: 53-24-23-18; fax: 53-24-20-89).

L'ETRIER DU MONT-HEDIN, Signy Le Petit, Ardennes: Is there any more romantic name in France than Champagne? As it turns out, this beautiful region is exceptionally well supplied with riding facilities. From *Easter* to September, this one offers accommodations in rustic but comfortable quarters, and in addition to a complete program of riding instruction and excursions, there's glorious champagne to make every adventure just that much more effervescent. Information: *L'Etrier du Mont-Hedin,* Tarzy, Signy le Petit 08380 (phone: 24-54-32-52).

For those with a yen to canter (or walk) a horse along a beach, Brittany, with its miles of mainly unspoiled, uncrowded beaches and numerous *centres équestres* (riding centers) allows for an unusual holiday experience for beginners or experienced riders. One possibility is the *Centre Equestre du Trégor* (Kerianou 56193; phone: 96-95-67-41) on the outskirts of the north-coast town of Tréguier, which offers rides along the nearby Presq'île Sauvage (wild peninsula) or to the Point du Château at the tip of another peninsula for splendid views of the Côte du Granit Rose (pink granite coastline). For riding centers elsewhere in Brittany, contact the *Ligue de Tourisme Equestre de Bretagne* (8 Rue de la Carrière, Josselin 56120; phone: 97-22-22-62).

And for those who want to experience the luxuriant French countryside at a slower pace (around 4 miles per hour), the Dordogne Tourist Board has organized *roulotte à cheval* (horse-drawn cart) rentals. The *roulottes,* which are wooden trailers, accommodate four people and are equipped with a portable stove, kitchen utensils, and bed linen (there's no electricity, however). They can be rented by the weekend or week from April to October, and depart from Bergerac along a *bastide* (fortified village) route or from Quinsac through the unspoiled, agricultural Périgord vert (green Périgord). Planned nightly stops are in special areas where water and shelter for the horse and bathing facilities for the passengers are provided. A week's rental (which includes a training session in operating the *roulotte,* food for the horse, and insurance) costs around $800 during the high season, less at other times. Information: Contact the *Maison du Périgord,* 6 Rue Gomboust, Paris 75001 (phone: 47-42-09-15) or the *Office Départemental du Tourisme de la Dordogne,* 16 Rue Wilson, Périgueux 24009 (phone: 53-53-44-35; fax: 53-09-51-41).

■**Carriage Trade:** Lessons in the genteel art of carriage driving (*"attelage"* to the French) are offered in the exceedingly pleasant and refined surroundings of the Loire Valley and Château Le Fresne, home of the Marquis de Brantes, president of one of France's principal Carriage Driving Association chapters. Instruction is given by Mireille Escavi, a carriage champion and certified instructor, and a flexible schedule can be tailored to individual requests. Accommodations can be arranged at nearby country inns and bed and breakfast establishments. Information: Sue de Brantes, *Le Fresne,* Authon 41310 (phone: 54-80-33-04; fax: 54-80-34-41).

HORSE RACING

With Pigalle turf touts rubbing jodhpurs with the *beau monde* of the elegant Faubourg-St-Honoré, the *Hippodrome d'Auteuil* in the Bois de Boulogne supplies a supremely Parisian day at the races; open year-round. Also worth attending are the evening races at the *Champs des Courses de Vincennes.* The restaurant here, *Le Paddock,* affords diners a splendid view of the track (phone: 43-68-64-94).

From June to mid-September, stately old Vichy offers the ultimate in stylish horse racing in an atmosphere of thermal baths, palm-lined promenades, and twirling white parasols. The *Grand Prix de Vichy* in late July is one of the high points.

And the August racing season at Deauville on the Normandy coast, France's answer to England's Ascot, is one of the country's major social and sporting highlights. The *Grand Prix de Deauville,* at the end of the month, is a highlight.

Some of the year's other major racing events include the *Grand Prix d'Amérique,* a late January annual in Paris (*Vincennes*); the *Prix du Président de la République,* in Paris (*Auteuil*) in the middle of April; in Chantilly, the elegant *Prix du Jockey-Club* in early June, and the *Hermès*-sponsored *Prix de Diane* in mid-June (wear your fanciest hat); late June's *Grand Prix de Paris* in Paris (*Longchamp*); and the *Prix de l'Arc de Triomphe,* in early October in Paris (*Longchamp*).

Visitors to Paris also can pick up the flavor of the track by reading *Paris-Turf* (in French), available at kiosks, or by dropping in at the *Champs-Elysées Horse Club* (34 Av. des Champs-Elysées; phone: 42-25-12-60), where all the action is on television and all the jockeying at the bar.

Horse racing in France is divided into three disciplines — steeplechasing (*courses d'obstacles*), flat racing (*courses de plat*), and trotting races (*course de trot,* both mounted and with sulkies) — with a special racecourse (hippodrome) for each kind of race. In Paris, both the steeplechase course, the *Hippodrome d'Auteuil,* and the flat course, the *Hippodrome de Longchamp,* are located in the Bois de Boulogne. The chicest race of the year by far is the *Arc de Triomphe* at *Longchamp* in October, with its mix of turf touts and colorful *beau monde.* Children can even run freely through the grassy areas in the middle of the course, where families often picnic on fine days as the horses thunder past over the jumps. The steeplechase seasons are in the autumn and spring, culminating in the *Grand Steeplechase de Paris* in June. Evening trot races attract crowds at the *Hippodrome de Vincennes* at the *Vincennes* track (on the eastern edge of Paris), as does *Le Paddock* restaurant (phone: 43-68-64-94), with its splendid view of the track.

While racing in Deauville is chic, at other provincial courses it's a family affair, where the locals of all ages turn out for a day at the races. While the racing itself is serious and varied (steeplechasing, flat, and trotters all compete at country courses), the atmosphere for spectators is much more casual than at Paris tracks. It's possible to wander among the horse vans and watch trainers saddling up their charges, and there are always numerous stands selling delicious *frites* (French fries), crêpes, sandwiches, and sausages. Some of the main provincial racing events are at Pau (Pyrénées-Atlantiques) throughout the winter, Craon (Mayenne) in August and September (especially the first weekend in September, the main meeting for the west of France), Corlay (at a particularly scenic location on a hill in central Brittany southwest of St-Brieuc) in June and July, and at Saumur and Lion d'Angers (Maine-et-Loire) in spring and summer. Lion d'Angers also has a 3-day-event course that attracts some of the top equestrians in the sport worldwide. For information, contact the *Fédération Nationale des Sociétés de Courses de France,* 22 Rue de Penthièvre, Paris 75008 (phone: 42-25-96-71) or check with local tourist offices.

Freewheeling by Two-Wheeler

 To understand just how seriously the French have always taken the sport of bicycling, a visitor has only to consider the annual *Tour de France* (won by an American three times in the last 5 years). The world's premier bicycle competition, it has the French people cheering from the valleys of the Loire to the mountain passes of the Alps. But though this competition is reserved for professional cyclists, the passion that spawned it is felt by many, and there are all kinds of other activities and competitions for less serious cyclists at every level. Among them, there also is a distance program, with merit certificates to recognize accomplishment in a variety of categories; those who cover a stipulated territory, and pass through certain checkpoints in the various *départements,* complete certain short but difficult itineraries, or make certain long-distance trips, and the like, may earn special certificates.

However, most visitors, who just want to pedal through the French countryside in a leisurely fashion, merely take advantage of the itineraries provided through the various regional societies of the *Fédération Française de Cyclotourisme (FFCT;* 8 Rue Jean-Marie-Jégo, Paris 75013; phone: 45-80-30-21). These (easy to hard) *Randonnées Permanentes,* which can be taken by individuals or by groups at any time of year and normally cover several hundred miles over country roads, are designed to be completed over a period of days or weeks, with stops specified at intervals of a dozen or so miles. While written in French, the place names, route numbers, and distances are comprehensible even to those who do not speak the language. The *FFCT* will supply specific information for all of the routes listed below.

BASQUE PROVINCES: Using the seaside resort of Biarritz as the starting point, this excursion passes through the green hills of the French and Spanish Basque country to Bayonne, where there is a Basque museum, and to Bonloc, a popular rest stop along the pilgrimage to Santiago de Compostela. After crossing into Spain at Arnéguy, it takes in Santesteben, known for its picturesque houses, and San Sebastián, which has a magnificent beach. In Fuenterrabía there is a fine *parador,* once a medieval fortress and now an inn (phone: 943-642140), which makes a pleasant overnight stop before the route turns once again to France and the house of the composer Maurice Ravel in Ciboure. 337 miles (539 km).

BOURBONNAIS: The ancient province of Bourbonnais, famous for its landscape, lies almost in the dead center of the country west of Burgundy. In the *département* of Allier, the area covered on this tour begins and ends in Vichy, famous for its mineral water and for having been the collaborationist government headquarters during World War II. Traveling west and then clockwise around the *département,* the ride shows off soft mountains, an 11th-century church at Veauce, the Forêt Château-Charles, the Tartasse Valley near Ronnet, the ancient market town of Hérisson and its splendid ruined 14th-century château, the spa at Bourbon-l'Archambault that has been serving rheumatics since Roman times, the magnificent Romanesque church at Château-Montagne, and the museum of prehistory at Glozel. One of the most interesting areas is the Forêt-de-Tronçais, whose 26,000-acre oak grove is reputed to be the most beautiful in the country. In old French, *tronce* referred to huge oak trunks, hence Tronçais. 325 miles (520 km).

BRITTANY: Beginning in cosmopolitan Nantes, where Jules Verne was born in 1828, this itinerary quickly takes you to more rural scenery, taking in the fishermen's hamlet of Pont-St-Martin, the fortified city of Guérande, the eerie megaliths at Carnac, the rocky and surf-pounded coast at Quiberon, and the folkloric center of Brittany at Quimper. Modern Brest and the famous islet of Mont-St-Michel — perhaps France's best-known monument after Notre-Dame and the Eiffel Tower — also is on the tour. 852 miles (1,363 km).

BURGUNDY: Setting out from Dijon, the ancient capital of the duchy of Burgundy with its Louis XIV palace, this trip meanders along winding country roads, through villages full of flower-bedecked stone buildings that date from the 16th century, past immense cathedrals and imposing abbeys and châteaux. There is an undeniable tranquillity to it all. In Dijon proper, it takes in the Hôtel Chambellan and the typically Burgundian old Rue des Forges, the pure Gothic Cathédrale St-Bénigne, the curious 15th-century Eglise St-Michel, the Renaissance Palais de Justice, and the Palace of the Dukes of Burgundy. It skirts a crannied quarter of picturesque old streets and passes the Clairvaux wine cellars, which were built by 13th-century monks. Heading northwest and continuing roughly counterclockwise around Burgundy, it subsequently encompasses St-Germain-Source-Seine, where the famous river begins, the ruins of a 12th-century château at Maisey-le-Duc, and Ancy-le-Franc, where one of the most magnificent Renaissance châteaux in Burgundy is open to the public. Tonnerre, a comfortable small town on a hill full of vines and greenery, is another stop, as is Noyers, a handsome fortified city that has changed little since the Middle Ages, right down to the twisty outdoor stairways, the ancient stone walls, and the half-timbered architecture. Beaune, famous for its wine, is one of some 3 dozen other towns on the tour. 750 miles (1200 km).

CALVADOS: Best known for its apple cider, this area of Normandy appeals to cyclists because of its diverse geography. The *FFCT* itinerary runs along the coast through the picturesque old port of Honfleur, takes in the splendid beaches of Deauville and Arromanches, visits the Louis XIII château and the beautiful, peaceful Cérisy-la-Forêt (Cerisy Forest), the Orne Valley, and the caves and high rocky cliffs of "Swiss" Normandy, which center on Clécy. 287 miles (459 km).

CATHARIST SITES: This region in south-central France is known for its many fortresses and other remains from the 12th and 13th centuries, when it was inhabited by a group of Catharists, one of the medieval Christian sects who believed that Christ was of angelic and not human origin. The tour begins in Toulouse, known for its many churches and its famous Hôtel de Ville (Town Hall), and continues through Carcassonne, the 13th-century walled city that remains Europe's largest fortress. Subsequent stops include the ancient blockhouse of Mirepoix, the ruins of the Puilaurenx Château, the fortified 14th-century village of Lagrasse, and the wine city of Béziers. 482 miles (771 km).

CHÂTEAUX OF THE LOIRE: Probably no region of France is better suited to quiet pedaling than this area surrounding the quiet Loire River. The lazy stream, the colorful villages, the spectacular valleys, and the beautiful châteaux combine to draw thousands of tourists each summer. The *FFCT* recommends four itineraries, all beginning in La Folie. The first takes in Balzac's birthplace at Tours and the châteaux near Vallière, Langeais, La Gaudinière, and Le Lude. A second travels southeast to Montbazon, famous for its ancient dungeon, and includes the châteaux near Azay-sur-Indre, Montrésor, Valençay, Orbigny, and Montpoupon. The third heads west to the châteaux near Candé, Pont-de-Ruan, Chinon, Saumur, and Montsoreau. And the fourth follows an easterly route through Montrichard, Fougères-sur-Bièvre, Chambord, and St-Gervais-la-Forêt. 443 miles (709 km).

DORDOGNE: That there are more than 1,000 châteaux and country manors in this lush area of rolling hills, fern-carpeted forests, and cliff-edged rivers — more than in any other *département* in France — is just one of the charms of this tour. It begins in Périgueux, the capital of truffles and foie gras, and proceeds through one of the sections of the country that is richest in ruins and religious art. Splendid vistas are the norm and there are innumerable small villages full of mellow stone churches and old houses dating to the Middle Ages. Serenely set Brantôme is one of the highlights, for its abbey founded by Charlemagne, its brace of excellent restaurants, and the hyacinth-choked Dronne River that meanders through it. 370 miles (592 km). See also the *Périgord* tour route, DIRECTIONS.

EDELWEISS ARIEGEOIS: Ariège, in the Pyrénées, is perfect for the conditioned cyclist. Surrounded by these vast, beautiful mountains, the tour begins in the heart of the Pyrénées in tiny Pamiers and includes prehistoric sites, pine forests, and a moving 12th-century monastery at Montjoie. 538 miles (861 km).

GIRONDE: Anyone familiar with fine wine will recognize many of the stops on this tour of the green Bordeaux region, immediately southwest of the Dordogne: attractive little Pauillac, St-Emilion, Monségur, and the walled city of Blaye. Beginning in Bordeaux proper and moving through the Dordogne Valley before circling westward again, the tour spends a good deal of time southwest of the city in the quiet Landes forest, an amazing trail-crossed tract of regal conifers. Especially in the Médoc, the terrain often is flat, and the parallel rows of vines, with every plant trimmed to the same height, is a study in elegant precision. 478 miles (765 km).

HAUTE-PROVENCE: Covered with lavender fields and olive groves, this dry, mountainous region in the extreme southeast of France offers exceptionally scenic terrain for the cyclist. The route begins at Dignes, the capital of "the Lavender Alps," and extends spoke-like in four directions. The southern spoke travels through Moustier-Ste-Marie, an ancient village whose maze of alleys is set in the shadows of some fantastic boulders. East, there is picturesque Castellane, a village noted for Romanesque churches and magnificent views. To the north, there's Seyne-les-Alpes, where Louis XIV built an interesting citadel; the view from its ramparts now is a favorite with visitors. And the western route leads to the ancient fortress town of Sisteron, to Forcalquier, noted for its 16th-century Gothic fountain, and to the old market town of Manosque. 325 miles (520km).

JOAN OF ARC ROUTE: This pilgrimage, which runs from Lorraine through the Loire country to Normandy, begins in Domrémy-la-Pucelle, where the national heroine was born in 1412, and continues on a line through Tonnerre and Auxerre in Burgundy, passes through Chinon, and takes in Troyes, Reims, sections of Normandy, and Rouen, where she was executed in 1431. 934 miles (1,494km).

MONT-BLANC TOUR: A demanding route that circles Mont-Blanc, the highest peak in the Alps, this itinerary begins in medieval Albertville at 1,132 feet, continues through the popular ski resorts of Megève and Chamonix, and penetrates into Switzerland, where, in the village of Col de la Forclaz at 5,009 feet, it descends rapidly — with the Rhône Valley always in view — to the small Swiss town of Martigny at 1,561 feet.

This marks the beginning of a steep climb into Italy via an 8,100-foot mountain pass that has been well traveled since the Bronze Age. Aosta, founded by Caesar Augustus in 25 BC, and Bourg-St-Maurice are among the final stops. 200 miles (320 km).

FOR MORE INFORMATION

The main *FFCT* office (8 Rue Jean-Marie-Jégo, Paris 75013; phone: 45-80-30-21) can provide bicycling route maps as well as information about where to rent multi-speed bicycles; also available is a list of the train stations in France where simple one-speed bicycles may be rented and returned to another station. For information about organized biking tours all over France, contact *Bicyclub* (8 Pl. de la Porte Champerret, Paris 75017; phone: 47-66-55-92). Also see "Camping and RVs, Hiking and Biking" in *When and How to Go,* GETTING READY TO GO.

Great Walks and Mountain Rambles

 While no European terrain can rival the vast reaches of open land so abundant in the United States, Europe does offer an enormous range of scenic country close to wherever you happen to be visiting. This is particularly true of France.

Here the hiker will discover varied terrain suitable for all kinds, and angles, of walking. There are the high mountain ranges of the Alps and the Pyrénées, the green volcanic outcrops of the Massif Central, the forests of Burgundy and the Ile-de-France, and the gently rolling countryside of Brittany and Normandy. Add to this a climate that generally is benign and (south of the Loire) warm in summer, plus excellent food and wine whose consumption can be even more easily justified after a day on the trail, and, once you get into the *arrière pays* (the backcountry), very low prices. And although it was a Frenchman who coined the phrase "*une journée de sentier, huit jours de santé*" ("one day on the trail makes for eight healthy days"), the nation's footpaths are more or less empty — except, that is, during the month of August, France's peak holiday time.

France's star treks are the Sentiers de la Grande Randonnée, the more than 18,000 miles of footpaths that wend their way into even the most remote corners of the country. Each Grande Randonnée (GR) trail is numbered, and each is marked with distinctive red and white blazes on trees, telegraph posts, rock faces, walls, gateposts, and the like, wherever there is a shift in direction or point of ambiguity. Some are straight routes and some are circular, and the network covers an immense variety of landscapes. The GR5 alone spans the Alps from Lake Geneva down to the Mediterranean. The GR10, a 400-mile (640 km) hill walk that will take even the fittest hiker many weeks to complete, covers the Pyrénées. The GR3 meanders along the Loire through the château country. The GR65 follows the famous 620-mile (992 km) pilgrims' road from Le Puy to Santiago de Compostela and the Spanish frontier. In addition, there are six Trans-European footpaths like the 1,240-mile (1,984 km) E2 from Ostend to Nice, a little over half of which lies within France.

These are the long walks, several lasting for many weeks, but the French trail network offers a little something for everyone. Even the long trails contain a number of cutouts or feeder trail variations by which the route can be shortened to the needs of a brief vacation or weekend break. In addition, every province has at least one perfect center for hikes and its nearby *sentiers de pays* (country trails). In Brittany, for example, Huelgoat in wooded Finistère has an abundance of them, as do the Seine Valley and the hilly Suisse Normande area near Alençon in neighboring Normandy. In the Pyrénées, Ascain in the green Borique country is good, as are Luchon, which has walks across the border into Spain; Luz-St-Sauveur, south of Lourdes and close to the spectacular Cirque de Gavarnie; or, in the east, Font-Romeu on the high plateau of the Cerdagne. In each case, you'll find spectacular scenery, plenty of inexpensive accommodations, and good, good walking.

Before choosing a specific area of the country for hiking, look at a general map of France that shows physical characteristics, so as not to opt for terrain too demanding for your level of fitness. For those who are sedentary, the choice of a mountainous region would be foolhardy; far more sensible are areas such as the Brittany heathlands, the open plateau of the Causse country south of the Massif Central, and the green Basque foothills of the southwest.

Since hot weather is not necessarily a welcome companion on a walk, it's best to avoid the southern half of the country in midsummer. And since it can get extremely warm anywhere south of the Loire between May and September, the wise walker will get most of his day's journey done before midday. Although it is possible to get caught in a snowstorm as late as April in the northern areas, the essential pieces of equipment are a hat, shorts, plenty of sunblock, rainwear, and something warm, just in case.

In more remote areas, a backpack, sleeping bag and pad, cookstove, food, and other gear are requisites. It's possible to camp out in the wild except in high summer, when certain sites are restricted because of the considerable risk of fire. In general, although *camping sauvage* never is actively encouraged (and actually is forbidden in the national and regional parks), the French tend to turn a blind eye to small tents in remote areas that are placed discreetly above 5,000 feet and in areas that are an hour or more away from alternative accommodation.

Throughout France, a hiker will have little difficulty finding simple, inexpensive accommodations in villages along the way. In fact, since French walkers prefer a real roof rather than mere canvas at night, GR trails are equipped, at intervals of 5 hours or so, with *gîtes d'étape* — small, usually unmanned hostels in a converted barn or other farm building that are fitted out with dormitory accommodations for around 20 people, but no bedding, and kitchen facilities (inexpensive and in demand; reserve by telephone a day in advance in summer). In mountainous regions, the *gîtes'* counterparts are the basic huts called *abris,* some staffed and some not — warm and dry, but not much more (free). Locations are noted invariably on the *Topo Guides* and on the IGN 1:50,000 or 1:25,000 series of maps (described at greater length below). Here's a sampling of some of the better areas for hiking in France.

ALPS: The Alps is the area where walking turns into scrambling, climbing, and mountaineering; where the times given in trail guides are as important as the distances; and where the best of the trails demand fitness, outdoor skills, and proper equipment. It should not be forgotten that every year the mountains claim the lives of hundreds of hikers, many of whom should never have ventured from the security of easy footpaths. Yet some of France's classic walks are in the Alps, and they are as irresistible to the committed hiker and climber as the *Louvre* is to lovers of fine art. Consider the best-known route, the Tour du Mont-Blanc; a 14-day adventure around Western Europe's tallest mountain, it offers plenty of scrambling and, for the upwardly mobile, a complement of climbing as well. The 240-mile (384 km) Grande Traversée des Alpes Françaises, GR5, dotted by 100 mountain refuges, is another major walk. And in the Vanoise, France's first national park, hikers can tackle the Tour Pédestre, which runs from the Tarentaise across to Maurienne, with winter ski resorts as stopovers. Huge numbers of day hikes complete the picture. Mondane, Val d'Isère, and Plan d'Amont give access to the 300 miles of trails in this park, and the summer and winter resort of Chamonix boasts an additional 180 miles of marked trails into the mountains around it. Local *Syndicats d'Initiative* and branches of the *Club Alpin Français* are the best sources of information for the surrounding areas. For other details: *Comité Régional du Tourisme (CIMES)*, Maison du Tourisme, 14 Rue de la République, Grenoble 38019 (phone: 76-54-34-36); and the *Syndicat d'Initiative*, Bonlieu, 1 Rue Jean-Jaurès, Annecy 74000 (phone: 50-45-00-33). See also *The Alps*, DIRECTIONS.

AUVERGNE: The very center of France, this northern corner of the Massif Central provides an excellent introduction to France's spikier landscapes. The area's finest scenic assets lie in the domain of the fairly energetic backpacker. But because the land is predominantly rural and dotted with small market towns that serve the needs of the wheat farming, sheep raising, and vineyard tending population, the hiker will find a good variety of walks of all grades in each of its four *départements:* Allier, which the Bourbons called home, the least rugged quarter, with modest hills covered by forests and farmlands; the Haute-Loire, the source of its grand namesake river (no more than a trickle in summer); remote Cantal, with gorgeous valley scenery; and the volcanic core known as Puy de Dôme, whose 500-million-year-old green hills are hard to beat for anyone planning to day-hike out of a home base. GR routes, as well as sections of long-distance trails, ribbon the whole of the Auvergne. Particularly rewarding is GR40, the 96-mile (154 km) Tour du Velay, which circles some moderately hilly terrain in the Haute-Loire and Le Puy de Dôme. The GR400, known as the Tour des Volcans du Chantal, offers 87.6 (140 km) additional scenic miles. The GR65, covering 84 miles (134 km), was named the Sentier de St-Jacques-de-Compostelle after the old pilgrims' trail that some of its sections follow. And GR441, called the Tour de la Chaîne des Puys, takes in more than 3 dozen extinct volcanoes as it makes the circuit of the Volcanoes National Park, one of a pair in the area. Morvan, the second, is full of woods, rivers, and primarily artificial lakes. Summers are hot and dry, though with an occasional thunderstorm and generally chilly nights. Information: *Maison de l'Auvergne*, 194 *bis* Rue de Rivoli, Paris 75001 (phone: 42-61-82-38); *Comité Régional du Tourisme*, 43 Av. Julien, Clermont-Ferrand 63011 (phone: 73-93-04-03).

BRITTANY AND NORMANDY: Good, fairly gentle trails, coupled with plenty of historical sights and good food, make this northwest corner of France a sensible choice for the less ambitious walker in need of wayside distractions. Both Normandy and Brittany primarily are fishing and agricultural regions, and the landscapes and the high quality of the cuisine reflect the fact. Normandy's most popular corner for walkers is the Cotentin Peninsula, the broad finger of land that pokes the English Channel; its delightful coastline is peppered with tiny fishing harbors such as Barfleur, St-Vaast, and St-Pierre-l'Eglise, which are linked by the 141-mile (226 km) GR223 coastal footpath. In Brittany, the prime terrain is in Finistère, the *département* where you'll find Breton culture at its most intense. For a breezy look at Brittany's rocky coast carved by the Atlantic, and the equally rugged Point du Raz west of Quimper, there are hikes along the Presqu'île de Crozon south of Brest; the trails there overlook a stretch of water known as the Raz de Sein, where *nul n'a passé sans peur ou sans douleur* (no one has passed through without fear or pain), according to Baudelaire. Delightful Huelgoat (an ideal center for tours), the Parc Naturel d'Amorique, and several Grands Sites (officially designated as such due to their natural beauty) are the other chief lures for the walker in Brittany. Although both provinces offer plenty of easy short walks, no fewer than 21 GR trails are found here, including GR34, which is known as the Tour de Bretagne since its 521 miles (834 km) cover the entire province, and a section of GR36, which runs from the Channel coast to the Pyrénées. Information: For details about walks in Normandy, write to the *Comité Régional du Tourisme de Normandie*, 46 Av. Foch, Evreux 27000 (phone: 32-33-79-00); for walking information about Brittany, contact the *Comité Régional du Tourisme*, 3 Rue d'Espagne, Rennes 35041 (phone: 99-50-11-15). Also, for details about towpath trails that follow the more than 930 miles of canal, write to the *Comité de Promotion Touristique des Canaux-Bretons*, 12 Rue de Jemmapes, Nantes 44000 (phone: 40-47-42-94).

CÉVENNES: Those who enjoy backpacking in remote territory will particularly enjoy the five *départements* of the Languedoc-Roussillon region to the west of the Rhône Valley — Aude, Gard, Hérault, Lozère, and the Pyrénées-Orientales. Each has its merits, but for those with limited time, the best choices are Lozère and the Cévennes range. Full of steep, wooded hills and lovely, lonely rivers, it is mostly enclosed by the Cévennes National Park, the country's largest. Of the several miles of trails here, the most famous is the one that its namesake, Robert Louis Stevenson, followed with his donkey in 1878; it runs between Le Monastir, near Le Puy, and St-Jean-du-Gard, and links this region with the Auvergne. Other GR routes include the 94.8-mile (152 km) GR67-67A, the Sentier du Tour des Cévennes; and the 48-mile (77 km) GR71, the Chemin des Templiers et Hospitaliers, which follows the routes once patrolled by the Knights Templar. Since the region is so large, a hiker should be prepared for a variety of climates, including snow as early as October. Information: *Comité Régional du Tourisme,* 20 Rue de la République, Montpellier 34000 (phone: 67-92-67-92); *Office du Tourisme,* 2 Rue Michelet, Alès 30100 (phone: 66-78-49-10); or from *Easter* to November 1, Pl. Gabriel Peri, Alès 30100 (phone: 66-52-32-15).

CORSICA: Easily overlooked when poring over a map of France with walking in mind, this island — the largest in the Mediterranean — lies about 100 miles from the southern coast of France (and is in fact far closer to Italy). So covered by myrtle, gorse, and heather that Napoleon reckoned he could recognize the place by its smell alone, it is rugged and mountainous, and its best-known trail, GR20, represents 103.8 (166 km) miles of hard, isolated going that should be tackled only by the extremely fit. Information: *Comité Regional du Tourisme de Corse,* 17 Bd. Jérôme, BP 19, Ajaccio 20176 (phone: 95-21-56-56).

ILE-DE-FRANCE: Despite its proximity to Paris, the many miles of marked trails here, all with gentle gradients, thread their way through some of France's finest forest scenery, the old hunting terrain of the Bourbon kings. The area's classic route is the GR1, a 372-mile (595 km) circle around Paris that begins and ends at the Parc de Saint-Cloud. But the single most attractive terrain undoubtedly lies to the east in the Ardennes, a region of lush woodlands, steep valleys and magnificent castles, all strung together like beads on the network of footpaths. Most of these are suitable for day trips, but a few cover real distances; witness the 186-mile (298 km) GR12-12a, which crosses the Oise and Aisne rivers. The best centers for day hiking include Charleville-Mézières and Sedan, a town on the Meuse that boasts the largest castle in Europe. The *FFRP-CNSGR* describes 30 marked trails in its two-volume *Petite Randonnée en Ile-de-France.* And the Comité Départemental des Ardennes in Charleville-Mézières covers several attractive routes in its *Sentiers de Grande Randonnée et Sentiers Pédestre.* Information: *Centre d'Information de la Randonnée Pédestre,* 64 Rue de Gergovie, Paris 75014 (phone: 45-45-31-02).

MIDI-PYRÉNÉES: Stretching from the Auvergne in the northeast to the Basque country in the southwest and to Languedoc-Roussillon in the southeast, this vast region in the south comprises no less than eight *départements.* The population is sparse and the scenery is spectacular — defined as it is by the mountains of the Pyrénées and its foothills and by the courses of several rivers, including the Aveyron, Blais, Garonne, Gers, and Tarn (which also has stupendous gorges). Consequently, for walkers of all abilities — particularly backpackers and long-distance day hikers who don't need villages at frequent intervals to supplement the pleasures of the trail — the area is a natural. Most of the region's *Syndicats d'Initiative* are sympathetic to a walker's needs, and towns like Aveyron, St-Bléat, and Luchon boast an impressive density of footpaths on their very doorsteps; the last, for instance, is the departure point for 25 marked trails. In addition, there are a number of GR routes in the area. The GR60 (58 miles/93 km) follows an old trail along which herds of animals used to be driven to market. The GR65 and GR65-651 continue the Sentier de St-Jacques-de-Compostelle, the historic

Western European footpath that Christian pilgrims have been following for 1,500 years. Generally speaking, the walking gets easier as you move north through the area, though even in the south, the river valley trails don't demand anything like a bionic constitution. The summer months are extremely hot, so the optimal seasons are spring and fall. Information: *Comité Régional du Tourisme,* 12 Rue Salambo, Toulouse 31222 (phone: 61-13-55-55).

PYRÉNÉES: Several of the routes in the Pyrénées demand a fair measure of scrambling and even climbing ability, and crampons (spiked steel frames that attach to boots) and an ice ax are essential. But there are many miles of more amenable trails in addition to those involving rock faces. The Pyrénées National Park, which runs along the Spanish frontier, has 240 miles of marked trails; they range from comfortable valley walks that follow the courses of the Aspe or Ossau River to the more rugged treks in the Pays Toy area around Luz-St-Saveur and take in such attractions as the *cirques* of Gavarnie and Troumouse, spectacular glacial amphitheaters. There also are the two famous long-distance walks — the 420-mile (672 km) GR10, between Hendaye on the Atlantic and Banyuls on the Mediterranean, and the Haute-Route, a demanding hike requiring as much as a couple of months on the trail. Luchon in the Haute-Garonne, Aix-Les-Thermes in Ariège, and Font-Romeau in the Pyrénées-Orientales make good centers for day hiking. *Département* information offices are at Carcassone, Foix, Paul, and Tarbes; and the *Club Alpin Français* has branches in many towns and villages. Information: *Comité Régional du Tourisme,* 12 Rue Salambo, Toulouse 31200 (phone: 61-13-55-55).

PLANNING A HIKE

As the popularity of walking has increased in France, the French have improved upon their natural advantages by providing well-organized facilities at both the national and local level. An abundance of literature also exists, and before ever setting foot on the trail, savvy hikers will investigate their routes through both avenues.

ORGANIZATIONS: The principal organization for walkers in France is the magnificently titled *Fédération Français de la Randonnée Pédestre–Comité National des Sentiers de Grande Randonnée.* The *FFRP-CNSGR* has branches throughout France and, from its main office in Paris (8 Av. Marceau, Paris 75008; phone: 47-23-62-32), organizes the marking of long-distance trails, negotiates rights of way, urges local authorities to maintain and blaze their own paths with the assistance of *FFRP* members, and produces an excellent series of *Topo Guides* — one for every trail in the Grande Randonnée network and some for regional and local footpaths as well. The *FFRP* also has produced a series of *Topo Guides* for the regional long-distance footpaths known as the GR de Pays and for the shorter day walks of a particular region, such as the forests of the Ile-de-France near Paris. The *FFRP-CNSGR* magazine, *Randonnée GR,* not only details new trails but also has tear-out pages with which to update the *Topo Guides.* The *FFRP*'s efforts are supplemented by those of the many walking groups such as *CHAMINA,* in the Auvergne; *ADDRAM,* for the Alpes-Maritimes; the *Randonnées Pyrénéan,* which looks after the interests of hill walkers in the hot, high mountains of the south; and the *Club Vosgian,* France's oldest walking organization, which maintains an excellent network of paths and hostels in the green Vosges hills and the Moselle River valleys.

The *Club Alpin Français* (24 Av. Laumière, Paris 75019; phone: 42-02-68-64) oversees matters relating to strenuous walking and climbing.

It's also useful to know about the *Fédération Française du Camping-Caravaning* (78 Rue de Rivoli, Paris 75004; phone: 42-72-84-08) and the *Fédération Unie des Auberges de la Jeunesse* (French Youth Hostel Association; 10 Rue Notre-Dame de Lorette,

Paris 75009; phone: 42-85-55-40). Unfortunately for walkers, most of this group's 200-odd hostels are in large towns, not in country districts.

MAPS AND GUIDES: Each of the GR routes is described fully in one of the excellent *Topo Guides*. The only snag with these, and with the bulk of the information provided by the various organizations noted above, is that nearly everything is in French. But the maps are clear, regardless of language, and, with the aid of a smattering of high school French, plus a small dictionary, the text, too, can be followed.

That said, the maps in the *Topo Guides* clearly indicate the route of the trail on a 1:50,000 scale as well as provide information on shelters, campsites, transportation, food replenishment, points, timings, and distances. The various timings and stages assume 7 hours' walking a day as a fair average, at a speed of roughly 2 or 3 miles per hour.

The most popular series of topographical maps for walkers is the series published by the *Institut Géographique National* (*IGN*, 107 Rue La Boëtie, Paris 75008; phone: 42-25-87-90). Its shop, just off the Champs-Elysées, is well worth visiting.

As for inspiration, the best single source is the IGN 1:1,000,000 Map 903, *Sentiers de Grande Randonnée,* which shows all the GR trails. The *FFRP-CNSGR* also produces a guide called *Randonner,* which includes a general map and a list of the *Topo Guides* that describe the GR trails. The IGN series of 1:50,000 maps (roughly 1¼ inches to the mile) and 1:25,000 maps (2½ to the mile) are detailed enough for trail use. Showing both the marked trails and local paths, these maps are available all over France.

The series published by the *Editions Didier et Richard* of Grenoble, especially those covering eastern France, the Alps, and the Jura, are also good.

Since there are roughly three times the number of *sentiers de pays* as there are GR routes, you'd be well advised to call at the local tourist office of the *Syndicat d'Initiative,* for maps of the shorter trails in the immediate vicinity as well as general background information on the region.

If the area receives a large proportion of British or American visitors, these materials usually will be in English.

WALKING HOLIDAYS: Since the British are among the most enthusiastic walkers in France, it is hardly surprising that the largest number of accompanied walking holidays are led by English-speaking guides and are based on the opposite shore of the Channel. Two of the best are the following:

> *Ramblers Holidays,* 13 Longcroft House, Fretherne Rd., Welwyn Garden City, Hertfordshire AL8 6PQ, England (phone: 70-733-1133)
>
> *Waymark Holidays,* 44 Winslow Rd., Slugh SL1 2EJ, England (phone: 75-351-6477; fax: 75-351-7016)

Also see "Camping and RVs, Hiking and Biking" in *When and How to Go,* GETTING READY TO GO.

THE LAW AND THE WALKER: Apart from the official trails, walkers are free to walk on all footpaths and unmade tracks. You may find a path barred to prevent animals straying, but although the obstruction is inconvenient, you still are allowed to pass along the route. Similarly, the frequently spotted "Chasse Privé" signs or "Réserve de Chasse" refer to shooting rights and do not exclude access by walkers. Private land is encircled by a wall, fence, or boundary ditch and usually has a "Proprieté Privée" or "Défense d'Entrer" sign at frequent intervals around the perimeter. You are not allowed to walk across such property, nor over cultivated land, which includes orchards, mushroom fields, chestnut groves, and snail "fields" — all less obvious than fields of wheat or barley. (Snails, please note, are cultivated under piles of stones.)

Although not entirely backed by the force of law, the Country Code, as the country's environmental rules are called, should be respected by all walkers in France. This code prescribes that all hikers should love and respect nature; avoid unnecessary noise; destroy nothing; reclose all gates; protect and preserve the habitat; refrain from smoking or building fires in the forests (the one rule that is actively enforced); stay on the footpath; respect and understand the country way of life and the country people; think of others as they would think of themselves. In addition, hikers should not leave litter; should not pick flowers or plants; and should not disturb wildlife.

CLIMBING

ALPS: Among the more than 2,000 trails in this massive chain of mountains, there is climbing for everyone from the expert to the rank beginner (although the latter will not be able to notch up all that many peaks). Though there are some 40-odd huts and bivouac spots so the climber does not have to pack a tent, even relatively easy climbs demand a high degree of fitness, plus navigational and rope handling skills. Sometimes a climb can be tackled in a single day; in other cases, a party goes as far as a climbers' hut on the first afternoon, then makes the final ascent beginning early the next morning, in time to assault the peak and return to the base by dusk.

The 15,771-foot Mont-Blanc and its surrounding peaks offer climbers innumerable Himalayan challenges and require the highest level of competence. Sometimes the climb requires primarily technical skills; sometimes, as in the case of Mont-Blanc itself, the challenge lies primarily in the mountain's well-known sudden weather changes, which can render the visibility close to zero, and the danger of avalanches. The main center for climbs on the popular north ridge is Chamonix; the favorite ascent from there begins with a trip via cable car and train to Nid d'Aigle and then on to the Aiguille du Gouter hut for an overnight before the peak assault on the following day.

The Swiss cartographers Kummerly and Frey produce a pair of maps of the Alpine region as a whole. Individual sections of the Alps are best covered in the Didier et Richard 1:50,000 and 1:25,000 series. The *Vallot Guides,* published in French, assess the difficulty of all climbs on a scale that runs from *facile* (F), easy, through *extrêmement difficile* (ED), extremely difficult.

Further information is available from the *Fédération Française de la Montagne — FFM —* (16 Rue Louis Dardenne, Vanves 92170; phone: 41-08-00-00), the umbrella organization for the Alpine associations for the various individual regions; and the *Club Alpin Français* (24 Av. Laumière, Paris 75019; phone: 42-02-75-94), which coordinates 80 local divisions in the main French towns and mountain resorts and administers nearly all the high-altitude shelters.

PYRÉNÉES: Though this wall of mountains dividing France from Spain is one of Europe's most challenging ranges for the able climber, it is also ideal for the less experienced climber. That is in large part a result of the weather, which tends to be more reliable than in the Alps. But it is also because most of the summits are both relatively modest in stature and comfortably reached from the more than 50 huts operated by the *Club Alpin Français* and by the government authority that manages the 75-mile stretch of the mountains between the Col du Somport and the Cirque de Gavarnie.

The most popular of the rock climbs for which the Pyrénées are particularly noted are the walls around the Cirque de Gavarnie, a hollow measuring about half a mile in diameter with a floor at about 5,400 feet and peaks at 9,900 feet — the ascents here can challenge even the most competent mountaineers. The granite faces of the Balaitous, particularly in the west, the north face of the Vinnemale, the Pic du Midi d'Ossau, and the Pic Long are also good.

The best books on the area are *Pyrénées East* and *Pyrénées West,* published in Great Britain by West Col Productions and in France by the Ollivier/FEM series.

Boating:
France's Wonderful Waterways

Given France's vast coastline and its 5,000 miles of inland rivers, canals, and lakes, it's little wonder that when the weekend rolls around, scores of French pleasure-seekers roll back the tarps of their boats and head out for some serious cruising. Avid sailors can challenge the waters of the Atlantic or Mediterranean and dock overnight in a charming old port town for a fine seafood meal in a waterside café. Or they may relax on the tame inland lakes. The canoe or kayak enthusiast can find adventure on the Loire, Rhône, and Vézère rivers or in the whitewater of the Alps and Pyrénées. And then there are the leisurely cruises on hired craft through the canals of Burgundy, Bordeaux, and the south of France. Boating novices can sign up for any number of sailing, cruising, or canoeing courses of varying duration.

Foreigners sailing their own boats in France must have a *permis de circulation,* a license that is available free of charge at French government tourist offices in foreign countries; depending on the size and type of vessel, other permits may be necessary as well, so it's wise to check with the French tourist authorities before sailing to France. Communities along the French rivers usually have canoeing and kayak clubs to advise on conditions and arrange lessons and group outings.

Here are some choice destinations for boat-lovers of every sort.

SAILING

BRITTANY COAST: Many sailors rave about the Raz de Sein, that stretch of rugged water off the westernmost point in France between the Pointe de Raz and the stony, isolated Ile de Sein. The rocky scenery is unequaled anywhere, but the wind can be fierce, and widows on the island call these waters "the Sailors' Graveyard" — be prepared. Farther down the coast in the Baie de la Forêt are the lovely fishing ports of Pont-Aven, a favorite retreat of the painter Gauguin, and Concarneau, where 1- and 2-week sailing courses are available throughout the year. The island-filled Golfe de Morbihan west of Vannes offers an opportunity to go for a sail in a *sinagot,* a traditional coastal fisherman's boat. For sailors or those who simply like to watch sailboats, the *Tour de France à la Voile* (Sailing Tour of France) race has a stop in Perros-Guirac, on Brittany's north coast, in July. Many ports in Brittany offer sailing lessons. Information: Contact the *Fédération Française de Voile,* 55 Ave. Kléber, Paris 75016 (phone: 45-53-68-00) or the *Ecole de Voile les Glénans,* 1 Quai Louis-Blériot, Paris 75016 (phone: 45-20-01-40).

EASTERN MEDITERRANEAN COAST: The Port de Fos, just west of Marseilles, handles large commercial ships and is usually closed to pleasure craft. But on the other side of the peninsula west of the gulf is the mouth of the Grand Rhône, and from Port St-Louis-du-Rhône it's possible to drive on up to Arles, Cézanne's favorite hideaway. En route, just shy of the fork of the Petite Rhône, there's the exceptional bird sanctuary of the Camargue National Park. Near Sète at St-Gilles along the Petite Rhône is the fortification of Aigues-Mortes, whence St-Louis departed on an Egyptian crusade in 1248. Farther toward Sète and the Etang de Thau, a small bay, are the picturesque ports of Balaruc, Bouzigues, Marseillan, and Mèze, where there are sailing courses year-round. Information: *Comité Régional du Tourisme de PACA,* 2 Rue Henri-Barbusse, Marseilles 13006 (phone: 91-39-38-00).

NORTHERN COAST: The small port of St-Valéry-en-Caux, about 20 miles (32 km) west of Dieppe, just a bit removed from the heavy Channel traffic, makes a good starting point for northeasterly sails under the spectacular white cliffs that edge the English Channel. Before setting out, visit Notre Dame du Port, a 13th-century church and the former residence of Henri IV next door. In busy Dieppe, visit the bustling farmers' market on Saturday. The Somme estuary, farther along, is enlivened by the many varieties of birds that emigrate there; on one side, there's the beach-blessed Le Croitoy, and on the other, St-Valéry-sur-Somme, a recommended port of call and one of the many points from which you can navigate by canal to Paris. Sailing lessons are available in July and August. Information: *Comité Régional du Tourisme,* 46 Av. Foch, Evreux 27000 (phone: 32-33-79-00).

RIVIERA: The coastline of the Mediterranean teems with sailboats in summer, and it is easy to navigate the entire French coastline — perhaps stopping in Monte Carlo for an evening at the casino and then setting out for a couple of days in Corsica. However, the loveliest section is the stretch between Cap Croisette and Cassis, where there are scores of secluded *calanques,* the Mediterranean creeks with ports that are accessible only by water. The opportunity that these destinations offer to escape the madness of Marseilles and the other large Riviera harbors may well justify wrestling with a stiff eastern wind or even the mistral to reach them. Cassis is a charming port, with sand and pebble beaches, and in July and August, sailing courses lasting from 1 to 3 weeks are available. Information: *Maison de Cassis,* Pl. Pierre-Baragnon, Cassis 13260 (phone: 42-01-71-17).

SOUTHERN ATLANTIC COAST: The 125 miles of coastline along the Landes forest south of Bordeaux offer very few ports for yachts, and the Atlantic is generally rough and dangerous. However, there is nice, leisurely boating in the Bay of Arcachon and near St-Jean-de-Luz not far from the Spanish border. The former is relatively calm, and the port itself has fine beaches and oyster beds. The rocky coastline outside the latter is more challenging, but the port at Ciboure is small enough that it may be necessary to sail on into Spanish waters to find docking facilities. Information: *Comité Régional du Tourisme d'Aquitaine,* 21 Rue Grassi, Bordeaux 33000 (phone: 56-44-48-02).

CANOEING AND KAYAKING

Possibly because canoes and kayaks are so easily transported and because it's possible to take them out on so many waterways, canoeing and kayaking are extremely popular in France. As in North America, streams are graded in order of difficulty from classes I through VI, with category VI being the most difficult and therefore suited to only the most accomplished sportspersons.

AVEYRON: The Aveyron is only one of several fast-flowing rivers in the forested northwestern section of the *département* of Tarn; the Tarn and the Agôut also are recommended. Information: *Comité Régional du Tourisme,* 12 Rue Salambo, Toulouse 31200 (phone: 61-47-11-12).

DORDOGNE: The trip on the Dordogne River toward the Garonne is magnificent, especially the 75 miles or so before Sarlat-le-Canéda, with its forested gorges and limestone rocks. From Argentat to Trémolat, the water is category I and II. The only non-navigable point is at Beaulieu, about 15 miles downstream from Argentat, where it is necessary to portage past an obstruction. La Vézère, a tributary of the Dordogne, also is well-suited to canoeing; the usual trip is from Montignac to Les Eyzies. For white-water trips, with or without instruction, the Gorges de Vézère has sections classed I and II for beginners and II, III, and IV for experienced kayakers. Information: *Office Départemental du Tourisme de la Dordogne,* 16 Rue Wilson, Périgueux 24000 (phone: 53-53-44-35); or the *Maison du Périgord,* 6 Rue Gomboust, Paris 75001 (phone: 47-42-09-15).

LOIRE: France's longest river, which runs from its source high in the Massif Central to Nantes in Brittany and its mouth in the Atlantic, offers a wealth of possibilities. There are some lovely ruins of a château not far from the source, between Arlempdes and Goudet, and there are torrential waters farther downstream at the Gorges de Peyredeyre. The river is navigable all the way to the Atlantic and is rated category I from Roanne to Nantes. Information: *Comité Régional du Tourisme,* Pl. Commerce, Nantes 44000 (phone: 40-48-24-20).

RHÔNE: One of the most popular rivers among French canoeing and kayaking enthusiasts because it is navigable for almost 500 miles, from the Swiss city of Brig all the way to the Mediterranean. Anyone who manages to go the distance ends up on the Riviera — a suitable reward. The water is category II from Geneva to Lyons, category I the rest of the way.

VÉZÈRE: This tranquil river in the Dordogne is perfect both for newcomers to the canoe-kayak scene and for experienced boaters who are looking for not too strenuous good times. Except just after a storm, when the waters swell and the current speeds up, the waters are swift but not dangerous. Points of interest en route include the unusual caves in the hills around Les Eyzies and the charming medieval village of Sarlat farther downstream. Information: *Office Départemental du Tourisme de la Dordogne,* 16 Rue Wilson, Périgueux 24000 (phone: 53-53-44-35).

RIVER CRUISING

There hardly exists a finer way to see the French countryside than to travel on a slow boat along some section of the nation's thousands of miles of river. Dozens of companies in France rent riverboats for leisurely cruises, with or without captains and accommodations. A handful of American firms also offer cruising through specified areas.

Below are five organizations that can provide information and ideas:

Blue Lines (Le Grand Bassin, BP21, Castelnaudary 11400; phone: 68-23-17-51). Rents hundreds of boats, all with sleeping quarters, on waterways all over France.

Floating Through Europe (271 Madison Ave., New York, NY 10016; phone: 212-685-5600). Operates leisurely cruises complete with guide, comfortable sleeping quarters, and wonderful meals.

Maine-Anjou Rivières (Chenillé Changé, le Lion d'Angers 49220; phone: 41-95-10-83; fax: 41-95-10-52). A reliable and friendly operation based in the Loire Valley north of Angers that organizes boat rentals throughout France. Crafts are available in all sizes and are all luxuriously fitted; no permit is required to pilot the boat yourself.

Rives de France (172 Bd. Berthier, Paris 75017; phone: 46-22-10-86). Rents self-pilot boats throughout France.

Syndicat National des Loueurs de Bateaux de Plaisance (Port de la Bourdonnais, Paris 75007; phone: 45-55-10-49). Can advise about riverboat rentals with or without sleeping quarters.

BRITTANY: The Nantes–Brest Canal, which ribbons through the heart of Brittany, provides access to many fine country hotels. But since the cruising speed on all canals in Brittany is limited to 3.5 mph (5.5 km), be prepared to take your time. The River Vilaine, which flows north to St-Malo, is another good destination. Information: *Comité de Promotion Touristique des Canaux Bretons,* 12 Rue de Jemmapes, Nantes 44000 (phone: 40-47-42-94) or the *Comité des Canaux Bretons et des Voies Navigables de l'Ouest,* 7 Rue de la Clavurevie, Nantes 44000 (phone: 40-20-20-62).

BURGUNDY: The Canal du Nivernais provides a window on the beauties of Burgundy. Stopping every half hour or so to pass through the locks and exchange pleasantries with the lockkeepers, tasting the marvelous wines and cheeses of the region, and docking in the afternoon to visit an interesting old Roman church or a charming medieval town like Corbigny make for an unforgettable cruise. A good starting point is Auxerre, which has a splendid Gothic cathedral. Most boats have full living accommodations. Information: *Office du Tourisme,* Pl. Darcy, Dijon 21022 (phone: 80-43-42-12).

PARIS: Everyone knows about the *bateaux-mouches* that parade from morning to evening along the Seine. Less well known, but perhaps even more charming, are the morning and afternoon cruises along the Canal St-Martin, between the métro stops at Jean-Jaurès and Bastille, and the full-day excursions on the Canal de l'Ourcq, which take in some lovely green areas starting at the Paris-Bassin de la Villette near the métro stop at Jean-Jaurès. Information: *Office du Tourisme,* 127 Champs-Elysées, Paris 75008 (phone: 47-23-61-72).

THE SOUTH: The Canal du Midi, which runs southeast from the center of Toulouse through the corn and wheat fields of the Lauragais to Carcassonne, Béziers, and the Languedoc coast, gives you a real feeling for the south of France, with its red tile rooftops, its powder blue sky, and its dark green cypress trees at every turn. Most boats in the area offer accommodations and meal facilities to allow for extensive cruises. Information: *Syndicat d'Initiative,* Donjon du Capitole, Rue Lafayette, Toulouse 31000 (phone: 61-23-32-00).

FOR MORE INFORMATION

The following organizations can provide countrywide information on a variety of on-the-water subjects. (For further information, see *Traveling by Ship* in GETTING READY TO GO.)

Fédération Française de Canoe/Kayak, BP 58, Joinville-le-Pont 94340 (phone: 48-89-39-89). Specifics on local canoeing and kayaking clubs.

Fédération Française de la Voile, 55 Av. Kléber, Paris 75016 (phone: 45-53-68-00). Details about sailing in France.

For the Mind

Memorable Museums and Monuments

 The stunning achievements of French art are an exhilarating hymn to human possibility, from the halls of Mont-St-Michel to the shores of Cap d'Antibes, from the prehistoric cave paintings of Les Eyzies to the science fiction Tinkertoy that is Paris's *Centre Georges Pompidou.* There is a breathtaking elegance to French artistic endeavors, whatever the century. It can be seen in the intricate weave of an Aubusson tapestry, in the airy geometry of the Eiffel Tower, in the angular grace of a Lautrec chanteuse; everywhere, the cool complexity of the Gallic mind is in evidence, together with that exquisite sense of taste, as orderly and yet as exuberantly fruitful as a Burgundy vineyard.

Sip these pleasures — don't gulp them. Mix monuments with merriments. Try a few casual nibbles at a museum rather than a single marathon banquet. As soon as you feel a sense of duty creeping over you, it's time to look for the nearest glass of beaujolais. And always remember that a rainy Monday in February is far better for quiet contemplation than tourist-mad midsummer. But if you must travel in August, at least present yourself at the gates for their early morning opening — or visit at lunch hour, when the hordes usually forsake Leonardo da Vinci for pâté.

MUSÉE FESCH, Ajaccio, Corsica: This early 19th-century palace belonged to Cardinal Fesch, Napoleon's uncle, and is home to some 16,000 paintings assembled by this ecclesiastical man. Reopened in 1990 (the museum was inaugurated in 1852) after many years of extensive renovation, it now is among France's best museums. It looks out onto the Bay of Ajaccio and its white, modern setting is perfect for some of the finest Italian primitive and Renaissance paintings found outside the *Uffizi* and *Pitti Palace* museums in Florence and the *Louvre.* Especially noteworthy are Botticelli's *Madonna and Child,* and Tura's *Madonna and Child with St. Jerome.* Closed Tuesdays. Information: *Musée Fesch,* 50 Rue Fesch, Ajaccio, Corsica 20000 (phone: 95-21-48-17).

MUSÉE TOULOUSE-LAUTREC, Albi, Tarn: Born of noble family in this charming town on the banks of the Tarn, Henri de Toulouse-Lautrec, that crippled and tormented genius, became a creature of the Parisian night and immortalized its prostitutes, cabaret dancers, and café dwellers. The museum installed within the austere, brooding walls of the 13th-century Palais de la Berbie bursts with the multicolored animation of Lautrec's special world. The more than 500 works here, including the famous posters that marked the beginning of a whole new art form, make this the richest Lautrec collection anywhere. Nearby, you can visit the artist's family's house, the Hôtel du Bosc (open in July and August). And don't miss the red brick monolith of the Basilique Ste-Cécile, on the same square as the museum (see *Celebrated Châteaux and Cathedrals,* below). Closed Tuesdays in off-season. Information: *Musée D'Albi,* Palais de la Berbie, Albi 81000 (phone: 63-54-14-09).

MUSÉE PICASSO, Antibes, Alpes-Maritimes: Picasso lived and worked at the 16th-century Château Grimaldi in 1946 — one of the most prolific years of his career — and later donated the entire production of that happy period to the town of Antibes on the condition that the works remain forever at their birthplace. The 23 major paintings of the collection, displayed in a stunning site overlooking the sea, fairly sing with the Mediterranean's marine joys; there are also lithographs, drawings, etchings, and a fine assortment of ceramics. Wander out on the exotic, flower-filled terrace to gawk at the gull's-eye view that kept Picasso inspired. Closed Tuesdays and November. Information: *Musée Picasso,* Château Grimaldi, Pl. du Château, Antibes 06600 (phone: 93-33-67-67).

TAPESTRIES OF AUBUSSON, Aubusson, Creuse: During the Renaissance, the methods and products of this ancient Limousin town, which had been an important center of tapestry weaving as early as the 9th century, were world-renowned; during the 20th century, they have had their own renaissance at the hands of master weaver Jean Lurçat. On the Avenue des Lissiers, the *Centre Culturel et Artistique Jean Lurçat,* a tapestry museum, documents the art from ancient days to the present; there are also films and animated demonstrations. And in the Rue Vieille, it's possible to visit an ancient weaver's studio, the *Maison du Vieux Tapissier,* and a score of private galleries full of tapestries to buy — or just ogle. Information: *Syndicat d'Initiative,* Rue Vieille, Aubusson 23200 (phone: 55-66-32-12).

CITÉ DE CARCASSONNE, Carcassonne, Aude: This fortress-village perched on a hilltop above the Garonne Valley, a movie-set forest of turrets, battlements, and drawbridges, is Europe's most perfect example of medieval military architecture. Romans, Gauls, Visigoths, Arabs, Franks, and the royalty of France assembled it over a period of some 13 centuries, and the celebrated architect Eugène Viollet-le-Duc restored it lovingly in the 19th century. For the best views of its 52 towers, make the promenade around the Lices between the inner and outer ramparts, starting from the Porte Narbonnaise. Don't fail to see the Basilique St-Nazaire, a wonderful marriage of Romanesque and Gothic blessed by Renaissance stained glass. Whatever you do, stay until nightfall; the illumination of the Cité is high drama. Information: *Syndicat d'Initiative,* 15 Bd. Camille-Pelletan, Carcassonne 11012 (phone: 68-25-07-04).

CAVES OF LES EYZIES, Les Eyzies-de-Tayac, Dordogne: Ever since the caves at Lascaux were closed to the public, sleepy little Les Eyzies, at the confluence of the Vézère and the Beune rivers, has been France's center for the prehistoric. Of the huge numbers of cave dwellings unearthed by extensive excavations in the cliffs that rise above the town, most fascinating are the Grottes de Font-de-Gaume, with their 200 remarkably fluid wall paintings of 15,000-year-old bison, deer, mammoths, and horses colored with red and black oxides; the Grotte des Combarelles, for the 300 engravings; the Abri du Cap-Blanc, for its superb frieze of horses; and the Grotte du Grand Roc, which is rich in stalactite formations and offers, from its entrance, a panorama of the entire valley. The way so-called primitive man used the contours of the cave walls to convey the shape and bulk of the animal he was painting is particularly fascinating. The *Musée National de la Préhistoire,* installed in an 11th-century castle, houses one of the world's most important collections of prehistoric tools and weapons, tombs, ornaments, and Cro-Magnon skeletons — and models and explanations enough to help you understand what you saw in the caves. Note that the best caves are closed on Tuesdays and from November 25 to December 25 annually. The caves of Lascaux, one of the greatest prehistoric finds in Europe, have been re-created by artists from the *Beaux-Arts* in Paris, using the same vegetable dyes and oxides used by primitive man, in the hills above Montignac, about 12 miles (19 km) from Les Eyzies. In nearby Thonac is the *Centre d'Art Préhistorique du Thot/Espace Cro-Magnon,* where outdoor re-creations of scenes from the daily life of Cro-Magnon man are exhibited. Information: *Syndicat d'Initiative des Eyzies,* Les Eyzies-de-Tayac 24620 (phone: 53-06-97-05).

MUSÉE NATIONAL ADRIEN-DUBOUCHÉ, Limoges, Haute-Vienne: For centuries, this town has been Europe's most celebrated center of the porcelain and enamel crafts, and its museums are consecrated to their glories. The *Musée National Adrien-Dubouché* has the world's most extensive porcelain collection, more than 10,000 pieces in all. Delft and Wedgwood and the work of China and France — modern and ancient alike — are all represented. The *Musée Municipal de l'Evêché* shows off 300 of the finest Limoges enamels from the 12th century to just yesterday; and the Syndicat d'Initiative will arrange a visit to the studio of an artisan currently working in the discipline. The *Biennale Internationale de l'Email,* a summer-long porcelain fair held in even-numbered years, attracts artists from all over the globe. Information: *Musée National Adrien-Dubouché,* Pl. Winston-Churchill, Limoges 87000 (phone: 55-77-45-58); or *Syndicat d'Initiative,* Bd. Fleurus, Limoges 87000 (phone: 55-34-46-87).

LOURDES, Hautes-Pyrénées: Every year, more than 4 million people, the faithful and the curious alike, flock to this mountain village where, in 1858, a 14-year-old farm girl named Bernadette Soubirous had her famed visions of the Virgin Mary. The official recognition of this miracle by the Catholic church has made Lourdes one of the world's major pilgrimage sites. Thousands of pilgrims — particularly the ill and the handicapped — join in passionate group prayer. Cast-off crutches dangle at the entrance to the Cave of Apparitions. Although the town is full of religious supermarkets stocked with windup Virgins and Holy Water hip flasks, Lourdes is unique and unsettling, whatever your faith — or lack of it. Information: *Syndicat d'Initiative,* Pl. du Champ-Commun, Lourdes 65100 (phone: 62-94-15-64).

LE MONT-ST-MICHEL, Manche: Normandy's answer to the Pyramids, this 11th-century Benedictine monastery carved out of natural granite is one of France's — and the world's — most spectacular sights. On what was once an island separated from the mainland by quicksand shoals, the Bishop of Avranches built a shrine in the 8th century. Later, the original Romanesque church flared up into a Gothic riot of spires and flying buttresses that all seem to swirl and spiral heavenward. Since 1879, a 2,000-yard causeway has connected the mainland and the island's single main street, thereby permitting visitors to flock to the island in droves. Be sure to sample the special *omelettes Mère Poulard* at the restaurant of the same name, on the way up to the abbey gates. Better still, plan in advance to stay overnight in one of the unpretentious small inns on the island itself. Once the day tourists are gone, the place has a resonant silence that speaks more eloquently of its long history than all the tourist literature ever written. Information: *Syndicat d'Initiative,* Porte du Roi, Le Mont-St-Michel 50116 (phone: 33-60-14-30).

MUSÉE NATIONAL DE L'AUTOMOBILE, Mulhouse, Haut-Rhin: The *National Automobile Museum* documents the history of the automobile with some 500 cars representing nearly 100 different makes, from an 1878 Jacquot to a freshly minted Formula I Ferrari — a collection that two Swiss industrialists forfeited in lieu of paying taxes owed to the French government. Ranged between mile-and-a-half-long rows of antique lanterns, the jam-packed exhibition contains Hispano-Suizas, vintage Rolls-Royces (including a 1910 Silver Ghost with silver-plated fittings), and gems like the Dion Bouton (like an open stagecoach on wheels) and the Bugatti T16 Garros, which the French aviator had built with a transparent plastic body that reveals the motor, not to mention the vehicles that once belonged to Charlie Chaplin, Juan Fangio, and the Emperor Bao-Dai — all in perfect, gleaming condition. See also *Alsace,* DIRECTIONS. Information: *Musée National de l'Automobile,* 192 Av. de Colmar, Mulhouse 68100 (phone: 89-42-29-17); or the *Office du Tourisme,* 9 Rue Maréchal-Foch, Mulhouse 68100 (phone: 89-45-68-31).

MUSÉE NATIONAL MARC CHAGALL, Nice, Alpes-Maritimes: A collection of 17 major canvases, enriched by all of their preparatory sketches, as well as hundreds of gouaches, engravings, lithographs, sculptures, mosaics, and tapestries make this wonderful institution a concentrated communion with the spirit of one of our century's most original creators. The unity of Chagall's poetic vision of man, nature, and the Bible is clear and present in every room. And the lovely grounds and gardens, the reflecting pool, and the chapel glowing with stained glass all enhance the experience. While in the area, consider making a side trip to visit the *Fondation Maeght,* a splendid modern art museum that contains yet other works of Chagall and his contemporaries, and to the nearby hill town of St-Paul-de-Vence (see also "Special Places" in *Nice,* THE CITIES). Information: *Musée National Marc Chagall,* Av. du Docteur-Ménard, Nice 06000 (phone: 93-81-75-75).

ROMAN AMPHITHEATER, Nîmes, Gard: A virtual twin of the arena in nearby Arles, the Nîmes amphitheater, which dates from the 1st century AD, is one of the most stunningly preserved Roman remains in Europe. Used as a fortress by the Visigoths, it had long since degenerated into ghetto dwellings pieced together with chunks of Roman rubble when it was rehabilitated in the 19th century. But now, every spring and summer, more than 20,000 spectators jam its elliptical grandstands for bullfights. Equally well preserved is that other jewel of Nîmes, the *Maison Carrée,* a Greek temple from the 1st century BC that looks like a piece of the Acropolis on permanent loan. Information: *Office du Tourisme,* 6 Rue August (phone: 66-67-29-11) or *Comité Départemental du Tourisme du Gard,* 3 Pl. des Arènes, Nîmes 30000 (phone: 66-21-02-51).

LE PONT DU GARD, Remoulins, Gard: Another wondrous and perfectly preserved relic of ancient Rome's far-flung empire: a 3-tiered, 180-foot-high, 2,000-year-old stretch of the aqueduct that once brought water to Nîmes from the mountain springs near Uzes. The pastoral setting in the middle of the Gardon Valley has a way of putting you in closer contact with the grandeur that was Rome than the more obvious and far more frequented sites in Italian cities. It's even possible to walk across the bridge where the Roman waters once ran, although it's very dangerous (particularly the top tier) when there are strong winds. About 14 miles (22 km) northeast of Nîmes on the way to Avignon. Information: *Comité Départemental du Tourisme du Gard,* 3 Pl. des Arènes, Nîmes 30000 (phone: 66-21-02-51).

CENTRE GEORGES POMPIDOU, Paris: Known to Parisians as "the Beaubourg," this potpourri of multicolored geometry was a source of great controversy when it first splashed onto the sober Gothic cityscape in 1977. Since then, its annual admissions have been more than double that of the staid Louvre, as French and foreigners alike come to savor its quixotic feast of exhibitions with the basic theme of "the art and culture of the 20th century" — anything from Einstein memorials and the development of the pinball machine to solar heating and disco dancing. The Beaubourg also has a vast library and a regular program of concerts, poetry readings, and dance recitals. But it would be worth a visit if only for the sci-fi architecture, the fishbowl escalators, and the plaza outside, where swords are swallowed, fire is eaten, and commedia dell' arte is enacted by roving mimes. Open weekdays, except Tuesdays, from noon to 10 PM; weekends from 10 AM to 10 PM. Information: *Centre National d'Art et de Culture Georges Pompidou,* 120 Rue St-Martin, Paris 75191 (phone: 42-77-12-33).

JEU DE PAUME, Paris: Renovated and reopened as a gallery for contemporary art in 1991, this is the latest expansion in the "Grand Louvre" project that began with the opening of the I.M. Pei pyramids. One of the most historic buildings in Paris, the Jeu de Paume was originally an indoor tennis court for royalty; it gained a place in history when, in 1789, delegates met here to declare their independence, marking the beginning of the French Revolution. Extensively modernized, the museum now houses exhibitions of contemporary works from the last 20 to 30 years, including those of Takis, Broodthaers, and Dubuffet. Previously home to the Louvre's overcrowded Impressionist collection (now in the Musée d'Orsay), it has video and conference areas available. Open

Tuesdays through Fridays from noon to 7 PM (Tuesdays until 9:30 PM); weekends from 10 AM to 7 PM. Information: *Jeu de Paume,* Pl. de la Concorde, Paris 75001 (phone: 47-03-12-50; fax: 42-60-39-05).

MUSÉE DU LOUVRE, Paris: This colossus on the Seine, born in 1200 as a fortress and transformed over the centuries from Gothic mass to Renaissance palace, served as the royal residence in the 16th and 17th centuries until it was supplanted by suburban Versailles, becoming a museum when François I donated a dozen masterpieces from his private collection. Napoleon later turned it into a glittering warehouse of artistic booty from the nations he conquered. Today its 200 galleries cover some 40 acres; to view all 297,000 items in the collections in no more than the most cursory fashion, it would be necessary to walk some 8 miles. In addition to the *Mona Lisa, Venus de Milo,* and the *Winged Victory of Samothrace,* it has many delights that easily are overlooked — Vermeer's *Lace Maker* and Holbein's portrait of Erasmus, for instance; not to mention Van der Weyden's *Braque Triptych,* Ingres's *Turkish Bath,* Dürer's *Self-Portrait,* Cranach's naked and red-hatted *Venus,* and the exquisite 4,000-year-old Egyptian woodcarving known as the *Handmaiden of the Dead.* More of our favorites include Michelangelo's *The Slaves,* Goya's *Marquesa de la Solana,* Watteau's clown, *Gilles,* and his *Embarkation to Cythera,* Raphael's great portrait, *Baldassare,* Veronese's *Marriage at Cana,* Titian's masterpiece, *Man with a Glove,* both *Mary Magdalen* and *The Card Sharps* by Georges de la Tour, Rembrandt's *Bathsheba,* and Frans Hals's *Bohemian Girl.* Try to save time for any one of David's glories: *Madame Recamier, The Oath of the Horatti, The Lictors Bringing Back to Brutus the Body of His Son,* or *The Coronation of Napoleon and Josephine.* And don't miss *Liberty Leading the People* and *The Barque of Dante,* both by Delacroix, and Courbet's *The Artist's Studio, Burial at Ornans,* and *Stags Fighting* — just for openers! I. M. Pei's controversial glass pyramid (there are actually three), which was unveiled in time for the celebrations of the bicentennial of the French Revolution in 1989, opened subterranean galleries and constituted a step toward expanding gallery space by about 80%. Open Mondays and Wednesdays from 9 AM to 9:45 PM; Thursdays through Sundays from 9 AM to 6 PM. Information: *Musée du Louvre,* Palais du Louvre, Paris 75058 (phone: 40-20-51-51 for a recording in both French and English or 40-20-50-50 for more detailed information).

MUSÉE D'ORSAY, Paris: The Impressionist paintings that once crowded intimately into the joyfully informal *Jeu de Paume* museum have found a more spacious and sober home. The brilliant transformation of a vast turn-of-the-century glass and cast-iron train station into a museum has brought the best artistic production of France from 1848 to 1914 under one vaulted, translucent roof. Now Degas, Lautrec, Monet, and Renoir are gloriously displayed in specially designed spaces within this former railroad-cathedral, along with the works of 600 other painters and 500 sculptors. No detail of light, humidity, or acoustics has been left to chance, making this voyage around the art world a very comfortable one. Don't miss the museum's pièce de résistance — the Van Goghs on the top floor, glowing under the northern Parisian skylight. Open 10 AM to 6 PM daily, except Mondays; Sunday mornings and in summer the museum opens at 9 AM, and Thursday evenings it stays open until 9:45 PM. Information: *Musée d'Orsay,* 1 Rue de Bellechasse, Paris 75007 (phone: 40-49-48-14).

MUSÉE PICASSO, Paris: Showing works still amazingly modern, this museum is in a 17th-century mansion in Paris's oldest neighborhood. It houses a part of the collection with which Picasso could never bring himself to part, and gives a panoramic view of the versatile doyen of this century's art. His varied career went from the contemplative self-portrait painted in shades of blue in 1921, through the cubist newspapers and guitars, to the 1961 iron-sheet sculpture of a soccer player looking like an ice cream on a stick. Especially interesting is the master's collection of works by other artists. Open Mondays and Thursdays through Sundays from 9:15 AM to 5 PM; Wednesdays from 9:15 AM to 10 PM. Information: *Musée Picasso,* 5 Rue de Thorigny, Paris 75003 (phone: 42-71-25-21).

MUSÉE RODIN, Paris: This is one of France's most complete and satisfying museum experiences. Ambling in a leisurely way through one of the great 18th-century aristocratic homes and its grounds, it's possible to follow the evolution of the career of that genius of modern sculpture Auguste Rodin. Among the broad terraces and in the serene and elegant gardens are scattered fabled statues like the *Thinker,* the *Bourgeois de Calais,* the superb statues of Honoré de Balzac and Victor Hugo, and the stunning *Gate of Hell,* on which the master labored a lifetime, and *Les Bavardes,* a sculpture by Rodin's mistress Camille Claudel, along with much, much more. The master's celebrated *Ugolin* group is placed dramatically in the middle of a pond. The museum boutique sells reproductions of the major works. Open daily except Mondays from 10 AM to 4:30 PM. Information: *Musée National Auguste Rodin,* 77 Rue de Varenne, Paris 75007 (phone: 47-05-01-34).

LA STE-CHAPELLE, Paris: Tucked away in the monumental complex of the Palais de Justice, the 13th-century Ste-Chapelle was built by the monarch Louis IX (St-Louis) on the site of the former palace of the early kings of the Capetian dynasty as a reliquary for the recently obtained Sacred Crown of Thorns. The 15 soaring stained glass windows, with more than 1,100 brilliantly colored and exquisitely detailed miniature scenes of biblical life, are one of the unquestioned masterpieces of medieval French art, and the graceful, gleaming spire is one of the city's most beautiful and understated landmarks — particularly stunning on a sunny day. Open daily from 10 AM to 4:40 PM. Information: *La Ste-Chapelle,* 4 Bd. du Palais, Paris 75004 (phone: 43-54-30-09).

LA TOUR EIFFEL, Paris: Measuring 1,056 feet in height, 412 feet in breadth, and 8,500 tons in weight, this famous pre-fab — the world's first, whose 18,000 pieces are joined by 2,500,000 rivets — was built to commemorate the centenary of the French Revolution. At the time of its March 1889 inauguration, it was the world's tallest structure; early critics predicted it would keel over in the first high wind, reviling it as a grotesque edifice that marred the city's skyline. From the very start, it was destined to be dismantled, and when its lease expired in 1909, it escaped destruction only by a narrow margin. Since then, it has been scaled by alpine climbers, a plane has flown through it, and an elephant was hoisted up into it. To celebrate its centennial, the lights that illuminate it at night were reworked — a dazzling success. Hundreds upon thousands of visitors have braved the 1,789-step climb to its summit (although most take the elevator), and it is safe to say that visiting Paris and missing the E.T. is like visiting France and skipping Paris. There are three snack shops as well as three restaurants in the tower. Open daily from 10 AM to 11 PM; in the summer from 10 AM to 11 PM. Information: *La Tour Eiffel,* Champ-de-Mars, Paris 75007 (phone: 45-55-91-11).

ROCAMADOUR, Lot: This ancient shrine-city in the south of France, a reputed source of miraculous cures whose origins are wrapped in a tangled cloth of legend, has been a goal of pilgrims for 900 years. Breathtakingly built onto the face of a sheer rock canyon wall some 500 feet above the gorge, the town has seven churches teetering on its blade of limestone cliff, a cluster of houses clinging precariously to its rock, massive fortified gates, a citadel, and a château, all stacked on top of one another as if to ascend to the azure Périgord sky. When seen at dawn in spring or at sunset in summer, Rocamadour is almost as intoxicating as the tantalizing quail steeped in gin that the local restaurants brew. Since the village likes to call itself the "Deuxième Site de la France" — the second best tourist attraction in the country after Le Mont-St-Michel — there are a few too many souvenir vendors along the sloping main street. But if you use your imagination you will not be disappointed. Information: *Syndicat d'Initiative,* Hôtel de Ville, Rocamadour 46350 (phone: 65-33-62-59).

The Liveliest Arts:
Theater, Opera, and Music

 When a Frenchman utters the word *province,* usually with a certain wrinkling of the nose, he is referring to any part of the country that isn't Paris. Nothing of any significant artistic interest was deemed to occur there, for the capital held an unquestioned monopoly on culture. But the byword of the past decade has been *décentralisation,* and the theatrical-musical map of France has undergone some startling changes. *Province* now fairly bristles with first-rate repertory companies and orchestras financed by generous subsidies from the central and regional governments. Top French directors like Patrice Chéreau and Roger Planchon chose working class areas in Nanterre and Lyons as their base of operations. The renowned center for electronic music is situated in the otherwise quiet town of Bourges. The operas of Nancy, Toulouse, and Strasbourg have been outdoing their staid Parisian cousins in critical acclaim.

Many of these companies spend a good part of their season on tour, bringing the word and the note to other parts of the country and to smaller towns in their region. So keep an eye on kiosks and wall posters; if you miss the *Théâtre de la Salamandre* in Lille, you might still catch it in some Breton upland village.

And don't bypass an evening in the theater just because your French is a high school relic, because it's a fine way to become a part of local life. In your favor is the current style for splashy, highly visual productions where spectacle trumps text. Where classics are concerned, English copies generally can be found in a city of any size — and at any rate, France's most-performed playwright is the *formidable* Guillaume Shakespeare.

CATHÉDRALE NOTRE-DAME, Chartres, Eure-et-Loir: Some 20 years ago, a massive restoration of the cathedral's 14th-century organ once again placed it among Europe's noblest instruments. Frequent recitals, masses, an organ festival held in the spring, and an international competition should give most visitors plenty of opportunity to hear the instrument's rich and majestic tones swelling and rising into the cathedral's celestial heights. And only about 58 miles (93 km) away, at that other Notre-Dame in Paris, there are concerts by France's foremost organists every Sunday afternoon. Information: *Syndicat d'Initiative,* Place de la Cathédrale, BP 289, Chartres 28007 (phone: 37-21-50-00).

CENTRE DRAMATIQUE NATIONAL DES ALPES, Grenoble, Isère: Grenoble was one of the first of the provincial cities to be alloted one of the cultural centers known as Maisons de la Culture during the reign of de Gaulle's renowned minister André Malraux. The *Centre des Alpes,* like many another of the more successful centers, eventually became a flourishing theater group. The elegant and original productions often dismantle and reassemble traditional works like *Lorenzaccio* and *King Lear* with a flashy theatricality; the productions are always lively, often controversial, and never predictable. Information: *Centre Dramatique National des Alpes,* 4 Rue Paul-Claudel, Grenoble 38000 (phone: 76-25-54-14) or 61 Rue Leconte-de-l'Isle, Grenoble 38000 (phone: 76-09-03-65).

ORCHESTRE NATIONAL DE LILLE, Lille, Nord: The thriving commercial-industrial complex of Lille-Roubaix-Tourcoing, just at the Belgian border, enjoys one of the richest cultural lives outside Paris. This excellent young orchestra is under the direction of Jean-Claude Casadesus of the famous French musical dynasty, and he has stocked it with the finest new talent. If you have trouble hearing them on their home ground, you may just as well find them performing at major music festivals like the one at

Aix-en-Provence. Information: *Orchestre National de Lille,* 3 Pl. Mendès-France, Lille 59000 (phone: 20-54-67-00).

THÉÂTRE DE LA SALAMANDRE, Lille, Nord: One of the first-ranking provincial theaters subsidized by the national government, this company of 15 performs under the direction of the exciting Gildas Bourdet. The repertoire may include anything from works by Racine and Corneille, those twin pillars of French classical theater, to Gorky's *Lower Depths* or stage versions of Jack London stories. An offer to perform with this troupe is prestigious enough to pull first class talent away from Paris. Information: *Théâtre de la Salamandre,* Pl. Général-de-Gaulle, Lille 59200 (phone: 20-40-10-20).

AUDITORIUM MAURICE RAVEL, Lyons, Rhône: Part of an architectural complex that also includes a huge tower-shaped hotel and a shopping center, this auditorium is an enormous, ultramodern music palace whose stage is surrounded by a horseshoe-shaped seating area. Concertgoers might hear anything from a flute sonata to Beethoven's "Ninth" — the spaces and the acoustics are equally suited to both — and all the top names in French music appear in the course of any year. In September of odd-numbered years, the auditorium hosts a *Biennale de la Musique Française.* Information: *Auditorium Maurice Ravel,* Pl. Charles-de-Gaulle, Lyons 69003 (phone: 78-60-37-13).

THÉÂTRE NATIONAL POPULAIRE, Villeurbanne-Lyons, Rhône: In the working class suburb of Villeurbanne, the *TNP* has been France's most successful experiment in bringing dynamic theater to a wider, less educated audience, and with the support of local management and labor agencies, it has built a huge permanent roll of subscription holders that includes patricians and proletarians alike. Director Roger Planchon, one of the boy wonders of French theater, alternates easily between startling new visions of classics like Molière's *Tartuffe* and freshly minted works by young unknowns. Whatever happens in Lyons is usually the talk of Paris. Information: *Théâtre National Populaire,* 8 Pl. Docteur-Lazare-Goujon, Villeurbanne-Lyons 69627 (phone: 78-03-30-30).

COMPAGNIE ROLAND PETIT, Marseilles, Bouches-du-Rhône: France's best-known dance company, which makes its home in Marseilles but travels incessantly both at home and abroad, presents dance pieces that cross the austerity of the classical tradition with American musical comedy brashness to produce a personable style all its own that is never dark, stark, or aggressively experimental. Since all of this is further enlivened by Zizi Jeanmaire (Madame Petit), the ageless and inimitable prima ballerina (although she now only dances about twice a year), the *compagnie* provides a fine introduction for people who secretly are worried that they may be bored by ballet. Don't miss the marvelously original *Coppelia,* in which the character that most companies portray as a lonely old man is a decadent roué in white tie and tails who attempts to bring to life the doll he has created, not to be the daughter he never had — but as a lover. Information: *Ballet National de Marseille Roland Petit,* 1 Pl. Auguste-François-Carli, Marseilles (phone: 91-42-43-43 or 91-47-94-88).

ORCHESTRE PHILHARMONIE DE LORRAINE, Metz, Moselle: The entire population of this stately town on the banks of the Moselle is music-mad and music-proud, and at any given performance at the ornate, 19th-century *Théâtre Municipal* those who manage to procure a ticket will find themselves surrounded by an audience of both long-haired, tight-jeaned high schoolers and elders of the Légion d'Honneur — and a great many others in between. The orchestra excels especially at works by composers in the royal family of the French repertoire — Berlioz, Bizet, Debussy, Fauré, Franck, Gounod, and Saint-Saëns. Information: *Orchestre Philharmonie de Lorraine,* 57 Rue Chambière, Metz 57000 (phone: 87-32-66-30) and the *Théâtre Municipal de Metz,* Pl. Comédie, Metz 57000 (phone: 87-75-40-50).

THÉÂTRE DES AMANDIERS, Nanterre (near Paris), Hauts de Seine: Known for its continually evolving and inventive style, the theater is now under the hands of impressario Jean-Pierre Vincent, whose career has taken him all the way from actor with the theatrical school at the Lyçée Louis-le-Grand, in 1959, to administrator of the *Comédie Française* in 1983. Recent presentations have included such time-honored classics as the Greek trilogy *Oedipe et les Oiseaux, Oedipe Tyran,* and *Oedipe à Colone* by Sophocles, but a trip to the box office can turn up any number of theatrical surprises. About 20 minutes by the *RER* city-rail from downtown Paris. Information: *Théâtre des Amandiers,* 7 Av. Pablo-Picasso, Nanterre 92022 (phone: 46-14-70-70).

LA COMÉDIE-FRANÇAISE, Paris: The undisputed dowager queen of French theater, as much a national monument as the Eiffel Tower, this dramatic doyenne presents a steady diet of lavish productions of great classics by Corneille, Racine, Molière, Rostand, and the happy few 20th-century playwrights like Anouilh, Giraudoux, and Sartre who have been received into the inner circle of French culture. The *CF* is streamlining its fin-de-siècle image, but even at its stodgiest, it's well worth seeing. Information: *La Comédie-Française,* 2 Rue de Richelieu, Paris 75001 (phone: 40-15-00-15).

IRCAM, Paris: The versatile musicians of this *Institut de Recherche et de Coopération Acoustique Musique,* France's current center of contemporary music activity, perform in the various auditoriums of the *Centre Georges Pompidou* — including the *Salle Polivalente,* whose rotating walls, rising floor, and lowering ceiling make it the last word in acoustical acrobatics. Computers are as common as clarinets, and the whole enterprise is under the aegis of Pierre Boulez, who conducts some of the major *IRCAM* concerts. Information: *IRCAM, Centre Georges Pompidou,* 31 Rue St-Merri, Paris 75004 (phone: 42-77-12-33).

MAISON DE RADIO FRANCE, Paris: This round white fortress on the banks of the Seine is mission control for French radio and television. It also is the principal residence of two of the country's finest orchestras, the *Orchestre National de France* and the *Nouvel Orchestre Philharmonique,* which subdivides into a number of smaller ensembles specializing in various instrumental combinations or musical periods. Consequently, there is some vintage music making at this *maison* virtually every day of the week. Watch kiosk posters for appearances of the two orchestras in the capital's other major concert halls. Information: *Maison de Radio France,* 116 Av. du Président-Kennedy, Paris 75016 (phone: 42-30-15-16).

OPÉRA DE PARIS, Paris: In a futuristic opera house on the Place de la Bastille, *L'Opéra Bastille* began regular performances in 1990 under the baton of Myung-Whun Chung, and the grand *Palais Garnier* (former home of grand opera) at the melodramatic end of Av. de l'Opéra is the site of the best in ballet. The other mainstays of Paris opera are the *Théâtre Musical de Paris,* in the old *Châtelet Theater,* and the *Opéra Comique,* at the *Salle Favart.* The latter isn't especially comic. The theater is smaller, the performers, as a rule, less well known; but the administration is the same, and the repertory is comparably vast. The *Théâtre Musical de Paris,* once the stronghold of the frothy operetta, now does everything from early Offenbach to late Verdi, importing productions from other European operas as well. The touch is light and stylish, the accent utterly French. Information: *L'Opéra Bastille,* 120 Rue de Lyon, Paris 75012 (phone: 40-01-17-89 or 40-01-16-16); *Théâtre National de l'Opéra,* 8 Rue Scribe, Paris 75009 (phone: 47-42-57-50); *Théâtre National de l'Opéra Comique,* 5 Rue Favart, Paris 75002 (phone: 42-86-88-83); *Théâtre Musical de Paris,* 1 Pl. du Châtelet, Paris 75004 (phone: 40-28-28-40).

SALLE PLEYEL, Paris: Often called the *Carnegie Hall* of Paris, the renovated *Pleyel* is so admirably suited to all types of music that it has even been the site of jazz concerts. The greatest names in European music visit here, and the superb *Orchestre de Paris* lives at this elegant address on the Faubourg-St-Honoré. Other temples of Parisian music include the smaller, charming *Salle Gaveau* on nearby Rue La Boëtie; the

Théâtre des Champs-Elysées on Av. Montaigne; and the massive *Palais des Congrès* at Porte Maillot. Any of the city's major orchestras may perform at the latter two, but if you turn up at the *Palais* on the wrong night, you may trade sacred Bach for punk rock. Information: *Salle Pleyel,* 252 Rue du Faubourg-St-Honoré, Paris 75008 (phone: 45-61-06-30; and, for the *Orchestre de Paris,* 45-63-07-40).

L'ODÉON–THÉÂTRE DE L'EUROPE, Paris: The chameleon-like *Odéon* has, for years, been the joker in the French theatrical pack. After the turbulent period when it housed the fabled company under Jean-Louis Barrault and Madeleine Renaud and ranked among the most popular houses in the city, it became an annex of the *Comédie-Française.* Now it can be seen in yet another incarnation, as the *Théâtre de l'Europe.* Under the direction of one of Europe's foremost men of the theater, Giorgio Strehler of Milan's *Piccolo Teatro,* it became a kind of theatrical Common Market, with original-language productions from all over Europe. It presently is under the direction of a Spaniard, Luis Pasqual. But there's no telling whether, by the time we go to press, the *Odéon* will be transformed once again — perhaps into a circus arena or a House of Parliament. Information: *L'Odéon–Théâtre de l'Europe,* Pl. Paul-Claudel, Paris 75006 (phone: 43-25-70-32).

THÉÂTRE NATIONAL DE CHAILLOT, Paris: The rightful heir to the great *Théâtre National Populaire* created by the legendary Jean Vilar in the same building, this three-ring theatrical circus consists of a large room, a small room, and Grand Central Station–size corridors that themselves can be transformed into performance spaces. Everything happens here, from *Hamlet* and *The Three Sisters* to *Faust* for children — performed by marionettes — to new texts by Algerian workers, and contemporary musical happenings. New formats, odd curtain times, and a constant redefining of theater and its audience are the watchwords. Information: *Théâtre National de Chaillot,* Pl. Trocadéro et du 11-Novembre, Paris 75116 (phone: 47-27-81-15).

THÉÂTRE DU SOLEIL, Paris: In the Cartoucherie de Vincennes, an old cartridge factory on the outskirts of Paris, this theater always has had a colorful, sweeping style with a popular mood and political overtones. That was true in the dazzling *1789,* which made the troupe's international reputation during that other year of French upheaval, 1968, and in the more recent Shakespeare series as well. Information: *Théâtre du Soleil,* La Cartoucherie de Vincennes, Bois de Vincennes, Paris 75012 (phone: 43-74-24-08 or 43-74-87-63).

THÉÂTRE NATIONAL DE STRASBOURG, Strasbourg, Bas-Rhin: Today, this Strasbourg theater, an outgrowth of the general government effort to make Alsace completely French after the war, has a decidedly international flavor and outlook. One week you'll see *Tartuffe* with François Périer and Gérard Dépardieu; the next, a play by Pirandello directed by an Italian and performed in French. At the same time, the group also has tried to move out of conventional theatrical spaces; recent productions have been presented at a horse stud farm, in an 18th-century military barracks, and on the roof of the city's cathedral. Information: *Théâtre National de Strasbourg,* Pl. de la République, Strasbourg 67000 (phone: 88-35-44-52). The address of the administrative office is 1 Rue du André Malraux (even though it's located in the same building).

THÉÂTRE DU CAPITOLE, Toulouse, Haute-Garonne: A longtime rival for national preeminence with the *Opéra de Paris,* it has often been a proving ground for the finest new singers in French opera. The orchestra, which usually plays for both opera and concert seasons in the stately 19th-century *Capitole,* even did a triumphal tour of the United States, and has brought both operas and a memorable Beethoven's "Ninth" to sellout audiences in the city's sprawling *Palais des Sports* as well. All of France is in the throes of a frantic opera renaissance, so to avoid all-night lines of sleeping-bagged *mélomanes* (music lovers), it's wise to book seats well in advance. Information: *Théâtre du Capitole,* 687 Pl. Capitole, Toulouse 31000 (phone: 61-22-80-22).

Festivals à la Française

 Festivals, direct descendants of the Greek drama marathons and the first *Olympic* games, are annual celebrations of the pleasures of creating, competing, or just plain existing. They let a visitor cram the best and most of any given experience into the shortest possible time — whether it's auto racing or chamber music, wine tasting or bullfighting.

A word of sober caution to those planning to hurl themselves into the merriment at one of France's frothiest celebrations. Crowds are very much a part of most festivals, so be prepared for crowded hotels, crowded restaurants, crowded auditoriums, and crowded toilets. Though advance planning will ward off much of the discomfort (reserve rooms ahead of time and write ahead for seats), it's still necessary to prepare yourself mentally for being jostled, for waiting in line, and for paying $5 for a can of warm cola — all part and parcel of festival going. Just remember that you and your fellow merrymakers share a common passion and that everybody is in the same boat. Also keep in mind that festivals tend to offer some of France's most savory street eating, so avoid the meals offered in jammed, festival-priced restaurants in favor of crêpes stands, oyster bars, and wine booths. You'd be surprised how well Beethoven's "Ninth" goes with French fries.

FESTIVAL D'AIX-EN-PROVENCE, Aix-en-Provence, Bouches-du-Rhône: Of France's 250-odd music festivals, this one ranks among the best since it combines a high musical level with meticulous organization and a delightful setting in a leafy town in the south of France. From mid-July to early August, the festival offers works of all vintages, from early Rameau to late Berio, and of all instruments, with a special emphasis on voice. Operas are performed in any one of three theaters, and concerts make lyrical use of the beautiful Cathédrale St-Sauveur and its cloister. A recent festival featured performing groups from the English *Baroque Soloists* to the *Ensemble Intercontemporain,* with Pierre Boulez wielding the baton. Information: *Festival International d'Art Lyrique et de Musique,* Palais de l'Ancien Archevêché, Aix-en-Provence 13100 (phone: 42-23-37-81 or 42-17-59-00; for reservations, 42-23-11-20).

FESTIVAL D'AVIGNON, Avignon, Vaucluse: This rendezvous for the most active stage people from all over France turns a modest provincial town of 90,000 into a polyglot United Nations of theater from early July to early August. Groups from all over the world — from Stuttgart's *Staatstheater* and England's *Footsbarn Travelling Theatre* to Milan's *La Scala* and a Japanese ritual dance troupe — perform in more than a dozen different sites such as the Cour d'Honneur of the Palace of the Popes, the Chapel of the White Penitents, and the courtyard of the Faculty of Science. Dance, music, debates, and creative electronics are the daily side orders. Information: *Office du Tourisme,* 41 Cours Jean-Jaurès, Avignon 84000 (phone: 90-82-65-11).

FESTIVAL INTERCELTIQUE, Lorient: One of France's liveliest festivals is a celebration of Celtic culture held annually during the first 2 weeks of August in this town in western Brittany. Participants from all over Europe — including Ireland, Scotland, Wales, Galicia, Asturias in Spain, and Brittany itself — gather at Lorient's Port de Pêche (Fishing Port) for theater and dance performances, sea shanties, tales told by professional storytellers, and food and drink, all with a Celtic accent and flavor. The

"Celts" of today are often Europe's outsiders, heirs to traditions and dialects that were gradually supplanted by the dominant ones in their countries but traces of which still survive. Information: *Office du Tourisme,* Maison de la Mer, Quai de Rohan, Lorient 56100 (phone: 97-21-07-84).

LES TROIS GLORIEUSES, Beaune, Clos-de-Vougeot, and Meursault, Côte d'Or: The event whose name translates as "the three glorious days" — France's most important wine festival — takes place in three different Burgundian towns on the third Saturday, Sunday, and Monday in November. The weekend begins with the great banquet of the oenophiles of the Chevaliers du Tastevin at Clos-de-Vougeot; it continues on Sunday with the famed *Les Hospices de Beaune* wine auction, which attracts merchants and bon vivants from all over the drinking world; and its grand finale is *La Paulée,* a celebration in Meursault, the village that produces some of the world's most exquisite white wines. Some of the activity is for professionals, and tickets for the banquets often disappear a year in advance. But there is plenty of wine tasting, folk dancing, and general merrymaking for casual visitors — and in any case, this is a fine opportunity to visit some of the region's legendary vineyards. Information: *Conseil Régional Bourgogne,* 1 Rue Nicolas-Berthot, Dijon 21035 (phone: 80-55-24-55); or *Office du Tourisme,* Beaune 21200 (phone: 80-22-24-51).

FESTIVAL DE MUSIQUE DE BESANÇON ET DE FRANCHE-COMTE, Besançon, Doubs: Based in an ancient town tucked into a lyre-shaped bend of the Doubs River, this September festival begun after World War II has spread to a whole cluster of other towns in the region. Chamber music has a special preeminence. A number of the charming settings here cannot accommodate a full symphony orchestra but seem to have been created for the string quartet. New York's distinguished *Beaux-Arts Trio* has been a highlight along with pianist Claudio Arrau and soprano Teresa Berganza. The international competition for young conductors that is a festival tradition has all the drama of a musical Wimbledon. For an unforgettable philharmonic orgy, try the Abonnement Complet, a subscription ticket that provides admission to every one of the festival's concerts. Information: *Festival de Musique de Besançon et de Franche-Comté,* 2-d Rue Isenbart, Besançon 25000 (phone: 81-80-73-26).

MAI MUSICAL DE BORDEAUX, Bordeaux, Gironde: Quite apart from its fine artistic value, the *May Musical Festival* also provides a lovely opportunity to get to know the Aquitaine in the spring. The concerts alternate between town and country: Venues include Bordeaux's 18th-century *Grand-Théâtre,* one of Europe's most beautiful halls; the Cathédrale St-André; the 13th-century Château de la Brède, on Bordeaux's outskirts; a cruise boat on the Garonne; and castles and churches in the wine-rich villages of the Bordeaux countryside. It's particularly tempting here to uncork a bottle of St-Emilion before a madrigal concert in the town's ancient Collégiale and, between performances in the city, to visit the Maison du Vin and taste enough wine to make Wagner sound like Gilbert and Sullivan. Information: *Mai Musical de Bordeaux, Grand-Théâtre,* Pl. de la Comédie, Bordeaux 33000 (phone: 56-90-91-60) or the tourist office (phone: 56-44-28-41).

FESTIVAL INTERNATIONAL DU FILM, Cannes, Alpes-Maritimes: The suntanned starlets in leopard skin sunglasses, the stogied producers, and the phalanxes of tuxedoed moguls who are always portrayed in the tabloids are indeed all part of the *Cannes Festival.* But that's only the glamorous tip of the moviedom iceberg. The festival also is a 24-hour-a-day bazaar where moguls hailing from as far away as Hong Kong and Ankara and New Delhi peddle and purchase hundreds of items like *Rocky X vs. the Teenage Mutant Ninja Turtles.* Some 40,000 cinema pros throng the *Palais du Festival* and the dozens of theaters and screening rooms between Rue d'Antibes and the sea. Some 400 pictures are shown that are not even competing for the coveted Golden Palm. For just plain film fans, the mid-May fantasia is a chance to see everything that is old, new, borrowed, and especially blue in an atmosphere that blends

Hollywood, the Riviera, and the souks of Damascus. Information: *Office du Tourisme,* Palais des Festivals-La Croisette, Cannes 06400 (phone: 93-39-24-53).

LE QUATORZE JUILLET, Carcassonne, Aude: July 14, *Bastille Day* — France's biggest and most colorful holiday — is celebrated in especially high style at the medieval citadel of Carcassonne. The nighttime fireworks spectacular known as "*L'Embrasement de la Cité*", literally, "the setting on fire of the ancient fortress-town," conjures up visions of boiling oil, flaming arrows, and besieging Crusaders as it illuminates the city's 50 fantastic towers like a stupendous blaze. The holiday also is the centerpiece of the *Festival de la Cité,* a 2-week feast of ballet, music, and theater; Ray Charles, Yehudi Menuhin, Rudolf Nureyev, and the major orchestras of France have all made appearances. Here, as in the rest of France, there really is dancing in the streets. Information: *Syndicat d'Initiative,* Bd. Camille-Pelletan, Carcassonne 11012 (phone: 68-25-07-04); *Festival de la Cité, Théâtre Municipal,* BP 236, Carcassonne 11000 (phone: 68-71-30-30); or the *Mairie de Carcassone* (phone: 68-71-11-11).

FOLKLORIADE INTERNATIONAL, Dijon, Côte d'Or: Really a double-feature festival, this international bacchanal combines folklore with wine lore the first week in September. Some 20 foreign traditional singing and dancing groups from countries such as Israel, Japan, Romania, Sri Lanka, Turkey, Russia, and points east and west join 2 dozen of their French counterparts to make merry through all the wine-dark vineyard villages of the Côte de Nuits and the Côte de Beaune. A concomitant wine exposition allows for endless *dégustations* (tastings) — on the spot and in all the villages and châteaux nearby. Information: *Office du Tourisme,* Pl. Darcy, Dijon 21000 (phone: 80-43-42-12).

SON ET LUMIÈRE, Loire Valley, Indre-et-Loire and Loir-et-Cher: Invented in the Loire Valley in the early 1950s, these 30-to-90-minute sound and light pageants are offered today by virtually every major château. Undeniably corny yet undeniably gripping, they are an ingenious weave of mellifluous voices, music, and roving floodlights — part slick spectacle, part crash course in French history. Some start as early as *Easter* week, and most run until mid-September, with several châteaux offering performances in English on alternate nights. The best are held at the castles of Chambord and Chenonceau, described at length in *Celebrated Châteaux and Cathedrals,* in this section. Information: *Syndicat d'Initiative,* 3 Av. Jean-Laigret, Blois 41000 (phone: 54-74-06-49); or *Office du Tourisme,* Pl. de la Gare, Tours 37042 (phone: 47-05-58-08).

LES 24 HEURES DU MANS, Le Mans, Sarthe: June's *24 Hours of Le Mans,* a grueling 2-day endurance contest at which speeds can reach 210 mph — one of the great events of European auto racing since its debut in 1923 — is actually only the centerpiece of a week-long celebration of man and motor that begins with *le pesage* (the weighing in) and gathers steam with the trial heats. A ticket for the Enceintes Générales gets you inside the 7.8-mile circuit, where there is space for cars and camping; the classiest observation post is a loge seat in the Tribune Citroën beside the dignitaries of the *Automobile Club de l'Ouest.* During the festivities, don't fail to visit the *Musée de l'Automobile,* inside the circuit, which has 150 stunning vintage vehicles starting with an 1884 De Dion Bouton. Information: *Automobile Club de l'Ouest, Circuit des 24 Heures, Office du Tourisme,* Hôtel des Ursulines, Rue des Ursulines, Le Mans 72040 (phone: 43-28-17-13).

CARNIVAL, Nice, Alpes-Maritimes: The history of the Nice *Carnival* goes back to the 13th century, but it was the city's emergence as a fashionable winter resort during the last century that brought it to the full flower that visitors encounter today, beginning 3 weekends before *Shrove Tuesday* with the first of the Saturday night torchlight processions. The following Sunday afternoon's parade, the *Grand Corso Carnavalesque,* features fabulous floats and huge, leering dummies. On Wednesdays, there are the famous *Batailles des Fleurs* — the battles of flowers. And every week is crammed to the gills with all manner of regattas, masked balls, confetti wars, and fireworks until the very moment on that riotous *Mardi Gras* when King Carnival is burnt in effigy. With its throbbing music, its steaming street food, the prancing drum majorettes, and all those emphatically thronging throngs, Nice's *Carnival* is not a party for the faint of heart or, for that matter, for the faint of eardrum. Information: *Comité des Fêtes,* 5 Promenade des Anglais, Nice 06000 (phone: 93-87-16-28).

GRANDE PARADE DU JAZZ, Nice, Alpes-Maritimes: The biggest and brassiest riff in Europe, this Nice event held annually for 10 days in July attracts just about every major jazz musician from America and the Continent. Chick Corea, Fats Domino, Ella Fitzgerald, Dizzy Gillespie, Lionel Hampton, Woody Herman, Sonny Rollins, Muddy Waters, and a whole hall of fame's worth of others have performed, in styles ranging from the best vintage New Orleans Dixieland to the last 12-tone word, from hot and bop to blue and mod and cool. And the music never stops: From late afternoon until midnight, a music lover can hear concerts in the gardens of the Roman amphitheater at Cimiez and after that can track down all-night jam sessions in the city's jazz joints. Food stalls dish out shrimp creole and *salade niçoise* in appropriately marathon fashion. Information: *Office du Tourisme,* at the *SNCF* (railway) station, Av. Thiers, Nice 06000 (phone: 93-87-07-07) or (open in season only) 5 Av. Gustave-V, Nice 06000 (phone: 93-87-60-60).

FOLK-EPIC SPECTACLE, Puy du Fou, Vendée: A remarkable marriage of oral tradition and high-tech computer sound and light effects, this outdoor spectacular is a retelling of the history of France from the Middle Ages to the present, through the eyes of a Vendean peasant family named Maupillier. A modern descendant of the son-et-lumière (sound and light) shows developed in the Loire, it is set against the stark background of a ruined château, but the hundreds of local actors and superb effects — as well as the renewal of area folk traditions — make this a unique experience. Performances take place Fridays and Saturdays from mid-June through July and from mid- to the end of August. Thousands attend each show, so it is advisable to reserve ahead. Information: *Secretariat Puy du Fou,* 30 Rue Georges-Clemenceau, Les Epesses 85590 (phone: 51-57-65-65).

FESTIVAL ESTIVAL AND FESTIVAL D'AUTOMNE, Paris: The former, which begins in mid-July and lasts until mid-September, brings a musical kaleidoscope of Gregorian chants, Bartók string quartets, Rameau opera, and more to the city's most picturesque and acoustically delightful churches. The *Festival d'Automne* takes up where the *Estival* leaves off and concentrates on the musically contemporary, generally focusing on one or two main themes or composers and including a certain number of brand-new works. Its moving spirit is Pierre Boulez, France's top musical talent. Information: *Festival Estival de Paris,* 20 Rue Geoffroy l'Asnier, Paris 75004 (phone: 48-04-98-01); and *Festival d'Automne,* 156 Rue de Rivoli, Paris 75001 (phone: 42-96-12-27).

GRAND PÈLERINAGE DE MAI, Les Stes-Maries-de-la-Mer, Bouches-du-Rhône: On every May 23, 24, and 25, some 15,000 Gypsies from all over Europe flock to the Mediterranean village of Stes-Maries-de-la-Mer in the Camargue to honor their patron saint, Sarah of Egypt, who was the servant of two legendary followers of Jesus, Mary Salome and Mary Jacobe. According to the story, the two Saint Maries were expelled from the old kingdom of Judea and cast adrift with their serving girl, but they miraculously were washed ashore at this site that now bears their name. The colorful ceremonies include a candlelight vigil in the church crypt and an exuberant procession to the sea with the sacred statues of the saints borne aloft in a sculpted boat. For 3 days, the whole town — itself already richly atmospheric with its bullfights, flocks of flamingos, marshes, and legends of wild white horses — fairly vibrates with the gaudy rhythms and colors of Gypsy life. Information: *Syndicat d'Initiative,* Av. Van-Gogh, Stes-Maries-de-la-Mer 13460 (phone: 90-47-82-55).

An Odyssey of the Old: Antiques Hunting in France

 The history of France may best be seen in fortresses and châteaux and the Bastille, but it is best felt by holding a fragment of a sculpted choir stall or an Art Deco soup ladle, by touching the satiny surface of a marquetry wedding chest or by slipping on the signet ring that once belonged to a scheming marquise. Such morsels of the nation's past can be savored at some 13,000 French antiques shops and auction houses or at a countrywide and year-long array of fairs and markets from Abbeville to Zonza.

SOURCES FOR ANTIQUES NATIONWIDE

SHOPS: No little village in France would be complete without its *Petite Galerie* (Little Gallery) or its *Au Bon Vieux Temps* (In the Good Old Days). Some are true *antiquaires,* antiques dealers, who handle pieces of established value and pedigree. Others are *brocanteurs,* secondhand shops, whose stock may run the gamut from Second Empire snuffboxes to broken 78 rpm Edith Piaf records. Many dealers belong to either the *Syndicat National des Antiquaires* (National Antique Dealers' Association) or the *Syndicat National du Commerce de l'Antiquité* (National Association of Antique Businesses), two highly reputable guilds whose members have pledged to tell the truth about all items they are selling.

For an important purchase, the wise buyer will request a certificate of authenticity. With furniture, in particular, the dealer should be precise about just which parts have been restored and how; a number of "antiques" are really superbly carpentered composites of partly salvaged pieces, and there is a thriving industry in the recycling of genuinely ancient wood into pieces of "antique" furniture that were actually born yesterday.

A trend of the past decade has been the clustering of individual shops into *villages d'antiquaires,* which are something like shopping centers for antiques, with dozens of dealers housed under a single roof. The prototype is the giant *Louvre des Antiquaires* (2 Pl. de Palais-Royal), whose 250 different shops are in an old Paris department store. But there are others: *La Treille des Antiquaires,* 23-25 Rue des Chats-Bossus, Lille; the *Cour des Antiquaires,* 7 Rue de l'Industrie, Nantes; the *Village Ségurane,* 2 Rue Antoine-Gauthier, Nice; the *Marché des Antiquaires,* between Cannes and Antibes at Vallauris. Most are open on weekends and make a pleasant excursion — even if you are only in the market for a very contemporary sandwich and a beer.

The richness and tradition of the French antiques trade has spawned a high degree of specialization, both by genre and by period. Some shops deal exclusively in dolls, maritime instruments, chimneys and mantelpieces, locks and keys, and postcards. Several antiquarians in Paris stock only items from the 1950s. Passionate collectors with a one-track mind should consult the *Guide Emer* (50 Rue-Quai de l'Hôtel-de-Ville, Paris 75004; phone: 42-77-83-44) for information about where in the whole of France to indulge their most exotic whims.

EXPOSITIONS, FAIRS, AND SALONS: These are three words for roughly the same ritual — an annual antiques fair that lasts a week, give or take a few days, and attracts dealers from all over the region, the nation, or Europe, depending on its importance in the trade. There are so many salons in France now that many dealers have no home base at all; they simply travel the circuit from one fair to the next, selling, buying, trading, and sizing up the competition.

One of the biggest and best is the *Salon des Antiquaires Languedoc-Midi-Pyrénées* at Toulouse. For 10 days, usually beginning the second week in November, more than 400 dealers spread their wares throughout the giant *Parc des Expositions.* The merchandise is some of Europe's finest, and the crowd includes all of the country's top professionals. It's a bit like ambling through an out-of-town *Louvre* where everything is for sale.

A few other three-star salons include: *Salon des Antiquaires du Sud-Ouest,* an early February annual at the *Parc des Expositions,* Bordeaux-Lac; *Salon Européen des Antiquaires,* staged in late January or early February at *Alpexpo,* Grenoble; *Salon Indépendent des Antiquaires de Marseille,* held the last week in October at the *Parc Chanot* in Marseilles; and the *Salon des Antiquaires et Brocanteurs,* which takes place in late April in Nancy.

FLEA MARKETS: The range of France's countless *marchés aux puces* — literally, "markets with fleas" — extends from the vast, sprawling bric-a-brac city that is Paris's *Porte de Clignancourt* flea market to two folding tables in the town square in Poubelle-les-Bains. The merchandise varies from lower-echelon antiques to very rare rubbish, and it may be necessary to comb your way through ten boxes of bent spoons and a decade of back copies of *Paris-Match* before finding the Picasso of your dreams.

But dealers stock up in precisely this fashion, and flea markets are where everybody in Paris or Poubelle seems to be on nearly every sunny Saturday. The Syndicat d'Initiative in whatever town you may be visiting can tell you the time and the place of the nearest *marché.* A dozen of the most delightfully dilapidated are in the following towns at the following times:

Aix-en-Provence, Tuesday, Thursday, and Saturday mornings, Pl. de Verdun
Antibes, Thursdays and Saturdays, Pl. Aubertini
Avignon, Saturday mornings, Place Crillon; Sundays, Pl. des Carmes
Cannes, Saturdays, Allée des Fleurs
Lille, Sunday mornings, *Marché Wazemmes*
Lyons, Thursdays and Saturdays, and Sunday mornings, *Brocante Stalingrad*
Nantes, Saturday mornings, Pl. Viarme
Nice, Daily except Sundays, Mondays, and holidays, Vieux Port
Nîmes, Monday, Rue Jean-Jaurès
Reims, First Sunday of the month (except August), Pl. du Boulingrin
St-Tropez, Tuesday and Saturday mornings, Pl. de Lices
Toulon, Sunday mornings, Quartier Ste-Musse
Toulouse, Saturdays, Sundays, and Mondays, *Marché Saint-Germain*

AUCTIONS: Once something of a professional club for dealers only, auctions — known in French as *ventes aux enchères* — have become the favorite indoor sport of the *haute bourgeoisie* in the last few years, and in the *salles des ventes* (salesrooms) of France, there are fewer bargains around than there used to be. However, those who know their market may still save as much as a third of the retail price; and even for those who don't, auctions are hard to beat for pure theater.

But the auction situation in France is a bit different than those in the US, Great Britain, and Ireland, for all sales take place under the aegis of a government-authorized auctioneer known as the *commissaire-priseur.* And the auction houses in the various cities, including Paris's venerable *Hôtel Drouot,* are basically cooperatives managed by the local guild of *commissaires-priseurs,* and it is they who are known for their probity and expertise rather than salesrooms or specific companies. By law, French auctioneers are responsible for the authenticity of any item they sell for 30 years after the sale.

Besides the houses in Paris, the most important *salles des ventes* are in Angers, Brest, Cannes, Chartres, Dijon, Enghien, Fontainebleau, Lille, Lyons, Morlaix, Toulouse, Versailles, and L'Isle-Adam.

The weekly *Gazette de l'Hôtel Drouot* (on sale on newsstands everywhere) prints a calendar of auction sales all over France as well a running tally of the results (10 Rue du Faubourg-Montmartre, Paris 75009; phone: 47-70-93-00). Remember that provincial sales, often held on Sundays, can help liven up a rainy day in a place like Rouen.

HOT SPOTS FOR ANTIQUERS

With the possible exception of those in the mountain regions like the Haute-Savoie and the Pyrénées, all roads in France lead to antiques. The city of Paris plus the four regions described below are perhaps the richest, both historically and commercially. A word to the wily: The Riviera has the thinnest stylistic traditions and the thickest prices in the country. Save your money for areas where the local antiques were once household objects rather than bathing season baubles.

PARIS: Just as Vienna specializes in *Carnival* balls, the French capital is a feast of antiquing activity.

The greatest concentrations of antiques shops are at the *Louvre des Antiquaires* (2 Pl. du Palais-Royal; phone: 42-97-27-00), open daily except Mondays, and Sundays in the summer; at *Le Village Suisse* (78 Av. de Suffren and 54 Av. de la Motte-Picquet; phone: 43-06-69-90), open daily except Tuesdays and Wednesdays; at *La Cour aux Antiquaires* (54 Rue du Faubourg-St-Honoré; phone: 42-66-38-60), open daily except Sundays and Monday mornings. Then there's *Le Carré Rive Gauche,* an association of more than 100 antiques shops in the square of streets formed by Quai Voltaire, Rue de l'Université, Rue des Sts-Pères, and Rue du Bac.

Other good hunting grounds include Boulevard. St-Germain, Rue Bonaparte, and Rue Jacob on the Left Bank; and Rue du Faubourg-St-Antoine, Rue St-Honoré, Rue du Faubourg-St-Honoré, Avenue Victor-Hugo, Rue La Boétie, and Rue de Miromesnil on the Right Bank.

As for the Paris auction world, the center is the *Hôtel Drouot* on the Right Bank, not far from Bd. Montmartre. Some 600,000 lots go through its 16 salesrooms every year, and the activity is frantic. If you find yourself in a room full of plumbers' fittings or vintage cognacs when what you really wanted was antiques, just go up to the next floor. Information: *Drouot-Richelieu,* 9 Rue Drouot, Paris 75009 (phone: 48-00-20-20). Sales also are held at the *Drouot-Montaigne,* 15 Av. Montaigne, Paris 75008 (phone: 48-00-20-80 or 48-00-20-20).

A new bidding-free variation on the auction theme is the *dépôt-vente,* a salesroom where private sellers leave lots on consignment with a dealer who sets the price and takes a 15% commission. These generally are well patronized by bargain-hunting professionals. The largest is the immense *Dépôt-Vente de Paris,* 81 Rue de Lagny, Paris (phone: 43-72-13-91).

Among flea markets, the best known is the *Marché aux Puces de St-Ouen* at the Porte de Clignancourt, open Saturdays, Sundays, and Mondays from 8 AM to about 5:30 PM. *St-Ouen* actually comprises a number of submarkets — the *Biron,* the *Paul Bert,* the *Vernaison,* and the *Serpette* among them — and there are some 3,000 stalls, ranging from the equivalent of chic boutiques to rickety tables to blankets on the curbstone. You may have to hack your way through a million pairs of Taiwan Levi's to get to the Marie-Antoinette miniatures.

Lesser known and lower brow are *Les Puces de Montreuil* (literally, "the fleas of Montreuil"), held on Saturdays, Sundays, and Mondays at the Porte de Montreuil; and *Les Puces de Vanves,* held on Saturdays and Sundays at the Porte de Vanves. Both run from early morning to about 5 PM.

And then there are the salons and expositions. The classic is the *Biennale International des Antiquaires,* held astride September and October in even-numbered years in the *Grand Palais.* With its stock of the finest pieces available in Europe and a range of exhibitors that includes all the top dealers from France and abroad, the *Biennale* may set the tone of the market for the following 2 years.

The *Grande Foire à la Ferraille et au Jambon* is a curious event that takes place in March and September every year and mixes antiques, handicrafts, and regional foods from all over France; fairgoers do lots of wine tasting, cheese nibbling, and bric-a-brac browsing.

The *Foire Nationale à la Brocante* at Ile de Chatou, 10 minutes from Paris, also is held twice a year — in early March and late September. This party is organized by *SNCAO*, 18 Rue de Provence, Paris 75009 (phone: 47-70-88-78).

In Ivry-sur-Seine, the new *FIBA* (*Foire Internationale Brocante Antiquité*) attracts over 1000 exhibitors every March, June, and September. Organized by *SODAF*, 2 Placette Fauconnières, Ivry-sur-Seine 94200 (phone: 46-71-66-14).

BURGUNDY: In addition to antique vintage burgundy wines, you'll find the flower of French furniture and sculpture in Burgundy. The town of Beaune is a good bet, and, especially for those in search of an antique mantelpiece, the villages of Mâcon and Nevers also can yield treasures.

Dijon – One big deal is the *Salon des Antiquaires et de la Brocante,* which takes place every May at the *Parc des Expositions.* But for those who travel at other times of the year, there's the flea market on Rue Delaborde the last Sunday of each month. And there are a handful of shops on Rue Verrerie and Rue des Forges.

LOIRE VALLEY: The forest of princely châteaux here was synonymous with France itself in the 16th and 17th centuries, and many of its treasures have remained in the region. Drive from Blois to Orléans along one bank of the Loire and back along the other, and you'll find dozens of shops in all the villages en route.

Chartres – There's a flea market held in the Place St-Pierre on the fourth Sunday and Monday of each month from May to October.

Tours – The most rewarding browsing is at the *Salle des Ventes* (20 Rue Michel-Colombe); at the *Salon des Antiquaires* (*Parc des Expositions*), held annually on the fourth weekend in March; and in the shops along Rue de la Scellerie. Wednesdays and Saturdays are flea market days at Place des Victoires.

PROVENCE: An antiques hunter will turn up all manner of oldies but goodies in the south of France at a handful of exceptional locations.

Aix-en-Provence – After the 80 antiques shops in town, the *Village des Antiquaires,* 5 miles (8 km) from Aix on RN7 toward Avignon, and the *Marché aux Puces,* held on Tuesday, Thursday, and Saturday mornings on the Place de Verdun, are the best bets.

Avignon – Dedicated browsers here haunt the flea markets on Saturday mornings on Pl. Crillon and on Sunday mornings on Pl. des Carmes; and auction mavens patronize the regularly scheduled auctions at the *Hôtel des Ventes,* 2 Rue Rempart St-Lazare. And, about 13 miles (21 km) southeast of Avignon, there are a handful of good shops in the *Village d'Antiquaires* at l'Isle-sur-Sorgue, open Saturdays through Mondays. Twice yearly, in May or June and August or September, there's the big *Foire à la Brocante.*

Montpellier – On Saturday mornings, the town's antiques lovers all can be found prowling through the *Marché aux Puces* on the Place des Arceaux. And every year in late April or early May, all eyes turn to the good-size *Salon des Antiquaires et de la Brocante* at the *Parc des Expositions.*

Nîmes – On Mondays, dealers congregate at the *Marché à la Brocante* in the Allée Jean-Jaurès. On Sundays, there's the little flea market in the Pl. des Carmes. And the year's activity climaxes in December with the *Salon des Antiquaires* at the *Parc des Expositions.*

NORMANDY: Wonderful Norman carvings in oak are among the more splendid finds in this corner of France.

Caen – There's often a treasure or two at the *Marché aux Puces,* held on the first Saturday of every month on Rue du Vaugueux and the shops on Rue Ecuyère. The *Salon des Antiquaires,* held in mid-June at the *Palais des Expositions,* brings new dealers and new wares.

Honfleur – Antiques shops are a special attraction of this picturesque port town. The greatest concentration is around Place Ste-Catherine and in the half-timbered houses along its side streets.

Rouen – Supplementing the city's roster of shops, which are concentrated on Rue Damiette, are the auctions scheduled regularly at the *Salles des Ventes* (at 25 Rue du Général-Giraud and at 10 Rue Croix-de-Fer). And during the second half of October, the *Parc-Expo* hosts the big *Salon National des Antiquaires.* Look for the flea market on Thursdays at Place des Emmures, and on Saturdays and Sundays at Place St-Marc.

RULES OF THE ROAD FOR AN ODYSSEY OF THE OLD

Buy for sheer pleasure and not for investment. Forget about the carrot of supposed resale values that French dealers habitually dangle in front of amateur clients. If you love something, it probably will ornament your home until the next Revolution.

Don't be afraid to haggle. This is true even in the most awesomely elegant boutique on the Rue du Faubourg-St-Honoré. Everything is negotiable, and the higher the price, the harder (and farther) it falls.

Buy the finest example you can afford of any item, in as close to mint condition as possible. Chipped or broken "bargains" will haunt you later with their shabbiness.

Train your eye in museums. These probably are the best schools for the acquisitive senses, particularly as you begin to develop special passions. Collections like those of tapestries at Aubusson, of porcelain at Limoges, and of furniture in the *Louvre* will set the standards against which to measure purchases.

Peruse French art and antiques magazines. French newsstands abound in them. The best include *Connaissance des Arts, L'Estampille, Beaux-Arts,* and *L'Oeuil. Trouvailles* deals with bric-a-brac and flea markets. The weekly *Gazette de l'Hôtel Drouot* details auction action.

Get advice from a specialist when contemplating a major acquisition. Members of the various national guilds of antiques experts are well distributed throughout the country. For more information, contact the *Chambre Nationale des Experts Specialistes en Antiquités* (4 Rue Longchamp, Nice 06000; phone: 93-82-21-40) or the *Syndicat Fran- çais des Experts Professionnels en Oeuvres d'Art* (81 Rue St-Dominique, Paris 75007; phone: 47-05-50-26).

Celebrated Châteaux
and Cathedrals

For half a millennium, the Gothic cathedral and the Renaissance château reigned as the most sublime reflections of the French spirit. As their massive stone shadows colored the life of the whole town and the surrounding countryside, these structures were the peaceful statements of the power, both religious and secular, that was France.

The Gothic mode took shape in the northern part of the country during the middle of the 12th century and then spread throughout Western Europe. With its vaults and spires straining heavenward and its pointed arch, which the sculptor Rodin called "a pair of hands in prayer," the cathedral was a celebration of both God and engineering.

Searching for ever greater elevation and ever more light, its architects replaced the massive walls of earlier styles with airy windows and raised the vaulting higher and higher like stakes in some Olympian poker game. The result was a whole new system of stress and support, characterized most obviously by the famous *arc boutant,* flying buttress.

The onset of the Hundred Years War in 1337 put an end to the golden age of Gothic cathedral building. But the end of the conflict in the middle of the 15th century marked the beginning of the château building years, when new generations of royalty subjected the placid Loire Valley to an orgy of regal real estate development. And as decoration replaced defense as a prime architectural motivation, the once stolid and brooding medieval fortress gave way to the fanciful wonder that became the Renaissance château.

One brief caution: Since cathedrals and châteaux share a number of stylistic features, there's a risk of aesthetic indigestion if you try to see a great group of them on successive days. So to get the most out of your visits, vary your sightseeing menu as much as possible. Take in an evening organ concert at one cathedral and attend early morning mass at another, for instance, or try bicycling between a pair of Loire castles and tour the interior of one and visit only the gardens of another; stop at Azay-le-Rideau after an icy bottle of vouvray, then see Chambord dramatically lit at night. It is also less than original sin to leave a few stones unturned.

CATHÉDRALE STE-CÉCILE, Albi, Tarn: This great crimson citadel — together with the Palais de la Berbie across the square — was built for defense as well as worship beginning with the laying of its cornerstone in 1282 by the Archbishop of Albi. Set in a corner of France where the Church had led holy wars against the heretical Cathars, it is the country's finest example of the simple, bare Midi Gothic. Characterized by a column-free nave whose 100 feet of elevation equals the span of its base, the interior was richly decorated at the beginning of the 16th century by a team of sculptors from Burgundy and painters from Bologna. The breathtaking view from the tower over the town and the River Tarn is worth the heavenward trudge. Information: *Office du Tourisme,* 19 Pl. Ste-Cécile, Albi 81000 (phone: 63-54-22-30).

CATHÉDRALE NOTRE-DAME, Amiens, Somme: While its 261,400 cubic yards make this cathedral at Amiens the largest in France, its harmony of style and the airy grace of its immense spaces make it one of the most beautiful as well, and the statuary of the west portal is one of the high points of Gothic art. Inside, don't miss the oaken choir stalls, where some 3,600 carved figures depict scenes from the Old and New Testaments, and be sure to see the unique bronze reclining statues of the two bishops who spent their part of the 13th century supervising the construction of these precious stones. Information: *Office du Tourisme,* Rue Jean-Catelas, Amiens 80000 (phone: 22-91-79-28).

CATHÉDRALE ST-PIERRE, Beauvais, Oise: At Beauvais, an easy hour's journey from Paris, the Gothic architects' ceaseless quest for ever more height and light ended in disaster. With too much space between the support piers and too little mass in the ribbing, the choir collapsed in 1284. Reconstruction, begun shortly thereafter, was ultimately broken off until the 16th century, when the tower above the transept crashed. It was never repaired. As a result, the 20th century's inheritance at Beauvais is an unfinished symphony of Gothic art with splendid stained glass windows and a priceless collection of Beauvais, Gobelin, and Flemish tapestries. Information: *Office du Tourisme,* Rue St-Pierre, Beauvais 60000 (phone: 44-45-25-26).

PALAIS DES PAPES, Avignon, Vaucluse: The residence of the popes during the 14th-century schism in the Catholic church, this massive, imposing sprawl is a kind of French Vatican City. By turns military, religious, and residential, it sometimes seems like some fanciful sand castle that any one of half a dozen capricious popes might have built during a long stay at the beach. The cavernous frescoed interior may be visited on guided group tours, and the cloisters and the courtyard hold dramatic musical and theatrical productions during Avignon's summer festival. Information: *Syndicat d'Initiative,* 41 Cours Jean-Jaurès, Avignon 84000 (phone: 90-82-65-11).

AZAY-LE-RIDEAU, Azay-le-Rideau, Indre-et-Loire: Often described as the most "feminine" of French châteaux, Azay-le-Rideau was built between 1518 and 1529 under the supervision of a woman, the wife of the great financier Gilles Berthelot. A cheerful white manor, military in style but not in spirit, it stands gracefully astride a branch of the Indre and is reflected in its waters; with its surrounding English gardens and its beautiful avenue of trees, it has a certain domesticity that seldom fails to inspire thoughts of how lovely it would be to live there. In fact, François I liked it so much he confiscated it. Those who tire of lounging about the luxuriant grounds should note the fine collection of Renaissance furniture and tapestries inside. Information: *Syndicat d'Initiative,* Rue Nationale, Azay-le-Rideau 37190 (phone: 47-45-44-40) or *Office du Tourisme,* Pl. du Maréchal-Leclerc, Tours 37000 (phone: 47-05-58-08).

PALAIS JACQUES COEUR, Bourges, Cher: A banker to King Charles VII and one of the 15th century's most powerful merchants, Jacques Coeur built his palace at Bourges with profits, not an inheritance, and for many years the *palais* functioned as much as a warehouse as a sumptuous bourgeois dwelling. The practical burgher spirit is evident in everything from the efficient modern plumbing to ornamental details like the embellishments of cattle and turnips instead of the more usual unicorns and fleurs-de-lis. The ample courtyard is the site of June's annual *Festival of Experimental Music,* a major international event on the busy French contemporary music calendar. Information: *Syndicat d'Initiative,* 21 Rue Victor-Hugo, Bourges 18000 (phone: 48-24-75-33).

CHÂTEAU DE CHAMBORD, Chambord, Loir-et-Cher: This quintessentially elegant, marvelously balanced 440-room creation in the Italian Renaissance style was the brainchild of the château-mad François I, who, at the outset of the 16th century, diverted a river to make way for it and emptied church coffers and melted down silverware to finance it. On the site of an old hunting lodge in the middle of the great forest domain of the Counts of Blois, it is the largest castle in the Loire Valley and is renowned for its roof terrace that is crowded with black slate turrets, chimneys, dormers, and buttresses ornamented with an almost frenzied array of pediments and capitals and statues, and for the double spiral staircase that twists from the central lantern turret at the top to the ground floor. There are 84 additional staircases within its maze-like interiors as well as 365 chimneys. Molière was a house guest of Louis XIV here, and *Le Bourgeois Gentilhomme* had its world premiere at Chambord. The castle was sacked during the Revolution, and since many of the rooms have not yet been refurbished, much of it is empty. Be sure to stroll on the splendid roof terrace, the lookout from which the royal court stargazed, watched falcons, and applauded the jousting of the tournaments below. The lawns that edge the château are broad and green, and the surrounding 14,000-acre deer park, rimmed by a 20-mile-long wall, may be seen on rental horses — a special delight in the golden light of late afternoon and when a bluish mist fogs the château's base. The château also was the site of the world's first son et lumière performance, set to the music of Jean-Baptiste Lully, who composed and performed here in the 17th century. The château is open daily except *Christmas* and *New Year's Day,* from 9:30 AM to 1:45 PM and 2 to 4:45 PM in winter; from 9:30 AM to 5:45 PM in summer, except August when it stays open until 6:45 PM. Information: *Château de Chambord,* Chambord 41250 (phone: 54-20-31-31 or 54-20-31-50).

CATHÉDRALE NOTRE-DAME, Chartres, Eure-et-Loir: When an 1194 fire destroyed an earlier Romanesque church on the same site, a vast community effort produced this masterpiece of the human spirit in only 30 years — record time for a Gothic cathedral. As a result, this medieval marvel at Chartres has an architectural unity unrivaled by any of its sisters. The intricate webbing of flying buttresses so lightens the stone colossus that it seems almost poised for flight; the Royal Portal is one of the pinnacles of medieval French sculpture; and the stained glass windows in famed "Chartres blue" bathe the interior in subtle shades that modulate with the time and tonality of the day. Try to hear one of the frequent recitals on the restored 14th-century organ, which is among the best in Europe. Information: *Office du Tourisme de Chartres,* Pl. de la Cathédrale, Chartres 28000 (phone: 37-21-50-00).

CHÂTEAU DE CHENONCEAUX, Chenonceaux, Indre-et-Loir: A haunting way to see this most majestic and graceful of French castles is the son et lumière spectacle performed on the grounds on summer evenings from June 15 to September 15 at 10:15 PM. As the languid River Cher whispers under the enchanting gallery built on a bridge by Catherine de Médicis, Renaissance music and courtly voices emerge from the woods, and lights dart on and off in the bedchamber where Diane de Poitiers amused Henri II. Wife and mistress respectively to the king, these two women ruled and embellished the castle during its heyday in the mid-16th century, and their rival gardens still face each other across an ancient drawbridge. Built in the first part of that century by a royal tax collector named Thomas Bohier, who died with his debts to the throne unpaid, Chenonceaux came under the ownership of the French Crown, and Henri II gave it to his mistress upon his coronation in 1547; Catherine de Médicis confiscated it after Henri's death 12 years later. The interior, unlike that of Chambord, is largely intact, if somewhat worn, and there is a warm feeling about the place that makes it especially pleasant to visit. This is also one of the few Loire châteaux where visitors are permitted to amble about without a guide; there's a small café for coffee or lunch. Information: *Syndicat d'Initiative,* 13 Rue Château, Chenonceaux 37150 (phone: 47-23-94-45) or call the château directly (phone: 47-23-90-07).

CHÂTEAU DE FONTAINEBLEAU, Fontainebleau, Seine-et-Marne: Set in the midst of a verdant forest 39 miles (63 km) south of Paris, Fontainebleau was built, expanded, redecorated, or otherwise touched by all the greats of French royalty. François I transformed it from hunting lodge to palace, Henri IV created its lakes and carp-filled pond, Louis XIII was born here, Louis XV was married here. And Napoleon turned Louis XIV's bedroom into his own throne room, signed his abdication here, and bade farewell to his Old Guard from the great Horseshoe Staircase. The most beautiful sections of the interior are the Gallery of François I and the Ballroom — but Josephine's bedroom and Marie-Antoinette's boudoir are worth a look as well. Open daily except Tuesdays from 9:30 AM to 12:30 PM and from 2 to 5 PM. Information: *Syndicat d'Initiative,* 31 Pl. Napoléon-Bonaparte, Fontainebleau 77300 (phone: 64-22-25-68) or the *Château* (phone: 64-22-27-40).

CATHÉDRALE NOTRE-DAME, Paris: Along with the Eiffel Tower, Paris's other great perpendicular, this noble structure rising above the Ile de la Cité in the middle of the Seine rules the skyline with all the accumulated authority of Church and State — who, in fact, split its original cost. Built on the site of a Gallo-Roman temple that dated back to the earliest pre-Christian days of Paris, it took more than 200 years to erect, from the middle of the 12th century until the middle of the 14th, and was built from the plans of a single anonymous architect. Napoleon was crowned emperor here in 1804 by Pope Pius VII, and the distances from the rest of France to Paris are measured from the Place du Parvis in front. Among its myriad wonders are the main portals, the portal to the cloister, the portal of St. Stephen, the 13th-century rose windows, the "flying buttresses" which support the whole edifice, and the heart-stopping view from the tower. Information: *Cathédrale Notre-Dame,* Pl. du Parvis de Notre-Dame, Paris 75004 (phone: 43-26-07-39).

CATHÉDRALE NOTRE-DAME, Reims, Marne: The history of Notre-Dame de Reims is intimately bound up with that of the French monarchy. On *Christmas* night in the year AD 496, Clovis, the first Christian King of France, was baptized on the site by that pious politician, the Bishop St-Remi, and from its construction in the early 13th century until the Revolution, virtually every sovereign was crowned in this cathedral.

It was here that Joan of Arc, having driven out the hated English, presided over the coronation of Charles VII to the strains of the *Te Deum*. Badly damaged in World War I, Notre-Dame has been painstakingly restored, and the simple and elegant interior contrasts strikingly with the Flamboyant Gothic exterior. Be sure to admire the walls full of 15th-century tapestries, the lapis lazuli rose window, and the stained glass windows by Marc Chagall. Information: *Office du Tourisme de Reims,* 2 Rue Guillaume de Machault, Reims 51100 (phone: 26-47-25-69).

DOMAINE DE VAUX-LE-VICOMTE, Melun, Seine-et-Marne: On the evening of August 17, 1661, Louis XIV's superintendent of finance, Nicolas Fouquet, proudly welcomed his 23-year-old king to see the new castle on whose construction he had just spent his entire personal fortune. Serenades especially composed by the renowned Lully, a new stage production by Molière, a fabulous five-course banquet, and a fireworks display all heralded the occasion. Three weeks later, the jealous and fearful Louis XIV had Fouquet clapped into jail for life on trumped-up charges and hired his former superintendent's architect, painter, and landscapist to whip him up a pied-à-terre called Versailles. Vaux-le-Vicomte, Fouquet's castle, is today the largest private property in France; its magical, stylized gardens alone cover more than 125 acres. And it is full of lovely fountains, placid pools, sculpted lawns, and fields of flowers that look like giant illuminated medieval manuscripts. The Vaux-aux-Chandelles (Vaux-by-Candlelight) tours show off all of the château's splendors at their most dramatic. The tours take place on Saturdays at 9:30 PM from June through September. Information: *Service Touristique,* Domaine de Vaux-le-Vicomte, Maincy 77950 (phone: 60-66-97-09).

CHÂTEAU DE VERSAILLES, Versailles, Yvelines: In 1682, 2 decades after its founding, the town and castle of Versailles became the French court's new suburban home. Besides a nucleus of a thousand nobles, Louis XIV's retinue consisted of some 9,000 men-at-arms and an equal number of servants. At any given moment between 5,000 and 6,000 people were living here, which only begins to suggest the scale of this royal commune, and seeing it all in one visit is about as relaxing as running the *Boston Marathon*. But before you drop, be sure to squeeze in the cream and gold chapel where the kings said mass, the State Apartments, the fabled Hall of Mirrors, the Royal Suites, and, on the grand green grounds, the Petit Trianon, Marie-Antoinette's rustic small castle. Between May and September, on specified afternoons, the 600 jets of water in the 50-odd fountains and pools in the park outside the palace are all turned on; it's a spectacular sight. Versailles is accessible by public transportation from downtown Paris. For further information, see "Versailles" in the *Ile-de-France* route, DIRECTIONS. Information: *Office du Tourisme,* 7 Rue des Réservoirs, Versailles 78000 (phone: 39-50-36-22).

DIRECTIONS

Introduction

As the largest country in Western Europe, France lends itself to an infinite variety of driving tours. While visits to the major French metropolitan areas reveal something of this diverse country and its people, there are other aspects of Gallic life that can only be experienced outside city limits — in small fishing villages in Brittany or mountain campsites in the Pyrénées, on rocky beaches on the Côte d'Azur or along hairpin turns in the Alps, along the lush valley of the Loire or the rugged terrain of Corsica, or through the wildlife preserve of the Camargue National Park.

France has captured the imagination of travelers for decades. Drawn to this land that offers a range of climates, scenery, and cultures, there is much for visitors to absorb beyond its urban centers — museums, monuments, churches, and châteaux, to name the most obvious. Outdoor activities — from swimming on the beaches of the northern, western, and southern coasts to skiing down the slopes of the Alps — also are part of the French experience. And the construction of new and improved routes for last year's *Winter Olympics* in the Savoie region of the Alps has resulted in easier access to the area through improved roads and highways.

On the following pages are 18 driving tours through France's very varied provinces. From Normandy to Provence, they traverse the country's most spectacular routes and roads, most arresting natural wonders, and most magnificent historical sites, offering unforgettable views of azure lakes, winding rivers, dramatic mountain peaks, and virgin forests. They travel through not only the most distinctively French regions of the country, but into areas where other heritages thrive. In Alsace and Lorraine, German dialects are spoken; in Brittany, Breton; in the Pyrénées, Basque; and in the Languedoc, an old Provençal tongue. There are journeys, too, into France's past. Routes enable travelers to follow in the footsteps of the inhabitants of La Belle France, from the early cavemen of Lascaux in the Dordogne to the Résistance fighters in the mountains of Corsica.

Descriptions of each of the routes begin with an introduction to the region, then describe suggested driving tours, each designed to take 5 to 7 days of traveling. It is possible to string together several routes to form longer itineraries, but if you are pressed for time, you will find that by following any single itinerary you will see most of the sites and sights (and enjoy the best restaurants and accommodations) in the area. Each route offers suggestions for the best hotels and restaurants along the way, from simple pensions to deluxe châteaux, from cozy bistros to three-Michelin-star dining rooms (hotels are listed first, in order of expense, followed by restaurants).

These tours are not exhaustive — there is no effort to cover absolutely everything in each region. But the places recommended and activities described were chosen to make your drives memorable ones.

The Ile-de-France

The first thing to know about the so-called Island of France (l'Ile-de-France) is that it is not an island at all. It is the region surrounding Paris to a radius of roughly 50 miles, and its name alludes to the fact that its boundaries are delineated by rivers and waterways — The Epte, the Aisne, the Eure, the Ourcq, the Autonne, the Essonne, and others form an irregular circle around the area, while the mighty Marne and the regal, ubiquitous Seine coil and curve through its heart.

In fact, it's the rivers that define the land here, lending their names to the valleys that lie between them. Officially, the Ile-de-France can be divided into eight subregions: Paris and seven other *départements* (Seine et Marne, Yvelines, Essone, Hauts de Seine, Seine St-Denis, Val de Marne, and Val d'Oise) that wrap snail-like around the French capital, cradling it in a temperate basin.

Richly blessed with both natural and manmade treasures, the Ile-de-France constitutes what art critic and author John Russell described as "one vast national park of fine living." Russell added, "I doubt, indeed, if there is anywhere in France a greater abundance of unexplored marvels." This is the region of the French kings, of their regal châteaux, and the châteaux of their ministers and mistresses. The special quality of the light has inspired nearly as many painters (and often the same ones) as those who worked in Provence, while writers and poets have found their inspiration in the region's character.

Through this area passed Charlemagne, St-Louis, Joan of Arc, and Napoleon, each leaving an imprint. Almost every illustrious Frenchman or woman has ties to the Ile-de-France. The homes of historical, literary, and artistic notables are here, many of these now memorials or museums honoring their famous former occupants.

No other region of France has a higher concentration of cathedrals and abbey churches, exquisite Gothic stone witnesses to a fervent religious past played out over centuries. The same locally quarried stone chiseled for these masterpieces also defines the châteaux — not just Versailles and Fountainebleau — and the other countless small gems that dot the countryside.

The modern landscape of the Ile-de-France is full of sometimes jarring contrasts: quaint market squares, medieval fortresses, deep woods, and the ever-present serpentine rivers juxtaposing the bleak industrial pockets and urban sprawl that can dishearten the casual traveler. But, despite the encroachment of modern times and suburbanization, nature still firmly holds its own. And there are places within minutes of the Paris periphery that are secret havens — so near and yet seemingly so far removed from the capital's crowds and traffic.

Apart from the rivers and their soft green valleys, the most characteristic natural feature of the region are its tens of thousands of acres of majestic forests, including Fontainebleau, Compiègne, Chantilly, and Rambouillet, as well as small, lesser known woods, such as Fausses Reposes. Head out of Paris in almost any direction and you're likely to run into one of these woodlands, some tended and tamed, others wild and untouched by time. Once princely hunting grounds, these forests, and the peaceful country-style inns that frequently can be found in their shadows, are rare pleasurable retreats for modern travelers.

We suggest that you make Paris your base for forays into the region, particularly if your time is limited. The route suggested here begins at St-Denis in the north, then winds clockwise around the capital, occasionally spilling over into areas that are outside the official boundaries of the Ile-de-France. Every site on the route makes a comfortable day trip or can be combined with other stops to fill out a weekend jaunt. To strangers, Paris — the City of Light — can seem rather dark on Sundays and Mondays, when its shops and many restaurants are closed. These are ideal days to take advantage of the nearby countryside. For tourist information on sights of interest and accommodations in the Ile-de-France, write the *Comité Régional d'Ile-de-France* (73 Rue Cambronne, Paris 75015; phone: 45-67-89-41), or visit the Ile-de-France booth at the Paris Tourist Office (127 Champs-Elysées; phone: 47-23-61-72 or 47-20-60-20).

Because of their proximity to Paris, country inns in the Ile-de-France tend to have city prices. Reservations almost always are required. Expect to pay $105 and up per night for a double room in hotels listed as expensive; $60 to $105 in those listed as moderate; and under $60 for inexpensive rooms. The restaurants range in price from $105 and up for a dinner for two in the expensive category; $60 to $105 in the moderate range; and under $60 for an inexpensive meal. Prices do not include wine or drinks, although service usually is included.

ST-DENIS: Worth a visit to this otherwise dreary suburb is the Basilica of St-Denis. Located at the northern gate of Paris (off the A1 autoroute, less than 2 miles/3 km north of the Porte de la Chapelle), it is perhaps one of the greatest, albeit one of the least visited, of the Ile-de-France's greatest ecclesiastical monuments. Considered the cradle of French Gothic style, it is noteworthy not only as an architectural milepost, but also for its magnificent tombs. French kings and queens have been buried here for 12 centuries, since St. Louis commissioned the chiseling of a series of effigies to commemorate his ancestors — rulers of France going back to the 7th century.

A church has stood on this holy ground since before the 5th century. St. Denis, who is depicted repeatedly in the church in stained glass and stone with his severed head in hand, was an evangelist. Along with two fellow missionaries, he brought Christianity to pagan Lutetia (later named Paris) in about 250 AD. So successful were the trio's preachings that they were decapitated at Montmartre (named the Martyr's Mount in their honor) by leaders jealous of their influence. Legend has it that the decapitated St. Denis rose, picked up his head, and walked north into the countryside until he collapsed. The spot where he fell and was buried became a pilgrimage sight, where a modest abbey eventually was erected.

At the behest of Ste. Geneviève, work on a larger church began in the 5th century, and in 638, King Dagobert sponsored the construction of the abbey church. Nearly 600 years later, the Abbot Suger, Louis VII, and architect Pierre de Montreuil conspired to promote a new style that included the first rose windows, ogival arches, and buttresses (concealed at this early stage), marking the earliest manifestations of Gothic architecture. Much of what the visitor sees today is a result of excellent 19th century restorations undertaken by Viollet-le-Duc in an effort to correct the ravages of time.

Note the restored central portal representing the last judgment. The one on the right depicts the last communion of St. Denis, and the portal on the left shows the torture of the saint and his fellow missionaries, Rustique and Eleuthere.

St-Denis's early Gothic architectural grandeur notwithstanding, an equally impressive wealth is represented by the tombs grouped around the transept, a sketchbook in stone of France's monarchs and their loved ones. Among those buried here were Clovis, the first King of France, Dagobert, Charles Martel, and Pepin the Short. Elaborate Renaissance structures, many of them created by the sculptor Germain Pilon, represent Catherine de Médicis and Henri II, Louis XII and Anne de Bretagne, and, most moving of all, Louis XVI and Marie-Antoinette. Most of the tombs now are empty — the royal remains were exhumed during the revolution and heaped into a nearby communal grave. There are other tombs in the crypt, as well as excavations of the churches that preceded the present one on this site. Regular guided tours (for a fee) of the transept are available. Visitors also may rent headphones with commentary in several languages. Open daily from 10 AM to 5 PM; Sundays from 2 to 5 PM (phone: 48-09-83-54).

EATING OUT: _Mets du Roy_ – An inviting, creamy stone façade fronts this rather formal restaurant serving traditional fare. Located directly across the square from the cathedral. Closed Saturday lunch, Sundays, 2 weeks at _Easter,_ and 2 weeks in July. Reservations advised. Major credit cards accepted. 4 Rue de la Boulangerie, St-Denis (phone: 48-20-89-74). Expensive.

Cour de l'Abbaye – Also within walking distance of the cathedral, this casual restaurant leans heavily on the hearty fare of France's southwest. The prices are reasonable and the service is friendly. Open daily for lunch, and for dinner Fridays only. Reservations unnecessary. Major credit cards accepted. 8 Rue de Boucherie (phone: 48-09-84-13). Inexpensive.

ECOUEN: Travel north from St-Denis about a dozen miles (19 km) on N16 to reach Ecouen, a rather drab town of about 5,000 inhabitants that easily could be bypassed if it weren't for the superb Château d'Ecouen and the _Musée National de la Renaissance_ (National Museum of the Renaissance; phone: 39-90-04-04) that it houses. Dating from the early 16th century, perched on a hill and surrounded by a park, Ecouen rivals Chenonceaux — one of the great Loire Valley châteaux — in elegance, though far fewer travelers visit it. Its columned interior porticoes, delicately chiseled stone, and ribbed vaulting exhibit elements of the Renaissance. Anne de Montmorency, a powerful adviser to François I, commissioned two of the epoch's masters — Jean Goujon and Jean Bullant — to construct this palace for the king.

It would be hard to imagine a more appropriate home for the museum devoted entirely to the Renaissance. Its collection, much of it formerly stored at Paris's _Musée de Cluny,_ represents an outstanding assemblage of 16th and early 17th century pieces, particularly works from the decorative arts — furniture, carved wood panels, tapestries, ceramics, and enamels. Not to be missed is the 250-foot long series of tapestries depicting the story of David and Bethsheba. Woven in silk, wool, and silver threads, it dominates the west wing of the museum's first floor and ranks among the most beautiful 16th-century tapestries in France. Note also the painted mantelpieces depicting biblical scenes in the style of the Fontainebleau School. The museum is open daily, except Tuesdays and holidays, from 9:45 AM to 12:30 PM and from 2:00 to 5:15 PM. Admission charge.

Before leaving Ecouen, visit the Church of St-Acceul near the center of town. Its remarkable stained glass windows, attributed to Jean Cousin, date from 1545. Italian influences can be detected in the windows devoted to the life of the Virgin, while those depicting members of the Montmorency family and the church's benefactors clearly follow the French style. Jean Bullant, who was responsible for much of the design of the Château d'Ecouen, is thought to be the architect of this church.

En Route from Ecouen – On the way to Chantilly, wander north on N16 about 4 miles (6 km), and then turn west on to D922 and D909 to visit Royaumont, one of the best preserved medieval abbeys in France. Founded in 1228 by Blanche de Castille, then Regent of France, and her 12-year-old son, the future Louis IX (St. Louis), this immense Cistercian abbey has a regal character that is reflected in its name. The wealth and beauty that still are apparent here attest to the protection and interest lavished on Royaumont by kings after Louis IX. Visit the vaulted refectory with its five monolithic columns and the tomb of Henri of Lorraine sculpted by the artist Coysevox.

CHANTILLY: Only a few miles northeast of Royaumont via N16, Chantilly is famous for its château, its park, and of course, the track where horse races have taken place since 1836. The surrounding 5,187-acre Chantilly Forest is crisscrossed by roads and horse trails, many of them closed to automobiles. Over the last 2,000 years, five different châteaux have stood on this site. The Montmorency family owned Chantilly's château until it passed into the possession of the noble French family, Grand Condé, in 1632. The present one was built between 1875 and 1881 by Nicolas-François Mansart at the behest of the Duke of Aumale, a son of King Louis-Philippe. Resembling an island rising out of the surrounding moat, the château is small by French standards, but exceptionally elegant. It now houses the *Musée Condé,* an excellent museum with over 2,000 artworks, including more than 600 oils by French, Flemish, and Italian masters of the 16th–18th centuries, and some superb illuminations from the 15th and 16th centuries. Open from 10 AM to 6 PM, March 1 to October 31; and 10:30 AM to 12:45 PM and 2 to 5 PM, November 1 to February 28; closed Tuesdays; (phone: 44-57-03-62 or 44-57-08-00). Admission charge. Tour the interior of the château to see the library, with its prodigious collection of rare books.

The 18th-century stables have been transformed into the *Musée Vivant du Cheval* (Living Museum of the Horse; phone: 44-57-40-40). From April to October, it is open weekdays except Tuesdays from 10:30 AM to 5:30 PM, to 6 PM on weekends and holidays; from mid-November through March, open weekdays from 2 to 4:30 PM, and 10:30 AM to 5:30 PM on weekends and holidays. Admission charge. Also visit the chapel where — to this day — the descendants of the last owner gather for Sunday services. Take time, as well, to wander through the 17th-century gardens and park, created by the renowned royal landscaper, Le Nôtre. There are several additional buildings of interest in the park, including the Maison de Sylvie, named for the Duchesse de Montmorency, who hid Théophile de Viau after he was condemned to death for his licentious poems. The house, rebuilt in 1684, later was the site of a mysterious romantic liaison that ended in the death in a "hunting accident" of the Duc de Joyeuse, Louis de Melun. Connected to the main château is the Petit Château, a lovely castle built in 1560 by Jean Bullant.

CHECKING IN: *Hostellerie du Lys* – A modest 35-room hotel in a calm, beautiful park. Major credit cards accepted. 63 Av. Septième, Lys-Chantilly (phone: 44-21-26-19; fax: 44-21-28-19). Moderate.

EATING OUT: *Le Relais Condé* – Small and bright, with a beamed ceiling and huge stone fireplace, this restaurant serves classic fare, including sweetbreads and a good selection of fish. Open year-round. Reservations advised. Major credit cards accepted. 42 Av. du Maréchal-Joffre, Chantilly (phone: 44-57-05-75). Moderate.

En Route from Chantilly – St. Leu-d'Esserent lies 3 miles (5 km) northwest of Chantilly via N16 on D44. Renowned for its architectural excellence, its mellow and beautiful 12th-century stone church sits on a commanding site overlooking the Oise River.

Route N924 east leads to the charming town of Senlis, dominated by the Ancienne Cathédrale de Notre-Dame (Pl. Notre-Dame) that was begun in 1153. Of particular interest is the portico, dedicated to the Virgin and used as the prototype for the porticoes of Chartres, Notre-Dame-de-Paris, and Reims. Also worth a visit are the ancient Eglise St-Pierre (Pl. St-Pierre), the Château Royal (for its Gallo-Roman walkway), and the *Musée de la Venerie* (Hunting Museum) in front of the château. The Gallo-Roman walkway, a defense wall on the château's perimeter, provides a good vantage point from which to view all the principal monuments.

COMPIÈGNE: On the banks of the Oise, 49 miles (79 km) north of Paris via N17, is this village justly famous for its palace (Pl. du Palais). The exterior is somewhat austere, but the rich and exquisite interior is preserved beautifully.

Compiègne has played a significant and paradoxical role in French history: Most of the Kings of France visited it at one time or another, and Joan of Arc was taken prisoner here in 1430. More recently, the armistice of November 11, 1918 was signed here (the exact site — Clairière de l'Armistice — is marked in a clearing in the woods surrounding the palace). Sadly, from 1941 to 1944, Compiègne served as a deportation center for some members of France's Jewish community en route to concentration camps.

The forest of Compiègne, with nearly 35,000 acres, has majestic avenues, ponds, and picturesque villages, such as Vieux-Moulin and St-Jean-Aux-Bois. Just beyond the forest, via D85, is the splendid 12th century château-fortress of Pierrefonds, once the property of Napoleon.

 CHECKING IN/EATING OUT: *Auberge à la Bonne Idée* – A peaceful setting surrounds this 24-room hostelry with a fine restaurant. Major credit cards accepted. St-Jean-aux-Bois, Compiègne (phone: 44-42-84-09). Moderate.

En Route from Compiègne – Retrace your route back to Senlis, turn east onto N330 toward Meaux. Seven miles (11 km) south of Senlis in the town of Châalis are the picturesque ruins of a 13th-century abbey, a château, a park north of the entrance to the château, and a museum — with three rooms devoted to the works of Jean-Jacques Rousseau, who died in 1778 in Ermenonville (2 miles/3 km) south. The countryside is dotted with numerous ponds. The Mer de Sable (Sea of Sand) — a mini-desert and a small zoo — is at Ermenonville.

MEAUX: Continue on N330 about 15 miles (24 km) south to Meaux (pronounced *Mow*), a market town of about 50,000 in the center of the wheat fields of the Brie plain — Paris's breadbasket. Meaux is renowned for its rich, creamy brie cheese and a bishop named Bossuet (known for his controversial oratories). Though just 25 miles (40 km) from Paris, it is quite removed from the frenzied hubbub of the French capital.

A diocesan see since the 4th century, Meaux has a significant religious importance. Its 14th-century Cité Episcopale is one of the rare bishopric ensembles in France that remain almost entirely intact. The complex consists of St-Etienne Cathedral, the Episcopal Palace, the chapter house, and a garden laid out in the form of a bishop's miter by the famous landscape artist, Le Nôtre.

Not to be missed on even the shortest visit to Meaux, the Cité Episcopale is located in the heart of the Old City. Start at the St-Etienne Cathedral. Constructed between the 12th and the 13th centuries, it illustrates the evolution of the Gothic style: The elegant south façade is radiant Gothic, while the main façade is Flamboyant Gothic.

Connected to the cathedral is the 13th-century chapter house with its covered 16th-century staircase.

The Ancien Evêché (Episcopal Palace) forms a rectangular courtyard with the chapter house and the cathedral. Today the palace (built during the 12th century and modified in the 17th century) houses a museum that displays Bossuet's personal effects and writings. The chapel has a collection of sacred art, including medieval sculpture, fabrics, and religious relics. Part of the palace is devoted to local history and displays works of art by regional painters and other artists including Millet, Courbet, and Van Loo. From here, visit Le Nôtre's beautiful miter-shape garden and the old ramparts, parts of which date from the 4th century. The terrace affords a beautiful view of the garden, the palace, and the cathedral.

One of the city's most illustrious citizens was Jacques-Bénigne Bossuet, an intellectual who served as the dauphin's tutor for 12 years, and subsequently was named Bishop of Meaux in 1682 by a grateful Louis XIV. Bossuet held the post for 22 years and his religious and moral convictions, as well as his gift for rousing oratory, earned him a place in posterity under the title of L'Aigle de Meaux (the Eagle of Meaux). In his vast library, Bossuet composed five famous eulogies — most notably the funeral oration for Marie-Thérèse, Louis XIV's wife. To commemorate the tricentennial of Bossuet's appointment as bishop, Meaux inaugurated a spectacular son-et- lumière (sound-and-light show) with over 1,000 performers that takes place in the summer on Friday and Saturday evenings in the court of the old chapter house. Check with the local tourist office (2 Rue Notre-Dame; phone: 64-33-02-26) for times and days of performances.

Meaux's bishopric weathered the Revolution better than most, though in 1792 it was the sight of the bloody "Massacres de Septembre," where 14 prisoners and several priests were killed in the palace courtyard. On his flight to La Varennes, Louis XVI spent the night in this palace, and Napoleon also stayed here.

The city was spared destruction during the German invasion of 1914, though the area directly north of it was the sight of devastating and decisive battles.

Before leaving town, visit the nearby market area and the core of medieval streets that wrap around it. The first *halle* (market) was built here in 1722. The current structure — a metal-frame, covered market reminiscent of Paris's central *halles* (torn down in the 1960s) — is stocked with the best food products from the generous Brie plain. Be sure to pick up a wedge of the area's famous brie — a fragrant, runny cow's milk cheese.

 EATING OUT: *Champs de Mars* – Locals recommend this traditional establishment for its consistent good quality and pleasant ambience. Closed for Tuesdays and Sundays for lunch, Friday evenings, and Saturdays. Reservations advised. Major credit cards accepted. 16 Av. Victoire, Meaux (phone: 64-33-13-96). Expensive.

En Route from Meaux – Take A4 west to *Euro Disneyland* (the exit is signposted; Marne-La-Vallée/Val d'Europe; phone: 49-41-49-41), which opened in April of last year. More than 11 million visitors are expected to pass through the $4.5 billion European home of Mickey, Minnie, Donald, et al., in its first year alone. Familiar Disney attractions include Main Street USA, Frontierland, Adventureland, Fantasyland, and Discoveryland (known as Tomorrowland in the US parks), although there are some French additions, such as a fire-breathing dragon at Sleeping Beauty's castle and a theater which features both videos and live entertainment (it turns into a disco at night). Disney aficionados can enjoy such facilities as six theme hotels, plus a campground (see *Checking In*), restaurants, shops, an 18-hole golf course (an additional 9 holes were being added as we went to press), and *Festival Disney,* a nighttime entertainment center and the site of the *Buffalo Bill Wild West Show.* Long-range plans include the opening of movie and television production facilities and a motion picture theme park, a convention center, and a water park. The site also can be reached by a 35-minute *RER* (regional express train) ride from Paris. There is a shuttle service from Charles de Gaulle and Orly airports (the park site is in between the two) to carry visitors to the park's hotels, and the *TGV* is expected to serve the park from Paris next year. Note: This *Disney* park and its hotels are much pricier than their US counterparts. It's open year-round.

Note: For hotel reservations information (in English), call 49-41-49-10 or send a fax to 49-30-71-00. You can make reservations in the US by calling 407-352-3254. All hotels have specially adapted rooms for the handicapped, as well as rooms for non-smokers. All rooms accommodate up to four people, and the log cabins at Camp Davy Crockett can bed down six people. For the region, prices are very high. At *Disneyland,* expect to pay $350 per night for a double room in hotels listed as very expensive; $250 in those listed as expensive; and $150 for moderate rooms.

CHECKING IN: *Disneyland* – This deluxe gingerbread-style hotel, with 500 rooms and 21 suites, is reminiscent of a turn-of-the-century Victorian hostelry. There are 4 restaurants, a bar, lounge, health club, an indoor heated swimming pool, a convention center, and shops. Major credit cards accepted. (phone: 60-45-65-00; fax: 60-45-65-33). Very expensive.

***New York* –** Constructed to look like a cluster of Manhattan buildings — towers, rowhouses, and brownstones — this 574-room, 36-suite property's interiors are pure Art Deco — as designed by Michael Graves — and are decorated in lugubrious colors. There are 2 restaurants, a huge convention center, a health club, 2 tennis courts, a swimming pool, and a skating rink designed to resemble the one in Rockefeller Center. Major credit cards accepted (phone: 60-45-73-00; fax: 60-45-73-33). Very expensive.

***Newport Bay Club* –** This re-creation of a Rhode Island seaside resort, with 1,098 rooms and 15 suites, has everything from dormer windows and awnings to an expansive front porch. There is even a croquet lawn, where you can practice your game. Other amenities include indoor and outdoor swimming pools, a health club, 3 restaurants, and convention center. Major credit cards accepted (phone: 60-45-55-33; fax: 60-45-55-00). Very expensive.

***Sequoia Lodge* –** There are 1,011 rooms and 14 suites set in what looks like a national park in the US — it has 6 lodges, 3 restaurants with garden views, a "winter room" with a fireplace, indoor and outdoor swimming pools, and 2 rivers. Rooms are simply decorated with patchwork quilts and checked curtains to re-create the atmosphere of a hunting lodge. The overall atmosphere is more than somewhat severe. Other amenities include a health club, bar, a convention center, and shops. Major credit cards accepted (phone: 60-45-51-00; fax: 60-45-51-33). Expensive.

***Camp Davy Crockett* –** Those longing for pine trees and squirrels can stay in one of the 181 campsites specially designed to resemble the great outdoors. This re-created forest offers secluded wooded areas studded with log-cabin-style trailers, and there are also many areas where you can simply pitch a tent. Each of the 414 log cabins accommodates up to six people, and is equipped with a TV set and telephone. Comfort stations with showers and rest rooms are located nearby, as is an indoor swimming pool and a laundromat. Throughout the campsite, there are winding nature trails, as well as bicycle and jogging paths. Major credit cards accepted (phone: 60-45-69-01; fax: 60-45-69-37). Moderate.

***Cheyenne* –** More family-oriented (and lower-priced) than the other Disney properties, it has 1,000 rooms and simulates a frontier town in the Wild West — there is a log fort with an observation tower, a corral, and a covered wagon. Each room has bunk beds for children, and 2 restaurants and a bar complete the picture. Major credit cards accepted (phone: 60-45-62-00; fax: 60-45-62-33). Moderate.

Santa Fe – The architecture of this 1,000-room (they're on the smallish side) property is adobe-style. Four complexes are reached by trails landscaped with New Mexican flora, and the decor uses artifacts and desert tones that reflect the US Southwest. No restaurant. Major credit cards accepted (phone: 60-45-78-00; fax: 60-45-62-33). Moderate.

Take A4 (east) to Provins.

PROVINS: Roses thrive throughout the Ile-de-France, but nowhere are they more prevalent than in Provins, dubbed the "town of roses." According to legend, it was Thibaud IV, King of the Navarre, Comte de Champagne, and religious crusader, who imported the first rose to France on his return to Provins from the Holy Land in the 13th century. He brought it as a gift to Blanche de Castille, his cousin, and the mother of St. Louis. The red "rose Gallica," later "*La Rose de Provins,*" flourished in the fertile Brie plain and became the object of cults. It symbolized the prosperity and flowering of this town, which remains one of France's most important (and least discovered) relics of the Middle Ages.

Today, Provins has barely 13,000 inhabitants, but during the Middle Ages, it boasted some 80,000 residents and was the third largest city in France after Paris and Rouen. Behind the city's wealth was the *Foire de Champagne,* a twice-yearly trade fair sponsored by the powerful Counts of Champagne that attracted merchants from all over Europe.

The Ville Haute (Upper Town), a fortification on a promontory jutting out over the valleys of the Voulzie and the Durteint rivers, already was a key post in 800 when Charlemagne sent his governors to oversee the settlement. The Lower Town was founded later in 1049, when one of the Counts of Champagne built a chapel in the chestnut forest below. Provins gained power and prestige, and by the 10th century, it was minting its own currency and was one of France's most powerful cities.

Numerous vestiges of Provins's former prominence remain. The wide stone ramparts of the Upper Town — which date from the 12th and 13th centuries — are reminiscent of the famous walled city of Carcassonne. Visit the St-Jean and the Jouy gates, and walk along the ramparts or stroll down the quaint, interior cobbled streets. Near the edge of the Ville Haute is the pride of Provins, the Tour César, a curious 150-foot high stone tower built over the foundations of a 12th-century dungeon. The wall at its base, added by the British in 1432 when they occupied the tower, was dubbed "English Pie." When the French recaptured the tower, they hurled the executed English into the moat, which henceforth became known as the "English Pit."

Nearby is the Church of St-Quiriace. Work on the present structure began in the 12th century, and although church canons had hopes of creating a cathedral to rival the one in Reims and other great edifices, its completion was plagued by lack of funds; the façade wasn't added until nearly 4 centuries later. Shortly afterward, a fire destroyed many of St-Quiriace's early treasures, though the 12th-century choir stalls remain, as well as the north and south doorways (built during the 12th and 13th centuries).

Provins has an exceptional number of underground passages, some of which are open to visitors. Dug over 1,000 years ago, these passages formed a bizarre labyrinth, winding from the Lower to the Upper Town. Whether these were used as simple refuges, places of worship, or for meetings of the secret societies (whose symbols are carved in the earthen walls) is unknown. Guided tours in English of one portion (the only one open to tourists) of the passages begins at the 12th-century palace of the Comtesses de Blois and Champagne, which was later transformed into a hospital, and now is empty. Note the 13th-century portal and the Renaissance stone altarpiece, donated by the Seigneurs de Chenoise in 1506. Below is the vast vaulted gallery from which tours exit. Check with the tourist association (Pl. Honoré Balzac; phone: 64-00-16-65) for details on days and times.

Also worth visiting is the Church of St-Ayoul, which stands on the site of the first chapel built in the Lower Town. Portions date from the 12th century, though much of it was rebuilt during the 16th century. The damaged Romanesque doorway recently has received a bronze tympanum, the subject of considerable local controversy. If you visit in June, be sure to attend the colorful medieval festival that takes place every year in the Upper Town. (Check with the tourist office for dates.)

En Route from Provins – Before leaving the area, drive 5 miles (8 km) southwest of Provins to see the St-Loup-de-Naud church. A beautiful little building, it has a magnificent 12th-century main door and is surrounded by sculpture that rivals Chartres's cathedral portals. In 1432, the English destroyed the monastery that stood here.

CHECKING IN/EATING OUT: *Aux Vieux Remparts* – Reputed to offer the "best table in town," this hotel in the Upper Town has a garden and 25 modern rooms. The rustic, beamed restaurant is in the older part. Its menu features refined interpretations of local specialities, with a strong emphasis on fish. Reservations advised. Major credit cards accepted. 3 Rue Couverte, Ville Haute, Provins (phone: 64-08-94-00); hotel, moderate to inexpensive; restaurant, expensive to moderate.

Croix D'Or – Claiming to be the "oldest inn in France," this 13th-century stone hostelry has 5 spacious old rooms. It also has 2 dining rooms, each warmed by a great hearth. Restaurant closed Sunday evenings and Mondays. Visa and Carte Bleue accepted. 1 Rue des Capucines, Provins (phone: 64-00-01-96). Moderate to inexpensive.

En Route from Provins – Return via N19 to the junction of N36 and follow it south to Vaux-le-Vicomte, a 17th-century château and park that ranks among the most beautiful in Europe. The château was commissioned by Fouquet, minister of finance under Louis XIV. Unfortunately, Fouquet's exquisite taste required greater resources than his personal fortune could accommodate, and his access to state funds was convenient. To build Vaux-le-Vicomte, Fouquet hired the greatest talents of the day: Le Vau as architect, Le Brun as Decorator, Le Nôtre as landscape architect. A total of 5 years, 18,000 laborers, and the equivalent of $10 million later, his château was finished. But Fouquet had committed the fatal error of being grander in scope than his sovereign. In August 1661, he gave a fabulous dinner for Louis XIV. The decoration, the food, and the entertainment were so dazzlingly elegant that they provoked the king's jealous curiosity, and in no time Fouquet's embezzlement was exposed. A few days later, Fouquet was in prison and his property confiscated. But the magnificent château had whet the self-indulgent king's appetite, and in the mid-17th-century, Louis XIV employed the same people to build his own dream palace at Versailles, the site of his father's hunting lodge. Many of the splendidly decorated rooms of Vaux-le-Vicomte are open to the public daily from 10 AM to 6 PM April through October; 11 AM to 5 PM in November, February, and March. Closed in December and January. Special candlelight visits are offered on Saturday evenings from 8:30 to 11 PM from May through October. Admission charge (phone: 60-66-97-09).

FONTAINEBLEAU: Continue south via N36 past Melun to the forest and town of Fontainebleau — the fabulous Renaissance palace that is set within 50,000 acres of forest and was the ancient hunting preserve of the Kings of France. Today the grounds are open to the public, and picnicking, hiking, or horseback riding among the trees, ravines, and ponds makes a perfect counterpoint to a day of city sightseeing. (Some energetic folks even travel here to enjoy a strenuous afternoon of rock climbing.) There are references as early as 1137 to Fontainebleau as a royal hunting site. Philippe IV was born and died here, but it wasn't until the early 16th century that the palace itself was transformed by François I — with the help of some of Italy's most talented artists — from a 12th-century medieval château to a Renaissance palace. Later kings made further alterations and added wings. Louis XIII was born here and Louis XIV signed the Revocation of the Edict of Nantes here in 1685.

Napoleon lived in Fontainebleau during most of his reign. He abdicated on April 6, 1814, but that wasn't his final good-bye. He returned from Elba in March 1815 to rally his troops again.

In August 1944, following 3 years of German occupation, US General Patton liberated Fontainebleau; the château then was used as headquarters for the Allied army.

Some people find Fontainebleau more beautiful than Versailles. It certainly is more intimate, full of surprising little corners. It's open daily except Tuesdays from 9:30 AM to 12:30 PM and 2 to 5 PM (the ticket booth closes at 4:15 PM); closed *Christmas, New Year's Day,* and May 1 (admission charge; phone: 64-22-27-40). Be sure to visit the Throne Room, the Queen's Bedroom, which was redone for Marie-Antoinette, the splendid Royal Apartments with their Gobelin tapestries, the Council Room, and the Red Room, where Napoleon abdicated in 1814.

The Cour des Adieux or Cour du Cheval Blanc – The Court of Farewells, or Court of the White Horse, was named for the site of Napoleon's farewell to his guard on April 20, 1814, and for the equestrian statue of Marcus Aurelius that formerly stood here, respectively. An elegant horseshoe shaped staircase leads to the first floor.

Salle de Bal – The work of Philibert Delorme, this splendid 100-foot long ballroom, the site of feasts and celebrations, includes mythological paintings conceived by Primaticcio and painted by Dell'Abate.

Chapelle de la Ste-Trinité – The medieval château's original chapel was consecrated by Thomas Becket in 1169. Its replacement, located to the left of the vestibule, was built by Philibert Delorme and was the site of the marriage between Louis X and Marie Leczinska in 1725.

Galerie de François I – Named for the king responsible for the transformation of Fontainebleau, this long gallery dates from the 1530s and includes the original works of Italian masters such as Rosso and Scibec de Capri.

Appartments Royaux – These regal apartments are composed of several rooms, notably the Salon Louis XIII, the Appartements de la Reine, decorated by Marie-Antoinette, and the Salle de Trône, the king's bedroom from the reign of Henri IV to Louis XVI — transformed into a throne room by Napoleon.

In addition, don't miss the Salle du Conseil, the Appartment de l'Empereur (including Napoleon's bedchamber and abdication room), and the Appartements des Reines Mères et du Pape. Before leaving, visit the *Musée Napoléon* and the extensive and beautiful gardens — particularly the Jardin de Diane created for Catherine de Médicis.

CHECKING IN/EATING OUT: *L'Aigle Noir* – An elegant, family-run establishment facing the château gardens and near the heart of the city. The style is Napoleonic — fittingly grand lodgings for visitors to the château of which the emperor was so fond. There are 57 rooms, including 5 suites; an elegant restaurant (a recent recipient of its first Michelin star), an indoor pool, a workout room, meeting rooms, and an interior garden. Major credit cards accepted. 27 Pl. Napoléon-Bonaparte, Fontainebleau (phone: 64-22-32-65; fax: 64-22-17-33). Expensive.

En Route from Fontainebleau – Just on the edge of the forest lies Barbizon, made famous as an artists' colony in the 19th century by the likes of the painters Honoré Daumier and Constant Musset, the poet Alfred de Troyon, and the writer George Sand. You can visit Rousseau's house at 55 Grand-Rue, just behind the Monument aux Morts (phone: 60-66-22-38). It is open weekdays except Tuesdays from 10 AM to 12:30 PM and 2 to 6 PM from April through September, and from 2 to 5 PM October through

March; on weekends and holidays there is no midday closing. Stop for lunch or a drink at the celebrated, half-timbered inn *Bas-Bréau* (see below), an elegant second home to many Parisians.

 CHECKING IN/EATING OUT: *Hotellerie du Bas-Bréau* – An elegant hotel (a member of the Relais & Châteaux group) that welcomes fashionable — and well-heeled — Parisians. In existence since 1867, it has housed such celebrities as Robert Louis Stevenson and Napoleon III. With modern bathrooms, an intimate bar, and a superlative haute cuisine restaurant (one Michelin star), this place is expensive but worth it. An absolutely perfect place for a Sunday drive from Paris. Closed January. Reservations necessary. Major credit cards accepted. 22 Rue Grande, Barbizon, via N7, N37, and D64 from Fontainebleau (phone: 60-66-40-05; fax: 60-69-22-89). Very expensive.

From here travelers can opt for several different routes depending on their interests and the time available. Nearly due west by some 70 miles (113 km) is Chartres. (For a detailed report on the city, its sights, and restaurants, see *Chartres*, THE CITIES.) Returning toward Paris via A6, then turning west on N446 will lead you through an area that many of the French consider the prettiest countryside in the Ile-de-France — the Vallée de Chevreuse. Picturesque villages abound: Châteaufort, with its 12th-century fortress; St-Rémy-lès-Chevreuse; St-Lambert; Dampierre, the site of a 16th-century château; and Les Vaux de Cernay, one of the loveliest valleys in France. Just south of Les Vaux de Cernay on N306 is Rambouillet, the château that served as a rural retreat for Louis XVI and Napoleon and is used today by President François Mitterand. Originally a medieval fortress, it retains its impressive 14th-century tower. President Mitterand uses the château for some political meetings and visits on Mondays, Wednesdays, Fridays, and Saturdays. Tourists can tour the château (admission charge; phone: 34-83-00-25) when he is not there. It is open daily except Tuesdays from 10 to 11:30 AM and 2 to 4:30 PM. In nearby Chatenay-Malabry (via N186) is the home of the writer Chateaubriand (*Maison de Chateaubriand;* 87 Rue de Chateaubriand, Vallée aux Loups; phone: 47-02-08-62). It has been transformed into a museum in tribute to the author and his fellow Romantics. It is open Wednesdays, Fridays, Saturdays, and Sundays from 2 to 5 PM; Tuesdays and Thursdays are reserved for group visits. Admission charge.

 CHECKING IN: *Château d'Esclimont* – Built in 1543, this turreted feudal castle was restored and now is a luxury hotel (and a member of the Relais & Châteaux group). Its 48 rooms and 6 suites are furnished beautifully with period pieces; their shape varies depending on whether they're in the castle, dungeon, stables, or a separate pavilion. The restaurant overlooks a 150-acre walled park that surrounds the hotel. Tennis, swimming, and hunting are available. Reservations necessary. Major credit cards accepted. St-Symphorien-le-Château, off N10 between Rambouillet and Chartres (phone: 37-31-15-15). Expensive. Continue west on N186 to reach Versailles.

VERSAILLES: The construction of Versailles nearly bankrupted France. About 6,000 people once lived in this incredibly lavish palace, and its vast gardens, designed by the famous royal gardener Lenôtre in the formal French style, are spread over 250 acres. A river was diverted to keep the 600 fountains flowing. A gleaming monument to the French monarchy at its most ostentatious, Versailles epitomizes the excesses that sparked a revolution that changed the course of history.

Its beginnings were modest enough. In 1624, Louis XIII ordered a hunting lodge to be built on a hill above the small village of Versailles, 14 miles (22 km) west of Paris. Versailles's evolution from this simple lodge to the grandiose palace of the Sun King and the seat of the French government from 1682 to 1789, was the result of a complex, and ultimately condemning, set of circumstances.

There is so much to see at Versailles that a full day is almost the minimum required for a visit. If time allows, plan to spend 2 days. The château is under continuous restoration, so be prepared for temporary closings of certain rooms from time to time. The château is open daily, except Mondays, from 9 AM to 5:30 PM; and from 9 AM to 7:30 PM April through September (phone: 30-84-76-76). Admission charge for the château; no charge for the gardens.

Before crossing the wide avenue that passes in front of the château, notice the king's stables (*écuries royales*) and carriage house constructed by Jules Hardouin-Mansart. Once past the Louis XVIII gates, three successive courtyards lead up to the visitors' entrance: the Minister's Courtyard and the Royal Courtyard, separated by a bronze statue of Louis XIV on horseback, which give way to the internal Marble Courtyard.

The main entrance to the right of the Royal Courtyard leads to a vestibule and ticket booth through which some 4 million visitors pass annually. To get the most from your visit, join an English-language lecture tour (leaves every 20 minutes from Gate C) or read up in advance.

The Chapel – Built between 1699 and 1710 by Mansart, this masterpiece of white stone and multicolored marble — punctuated by great gilded doors and the bas-reliefs of masters such as Puget and Vasse — was dedicated to St. Louis. Its construction was vehemently opposed by Mme. de Maintenon (mistress and subsequently second wife of Louis XIV) who, according to Voltaire, was preoccupied with the poverty of the people. This did not deter the Sun King, whose aim was to offer God the most magnificent of all chapels. Note the elaborate ceiling paintings dedicated to the Holy Trinity and the magnificent gilded organ loft.

Grand Apartments – Some of the château's most extraordinary rooms are found in this first floor wing. Start at the Salon d'Hercule, named for François Lemoine's ceiling painting, the *Apotheosis of Hercules*. Next is the Salon de l'Abondance, which marks the beginning of the king's State Apartments. Each of the following five rooms was dedicated to a Greek god: the Salons of Venus and Diana, with their Italianate marble decors; the Salon of Mars, with an early Gobelins tapestry depicting the life of the king; the Salon of Mercury, a card room where Louis XIV lay in state for 8 days after his death; and the Salon of Apollo, the former throne room and the last of the king's state apartments.

The Hall of Mirrors – Flanked on either side by the Salon de la Guerre and the Salon de la Paix, the Galerie des Glaces is, for many visitors, the most memorable of all of Versailles's rooms. Extending along the west façade of the château, it measures 240 feet long, 33 feet wide and 40 feet high. Seventeen tall, arched windows facing east are reflected in 17 sparkling mirrors on the opposite wall, each separated by red marble and gilt bronze pilasters. Gilded scrolls and cherubs, ornate candlesticks, crystal chandeliers, and a celebrated ceiling painting by Le Brun add to the pomp and splendor of this hall, once the scene of magnificent balls and the place the Sun King chose to grant audiences to ambassadors from Persia, Siam, and other distant lands. The Treaty of Versailles was signed in this gallery on June 28, 1919, putting an end to World War I. In 1923, John D. Rockefeller donated funds for repairing the roof of the Hall of Mirrors, thus initiating the restoration of this great monument.

Queen's Apartments – The queen's bedchamber, her private suite, antechamber, and guard room were created for Marie Thérèse, first wife of Louis XIV. Most outstanding is the sumptuous bedchamber, unveiled in 1975 after an intensive 30-year restoration. The elaborate floral motifs amid rococo ornamentation reflect the queen's love of flowers. It is said that royal gardeners replanted the garden outside these windows daily so that the queen would see a new assortment of blossoms each morning. Nineteen royal children were born in this room, including Louis XV and Philippe V of Spain, and it was here that Marie-Antoinette spent her last night at Versailles.

King's Apartments – The king's state and private chambers comprise a series of some 15 rooms arranged in a "U" around the Marble Court on the east façade of the palace. Completed in 1701, these rooms clearly illustrate the evolution of the decorative style known as Louis XIV. Included are the "public" bed chamber where the king's waking and retiring were attended by members of the court and the public, as well as his private bedchamber and rooms — the king's most secret quarters.

Museum of French History – Louis-Philippe converted the palace's south wing — the apartments of Louis XIV's brother and some of the royal children — into a museum. The centerpiece of the museum is the Hall of Battles where huge paintings, busts, and bronze plaques constitute a survey of French history from the 17th to the 19th century. Other parts of the palace museum include the 16th through the 19th-century rooms, including many royal apartments which have been reopened to the public.

Royal Opera – Louis XV commissioned this dazzling display of carved and gilded wood, colorfully painted imitation marble, and glittering crystal in honor of the marriage of his grandchildren, in particular that of the dauphin to Marie-Antoinette on May 16, 1770. It was the first theater in France to have an elliptical shape and levels graded in tiers. Built in just 21 months, it was designed by Gabriel with decorative motifs by Pajou. It was stripped during the Revolution and later used for Assembly and Senate meetings from 1870 to 1875; it was restored to its original splendor in the 1950s.

Gardens – Lenôtre created the gardens between 1661 and 1668, with mechanical assistance for the fountains by Mansart and magnificent sculpture by Le Brun. The gardens spread over 2,470 acres and represent the pinnacle of French formal landscaping. An in-depth visit requires nearly as much time as a tour of the château and can uncover a multitude of delightful surprises. On summer·Sundays, the fountains dance to a son et lumière presentation. (For information, check with the Versailles Tourist Office, 7 Rue des Réservoirs; phone: 39-50-36-22.)

Grand and Petit Trianons – Apparently not content with the size of the domain encompassed by Versailles's palace and its immense gardens in 1668, Louis XIV bought the small village of Trianon located at the edge of his gardens and ordered his architects to construct a pavilion for casual gatherings and rustic fetes. The resulting House of Porcelain, completed in 1670, was covered with blue and white Delft tiles. However, it proved too small and quaint for the king and in 1687, he commissioned a more glamorous, marble palace — the Grand Trianon — that remains today. Nearby is the Petit Trianon, a small masterpiece by Gabriel set in the midst of a botanical garden and a sort of experimental farm, commissioned by Louis XV in 1761. After the king's death, his son gave the Petit Trianon to Marie-Antoinette, who went there frequently in an effort to escape the pressures and confusion of Versailles. She decorated its rooms in the style of the period. Several other structures also are grouped in this area, including Le Hameau, a collection of cottages emulating the small hamlet of Chantilly. Though legend has it that Marie-Antionette amused herself here by playing the peasant, most sources refute this, saying that the queen's sense of propriety would have prevented such behavior. What seems certain is that she enjoyed the simplicity and privacy afforded by this hidden hamlet. Both the Grand Trianon and the Petit Trianon are open weekdays except Monday from 10 AM to 12:30 PM, and from 2 to 5:30 PM; open from 10 AM to 7:30 PM on Saturdays and Sundays.

 CHECKING IN/EATING OUT: *Le Trianon Palace* – Versailles's most prestigious hotel, in operation since 1911, has been transformed into an even more glorious weekend retreat. The 130 rooms are furnished with antiques, and there is a covered swimming pool and 2 terraces facing the chateau's park, where a flock of docile white sheep keep the lawn tidy by nibbling the grass. Newly installed, the elegant yet intimate *Trois Marches* offers perfect service and highly original cooking — celebrated by two Michelin stars — which would be worth the trip even if you weren't visiting Versailles. Chef Gérard Vié invents new recipes daily, but his foie gras is famous, as are his oysters and wild goose. The wines here, especially the burgundies, are excellent, too. Restaurant closed Sundays and Mondays. Major credit cards accepted. 1 Bd. de la Reine, Versailles (hotel phone: 39-50-34-12; restaurant phone: 39-50-34-12). Very expensive.

SCEAUX: Even in this region of lush woods and kings' gardens, Sceaux (pronounced *Sew*) — located 10 miles (16 km) east of Versailles via N12 — with its cascading fountains, reflecting pools, grand canal, and precisely manicured emerald lawns, stands out. A park worthy of any monarch, Sceaux's gardens and château were commissioned not by the king, but by his audacious minister of buildings, Colbert.

In 1670, Colbert called on the greatest architectural and landscaping talents of the epoch, including Claude Perrault, Le Brun, Girardon, Coysevox, and Le Nôtre, to collaborate in the realization of his grandiose project. The inauguration in 1677, before honored guest Louis XIV, was a spectacular affair during which Racine's *Phèdre* first was presented.

Transformed from a small, anonymous hamlet in the center of vineyards to a de rigueur stop for royalty and nobility, Sceaux entered its golden age. About 2 decades after the Sun King and his mistress (later wife) Mme. de Maintenon were received at Sceaux, their son, the Duc de Maine, bought the château and its gardens. His ambitious wife, the Duchesse de Maine, added to Sceaux's renown with her lively salons and spectacular *nuits de Sceaux* (festive evenings) that drew *tout* Paris and Versailles. Habitués included Voltaire, Racine, and Molière, some of whose works were performed in the Orangerie (northeast of the château) constructed by Jules Hardouin-Mansart in 1684. To the right of the Orangerie is the Pavillon de l'Aurore, built by Perrault, and behind it a series of neatly kept French gardens.

Colbert's sumptuous 17th-century château was replaced in the 19th century by the more modest one that still stands today and nearly is overwhelmed by the park's grandeur. Since 1937 the château has housed the *Musée de L'Ile-de-France* (Museum of the Ile-de-France; phone: 46-61-06-71) documenting the history and topography of the region through drawings, photographs, and objects such as the ceramics of Sceaux, St-Cloud, and Sèvres. Open daily from 10:30 AM to 6 PM; open until 5 PM in winter. Admission charge.

After a visit to the museum, wander through the grounds to the west and south. Laid out by Lenôtre, it is one of the most beautiful public parks in the Paris region. Most spectacular is the Allée de la Duchesse leading to the Grandes Cascades, where ten broad platforms of tumbling water and fountains empty into the sculpture-flanked, octagonal pool. To the west is the Grand Canal and beyond a putting-green-perfect lawn is the curious Pavillon de Hanovre. Constructed in 1760 on Paris's Boulevarde de Capucines, with funds extorted from Hanoverians during the Seven Years War, the structure was picked up and moved to Sceaux in 1832. (It is not open to the public.)

Exit the park at the northwestern gate to visit the town. The French fabulist Florian is buried in the Jardin des Félibres behind the church where there are busts of Mistral and other provincial poets. In the local cemetery are the tombs of Pierre and Marie Curie. Also visit the 16th-century Eglise St-Jean-Baptiste, which houses some mementos of the Duc and Duchesse du Maine, as well as a medallion of the Virgin attributed to Coysevox. Nearby is yet another garden, the Jardin de la Ménagerie.

The winding little main street of Sceaux is a quaint pedestrian walkway lined with shops — many selling cheese, meat, and bread perfect for a picnic. Beautifully displayed cheeses, *pain poîlane* (a French country bread), *tourtes* (savory tarts), and prepared dishes that use cheese, are among the offerings in *Le Fromagerie*, a jewel-like boutique (37 Rue Houdan; phone: 46-61-01-50). They also sell excellent wines. Also try *Au Porcelet Rose* (41 Rue Houdan; phone: 46-61-01-71), a rosy-hue, high-tech charcuterie, featuring everything from roast chicken and prepared salads to foie gras and steamed lobsters.

En Route from Sceaux – Northeast of Sceaux via N13 is the château of Malmaison, bought by Josephine Bonaparte in 1799, 3 years after her marriage to Napoleon. It became the empress's favorite residence; she settled here after her divorce in 1809 and stayed until her death in 1814. It now is a museum (phone: 47-49-20-07) containing many impressive artworks of the Napoleonic period as well as some of the house's original furnishings and a survey of the era's history as seen through war documents and mementos. It is open daily except Tuesday from 10 AM to noon and from 1:30 to 5 PM. Admission charge.

ST-GERMAIN-EN-LAYE: Return to N13 and travel 5 miles (8 km) farther west to reach St-Germain-en-Laye. This former home of kings is today a favorite weekend retreat for Parisians. The château was begun during the 12th century but completely rebuilt in the 16th century to bring it up to Renaissance standards. Two floors now are occupied by the *Musée de Antiquités Nationales* (phone: 34-51-53-65), which displays tools, jewelry, ceramics, and other objects through the time of Charlemagne as well as prehistoric and Celtic artifacts. It is open daily except Tuesdays from 9 AM to 5:15 PM; admission charge. The gardens and terraces are splendid, and the extensive forest surrounding the town offers all manner of recreational activity.

The town itself is one of the chicest and best-heeled in the environs of Paris. The pedestrian shopping street that curves away from the château (Pl. Charles de Gaulle) leads to more boutiques-lined streets that are worth exploring. Also visit the *Musée du Prieuré* (2 *bis* Rue Maurice-Denis; phone: 39-73-77-87), a few minutes' walk southwest of the main shopping streets. Dedicated to the works of artists from the Symbolist and the Nabis schools, and particularly to the museum's benefactor, artist Maurice Denis, who made this former hospital his home and studio from 1914 to 1943, the museum has a noteworthy collection of works from the mid-19th to the mid-20th century. Be sure to see La Chapelle St-Louis, the chapel of the old hospital, decorated in blue frescoes and stained glass by Denis. Open Wednesday through Friday, 10 AM to 5:30 PM; weekends and holidays from 10 AM to 6:30 PM. Admission charge.

CHECKING IN: *La Forestière* – A charming, traditional country inn with modern conveniences; set among beautiful gardens, it also has a fine restaurant, *Cazaudehore,* which serves classic cuisine as well as several Basque specialties such as *pipérade* (eggs cooked with peppers, ham, and hot sausages). Closed Mondays except holidays. Major credit cards accepted. 1 Av. Président-Kennedy, St-Germain-en-Laye (phone: 39-73-36-60; fax: 39-73-73-88). Expensive.

Pavillon Henri IV – An old-fashioned hostelry with 42 plush rooms and apartments, a delightful atmosphere, and a pleasant restaurant overlooking the Seine Valley. This is where béarnaise sauce was created. Major credit cards accepted. 21 Rue Thiers, St-Germain-en-Laye (phone: 34-51-62-62; fax: 39-73-93-73). Expensive.

Auberge Morainvilliers – This very attractive country inn and restaurant are set in private gardens with a swimming pool. Major credit cards accepted. Morainvilliers-Orgeval, via N13 and D198 from St-Germain-en-Laye (phone: 39-75-87-57). Moderate to inexpensive.

EATING OUT: *L'Esturgeon* – Sturgeon no longer are served here (they no longer frequent the Seine), but there is a good *coulibiac* of salmon, the house specialty, and a variety of delicious crêpes. Sadly, though, the dining room has lost its Michelin star. Closed Thursdays and August and 1 week in February. Reservations advised. Major credit cards accepted. Seventeen miles (27 km) northwest of Paris via N190, at 6 Cours du 14-Juillet, Poissy (phone: 39-79-19-94 or 39-65-00-04). Expensive.

Brasserie du Théâtre – The front room of this bustling archetypal eatery provides a great view of the château, located just across the square. The decor is Art Deco and the service friendly. The food is classic brasserie fare, including a fresh raw bar, grilled meat, steak tartare, and *choucroute* (sauerkraut with pork, sausages, and ham). Open daily until 1 AM. Closed *Christmas*. Visa accepted. Pl. Charles-de-Gaulle, St-Germain-en-Laye (phone: 30-61-28-00). Moderate.

En Route from St-Germain En Laye – North of St-Germain-en-Laye via D927 is *Mirapolis* (outside Pontoise), France's first theme park. If you have children along, it's worth a visit. Open year-round (phone: 30-75-14-91).

But if art and gardens are more to your liking, take a detour to the west (via A13) for a visit to Giverny and the *Museum of Claude Monet*. (For a complete description, see "Vernon" in *Normandy*, DIRECTIONS.) If time still allows, continue north to Beauvais — 45 miles (72 km) from Paris via A15 and D927. Although technically it too lies outside the boundaries of the Ile-de-France in a less-than-attractive area, a visit to the imposing Cathédrale St-Pierre makes the trip worthwhile.

The cathedral, whose Gothic style is in rather jarring contrast to that of the rest of the city, has had an erratic history, plagued by overambition and underfinancing. The soaring choir section, begun in 1247, was a challenge to architects throughout Europe. They did not prove equal to the challenge, and in 1284 the choir collapsed. In 1500, another generation of bishops decided to continue the work and undertook to finance it by the expedient sale of indulgences. But again the architects literally let Beauvais down: An experimental cross tower was constructed, but the supporting pillars gave way in 1573. Since then, the cathedral of Beauvais has remained a magnificent, if unfinished, monument.

The vaulted interior of the cathedral appears to rise to startling, almost dizzying, heights. Through the well-preserved stained glass windows streams a luminous light in which to view the church's magnificent tapestries, attesting to the city's renown as a center of weaving.

Before leaving the city, also look at the Eglise St-Etienne (Rue de L'Etamine and Rue de l'Infanterie). The stained glass of the Choir section has some of the most beautiful examples of Renaissance windows.

 CHECKING IN: *Mercure Beauvais* – Modern facilities and an outdoor pool are offered at this comfortable hotel. Major credit cards accepted. Av. Montaigne, SAC Quartier St-Lazare, Beauvais (phone: 44-02-03-36; fax: 44-02-12-50). Moderate.

N1 leads to Paris.

The Loire Valley

The Loire Valley is one of the most strikingly beautiful portions of a country renowned for its beauty. Here the turrets of a medieval castle soar above the deep green branches of a forest in which the Kings of France once hunted wild boar; there the bright waters of a broad river part to curve around a lushly wooded island with children splashing on its shore; and everywhere neatly tended vineyards, orchards, and vegetable fields stretch between water and rolling slopes under a wide, pale blue sky that is almost always speckled with a few puffs of cloud. "Peaceful" is the word most often used over the centuries to describe the Loire Valley, and that it still is — gentle, tranquil, and calm. An important element in this mildness is the climate, tempered by winds blowing inland from the Atlantic, into which the Loire — at 625 miles the longest river in France — flows 100 miles (160 km) west of the city of Angers, by general agreement the western limit of the Loire Valley. Spring comes early here — Loire Valley gardeners send asparagus and strawberries to Paris street markets before Parisians are out of their winter coats — and summer often lingers late.

But for all this sweetness and softness that the French term *douceur,* the Loire Valley has seen considerable drama, intrigue, and outright bloodshed. Kings and counts have fought over each piece of high ground here — and over the affections and dowries of a long list of wealthy, titled, sometimes beautiful, and often scheming women — obtaining naturally well defended positions and, in the process, spectacular views.

Today the people you meet in the Loire Valley are warm and charming 20th-century innkeepers, restaurateurs, and vintners, but you are likely to come away with equally vivid impressions of dramatic, sometimes blood-thirsty characters who lived, and in some cases died, long ago in the châteaux and abbeys of the valley, among them Richard the Lion-Hearted, François I, Marie de Médici, Honoré de Balzac, and Leonardo da Vinci. It was here that Joan of Arc won the allegiance of the dauphin and rode into history and immortality under his banners. To walk the Loire Valley's heavy stone corridors and ancient flower gardens is to be touched by hints of what life must have been like for these fascinating people centuries ago.

Going back some 5,000 years, you also can visit remarkable prehistoric stone monuments called dolmens and menhirs, especially in the Saumur-Gens area. Everywhere you will see troglodyte dwellings and cave homes, often large and comfortable, dug right into the region's soft cliffs; people live in them (though they must seem very unusual "basement" apartments) or use them for garages or wine cellars.

Gentle as well as more vigorous sports are available here for visitors. Much of the area is flat, with well-surfaced country roads meandering through pretty fields and along enchanting waterways, so bicycling has become popular. Bicycles can be rented in several towns and at three locations in Tours, in the heart of the region: the train station (Pl. de la Gare; phone: 47-20-50-50), *Au Col de Cygne* (46 *bis* Rue Docteur-Fournier; phone: 47-46-00-37), and *Grammont Motocycles* (93 Av. de Grammont; phone: 47-66-62-89).

You can canoe, kayak, and even windsurf on the Loire and its tributaries; fishing is so popular that places like Chinon and Langeais are full of shops selling *articles de pêche* (fishing tackle). The truly adventurous can fly over the Touraine region in hot-air balloons; tours are organized by a number of companies, including *B. Bombard* (phone: 80-26-63-30; fax: 80-26-69-20) or *Polisphair* (phone: 47-58-89-58; fax: 47-58-85-39).

For most visitors, though, the Loire Valley is a place simply to slow down and enjoy the exercise inherent in climbing château steps (some have many) and in strolling across flowery fields under a gentle noonday sun to find an ideal picnic place. Evening entertainment here is correspondingly quiet: perhaps a son et lumière at the closest castle or a chamber concert in a nearby cloister.

Many of the churches and châteaux have superb acoustics, and many musical events are scheduled, especially from July through September. The best-known musical festival in the Loire Valley is probably the 29-year-old *Fêtes Musicales en Touraine* (see the city of Tours, below).

Mealtime is a particular pleasure in the Loire Valley. Not surprising in a region laced by sparkling rivers and bursting with agricultural abundance, you will find delicious fish, tasty sausage, and fine meat of all kinds, often exquisitely sauced and accompanied by excellent vegetables and fruits, the freshest of local cheeses, and delightful wines. Regional dishes include *saumon à l'oseille* (salmon with sorrel sauce), *andouillette* (sausage made from chitterlings) from Tours or Angers, coq au vin (chicken cooked in wine sauce) made with regional bourgueil or chinon red wines or even white vouvray, *matelote d'anguille* (stewed eel), and *rillons* (spicy, cubed pork) and *rillettes* (minced pork usually spread on crisp bread) from Tours. The house specialty in the Loire Valley may be a terrine made from deer, pheasant, or boar from a nearby forest, freshly caught fish (such as the tasty Loire River *sandre*), or vegetables from a nearby garden. Pâtés usually are worth sampling, as are *chèvres* (goat cheeses) and fruit tarts. For all of these, prices usually are very reasonable.

Travelers brought up on the idea that a hotel restaurant equals a bad restaurant should prepare to change their thinking in the Loire Valley. First of all, if you decide to stay in some of the charming small towns (strongly recommended) rather than in Orléans, Blois, Tours, or Angers, there may be few restaurants other than hotel dining rooms. Luckily, some of the finest restaurants *are* connected with hotels. And what a pleasure after a rich meal and good wine simply to climb the stairs to a comfortable bed instead of driving on dark and unfamiliar roads.

In 1882, Henry James said: ". . . it is half the charm of the Loire that you can travel beside it. A wide river, as you follow a wide road, is excellent company." The Loire Valley route covers about 300 miles (480 km), beginning at Blois, 113 miles (181 km) and 2 hours by autoroute south of Paris. It progresses generally west past châteaux, through forests, and along rivers on the southern side of the Loire to Angers, then turns east, following the northern bank of the river back to Tours, where you can take the autoroute north to Paris or south toward Bordeaux. It's also possible to zigzag back and forth across the river west of Tours and end the route at Angers in order to continue into Britanny. Michelin map No. 64 contains all but a short southern dip of the route.

A caveat: To cover all the stops mentioned in a single trip might be wearying and could lead to the malady known as being "châteauxed out." Distances between one point of interest and the next are short — Blois and Angers are only 100 miles (160 km) apart, and the direct distance from Angers to Tours is a scant 66 miles (106 km) — so it is highly possible to cover the entire route, with stops, in 3 or 4 days. You may, however, choose to concentrate on the sections of the route that most intrigue you and save the rest for return trips.

Other tips: Reserve as early as possible for hotels and special restaurants; this area is as popular with Parisians as it is with tourists, and some towns have only one or two specially pleasant hotels. Hotels usually charge extra for breakfast; check the card on the back of your hotel room door for both room and breakfast rates. Some châteaux and museums close 1 day a week, most commonly Monday or Tuesday, and many are closed daily from noon to 2 PM. You may welcome a lunch break yourself, but if you are trying to squeeze in as much sightseeing as possible, study brochures from the regional tourist offices ahead of time. Be forewarned, though, that closing dates, not only of châteaux and museums but also of restaurants and hotels, may change.

Admission prices to the châteaux vary dramatically. Some are run by the government; others are privately owned and are usually more expensive; still others include visits to adjacent museums in the cost.

For up-to-date information on all aspects of life in this area, consult regional and local Syndicats d'Initiative, or tourist offices. The main tourist office in Tours, opposite the train station, is an especially dynamic operation, publishing each year a detailed series of brochures in English covering food and wine, hotels, monuments and museums, concerts and son et lumière performances, routes for tourists, and even unusual things to do and see in Touraine. Write to the Office du Tourisme de Tours, Bd. Heurteloup, Tours 37042 (phone: 47-05-58-08; fax: 47-61-14-22).

Expect to pay $160 and up for a double room in a very expensive hotel; $100 to $160 in an expensive one; $50 to $100 in one listed as moderate; and less than $50 in an inexpensive place. A meal for two with a bottle of regional wine will cost $100 and up in an expensive restaurant; $50 to $100 in a moderate one; and under $50 in an inexpensive restaurant. Service usually is included.

ORLÉANS: No one has received quite the rousing welcome Joan of Arc did when she liberated this city from the English in 1429, but it is still often chosen as the beginning of a tour of the Loire Valley. World War II was not kind to Orléans, now as in centuries past an industrial center and with a current population of 130,000; yet a few treasures remain, and the city is a good point from which to explore the surrounding Loire region. Though not as stunning as its castle-flecked counterpart to the west, it still is special in its own right. The tourist office is located at Pl. Albert-Ier (phone: 38-53-05-95; fax: 38-54-49-84).

A visit to Orléans should include the following three sights, all conveniently on or just off Rue Jeanne-d'Arc: First, the Gothic Cathédrale Ste-Croix, as large as Notre-Dame in Paris, which was begun in the 13th century. Partially destroyed by the Huguenots (who made Orléans their headquarters briefly in 1568), it was not completed until the 19th century. Its chancel contains outstanding woodwork from the early 18th century executed by Jules Degoullons, who also designed the stalls in Notre-Dame and contributed to the decoration of Versailles. Near the splendid old Town Hall, which dates from the 15th century (1 Rue Fernand Rabier; phone: 38-53-39-22) is the *Musée des Beaux-Arts* contains some outstanding works of primitive art from the 15th century, pastel and oil portraits from the 18th century, and 19th- and 20th-century art, including works by Gauguin and Max Jacob. It is open daily except Tuesdays from 10 AM to noon and 2 to 6 PM; no admission charge. The *Musée Historique et Archéologique,* in the restored 16th-century Hôtel Cabu (Pl. de l'Abbé-Denoyers; phone: 38-53-39-22), is small and lovely, with examples of local arts and crafts from the 17th through the 19th century. It is open daily except Tuesdays from 10 AM to noon and 2 to 6 PM. Admission charge.

A statue of Joan of Arc on horseback, erected in 1855, dominates Place du Martroi, into which Rue Royale dead-ends. Every May 7 and 8, the city celebrates its Maid with great pageantry.

From Orléans, excursions can be made easily into the Forêt d'Orléans, 124,000 acres of pine and oak, and beyond it to the Basilique St-Benoît-sur-Loire, 19 miles (30 km) upstream from Orléans on the north bank of the river. This exquisite Romanesque structure, perhaps the finest in France, stands on foundations that date to 806 and is crowned with a beautifully carved belfry on the 11th-century chancel; a Roman mosaic brought from Italy in 1531 graces the floor, and the restored crypt looks the same as it did 8 centuries ago.

A few miles south of Orléans via RN20 is the Château La Ferte Saint-Aubin, a private castle open to the public. Though there has been a château on this site since the 11th century, most of this exceptional building was built in the 17th century by Henri de Saint-Nectaire. Open daily from 10 AM to 7 PM from mid-March to mid-November (phone: 38-76-52-72).

Follow N152, or the speedier A10, west for 37 miles (59 km) to Blois.

CHECKING IN: *D'Arc* – One of Orléans's most comfortable hotels, it has 35 rooms that are decorated with rattan furniture. Located opposite the plaza in front of the train station. Major credit cards accepted. 37 Rue de la République (phone: 38-53-10-94; fax: 38-81-77-47). Expensive to moderate.

EATING OUT: *La Crémaillère* – This lovely place delights guests with its tempting three-fish platter, *coquilles St-Jacques,* and cold fruit soufflé, among other popular dishes (although it recently lost its one-star status). Closed Sunday evenings and Mondays. Reservations necessary. Major credit cards accepted. 34 Rue Notre-Dame-de-Recouvrance, Orléans (phone: 38-53-49-17). Expensive to moderate.

BLOIS: Rising above the right bank of the wide Loire River, its skyline dominated by a historic château, this pleasant city of 50,000 is mainly a business center for the surrounding farming region. Blois prides itself on its complex history as a residence of French kings and on its rich architecture from the 13th to the 17th century, expressed most dramatically in the château itself. The multi-winged whole reads like a summary of the evolution of French architecture over 400 years: its separate sections date from the 13th-century feudal period, the 15th-century Gothic-Renaissance transition period, the Renaissance of the 16th century, and the 17th century's Classicism. Dastardly deeds and intrigues aplenty are evoked on a visit here: The Duc de Guise was assassinated in King Henri III's bedroom on the second floor in 1588; Marie de Médici, as a stout, middle-aged woman, inched down a rope ladder into the moat by night in 1619 to escape after 2 years of banishment here ordered by her son, Louis XIII; and 237 carved wooden panels in Catherine de Médicis's study still conceal her secret cupboards.

Other places to visit in Blois include the fine Eglise St-Nicolas, the Cathédrale St-Louis, and the picturesque streets stretching down from it toward the Loire, and the former Bishop's Palace, now the Hôtel de Ville (Town Hall), with a terrace overlooking the river and an 18th-century humpbacked bridge across it. The statue of Joan of Arc on the terrace is the work of an American sculptor, Anna Hyatt Huntington. There also is a statue of Denis Papin, Blois's most famous son, who discovered the principle of the steam engine in 1707 and also invented what he called a "digester," the forerunner of the pressure cooker. Follow D951 and D84 upriver to Chambord.

On a clear day in the summer, a flight by helicopter, lasting from 10 minutes to an hour leaving from the *héliostation* (phone: 54-74-35-52), can be organized at the tourist office in Blois (3 Av. Jean-Laignet; phone: 54-74-06-49; fax: 54-56-04-59).

CHECKING IN: *Hostellerie la Malouinière* – Formerly the residence of Bernard Lorjou, a Loire Valley painter, this white stucco and red brick building has been transformed into an elegant country inn and restaurant. The 8 guestrooms — each named for a Loire château — are decorated with antique furniture, and floral-print fabrics from Pierre Frey, one of France's foremost designers. The bathrooms are large and luxurious. A sunny terrace, garden, park, pool, and a rose-filled, one-star dining room add to the pleasure. Chef-owner Claude Berthon's specialties include *consommé aux truffes* (truffle consommé), grilled Brittany lobster, and roast rack of lamb with garlic butter. Closed from January 2 through early March. Reservations advised. Major credit cards accepted. About 3 miles (5 km) east of Blois via N152. 1 Rue Bernard-Lorjou, St-Denis-sur-Loire (phone: 54-74-76-81; fax: 54-74-85-96). Expensive.

Le Médicis – A homey atmosphere prevails in both the hotel and its restaurant, located just behind the train station. Some of its 12 individually decorated rooms have Jacuzzis. 2 Allée François I, Blois (phone: 54-43-94-04; fax: 54-42-04-05). Moderate.

EATING OUT: *L'Orangerie du Château* – Installed in elegant, historic quarters near the château, this restaurant serves classic but light cuisine and there's a pleasant terrace for outdoor dining in summer. Closed Sunday evenings and Mondays. Reservations advised. Major credit cards accepted. 1 Av. Dr.-J.-Laigret, Blois (phone: 54-78-05-36; fax: 54-78-22-78). Expensive to moderate.

La Bocca d'Or – Set in a 14th-century vaulted cellar, this dining spot is run by well-known chef Patrice Gallard and his Californian wife. Closed Sundays, Mondays, and February or March. Reservations advised. Major credit cards accepted. 15 Rue Haute, Blois (phone: 54-78-04-74). Moderate.

En Route from Blois – Cross Blois's main highway bridge over the Loire, with lovely views of sandbars and sometimes small boats, toward Chambord, turning right just at the south end of the bridge and then right again under it to follow D951 along the picturesque south bank of the river. Like many in the Loire region, the road has only two lanes but a good surface. It passes well-tended fields, pretty camping areas, and the remains of an old aqueduct on the right, and then on the left there's an excellent view across the river of the Château of Menars and its terraces. Turn south on D84, which curves gently through cornfields and tiny villages, until you reach a sign warning you to limit your speed since deer and wild boar roam freely through the forest of Chambord.

CHAMBORD: The largest of all the Loire Valley châteaux, this is also one of the most spectacular. To reach it, you pass through a gateway in the longest wall in France — 20 miles around! — into the immense national game reserve of 13,600 acres that surrounds the château, then proceed straight down a long alley carved through the forest to frame the central spire of the château until the road at last opens onto the whole magnificent structure. François I built this extravagant 440-room hunting lodge in the 16th century; the Renaissance inspired the fantastic terrace atop the château, a forest of spires, gables, turrets, and chimneys decorated with black slate, which offers visitors an extraordinary view. A remarkable interior feature is François I's ingenious double staircase, which soars from ground floor to roof terrace in two spirals superimposed on one another so that one person can ascend and another descend simultaneously without meeting. The apartments of the château, long nearly bare, have been refurnished. The world's first son et lumière performance was presented here in 1952, set to the music of Jean-Baptiste Lully, who composed and performed in this very château. For information, call the château at 54-20-34-86. The château is open daily except holidays from 9:30 to 11:45 AM and 2 to 4:45 PM; in summer, it is open from 9:30 AM to 5:45 PM (6:45 PM in July and August).

CHECKING IN/EATING OUT: *Grand St-Michel* – An old rambling establishment with bright flowers in the windowboxes and a pleasant staff, this would be a comfortable place to stay anywhere, but it happens to be idyllically located directly across a narrow road from Chambord castle, far from any town and surrounded by Chambord's vast, game-filled forest. Stay here and at dusk, after the busloads of tourists have gone, drive to an observation platform to spy on deer and perhaps even boar. Return to the hotel's spacious dining room, which specializes in game during the hunting season and also offers such Loire specialties as *rillons* (spiced, cubed pork) and poached salmon and trout. Then, in season, watch a son et lumière performance (if they are on) from your bedroom window, or simply gaze at the château as it glows silver by moonlight or rosy with dawn. Both hotel and restaurant are closed from mid-November to late December. Major credit cards accepted. Chambord (phone: 54-20-31-31). Inexpensive.

CHEVERNY: Only 10 miles (16 km) south of Chambord via D112, which cuts through the cool forests of Chambord and Boulogne, then west on D102 from the pleasant little town of Bracieux, the Château de Cheverny is a lordly mansion, unusual in the Loire for having been built all in one piece in the 17th-century classical style. Many of its handsomely furnished rooms can be toured. Even more memorable is the hunting museum, in an outbuilding with one room containing 2,000 sets of stag antlers, and the kennel, where you can see a pack of 70 hounds that are a crossbreed between the English foxhound and the French poitevin. Your ears will guide you right to it. There are weekly stag hunts in the surrounding forests during hunting season.

From Cheverny, head south on D102 for just under 30 miles (48 km), cutting across an edge of the Cheverny forest; at Contres, pick up D956, which crosses the Cher River at Selles-sur-Cher, whose château towers are reflected in the water. Then on to Valençay.

CHECKING IN/EATING OUT: *St-Hubert* – Close to the Château de Cheverny, this 20-room quiet inn has been in the same family for 45 years. The restaurant specializes in game. Closed on Wednesdays and during January. Major credit cards accepted. Rue Nationale, Cour-Cheverny (phone: 54-79-96-60). Restaurant, moderate; hotel, inexpensive.

Trois Marchands – A former coaching inn, this pleasant restaurant bustles, especially at noon, and the food (lots of fish specialties) is fresh and good. There also are 39 rooms. Closed from late January to mid-March and Mondays from October to mid-January. Major credit cards accepted. Cour-Cheverny (phone: 54-79-96-44; fax: 54-79-25-60). Moderate to inexpensive.

VALENÇAY: Just far enough off the main route of Loire Valley tour buses to preserve its tranquillity even at the peak of summer, Valençay is small and pleasant, with tree-shaded avenues that lead to a château whose builder, Jacques d'Estampes, was inspired by Chambord. Dating from 1540, the château was owned in the early 19th century by Talleyrand. King Ferdinand VII of Spain was comfortably confined here by Napoleon from 1808 to 1814. And you can see the table used for the Congress of Vienna in 1814–15, when a new map of Europe was drawn up. Its elegantly furnished 17th-century west wing can be visited, now the scene of musical and theatrical productions in the summer (Information: Château de Valençay, Valençay 36600; phone: 54-00-10-66).

Probably its most unusual feature is its large park filled with deer, llamas, buffalo, peacocks, swans, and flamingos, a joy especially for youngsters. There is a museum filled with souvenirs of Talleyrand as well as a well-kept automobile museum on the grounds.

CHECKING IN/EATING OUT: *Espagne* – A beautiful old coaching inn, its main connection with Spain seems to be that the staff of King Ferdinand VII was housed here while he was confined to Valençay's château, a few steps away. Since 1875, four generations of the Fourré family have welcomed guests to the elegant lodgings (8 rooms and 8 suites, many with private balconies) built around a flower-filled courtyard. The one-star dining room serves specialties including *ris de veau aux morilles* (sweetbreads with morels), lamb filet with tarragon, *sandre* (pike perch), and flambéed peaches. This is one of the many little towns in this area that produces its own wine, so you may want to try a bottle of the rather nondescript dry white valençay just for the fun of it. A member of the Relais & Châteaux group. Closed January and February. Reservations advised. Major credit cards accepted. 9 Rue du Château, Valençay (phone: 54-00-00-02; fax: 54-00-12-63). Expensive.

En Route from Valençay – Head west along pretty, sunflower-bordered D960 for 14 miles (22 km) to the tiny village of Nouans-les-Fontaines; watch for its strangely shaped church spire, which looks something like a rocket soaring over the fields, or you may drive through without realizing it. Oddly enough, this unassuming village church contains one of the finest French works of art of the late 15th century, a moving *Descent from the Cross,* also called the *Nouans Pietà,* painted on wood in somber colors by artists from the school of Jean Fouquet. A 5F piece placed in a slot illuminates the painting and sends a detailed commentary in French, English, or German echoing through the usually empty church.

MONTRÉSOR: In this pretty town on the right bank of the Indrois River, 5 miles (8 km) west of Nouans-les-Fontaines across rolling fields of sunflowers, are an interesting church and château, and somebody has gone to the trouble of lining the main road with trees of alternating red and green foliage. The church is known for its fine doorway and the 16th-century tomb of the Basternays, overlords of Montrésor. The castle is one of 20 in the Loire Valley built by Foulques Nerra (971–1040), a Count of Anjou and one of the most dramatic and violent personalities in the region's history. He spent his life battling the Counts of Blois, building fortresses to use in this fight; then, during periodic fits of repentance for his unscrupulous and sometimes criminally violent acts, he raised churches and went on pilgrimages to Jerusalem. You can walk around the fortified promontory on which the château is perched, high above the Indrois.

Follow D760 5 miles (8 km) west to the long wall that denotes the Chartreuse du Liget.

CHARTREUSE DU LIGET: Though these are only the ruins of a Carthusian monastery founded in the 12th century, supposedly by Henry II of England in expiation for the murder of Thomas à Becket, Archbishop of Canterbury, impressive ruins they are. Park near the monumental 18th-century gateway, walk through it, and obtain permission from the caretakers to visit the open, grass-floored ruin of the 12th-century chapel and, near the brook called the Liget, the vast cloisters, where now a child's swing is set up. Chapelle St-Jean-de-Liget, standing alone in a field west of the monastery, contains interesting 12th-century frescoes. You can stage a memorable picnic amid tiny wildflowers just outside the walls of the monastery.

Continue west on D760 west for 16 miles (26 km) to Loches.

LOCHES: Relatively unknown, yet one of the special treasures of the Loire Valley, this attractive little town on the Indre River, with modern stores and friendly inhabitants, has preserved a large and fascinating medieval quarter, the Cité Médiévale, on the heights in its center, with a château full of history and dungeons with grim memories. Loches has been fortified from its earliest history; captured in a 3-hour surprise attack by Richard the Lion-Hearted in 1195, it was regained for France 10 years later by Philippe-Auguste after a year-long siege. Loches then became the state prison of the Kings of France. In the keep, a group of fortified towers at the southern end of the medieval city, are some of the most gripping dungeons you are ever likely to see, complete with torture instruments and inscriptions carved or painted on the walls by the prisoners. During World War II, Nazi collaborators were jailed here. Also interesting in the medieval city are the *Musée Lansyer* (1 Rue Lansyer; phone: 47-59-05-45; open daily from 9 AM to noon and 2 to 6 PM from April through September; open daily except Fridays from 9 AM to noon and 2 to 5 PM from October to March) and the *Musée du Terroir* (Folklore Museum; same address, phone number, and hours of operation). The former is devoted to the works of a local landscape artist; the latter affords a lovely view of Loches, both on Rue Lansyer. Eglise St-Ours has two unusual pyramids rising between its towers; and the château, at the northern end of the promontory, holds the lovely, sculpted tomb of Agnès Sorel, mistress of Charles VII. The remains of *"la dame de beauté,"* as she was known, are no longer here; originally buried in St-Ours, they were scattered to the winds during the French Revolution by soldiers who mistook Agnès for a saint. Loche's château and dungeon are closed Wednesdays off-season and all of December and January. —

Head north from Loches on D31 for 17 miles (27 km) through fields and vineyards, then twist through the busy little town of Bléré and turn east on N76 toward Chenonceaux, 4 miles (6 km) away.

CHENONCEAUX: Leapfrogging splendidly across the Cher River like a fantasy bridge, with views of decorative gardens and water from almost all of its beautiful furnished rooms, Chenonceaux, perhaps the most photographed of all the region's châteaux, is not to be missed even on the briefest tour of the Loire Valley. You approach it down a long avenue shaded by plane trees, with ducks and swans swimming in canals alongside, then cross a drawbridge onto a terrace surrounded by moats. To the left is the Italian garden of Diane de Poitiers, who was given the château in 1547 by her lover, King Henri II, 20 years her junior; to the right, that of Catherine de Médicis, the king's wife, who evicted Diane and took over Chenonceaux herself after Henri II was killed by a lance thrust in a tournament in 1559. Several other women played major roles in the history of the beautiful château, including Catherine Briçonnet, who supervised its building from 1513 to 1521, and Louise of Lorraine, daughter-in-law of Catherine de Médicis, who retired to Chenonceaux to mourn after the assassination of her husband,

Henri III. Louise became known as "the White Queen" because she wore white, widow's clothes until her own death 11 years later. One of the special pleasures of Chenonceaux is that you can stroll through it on your own, without the guided tour that is obligatory in most châteaux, reading full descriptions of each room from a free brochure available at the ticket booth. An English version is available.

The entire château is fascinating, but make a special effort to see the tiny library, with windows overlooking the Cher, that was used by Catherine de Médicis; the downstairs kitchens, a labyrinth of rooms set almost at water level into the château's piers; and, above the kitchens, the beautiful gallery spanning the river, built by Catherine on top of a bridge previously constructed by Diane de Poitiers. A plaque informs you that in the bright, 65-yard-long gallery, where today taped Renaissance music plays softly, 2,254 wounded people were given medical care during World War I; the château was turned into a temporary hospital by its owners, members of the Menier chocolate manufacturing family. Follow signs to the *Musée de Cires* (Waxworks Museum), where 15 scenes depict château life. The château (phone: 47-23-90-07) and museum are open daily from 9 AM to 4:30 PM in winter and from 9 AM to 7 PM in summer. Admission charge.

The most scenic route for the approximately 8 miles (13 km) from Chenonceaux north to Amboise is D81, which passes through vineyards and countryside dotted with hay in big round bales at harvesttime and under the overhanging greenery of the Forest of Amboise.

CHECKING IN/EATING OUT: *Château de Chissay* – Between Chenonceaux and Montrichard, this 12th-century castle was converted into a luxury hotel in 1986, complete with mosaic bathrooms and a heated swimming pool. Closed January and February. Major credit cards accepted. 4 miles (6 km) east of Chenonceaux on D176, Chissay en Touraine (phone: 54-32-32-01; fax: 54-32-43-80). Expensive.

Domaine des Hauts de Loire – Less than 10 miles (16 km) north of Amboise on N152, this gracious 18th-century manor set in a 75-acre park was once the hunting lodge of the Count de Rostaing. Most of the 22 rooms and 4 suites, in a newer but equally charming annex, are exquisitely decorated with antiques and have modern bathrooms. The elegant dining room more than deserves its one Michelin star; fresh salmon, parsley mousse in hazelnut oil, and hot apple tart star among the house specialties. There also is a tennis court and an 8-acre lake stocked with pike and carp. A member of the Relais & Châteaux group. Closed December to March. Reservations advised. Major credit cards accepted. Outside Onzain on N152 (phone: 54-20-72-57; fax: 54-20-77-32). Expensive.

Château de Gué Péan – Stop by just to visit or stay on a while in this 27-room, 17th-century castle, which is set in a private forest and furnished in the style of the 18th century. It has an elegant dining room. Open year-round. Reservations advised. No credit cards accepted. Less than 10 miles (16 km) east of Chenonceaux, Monthou sur Cher (phone: 54-71-43-01). Expensive to moderate.

Hostellerie de l'Isle – Relax in the warm family atmosphere of this cozy 18th-century manor house with 8 rooms. The well-prepared meals are served by the fire on chilly days or under the trees in the surrounding garden-park on warmer ones. Open year-round. Major credit cards accepted. On scenic D176 at Civray de Touraine, 1 mile (1.6 km) before Chenonceaux (phone: 47-23-80-09; fax: 47-23-82-91). Moderate to inexpensive.

Bon Laboureur et Château – *The* place to stay in tiny Chenonceaux. A short walk from the château and the son et lumière performances, it is as charming as its name, *Hotel of the Good Plowman.* Low and vine-covered, it proffers windowboxes bright with flowers and a dining room that serves an abundance of well-prepared Loire Valley fish, other specialties, and good regional wines. A breakfast of fresh croissants and jam served in the 36 rooms (some in an annex) is especially pleasant. There is also an outdoor pool with a bar and a grill-style restaurant. Closed from mid-December to mid-February. Major credit cards accepted. Chenonceaux (phone: 47-23-90-02; fax: 47-23-82-01). Hotel inexpensive; restaurant moderate to inexpensive.

AMBOISE: The village of Amboise offers a fine château perched high on a promontory, magnificent views over the Loire and surrounding countryside, and a lovely 15th-century clock tower. It also has a rich history, featuring 15th- and 16th-century kings (this was the birthplace of the dauphin) and even a massacre — of the Huguenots (French Protestants), who were hanged from its castle walls or thrown from its battlements into the river in 1560. Its most illustrious resident was Leonardo da Vinci, who spent his last years working here and was buried here (his remains are in the château's Chapelle St-Hubert, in the north transept). After touring the château (open daily from 9 AM to 6:30 PM in summer; 9 AM to noon and 2 to 5 PM from late September to mid-April; open to 6:30 PM in spring and fall; admission charge), stroll about a third of a mile east along Rue Victor-Hugo to the Clos Lucé (open daily from 9 AM to 7 PM from mid-March to mid-November and 9 AM to 6 PM from mid-November to mid-March), the charming 15th-century manor house that François I, a patron of the arts, turned over to Leonardo after bringing him here from Italy in 1514. Pass through a gateway under a pretty little gallery with wooden arches, the oldest part of the red brick house, and by a lovely park with paths and benches to find this quotation from Leonardo just inside the front door: "A well-filled day gives a good sleep. A well-filled life gives a peaceful death." Past 60 when he arrived here and with a paralyzed right hand, the artist nevertheless painted and sketched actively until his death on May 2, 1519, in an upstairs bedroom with a view of rose gardens and, in the distance, the château. Some say François I was with him when he died. The lowest floor of the Clos Lucé holds a fascinating collection of 40 models of intricate machines constructed by IBM from plans by Leonardo, demonstrating his engineering genius in precursors of the first airplane, helicopter, military tank, and bridge designed to swing open. For information, contact the Syndicat d'Initiative (phone: 47-57-09-28).

Tours lies only 15 miles (24 km) downriver from Amboise and good roads lead to it on both sides of the Loire; D751 on the south bank and N152 on the north provide good views of the river, its islands, and sandbars.

CHECKING IN: *Au Lion d'Or* – Choose one of the back rooms in this comfortable 23-room dwelling, for an undisturbed quiet spot with shuttered windows that open onto the wall of the château. The dining room, long and spacious, exudes the atmosphere of a hunting lodge: A large fireplace fills one end and game trophies line the walls. Try the *foie gras frais de canard* (fresh duck foie gras), *pain d'épinards à la crème* (spinach soufflé covered with a delicate cream sauce), or *navarin de cidre* (pork stew with potatoes, turnips, and a pungent cider sauce). Closed Sunday evenings and Mondays in off-season, and early January to mid-February. Major credit cards accepted. 17 Quai Charles-Guinot, Amboise (phone: 47-57-00-23). Moderate.

L'Auberge du Mail – This calm, comfortable 12-room inn is on the Loire River, near the Amboise château. The restaurant has an old-fashioned atmosphere, with wooden beams, an iron candle chandelier, high-backed chairs, and a sideboard laden with wines and cognacs. The house specialties include salmon mousse, asparagus with a mousseline sauce, and fish stew with baby eel. Closed Fridays and mid-November to mid-December. Reservations advised. Major credit cards accepted. 32 Quai du Général-de-Gaulle, Amboise (phone: 47-57-60-39). Moderate to inexpensive.

Château de Pray – Less than 2 miles (3 km) northeast of Amboise via D751 on a bluff overlooking the Loire, this picturesque old château with 15 rooms has a dining room with a fireplace and a beamed ceiling and, for pleasant summer lunches, a terrace overlooking part of its own walled-in garden and the Loire — the perfect spot to linger over salmon in sorrel sauce. Adjoining the more formal garden with its graveled paths and geraniums in big pots is a wild, woodsy park with leafy trails and even a swing set in a clearing. Closed from early January to mid-February. Major credit cards accepted. D751, just northeast of Amboise (phone: 47-57-23-67; fax: 47-57-32-50). Hotel moderate to inexpensive, restaurant moderate.

EATING OUT: *Le Manoir St-Thomas* – A Renaissance manor house that has the best reputation in town, and deservedly so. Its excellent menu and fine selection of wines have earned it a Michelin star. Closed Sunday evenings, Mondays, and mid-January to mid-March. Reservations advised. Major credit cards accepted. Pl. Richelieu, Amboise (phone: 47-57-22-52; fax: 47-30-44-71). Expensive to moderate.

La Bonne Etape – Near the Château de Pray, this quaint little restaurant has lovely gardens with a graceful willow, winding paths, and neat hedges. The dining room is warm and informal, and potted geraniums decorate its terrace. The specialties here are seafood, such as *friture* (small fried fish served with lemon) and *sandre* (pike perch). There also are 17 modern rooms. Closed late December to early January and February 17 to March 4. Major credit cards accepted. Rte. 2, about a mile east of Amboise (phone 47-57-08-09). Inexpensive.

En Route from Amboise – One advantage of taking the northern route, N152, to Tours is that you can make a short detour to follow a marked Route du Vouvray past vineyards and through the hamlets of Noizay and Vernou to the little town of Vouvray, which produces the best-known white wine of Touraine. Watch for the signs of wine producers offering visits and tastings.

TOURS: The major city of a region rich in magnificent châteaux, fine food and wine, and some of the most beautiful countryside in France, Tours has been an important metropolis since Gallo-Roman times. It was bombed heavily in World War II, so it greets you with ugly 20th-century apartment towers instead of the elegant château towers of its Loire neighbors. Yet Tours, the home of 136,000 people (and another 114,000 in the outlying areas), is an ideal base for visitors who prefer to sleep in the same bed every night while exploring the Loire Valley, and it is easy to reach from Paris, 3 hours by autoroute or just 70 minutes by rail via the *TGV Atlantic.* The charms of this city must simply be sought out. Stop at the large and well-run tourist office in front of the train station (Bd. Heurteloup; phone: 47-05-58-08; fax: 47-61-14-22), then visit Cathédrale St-Gatien, which could illustrate an art history text on the evolution of the Gothic style; it was begun in the early 13th century and not finished until the 16th. Be sure to see the fine stained glass windows that date from the 13th to the 15th century. The cathedral's cloister was the setting for native son Honoré de Balzac's novel *Le Curé de Tours* (The Vicar of Tours). Nearby, in the *Musée des Beaux-Arts* (18 Pl. François-Sicard; phone: 47-05-68-73), formerly the archbishop's palace, hang paintings by Mantegna, Rubens, Rembrandt, Degas, and Delacroix. Open daily except Tuesdays and major holidays from 9 AM to 12:45 PM and 2 to 6 PM; admission charge. A few blocks to the west, on Rue Nationale, are the Eglise St-Julien, part of a former Benedictine abbey, whose cellars now house a Touraine wine museum that includes a 12th-century cellar, and the *Musée du Compagnonnage* (Museum of the Craft Guilds), where the work and tools of a variety of craftspersons are displayed (8 Rue Nationale; phone: 47-61-07-93). Open daily except Tuesdays and major holidays from 9 to 11:30 AM and 2 to 4:30 PM, until 6:30 PM in summer; admission charge. Keep walking west to reach Vieux Tours (Old Tours), with half-timbered houses that lean into charming narrow streets. The *Musée du Gemmail* (Rue du Mûrier; phone: 47-61-01-19), which focuses on the "gemmail" artistic technique of superimposing pieces of glass to produce painting-like works, is in this area (open daily except Mondays from 10 to 11:30 AM and 2 to 6 PM from March to mid-October), as is a honeycomb of little streets called Les Artisans du Petit St-Martin, featuring painted jewelry, marionettes, lampshades made to measure, and many other items of silk, wood, and leather. One of Tours's newest museums, the *Musée St-Martin* (3 Rue Rapin), is devoted to the life and works of the saint who was born in this city.

Especially in the summer, there are frequent concerts. A classical music festival, the annual *Fêtes Musicales en Touraine,* is held the last weekend in late June at the Grange de Meslay, a vast, 13th-century barn that was part of a fortified farm; it is about 5 miles (8 km) north of Tours on N10, toward Château-Renault. Another festival, the *Semaines Musicales de Tours,* takes place in churches and halls in Tours itself, usually during July. The city also stages a folksy *Garlic and Basil Fair* each summer on *St. Anne's Day,* July 26.

Follow D7 12 miles (19 km) west to Villandry.

CHECKING IN: *Jean Bardet* – Installed in a grand old mansion set in a park near the center of Tours, Monsieur Bardet established his hotel-restaurant as one of the most outstanding in a region rich with luxurious hostelries. Dining specialties include fresh steamed salmon in soy sauce, farm rabbit with artichokes, and oven-roasted lobster. The hotel is a member of the Relais & Châteaux group, and the dining room has been awarded two Michelin stars. Restaurant closed Sunday evenings and Mondays in winter; hotel and restaurant closed early February to late March. Reservations necessary. Major credit cards accepted. 57 Rue Groison, Tours (phone: 47-41-41-11; fax: 47-51-68-72). Very expensive.

Les Hautes Roches – Luxurious rooms cleverly carved into the soft limestone cliffs of the Loire riverbank make this one of the region's (and the country's) most original hotels. Eight of the 11 rooms are like caves, with cool, mellow stone walls, vaulted bathrooms, and striking views of the water. There is a riverside terrace and a one-star restaurant featuring local fish in the pretty 19th-century château perched on a natural stone cliff in front of the cave dwellings. Closed from mid-January to mid-March. Reservations advised at the restaurant. Major credit cards accepted. 86 Quai de la Loire, Rochecorbon (phone: 47-52-88-88; fax: 47-52-81-30). Expensive.

L'Hôtel de Groison – In a quiet neighborhood across the Loire from the heart of Tours is this 18th-century townhouse that has been transformed into a lovely hotel. Most of the 10 individually decorated rooms overlook a garden and the restaurant, *Le Jardin du Castel,* has one of the city's prettiest dining rooms. Restaurant closed Wednesdays, Saturday lunch, and mid-January to mid-February. Reservations advised. Major credit cards accepted. 10 Rue Groison, Tours (phone: 47-41-94-40; fax: 47-51-50-28). Expensive to moderate.

Hôtel du Cygne – On a quiet street near the center of town, this 19-room hostelry claims to be one of Tours's oldest. The 17th-century building has geranium-filled balconies and there's a cozy fireplace in the lounge. The management is friendly. Open year-round. Major credit cards accepted. 6 Rue du Cygne, Tours (phone: 47-66-66-41; fax: 47-20-18-76). Inexpensive.

Near Montbazon, 8 miles (13 km) south of Tours on N10, are two elegant hotels that allow you to fulfill the fantasy of "living" in a luxurious Loire Valley château after a day of touring others.

Château d'Artigny – This world-famous château (a Relais & Châteaux member), once the property of the perfumer François Coty, perches in a fairy-tale setting of gardens and woods above the Indre River. You can swim in a heated pool, play tennis, fish, or even listen to a string quartet if you arrive for one of the "Soirées Musicales" during the winter; golf and horseback riding are nearby. The dining room rates one Michelin star; try the sweetbread casserole and fish specialties. Closed from late November to mid-January. Reservations essential. Major credit cards accepted. (See also *Romantic French Hostelries*, DIVERSIONS.) A little more than a mile (1.6 km) southwest of Montbazon via D17 (phone: 47-26-24-24; fax: 47-65-92-75). Expensive.

Domaine de la Tortinière – Smaller and slightly less illustrious than its neighbor across the valley of the Indre, this storybook château can provide an equally memorable stay. Romantic but small rooms (there are 21 in all) surrounded by towers and turrets overlook grounds that slope gently toward the river. A garden-style restaurant adds to the pleasure, with fine fish and good sauces. The chef sometimes holds week-long cooking classes for groups of 10 or more at the hotel; English translation is provided as needed by Americans living in this area. The château is closed from December 20 to March 1. Reservations necessary. Major credit cards accepted. A mile (1.6 km) north of Montbazon on N10 to D287 — watch for signs on the right if you're driving south from Tours (phone: 47-26-00-19; fax: 47-65-95-70). Expensive.

EATING OUT: Charles Barrier – This venerable chef has garnered top culinary ratings in Tours for decades and continues to merit two stars from Michelin for his refined versions of regional specialties. A reasonable fixed-price menu puts the pleasures of *Barrier's* elegant dining room within reach of those of moderate means. Also a member of the Relais & Châteaux group. Closed Sunday evenings. Reservations necessary. Major credit cards accepted. 101 Av. de la Tranchée, Tours (phone: 47-54-20-39; fax: 47-41-80-95). Expensive.

Le Bistrot des Halles – True to its name, this wood-paneled spot with crisp white tablecloths and walls lined with gilt-framed pictures, delivers just what one would hope to find in a bistro on the main market square in a city like Tours. The ambience is cozy but sophisticated, the food traditional bistro fare, with an emphasis on fish, and the service professional, if characteristically curt. Closed *Christmas Eve* and *New Year's Eve.* Reservations advised. Major credit cards accepted. 31 Pl. Gaston Paillhou, Tours (phone: 47-61-54-93; fax: 47-66-19-98). Moderate.

La Poivrière – Romantically situated in a beautiful 15th-century house in Vieux (Old) Tours, this spot specializes in fish. Closed Saturday lunch and Sundays. Reservations advised. Major credit cards accepted. 13 Rue du Change, Tours (phone: 47-20-85-41). Moderate.

Rôtisserie Tourangelle – A longtime favorite of residents, this brasserie has been completely remodeled. The decor remains rustic and house specialties include homemade foie gras, snails in red wine, and local fish in a *beurre blanc* sauce. Closed Sunday evenings, Mondays, and in February. Reservations advised. Major credit cards accepted. 23 Rue du Commerce, Tours (phone: 47-05-71-21). Moderate.

Les Tuffeaux – Highly regarded, it boasts a special location in the old quarter, near the cathedral. Loire fish are especially good here, as well as puff pastry desserts. Closed Sundays, Monday lunch, and the last 2 weeks in July. Reservations advised. Major credit cards accepted. 19 Rue Lavoisier, Tours (phone: 47-47-19-89). Moderate.

Brasserie Buré – Dark wood, brass, smoked glass, and a sweeping staircase add to the charm of this modern interpretation of the traditional brasserie. The menu includes a wide array of oysters and shellfish, as well as *choucroute* (sauerkraut) accompanied by the local *rillons* (spicy, cubed pork). Open daily until midnight. Reservations unnecessary. Major credit cards accepted. 1 Pl. de la Résistance (phone: 47-05-67-74). Moderate to inexpensive.

Les Trois Rois – A pleasant pub that serves lunches of toasted sandwiches and salads, but no evening meals, in a 15th-century house on the most charming square in Vieux Tours. It's a wonderful place to sip a cold drink on a hot summer afternoon. Open daily. No reservations. No credit cards accepted. Pl. Plumereau, Tours (phone: 47-20-61-20). Inexpensive.

En Route from Tours – For those interested in such curiosities, the three-quarter mile "petrifying grottoes" are 10 miles (16 km) west, on D7 at Savonnières, less than 2 miles (3 km) from Villandry. The caves, which are connected to the Villandry château by an underground passage, are the scene of continuous dripping that allegedly petrifies objects left there in a matter of months. Hour-long guided tours are available daily except from December 16 to February and Wednesdays from February 1 to March 31, and from mid-November to mid-December; bring along a sweater to ward off the 57F chill.

VILLANDRY: This is the one place in the Loire Valley where the gardens are much more spectacular than the château they adjoin, and these are amazing: 3 tiers of large, superimposed terraces that include a lake, hedges, and bushes trimmed into precise patterns representing, among other things, different kinds of love (tender, passionate, adulterous), an extensive garden of herbs and medicinal and aromatic plants, and, most unusual, a large 16th-century kitchen garden whose beautiful patterns in a wealth of colors are formed by carefully planted ordinary fruits and vegetables. Villandry, the hamlet of the same name, faces the Cher River near the point at which it joins the Loire; it was the last great Renaissance château to be built in this area, and Jean le Breton, a financier and minister to François I, finished it in 1536. Unlike many neighboring châteaux, Villandry has always been privately owned, and the interests of its owners have given it a special flavor. Le Breton had served as the French ambassador to Italy and was knowledgeable in both architecture and garden design. His château, attractive and of moderate size with a moat and elegant courtyard, is purely French in style, but the gardens, which manifest both French and Italian influences, were always the more famous. The Cardinal of Aragon is said to have visited Villandry's kitchen garden around 1570 and wrote to the pope that there he had seen "finer salad vegetables than in Rome." The 16th-century gardens were lost temporarily when the 19th-century owners tore them out to follow the fashion by planting a garden landscaped in the English style. Happily, they were replanted according to old plans and drawings early in this century by Dr. Joachim Carvallo, whose grandson now owns and lives in the château with his family. The part of the château open to the public includes a fine collection of Spanish paintings and even an intricate Moorish ceiling brought from Spain by Dr. Carvallo. Visitors ultimately should climb to a vantage point over the gardens and then wander through them at leisure. The château is open daily from mid-March to November 12, the gardens from 9 AM to nightfall year-round.

Follow D39 due south to Azay-le-Rideau.

CHECKING IN/EATING OUT: *Cheval Rouge* – An extremely pleasant provincial 20-room hotel and restaurant, a short stroll from the château gardens. The menu offers homemade foie gras and smoked salmon, Loire fish, including *sandre* (pike perch), and good regional wines on the menu. Meals are served until 9 PM. Closed Mondays in winter, and January to mid-March. Major credit cards accepted. Villandry (phone: 47-50-02-07; fax: 47-50-08-77). Moderate.

AZAY-LE-RIDEAU: Pocket-sized and charming, Azay boasts a handful of picturesque old streets, some interesting shops, and in its heart, a Gothic château so visually satisfying in its setting of woods and water that it is considered one of the jewels of the Loire Valley. Because it stands where the road between Tours and Chinon crosses the

Indre River, Azay was fortified early in its history. Named for one of its overlords, Ridel, or Rideau, of Azay, the village today contains immense trees and expanses of greenery. It is hard to believe that it was known as Azay-le-Brulé (Azay-the-Burnt) from 1418 — when Charles VII, then dauphin, retaliated after a verbal insult from a guard by executing 350 soldiers and torching the town — until the early 16th century, when the present château was built. Although it was owned by a financier, Gilles Berthelot, the château, built partly over the Indre and surrounded by water, actually was constructed under the supervision of his wife, Philippa Lesbahy, and she usually is given credit for its grace. The son et lumière performance here is especially striking, with woods and water dramatically illuminated and the château perfectly mirrored in its moat as spectators follow elaborately costumed youths carrying tall torches on a 1-hour stroll around the grounds.

Saché is about 4 very pleasant miles (6 km) from Azay-le-Rideau; take D84 east past tall stands of trees, then turn south on D9 across four very narrow bridges.

CHECKING IN/EATING OUT: *Grand Monarque* – If a stay here doesn't relax you, probably nothing can. Located in the center of town, the hotel and its outbuildings ramble around a large, graveled, tree-shaded courtyard, where tables are set up for summer lunch. The 27 rooms are old-fashioned, quiet, and comfortable. The dining room, prettily decorated and filled with flowers, serves tasty meals, with the *andouillette* (chitterling sausage) and several good fish dishes especially recommended. The château is a 3-minute walk away, and for a treat after the son et lumière, return to the hotel lobby for a cognac or raspberry liqueur. The hotel is open, and serves breakfast, all year except from mid-December to mid-February; the restaurant is closed from mid-November to mid-March. Reservations necessary. Major credit cards accepted. Pl. de la République, Azay-le-Rideau (phone: 47-45-40-08; fax: 47-45-46-25). Hotel moderate; restaurant expensive to moderate.

SACHÉ: This tiny village has served as the home of two very creative men. A striking stabile with blue and red arms outside the Town Hall testifies to the presence of Alexander Calder, whose home and workshop were near the village, and a block away, at the Château de Saché, in a park by the Indre River, the bedroom of Honoré de Balzac remains as it was when he lived and wrote here from 1829 to 1848. That and other rooms have been turned into a Balzac museum.

From Saché, zigzag west and south (D17 to D217) for 3 miles (5 km) to Villaines-les-Rochers.

VILLAINES-LES-ROCHERS: An entire village of basket makers, little Villaines has long been known for its wickerwork. Some 80 families, many working in troglodyte homes dug into walls of rock, belong to the wickerwork cooperative that was founded here in 1849 by a village priest. The cooperative's big showroom is an excellent place to buy baskets of all shapes and sizes, wicker furniture from baby chairs to large sofas, and even cleverly designed wicker babies' rattles with pebbles woven inside the wicker. In an adjoining workroom, you can watch craftspeople at work on similar objects. Individual artisans invite visitors to their own workrooms as well; the shop of Joël Metezeau, with a big sign on the right as you enter the village from Saché, is a pleasant place with a clutter of picnic baskets, cradles, armchairs, and bracelets, all produced by amiable men weaving skillfully on the floor in the back room. They seem happy to break the monotony of their routine by chatting with visitors.

Return to Azay-le-Rideau, then head southwest on D751 to Chinon. The 13 miles (21 km) to Chinon literally are straight as an arrow on the map; they are indeed straight but the road includes long, roller coaster dips through the green Chinon Forest.

CHINON: The mention of Chinon makes one think first of the delightful red wine that is produced here and only later of this pleasant town astride the Vienne River. In its castle, Joan of Arc recognized the dauphin, Charles VII, in 1429 as he tried to hide himself in a crowd of followers, and here she persuaded him to trust her. Chinon was the site of the deaths of the English King Henry II, in 1189, and his son Richard the Lion-Hearted, in 1199, and in 1321 of all the Jews in the town (by fire) on Ile de Tours, the island in the Vienne River opposite the town, after a local uprising and accusation of well poisoning, only a year before all the Jews were expelled from France. François Rabelais was born just outside Chinon, in La Devinière, in 1494, and spent his early years in this area; his birthplace, a mile (1.6 km) from Chinon, is open to the public.

The château is mostly in ruins on a hilltop spur that dominates the town; you enter them through a clock tower that contains a small Joan of Arc museum. Peacocks stroll near historic walls, and there is a deep moat and good views of the countryside. From the château, a short walk brings you to the wine-tasting shop of the Couly-Dutheil vintners; their Clos de l'Echo is among the best of all chinons. A few dozen yards more, down a road marked cryptically "To the Echo," you can try one of the most amusing simple pleasures of the Loire Valley. A small sign adjacent to a vineyard denotes "l'Echo." Climb up on a concrete platform, face the walls of the castle (which stands across a ravine), give a few shouts of different pitches, and enjoy the fun. When the weather is clear and there aren't too many people around to muddy the acoustics, the echo is amazingly clear and strong. If possible, try the rhyme that generations of residents have relied on to tease their wives and girlfriends:

"Les femmes de Chinon, sont-elles fidèles?"
Echo: *"Elles?"*
"Oui, les femmes de Chinon."
Echo: *"Non."*

(The women of Chinon, are they faithful? Echo: Them? Yes, the women of Chinon. Echo: No.)

Below the castle, "taste" medieval Chinon with a walk down Rue Voltaire, where red and yellow banners stretch between old stone buildings and rosebushes bloom in lovely courtyards. Pedestrians have priority on the narrow street and can admire at leisure the pretty 17th-century Hôtel du Gouvernement and the *Maison des Etats-Généraux,* now an interesting museum, in which, according to local tradition, Richard the Lion-Hearted died of a wound he received at Châlus. A few steps farther is the reconstruction of a well on whose rim Joan of Arc supposedly placed her foot while dismounting from her horse. Chinon holds a medieval fair the first weekend in August, when residents dress in period costumes and everybody makes merry.

Take D751 west 14 miles (22 km) to Fontevraud-l'Abbaye.

CHECKING IN: *Château de Marçay* – This 15th-century fortress has metamorphosed into a luxury hotel (a member of the prestigious Relais & Châteaux) with 32 elegantly appointed rooms and 6 suites. Surrounded by its own park, the château also has a swimming pool and tennis courts. In the one-star dining room, try the soft-boiled eggs with puréed morels. Wealthy Parisians relax here on weekends, so be sure to make reservations. Closed from January to mid-March. Restaurant closed Sundays evenings and Mondays from November to January. Reservations essential. Major credit cards accepted. 4 miles (6 km) south of Chinon by D749 and D116 in Marçay (phone: 47-93-03-47; fax: 47-93-45-33). Expensive.

La Poitevinière – A touch of the US in the Loire Valley, this château was purchased and renovated by Americans in love with France. Stay in one of the 5 large rooms, each with its own bath, or if you prefer, rent the entire château for about $6,000 a week. No restaurant. No credit cards accepted. Huismes 37420, Avoine (phone:

47-95-58-40; fax: 47-95-43-43; in the US, phone: 415-922-1496; fax: 415-928-2863). Expensive.

Hostellerie Gargantua – A charming 15th-century hotel, in the heart of Old Chinon just beneath the château. All 18 rooms have been entirely redone, as has the kitchen. On Friday evenings, guests are received by staff dressed in medieval costume. The house specialty is the *omelette Gargamelle,* with herbs and mushrooms. Closed Wednesdays, Thursday for lunch in off-season, and mid-November to mid-March. Major credit cards accepted. 73 Rue Voltaire, Chinon (phone: 47-93-04-71). Moderate.

La Giraudière – In the attractive countryside just to the west of town, by the road to Bourgueil and the turnoff to Savigny, this picturesque manor house offers simple charm and the convenience of kitchenettes in some of its 25 rooms. There is also a restaurant. Swimming, tennis, and horseback riding are available nearby. Hotel open year-round. Restaurant closed Tuesday evenings in off-season and in January. Reservations advised. Major credit cards accepted. 3 miles (5 km) west of Chinon (phone: 47-58-40-36). Moderate to inexpensive.

En Route from Chinon – Shortly before the turnoff for Fontevraud-l'Abbaye, D751 becomes especially pretty; tree-shaded, it passes fields, small châteaux, and the scenic Vienne River close on the right. The stretch through La Chausée and St-Germain-sur-Vienne is most charming and you may want to pull off the road for a picnic. At the very least, slow down a bit, both to admire the flowers in the windowboxes of the storybook houses and to be prepared for the occasional herd of cattle or flock of sheep crossing the road.

FONTEVRAUD-L'ABBAYE: Another relatively unknown treasure of the Loire Valley, the vast Royal Abbey of Fontevraud gives visitors a chance to explore one of the most intact complexes of monastic architecture standing today in France. Founded in 1099 by Robert d'Arbrissel, a Breton hermit, the Fontevraud order was remarkable for its aristocratic nature, for having been ruled over by a succession of 36 abbesses, all members of noble families, and for opening the doors of five separate monasteries to monks, nuns, lepers, the sick, and aristocratic women who wished to withdraw to a life of prayer and contemplation. The abbey church, consecrated in 1119 by Pope Calixtus II, is a huge Romanesque structure with a single nave. It contains the tombs of Henry II Plantagenet, Count of Anjou, who became King of England in 1154 and who asked on his deathbed to be buried at Fontevraud; Eleanor of Aquitaine, his widow, who withdrew to the abbey for the 15 years preceding her own death; Richard the Lion-Hearted, their son, who also requested that his remains be buried here; and Isabelle of Angoulême, the second wife of Richard's brother, King John Lackland. Their four beautiful, recumbent statues lie just to the right of the nave. There also are tranquil cloisters with noteworthy Renaissance and Gothic carving and an extremely unusual octagonal tower that served as the abbey kitchen, said to be the only one from the Romanesque period remaining in France. French revolutionaries destroyed some monastery buildings in 1793 and put an end to the monastic life. In 1804, Napoleon converted most of the remaining buildings into a cloister of another kind, a national prison, which functioned until 1963. Today the French government and regional cultural agencies administer Fontevraud and use it for concerts, art exhibitions, and theatrical productions. Also of note in the small town are St. Michael's parish church, across Place des Plantagenets and Rue du Logis Bourbon from the abbey, and the 13th-century chapel of St. Catherine, off a pretty avenue of lime trees leading from the church.

Route D947 follows the river west to Saumur.

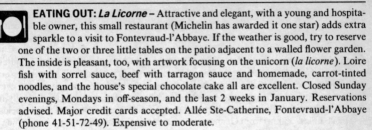

EATING OUT: *La Licorne* – Attractive and elegant, with a young and hospitable owner, this small restaurant (Michelin has awarded it one star) adds extra sparkle to a visit to Fontevraud-l'Abbaye. If the weather is good, try to reserve one of the two or three little tables on the patio adjacent to a walled flower garden. The inside is pleasant, too, with artwork focusing on the unicorn (*la licorne*). Loire fish with sorrel sauce, beef with tarragon sauce and homemade, carrot-tinted noodles, and the house's special chocolate cake all are excellent. Closed Sunday evenings, Mondays in off-season, and the last 2 weeks in January. Reservations advised. Major credit cards accepted. Allée Ste-Catherine, Fontevraud-l'Abbaye (phone 41-51-72-49). Expensive to moderate.

En Route from Fontevraud-l'Abbaye – The 7-mile (11-km) stretch of D947 west along the Loire to Saumur starts at Montsoreau, with a pretty château and the *Musée des Goums* (French cavalry units recruited in Morocco; the museum contains souvenirs of the Moroccan conquest), and includes a string of charming villages. Watch for picturesque troglodyte houses, an old windmill on a ridge, and cellars in which to taste wine, mainly Saumur.

SAUMUR: With a many-arched old bridge over the Loire, attractive shops, and busy streets, Saumur is famous for its wines, especially the sparkling mousseux variety, and its riding school, the Cadre Noir (Black Squadron), which draws eager crowds to a military tattoo and riding spectacle at the end of July each summer. Tasting the wine is no problem; a Maison du Vin run by the wine producers' association is next door to the tourist office (Rue Beaurepaire; phone: 41-51-03-06) on Place de la Bilange. Open Tuesdays through Saturdays from 9 AM to 12:30 PM and 2 to 6:30 PM. You also can visit the Ecole d'Application de l'Armée Blindée de la Cavalerie (Cavalry and Armored Corps School), founded when the best horsemen in the French army were sent in an elite regiment to Saumur in 1763 to become the original *Cadre Noir.* Saumur has a dramatic castle that soars high above the town on a sheer promontory. Several fortresses have stood here; the present one dates from the late 14th century and contains both a museum of decorative arts and one tracing the history of — what else? — the horse.

En Route from Saumur – Route D751 snakes along for 32 miles (51 km) to Angers. For an interesting detour, follow N147 through Saumur, over the Thouet River and into the suburb of Bagneux, which has one of the largest dolmens (prehistoric stone structures with side and roof slabs) in France. Standing in a yard by a café at the end of Rue du Dolmen, the monument, built some 5,000 years ago, is 70 feet long and divided into two chambers. The granite slabs that make up its sides and roof weigh as much as 35 tons.

Another Loire Valley curiosity is just west of Saumur's northwest suburb of St-Hilaire-St-Florent: the *Musée du Champignons,* a mushroom museum. Here you can take a half-hour tour of a labyrinth of caves carved out of the porous limestone called tufa during which you see all the stages of growth of the white mushrooms known as *champignons de Paris.* Just inside the entrance to the caves is an exhibit of the old and new ways in which the famous tufa (Westminster Abbey in London is made from this stone) is extracted. According to the guide, 40% of the world's canned mushrooms come from the Saumur region, where a full 500 miles of caves are used to grow mushrooms. One of the secrets of their successful cultivation here is that much of the manure in which they thrive comes from the nearby riding school. You can buy your own mushrooms, fresh or canned, at the museum entrance (Routes de Gennes, Saumur; phone: 41-50-31-55). Open daily from 10 AM to 6 PM from March to mid-November; open daily from 10 AM to 8 PM from May through September.

A beautiful church dating from the 11th to the 13th century graces the very pleasant village of Cunault, 3 miles (5 km) west of Chênehutte-les-Tuffeaux on D751. The belfry is Romanesque; the west front is fortified, with a fine 13th-century sculpted portrayal of the Adoration of the Virgin. Inside are traces of the painted decoration used to emphasize the main architectural lines of medieval churches: the richly carved capitals and a rare painted wooden shrine from the 13th century, riddled with wormholes but still lovely. The nave of this large church is tapered slightly to make it appear even longer than it is. In Gennes, just beyond Cunault, four dolmens rise dramatically in the hills behind the village; several upright stones called menhirs stand in nearby fields.

The 20 miles (33 km) from Gennes to Angers along D751 is a pastoral jaunt through sleepy villages where little seems to stir except the church bells that mark the hours. Fields of corn and sunflowers, vineyards, and old windmills, some of them overgrown with vegetation, beckon the wanderer to follow.

CHECKING IN/EATING OUT: *Le Prieuré* – One of the most splendid hostelries of the Loire Valley, famous for its quiet, wooded setting with a sweeping view of the Loire, elegant rooms in a 12th- and 15th-century priory, and an excellent dining room, it sits on a bluff above Chênehutte-les-Tuffeaux. (A member of the Relais & Châteaux group.) There is a tennis court, a heated swimming pool, and 35 rooms, with 15 in the château itself ("Americans prefer these," says a staff member) and the rest in bungalows scattered over the grounds. Reserve several months in advance for the summer and as early as possible the rest of the year. The dining room features *foie gras de canard* (duck foie gras), a *panaché,* or mix, of *sandre* and turbot served with wild rice and curry, *magret de canard* (duck breast) with raspberry vinegar, and a *menu dégustation* (tasting menu), with small portions of many specialties. The view from your table will be spectacular, especially at sunset. Closed January 25 to March 7. Reservations advised. Major credit cards accepted. Chênehutte-les-Tuffeaux, 5 miles (8 km) west of Saumur by D161 and D751 (phone: 41-67-90-14; fax: 41-67-92-24). Expensive.

Hostellerie de la Loire – Some 11 rooms are available here, and for a copious, tasty meal in cheerful surroundings, the restaurant is an excellent choice. Especially on weekends, you're likely to be among happy local families, which means children will feel at home here, too. Try the menu (the prix fixe meal), starting with the mushrooms in a pastry shell — irresistible if you've just toured the mushroom caves — and progressing to fish, steaks, or chicken, then salad, cheese, and dessert. The hotel and restaurant are closed Monday evenings, Tuesdays, and January. Reservations advised in summer. Major credit cards accepted. Gennes (phone: 41-51-81-03; fax: 41-38-05-22). Inexpensive.

ANGERS: Although the Loire River flows on for another 80 miles before reaching Nantes and the Atlantic Ocean, the city of Angers, population 143,000, is generally considered to mark the western end of the Loire Valley. Conquered by the Romans and later by the Normans in its early history, Angers lived through an especially brilliant period under the Counts of Anjou, from the 10th to the 12th century. A major city today, though not noted for its charm, Angers boasts an imposing castle in a feudal architectural style patterned on the crusaders' castles of Palestine; its 17 large towers are connected by a high curtain wall, and deer grazing in the dry moat add a whimsical note. Displayed in the castle is the huge Apocalypse Tapestry, woven in Paris between 1373 and 1380 for Louis I of Anjou. The Cathédrale St-Maurice, the other sightseeing highlight in Angers, claims a single nave with the first Gothic vaulting constructed in Anjou, an impressive late Romanesque façade with fine sculptures surmounted by three towers, and a good collection of original stained glass windows. The oldest window, in the north aisle, dates from the 12th century. Angers also has a fine arts museum — the *Musée Beaux Arts* (10 Rue du Musée; phone: 41-88-64-65; fax: 41-88-09-04; open daily from 9:30 AM to 12:30 PM and from 2 to 7 PM from June 10 through September

15; open from 10 AM to noon and 2 to 6 PM off-season), located in the Logis Barrault —
and, on the streets around Hôtel Pincé on Rue Lenepveu, some interesting 16th- and
18th-century buildings. The popular *Festival of Anjou,* held here in July, includes
ballets, concerts, plays, and other cultural activities.

Backtrack east from Angers along the Loire's northern bank on D952, N152, and
D749 to Bourgueil.

CHECKING IN: *Concorde* – This modern hotel in the center of town has 78
rooms and a pleasant restaurant open until 11:30 PM. Major credit cards
accepted. 18 Bd. Maréchal-Foch, Angers (phone: 41-87-37-20; fax: 41-87-49-
54). Moderate.

France – Opposite the train station and the tourist office, this hostelry has 56
attractive rooms and a restaurant, *Plantagenets,* that offers fine food and service.
The restaurant is open daily, except Saturdays. Major credit cards accepted.. 8 Pl.
de la Gare, Angers (phone: 41-88-49-42; fax: 41-86-76-70). Moderate to inexpensive.

EATING OUT: *Le Toussaint* – A comfortable place that features simple and
creative cooking such as vegetable cake, *foie gras au Layon,* and fresh fruit
sherbets. Closed Sunday evenings and Mondays, late February, and 1 week in
August. Reservations advised. Major credit cards accepted. 7 Pl. Kennedy, Angers
(phone: 41-87-46-20). Expensive to moderate.

L'Entr'acte – Popular, rustic, and near the post office, it is notable for its *coquilles
St-Jacques au champagne* (scallops in champagne) and *saumon du Bourgueil*
(salmon). Closed Saturday lunch, Sundays, and from mid-July to mid-August.
Reservations advised. Major credit cards accepted. 9 Rue Louis-de-Romain, Angers (phone: 41-87-71-82). Moderate.

Le Logis – Endowed with one Michelin star, it specializes in seafood. Closed Saturday nights from July to October, Sundays, the last 2 weeks of July, and the first
2 weeks in August. Reservations advised. Major credit cards accepted. 17 Rue
St-Laud, Angers (phone: 41-87-44-15). Moderate.

Le Vert d'Eau – Well known in the area, it serves original dishes that include *poissons
de Loire beurre blanc* (fish with a white butter sauce), *fricassée de poulet à l'ange-
vine* (chicken fricassee with anjou wine), and strawberries in season. It's closed
Sunday evenings, Mondays, and 1 week in February. Reservations advised. Major
credit cards accepted. 9 Bd. G.-Dumesnil, Angers (phone: 41-48-52-86; fax: 41-72-
01-63). Moderate.

En Route from Angers – Route D952 provides enchanting views of the river and
its tree-covered islands as well as glimpses of towns and villages with big stone quays
that were once prosperous river ports. The highway hugs the edge of the river through
Saumur, where it becomes N152 to continue its scenic route eastward. Follow it to
Port-Boulet, across the Loire from the enormous stacks and globes of the Avoine
nuclear power plant, begun in 1957 and one of the first in France. Then turn north for
3 miles (5 km) on D749 to Bourgueil.

BOURGUEIL: A charming little town containing the remains of a powerful Benedictine abbey founded in 990, Bourgueil produces one of the two acclaimed red wines of
the Loire Valley (the other being that of Chinon, 10 miles/16 km south). You can drive
for miles past vine-covered slopes and find innumerable wine merchants happy to let
you taste their full-bodied ruby red bourgueil and to sell you as many bottles as you
wish. It was in Bourgueil that the deaf French poet Pierre de Ronsard met the object
of the inspiration for his famous love poems.

CHECKING IN/EATING OUT: *Château des Reaux* – This charming 15th-
century château originally built by the Briconnet family, who later built the
châteaux of Chenonceaux and Azay-le-Rideau, has been opened as a small

hotel. All 8 guestrooms and 4 suites are charmingly appointed with antiques. Guests have access to nearby tennis courts. There is a small restaurant on the premises. Open year-round. Reservations advised. Most major credit cards accepted. Bourgueil (phone: 47-95-14-40; fax: 47-95-18-34). Expensive.

Route D35 east connects with N152, which leads to Langeais.

LANGEAIS: This crowded town 12 miles (19 km) east of Bourgueil boasts store windows filled with enough fishing gear to tempt any visitor into testing the waters of the Loire, a few steps away. In its center reposes another of the region's idiosyncratic and memorable castles. Although much smaller than those of Chambord and Blois, the Château of Langeais is unusual in having all been built by Louis XI within a 5-year period in the 15th century and for having remained unaltered since then. The building, which you enter by a drawbridge between two solid towers, looks like a powerful medieval fortress. It was intended to serve as a strong defensive position in case of an attack from Bretons heading from Nantes up the Loire Valley toward Touraine. Such worries were put to rest on December 16, 1491, when the son of Louis XI, Charles VIII, married Anne of Brittany in this very castle, thereby uniting Brittany and France. Viewed from the inner courtyard, the château clearly is the residence of a 15th-century lord. Its apartments are furnished with an excellent collection of 15th- and 16th-century antiques, the marriage chest of Anne of Brittany among them.

Continue 3 miles (5 km) east on N152 to Cinq-Mars-la-Pile.

CHECKING IN/EATING OUT: *Hosten* – This charming, comfortable country inn is only a short stroll down the street from the château in Langeais. Most of the 11 rooms are on winding corridors over an inner courtyard, well isolated from traffic noise. The rustic decor of chintz and country furniture is confined to the cozy bedrooms; bathrooms are completely modern and include such amenities as shower caps and scales. Its restaurant, elegant and comfortable with dark wood and fresh flowers, has one Michelin star and it serves specialties like lobster salad with foie gras, sole with *cèpes* (mushrooms), and duck cooked in bourgueil wine. Reservations are advised. The hotel and restaurant both are closed Monday evenings and Tuesdays, from mid-June to early July, and mid-January to early February. Reservations advised. Major credit cards accepted. 2 Rue Gambetta, Langeais (phone: 47-96-82-12; fax: 47-96-56-72). Hotel moderate, restaurant expensive to moderate.

CINQ-MARS-LA-PILE: This tiny village has two noteworthy monuments: its château and "La Pile," a unique Gallo-Roman tower. The château, now only two movingly overgrown 11th- and 12th-century towers, provides a fine, clifftop view over the Loire and its south bank. It was once the property of a favorite courtier of Louis XIII, Henri d'Effiat, the Marquis de Cinq-Mars, who was convicted of conspiracy against Richelieu and beheaded at the ripe age of 22. La Pile, visible from the highway, is a square masonry structure 98 feet high surmounted by four small pyramids. A path leads up a ridge to its base, but its solid interior doesn't invite climbing. Its purpose remains a mystery, as does the name of the town, which in earlier times was called St-Mars.

To get to Luynes, the last stop on this route and only 8 miles (13 km) west of Tours, turn off N152 onto D76, a little more than 2 miles (3 km) beyond Cinq-Mars.

LUYNES: This town lies under the shadow of a strictly feudal 13th-century castle. Privately owned and occupied (by the same family since 1619), the castle can be viewed only from below. There are many troglodyte houses in this area, and signs lead through the pretty countryside behind and above the town, past horses pulling wooden farm carts, to the ruins of a Roman aqueduct.

CHECKING IN/EATING OUT: *Domaine de Beauvois* – Another luxurious Loire Valley château, this one 2 miles (3 km) northwest of Luynes via D49 is both a hotel with 42 rooms, surrounded by woods and offering amenities such as a swimming pool and a tennis court, and a restaurant. Specialties include a terrine made of eel, bass cooked with truffles and leeks, and *beuchelle à la Tourangelle,* a Touraine dish combining sweetbreads and kidneys served in a delicious sauce. The hotel and restaurant are closed from early January to mid-March. Reservations advised. Major credit cards accepted. Luynes (phone: 47-55-50-11; fax: 47-55-59-62). Expensive.

Normandy

Normandy owes its name to the Northmen, or Norsemen, those Scandinavian invaders who swept down the Seine Valley in AD 820. It was neither the first nor the last time invasions would play a momentous part in the province's history.

Whether the early Celts, whose descendants remain in neighboring Brittany, were settlers or conquerors is unsure. The Romans who sent many of them fleeing to the west were certainly the latter, though the legions stayed long enough to build towns where Evreux, Rouen, and Coutances now stand and to leave evidence of their presence in the ruins at Lillebonne. Saxon and German raiders disturbed the Roman peace, and toward the end of the 4th century the legions withdrew, leaving Normandy as a battleground between warring factions, a condition that was to be repeated on several occasions.

Under Frankish domination from 500 to the early 9th century, the foundation was laid for Normandy's major religious houses such as those at Mont-St-Michel, Fécamp, and Jumièges, which, rebuilt and refashioned in later years, became part of the architectural glory of France.

Although the Norsemen plundered and sometimes destroyed many of these establishments, by the early 10th century the invaders had become settlers, and in 911 at the Treaty of St-Clair-sur-Epte the Norman chieftain, Rolf the Ranger, became Rollo, Duke of Normandy. He subsequently was baptized at St-Ouen in Rouen.

The most famous of all the dukes descended from Rollo was William the Bastard, the illegitimate son of Robert the Devil and a tanner's daughter. After William's successful invasion of England in 1066 history accorded him the sobriquet William the Conqueror. It is to him and his wife, Matilda of Flanders, that we owe the two great religious houses at Caen, the Abbaye aux Hommes and the Abbaye aux Dames.

Normandy's potential as a threat to the French throne and realm dominated its history for the next 138 years, especially after the English King Henry II added to his empire the vast territories of Aquitaine by his marriage to the colorful duchess Eleanor. Henry's son Richard, realizing that the duchy's position not only was threatening but also vulnerable, built the formidable Château Gaillard on the Seine, close to the border of the French territories. Its romantic ruins still can be seen. Richard's foresight notwithstanding, his brother, the unloved and unwise John Lackland, managed to lose Normandy in 1202 when Philippe Auguste invaded the duchy to avenge John's murder of his nephew Arthur of Brittany at Rouen.

From 1204, Normandy was united with the French crown, first as a duchy held by the sovereign and later as a province with its own governing body at Rouen. However, it still served as a battleground during the dynastic quarrels of the French and English kings, especially in the Hundred Years War

(1337–1453), when parts of Normandy were occupied by the English for 30 years.

The English finally were driven out in 1453, and Normandy enjoyed a period of peace and prosperity until the religious wars of the late 16th century. During this time of calm, great châteaux, such as those of O (*sic*) and Fontaine-Henry, were built, not just as fortifications but as country residences. Ornate and sumptuous mansions such as the Parlement de Rouen (now the Palais de Justice) and the Hôtel de Bourgtheroulde in the same town gave expression to the Renaissance passion for elaborate architectural design in the province's capital. Rouen and Caen became free cities during this period, and the increasingly important merchant classes began to construct the lovely half-timbered houses that still line the old streets of Rouen (but were destroyed in Caen in World War II).

The Wars of Religion did little to alter the face of Normandy, though they are recalled in the names Arques-la-Bataille, near Dieppe, and Ivry-la-Bataille, near Dreux. The great cathedrals at Evreux, Rouen, Bayeux, and Coutances and the abbeys at Fécamp, Mont-St-Michel, Jumièges, Cérisy-la-Forêt, and Caen remained almost completely unscathed. The first mindless acts of destruction came during the French Revolution, when few cathedrals or churches escaped some form of desecration, particularly Mont-St-Michel and Fécamp, which were stripped of their treasures, and Cérisy, which had some of its bays removed.

Worse destruction was to come in June, July, and August 1944, when in the battle to liberate France from the Nazis more than 200,000 buildings and 586 towns and villages, among them Le Havre, St-Lô, Caen, Lisieux, and Evreux, were almost totally destroyed. Of all the great, ancient Norman cities, only Bayeux and its two great treasures, the cathedral and the *Tapisserie de la Reine Mathilde* (Queen Matilda's Tapestry), remained virtually intact.

The war changed the urban face of Normandy radically and in a way that only the patina of a century or so will make palatable. The landscape, more resilient, retains much of the lush green pasturage and forest that must have attracted the early Norsemen.

Normandy is bordered on the west by Brittany and the English Channel, on the north by the Channel as it narrows toward the Straits of Dover, on the northeast and east by the ancient region of Picardy, the Ile-de-France around Paris, and on the south by the Loire Valley.

Although a small area by American standards, the province is divided by geography and tradition into quite distinct regions. The Cotentin Peninsula in the northwest, stretching to the Channel around Cherbourg, is famous for horse breeding and dairy farming. Dairy farming also is important in the Bessin, the area between Bayeux and the coast, a region famous also for its handsome, fortified, gray stone farmhouses. The town of Isigny-sur-Mer, between the Cotentin and Bayeux, gives its name to a butter that is a household staple throughout France. In the Norman *bocage* ("open woodland," literally, but usually stone walls thickly overgrown with hedges) south of the Bessin there is more dairy farming and some celebrated cider from the apples that blossom with an astonishing beauty all over the region during April and May. On the prairie-type terrain around Caen, cereals have become a major postwar crop. East of Caen, in the Pays d'Auge are more apple orchards, often surrounded by half-timbered farms and run-down barns that make this part of France seem particularly idyllic. The dairy farms in the Pays d'Auge provide the milk that is turned into three celebrated cheeses, camembert, livarot, and pont-l'evêque. South of the plains around Caen, tributaries of the Orne have dug deep into the hilly pastures and woods around Flers, Clécy, and Falaise to form dramatic gorges. Ambitious promoters have dubbed the region Suisse Normande (Norman Switzerland), a name that even the spectacular view from La Roche d'Oëtre does not quite make plausible. Across the Seine, in the triangle formed by Dieppe, Le Havre, and Rouen, are the rolling hills and valleys of the Pays de Caux, bordered on the Channel by great white chalk cliffs that drop precipitously into the sea. The main cash crops of the hinterland are flax and sugar beet.

The Seine, which curves through Normandy in a half-dozen or so serpentine loops, is the region's economic lifeline. Its strategic position between the English Channel and Paris and its navigability have drawn major industries such as paper and textile manufacturing to Rouen and have caused huge petrochemical works to flourish along the river between Rouen and Le Havre, where there also are important shipbuilding and iron industries. The old cottage industries have all but disappeared. Ivory, for which Dieppe was famous, lace, wrought iron, and faïence de Rouen (ceramicware) now are mostly seen in museums, although there still are lace schools with small boutiques at Alençon and Bayeux, and ironwork still can be bought from small foundries at Gaillon and Monceau.

The one ancient activity other than farming that survives is commercial fishing, most of it local, but some in waters as far off as Newfoundland, where fishermen from Dieppe, Fécamp, and Honfleur harvest the cold North Atlantic for cod. The fruit of their labors graces the tables of most Norman restaurants and homes. The regional specialty, *assiette de fruits de mer* — a platter of fresh shellfish — is a visual and culinary delight and might include crayfish, crabs, several kinds of shrimp, oysters, clams, cockles, mussels, and winkles, often served on a bed of damp seaweed. Another favorite, *marmite dieppoise*, is served along the coast as far south as Isigny-sur-Mer; it can consist of a mixture of sole, turbot, brill, mackerel, whiting, shrimp, and crab, all simmered in their own juices to make a substantial half stew, half soup, to which is added another Norman staple, fresh cream. Rich, fattening, and irresistible — cream is used to enhance almost every type of dish found on the Norman table, from vegetables to poultry, game, and fish to fresh fruit and pastry.

Often what is not cooked in cream in Normandy is cooked in cider — not apple juice but a hard cider with an alcoholic content. Ham, chicken, duck, rabbit, and hare braised this way can be unforgettable. Although cider is bottled and can be purchased, most of it sold this way is *doux*, on the sweet side, and its consumption is considered effete. Cider bought from farmers who brew their own is dry, still, and has a powerful bite. Normandy's other famous beverage is calvados, a kind of applejack with class that takes 12 to 15 years to mature. It usually is served as a liqueur, although there are places, especially in and around Caen, where chefs cook tripe in it.

Tripe is a gastronomic specialty of the Caen region. Other regional delicacies are oysters from St-Vaast-la-Hougue; *agneau pré salé,* lamb fed on saltwater grasses near Mont-St-Michel; and another Mont-St-Michel specialty, *omelettes Mère-Poulard,* named for a famous restaurateuse on the island who created these enormous, soufflé-like concoctions.

Normandy cheeses are savored all over the world, although pont-l'evêque never tastes quite as good as when eaten in or near the small village of lovely half-timbered houses for which it is named; and camembert is not camembert if it is made anywhere else.

This concentration on the culinary arts is not to suggest that the fine arts have been neglected in Normandy. Often the former has inspired the latter. The painters Gustave Courbet and Eugène Boudin were frequent visitors at the *Ferme St-Siméon* (see *Romantic French Hostelries,* DIVERSIONS) near Honfleur, where they came to drink cider and sample the cooking of Mère Tatin, the proprietress. Boudin brought along his painter friends whose experiments with light led them to be called Impressionists. Jean Renoir was one, Alfred Sisley another, but the most notable visitor was Claude Monet, whose pictures of the cliffs at Etretat and studies of Rouen Cathedral are among his most famous works. Monet bought a villa at Giverny (just inside Normandy's border with the Ile-de-France), which is now a museum open to the public. Norman painters and subjects are well represented in the art museums at Rouen, Le Havre, and Caen as well as in some smaller galleries.

Some of Normandy's cathedrals, monasteries, and châteaux may be considered artistic masterpieces as well, including such buildings as the abbeys at Jumièges, Cérisy-la-Forêt, and Caen. In fact, medieval Norman architecture became so widespread and idiosyncratic that it was called the Norman style in England, which can be discerned in certain details at Canterbury, Westminster, and Durham.

Normandy also has its literary lights. Pierre Corneille, one of France's great tragedians, was born in Rouen in a house that still can be visited and practiced law in the Palais de Justice. Gustave Flaubert also was born in Rouen and describes his father's apartments in the hospice there in the novel *Madame Bovary.* Guy de Maupassant, another Norman, went to a school in Rouen, now called the Lycée Corneille, and used to relax at Etretat, one of his favorite resorts. Marcel Proust often stayed at the resorts on the Côte Fleurie, especially Cabourg.

This tour starts at Vernon, leaving autoroute A13 from Paris to cross the Seine for a visit to Monet's home at Giverny. The route continues via Rouen on D982 to Lillebonne and then goes across the Pays de Caux to Dieppe. It then travels down the coast to Le Havre, backtracks a short way along the Seine, and crosses the river by the great bridge at Tancarville heading for Honfleur, Trouville-sur-Mer, Deauville, and Cabourg, where it turns inland to Caen. There, a detour can be made to visit the Normandy beaches that were made famous on *D-Day* before returning to Caen and continuing the main itinerary via Bayeux, St-Lô, and Coutances to Granville on the west coast of the Cotentin Peninsula. The route then takes the coast road along Mont-St-Michel Bay to Avranches and the mount itself.

Expect to pay $180 and up for a double room in hotels listed as very expensive; between $120 and $180 in an expensive one; $70 to $120 in places listed as moderate, and less than $70 in those listed as inexpensive. Note that hotels in Deauville and Cabourg are very expensive in July and August, often charging closer to $200 for a double room, and in any season, all along the Norman coast, a sea view can add $30 to $40 to a room's price. Note, too, that there still are many inexpensive *auberges* (inns) and small hotels in Normandy where clean rooms with a minimum of amenities — usually just a sink; not always that — can be found for under $55. Dinner for two in the restaurants listed as very expensive is $160 and up; in the expensive category, $110 to $160; in the moderate range, $65 to $110; and in the inexpensive range, less than $65. Prices do not include wine or drinks, though service usually is included. A caveat: An *assiette de fruits de mer* — which everyone not allergic to shellfish should try at least once — will cost double if it is crowned with a lobster.

VERNON: Although much of the town was destroyed in World War II, its site on the left bank of the Seine backed by the forest of Bizy and opposite the great forest of Vernon has attracted visitors ever since the 12th century, when Louis IX (St. Louis) used to come here to escape the heat of Paris. So enamored of the place was that most likable of princes that he allowed Vernon to add the fleur-de-lis, the Capetian family emblem, to the three bunches of watercress on its escutcheon. The collegiate Church of Notre-Dame, which largely escaped damage in the war, was originally built in the 12th century and was added to and modified in the 15th and 16th centuries. There is a splendid rose window on the west front, adorned on both sides by galleries with flying buttresses. The 15th-century nave, taller than the transept, is lofty and narrow, its cool lines enhanced by the grace of the triforium and the elegance of the high windows. In the precincts of Notre-Dame are a few 15th-century half-timbered houses that escaped the devastation caused by the bombing, including one next door to the church and others on Rue Carnot.

About a mile (1.6 km) outside the town, hidden behind stately trees, is the Château de Bizy (open April through October; closed Fridays), which still is the home of the Duke of Albufera. The exterior has no great distinction, but the interior is decorated handsomely in the Empire style and contains some splendid tapestries and paneling as well as a collection of souvenirs of the Napoleonic era. The gardens, laid out to provide a suitable context for the original château (1740), are adorned with waterfalls and baroque fountains that suggest Italy rather than northern France. From the bridge linking Vernon to the suburb of Vernonnet, across the Seine, there is a pleasant view of forested islands upstream and down. You also can see the remains of the original 12th-century bridge and the *donjon* (keep) of the small fortress that guarded it on the right bank.

Just over a mile (1.6 km) upstream from the bridge on D5 is Giverny, a charming little village nestling against the hillside, where Claude Monet lived from 1883 to 1926. Monet's house, now the *Musée Claude-Monet* (open daily, except Mondays, from April through October; phone: 32-51-28-21), is a delightful, homey contrast to the great residential châteaux and manor houses of Normandy; beautiful though they undoubtedly are, they tend toward a certain monumental quality even in their most domestic moments. Apart from the great studio where Monet painted some of his most famous works, everything about the artist's house is intimate and serene. It owes its present condition, which is a somewhat idealized version of the way it was when Monet lived here, to an international group of sponsors who rescued it from decay and dilapidation and subsidized the founding of the museum under the auspices of the Institut de France.

The painter's love affair with color can be appreciated from the exterior's pink walls, white highlights, and green jalousies to the blue motif of the old-fashioned country kitchen and the wonderful primrose yellow dining room. The interior — platters on the walls, dressers in the dining room, and pots on the yellow chimneypiece — has all been restored to look as it did when Renoir, Sisley, Cézanne, Manet, and Pissarro dropped by for a bite and a chat. Monet's much-loved Japanese prints have been restored as far as possible to the places he allotted them. His bedroom is an unexpectedly elegant enclave, with none of the Bohemian ambience one associates with 19th-century painters. Most appealing is his drawing room/studio, complete with couch, armchairs, and basketwork chairs, which conjures up the atmosphere of good talk, cigar smoke, wine, and absinthe that must have prevailed.

One of Monet's great passions, again associated with color, was his garden. This too has been re-created, and what one sees at any time of the year is, as far as possible, what he saw, down to the particular flowers growing in a particular place. The gardens were a frequent theme of his paintings after 1900, and in later years his only theme. Anyone who has seen pictures of the water lily pool with its Japanese bridge will recognize the original immediately, now regrettably separated from the main gardens by a road. The irises, peonies, heliotropes, and Judas trees — not to mention the willows and the water lilies — are all here just as they are on canvas. In spring, wisteria blooms over the bridge, and in the extensive gardens closer to the house, fruit trees burst into a blizzard of white and pink flowers not far from great masses of daffodils. In summer, morning glories appear, along with snapdragon, nasturtium, foxglove, sweet pea, stock, columbine, phlox, gentian, and sage — virtually the whole inventory of flowers found in the gardens of northwestern Europe at this season. In fall, the garden is ablaze with the gaudy, outrageous colors of the teeming autumn, brazen dahlias and sunflowers, subtler asters, and lofty hollyhocks. Seen in any of the three flowering seasons, Giverny leaves an indelible impression.

A new attraction, the *Musée Américan Giverny,* opened last spring. This collection, which celebrates the French Impressionist connection, showcases important American Impressionists who were strongly influenced by Monet and other great French painters a century ago. The 3½-acre museum is located at 99 Rue Claude Monet next to the Monet gardens. Exhibition galleries are open daily except Mondays from 10 AM to 6 PM from April through October; admission charge; phone: 32-51-94-65.

CHECKING IN/EATING OUT: *Hôtel d'Evreux* – This 18th-century townhouse became an inn more than 100 years ago. Today, it's a typically French family-run hotel/restaurant with homey touches, fine food, and friendly service. The recently renovated hotel is open year-round, and the restaurant is closed Sundays. Major credit cards accepted. 7 Pl. d'Evreux (phone: 32-21-16-12; fax: 32-21-32-73). Moderate.

En Route from Vernon – Take route D313 to Les Andelys to see Château Gaillard, the remains of a beautiful 12th-century fortress built by Richard the Lion-Hearted overlooking the Seine. The view over Les Andelys along the river, romantically dominated on the left bank by cliffs, is spectacular. From Les Andelys take D1 north to D2 and Ecouis, where there is one of the most famous churches in the Vexin (as the surrounding territory is known); it was built in 1310 and contains a 14th-century wooden sculpture of St. Veronica and an unusual statue supposedly of St. Agnes, whose robe is formed of her own flowing hair. Farther along D2, the church at Lisors is worth a stop to see the beautiful 14th-century statue of Our Lady, Queen of Heaven. A right turn onto D715 leads to the picturesque ruins of the Cistercian Abbaye de Mortemer, surrounded by trees and lawns.

Turning left on D6, you pass through Lyons-la-Forêt, the center of a beech forest, once the favorite hunting grounds of the Norman dukes and still the site of formal hunts with much scarlet livery and black velour headgear in evidence between April and September. The town's 15th-century church contains several huge wooden statues. Another left turn, this time onto D321, leads to the Abbaye de Fontaine-Guérard, on the banks of the River Andelle. This Cistercian foundation for nuns, initially sponsored by Robert, Earl of Leicester, in 1132, eventually came under the protection of John Lackland and Louis IX (St-Louis) and now is owned by the Salvation Army. There are interesting early Gothic features in what remains of the abbey church, chapter house, nuns' parlor, and the study hall. (Open daily, except Mondays, from April through October; phone: 32-49-03-82.)

Backtracking about a mile (1.6 km) along D321, one comes again to D1, which passes the restored Château de Vascoeuil (open April through October, weekends only in winter; phone: 35-23-62-35), where one finds — surprisingly — sculptures by Braque, Léger, and Calder as well as works by David and Bernard Buffet. A few yards north of Vascoeuil off D1, N30 leads to Martainville and its château, a somewhat small, red brick affair built by a Rouen merchant. This sensible-looking house with stout turrets (which do not remotely suggest fortifications) has been turned into a showplace of Norman arts, crafts, and traditions. The kitchen, with its huge brick fireplace and dozens of implements, is a joy. (Closed Tuesdays and holidays; phone: 35-23-40-13.) Route N31 continues west to Rouen.

ROUEN: For a detailed report on the city, its sights, hotels, and restaurants, see *Rouen* in THE CITIES.

En Route from Rouen – Take D982 to Canteleu, where there is a good view along the Seine from the top of the hill. You can reach St-Martin-de-Boscherville by crossing the corniche on D982, but a more interesting though circuitous route is via the turnoff on D51, running along the cliff top above the river to Sahurs, then turning right on D351 to drive through the Roumare Forest. St-Martin boasts the first of the great abbeys along the Seine between Rouen and Le Havre. The abbey Church of St. George was founded in 1050 by Raoul de Tancarville (who first was tutor and later chamberlain to William the Conqueror) and is one of the finest examples of Romanesque art in Normandy. The church is astonishingly pure in design, with a minimum of Gothic trappings to distract from the simple Romanesque arches. Two jousting knights, typical of the era in which the church was constructed, adorn the capitals in the south transept.

From St-Martin it once again is possible to skirt the looping Seine by taking a road that becomes D65 at Duclair, to swing round to Jumièges, or to continue on D982 and make a short left backtrack to the Jumièges Abbey from Yainville. The ruins of the great Benedictine abbey of Jumièges are among the most romantic in France. The monks were here from the 7th century until the Revolution, during which time Jumièges was one of the great church establishments controlling life along the Seine, materially as well as spiritually. The remains include the entire nave and parts of the transept and chancel. In the center of the square cloister is an ancient yew tree, which romantics claim is almost as old as the abbey. (Open daily, 10 AM to noon and 2 to 4 PM, in winter; 9 AM to noon and 2 to 5 PM in spring; 9 AM to 6 PM in summer; phone: 35-37-24-02.)

Route D928 continues past Le Triat to St-Wandrille, a splendid abbey whose Benedictine community still thrives. The monks have been here, with interruptions, since the 7th century. St. Wandrille was a count at the court of Dagobert who decided just after his marriage to become a monk. He was ordained at St-Ouen in Rouen and eventually founded the abbey named for him. Because of his angelic qualities and his physical carriage, he was known as "the athlete of God." The cloister, seen only on a guided tour (offered daily at 3 and 4 PM), has an interesting 16th-century lavabo. The monks still use a medieval barn brought stone by stone from the department of Eure and reconstructed here as the abbey church. Mass is said and vespers sung in Gregorian chant each day (phone: 35-96-23-11).

 CHECKING IN/EATING OUT: *L'Auberge du Bac* – A Normandy farmhouse transformed into a fine country inn at the ferry crossing. On sunny days you can dine on the terrace and watch the ships go up and down the Seine. The food and service are very good. Closed Tuesday evenings and Wednesdays. Major credit cards accepted. Jumièges (phone: 35-37-24-16). Moderate.

Auberge des Ruines – This hotel/restaurant is wonderfully rustic, with a charming fireplace for winter dining, a romantic arboreal bower for summer, and those exquisite ruins nearby. The fare is not particularly imaginative — duck *à l'orange*, turbot with hollandaise — but it is good and no one minds if you linger. There are 4 inexpensive rooms. Visa accepted. 1 Pl. de la Mairie, Jumièges (phone: 35-37-24-05). Moderate.

CAUDEBEC-EN-CAUX: An extraordinary view over the Seine makes Caudebec an attractive spot, even though only a few of the half-timbered houses that lined its streets before the Germans set fire to the town in 1940 remain. The panorama over the river is best seen from the steps of the Hôtel de Ville (Town Hall). Occasionally a huge merchant ship plying between Le Havre and Rouen obliterates the vistas on the opposite bank; to see these large boats against such an idyllic setting can be awesome.

The fine Flamboyant Gothic Church of Notre-Dame, with its celebrated organ, dates from the 15th and 16th centuries. Sculpted on the balustrade surrounding the church are some of the words from the Magnificat and the Salve Regina. The 15th-century window over the north door is of English glasswork, rare in France. The *Musée Biochet-Bréchot* (phone: 35-96-00-21), in the wonderful old building known as the Maison des Templiers (Templars' House), has pictures and artifacts of local history from prehistoric times to the present. It is open June 15 to September 15. For information in off-season, contact the Syndicat d'Initiative (phone: 35-96-20-65.)

VILLEQUIER: Take D81 out of Caudebec to this charming riverside spot sheltered by wooded hills where the road reaches down off the cliff to the water's edge. Victor Hugo stayed here often at his son-in-law's family home overlooking the river. It is now the *Musée Victor-Hugo* and contains manuscripts, autographs, and letters by or concerning the author as well as portraits and furniture. Open daily from 10 AM to noon and 2 to 6 PM (phone: 35-56-78-31.)

LILLEBONNE: The Romans called this town Juliobona and, in the days when they controlled Gaul, it was a major city. Today only the grass-covered remains of the Roman theater recall its early importance. Apply to the *Café de l'Hôtel de Ville* (Place Félix Square, Lillebonne, 76170) for permission to wander through the site. William the Conqueror also found Lillebonne strategically useful, and he built a fortress here; the formidable walls of the keep and several towers remain. It was here that William gathered his barons before crossing to Hastings in the eventful year of 1066.

En Route from Lillebonne – Take D173 to Bolbec, where there are four handsome 18th-century houses on Rue de la République, then take meandering D149 into Dieppe. The road passes through typical Pays de Caux countryside, which is characterized inland by large half-timbered farmhouses, with barns and outhouses around a central courtyard. These in turn often stand in orchards, with the whole farm sometimes ringed by windbreaking rows of oak and beech trees. Here and there, barns have been remodeled with chic doors and windowboxes testifying to their new role as country retreats for city dwellers.

At Longueville there is a ruined castle that once belonged to Dunois, the Bastard of Orléans, who appears sympathetically in Shaw's *Saint Joan*. Farther on, at Arques-la-Bataille, poised high on a rock are the remains of a much larger castle, dating from the 12th century and surrounded by a moat. There are good views over the valley from the keep, the highest point of the castle, though the temptation to wander inside the walls should be avoided since crumbling masonry can be a danger.

CHECKING IN/EATING OUT: *Auberge du Clos Normand* – Regional specialties, the order of the day here, are served either in the wood-beamed and copper decor of the dining room or in the garden, which has a footbridge-laced stream running through it. Quiche lovers should request the *tarte aux moules,* with mussels. There are 9 rooms available. The restaurant is closed Monday nights and Tuesdays off-season and from mid-November to mid-December. Martin-Eglise, 22 Rue Henri-IV (phone: 35-82-71-01). Moderate.

***Auberge de la Durdent* –** This small inn has a wooden balcony out front, lots of oak beams, plenty of chintz — and a river running through that divides the bar from the dining room. Trout, not surprisingly, is a specialty and good in any of the several ways in which it is prepared. In typical Norman fashion, cream is used with just about everything. There are 15 rooms with showers. Both the rooms and the cooking are traditional. Closed Wednesdays, 2 weeks in February and 3 weeks in November. Major credit cards accepted. At the crossroads of D149 and D131. Héricourt-en-Caux (phone: 35-96-42-44). Inexpensive.

DIEPPE: The main attraction of this major Channel seaport is the beachfront, which stretches for nearly a mile between cliffs dominated at the west end by a castle and at the east by the port itself. The basins of the port, lined here and there with 18th-century houses, extend deep into the town along the Quai de Quesle and the Quai de Norvège. Dieppe became a fashionable seaside resort in the 19th century when it was visited by Duchesse de Berry as well as by Empress Eugénie and her consort, Napoleon III.

Eglise St-Jacques, dating from the 13th century but with later additions, is the most interesting of the town's churches. In its Flamboyant Gothic Sacred Heart Chapel, a frieze shows Brazilian Indians, recalling the time in the 16th century when Dieppe was an important point of embarkation for Atlantic explorers. There still are some picturesque old houses in the neighborhood of St-Jacques, especially along Grande-Rue leading to Dieppe's other interesting church, the part Gothic, part Renaissance St-Rémy. Beyond St-Rémy via Rue de Chastes is a much-restored but still imposing 15th-century castle, offering excellent views of the town and its surroundings from the terraces. The château-museum is notable for its extensive collection of ivory carvings. (Open daily, June through September; closed Tuesdays the rest of the year; phone: 35-84-19-76.)

On August 19, 1942, Dieppe was the scene of the first Allied landing after the retreat from Dunkirk when 7,000 men, mostly Canadians, crossed the Channel in Operation Jubilee, hoping to secure a foothold on the northern shore of the continent. But the Allies did not know how strongly the port was defended, and the operation was a failure, costing the lives of 5,000 soldiers. However, the Dieppe Raids, as they became known, taught the Allies two major lessons: first, that the Germans expected any major attack to come via the ports and that, therefore, plans should be made to attack via the beaches and cliffs; second, that aerial and naval bombardment would be essential before land forces could gain a foothold. Almost 2 years later, these lessons were put into effect successfully on *D-Day* to the west of Dieppe, beyond the River Orne.

CHECKING IN: *La Présidence* – This inviting place has 88 comfortable rooms and a fourth-floor restaurant, *Le Queiros,* that offers good seafood dishes and wines, and a fine view of the water. Major credit cards accepted. 1 Bd. Verdun, Dieppe (phone: 35-84-31-31; fax: 35-84-86-70). Moderate.

***Univers* –** A small and very popular hotel, its 28 rooms are decorated with beautiful antiques; a restaurant is on the premises. Be sure to make reservations. Major credit cards accepted. 10 Bd. Verdun, Dieppe (phone: 35-84-12-55; fax: 35-40-20-40). Moderate.

EATING OUT: *Auberge de la Bucherie* – On the road to Rouen, this is the best dining spot in the Dieppe region. Small and flower-filled, it features traditional fare. Closed Sunday evenings and Mondays. Reservations advised. Major credit cards accepted. Rte. de Rouen, Offranville (phone: 35-84-83-10). Moderate.

Marmite Dieppoise – The obvious choice here is the *marmite dieppoise,* mussels, crayfish, crabs, sole, and turbot in a cream sauce of potatoes and leeks with fennel. There also are other delicious seafood dishes and Norman classics. Closed Sunday and Thursday nights, Mondays, and from *Christmas* to *New Year's Day.* Visa accepted. 8 Rue St-Jean, Dieppe (phone: 35-84-24-26). Moderate.

En Route from Dieppe – D75 climbs the cliff just beyond the castle and runs for a little over a mile along the coast before it turns inland to reach Varengeville-sur-Mer. There one can visit the Manoir d'Ango, the country home of a famous Dieppe merchant-adventurer whose privateers broke the Portuguese trade monopoly on the west coast of Africa in the 16th century. The manor house, dating from 1530, is a wonderful asymmetrical pile of brick and stone with sturdy Romanesque arches and a famous circular dovecote of ornate red and black brickwork. (Open Tuesdays, Thursdays, weekends, and holiday afternoons from *Easter* to October 31.) Varengeville itself contains some fine old houses on wooded hillsides and the Eglise St-Valéry. Dating from the 12th century but much modified, the church stands in a rather lonely spot on the cliff's edge, bordered by a cemetery in which the painter Georges Braque is buried. The Tree of Jesse window inside the church was designed by the celebrated Cubist.

From the Phare d'Ailly (Ailly Lighthouse), at nearby Ste-Marguerite, it is possible to see about 40 miles up and down the cliff-lined coast. The lighthouse is open from 8 AM until about an hour before dusk, and the lighthouse keeper who admits visitors to the first-floor platform is not averse to accepting a small tip. The 12th-century church at Ste-Marguerite, much altered in the 16th century, is notable for its high altar, dating from 1160. Turn left off D75 at St-Aubin-sur-Mer to make a delightful detour along the Dun Valley to Bourg-Dun to see the unusual spire on the church tower: It's shaped like the head of an ax. Return on the same road and turn left onto D68, the coast road, for Veules-les-Roses, picturesquely situated in a wooded valley through which runs what is supposed to be the shortest river in France.

EATING OUT: *Les Galets* – Its name means "the shingles," and this small, modern restaurant could hardly be closer to the shingled beach. Its seafood specialties, desserts, and superb selection of local cheeses have won it a Michelin star. Closed Sunday evenings off-season, Tuesday lunch, Wednesdays, and most of January. Major credit cards accepted. 3 Rue Victor-Hugo, Veules-les-Roses (phone: 35-97-61-33). Expensive.

ST-VALÉRY-EN-CAUX: Like many other coastal towns, the fishing port of St-Val, as it is locally known, is a breach in the great chalk cliffs, and most of its arterial streets run more or less parallel to the colorful yacht and fishing basin that penetrates deep into the town. St-Val was badly damaged in 1940, during the retreat of the British 10th Army, but was rebuilt and became a popular seaside and sailing resort. A few old houses remain on the left bank, but most of the villas and small hotels date from the 1950s. Take the clifftop road D79 to Fécamp.

EATING OUT: *Port* – Unusual combinations of fish and sauces make this restaurant overlooking the port an occasionally esoteric culinary experience. For example, the chef-owner may cook fish in red wine. Closed Sunday evenings and Mondays. Major credit cards accepted. 18 Quai d'Amont, St-Valéry (phone: 35-97-08-93). Moderate.

FÉCAMP: Set between great white cliffs where the Pays de Caux meets the sea, this town is France's fourth-largest fishing port. The colorful boats lying placidly at anchor along the quays may be waiting for a tide that will take them to the cold, rough fishing grounds off Newfoundland. Fécamp also is a seaside resort, with a gambling casino and a shopping center for people from surrounding villages.

The most interesting sight here is La Trinité, an early Gothic abbey church. The present structure, built between 1175 and 1225 and subsequently embellished, is the successor to earlier buildings. Apart from the application of a baroque façade in the 18th century, the church is impressive. Its massive lantern tower, 210 feet high, dominates the valley of Fécamp. The interior is no less commanding: At 416 feet in length, it's one of the longest churches in France. The ten awesome bays in the nave are marvelously free of ornament. Decoration, when present, is elaborate, especially in the sumptuous gilded baldachin, which hovers above the high altar poised on marble pillars. The cross on the altar is bronze and has an unusually poignant figure of Christ. The chapels in the ambulatory are hidden behind splendid stone screens playfully sculpted with classical vases, chimera, palms, hearts, and olives. In the Lady Chapel are four famous medallions carved in wood, including one with a veiled figure of Christ on the cross. Opposite the Lady Chapel at the back of the high altar is the Tabernacle of the Precious Blood, carved in white marble in 1505. People still come in large numbers to venerate the relic on the Tuesday and Thursday following *Trinity Sunday.* In the Chapelle du Calvaire you can see fragments from the old rood screen: John and Peter asleep during Christ's watch at Gethsemane; James with his face turned to the wall; Judas shaking his fist. In the south transept there is a remarkable Dormition of the Virgin with nine saints and friends in attendance, all sculpted in wonderful detail. In the humanistic tradition of the early Renaissance — it was worked in 1495 — the attending figures are all idiosyncratic personalities, suggesting that real models were used.

This abbey was the home of the Benedictine Brother Vincelli, who in 1510 experimented with the herbs he found on the nearby cliffs to produce a soothing distillation in the form of a liqueur. The secret recipe, closely guarded by the monks, was lost during the Revolution. However, searching through family papers one day in 1863, a local businessman named Alexandre Le Grand came upon an ancient manuscript with scarcely decipherable writing that turned out to be a recipe for a concoction based on herbs and spices. After lengthy experiments, Le Grand produced an elixir to his taste and called it Bénédictine. The factory where it is made, *Le Musée de la Bénédictine* (110 Rue Alexandre-Le-Grand; phone: 35-28-00-06), is open to the public daily from 9:30 to 11:30 AM and 2 to 5:30 PM (winter hours are shorter). It houses a sweet-smelling room piled with sacks of dried herbs and lined with bottles from all over the world. In the distillery, there are handsome old copper vats, and in the cellars, casks where the liqueur matures. And there is much more: Le Grand, who collected paintings and objets d'art, commissioned a part Renaissance, part Gothic palace adjoining his distillery in which he could display his burgeoning collection. The building is a rather ugly and pretentious piece of architecture, but Le Grand's collection, predominantly religious in theme, contains some extraordinary pieces — an ivory Spanish triptych of the life of Christ; an ivory, wood, and marble bas-relief of the Presentation at the Temple; and a 12th-century missal that alone would merit a visit to the museum. There also are scores of other bas-reliefs, statues, and a variety of items rescued from the abbey at the time of the Revolution as well as a fine ironwork collection and 600 oil lamps from the days of the Roman Empire.

CHECKING IN: *L'Universe* – A small, family-run hotel in the center of town, it offers a warm welcome to travelers who'd like to spend a night or two in Fécamp. Some of the 16 rooms have television sets. Visa accepted. 5 Pl. St-Etienne (phone: 35-28-05-88). Inexpensive.

EATING OUT: *La Marine* – There is nothing spectacular about this brasserie except the value. As the name suggests, seafood dishes are best: simply and expertly prepared and certainly ample. There is a fine view of the bay and the yacht basin from the first floor. Closed in January. Major credit cards accepted. 23 Quai Vicomté, Fécamp (phone: 35-28-15-94). Moderate.

En Route from Fécamp – At St-Léonard on D940, just at the top of the hill, there are some beautiful old half-timbered cottages and farms on the right. Take the coast road D211 down to Yport, which passes tidy middle class homes with neat yards and gardens lined with rows of vegetables. From Yport, the road to Etretat climbs over cliffs that look like moorland, covered with gorse, ferns, and brambles and often shrouded in mist. Along the way, look for signs offering fresh fruit and *chèvre* (goat cheese) for sale.

ETRETAT: Etretat is a small quiet resort that's barely more than a cleft between the precipitous Falaise d'Aval (Aval Cliff), to the left as you face the ocean, and the Falaise d'Amont (Amont Cliff), to the right. The famous opening in the cliff to the left, which looks like a flying buttress, is known as the Porte d'Aval (the Aval Gate), and jutting from the sea close by is the needle rock. Claude Monet painted these cliffs many times.

By taking the stairway and path from the Aval end of the beach you can see the cliffs from above, a much more thrilling perspective, especially when the fog swirls and eddies below, around, and above you. The path (which is steep and not recommended for anyone who has difficulty walking) leads past grim gun emplacements from World War II over firm, springy turf and past an enormous bramble bush, which in September is laden with luscious blackberries. Beyond the brambles, you reach the edge of the cliff and on a clear day can see to another "gate," the Manne, to the left, and the lighthouse atop the Cap d'Antifer. At the cliff's edge a very narrow pathway, which falls away treacherously on either side, permits you to reach what looks like ramparts on the cliff. The flat, milky, blue-white of the ocean here explains why this is known as the Côte d'Albâtre (Alabaster Coast). A warning about the path: It is narrower on the inland side than on the ocean side; jumping from the narrow side to the cliff's edge, where it is broader, is not too difficult; jumping back, especially in a high wind, can be very dangerous.

The Amont Cliff, on the other side of Etretat, is accessible by car. It is less dramatic than the Aval Cliff, although the nearby Chapelle Notre-Dame-de-la-Garde is worth seeing. On the beach at Etretat there's a small open-air bar where the fishermen may be found in the late morning, sometimes breaking into song, sea chantey-style, though they tend to be inhibited if they think they are attracting too much attention.

 CHECKING IN: *Dormy House* – A small, tranquil inn in which the rooms offer an exceptional view of the Etretat cliffs. Closed March to mid-April. Visa accepted. Rte. du Havre (phone: 35-27-07-88; fax: 35-29-86-19). Moderate.

LE HAVRE: About 90% of this port, the second largest in France, was destroyed in World War II. Its proximity to the English coast made it the target of a series of RAF bombings meant to preclude a German invasion of Great Britain, and by 1945 it was the most damaged port in Europe. After the war, the architect Auguste Perret rebuilt the center of the city following the grid pattern of the old, 18th-century town, although the present concrete buildings do not convey the charm of the original. The *Musée des Beaux-Arts André-Malraux* contains paintings dating from the 16th century, but the outstanding collections are of works by Eugène Boudin (296 pieces, of which 50 are on permanent display) and Raoul Dufy, who was born in Le Havre. There also are important paintings by Corot, Sisley, Monet, and Pissarro (closed Tuesdays and holidays; Bd. John-F.-Kennedy; phone: 35-42-33-97). Also interesting is the Cathédrale Notre-Dame on Rue de Paris. Although it was devastated in the war, it has been almost completely and attractively restored. As a result, it has a certain pristine quality that one does not sense in some of the more ornately decorated churches in Normandy.

Another ecclesiastical site worth visiting is the Abbaye de Graville (Vierge Noir; phone: 35-47-14-01; closed Mondays and Tuesdays), in what is now a suburb of Le Havre. There has been a church here since the 6th century, but the present edifice is a restoration of the one built in the 12th and 13th centuries as an adjunct to the abbey. The buildings to the right, where Henry V stayed during the siege of Harfleur in 1415, are now a museum (also closed Mondays and Tuesdays). On view are beautiful medieval pieces and fragments of the original abbey, along with religious statues, gravestones, bas-reliefs, documents, and processional crosses.

Ste-Adresse, on the cliffs northeast of Le Havre, is a suburb with cliff top villas from the Edwardian period. There also is a tiny chapel, Notre-Dame-des-Flots (Our Lady of the Tides), which is lined with plaques thanking the Virgin for guiding a loved one to a safe harbor. Ste-Adresse was the provisional capital of Belgium during World War I, and the Belgian coat of arms is incorporated into that of the village.

Another de facto suburb of Le Havre, even though it still boasts its own Town Hall, is Harfleur. Like the similar-sounding Honfleur on the Seine Estuary, Harfleur was a port of considerable importance until François I's edict created "Le Havre de Grace" in the 16th century. In grisly testimony to its stature, during the Hundred Years War the English laid siege to the town no less than nine times, though successfully only once. This was in 1415, when Henry V was a guest at Graville and the walls finally were penetrated. In Shakespeare's *Henry V,* the king says, "Once more into the breach, dear friends, once more, or close the wall up with our English dead." By the bard's time, the Breach (la Brèque) was the common name for the neighborhood of Harfleur where the wall was broken through.

The striking bell tower, 272 feet high, that dominates Harfleur belongs to the Eglise St-Martin, built in the 15th and 16th centuries. Inside, the decorative capitals on the pillars on the north side and the Renaissance organ are worth noting. Parts of the old wall of Harfleur are visible near the Porte de Rouen (Rouen Gate). Among the not always attractive 19th- and 20th-century buildings, you still can glimpse parts of the Old Town; the Rue des 104, Rue de l'Eure, and Rue Thiers are likely to be the most rewarding.

CHECKING IN: *Bordeaux* – This hotel is modern, quiet, and comfortable, with a minimum of service (in the American motel fashion). All 31 rooms have a bath or shower, refrigerator-bar, TV set, and telephone, and some rooms overlook the marina. Major credit cards accepted. 147 Rue Louis-Brindeau, Le Havre (phone: 35-22-69-44). Expensive.

EATING OUT: *Cambridge* – The dark blue decor actually suggests Oxford, but since the coat of arms is Cambridge's, why quibble? Try the Norwegian smoked salmon, brill in sorrel, warm apple tart and Normandy cream. Not surprisingly, this restaurant is very popular with visiting Britons. Closed Sundays, Monday lunch, and most of August. Major credit cards accepted. 90 Rue Voltaire, Le Havre (phone: 35-42-50-24). Moderate.

Nice-Havrais – The best eating in Le Havre is here, in a seaside suburb. This restaurant is noted for its menu selections and their presentation. Seafood and other regional specialties abound, among them turbot in raspberry vinegar, sweetbreads and lobster in tarragon sauce, shrimp and lobster crèpes, and steaks with oysters cooked in champagne. Closed Sunday and Monday evenings year-round. Visa accepted. 6 Pl. F.-Sauvage, Ste-Adresse (phone: 35-46-14-59). Moderate.

En Route from Le Havre – Take N182 to Tancarville and cross the spectacular Pont du Tancarville, a suspension bridge completed in 1959 to replace the slow ferry service across the Seine. The bridge is almost a mile long and never less than 158 feet above the river at high tide. The south side of the Seine here is known as the Marais Vernier (Vernier Marsh), which was drained by Dutch engineers and laborers during the reign of Henry IV. It is surrounded by an amphitheater of wooded hills that mark the old course of the river before it found a new channel eons ago. The marshy plain left behind is today a rich alluvial pastureland crisscrossed by canals and dotted with cattle and fruit farms. Both the plain and the surrounding hills can be seen to great advantage from the Pointe de la Roque, just off route D178 between Tancarville Bridge and Foulbec, from where a coast road takes you into Honfleur.

HONFLEUR: Imagine a bright blue sky in the west and nervous gray clouds in the east, and where they blend, luminous edges shedding a watery, silver light. See, illuminated by this, a small old port where picturesque fishing boats, their nets drying, lie at anchor, and tall narrow houses, their sides lined with gray slates, loom over the quays. This is Honfleur, a colorful antique, but a working one. The boats may be decorative but they also are functional, and their casual comings and goings may be to and from places as remote as St-Pierre and Miquelon, off Newfoundland. Honfleur on a Sunday is quiet and still, but on weekdays the fishermen, ships' engineers, and carpenters lend a sense of urgency.

The painter Eugène Boudin was born here and brought Monet, Renoir, Sisley, Pissarro, and others to Honfleur, where they experimented with the light in painting that eventually gave the world Impressionism. Honfleur also was the birthplace of some famous explorers, including Paulmier de Gonneville, who sailed the South Seas, and Samuel de Champlain, who set off from here in 1608 on an expedition that resulted in the discovery of Quebec. The Vieux Bassin (Old Dock), from which he sailed, still is the most celebrated sight in Honfleur.

The *Musée du Vieux-Honfleur* (Rue de la Prison, 14600 Honfluer; phone 31-89-14-12), in the former Eglise St-Etienne, contains antique arms, costumes, ceramics, and furniture illustrating the town's past back to Gallo-Roman times. (Open July to mid-September, weekends off-season, and holidays).

The most celebrated curiosity in Honfleur is the double-naved Eglise Ste-Catherine, shaped like an upturned keel, an ancient concept that has special poignancy here because the ceilings of its two naves were built by shipwrights, not masons. Even though the naves are unequal in length and there is a makeshift quality to the church (though it has been here for 500 years), the church is exceptionally appealing. Chief among the decorative items are a number of wooden statues, which harmonize beautifully with the rustic atmosphere of the church. Seventeen carved panels on the 16th-century banister of the organ loft show mythological figures playing what amounts to an inventory of the musical instruments of the period. The church belfry, also of wood, was built across the road from the church and now seems to exist almost independently as a small museum, *La Tour Ste-Catherine* (St. Catherine's Tower), with liturgical objects and the records of the Confrérie de St-Léonard, a local guild. The church and tower frequently appear in paintings by Boudin, Monet and others. (Open *Palm Sunday* through September, except Tuesdays.)

The *Musée Eugène-Boudin* (Pl. Erik-Satie) is a modern, 3-story building that shares a courtyard with a typical 19th-century apartment house. Oblivious to the high-minded tourists coming and going below, residents put eiderdowns and colorful bedspreads out to air on their windowsills — a delightful scene — just as they would have in Boudin's day. Besides the work of Boudin, Monet, and other Impressionists, the museum displays antique lace caps, children's bonnets, and collars as well as the instruments used in making them. From the third-floor gallery there is a good view over the town, showing just how it is placed in relation to the Seine Estuary and the Channel. (Closed during January and February, Tuesdays from mid-March through September, and weekday mornings in winter; phone: 31-89-16-47, ext. 27.) There are some fine old houses within easy walking distance of one another; apart from those surrounding the Vieux Bassin and the church, the Rue Haute and the Rue de Puits are especially rewarding.

CHECKING IN: *Ferme St-Siméon* – This half-timbered 17th-century inn (a member of the Relais & Châteaux group), overlooking the Seine estuary, was much frequented by the Impressionists. Now a modern, 19-room annex has been built, but the original 19 rooms are charming and cozy, and the kitchen turns out such well-prepared specialties as lobster stew, which won it a star from Michelin. Aperitifs are served on the terrace amid flowerboxes and under colorful umbrellas. A fitness center, which includes a swimming pool and sauna, was recently added. Open daily. Major credit cards accepted. Rue A.-Marais, Honfleur (phone: 31-89-23-61; fax: 31-89-48-48). Very expensive.

Le Cheval Blanc – On the quai overlooking Honfleur's port, this half-timbered 15th-century inn has a traditional style about it and attractively refurbished rooms. Winter weekend packages include painting courses taught by Beaux Arts instructors. Closed in January. Major credit cards accepted. 2 Quai des Passagers, Honfleur (phone: 31-89-13-49; fax: 31-89-52-80). Moderate.

EATING OUT: *L'Auberge du Vieux Puits* – Leave the task of selecting the buttery, creamy components of your meal in the hands of the immensely charming proprietors of this establishment in a rustic old Norman house (though it is a good idea to let on that a taste of the bewitching local trout would be most welcome). Closed Mondays evenings and Tuesdays, early July, and from mid-December to mid-January. Reservations advised. Major credit cards accepted. Sixteen miles (25 km) south of Honfleur on A13. 6 Rue Notre-Dame-du-Pré, Pont-Audemer (phone: 32-41-01-48). Expensive.

Le Bistrot du Port – Although it looks out on the port rather than the Vieux Bassin, the view can be delightful when fishing boats are chugging to and fro along the quays. Indoors, the exposed beams and fireplace provide a congenial setting for this restaurant's spectacular *assiette de fruits de mer,* a platter of mixed seafood that includes oysters, mussels, shrimp, crab, and other crustaceans. Closed Monday evenings, Tuesdays, and November 11 to early February. Major credit cards accepted. 14 Quai de la Quarantaine, Honfleur (phone: 31-89-21-84). Moderate.

En Route from Honfleur – Take D513 for a scenic ride past old farms and views of the Channel through the apple orchards. The apple trees and flowers blooming on the cliffs that bracket the fine sandy beaches in this region, together with the sometimes exotic plantings by hillside villas and seaside homes, have given this corner of Calvados the name Côte Fleurie (Flowered Coast). At Cricqueboeuf, just before entering Villerville, look for a romantic, ivy-covered, 12th-century church next to a pond. Villerville itself is little more than a cleft in the cliffs, which shelter a small, attractive beach.

EATING OUT: *Le Moulin à Grains* – The dining room in this old Norman grain mill, with exposed beams and two fireplaces, is known for its generous portions of meat and seafood. The tripe in white wine and calvados and the *cochonnailles* (an assortment of sausage, pâté, and sliced ham) platter are very popular locally. A special prix fixe dinner includes lobster, scallops and shellfish pies, a seafood shish kebab, crab sausage, black pudding, tripe, and dessert crêpes with apple brandy. Closed Sunday nights and Mondays. Major credit cards accepted. Trouville-Aliquerville (phone: 35-38-04-46). Moderate to inexpensive.

TROUVILLE-SUR-MER: In the heady days of Napoleon III, the affluent *boulevardiers* (men about town) of Paris brought their wives, children, and children's nannies to this fishing village–turned–resort for the season while they disported themselves with their mistresses a stone's throw away, across the River Touques at Deauville. Boudin's masterly drawings and paintings of the beach at Trouville, showing women with bustles and parasols, illustrate what it must have been like when Empress Eugénie made it the most fashionable beach in France. The *Montebello Municipal Museum* (64 Rue Maréchal Leclerc; phone: 31-88-16-26) exhibits paintings by Boudin and others. Open daily from 2:30 to 11 PM April to October.

Today, Trouville stays busy long after Deauville has put up its shutters and started to doze for the winter. The fishing boats still go out in the morning; and at day's end, the nets still hang out to dry along the wall by the side of the river while the fishermen, in dungarees and navy sweaters, smoke their pipes and chat.

Bearing right at the Trouville seafront and walking toward the yacht club, you will find several blocks of villas, most of them still privately owned, which add up to an extravaganza of Gothic, Norman, and half-timbered follies that vie to outdo one another in turrets, towers, arches, and fantastical windows. The golden sand beach beyond the yacht club at the end of Rue Lieutenant-R.-Morane lies under a low cliff and is much quieter than the Deauville end of the beach. Toward the end of July there is a sandcastle contest at the Deauville end, in front of the casino, in which amateur architects attempt to reproduce some of the more dramatic buildings in the neighborhood. Also in July is Trouville's most important festival, the annual *Fête de la Mer,* and in May and November, the city hosts antiques shows.

There is still gambling at the *Casino Municipal de Trouville* (14360 Pl. Foch; phone: 31-87-75-00) — its atmosphere is decidedly less snooty than that of Deauville — though part of the building has been turned into a cinema and a concert hall where entertainers from Paris sometimes perform during the season. The fish market on the riverbank is open daily; try *Chez Saiter* (phone: 31-88-13-55) for take-out *soupe de poisson* (fish soup) and *bisque de homard* (lobster bisque).

EATING OUT: La Roches Noires – For fine fare, locals recommend this slightly out of the way restaurant, perched above a sandy beach on the road to Honfleur near an old mansion of the same name. Arrive in time to watch the sun set over the channel. Closed Tuesday evenings and Wednesdays. Major credit cards accepted. 16 Bd. Louis-Bréguet, Trouville (phone: 31-88-12-19). Moderate.

Les Vapeurs – The name means "the steamships," which are represented in red and white Art Deco tiles. This brasserie has a dedicated jet set following for several reasons: The service is exceptionally friendly, the *moules marinières* (marinated mussels) generous, and the *saucisse de Morteau* (sausages served warm with potatoes in oil and vinegar) satisfying. Closed Tuesdays, Wednesdays, the last half of November, and January. Major credit cards accepted. 160 Quai Fernand-Moureaux, Trouville (phone: 31-88-15-24). Moderate to inexpensive.

DEAUVILLE: It was Napoleon III's half-brother Charles, Duc de Morny, who established Deauville as the summer headquarters for the smart set, and its cachet lingers even today. This fashionable resort has a very short season — mid-July through September — during which visitors flock here to shop (in the town center are such famous designer boutiques as *Cartier, Chanel, Hermès, Yves Saint Laurent*); sail in regattas; golf on two fine courses; gamble in an elegant casino; and gambol on the beaches. The highlight of the season is the *Grand Prix de Deauville,* a horse race in late August that draws some of the most famous breeders and punters from around the world. Anyone interested in ogling celebrities will certainly find them here then; the Aga Khan and the Rothschilds are just a few of the fancy folk who may have reservations for lunch at the "in" spot, *Le Ciro's* (see *Eating Out*). Besides the casino, the racetrack, and *Ciro's,* the place to be seen is on the *planches,* the wooden walkways along the beach, or on the beach itself, which is filled with the innumerable, brightly colored beach umbrellas of sunbathers. For a less rarefied experience, walk along the jetty in town on the west side of the Port-de-Deauville; it's especially nice at sunset, when pleasure craft make their way through the buoys into the harbor. Or take a moment to gaze at the Villa Strassburger, the lavishly detailed Belle Epoque building that recalls an architectural era of turrets, spreading balconies, overhangs, and dormers.

Deauville's casino is grander and more sparkling than ever, following a major face-lift, polish, and remodeling in 1988, and now remains open year-round. The winter casino is closed indefinitely.

CHECKING IN: *Normandy* – Its half-timbered gables and balconies make this property one of Deauville's focal points. Inside it's as sumptuous as could be: huge plump pillows and soft velvet spreads adorn the beds in the 300 rooms and 20 suites. The tables and easy chairs are elegant reproductions of the Louis XVI era, and the bathrooms are spacious. Although the place has a reputation for snobbery, the staff seems pleasant enough. (See also *Romantic French Hostelries,* DIVERSIONS.) Open year-round. Major credit cards accepted. 38 Rue Jean-Mermoz, Deauville (phone: 31-98-66-22; fax: 31-98-66-23). Very expensive.

Hostellerie de Tourgeville – A steeply pitched roof and half-timbered walls give this modern hotel a traditional Norman look. Inside, the bedrooms also are modern and comfortably furnished, decorated in earth tones, and have lovely picture windows and large baths. There is a pool, a sauna, and tennis facilities. Major credit cards accepted. Chemin de l'Orgueil, Tourgeville-Deauville (phone: 31-88-63-40; fax: 31-98-27-16). Expensive.

Royal – The other traditionally luxurious hotel in town, its 293 rooms and 17 suites are decorated comfortably yet somewhat formally in mock French Provincial-style. This slightly stiff note is carried into the restaurant and lobby, both dominated by floor-to-ceiling windows, crystal chandeliers, ornamental plasterwork, and a gold and white color scheme. A heated swimming pool, a sauna, and parking all are available. Closed December to mid-March. Major credit cards accepted. Bd. Eugène-Cornuché, Deauville (phone: 31-98-66-33; fax: 31-98-66-34). Expensive.

Le Trophée – It offers 24 modern rooms (some with balconies), a rooftop sun deck, a pleasant restaurant, and a complete range of services for a moderate price. Conveniently located in the center of town, just a short walk from the beach. Major credit cards accepted. 81 Rue du Général-Leclerc (phone: 31-88-45-86; fax: 31-88-07-94). Moderate.

EATING OUT: *Le Ciro's* – Make no mistake about it, this is *the* place to eat during the high season when the jet setters are in town from Paris, London, and Hollywood. Crisp white napery and well-polished silver and glassware provide an appropriate setting for the classical dishes served. And it is right on the *planche,* so tables have fine views of the sea. Open daily until 9:30 PM. Major credit cards accepted. Promenade des Planches, Deauville (phone: 31-88-18-10). Expensive.

La Kraal – A second-floor restaurant overlooking the market that serves simply prepared local seafood including fresh lobster and a mousse made with Normandy apples. Open daily. Major credit cards accepted. Pl. du Marché, Deauville (phone: 31-88-30-58). Moderate.

Le Spinnaker – If *Le Ciro's* is the place to be seen, this increasingly popular spot near the main drag is the place to dine. The young chef shows considerable promise; his preparations have earned the establishment a Michelin star. Closed Wednesdays. Major credit cards accepted. 52 Rue Mirabeau (phone: 31-88-24-40). Moderate.

Chez Miocque – Noisy, friendly, and unpretentious, it's the kind of place where people talk across tables, bring their dogs and children, and taste one another's dishes. Order *moules marinières* (marinated mussels) to start (you'll receive at least 100 per person). Follow that with steaks and a large platter of perfectly cooked *pommes frites* (French fries). Other standard Norman fish and poultry dishes, as well as tripe and pigs' feet, also are served. Closed Tuesdays and Wednesdays in off-season, and January. No credit cards accepted. 81 Rue Eugène-Colas, Deauville (phone: 31-88-09-52). Moderate to inexpensive.

En Route from Deauville – Blonville, Bénerville, Villers-sur-Mer, and Houlgate are four popular Norman resorts that D513 passes through on the way to Cabourg. Blonville and Bénerville nestle at the foot of pleasant, wooded hillsides studded with summer homes and are the quietest of this quartet of seaside spots. The beach at Villers is long but crowded in summer, with a promenade along much of it. Houlgate is the brassiest of the bunch and is much favored by the citizens of nearby Caen. Between Villers and Houlgate is one of the chief sights of the Côte Fleurie, the Falaise des Vaches Noires (Black Cow Cliffs), which, unlike the almost sheer chalk cliffs of the Pays de Caux, seem to tumble like a series of canyons down to the water. Geologically they consist of dark clay and marl and are famous for yielding fossils. It is possible to walk underneath the cliffs from Villers to Houlgate or vice versa (remembering to start when the tide is going out) or to walk on top of them from Auberville, a tiny hamlet between the two resorts.

 EATING OUT: *Auberge de l'Escale* – Rustic Norman furniture and walls lined with fishnets suggest the menu here: seafood Norman-style, abundant and good. Closed Monday evenings, Tuesdays, Wednesdays, 2 weeks in December and the month of January. Major credit cards accepted. Pl. de l'Hôtel-de-Ville, Blonville (phone: 31-87-93-56). Moderate.

CABOURG: A long stretch of beach and the most pleasant formal promenade of the Côte Fleurie are Cabourg's chief charms. The center of the promenade is dominated by the *Grand* hotel (see below) and the *Cabourg* casino. Proust loved Cabourg and often stayed at the *Grand* as a child; he used Cabourg as one of the prototypes for Balbec in "A l'Ombre des Jeunes Filles en Fleurs," the "Within a Budding Grove" section of *Remembrance of Things Past.* There is a pleasant walk at the east end of the beach along dunes above the estuary of the River Dives.

CHECKING IN: *Grand Hôtel Pullman* – Dripping with lavish, turn-of-the-century details — marble columns, crystal chandeliers, elaborate plasterwork, plush draperies — this hotel has 68 bedrooms, all of which overlook either the sea or the adjacent casino gardens. Its fine restaurant, *Le Balbec,* also rich in decor, serves well-prepared basics such as lobster, tournedos, rack of lamb, shrimp and avocado salad, and lush desserts. Restaurant open till 10 PM. Parking available. Major credit cards accepted. Promenade Marcel-Proust, Cabourg (phone: 31-91-01-79; fax: 31-24-03-20). Expensive.

EATING OUT: *L'Amiral* – The white tables and chairs with blue umbrellas outside this beachfront bar-restaurant look quite inviting, as does the interior — light, modern, and airy, with exposed, bleached beams and some tiles of Norman and Breton women in traditional dress. *Fruits de mer* (seafood), tripe in cider, and shrimp in butter sauce are among the specialties. The food is well prepared and, except on crowded Sundays, the service is good. Closed mid-November to *Easter.* Major credit cards accepted. Promenade Marcel-Proust, Cabourg (phone: 31-91-50-66). Moderate.

CAEN: Of all the French towns ravaged by the bombs of World War II, none was so severely wounded as Caen. Its old central quarter, which burned for 10 days, was completely destroyed; some buildings have been nicely restored. Fortunately for Caen, its two restored great churches, the Abbaye aux Hommes, also known as Eglise St-Etienne, and the Abbaye aux Dames, also known as Eglise de la Trinité, survived. These, together with Caen's *Museum of Peace* (open daily from May through September; closed Mondays from October through April) and the ruins of William the Conqueror's castle, are most of what is worth seeing in the town.

Abbaye aux Hommes is best viewed from Place Louis-Guillouard, across a broad vista of lawns and formal gardens, beyond which are the 18th-century residential quarters of the abbey, now the Hôtel de Ville (Town Hall). Crossing the Place and turning into the Rue Guillaume-le-Conquérant and then left again brings you around the church to a point right under the domineering west front, its simple Romanesque lines almost, it seems, as massive and forbidding as the cliffs at Etretat. The lovely 14th-century apse and choir are early Gothic but blend subtly with the earlier parts of the church to form a monumental whole. In front of the pink marble high altar is the tombstone of William the Conqueror, who was buried ignominiously in the abbey in 1087. His wife, Matilda, was buried in the Abbaye aux Dames, the sister foundation. The couple built the abbeys as a penance following their marriage without papal dispensation for an impediment of consanguinity: They were cousins.

Abbaye aux Dames is smaller and appears more human in scale despite the great arches over the nine lordly bays. There is a delightful 13th-century Gothic chapel in the south transept, with delicately worked ribs and columns and female heads carved on the supporting arches. The 16 pillars in the 11th-century crypt make it look like a stone copse. A slab marking the spot where Matilda was buried can be seen in the choir, although the tomb itself was desecrated during the Revolution.

Caen's castle, built by William in 1060 and now a truly magnificent ruin, encloses lawns and sylvan walkways where its great towers once stood. A platform provides a pleasant view over the city, but the chief attraction is the splendid *Musée des Beaux-Arts.* Open 10 AM to noon and 1:30 to 5:30 PM daily; 10 AM to 12:30 PM and 2 to 6 PM Sundays. Closed Tuesdays and holidays. Esplanade du Château (phone: 31-85-28-63.) Few modern buildings sit so well in ancient surroundings; here the great gray stone slabs of the museum building merge handsomely with the medieval battlements. The collection is quite impressive and includes many pieces plundered by Napoleon in his forays across the Continent. Highlights include a magnificent *Marriage of the Virgin* by Pietro Vannucci (who called himself Perugino) and Bordon's *Annunciation.* Veronese, Titian, Tintoretto, and Van Ruysdael all are notably represented. The museum also houses the Mancel Collection, more than 40,000 prints including works by Rembrandt, Callot, Van Dyck, and Rubens.

The *Caen Mémorial Musée Pour la Paix* (Museum of Peace), which opened in 1988, was built on the site of a German underground command post to commemorate the 1944 *D-Day* landings and the ensuing battles. Its sobering exhibits emphasize not the military victories but the suffering of people in wartime. It's open from 9 AM to 7 PM daily, except *Christmas, New Year's,* and the first 2 weeks of January. Bd. Montgomery (phone: 31-06-06-44).

 CHECKING IN: *Hôtel Saint Pierre* – A simple traditional-style place in the heart of Caen at Place Courtonne, purchased by a couple whose sincere welcome sets this apart from other hostelries in its class. Ten of the 19 rooms have private baths. 40 Bd. des Alliés, Caen (phone: 31-86-28-20). Inexpensive.

EATING OUT: *La Bourride* – In this 400-year-old dwelling, chef Michel Bruneau has earned two Michelin stars for his cooking, which features the best and freshest ingredients from Normandy's farms and fishing ports. Closed Sundays, Mondays, January 3-23, and 2 weeks in August. Major credit cards accepted. 15 Rue Vaugueux, Caen (phone: 31-93-50-76; fax: 31-93-29-63). Expensive.

Relais des Gourmets – Silver candelabra, gleaming glassware, and fresh white napery set the scene for some very fine Norman cooking and a superlative wine cellar. Try the *rognons grillés au bacon* (grilled kidneys with English-style bacon) or the *turbot fourré de langouste* (turbot stuffed with crayfish), and a chocolate cake so rich it's almost pudding. There also are 26 clean, very comfortable rooms and 2 suites with bath upstairs. Restaurant open daily. Major credit cards accepted. 15 Rue de Geôle, Caen (phone: 31-86-06-01; fax: 31-39-06-00). Expensive to moderate.

Alcide – The place most recommended for sampling Caen's famous *tripe à la mode:* tripe simmered in calvados, the region's apple brandy, and served with boiled potatoes and a calvados chaser. Closed Saturdays and holidays. Major credit cards accepted. 1 Pl. Courtonne (phone: 31-44-18-06). Moderate to inexpensive.

D-DAY INVASION BEACHES: From Caen it is easy to make a detour to Sword, Juno, Gold, Omaha, and Utah beaches, the 50 miles of shore that played such an enormous role in the events of *D-Day,* June 6, 1944. Take D515 out of Caen to Bénouville and Pegasus Bridge. Here the road becomes D514 and continues to Ouistreham and Riva-Bella, where you turn left to follow the coastline via St-Aubin-sur-mer, Arromanches-les-Bains, Port-en-Bessin, Pointe du Hoc, and Grandcamp-les-Bains. The route then turns inland to join the N13 highway just before Isigny-sur-Mer, passes through Carentan, leaves N13 after a few miles to follow D913 past Ste-Marie-du-Mont, then heads north along the coastal D421 to Quinéville. Return inland to Montebourg on D42, making a left back onto N13 through Ste-Mère-Eglise and continuing to Caen.

Virtually no one comes away from a visit to these famous beaches on Normandy's Calvados coastline without at least some twinge of patriotism. Looking out over sweeping stretches of seascape, now so picturesque and serene, it's difficult to imagine the devastation that took place on *D-Day.*

First it might be useful to contemplate some of the events of that period. It had been agreed at meetings between Winston Churchill and Franklin D. Roosevelt in 1942 and 1943 that an Allied invasion of Europe through France would be launched somewhere in the north of the country at some propitious time. Following the abortive attempt to seize Dieppe in 1942, it became clear that the beaches of Calvados were ideal. They were considered the least likely landing spot from the German viewpoint, for the Allied troops would have to overcome unreliable weather patterns, strong sea currents, and steep cliffs in order to succeed. The umbrella name for the invasion was Operation Overlord; General Dwight D. Eisenhower was appointed Supreme Commander of the Allied Expeditionary Forces in charge of strategic planning, and tactical coordination of all ground troops fell into the hands of General Bernard Law Montgomery of Great Britain. The unusual preparations for the invasion included training special British Commando and American Ranger units in cliff climbing; building vast floating docks for an artificial port; and creating an elaborate intelligence plan to convince the Germans — successfully, as it turned out — that the action would take place at Calais. The invasion was projected for the early part of June, when the weather could be expected to be good, the tides would be right, and the moon would be full enough to provide light for the airborne troops scheduled to be dropped behind the German coastal defenses ("the Atlantic Wall") a few hours before the landings.

In the early hours of June 6, the US 101st and 82nd and the British 6th Airborne divisions dropped into France, the first two on the western flank of the beaches just north of Carentan, the latter on the eastern flank around Bénouville, on the Orne River. Their mission was to divert the enemy as much as possible from the seaborne assault troops steaming across the English Channel: General Omar Bradley's 1st American Army, headed for Utah and Omaha beaches, where they landed at 6:30 AM; and the British 2nd Army under General Miles Dempsey (whose forces also included the 3rd Canadian Division), headed for Gold, Juno, and Sword beaches. Low-lying Utah Beach proved fairly easy to capture. By about noon on June 6 it was taken, and the 3rd Battalion of the 8th Infantry Regiment had managed to forge a unit inland about 8 miles to meet up with the 82nd Airborne. By the end of the day, 23,250 men and 17,000 vehicles had come ashore there.

Of all the Normandy beaches, Omaha was the hardest to conquer. The cliffs along its shoreline proved a predictably tough barrier, especially with rough seas at their foot.

These harsh conditions became even worse for the troops that followed the initial landing force, since by then the Germans had opened fire. Losses were heavy. Nevertheless, 225 US Rangers managed to scale and capture Pointe du Hoc and hold it against heavy counterfire until they were relieved on June 8. The almost legendary Northumberlands, the 50th British Infantry Division, were part of the British 2nd Army that landed at Gold Beach around 7:25 AM, and the Royal Marine Commandos pushed west to Port-en-Bessin where they joined the American troops on June 8. The Canadian 3rd Infantry Division landed at Juno Beach around 7:10 AM, and by 5 PM the 7th Brigade had taken the beautiful hamlet of Creully, a few miles inland. The British 3rd Infantry Division, its objective Caen, came ashore on the part of Sword Beach between Lion-sur-Mer and Riva-Bella at about 7:30 AM. They captured a few small villages but met heavy resistance from the German 21st Panzer Division after 4 PM. A Franco-British Commando unit under Commander Philippe Kieffer managed to take Riva-Bella and continue on to Bénouville, where they met up with the British 6th Airborne.

June 6 was an extraordinary day's work, pivotal in mankind's history. The Battle of Normandy lasted about 11 weeks more, finally ending shortly after the capitulation of the German 7th Army on August 19 at Chambois.

Route D515 out of Caen leads to Bénouville, where a sign with a blue flying horse marks Pegasus Bridge on the Orne. This important crossing was liberated in the early hours of *D-Day* by members of the British 6th Airborne Division, who landed near the swing bridge in three gliders that had been towed across the Channel by Halifax bombers. The Town Hall of Bénouville was the first in France to be liberated. Details of what happened can be seen at the *Musée des Troupes Aéroportées* (Airborne Museum; 10 Av. Commandant-Kieffer; phone: 31-44-62-54), which is open daily from mid-March. Bénouville also has an interesting 18th-century château, famous for its monumental staircase.

Ouistreham and its neighbor Riva-Bella formed the ancient port of Caen. Now this is a popular pleasure boating center, and in summer the harbor is filled with the colorful sails of yachts from many northern European countries. British frogmen swam ashore here just before the invasion to clear the canals of obstacles. The *Musée du No. 4 Commando* (Pl. Alfred-Thomas; phone: 31-97-18-63) is open weekends from *Palm Sunday* through May; daily from June through mid-September. It concentrates on the French involvement in the invasion under Commander Kieffer with displays of arms, equipment, documents, uniforms, and photographs.

At Lion-sur-Mer, halfway along Sword Beach, there is little evidence of the chaos of *D-Day*. It is a typical Côte de Nacre resort, with a sandy beach, small hotels, tennis courts, and beachfront cafés. At Bernières-sur-Mer, a little farther on, two monuments commemorate the Canadian forces that created one of the essential bridgeheads in the operation. The 13th-century belfry of the church, with charming corner turrets over a small porch, is exceptionally fine, rising to a height of 220 feet. At Courseulles-sur-Mer, known for its oysters, ships were deliberately sunk during Operation Overlord to form a temporary harbor. Early in the operation, Winston Churchill, George VI, and Charles de Gaulle landed here to visit the battlefields. Just before entering Arromanches, there is an orientation table at the point called St-Côme-de-Fresne, high on the cliff. It still is surrounded by German gun emplacements. The table, at the top of a flight of steps, provides the visitor with a perfect perspective of the beaches from Sword to Utah. In front are the remains of the breakwaters of the great artificial port that was built at Arromanches and still ranks as one of the most extraordinary examples of military marine engineering in the history of warfare.

Arromanches, set between cliffs around a sandy beach, has the finest of all the museums in Normandy commemorating Operation Overlord: the *Exposition Permanente du Débarquement* (Permanent Exhibition of the Landings; Pl. du 6-Juin; phone: 31-22-34-31), closed *Christmas, New Year's Day,* and the first 3 weeks of

January. The museum is famous for its vivid models and dioramas. Chief among them is one of the great artificial ports called Mulberry Harbor B, which was built because the coast had no natural protection. Eighteen old merchant ships were scuttled to form the first shelter behind which smaller units could unload their cargoes. Soon after the ships were scuttled, more than 100 concrete pontoons each weighing between 3,000 and 6,000 tons were towed into position by tugs, and they too were sunk, forming a breakwater 7 miles long. (Forty of them remain more or less intact, although their life expectancy in the rough seas of the Channel was estimated at less than 2 years; they can be seen in a semicircle offshore.) Pierheads, floating steel platforms, also were established for unloading purposes. These were linked to the shore by floating roadways made of small pontoons connected by "Bailey" bridges, each about 4,000 feet long and capable of withstanding the weight of jeeps and other heavy cargo. Just 6 days after the invasion had begun 326,000 men and 54,000 jeeps had been put ashore. A model of this stupendous operation can be seen at the museum. Also on view are parachutes of the 101st and 82nd Airborne divisions, aerial bombs, high explosives, uniforms of various regiments and squadrons, and other items such as General Matthew Ridgway's jump boots. A Royal Navy film shot on June 6, 1944, shows what took place around Arromanches that day.

A few miles beyond Arromanches, a turnoff to the right leads down to the fishing harbor of Port-en-Bessin, a cleft in the cliffs at the mouth of the Drôme River, where American and British forces finally made contact on June 8. Even in summer, Port-en-Bessin is relatively quiet, although the granite jetties occasionally are jammed with fishermen, and the action at the early morning fish auctions on Mondays, Wednesdays, and Thursdays can be colorful.

A road to the right off D514 between Colleville-sur-Mer and St-Laurent-sur-Mer leads to the Normandy American Military Cemetery and Memorial, on a cliff right above Omaha Beach and the Channel. An overlook with an orientation table details the landing beaches. The 172½-acre cemetery contains the graves of 9,386 military personnel, including 307 unknown, each marked by a plain white marble cross or Star of David. The sight of these simple headstones in crisp, sharp rows on neatly clipped lawns is very moving. In one instance they mark where a father and son lie side by side; in about 30 others, where brothers lie next to one another.

There is another right turn off D514 at St-Laurent onto a small road that follows the beach at sea level as far as Vierville-sur-Mer, about 1 mile (1.6 km). At the east end, a post marks the spot where the first American casualties were buried originally. The western end of this pleasant seafront road was called Dog Green on *D-Day*. This is where the heaviest casualties on Omaha took place, with the majority of the 116th Regiment killed or injured.

The church at Vierville-sur-Mer is worth noting. Its current belfry replaces one that was an important German lookout and stronghold; it was destroyed on *D-Day* by offshore shelling in order to assist the American Rangers who scaled the nearby cliffs to Pointe du Hoc.

Pointe du Hoc is reached by a short side road off D514. On *D-Day*, 225 American Rangers under Colonel James Earl Rudder climbed the 9-story-high cliffs using grappling hooks and firemen's ladders (among other equipment) amid smoke from offshore barrages and constant German fire from the cliff top. General Bradley called the operation "the most difficult assignment I ever had to give anyone." Today the clifftop that was taken and held by these men is still shell-scarred. There are potholes and gun emplacements, though they are now covered with grass, gorse, and brambles, and linnets and larks twitter and trill where guns blazed. At the cliff's edge is a modest stone column that reproduces the rock needle just offshore that gives the *pointe* its name. The dedication reads: "To the Ranger Commandos of the 116th Infantry."

About a mile (1.6 km) after D514 runs into N13 is Isigny-sur-Mer, which was liberated on June 9, 1944. Today, the town is famous throughout France for its butter. Carentan, the next town on the route, another prosperous dairy farming market town, is bordered by the marshes typical of the southeastern corner of the Cotentin Peninsula. There is a memorial to the 101st Airborne Division near the Hôtel de Ville (Town Hall).

Beyond Carentan, turn off N13 onto D913, passing Ste-Marie-du-Mont to reach the monument at La Madeleine at the south end of Utah Beach on route D421. The memorial consists of a former German blockhouse honoring the 1st (American) Engineer Special Brigade. Route D421 follows the coast, though the sea is often obscured by dunes. Utah Beach stretches for nearly 2 miles, as far as Les Dunes-de-Varreville. This is where the 4th American Division met tough German resistance on *D-Day*, although before nightfall they were able to meet up with the paratroopers who had been dropped inland around Ste-Mère-Eglise. Just off the road marked Route des Alliés at Les Dunes-de-Varreville, a pinkish granite marker, similar in shape to the forward part of a ship, is a reminder of French General Leclerc's arrival on August 1, 1944, with his 2nd Armored Division.

A little beyond Varreville, turn left and pick up D15 to Ste-Mère-Eglise, where parachutists of the 82nd and 101st Airborne dropped just before dawn on *D-Day*. Unfortunately, this air drop wasn't the surprise it was meant to be, since a fire had awakened just about everyone in town, including the German soldiers. Many American soldiers were shot as they touched the ground. The best known of these soldiers was John Steele, who came down on top of the church spire and dangled there for hours, pretending to be dead. Outside the Town Hall there is the first milestone of Liberty Way, marked out by the American troops as they crossed France. The *Musée des Troupes Aéroportées* (Airborne Troops Museum) contains documents, photographs, arms, uniforms, and, outside, a Sherman tank — all part of the story of the early morning hours of the invasion. Some of the exhibits give a special, almost intimate flavor to the events of those historic days: dog tags, a chocolate vitamin ration, a French phrase book, and a photograph of a soldier reclining in front of a wooden sign reading Ste-Mère-Eglise. (Open daily April through September, weekends in winter; closed mid-December to mid-January; Pl. du 6-Juin; phone: 33-41-41-35.) The town has commemorated *D-Day* with a stained glass window over the main portal of its 13th-century stone church that depicts the Virgin Mary and Child surrounded by American soliders parachuting from the sky to liberate Ste-Mère-Eglise. From here you either can take an hour's drive back to Caen via N13 or stop at Bayeux along the way.

EATING OUT: *Manoir d'Hastings* – At this restored 17th-century country manor a few miles from Caen, the emphasis is on seafood and on a "lightened" version of Norman cuisine. Local ciders also are served and used in many dishes. One Michelin star. There also are 11 comfortable rooms. Closed the first week of February. Major credit cards accepted. 18 Av. de la Côte de Nacre, Bénouville (phone: 31-44-62-43). Expensive.

La Marine – Not promising from the outside, this restaurant is comfortable and relaxing, with views of the sea through huge picture windows. It is as good a place as any to try a *marmite*. Depending on what's available that day, the stew may contain sole, turbot, *lotte* (monkfish), crab, mussels, and scallops. The fish soup is scarcely less substantial, and one serving usually is enough for at least three helpings. Closed December through the first week of February. Major credit cards accepted. 5 Quai Letourneur, Port-en-Bessin (phone: 31-21-70-08). Expensive to moderate.

Auberge Normande – Brill with oysters is among the specialties that draw people again and again to this Norman restaurant with one Michelin star. Guests also appreciate the fire that is kept roaring whenever there is a nip in the air. Closed Sunday nights and Mondays. Major credit cards accepted. 17 Bd. de Verdun, Carentan (phone: 33-42-02-99). Moderate.

BAYEUX: Few towns in the world are famous for a piece of embroidery, but such a possession has indeed made this beautifully preserved town in the north of France celebrated for centuries. Bayeux could claim notice for other reasons. It has a fine cathedral, ancient streets, and it is the only town close to the Norman coast unscarred by the devastation of World War II. It also has a colorful history. Bayeux was an important city in Caesar's day, and successive waves of Celts, Saxons, and Vikings later came to occupy the city. Around 1050, William the Conqueror gave the episcopal land here to his half-brother Odo, who, as bishop, built the original cathedral. In ensuing years, the Conqueror's three sons engaged in various power struggles for the English throne and the duchy of Normandy. It was during one of these conflicts that Henry I came to Bayeux and burned the cathedral along with the rest of the city (most of the present structure dates from the 13th century). Much later, in the 19th century, the novelist Honoré de Balzac used to enjoy well-earned respites in Bayeux, and on June 7, 1944, Bayeux became the first town in France to be liberated by the Allies.

But it is the tapestry that draws most people here — justifiably, since it is one of the great treasures of France. Called in France *La Tapisserie de la Reine Mathilde* (Queen Matilda's Tapestry, or sometimes simply the Bayeux Tapestry), it is on display daily at *Centre Guillaume-le-Conquérant* (Rue de Nesmond; phone: 31-92-05-48). The tapestry, 19 inches wide and 231 feet long, tells the story of the events surrounding the Norman conquest of England, including the flight of the English after King Harold's death in the Battle of Hastings. Legend has it that the tapestry was commissioned by Bishop Odo and worked by William's wife, Matilda, and her ladies-in-waiting, although more prosaic minds have insisted that the stitching suggests it was sewn by Saxon women in England. Regardless, the tapestry is a remarkable and lively document consisting of 58 distinct scenes, each with a Latin legend summarizing the picture. The costumes, uniforms, food, boats, furniture, and pets of the period are all vividly illustrated, and the borders are decorated with an awesome bestiary of real and imaginary monsters. The tapestry is laid out in a glass case and can be followed section by section with an excellent commentary in English on a listening device. It originally was kept in the cathedral, one of the few major churches in lower Normandy to escape damage in World War II. Today's few remaining lacemakers can be seen at their craft — creating bobbin lace, for example — at the *Atelier du Centre Norman de la Dentelle aux Fuseaux* (5 Pl. aux Pommes; no phone).

The two Romanesque towers with 13th-century Gothic spires that dominate Bayeux and the surrounding countryside belong to the Cathédrale Notre-Dame on Rue du Bienvenu. Entering the cathedral from the west door, one is immediately struck by the formidable Romanesque arches of the nave contrasting with the light, airy Gothic arches directly below. The walls of the nave are profusely decorated with saints, leaves, flowers, and abstract designs as well as with various creatures both exotic and mythical. The nine chapels all date from the first half of the 14th century. In the Chapelle de Bonne Nouvelle, an extraordinary stone tableau shows the Virgin with all the sacred symbols connected with her. The Chapelle de St-Michel has a 15th-century fresco worked in a variety of blues and pinks showing Mary's Visitation to Elizabeth following the Annunciation.

Behind the cathedral is the *Musée Baron Gérard* in the charming Place des Tribunaux (open daily; phone: 31-92-14-21). Lacework, for which Bayeux was famous, and local porcelain are important among the museum's collections.

On Saturdays, Bayeux is enlivened by brightly dressed shoppers on Rue St-Jean, the town's main shopping street, as well as on Place St-Patrice, which is transformed into a bustling market with stalls selling clothes, bric-a-brac, finely bound old books, and especially food. From the beautiful, fortified farms of the surrounding Bessin countryside and from the nearby channel ports come farmers and fishermen with refrigerated trailers laden with cheeses, especially Normandy's own camembert, pont l'évêque, and livarot, seafood, charcuterie, and vegetables and fruit — predominantly apples in the fall.

The countryside east of Bayeux, between highway N13 and the coast, is considered one of the most beautiful and serene parts of Normandy. Along N13 near Caen the landscape tends to be flat — acres and acres of fields of grain; closer to the coast, tiny roads undulate through gentle valleys and around modest hills and twist through copses. An interesting architectural note is that the farmhouses are not half-timbered as in the neighboring Pays d'Auge around Lisieux and in the Pays de Caux, but are built of stone. Often these farmhouses are quite large, with arched stone gateways and barns that look like small fortified châteaux.

From Bayeux, it is possible to wander along dozens of very appealing country roads that ramble from Bayeux to points north and east, but we suggest taking N13 southeast for a short distance, then picking up D35 and following it to St-Gabriel-Brécy. Here is an 11th-century priory, a delightfully haphazard conglomeration of buildings with towers, turrets, arched windows, and stone entrances, staircases, and balconies. It is now a horticultural college for the region, but permission to look around can be obtained at the reception office. About a mile (1.6 km) farther is Creully, one of the most perfectly preserved feudal villages in Normandy. At the adjacent community of Creullet is a charming manor house in a pasture, where General Montgomery established his headquarters in a trailer just after *D-Day*. In Creully itself is a château (with parts dating from the 12th through the 16th century), which was the BBC's headquarters just after the invasion. This building, standing in lordly fashion on a hill above the River Seulles, is now the Town Hall and can usually be visited every day.

From Creully, continue south on D22 and pick up D141 to Château Fontaine-Henry, home of the family d'Harcourt for centuries and one of the triumphs of Renaissance domestic architecture in Normandy. The château is most notable for its steeply pitched roof, which is actually taller than the buildings it caps. Inside is a fine Gothic staircase dating from the reign of François I, and a charming private chapel is on the grounds. In the main room there is a portrait by Mignard of the infant Louis XIV. (Open Wednesdays, weekends, and holidays from *Easter* through May and mid-September through October; daily except Tuesdays and Fridays from June through mid-September; closed November through *Easter;* phone: 31-80-00-42.)

CHECKING IN: *D'Argouges* – This 18th-century mansion has become a comfortable hotel combining Old World charm with modern amenities. The 25 rooms and suites face either the inner courtyard or the back garden. Breakfast is served in the dining room, but there is no restaurant. Television set available on request. Major credit cards accepted. 21 Rue St-Patrice, Bayeux (phone: 31-92-88-86; fax: 31-92-69-16). Moderate.

EATING OUT: *Lion d'Or* – The best restaurant in Bayeux, perhaps in Normandy, it has been open since 1640 and in the same family since 1929. The entrance is through a cobblestone courtyard overlooked by windows with red awnings and boxes of red geraniums. A menu of classic Norman cooking features brill, lobster, sole, salmon, and other favorites. Service is friendly and unhurried. There are 30 clean, airy rooms upstairs, all with bathrooms; in summer, half board only. One Michelin star. Closed mid-December to mid-January. Major credit cards accepted. 77 Rue St-Jean, Bayeux (phone: 31-92-06-90; fax: 31-22-15-64). Moderate.

En Route from Bayeux – Take D572, turning almost immediately onto D67 for about 3 miles (5 km) to the sign on the left saying Abbaye de Mondaye. Although this 18th-century abbey of the Prémontré's order (phone: 31-92-58-11) is open only for guided tours on Sunday afternoons, the classical church and conventual buildings can be seen at any time. In the manner of the period they form a graceful unity, often offset by cows grazing almost up to the abbey walls. Continue along D67 until it meets D13, then turn right to the Château de Balleroy, built in the early 1600s by François Mansart, for whom the mansard roof is named. The symmetrical main buildings are built of brick and stone, with gardens by Le Nôtre adding to the overall formality. The painted ceiling in one of the halls shows classical allegories of the four seasons and contains portraits by Mignard of Louis XIII, Anne of Austria, Louis XIV, and Madame de Maintenon. The château also houses the *Musée de Ballons* (Museum of Balloon Flight), with old prints, blueprints, maps, documents, and instruments pertaining to lighter-than-air flight from the experiments of the Montgolfier brothers in the late 1700s to the present. Among the interesting dioramas is one showing the part dirigibles played in the *D-Day* invasions. (Open daily except Wednesdays from 9 AM to noon and 2 to 6 PM from mid-April through October; phone: 31-21-60-61.)

Continue on D13 through Cérisy de Forêt (phone: 33-56-10-01) to the ruins of the 11th-century abbey (open Sundays and holidays from April through October), which has son et lumière (sound and light) shows on Saturday evenings from mid-July through August. Since the Revolution the church has had only three bays (there were once seven), but it still is imposing, especially when seen through the trees across the nearby meadows. Inside, the Romanesque choir with its simple oak stalls is considered by experts to be the finest in Normandy. The 13th-century conventual buildings, the chapel, the porter's lodge, and the hall of justice have been converted into a museum containing 14th- and 15th-century religious manuscripts and books and 16th- and 17th-century furniture. Retracing route D13 from Cérisy toward Balleroy, turn right on D572 (which becomes D972) into St-Lô.

ST-LÔ: So devastated was this ancient town in the 1944 Battle of Normandy that it was dubbed "the capital of the ruins." One of the very few buildings to escape complete destruction was the Church of Notre-Dame, which today has been almost completely rebuilt, although some portions were left damaged as a memorial to those terrible times. For centuries St-Lô was an important fortified city, and the ramparts — ironically, beautifully exposed now as a result of the bombardments — are a favorite promenade from which to view the rebuilt town. The museum in the basement of the Hôtel de Ville (Town Hall) is worth a visit for a series of eight Flemish tapestries worked in Bruges in the 16th century. They provide a humorous, down-to-earth glimpse of peasant life, showing the flora, fauna, work implements, and musical instruments that would have been part of the contemporary Flemish scene. The museum also has a collection of portraits of the Matignon-Grimaldi family, ancestors in a circuitous line of the Prince of Monaco. There also are paintings by Corot, Rousseau, and Boudin. (Closed Tuesdays; Pl. du Général-de-Gaulle; phone: 33-57-43-80.)

Continue along D972 to Coutances.

CHECKING IN/EATING OUT: *Crémaillère* – Close to the ramparts, this restaurant sticks to a fairly simple menu. There also are 16 clean and modestly furnished rooms. Closed Saturdays and mid-December to mid January. Major credit cards accepted. 27 Rue du Belle, St-Lô (phone: 33-57-14-68). Moderate.

COUTANCES: This city on a hill is dominated by a cathedral that can be seen from whichever direction you approach: a gray stone beacon that appears almost silver in sunlight. Go to the Place du Parvis for your first close look at the west façade, which has two towers with spires and pinnacles. The cathedral was begun in 1030 but ravaged by fire in 1218, and soon after a Gothic structure was superimposed on the original shell. The result is a fine example of Norman Gothic, notable for its harmonious proportions. Especially interesting is the large octagonal lantern tower, which crowns the transept and reaches a height of about 135 feet, and the chapels, which are separated from one another by delicately worked stone screens. The central chapel in the apse is much revered locally as the setting for the 14th-century statue of the Virgin known as Our Lady of Coutances. The St. Francis Chapel has a 17th-century woodcarving showing Judas's betrayal of Christ with a kiss. The three 13th-century windows in the north transept depict St. George, St. Blaise, and St. Thomas à Becket.

The Jardin Public (Public Garden) is quite fine, with terraces and rose-filled flowerbeds, stone staircases leading down grassy slopes, and lots of trees. The gardens are open from 8 AM to 8 PM in summer, when there is a son et lumière involving the gardens and the cathedral, and from 9 AM to 5 PM in winter. The town's small museum (2 Rue Quesnel-Morinière, Coutances; phone: 33-45-11-92; generally closed Sunday mornings and Tuesdays) has an interesting bust of Emperor Hadrian, and among what remains of its collection of paintings (much damaged in World War II) is a Rubens.

Follow D971 south to Granville.

GRANVILLE: Granville is basically a town with a split personality. The old upper town, planted firmly on a promontory surrounded by ramparts, is seen to its best advantage on a sunny day (it looks rather grim and gray otherwise). The Church of Notre-Dame, on the summit of the Roc de Granville in the upper town, looks out over the ocean with all the certainty of canonized granite. The seaward views from the upper town are stunning. The newer lower town, with its port and 19th-century resort hotels, is less appealing.

EATING OUT: *Le Phare* – This eatery has a terrace and a view of the hustle and bustle of Granville's harbor, and the food has hints of nouvelle cuisine about it. The seafood mousse and lamb chops in tarragon sauce are among the tastiest dishes. Closed Tuesday evenings and Wednesdays except in July and August, December 20 through January, and the last 2 weeks of September. Major credit cards accepted. 11 Rue du Port, Granville (phone: 33-50-12-94). Moderate.

En Route from Granville – The most picturesque route is the turning and twisting coast road, D911, which occasionally has splendid views over Mont-St-Michel Bay and distant prospects of the abbey itself, especially from Cabane Vauban. It is a favorite spot for viewing the mount and the coast of Brittany.

AVRANCHES: Avranches is chiefly famous for having such a splendid view of Le Mont-St-Michel, especially at sunset in late spring or early fall. It is most romantic by moonlight, when the great rock and its crowning glory, La Merveille (the Marvel), swim against a shimmering silver backdrop of sea, sand, rivulets, and tides. The best spot for seeing what is certainly one of the world's most famous silhouettes is from the viewing table on the terrace of the Jardin des Plantes (Botanical Gardens), on Place Carnot. It was a Bishop of Avranches, St. Aubert, who was initially responsible for establishing a place of worship on the nearby rocky islet in the bay, though only after some prodding — literally speaking, if legend is to be believed — by St. Michael the Archangel. Aubert's skull, with a dent in it where Michael somewhat zealously drove home his point, is one of the relics now housed in the St. Gervais Basilica (Pl. St-Gervais). This, together with some superb relics of the Middle Ages, can be seen by contacting the sacristan. Manuscripts from or connected with the monastery of Le Mont-St-Michel and dating from the 8th to the 15th century are some of the principal holdings of Avranches's museum (closed Tuesdays and November through March; Pl. Jean de St-Avit; phone: 33-68-31-89). Among these are Abélard's famous *Sic et Non* (a collection of religious writings by the church hierarchy), an account by Abbot Robert de Torigni on the founding of Le Mont-St-Michel, and wonderful illuminated manuscripts. The museum also has rooms and artifacts illustrating the life and work of the people of rural Normandy, including the interior of a farm kitchen, with benches, tables, dressers, and armoires.

Avranches also is where Henry II of England did his first public penance (in 1172) for the murder of Thomas à Becket, a deed performed on the orders of Abbot Torigni of Le Mont-St-Michel. The scene took place at the old cathedral. Though the cathedral was destroyed in 1794, the stone where he knelt in repentance can still be seen in La Plate-forme, near the police station, off Boulevard des Abrincates.

LE MONT-ST-MICHEL: Victor Hugo called it "the pyramid of the seas" while to Guy de Maupassant it was "a fantastic manor"; indeed, it is hard to talk about the abbey on the island mount without resorting to simile or metaphor. Whether you see Le Mont-St-Michel first from Granville, from the public gardens at Avranches, or from any number of side roads that extend toward it from the coasts of Normandy and Brittany, it looks magical and mystical; profane and sacred; something from a fairy tale or an ancient saga.

It can be reached by car via the causeway that leads from La Digue, the small mainland village opposite the rock; but the ideal approach is to walk across the causeway, stopping first to look at the mount and its extraordinary assemblage of buildings from the bridge over the Couesnon River on the landward side of the causeway. There, when the tide is in, you can see Le Mont-St-Michel twice, as a jagged and formidable reality and as a shimmering, mysterious watery reflection. The walk across the causeway, slightly less than a mile, is an essential part of experiencing the island and its history. At first the path is a bit rocky, but it soon levels out so that one can concentrate on the shades and shadows as it comes more and more into focus, the vague gray shapes slowly turning to precise forms and lines.

Legend has it that Michael the Archangel himself wanted a chapel or oratory built on what was then known as Mont-Tombe, a rocky outcrop in the forest. With the casual facility ascribed to such luminaries, he appeared in 708 to St. Aubert, Bishop of Avranches, suggesting that a sanctuary be built on the mount in his honor. Aubert, it is said, was somewhat skeptical about the project, and it was only after the archangel had prodded him hard enough to leave a dent in his skull that he decided that, the forest notwithstanding, a small church might not be impossible. Accordingly, St. Aubert dutifully constructed a small oratory on the island. (Geologists say some phenomenon, probably tidal waves, occurred in the region during the first part of the 8th century, which would explain the sinking of the forest around the mount.)

But the abbey had its real beginnings in 966 when Richard I, Duke of Normandy, brought Benedictine monks to the site and began building a grander Le Mont-St-Michel. Most of what remains of the Norman Romanesque parts of the abbey were completed during the 11th and 12th centuries (much was destroyed in a 13th-century fire). This was also the period in which the monastery became a powerful force in Normandy; the abbot soon became the feudal lord over dozens of nearby villages and other fiefdoms and usually played an important role at the ducal court. While a reputation for sanctity was not always prevalent, a reputation for learning and miracles soon attached itself to the mount and its denizens.

The attention and fame that Le Mont-St-Michel enjoyed meant that ideally its buildings should be monumental, beautiful, and in harmony with the latest taste, so Flamboyant Gothic was built upon Gothic, which was built upon Romanesque, which has Carolingian foundations. Under the great Abbot Torigni, scion of a Norman noble family and chronicler of the island's history, the abbey reached the zenith of its fame and influence. Torigni's assets were worldly rather than spiritual, and he obtained royal confirmation of the abbey's fiefdoms and holdings in France and England. He received Henry II of England and was instrumental in persuading him to do penance for the murder of Thomas à Becket in front of the cathedral at Avranches. Less than 20 years after Torigni's tenure as abbot ended, Normandy had passed into the hands of the Kings of France. To ensure the good will of the abbey and those whose spiritual and temporal allegiance it commanded, Philippe Auguste showed that Capetian favor could be just as generous as Plantagenet. His munificence was instrumental in starting the construction of La Merveille (The Marvel) — as the French call the abbey church and buildings on the mount's north side, the Gothic crown on top of earlier Gothic and Romanesque buildings underneath — which was completed by 1230. The abbey continued to gain in political power, and although canonical hours were observed and mass was said daily, the monks' tasks often seemed more for the glory of the abbey than of God, and the abbey was managed not just as a community of brothers but as a small city with a comptroller, chancellor, and administrator for the vast tracts of forest in the abbatial domains.

During the 13th century, Le Mont-St-Michel's potential as a military stronghold became increasingly apparent; fortification began in earnest in the 1250s with the help of Louis IX (St. Louis). When it was completed, a garrison was maintained by the abbot with at least a token presence of soldiers of the crown always on hand to uphold the king's rights as the prelate's feudal overlord. During the long and dreary skirmishes of the Hundred Years War, its military role often seemed to supersede its spiritual one. Clearly, the close relationship between the monastery and the French could not escape the notice of the marauding English, and the island was the object of three major assaults in the early 1400s, all of which were repulsed even though most of Normandy was in the hands of the King of England.

Later, during the Revolution, most of Le Mont-St-Michel's treasures, pictures, and furniture were destroyed, leaving the abbey scarred and empty except for prisoners; "the Marvel" dedicated to God became a jail. Despite the mindless ravages that took place, enough remains today to satisfy even the greatest hunger for the past.

A day — at least — is needed to begin to appreciate the island and its wonders. Turning left through the Porte de l'Avancée, the outer gate, which is the only opening through the ramparts, one passes the Guardhouse and goes through a second gate called the Porte du Roi (King's Gate) onto the Grande-Rue. This narrow street of granite houses, some with mullioned windows and windowboxes full of geraniums, is the secular heart of Le Mont-St-Michel. A proliferation of souvenir shops and restaurants has not destroyed the street's charm, although the summertime throng can be unnerving. The street climbs past small garden plots nestling behind low stone walls to the medieval Eglise St-Pierre, the island's parish church. The church is totally overshadowed by the abbey physically and historically, but it is well worth a stop. Inside, it is dim and damp, with the smell of the sea permeating the solid stone walls. In the morning you may see pilgrims singing hymns in front of a burnished and bejeweled statue of St. Michael battling a dragon. The street climbs up past more terraced lawns and rose gardens to the Ramparts, where there is a fine view over the great tidal flats to the Grand Degré (Great Stair), which leads in turn to the only entrance to the abbey. Past the fortified gateway under the Châtelet, stairs lead to the Salles des Gardes (Guards' Room), where a small entrance fee is paid. More steps leading up pass the abbey lodgings, the cistern, and then finally reach Gautier's Leap. Just beyond is the West Platform, an open terrace with wonderful views south to La Digue and west to Brittany.

It is here that guided tours begin (in English at 10:30 AM and 2:30 PM). For anyone unfamiliar with the abbey buildings, it is foolish to proceed without a guide since the interior is labyrinthine. From the terrace, the tour leads into the abbey church. The stained glass windows, ornaments, and furniture are gone, but the mellow pink stone of the Romanesque arches in the nave and the spartan bareness of the Flamboyant Gothic choir add up to a whole that is exceedingly graceful. In the traditional Norman Romanesque manner, the roof is supported not by vaults but by a timber ceiling. From one of the 16th-century chapels in the chancel — the second on the right — a doorway opens onto the *escalier de dentelle* (lace stairway), which leads up between elaborately carved stone balustrades to a gallery 394 feet above the sea, from which one can look across the sands and streamlets to the mainland over the heads of snarling gargoyles. Leading out of the church is a favorite spot for many people, the cloister. The garden-side perimeter here is lined with two rows of columns staggered evenly on a low wall. The garden-side capitals are plain and unadorned, but on the enclosed side there are sculpted flourishes of flowers, leaves, and vines occasionally enclosing figurines. The cloister's most interesting feature, however, not visible from inside, is that it is constructed above the Knights' Hall on the level below and not, as the center garden might suggest, on rock.

Similarly, the adjacent refectory is built over the 13th-century Guests Hall. About 50 slit windows in the refectory provide an effect of suffused light that is hard to forget. It is easy to imagine a monk reading the day's lesson from the lectern at the southern end of the hall as the brethren ate the midday or evening meal in this serene, otherworldly atmosphere. Descending to the old cloister on the next level down, one can see where the 7-foot-thick walls meet the cold, damp rock. Also on this level is the catacomb-like chapel of Notre-Dame-sous-Terre, the Chapelle de St-Martin, with its spartan altar and simple crucifix, and the Crypte des Gros Piliers, directly underneath the chancel of the church. The two major rooms on the middle level are the Salle des Hôtes (Guests' Hall) and the Salle des Chevaliers (Knights' Hall). Although the abbey closes at 11:30 AM for 2 hours, anyone wishing to remain for the noon mass may do so. If the number of visitors is not large, they are invited into the sanctuary for the service with the Benedictine monks and sisters.

Leaving the church by the Grand Degré one passes a gate and a small souvenir shop, on the other side of which are the abbey gardens. The west end of the lower garden, above St. Aubert's Oratory (on a rock just above the beach), is the best spot from which to watch the incoming tide. It comes first as a trickle, then streamlets merge to become rivulets, pools join pools and become lagoons, until all the island except the causeway is surrounded by rippling water. Because of silting in the bay, only the highest tides of the year produce the spectacular effect for which the mount was long famous. The best times are in March, September, and sometimes October. Tide tables are available at most tourist offices along the Norman coast. As the tide comes in, improperly parked cars are sometimes inundated with salt water. To obtain a parking spot on high ground, arrive before 8 AM. (High tide warnings are always posted to advise visitors where and for how long they may park.) Le Mont-St-Michel is open all year from 9 to 11:30 AM and from 1:30 to 4 PM mid-May through September. Additional summertime hours (10 PM to 1 AM, nightly except Sunday from mid-June through September) now allow tourists to visit the abbey at night. The 50-minute guided tour features a sound and light show along the 1-mile walk. For more information, contact the tourist office (phone: 33-60-14-30 or 33-60-14-14).

The tide also cuts off the St. Aubert Oratory, which is outside the ramparts. To reach it (after making sure that the tide is well and truly out), walk around the rocks to the left of the Gabriel Tower. It is a simple stone edifice with a small, humble altar that can be seen through an aperture in the door. It may have been all that the archangel wanted.

There are a handful of small guesthouses right on the mount, which are delightful for an overnight stay — not particularly for their fine accommodations and amenities, but simply because Le Mont-St-Michel minus the daytime crowds is a completely different experience. Hearing your footsteps echo on medieval cobblestone streets while beholding the abbey washed in moonlight is unforgettable.

CHECKING IN: *Altéa K* – The best motel of its kind near the mount. The beds are quite comfortable and the long white Formica desks fitted against the walls are ideal for spreading out all the accumulated bric-a-brac of travel. Closed from November to February. Major credit cards accepted. Rte. D976 at Le Pré Salé (phone: 33-60-14-18). Moderate.

Relais du Roy – Just on the mainland side of the causeway to the mount, this is the best of three or four motel-type hostelries in the immediate neighborhood. An old gray stone part of the building lends the place some character. The 27 bedrooms (some overlook Le Mont-St-Michel Bay), all with bath, shower, and toilet, though sparsely furnished, are attractively decorated in off-white tones. Fresh flowers usually are added for a touch of color. Two large stone fireplaces (there's a third in the bar) dominate the dining room, in the middle of which is a refectory table generously laden with fresh fruit, tarts, and other desserts. The *agneau pré-salé* (lamb grazed in saltwater marshes) is splendid, served with green beans and potatoes au gratin. Also good are the *omelettes à la Mère Poulard* and the *assiettes de fruits de mer* (platter of mixed seafood). Closed mid-November through mid-March. Major credit cards accepted. Rte. D976 at La Digue (phone: 33-60-14-25; fax: 33-60-37-69). Moderate.

EATING OUT: *Mère Poulard* – This restaurant is famous for its huge omelettes, which are actually more like soufflés; the most dramatic version of *les omelettes à la Mère Poulard* is flambéed, for dessert. Another specialty is *agneau pré-salé* (lamb grazed in saltwater marshes) served with *flageolets* (beans). The dining room lives up to its location, with flagstone floors, a fireplace, and gleaming glassware, even if word is that the welcome can be indifferent. Open daily till 9:30 PM. Major credit cards accepted. Le Mont-St-Michel (phone: 33-60-14-01; fax: 33-48-52-31). Expensive to moderate.

Brittany

Surrounded on three sides by water, Brittany always has been something of an anomaly with respect to the rest of France. Something quiet and mysterious in the nature of the land itself, the dark mountains and the forests that once covered the inland sections, and the sea that crashes on the shoreline boulders and cliffs inspired a deep mysticism in the people from the very beginning, as early as 3500 BC, when a race of early men began constructing huge monuments of rough stone slabs weighing several tons each. The population claims as ancestors the Gauls, who arrived in the 6th century BC and called the country Armor (the country by the sea) and Argoat (the country of wood); the Romans, who came at about the time of Christ; and the Celts, who were fleeing the Angles and the Saxons in Britain in the 5th century. The Celts brought their keenly felt Catholicism, their saints (whose numbers they increased by granting sainthood to some of their own leaders), the seeds of a religious approach to life that found fertile ground in the Breton spirit, and a Celtic language not unlike Welsh, which immediately opposed itself to early French and reached its zenith in the wake of one Nominoé, who established a dynasty that controlled the area for a century.

Thus established, Breton independence from the then nascent French monarchy was guarded fiercely against further onslaughts for 400 tumultuous years. But in the end, it was no match for the tremendous power of the throne. Anne of Brittany married two French kings, Charles VIII and his successor, Louis XII, but maintained control of the duchy for herself. Her daughter Claude was another matter entirely. More interested in gardening than politics (she gave the world the species of plum known as the Reine Claude), she married Anne's husband's successor, François de Angoulême, and quickly was persuaded to allow the duchy to become part of the legacy of their son Henri II, the future King of France. Brittany was lost.

Yet, even as a part of France, the province always stood apart. Habitually resistant to any central control, the Bretons banded together against the throne in the 18th century and fomented the Revolution in its early years; then, when the rest of France arose, they fought passionately on the other side; anti-Revolutionary Breton peasants known as the Chouans were engineering revolts as late as 1832. During World War II, the Bretons again resisted control by outsiders — this time the Germans. World War II was a great turning point in the history of the area. Young men for the first time in Breton history left the province by the thousands, and when they came back, it was with a broader worldview that seemed to dim the clarity of the folk legends of Brittany's past. At the same time, young people began leaving their homes to seek their fortune in the large cities, further eroding the culture, and large-scale commercial fishing began to threaten the region's local fishermen. The cost of traditional Breton furniture and clothing rose;

modern clothing and modern furniture were inexpensive and efficient by comparison. Thus the traditional became a luxury rather than the outgrowth of a simple lifestyle. Nowadays, travelers seldom see the traditional lace headdresses known as *coiffes* except on great holidays, even in rural hamlets and villages.

Yet the legacy of the past remains. Most obvious to the first-time visitor are the strange Breton place names, comprised in part of Celtic words — *coat, goat, goët,* and *hoët,* which signify "wood" (as in Huelgoat, high wood, and Penhoët, end of the wood); *ker,* which means "village" or "house" (as in Kermaria, Mary's village); *loc,* which means "holy place" (as in Locmaria, Mary's place), or Locronan, St. Ronan's place); *pleu, plo, ploe,* and *plou,* which mean "parish"; *tre* or *tref,* which means "parish subdivision"; *ty,* which means "house"; and *fest noz,* which means "night festival", a village celebration held at night. And Breton regional loyalties are strong, particularly concerning the Breton language. Gradually displaced by French, both through usage and government edict, the Breton dialect began a resurgence in the 1970s; it's now taught in schools, appears on sign posts, is heard on TV and radio stations, and is spoken by an estimated 800,000 people. Breton songs and dances have become popular again as well, and BZH (which stands for Breizh, or Brittany) on cars' license plates is an additional sign of regional pride.

Then there are the legends, which the people nourish by the score. The story of Tristan and Iseult is said to have taken place here. And it was in the Forest of Brocéliande, now known as the Forest of Paimpont, that Christ's disciple Joseph of Arimathea is believed to have vanished with the Holy Grail. In the same forest, the renowned Merlin is said to have met and been inflamed by love for the fairy Viviane, who enclosed him in a magic circle in order to keep him forever. Then there is the story of the good King Gradlon, who reigned over a section of Brittany known as Cornouaille in an exquisitely beautiful capital city, Is, which was contained from the sea by a dike. Seduced by the devil in the form of a suitor, his beautiful but dissolute daughter stole the key to the seawall and flooded the city. Gradlon escaped on horseback and was saved only after he tossed his offspring into the sea — but Is was lost, and Gradlon went to Quimper to rebuild his kingdom. His daughter turned into a mermaid and charmed sailors to their deaths.

The people's considerable religious fervor, which went hand in hand with their belief in such legends, found an enduring expression in stone. Nine cathedrals, some 20 large churches, country churches and chapels by the thousand, and even greater numbers of calvaries and simple crosses were erected at crossroads throughout the province as expressions of thanks for prayers answered. The native building material, granite, was so hard as to be nearly impossible to cut. Yet, motivated by their faith, artisans wrought wonders with the substance.

When the desired effects could not be achieved in stone, they turned to wood and carved organ casings, pulpits, baptistries, choir screens, rood screens, rood beams, confessional enclosures, and other structures in the church; not a square inch was left unadorned. Thus, in many Breton houses of worship, there is a striking contrast between the simplicity of the stonework and the profusion of wooden ornament. The liveliness of the individual sculptures in both stone and wood further distinguishes Breton cathedrals and churches from their Norman counterparts, as do their ornate and imposing belfries and handsome porches on the south wall (used in the past for meetings of parish notables), which can be found even on small chapels.

In some communities, there are the uniquely Breton parish closes as well. Built primarily in the 15th and 16th centuries, these consist of the church; a calvary carved with episodes from the Passion, a type of monument that harks back to the menhirs of Brittany's earliest inhabitants; a cemetery; a triumphal arch guarding its entrance and heralding the arrival of the just into heaven; and, adjoining the cemetery, a charnel house, used to house bones that were exhumed when a cemetery ran out of room. (Its proximity to the church vividly recalls how close death was to life in those days of plagues and wars.) That Bretons saw it not without a sense of humor is revealed in an inscription near a bas-relief that portrays death menacing a group of figures from all walks of life on one of Brittany's largest ossuaries: "I'll kill you all," it reads.

Perhaps the belief in such legends is not what it once was, but neither does disbelief hold sway. Many Breton churches and chapels are the scenes of great religious processions known as *pardons,* and they still draw huge crowds for long walks, masses, and bonfires. If the celebrants do not believe as unreservedly as their grandparents, neither do they turn their back upon the blessings that their participation may bring, so they join the throngs and make a holiday of it. If the saint to which the *pardon* is devoted can heal colic or headaches, bring justice or wealth, or satisfy other earthly needs, so much the better.

A visitor sees this tapestry of fact, folkway, legend, and belief against the backdrop of one of the greatest landscapes in France. Fringing Brittany is a seacoast so notched and indented, so cliffbound, gorge-riven, and sea-pounded that the simple word "rocky" does not do it justice. Formed by movements of the earth that took place millions of years ago and by the tidal erosion, the action of the rivers, and the storms of the centuries, the coast consists of huge piles of rocks, tall escarpments, grand peninsulas, and bizarre rock formations. Inland, the woods that the Gauls called Argoat have been effectively decimated, but in a few spots it's possible to envision the dark mystery of the country that nourished the legends. The patchwork of fields and pastures separated by thickly overgrown hedgerows known as *bocages* lends a serenity to the place that makes for exceptionally restorative touring.

Neither is the food designed to exhaust the digestive tract. Breton fare is plain, by and large. But here the ingredients are so fine as to require little in the way of elaborate cooking. The lambs that graze on the salt meadows within sight of the sea, the cauliflowers and artichokes, onions, peas, strawberries, and string beans that grow on the edge of the escarpments along the north coast, draw an additional tang from the salt air. There are excellent lobsters — *homards,* which resemble the Maine crustaceans, as well as *langoustes,* which are more like the creatures of the Pacific coast. Oysters (*huîtres*) abound. They show up on menus (usually raw, on the half shell), at roadside stands, and in every fishing port. *Belons,* one of the two main varieties, are mild, smooth-shelled, firm, and subtly flavored — the truffles of oysterdom. *Portugaises* have rough shells and a briny taste. Both are bred in the oyster beds in the Gulf of Morbihan, and then shipped for fattening to estuaries in other sections of Brittany and nearby areas, where they gain a distinctive flavor from the mix of food substances in the water — and at the same time acquire the name by which they are known in the market. (*Cancalaises,* for instance, are oysters fattened around Cancale.) Fish generally is broiled or poached or served with a straightforward sauce. The simple soup known as the *cotriade* — Brittany's answer to bouillabaisse — is about as elaborate as the local cuisine gets. The crêpes also are worth noting. These thin Breton pancakes are served in *crêperies* in almost every small town, and it's easy to make a meal of them — with those made of buckwheat flour and stuffed with cheese or tomatoes or bacon or other hearty ingredients as a main course (called *galettes*), and with the more delicate ones made of wheat flour and stuffed with butter and sugar or jam, perhaps flamed with a liqueur, as dessert (called *crêpes*). The cost is low, and the meal filling and delightful — especially when consumed with a bottle of Breton cider, which is mildly apple flavored, not very sweet, and gently alcoholic. Breton butter is, as befits a maritime region, generally mildly salted, unlike butter elsewhere in France. Breton pastries are generally simple rather than elaborate — the most typical is the *far breton,* a sturdy cake-cum-flan made with plenty of milk, eggs, and prunes soaked in rum, and *kouign-amann,* a flaky yeast cake.

The route outlined below shuttles between Armor and Argoat and takes in fishing villages and inland market towns, sophisticated resorts and backwoods farming centers. With the exception of Nantes, which provides an introduction to the folk art of the past and to some of the more interesting periods in Breton history, the tour avoids big cities — including Rennes and Brest, which are on the whole less rewarding for visitors than the countryside. Our suggestion is that you use the route as an outline. Then, with a detailed map, follow the unnumbered byways to the *artisanats* (craft shops), *moulins* (mills), *chapelles* (chapels), or châteaux signposted off the main roads. In general, the smaller and more obscure the road, the more appealing the scenery, and detours help avoid the congestion of primary routes at the height of the season. Note: The *TGV-Atlantic* high-speed train has reduced travel time from Paris to Rennes or Brest to just over 2 hours — a good reason to think about taking a train to either of these cities and, on arrival, renting a car to begin a Breton circuit. (Major car rental companies have kiosks at or near the train stations.) Before leaving Paris, stop by the *Maison de la Bretagne* (17 Rue Arrivée; phone: 45-38-73-15). They organize some particularly interesting packages, including the *Bienvenue au Château,* which offers travelers the possibility of staying at some of the region's private châteaux and manor houses. *Ti Ar Vretoned* (22 Rue Delambre, Paris 75014) and the Librairie Breiz (10 Rue du Maine, Paris 75014) offer additional information, including a selection of post cards, souvenirs, and Breton magazines. It's also possible to tour Brittany by bicycle or on foot. Cyclers can write to the *Ligue de Bretagne de Cyclotourisme* (5 Belle-Vue, St-Nolff; phone: 97-45-42-54) or *Bretagne Vélo Tout-Terrain* (2 Pl. de Locminé, Rennes; phone: 99-63-73-31) for information about bicycles. Brittany is a paradise for hikers; in the Middle

Ages, a Breton who made the Tro-Breizh (tour of Brittany) on foot was sure to reach heaven, and today there are over 1,600 miles (2,500 kms) of hiking trails throughout the region. Contact the local *syndicats d'initiatives* (tourist offices) for maps and other information.

May and September are ideal times for visiting Brittany — the weather is fine and there are no crowds. From October through March, increasing numbers of hotels and restaurants post signs proclaiming *fermeture annuelle* (annual closing), so that it sometimes seems that whole communities have turned into ghost towns. However, there usually are a few tourist facilities open in every town. In summer, reserving hotel rooms and seatings at well-known restaurants far in advance is a must. No matter when you travel, expect to pay $90 and up for a double room in hostelries listed as expensive, from $65 to $90 for those described as moderate, and under $65 at places classed as inexpensive. A meal for two will run $100 and up in an expensive restaurant, $65 to $100 in a moderate one, and under $65 in one that is rated inexpensive. Prices do not include wine or drinks. Service usually is included.

NANTES: Its outskirts now predictably full of auto dealers and apartment towers, Brittany's largest city (pop. 44,000) became a prosperous shipping center thanks to its location about 30 miles from the point at which the Loire River flows into the ocean. During the 18th century, before the abolition of the lucrative slave trade between West Africa and the Antilles after the Revolution and before the later tonnage increases made it impossible for ships to travel upstream as far as Nantes, the town laid out gracious boulevards edged by stately rows of trees, and wealthy merchants built themselves fine mansions. A walk that takes in the Place du Pilori, the Place Royale, the Rue Crébillon (Nantes's answer to Paris's exclusive shopping street, the Rue du Faubourg St-Honoré), the Place Graslin, the octagonal Place Mellinet with its eight identical townhouses, and the Cours Cambronne, a smaller version of Paris's Jardin du Luxembourg, will show off a number of mansions. It also passes scores of glossy shops; the 19th-century *Palais Dobrée,* now a museum filled with its wealthy builder's collections of prehistoric and medieval antiquities, religious relics, and paintings; and the Passage Pommeraye, a mid-19th-century shopping arcade with polished wood floors, a glass roof, pedestrian bridges, and much ornate cast ironwork. A walk around the area of the 17th-century Ste-Croix Church will reveal a medieval district with narrow, winding streets and half-timbered houses.

In addition, Nantes offers the Cathédrale de St-Pierre et St-Paul, which also is in the center of the city on the Place St-Pierre. This truly is a fabulous structure, from its elegantly carved façade to its soaring interior. Unlike most Breton cathedrals, which are built of granite, Nantes's is constructed of Vendée stone; its lightness allowed the vaults to soar to 120 feet, about twice that of other large cathedrals in Brittany and even higher than that of Notre-Dame in Paris. The softness of the stone permitted the sculptors to give sharp definition to every bit of Flamboyant Gothic ornamentation and to outline the slender ribs and groins with a crispness difficult to achieve in granite. And unlike most other cathedrals in France built over the centuries as this one was (between 1434 and 1893), it is architecturally harmonious, its pure Gothic lines undarkened by any shadow of other building styles. There is a fine tomb for François II and his second wife, Marguerite de Foix, a memorial ordered by Anne of Brittany for her father and carved by the Breton sculptor Michel Colombe between 1502 and 1507. Note its interesting statue of Prudence, one of four corner sculptures. She is depicted holding a mirror, which stands for the future and in which is reflected the visage of an old man, representing the past (the idea being that sagacity comes from consulting the past before determining a course for the future). Also note the fine modern windows: one, 80 feet high and 17 feet wide, portrays various Breton saints in unusually intense hues of scarlet and gold; others, ingenious and surprisingly beautiful, are done in oddly shaped glass pieces shading from pale to dark gray, which give the scenes the appearance of Cubist paintings from outside. The lovely garden surrounded by Renaissance houses to the right of the cathedral, the Place de la Psallette, is a rejuvenating respite from a long walking tour.

The cathedral — like the excellent *Musée des Beaux-Arts,* one of the best of its kind in the country (closed Tuesdays; 10 Rue Georges-Clemenceau) — is very far from the little harbor towns, simple chapels, pastures, and woodlands that most people expect of Brittany. But the city's tenacious attachment to its Breton identity is not as far-fetched as first appearances would indicate. The 15th-century Château des Ducs de Bretagne (closed Tuesdays), with round towers and a placid moat edged by graceful willows in front, makes this apparent. One of the most important Breton historical structures, it was first of all the birthplace of Anne of Brittany. Rebuilt in 1466 from a 9th- or 10th-century structure by her father, it was luxurious and full of intrigue as ministers, councils, chamberlains, majordomos, secretaries, equerries, and footmen danced attendance on him and each other. In 1598, Henri IV came here to discuss the epochal Edict of Nantes, which granted freedom of worship to French Protestants. Today, the château houses three museums accessible through a spacious courtyard. Most interesting as an introduction to a tour of Brittany is the one devoted to local popular arts; *coiffes,* embroidered costumes, pottery, ironwork, and carved oak box beds and chests can be seen here in numbers not encountered elsewhere in the province. Displays are organized by region to facilitate methodical study, but even a cursory perusal turns up dozens of interesting exhibits like the array of carved wooden marriage spoons and the bright yellow mourning costumes of the Bigouden area. Also on the premises are a decorative arts museum displaying modern textiles and a maritime museum.

The Syndicat d'Initiative on the Place du Change (closed Sundays; phone: 40-47-04-51) has maps and a wealth of other material, including an inexpensive, liberally illustrated book of walking tours. It also can provide information for events such as the *Festival des Arts et Traditions Populaires,* which takes place during the first 2 weeks of July every year.

CHECKING IN: *Le Domaine d'Orvault* – Ten minutes from the center of Nantes in an attractive residential area, this luxurious establishment (a member of the Relais & Châteaux group) with 29 rooms is the logical choice for peace and quiet. The restaurant, which merits a Michelin star, is closed Monday lunch and during February. Major credit cards accepted. Chemin des Marais-du-Cens, Nantes (phone: 40-76-84-02; fax: 40-76-04-21). Expensive.

EATING OUT: Pike, a local specialty, is found on many Nantes menus, either poached or in the form of the small dumplings known as *quenelles* and often doused with white butter sauce called *beurre blanc.*

L'Atlantide – Fresh seafood served in a light, modern dining room. The chef loves to experiment, and dishes such as *langoustines* (actually Dublin Bay prawns) sautéed in aquavit win resounding praise from the locals. Reservations advised. Closed in August. Major credit cards accepted. Centre de Salorges, 16 Quai E. Renaud, Nantes (phone: 40-73-23-23; fax: 40-73-76-46). Expensive to moderate.

Le Gavroche – This fashionable restaurant offers excellent traditional dishes with an emphasis on local seafood. Reservations advised. Closed Sunday evenings and Mondays. Credit cards accepted. 139 Rue Hauts Pavés, Nantes (phone: 40-76-22-49). Expensive to moderate.

La Cigale – Chic Nantais throng to this warm, busy museum piece of a café-brasserie not so much for the food, which is simple, but for the sumptuous turn-of-the-century surroundings — heavy iron-edged doors filled with beveled glass, walls partially faced with turquoise tiles, ceilings full of gilt plaster, rosy-cheeked cherubs, and buxom damsels with masses of hair and angelic robes. Open daily until 12:30 AM. Major credit cards accepted. 4 Pl. Graslin, Nantes (phone: 40-69-76-41). Moderate.

La Rôtisserie de Palais – Small and unprepossessing but very popular, with a fairly substantial menu that changes with the market's offerings. Closed Sundays. Major credit cards accepted. 1 Pl. Aristide-Briand, Nantes (phone: 40-89-20-12). Moderate to inexpensive.

LA BAULE: This full-blown basically middle class French resort boasts discos, a recently rebuilt casino, a yacht harbor, villas perfumed with honeysuckle and jasmine, the pine forest known as the Bois d'Amour, and dozens of boutiques just as sophisticated as those in the South of France. It is the most famous part of this short stretch of coast west of Nantes thanks to a wide crescent of white sandy beach that stretches for some 3 miles from end to end. Protected from the wind by the pines on the dunes to the north, by the Pointe de Penchâteau on the east, and by the Pointe du Croisic on the west, it is thronged with vacationers packed bikini to bikini in season and bounded with nearly identical white high-rise hotels jammed edge to edge like giant bricks in a fortress wall. These are a sight to be sure — especially in the off-season, when tightly closed shutters conceal any evidence of human life.

CHECKING IN/EATING OUT: *Castel Marie-Louise* – In a handsome villa, complete with gables and towers, this stylish 31-room hostelry strikes a note of Edwardian grace in the nondescript symphony of contemporary beachfront high-rises that flank it on either side. The restaurant's cuisine is elegant and inventive enough to satisfy even that bon vivant François André, who founded La Baule in the 19th century. Michelin has awarded it one star. Tennis, a saltwater swimming pool, golf, and bicycling are available at this member of the Relais & Châteaux group. Major credit cards accepted. Esplanade du Casino, 1 Av. Andrieu, La Baule (phone: 40-60-20-60; fax: 40-24-33-65). Expensive.

En Route from La Baule – For huge Breton cliffs, tiny new moons of beach, and sweeping ocean vistas, you have to leave La Baule and make the superscenic drive along D45, which skirts the Grande Côte between the Pointe de Penchâteau and the Pointe du Croisic. Salty Le Croisic, whose port shelters fishing boats and pleasure craft alike, has a colorful fish market, with auction action from about 7 to 10 in the morning; you can get a fine view of the coast and the *marais salants* (salt marshes) to the north from the top of Mont-Esprit, a hill constructed from ships' ballast.

From there, follow D774 through Guérande to La Roche-Bernard, an erstwhile shipbuilding center that overlooks the Vilaine River. Turn west on N165 toward Vannes and you will cross the river on a 160-foot-long suspension bridge that fairly leaps out of the cliffsides.

CHECKING IN/EATING OUT: *Domaine du Château de Rochevilaine* – This luxurious 27-room hostelry sprawls over a rockbound nipple of land, a former estate, which thrusts into the English Channel near the mouth of the Vilaine River. Since the guest quarters are in the old manor house and its outbuildings, each is different; some are huge, with lofty ceilings, crystal chandeliers, velvet-covered furniture, tapestries, and Oriental rugs, spacious bathrooms, and fantastic views out over the sea-pounded boulders. The dining room (one Michelin star) is particularly gracious, with its beamed ceiling, dark floors, and linen tablecloths. Closed mid-January to mid-February. Major credit cards accepted. Pointe de Pen-Lan, Billiers-Muzillac (phone 97-41-69-27). Expensive.

QUESTEMBERT: Zigging and zagging between *armor* and *argoat* — between sea and woodland — a traveler's next logical stop after Nantes is this minuscule town full of buildings constructed of a steely gray granite that seems hard and implacable even by Breton standards. The 16th-century covered market pavilion that dominates the town, crowded on all sides by more stores, is particularly attractive inside, where you can see the massive timbers that support the steeply pitched roof that sweeps practically to the ground.

CHECKING IN/EATING OUT: *Le Bretagne Georges Paineau* – By the time a diner discovers that there are around 900 calories in the special "dietetic" menu that chef Georges Paineau offers at this Relais & Châteaux establishment, he probably is ready to throw caution to the wind and gobble every bite of the meal, from the feather-light *galettes de pommes de terre aux épices* (spiced potato pancakes) and barely-cooked oysters to the last drop of espresso. Michelin has awarded it two stars. The old stone structure wrapped in a tight net of vines is sheer visual delight inside, with its tapestry covered chairs, gleaming silver, and polished walnut paneling. The 6 guestrooms overlooking a small garden bring to mind the phrase *tout confort* (every comfort) with their modern bathrooms and firm double beds. Restaurant closed Sunday evenings and Mondays except in July and August; hotel closed from January to mid-March. Major credit cards accepted. 13 Rue St-Michel, Questembert (phone: 97-26-11-12; fax: 97-26-12-37). Expensive.

MALESTROIT: The small bridge over the River Oust on the fringes of town is the best introduction to this charming, decidedly untouristy village. From here, the visitor sees a fine view of the stream, the *allées* of trees reflected in its still waters, and the town's mountain range of rooftops bristling with antennas, chimneys, and steeples. Curiously, in this land of steely gray granite, the town has done its building in a stone that is vaguely rust-colored streaked with shades of gray, green, and brown. Many structures along the narrow streets near the 12th- and 16th-century Eglise de St-Gilles have carved beams adorned with folksy carvings, like the one of the bourgeois flailing an errant wife.

JOSSELIN: The Rohan family has been a force in this attractive village full of half-timbered houses for more than half a millennium. The Rohan coat of arms can be seen in an intensely colored stained glass window in the Basilique Notre-Dame-du-Roncier, a simple but elegantly detailed structure in the center of town; and towering over the Oust River nearby is the imposing fortress-mansion that has been the family seat for 600 years.

Constructed in the 11th century as a palace, the Josselin château was fortified with nine perfectly cylindrical towers and 12-foot-thick walls by Olivier de Clisson in 1370. The Rohans, the family of de Clisson's wife, Marguerite, acquired it upon his death in 1407. In 1488, the castle was partially destroyed on the orders of the Duke of Brittany, François II, after Jean II de Rohan had fought against him, on the side of the French crown, in the struggle for national unification. Subsequently, François II's daughter Anne of Brittany (who had married the King of France) made funds available to her husband's Rohan supporter to restore the castle. It was then that the façade of the mansion inside the walls was endowed with its granite carvings, as ornate and profuse as if they had been worked with wood, that are one of the château's distinctions. Of de Clisson's towers, only three survived the often bloody years since then. The satiny gloss to which the conical slate roofs have been burnished by the centuries, together with the wedding-cake carvings outside and the regal interiors (seen on guided tours), are the chief attractions of the château. A great *pardon* takes place here annually on the second Sunday in September. (Closed in winter; phone: 97-22-22-50.)

En Route from Josselin – Worth a small detour is the town of Elven to see the spectacular son et lumière show inspired by the legend of Tristan and Iseult. It is presented on Friday and Saturday evenings from mid-July to September at Tours de Largoet in Elven (7 ½ miles/12 km from Vannes). For information and exact times, get in touch with its office at Rue Robert de la Noë (phone: 97-53-52-79).

VANNES: Though the real joy of a tour of Brittany lies in picturesque villages like Josselin, the larger towns offer their pleasures, too. Vannes, an agricultural center with a population of about 45,000, is worth noting for its particularly handsome and extensive Old Quarter, which dates back to BC 200, when it was known as Men-Gweur (Stone of the Goat). The Kings (later the Dukes) of Brittany headquartered here. Extending on all sides of the Cathédrale de St-Pierre, a particularly infelicitous architectural hodgepodge noted primarily for its soaring 16th-century Italian Renaissance chapel, this area is edged on one side by the town ramparts and, at their base, by gardens full of sharply clipped hedges laid out with geometrical precision. One of the most stunning sights in Vannes, seen from the Rue Alexandre-Le-Pontois near the Porte Poterne, is the view of these gardens and a cluster of ramshackle old washhouses, their terra cotta tile roofs punctuated whimsically with chimneys and reflected in a placid little river with the ramparts and the cathedral's steeple looming behind.

The Old Quarter proper, reached by crossing a narrow bridge just above the washhouses, is a labyrinth of narrow pedestrian streets crowded by half-timbered houses. Particularly attractive are the Rue St-Guenhaël, which skirts the mossy-walled cathedral, the Rue de la Monnaie, and the Place Henri-IV, an enclave of gabled 300-year-old houses. The 15th-century Gaillard Château (2 Rue Noë; phone: 97-47-24-34) displays archaeological relics from the paleolithic period to the Iron Age. It is open daily, except Sundays (afternoons only in winter). The explanatory notes in the cases (in French) give a cursory overview of the finds at the excavations at Carnac, a later stop on the tour. The *Musée de la Cohue* (from the Breton *cochug,* meaning "market"), located opposite the cathedral (phone: 97-47-35-86), has two exhibitions: seascape paintings and other sea-related subjects, and an explanation of oyster cultivation — a subject that will take on increased interest after several days of watching fishermen unload their harvest in little Breton harbor towns. Closed Sundays and Tuesdays. Also worth a visit is the *Aquarium Océanographique et Tropical de Vannes* (Parc du Golfe, Vannes 56000; phone: 97-40-67-40). Open daily from 9 AM to noon, and 1:30 to 7:30 PM; July and August from 9 AM to 7 PM. Summer events in Vannes include a *Festival de Jazz,* held in early August (phone: 97-01-80-00).

CHECKING IN/EATING OUT: *La Marébaudière* – Set back from the road a bit and therefore quieter than other town hostelries, this establishment is only a couple of decades old (and the premises are accordingly up-to-date). But the pretty wallpaper, draperies, brass or antique bedsteads, and other handsome furniture in its 42 rooms give the place rather more character than most of its vintage. Seafood, straightforwardly prepared, is offered in the hotel's simple, modern restaurant *La Marée Bleue,* in its own building across the street (8 Pl. Bir-Hakeim; phone: 97-47-24-29). Closed Sunday evenings off-season and from mid-December to mid-January. Major credit cards accepted. 4 Rue Aristide-Briand, Vannes (phone: 97-47-34-29). Moderate.

Le Richemont – This simple hotel opposite the train station is done up with quasi-medieval beams and chandeliers that recall the château where its 14th-century namesake, Arthur de Richemont, the Constable of Brittany, was born. It has 29 very comfortable old-fashioned rooms with enough charm to overcome the occasional quirks of the older structure that houses the guest quarters. In the one-star restaurant next door, *Régis Mahé,* low beams, stained glass windows, a carved stone fireplace, and Genoese velvet chairs produce an air of luxury quite in keeping with Chef Mahé's menu of seafood, grills, and refined versions of Breton specialties, such as *filets de rougets safranés* (red mullet filets in saffron sauce) served with a *galette de blé noir* (a buckwheat crêpe). Closed Sunday evenings,

Mondays (except holidays) and 2 weeks in February and November. Major credit cards accepted. 26 Av. Favrel et Lincy, Vannes (phone: hotel, 97-47-12-95; restaurant, 97-42-61-41). Hotel, inexpensive; restaurant, moderate.

GULF OF MORBIHAN: This nearly circular body of water, very much "the little sea" to which its name refers, measures 12 miles across and 10 miles (16 km) from Vannes on the northern end to Port Navalo, on the south. It is a pretty area, flatter than an oyster shell and known for its rosy sunsets, its subtle light, the oyster beds in the rivers that open onto it, and its dozens of islands of all shapes and sizes, some woodsy and natural, some immaculately landscaped.

The best way to experience the area is by boat. Pack a picnic lunch and climb aboard one of the *Vedettes Vertes* boats at the Gare Maritime (Maritime Station) in Vannes (phone: 97-63-79-99). These craft call at most of the major islands, where passengers can stroll on landfalls like the 4-mile-long Ile-aux-Moines (Monks' Island), where dolmens guard heather moors and fishermen pedal home to thatch-roofed cottages along quiet roadways. You can also rent a small motorboat from *Le Blan Marine,* at Port d'Arradon (phone: 97-44-06-90) to explore the interesting environs. But the ideal way to tour the gulf is in a *sinagot,* a small sailing craft once used extensively by coastal fishermen which are now piloted by local seamen. Contact the Office du Tourisme de Vannes for information (1 Rue Thiers; phone: 97 47 24 34).

Skirting the shoreline by car, with glimpses of the sea here and there, is another alternative. South and east of Vannes, a tour might take in St-Armel; St-Colombier; the grand, windswept ruins of the 14th-century Suscinio château, where the Dukes of Brittany once summered; and St-Gildas-de-Rhuys, the site of the church of the abbey to which the learned 12th-century philosopher Pierre Abélard repaired after his forced separation from his beloved Héloïse.

Moving west from Vannes, several highways connect small roads that reach to the very tip of the little points of land that notch the coast. In the Marais de Pen-en-Toul, a visitor might spot a lonely heron standing sentry over a sawtoothed patch of grass, and in harbors like the ones at Arradon and Larmor-Baden, a traveler might spy fishermen unloading their day's harvest in the dark blue twilight that follows a particularly scarlet sunset. Near Moustoir, where a handful of signs point to obscure villages along lanes more suited to bicycles than to cars, cows being herded from field to barn block the road. At Port-Blanc, there are boats to the Ile-aux-Moines, and Larmor-Baden has service to the Gavrinis Tumulus, one of the most interesting megalithic monuments in Brittany due to the extent and preservation of the chambers.

CHECKING IN: *Les Vénètes* – White, modern, and very small, this 12-room hostelry occupies a pleasant spot on the harbor at Arradon, just a short walk along the base of the cliffs from Arradon Point, where there are fine views of the sunset. Closed October through March. Major credit cards accepted. On the point in Arradon (phone: 97-44-03-11). Expensive to moderate.

AURAY: Much smaller than Vannes and far more manageable, Auray also has a charming Old Quarter. Occupying a point created by a bend in the Auray River and connected to the town proper on the opposite bank of the stream by a one-lane bridge, it has cobbled streets compressed to one lane by shuttered stucco and stone houses dating from the 15th century. The heart of the area is Place St-Sauveur, which is full of brasseries and cafés whose site by the river makes them especially charming for afternoon coffee. Be sure to note the quay that leaves the square. Benjamin Franklin, sailing to France in 1776 to enlist aid for the Revolutionary cause, spent the night in a house 150 yards away when stiff headwinds stopped his ship from traveling up the Loire to Nantes.

CHECKING IN: *Fairway* – Golfers especially should take note of this addition to Brittany's lodging places, some 4 ½ miles (7 km) outside Auray. Though its modern facilities and rooms lack the charm of the region's old stone inns, it has a pristine 27-hole golf course. There also is a pool, a gym, and tennis courts. Closed mid-December to mid-January. Major credit cards accepted. Mailing address: *Golf St-Laurent,* Auray (phone: 97-56-88-88; fax: 97-56-88-28). Moderate.

En Route from Auray – Ste-Anne-d'Auray, a few miles north, is the setting not only for some of Brittany's most important *pardons* in late July but also for the more minor pilgrimages that take place from Monday to Thursday nearly weekly between *Easter* and October. The elaborate costumes of the faithful are as impressive as the fervor with which they undertake their journeys; some will struggle up the double staircase known as the Scala Sancta, leading from the square to the basilica, on their knees.

CARNAC: Megalithic monuments may seem dull stuff, but not at Carnac, whose concentration of these rough-hewn stones has few equals in all of Europe. Here they stand, some 3,000 of them, aligned with the points of the compass or with stellar and solar trajectories — a silent testament to the ingenuity of man in service to his gods, eerie mementos that vibrate with a piety that, however antique, is fully the equal of that of the Ste-Anne pilgrims. To get a sense of the magnitude of the force required to erect them, consider that when the 220-ton Luxor obelisk was set up in the Place de la Concorde in 1836, Parisians hailed it as an extraordinary feat. Yet megaliths typically weigh as much as 350 tons.

Sometimes the stones are impressive for sheer size. Witness the Tumulus St-Michel, a huge mound of earth that conceals several burial chambers (accessible near Carnac's *Tumulus* hotel, off N781). Or the almost mystical allure derived from the stones' number, as in the case with the Ménec Lines, on the left of D196 as it heads north from Carnac, where more than a thousand stones of varying heights punctuate the fields of golden broom in several straight lines for about three-quarters of a mile. A visitor scarcely has time to absorb this sight before the Kermario Lines — still more of the same — appear along the road. The Kercado Tumulus, off the beaten path on the grounds of a private château, is only a bit farther. To see the tumulus, go down a long, straight, tree-lined lane that shoots off to the right past the Kermario Lines, stop at the gatehouse and speak to the gatekeeper, pay the small fee, and pick up the key to the barrow's locked door, a flashlight, and an information sheet. The turnoff is not marked by a sign, so the site is nearly always deserted and feels every bit the tomb that it probably once was. At the Kerlescan Lines farther along, the stones are taller than a man and even more mystically powerful.

The *Musée de Préhistoire,* a museum in town, displays the prehistoric findings of the excavations of the Carnac monuments — necklaces, axheads, vases, and the like. Open daily except Tuesdays from 10 AM to noon and 2 to 5 PM. 10 Pl. de la Chapelle, Carnac 56340 (phone: 97-52-22-04.)

 CHECKING IN: *Hôtel du Tumulus* – Calm and quiet with a heated pool and a pleasant garden, this 26-room hostelry is filled with antiques and ideally located between the beach and the famous megaliths. Closed October to *Easter.* Major credit cards accepted. 41 Rue Tumulus, Carnac (phone: 97-52-08-21). Moderate.

Lann Roz – From the small, cheery garden to the salon full of pretty caged birds to the 13 daintily wallpapered rooms upstairs, this inn is a delightful spot to spend a night or two, though we've heard echoes of late that the owner can be less than welcoming. Closed January. Major credit cards accepted. 36 Av. de la Poste, Carnac (phone: 97-52-10-48). Moderate.

EATING OUT: *Chez Yannick* – Breton *crêperies* usually are staid, plain affairs, but not this quirky, appealing place. Ivy creeps over nearly every inch of the ceiling, and the menu includes crêpes filled with *crème fraîche* and smoked Scotch salmon or, for dessert, blueberry jam flamed with chartreuse. A must. Closed Sunday evenings, Mondays off-season, and during January. Major credit cards accepted. 8 Rue du Tumulus, Carnac (phone: 97-52-08-67). Inexpensive.

QUIBERON: This busy resort center, extending landward from its beach and its harbor, is something of a carnival in season and has hotels, villas, a casino, bars, discos, tearooms, fishing supply stores, and boutiques by the dozen. Some are modern and some old-fashioned, so the place has an appealing mixed quality. What makes it particularly noteworthy, however, is the coastline all around it, which is some of the most spectacular in southern Brittany. Near town at the Pointe du Conguel, the waves hurl themselves onto low-lying rocks that afford a fine view of Belle-Ile (Beautiful Island) and the islands of Houat and Hoëdic. To the north of town, they crash upon tiny beaches at the base of tall cliffs. It is easy to understand why this stretch of shoreline was dubbed the Côte Sauvage (the Wild Coast).

Much of it is visible from the road that twists and climbs and rolls through the moors at the top of the cliffs. For a better view, park the car and walk the 2 miles (3 km) of coast between Port-Pigeon, midway along the peninsula's west coast, and Portivy, just north of the Pointe du Percho on the north. *Note:* Strong currents make swimming dangerous.

 CHECKING IN: *Ker Noyal* – Well-kept and modern, this luxurious club-like establishment a short walk from the beach has two square buildings that face each other across a courtyard. Most of the 100 modern rooms have terraces with views of either the sea or a well-tended garden massed with bright flowers and pine trees. Closed from November to March. Major credit cards accepted. Rue de St-Clément, Quiberon (phone: 97-50-08-41; fax: 97-30-58-20). Expensive.

Sofitel – For every comfort, including a saltwater spa, plus pool and tennis courts, this 116-room modern hotel, which has been completely renovated, is a good bet even if it lacks local charm. Closed in January. Major credit cards accepted. Quiberon (phone: 97-50-07-34). Expensive.

Gulf Stream – An older hostelry, this simple 20-room inn on the harbor gets its charm from the classic balustrades and windowboxes splashed with color. The whole place seems to gleam. Closed mid-November to early February. Major credit cards accepted. 17 Bd. Chanard, Quiberon (phone: 97-50-16-96). Moderate.

Le Neptune – Small, modern, and right on the harbor, this establishment is not long on charm, but the 22 rooms have decent beds and small-patterned wallpaper, and the view from the terraces of the quarters facing the harbor and the gleaming bathrooms, sometimes done in handsome dark blue tiles, are a genuine pleasure. Closed from late December to mid-February, and Mondays off-season. Major credit cards accepted. 4 Quai de Houat, Quiberon (phone: 97-50-09-62). Moderate.

BELLE-ILE: Of all the islands off the Breton coast, Belle-Ile, once frequented by Sarah Bernhardt and Monet, among celebrated folk, is most often mentioned as a must. It is accessible by steamer from Port-Maria, which dominates 10-mile-distant Quiberon. The scenery is impressive — the shoreline cliffs, the deep valleys, the verdant pastures, the wheat and potato fields interspersed with patches of weeds and stately trees, and the small complexes of whitewashed farmhouses and barns. From several of the small villages there are fine walks to places on the coastline where the sea has carved caverns and odd shapes out of the cliffs. Don't miss the Grotte de l'Apothicairérie (Apothecary Grotto), named for the cormorant nests that used to be lined up along niches in the cave walls like bottles in a pharmacy. Especially in the late spring and early fall, there is a delightful serenity to this island that is hard to beat. (For steamer information, call 97-31-80-01.) Touring by bicycle can be a lovely way to enjoy the remarkable scenery. Cycles can be rented from *Didier Bonnet* (Quai l'Acadi, Le Palais; phone: 97-31-84-74).

CHECKING IN: *Castel Clara* – Boasting bathrooms paved with marble and balconies opening onto the sea, this comfortable, gleaming white 43-room member of the Relais & Châteaux group occupies a secluded hillside on the peaceful west coast of the island. There also is a terrace, a heated saltwater pool, tennis facilities, and a state-of-the-art saltwater spa. Closed from mid-October to mid-March. Major credit cards accepted. Port-Goulphar (phone: 97-31-84-21; fax: 97-31-51-69). Expensive.

La Désirade – A collection of sparkling white stucco bungalows are set around a swimming pool at this refreshingly simple, 24-room establishment near Bangor and Port Coton. No restaurant, but breakfast is available. Closed January and February. Major credit cards accepted. Rte. Port Goulphar, Belle-Ile-en-Mer (phone: 97-31-70-70; fax: 97-31-89-63). Moderate.

Manoir de Goulphar – Thanks to its fine views and chic decor, this posh white structure with 53 rooms on the peaceful coast has far more character than its modern construction might suggest. Closed from November to mid-March. Major credit cards accepted. Port-Goulphar (phone: 97-31-80-10). Moderate.

KERNASCLÉDEN: The care with which pious Bretons decorated their simple churches immediately is apparent in the 15th-century, lichen-splotched house of worship that dominates this little town about 10 miles (16 km) north of Hennebont. The slender belfry is elegantly proportioned and finely embellished with small ornamental motifs, as are the tops of the buttresses. The archway above the front door is topped with one layer after another of decorative grooves. And the porch is lined with niches, each one edged with a wealth of lacelike details that frame realistic statues of the apostles.

Of particular interest inside this church (which has been restored) are its frescoes — some depicting musical angels and scenes from the life of Christ and the Virgin; others, underneath a beautiful rose window, showing macabre images like the Dance of Death between skeletons and courtiers and the weird pictures of horned devils in hell smashing anguished sinners into pots of boiling oil with pitchforks.

CHECKING IN/EATING OUT: *Château de Locguénolé* – Visiting this stately castle, now an inn, owned by the same family for more than 500 years, is like attending a courtly house party in some past century. The restoration of the 37 rooms and apartments has been masterfully done; those on the second story, originally consecrated to the gentry, have high ceilings, velvet curtains, soft rugs, and refined furniture, while those on the floor above, under the eaves, are handsomely rustic, with country prints and exposed beams. Views over the well-tended grounds, which slope down to the edge of the river Blavet in the rear, are stupendous. Antiques, paintings, and tapestries collected over the centuries ornament the salons, which manage to be comfortable and welcoming despite their formality. People come for miles around to sample the well-conceived and finely executed nouvelle specialties on the menu (rated one Michelin star), which changes regularly from one season to the next but remains innovative — witness the red mullet cooked in a salt crust, the sweetbread salad flavored with sorrel, and the light crayfish bisque served with a vegetable mousse and fresh mint. A member of the Relais & Châteaux group. Closed Mondays, off-season, and January. Major credit cards accepted. About 2½ miles (3 km) south of Hennebont, just off D781 (phone: 97-76-29-04; fax: 97-76-39-47). Expensive.

LORIENT: Originally spelled "L'Orient" (the Orient), the town was founded in 1666 as the base of the Compagnie des Indes, a royal monopoly established by Louis XIV that dealt in spices and other Far East merchandise. The French Revolution put an end to this enterprise, which had been very profitable for the crown, but Lorient survived as a fishing center and, from the 19th century, as a naval base. The city suffered heavy bombing during World War II of its port and ancient city center, which have now been replaced by modern buildings. But what Lorient lacks in architectural charm is made up for by hosting one of the world's largest celebrations of Celtic culture, the *Festival Interceltique,* held annually during the first 2 weeks of August. Music, dance, folk art and foods from Celtic regions throughout the world are featured, with participants from Ireland, Wales, England, and Spain, as well as Brittany. For a program of events, call the *Festival Interceltique* (phone: 97-21-24-29) or contact the Office du Tourisme (Maison de la Mer, Quai de Rohan; phone: 97-21-07-84). In addition to the *Festival Interceltique,* Lorient hosts another event, *Les Océanes,* the week before *Bastille Day* (July 14) every year, which features sea tales told by storytellers, sea chants, and plays with maritime themes. For information about the program, contact the Office du Tourisme or call *Les Océanes* (phone: 97-65-63-01).

CHECKING IN: Mercure – All 58 guestrooms at this modern, airy establishment have recently been renovated, so everything is in pristine condition. There is also a cozy bar, a perfect spot in which to lounge and imbibe a post-prandial cognac. Open all year. Major credit cards accepted. 31 Place J. Ferry (phone: 97-21-35-73; fax: 97-64-48-62). Expensive to moderate.

Victor Hugo – This little charmer is conveniently located between the port and the town center. While the 30 guestrooms may not be the epitome of luxury, they are extremely comfortable and cheery, and the management is unusually friendly and helpful. Open all year. Major credit cards accepted. 36 Rue Lazare-Carnot (phone: 97-21-16-24). Inexpensive.

EATING OUT: Le Poisson d'Or – A seafood restaurant with a very friendly manager and local seafood in many guises, all of it delicious. Closed Saturday lunch, Sundays, 2 weeks in February, and November 1. Major credit cards accepted. 1 Rue Maître Esvelin (phone: 97-21-57-06). Expensive to moderate.

Le Jardin Gourmand – An excellent and very reasonably priced restaurant with its own garden, run by a young couple, the Pelletiers. Madame proves to be a top-notch chef, and her recipes are traditional Breton fare enhanced by fresh vegetables and seafood. Try the *cotriade* (a traditional Breton seafood stew), the *blanquette de jarette de veau* (veal-shank stew in a cream sauce), or, if you like tripe, the *galette de pommes de terre à l'andouille de Guémené* (a potato pancake containing tripe sausage from Guémené, a town in Brittany renowned for its *andouille*). The cave concentrates on Loire Valley wines; the white Savennières (an Anjou wine) and the inexpensive red Gamay de Touraine are excellent. Closed Sundays. Major credit cards accepted. 46 Rue J. Simon (phone: 97-64-17-24). Moderate.

LE FAOUËT: An old town with a 16th-century covered market building not unlike the one at Questembert, with a veritable forest of pillars inside, Le Faouët is well worth visiting for the two fine chapels nearby and the beautiful countryside in between the district's Inam and the Ellé rivers.

By far the better known of the two is the one devoted to the Irish hermit St. Fiacre, the patron saint of gardeners. Somewhat asymmetrical but nonetheless balanced on the outside, this rather simple structure set alongside a simple farm is ornamented inside with a carved Gothic choir screen; its lifelike carvings, though executed in a rather primitive style, demonstrate the heights to which the Breton woodcarvers' skill eventually rose. On the nave side, note the thieves contorted on their crosses and, along the border, the crowd of curious faces, looking and leering and grinning. Facing the chancel, don't miss the pie-eyed peasant vomiting a fox (an image that represents drunkenness) and the man with the woman lifting her skirts flirtatiously (symbolizing lust).

The Chapel of Ste-Barbe, a few miles on the other side of Le Faouët, is remarkable not so much for its interior, which is small, as for its site; it clings to the side of a cliff just beneath the crest of a hill whose summit overlooks the fields and forests of the Ellé Valley. To get to the chapel, it's necessary to walk through the woods for about 10 minutes up a switchbacked trail that begins immediately across the road from the *Café de l'Ellé*. There are two ways to go, one considerably steeper than the other, and the signs are no help. Inquire before starting out. The trail ends at a finely proportioned Renaissance stairway, which in turn leads to the chapel and the viewful hilltop where the only sounds may be the roaring of the wind across your ears or the occasional bark of the caretaker's fierce dogs. It is of such apparently inconsequential sites that the best Breton memories are made. *Pardons* are held here on December 4 and on the last Sunday in June.

QUIMPERLÉ: This unprepossessing hill town is well known to the fishermen who come for the salmon and trout in the placid little Isole and Ellé rivers, which here form the Laïta. But it is more interesting for the variation it offers on the Gothic church theme, the Romanesque Eglise de Ste-Croix, which is laid out not in the shape of the rectangular, Latin cross but in that of the square Greek cross, like the Holy Sepulcher in Jerusalem. The round arches, the barrel vaulting, the small apse with its vividly colored windows, and the cool crypt supported by capitals carved with vaguely Celtic designs make this a spot to remember.

Not far from the church, along the Rue Brémond-d'Ars and the narrow, alley-like Rue Dom-Morice, there are some pretty half-timbered houses with walls that lurch and lean with the abandon of a drunkard.

 CHECKING IN: *Ermitage* – Occupying an old manor house and several stone outbuildings, this 28-room establishment is notable for its setting on the edge of a forest, its gardens full of rosebushes and hydrangeas, and the sounds — mainly of the wind rushing through the pines that crowd the complex and edge the small slate-terraced swimming pool. Major credit cards accepted. On D49, Rte. du Pouldu, about a mile (1.6 km) south of Quimperlé (phone: 98-96-04-66; fax: 98-39-23-41). Moderate.

FOREST OF CARNOUET: Legend has it that this 1,852-acre preserve, which flanks D49 south of Quimperlé, once was inhabited by the Count of Comorre, a fearsome fellow who, under the spell of a prophecy that he would be murdered by his son, killed four wives, one after another, as soon as they became pregnant, then slaughtered the son of a clever fifth wife who had managed to bear her child. But the prophecy was fulfilled, nonetheless: St. Trémeur, as the son was later known, lived long enough to pick up his head and toss a handful of dirt at the count's castle with a force that made the building collapse. The fearsome Bluebeard of Cornouaille was buried alive in the rubble.

The reverberations of this legend add an extra dimension to the vision of the beautiful tall, straight trees, and many Bretons make a point of taking a walk along the many footpaths that shoot into the woods from the road — perhaps to the ruins of the Abbaye St-Maurice (accessible via D224, off D49); to the Rocher Royal, a ridge that overlooks the serene Laïta River (a little over a mile/1.6 km from D49 via a footpath); or perhaps to the Château de Comorre itself.

 CHECKING IN: *Les Moulins du Duc* – A tiny lake, swans, white doves, a waterwheel velvety with moss, comfortable quarters in a handful of rustic houses, a swimming pool, and a woodsy valley setting make this 22-room, 5-suite establishment one of the most inviting in the province. Nearby cascades the Belon River, which is famous for its oysters. Closed mid-January through February; restaurant closed Wednesdays for lunch off-season. Near Moëlan-sur-Mer, about 5 miles (8 km) from the southern edge of the Carnouet Forest (phone: 98-39-60-73). Expensive to moderate.

EATING OUT: *Chez Jacky* – This is not just another rustic restaurant, but a seafood lover's paradise. Grilled lobster served with a creamy house sauce is the specialty, and Belon oysters are available. Appetites can be appeased from 10 AM to 10 PM. Closed Mondays and October through *Easter*. Major credit cards accepted. Port de Belon, Riec-sur-Belon (phone: 98-06-90-32). Moderate.

PONT-AVEN: It was in yet another simple Breton chapel, Chapelle Trémalo, that the Impressionist Paul Gauguin found the 16th-century wooden Christ on which he modeled his well-known *Yellow Christ*. The chapel can be seen today just less than a mile from this pleasant little town by following D24 and a climbing, twisting side road through the cow pastures edged by romantic lines of tall, straight trees. The celebrated carving is still there, but the real allure of the place is the granite structure itself — simple and asymmetrical and seemingly at the top of the world. The scene is especially beautiful at dusk, when the light makes the cows nearby look almost like statues and imbues the whole scene with a mystical quality.

In fact, it was this very quality of light that attracted Gauguin before his voyage to Tahiti, along with Maurice Denis, Paul Sérusier, Emile Bernard, and other painters, who together were known as the Pont-Aven School. The town is said to have been particularly picturesque then, with its valley setting, its little white houses, and its numerous mills driven by the Aven River.

But it is no less so today. There are several galleries and a town museum that mounts art exhibitions. Visit the *Musée de Pont-Aven* (Pl. de l'Hôtel de Ville; phone: 98-06-14-43) to see works by artists from the Pont-Aven School, as well as temporary exhibits of contemporary painters. Open 10 AM to 12:30 PM and 2 to 7 PM, from April through December. A few shops that sell the absolutely delicious butter cookies for which Pont-Aven is known, and some antiques shops and boutiques of more than usual interest; the clientele is as apt to be clad in suede trousers and one gold stud earring — male and female alike — as in blue jeans and T-shirts. Even the simplest bars and *crêperies*, with their whitewashed stucco walls, beamed ceilings, and polished antique furnishings, have atmosphere to spare. And, though the mills no longer are operating, the sound of the rushing waters that powered them still reverberates between the stone walls.

CHECKING IN: *Le Manoir du Ménec* – This hotel and leisure center installed in a gracious 15th-century stone manor northeast of Pont Aven has cozy individual cottages, each named for a famous painter, as well as 10 deluxe guestrooms. The restaurant, with ancient stone walls and elegant chandeliers, is in the oldest part of the manor, while the heated pool, Jacuzzi, sauna, and gym are in the newer addition. There are also facilities for small conferences. Major credit cards accepted. Bannalec (phone: 98-39-47-47; fax: 98-39-46-17). Expensive to moderate.

EATING OUT: *Moulin de Rosmadec* – The sounds of the mill stream that borders it on three sides are only part of the reason that this reconstructed 15th-century stone mill is such a delightful dining spot. Consider also the antiques scattered around the cozy dining rooms inside and the profusion of honeysuckle and roses and rhododendrons crowding the mill walls and edging the terrace outside. Then look at the menu itself, which offers a lemony *soupe de poisson* (fish soup), *palourdes farcies* (stuffed clams), *homard grillé à l'estragon* (grilled lobster flavored with tarragon), *pigeonneau sauce foie gras* (young squab in foie gras sauce), and more — all rated one Michelin star. There are also accommodations upstairs, all with views of the river. Closed Sunday evenings, Wednesdays, the last 2 weeks in October, and all of February. Major credit cards accepted. Near the center of Pont-Aven (phone: 98-06-00-22; fax: 98-06-18-00). Expensive.

La Taupinière – Surrounded by a beautiful garden and coiffed with a straw roof, this restaurant serves giant crayfish grilled in the fireplace, raw tuna marinated in lime, angler fish in butter, and farmers' cider. Michelin has awarded it one star. Closed Monday evenings, Tuesdays, and from mid-September to mid-October. Major credit cards accepted. Rte de Concerneau, 1½ miles (2 km) from Pont-Aven (phone: 98-06-03-12). Expensive.

CONCARNEAU: This walled port, an erstwhile coastal fortress town, wears two faces — one as a popular summer resort, with a long stretch of beach and a *ville close* (walled city), where cars usually are prohibited; the other as a fishing center whose boats, which can be seen in all sizes in the *nouveau port* (new port) behind the Old City, haul in some of the biggest tuna catches in France between midnight and dawn.

The *ville close* has narrow streets attractively crowded by high, shuttered houses, but it also has souvenir shops that tend toward the trinkety and galleries where seascapes are the staple; some people find their tolerance for such fare limited. But when fishermen are unloading their catch by the basket and buyers are scrambling to bid for the best, even travelers who can't stand tourism are fascinated. And as a result of the continual influx of sailors, the city's middle class side is balanced appealingly by a certain raunchiness.

Don't miss the drive along the Boulevard Katerine-Wily, which wends its way between a wall of nondescript apartment towers and a glorious postcard sweep of bay. Buy a ticket at the clock tower just over the bridge at the entrance to the *ville close* and climb the ramparts for another view of the harbor. And explore the *Musée de la Pêche* and its exhibits on commercial fishing. On the next-to-last Sunday in August each year, the *Fêtes des Filets Bleus* (Festivals of the Blue Nets) is held, featuring singers, dancers, and craftspeople who don traditional Breton costumes, as well as concerts of Breton music.

CHECKING IN: *Manoir du Stang* – This particular one of Brittany's handful of 16th-century château-hotels, on the outskirts of sleepy La Forêt-Fouesnant, proclaims the stateliness of the early life here, from the tall *allée* of trees to the neatly clipped lawns beyond them, from the imposing stone gate to the formal square of the graveled courtyard beyond it. The interiors are absolutely seductive — all paneling and crystal and velvet and silk and antiques. Closed September through May. No credit cards accepted. Off D783, 6 miles (10 km) from Concerneau, near La Forêt-Fouesnant (phone: 98-56-97-37). Expensive.

Ferme du Letty – Near the small village of Bénodet is an ancient farmhouse by a stream that the Builbault family has converted into one of Brittany's finest restaurants. The chef's trademark are his inventive sauces that accompany seafood so fresh that the hook has barely been wrenched from its mouth. Closed Wednesdays (except for lunch in July and August), Thursdays for lunch, and mid-October through February. Major credit cards accepted. In Letty, about 1½ miles (3 km) southeast of Bénodet (phone: 98-57-01-27). Expensive to moderate.

Grand – Of the various Concarneau hostelries, this old-fashioned 33-room inn, on a busy corner overlooking the port bristling with ships, is most convenient to the *ville close.* Closed from October to *Easter.* Major credit cards accepted. 1 Av. Pierre-Guéguin, Concarneau (phone: 98-97-00-28). Inexpensive.

EATING OUT: *Le Galion* – The velvet curtains on the windows and the white linen and silver and crystal on the tables contrast strikingly with the low rough beams and rugged granite walls of this lovely, one-Michelin-star establishment. But attractive though the atmosphere may be, it's the food that constitutes the real draw — mainly seafood that seems to have come straight out of the surf. The chef excels when he uses his imagination, as in the *civet de lotte* (a stew made from monkfish), the *fricassée de langoustine* (lobster stew), the *coquilles Saint-Jacques grillé au cumin* (sea scallops grilled with cumin), and the *turbot braisé avec* *champagne* (turbot with champagne). Closed Sunday evenings and Mondays except in summer, and also 3 weeks in November and mid-January to March. Major credit cards accepted. In the *ville close*, 15 Rue St-Guénolé, Concarneau (phone: 98-97-30-16; fax: 98-50-67-88). Expensive to moderate.

QUIMPER: Sprawling though it is, with a population of nearly 61,000, there still is something of the sleepy Breton village in this city, whose name in Breton (*kemp-er*, "junction") refers to the meeting point of the placid Steir and the Odet rivers in the town. Narrow streets miraculously spared damage during the war angle this way and that between tall half-timbered houses whose second stories are cantilevered out over the street. Walk through the old section of the city, following the Rue Elie Fréron, the Place au Beurre, the Rue du Sallé (with many restored structures), the Rue de Kerguelen, the Rue Valentin, the Place Mesgloaguen, the Rue St-Nicolas, the Rue des Gentilshommes, the Rue des Boucheries (Butchers' Street, which once ran with the blood of slaughtered animals), and the Rue du Guéodet (distinguished by a house whose ground floor is guarded by caryatids in antique costumes). Fairly detailed maps and guided walking tours (in warm weather) are available at the town's tourist office (Pl. Résistance; phone: 98-93-04-05). The whole area is full of boutiques purveying carved wood, embroideries, Breton musical instruments, regional clothing, handwoven cloth, its world-famous *faïence*, and more. If nothing else, Quimper is Brittany's best regional shopping center outside the major cities.

At the heart of the town and only a block from the graceful tree-lined quais of the Odet and the Rue Ste-Catherine, where one of a half-dozen bridges lace together the riverbanks is the Cathédrale St-Corentin, rather clunky and awkwardly proportioned compared to the one in Nantes but worth seeing nonetheless. The structure is named for the legendary spiritual adviser of the good King Gradlon, who is said to have subsisted on the meat of a single perpetually regenerating fish; he also is, incidentally, one of a handful of Breton saints not recognized by Rome. The church was erected between the 13th and the 15th century except for its pair of 250-foot towers, which were built in 1856 with funds provided by some 600,000 diocesans — each paying one *sou* annually for 5 years. Inside, note that the choir and the nave are out of alignment — possibly a result of some construction problem, though no one knows for sure. There are some richly colored stained glass windows. Sunday visitors are in for a treat: The organ is one of the best in Brittany, and after high mass, the air fairly vibrates with its chords.

Immediately adjacent, in the 16th-century bishop's palace, is the *Musée Départemental Breton* (1 Rue Roi Gradlon; phone: 98-95-21-60; closed Mondays and Tuesdays in low season, and from October to late March), with displays of Breton pottery, musical instruments, embroidered regional dresses and starched *coiffes,* and furnishings of lower Brittany. The carvings on the furniture demonstrate the considerable skill attained by rude Breton woodworkers; the resemblance of the ornamentation on a 19th-century *coffre à blé* (wheat storage chest) near the entrance to that often found in Great Britain and Ireland emphasizes Brittany's ties to Celtic culture — and is uniquely appropriate to an institution based, as this one is, in the capital of the region named La Cornouaille by its original settlers, who came from Cornwall, England. Also interesting is the Quimper ceramics display, which shows its development from the very crude to the extremely refined and illustrates the evolution of the *petits bretons* (little Bretons) which have been found on almost every traditional Quimper plate from their debut in the 1880s to the present.

This white ceramicware, painted in blue and yellow with Breton figures and flowers and fruits, has been one of the city's primary claims to fame since the 17th century, when artisans came from Rouen and elsewhere to work in the Quimper potteries, and it is featured in nearly every prominent shop window in the older part of town. Guided tours of the factories that produce them also are available. Contact the *Faïenceries de Quimper Henriot* (Rue Haut; phone: 98-90-09-36) or the *Faïenceries Keraluc* (71 Rue du Président Sadat; phone: 98-53-04-500. Both are closed on weekends except in July and August, when *Keraluc* is open on Saturdays.

It's also pleasant to board a boat for the 3-hour round trip down the forest- and cliff-edged Odet as far as the slick resort of Bénodet at its mouth. Also note that the restored *Musée des Beaux-Arts* boasts one of the best collections of paintings in provincial France; works from the Italian, Spanish, Flemish, and Dutch schools hang next to paintings by members of the Pont-Aven School and others who took their inspiration primarily from Breton scenes. (Closed Tuesdays; Pl. St-Gorentin; phone: 98-95-45-20.)

Visitors expecting to arrive the week ending the fourth Sunday in July should plan to attend the important week-long *Festival de Cornouaille,* which has been preserving and promoting Breton music and dance since 1923.

 CHECKING IN: *Tour d'Auvergne* – A block from the Odet River, this older but renovated establishment boasts a subdued 1930s look that has been updated in many of the 45 guest quarters by warm, country-like red wallpaper. Bathrooms generally are commodious. There also is a restaurant. Closed over the *Christmas* and *New Year* holidays. Major credit cards accepted. 13 Rue des Réguaires, Quimper (phone: 98-95-08-70; fax: 98-95-17-31). Moderate to inexpensive.

EATING OUT: *Les Acacias* – One of Quimper's newer restaurants, this is a good place for solid, substantial seafood dishes. The prix fixe menus are a bargain. Major credit cards accepted. Closed Sunday evenings and Mondays. 88 Blvd. Créach-Gwen (phone: 98-52-15-20). Moderate.

PONT-L'ABBÉ: The area around this town of about 7,700 offers plenty of exceptions to the rule that traditional Breton costumes — the richly embroidered velvet skirts, lace aprons, and starched white *coiffes* — seldom are seen nowadays, even in the country. Here, not only do the old women wear their Bigouden costume to the town's *pardon* in mid-July, but they also can frequently be seen pedaling bicycles down lonely lanes at dusk, piling fruits and vegetables into net shopping bags on market day, or trudging to Mass on a Sunday, their black velvet skirts swishing and their wondrously tall headdresses bobbing with their every movement. The town's 14th-to-17th-century fortress-château has a museum that displays a collection of the historical versions of these colorful outfits. (Closed from October to May; admission charge; phone: 98-87-24-44.) *La Maison du Pays Bigouden,* at the edge of Pont-L'Abbé, is an outdoor museum that is a reconstruction of a turn-of-the-century Bigouden farm. Closed Sundays, holidays, and from October through May. Admission charge (phone: 98-87-35-63).

CHECKING IN: *Bretagne* – When 18 rooms were installed on the upper floors of this longtime favorite local restaurant a few years ago, the friendly proprietors let themselves be guided by their excellent taste and paid great attention to details such as flowered wallpapers and spacious bathrooms. Simple, but a real find. Closed 2 weeks in January. Major credit cards accepted. 24 Pl. de la République, Pont-L'Abbé (phone: 98-87-17-22). Moderate to inexpensive.

Château de Kernuz – Reached by a winding, tree-lined lane with stone farm buildings huddling up next to the stone wall that bounds the property on one side, this comfortable 16th-century establishment with 16 recently renovated rooms and a pool has wonderful salons full of antiques, chandeliers, beamed ceilings with refined paneling, and massive hearths big enough to make a playhouse for a fourth-grader. Closed October to April. Demi-pension is required in July and August. Major credit cards accepted. 1½ miles (2 km) from Pont-L'Abbé on N785, Route de Penmarch (phone: 98-87-01-59). Moderate.

Ker Ansquer – A traditional stone house with a rustic, familial charm, this inn has 11 rooms, a dining room, and a roaring fireplace. The sea is only a few miles away. Closed October to May. Major credit cards accepted. Pouldreuzic-Lababan (phone: 98-54-41-83). Moderate to inexpensive.

EATING OUT: *Relais de Ty Boutic* – Light, fresh foods, such as *langoustines à la fondue de poireau* (Dublin Bay prawns with leek sauce), served by an innovative chef about 2 miles (3 km) from town. Closed Mondays and February. Major credit cards accepted. Rte. de Plomeur, Pont-L'Abbé (phone: 98-87-03-90). Moderate.

En Route from Pont-L'Abbé – The west coast of Brittany offers a study in the many meanings of the word "shoreline." Le Guilivinec, a fairly undistinguished commercial fishing port, is worth a detour around 5 PM, when the sardine and tuna boats come into port and the fishermen unload their catch. There is no question that fishing is important throughout the area; that it has been so historically is evident in Penmarch, where the doorways of the 16th-century Flamboyant Gothic St. Nonna's Church are embellished with carved reliefs of the ships of the wealthy merchants who built it. The Pointe de Penmarch, when low tides reveal a liberal scattering of smooth, sea-pounded rocks that might be cliffs squashed flat as pancakes, offers a vision of one of the types of coastline with which Breton sailors have always had to contend. Rising above it are the two lighthouses that have been warning sailors to steer clear of these waters ever since the 19th century; one of them, the Phare d'Eckmuhl, can often be toured. From its 213-foot-high gallery, it's possible to see nearly the length of the coastline in fine weather; half a dozen lighthouses can be seen in a single glance.

From here, D80 hugs the water's edge as far as the resort of St-Guénolé, where there still are more boulders along the shore. At high tide, when the surf is beating against them, it's easier to envision that a great wave could come along and sweep away a whole family, an event of 1870 commemorated by an iron cross attached to one of the rocks. The road turns inward, and the sea becomes accessible only by spur roads from a larger highway like D57 until Pouldreuzic, where D40 turns westward to Penhors. Site of the annual *pardon* of Notre-Dame-de-Penhors on September 8, one of the largest in Cornouaille, the area is thronged with the faithful, who join a procession through the countryside to the shoreline for a blessing of the sea. The unnumbered northbound continuation of D40 passes through charming tiny villages like Keristenvet, Plozévet, and Ports-Poulan before turning inland again.

At Audierne, an attractive small fishing port at the base of a woodsy hillside on the Goyen River estuary, lovers of Breton folklore will want to stop on the Quai Pelletan, not far from the beach, to see La Chaumière (the Thatched Cottage), where wonderful 17th- and 18th-century carved oak furniture has been set up to suggest the interior of an old Breton cottage (open in July and August; 5 Rue Amiral Guepratte; phone: 98-70-12-20). Here, too, a traveler anxious to get far away from it all can catch the 90-minute boat trip (there is at least one daily trip if the weather permits, with three trips daily during July and August) to the wild, bare, and rocky Ile de Sein (Island of the Breast). The reclusive islanders are known for their bravery, not only for confronting the often treacherous sea and carving a living out of this bare island, but for their steadfast patriotism. During World War II, when General de Gaulle, then in London, broadcast an appeal for volunteer French troops to join him to mount an assault on the occupying German forces in France, all 150 able-bodied men of the Ile de Sein (except for the mayor and the curé) left for England. When De Gaulle later gave a roll call of his 600 new volunteers, asking where each was from, 150 answered "Ile de Sein." De Gaulle responded *"Sein, est-il-donc le quart de la France?"* (Does Sein make up a quarter of France?).

CHECKING IN/EATING OUT: *Le Goyen* – This gracious, 34-room establishment (another member of the Relais & Châteaux group), right on the harbor in Audierne and decorated in fine French style, is clean, well-kept, and very comfortable. Out in front there is a long front porch, brightened with pots of geraniums and plenty of white chairs, on which to while away a summer afternoon. It also boasts a first-rate restaurant that earned one Michelin star for specialties like mushrooms in walnut oil sauce and lobster sautéed with mushrooms or in tarragon sauce. The chef follows his whim and the market offerings, so there's always something new. Closed from mid-November to February; closed Mondays and Tuesday lunch off-season. Major credit cards accepted. Pl. Jean-Simon, Audierne (phone: 98-70-08-88). Hotel, moderate; restaurant, expensive to moderate.

POINTE DU RAZ: A far more common destination for travelers leaving Audierne is the Pointe du Raz, a mass of craggy, tumbled cliffs and rocks assembled to look like the fin of a prehistoric animal. It is habitually battered by the sea with a ferocity that prompted Baudelaire to exclaim: *"Nul n'a passé le Raz sans peur ou sans douleur"* ("No one has passed through the Raz without fear or pain"). The two good sized parking lots and the square full of rinky-tinky souvenir shops only begin to suggest the popularity of the spot. But even when there is not a single free space and the area guides have their hands full of tourists wanting to sign up for one of the walking tours along the footpaths that squiggle to the sea, the grandeur of the scene is undeniable. The Baie des Trépassés (Bay of the Dead), to the right of the headland, is believed to have been the point of embarkation for druids bound for the Ile de Sein to bury their dead. Legend has it that the town of Is, the beautiful capital of Cornouaille at the time of the good King Gradlon, was inundated offshore.

En Route from Pointe du Raz – There are equally scenic points at the end of the spur roads from D7 to Douarnenez — notably the Pointe du Van, less overwhelming than Raz and accessible only by a half-hour's walk, but a good deal more peaceful; and the Pointe de Brézellac, farther along, where the viewing area is close to the road.

DOUARNENEZ: Businesslike Douarnenez, a town of about 18,000 with packing plants and efficient docks, offers a certain respite from touristy Raz. The quays are lined with straightforward bars with names like *Le Voyageur* and *Le Navigateur,* meant for sailors. A stop at the New Port, which looks more industrial than nautical with its seawalls, ramps, and warehouses, offers another look at the seafaring life while its jetty provides a broad view of the town's namesake bay. Visitors who pass through Douarnenez in the morning should make a point of pausing at the open-air market near the Place Gabriel-Péri, where ladies in *coiffes* sometimes can be seen. Boat lovers should not miss the *Musée du Bateau* (Pl. de l'Enfer; phone: 98-92-65-20), with its fascinating marine memorabilia. Open daily from 10 AM to noon and 2 to 7 PM.

Offering another view of the craggy coast to the west are the harbor cruises (phone: 98-27-09-54 or 98-92-10-38), available from June through September, which visit the seabird refuge, the Réserve de Cap Sizun; pass by the Grottes de Lanvilo, hollowed out by the sea; and take in Ile Tristan, the legendary setting for the palace of King Mark of Cornwall. His nephew, Prince Tristan, was sent to Ireland to fetch his bride, Iseult. But the pair accidentally consumed a love potion intended to cement Mark's own union. Breton fancies embroider the end: Some people say that Tristan is murdered by Mark. Others marry off Tristan and Iseult and let them live happily ever after.

CHECKING IN: *Auberge de Kervéoc'h* – On the fringes of a decidedly workaday town such as Douarnenez, this snug and very attractive 14-room hostelry in an old stone farmhouse, deep in a country where the only sound is the twittering of the birds, comes as quite a surprise. The adaptation was executed in the best 20th-century style — juxtaposing the beauty of the stone walls, great beams, and massive fireplaces with the most up-to-date oatmeal-colored Berber carpet, slanted ceilings, and skylights. Good hard beds are the frosting on the cake. Closed from mid-October to *Easter*. Major credit cards accepted. Rte. de Kervéoc'h, 2½ miles (4 km) from Douarnenez on the Rte. de Quimper (phone: 98-92-07-58). Moderate to inexpensive.

LOCRONAN: Some visitors find this little inland town too pretty to be real; others lament the number of tourists who clog its narrow lanes and tiny craft stores and boutiques throughout the season. Nonetheless, if you have time to visit only one of Brittany's inland towns during your stay, it probably should be this one.

It is an enchanting village, a real gem. Its perfectly preserved 16th-to-17th-century square is rimmed by old houses built of granite gone mossy with age, brightened with pots of geraniums, and punctuated by a small old well where a handful of children usually can be seen peering over the edge. And the 15th- to 16th-century Eglise et Chapelle du Pénity forms a relatively simple ensemble that strikes just the right note in the setting.

Inside are several statues, some carved out of relatively soft Kersanton granite by a busy local workshop of the 17th century, and others made from wood — Christopher the ferryman with the baby Jesus on his strong shoulders, Barbara and her tower, Fiacre with his spade, the Virgin Mary, and others; the most notable is the one sculpted in Kersanton granite on the tomb of St. Ronan, an Irish bishop who came to the area (and gave it his name) in search of a solitary environment in which to lead a life of self-denial and mortification during the Viking invasions of the 9th century. Tradition has it that passing underneath the statue, which is supported by a sextet of yard-high figures also carved from granite, will suppress symptoms of arthritis. On the pulpit, be sure to note the series of paintings that tell the story of St. Ronan's arrival in the area, his conversion of a peasant, his persecution by neighbors and by the peasant's wife, his rescue of a child from the dead, and his ultimate defeat of the devil. The very fortunate traveler will arrive at the church when the rich, sonorous organ is being played.

Just as much of the history of Locronan is bound up with St. Ronan, so too the physical town owes its current appearance to the weaving business that flourished here between the 16th and 18th centuries. The architectural harmony of the square and the richness of the ecclesiastical embellishments are the legacy of the prosperous times — when literally acres of sailcloth were shipped to England, Spain, and Holland, among other places — and their preservation is mainly a result of the poverty of the village in the intervening years. The town was so poor by the beginning of the 19th century that when the church steeple collapsed, struck by lightning, the villagers could not afford to rebuild it and had no recourse but to finish pulling it down. This abject poverty has been eroded by the influx of tourists, and the old houses and other granite structures have now been given over to shops where the merchandise, mainly handwovens and hand-knits and other one-of-a-kind wares, is decidedly above average. These, together with a handful of studios where craftsmen can be seen at their looms and workbenches, are scattered on the perimeter of the main square and along the streets and narrow alleyways leading from it.

Locronan is also the site of an elaborate *pardon* at which pilgrims follow the path to the top of the Mountain of Locronan that St. Ronan, barefoot and fasting, used during his life in the area. Cars can drive up the mountain throughout the year, and there's a small chapel with pretty stained glass windows and a fine view over the area at the top. But it is more colorful during the *pardons* — both the minor ones held on the second Sunday in July most years and the larger "Grande Troménie," as the procession is called, when the route is extended to 7 miles and broken up with 12 stops, held in mid-July every 6 years; the next will take place in 1995.

CHECKING IN/EATING OUT: *Hôtel au Fer à Cheval* – "The Horseshoe" is handsome and contemporary if not particularly endowed with charming atmosphere of the establishment's sister restaurant on the Locronan square — itself quite acceptable and decidedly friendly, considering its location in the heart of one of the most heavily visited villages in Brittany. All 35 rooms are modern and have a television set. Closed Mondays. Major credit cards accepted. Rte. du Bois-de-Nevet-Locronan, Locronan (phone: 98-91-70-67). Moderate.

Hôtel du Prieuré – Part of the Logis de France group of rural *gîtes* and *auberges*, this typical Breton 14-room inn has rugged wood beams, flowered wallpaper, chenille bedspreads and a restaurant. Closed Mondays in off-season and October. Major credit cards accepted. 11 Rue Prieuré, Locronan (phone: 98-91-70-89). Moderate to inexpensive.

Manoir de Moëllien – Just outside Locronan to the northwest is this charming hotel and restaurant, snugly situated in the peaceful countryside. All 10 finely furnished rooms look out upon bucolic settings, and the restaurant specializes in simple yet elegant seafood dishes. Closed Wednesdays in the off-season, and January through March. Reservations advised. Major credit cards accepted. Plonerez-Porzay (phone: 98-92-50-40; fax: 98-92-55-21). Moderate.

En Route from Locronan – Follow D63 to Plonévez-Porzay, then take D61 to Ste-Anne-la-Palud, where a 19th-century chapel peers out over the flattest of seaside meadows, gilded beautifully in summer by little yellow flowers. Every year, on the last Sunday of August, the area is the setting for a massive Breton *pardon* to which the faithful come in such numbers that the narrow roads become nearly impassable. From here, go inland again to Ploeven and turn toward the sea and travel through St-Sébastien to Lestrevet, the southernmost crossroads settlement along the Lieu de Grève (Place of Seashore), where there is a remarkable long, wide, straight, flat, Atlantic-pounded strand on one side of the road and an expanse of green pastures on the other.

Next, turn toward St-Nic and travel through some wide open country patched with fields and strips of trees. Then take D108 for about 2 miles (3 km) and D887 for about a third of a mile in the direction of Châteaulin to the turnoff for the steep D83, which ascends the Menez-Hom; its utterly bald, windswept, 1,082-foot summit is one of the finest viewing points in the province. On cloudy days, you won't see a thing; don't even bother to leave the main road. The rest of the time, it is possible to see Locronan Mountain, Douarnenez, Van Point, and more. A viewing table identifies them all.

CHECKING IN/EATING OUT: *Hôtel de la Plage* – Embraced on one side by the gorgeous Lieu de Grève and nuzzled by a garden and a couple of handsome cypress trees, this charming white stucco hostelry (a Relais & Châteaux member) is tranquil as can be. There's a pool and tennis and sunsets to admire (right from your room if it faces west). The good food (one Michelin star) — lamb with a tarragon cream sauce, frozen raspberry soufflé, and other items according to the chef's inspiration — is the bonus. Closed from mid-October through March. Major credit cards accepted. On the beach in Ste-Anne-la-Palud (phone: 98-92-50-12; fax: 98-92-56-54). Expensive.

Relais de Porz-Morvan – Staying at this hostelry, whose clean and comfortable if not particularly stylish 12 rooms were installed in a granite farmhouse and the neighboring stables, is a reason for winnowing your way into the most rural heart of the Breton countryside. Absolute quiet reigns. Tennis, too. The adjacent *crêperie*, which displays a collection of Breton antiques that only adds to the coziness, serves fine crêpes. The specialty of the house, crêpes stuffed with apples and flamed with calvados, is worth a try. Closed October to *Easter*. Visa accepted. 1¼ miles (2 km) from Plomodiern (phone: 98-81-53-23). Moderate.

CROZON PENINSULA: Route D887 — a fine road that races through sweeping fields and pastures full of black and white cows — leads west onto this peninsula, another grand Breton meeting ground for sea and sky. Each of the handful of rock-bound points begs to be explored: the most southerly, the Cap de la Chèvre (the Headland of the Goat), which pushes across Douarnenez Bay toward the Pointe du Van and the Pointe de Brézellac and their neighbors on the Raz peninsula; the somewhat more impressive Pointe de Dinan, which ends in a rather castle-like rock formation; and the most northerly, the Pointe des Espagnols, on the end of a peninsula that boasts shoreline roads with exceptional scenery.

Those who have time to see only one should head toward the Pointe de Penhir, where there are high cliffs from whose edge the sea is 229 feet away — straight down. It is perpetually windy on these heights, the view is nothing but grand, and it would be easy to spend a couple of hours here clambering over the rocks or, on a weekday in the off-season, celebrating life with a picnic.

Of the trio of small towns on the peninsula, Camaret is most notable. It seems a random little place, neither rich nor obviously poor but simply utilitarian. It is well known as one of the most important French lobster ports, a fact confirmed by the abundance of boats in the harbor, although a dramatic decline in the catch has been reported for the past few years, and the town is turning more and more to tourism for its livelihood. There also is a building by the 17th-century military architect Vauban, a castle-like, red stucco structure full of slits that now houses a naval museum, and, nearby, a very simple, yellowish chapel, the Chapelle de Notre-Dame de Roc'h-Ama-dour, where a *pardon* is held every year on the first Sunday in September. With the rotting wooden ships left foundering on their sides like beached whales by the low tide, the whole scene is picturesque enough to warrant a detour. On the outskirts of town are the Lagatiar menhirs, megalithic standing stones arranged in a semicircle. Even awkwardly situated opposite some nondescript vacation houses, these boulders exert a deep Celtic power. A visit to the beaches at Toulinguet and Very'ach will reveal particularly beautiful and unspoiled vistas.

En Route from the Crozon Peninsula – Head back to D887 and thence to D791. This fast road ribbons through the woods, crosses the Aulne River and follows the coast (plenty of good views), and traverses tiny Le Faou, where you should watch for D42 in the direction of Rumengol, where *pardons* are held throughout the year. Route D42 then winds through the hilly Forêt de Cranou, whose oak and beech woods eventually give way to the great windswept plateaus of the Parc Naturel Régional d'Armorique, which preserves the Arrée Mountains. These are not high — only 1,200 feet at the most, their once lofty peaks ground down and eroded to hills by the ages — but they seem elevated enough thanks to their barren windswept summits and the wide open vistas they provide when clouds are not swirling around their summits.

At Croas-ar-Go, turn left onto D342 and make your way to Sizun, which has the first of a handful of parish closes. This one has an organ (1683–84) whose carved and gilded case compares favorably with the most beautiful baroque instruments in central Europe. Its builder, the Englishman Thomas Dallam, had come to work in Brittany with his father, Robert, who was fleeing persecution by Queen Elizabeth I. Go north on D764 as far as Lanviguer, then turn north toward La Roche-Maurice. At La Martyre there is another parish close, where *pardons* are held on the second Sunday in May and July. Note the angels carved on the archway that frames the Nativity scene above the porch. Next, turn right on D35 toward Ploudiry, whose parish close has a bizarre ossuary on whose façade a Dance of Death is carved in relief.

LAMPAUL-GUIMILIAU: The parish close in this otherwise insignificant inland town is most notable for the incredible richness of the decoration inside the 16th-to-17th-century church. The idea seems to have been to cover every square inch of wall with ornamentation — not merely idle decoration but also a sort of bible for the poor. Woodcarving, for instance, covers both sides of a 16th-century rood beam overhead, where angels catch the blood dripping from the feet of the crucified Christ; blankets the 18th-century pulpit; and overlays two panels flanking the altar. Particularly notable is an altarpiece divided into eight compartments, each one containing a scene from the Passion packed with figures carved with such skill that they almost seem to move. In addition, at the front of the church are lively paintings that portray square faces distinctive enough, one from the other, to suggest that they were modeled from life, and with formidable skill.

GUIMILIAU: This former weaving center is named for a good and pious 8th-century prince who was decapitated after 7 years on the throne at the instigation of his evil brother. With a population of only about 800, it is even smaller than Lampaul-Guimiliau. But its parish close, which includes a 16th-century church whose style foreshadows the Renaissance as well as several other structures, is even more striking. There literally are dozens of statuettes in the church. On the Renaissance porch, the arch that forms its entrance is articulated with three rows of figures representing angels and saints, and the corners seem to be sprouting curious gargoyles that look like bearded dragons. Inside the porch, both walls are lined with niches occupied by statues representing the 12 apostles; other figures, depicting scenes from the Old Testament, alternate with rose medallions in an ornamental frieze below. In one, a monk-exorcist stands near a grimacing sinner above whose head is a horned devil; in another, God can be seen pulling Eve by the arm out of the side of a sleeping Adam.

The large 16th-century calvary is adorned by some 200 figures. Many depict scenes from Christ's life, but there also are local motifs such as the story of Catell-Gollet or Catherine la Perdue (Catherine the Lost), a servant girl who steals a consecrated Host as a present for her lover, actually the devil in disguise, and is subsequently condemned to all manner of hellish tortures. Young women with flirtation on their minds were meant to take note. The images are arranged on two levels, each of which seems to have been sculpted by a different artisan; the bodies of the lower statues seem dry and rigid and a bit naive, particularly in comparison to those outlined against the sky on the upper level, which are so full of curves and so dynamic that they seem almost ready to march off.

Be sure to note the late-17th-century baptismal font inside the church, one of the most exuberant pieces of carved oak anywhere in Brittany. Garlands, leaves, vines, tiny birds pecking at berries, saints, evangelists, angels, and more, embellish the structure. The organ and the pulpit, supported by a column comprised of four cherubs, are also elaborately ornamented. A visitor might find the same sumptuous carving in a great cathedral. But here, as at Lampaul-Guimiliau, the profusion of work is concentrated in a relatively limited space, so a sense of the talent and energy of the artists who wrought the wonders is brought home all the more clearly.

ST-THÉGONNEC: Another magnificent Breton parish close can be found in the center of this little town. Note the calvary, built in 1610; the Passion is depicted on the base. The figure in the niche underneath is of St. Thégonnec, who is portrayed with a cart to which he harnessed a wolf after his donkey had been consumed by its fellows. The town's namesake also is portrayed over the porch of the church and in a niche above the pulpit inside. The figure bearing a trumpet atop the canopy is the Angel of Judgment.

The organ has been classed as a historical monument since December 1973. Ordered in 1670, it was the subject of a pair of suits — one by a local noblewoman, who insisted that her coat of arms be put on the organ case rather than on the bay window at the rear of the church, the other by the men of the church, who complained that the factory had not delivered a satisfactory instrument. The suits only increased its cost, and the organ had to be rebuilt by another manufactory before finally being installed in 1684. It was restored and transformed on a regular basis for the next 2 centuries. Far from harming the sound, these restorations, together with the most recent one (1978), only enhanced the original, so that now the instrument has a sonority all its own, as rich as the gilded carvings that encase it. Lucky are the travelers who arrive when an organist or a student is playing. Note the images on the console — among them Ste. Cécilia, the patroness of musicians.

CHECKING IN: *Chez Madame Kergadallan* – A comfortable bed and breakfast establishment with 3 neatly appointed rooms. Closed 1 month in winter. Most major credit cards accepted. 20 Av. Kérizella, St-Thégonnec (phone: 98-79-63-86 or 98-79-65-30).

EATING OUT: *L'Auberge St-Thégonnec* – *Mille-feuille de coquilles St-Jacques au safran* (scallops with saffron in puff pastry) and *homard à la crème* (lobster in cream sauce) are just a few of the dishes that have established this inn's culinary reputation. There also are 20 rooms. Closed Sunday evenings and Mondays in off-season and from *Christmas* to mid-January. Reservations essential in summer. Major credit cards accepted. St-Thégonnec (phone: 98-79-61-18; fax: 98-62-71-10). Moderate to inexpensive.

Crêperie Steredenn – Large photographs of Breton scenes decorate the stone walls here. A fire crackles in the huge hearth and, at dusk, throws a warm, flickering light on the low beamed ceiling. Breton and Irish music play on a sleek stereo tucked away in a vast oak armoire. Without question, this neat, friendly establishment rates kudos as one of the most pleasant *crêperies* in the province. Particularly tasty is the *crêpe druidique* — slathered with bitter orange marmalade and almonds flavored with Grand Marnier. Just up a hill on a street leading from the parish close. Open Fridays, Saturdays, and Sundays off-season. Major credit cards accepted. 6 Rue de la Gare, St-Thégonnec (phone: 98-79-43-34). Inexpensive.

En Route from St-Thégonnec – Take N12 west and D230 and D30 north to the coast. In contrast to the wild shoreline terrain in southern Brittany, this area is fertile — with fields of cauliflowers and artichokes that stand up straight as if looking out to sea. Sometimes you even can smell the vegetables in the fields. The unnumbered coast road takes in farm settlements like Forban, Poulfoën, Kervaliou, Moguériec, and Santec. Even these insignificant hamlets seem to have their imposing granite churches, their perforated belfries shooting high into the horizon. Even a slight rise in the road opens up a huge panorama. In Roscoff, an attractive resort center with shops selling *vêtements marins* (seafaring clothes) and a pretty harbor fixed up with new landscaping and contemporary lampposts, there is regular ferry service to the Ile de Batz, itself little more than a quaint village undiscovered by tourists, with huge stretches of coastline that cry out for picnickers. Ferry service to Cork, in the Irish Republic, and to Plymouth, England, is also available from Roscoff. Bonny Prince Charlie took refuge here after his abortive attempt to gain the English crown in 1746.

CHECKING IN/EATING OUT: *Brittany* – The dining salon has stone floors, walls made of huge granite blocks, and a baronial fireplace; the bar is done up with red tartans; there are crystal chandeliers and an overall air of stateliness about the lobby; and the 23 rooms, in a tower in the back, have balconies, views, and the 20th-century comforts appropriate for a middle class clientele. This property adjoins a small pebbly beach. Closed off-season. Major credit cards accepted. Bd. Ste-Barbe, Roscoff (phone: 98-69-70-78; fax: 98-69-23-74). Expensive to moderate.

Gulf Stream – Fresh seafood, often innovatively sauced with something like a cucumber purée or made into a terrine encased in aspic, is the specialty at the restaurant of this recently renovated, 32-room establishment, which overlooks a great sweep of Roscoff's bay. Closed from late October to April. Major credit cards accepted. Rue Marquise-de-Kergariou, Roscoff (phone: 98-69-73-19; fax: 98-60-11-89). Hotel, moderate; restaurant, expensive to moderate.

ST-POL-DE-LÉON: Between January and September, the modern market here bustles with activity as tractor trailers, vans, carts, and vehicles of all descriptions haul in artichokes, cauliflowers, onions, potatoes, and other vegetables from the fertile fields that surround the town. This is France's largest wholesale vegetable market. This commerce adds another dimension to what is already a very worthwhile place to visit.

The chief attractions of the town, which was named for a Celtic religious leader who came here from Britain in the 5th century, are two ecclesiastical structures. The Cathédrale de St-Pol-de-Léon, built between the 13th and the 16th century, is especially elegant, in part because of its fine proportions, in part because of the use of Norman limestone, whose pale hue lends a lightness to the interior. There is a beautiful 15th-century rose window, whose bright colors often are thrown on the polished wood floor of the sanctuary. Note the wooden statue of Ste. Apolline, now the patron saint of dentists, whose torturers pulled out all her teeth. Just to the rear of the sanctuary are a few rows of skulls, collected by families to keep relics of the dead formerly buried in the cemetery; some are enclosed in boxes ornamented by heart-shaped perforations that reveal a bit of bone inside. The carved oak bishops' stalls are also very fine. The organ dates from the 17th and 19th centuries.

The Kreisker Chapel, down the road a short distance and now part of a boys' school, is known for its tall belfry set at the transept crossing, made to seem even taller than its 246 feet by the vertical tracery articulating the windows. Inspired by the spire of St. Peter's in Caen, Normandy, which was destroyed during the war, it has itself been the inspiration for many others. The tall steeple at the top is stabilized by four bell towers; the whole structure is supported inside by a stone vault joining four massive uprights. The rest of the roof inside is of wood.

En Route from St-Pol-de-Léon – The narrow roads that hug the coast, with their vistas of ocean and artichokes, are the most scenic way to travel south. Farm compounds and resort communities, which nudge each other like the black and white squares of a chessboard, add still more variety. Particularly on a sunny day, a traveler making a hurried tour of Brittany yearns for an extra couple of days in which to sprawl in the sun on a pretty stone terrace or to stroll along a promenade by the sea. Carantec, on a point well off the highways and all the more pleasant as a result, is particularly delightful (although the lovely beaches here can become quite crowded in July and August). The roads that wind through the residential areas are almost too narrow for even a single tiny French vehicle. Houses crowded with hydrangeas are angled this way and that to maximize the minuscule amount of space. There are fine views, like the one from the Pointe de Pen-Lan.

Going south, D73 toward Locquénolé hugs the west shore of the Morlaix estuary, crossing gently rolling countryside occasionally patched with trees. Now and then you can see a sailboat chugging back to its moorings at Morlaix or out to sea for a day on the water. By the time D73 joins D769, the estuary has narrowed to the dimensions of a stream. High cliffs line it on one side and a wooded slope plunges on the other.

CHECKING IN: *La Falaise* – The yachtsmen who often patronize this small stucco and brick hotel set quietly on a high cliff above the Bay of Morlaix give the place a particularly relaxed air, and the rosy-cheeked proprietor adds the perfect touch of friendliness. The 24 guestrooms are simple and clean with high ceilings. Closed from mid-September to mid-May. No credit cards accepted. Plage de Kélenn, Carantec (phone: 98-67-00-53). Inexpensive.

***Pors-Pol* –** This very simple family hotel, set in a residential neighborhood, provides

30 rooms with sea views and a small beach nearby. Closed from late September to late March. No credit cards accepted. 7 Rue Surcouf, Carantec (phone: 98-67 00-52). Inexpensive.

MORLAIX: Typical of many towns of the same size (pop. 20,000), this erstwhile port dominating the estuary of its namesake river boasts an extremely handsome Old Quarter with narrow, twisting streets and lanes, row upon row of houses dating from the days of half-timbers through the 19th century, and fashionable shops purveying shoes, faïences (ceramic ware), clothing, and antiques. Especially noteworthy are the Grand'-Rue, the Place Salvador Allende, the Place des Jacobins, and the Place des Viarmes. The corbelled 16th-century Maison de la Reine Anne, whose overhanging half-timbered second story seems to be supported by caryatids carved in the form of saints, is on the Rue de Mûr, which parallels the Grand'Rue.

What makes Morlaix different is its topography — immense hills that demand perpetual downshifting in the car. From the topmost of the city's tiers, there are fine views of the estuary and the Old Town not far away. There is also a mammoth 2-story viaduct across the Morlaix. Measuring 190 feet in height and 935 feet in length, it can be seen from most open areas in the city.

CHECKING IN: *Europe* – A traditional, recently renovated 66-room hotel, with a restaurant whose chef, Olivier Brignou, is considered one of France's most promising young talents. His preparations are classical, yet original, served in elegant surroundings. Major credit cards accepted. 1 Rue Aiguillon, Morlaix (phone: 98-62-11-99; fax: 98-88-83-38). Hotel, moderate; restaurant, expensive.

EATING OUT: *La Marée Bleue* – In an old stone building that has been renovated to reflect contemporary design, the food is fully the equal of the extremely gracious reception accorded to guests. Seafood and fish are presented either plain or with the kinds of sauces that are simply not found in every Breton restaurant. The lengthy, detailed wine list is an education in its own right. Closed Sunday evenings, Mondays and February. Visa accepted. 3 Rampe St-Mélaine, Morlaix (phone: 98-63-24-21). Moderate.

One unusual attraction in Morlaix is the local beer, Coreff, a dark beer made in the old-fashioned way and sold in several cafés. The brewery can be visited on wednesdays and Thursdays all year; call ahead for an appointment. *Brasserie des Deux Rivières,* 1 Place de la Madeleine (phone: 98-63-41-92).

HUELGOAT: Breton scenery lovers come here by the score to walk through the forests to which the woodsy scenery along D769 from Morlaix provides a good introduction, and to see the unusual arrangements of huge sandstone and granite boulders, some coated with intensely green moss, which are tumbled through the woods and along the little Argent River in ways that have suggested names like Chaos du Moulin (Mill Rock Chaos), Grotte du Diable (Devil's Grotto), Ménage de la Vierge (Virgin's Household), Roche Tremblante (Trembling Rock), and others. The latter, which weighs in at about 100 tons, can be made to sway on its base if you push hard enough. Great oaks, beeches, and spruce and pine trees tower over these landmarks, which are reached by well-marked footpaths. Because the forest floor has no underbrush, the area has an unusually open feeling.

There also is a little lake, where anglers try for carp and perch, and a handsome square, the Place Aristide-Briand.

However, the whole area abounds in hiking trails that take in fine scenery, and it would be easy to spend more than the hour and a half that it takes most visitors to whiz in and out of Huelgoat. In nearby Locmaria-Berrien, a pretty chapel is fronted by two immense oak trees, one of them completely hollow inside and bound together by rusting bands. Nearby, a caravan center in the old railroad station, *Rouloete Bretagne,* rents cozy, bright carriages reminiscent of Gypsy wagons and the gentle horses to pull them for anywhere from a few days to weeks at a time. The proprietors will help plan the route to include as many of the local calvaries, chapels, manors, farms, and granite hamlets as you have time to see. A carriage costs about $700 per week. April through late September. (Gare de Locmaria-Berrien, Huelgoat 29218; phone: 98-99-73-28.)

CHECKING IN/EATING OUT: *Auberge de la Truite* – This comfortable inn has 6 pleasant rooms, a fine wine cellar, and a good restaurant, where the *truite maison* (house-style trout) comes with a *beurre blanc* (white butter) sauce flavored with lemon and chives. Closed January and February, Sunday evenings and Mondays except in July and August. Major credit cards accepted. Locmaria-Berrien, 4¼ miles (7 km) from Huelgoat at the intersection of D769 and the small road descending from the village (phone: 98-99-73-05). Hotel, moderate; restaurant, expensive to moderate.

En Route from Huelgoat – The fields and forest scenery of the Argoat is at its best to the east, especially off the main roads. Follow the signs along the swooping curves of D769 through Poullaouen; then head along D154 to beautiful St-Gildas, where there is a picturesquely situated chapel just at the base of a hill where the Romans once camped — ideal for picnics. Follow the signs south through Carnoët to D787, then turn north toward Callac. From there, follow D18 to St-Servais, then go north on D31 to Burthulet, in whose lonely chapel the devil is said to have died of cold, and Bulat-Pestivien, whose 15th-to-16th-century church is one of the oldest in the Renaissance style in Brittany.

Retrace your steps along the beautiful D31 as far as Ty-Bourg and D28, then continue south on D31. At Croas-Tasset, there is a turnoff on D20 for the Gorges du Corong. Large trees planted atop the hedgerows arch over the road to the south. At N164, about 9 miles (14 km) farther south on D31, turn east toward Rostrenen.

From here it's possible to follow many beautiful country roads, turning this way and that, to skirt the massive impoundment of the Blavet River known as the Lac de Guerlédan. Routes D15A and D15 both cross the woods and heath plateau country of the 6,916-acre Forêt de Quénécan. For a more direct route, head directly toward Gouarec along N164. A short distance from town are the deep Gorges du Daoulas, some almost vertical, formed where the Daoulas River joins the Blavet. Just off the N164 bis about 3 miles (5 km) shy of Gouarec are the exciting ruins of the 12th-century Abbaye de Bon Repos, where the ivy grows thick as plush on the granite stones and ferns feather the broken tops of the walls.

At Gouarec, turn north along D8 for more exploring in the Argoat. At the Gorges de Toul Goulic, about 8 miles (13 km) north, a rather steep footpath leads to the point at which the sizable Blavet River totally disappears into a cleft. About 3 miles (5 km) farther, the Chapelle de Notre-Dame-de-Guiaudet suddenly appears almost out of nowhere, its immense belfry crammed with bells outlined against the sky. Accessible via a road lined on both sides with straight rows of trees, it occupies a piece of property that itself is laid out in a cruciform with the Stations of the Cross, a fountain, and a war monument.

CHECKING IN/EATING OUT: *Blavet* – For peace and quiet, this *auberge* on a sometimes busy highway is not ideal. But the simplest rooms have real charm with their old-fashioned wallpaper, Breton armoires, antique headboards, high ceilings, and modern bathrooms; and some of the rooms are quite elaborate, with four-poster beds and such. (One wishes that the rather soft mattresses were equally satisfactory.) There is a homey quality about the hairless doll, the high chair, and other debris of children that may occupy a corner of the breakfast room during the off-season. The dining room, with its rosy pink linen tablecloths, is elegant, as is the food — such as *huîtres chaudes aux poireaux* (warm oysters with leeks) or tournedos topped with wild mushrooms. Closed Sunday evenings and Mondays (except in July and August), a week in December, and during January. Visa accepted. N164 *bis,* Gouarec phone: 96-24-90-03). Moderate.

Hostellerie de l'Abbaye – Set at the end of a path of sycamores within a few hundred yards of the ruins of the Abbaye de Bon Repos, this longtime restaurant has acquired 5 rooms that can't be beat for tranquillity. Closed Tuesdays evenings, Wednesdays, and 2 weeks in winter. Visa accepted. Just off N164 *bis,* St-Gelven, west of Gouarec (phone: 96-24-98-38). Moderate to inexpensive.

GUINGAMP: This erstwhile feudal city is another one of those beautiful Breton towns with a tree-bordered square, a batch of half-timbered houses, and a fine Gothic church. Here, though, there also is a wonderful tiered fountain full of carved horses with goose wings, dragon tails, and goat faces. And the Basilique de Notre-Dame de Bon-Secours (Basilica of Our Lady of Perpetual Help) is Gothic only on one side. When the south side collapsed in the 16th century, the town held a competition and awarded the commission to a young architect whose plans were in the Renaissance style. Inside and out, the two faces are obvious — the round Renaissance arches with their keystones and pilasters on one side, and the Gothic ogives on the other. The best views are from the side yard (the opposite side of the church from the one edged by the Rue Notre-Dame). The Black Virgin, the basilica's patroness, has a chapel of her own opening into the Rue Notre-Dame; her altar is always massed with flowers. A *pardon* held annually on the second weekend in July attracts thousands.

CHECKING IN/EATING OUT: *Le Relais du Roy* – The presence of this hostelry in an old house on the main square is reason enough for travelers to seek out Guingamp. The 7 rooms, reached by climbing a 16th-century stone-walled stairwell, are decorated in the best of taste, with oh-so-French furnishings and appropriate wallpapers, generally striped or flowered. The same is true of the small and intimate dining room, where several carefully conceived *table d'hôte* dinners usually are available. The cozy bar, all polished mahogany and brass with Empire-style armchairs and walls of a golden brown raw silk that lends a certain formality, is a fine place for a quiet afternoon coffee. Be sure to note the Renaissance doorway in the courtyard, edged with carvings of many droll faces. Closed Sundays from September to mid-June, hotel and restaurant closed from *Christmas* through mid-January. Major credit cards accepted. 42 Pl. du Centre, Guingamp (phone: 96-43-76-62). Expensive to moderate.

En Route from Guingamp – Lannion and the coast can be reached in a flash by D767, but it's far more pleasant to make the trip along meandering country roads. Take N12 to the turnoff to the Menez-Bré, where a narrow, bumpy road climbs to lush meadows, where there is a simple stone chapel, like one a child might draw, and a fine view that stretches for miles. Return to N12, and turn right toward Gollot and Manaty. Then make your way to D11 following D31A, D31, and D30.

From D11, you can turn off for the Kergrist castle, whose gardens may be toured. Farther along, signs point to the moss-splotched Chapelle de Kerfons, which sits on a rutted road opposite a stone barn where the pigeons bill and coo as if to fill the quiet countryside with noise, and to the ruined 15th-century Château de Tonquédec, a hulk of granite topping the crest of a precipitous hill surrounded by beautiful woods. The keep has walls 13 feet thick.

CÔTE DU GRANIT ROSE: This stretch of shore, which runs between Morlaix and St-Brieuc, is aptly named for the beautiful rosy hue of the rocks. This route explores it beginning at Trébeurden.

From this little beach town to the larger resort city of Perros-Guirec, the ocean has carved and chiseled the granite rocks offshore into fabulous shapes. Any drive in this area turns up a handful of signs pointing to boulders that only occasionally resemble the armchairs, corkscrews, elephants, gnomes, horses, rabbits, rams, thimbles, turtles, umbrellas, whales, witches, and such for which they are named; viewing points like the high, windy Pointe de Bihit at Trébeurden provide a panorama of such rocks both up and down the coast. In Trégastel, there is the Tire-Bouchon (Corkscrew), which looks much like a pile of cow dung, and an improbable Roi Gradlon (King Gradlon). The hour-long walk along the Grève Blanche (White Seashore), roughly between the beach at the end of the Rue Grève-Blanche and the far end of the Plage de Coz-Pors (Coz-Pors Beach), skirts the coast, where imaginative travelers can make up a few names for the rock formations along the way. Still others — the Tête de Mort (Death's Head) and the Tas de Crêpes (Pile of Pancakes) — lie just beyond.

Ploumanac'h, a not particularly scenic fishing port and seaside resort farther along, has its own spate of rock formations, which surround a lighthouse a few yards from the sea. A platform close to the top provides a bird's-eye view of the coast. Nearby, the rocky landscape has been preserved as a municipal park. The Pointe du Squewel shows off the sawtoothed, rockpiled shoreline at its best. Those with a penchant for walking can follow the celebrated Sentier des Douaniers (Customs Agents' Footpath) along the tops of the 100-foot-high red and black stone cliffs within sight of more of these bizarre formations all the way to Perros-Guirec (about 2½ hours round-trip); sometimes there are berries to pick en route. Offshore are the Sept-Iles, a sanctuary for the auks, cormorants, gannets, gulls, guillemots, and puffins that nest on the island cliffs. Bird watchers interested in coming here should contact the Office du Tourisme in Perros-Guirec (phone: 96-23-21-15).

Every rocky point along this shoreline offers similar scenery. Sometimes there are grand vistas from the road or from a viewing point with a parking lot; sometimes a short walk is required. Adventure-minded travelers can follow their own whims, twisting through the crannied lanes of the residential neighborhoods that always seem to cluster near the shore, glimpsing bits of sea and sky between the houses, or swooping and soaring along as the road rises and falls with a full panorama of rocks and ocean off to the side. Often the road will end within a few feet of a beach. The long crescent of sand at Perros-Guirec, presided over by a casino that looks like a Moorish temple without the minarets, is wide and long and usually moderately to extremely crowded; but others that are quieter, less heavily endowed with facilities like trampolines and changing tents, are not hard to find. Sometimes, as in the area near Porz-Hir and the Pointe du Château, people are selling *homards* (lobsters) and *huîtres* (oysters). The whole landscape is littered with boulders, and often the houses are built right up beside them. On these roads, it is impossible to hurry.

Tréguier, the site of an extravagant *pardon* on the third Sunday in May honoring Brittany's beloved St. Yves, is another pretty Breton town. Its Cathédrale de St-Tugdual is unusual for its handsome cloister and its relatively unspoiled vertical lines, and the inside walls are full of simple carved plaques thanking the saint for miraculous rescues. "Merci à St-Yves," they read. Known for righting wrongs, this legendary figure once heard a suit in which a wealthy man complained about a beggar who loitered at his kitchen window to sniff the odors of the food cooking inside. Tossing a coin on the bench, Yves informed the plaintiff that the ring of the coin was his recompense for the smell of the food.

Particularly beautiful among the rocky viewing spots is the Pointe de l'Arcouest, where the shoreline slopes gently to the sea with a jumble of rocks whose hollows are filled with little pools of water that sparkle like sequins in the sun. The view is of the Ile de Bréhat, a mile long and twice that in width, where there are parks and gardens and villas, fields crossed by footpaths, and lots more rocky, cove-notched coast. It is beautiful, silent, and incredibly pastoral — well worth a trip. According to local legend, Christopher Columbus learned about the existence of the New World, nearly a decade before his milestone voyage, from a seafaring man from Bréhat whose fellow fishermen had been traveling there for years.

South of Paimpol are the farm-ringed ruins of the 13th-to-14th-century Abbaye de Beauport, built of warm, rose-colored granite furred with ivy, ferns, and other greenery. The beautifully articulated rose window is worth noting even without stained glass.

Binic, once a codfishing center, still is a seagoing place, with its serviceable jetty and a plethora of marine stores that really mean business. Some of the buildings that edge the harbor are modern and not particularly picturesque, but the town is not overbuilt and seems more relaxed than most. Notre-Dame-de-la-Cour, named for the small 15th-century chapel at its center, lies inland; it has harmonious proportions, elegant detailing, and a dollhouse quality that is particularly appealing.

On D786 from here to St-Brieuc, tiny spur roads run down to the sea. There are no obvious stops, no musts except the sunrises over the Baie de St-Brieuc, which are well worth the trouble it takes to see them. The point of this coast is to follow your hunches, to pick a road and follow it to the end just to see what's there.

CHECKING IN: *Château de Coatguélen* – This mid-19th-century château with 17 rooms and 3 suites rises like a fairy tale fantasy in the middle of an expansive park. Tennis, swimming pool, fishing, and golf. Closed from mid-November to *Easter*. Its highly touted restaurant serves such elegant dishes as *millefeuille de foie gras et d'épinard* (foie gras and spinach layered in puff pastry). Reservations advised. Major credit cards accepted. On D7, between Lanvollon and Paimpol (phone: 96-22-31-24; fax: 96-22-37-67). Expensive.

Manoir de Lan-Kerellec – This 13-room hotel (a member of the Relais & Châteaux group), whose restaurant has recently lost its one Michelin star, occupies a handsome old stone building with smartly squared hedges twice the height of a man and comfortable rooms with ocean views. The dining salon, with its vaulted ceiling and baronial paneling, is especially striking. Closed from mid-November to mid-March. Major credit cards accepted. Trébeurden (phone: 96-23-50-09; fax: 96-23-66-88). Expensive.

Ti al-Lannec – Rarely in Brittany do you find a hostelry like this one, in which the conversion from bourgeois mansion to hotel has been executed with such taste and attention to detail. Lively wallpapers add cheer to bedrooms, which already have sloped ceilings or fine views or even terraces to their credit. There might be eyelet embroidery edging the sheets, or an antique white coverlet on the bed, a quaint hooked rug on the floor, or a handsome bouquet on the dressing table. Bathrooms are capacious as can be, with plenty of big, thick towels. As if that's not enough, the management sparkles with friendliness, and there are salons where guests can play Bach on an excellent stereo and enjoy after-dinner coffee and chocolate truffles over a game of cards or Scrabble. The food is excellent in the best nouvelle manner. Consider, for instance, the seafood terrine with two sauces, a symphony of pinks and whites that is almost fragile to the fork, or any other fish on the menu, whose English names the waiters are only too glad to share. Restaurant closed Monday lunch except in season; hotel closed from mid-November to mid-March. Demi-pension (breakfast and either lunch or dinner) required in high season. Major credit cards accepted. Allée de Mézo-guen, Trébeurden (phone: 96-23-57-26; fax: 96-23-62-14). Expensive.

Le Barbu – Many a beautiful point in Brittany has its hotel, but few are as pretty as this old-fashioned, 19-room establishment, with its panoramic restaurant above the sea, its small swimming pool, its hedge of hydrangeas, its chandeliered salon, and its lace curtains. Consider a plate or two of their oysters, which are excellent. Visa accepted. On the Pointe de l'Arcouest, about 3½ miles (6 km) from Paimpol (phone: 96-55-86-98). Expensive to moderate.

La Colombière – Spectacularly set on a pine-fuzzed cliff overlooking a swooping curve of beach and acres of blue water, this is a friendly place. Though close to the highway, it is in a hollow so that the chief noise is not of traffic but of the crash of the surf. The garden is full of hydrangeas, paths run down to the sea, and bleating goats roam a section of the lawn. The comfortable rooms vary from antique to contemporary in style, and many have fine sea views. The menu is mainly seafood. Closed Sunday evenings and Mondays in off-season and the first 2 weeks of October. Major credit cards accepted. Bd. du Littoral, Etables-sur-Mer (phone: 96-70-61-64; fax: 96-70-72-76). Expensive to moderate.

Printania – The atmosphere at this half-century-old establishment straddles the fine line between being very outmoded as a result of its age and very contemporary thanks to stylish refurbishings. Some rooms have balconies and narrow doors, and others have huge round windows. Closed from mid-December to mid-January. Major credit cards accepted. 12 Rue des Bons-Enfants, Perros-Guirec (phone: 96-23-21-00; fax: 96-91-16-36). Expensive to moderate.

EATING OUT: *La Cotriade* – A former cook from New York City's *Lutèce* now holds forth in a tiny harbor establishment named for Brittany's fish stew; he offers some of the most inspired cooking in Brittany and has elevated regional dishes to works of art by his deft touch. His *homard grillé* (grilled lobster) and *turbot au beurre rouge* (turbot in red butter) are just two of the dishes for which he has earned one Michelin star, although some have complained that the portions are too small and the prices too high. Closed Monday nights, Tuesdays, and mid-January to mid-February. Visa accepted. Port de Piégu, about ½ mile (1 km) from Pléneuf-Val-André (phone: 96-72-20-26). Expensive.

Lorand-Barre – The decor is country, the menu lengthy and well balanced (with one Michelin star), and the *homard grillé* (grilled lobster), the *ris de veau au porto* (sweetbreads in port), and the *poulet sauté à l'estragon* (chicken sautéed with tarragon) as professionally presented as they are delicious. Closed Sunday nights, Mondays, and winter. Visa and American Express accepted. Les Ponts-Neufs, about halfway between St-Brieuc and Lamballe (phone: 96-32-78-71). Expensive.

La Vieille Tour – Seafood is the specialty at this highly regarded establishment with one Michelin star near St-Brieuc, and it is as innovatively prepared as it is fresh. Unusual sauces, lobster cooked with herbed oysters, and light dessert pastries with caramelized strawberries (in season) are among the culinary stars here. Closed Sunday evenings and Mondays. Major credit cards accepted. 75 Rue de la Tour, Port de St-Brieuc-Le-Légué, about 2 miles (3 km) from St-Brieuc on D24 (phone: 96-33-10-30). Expensive to moderate.

CÔTE D'EMERAUDE: Reaching from St-Brieuc to Dinard, this scalloped coastline takes in a string of pretty resort and harbor towns along D786. At both points of every scallop, there are fine views and pleasant walks.

At Le Val-André, which is noted for its beautiful long beach, a visitor might stroll along the cliff path high above the Bay of St. Brieuc to the Pointe de Pléneuf, or on the Promenade de la Guette (Watchman's Walk), where there are still other sea views. At Erquy, a cluster of beautiful little houses wrap around a huge bay where a small scallop fishing fleet anchors at night, and an evening walk might lead along the harbor, where the sun can be seen setting through a grid of masts. There are beaches to explore at Sables-d'Or-les-Pins, which is full of hotels, and at Le Vieux Bourg.

But there are two particularly fine experiences — the ride from here to Cap Fréhel, on a road that skims the cliff-tops along the fringes of the gold-tinged fields, then drops off to perfect little beaches; and a walk on the cape itself, across moors flecked with tiny golden flowers where the constant wind has bent the heather to its will. The cliffs are rocky and high, reaching to some 229 feet, and the panorama stretches from the Ile de Bréhat on the left to the Pointe de Grouin on the right. When the weather is very clear, it's possible to see all the way to the Channel Islands. The whole area is crossed by paths; be sure to view the seagulls and cormorants crowded on the Fauconnière rocks just offshore, and at dusk, when the light transforms the landscape into a study in pastels, try to get off by yourself for a while to muse on the grandeur of the spectacle. Just to the east on this hefty notch of land, it's possible to see Fort La Latte, a massive 13th-to-14th-century stronghold — everyone's idea of a medieval fort. You can visit the fort (signs near Fréhel point the way), and it's well worth the long walk from the parking lot to the drawbridge, for here the thick stone walls that make so many French castles so impressive frame not ordinary scenery but some of Brittany's most stunning sea views. Incredible as it may seem, sections of the structure still are inhabited.

Dinard, which marks the eastern end of the Emerald Coast, is tame by comparison. But its own charms, representing the civilized side of the province, are considerable: high Victorian villas that crane toward the view; narrow lanes and pine-shaded residential neighborhoods; a large casino; a beach pinned at one end by a ruined priory; and a glittering round of resort life to be lived in dozens of hotels. (See *France's Best Beaches* in DIVERSIONS.)

DINAN: Of the many medieval towns in Brittany, this rampart-bound town of 14,000 stands out among the prettiest. It is guarded by a handsome castle and laced by winding streets lined with half-timbered houses in a quantity unusual even in Brittany. Certainly, if you see no other inland towns during your stay, it should be this one. And you should allow at least a couple of hours if you intend to dally among the shops in the picturesque Old Quarter.

The best place to begin is the Jardin Anglais, which snuggles up against the ramparts and offers a fine view of the valley of the Rance River and the 250-foot Romanesque bridge that spans it. The Promenade de la Duchesse Anne, shaded by beautiful rows of chestnut trees and punctuated with benches that would be perfect for a picnic, skirts the ramparts, then descends to the street, which eventually leads to the 14th-century castle, a section of which contains a museum of local history. Yet another gracious walkway, the Promenade des Petits-Fossés (Walk of the Little Ditches) skirts the base of the castle.

From the statue of the great 14th-century Breton soldier Bertrand du Guesclin, which stands at the midpoint of this Promenade, it's only a short walk via the Rue Ste-Claire and the Rue de l'Horloge into the Old Town, one of the chief charms of Dinan. The Place des Merciers, the Place des Cordeliers, the Rue de la Lainerie and its extensions, the Rue du Jerzual and the Rue du Petit-Fort, which are bounded by shops where artisans usually can be seen at work (but seldom on Mondays), all evoke another age. The Eglise St-Sauveur, where Romanesque and Gothic are in gentle counterpoint, shelters the heart of du Guesclin, whose body was buried at St-Denis, near Paris.

CHECKING IN/EATING OUT: *D'Avaugour* – A pleasant 27-room hotel, with a parrot who squawks "Bonjour" in the lobby. It overlooks the square in the front and a garden in the rear. The restaurant, presided over by a chef who ventures beyond the usual *plat de fruits de mer* (cold seafood platter) into the nouvelle, in which diners might find their salads flavored with walnut oil and fruit or studded with turnips and oranges, or their platter of hot oysters served with curried carrot mousse. Closed Monday evenings in off-season. Major credit cards accepted. 1 Pl. de Champs Clos, Dinan (phone: 96-39-07-49). Expensive.

Manoir du Vaumadeuc – Built of Breton granite and fitted out with objets d'art from around the world, this former manor house is surely one of Brittany's most sumptuous hostelries. Its site deep in the quietest country is only part of the attraction. There are 12 elegant rooms and 2 suites, each with a fireplace and some with massive overhead beams. And the cuisine is classic and ambitious, with lobster *gratiné* keeping company on the menu with *quenelles de brochet nantua* (pike dumplings with a lobster sauce). Closed early January to mid-March. Major credit cards accepted. Pléven, near Plancoët, about 14½ miles (23 km) from Dinan (phone: 96-84-46-17; fax: 96-84-40-16). Expensive.

La Caravelle – The young J. C. Marmion, the chef at this comfortable 11-room establishment, lets the market determine his menu to a great degree. Tomato and fresh green peas might figure in the summer, while hare and rabbit might appear in the fall in his fricassees, mousses, terrines, sauces, and salads. Closed Sunday evenings and Wednesdays off-season, and mid-November to early December. Major credit cards accepted. 14 Pl. Duclos, Dinan (phone: 96-39-00-11). Hotel, inexpensive; restaurant, expensive.

ST-MALO: Many a fine town would lose its charm altogether if forced to endure the onslaught of visitors to which this one-time privateering and shipbuilding center is subjected nowadays — throughout the season and on weekends the rest of the year. But the crowd is a mixed lot: Americans who visit St-Malo if they stop nowhere else in Brittany; Englishmen who arrive on their yachts or on huge, sleek white ferries from Portsmouth, Guernsey, Jersey, or Sark; and the professional seamen from the French navy or merchant marine who tie up here periodically. The mix gives the old city an air of festive good cheer such as that more commonly found at a *Mardi Gras* or a house party. The bars, most notably the one at the *L'Univers* on the Place Chateaubriand, are gleaming studies in brass and wood, with photographs of famous racing yachts. The restaurants are the kinds of comfortable and appealingly decorated eateries, seldom all that formal, that people like to find on vacation. And there are plenty of attractive shops in which to while away an afternoon or two. Not to mention the natural beauties: the scenery of rooftops and water seen from the ramparts, which are remnants of when St-Malo was a republic in its own right and stayed aloof from attacking Normans, French, and English alike. (In fact, though St-Malo seems very old, the structures themselves are restorations, since the *ville close* was largely destroyed during the war.)

The center of town is the Place Chateaubriand, named for the Romantic novelist who was born here. There is a museum devoted to Malouin history on the right, built into the ramparts; the exhibits, which include pirate paraphernalia like treasure chests and cannon, memorabilia of Chateaubriand and of the French explorer Jacques Cartier, are handsomely lighted and displayed elegantly enough to warrant a visit. A stairway nearby leads to the breezy ramparts for which the city is famous. Also worth visiting is the handsome Cathédrale de St-Vincent, which has a 12th-century nave and a set of stunning, almost fiery, modern windows.

If there's time, take the 25-minute breezy walk out to the islets of Grand and Petit Bé, where Chateaubriand wished to be buried. (Check the tide tables, go at low tide, and plan to return before the tide rolls in again.)

CHECKING IN: Central – The Best Western chain's associate in the Old Town has 46 large, attractively furnished (if somewhat spare) rooms that substantiate its status as one of the premier hotels here, not to mention a creditable if somewhat formal restaurant. It is not long on warmth, however. Major credit cards accepted. 6 Grande-Rue, St-Malo (phone: 99-40-87-70; fax: 99-40-47-57). Expensive to moderate.

Grand Hôtel des Thermes – Facing the majestic bay of St-Malo, this hostelry, including a good restaurant, *Le Cap Horn,* opened next to the city's famous saltwater spa, the *Termes Marins de St-Malo.* Its 189 guestrooms range from simple to super-luxurious, with prices to match. Charm is not its strong point, but it is a useful address when other hotels are full in summer. Closed most of January. Major credit cards accepted. 100 Bd. Hébert (phone: 99-40-75-75; fax: 99-40-76-00). Expensive to moderate.

Elizabeth – Notable for its small but attractive rooms, this snug 17-room establishment off the beaten path is certainly the most atmospheric and comfortable in the old city — a gem in a town where the polished exteriors too often conceal run-down guest quarters. No restaurant. Major credit cards accepted. 2 Rue des Cordiers, St-Malo (phone: 99-56-24-98; fax: 99-56-39-24). Moderate.

La Korrigane – A graceful 19th-century mansion in the southern part of St-Malo has been transformed into an intimate, refined 10-room hotel. There's a garden, parking, and English-language cable television programs. Closed mid-November to mid-March. Major credit cards accepted. 39 Rue le Pomellec, St-Malo (phone: 99-81-65-85). Moderate.

EATING OUT: *Duchesse Anne* – Charming, brightly lit, and done up with reddish walls, this polished place with one Michelin star in the center of town serves fine fish and shellfish, including plain oysters from Cancale and occasional surprises like *pétoncles farcies* (garlicky buttered bay scallops sizzling on the half shell). Closed December, January, and Wednesdays. Major credit cards accepted. 5 Pl. Guy La Chambre, St-Malo (phone: 99-40-85-33). Expensive to moderate.

Robert Abraham – Splendid views of the sea, fresh seafood, and inventive appetizers such as a smooth cherry soup keep the customers coming. Reservations advised. Closed Sunday evenings and Mondays (except in July and August), and mid-January to the end of February. Major credit cards accepted. 4 Chaussée Sillon, St-Malo (phone: 99-40-50-93; fax: 99-40-19-19) Moderate.

En Route from St-Malo – Don't miss the Pointe du Grouin, accessible from the scenic D201, which squiggles along the coast eastward. Along with the Grouin du Sud (on the Normandy side of the bay near Avranches), this is considered the best spot for viewing the astonishingly high tides. The locals swear that the tides in the Baie du Mont-St-Michel rise at the speed of a galloping horse during the spring and fall equinoxes, which is no exaggeration. A chart listing dates, times, and levels of tides is available from any Maison de Presse in the area.

CANCALE: This port of 5,000 has been famous for its oysters for centuries. And though the native shellfish population was decimated by a disease whose origins have never been pinpointed, Cancale has maintained its claim by using the oysterian equivalent of seedlings (*spats*), imported from the community of Auray in the south. The *spats* are shoveled into bags made of tough netting, taken out to sea, and left to grow for a couple of years before harvesting. Late in the afternoon, visitors gather along the port to watch the oyster boats come in and unload their huge sacks full of the delicacies, and shopkeepers display baskets of oysters in all shapes and varieties. No need to bemoan the lack of a picnic table: They can be opened and consumed with a squeeze of lemon on the spot, and the juices left to drip on the pavement.

EATING OUT: *Bricourt* – Situated in a charming village, this is the perfect place to savor the sea's best bounty (Michelin has awarded it two stars, and it is a member of the Relais & Châteaux group). The chef, Olivier Roellinger, born in Cancale, is considered by many food critics to be one of the most inventive seafood chefs in France. His specialties — such as a soup of Belon oysters with local herbs — involve intensely flavored reductions of fish broths and unusual combinations of herbs and spices. There are 6 luxurious rooms currently available in the adjoining hotel, and the Roellingers have recently opened a 15-room annex in the nearby Château Richeux, located directly on the beach. Closed Tuesdays, Wednesdays, Thursdays during July and August, and from the end of December to March. Make reservations well in advance. Major credit cards accepted. 1 Rue Duguesclin, Ille-et-Vilaine, Cancale (phone: 99-89-64-76; fax: 99-89-88-47). Expensive.

The Atlantic Coast

"The Green Venice." "The Coast of Beauty." "Bright Island." "The Savage Coast." "The City Built on a Balcony." All are tag names for places lying along this route through the Charente and Charente-Maritime departments of France. About 400,000 people live in the Charente, more than 500,000 in the Charente-Maritime. Just across the Gironde estuary from Bordeaux, they are accessible to travelers via autoroute A10, which goes from Paris to Bordeaux. The region attracts oyster lovers, cognac lovers, lovers of history and pastoral beauty — lovers period (they should go directly to La Rochelle and Ile de Ré). Though residents are quick to defend the distinction between the two departments, there is one unifying thread: The 220-mile Charente River, which Henry IV once called "the most beautiful stream in my kingdom," meanders past Angoulême and Cognac, in the Charente department, through Saintes and on to the sea at Rochefort, both in the Charente-Maritime.

Beginning at Angoulême, the route through the region heads west to Royan, then north to La Rochelle and the Marais Poitevin. It passes open meadows, rolling hills covered by lush vineyards, fields of corn or cows, rocky coastlines, enticing beaches, and more than its fair share of charming towns that history left in its wake. The French president François Mitterrand was born in the Charente-Maritime, in Jarnac, as well as Samuel de Champlain, the founder of Quebec who was born in Brouage. It was from this area that French pioneers set sail for the new land in Canada and America. Huguenot emigrants departed from La Rochelle and settled just north of New York City in a town they named Nouvelle Rochelle (New Rochelle). Settlers of Prince Edward Island, New Brunswick, and the rest of what became known as Acadia (in Canada), also hailed from here.

Still centuries after these adventurers helped tame the New World, many modern voyagers have yet to discover the charms of the area the Charentais left behind — one of France's most varied and fascinating regions. Too many travelers tend to dash through its mellow landscape en route to southern Atlantic seaside resorts. But those who take the time to linger find no lack of pleasures in this gentle countryside.

Nestled snugly between Brittany and Bordeaux, Charente and Charente-Maritime share characteristics with both neighbors, particularly the fishing culture of the north and the vineyards of the south. The landscape is dotted with marshlands and pastures and touched by sea breezes. Wealth derives equally from land, sea, and the estuaries in between. Stately châteaux stand as monuments to the prosperity the region has enjoyed. The most outstanding among them are the 15th-century Château de la Roche Courbon near Saintes and the 12th-century and Renaissance Château de la Rochefoucauld, where weekend son et lumière shows during the summer months trace 1,000 years of history.

Art and architecture tell the region's history — read it in the whimsical façade of Cathédral St-Pierre, the amphitheater in Saintes, or the fairy-tale stone towers guarding the entrance to La Rochelle's little port.

The regional character also is expressed eloquently through the food, which is simple and relies on the fine-quality products of land and sea, rather than on culinary sleight of hand. The famous oysters of Marennes-Oleron are eaten *au nature* or accompanied by small eels and escargots, the latter prepared with wine, onions, and garlic. Another specialty is *chaudrée,* a fish soup made with white wine and the fresh catch of the day (such as pike, merlan, or sole). Rich pasturelands produce beef, pork, and the succulent *pré-salé* lamb, named for the saltwater-washed feeding grounds that give the meat its special flavor. The butter of the Charente is prized by purists for its delicate flavor. And then there is cognac.

A substantial 236,000 acres in the Charente and Charente-Maritime produce the white grapes from which cognac, France's famous elixir, is made. The highest-quality grapes and resulting eau-de-vie come from the area immediately surrounding the towns of Cognac and Segonzac, named Grande Champagne. Cognac is a brandy, but most brandy is not cognac and cannot bear the name unless it is from this region and has been distilled twice, then carefully aged in oak barrels. The cognac industry began in the 17th century, and today more than 300 firms produce cognac; fewer than half of them export it, however. The large firms offer free tours and tastings and go out of their way to cater to tourists. Before tasting cognac, it is traditional to hold the bulb-shaped glass in your palm for a few minutes to warm it and release the spirit's vapors; sniff and then sip. Drinking cognac is a smelling and tasting experience, one to savor slowly.

Pineau, a regional drink rarely found elsewhere in France, is a mixture of one-third cognac and two-thirds unfermented grape juice, with an alcohol content of 16% to 22%. It remained a home brew from the 16th century until 1935, when it was first sold commercially.

The Charente River is navigable from Angoulême to Rochefort, with 21 tidegates over the 100-mile stretch. From April to July, boats carrying 70 to 180 people depart from Angoulême or Châteauneuf; from April to October, they leave Rochefort, St-Savinien, Saintes, Cognac, and Jarnac. For information, contact the regional tourist office (2 Pl. St-Pierre in Angoulême; phone: 45-95-16-84). Barges also can be hired for 4- to 7-day cruises. For information, contact *Maison Poitou-Charentes* (68-70 Rue de Cherche Midi, Paris 75006; phone: 42-22-83-74).

There also are quite a few land activities in the region. The Charente area now offers a total of 12 golf courses, the majority of which opened in the last 3 years (for information, contact the regional tourist office in Poitiers at 2 Rue St-Opportune; phone: 49-88-38-94). Add zoos, parks, aquariums, bird preserves, peaceful islands, and Venice-like canals winding through marshlands, and there's more than enough to justify an extended visit here.

The Charente and Charente-Maritime regions have a vast selection of good hotels at reasonable prices. Though good restaurants aren't as plentiful except in La Rochelle, they do exist, and the regional dishes they prepare deserve ample tasting. In hotels listed as expensive, expect to pay $65 and up for a double room; $45 to $65, moderate; and less than $45, inexpensive. In an expensive restaurant, you will pay $75 or more for a meal for two, without wine; between $45 to $75, moderate; and less than $45, inexpensive. Service charge usually is included.

ANGOULÊME: Nicknamed "the town built on a balcony," Angoulême is perched on a rocky ridge overlooking the Charente Valley. The principal town and the administrative center of Charente, as well as the center of France's paper industry, it has a population of 50,000, with another 100,000 people living in the outlying area. Finding the center of town is easy: Just keep climbing until you can't go any higher. All the sites are well marked, and the tourist office has two handy locations (2 Pl. St-Pierre; phone: 45-95-16-84), and in a kiosk across from the train station; closed Mondays (Place de la Gare; phone: 45-92-27-57). Each year the city holds an international comic book festival at the end of January and an international jazz festival at the end of May and the beginning of June. The main post office, open weekdays and Saturday mornings, is at Place du Champs de Mars; another, a more convenient one is at Place Francis-Louvel. A large covered market is held every morning at Place Guillon; Rue des Postes and Rue Beaulieu are pedestrian streets conducive to strolling and browsing.

The crowning glory of Angoulême is Cathédral St. Pierre, just off Rue de Friedland. The fourth building on this site (the first was built in AD 560) and the work of Bishop Gérard II, it was consecrated in 1128 and remains one of the oldest and most venerable cathedrals in France. Its façade, unique to the point of whimsy, contains 114 figures depicting not only the Last Supper and the Ascension of Christ but also Samson and the lion, St. George slaying the dragon, and scenes from the "Song of Roland." Monsters, birds, and winged horses all are part of the decoration. Across the street is a fine promenade along the ramparts of the city. The views both near and far are splendid. Two small churches in Angoulême deserve a look: Eglise St-Martial, a Gothic structure that is lovely inside, and the 12th-century Roman Eglise St-André (rebuilt in 1585 to 1660 in Plantagenet style), which has a 19th-century façade, three naves, and a tranquil garden.

The excellent *Musée des Beaux-Arts* (1 Rue de Friedland; phone: 45-95-07-69) is tucked away in what used to be the bishop's palace. It has striking ceramics by Alfred Renolleau, a master potter from the Charente during the late 19th and early 20th centuries. One gallery is devoted to the works of another Charente artist, Léonard Jarraud, and two other rooms display stunning art from west and central Africa and a number of Pacific islands. There is even a comic strip hall of mirrors. Not to be missed is a haunting painting by Pierre Vafflard, *Richard Young Burying His Daughter* (1804). It is open daily except Tuesdays and holidays (in off-season) from 10 AM to noon and 2 to 6 PM. Renolleau's work also can be viewed in a shop, *Faïencerie d'Art D'Angoulême* (5 Rue Renolleau; phone: 45-95-01-75; open Sundays and Tuesdays through Fridays from 8 AM to noon and 2 to 7 PM; Saturdays and Mondays from 2 to 6 PM).

In what used to be the old *Renaissance* hotel, the *Maison St-Simon,* dating from 1550, now houses the *FRAC* (*Fond Régional d'Art Contemporain;* 15 Rue de la Cloche-Verte; phone: 45-92-87-01) of Poitou-Charentes which displays the work of up-and-coming artists. It is open Wednesdays through Fridays from noon to 5 PM, Thursdays from noon to 8 PM, Saturdays from 2 to 7 PM, and Sundays from 3 to 6 PM. The *Association du Centre d'Arts Plastiques* is installed in the *Atelier Musée du Papier* (134 Rue de Bordeaux; phone: 45-95-87-20 or 45-92-34-10), which also is interesting for its exhibits on paper production. The cultural center, or *CAC* (*Centre d'Action Culturelle*), presents concerts, cinema, video, exhibitions, theater, dance, and much more (Bd. Berthelot; phone: 45-95-43-45). The *Musée Archéologique,* an archaeology museum, provides information about the history of the Charente region (closed Mondays; 44 Rue de Montmoreau; phone: 45-38-45-17). Open 3 years ago, the *Centre National de la Bande Desinée et l'Image* (121 Rte. de Bordeaux; phone: 45-95-87-20) is devoted to the world of comic strips, and has, in addition to a permanent collection of over 8,000 original works, many excellent temporary exhibits. Open Wednesdays through Saturdays, noon to 7 PM, and Sundays 2 to 7 PM. The city's theater is on Avenue des Maréchaux beside tree-lined Place New-York (phone: 45-95-38-40).

For a sweet-tooth fix, *Pinoteau* is good. It's a *pâtisserie–salon de thé* on a pedestrian walk (32 Rue St-Martial). Ask for a *gâteau ganage,* a small cake with chocolate icing and a layer of semisweet chocolate inside, or a regional cake filled with cognac called *Le 16.* Some say an even better *pâtisserie* is *Geslin* (on Pl. F.-Louvel; phone: 45-95-00-73).

Be sure not to overlook the Old Town; it's filled with very short, interesting streets: Rue du Soleil, Rue des Trois-Notre-Dame, Rue de la Cloche-Verte, as well as Rues Marengo, Genève, Massillon, Trarieux, and Taillefer. Place du Palet, a renovated square with a fountain, is one entrance to the Old Town. Also check out the beautiful view from the ramparts of the Charente River valley.

CHECKING IN: *Hostellerie du Moulin du Maine Brun* – Comfortable and chic, this member of the Relais & Châteaux group has 20 rooms, a fine one-star restaurant, a swimming pool, and its own park. Closed November and December. Major credit cards accepted. Five miles (8 km) west of Angoulême on N141, in La Vigerie, near Asnière-sur-Novère (phone: 45-90-83-00; fax: 45-96-91-14). Expensive.

***Altéa Hôtel de France* –** Right in the center of town with a good view of the valley and an exquisite garden, this great old hotel, acquired by the Altéa chain, has 90 rooms, a large terrace built on 12th- and 13th-century ramparts, a restaurant, and a garage, and claims to be "the best place to stop between England and Spain." Major credit cards accepted. Pl. des Halles, Angoulême (phone: 45-95-47-95; fax: 45-92-02-70) Moderate.

***Palais* –** In the center of the Old Town, it has 52 rooms on 3 floors and a comfortable sitting room. This is a clean, quiet place in a great location. Major credit cards accepted. 4 Pl. F.-Louvel, Angoulême (phone: 45-92-54-11 or 45-92-55-10; fax: 45-92-01-83) Moderate.

***Trois Piliers* –** Convenient to both downtown and the train station, this pleasant hotel has 50 rooms, a bar, a terrace, and a garage. Visa accepted. 3 Bd. de Bury, Angoulême (phone: 45-92-42-11; fax: 45-95-77-07). Moderate.

■ **Note:** Excellent municipal camping is available on the Ile de Bourgines, a quick bus ride (No. 7) from downtown or half an hour's walk (phone: 45-92-83-22); there also is an open-air municipal pool. In addition, the island has a very nice youth hostel; though it only has 16 rooms, it looks like a small motel (phone: 45-92-45-80). Ile de Bourgines also offers canoeing, kayaking, and other sports.

EATING OUT: *La Ruelle* – Exposed ceiling beams and ancient stone walls lighted by a blazing fire in the hearth set the stage for preparations by Jean François Dauphin and his daugher Véronique. Their style is traditional but original. There's a good, well-priced wine list, and wines are served by the glass. Closed Saturday lunch, Sundays, and February. Major credit cards accepted. 6 Rue des Trois-Notre-Dame (phone: 45-92-94-64). Expensive.

***L'Amandier–Ecole St-Joseph* –** For a wonderful lunch and a special travel experience, dine at this private French cooking school, where the meal is prepared and served by students who are supervised very closely. Menus for the week are posted; on the day (open weekdays only) you want to visit, call before 10 AM and arrive between 12:15 and 12:30 PM. The formal dining room serves 100 people — teachers, students, and visitors — daily. The food is very good, and wine is available. No credit cards accepted. In St-Iyreix, just outside Angoulême (phone: 45-95-11-45). Moderate.

Le Margaux – Traditional dishes prepared with contemporary finesse make this a favorite among locals. An extremely appealing decor adds to the pleasurable experience of dining here. Closed Sundays and 2 weeks at *Christmas.* Major credit cards accepted. 25 Rue Genève (phone: 42-92-58-98). Moderate.

En Route from Angoulême – Before heading to Cognac, the traveler who truly wants to savor the environs of Angoulême should consider two possibilities: one, a pleasant afternoon outing of a couple of hours, the other, a summertime day trip. If you have a free afternoon, take D674 south to D104 (go toward Libourne through the tunnel under the town) to the tiny town of Puymoyen, about 16 miles (26 km) away. Then follow the signs to the Verger paper mill, Moulin du Verger, about 3 miles (5 km) along a narrow, winding, forested road through the Eaux Claires Valley. The mill has been in operation since 1539 and continues to be self-supporting, selling its fine hand-made paper to buyers in the United States, England, and Europe (there are only two other mills that aren't subsidized in France — in Couze in the Dordogne and in Auvergne). You actually can watch the paper being made — a mixture of fibers (cotton, manila, and linen, with flowers or straw sometimes added for decoration) and water; in one year this mill produces the same amount of paper it would take a machine to make in half an hour, but this paper will last for 500 or 600 years. Tours of the mill and explanations (in English) of the process are given daily at no charge (afternoons only on Sundays). There is a shop that sells paper. If you have no car, take bus No. 8 from Place du Champs de Mars and walk the mile (1.6 km) to the mill (phone: 45-61-10-38). Another mill in the area, Moulin de Fleurac, on D699 near Nersac, is government-subsidized; it has a museum with exhibitions of old documents as well as an explanation of the history of paper and writing. (Closed Tuesdays; phone: 45-91-50-69.) Also of interest is the *Atelier Musée du Papier* (see *Angoulême* above).

An excellent day trip out of Angoulême follows N141 about 14 miles (22 km) northeast to the 1,000-year-old town of La Rochefoucauld (pop. 4,000). It has a 9th-century castle with an 11th-century keep, a 15th-century tower, and a 16th-century galleried staircase and chapel. It is open only in July, August, and the beginning of September. In July and August a historical son et lumière festival is held in the garden. Some 500 costumed citizens, including 60 horseback riders and coachmen, relate 11 centuries of local history in 11 tableaux. The show is held on Friday and Saturday nights; an admission fee is charged.

Another pleasant detour is the 15th-century Château de l'Oisellerie, where visitors can taste and buy *pineau* and cognac (3 miles/5 km south of Angoulême on N10). A bit farther is the 11th-to-13th-century abbey of La Couronne; an adjacent 18th-century building boasts a beautiful, ironwork Louis XV door.

The tourist office in La Rochefoucauld is in a 14th-century cloister (on Rue des Halles; phone: 45-63-07-45; open from June 15 to September 15). During July and August, there are sound and light shows here; check with the tourist office for place and times. At 39 Grande-Rue, Jacques and Mady Brun run a *salon de thé* that was started by his father in the late 1940s. M. Brun the elder created a delicious chocolate candy, unique to this town, called *pichottes;* of course, there is a story behind the name. In the 17th century, the monks used to grow mulberries, but migratory birds called *pichottes* would swoop down on them every year. The already weary birds would fall to the ground because of the small amount of alcohol in the fruit, and the monks would collect them and give them to hunters. The hunters then carried them to neighboring towns to sell, crying *"Voilà la pichotte; la pichotte est arrivée!"* People from La Rochefoucauld became known as *pichottiers,* and today they eat *pichottes* of the featherless variety. M. Brun the younger created a candy, as well: *calines,* dark chocolates made with cognac and wrapped in gold paper. The store is closed Mondays and Tuesdays, and at lunchtime.

A quick connection with D939 at Mareuil takes you back to Angoulême; from there N141 leads west for 26 miles (42 km) to the small town of Cognac.

CHECKING IN/EATING OUT: *La Chouette Gourmande* – For those who will go out of their way for a good meal, drive 22 miles (35 km) southeast of La Rochefoucauld via the road to Nontron (D6 to D65 to D4) to the small village of St-Front-sur-Nizonne. This restaurant may be in the middle of nowhere, but you need a reservation to get in. There also are 3 guestrooms. Open daily. No credit cards accepted. St-Front-sur-Nizonne (phone: 53-56-14-70). Moderate.

La Vieille Auberge – A visit to La Rochefoucauld should include lunch or dinner (and perhaps a night) at this 32-room inn, which serves regional dishes. You even can call and place your order. Open daily. Major credit cards accepted. 13 Faubourg de la Souche, La Rochefoucauld (phone: 45-62-02-72; fax: 45-63-01-88). Moderate to inexpensive.

COGNAC: To look at the unassuming town of Cognac (pop. 23,000), you'd never guess that the equivalent of more than a billion bottles of cognac was aging in its warehouses. The town is a virtual storehouse for the coveted brew, and it's possible many days to catch a whiff of it in the air. The equivalent of 20 million bottles evaporates from the porous oak aging casks each year; people call this "the angels' share" and perhaps it accounts for the advanced age some of the residents attain. The vapors may contribute as well to the softness of the light in the afternoons, so beautiful that even the busiest sightseers are bound to stop to admire it. The light and the cognac firms, all of which give free tours (and most offer tastings), are why most visitors stop here. The town itself has become commercial; billboards mar its walls and the roads leading into town. The town looks dingy because of a black fungus that lives on the fumes of the evaporating cognac and turns buildings gray. (It's impossible to store cognac illegally and get away with it!)

Cognac was the birthplace, in 1494, of François I, whose image and name appear around town as much as the word "cognac;" the town square features an equestrian statue of him, the municipal park (which has a swimming pool) is a woodsy 138 acres named after him, and the best hotel in town claims his name (see *Checking In*). François I was born in the Château Valois, which is beside the Charente River and now is the home of the Otard cognac firm (there also is a sound and light show here). Nearby is the 15th-century Porte St-Jacques, all that's left of the old fortifications around the town, and beyond it, the Hennessy company, whose main building is a 17th-century abbey. The gate marks the entrance to the oldest part of town, which has dwellings from the 15th to the 18th century, many of them now restored. In the Old Town, near the tourist office, you can buy regional drinks, glasses, and cognac drenched chocolates from *La Cognathèque* (Pl. Jean-Monnet; phone: 43-82-43-31). Try its "cigar-drink," a test tube with a tobacco leaf wrapped around it like a cigar but with cognac inside.

The tourist office (phone: 45-82-10-71), between Place Jean-Monnet and Place François-I in the center of town, has a map of the cognac firms and their tour hours (or see the list below). Some have multilingual guides. These include Hennessy (whose tour features a visit to its barrel museum and its warehouse and bottling plant across the river), Martell, Camus, Rémy-Martin, and Otard. Most are open only on weekdays and some are by appointment only. The Courvoisier company is in Jarnac, 9 miles (14 km) east of Cognac along N141; as you cross the bridge into town, the building looms majestically to your right. (In 16th-century Jarnac, the Catholics lived on one side of the river and the Huguenots on the other.) For more information about visiting the firms, contact the following:

Bisquit, Domaine de Lignères, Rouillac (phone: 45-21-88-88)
Camus, 29 Rue Marguerite de Navarre, Cognac (phone: 45-32-28-28)
Courvoisier, 21 Pl. du Château, Cognac (phone: 45-35-55-52)
James Hennessy & Co., 1 Rue de la Richonne, Cognac (phone: 45-82-52-22)
Martell & Co., Pl. E. Martell, Cognac (phone: 45-82-44-44)
Otard, Cognac, SA, Château de Cognac, Cognac (phone: 45-82-40-00)
Rémy-Martin & Co., 20 Rue de la Société Vinicole, Cognac (phone: 45-35-76-66).

The priory Church of St. Léger, at 55 Rue Aristide-Briand in Cognac, was built between 1130 and 1140; its tower makes it the tallest edifice in town. The façade, walls of the nave, and base of the bell tower remain from the 12th century. The rose window dates from the 15th century, and if you look closely at the outermost section of the sculpted doorway, you'll recognize the signs of the zodiac. Cognac has a good museum, *Musée Municipal,* with exhibitions of wine making tools and regional ethnography. The museum is in the Jardin Public, 25 acres of shaded walkways and quiet ponds (no admission charge; open daily except Tuesdays from 2 to 5:30 PM October through May; open daily from 10 AM to noon and 2 to 6 PM June through September. 48 Bd. Denfert-Rochereau; phone: 45-32-07-25).

The municipal theater has film festivals, classical concerts, and theatrical productions of classical and modern works (Pl. Robert-Schuman; phone: 45-82-17-24). The *Convention Center,* near the tourist office, has changing exhibitions; there is no admission charge and it's open daily. A statue depicting a grape harvester at work is in front of the Palace of Justice (Pl. Charles-de-Gaulle) and is worth a look, especially if you miss seeing the real thing in October.

For nightlife, there's an inviting atmosphere at *Pub Victor-Hugo* (Av. Victor-Hugo; phone: 45-32-28-11) which has a piano bar.

For a down-home experience, try to arrive on the weekend of the *Fête de la Vendange* (Harvest Festival). The town's streets, closed to traffic, fill up with colorful floats, majorettes, and marching bands to kick off the harvest. There is an admission charge for the festival. Cognac's grapes are among the last to be picked in France, and the harvest usually begins around the middle of October. In June and July, a sound and light show and a *Spectacle Historique* (Historical Pageant) are presented at the Château St-Brice about 3 miles (5 km) from Cognac. Check with the tourist office for dates and times, or call (phone: 45-35-57-53) for reservations.

CHECKING IN: *Moulin de Marcouze* – Definitely worth the 25-minute drive south of Cognac, is this charming old mill converted to a first class inn and restaurant by Dominique Bouchet, former head chef of Paris's famous *Tour d'Argent.* It has been awarded two Michelin stars. From Cognac, take D732 south to Pons, then N137 to Belluire and Mosnac. Closed Tuesdays, Wednesday lunch, and February. Major credit cards accepted. Mosnac/St-Genis de Saintonge (phone: 46-70-46-16; fax: 46-70-48-14). Expensive.

Moulin de Cierzac – About 8 miles (13 km) from Cognac via D731, this 10-room inn is located at the water's edge in a park. Its restaurant has earned one Michelin star for specialties such as *navarin de sole aux herbes de Marennes* (ragout of sole with vegetables and herbs). Closed Sunday evenings from November to March and Mondays. Major credit cards accepted. Cierzac (phone: 45-83-01-32). Expensive to moderate.

Le Valois – Near the post office, it offers 30 rooms with mini-bars as well as one large bar and parking. Closed December 22 to January 2. Major credit cards accepted. 35 Rue du XIV-Juillet, Cognac (phone: 45-82-76-00; fax: 45-82-76-00). Expensive to moderate.

L'Auberge – A small, 2-story hotel that is on a quiet side street near Place François-I. Recently renovated, the quality of the 24 rooms varies, but some are very nice; the large bathrooms are a treat. Major credit cards accepted. 15 Rue Plume-jeau, Cognac (phone: 45-32-08-70). Moderate.

François I – This historic hostelry where General de Gaulle once stayed overlooks the town square and has 29 rooms on 3 floors. It used to be an inn, and what now is the garage was a stable. Ask for a room facing the plaza. Major credit cards accepted. Pl. François-I, Cognac (phone: 45-32-07-18). Moderate to inexpensive.

EATING OUT: *L'Echassier* – Under the supervision of one of the finest chefs of the region, this turn-of-the-century dwelling was transformed into an elegant dining spot where rich local food (one Michelin star) marries well with bordeaux wines. Closed Sundays. Major credit cards accepted. 72 Rue de Bellevue, Cognac-Châteaubernard (phone: 45-32-29-04; fax: 45-32-22-43). Expensive to moderate.

Pigeons Blancs – In a lovely, wooded setting, this excellent dining room in a château-hotel (6 rooms) of the same name offers nouvelle cuisine, including a good *sole à la vapeur de cognac* (steamed sole). Don't miss cocktails on the terrace, overlooking the garden. Follow D731 north a short distance, toward Cherves. Closed Sunday evenings. Major credit cards accepted. 110 Rue Jules-Brisson, Cognac (phone: 45-82-16-36; fax: 45-82-29-29). Expensive to moderate.

La Ribaudière – Only 5½ miles (8 km) from Cognac on the road to Angoulême, this restaurant offers a variety of grilled dishes and meat. It has a terrace facing the Charente River. Closed Mondays and January. Major credit cards accepted. Follow N141 east to Bourg-Charente; the restaurant is on the left-hand side of the road (phone: 45-81-30-54). Moderate.

SAINTES: Route N141 heading west from Cognac very quickly leads to the charming town of Saintes, reminiscent of St-Emilion in Bordeaux, with its cathedral and houses with red tile roofs. Everything about Saintes has a gentle quality — the people, the curve of the river, the arch of the two bridges in the center of town, the shape of the plantain trees shading the sidewalks along Cours National. It might be called the city of markets and museums, of petunias and marigolds. It's the kind of place that is perfect for wandering aimlessly. Turn almost any corner and you're bound to happen upon a quaint street or an ancient landmark such as the 1st-century Roman arch (the votive arch of Germanicus) and amphitheater. The elliptical amphitheater, a large green basin between two hills, is amazingly well preserved, though it is said that unthinking citizens were in the habit of taking some of the evenly cut stones to build their own homes until the middle of the last century. Once, as many as 20,000 spectators could sit and watch gladiator battle gladiator or beast. Its outer dimensions are 336 by 415 feet; the arena itself is 129 by 211 feet.

Saintes is a grand place to shop; walk along the small pedestrian Rue St-Michel or the larger Rue Victor-Hugo or Rue Alsace-Lorraine. The prices for food and clothing are more reasonable than anywhere else in the region. There are plenty of markets to stroll through. The one beside the cathedral is open Wednesdays and Saturdays; there is an open-air market on Tuesdays and Fridays at Cours Reverseaux and Rue St-Macoult and one on Thursdays and Sundays, near the train station. The first Monday of each month, a merry band of sellers comes into town and the streets fill up with vendors; look for them particularly near the arch at the abbey. To have a drink and listen to music, drop by *Le Vaudeville* at Quai de la République (phone: 46-93-11-91).

The tourist office (Villa Musso, 62 Cours National; phone: 46-74-23-82) provides a map with a walking tour of the city; it is open Mondays through Saturdays as well as the Monday the vendors come to town (closed the day after) and daily in summer.

The local food specialty is a *galette charentaise,* a glazed sugar cookie. It's usually the size of a small pizza (some places make smaller ones, but they're hard to find) and impossible to eat without the help of half a dozen friends. To actually sample cognac where it is produced, visit M. Bossuet, who welcomes visitors at "Logis de la folle blanche," Senouches (Chaniers on N141; phone: 46-91-51-90). If you want to take home samples of pottery from Saintes and Angoulême, visit Mme. Bovet in the little town of St-Porchaire (on the main road); for a less traditional sampling, go to *Alexiu* (La Chapelle des Pots, 5 miles/8 km from Saintes, near Brizambourg; phone: 46-91-51-04).

Cathédrale St-Pierre has been built and destroyed a number of times. It originally was built in the late 12th century, then reconstructed in the Ogival Gothic style in the 15th century. Most of what remains today is from that period — the western portal at the base of the steeple, for instance, which is a beautiful piece of sculpture and deserves special attention. (The north and south walls of the base of the clock tower, on the other hand, appear to be part of the pre-Roman church.) The 240-foot clock tower dates from the 17th century, while the southern part of the transept and its dome date from the 12th century. Note the Renaissance chapel, the spiral staircase, and the ancient cloister of Chapitre St-Pierre, next to the cathedral. The inside of the cathedral is surprisingly well lit by the sun during the day.

The Abbaye des Dames, a Romanesque church dating from the 12th century, was administered for 7 centuries by abbesses from distinguished French families, from among whom will come the future Marquise de Montespan. Converted to a prison during the French Revolution, it was used as a barracks until 1926, and its reconstruction began 50 years later. Today the abbey houses a vibrant, living church; modern tapestries hang on the walls, and concerts of medieval music are held here in July. The central portal is intricately carved and the bell tower is worthy of note.

The remarkable Eglise St-Eutrope was built on the road to Santiago de Compostela on the spot where St. Eutrope became a martyr. Consecrated in 1096, the vast crypt, which contains St. Eutrope's tomb, is the most interesting part of the church. The bell tower, the spire of which is almost 200 feet high, was built in the late 1400s. Across the street is a small, inviting park as well as a good *salon de thé*.

The *Musée des Beaux-Arts,* in a restored, 3-story, 17th-century hotel (Rue Victor-Hugo; phone: 46-93-03-94), is worth a visit if only for the building. The collection includes pottery from the 16th to the 18th century, including some of the work of the famous 16th-century artisan Bernard Palissy. There is an interesting framed fragment of a tapestry from the 17th century portraying St. Peter holding the keys to heaven. Nearby, the *Musée de l'Echevinage* (Rue Alsace-Lorraine; phone: 46-93-52-39) has a dozen noteworthy paintings from the 19th and 20th centuries as well as Sèvres china. Neither museum has an admission charge and both are closed Tuesdays; during the winter, closed Mondays.

If you have time for only one museum, let it be the *Musée d'Art Régional Dupuy-Mestreau,* in the former townhouse of the Marquis de Monconseil, which was built in 1738 and completely renovated in 1974 (Rue Monconseil; phone: 46-93-36-71). It has one of the best collections of French folklore anywhere, with excellent exhibitions of clothing, lace, and peasant and upper class headdresses (including the *quichenot* — "kiss me not" — that occasionally still is worn by women to gather oysters but was supposedly used originally to keep the English soldiers from trying to kiss the maidens). It also has 18th- and 19th-century dolls, jewelry from the reign of Marie-Antoinette, ceramics, furniture, and a re-creation of a 19th-century bedroom and kitchen in a Saintonge house as well as the bedroom of the Marquise de Monconseil. Don't overlook the tarot cards from 1854 and the tiny mustache brush. A guided tour is included with the admission charge. Open afternoons only, except Tuesdays in summer and Sundays, Mondays, and Tuesdays in winter. There also is the *Musée du Folklore* (89 Rue St-Palais; phone: 46-93-67-09), open daily, except Sunday afternoons, from June to October.

The *Musée Archéologique,* beside the tourist office on the east side of the river on

Esplanade Malraux, has been around since 1815 but now is more a warehouse for Roman relics than a museum; it's free and should be (closed Tuesdays; phone: 46-74-20-97). Nearby is a pleasant public garden with a gazebo and large dovecote. The municipal library, in the old Hôtel Martineau at Place de l'Echevinage, houses the extensive collection of Maurice Martineau, more than 75,000 volumes. Notice the beautiful wood door; the entrance is through the courtyard. Open Tuesday to Saturday afternoons from 1:30 to 6 PM; Wednesday and Saturday mornings from 9:30 to 11:30 AM. Closed the first 2 weeks in August (phone: 46-93-25-39).

CHECKING IN: *Le Mancini* – Centrally located, this stately hotel (actually several adjoining houses) has 44 stylish rooms, a bar, a breakfast room, and a seafood restaurant. Diners can pick their lobster fresh from a tank, or try one of the duck or oyster specialties. Major credit cards accepted. Rue des Messageries, Saintes (phone: 46-93-06-61; fax: 46-92-23-37). Expensive to moderate.

Le Relais du Bois St-Georges – This inn, which looks like a country estate at the end of a tree-lined drive, has 27 rooms and 3 suites, all delightful and tastefully decorated, from the antique furniture to the teal blue carpeting and wallpaper. Each of the 20 tables in the restaurant has a view of the lawn, since the walls are all glass; the room also has a raised ceiling, Oriental rugs, and a fireplace faced by comfortable leather chairs. Bass and turbot dishes are the house specialties; vegetables come straight from the garden. Indoor pool. Major credit cards accepted. About a mile (1.6 km) outside Saintes on Rue Royan and Cours Genêt (phone: 46-93-50-99; fax: 46-93-50-99). Expensive to moderate.

France – Across from the train station, this cozy hotel is a little removed from the downtown area but is a very pleasant place to stay. It has 25 rooms; request one facing the garden. There is a seafood restaurant, *Le Chalet,* and in summer you can dine outside under the trees. The hotel is closed in November; the restaurant is closed Fridays from December to *Easter.* Major credit cards accepted. Pl. de la Gare, Saintes (phone: 46-93-01-16). Moderate to inexpensive.

EATING OUT: *Le Logis Santon* – Self-taught chef Alain Sorillet has turned the family residence into one of the best restaurants in the region, combining tradition (local specialties) and creation (particularly the sauces) in a charming setting that accommodates only 20 guests. Closed Sunday evenings, Mondays, and the last week in February. Visa and Carte Bleue accepted. 54 Cours Genêt, Saintes (phone: 46-74-20-14). Moderate.

Le Jardin du Rempart – This pleasant piano bar-dining spot, filled with hanging plants and skylit during the day, offers a fine salad bar as well as beef, duck, and grilled dishes. Open daily for brunch and dinner. Music nightly. Major credit cards accepted. 36 Rue du Rempart, Saintes (phone: 46-93-37-66). Moderate to inexpensive.

Le Procopio – At this large Italian eatery, the best seating is upstairs, in the garden, and on the enclosed terrace. Almost anything you order is large enough to be shared by two. Closed Sundays and Mondays. Major credit cards accepted. Near the cathedral, at 5 Rue de la Comédie, Saintes (phone: 46-74-31-91). Inexpensive.

En Route from Saintes – Before continuing west on N141, consider a 10-mile (16-km) detour north on N137 to St-Porchaire to see the most elegant of the handful of large châteaux in this region that are open to the public. This one, La Roche Courbon, with two towers, manicured lawns, and a large reflecting pool, is a real beauty. Built during the 15th century and renovated 2 centuries later, the impressive structure is in a forest on a riverbank; within walking distance are prehistoric caves that can be explored. The interior of the château is ornate and filled with furnishings from a number of periods; one room is full of paintings on wood dating from 1662, and the Louis XIII room has noteworthy painted beams. The gardens are open daily year-round; the château is open daily from 10 AM to noon and 2:30 to 6:30 PM mid-June to mid-September, and daily except Thursdays from mid-September to mid-June. Closed February 15 to March 15 (phone: 46-95-60-10).

The environs of Saintes are filled with tiny 15th- to 18th-century churches and chapels, usually off the main road, but the turnoffs are well marked. You can take pot luck or, one suggestion, follow D129 south to Rioux, a tiny Roman church 10 miles (16 km) from Saintes; the carvings make the detour worthwhile. Route N150 leads from Saintes to Royan, 23 miles (37 km) southwest.

ROYAN: A resort town that has known better days, Royan (pop. 18,000) was destroyed in World War II and has been completely rebuilt, leaving it with a mishmash of buildings, streets glutted with traffic, and none of its former charm. People still flock to its beaches every summer, but better spots lie to the south and north. The only real attraction here is Eglise Notre-Dame, designed by Guillaume Gillet and built in the late 1950s. It's impossible to miss it, rising like the hull of a great ship moored at the highest point in the city. Inside, it is even more boat-like, and you should stand in the center as well as at either end to get the full effect. The church is in the shape of an ellipse, and the ceiling soars high overhead, with nothing — neither column nor arch — obstructing the inner space. Vertical strips of pale stained glass set into slabs of reinforced gray mortar add to the unexpected beauty of the church. In summer an organ festival is held here. Signs point the way to the church from the center of town; it's uphill all the way.

Good maps of the Charente-Maritime region are available at the Royan Tourist Office (Palais des Congrès; phone: 46-38-65-11) and in a kiosk to your left just as you come into town (Rond-Point de la Poste; phone: 46-05-04-71). Regular ferries (phone: 56-09-60-84) travel from Royan to Pointe de Grave, where routes can be picked up either along the Atlantic coast or through the wine producing region of the Médoc.

CHECKING IN: *Residence de Rohan* – A few miles north of Royan is this elegant 19th-century manor house that has been converted into a tranquil 40-room country inn. Closed mid-November to *Easter*. Major credit cards accepted. Conche de Nauzan (phone: 46-39-00-75; fax: 46-38-29-99). Moderate.

En Route from Royan – Before heading north to the more interesting town of Rochefort, take time to follow the beach road, banked by pine-covered boulders plunging into the sea, a few miles south to the small, peaceful beaches of Meschers. Then continue 7 miles (11 km) farther south to Talmont. The sight of the tiny 12th-century church clinging to a wall by the side of the sea is what travel, and prized travel photographs, are all about. Built by Benedictine monks and damaged over the years by sea, wind, and war, this simple church, called Ste-Radegonde, has retained its dignity and beauty and now is designated a national monument.

Route D733 leads directly from Royan to Rochefort, 25 miles (40 km) north, but it would be a shame to miss Marennes, the most important center for oyster cultivation in France, and the 17th-century fortified town of Brouage along the way. On a clear day, going to Marennes via the coastal road, D25, is especially worthwhile. There is a zoo along this route, in La Palmyre. Open year-round from 9 AM to 7 PM, it has 900 birds and animals in 24 acres of hills and valleys (phone: 46-22-46-06). Stop at Pointe de la Coubre to admire the lighthouse, and its spectacular view of Ile d'Oléron and the cliffs to the south; just south of the lighthouse is a nude beach, but be warned that the water can be treacherous here. North of the lighthouse stretches the Côte Sauvage (Savage Coast); let the name alone, with its inherent images of beauty, desolation, and danger, be enough to discourage a quick dip, no matter how refreshing it might seem.

Try to plan a stop in Marennes as close as possible to the outgoing tides in order to see the huge oyster beds and the people gathering the delicacies from the sea.

Purportedly the finest oysters in all of France, they are green due to the algae in the water in which they thrive. Parisians are said to prefer these expensive, green oysters, though the people from the Charente-Maritime stick to the flat or long varieties that are a "normal" color. Stop to enjoy fresh oysters, mussels, and other seafood in La Cayenne, the oyster-fishing harbor at Marennes. There is an oyster museum here in the 17th-century Fort Louvois (also called Fort du Chapus), which is open only from June to mid-September. In Marennes it also is possible to visit the elegant Château de la Gataudière, part of which is now a maritime museum; the architecture and furnishings remain as they were when the château was built, in the mid-18th century, by François Fresneau, also known as "the father of the raincoat." The château is open March through November from 10 AM to noon and 2 to 6:30 PM (phone: 46-85-01-07). You can reach Marennes on D728 (turn left on D733 from Royan) if you don't take the coast road.

A country road full of hairpin turns, D3 leads from Marennes 4½ miles (7 km) to Brouage, whose walls rise up out of the road like a medieval mirage.

BROUAGE: Founded in 1555, Brouage was a port city until land encroached upon the sea and changed its history. It was here that Samuel de Champlain, the founder of Quebec, was born, in 1570, and from here French colonists set sail for the New World. The ancient ramparts, built in the 1630s by order of Richelieu, still encircle the town, which seems to have fallen asleep several hundred years ago. The walls, 3 miles of them punctuated with 22 watch towers, are still beautiful though crumbling in places. The best way to see the town and the surrounding area is to walk halfway around the ramparts; go up the stairs to the left of the tourist office (beside the northern entrance) and come back down again when you reach the main street, Rue du Québec, which passes by the town's early-17th-century church. Once you look out over the ramparts, it's easy to imagine the water that once lapped these walls, the workers loading salt for export onto waiting ships, and the tragic heroine Marie Mancini bidding farewell to Louis XIV, the lover she was never to see again, as he sailed south to marry Maria Teresa for political reasons in 1659. Driving through the portals of Brouage is like stumbling into a hidden garden, and an hour's visit here will leave you feeling peaceful and nostalgic for something not quite definable.

The 8 miles (13 km) of road, still D3, are pastoral and winding; on either side, sea grass grows profusely and cows are kept penned in by narrow moats rather than fences.

ROCHEFORT: The friendliness of this place and its people is apparent immediately. Today a bustling city of 30,000, Rochefort was founded in the 17th century as a military port, and it contains one of the greatest pieces of architecture from the reign of Louis XIV, the Corderie Royale, an incredible 1,236-foot arsenal. It burned in May 1944 and has been almost completely restored. The Corderie extends majestically along the Charente River, beginning at the Jardin des Retours (Garden of Returns) and ending at the boat basin. Today it is a living museum to the seafaring life (Centre International de la Mer; open daily; phone: 46-87-01-90), complete with exhibitions and videotapes.

The city has a transporter bridge dating from 1900, the last of its kind in France. It ceased service in 1967, when its duties were taken over by the neighboring Pont à Travée Levante. The bridge allows the number of vehicles that cross the Charente to expand from 2,500 to 25,000 a day.

Place Colbert, in the center of town, is an open, graceful plaza. A few blocks away is the tourist office (Av. Sadi-Carnot; phone: 46-99-08-60), which is open daily. Also nearby is the only store in the region where cameras with serious problems can be repaired, *Vidéophot,* where M. Deserson offers reliable service and reasonable prices (111 Rue de la République; phone: 46-99-63-84; fax: 46-99-52-64).

On Tuesday, Thursday, and Saturday mornings, Avenue Général-de-Gaulle and

Avenue Lafayette become a street fair, where vendors of prepared foods and produce, not to mention hamsters and chickens, file into town. This is one of the largest, liveliest, and most colorful markets in the Charente region. Use it as a chance to sample a regional specialty, *tourteau fromagé,* a round cake made with cottage cheese and oddly charred on top.

One of France's greatest novelties and best-kept secrets — at least to outsiders — is in Rochefort: the Maison de Pierre Loti, the birthplace and lifelong home of the famous French writer, soldier, and adventurer who collected an impressive number of souvenirs in his travels. The house can best be described as an extravagant curiosity inside; it contains, among other things, a medieval room, a Turkish room, a Renaissance room, an Islamic mosque with a sunken floor, an exquisite ceiling, and marvelous tiles and Oriental rugs. These rooms were backdrops for Loti's lavish parties, to which guests came decked out in magnificent costumes, many of them provided by their host. The weapons randomly placed throughout the house are works of art. (Open daily except Sunday mornings and Tuesdays from 10 AM to noon and 2 to 5 PM; 141 Rue Pierre-Loti; phone: 46-99-16-88. Tours are included in the admission charge.)

The *Musée de la Marine* is in the 17th-century Hôtel de Cheusses and pays homage to the sea, its vessels, and their crews. Downstairs are enormous models of ships from the 17th through the 19th century; upstairs, a modern section includes replicas of an ocean liner, a submarine, and much more. On the ground floor but with its own entrance is the Grand Salle, which has an exhibit of nautical knots (47 in all). The museum is next to the Porte du Soleil (Sun Gate), the principal entrance to the ancient marine arsenal. (Closed Tuesdays and holidays; Pl. de la Galissonnière; phone: 46-99-86-57.)

There also is the *Musée d'Art et d'Histoire de la Ville de Rochefort* (closed Sundays and Mondays; 63 Av. Général-de-Gaulle; for information, phone 46-99-83-99) with paintings and ethnographic collections from the 16th through the 19th century. The city's theater, the 18th-century *Théâtre de la Coupe d'Or,* has concerts and plays year-round, including light opera and the works of such playwrights as Pinter and Anouilh; in the summer it sponsors open-air concerts and in the spring, lyric art festivals (101 Av. de la République; phone: 46-99-03-32).

Rochefort has gained a reputation in recent years for its thermal springs, sought out by those seeking relief from rheumatism, circulatory ailments, and skin problems. Visitors who come for treatment — some 5,000 a year — need to have a reservation; there is a hotel for their convenience. For more information, write to the *Etablissement Thermale de Rochefort* (Av. Camille-Pelletan, Rochefort 17300; phone: 46-99-08-64).

Route N137 leads to La Rochelle, 20 miles (32 km) north of Rochefort.

CHECKING IN: Corderie Royale – Regally housed in a 17th-century building, this establishment offers 50 modern rooms with baths and a mini-health club for guests (no additional charge). Each room has a TV set, a direct-dial phone, and a mini-bar. Major credit cards accepted. Rue Audebert, Rochefort-sur-Mer (phone: 46-99-35-35; fax: 46-99-78-72). Expensive to moderate.

Le Soubise – This comfortable hotel has 22 rooms and an outstanding restaurant (closed Sunday nights and Mondays) that specializes in regional dishes. It's in the little town of Soubise, 5 miles (8 km) southwest of Rochefort on D238E. Closed during October. Major credit cards accepted. 62 Rue de la République, Soubise (phone: 46-84-92-16). Hotel, expensive to moderate; restaurant, expensive.

La Belle Poule – An attractive hostelry on the Royan road into Rochefort, it has 22 rooms and a fairly expensive restaurant. Closed Sunday evenings. Major credit cards accepted. Rochefort (phone: 46-99-71-87). Moderate.

Roca-Fortis – Near the center of town and only a short walk from the boat basin, this spacious hotel has 16 rooms. Major credit cards accepted. 14 Rue de la République, Rochefort (phone: 46-99-26-32). Moderate to inexpensive.

Le Bassin III – This little inn with lace curtains on the windows is certainly *charmante*. You'll find it just before the bridge on the road to Saintes out of Rochefort (near the boat basin). It has only 8 rooms, and there is a good, small restaurant with regional specialties such as *entrecôte à l'ardoise* (steaks cooked on slate). Major credit cards accepted. 6 Av. William-Ponty, Rochefort (phone: 46-99-01-88). Inexpensive.

EATING OUT: *Le Tourne-Broche* – Meat is grilled over a wood fire, but regional fish dishes are the real specialty here. Closed Sundays, Mondays, and July 1–15. Major credit cards accepted. 56 Av. Général-de-Gaulle, Rochefort (phone: 46-99-20-19). Moderate.

Café "Le Flore" – Snuggled up against the boat basin, this is the local spot for a daily special of steaks with fries, seafood, a burger, or drinks. Weather permitting, you can sit on the porch in one of the ten rocking chairs. Closed Wednesdays. Major credit cards accepted. Bassin de Plaisance (Pleasure Boat Basin), Rochefort (phone: 46-87-21-06). Inexpensive.

LA ROCHELLE: Called "the City of Lights," this is a dazzling town, night or day, and it also is the cultural and administrative center of the Charente-Maritime *département*. La Rochelle was a fishing village that was developed in the 12th century between two points of land jutting into the Atlantic, Minimes Point and Pallice Point. Two commanding towers — Tours St-Nicolas and de la Chaîne — guard the entrance to the old port, as they have done for 6 centuries, and make entering this city of 85,000 all the more dramatic. And La Rochelle has the largest number of streets with covered archways in France as well as many houses dating from the 15th century, including Revival timbered houses. To add a modern note, it also has impressive high-rise condominiums and the biggest pleasure boat basin in all of Europe. The unflagging interest in ecology of Mayor Michel Crepeau, who used to be France's minister of the environment, is apparent throughout the city.

The old port has existed since the 13th century and probably was always fortified. The St. Nicolas and the Chain towers actually used to have a chain stretched between them to keep out unknown ships as well as to keep others from leaving without paying taxes. Tour de la Chaîne is connected by a rampart to yet another tower, Tour de la Lanterne (The Lantern, or Four Sergeants, Tower); it was used as a lighthouse as well as a prison and for defense. The names of former inmates still are visible where they were carved on the walls. This tower, with its Gothic spire, offers an impressive view of the city and the harbor. All three towers are open for visits.

Plentiful free parking is available at the old port. On Saturday and Sunday nights in the summer the main street of the port is closed to traffic, making it even more pleasant to stroll and admire the beautifully lit sweep of buildings along the seafront, with the medieval gate to the old town, the Porte de la Grosse Horloge, right in the center, beckoning wayfarers into the heart of town. The faint music of the 100-year-old carousel on Valin Square fills the air, advertising a free ride for anyone in the mood. Bicycles are provided (with proof of ID) at Valin Square and the Esplanade des Parcs at no charge every morning and afternoon except on Sundays, Mondays, and holidays, and are especially fun to take to Parc Charruyer, a mile-long, 660-foot-wide strip of green with a stream running through it.

The tourist office is at Place de la Petite-Sirène, Le Gabut, near the port (phone: 46-41-14-68; generally closed Sundays and holidays). The *Musée du Nouveau Monde* (10 Rue Fleuriau; open daily except Tuesday and Sunday mornings; closed lunchtime; admission charge) is housed in the superbly restored 18th-century *Hôtel Fleuriau,* itself a marvelous exhibition piece. It has 17 rooms on 4 floors open to the public, 10 galleries, and 7 period rooms with beautiful wainscoting and fireplaces. This museum describes the opening of Louisiana by Louis XIV and depicts the lives of the early French settlers there. Objects on display date from the 16th through the mid-19th century and were chosen for their historic as well as artistic value. One room is devoted to the American Indian. For Americans especially, a visit to this museum is a chance to learn more about a very rich part of our heritage (phone: 46-41-46-50).

Rue Dupaty leads to a small square where you will find the central post office and the Hôtel de Ville (Town Hall), a striking building with a Gothic surrounding wall dating from the 15th century. The main part of the building dates from the 16th century and is very decorative; the façade and staircase are Henri IV. Throughout, visitors will see many mementos from the siege of 1628 as well as Jean Guiton's study with its marble table. Guided tours are given every 20 minutes during the summer; off-season, afternoons only.

Coursive (Rue St-Jean at Cours des Dames, beside the old port; phone: 46-51-54-00) has a full and ever-changing agenda of films, music, dance, art exhibitions, and theater. The *Carre Amelot* (Municipal Youth Center) has similar offerings, but the acoustics aren't as good (closed Mondays; 10 *bis* Rue Amelot; phone: 46-41-45-62).

The *Musée d'Orbigny-Bernon* has quite a menagerie; of special note are the 18th-century apothecary and the carved, oval Oriental bed on the third floor. (Open daily except Sunday mornings and Tuesdays; 2 Rue St-Côme; phone: 46-41-18-83.) The aquarium, France's largest, with fish from all over the world, is between the harbor and the beach (open daily; phone: 46-44-00-00). Right across from the harbor, on Rue de la Désirée, in a small section of wooden houses, is an automaton museum filled with 300 robots (open daily; phone: 46-41-68-08). The *Lafaille Museum of Natural History* is a bit of a hike from the center of town, but it has a nice garden where you can rest once you get there (closed Mondays; 28 Rue Albert-I; phone: 46-41-18-25). Finally, there is a *Musée des Beaux-Arts* (Rue Gargoulleau; phone: 46-41-64-65) with paintings from the 16th through 20th century (closed Tuesdays). One ticket gains admission to the *Beaux-Arts, D'Orbigny,* and *Nouveau Monde* museums.

There's more to do in La Rochelle at night than simply admire the city lights. *Le Crystal* (54 Cours Dames), the Art Deco café and piano bar with a striking chartreuse interior, is next to the Tour de la Chaîne. It serves cocktails, ice cream, and tea, and the concoctions dreamed up here are delightful (phone: 46-41-43-10). *Le Café de la Paix* sometimes has live jazz or classical music (54 Rue Chandrier, Pl. de Verdun; phone: 46-41-39-79). A local hangout that tourists might not ordinarily happen upon is the intimate *Piano Pub;* it's the epitome of "out-of-the-way" (12 Cours du Temple, just off Rue du Temple via Petite Rue du Temple; closed Sundays; phone: 46-41-03-42). Numerous nightclubs are scattered around the old harbor.

La Rochelle is a good city for shopping (especially for sailor-type togs) and eating out, though prices often are high. For local pottery, there is *Poterie de la Rochelle* (29 Quai Maubec; phone: 46-41-38-14). Gastronomic pleasures revolve around seafood, of course, and regional specialties on most menus include *mouclade* (mussels in a curry cream sauce), *chaudrée* (fish chowder), and *cagouilles* (small snails). For scrumptious chocolates and other sweets, visit *Boutet* (5-7 Rue du Temple).

For a real bird's-eye view of the city and surrounding area, you can take a sightseeing trip in a small airplane. The planes also go to Ile d'Oléron or Ile de Ré (the latter is the preferred stop — despite the new bridge that moors it to the mainland — because Oléron has become very populated in recent years and has lost much of its charm). For more information, call *AéroClub Charente-Maritime* (phone: 46-42-54-74). You also can get a couple of breathtaking views without ever leaving the ground: Stroll along the walkway around the old port at sunset, or drive out for a look at the new pleasure boat basin.

There is a produce market on Wednesday and Saturday mornings at Place du Marché and a Saturday flea market in Quartier St-Nicolas. In September there is a sailboat festival; in late June and early July, an international film festival; also in July, *Francofolies,* a festival of French songs; and in November, a car rally.

CHECKING IN: La Monnaie – In a stately stone building that once served as 17th-century Paris's mint and treasury, this hotel offers plush modern rooms and proximity to both the sea and the old port. Major credit cards accepted. 3 Rue de la Monnaie (phone: 46-50-65-65; fax: 46-50-63-19). Expensive to moderate.

Le Yachtman – Facing the old port, this hotel offers 40 rooms that look out on either the port or its swimming pool, which is enclosed by ivy-covered walls. Each room has a refrigerator, TV set, and direct-dial phone. Open year-round. Major credit cards accepted. 23 Quai Valin, La Rochelle (phone: 46-41-20-68; fax: 46-41-81-24). Expensive to moderate.

St-Jean d'Acre – This pleasant place, with 77 soundproof rooms (some overlooking the port) is tucked behind the Tour de la Lanterne. It has a good restaurant, *Au Vieux Port,* with a terrace on the wharf. Among the regional specialties are grilled lobster, salmon, and turbot. Major credit cards accepted. 4 Pl. de la Chaîne, La Rochelle (phone: 46-41-73-33; fax: 46-41-10-01). Moderate.

St-Nicolas – Quiet, and only a few blocks from the flow of traffic and activity, this 74-room establishment is still within walking distance of everything. Though totally redecorated in an ultramodern style, the friendly staff makes staying here still seem more like being in a home than in a hotel. Major credit cards accepted. 13 Rue Sardinerie, La Rochelle (phone: 46-41-71-55; fax: 46-41-70-46). Moderate.

EATING OUT: La Marmite – Another Michelin star holder, its chef holds to traditional bourgeois cooking and does it well, with the accent on quality of preparation and richness of ingredients. Closed Wednesdays and mid-February to mid-March. Major credit cards accepted. 14 Rue St-Jean-du-Pérot, La Rochelle (phone: 46-41-17-03). Expensive.

Le Pavillon – Owned by a chef from Lyons, this eatery gets high ratings for extremely refined cooking. Housed in a new building overlooking the Ile de Ré, it specializes in fish and seafood. Try the salmon filet and the fish terrine (pâté). Closed Sunday evenings and Mondays. Major credit cards accepted. Le Belvédère, La Repentie at Pont L'Ile de Ré, 4 miles (6 km) from La Rochelle (phone: 46-42-62-62). Expensive.

Richard Coutanceau – With two Michelin stars, it has a view of the sea to accompany such specialties as *salade de goujonnettes de sole et langoustine aux senteurs de Provence* (sole and lobster salad with Provençal herbs) and *bar en feuilles vertes au fumet de St-Emilion* (bass in green leaves with St-Emilion). There is a pleasing dessert selection and myriad white wines from which to choose. A member of the prestigious Relais & Châteaux group. Closed Sundays and Monday evenings. Major credit cards accepted. Behind Tour de la Chaîne, Plage de la Concurrence, La Rochelle (phone: 46-41-48-19). Expensive.

La Maison des Mouettes – In summer, grab a table on the terrace and order *langoustines au court bouillon d'algues* or *l'effilade de volaille au crabe.* The selection is as expansive as the seaside view. Closed Mondays. Major credit cards accepted. Route de la Plage, in Aytre, 3 miles (5 km) south of La Rochelle via D937 (phone: 46-44-29-12). Expensive to moderate.

Serge – Well-known, with one Michelin star, it is surprisingly small and cozy, with a wood ceiling and walls and lace curtains at the windows. Seafood delights include lobster, crab, prawn pâté, and oysters on the half shell, served on silver platters on a bed of ice. Everything is accompanied by mayonnaise and butter, *à la charentaise.* The restaurant is open for lunch and dinner; closed Tuesdays in off-season. Major credit cards accepted. Facing the old port, at 46 Cours des Dames, La Rochelle (phone: 46-41-18-80). Expensive to moderate.

En Route from La Rochelle – From La Pallice Point, you can cross the bridge to Ile de Ré, a 48-mile-long treasure of tiny villages, small whitewashed cottages, beaches, and mostly uninhabited land except in summer, with the tourist migration. A bird sanctuary is at the northern end of the island. In the summer you can rent a bike near the bridge, as well as in other locations, for some personal exploration; bike paths are plentiful.

■ **Note:** It is dangerous to swim in the inlet, called Fiers d'Ars, at the northeast end of the island, but there are plenty of safe, well-marked beaches elsewhere. Ile de Ré is rightfully called "the white island" because of the bounteous sunlight that reflects off its white houses. Route N11, the road to Niort, leads north from La Rochelle to "the Land of the Great Green Silence," the Marais Poitevin.

MARAIS POITEVIN: Also called "the Green Venice," the unique Marais Poitevin comprises 212,000 acres, some 40,000 of which are filled with canals and islands, flooded areas interspersed with clumps of forest, houses with thatch roofs, and friendly country people. The Parc Naturel Régional du Marais Poitevin is a protected area, and within it lie many diversions, among them 34 miles of hiking trails, a "zoorama" containing 600 animals on 62 acres in Chizé Forest, 15 miles (24 km) south of Niort, ethnography museums, castles, and abbeys. Only a flat-bottom boat can maneuver you deep into this region, however, where lime green algae blankets the water and trees intertwine overhead to give all the nicknames credence. People who live here year-round depend on boat travel to get them to solid ground to buy groceries or mail a letter. Boat rentals and guided tours are available in several towns in the area: In La Garette, try *Largeaud-Bouyer* (phone: 49-35-93-35); in Magné, *A. Cardinaud* (La Repentie; phone: 49-35-90-47), in Damvix, *Germaneau* (phone: 51-87-15-18), and in La Ronde, *Rabatière* (phone: 46-01-17-16). They're also available in Arçais at *Bardet* (phone: 49-26-31-80) and at the old Abbey of Maillezais. Now in ruins and lost in the moors, Maillezais was the home of the writer Rabelais from 1523 to 1527. The drive from Arçais to Coulon, 6 miles (10 km), follows a canal; La Garette is 1½ miles (2 km) from Coulon. To get to Coulon, go via Courçon, Frontenay-Rohan-Rohan. The canals are named and well marked on maps;take a picnic, tie up your boat along the way, and go ashore for a secluded feast in France's "green land." For information, call 46-27-82-44, or visit the information center in the town of La Ronde, near Courçon.

Bordeaux
and the Médoc

The Bordeaux region in southwest France stretches from the tip of the Médoc Peninsula — located between the Gironde River and the Atlantic Ocean — east to the border of neighboring Périgord, and south to the splendid Arcachon Basin and the forests of the Landes. It contains the Médoc, some of the richest wine country in the world, glorious unsung beaches, two huge lakes and the Basin itself, 2 million acres of serene, trail-covered pine forest, and seaside towns and tiny fishing villages that entice even the most blasé travelers. The best part is that this bounty, in all its diversity, is only an hour or less from Bordeaux, no matter the direction chosen: north to the Médoc, south to the Basin, or west to the Côte d'Argent (Silver Coast).

The Médoc extends with hardly even the suggestion of a hillock along the bank of the Gironde from Bordeaux to Pointe de Grave, where the river enters the ocean. Its flat terrain may not be the most interesting, but many people find beauty in the elegant precision of the parallel rows of burgeoning vines, every plant trimmed to identical height. The all-encompassing greenness is punctuated by red roses planted at the roadside ends of the rows (now just a nice touch, but at one time a sort of early warning system against fungus attacks, since the weaker roses would be the first to succumb). From one end of the Médoc to the other, the villages along the vineyard road derive their sustenance from wine: In workshops around the town square, joiners put together the wine cases for the châteaux, and vineyard workers bicycle from their cottages to the fields; even the printing of wine labels is an important subsidiary trade. Although the wines of the Médoc make up only about 8% of those produced in the Bordeaux region, these thoroughbreds set the standard to which the remaining 92% aspire.

An old Médoc saying has it that if you can see the river and feel the pebbles under your feet, you can make good wine. The proximity of the river moderates the winter cold and softens the impact of the spring frosts. In this temperate climate, cool nights follow mild days, and abundant sunshine in the summer inspires the development of natural sugars that produce fermentation. The sand and gravel that the river has tossed onto its banks — no rich alluvial silt here — are perfect for drainage and the development of good wine producing grapes. Pebbles on the soil surface reflect the sunlight to help ripen the grapes. The vines of the Médoc are extremely strong and hardy and can live up to 80 years, with roots that delve as far as 10 to 15 feet down toward the water table. The finest wines come from old stock, and 8 to 10 years of age, corresponding to the maximum of root development, is considered the absolute minimum for top quality. In fact, local law forbids making wine from vines less than 4 years old.

In most wine making districts, the cellar master will invite you into a cool, low-ceilinged *cave* hewn out of bedrock. In Bordeaux, where the soil is sand rather than rock and where, because of the proximity of the river, the water table is high, traditional wine cellars are impractical. With few exceptions, the Médoc wine maker goes about his business in the *chai,* a long shed with a sloping roof of sunbaked terra cotta tiles. The *chai* resembles a kind of warehouse, with whitewashed walls and good ventilation. There usually is a central row of columns supporting the roof over the earthen floor, and the barrels are stacked two or three high in orderly rows that run the length of the *chai.*

The terms first growth (or *cru*), second growth, third growth, and so on, refer to a system of ranking the top wines of the Médoc that was formulated more than a century ago. In 1855, Napoleon III ordered a classification of bordeaux wines by quality for the *Exposition Universelle de Paris,* a kind of world's fair. This classification still is used, and although it remains accurate in its assessment of the very top of the great growths, there are many who argue that some wines deserve to be upgraded by rank and others lowered. The fun is to compare the wines from the various *crus* and other excellent selections that may not have a ranking (remember, the classification was of the best of the best), find those that particularly appeal to your taste and pocketbook, and perhaps return home with a case of your favorite. Some 25% of all Médoc wines are *crus classés,* while nearly 50% are *crus bourgeois,* a classification first developed in the early 1930s and one that is unique to the Médoc.

There is no great mystery to tasting wines at the Médoc vineyards (or anywhere else, for that matter). You'll find the people who work with wine completely free of the jargon and pretension that wine snobs like to invoke to intimidate lesser mortals. Just hold the glass by the stem or the base, not by the bowl, and raise it to the light. The wine should be a rich, vibrant red, perfectly clear and limpid. Swirl it gently in the glass, then smell it. Take a small sip and hold the liquid in your mouth. Let the wine tumble about the tip and sides of your tongue while you think about the taste. Then spit it out, especially if you're trying several different wines. This may be embarrassing at first, but it is a common practice. In the first place, young wine is not the most digestible drink, and for another, if you want to continue your tour by car and visit several châteaux in the course of the day, common sense will tell you that you can't afford to drink. Some châteaux provide sawdust-filled tubs for spitting; at others, use the floor as professionals do, but remember to turn your head to the side to avoid unnecessary dry cleaning bills for your fellow tasters. Even the best-brought-up tyro soon will be spitting with the rest.

Opposite the Médoc, along the western side of the peninsula jutting out from Bordeaux, a string of unsung beaches lazes in the French sunshine. The stretch of Atlantic from Soulac-sur-Mer, just below the mouth of the Gironde River, to Cap-Ferret, at the entrance to the Arcachon Basin — 60 miles of beautiful coastline backed by towering pine trees — has long been enjoyed by vacationing Bordelais and visiting Germans, Belgians, Dutch, and Swiss. The British are beginning to take advantage of its proximity, and soon other travelers are bound to follow — with good reason. These beaches, though certainly popular, are not as crowded as those along the southern expanse of the Côte d'Argent around Biarritz, and they rub elbows with two large freshwater lakes that offer boating, sailing, and swimming with no waves or undertow to battle. And the bountiful pine forest of the Landes (pronounced *Land*) — what one sees here is merely a hint of its vast acreage — has many convenient trails for hiking and biking.

Bordeaux's backyard beaches make up almost a third of the largest coastline in the world, the Côte d'Argent, and they are rapidly being developed, especially in Soulac-sur-Mer, in Lacanau-Océan, and — a brief hop inland — at lakeside Maubuisson, to provide hospitality, good food, and comfortable lodging for wayfarers. At the same time, parts of the coast are deliberately being left alone, a tribute to the foresight of environmentally minded regional planners.

Always keep in mind that these beaches suffer from a strong undertow; be especially attuned to flags posted to indicate the safety of the waters on any given day. A green flag means you can swim safely and that a lifeguard is on duty; a yellow flag warns you to proceed with caution; a red flag orders you to limit yourself to sunbathing and reading. Don't expect to collect shells when the waves are off-limits, however; you'll usually find only smooth stones and pebbles and occasionally ravenously hungry insects (carry repellent). Some beaches are especially designated *naturiste,* meaning that bathers *must* be nude. However, swimming and sunning in the buff occur openly at most places, though somewhat off to one side or the other of the central cluster of swimmers. Topless bathing is a common phenomenon wherever sand and water exist in tandem; those from countries where this is not the custom should gawk as unobtrusively as possible.

Almost directly west of Bordeaux lies the tidy triangle called the Arcachon Basin: a mooring spot for thousands of sailboats; an important breeding ground for several varieties of oysters; a source of livelihood for a handful of small fishing villages and beach communities; and an exquisite backdrop for the resort town of Arcachon, which still bears vestiges of the Belle Epoque days when it was Queen of the Ball, wooed by English gentry and French artists alike.

The largest sand dune in Europe, Pilat Dune, sprawls a few miles south of Arcachon, at Pyla-sur-Mer. Scale its 380-foot height (and still growing!) for the best view of the region's odd juxtaposition of pine trees, sea, and dunes.

The regal conifers of the Landes, so evident along the coastal area to the north, become even more prevalent around the Basin. In fact, the Parc Régional des Landes de Gascogne (Gascony Moors Regional Park) begins at the southeast corner of the Arcachon Basin and extends about halfway to Biarritz. But it is only a 515,000-acre part of the Landes area. If you were simply to extend the sides of the peninsular triangle formed by Bordeaux, Arcachon, and Pointe de Grave (at the mouth of the Gironde River) down to Biarritz along the coast on the west and along the route of the Garonne River on the east, a new and larger triangle, its base falling just north of Gascony, would be created to encompass the 3 million acres of the Landes.

Until the end of the 18th century, the coastline here was barren and the Landes region was desolate, disease-harboring, swampy moorland. Even worse, strong Atlantic winds were blowing coastal sand farther and farther inland yearly, threatening to turn the inhospitable moor into a more inhospitable desert. The amazing metamorphosis of this tract into the biggest and most important forestland in France began in 1788, when engineer Nicolas Brémontier devised a plan to barricade the coastal dunes with wooden planks, ground cover, and pine trees. Once the dunes had been fixed in place, the swamp inland could be drained, a problem that was settled by 19th-century engineers. The job was completed with the large-scale planting of trees on the former swamp. Landes was once an area where people eked out a meager living herding sheep, which they did quite adroitly on stilts because of the soggy terrain. Now the inhabitants are more gainfully employed in the timber and paper industries and in the cultivation of corn, trout, and chickens. The tastiness of the poultry comes from the fact that it is allowed to roam free in the Landes forest, dining on the delicacies it finds there.

By no means a private preserve, the forest is very much open to and used by the public. In the bird sanctuary in Le Teich, at the southeast corner of the Basin, the land has been left in its natural, unforested state. Here it's possible to commune with the feathered residents and go back in time to see just how forlorn this part of France used to be.

Fire has proved a serious hazard here. From 1944 to 1949, it wiped out more than a third of the forest (fortunately, it has been replanted). Needless to say, campsites are regulated carefully. For more information about the Landes regional park, see tour routes in *Gascony* and *The Pyrénées,* also in this section.

Hotels in each of Bordeaux's three quick getaway regions — the Médoc, the Coast, and the Arcachon Basin — charge about the same rates as the city: $100 and up for an expensive double room; $65 to $100 for a moderately priced one; and under $65 for an inexpensive but adequate room. In restaurants, expect to pay $110 or more for a meal for two (not including wine or drinks) in the expensive category; between $75 and $110, moderate; and under $75 for an inexpensive meal. Service usually is included.

THE MÉDOC

Most of the châteaux in the Médoc make sure that an informed representative is available to greet visitors, take them on a tour of the *chais,* explain the processes involved in making the wine, and perhaps invite them to taste the most recent vintage from the barrel (there is a fee for some tastings). An appointment often is necessary — most châteaux are open from 9 or 10 AM to noon and from 2 to 5:30 PM, but it's strongly recommended to call ahead. Tours generally include visits to the *chais* only, not to the châteaux themselves. Contact French Government Tourist Offices in major US cities (for addresses, see "Tourist Information" in GETTING READY TO GO) before leaving for France and ask for the brochure, *Découverte Médoc,* an excellent guide to châteaux and accommodations in the region. It is published annually by the Conseil des Vins du Médoc. Or drop by the Maison du Vin in Bordeaux (1 Cours 30-Juillet; phone: 56-00-22-66) weekdays and get a list of châteaux that are open to the public; this includes the times they are open as well as which ones have English-speaking guides. Be forewarned that the *maître de chai* probably won't speak English, although your tour guide may, and that most châteaux do not allow visits during the grape harvest. The Maison du Vin also offers tastings of the region's wines on weekdays from 10:30 to 11:30 AM and 2:30 to 4:30 PM. Bottles or cases of recent vintages usually are available for purchase at the châteaux, but if you intend to make a substantial purchase, consult reliable vintage charts ahead of time and ask the advice of a reliable wine dealer. If you are interested in buying wine, visit the Maison du Tourisme et du Vin de Médoc in Pauillac (Quai Léon-Perrier, La Verrerie; phone: 56-59-03-08), the only place in the region where Médoc wines can be purchased at slightly over wholesale prices. The Maison's list includes over 180 choices; be aware that there are no tastings and they cannot ship wine overseas.

Despite its importance to the city, the Médoc is poorly marked from Bordeaux. Follow the signs for Verdon, or find the directions to the Barrière du Médoc. The vineyard road, D2E, branches off to the right about 2 miles (3 km) beyond the turnoff for the Paris autoroute. At this point it's impossible to get lost — especially with ample signs that say Route Touristique du Médoc Nord (or Sud) pointing the way. All the châteaux, large and small, are individually marked right along with the towns. This is the way to all the greatest châteaux and some of the wonderful wines of the region — truly the road to happiness.

Before heading up the vineyard road, golfing enthusiasts can detour west via D211 to the *Golf du Médoc* (Le Pian-Médoc, Blanquefort; phone: 56-72-01-10), a course that vies for honors as France's most deluxe tee-off facility. Each of its 18 holes is sponsored by a different château in the region. The clubhouse and restaurant serve wines from these and other Bordeaux châteaux at very reasonable prices.

The first noteworthy property comes into view on D2E in about 11 miles (18 km).

Château La Lagune – The house and *chai* of this château are visible behind a lacy wrought-iron gate to the right of the vineyard road. The third-growth château, which was built in 1730 by Victor Louis, the architect of the *Grand Théâtre* in Bordeaux, is in the Chartreuse style typical of the 18th and early 19th centuries in the Bordeaux region. The château produces about 25,000 cases of high-quality wine yearly. Closed in August. Visits are by appointment only and generally reserved for wine professionals (Ludon; phone: 56-30-44-07).

Château Cantemerle – About a mile (1.6 km) up the vineyard road from Château La Lagune, the handsome stone manor house of Château Cantemerle nestles deep amid grand old trees in a beautiful parkland setting. The fifth-growth wine of this château enjoys continuing popularity. By appointment only (call the château, 56-30-41-52, or Domaines Cordier, 56-31-44-44).

MARGAUX: No fewer than 21 classified growths as well as a good many unclassified labels are found among the 2,625 vineyard acres of Margaux that produce 5.5 million bottles of wine a year. This world-famous village allows its name to be hyphenated to those of four neighboring hamlets: Arsac, Labarde, Cantenac, and Soussans. Half a million cases of wine entitled to sport the name Margaux are produced here each year, 65% of which are classified growths. About 75% to 80% of the total is exported to eager foreign buyers. Margaux boasts the deepest beds of pebbled earth in what is known as the Haut-Médoc, which includes the townships of Margaux, St-Julien, Pauillac, St-Estèphe, Moulis, and Listrac. For more information, visit the Maison du Vin de Margaux (closed Sundays and Monday mornings); Pl. la Trémoille, Margaux (phone: 56-88-70-82).

Château Giscours – This is a third growth that, like many Bordeaux properties, lay in virtual desolation from the German occupation until the mid-1950s. Under the supervision of the father-son team that has owned the property in the succeeding decades, the vineyards have been restored to full production and the quality of the wine has been recaptured. Land unsuitable for vine cultivation has been planted with many varieties of rhododendrons, which make a magnificent display of bloom in the parkland behind the château. By appointment only; English is spoken (Labarde; phone: 56-88-34-02 or 56-30-06-66).

Château Prieuré-Lichine – At the bend in the vineyard road where D2E becomes

D2, you'll catch your first sight of the fourth-growth Château Prieuré-Lichine, whose late owner, American Alexis Lichine, also was the author of the informative *Guide to the Wines and Vineyards of France*. Sacha Lichine, Alexis's son, currently manages the vineyard. The original part of the château was built as a Benedictine priory (*prieuré*), which served the village of Cantenac through the adjacent church until the dissolution of religious houses at the time of the Revolution. To visit, leave your car on the side of the road opposite the gateway and walk through the arch into the courtyard. The remains of the old cloister are decorated with the fanciful designs of antique cast-iron firebacks collected by the owner from all over Europe. At the office at the end of the gravel walk, you'll find an English-speaking guide who will take you through the *chai*. The vat room, which was built by the monks who tended the vines for centuries, features the original 16th-century beams, but the gleaming stainless-steel vats and wine making equipment are among the most modern in the Médoc. The *maître de chai* may invite you to sample wines in the attractive tasting room (for a fee); purchases are easily arranged. Unlike most châteaux, Prieuré-Lichine is open every day from 9 AM until 7 PM in spring and fall; until 8 PM in summer; until 6 PM in winter (Cantenac; phone: 56-88-36-28).

Château d'Issan – A stroll from Château Prieuré-Lichine along a grassy avenue of stately plane trees leads to this 16th-century château, which, with its pepper pot turrets and a moat, looks like some honey-colored castle bewitched in a fairy tale. In the spring, the grounds are carpeted with wildflowers. One of the *chais* is so magnificent that it has been designated a historic monument; it should not be missed. The property is owned by a prominent Bordeaux family of wine shippers, and visits to the château are not permitted. To arrange a visit to the *chai*, call 56-44-95-45.

Château Palmer – The compact and attractive Château Palmer, on the right side of the vineyard road, flies a flag to honor each of its three proprietors, who are English, French, and Dutch. A pretty feature of the 19th-century château is the rose border at the base of the courtyard walls. Open to the public on weekdays; appointments recommended (Cantenac; phone: 56-88-72-72).

Château Margaux – Take the vineyard road three-quarters of a mile to the marked turnoff to Château Margaux, which, along with its *chai* and grounds, has been classified a historic monument. The grand house with its Ionic columns was built in 1802 and remains an acknowledged perfect example of the Empire style. An intensive program of restoration of the house and modernization of the vineyards and wine making areas has been undertaken since 1977, when the first-growth property was bought by a couple who headed one of France's largest supermarket chains. Widowed and remarried since the purchase, the owner has sought the advice of the country's leading authorities on architecture and decoration to return the house to its Empire splendor; she has applied the same meticulous care to the production of Margaux's fabulous wines.

The enormous *chai* is a most impressive sight: Visitors enter by a kind of dais that is raised slightly above the earth floor to look out over row upon row of barrels, their glass bungs (stoppers) aligned in perfect precision. All splatters and droplets falling onto the wood in the course of sampling are wiped off by workers whose job it is to maintain the order and neatness of the *chai*.

Château Margaux is one of the few places whose production is large enough to justify making its barrels in the property's own cooperage. This is a vast room, with walls of the characteristic pale gold stone of the region, heated by flames leaping from crackling vine clippings in a fireplace large enough to roast an ox and illuminated by daylight streaming in through clerestory windows. In front of the fireplace, burly coopers wrestle the hoops down over the barrel staves in a scene that gives you the sensation of entering the world of medieval woodcuts instead of touring France by car in the 1990s.

The château itself is not open to visitors, but an English-speaking guide is available by appointment to take you through the *chai* (Margaux; phone: 56-88-70-28). In the tasting room are displayed interesting documents and photographs covering the history of the property.

CHECKING IN: *Le Relais du Margaux* – Luxury is the key in the 27 rooms and 3 suites of this well-equipped hotel. It has tennis courts, a swimming pool, and a beautiful, serene park. Its restaurant offers specialties such as asparagus with truffles and fish filet with herbs. Closed late December to February. The restaurant is open daily when the hotel is open. Major credit cards accepted. About 1 mile (1.6 km) north of Margaux (phone: 56-88-38-30). Expensive.

EATING OUT: *Lion D'Or* – A lively, rustic bistro a few miles south of Margaux, where many local wine producers congregate for friendly lunches. You can bring your own wine. Closed Sunday evenings, Mondays, 1 week in January, and all of July. Reservations advised. Major credit cards accepted. Take D2 to Arcins (phone: 56-58-96-79). Moderate to inexpensive.

Relais du Médoc – It has good home cooking, Bordeaux style. There also are 7 simple rooms. Open for lunch and dinner. Closed Monday and Wednesday evenings and in October. Visa accepted. A few miles north of Margaux in Lamarque; turn right off D2E onto D5 and you're as good as there (phone: 56-58-92-27). Moderate to inexpensive.

Le Savoie – This inn serves straightforward cooking and offers a wide variety of local wines. Eat in the garden in season. Closed Sundays and holidays. No credit cards accepted. Pl. la Trémoille, Margaux (phone: 56-88-31-76). Moderate to inexpensive.

ST-JULIEN: As you continue on the vineyard road toward St-Julien, note the contrast between low-lying fields of rich, loamy soil, where fat, contented dairy cows amble about the pasture, and the raised vineyard plantations, where the fast-draining, pebbly soil fosters a king's ransom in wines but could hardly feed a cow for a week! Here, 1,875 acres produce 4.2 million bottles of wine every year.

Château Beychevelle – The first vineyard in St-Julien, this was once, like Château Prieuré-Lichine, a monastery. It was rebuilt in 1757, and the long, low, elegant château is considered a particularly lovely example of the Chartreuse style. At the end of the 16th century, the property belonged to the Chief Admiral of France. Mariners plying the river saluted him by dipping their sails, and the name Beychevelle (*baisser voile,* to lower the sail) commemorates that salute. Open Mondays through Fridays from 9 to 11 AM and from 2 to 7:30 PM. Guided tours, in English in July and August, of the *chais* and parklike gardens are given, though appointments are necessary (phone: 56-59-23-00).

Château Ducru-Beaucaillou – The vineyards of this château, a second *cru,* adjoin those of Beychevelle. The name *beau caillou* (beautiful pebble) honors the soil on which the life of the château depends. The *chais* have been sunk slightly into the ground and have a cool, damp atmosphere that is especially conducive to the preservation of old wines. In surroundings that are too dry, corks will dessicate and crumble, allowing air to enter the bottle and oxidize the wine as well as letting precious wine evaporate. English is spoken. Visits by appointment only; closed weekends, August, and at harvest time (phone: 56-59-05-20).

PAUILLAC: This attractive little town (pronounced more or less *Po*-yak) is one of the oldest in the Médoc and certainly the most central, lying halfway between Bordeaux and Pointe de Grave. The Médoc is not known for great lodgings, and the available hotels are generally modest, with a few notable exceptions. Still, it's nice not to have to turn around and go back to Bordeaux or rush to Soulac-sur-Mer if you're caught up in the spirit and the beauty of the area. Pauillac has several things going for it: a tourist office and Maison du Vin (which sells local wines at just over wholesale prices) that are open daily (Quai Léon-Perrier at La Verrerie; phone: 56-59-03-08); the stationery store of *M. Lafon,* on Quai Léon-Perrier, which sells a number of English newspapers as well as good maps and postcards; and a handy camera store just up the street. The post office is at Place Gachet, and there are several quick-service dry cleaner–laundries. For a break from driving, go for a swim at the town pool or drive 11 miles (18 km) to Lamarque, leave the car, and take the ferry over to the walled city of Blaye (see *Bordeaux* in THE CITIES). Or for a unique opportunity to spend some time in a real Bordelais château, go to Moulis and visit the *Musée des Arts et Métiers de la Vigne et du Vin,* at Château Maucaillou (phone: 56-58-01-23). Dedicated to the art of the vine and wine, the museum is open daily from 10 AM to 6 PM. There is a fee for tastings. Back in Pauillac, stroll along the promenade by the river or out onto the piers, admire the pleasure boats, and, of course, visit some of the most famous châteaux in the world, whose mailing address is this quiet little town, where 2,750 acres produce 5.2 million bottles of wine a year.

Château Latour – This great first-growth château, surprisingly modest in appearance, is the last vineyard in St-Julien or, in some eyes, the first in the district of Pauillac, straddling the boundary as it does. The fortress that once stood on the site was built to repulse the river pirates and bands of pillaging mercenaries who roamed Europe in the wake of medieval wars. By the end of the Hundred Years War, which pitted England and France against each other until 1453, the fort was little more than a heap of rubble. The sole vestige is the tower (*la tour*), which stands today like a sentinel keeping watch over the vineyards. Château Latour will accept visitors by appointment only, on weekdays; it's closed in August (phone: 56-59-00-51).

Château Mouton-Rothschild – Classed as a second growth in 1855, only 2 years after the Rothschild family bought the property and before they had time to restore the vines, this has been ranked with the first *crus* of the Médoc since 1973 thanks to the unremitting efforts of the now deceased owner, Baron Philippe de Rothschild. The grounds here are kept meticulously, and the château is surprisingly small, because it was the last of the existing buildings to be added and there wasn't much room left except in the courtyard. An appointment is required (and difficult to get) to visit the *chais*, where the rows of barrels extend for about 3,000 feet, and the *Musée du Vin.* The museum, set up by the baron's late wife, Pauline, an artistic and creative American, is in former wine cellars. Here paintings, tapestries, finely wrought silver, and all manner of antique and contemporary works of art collected by the Rothschilds celebrate the history and pleasures of vines and wines. Closed in August. English is spoken (call Miss Parinet at 56-59-22-22).

Château Pontet-Canet – Right across the road from Château Mouton-Rothschild is the largest vineyard, at 170 acres, and one of the loveliest properties in the Médoc: Château Pontet-Canet. A narrow driveway leads through the shade trees to the simple 18th-century stone château, with its white shutters and clean lines. The rose garden and gray, vine-covered outbuildings with claret-colored shutters only add to the beauty of the place. The château was owned by the same family, the Cruses, for a century before it changed hands in 1975. Unlike most châteaux in the region, this one is lived in year-round. Many believe that the wine produced here deserves far better than its fifth-*cru* status. Visits by appointment on weekdays (phone: 56-59-04-04 or 56-52-15-71).

Château Lafite-Rothschild – The word "Lafite" is a corruption of the local dialect term *la hite* (the height), referring to the elevation on which the château, with its medieval tower, is built. Since 1868, the owners of Château Lafite have been another branch of the Rothschild family, cousins of Baron Philippe de Mouton-Rothschild. The reputation of Château Lafite extends far back beyond the Rothschilds, however; wine making has been carried on here for as long as 800 years, by some accounts. The wine of Château Lafite is said to have been the favorite of two royal mistresses: Mme. de Pompadour served little else to Louis XV, and Mme. du Barry put away a few cases while she helped to while away the evenings for Louis XVI. The Nazi field marshal Hermann Göring declared his intention of taking the first-growth Lafite, with its exquisite vaulted *chais,* as his share of the spoils of France after Germany's inevitable victory in World War II. It is our good fortune, and France's, that matters didn't turn out quite the way he planned. Closed from September 15 to November 1; visits by appointment only on weekdays can be arranged by calling the Paris office (phone: 42-56-33-50).

CHECKING IN: *Château Cordeillan-Bages* – Extensive renovation has turned this 17th-century château into a deluxe 18-room hotel, a new member of the Relais & Châteaux group. The Ecole du Bordeaux, which offers weekend and short-term wine training and tasting sessions for professionals and novices, has its base here. There also is a restaurant known for specialties such as *lamproie en rémoulade bourgeoise* (lamprey eel in an herb and anchovy-mayonnaise sauce) and *noisette d'agneau de Pauillac à la citronelle* (medallions of Pauillac lamb with lemon grass). Closed Mondays and the month of January. Major credit cards accepted. BP 90, Pauillac (phone: 56-59-24-24; fax: 56-59-01-89). Expensive.

***Hôtel de France et d'Angleterre* –** This modern 29-room hotel is an excellent bargain; a plus, too, is that English is spoken. The restaurant specializes in the famous lamb of Pauillac. Closed December 22 to January 13. Major credit cards accepted. 3 Quai Albert-Pichon (phone: 56-59-01-20; fax: 56-59-02-31). Moderate.

***Hôtel-Restaurant de la Renaissance* –** The views from this modern 11-room hotel make it worth a stop. Its restaurant serves traditional French food. Closed Sundays. St-Laurent-Médoc (phone: 56-59-40-29). Inexpensive.

EATING OUT: *Relais du Manoir* – Set in an old manor house, the kitchen prepares regional foods in original ways; be sure to try the assortment of salads with foie gras. It also has 8 reasonably priced rooms. Closed Sunday evenings. Major credit cards accepted. Just outside Pauillac, on Rte. de la Shell (phone: 56-59-05-47). Moderate.

***La Salamandre* –** The price is right and the food's good at this little brasserie. Open daily for lunch and dinner, June to August; open daily for lunch only and dinner on Saturday and Sunday evenings, September to April. Major credit cards accepted. Pauillac (phone: 56-59-08-68). Inexpensive.

ST-ESTÈPHE: Some 6.9 million bottles of wine are produced on 2,750 acres in this tiny village yearly, although less than 20% percent of the total is from classified growths. The soil of St-Estèphe has the least gravel of the Médoc areas, and its heavier, moisture-retaining clay imparts a somewhat "heavier" quality to the wine. The Maison du Vin sells all the wines from the region and presents an audiovisual show; it also exhibits a collection of old wine cellar tools. Open Mondays through Saturdays from 10 AM to 7 PM June through August; Sundays from 2 to 6 PM; open Mondays through Saturdays from 10 AM to noon and from 2 to 6 PM during the off-season. Closed Sundays off-season, and February (phone: 56-59-30-59).

Château Cos d'Estournel – The second-growth wine produced here is first class, but you're likely to remember Cos d'Estournel for its bizarre architecture. The château, whose first owner traveled in the Far East, was put together in the 19th century with such incongruous details as pagoda towers and massive carved wooden doors from the palace of the sultan of Zanzibar. Of all the châteaux, it casts the most exotic outline against the already dramatic Médoc sky. Open to the public afternoons only (except Mondays) in July and August; tours are available in English, Dutch, and German, and an audiovisual show (also multilingual) is presented. This château is very popular in season (phone: 56-59-35-69).

Château Montrose – This château has the distinction of being run by a mother-and-son team in a business where father-and-son teams are the norm. They maintain the brilliant standard of the full, long-lived wine that was recognized as a second growth back in 1855. Open by appointment only. Closed from mid-July to mid-August. (phone: 56-59-30-12).

Château Calon-Ségur – A third *cru,* this is the northernmost classified growth of the Médoc. "Calon" refers to the small boats that were once used extensively by ferrymen to transport timber across the Gironde from the heavy forests of St-Estèphe. The name Ségur recognizes a man who was not only a president of the Parlement de Bordeaux in the 18th century but also proprietor of both Château Lafite and Château Latour, along with his property here. The heart design on Calon-Ségur's label commemorates Ségur's great love for this property, and the motto carved in stone at the arched entrance to the château echoes this sentiment: "I make wine at Lafite and Latour, but my heart is at Calon." Open by appointment only; tours given in French (phone: 56-59-30-27).

 CHECKING IN: *Vieux Acacias* – This pleasant 14-room hostelry amid a peaceful park and gardens provides a good stopping point between the vineyards of the Médoc and the Atlantic Coast. Major credit cards accepted. Queyrac, Lesparre (phone: 56-59-80-63). Moderate.

 EATING OUT: *Château Layauga* – An 18th-century château that was converted into a small luxury hotel with 7 rooms, decorated in Louis XV style. Its restaurant (Michelin awarded it one star) serves updated French classics prepared by chef/owner Philipe Jorand. The wine list is excellent. Open daily. Major credit cards accepted. Gaillan en Médoc (phone: 56-41-26-83). Hotel, moderate; restaurant, expensive to moderate.

En Route from the Médoc – After looking at nothing but straight vine rows along most of the vineyard road, travelers may find its northern remnant a surprising, perhaps welcome, change. The flatness of the lower reaches gives way to wooded slopes and fields of more conventional farm crops — such as corn — and grazing land. A salty breeze is a reminder that this last stretch of the Gironde is the estuary where fresh water meets the Atlantic.

Note: Although D2E/D2 is known as the *route des châteaux* because it leads to a remarkable number of great châteaux, smaller roads, notably D5, also will take you to a number of châteaux that produce sound, reliable wines that often equal the products at least of the lesser Margaux, St-Julien, Pauillac, and St-Estèphe vineyards. In a few cases, the wines are really distinguished. Two of the most outstanding châteaux along D5 are Château Chasse-Spleen, "banish blues," i.e., by drinking the wine (phone: 56-58-02-10), and Château Maucaillou, "bad pebbles" in contrast to the *beaucaillou* back in St-Julien (phone: 56-58-01-23). Both châteaux are in the township of Moulis, northwest of Margaux.

Also worth visiting is the Château Loudenne (phone: 56-09-05-03), a working château where a British staff offers weekly wine courses and tastings. There also is a museum, the *Musée des Outils de la Vigne et du Vin* (no phone), that exhibits tools used in wine making. There are many other *cru bourgeois* châteaux in the area that are noteworthy: Château Lanessan (in Cussac, Fort Médoc; phone: 56-58-94-80); Peter Sichel's Château D'Angludet (in Cantenac; phone: 56-88-71-41); and Château La Tour de By (in Begadan; phone: 56-41-50-03). Their wines are less expensive than those of the *grands châteaux,* and the welcome is often more sincere.

THE COAST

The opposite side of the Bordeaux peninsula from the Médoc, and the northern third of the increasingly popular Côte d'Argent (also known here as the Côte Aquitaine), this string of beaches is easily accessible from Bordeaux and still refreshingly under-populated. A small coast road links most of the beach communities, which are about half an hour's drive apart. If you're in a hurry or don't want to explore each beach, it's quicker to take the more inland route, D101, from Soulac-sur-Mer as far as Hourtin and then D3. This route passes just east of two large lakes, Lac d'Hourtin-Carcans and Lacanau, and links the forested towns of Soulac, Vendays-Montalivet, Hourtin, Carcans, Lacanau, Le Porge, and Lege-Cap Ferret; connector roads lead from the towns to their respective beaches. Good accommodations are available near the beach in both Soulac-sur-Mer and Lacanau-Océan as well as in Maubuisson and at the recreation area called Bombannes, both on Lac d'Hourtin-Carcans.

SOULAC: The largest town along this part of France's Atlantic coast, Soulac is a tidy, bustling place with brick houses that have especially colorful shutters and trim. The town has a market every morning, and there is a museum, the *Fondation Soulac-Médoc* (phone: 56-09-83-99), open from 3 to 7 PM, June to October, which features the paintings, drawings, and sculpture of more than 100 Aquitaine artists. There also is the *Musée d'Archéologie* (28 Rue Victor Hugo) which includes prehistoric, protohistoric, and Gallo-Roman pieces. Open daily May 1 to September 15 from 3 to 7 PM. Soulac also has a municipal swimming pool, 21 tennis courts (2 of them covered), a gym, a cinema, and a casino (open from June to September). Visitors can rent horses for rides or trips (call the *Club Hippique* at 56-09-71-93). Adventurous travelers can try parachuting with the *Centre Départemental de Parachutisme* (Aérodrome de Soulac; phone: 56-09-84-50). The nearby beach at L'Amélie-sur-Mer, just south of Soulac, is especially striking with its black rock formation and dunes. The town also has two nightclubs, *Memphis* (Bd. Charcot; phone: 56-09-82-74) and *Koale* (Rue de la Briquetterre; phone: 56-09-94-69). But the crowning attraction is the Eglise Notre-Dame de la Fin des Terres, a splendid 12th-century Roman church that was completely covered by sand in the 18th century and not unearthed until 1860. In July and August, a music festival takes place in the church. Soulac is close to the famous vineyards of the Médoc (N215 connects with the vineyard road, D2, at the village of St. Vivien du Médoc). It is also only 3½ miles (6 km) south of Le Verdon, where ferries depart every half hour or hour, depending on the time of day, for Royan from the end of June to the end of August; other months, every hour to hour and a half. For a city map, drop by the tourist office (Place du Marche, near the Eglise Notre-Dame; phone: 56-09-86-61); it's open year-round.

The first 19 miles (30 km) of the drive south from Soulac are especially pastoral and pleasant, the backside of beaches masquerading as farmland.

 CHECKING IN/EATING OUT: *Margaux* – Also known as "La Dame de Coeur," this is one of the handful of hotels that don't close in the off-season, and it's in the heart of downtown. All rooms come with a bath, and the restaurant serves hearty fare. Open daily. Major credit cards accepted. Pl. de l'Eglise, Soulac-sur-Mer (phone: 56-09-80-80). Moderate.

Pins – In the small community of L'Amélie, 2½ miles (4 km) from Soulac, it's about 100 feet from the beach. The hotel has 35 rooms and is open year-round, except January and February. Its restaurant closes on Fridays and Sunday evenings off-season. Major credit cards accepted. L'Amélie-sur-Mer (phone: 56-09-80-01). Moderate.

L'Hacienda – With its lush garden and terraces, this hotel looks as though it was transported intact from Spain. It has 12 bedrooms, and a restaurant under separate management — the *NovioMagus* (phone: 56-09-99-45) that serves traditional cuisine. Restaurant closed Sunday evenings and Monday lunch. Visa accepted. 4 Av. Du-Levrier-de-Larsan, Soulac-sur-Mer (phone: 56-09-81-34). Moderate to inexpensive.

Lescorce – This comfortable hotel has a gameroom for Ping-Pong and billiards, a tennis court (make your reservation in the hotel bar; you don't have to be a guest to play), a TV room, and a homey ambience. The owner speaks English. Open from April to October. Major credit cards accepted. 36 Rue Trouche, Soulac-sur-Mer (phone: 56-09-84-13). Moderate to inexpensive.

MONTALIVET-LES-BAINS: This long stretch of beach officially is designated *naturiste*. It is large enough to afford plenty of privacy and is used mostly by young couples with children. People simply park by the side of the road and walk across the dunes. Take along insect repellent and carry your valuables with you; it's not safe to leave them in the car.

EATING OUT: *La Clef des Champs* – Elegant and off the beaten track, this restaurant-farm is managed by a mother-and-daughter team, the *Mesdames* Lussagnet. Whatever game and vegetables are in season will appear on the menu. Closed occasionally in winter; call to make sure it's open. Reservations are necessary, for the word's out. Major credit cards accepted. Between Vendays and Montalivet, 3 miles (5 km) from Montalivet; watch for signs (phone: 56-41-71-11). Moderate.

CARCANS: The streets in this town of 500 people dead-end into a large sand dune 20 feet high; you have to climb over it to get to the ocean. This beach is more crowded than Montalivet and more conservative. There is a small museum of arts and crafts that is open daily in the late afternoons in July and August (phone: 56-03-36-65). For information, contact the Carcans–Maubuisson Tourist Office (phone: 56-03-34-94).

En Route from Carcans – If at this point you've had enough sun and salt water and want a break, if only for a few hours, visit Lac d'Hourtin-Carcans, a pebble's throw away on D3E. Maubuisson, a tiny resort town on its southern shore, has a couple of decent hotels and restaurants right across the street from the lake. If you want to play or lie in the shade of a pine tree, the lakeside resort complex of Bombannes, about 5 miles (8 km) north of Maubuisson, is a must. Apartments are available only for minimum 1-week rentals. Facilities include open-air and enclosed tennis courts, a gym, and picnic areas, and the ocean is a short drive away. Don't be surprised to find bright pink heather everywhere, blanketing the base of the pines and sweetening the air. The complex is open from 8 AM to 10 PM; closed December and January (phone: 56-03-31-01 or 56-03-31-03).

LACANAU-OCÉAN: This is the cleanest of all the beaches and the one best equipped for demanding travelers. It has a couple of large, seafront hotels as well as a tourist office (Pl. de l'Europe; phone: 56-03-21-01). The dwellings look like gingerbread houses made of brick. Sculpted dunes speckle the beach, and a "sandwalk" runs parallel to the ocean. Activity-prone vacationers will never want to leave: They can rent surfboards, windsurfers, and Hobie Cats from *Lacanau Lou* (phone: 56-03-23-54), take surfing lessons by the week at the *Lacanau Surf Club* (phone: 56-26-38-84), learn windsurfing at the surf club or the *Voile Lacanau Guyenne* (phone: 56-03-05-11), go horseback riding (phone: 56-03-52-74), undertake a 5-day tennis course, including one for children (phone: 56-03-24-91), or learn to water-ski (phone: 56-03-01-39 or 56-03-09-01). Lacanau Lake is nearby and there's an 18-hole (with 9 more holes underway) golf course, *Golf de Lacanau* (Domaine de l'Ardilouse, 1 mile/2 km from Lacanau on D6; phone: 56-03-25-60). During *Easter,* there is a festival of sports movies and sports medicine; there's also a 1-day *Mai Musical* (May Music Fest) at the Eglise St-Vincent, in the inland town of Lacanau. July brings a windsurfing day, an international tennis tournament, and a dance festival. The *Pro de Surf,* an international surfing competition is held in mid-August.

CHECKING IN: *Hôtel du Golf* – A modern hostelry at the edge of one of the region's best golf courses, it offers comfortable rooms and apartments with terraces overlooking the greens. It is surrounded by trees and is just a 4-minute walk from the ocean. Domaine de l'Ardilouse, Lacanau Océan (phone: 56-03-23-15). Moderate.

L'Etoile d'Argent – Right by the water, this impressive hotel has 14 rooms facing the beach and another 9 in the equally nice annex right behind it. Closed from December to mid-January. Major credit cards accepted. Pl. de l'Europe, Lacanau-Océan (phone: 56-03-21-07). Inexpensive.

EATING OUT: *La Taverne de Neptune* – Sit inside by the glow of candlelight or out on the porch by the glow of your fondue flame. (They do three kinds of fondue, plus other dishes such as duck, snails, lots of fish.) Service is slow but the food is delicious. English, Dutch, and German are spoken, and the menu is translated for you. Open daily for dinner, except October to mid-March. No credit cards accepted. Av. de l'Europe, Lacanau-Océan (phone: 56-03-21-33). Moderate.

LE PORGE-OCÉAN: This lovely beach has a well-kept 114-acre municipal campground nearby, not to mention a nudist colony called La Jenny. It's worth it to arrive via the inland road, D3, from Lacanau and then drive west to the ocean along D107 from Le Porge. This way you can truly appreciate the stately, dense pine forest and get a good sense of the peacefulness, even solemnity, it imparts. The drive to the beach may be the most serene 8 miles (13 km) of your trip, especially if you go in the morning when the mist still hovers in the forest.

Diehards who want a sample of the Atlantic coast between the Gironde River and the Arcachon Basin can continue south from Le Porge on D3, which links up with D106 to lead to Cap-Ferret.

CAP-FERRET: This beach town has two beaches, one facing the ocean, the other facing the still, safe waters of the Basin. A train trundles visitors back and forth, and bicycles can be rented for further exploration. For more information, see the Cap-Ferret listing in the Arcachon Basin route, below.

THE ARCACHON BASIN

The most popular close destination for Bordelais who have set their hearts on sunning, swimming, and sailing is a day or two at the Arcachon Basin, via N250 to N650 to D650. The Basin is trianglular and has a road that loops 112 miles around it, connecting a baker's dozen communities. The most appealing spots, however, all fall along the base (or southern part) of the triangle, on D650, from Le Teich to Arcachon. Cap-Ferret, across the channel from Arcachon, is a boat ride away and a pleasant day trip. No cars are allowed on the boats, so those who insist on four wheels can get there only by making the tedious, traffic-riddled trip around the Basin.

LE TEICH: The first point of interest southwest from Bordeaux is Parc Ornithologique, a bird park and sanctuary in Le Teich. The town (not to be confused with nearby La Teste) is in the southeast corner of the Basin, 25 miles (40 km) from Bordeaux. The park comprises 296 acres, 173 of which contain still, brackish water used as a fish preserve. In winter, more than 25,000 birds inhabit the park. Ducks, geese, swans, herons, storks, and flamingos are among the 280 species to be found here at that time of the year. Two hiking trails offer a 1- or 2-hour diversion, but the longer one, which follows a flat course with no shade trees, is of interest only to committed bird watchers, who visit in winter. Buy a small bag of grain at the entrance or the ducks waddling in your wake will probably make you feel very guilty. The paths are gravelly, so don't wear sandals. Observation booths, which are plentiful, contain useful information about yearly migrations. Open daily from from 10 AM to 6 PM, March 1 to September 30 (after September, it's open only on weekends and holidays), but if you don't arrive before 4 PM, you may not be allowed to enter; admission charge (phone: 56-22-84-89).

En Route from Le Teich – Just 2 ½ miles (4 km) west on D650 is *Ker Helen* (phone: 56-66-03-79), a lovely campground dotted with roses and striped with grapevines. The proprietors are especially helpful to visitors, and it's open year-round.

GUJAN-MESTRAS: Nicknamed "the oyster capital," this tiny village 11 miles (18 km) west of Le Teich on D650 contains no less than seven ports. A small tourist office on D650 is open daily, mornings only; look for it on the Basin side of the road. If you want to taste some of the local oysters, drop by *Castaing-Druart* or *Beynel-Daney* on the main road.

EATING OUT: *La Coquille* – Try the oysters at this restaurant with a cheerful black and white tile floor and tables covered with crisp white cloths. Other specialties include stuffed mussels and fish soup. Closed January 15 to February 15, and Sunday evenings and Mondays off-season. Major credit cards accepted. On the main road through Gujan-Mestras (phone: 56-66-08-60). Moderate to inexpensive.

LA HUME: Although La Hume is only about 6 miles (10 km) west of Gujan-Mestras, it seems eons away in time. In the summer, the restored medieval village here comes alive with craftspeople dressed as they would have been long ago: a leaded-glass worker, coppersmith, candle maker, clog maker, basket maker, caneworker, herbalist, bell maker, silk painter, blacksmith, cabinet maker, enameler — 40 artisans in all. After a few hours of wandering through the village, you'll be ready to stop by the tavern for a refreshing drink. La Hume is open from 10 AM to 7:30 PM daily from June 15 to September 15, as well as from 9 to 11:30 PM on Saturdays. Just follow the signs marked "Artisans d'Art." Nearby, close to the crossroad between N250 and D625, the Parc Aquatique Aquacity is open daily from June to September; the admission charge covers swimming and amusements.

ARCACHON: This seaside resort, once sought out for its curative waters, enjoyed its heyday in the middle to late 1800s, when European high society filled its streets, cafés, casino, hotels, and beaches. Arcachon also lured artists such as Manet and Toulouse-Lautrec and the composer Debussy. Today it enjoys continued popularity, primarily among the Bordelais and Germans. Especially appealing are the old beach-front hotels, sidewalk cafés, the promenade lined with feathery tamarisk trees, and the beach itself. The tourist office is open daily in season and weekdays off-season (Pl. Roosevelt; phone: 56-83-01-69). The casino, a white, castle-like building complete with turrets, is open afternoons and evenings in season; off-season it is open Friday and Saturday evenings and Sunday afternoons and evenings (Bd. de la Plage and Av. Général-de-Gaulle; phone: 56-83-41-44). The aquarium, on Rue Jolyet just off Quai D'Eyrac, has an exhibit on oyster cultivation and a number of local fish, including eels, on view. It is open daily, mornings and afternoons; there is an admission charge. The Ville d'Hiver (Winter City), behind the tourist office in the opposite direction from the Basin, is Arcachon's Old Town. It is a jumble of purposely winding streets (for protection from the wind) filled with 19th-century villas and chalets. Allées Alexandre-Dumas, Pasteur, Faust, Pereire, Brémontier, Velpeau, Docteur-Lalesque, and Avenue Victor-Hugo are notable. Oddly, a walking tour guide of the Ville d'Hiver can be purchased at the tourist office in Bordeaux; in season, the tourist office in Arcachon offers walking tours of the town. Small boats, *pinasses,* make regular trips between Arcachon and Cap-Ferret daily. Boat trips also are available to nearby Ile aux Oiseaux (Bird Island), to an oyster park, and for deep-sea fishing excursions. For information, contact the tourist office or, for groups, Union des Bateliers d'Arcachon (phone: 56-83-06-62 in season; 56-54-60-32 year-round).

CHECKING IN: *Grand Hôtel Richelieu* – This impressive establishment overlooks the Arcachon Basin and the Grand Pier, and has direct access to the beach. Centrally located, it has 43 rooms, a tearoom, a bar, and free parking. Closed November through mid-March. Major credit cards accepted. 185 Bd. de la Plage, Arcachon (phone: 56-83-16-50 or 56-83-16-51; fax: 56-83-47-78). Expensive.

***Les Ormes* –** A pleasant modern hotel a short distance from the center of town. It has 24 rooms, 12 with terraces overlooking the sea, and a restaurant. Open year-round. Major credit cards accepted. 77 Bd. de la Plage at Rue Hovy, Arcachon (phone: 56-83-09-27; fax: 56-54-97-10). Expensive.

***Roc* –** Cheerful brown-and-white-striped awnings beckon you inside to try one of the 54 modern, comfortable rooms. Near the casino. Closed December and January. Major credit cards accepted. 200-202 Bd. de la Plage, Arcachon (phone: 56-83-05-01; fax: 56-83-22-76). Moderate.

EATING OUT: *Chez Yvette* – Exceedingly popular through the the the entire region, this old inn has ceiling fans that lazily circulate the soft sea air. The specialty of the house is *lamproie à la bordelaise* (lamprey eel in red wine sauce); for the less adventuresome, the owner recommends delicious sole, turbot, and bass (*bar*) dishes. The bread, ice cream, and sorbets are homemade. Closed January. Major credit cards accepted. Across from the tourist office. 59 Bd. du Général-Leclerc, Arcachon (phone: 56-83-05-11) Moderate.

***La Guitoune* –** This commendable eatery is just a few kilometers away in Pyla-sur-Mer. It's also a small hotel (22 rooms). Open daily. Reservations unnecessary. Major credit cards accepted. 95 Bd. de l'Océan, Pyla-sur-Mer (phone: 56-22-70-10). Moderate.

En Route from Arcachon – People who live here praise the stretch of beaches south to Biscarosse. Take D112 south, stopping along the way at Pilat-Plage to be awed by the Pilat Dune. Like a gigantic glacier made of sand, this dune — 6½ miles long and about 35 feet high and still growing — encroaches on forest, town, and beach. Rugged beach buffs hike over it to get to the water; others take the stairs. Some 19 miles (30 km) farther south on D112, on the right-hand side of the road, is La Lagune, a quiet picnic area with a lovely, secluded beach where nude swimming is officially sanctioned.

CAP-FERRET: A quick boat ride across the Teychan Channel from Arcachon takes you to the seaside community of Cap-Ferret. A small train carries tourists from the town to the ocean, though the channel-side beach is by far recommended because it is both safer and cleaner. The tourist office is at 12 Avenue de l'Océan in Le Panier Fleuri Building in season; off-season it's harder to find — in a booth opposite the market, in the Town Hall (phone: 56-60-63-26). In fact, none of the streets here is clearly marked, so expect to be lost most of the time whether you are on foot or wheels. There is a splendid view from the Croix-des-Marins lighthouse, which is open daily from June through September; otherwise, by request. Bikes can be rented at 47 and 51 Avenue de l'Océan; sailboats, at 65 Avenue de Bordeaux. Ocean conditions are given daily in French on radio channel 102 at 1 PM.

Périgord

Wedged neatly between the high plateau and volcanic formations of the Massif Central, the plains of the Guyenne, and the sun-soaked lands of the Midi is the lush green province of Périgord, corresponding approximately to the modern *département* of the Dordogne (the second-largest in France). The Dordogne also encompasses parts of other ancient provinces, such as the Limousin and Quercy, but the geography and roads of Périgord make it natural to include certain sites in the Lot and Haute-Vienne *départements* in our itinerary here.

It is one of France's richest areas of both natural and manmade treasures and remains, if no longer undiscovered, at least still relatively unspoiled.

Coming into the Dordogne from the north, one notices a gradual change — not only in the terrain, but also in the rhythm and tempo of life. The autoroute gives way to tiny roads that wind their way through deep, cool, fern-carpeted forests, rolling hills, opulent valleys strewn with wildflowers, and tall white limestone cliffs that drop dramatically into deep river gorges.

Except in July and August, when increasing numbers of French and foreign tourists descend on the region, you can drive for miles on the smaller, picturesque roads without passing another soul — the only signs of life are an occasional group of grazing cows or a stray goose. At times it seems that the 20th century has passed over the region or, at most, touched down just long enough to deposit its telephone lines and TV antennas before moving on, leaving it in the calm of another era.

The region owes much of its beauty to its rivers, among them the Dronne, Isle, Auvézère, and the Vézère, all flowing into the majestic Dordogne, considered by many to be the most beautiful river in France. The river valleys are dotted with charming towns of mellow stone churches and houses dating from the Middle Ages. And firmly entrenched on the heights are the châteaux. Their proud military bearing, a sharp contrast to the elegance of the Loire Valley palaces, reflects a troubled, war-torn past.

Prehistoric man walked in these valleys some 40,000 years ago. The awesome proof of his presence is in the region's many cliff shelters and caves whose walls are decorated with beautiful, enigmatic symbols and paintings. Carbon dating places the majority of these incredibly advanced works in the Magdalenian era of the upper (late) paleolithic period. The discovery, only about a century ago, of the wealth of prehistoric sites in and around Les Eyzies, in the heart of Périgord, has earned it the title of the capital of prehistory, drawing anthropologists from all over.

About 35,000 years after their paleolithic predecessors, the Romans settled here, even before Caesar forced the Gauls to capitulate. The vestiges of their arenas, baths, and temples are signs of the prosperity of the Roman forerunners of Périgueux and the other principal cities. The province was in turn conquered by the Visigoths and then taken by Clovis.

These serene valleys were turned into battlefields during the Middle Ages thanks, in large part, to Eleanor of Aquitaine, whose divorce from Prince Louis, son of the King of France, freed her to marry Henry Plantagenet, who ascended to the throne of England 2 years later, in 1154. Eleanor brought her precious dowry, the ancient duchy of Aquitaine, to the British crown, thereby upsetting the already tenuous balance of power between the two countries and launching a bitter war for possession of the region that lasted for 300 years. During much of that period, Périgord suffered incredible devastation as the dividing line between the French and the British camps. It wasn't until the end of the Hundred Years War, in 1453, that the area reverted to French hands.

But the suffering didn't stop then; in the 16th century the Wars of Religion brought more conflict. Périgueux was a Protestant stronghold between 1515 and 1581 after being taken by Geoffroi de Vivance, the Huguenot leader. Neighboring Bergerac, at one time the headquarters of the Reformed church, was taken by Catholics in 1562, then lost and, in turn, recaptured.

Finally, in the 17th century, the political situation began to stabilize, and from the reign of Louis XIV on, the history of Périgord pretty much parallels that of the rest of France.

Not surprisingly, considering its history, the area is almost as rich in architecture as it is in natural beauty. Most of its churches are in the Romanesque style. Purely Gothic edifices are fairly rare, since the turbulence of the Hundred Years War discouraged the building of anything less practical than fortified castles and *bastides,* the defensive towns constructed under orders of the opposing Kings of France and England. Some of the humbler structures include low, conical huts with pointed roofs, called *bories,* composed entirely of stones, and *pigeonniers,* small square buildings perched on stilts with holes carved in the walls for nesting birds. According to some estimates, there are close to 1,500 châteaux in the region as well. Many of them combine different types of architecture, having been added to, embellished, and in some cases almost entirely rebuilt at various periods without regard to the original design.

In addition to the varied scenic, architectural, and historical appeal of Périgord, it has rich gastronomic traditions — by themselves reason enough for a visit. The specialties are known and loved throughout France and the world. This is the land of foie gras, *confit d'oie* (preserved goose), and *magret de canard* (sliced duck breast), truffles and *cèpes* (wild boletus mushrooms), walnut cakes and liqueurs, walnut oil, fresh river trout, beef *à la périgourdine* (in a red wine sauce similar to *à la bordelaise*), the hearty red wines of Cahors and Bergerac, and sweet white monbazillac, drunk chilled as an accompaniment to *foie gras.* The food is traditional and hearty — honest and refreshingly simple. Nouvelle cuisine has made few inroads here (though some chefs are lightening the classics somewhat), and the prices often match the downhome fare. A meal for two in an expensive restaurant can run to $80 and up. In the moderate range (most of the restaurants), the bill for two will average between $50 and $80, and in an inexpensive place (there are plenty) two can eat for well under $50. Prices do not include wine or drinks, though service usually is included. Hotel prices parallel those of the restaurants. A room for two in an expensive hotel will range from $80 and up; a moderate room, between $40 and $80; and an inexpensive room, less than $40. Although there are a few grand places, the majority of the hotels and restaurants in this region are cozy, comfortable, and traditional. In general, it's not an area for those who insist upon four-star luxury and modern conveniences such as air conditioning, television sets in their rooms, and overnight dry cleaning service.

Our tour route starts in Limoges, then curves southwest to Brantôme and Périgueux before turning into the heart of the region where the majority of the grottoes and prehistoric sites are found. Just a little to the east are the two most heavily visited towns, Sarlat and Rocamadour. The route then sweeps south to Cahors and the nearby grotto of Pech-Merle, then follows the wine route west of Cahors before turning north again, up to Bergerac and eventually back to Limoges. A trip through Périgord will soon reveal why Henry Miller once wrote, "One day France may cease to exist, but Périgord will survive, like dreams which nourish the human soul."

LIMOGES: "The men are noted for their wit and the women for their whiteness." Whether the author Jean de La Fontaine's portrait of the people of Limoges still holds true or not, there clearly is a special appeal to this busy city of some 150,000 inhabitants. About 250 miles (400 km) southwest of Paris in what is technically the Limousin, Limoges straddles the Vienne River on the site of the Gallo-Roman town of Augustoritum. It owes much of its modern strength and the title of "City of Art" to its world-renowned porcelain factories and enamel works.

Porcelain has been produced here since the end of the 18th century, when kaolin, the pure white clay from which it is made, was discovered 38 miles (61 km) south of the city, in St-Yrieix. (The Impressionist painter Auguste Renoir worked for a time in his native Limoges as a porcelain decorator.) The *Musée National Adrien-Dubouché* (open daily except Tuesdays from 10 AM to noon and 1:30 to 5:15 PM; Pl. Winston-Churchill; phone: 55-77-45-58) has more than 10,000 pieces of pottery and porcelain, tracing the evolution of china from antiquity to the present. More than 50% of all French porcelain is made in the factories here, some of which are open to visitors. (Ask at the tourist office on Boulevard Fleurus for information on tours; phone: 55-34-46-87.) Plenty of shops in the center of the city sell lovely porcelain. The best shops line the Boulevard Louis-Blanc, including *Prestige de Limoges* and *Charme du Logis.* Also worth a visit is the *Pavillon de la Porcelaine* (Rte. de Toulouse; phone: 55-30-21-86). Open daily from 8:30 AM to 7:30 PM from *Easter* to October; closed Sundays in winter. Also be sure to stroll the Boulevard Victor-Hugo or Rue Jean-Jaurès.

The art of enameling (called *émaux;* the various techniques are *émaux cloisonnés, émaux champlevés,* and *émaux peints*) has been practiced since antiquity, but it wasn't until the 12th century that Limoges's enamelers perfected their craft using the lead silicates and oxides of rare metals, including gold, silver, and cobalt, found in the primary faults of the area. Enamels still are made in tiny kilns at the rear of each enameler's workshop. Several of these shops are clustered around Place Wilson and in the old part of the city; visitors are welcome to wander in and observe the process. (For a frank and enlightening discussion on the current state of the art, stop in at 19 Rue des Tanneries, where Boris Veisbrot creates striking contemporary pieces. Both his work and his opinions are refreshing.) Two interesting shops for modern enamel are *René Restoueix* (2 Rue Haute Cité), and *Vincent Pécaud* (23 Rue Elie-Berthet). Appropriately, porcelain and enamel are the subjects of special exhibitions held in Limoges in July and August. The porcelain exhibition is held annually; an international exposition dedicated to the enamel arts is held in even-numbered years. For information on dates, contact the tourist office (phone: 55-34-46-87).

The *Musée Municipal,* in a beautiful 18th-century building that once was the bishop's palace (Palais de l'Evêché), has a wonderful collection of enamels dating from the 12th century to the present. It includes many pieces by Léonard Limousin, enameler to the Kings of France in the 16th century, and a fine group of post-Impressionist paintings. Open daily except Tuesdays from 10 AM to noon and 2 to 5 PM (Mairie de Limoges; phone: 55-45-60-00).

A short walk from the museum is Limoges's striking Cathédrale St-Etienne, begun in 1273 on the site of a Romanesque church, part of whose crypt and belfry remain. The cathedral is the only one in the Limousin to be completely in the Gothic style. Of particular interest are the Flamboyant Gothic St. John doorway, the delicately chiseled limestone screen inside at the end of the nave, and the three tombs flanking the chancel. The expansive gardens behind the cathedral are magnificent — neat rows of carefully tended flowers of all varieties and lanes of tall trees, all set against the backdrop of the cathedral and the river. Before leaving this area, wander the crooked streets of Vieux (Old) Limoges just to the north of the cathedral entrance. Especially charming is the Rue de la Boucherie, lined with half-timbered houses where the city's butchers have lived since the 10th century.

Also of interest are the Orsay Gardens, where the ruins of a Gallo-Roman arena were discovered during excavations in 1966. Near the tree-shaded Place de la République are two other churches, St-Michel-des-Lions, begun in 1364, and St-Pierre-du-Queyroix, its Flamboyant façade built in 1534. It was here, under the Place de la République, that the crypt of the former Abbey of St. Martial, dating from the 4th century, was found during excavations in 1960. Inside is the sarcophagus of St. Martial, the Limosin apostle who came to the area to convert people to Christianity in about AD 250. The abbey, destroyed in 1791, once was an important stop for pilgrims on the route to Santiago de Compostela.

CHECKING IN: *Royal Limousin* – A very comfortable, modern 75-room hotel that is one of the city's best. Major credit cards accepted. Pl. de la République, Limoges (phone: 55-34-65-30; fax: 55-34-55-21). Expensive to moderate.

Luk – On one corner of the Place Jourdan opposite Limoges's 19th-century replica of the Hôtel de Ville in Paris, this 56-room hotel offers modern comforts and a convenient location. In addition to an existing dining room, there is a "gastronomic" restaurant, the *Luk Epoch.* Breakfast is included in the room rate and parking is available. Major credit cards accepted. 29 Pl. Jourdan, Limoges (phone: 55-33-44-00). Moderate.

La Meule – A modest 10-room hostelry in the countryside with a rustic restaurant serving generous meals at very reasonable prices. The hearty breakfasts are sublime. Closed Tuesdays off-season and in January. Major credit cards accepted. On the N21 in Séreilhac about 10 miles (16 km) southeast of Limoges (phone: 55-39-10-08; fax: 55-39-19-66). Moderate.

EATING OUT: *La Chapelle St-Martin* – About 6 miles (10 km) northwest of Limoges in the Limousin countryside is this elegant inn with one Michelin star, a former 19th-century home, surrounded by a park with tennis courts and peaceful *étangs* (ponds). Everything served in the restaurant is excellent and original, including the *bar à la vinaigrette aux herbes* (bass in vinaigrette sauce) and *carré d'agneau du limousin à l'aïl confit* (rack of lamb with preserved garlic). In addition, owner Jacques Dudognon has furnished the inn's 13 rooms with lovely antiques, paintings, and porcelain. Restaurant closed Monday evenings; both inn and restaurant closed January and February. Visa accepted. St-Martin-le-Faux, near Nieul, on D35 (phone: 55-75-80-17; fax: 55-75-89-50). Expensive.

Le Champlevé – This eatery serves traditional cuisine presented on elegant porcelain with a touch of *La Belle Epoque.* Closed Sundays from July 1 through September; closed Wednesdays and Saturday mornings from October 1 through

June. Major credit cards accepted. Pl. Wilson, Limoges (phone: 54-34-43-34). Expensive to moderate.

Les Petits Ventres – The setting is a 15th-century house; the menu offers good, hearty food. Closed Sundays and for lunch on Mondays. Major credit cards accepted. 20 Rue de la Boucherie, Limoges (phone: 55-33-34-02). Moderate to inexpensive.

En Route from Limoges – Head south, turning onto D78 at St-Yrieix-la-Perche to reach Jumilhac-le-Grand, a romantic, turreted château on the rocks overlooking the Isle River. The core of this château was built during the 14th century, the two lateral wings added in the 17th century. Inside one of the wings is a great hall with wood carvings and a Louis XIV fireplace. Legend has it that the mistress of the castle, Louise de Hautefort, nicknamed La Fileuse (The Spinner), was locked up in the tower for life when her husband returned from the wars of Henri de Navarre to find his beautiful wife with a lover. Today you can visit the room where Louise is said to have sat spinning wool, making decorations, and painting her portrait on the door. In 1927, the château was purchased by Count Odet de Jumilhac, who gradually restored the badly neglected castle.

BRANTÔME: Continue on D78 to Brantôme, a peaceful little town on the Dronne River dominated by a Benedictine abbey founded by Charlemagne in 769. The abbey, which was sacked by the Normans and rebuilt in the 11th, the 14th, and again in the 18th and 19th centuries, once was presided over by Pierre de Bourdeille, better known as Brantôme, the chronicler whose literary fame derives mainly from his witty, spirited, and often cynical accounts of the lives of the *grands capitaines* and *dames galantes* of the late 16th century, an era rich in scandal.

Of particular interest here is the gabled Romanesque belfry, the oldest of its kind in the Limousin, erected in the 11th century. It stands apart from the abbey church on a 40-foot-high rock. Behind the abbey, in the caves that housed the monks' bakery and wine cellar, are huge 16th-century carvings in the rock of the Last Judgment and the Crucifixion. Every year, an exhibition of classical dance is held in these caves. Also noteworthy are the monastery buildings, with two 18th-century wings and a beautiful 17th-century staircase. The buildings house the Town Hall, the schools, and the *Musée Fernand-Desmoulin.* The museum has many prehistoric artifacts found in the area as well as the rather bizarre paintings of Desmoulin, produced while this 19th-century Périgord artist was under the influence of a medium.

But the real pleasure of Brantôme lies in its serene, storybook setting. It's a pleasure just to stroll among the willows on the banks of the Dronne, cloaked with white water hyacinths and spanned by asymmetrical stone bridges. Don't miss the Friday morning open-air food market, located in the central square near the abbey church.

CHECKING IN/EATING OUT: *Moulin de l'Abbaye* – Régis and Catherine Bulot have transformed an old mill on a gentle bend in the Dronne River into one of the most delightful spots in the entire region. Its 21 rooms and suites (elegantly furnished and decorated with French provincial fabrics) and the Louis XIII dining room, which opens onto a tree-shaded, riverside terrace, all contribute to the genteel, quiet luxury that charaterizes the inn, a member of the Relais & Châteaux group. Chef Rabinel's menu is an adroit blend of such up-to-date dishes as *dodine de barbue* (cold terrine of brill) and more traditional Périgord fare; his kitchen has been given one Michelin star. Closed from November to May. Major credit cards accepted. 2 Bd. Charlemagne, Rte. de Bourdeilles, Brantôme (phone: 53-05-80-22; fax: 53-05-75-27). Expensive.

Moulin du Roc – In a nearby village, on the verdant banks of the River Dronne, this 17th-century walnut mill has been converted by Solange and Lucien Gardillou into a romantic and peaceful inn. The 12 rooms are furnished with period pieces and have stocked mini-bars and television sets. The cozy but elegant dining room and sitting rooms are decorated with antiques as well as with objects from the old mill, and there are two terraces for outdoor dining and lounging. The imaginative regional cuisine, created by the talented Mme. Gardillou, has earned one Michelin star. Among the specialties are cod, guinea hen, preserved duck, and *pommes de terre aux truffes* (potatoes with truffles). The wine list features an extensive selection of fine bordeaux. Closed Tuesdays, mid-January to mid-February and mid-November to mid-December. Major credit cards accepted. The inn is about 3½ miles (5 km) northeast of Brantôme in Champagnac-de-Bélair (phone: 53-54-80-36; fax: 53-54-21-31). Expensive.

Chabrol – This refined and comfortable hostelry overlooking the Dronne is a particularly good value. The 19 rooms, some with river views, are small but charming; each comes with private bath and a TV set. The hotel is owned by the two Charbonnel brothers, who do the cooking while their amiable wives act as hostesses. Its one-star restaurant, *Les Frères Charbonnel*, offers a very satisfying three-course meal — for a very fair price — in a wonderfully appointed dining room with a river view. Try the scallops in shells with truffles, the squab, and, for dessert, sweet Dordogne strawberries marinated in champagne. Closed mid-November to mid-December, February 5–23, and Sunday evenings and Mondays from October 1 through June. Major credit cards accepted. 57 Rue Gambetta, Brantôme (phone: 53-05-70-15). Hotel, moderate; restaurant, expensive to moderate.

En Route from Brantôme – Take D78 southwest for about 6 miles (10 km) to reach Bourdeilles, one of the four feudal seats of ancient Périgord (Biron, Beynac, and Mareuil were the other three). This small town and its towering château on a cliff over the Dronne are perhaps more interesting than Brantôme, certainly worth a visit of several hours. What makes the castle here particularly intriguing is that it actually is two châteaux: a massive medieval fortress started in the 13th century next to a Renaissance palace filled with wonderful pieces dating from the 15th to the 17th century.

There are Flemish and Aubusson tapestries, Italian paintings and porcelain, and Spanish furniture inlaid with gold and ivory. The palace was started in the 16th century by Jacquette de Montbron, a sister-in-law of Pierre de Bourdeille (the famous Brantôme), in anticipation of a visit by Catherine de Médicis, but she never arrived, and so the castle was never completed. The contrast between the imposing 13th-century towers and ramparts and the airy, festive palace with its sculpted gardens and sparkling treasures is wonderful. One of the most magnificent features is the Golden Room, decorated by Ambroise Le Noble, one of the painters of Fontainebleau. There also is a 12th-century church nearby.

CHECKING IN: *Château de la Côte* – A superb 18th-century château converted to a hotel, high on a hill in its own park. All 12 rooms and 3 suites are luxurious; the adjoining restaurant offers regional cuisine. A swimming pool, ponies, and horses are all available to guests. Major credit cards accepted. On the D106 between Biras and Bourdeilles (phone: 53-03-70-11). Expensive.

Les Griffons – This cozy inn, just a short walk from the château, has 8 rooms and a restaurant; it's a good place to keep in mind. Closed from October to mid-April. Major credit cards accepted. Bourdeilles (phone: 53-03-75-61). Moderate.

ST-JEAN-DE-COLE: Located 12 miles (20 km) northeast of Brantôme, this is considered to be one of the most beautiful villages in France. Half-timbered and ochre-tinted houses crowd around a charming central square. Other sights include an 11th-century church, a medieval bridge, and a rustic covered market, which are located right in the middle of the village. Call the local Syndicat d'Initiative (phone: 53-62-14-15) for further information.

PÉRIGUEUX: The capital of the Dordogne, this modern town in the center of the fertile Isle Valley is one of the oldest settlements in France and retains ample evidence of its long and eventful history. There is scarcely a period of architecture that is not represented here. During Gallo-Roman times, Vesunna, as it was then called, was one of the most prosperous towns in Aquitaine. Remnants of the Tour de Vésone, a round temple dedicated to the deity for whom the settlement was named, can be seen today as well as the ruins of the 20,000-capacity elliptical amphitheater. Vesunna was sacked by the Alemans in the 3rd century AD.

During the Middle Ages, two rival cities shared the site — Puy St-Front, a commercial and monastic center on the hill, and the nearby Cité, where the aristocrats lived on the site of Vesunna. The two towns were reluctantly united under the name of Périgueux in 1251, but it was some time before these bitter rivals reconciled their differences and came together during the Hundred Years War under the motto "My strength is in the loyalty of my fellow countrymen." A good example of the early Périgord-Romanesque style is the Eglise St-Etienne de la Cité, built in the 12th century and topped with four domes (two of which were destroyed during the Wars of Religion), but the most arresting and curious sight is the Cathédrale St-Front, a sprawling, Byzantine structure built in the shape of a Greek cross and crowned with five cupolas similar to St. Mark's in Venice. The basilica was completed in 1173. Around 1755, the cathedral's five cupolas were covered to prevent water infiltration. They remained covered until 1852, when architects Abadie and Boeswillwald began restoring them to their original state, a project that wasn't completed until 1901. Visitors can see the cloisters — half Romanesque and half Gothic — as well as the crypt and confessionals. In summer you can walk around the domes of the cathedral roof, which has an excellent view of the old section. Back on the ground level, wander through the streets of the Puy-St-Front district, the Old Quarter, to discover remnants of Renaissance mansions. One of the most appealing streets is Rue Limogeanne, where 15th- and 16th-century houses have been renovated by their owners. Other picturesque streets are Rue de la Clarté and Rue de la Sagesse and streets of the Quartier Sauvegard. In the Cité district are the traces of the city's Gallo-Roman past, such as the remains of a vast amphitheater.

Well worth a leisurely visit is the *Musée du Périgord* (22 Cours Tourny) which has an impressive collection of prehistoric objects from all over the world, including ones found in the area. Included are tools from the paleolithic era, the skeleton of Chancelade man (late paleolithic), and engraved bones and mammoth tusks. A separate Gallo-Roman gallery on the main floor displays objects found during the excavation of the arena and the tower of Vésone, including mosaic floors that once flanked an altar on which bulls were sacrificed. Other sections of the museum are devoted to the paintings and arts of the region, such as enamels (open daily, except Tuesdays, from 10 AM to noon and 2 to 5 PM; phone: 53-53-16-42).

For a decadent detour, stop in at *La Chocolathèque* (2 Rue Taillefer; phone: 53-53-40-48) to sample *croquant du Périgord* (nougat and cognac covered with milk chocolate and almonds).

There's also a colorful local market every Wednesday morning in front of the cathedral. And the public market at Place Coderc can be of interest on a busy day, here in the heart of the area renowned for truffles and foie gras. On the street near the market there are plenty of unpretentious little restaurants in which to sample the regional specialties. During July and August, guided walking tours of the old section of Périgueux are offered in French and English, departing from the tourist office (1 Av. Aquitaine; phone: 53-53-10-63) at 2 and 4 PM, Tuesdays through Fridays.

CHECKING IN: *Château de Lalande* – A magnificent 18th-century château in a large park, which has been converted to a splendid hotel. The spacious rooms are tastefully appointed and comfortable, and the restaurant serves excellent regional cuisine. Closed mid-November to mid-March and Wednesdays for lunch except in July and August. Major credit cards accepted. Annesse-et-Beaulieu, Razac-sur-l'Isle, 1½ miles northwest of Périgueux on D3 (phone: 53-54-5-230; fax: 53-07-46-67). Expensive to mdoerate.

***Le Saint Laurent* –** Just outside of town and set in a private park, this modern hotel has 43 rooms, 13 of them duplexes that accommodate up to five people — perfect for families. A telephone and a color TV set are in every room, and the restaurant is noted for its regional dishes. Major credit cards accepted. St-Laurie-sur-Manoire, St-Pierre-de-Chignac (phone: 53-04-28-28; fax: 53-04-21-12). Hotel, moderate; restaurant, inexpensive.

***Hôtel du Périgord* –** Part of the Logis de France chain, this property has 20 rooms and a flower garden with a pond (with real fish). Its restaurant specializes in regional and Spanish fare (the chef is Spanish). Major credit cards accepted. 74 Rue Victor-Hugo (phone: 53-53-33-63). Moderate to inexpensive.

EATING OUT: *L'Oison* – A one-star dining room fills this old hosiery workroom in the old part of the city near the cathedral. Specialties include grilled fish with olive oil. Closed Sunday evenings, Mondays, 2 weeks in February, and 2 weeks in July. Major credit cards accepted. 31 Rue St-Front, Périgueux (phone: 53-09-84-02; fax: 53-03-27-94). Expensive.

***Le Tournepiche* –** A medieval structure in front of the cathedral is home to this rustic restaurant, which serves regional fare for reasonable prices under the vaulted stone arches. Closed Sundays and Monday evenings. Major credit cards accepted. 2 Rue de la Nation (phone: 53-08-09-76). Moderate.

En Route from Périgueux – Follow D5 about 24 miles (38 km) northeast to Hautefort, possibly the most handsome of Périgord's châteaux. This fine 17th-century palace has stately towers crowned with Renaissance domes and turrets.

The château that stood on this spot in the 12th century belonged to the Born family and was fought over by the two sons, Bertran (of troubadour-knight fame) and Constantin. Though he had the support of Henry II of England, Bertran eventually lost the château to Constantin, whose ally was Richard the Lion-Hearted. Years later, the property passed into the hands of the Gontaut family, who took the Hautefort name and crest and rebuilt the château during the early 1600s with the help of architect Nicolas Rambourg. Today the château looks much as it did more than 350 years ago, though it was restored following a serious fire in 1968.

Luckily, several important pieces — including 16th- and 17th-century tapestries and urns by the sculptor Torod — survived the fire and are on view. In the guard tower is a small museum dedicated to Eugène Le Roy, one of France's most respected authors, born here, the son of servants, in 1836. The 17th-century chapel contains 16th-century paintings on leather, the altar at which Charles X was crowned, and other noteworthy objects.

The château is surrounded by neatly manicured and sculpted gardens and a 99-acre park. Down below, in the town, is a charity hospital and church built in the same style as the restored château. A gift to the village from the Marquis d'Hautefort, it was designed to house 33 sick people, one for every year of Christ's life. Truffle fanatics will appreciate the *Ecomusée de la Truffe,* a small museum in Sorges 14 miles (24 km) outside Périgueux with exhibits lauding the elusive black truffle. Open 2 to 5 PM daily. Closed Tuesdays September through June; open 10 AM to noon and 2 to 5 PM in July and August. The Syndicat d'Initiative organizes truffle classes and truffle walks to areas where the prized fungus can be found. Call 53-05-90-11 for more information.

LES EYZIES-DE-TAYAC: "Few regions in the world are more rewarding to the visitor than the valley of the Vézère," wrote André Maurois in *A History of France.* "The river's murky waters flow between two walls of stone, and its high banks are pierced by black openings, the mouths of caves or shelters." It was in these caves near Les Eyzies, a sleepy little village at the confluence of the Vézère and the Beune valleys, that evidence of one of our most distant ancestors was found.

In 1868, when a path was being cut through the valley for the railroad, workers unearthed bones that, on examination by experts, proved to be the remains of Cro-Magnon man. There are at least a dozen grottoes and prehistoric sites in the vicinity of Les Eyzies, once dubbed "the cradle of history." It is, without question, one of the areas in the world richest in vestiges of prehistory. One of the most spellbinding grottoes (and one of the few to offer a tour in English once a day) is the Font-de-Gaume, a deep, narrow cave whose rock walls are decorated with beautifully fluid paintings of bison, deer, mammoths, and horses colored with black and red oxides. More than 200 drawings here date from the early paleolithic period, many of them, unfortunately, defaced by those who frequented the caves in the 18th and 19th centuries, unaware of the existence of the prehistoric art. In an effort to preserve the paintings from deterioration, the number of visitors is limited to 100 a day, so arrive early. In season, tickets are sold only in the morning. Closed Tuesdays.

In the nearby Combarelles Cave there are some 300 animal drawings, albeit very faint, dating from about the same period. Most intriguing is how "primitive" man used the rock contours in the caves to convey the shape and bulk of the animal. Again, entrance is limited, so arrive early to get your tickets.

The *Musée National de la Préhistoire,* in the restored medieval castle of Tayac halfway up a cliff near Les Eyzies's main street, houses one of the world's most important collections of prehistoric items (open daily except Tuesdays from 9:30 AM to noon and 2 to 6 PM; phone: 53-06-97-03).

Also nearby, at Abri du Cap Blanc, there is a superb frieze of horses, and there are many remarkable stalagmite and stalactite formations at Grotte du Grand Roc. Signs for both are clearly posted. For a contemporary equine excursion, visit the *Equestre de la Baronie* in nearby Tursac. This small, family-run operation arranges rides through the lovely countryside from their farm. The horses and ponies are so placid and gentle that even those skittish about equine beasts can feel safe atop them. Picnic lunches are also provided for day trips. On the D706 just outside Tursac. Open all year (phone: 53-06-93-83).

CHECKING IN/EATING OUT: *Le Centenaire* – At one end of the short main street is this sparkling hotel — more modern than the *Cro-Magnon* (below) but equally deserving of praise. The main building has 29 rooms; the old mill in the garden has been made over and now has 20 rooms. Amenities include a swimming pool, a sauna, and a gym. (A member of the prestigious Relais & Châteaux group.) Chef Roland Mazère, who apprenticed with such noted French chefs as the Troisgros brothers, Mark Haeberlin, and Jacques Manière, won his second Michelin star in 1981. His resolutely modern approach contrasts with the traditional kitchens in the area. Restaurant closed Tuesday lunch, both hotel and restaurant closed November to April. Major credit cards accepted. Les Eyzies (phone: 53-06-97-18; fax: 53-06-92-41). Hotel, moderate to inexpensive; restaurant, expensive.

Cro-Magnon – It is speculated that this wonderful, vine-covered inn stands where the Cro-Magnon skeletons were discovered in the 1860s. The hotel, which literally clings to the side of the massive, overhung rocks characteristic of the region, has been in the Leysalles family since 1910 and manages to provide modern luxury and efficiency without forfeiting a certain somnolent charm. There are 20 rooms and 4 suites, a swimming pool, and extensive grounds. The kitchen, rated one Michelin star, still can be counted on for the classic traditional fare for which it has been known, although these days the menu has begun to feature "some suggestions of the moment," such as *lotte aux morilles* (monkfish with wild morel mushrooms) or *foie gras de canard au poivre* (prepared duck foie gras). Closed from mid-October through April. Restaurant closed Wednesdays for lunch except on holidays. Major credit cards accepted. Les Eyzies (phone: 53-06-97-06; fax: 53-06-92-41). Expensive to moderate.

MONTIGNAC: In the hills above Montignac about 12 miles (19 km) from Les Eyzies (D706) are the Lascaux Caves, the site of one of the greatest prehistoric finds in Europe. These caves, which have been dubbed the Sistine Chapel of prehistory, contain magnificent friezes of bulls, horses, deer, and unicorn-like creatures, some larger than life and delicately shaded with black and red. The paleolithic drawings are remarkable not only for their quantity but for their grace and lifelike quality. Carbon dating indicates that the caves were occupied about 15,000 to 13,000 years before Christ, and it is thought that they were used for primitive rites and magic. The caves were discovered in the 1940s by four children attempting to rescue a dog that had fallen into a hole; they were opened to the public for about 20 years until it was realized that the atmospheric imbalance created in the small space by the carbon dioxide exhaled by large numbers of visitors was causing bacteria to grow and gradually destroy the paintings. As a result, Lascaux was closed to the general public in 1963 and now can be visited only with special permission from local authorities (about five people a day are admitted). But in July 1983, Lascaux II, an exact replica of the most interesting sections of the original, finally was completed after 6 years of work. Artists from the *Beaux-Arts* in Paris re-created the many hundreds of paintings in four chambers inch by inch (although most of the work was done by one artist, Monique Peytral), even using the same vegetable dyes and oxides that primitive man must have used. Lascaux II is open daily except Mondays from 10 AM to noon and 2 to 5:30 PM; in July and August, from 9:30 AM to 7 PM; closed January. Because of the heavy volume of visitors in July and August, tickets are sold in a kiosk next to the tourist office (on Pl. Bertran-de-Born; phone: 53-51-82-60). It's best to buy them early in the day. In the winter, tickets are sold at the entrance to the cave. Entry price includes admission to Le Thot, in nearby Thonac, which offers a video presentation on prehistoric man and an exhibition on the construction and painting of Lascaux II.

CHECKING IN/EATING OUT: *Château de Puy Robert* – A turreted storybook château in a wooded park about 1½ miles (2 km) from Lascaux, it has been converted into a deluxe hotel with 38 comfortably furnished rooms, a swimming pool, and a restaurant (rated one Michelin star) serving regional cuisine. The hotel is a new member of the Relais & Châteaux group. Restaurant closed Wednesday lunch; both hotel and restaurant closed mid-October to May. Major credit cards accepted. Montignac en Périgord (phone: 53-51-92-13; fax: 53-51-80-11). Expensive.

Soleil d'Or – This 32-room hotel, with a swimming pool, is set in a wonderful park. The restaurant features *cuisine bourgeoise*. Closed mid-January to mid-February. Major credit cards accepted. 16 Rue du 4 September, Montignac (phone: 53-51-80-22; fax: 53-50-27-54). Hotel, expensive to moderate; restaurant, expensive.

Hôtel-Restaurant des Iles – Overlooking a park on the Vézère River, this nicely located property offers 25 rooms, a swimming pool, and a restaurant. Closed January, February, and Mondays off-season except in July and August. Major credit cards accepted. Thonac (phone: 53-50-70-20). Moderate.

SARLAT-LA-CANÉDA: Take D704 to Sarlat, the capital of Périgord-Noir and one of the best-preserved medieval and Renaissance towns in France. The city was a religious center from the 14th to the 18th century, which accounts, in part, for its fine standard of architecture. Many of the old buildings are still standing thanks to the efforts of Prosper Mérimée, an inspector of historical monuments during the last century. And since 1964, Sarlat's appeal has been enhanced according to a plan sponsored in part by André Malraux and adapted by the city to restore and safeguard the Old Quarter. Not surprisingly, it is an irresistible destination for tourists; one hopes that the souvenir vendors won't break the spell cast by the ocher buildings and their crooked stone-covered roofs.

The first glimpse of Sarlat may not be impressive, particularly if you enter via Rue de la République, a "new" road built in the late 1800s and now lined with modern shops. It unfortunately cuts right through the center of old Sarlat, bisecting the medieval world. You'll enjoy the city more if you park the car, then wander aimlessly through the maze of curving streets and passageways.

You might want to start at Maison de La Boétie, the lovely Renaissance house in which Etienne de La Boétie, magistrate, poet, and close friend of the writer Montaigne, was born. Across the street is the 16th-century Cathédrale St-Sacerdos, which weds Romanesque and Gothic elements. Behind the cathedral past the terraced garden is the curious Lanterne des Morts (Lantern of the Dead), a 12th-century tower with a cone-shaped roof commemorating the miracle of healing performed here by St. Bernard in 1147. To the north on Rue Landry is the Présidial and its gardens, and farther on are Rue de la Salamandre and Place de la Liberté, which during July and August are transformed into open-air theaters where plays by Molière and Shakespeare are performed. On Rue des Consuls is the magnificent House of the Consuls, built between the 14th and 17th centuries and now a restaurant called *Le Jardin des Consuls* (phone: 53-59-18-77). Colorful Saturday and Wednesday morning markets are held in the Place du Marche and Place de la Liberté; there also are a number of shops selling foie gras, walnut oils, *cèpes* (wild mushrooms), and other Périgord delicacies. Nearby are several foie gras factories that can be visited, one of which even provides a tasting. Inquire at the tourist office for details; the office is open every day except Sundays all year. Closed noon to 2 PM. (Pl. Liberté; 53-59-27-67). During the summer, guided walking tours of the Old City start at the Place de la Liberté (next to the tourist office) at 10:30 AM and 10 PM Mondays through Fridays. Check with the tourist office for hours of weekend tours. Also of interest is the *Musée d'Art Sacré* (on Rue Jean-Jacques Rousseau; phone: 53-31-19-34) with displays of religious art of the area. Open daily except Sunday morning from 10 AM to noon and 3 to 6 PM.

CHECKING IN: *Hostellerie Meysset* – Just north of Sarlat, this ivy-covered manor house with 20 rooms and 6 suites also has a fine restaurant serving many duck dishes. Restaurant closed Wednesday lunch; hotel and restaurant closed mid-October to late April. Major credit cards accepted. Rte. des Eyzies, Argentauleau, Sarlat (phone: 53-59-08-29; fax: 53-28-47-61). Expensive.

La Couleuvrine – A charming hotel in a restored 12th-century structure. Its 25 rooms are decorated with antiques and reproductions. The restaurant serves regional cuisine. Closed the last 2 weeks of November and most of January. Major credit cards accepted. 1 Pl. de la Bouquerie, Sarlat (phone: 53-59-27-80; fax: 53-31-26-83). Moderate.

La Hoirie – Outside Sarlat, this 15-room hotel, a Périgourdine house set in a garden and with a swimming pool, is pleasant, very quiet, and reasonable. Closed mid-November to mid-March. Major credit cards accepted. About 1½ miles (2 km) south on Rte. 2, Sarlat (phone: 53-59-05-62; fax: 53-31-13-90). Moderate.

La Madeleine – A distinguished and traditional hostelry in the old part of town, its 19 rooms and 3 suites are air conditioned. The restaurant serves classic cooking, well prepared and presented. Try the *magret à la bordelaise* (sliced duck breast, Bordeaux-style) or *confit de canard en pot au feu* (preserved duck) but leave plenty of room for walnut cake, a house specialty. In high season guests are required to take breakfast and dinner at the hotel. Closed mid-November to mid-March. Major credit cards accepted. 1 Pl. Petite-Rigaudie, Sarlat (phone: 53-59-10-41; fax: 53-31-03-62). Moderate.

En Route from Sarlat – Take a short detour on D57 south to Beynac-et-Cazenac, another of the four feudal seats of the Périgord. The château here looms up magnificently some 500 feet above the Dordogne, like an extension of the rock on which it was built. In the 12th century, during the continuing struggle between the Plantagenets and Capetians, Richard the Lion-Hearted gave the fortress on this site to his defender, the bloodthirsty Mercadier. In 1214, it was demolished by the Crusader Simon de Montfort, who overran much of the South of France. The castle was rebuilt by the Barons of Beynac in the early 13th century and added to from the 14th to the 17th century. The panorama from the terrace here is superb. The sinuous course of the Dordogne seen below marked the dividing line in the struggles between the British and the French during the Hundred Years War. On the river's opposite bank are the Fayrac Castle (privately owned) and, beyond, the ruins of English-occupied Castelnaud, the bitter enemy of the French-controlled Beynac. Among the most interesting things to see here at Beynac are the 14th-century frescoes found in a small oratory in the impressive state hall, where the nobility of the four baronies of Périgord met once a year. The château is undergoing a meticulous restoration program that will continue until 1995.

Just a few miles away and worth another detour is the town of Domme, a well-preserved *bastide* (fortified town) on a rocky cliff with a panoramic view of the Dordogne Valley. Don't miss the well-preserved covered market and the spectacular view from the Terrasse de la Barre.

CHECKING IN/EATING OUT: *Hostellerie de la Guérinière* – This 17th-century noble's residence perched on a hill just south of Domme offers panoramic views of the lush Dordogne countryside; comfortable rooms in Louis XIV-, XV-, and XVI-style; and a rustic restaurant serving regional fare as well as French classics. Closed Wednesdays off-season. Major credit cards accepted. Cénac, Domme (phone: 53-28-22-44; fax: 53-28-26-79). Expensive to moderate.

Le Bonnet – A comfortable inn with a restaurant featuring regional cuisine overlooking the Dordogne river. The 22 rooms are rather small but aesthetically pleasing, especially those overlooking the beautifully tended garden. Closed mid-October to mid-April. Major credit cards accepted. Beynac-et-Cazenac (phone: 53-29-50-01). Moderate.

SOUILLAC: Much less sensational than its neighbors Sarlat and Rocamadour and about midway between the two, where the D703 meets N20, Souillac grew up around a Benedictine abbey built in the 12th century. The monastery was sacked by the English during the Hundred Years War and by the Protestants during the Wars of Religion, then destroyed by fire in 1572. The abbey church survived and still is the town's main attraction. Its domed Romanesque-Byzantine style is similar, though on a much smaller scale, to that of the cathedral in Périgueux. Inside, the bas-reliefs of the prophet Isaiah and St. Joseph on either side of the doorway are beautiful for their detail and motion — particularly the one of Isaiah, who appears to be dancing. Equally well executed is the bas-relief over the doorway, delicately chiseled scenes from the life of the monk Theophilus, framed by carvings of St. Peter and St. Benedict.

CHECKING IN/EATING OUT: *Château de la Treyne* – This lovely 17th-century château was transformed into a luxurious inn by a charming and enterprising Parisian, Mme. Michele Gombert-Devals. It has 12 beautifully furnished rooms, 1 suite, and sits on the edge of a cliff, attached to a 120-acre private park with a pool, tennis courts, and a sauna. The restaurant, which has a terrace garden, features classic cuisine such as *magret de canard au vin* (duck breast cooked in wine). Demi-pension (breakfast and dinner) required in high season. Closed mid-November to Easter. Major credit cards accepted. Lacave, 6 miles (10 km) southeast of Souillac, via D43 (phone 65-32-66-66; fax: 65-37-06-57). Expensive.

La Vieille Auberge – One of the nicest of several traditional inns near the center of old Souillac, it has 45 simply decorated rooms (20 in the original building), some of them down the street in an annex with a swimming pool. In the kitchen, owner-chef Robert Véril adds a delicate touch to local classics such as *émincé de pigeonneau aux figues* (squab with figs), *farandole de poissons* (an array of fish), or *chausson du "diamant noire"* (a "black diamond" truffle wrapped with ham and foie gras and baked in puff pastry). Closed January 1 to March 15. Major credit cards accepted. Pl. de la Minoterie, Souillac (phone: 65-32-79-43; fax: 65-32-65-19). Moderate.

Le Pont de l'Ouysse – In Lacave, close to *Château de la Treyne,* this establishment offers 12 cheerfully decorated rooms and 1 suite, with breakfast served in the garden if weather permits. The restaurant features a good but pricey à la carte menu. Specialties include foie gras and *magret de canard* (duck breast). Closed Mondays, and mid-November to March. Major credit cards accepted. Lacave (phone: 65-37-87-04; fax: 65-32-77-41). Expensive.

En Route from Souillac – The caves of Lacave are about midway between Souillac and Rocamadour on D23. Though less impressive in size and grandeur than the caves at Padirac to the northeast, the stalagmites and stalactites here have a more delicate beauty. It doesn't take much imagination to see the shapes of small people and animals in these fine crystalline deposits. Most intriguing is the Salle du Lac (Lake Chamber), which is suffused with the natural, dim, purple-white fluorescence of the formations still growing.

ROCAMADOUR: The first glimpse of Rocamadour from the L'Hospitalet road across the Alzou Canyon is unforgettable, particularly if you arrive in the morning when the sun shines on the rugged face of the cliff to which this village of medieval dwellings, towers, chapels, and ramparts clings. Its precarious position almost 500 feet above the river gorge seems to defy the laws of nature; however, Rocamadour has clung steadfastedly to this rock for centuries. In addition to its spectacular setting, Rocamadour has been an important point of religious pilgrimage for 900 years. In 1166, the remains of a man believed to be St. Amadour were unearthed near the threshold of the Chapel of the Virgin. Though the man's identity has long been debated, legend has it that he was Zaccheus, a disciple of Christ and husband of St. Veronica. As the story goes, after Christ's death, the couple was persecuted in Palestine and escaped to this part of France. When Veronica died, Zaccheus retreated to the rock high on the plateau and, when he died, was buried there.

Shortly after the discovery of the saint's remains, miracles began to occur, word spread, and the pious began to arrive in droves, among them the English King Henry Plantagenet. Until the 13th century, Rocamadour ranked in religious importance with Rome, Santiago de Compostela, and Jerusalem. Although it is still the site of an annual pilgrimage, the floods of worshipers have now been superseded by waves of tourists. The village, which has only about 800 permanent residents, bills itself as the "Deuxième Site de la France" (the second-best tourist attraction in the country; picturesque Mont-St-Michel is considered the first). Unfortunately, Rocamadour carries the scars and blemishes that accompany such renown. One can imagine how appealing the tiny, sloping main street guarded at either end by fortified gates might have been before any of its medieval structures were taken over by souvenir vendors. Nonetheless, if you make your way through it all and climb to the top of the 216 steps (called Escalier des Pèlerins and climbed by pilgrims on their knees), your effort will be rewarded by the sight of a lovely little square surrounded by no fewer than seven chapels. This is the Cité Religieuse, with several fine buildings: the fortified bishop's palace, Evêché; the 11th- to 13th-century Basilique St-Sauveur; the Chapelle St-Michel, known for its fresco of the Annunciation; St. Amadour's crypt; and, most entrancing of all, the Chapelle Miraculeuse. This last, the successor of the Chapel of the Virgin, was destroyed twice, then rebuilt during the 19th century; it houses the intriguing Black Virgin and Child, made of carved walnut covered with silver plate blackened by age and the elements. It is believed to have been carved in about the 9th century. Here also, suspended from the roof, is the miraculous bell that is said to ring of its own accord to foretell miracles.

On the wall outside the chapel are 13th- and 14th-century frescoes that depict St. Christopher and the Dance of Death between three living and three dead men. On the square near the Miraculous Chapel is the *Musée Trésor,* in which valuable religious items are displayed. Farther up the hill via a crooked dirt path is a fortress built in the 14th century to protect pilgrims. The adjacent 19th-century château now is inhabited by the chaplains of Rocamadour. The only part open to the public is the ramparts, from which there is a breathtaking view of the village and the surrounding countryside.

CHECKING IN/EATING OUT: *Château de Roumégouse* – This lovely Gothic Renaissance château, now an inn and a member of Relais & Châteaux group, has 14 luxurious rooms, 2 suites, and a restaurant. Ideal for those who appreciate elegance and isolation, it's in a wooded park and provides magnificent views of the Causse foothills. Restaurant closed Tuesdays for lunch; hotel and restaurant closed late October to mid-April. Major credit cards accepted. Off N140 at Rignac, almost 3 miles (5 km) from Gramat and 9 miles (14 km) from Rocamadour (phone: 65-33-63-81; fax: 65-33-71-18). Expensive.

***Beau Site et Notre-Dame* –** Wedged between souvenir stands on the sloping main street, the distinguished façade of this solid and venerable 55-room establishment offers a warm welcome to the modern pilgrim. Amazingly enough, it's been in the same family's hands for seven generations. There also is a reasonably priced restaurant, *Jean de Valon,* with a terrace that offers a beautiful view. Closed mid-November to December 26 and January to mid-April. Major credit cards accepted. Rue Roland-le-Preux, Rocamadour (phone: 65-33-63-08; fax: 65-33-65-23). Moderate.

***Ste-Marie* –** Perched on a landing about halfway up the Escalier de Pèlerins, this hotel with 22 comfortably decorated rooms is agreeably removed from the noise and traffic below. The cozy, well-appointed dining room and adjoining covered terrace (which has a fine vista of the Alzou Canyon) seem to be the best in town for trying the classics of the Quercy and Périgord. Some of the house specialties that should be sampled include *cassoulade d'escargots à la périgourdine* (snail casserole Périgord style), *truite à la crème de ciboulette* (trout with chive cream sauce), *omelette aux truffes* (truffle omelet), and walnut cakes, as well as one of the fine Cahors wines. Closed mid-October to late March. Major credit cards accepted. Pl. des Senhals, Rocamadour (phone: 65-33-63-07). Moderate.

GOUFFRE DE PADIRAC: About 9 miles (14 km) northeast of Rocamadour (via D673 and D90) is the famous Gouffre de Padirac (Padirac Chasm), one of nature's more dramatic feats in the region. This series of underground caverns dug out over the centuries by an underground river is adorned with fascinating limestone concretions. Start your journey by descending into the gaping hole 325 feet across and 328 feet deep, the natural entrance to this surreal underground world. Part of the journey is by boat on the cool, clear river and part on foot, up, down, and around the intriguing formations of stalagmites and stalactites. (Note that the tour is 1¼ miles long — a third of that by boat — and that the climbing is at times strenuous.) The most impressive features of the chasm are the Grande Pendeloque (Great Pendant), a giant stalactite overhanging and nearly touching the river's surface, and the Salle du Grande Dome (Hall of the Great Dome), which, at 250 feet high, is the largest and most beautiful of Padirac's chambers.

Not surprisingly, superstition surrounds this awesome natural phenomenon; according to legend, the great gaping hole in the earth was the work of the devil. It's said to have been the site of a showdown between St. Martin, returning from an excursion in search of souls to save, and Satan, who was toting a sack of souls condemned to hell. Satan offered St. Martin a deal. He would surrender the doomed souls if the holy man could make his reluctant mule cross an obstacle created by the devil. An agreement was struck, the devil stamped the earth with his hoof, and the great chasm yawned open. When St. Martin's mule heroically jumped clear of the hole, Satan was forced to give up the souls and retreated to hell through the mouth of the chasm.

En Route from Padirac – If time allows, make a special side trip north from Padirac via N140, D23, and D38 to Collonges-La-Rouge, an ancient red village lost in the rugged hills of the Corrèze. Its quaint, vine-covered houses and churches, some dating from the 12th century, are all built in striking red brick, a dramatic contrast to the somber gray stone of the surrounding towns. In recent years Collonges has been carefully restored by artists and local merchants, making it one of France's most beautiful villages, well worth the detour. Rejoin route N140 and follow it southeast before continuing to Cahors to visit one of the region's newest museums, the *Musée Champollion* (on Enpasse Champollion). Named after the French Egyptologist, this museum of Egyptian artifacts is in the house where Champollion was born.

CHECKING IN/EATING OUT: Le Relais St-Jacques de Compostelle – Arrive at dusk to sip an aperitif on the terrace as the sun sets over Collonges's red brick. The quaint inn has 12 simple rooms, a terrace, and a pleasant dining room which serves well-prepared regional dishes. Closed December, January, and Tuesday evenings and Wednesdays off-season. Major credit cards accepted. Collonges-La-Rouge (phone: 55-25-41-02). Moderate.

Le Prieuré – Generous servings of simple regional dishes such as ham omelettes and salad with walnut-oil dressing prove soothing and substantial to a palate wearied of fancy sauces. Closed mid-November to mid-March. Reservations advised. No credit cards accepted. Collonges-La-Rouge (phone: 55-25-41-00). Moderate to inexpensive.

CAHORS: South of the Dordogne Valley in a deep loop of the Lot River is Cahors, one of the main gateways to southern France (via D677, N20, or any number of wandering country roads). It is most famous for the red wine made from the grapes grown on the hills along the Lot west of the city.

Founded on the site of a spring (called Fontaine des Chartreux), the city was first known as Divona Cadurcorum and later as Cadurca; it grew prosperous under the Gauls and the Romans, acquiring the requisite forum, theater, baths, and temples. By the early Middle Ages, Cahors was already an important commercial and university center, but it reached its zenith in the 13th century when an influx of Lombard merchants and bankers earned it the reputation of the first banking city in Europe. The Lombard firms, known not only for their business acumen but also for their usurious lending habits, soon made Cahors world famous. However, the city's fortunes fell during the Hundred Years War, and eventually wine production replaced banking as the chief industry.

The two most compelling sights in Cahors are the Pont Valentré and the Romanesque Cathédrale St-Etienne. The first, one of the few surviving examples of a medieval fortified bridge, is still used. Its three crenelated towers rise for 130 feet and its narrow gateways allow only one modern vehicle to pass at a time. The best view of this proud, unusual structure (another construction that the devil had a hand in, according to legend) is from the right bank of the Lot, slightly upstream. It is particularly impressive when lighted at night. St. Stephen's Cathedral, in the old part of town, dates from the 11th century, when Bishop Géraud of Cardaillac began building here on the site of a 6th-century church. Particularly noteworthy is the north door, an intricate, Romanesque carving of the Ascension executed about 1140.

The Cahors Tourist Board (Pl. A. Briand; phone: 65-35-09-56) provides a map that outlines a pleasant walking tour of the old part of the city. It takes visitors past such medieval and Renaissance structures as the late-15th-century Roaldès Mansion, with crooked timberwork on one side and a rose window and mullioned doors and windows on the other. Also of interest is the *Musée Municipal* (Rue Emile Zola; phone: 65-30-15-13) in a former episcopal palace; its collection ranges from a Roman sarcophagus to 15th- and 16th-century sculpture to mementos of Cahors's most famous sons, including Pope John XXII, the French magistrate Léon Gambetta, and the 16th-century writer Clément Marot.

CHECKING IN: *Château de Mercuès* – In a turreted 12th-century castle perched above the Lot River, this inn has 25 rooms, 7 luxury suites, tennis courts, and a swimming pool. There also is an excellent, albeit overpriced, restaurant with commanding views. A member of the Relais & Châteaux group. Closed mid-November to mid-March. Major credit cards accepted. Located about 6 miles (10 km) from Cahors in Mercuès (phone: 65-20-00-01; fax: 65-20-05-72). Expensive.

***Terminus* –** Across from the train station, this traditional hotel with lovely stained glass windows from the early part of this century has 31 clean, bright rooms. The husband and wife team who run it are particularly friendly and helpful. The inexpensive restaurant features nouvelle fare. Major credit cards accepted. 5 Av. Charles-de-Freycinet, Cahors (phone: 65-35-24-50; fax: 65-22-06-40). Moderate.

EATING OUT: *Marco* – In an ancient vine-covered house, this restaurant serves local cuisine with a focus on foie gras in ravioli or accompanied by truffles. The wine list is definitely something to write home about, which boasts everything from a rare cahors to a superb 1983 Domaine Eugénie. Closed early January to early March and late October to early November, and Sunday evenings and Mondays in the off-season. Reservations necessary. Major credit cards accepted. Located about 5 miles (8 km) from Cahors in Lamagdelaine (phone: 65-35-30-64). Expensive to moderate.

ST-CIRQ-LAPOPIE: Wander along the course of the Lot east of Cahors via D662 to this picturesque village of less than 200 people. Dominated by its 15th-century church, it sits precariously on the top of a rocky escarpment, high above the meandering river. Albeit tiny, the village is not short on historical interest. This cliffsite, a natural stronghold for the valleys below, was long a source of strife. In the 8th century, it was the site of the Duke of Aquitaine's last stand against Pepin the Short. And in 1198, Richard the Lion-Hearted unsuccessfully attempted to seize it. St-Cirq was contested fiercely by the British and French during the Hundred Years War and by the Huguenots during the Wars of Religion. Both Louis XI (in 1471) and Henri de Navarre (1580) ordered the strategic castle destroyed. What remains of the castle sits at the highest point of the cliff (accessible by a dirt path), from which there is an inspiring view of the surrounding terrain. The half-timbered and stone houses of the village climb up the steep lanes (which are closed to traffic during the summer months). Many of them are inhabited by artisans, including potters, puppeteers, and a wood-turner, carrying on the former livelihood of the village.

CHECKING IN/EATING OUT: *Auberge du Sombral* – This particularly comfortable little inn, on one corner of the town's sleepy central square, has 10 rooms furnished in a delightful country style with private baths or showers. The spacious dining room provides a most pleasing setting in which to sample owner-chef Gilles Hardeveld's renditions of regional specialties. Closed Tuesdays, Wednesdays, and from mid-November to April. Major credit cards accepted. St-Cirq-Lapopie (phone: 65-31-26-08). Moderate.

La Pélissaria – Owned by François and Marie-Françoise Matuchet, this lovely 13th-century house has 7 rooms with whitewashed walls, exposed beams, and hand-turned wooden furniture, each with a private bath. All rooms, including the dining room, have views of the garden or village or, most spectacular, of the River Lot with its limestone cliffs. Mme. Matuchet now devotes most of her time to the hotel, so the restaurant (open for dinner only) offers a simple *menu gastronomique,* but the regional fare is quite good (terrines, desserts, and homemade bread). Closed mid-November to April. Major credit cards accepted. St-Cirq-Lapopie (phone: 65-31-25-14). Moderate.

GROTTE DU PECH-MERLE: The route north from St-Cirq to the caves at Pech-Merle is well marked, and it takes only a few minutes on the tiny back roads to reach this vast underground cave of tremendous geological and archaeological interest. These caverns, inhabited by prehistoric man some 20,000 years ago, were only discovered by modern man in 1922 when two boys happened to venture into the huge chambers. They found what you still can see today: marvelous and mysterious prehistoric paintings as well as weirdly beautiful stalagmites and stalactites. In the Galerie des Peintures are stunning, spotted horses and silhouetted handprints; and in the Salles des Hiéroglyphes, the outlines of feminine forms are just vaguely visible on the low clay roof of the cave. Nearby are the footprints of primitive man, petrified in the calcite-rich clay of the cave floor. The Salle des Disques contains more works of nature: strange, slanted disk-shaped formations as unexplained as the works of early man. Scientists don't know how or why these disks formed. In the hall of the broken column is a frieze of mammoths and bison believed to date from the Aurignacian age. The price of admission to this, one of the most intriguing of France's many grottoes, entitles the visitor to view a film before entering the cave and to visit the *Abbé Lemozi Museum,* where more prehistoric artifacts are on view.

En Route from Grotte du Pech-Merle – Follow the winding course of the Lot back to Cahors and drive west along the picturesque wine route; then head north on D710. Scattered through this area south of Bergerac are a number of *bastides,* the small feudal fortress towns constructed in the 13th century by both the French and the English when the two countries claimed sovereignty of the region. Monpazier, on D660, is perhaps the best-preserved *bastide* in France. Built by the English in 1284 in the name of Edward I, its layout is common to most *bastides.* The streets are arranged in a grid, with alleys between the houses to form fire breaks. (The alleys are called *andronne,* an old southwest term for man; it describes the width of these narrow passageways.) The central square and covered market are flanked by vaulted arcades and surrounded by houses, some with lovely Gothic bays. Nearby is the Eglise St-Dominique and the 13th-century Maison du Chapitre (Chapter House). Three of the six gates to the village still remain, protected by towers set in the ramparts. Other *bastides* of interest are at Lalinde, Villeneuve-sur-Lot, Villeréal, Puylaroque, Sauveterre de Guyenne, Domme, and Villefranche-du-Périgord.

BERGERAC: Take D660 back to Bergerac, a wine and tobacco center whose name will be familiar to lovers of wine and literature. The hills nearby produce the fine, dry bergerac reds and a sweet, white monbazillac, a perfect companion to foie gras. And, on the Place de la Myrpe, a statue of playwright Edmond Rostand's immortal hero, Cyrano de Bergerac, marks the town's literary connection.

Tobacco has helped make Bergerac prosperous, so it's fitting that it should have the only tobacco museum in France. In the old part of the town, the *Musée du Tabac* (10 Rue Ancien Pont) has a number of displays and exhibits on the history of the plant, how it's produced, and how it's consumed (open daily except Mondays from 10 AM to noon and 2 to 6 PM; phone: 53-63-04-13). Next door is a small municipal museum with prehistoric items, the works of Bergerac painters, and a section on local history.

Near the tobacco museum is the Couvent des Récollets (Monastery of Recollects), a former cloister built between the 12th and 17th centuries. A few doors away is the *Maison du Vin,* a small museum with exhibits on all the wines of the region, from hearty red bergeracs to the sauterne-like monbazillac. Open weekdays from mid-May to mid-October, afternoons only except in July and August. 2 Place du Docteur Cayla (phone: 53-57-12-57).

The Eglise Notre-Dame, built in the 19th century in an imitation Gothic style, has two Italian paintings from the early Renaissance and an immense Aubusson tapestry depicting the Bergerac coat of arms.

Leave town via the scenic Tobacco Route to take a small detour south (D13) to the lovely Monbazillac château and vineyard.

CHECKING IN/EATING OUT: *Bordeaux* – Though neither plush nor charming, this 42-room hotel is adequate, and it has a restaurant, *Le Terroir,* which excels in regional cuisine and overlooks a garden. Closed mid-December to February. Major credit cards accepted. 38 Pl. Gambetta, Bergerac (phone: 53-57-12-83; fax: 53-57-72-14). Moderate.

Le Cyrano – A charming little spot where Jean-Paul Turon directs the kitchen, generally sticking to the classics of the area — try his *escalope de foie chaud de canard grillotin* (slices of hot duck liver) and, for dessert, his *gratin de fruits rouges au sabayon de Monbazillac* (baked fruit in a warm custard sauce made with monbazillac wine). There also are 11 guestrooms. Closed Sunday evenings and Mondays in off-season, 2 weeks in June, and 2 weeks in December. Major credit cards accepted. 2 Bd. Montaigne, Bergerac (phone: 53-57-02-76). Moderate.

MONBAZILLAC CHÂTEAU AND VINEYARD: Set among the vineyards that produce the famous sweet white wine of the same name is this pristine, small gray stone château. The reputation of the monbazillac wine goes back centuries. Legend has it that when a group from Bergerac made the pilgrimage to Rome in the Middle Ages, they were asked by the pope where their home was. "Near Monbazillac" was the reply, to which the pope is said to have responded with the benediction *"Bonum vinum."*

Built in about 1550, the château is a pleasing amalgam of fortified castle and Renaissance palace. The surrounding grounds are well kept and the view of the Bergerac Valley below is superb. Today the château is owned and operated by the Monbazillac wine cooperative. Following a tour of the nobly decorated castle, guests are invited to visit the 17th-century wine cellar, now a tasting room, to sample (and, if they wish, purchase) both bergerac and monbazillac wines. Open Mondays through Fridays year-round. The cooperative will obligingly ship cases of wine overseas for you. It also runs a small restaurant (open for lunch only) in what were once the stables.

EATING OUT: *Closerie St-Jacques* – With one Michelin star, this restaurant features *aiguillette de canard au jus de noix verte* (sliced duck in green walnut sauce), *escalope de foie poëlée sauce raisin et monbazillac* (sliced liver in a monbazillac wine sauce). Closed Sunday evenings and Mondays (except June to

October). Major credit cards accepted. Monbazillac (phone: 53-58-37-77). Expensive to moderate.

En Route from Monbazillac – In an area such as Périgord, where splendid vistas of peaceful green valleys are as common as potholes in New York City streets, it's easy to become blasé about the scenery. There is, however, a particularly arresting view at the crest of a hill just outside Trémolat near D703 that's worth a detour. From here you can see the Cingle de Trémolat, a wide loop in the Dordogne River that encircles a resplendent valley of walnut orchards and soft, flat fields sprinkled with flowers.

CHECKING IN/EATING OUT: *Manoir Le Grand Vignoble* – Another elegant, quiet establishment whose 40 rooms are exquisitely appointed (barring the thoroughly modern annex). Its greatest claim to fame has little to do with the art of innkeeping, however; it is possibly the only place in France outside a zoo where llamas and zebras run riot through the nearby park. Horseback riding, tennis courts, a heated pool, and a putting green are all on the premises, along with a restaurant. An equestrian camp for children and teenagers is held in July and August. Closed late December to mid-January. Major credit cards accepted. About 7 miles (11 km) north of Monbazillac in Saint-Julien-de-Crempse (phone: 53-24-23-18; fax: 53-24-20-89). Expensive.

Les Ruines – The lofty aims of the chef to enhance regional dishes with unusual combinations of spices meet with wonderful success — the results are such fine dishes as *sauté de cèpes* and *foie gras* in a piquant yet spicy sauce. There is even (gasp!, in France) a separate room for nonsmokers. Closed Sundays evenings and Mondays. Reservations advised. Major credit cards accepted. In Le Peyrat, on the outskirts of Monbazillac (phone: 53-57-16-37). Expensive to moderate.

Gascony

For travelers with a passing knowledge of French literature, history, and gastronomy, reference to the province of Gascony is likely to conjure up vivid and romantic images. This is the land of d'Artagnan and the musketeers, Henri IV, the troubadours, and Blaise de Monluc. It was part of the province of Aquitaine, that area keenly contested and controlled alternately by the French and the English during the Middle Ages. It also is the source of some of France's best-loved dishes, including cassoulet (a casserole of beans, pork, and sausage), foie gras, *garbure* (a thick vegetable soup), *tourin* (garlic soup), duck and goose prepared in a variety of ways, including *confit* (preserved) and *magret* (sliced and grilled), and succulent game birds in heady dark sauces, as well as armagnac, the fiery brandy dubbed "the soul of Gascony." It's a proud and independent area that clings to old traditions and customs; the past is ever present here, the 20th century less insistent than in other areas.

In the heart of France's southwest, Gascony, as much a historical as an official appellation, does not have strict boundaries. It generally is considered to take up the modern *départements* of Gers and the Landes, bordered to the north by the mighty Garonne River, to the east by Toulouse, extending south into the foothills of the Pyrénées and all the way west to the Gulf of Gascony on the Atlantic coast.

The region is one of physical contrasts: The Gers is characterized by scenic rolling hills dotted with villages, vineyards, and neat fields of sunflowers and wheat. The Landes, to the northwest, is a flat, sandy expanse of sparsely settled land, a full two-thirds of which is a vast manmade forest. The two *départements* meet in an agricultural area that supplies this and many other regions of France with an abundance of fruit and vegetables.

When Roman armies penetrated these areas half a century before Christ, they found a large number of independent settlements whose people shared a physical stature and language that linked their origins more closely to those of the Basques in the Pyrénées than to those of the peoples in the rest of Gaul. The region prospered under Roman rule, as remnants of Gallo-Roman villas, particularly those in Séviac, unearthed near Montréal, bear witness.

The Vandals invaded in 410, followed by the Visigoths, and then by the Francs in 507. Around the beginning of the 7th century, the Basques moved north from their base in the Spanish Pyrénées, penetrating southwestern France and Gascony and imposing their will and ways on this kindred culture.

By the 10th century, Gascony had become a strong, almost totally independent duchy, but in 1062 the Count of Armagnac was forced to cede his realm to the Duke of Aquitaine. Ninety years later, Gascony was part of the dowry that Eleanor of Aquitaine presented to her new husband, Henry Plantagenet, heir to the British crown, and when he ascended to the throne 2 years later, in 1152, Gascony became part of England. For the next 300 years, Gascony and its neighbors to the north and west suffered continuous turmoil as the French and English battled for sovereignty. Several of the *bastides* (fortified villages) constructed by the opposing kings during this period still stand; particularly interesting are the remnants of these fortifications at Fourcès (near Montréal), Beaumarchés and Marciac (near Plaisance), and Bassoues (near Mirande).

Around the middle of the 14th century, the Counts of Armagnac regained control of their turf and for a time, under Bernard VII, champion of the French cause, Gascony's valiant soldiers controlled almost the whole of France.

During the Wars of Religion, the area once again was plunged into bitter conflict. Thanks to Jeanne d'Albert, mother of Henri de Navarre (the future King Henri IV), Nerac, in the north of Gascony, became an important Protestant stronghold and a frequent target of the Catholics. It was only after Henri ascended to the throne in 1589 that peace returned to the area, and in 1607 the lands of the counts of Armagnac were incorporated into the royal domain under his rule.

The Gascons did not, however, forfeit their independence to the French throne. The strong spirit and individuality of the region lives on today, embodied by the legendary d'Artagnan, certainly Gascony's most famous native son. Born Charles de Batz in 1615 near Auch (you still can see his birthplace at Castelmore), d'Artagnan presented himself at the court in Paris, taking his mother's family name to win royal acceptance more easily. After gaining the confidence of Louis XIII, he was appointed the first captain lieutenant of the king's company of musketeers, that gallant band of men whose swashbuckling exploits were immortalized (and certainly embellished) by Alexandre Dumas in *The Three Musketeers*.

Today, a visitor to this unspoiled area is likely to be charmed by the Gascon spirit, conveyed by the contagious warmth and bravado of its people. Though it frequently is overlooked by travel guides and foreign as well as French tourists, the region has a serendipitous appeal. Its attractions are subtle: narrow, tree-lined roads winding through sunflower-dotted landscapes; calm, inviting lakes; crumbling stone fortifications; and the arcaded squares of Gascony's countless pleasing villages that seem to exist in a time warp. It takes little imagination to suspend reality temporarily and let oneself drift back to another era.

Gascon cuisine also is reminiscent of another time — when portions were generous, food hearty and satisfying, and prices reasonable. The region is rich in family-run inns, where the quality of food is only outdone by the characteristic warmth of the Gascon welcome. They represent some of the best dining values in France today. The Gascons are serious about their food, a fact exemplified by an organization of chefs, "Ronde des Mousquetaires," whose members meet frequently at each other's establishments to share fine food, ideas, and comradeship. The gastronome will do well to seek out these restaurants, each with its own style and character but offering an extremely high level of cooking. Food lovers also will find guidance in a small paperback entitled *Le Guide Gascogne* (Guide to Gascony), available in most bookshops in the region; it lists undiscovered, out-of-the-way places of particularly good value.

A visit to this region can be particularly rewarding in summer, when the weather is warm and sunny and the sleepy little villages come alive with festivals and celebrations. It is even more enjoyable because it is less crowded than other rural areas in July and August, when practically the entire French population heads for the country. Plaisance is the site of an incomparable annual *Bastille Day* (July 14) goat cheese fair, *dégustation* (tasting), and judging (if you stop here, a meal at *La Ripa Alta,* a wonderful restaurant under the arcade of the main square, is a must; phone: 62-69-30-43). There's motor racing in Nogaro; an annual 3-day corrida in Vic-Fezensac in May, when bulls run through the streets before testing their might against Gascons in the arena; and in Marciac, an annual jazz festival in August. (For information about dates for these and other festivals, contact Mme. Baron at the Maison de Gers et Armagnac, 16 Bd. Haussmann, Paris 75009; phone: 47-70-39-61, or visit any of the local *Syndicats d'Initiatives* — almost any town big enough to have a hotel and a post office has one.) Mme. Baron also can supply you with information on the Gers's many pleasant lakes and other recreational possibilities.

This tour route starts in Auch, at the heart of the Gers; it then moves north to Lectoure and on to Condom, the center of Armagnac production. It continues west through the southern edge of the pine forests of the Landes, then over to the Gulf of Gascony and the seaside resorts of Hossegor and Capbreton.

Accommodations in Gascony range from the expensive, where rooms are $85 or more a night for two, to many moderate hotels, ranging from $45 to $85, to the bargain inns, where an inexpensive room for two is under $45. In the restaurant listings, the expensive category rates dinner for two at over $85; moderate, $55 to $85; and inexpensive, under $55. Prices do not include wine or drinks. Service usually is included.

AUCH: The administrative capital of Gascony, and the largest town (pop. 25,000) between inland Toulouse and Bayonne, Auch (pronounced *Osh*) is a lively market center on the banks of the Gers River. Its Old Town sits on a hill, grouped around the majestic, 16th-century, pale ocher cathedral that dominates the horizon for miles around.

People lived on this hill long before the arrival of Emperor Augustus in 25 BC. It became an important Roman town called Augusta Ascorum, a crossroads on the busy route from Toulouse to the Atlantic, and has continued to play a key role in the life and commerce of the region.

This is d'Artagnan's town, and it pays homage to its valiant musketeer, who was immortalized by Alexandre Dumas *père* in *The Three Musketeers,* with a swashbuckling statue perched midway up the monumental 232-step staircase that connects the lower, "new" town to the high ground on which the Old Town sits. At the top of the staircase is the serene, tree-shaded Place Salinis, overlooking the valley of the Gers and the rooftops of the ever-expanding modern part of town. Nearby rises the 15th-century Tour d'Armagnac, formerly a prison. In the same vicinity, picturesque narrow lanes (*pousterles*) wind steeply down the hill to the Gers past crooked structures dating from the Middle Ages.

More antiquities, such as the intriguing 15th-century structure that houses the tourist association (Pl. de la Cathédrale; phone: 62-05-22-89), line Rue Dessoles, a lively pedestrian street near the cathedral. On Saturday mornings the cathedral square is transformed into a colorful open-air market. Nearby is the prefecture, housed in a superb yellow brick, 18th-century structure that once was the archbishop's residence. Also of interest is the *Musée des Jacobins* (Pl. Louis-Blanc; phone: 65-05-74-79), a former cloister that now has a somewhat eclectic collection that includes Gascon furniture, old porcelain, a sizable grouping of pre-Columbian pieces, and the rather disquieting works of a local 19th-century painter, Jean-Louis Roumeguère. The Maison de Gascogne, on Rue Gambetta, exhibits regional foods and drinks, art, and crafts.

Auch's most precious treasures, however, are found inside the Cathédrale Ste-Marie. Construction of this magnificent work, whose twin bell towers are reminiscent of those of St. Sulpice in Paris, was started in 1489 by Cardinal de Savoie, Archbishop of Auch, and it was not completed until the 17th century. The Renaissance windows of the Gascon painter Arnaut de Moles are remarkable not only for their vivid colors but for the strikingly expressive, caricaturish faces of the elaborately clothed figures. Equally awesome are the 113 intricately carved choir stalls bearing more than 1,500 different figures. This masterpiece, sculpted out of oak that had been soaked in the Gers for a year, took more than 50 years to complete and represents some of the finest Renaissance woodcarving in France. The city's annual *Festival de Musique* includes classical concerts performed in the cathedral during June and July. It is also the location for *Les Lumières du Ciel*, a sound and light performance that is shown Wednesday and Saturday evenings at 9:30 during July and August. *Gascogne Expo* (Parc de Endoumengue), a 3-day agricultural fair, takes place the last week of September.

Other artworks worth the 40-mile (64-km) detour southwest of Auch to the town of Mirande are found in the *Musée des Beaux-Arts Décoratifs* (13 Rue de L'Evêché; phone: 62-66-68-10), which groups together paintings of the Italian, Flemish, and French schools from the 15th to the 19th century, along with a collection of French faïence. It's open daily except Sundays in summer from 9 AM to noon and from 2 to 6 PM.

 CHECKING IN: *Château de Larroque* – About 19 miles (30 km) from Auch, in Gimont, on the route to Toulouse, this stately pink brick château (a member of the Relais & Châteaux group) set in a park has 12 pleasant rooms, a serene terrace overlooking the gentle hills of Gascony, and a well-regarded restaurant. Restaurant closed Sunday evenings, Mondays, and during January. Major credit cards accepted. Rte. de Toulouse RN124, Gimont (phone: 62-67-77-44). Expensive to moderate.

France – This venerable establishment, the domain of the Daguin family since 1884, sits like a duchess benignly surveying the activity of Place de la Libération. It is a lively meeting place for French and foreigners alike, drawn here by the renown of chef-owner André Daguin's superb restaurant (see *Eating Out*), perhaps the best reason for an extended stay. Its 32 rooms, each individually decorated, have old-fashioned charm. Daguin and his wife, Jo, a witty and charming pair, create an atmosphere of elegance and familial warmth. Don't miss the impressive array of breads and jams that accompany *le petit déjeuner* (breakfast). Closed January. Major credit cards accepted. Pl. de la Libération, Auch (phone: 62-05-00-44; fax: 62-05-88-44). Expensive to moderate.

Relais de Gascogne – A modern hotel in the lower town, it has 32 comfortable rooms, each with a television set and direct-dial phone. There also is a restaurant and parking. Closed late December to mid-January. Major credit cards accepted. 5 Av. Marne, Auch (phone: 62-05-26-81). Moderate.

D'Artagnan – Once the residence of the Comtes de Monlaur, this terraced hotel between the old and new parts of the city offers 20 simple rooms, outdoor dining in summer, and a warm welcome. Pl. Villaret de Joyeuse, Auch (phone: 62-05-00-49). Inexpensive.

EATING OUT: *France* – Endowed with a d'Artagnan-like dash and bravado, André Daguin, founder of "La Ronde des Mousquetaires," is Gascony's biggest booster and one of its most loved and lauded chefs. His reputation — as well as two Michelin stars — is well earned. Dinner in this lush dining room, at once grand and homey, is a memorable experience whether you choose from among the traditional Gascon specialties — *magret de canard* (grilled duck breast) or *rôtie d'agneau aux anchois* (roast lamb with anchovy sauce) — or from Daguin's inventive variations on a theme — foie gras and rock lobster or a delicately sauced *feuilletté de saumon* (salmon in puff pastry) and *ris d'agneau* (lamb sweetbreads). Closed Sunday evenings, Mondays, and January. Major credit cards accepted. Pl. de la Libération, Auch (phone: 62-05-00-44). Expensive.

***Claude Laffitte* –** Tucked away near the cathedral, this cozy restaurant operated by Claude Laffitte offers regional character and a fine selection of well-prepared Gascon specialties: *la cuisse d'oie en daube* (leg of goose braised in wine), *salmis de palombe forestière* (pigeon with mushrooms, bacon, and potatoes), and an exceptional *croustade landaise* (bridal-veil-thin pastry laced with prunes and armagnac). Dine downstairs in the bistro atmosphere or upstairs amid wooden beams and flowers. Closed Sunday evenings and Mondays. Major credit cards accepted. 38 Rue Dessoles, Auch (phone: 62-05-04-18). Moderate to inexpensive.

En Route from Auch – To get the flavor of the Gascon countryside, drive northwest on D930, a pleasant tree-lined route that winds over verdant hills and dales before passing through Castéra-Verduzan, a somnolent thermal village of about 700 residents. The therapeutic properties of the town's two natural mineral springs were appreciated even in Roman times: The 3rd-century author Flagius Vegelius wrote about the Roman camp here called Castéra-Vivant. The Counts of Armagnac and French royalty came to take the cure; it was no doubt a livelier place during the reign of Louis XV, when going to take the cure reached its zenith. In modern times, this quaint village seems to have been all but forgotten, passed up for more dramatic attractions. Though it has no grand archaeological or architectural treasures, it's worth a stop, if only to take the waters (a visit to the pavilion housing *les sources* provides a glimpse of what thermalism is all about in France).

CHECKING IN: *Ténaréze* – Bernard Ramouneda, the chef at *La Florida* (below), and his family operate this hotel, just up the street from the restaurant. It has 23 modern, simple rooms and is a real bargain. Major credit cards accepted. Castéra-Verduzan (phone: 62-68-10-22). Inexpensive.

EATING OUT: *La Florida* – The dining rooms and chestnut-tree-shaded terrace are full of provincial charm, and chef Bernard Ramouneda serves a wonderful combination of the homey, traditional fare learned from his grandmother (the former chef) and dishes of his own contemporary cooking style. Try the foie-gras-and-*confit*-laced Gascon salad, the impeccable *terrine de légumes au coulis de tomate* (vegetable terrine with a light tomato purée), or his rich *cou d'oie farci* (stuffed goose neck in a prune-scented sauce). Closed Sunday evenings, Mondays, and most of February. Major credit cards accepted. Castéra-Verduzan (phone: 62-68-13-22). Inexpensive.

En Route from Castéra-Verduzan – Travel the vineyard-flanked D42 north to St-Puy, a tiny hillside village at the foot of Château Monluc. This hill was lost and regained by the French four times during their battles with the English, and the châteaux that stood here were repeatedly destroyed and rebuilt. Mostly what remains today is a small, welcoming château dating from the 15th and 18th centuries, though part of the crumbling stone walls around it date from the 12th century. Between 1502 and 1577 it was the property of Blaise de Montluc, a marshal of France who fought fiercely against the Protestants during the Wars of Religion and who later recorded his regrets at having done so in his famous memoirs, *Commentaires* (1592), called "the soldier's bible" by Henri IV. Only part of the château is open to visitors, as it is the home of M. and Mme. Lassus, producers of Monluc, a dry sparkling wine that is the base for the most Gascon of aperitifs, the *pousse rapière* ("the sword's thrust"), a mixture of sparkling wine and armagnac. The château tour includes a visit to the cellars, where the wine is aged under the old vaulting of an earlier château, and a tasting of the wine and the *pousse rapière*.

LECTOURE: Continue on D42 about 6 miles (10 km) to Lectoure, a town noted, even in this region filled with lofty villages, for the stunning vistas of the Gers Valley. On a clear day, the Pyrénées can be seen in the distance from the lovely tree-shaded Promenade du Bastion near the gardens of the Hôtel de Ville (Town Hall). This was the home of the Counts of Armagnac (a hospital now stands on the ramparts of their château), and it later became an important episcopal seat. Numerous *hôtels particulaires* and religious structures in the characteristic pale yellow stone of the region line the old streets; their scars bear witness to the town's stormy past. This was the site in 1473 of a terrible battle between the troops of Louis XI and the Counts of Armagnac. Jean V, the last count, was killed during this battle, which marked the fall of the house of Armagnac and the beginning of royal authority over the area. The old cathedral was badly hit during the siege of 1473 and suffered more abuse during the Wars of Religion. The remnants of the original spire were finally torn down in 1782. The oldest segments of the present cathedral, built in the Gothic style of the southwest, date from the 16th century.

Also of special interest here is the *Musée Municipal* in the Hôtel-de-Ville (Pl. Hôtel de Ville; phone: 62-68-76-98) which houses a famous collection of *tauroboles* (sacrificial altars) emblazoned with the head of a bull, and other mysterious objects and inscriptions. These marble altars, on which actual bulls were sacrificed in the purification rites of priests, are relics of the cult of Cybèle, believed to have existed 2,000 years ago. Twenty of the 40 *tauroboles* known to exist in France are assembled here. Open daily from 9 AM to noon and 2 to 6 PM.

CONDOM: A town of about 8,000 set on a hill above the Baïse River, Condom is the capital of the Ténaréze, the region between the Garonne and Adour rivers and one of the three armagnac producing areas in Gascony. It is an excellent base for excursions to the surrounding countryside, particularly rich in antiquities, including an old abbey, bishops' residences, *bastides* (fortified villages), and Gallo-Roman ruins.

The town itself has some interesting old structures, among them the 18th-century Hôtel de Cugnac and the Hôtel de Riberot, at 36 and 38 Rue Jean-Jaurès, respectively. The riverside quays here, in times past crowded with boats carrying armagnac to market in Bordeaux, are pleasant for a leisurely stroll. But the chief sight is the Cathédrale St-Pierre. Rebuilt between 1507 and 1531, it is one of the last large cathedrals constructed in the Gers and is certainly one of the most stunning examples of Flamboyant Gothic in the southwest. Particularly beautiful are the elaborate south doorway with its 24 statuettes, and the neo-Gothic choir enclosure, adorned in 1844 with the magnificently delicate, almost lacy terra cotta figures of saints and angels. The tourist office is across the street from the cathedral (Pl. Bossuet; phone: 62-28-00-80).

Condom also offers the *Musée de l'Armagnac* (Rue Jules Ferry) which displays antique tools and equipment, including alembics, used in the production of the brandy.

CHECKING IN: Hôtel des Trois Lys – Located in the heart of Condom, this hostelry in an 18th-century mansion has 10 rooms, each individually decorated in keeping with the period. There's a swimming pool, a bar, a terrace, parking, and seminar rooms. Major credit cards accepted. 38 Rue Gambetta, Condom 32100 (phone: 62-28-33-33; fax: 62-28-41-85). Expensive.

Cordeliers – A modern hotel with 10 simple rooms and a serene walled garden. Open year-round. Major credit cards accepted. Rue des Cordeliers, Condom (phone: 62-28-03-68). Moderate.

EATING OUT: Table des Cordeliers – This restaurant next to the *Cordeliers* hotel is set under the warm brick archways and vaulted ceiling of a 14th-century Gothic chapel. The ambience would make this place special even if the food were not so good. Closed Sunday evenings, Mondays, and January. Major credit cards accepted. Rue des Cordeliers, Condom (phone: 62-68-28-36). Expensive.

En Route from Condom – The first of several antiquities in the countryside here is the 12th-century Cistercian Abbaye de Flaran, a few miles south of town on D930. Set back from the road in an isolated, tranquil spot near the confluence of the Baïse and the Auloue rivers, this abbey, founded in 1151, is one of the most important remnants of the keen religious activity in the region in the 12th and 13th centuries. It consists of a predominantly Romanesque church of warm ocher stone, a small, elegant 14th-century cloister, and an adjoining, renovated 18th-century refectory. Particularly lovely is the small chapel on the east side of the cloisters; it has a low vaulted ceiling and columns of the black, red, and white marble of the Pyrénées. Damaged during the Wars of Religion, it later was neglected by private owners. Now owned by the *département* of the Gers, it is being restored and transformed into a regional cultural center. The cloister houses two exhibits: one on the abbey itself and the other on the pilgrimage routes to Santiago de Compostela, which passed through the Gascon region and included a stop here. Special changing exhibits are mounted in the refectory.

Life in this area revolves around armagnac, and you should be sure to visit one of the many cellars to taste this earthy brandy that in recent years has begun to chip away at the cognac market, even in the US. One of the most congenial places to taste and learn about it is Château Cassaigne (phone: 62-28-04-02), a handsome country château that once was the retreat of the Bishops of Condom. The original structure, built in 1247, was renovated at various periods. It retains architectural features of Gascony's three grand epochs: The thick-walled stone *cave* (cellar) where the armagnac is aged dates from the 13th century; the intriguing kitchen, whose vaulted ceiling was constructed like a bread oven, is 16th century; and the classic Renaissance façade is 18th century. It was here that the Gascon warrior Blaise de Monluc (from nearby Château Monluc) came to recuperate and write his memoirs after being injured in the Siege of Rabastens. One room is devoted to old documents of the bishops and other residents of the château, another to the explanation of local viticulture. If you are lucky enough to see Henri Faget, an armagnac producer and the present owner of the château, your visit will be enriched by this lively Gascon's evocative account of the history of the region and of armagnac.

Return to Condom to pick up D15 westbound, which will take you past Larressingle, perhaps the smallest fortified town in France. This dreamy, moat-encircled fortress overhanging the Osse Valley was also the work of the Bishops of Condom, who built it as a lookout and haven for the Barons of Armagnac traveling through the region. Inside its stone walls, square tower, and arched gateway is a Roman church, an inn, a flower-filled courtyard, and pretty little houses that still are inhabited.

Continue on D15 to Montréal, one of the first *bastides* in Gascony, completed in 1289 by order of the King of England. Although it seems to have held up well during the disputes between the French and the British, Montréal was almost completely destroyed during the Revolution. Today, only the ruins of Eglise St-Pierre-de-Genens, the ramparts, and one fortified gate remain.

CHECKING IN: *La Ferme de Flaran* – This old Gascon farm transformed into a provincial inn has a pool, a terrace, and a comfortable, rustic dining room serving regional cuisine. Less than a mile (1.6 km) from the Cistercian Abbaye de Flaran. Closed Thursdays from November to May and the first two weeks in March. Major credit cards accepted. Valence-sur-Baïse (phone: 62-28-58-22). Moderate.

EATING OUT: *La Gare* – Old French railroad posters and train schedules adorn this delightful restaurant in the old, until recently abandoned, train station of Montréal. It's a warm, amusing setting for Odette Jaurrey's homey specialties such as Gascon *garbure* (vegetable soup cooked in earthenware), *tête de veau vinaigrette* (braised calf's head with vinaigrette sauce), and *poulet grillé à l'échalote* (grilled chicken with shallots). Her husband, Michel, formerly a musician, is the cordial host and stationmaster. This is an excellent value; there also are 5 simple rooms in the nearby watchhouse. Closed Thursdays in off-season, Fridays, 3 weeks in January, and 2 weeks in October. Major credit cards accepted. Montréal (phone: 62-29-43-37). Inexpensive.

En Route from Montréal – About a mile (1.6 km) southwest on an unnumbered road is Séviac, the site of an important Gallo-Roman settlement. The rich carpet of mosaics here is a reminder of the opulent villa that stood on this plateau some 12 to 18 centuries ago. The first of the colorful, detailed mosaics was discovered in 1861. In 1911, further digs unearthed marble columns and, later, the remnants of the luxurious public baths. Today you can walk through the ruins, tracing the layout of the villa from its vast inner courtyard to the residential apartments with vestiges of an underground heating system, and on to the public areas and pools. Throughout, you'll see the rich and varied mosaic designs (even more brilliant when doused with water) that are the real treasures of Séviac. Digs still are under way here under the direction of Mme. Aragon Launet, a woman passionate about her work. Ask for her especially; her explanation of life in the villa is enlightening and memorable.

Follow D29 north from Montréal along the Auzoue River to Fourcès, another English *bastide,* whose curious circular plan makes it one of the most unusual in France. It was founded in the mid-1200s by Robert d'Anjou, Duke of Aquitaine, as a small and sturdy defense against the attempts of the French to regain their lost territory. Off the tourist route, it was all but forgotten in past decades and was threatened with destruction by modern developers. Mme. Launet, a self-appointed defender of regional antiquities, lobbied against the demolition and was the catalyst for the renovation now going on. In addition to the lovely circular core, flanked by stone and typically Gascon split-timbered houses, there is also a 15th-century château and a Gothic bridge.

CHECKING IN/EATING OUT: *L'Aubergade* – This 10-room château (a member of the prestigious Relais & Châteaux group) is worth a detour just to dine at the two-star haven of one of France's bright young chefs, Michel Trama. Specialties include *lasagne de homard au fumet de truffe* (lobster and truffle lasagna) and *cailles aux truffes* (quails stuffed with truffles). Restaurant closed Mondays except from *Easter* to September, and holidays. Reservations necessary. Major credit cards accepted. 52 Rue Royale, Puymirol (phone: 53-95-31-46; fax: 53-95-33-80). Expensive.

La Belle Gasconne – Food lovers can continue north of Fources to Mézin and a little beyond to the tiny town of Poudenas, where they'll find one of France's favorite female chefs, Marie Claude Gracia, at the stove of this quaint former wine cellar next to a mill. Specialties such as *civet de canard au Buzet* (duck braised in the wine of nearby Buzet), *agneau rôti et farci aux rognons* (roast lamb stuffed with kidneys), and *cèpes du pays en persillade* (wild local mushrooms sautéed with parsley and garlic) have earned this ebullient Gasconne one Michelin star. Marie Claude and her husband, Richard, who acts as host, have transformed the small mill next door into a cozy inn with 6 individually decorated rooms and 1 suite. A swimming pool was recently added. Closed Sunday evenings and Mondays in off-season, and from December 15 to January 15. Major credit cards accepted. Poudenas (phone: 53-65-71-58). Expensive to moderate.

BARBOTAN-LES-THERMES: This thermal station on D15 west of Montréal, on the wiggly border between the undulating hills of the Gers and the sparsely populated, majestic forests of the Landes, benefits from the distinct beauties of both regions. It's one of the region's most popular spas, attracting thousands of French each year, looking for cures. In fact, it seems there must be more inns and hotels here than permanent homes. Nonetheless, it retains an agreeable quaintness and flavor of times past, somewhat reminiscent of the holiday towns in the 1950s films of the late moviemaker Jacques Tati. Its natural springs, popular in Roman times, are particularly therapeutic for those with circulatory problems. There is a lovely park across from the thermal establishment as well as a handsome old stone and wood clock tower, the ancient gateway to the city, and an old church. The real charm of the place, however, is its provincial character and serene isolation.

 CHECKING IN/EATING OUT: *La Bastide Gasconne* – This 18th-century monastery, set elegantly among tall shade trees and terraces, has 35 comfortable rooms, a number of them decorated in a hokily appealing Gascon style. The atmosphere is refined and soothing and the staff particularly congenial. There also are thermal baths, a pool, and tennis courts. Even if you're not planning to spend the night, enjoy a meal in the charming, wood-beamed dining room, supervised by none other than three-star chef Michel Guérard, founder of the slenderizing *cuisine minceur* which helped make his nearby Eugénie-les-Bains spa famous. The menu has a strong regional character but reflects Guérard's fresh, light style. Member of the Relais et Châteaux group. Closed November to April. Major credit cards accepted. Barbotan-les-Thermes (phone: 62-69-52-09; fax: 62-69-51-97). Expensive to moderate.

En Route from Barbotan-les-Thermes – Travel west along D626 to D933 and D932, across the southern edge of the vast pine forests of the Landes; they start above Bordeaux, extend down the Atlantic coast to Biarritz, and east to where the Landes meets the Gers, near Nerac, and cover 5,500 square miles. *Lande* means "moor," and until the end of the 18th century the region was just that: desolate, inhospitable land, sandy at the coast and swampy inland. Swept progressively farther east by the Atlantic winds, the sand dunes of the coast threatened to turn the region into a desert until 1788, when a clever engineer named Nicolas Brémontier came up with a solution to stop the annual encroachment of the sands. After barricading the dunes with wooden planks, he planted them with hardy, strong-rooted ground cover. With the sands no longer a problem, the marshy areas inland could be drained and planted with pine groves, and this poor, barren region became the richest source of France's timber and resin for turpentine and varnish. As in earlier times, the region remains sparsely populated, dotted with tiny isolated villages, sawmills, and furniture factories. The most dramatic attraction here is the forest itself, part of which constitutes the 509,026-acre regional park, Landes de Gascogne.

If you are smitten with the forest, amble leisurely through the region above Mont-de-Marsan (D932), the capital of the Landes, on your way west to Hossegor and Capbreton, the Landes' coastal resorts and most popular tourist attractions. A few miles from Sabres, which is 22 miles (35 km) northwest of Mont-de-Marsan on N134, a 45-acre open-air museum, the *Ecomusée de Marquèze*, welcomes visitors. (It is named for the person first responsible for the reclamation of this region.) Created in 1969, this unique museum includes a sheep park, a mill, an outdoor oven for baking bread, Maison le Mineur (the Lesser House), which dates from 1772, Marquèze's house, which was built in 1824, and much more. A small train makes the trip between Sabres and the museum; the visit takes about half a day. The museum is open daily from mid-June to mid-September; otherwise, only on Sundays and holidays. Closed completely from October 30 to the Sunday before *Easter* (phone: 58-07-52-70). Those who want to extend their stay can try the inn in Sabres, *Auberge des Pins* (phone: 58-07-50-47). Its restaurant is closed Sunday evenings and Mondays except in July and August.

Continue west from Mont-de-Marsan along N124 to Hossegor and Capbreton on the Atlantic coast. En route you'll pass Dax, on the Adour River. Along with Mont-de-Marsan and Arcachon (about 90 miles/144 km to the north), it is one of the three major towns in the Landes and it has thermal springs (which used to ease the aches and pains of the Romans), a casino, a good assortment of hotels and restaurants, and lovely Parc Théodore-Denis, where vestiges from Roman days still can be seen.

Or, if you prefer, turn south at Mont-de-Marsan and travel the tiny roads (N124 to D11) through agricultural land to Eugénie-les-Bains, a tiny thermal village named for Empress Eugénie, who came here frequently to take the waters. Its name has become world-famous ever since Michel Guérard opened his elegant spa, *Les Prés et les Sources d'Eugénie* (see *Checking In/Eating Out*). There is not much of interest in the town itself, centered as it is around a short main street with only a few cafés and shops. Guérard's *Les Prés,* however, is a destination in itself. More than any other spa in the area (and perhaps more than any other in France), this establishment conforms to the American idea of a spa, offering not only the therapeutic hot springs treatments but also a full range of modern spa amenities, including saunas, gymnastic equipment, a swimming pool, mudbaths, massages, weight-loss programs, and beauty treatments. The cost of all this luxury is high, and the experience is definitely for those who like deluxe treatment and don't mind paying for it.

Pick up D924 at Grenade-sur-l'Adour about 6 miles (10 km) north of Eugénie-les-Bains and travel west to N124 and A63 to the coast. Hossegor and Capbreton lie just a couple of miles off A63 via D33 and D28, respectively.

CHECKING IN/EATING OUT: *Les Prés et les Sources d'Eugénie* – This white Second Empire mansion with its baroque lounge and tranquil, arcaded terrace sits back from the road; it is graced by a lush tropical garden and flanked by two newer white buildings. The 36 rooms are large, modern, and elegantly furnished with a pleasing mix of antique and contemporary pieces chosen by Christine Guérard. Those willing to pay three-star prices should not miss the pleasure of dining in the elegant but relaxed dining room. Those who have come to shed pounds can opt for Michel Guérard's *menu minceur,* refined and delicate dishes lightened somewhat of excess fat and calories, though by no means bare bones or lifeless. The more sybaritic will choose the *cuisine gourmande,* creative, beautifully presented dishes that have earned him the highest accolades from critics in France and abroad. Restaurant closed December 2–February 14. Hotel reservations necessary; restaurant reservations advised. Major credit cards accepted. Eugénie-les-Bains (phone: 58-05-05-05; fax: 58-51-13-59). Expensive.

HOSSEGOR: The pine forests of the Landes meet the sea here at wide sandy beaches and a tranquil blue lake fed by the tide through a canal built in 1886. Although Hossegor, and Capbreton like it, lacks some of the chic of the larger Atlantic resorts of Biarritz and St-Jean-de-Luz to the south, their beaches are cleaner and less crowded, their towns have a provincial charm, their hotels are more reasonably priced, and their surroundings are wild and unspoiled.

Until the turn of the century, the area around Hossegor's marine lake was little more than a sweep of desolate sand dunes, like much of the Landes coastline. It grew up somewhat haphazardly in the 1920s and 1930s, its pleasing climate and recreational potential attracting a quick following of nature lovers and sports enthusiasts.

Hossegor's town center, clean, white, and planted with flowers, has a lazy, relaxed holiday mood and lies between the lake and the ocean. Pretty little villas and quaint Basque hotels speckle the lakefront and nestle in the deep pine groves that stretch east from the beach and the lake. This place is ideal for those who would forgo sightseeing (there is little of historical interest here anyway) for sailing, windsurfing, golfing, tennis, hiking or horseback riding through the forests, or just basking in the sun.

Hossegor's sports casino (Av. de Gaujac) has a saltwater pool, five tennis courts, and a miniature golf facility. The town also has a jai alai arena, a yacht club, a surfing club, and a golf course. Each Wednesday there is a bullfight, with a wild cow playing the main role. The tourist office, in the center of town (phone: 58-43-72-35), has information about these and other sports activities and facilities.

CAPBRETON: Just a couple of miles south of Hossegor, Capbreton is so close that it seems almost an extension of its neighbor. Its past is a bit more colorful, though: Due to its location at the mouth of the Adour River, Capbreton grew into a lucrative fishing port and maritime city between the 10th and 16th centuries. Before the river changed its course and the harbor filled with silt, it was known as "the port of a hundred captains," and the 16th-century tower that guided navigators and fishermen to it still stands witness to its prosperous past. It was from Capbreton that seafarers set off for their new home on Cape Breton Island, in northeastern Nova Scotia (the island was a French possession from 1632 to 1763). A deep geological fault formed with the shifting of continents that produced the Pyrenean range tends to tame the force of the ocean here and, fortunately for visitors, makes the waves on this beach particularly gentle and pleasant for bathing.

The season in the resorts of Capbreton and Hossegor begins in June and runs through September 15, although a few hotels and restaurants stay open year-round.

CHECKING IN: *Océan* – A neat white hotel rimmed with balconies, it looks like a small ocean liner moored on the quay facing the colorful marina. Its rooms, many of which overlook the marina, are simple and comfortable, and the management is congenial. Closed October to April. Major credit cards accepted. Av. G.-Pompidou, Capbreton (phone: 58-72-10-22). Moderate to inexpensive.

EATING OUT: *Le Regalty* – A pleasant portside restaurant with a dining terrace where good Landes-style cuisine is prepared with a nouvelle touch. Closed Mondays, 2 weeks in January, and 2 weeks in November. Major credit cards accepted. Quai Pêcherie, Capbreton (phone: 58-72-22-80). Expensive to moderate.

La Sardinière – This rustic restaurant with seafaring motifs and an outdoor terrace facing the marina serves a good rendition of *ttoro,* a rich fish soup that is the Atlantic Coast's alternative to bouillabaisse. It also prepares plentiful seafood platters and a wide choice of other fish and meat dishes. Closed mid-November to December. Reservations unnecessary. Visa, Carte Bleue, and Eurocard accepted. 89 Quai Georges-Pompidou, Capbreton (phone: 58-72-10-49). Moderate.

The Pyrénées

The Pyrénées Mountains stretch from the rocky shores and sandy beaches of the Atlantic in the west of France to the lush Vermilion Coast of the Mediterranean in the east, forming a natural frontier between France and Spain and offering the most varied and enchanting panoply of scenery, culture, and history imaginable. Legend has it that the goddess Pyrene, the lover of Hercules, is buried somewhere in this range — whence, presumably, it derives its name.

The range extends some 275 miles from west to east, its highest peaks reaching about 10,500 feet, only slightly lower than those of the French Alps. These peaks still play second fiddle to the Alpine range, perhaps due to their greater distance from Paris (800 miles/1,280 km). All the better for the visitor: Their isolation has left them pristine and unspoiled and has allowed their peoples to hold strongly to old ways, preserving to this day the languages, customs, cuisines, architectural styles, and independence of their ancestors. In these ways they resemble their Gascon neighbors to the north.

So varied are the areas that make up the Pyrénées range that it is almost impossible to generalize about them. Physically they can be divided into three groups: The western Pyrénées are characterized by harmonious terrain, verdant hills rising inland from the ocean in roller-coaster fashion and growing into high, forested slopes. The central Pyrénées are the most dramatic. Magnificent, rugged mountains — the highest peaks in the range — are crossed by dizzying, barren passes and overlook glacial valleys that intrude like splayed fingers between the heights. In the eastern region, the peaks, still quite high at first, ease into the heavily wooded slopes and the chalky cliffs and gorges of the Ariège Valley, eventually giving way again to gentler terrain and tumbling down to the lush, semitropical vegetation of the Roussillon's red, baked soil.

Equally varied are the culture and history of these areas. To the west is Basque country, dotted with postage-stamp villages of split-timbered houses. The origins of the highly individualistic people, who share a language (l'Euskara), traditions, and physical characteristics with their neighbors on the Spanish side of the border, are still a mystery. According to some theories, their civilization goes back 25 centuries, starting with Homo pyrénéus, a contemporary of Cro-Magnon man. (But an abundance of caves in the Pyrénées gave shelter to even earlier inhabitants, whose traces were found — in the form of a human jaw 300,000 to 400,000 years old — near Montmaurin in 1949.) The Basque are a proud and keenly nationalistic people who sometimes, along with their cousins on the other side of the border in Spain, fight for self-determination. Their culture is worth thoughtful study. Their rustic, flower-bedecked inns are perfect Pyrenean retreats, and their hearty cuisine is the most distinctive in the entire region.

The central and eastern Pyrénées are a mix of modern ski resorts and lazy sun-warmed thermal spas, whose springs have been popular since Roman times. The impenetrable peaks behind these valleys protected them from attack from the south and allowed them to develop into strong, independent states during the Middle Ages, ruled over respectively by the Counts of Béarn, Bigorre, and Foix and later by the Kings of Navarre. Their strong stone châteaux still stand proudly on the heights, souvenirs of their lords' former power and glory.

Vestiges of prehistoric life are sprinkled throughout the numerous caves and grottoes that lie beneath the hills of the chain. Most notable, perhaps, are those at Niaux, whose well-preserved Magdalenian wall paintings rival those of the famous Lascaux in the Dordogne.

In 72 BC Romans founded Lugdunum Convenarum, a trading post and a small fortress, which later became St-Bertrand-de-Comminges. Sixteen years later, Crassus, Julius Caesar's lieutenant, conquered this area, establishing thriving settlements and the first spas. Remnants of their civilization can be seen at Montmaurin and St-Bertrand-de-Comminges. In the 3rd century, the region was invaded by Germanic tribes, followed by the Normans in the middle of the 9th century.

During the Middle Ages, the area was marked by keen religious activity. Scores of religious pilgrims from all over Europe regularly converged at St-Jean-Pied-de-Port and Sare in the Pays Basque (Basque Country) on their way to the important shrine of Santiago de Compostela in Spain. At about the same time, Romanesque churches and cathedrals were being erected in the central area (see St-Bertrand-de-Comminges, below), while farther east battles were being waged by the papacy and the ruling Capetians against the Cathari (or Albigensians), the religious dissenters who shunned the evils of earthly life and attacked the worldly ways of the established Church. At least four of the hilltop châteaux where the Cathari sought refuge before being wiped out by the Inquisition in the mid-14th century still can be seen around Foix. England gained control of the area in 1360, during the Hundred Years War. France won it back in 1463.

It wasn't until 1659 that the Peace of the Pyrénées was signed between Louis XIV and Philip IV of Spain at St-Jean-de-Luz, finally establishing this grand range as the official boundary between France and Spain. Only then did much of this territory come under French dominion. But 3 centuries of French rule have not erased the strong regional identity of the Pyrenean people. Indeed, many of its citizens consider themselves to be first Basque, Béarnais, or, to the far east, Catalonian, placing secondary emphasis on their membership in the French republic.

To appreciate fully the distinct charms of each area and the depth of its incredible natural beauty, it's necessary to get around by car and on foot. A good pair of sturdy walking or hiking shoes is mandatory. Not surprisingly, the recreational possibilities are vast here: camping, hiking, climbing, horseback riding, skiing, and fishing in clear mountain streams. If you happen to be in Paris first, stop at the Maison des Pyrénées (15 Rue St-Augustin; phone: 42-61-58-18), where several very helpful English-speaking employees will fill you in on upcoming events and sites of particular interest in the area. They also can arrange packages, such as 3- to 7-day hiking itineraries which include hotels and luggage transport from one destination to the next. (See "Great Walks and Mountain Rambles" in *For the Body,* DIVERSIONS.) Open Monday through Friday, closed in August.

As in many of the "undiscovered" regions of France, most of the hotels fall into the moderate and inexpensive price ranges. In a few, modern comforts such as air conditioning, TV sets, and room service are lacking, but they are compensated for by the rustic charm of flower-bedecked balconies, antique armoires, and down quilts.

The price categories for the hotels listed in this section are expensive, $80 and up per night for a double room; moderate, $40 to $80; and inexpensive, under $40. Dinner for two, including service, in an expensive restaurant is $100 and up; in the moderate category, between $50 and $100; and in the inexpensive category, under $50. Prices do not include wine or drinks.

The tour route starts at Bayonne, the gateway to the Basque Country and beautiful mountain vistas. It follows the coastline south to St-Jean-de-Luz before turning inland and starting to climb into the heart of the Pays Basque. After a short detour north to Pau, the cultural capital of the region, it climbs into the high Pyrénées, zigzagging from mountain ski resort to thermal spa, including stops at Lourdes and Cauterets. Finally it picks up the Route des Pyrénées, crossing three mountain passes before Luchon and then continuing into the lovely Ariège Valley and the romantic lands of the Counts of Foix.

If there's time at the end of this itinerary, you may choose to head south to the tiny mountain state of Andorra, Europe's last feudal protectorate, the main draw being its duty-free status, even now that the European Community has become a single market. Or you can continue east through the Pyrénées as they roll into the green hills, vineyards, and orchards of the Roussillon on their way to meet the Mediterranean at the beautiful beach resorts of the Vermilion Coast.

BAYONNE: This lively port just 4½ miles (7 km) inland from the white beaches and rocky precipices of Biarritz manages to combine a busy commercial life with a light-hearted holiday spirit. It is where Gascony meets the Pays Basque, the natural starting point for an itinerary through the Pyrénées, and it exhibits the distinct characteristics of both cultures. Its proximity to Spain adds yet another cultural dimension. A city full of personality and life, it is marked by a colorful past.

Like many of the cities in this part of France, Bayonne was inhabited in Roman times and called Lapurdum, from which the coastal Basque province of Labourd takes its name. As part of the province of Aquitaine, it passed into English hands in 1152 along with the rest of the southwest when Eleanor wed the British monarch Henry Plantagenet.

The city fared badly after the resumption of French rule in 1451. But in 1578, under Charles IX, canals were dug that reopened the silted-up port to the sea. In 1784 Bayonne was declared a free port and its already healthy trade tripled.

Bayonne's golden hour came in the 18th century, when it benefited from a brisk trade between Europe and the West Indies while its fishing fleet was bringing in salted cod from the waters near Terre-Neuve to be served at French Catholic tables every Friday. This was the port through which cocoa beans first entered France, and the city still is known for its fine chocolate. (It is equally famous for its smoked hams, which resemble Parma hams from Italy.) Bayonne also was known for its ironworkers and gunsmiths, who are credited with inventing the bayonet in the 17th century.

During the Revolution, Bayonne's fortunes once again turned downward with preemption of its free port status and the end of its trade with the British due to the blockade. When the Duke of Wellington trekked over the Pyrénées from Spain in 1813, leading an army of English, Portuguese, and Spanish soldiers, he dispatched a division to take Bayonne. But the city's garrison held out valiantly, capturing the English general. Again under siege in 1814, the garrison was equally heroic.

After the restoration, Bayonne did not return to its former position of glory. But the city experienced a renaissance in this century with the discovery of oil and natural gas at Lacq, 75 miles (120 km) to the east. By 1990, the port's traffic had passed the 3.5-million-ton mark, almost five times its volume in 1960.

Two of the best reasons to visit this city are its museums: the *Musée Basque* and the *Musée Bonnat*, both in Petit Bayonne, the area between the Nive and the Adour, the two rivers around which the city was founded. The *Musée Basque*, in a characteristically Basque structure on Rue Marengo by the bridge, is an excellent introduction to Basque culture, with traditional costumes, furniture, simulated interiors of Basque homes, and an exhibition of that very Basque sport *pelote,* which resembles jai alai. The *Musée Bonnat* (5 Rue Jacques-Lafitte) is built around the private collection of the painter Léon Bonnat, who willed it to his native city upon his death in 1922. A treasure trove of artworks from the 13th century to the Impressionist period, it includes the works of Van Dyck, El Greco, Goya, Degas, da Vinci, Raphael, Dürer, Rubens, Rembrandt, Fragonard, and Delacroix and is one of the finest and richest art museums in France.

On the opposite side of the Nive are the active pedestrian streets of the old city and, nearby, on Rue des Gouverneurs, the Gothic Cathédrale Ste-Marie, whose delicate spires dominate the horizon. The cathedral was begun in the 13th century and wasn't completed until the 16th. It has a 14th-century cloister, lovely Renaissance windows, and in one chapel, a curious plaque commemorating "the miracle of Bayonne," when a strange white light is said to have appeared in the sky, signifying the imminent surrender of the English in 1451.

Also on Rue des Gouverneurs is Château Vieux, a massive, square fortress with round towers that was once the home of the viscounts of Labourd. It was in this fort, which no longer is open to the public, that the Spanish collected the ransom of 1,200,000 *écus* (crowns) demanded for the release of François I. Before leaving town, walk down the pedestrian Rue du Pont-Neuf and drink hot chocolate (really chocolate sauce in a cup) under the arcades where the city's famous confectioners have been making their sweet delicacies for more than 300 years. Continue on to the animated Place de la Liberté and nearby public gardens (half of the area has been turned into a parking lot), the Hôtel de Ville (Town Hall), and the municipal theater; both are in the same building as the tourist office (phone: 59-59-31-31).

Each year at the beginning of August, the city holds a colorful week-long festival that includes bullfights, dancing, singing, and *pelote* games. The rest of the year rugby games are held on Sundays.

Just a quick hop to the Atlantic via D260 leads to the bright lights, lovely beaches, and beckoning waves of Biarritz.

CHECKING IN: *Le Grand-Best Western* – This renovated, graceful, traditional establishment flanked by the sidewalk cafés and shops of the main commercial street has 60 unassuming but comfortable rooms and a cozy little lounge, but no restaurant. Major credit cards accepted. 21 Rue Thiers, Bayonne (phone: 59-59-14-61; telex: 570794). Moderate.

Mercure – An ultramodern, almost high-tech hotel on the outskirts of town, it seems out of place in this old city full of split-timbered houses and ethnic charm. Nonetheless, it provides modern conveniences — TV sets, air conditioning — in its 105 comfortable, contemporary rooms, some of which are reserved for nonsmokers. Major credit cards accepted. Av. J.-Rostand, Bayonne (phone: 59-63-30-90; fax: 59-42-06-64; telex: 550621). Moderate.

EATING OUT: *Cheval Blanc* – Regional and fish dishes are offered at this eatery, housed in a half-timbered Basque house (ca. 1710) in the old part of town. The wine cellar is well-stocked with local varieties. Closed Sunday evenings and Mondays, except in July and August, and the last 3 weeks of January. Reservations necessary. Major credit cards accepted. 68 Rue Bourgneuf, Bayonne (phone: 59-59-01-33). Moderate.

Euskalunda – The decor and ambience at this cozy bistro on a narrow street in Petit Bayonne are as typically Basque as its name and its former chef, Geneviève Muruamendiaraz. She received laurels for almost 3 decades for her honest, inexpensive, and authentic Basque fare. Her daughter, Arroxa Aguirre, has taken over the kitchen and retained the food's high standards. Try the cuttlefish in its own sauce. A meal here is a perfect preface to an excursion into the Pays Basque. Closed Sunday evenings, Mondays, the last 2 weeks in May, and October 15 to November 1. Visa accepted. 61 Rue Pannecau, Bayonne (phone: 59-59-28-02). Moderate to inexpensive.

BIARRITZ: For a detailed report on the city, its sights, hotels, and restaurants, see *Biarritz*, in THE CITIES. Route N11 leads from Biarritz south to St-Jean-de-Luz.

ST-JEAN-DE-LUZ: If Biarritz is "the Queen of Beaches," then St-Jean-de-Luz, 9 miles (14 km) down the coast, certainly is the crown princess, whose casual, fresh, and impulsive character is in many ways more appealing than the distinguished charm of Her Royal Highness.

Its biggest attraction is the expansive, gracefully curving white beach. Sandy and wide, and usually very crowded, the beach is in a naturally protected horseshoe-shaped bay between the sea and the mouth of the Nivelle River. Year-round, the sunsets here are superb. In addition to being one of the most popular resorts on France's Atlantic Coast, it also is the principle fishing port of the Basque coast, and its restaurants always are supplied with an abundance of fine, fresh seafood — perhaps its second biggest attraction.

Like Biarritz, St-Jean-de-Luz was already an important whaling center in the 9th century. Its old name, St-Jean-de-la-Boue ("St. Jean in the mud"), leads us to believe that its environs were not always so inviting. When the whales disappeared from this area, the fishermen turned to cod; today the big catch includes tuna, sardines, and anchovies.

Its proximity to the Iberian border made the city a frequent target of the Spanish, who burned it to the ground in 1558 and again in 1635. Thus there are few ancient structures.

Without question, the finest hour of the city's history was in 1660, when Louis XIV married Maria Teresa, the daughter of King Philip IV of Spain, to fulfill one of the terms of the peace treaty signed by the two monarchs the previous year. The marriage took place on June 9, and the city still talks about and remembers the event. Today you can visit the Maison Lohobiague (Pl. Louis-XIV), where the Sun King stayed for 30 days before the wedding. It was the home of a wealthy shipbuilder and is filled with ornate furnishings and intriguing souvenirs of the king's stay. (The guided tour is in French, so ask for the English crib sheet to take along.)

The marriage ceremony (which lasted almost all day) was held in Eglise St-Jean-

Baptiste, not far from Place Louis-XIV, and the door through which the royal couple passed after the elaborate street processional was permanently walled over after the ceremony so that no other human would again cross this threshold. The church's interior is typically Basque, its walls stacked with three tiers of wooden galleries accessible only to the men of the congregation. Rebuilt after the fire of 1558 to replace the original 13th-century structure, this is perhaps the most sumptuous of Basque churches. Its magnificent retable, which dates from about 1670, contains large gilt statues of the popular saints of the Pays Basque.

Also of architectural interest is the gracious brick and stone Maison de l'Infante, where Maria Teresa stayed before the wedding, and, across the river in Cibourne, at 12 Quai Ravel, the 17th-century house in which the composer Maurice Ravel was born in 1875.

Explore the streets behind the port (Rue de la République and Rue Gambetta) and stop for a drink at one of the cafés on the lively Place Louis-XIV. On summer Sundays, there is Basque music and dancing here.

Route D918 leads southeast from St-Jean-de-Luz to St-Jean-Pied-de-Port.

CHECKING IN: *Chantaco* – A mile (1.6 km) or so south of town via D918, this genteel, peach-colored, turn-of-the-century Basque mansion has gracious archways and quiet gardens as well as 24 tranquil, pleasingly furnished rooms and a restaurant that matches the quality of the hotel. It has a swimming pool and is right across the street from a golf course. Closed November through *Easter*. Book well in advance. Major credit cards accepted. Rte. 918, St-Jean-de-Luz (phone: 59-26-14-76; fax: 59-26-35-97; telex: 540016). Expensive.

L'Hélianthal – This ultramodern 100-room addition to St-Jean-de-Luz's hotels near the beach offers *thalassothérapie* (health and beauty treatments) to its guests as well as a fine restaurant, *Le Mallet-Stevens*. Major credit cards accepted. Pl. M.-Ravel, St-Jean-de-Luz (phone: 59-51-51-51 or 59-51-51-60; fax: 59-51-51-54; telex: 573415). Expensive.

Le Madison – Conveniently located, this pleasant hotel features 25 attractive rooms, a sauna, a gym, and a very congenial management. Major credit cards accepted. 25 Bd. Thiers, St-Jean-de-Luz (phone: 59-26-35-02; fax: 59-51-14-76). Expensive to moderate.

Prado – A small, family-run place, the only one in town that stays open year-round. Six of the 38 rooms overlook the beach. Major credit cards accepted. Pl. de la Pergola, St-Jean-de-Luz (phone: 59-51-03-71). Moderate.

La Plage – Just a few steps from the beach, this homey, Basque-style family establishment has 30 simple rooms. During the summer, guests are required to take half- or full-board. Closed from mid-October to *Easter*. Visa accepted. 33 Rue Garat, St-Jean-de-Luz (phone: 59-51-03-44). Moderate to inexpensive.

EATING OUT: *Chez Margot* – On the opposite side of the bay, in front of the harbor, and below the fortress of Socoa, this country-style restaurant-bar offers a variety of simple and ample Basque food, especially fish. Closed Wednesday and Friday evenings in off-season and Friday lunch in season and the month of October. Visa accepted. Port de Socoa (phone: 59-47-18-30). Moderate.

La Taverne Basque – Seafood and tasty sheep's-milk cheese are the fare here, as well as the delicious light local wines. Located in the center of the city. Closed Wednesday lunch and Thursdays during off-season, and from January 15 to March 1. Major credit cards accepted. 5 Rue de la République (phone: 59-26-01-26). Moderate to inexpensive.

■**Note:** Two words sum up the restaurants in St-Jean-de-Luz: Basque and seafood. You can't go too far wrong in any of the dozens of warm, inviting places with wooden beams and colorful Basque linen tablecloths that line these narrow streets. Two such restaurants are the *Petit Grill Basque* (closed Fridays and December 20 to January 20; 4 Rue St-Jacques; phone: 59-26-80-76) and *Ramuntcho* (closed Mondays during off-season and November 15 to February 1; 24 Rue Garat; phone: 59-26-03-89); both are inexpensive.

En Route from St-Jean-de-Luz – You can follow the road (D912) around the bay to Socoa, along the Corniche Basque with its 16th-century fortress and magnificent vistas, and south to Hendaye, another popular resort, on the Spanish border. According to some, the beaches here are the French coast's most beautiful.

Or turn south on D918 and follow the Nivelle River into the heart of Basque country through tiny villages of split-timbered houses with rust-colored shutters and wooden balconies. Every town, no matter how small, has a *pelote* court where the Basque sport is played by young and old. If you are lucky enough to visit on a Sunday, you'll see the Basques dancing the fandango. Turn onto D4 and drive through Ascain, the village where Pierre Loti wrote *Ramuntcho* and continue on this curving route south to Sare, a storybook village huddled in the climbing hills that announce the ascent of the Pyrénées. (Just a couple of miles before this town is a curious little railroad car on a steep hillside; in summer it takes visitors up to the summit of La Rhune for an awesome view of the coast, including the beautiful Bay of San Sebastián in Spain.) Sare was a resting place for the 12th-century pilgrims who made the trek from all over Europe to Santiago de Compostela in Spain. As such it had, and still has, a tradition of welcoming hostelries.

CHECKING IN/EATING OUT: *Arraya* – This hotel is all wooden beams and stucco, with colorful fabrics and linen. Owner Paul Fagoaga upholds 400 years of Basque innkeeping tradition, and at the same time maintains a refinement and plushness rare in this province, where some comforts are forfeited for rusticity. The 20 rooms and 1 suite, most facing an interior garden, offer provincial luxury. The hotel's hearth-warmed dining room is particularly well-known for its preparation of game birds in the fall. The Basque specialties also are very tasty. Closed November to May 1. Reservations necessary. Major credit cards accepted. Sare (phone: 59-54-20-46; fax: 59-54-27-04). Expensive to moderate.

ST-JEAN-PIED-DE-PORT: Today's traveler wouldn't be at all surprised to see a bent, gray-cloaked, 12th-century pilgrim, staff in hand, emerge from behind the ramparts here, so convincing is the ambience of this Basque village, the last stop along the ancient road to the Spanish border. Its location required heavy fortification, and the old, or high, town, *ville haute,* is encircled by 15th-century stone ramparts that climb up the hill to a citadel. Inside the Old Town are steep, narrow stone streets, a church built into the ramparts, and Basque houses, their rickety, flower-entwined balconies overhanging the Nive River. This place is like a medieval stage set for a movie. Wander through the old streets and climb up to the 13th-century citadel built by the King of Navarre and let your imagination take wing.

Just outside the gates of the Old Town is the modern town, the capital and market center of the Basse Navarre, one of the three French Basque provinces. On Mondays the sloping main street, with lively Basque cafés and *auberges,* turns into a bazaar where vendors sell food, clothing, books, and just about anything you might need. Many of the shops here specialize in colorful Basque linen.

For a glimpse of Basque camaraderie, stop at the *Etche Ona,* a provincial *auberge* on the main street where bereted, ruddy-cheeked Basques take an animated afternoon break.

St-Jean-Pied-de-Port is an excellent point of departure for several excursions, north to the grottoes of Isturits and Oxocelhaya, with their prehistoric carvings, and south to the Iraty forest, one of the most lush in the Pyrénées.

CHECKING IN/EATING OUT: *Pyrénées* – A white stucco house with neat flower-bedecked balconies and a very pleasing tree-shaded dining terrace that looks out on the main street and the city's ramparts. It has 2 suites and 18 simply decorated, comfortable rooms and a fine restaurant, whose chef, Firmin Arrambide, prepares excellent fare. His reputation and his two Michelin stars are well deserved; a meal on his terrace can be memorable whether you order from such traditional offerings as an incomparably flavorful Basque fish soup or from Arrambide's slightly more *recherché* creations like roast pigeon with ravioli of wild mushrooms or cod-stuffed peppers. Try the iroulèguy wines from the vineyards nearby. A member of the Relais & Châteaux group. Closed mid-November to *Christmas,* and most of January, as well as Tuesdays during off-season. Reservations necessary. Major credit cards accepted. Pl. Général-de-Gaulle, St-Jean-Pied-de-Port (phone: 59-37-01-01; fax: 59-37-18-97; telex: 570619). Expensive.

Arcé – About 7 miles (11 km) west on D15, this is a perfect Pyrenean retreat — with 19 rooms, 6 suites, a swimming pool, and tennis court — secluded on the banks of a clear mountain stream. In the summer, guests dine on the garden terrace that overhangs the stream, the source of deliciously fresh trout that chef-owner Pascal Arcé, who rates one star in Michelin, puts on the table. Closed mid-November to mid-March. Reservations necessary. Visa accepted. St-Etienne-de-Baïgorry (phone: 59-37-40-14; fax: 59-37-40-27). Expensive to moderate.

En Route from St-Jean-Pied-de-Port – Leave by D933, turning onto D918 and crossing the Osquich Mountain pass before reaching the charming little town of Mauléon Licharre, which has a small, early 17th-century château worth seeing. The town also is France's largest producer of espadrilles, those comfortable rope-soled canvas shoes. Then continue on to Oloron-Ste-Marie via D24, D25, and D936. Beret lovers might recognize the name of this town at the junction of two swift mountain streams as that stamped inside most of the world's authentic Basque hats. The best reason for stopping here, other than to buy a beret, is to visit Eglise Ste-Marie, a small 13th-century cathedral with an incomparable Romanesque façade. Carved of Pyrenean marble that has mellowed to an ivory-like patina, its portal is peopled by scores of curious, intricately detailed creatures and deserves careful examination.

Up the hill in the Old Town are 15th- and 17th-century houses and the massive 13th-century Eglise Ste-Croix, the oldest Romanesque edifice in Le Béarn.

Route N134 leads from Oloron-Ste-Marie to Pau.

PAU: The largest and most cosmopolitan city of the western Pyrénées, Pau combines all the advantages of a metropolitan area with the genteel atmosphere of a mountain resort. Its graceful Boulevard des Pyrénées, the early 19th-century work of Napoleon I, offers magnificent vistas of the surrounding hills and the peaks of the high Pyrénées; to the east lies the 9,504-foot Midi de Bigorée peak and to the south, the slightly higher Midi d'Ossau peak. The peaks are especially magnificent summer mornings and at sunset.

Now the capital of the Pyrénées-Atlantiques *département,* it once was the capital of the historical Béarn region, land of the Kings of Navarre and of Henri IV, one of France's most colorful and best-loved monarchs. The best introduction to the history of the Béarn and to all the fascinating lore surrounding Pau's dear Henri is found in the magnificent château where he was born in the middle of the 16th century. Set on high ground at the end of the Boulevard des Pyrénées and overlooking the River Gave de Pau (or Pau's mountain torrent), it is surrounded by the narrow structures and streets of the old town.

The château has a wonderfully ornate Renaissance character, having been renovated in the 16th century by Marguerite of Angoulême, the beautiful and celebrated wife of Henri d'Albret, King of Navarre; she wrote the *Heptameron,* a collection of tales modeled after Boccaccio's. (The château also was embellished in the 19th century by both Louis-Philippe and Napoleon III.) Marguerite and Henri's daughter, Jeanne d'Albret, gave birth to Henri IV here on December 13, 1553, and the curious tortoise-shell cradle the infant slept in is on display. Other treasures here include richly carved Renaissance furniture, priceless artwork, and, most awesome of all, the world's richest and most precious collection of Gobelin and Flemish tapestries. On the third floor is a fascinating exhibit of the history and culture of the Béarn as well as a curator who will gladly explain the furnishings, art, models, and any other parts of the exhibit that interest you (phone: 59-27-36-22).

The massive square stone tower at the entrance to the château was built by Gaston Fébus, actually Gaston III of Béarn, who modestly dubbed himself *"fébus,"* which means "brilliant." This legendary hunter, poet, and military strategist managed to build the Béarn into a strong and independent state in the 14th century. (Many of his castles still can be seen throughout the Béarn.) The tower is all that remains of the militaristic medieval structure that once stood here.

At the opposite end of the Boulevard des Pyrénées is Beaumont Park, a graceful, verdant city park with a small lake and tawdry casino. Nearby, on Rue Mathieu-Lalanne, the *Musée des Beaux-Arts* (phone: 59-27-33-02) has important Italian, Dutch, Flemish, Spanish, and French works from the 17th to the 20th century. The *Musée Bernadotte* (phone: 59-27-48-42) is housed in the birthplace of and devoted to Marshall Jean-Baptiste Jules Bernadotte (1764–1844), who in 1818 became King Charles XIV of Sweden after being adopted as heir to Charles XIII. Closed Mondays. The tourist office is in the Hôtel de Ville (Pl. Royale; phone: 59-27-27-08).

The city's benign climate, made famous by a much-translated book by the Scottish doctor Alexander Taylor, made it a favorite destination after it was published in 1842. At one point, almost 15% of the town's population was British. Though the English left with the World Wars, some of their customs, such as afternoon tea, remain. *L'Isle au Jasmin* (28 Blvd. de Pyrénées) is a charming place to enjoy one of more than a dozen varieties of teas and half a dozen coffees. In May there is the *Grand Prix de Pau* car race, and in June and early July, Pau's streets come alive with music, dance, and theater festivals, many of the performances free.

CHECKING IN: *Continental* – A grand old establishment in the heart of Pau, most of its 110 rooms have been renovated in a modern functional decor. Ask for one of the four less modern, more charming rooms in the rotunda. Major credit cards accepted. 2 Rue Maréchal-Foch, Pau (phone: 59-27-69-31; fax: 59-27-99-84; telex: 570906). Expensive to moderate.

Gramont – On gracious Place de Gramont, this recently renovated, quiet, traditional hotel has 30 simple, spacious rooms and a breakfast room. Friendly staff. Major credit cards accepted. 3 Pl. de Gramont, Pau (phone: 59-27-84-04; fax: 59-27-62-23). Moderate to inexpensive.

EATING OUT: *Pierre* – Still considered by many to be Pau's finest for classic cuisine, service, and appointments, it has one Michelin star. Closed Saturday lunch, Sundays in off-season, and the last 2 weeks in February. Reservations necessary. Major credit cards accepted. 16 Rue L. Barthou (phone: 59-27-76-86). Expensive.

Au Panache d'Henri IV – A particularly welcoming bistro between Place Royale and the château, with a warm, wood-beamed interior and big windows flung open to the street in fine weather. Its menu consists of pleasing, simple, and solid regional fare. Closed Mondays in the off-season and in September. Visa accepted. Rue Adove, Pau (phone: 59-27-56-19). Moderate.

La Goulue – A tiny, rather curious little café near the château, its walls are plastered with art and theater posters and its crude wooden tables are covered with red paper. The menu includes southwest specialties, such as *magret* (grilled duck breast) and *confit* (duck or goose simmered in its own flavorful fat and aromatic spices). Try the jurançon wines produced near Pau. Closed Saturday lunch. Visa accepted. 13 Rue Henri-IV, Pau (phone: 59-27-44-44). Moderate to inexpensive.

En Route from Pau – Take D937 to Lourdes, stopping on the way at the Grottoes of Bétharram. A rickety aerial tram takes visitors up over a giant hill and down to the entrance of these stalactite- and stalagmite-filled caves where one travels almost 2 miles by boat, foot, and train past nature's awesome work.

Not far away is the curious 1661 Eglise Notre-Dame-de-Bétharram, where several miracles are said to have occurred, particularly between 1620 and 1640. Once an important pilgrimage site, it was overshadowed in the 19th century by nearby Lourdes. Most intriguing is the painted ceiling under the organ loft, depicting the ancestors of Christ according to the Gospel of St. Matthew.

LOURDES: On February 11, 1858, Bernadette Soubirous, the 14-year-old daughter of an impoverished Lourdes miller, claimed to have seen a vision of the Virgin Mary in a rocky grotto surrounded by woods near the Gave de Pau. More apparitions occurred in the girl's presence (18 in all), and on one occasion the vision was accompanied by the spouting of a spring when Bernadette scratched the dry ground with her fingers. Miracles were reported that were attributed to the healing power of the spring's waters; word spread and pilgrims began to flock here. In 1862 the church officially recognized this as a holy place, constructing a sanctuary at the grotto, and in 1933 Bernadette was canonized. Today the small grotto chapel by the mountain stream is overshadowed by a monstrous, double-decker basilica, its monumental semicircular staircase leading to the upper church and embracing a large open plaza.

Lourdes is the destination of more than 4 million pilgrims a year, many of them the sick and disabled, who come here to bathe in the waters of the miraculous spring in hopes of a cure. The pilgrims support this not so appealing town of 18,000, which seems to consist only of hotels and saintly souvenir shops selling blue and white plastic bottles in the shape of the Virgin (people fill them with water from the central fountain). There are more than 400 hotels here, modern structures stacked one next to the other on the hilly streets like so many pastel matchboxes. In fact, Lourdes has the largest number of hotel rooms of any French city except Paris. Despite that, don't try to get a room around August 15, the most important of six annual pilgrimage dates. (In 1983, Pope John Paul II came for the August pilgrimage and rooms were booked as far away as 100 miles.)

This is a city built on faith and hope — and, some say, on their exploitation — and it is certainly worth seeing, although many touristic pilgrims choose to pass it by, disturbed by the commercialism and the sad spectacle of the disabled and sick waiting patiently for miracles.

If you do stop, see the fortified château (pre-miracle) high on a hill above the town. It is an impressive piece of medieval architecture that served as a state prison in the 17th and 18th centuries, and has an interesting museum on the culture and traditions of the Pyrénées. You also can visit the house where Bernadette was born and see a film on her life or, on Sunday afternoons, watch a rugby game; the local club is one of the best in France.

Though there are, needless to say, plenty of hotels to choose from, you might do well to leave the crowded city via N21 south and drive for 10 miles (16 km) into the nearby valley, where there are many pleasing rural hotels near Argelès-Gazost. Or you may continue driving to where the flat valley suddenly climbs into the mountains to the resort of Cauterets, about 19 miles (30 km) from Lourdes.

CHECKING IN/EATING OUT: *Le Relais de Saux* – For those who choose to visit Lourdes, 1½ miles (2 km) north of the city this charming 17th-century hostelry and restaurant offer a splendid view of the mountains. The owners, M. and Mme. Héres, make their guests feel very welcome. Open daily. Major credit cards accepted. Hameau de Saux (phone: 62-94-29-61; fax: 62-42-12-64). Moderate.

CAUTERETS: This small, appealing resort compactly grouped at the feet of sharply rising peaks serves double duty, as both a ski resort and a health spa, and is as lively in the summer as in the winter. Its large thermal establishment attracts "curists" with respiratory ailments. (The waters also are said to benefit infertile women!)

The town is a pleasant base for excursions into the National Park of the Western Pyrénées, which begins a couple of miles beyond Cauterets. To reach the park, drive the scenically winding and climbing route to the Pont d'Espagne, where there is a magnificent waterfall. The road ends here, so you have to continue on foot into the forest, or you can take a chair lift to the lovely, clear lake of Gaube, about 6 miles (10 km) away. Hikers can continue through the mountains to another lovely work of nature, the Cirque de Gavarnie, a superb semicircular formation of mountains with tall, awesome waterfalls — the product of glacial erosion. The easier way, however, is to drive from Cauterets to Luz-St-Sauveur and then take the narrow roads to the town of Gavarnie. From here you have to walk or take ponies to the Cirque.

CHECKING IN/EATING OUT: *Trois Pics* – There's an alpine feeling about this cozy, modern little lodge with lacy wood balconies. It's almost always booked, so call in advance. The dining room is rather like a coffee shop, but the food is good. Closed from mid-November to mid-December. Reservations advised. Major credit cards accepted. 12 Bd. Leclerc, Cauterets (phone: 62-92-53-64; telex: 530337). Moderate.

Etche Ona – A friendly Basque hotel between the slopes and the thermal establishment, its rooms are modern and comfortable, the dining room and lounge very pleasant. The homey food with an occasional Basque flavor also is quite good. Closed November 1 to December 20 and mid-April to mid-May. Major credit cards accepted. Rue Richelieu, Cauterets (phone: 62-92-51-43). Inexpensive.

La Fruitière – This little *auberge* with 8 rooms in the mountains on the road to the Pont d'Espagne is the choice of regulars for creative, well-prepared fare. Closed Sunday dinner, first 2 weeks of May and from October to mid-December. No credit cards accepted. On N21, Cauterets (phone: 62-92-52-04). Inexpensive.

En Route from Cauterets – At Luz-St-Sauveur pick up the Route des Pyrénées (D918, then D618) again and follow its breathtakingly scenic path to Luchon, crossing three great mountain passes. These are in the high Pyrénées, ruggedly beautiful and dotted with quaint old spas and modern ski resorts. Cross the dizzying Col de Tourmalet (*col* means "pass"), south of the Pic du Midi de Bigorre (9,455 feet). Farther down the sinuous route is the Col d'Aspin, and finally you'll cross the Col de Peyresourd before reaching Luchon. This stretch is one of the most important stages of the annual *Tour de France* bicycle race that takes place in July. Traditionally the victor of this section wins the entire event.

LUCHON: Though it's billed as the premier spa of the French Pyrénées, and in fact it still may be, this quiet resort in a lush, flat valley shadowed by the highest of Pyrenean peaks seems to have lost some of its former cachet in recent years.

It does retain the vestiges of a premier spa, however: the park-encircled thermal establishment, its dimensions and façade reminiscent of a theater or opera house, and the elegant tree-lined main street with smart shops and cafés. The sulfur springs, named Ilixo by Romans who were the first bathers here, are particularly therapeutic for respiratory and throat problems. In the winter, Luchon welcomes skiers drawn to the steep, snowy slopes of the nearby Superbagnères ski station. If the weather is clear, you'll have a magnificent view of the surrounding valleys and the Maladetta range at the Spanish border.

Like many of France's thermal towns, this seems to be something of an anachronism and as such retains a certain flavor, charm, and tranquillity of times past that makes a stop here especially enjoyable.

Travel D125 north from Luchon to St-Bertrand-de-Comminges, 19 miles (30 km) away.

CHECKING IN/EATING OUT: *Corneille* – A gracious old white mansion in its own private garden, it provides 4 suites and 52 cozy rooms, each individually decorated. The staff here is extremely personable and the atmosphere familial and warm, and the food in the provincial dining room is good. Closed November to March 31. Major credit cards accepted. 5 Av. Alexandre-Dumas, Luchon (phone: 61-79-36-22; fax: 61-79-81-11; telex: 520347). Expensive to moderate.

Grand Hôtel des Bains – This traditional, turn-of-the-century hotel has 50 spacious rooms with high ceilings and wrought-iron balconies and 3 restaurants — Italian, Spanish, and French. Closed October 20 to *Easter*. Major credit cards accepted. 75 Allées-Etigny, Luchon (phone: 61-79-00-58; telex: 521437). Moderate to inexpensive.

ST-BERTRAND-DE-COMMINGES: Not far out of Luchon on D125 you can't help but notice an immense mellow stone cathedral surrounded by ramparts rising high on a hill in the distance and dominating the flat valley below. It compels one to draw nearer. The narrow, winding road leads to St-Bertrand-de-Comminges, no mirage, but a dreamy walled village of no more than 20 or 30 inhabitants. This practically deserted, storybook place above the Garonne River, and the town on the plain below (inhabited by another 200), were livelier 2,000 years ago. In its earlier life it was called Lugdunum Convenarum, apparently founded in 72 BC by Pompey on his return from a Spanish campaign. Because it was on the busy route from Toulouse to the popular baths of Luchon, the town grew rapidly and by the end of the 1st century had about 60,000 inhabitants. (According to the Jewish historian Flavius Josephus, it was here that Herod and his wife, murderers of St. John the Baptist, were exiled.)

In the 6th century the city was wiped out, by the barbarians according to some chroniclers, others say by the plague. The Roman city silted over, and archaeological digs have only recently unearthed remains of the old forum and some public monuments. The plain and the hillside apparently remained uninhabited until the 12th century, when Bertrand, Bishop of Comminges and later St. Bertrand, decided the magnificent acropolis was an ideal site for a cathedral, which he began building in 1120. At the end of the 13th century, Bertrand de Got, the future Clément V, first Pope of Avignon, began to enlarge the cathedral, completing the work in 1352. The Romanesque cloister, part of which was added in the 15th century, is lovely and provides a stunning view of the river and valley below. The cathedral's interior, embellished during various periods, is a fascinating lesson in religious architecture. It includes pure examples of Roman, Gothic, Renaissance, and baroque design. Perhaps its most beautiful treasures are the magnificent, intricately carved wood choir stalls. Sculpted by craftsmen from Toulouse in 1535, they tell the story of the redemption. Behind the altar is the frescoed stone tomb of St. Bertrand. There also is an exhibition of religious antiquities, such as richly embroidered bishops' capes dating from the 13th century.

Before leaving this lovely site, wander through the steep, curving, stone streets of the walled village surrounding the cathedral.

Travel east along N117 and D117 to Foix, the capital of the *département* of the Ariège.

En Route from St-Bertrand-de-Comminges – In the valley just north, at Valcabrère, is the 11th-century Basilica of St. Just. A graceful yellow stone example of early Romanesque design, it sits serenely in a cemetery surrounded by cypresses.

Nearby are the well-preserved remains of an opulent Gallo-Roman villa at Montmaurin (follow N125 and D633 north to D69C) and, close by, the Grotto de Gargas (northeast of D26), a cave inhabited by Aurignacien man, whose mysterious engravings of more than 231 mutilated hands, perhaps associated with some cult or ritual, have earned it the title of "Cave of the Cut Hands."

Traveling east on N117, then turning southeast on D117, the route soon passes into the department of the Ariège, the former domain of the Counts of Foix, an area whose romantic and colorful past is only outdone by the natural beauty of its glacial valley. This splendid wooded country is punctuated by chalky cliffs and commanding green mountains topped with the ruins of the medieval fortresses and stone strongholds of the 12th-century religious "heretics" known as the Cathari, or Albigeois.

The area also is rich in natural caves, where prehistoric man lived and left mystical clues to his activities drawn and engraved on the porous rock surfaces. One such cave is the Mas-d'Azil, north of St-Girons via D119. This curious tunnellike grotto, 1,400 feet long and 165 feet wide, was carved out by the Arize River under the Plantaurel range. It was inhabited by prehistoric man from 40,000 to 8,000 BC and bears graceful, scratched images of bison and horses. Digs have turned up a wealth of implements used by Magdalenian man. Later the early Christians hid here, followed in the 12th and early 13th centuries by the Cathari and by the Huguenots 4 centuries later. You can see the hiding place, the Salle du Temple, where the Protestants sought refuge in 1625 from the fierce attacks of Cardinal Richelieu.

Return to D117 and travel east about 25 miles (40 km) to Foix.

FOIX: This sleepy little town, the unassuming capital of the *département* of the Ariège, is notable for the 11th-century château of the Counts of Foix, set commandingly on a rock high above the town. (From the Middle Ages up to the 19th century, crowds used to pan for gold in the Ariège River at its base.) In 1002 Roger le Vieux, Count of Carcassonne, to the north, bequeathed this part of his realm to his son, who took the title of Count of Foix, the first in a line of illustrious characters such as the previously mentioned Gaston Fébus (see Pau, above). A famous battle took place here in 1272 when one of the counts refused to recognize the sovereignty of the King of France, Philip the Bold, who mounted a dramatic and victorious attack against the château. When the Counts of Foix acquired the Béarn in 1290, they lost interest in the town and the château. They returned under French jurisdiction during the reign of Henry IV in 1607. What remains of the château today — the central tower and the core of the original structure, flanked by two separate stone towers added later — is only a small part of the fortress that once stood here. The three towers, nevertheless, form an extremely romantic silhouette. In the 1800s they were used as a prison and the graffiti of political prisoners can still be seen on the walls of the round tower. Today, the three floors of the tower show collections of prehistoric, Gallo-Roman, and medieval artifacts found in the region. The central structure has an exhibit of the arts and traditions of the Ariège. A week-long festival, the *Journées Médiévales Gaston Phoebus,* takes place the second week of July, with parades of citizens in medieval garb, street fairs, and other festivities. Sound and light displays happen in an open-air theater in

July, August, and September. For details, visit the Foix Tourist Office (45 Cours G.-Fauré; phone: 61-65-12-12) or the regional tourist office (14 Rue Lazéma; phone: 61-65-29-00).

The potential for side trips, detours, and unexpected adventures is great along the winding roads between Foix and Collioure, a resort town on the Mediterranean coast, where good food and lodging and beaches await the weary wanderer.

En Route from Foix – Take N20 south to the Grotto of Niaux (near the town of Tarascon), one of the most superb repositories of prehistoric paintings in France. The graceful bison, horses, and deer-like animals, colored with oxides and manganese, that line the walls here date from 12,000 BC and represent the height of Magdalenian art. In recent years, authorities have started regulating the number of visitors to preserve the cave's atmosphere and to prevent the deterioration of these treasures. The caves are open all day from June through September and for limited hours from October through May. Groups are restricted to 20 people, so it's wise to arrive early and to make reservations (phone: 61-05-88-37).

Pick up D117 again, turning south on D9 to Montségur (about 19 miles/30 km from Foix), the last stronghold of the Cathari, the religious rebels whose doctrines so angered the church that Pope Innocent III mounted a vicious crusade against them. The infamous warrior Simon de Montfort, bent on eradicating the cultists in the name of his church and country, pursued them mercilessly, leaving a path of death and destruction from Toulouse to Montpellier and south to the Pyrénées. The final showdown was here, in 1244, when the last 207 "pure ones," as the spiritual leaders of the cult were called, had sought refuge in this high fortress on a seemingly impregnable mount against the Catholic army, almost 10,000 men strong. The siege began in July of 1243 and continued until the following March, when, according to some chroniclers, the château was set ablaze and the 207 Cathari burned alive. (Other accounts hold that they finally came out and surrendered.) Only the ruined stone walls and part of the square dungeon remain today. The ruins sit on a curious mount on top of a mountain pass above the small village of Montségur, where there is a Catharist museum. Though you can drive up to the pass, you have to climb the final mount on foot — no small task, as the trail is steep and rugged. It takes about 45 minutes to reach the château. Non-climbers can admire the crumbling stone walls from below. Those who do make the climb will be rewarded with a marvelous view of the surrounding valleys and mountains. There are two other Catharist châteaux in the area, one at nearby Roque-fixade (follow D9), also on top of a rocky mount; the other is at Puivert (D9 and, continuing east, D117).

Take D117 east from Lavelanet and pick up D613 southwest just before Quillan. At Ax-les-Thermes the road runs into N20, which follows the course of the Ariège River south into ruggedly beautiful mountain terrain, across the high pass of Col de Puymorens (open only in the summer). Continue southeast on N20 into the Roussillon region, picking up D618 past a string of winter resorts and mountain spas, including Font-Rameau, a high-altitude sports training center, Mont-Louis, a solar energy research center, and Prades, where in May the annual *Prades Music Festival* is held at the nearby Abbaye St-Michel-de-Cuxa. From nearby Vernet-les-Bains, a small winding road goes south to the magnificent 11th-century Abbaye St-Martin-du-Canigou, renowned for the grace and harmony of its church and cloister as well as its magnificent location — and resultant commanding view — on the slopes of towering Mont-Canigou. The abbey can only be reached on foot from the small town of Casteil. It is, however, a memorable sight, worth the almost-2-hour trek for those with comfortable shoes and time for an afternoon walk.

Return to N116 and travel east about 9 miles (14 km) to pick up D618, which winds slowly and picturesquely southeast to Amélie-les-Bains-Palalda, where the thermal springs have attracted people with respiratory and muscular ailments from Roman times to the present. This is the perfect starting point for some pleasant walks; a 30-minute stroll due south, for instance, leads to the impressive Mondony Gorges.

Only 5 miles (8 km) away, due east on D618, is Céret, a tiny Catalonian town set among orchards that once attracted the likes of Picasso, Braque, and others.

 CHECKING IN/EATING OUT: *Château de Riell* – Formerly a private mansion, this hotel affords spectacular mountain views from its 19 romantic guestrooms, complete with lovely antiques and the proverbial roaring fireplaces. There also is a swimming pool and tennis courts. Chef Marc Baudry presides over the one-star restaurant, specializing in Catalan-French fare. Finely prepared fare such as lamb with rosemary cream, filet of sole with poached oysters and caviar, and ice cream with fresh apricots and figs. Closed November to April 1. Major credit cards accepted. Molitg-les-Bains, Prades (phone: 68-05-04-40; fax: 68-05-02-91; telex: 500705). Expensive.

CÉRET: With a population of only 6,200 people, Céret, called "the Mecca of Cubism," is best known for the artists who used to live and work here (as well as in nearby Collioure, on the coast) and for the *Musée d'Art Moderne,* filled with their paintings and sculpture. Its collection includes works by Matisse, Picasso, Chagall, Juan Gris, Miró, Dalí, Maillol, and Manolo, the sculptor who is credited with luring the other artists here initially. One room is devoted to Picasso, and in the old part of town there is a plaza named after him, as well as a monument to this well-loved "adopted" son. Be sure to see the restored 14th-century Pont du Diable (Devil's Bridge), which rises 73 feet over the Tech River in a single arch. The tourist office is at 1 Av. G.-Clemenceau (phone: 68-87-00-53).

Continue east on D618 through the vineyards of the Tech Valley and, via N114, to the resorts of the Vermilion Coast.

COLLIOURE: This tiny fishing port about 12 miles (19 km) north of the Spanish border has been called "the Pearl of the Côte Vermeille"; it is certainly one of the most picturesque and pleasant bathing resorts on the Languedoc coast. The tranquil beauty of the spot, with its two tiny bays separated by an impressive fortified château, drew artists such as Dufy, Matisse, Picasso, and Braque around the turn of the century and became a favorite subject for them. Collioure is considered the birthplace of the Fauvist movement, the precursor of Cubism.

The sprawling brick château here was the summer home of the Kings of Majorca during their short but remarkable reign (ca. 1276–1344) over Perpignan and Catalonia. It is open to the public and has changing exhibits. A 17th-century church, Notre-Dame-des-Anges, set at the edge of the old port near the beach has a magnificent gilded retable (1698) by Joseph Sunyer, a Catalonian craftsman; the church's tower once served as the port's lighthouse.

Collioure, a port for Phoenician and then Roman merchants, was an important center of commerce during the Middle Ages, when the Catalonian coast dominated Mediterranean trade, but like many Languedoc ports, it lost commercial importance after the Peace of the Pyrénées in the mid-17th century and the later annexation of Provence to France. The French military architect of Louis XVI, Marshall Vauban, destroyed almost half of the city and gave it its present look. Today its principal attractions are sandy beaches, albeit relatively small and crowded, and the charm of tiny streets lined with inviting little outdoor restaurants serving such simple pleasures as tender, fresh anchovies and great iced platters of fresh seafood, accompanied by the wine of neighboring vineyards.

The winding coast road that leads south from Collioure is a magnificently scenic stretch, flanked on one side by the vine-covered slopes that produce the famous, sweet banyuls wine, on the other by a breathtaking expanse of clear blue sea. Port-Vendres and Banyuls-sur-Mer (the birthplace of the sculptor Aristide Maillol), both only a few miles from Collioure, are extremely enjoyable places in which to soak up the Mediterranean sun and relax after a trek through the Pyrénées.

CHECKING IN: *Hostellerie des Templiers* – This rustic inn on the quai facing the Château Royal was the gathering place for the Fauvists who lived and worked here around the turn of the century, and the walls of its charmingly cluttered dining room are lined with their sketches and paintings. Between the inn and its nearby annex, there are 52 simple rooms. Do stop for at least an aperitif to look over the intriguing art collection. The restaurant is closed Sundays for lunch, Mondays, and from November to mid-February, except for 2 weeks at *Christmas.* Visa accepted. Quai de l'Amirauté, Collioure (phone: 68-82-05-58). Moderate.

EATING OUT: *San Vicens et Vieux Remparts* – One of a number of simple, outdoor café-restaurants overlooking the beach, this place offers fresh anchovies, salads, and copious platters of fresh seafood for a very reasonable tab. Open year-round. Visa accepted. Av. Boramar, Collioure (phone: 68-82-05-12). Inexpensive.

The Languedoc

Just the name of this large, infinitely diverse, and colorful region in France's sunny southwest promises a certain magic. Languedoc literally means "the language of *oc*," *oc* meaning "yes" in the southern dialect — the tongue of the troubadours that long ago gave way to the official language of the north and its affirmative *oïl*, which became *oui*.

But even if the province today submits to the language and jurisdiction of the north, its heart and soul remain proudly independent, retaining the fiery spirit that underlies the language of *oc*, its art, culture, and traditions. This is France's deep south — a very Mediterranean province blessed with sun, a beautiful coastline of sandy beaches, lush valleys resplendent with vineyards and orchards, and, to the north, the rugged, mysterious terrain of the Causses and the Cévennes mountains, some of the wildest and most beautiful country in all of France.

The regional boundaries of the Languedoc, as much a historical as an official entity, are not distinct. However, the region generally is considered to take in the *départements* of Lozère, Gard, Hérault, Aude, Pyrénées-Orientales, and, historically, portions of Tarn and Haute-Garonne. The ancient region of the Languedoc was much larger. At one time the language of *oc* was spoken in nearly all the areas south of what might be considered the French Mason-Dixon Line, starting at the confluence of the Garonne and Dordogne rivers in the west and curving up to Angoulême, across to Vichy, St-Etienne, and the Italian border in the east. Physically cut off from the north by the Massif Central, this region had reached a much more advanced level of art and culture by the 9th and 10th centuries than the barbarian north. The seeds of this early development were planted by the Phoenicians, who colonized the Mediterranean coast in 600 BC. They were followed in the 1st century BC by the Romans, who settled in the Bas Languedoc around Narbonne, making it the capital of the rich province of Gaule Narbonnaise. The remnants of their stay here are most visible in Nîmes, which boasts one of the world's best-preserved Roman temples.

The Visigoths held sway over this territory from the 5th century until their defeat in the 8th century by Charles Martel. The 9th century saw the establishment of the Counts of Toulouse, who controlled much of the Languedoc until the Albigensian Crusade, combined with the assaults of the jealous Capetian rulers in the north, brought their dynasty to an end in the 13th century and marked the beginning of the north's preeminence. The short but terrifying crusade against the religious dissenters (who took their name from the city of Albi, where they found refuge early in their movement) left deep scars in the area. At the same time, other religious groups, among them Catholics and Jews, were massacred in Béziers. A period followed during which the church sought to underline its restored authority by constructing grand and powerful religious edifices such as those in Toulouse and Albi.

Farther south, the Roussillon, the southern coastal area that along with the adjacent northeast corner of Spain forms Catalonia, was alternately under the jurisdiction of France and Spain during this period. Perpignan's formidable Palais des Rois de Majorque (Palace of the Kings of Majorca) bears witness to the strength and glory of that dynasty. It wasn't until the Treaty of the Pyrénées in 1659 that this area came under French rule permanently. The process of making Languedoc and the rest of the southern part of the country French started with Louis XIV in the late 17th century and was reinforced by Napoleon during the 18th century. Religious upheaval violently rocked the lands of the Languedoc again during the Wars of Religion, which were particularly cruel and destructive here. Even today, an undercurrent of dissension against authority and northern rule seems to exist here, expressed from time to time in hazy separatist movements for a free Occitan state or, in Roussillon, a united Catalonian state. These are, to be sure, minority movements. Nonetheless, they reflect the strong and assertive sense of regional identity and independence you will soon discover. Along with this character and a warm southern style of hospitality, the Languedoc offers a range of cuisine: the much-heralded cassoulets of Toulouse, Carcassonne, and Castelnaudry; the traditional *cargolada* feast of Catalonia; bouillabaisse and a wealth of seafood along the coast; and rich, flavorful cheeses, including the famous roquefort, from the Causses area. The region's most important product is the grape — one *département* alone, Hérault, produces almost one-fifth of all the wines of France — and a visit would not be complete without tasting some of the many local wines.

In addition to precious souvenirs from its colorful past — the pink cathedrals of Toulouse and Albi, the Palace of the Kings of Majorca in Perpignan, the magnificent Roman arena and temple in Nîmes, to name a scant few — the region offers wonderfully diverse and dramatic countryside, the highlight of which certainly is the 30-mile-long Gorges du Tarn, one of France's natural wonders. There also are darkly wooded mountains, the arid plateau of the limestone Causses, the wild Cévennes range rolling down into *garrigues,* rugged, brushcovered areas, and, of course, the long Mediterranean coastline backed by sun-baked vineyards for as far as the eye can see (and much farther still).

This tour route starts at Toulouse, the ancient capital of the Languedoc and home of the troubadours, and moves east to the great walled city of Carcassonne, then loops north to Albi and Cordes. From Albi it continues east to the rugged Causses area, through the Gorges du Tarn and down the southern slopes of the Cévennes range to Nîmes, on the eastern border of the Languedoc. From Nîmes and its nearby Pont du Gard — a triple-deck 1st-century Roman bridge — it curves down to Montpellier and follows the Mediterranean coast to Perpignan. Though this area hardly can be considered undiscovered, it is less crowded than its Mediterranean neighbor, Provence, with its Côte d'Azur. Its hotels and restaurants, many of which are relatively new, are comfortable and still relatively reasonable — downright bargains compared to those on the Côte d'Azur. Our price categories for the hotels listed in this section are expensive, more than $100 for a double room; moderate, between $50 and $100 a night; and inexpensive, less than $50. For restaurants, the expensive category is more than $100 for dinner for two;

moderate ranges from $50 to $100; the inexpensive category is $50 or less. Prices do not include wine or drinks, though service usually is included.

TOULOUSE: A poetic observer once described Toulouse as "a city pink at dawn, red at midday, and mauve at dusk." His characterization of what others have called the pink brick city aptly captures the face of this warm, animated metropolis. Toulouse is a colorist's dream, owing much of its charm to terra cotta brick, red roof tiles, the Garonne River, translucent sky, and the southern sun that plays off them in so many hues. But the city has much more to offer than a magnificent façade: It is the old capital of the Languedoc, one of the largest French regions — larger, in fact, than Belgium but with only one-third the population. It now is the fourth-largest city in France, a cultural capital and university center, and the heart of the nation's aerospace and electronics industries (the *Concorde* and the *Airbus* are built here). It is, as well, one of France's most appealing *villes d'art.*

This spot at a ford in the Garonne River was settled even before Rome; its early inhabitants were a tribe called the Volques-Tectosages. Later colonized by the Romans, it grew and had become the third city of Gaul by the 3rd century AD. About this time the evangelist St-Sernin (to whom Toulouse's most magnificent cathedral is dedicated) arrived, converting much of the populace to Christianity. The Visigoths invaded in 410, making this the capital of their vast territory. Next came the Francs and a period of chaos. Order returned under Charlemagne in 778, when he created the kingdom of Aquitaine. When Louis le Pieux (the Pious) became King of Aquitaine, he designated advisers from his family to oversee the city, thereby starting the lineage of the great Counts of Toulouse. For centuries to come these counts, whose lands spread from the Pyrénées to Auvergne, ruled over one of the liveliest courts in Europe. The city itself was governed by the consuls — called *capitouls* — who advised the counts on matters of defense and taught them how to negotiate with their vassals. This was the home of the troubadours (who later founded France's first literary society here, the Académie des Jeux Floraux, around 1323 for the preservation of the *languedoc*). This brilliant and gay court was brought to its knees in the early 13th century during the bitter conflicts between the north and the south over the Cathari, or Albigensians, religious "heretics" against whom Pope Innocent III and the ruling Capetians of the north mounted a fierce crusade led by the notorious Simon de Montfort. Count Raymond VI of Toulouse, accused of complicity with the heretics, fought to defend his city against the attacks of de Montfort, who finally was killed here in 1218. In 1229, Raymond VII, demoralized by continued attacks from the north, agreed to abide by the clauses of the Peace of Paris, which marked the beginning of the gradual incorporation of this area into the royal domain. Following the Albigensian Crusade and the devastation of the Hundred Years War, Toulouse experienced a renaissance thanks to a small plant called *coquanhas.* The blue dye yielded by this plant became so popular and was in such great demand that its production brought great fortunes to the city. But when the indigo plant and the inexpensive dye derived from it was discovered in India in 1560 and brought to France by traders, it brought an end to the Toulouse monopoly on blue. Many of the superb palaces built by the newly rich *pastel* (dye) merchants in the early 16th century still remain.

You could spend several days wandering through the old quarters of Toulouse, most of them named after and grouped around the city's great churches; they abound in architectural gems from 11th-century stone dwellings to Renaissance *hôtels particuliers.* If time is short, you may want to concentrate on two districts, both near the heart of town and Rue d'Alsace-Lorraine, Toulouse's main commercial street. The first district centers around the Hôtel de Ville (Town Hall), a marble-pillared baroque marvel dominating the Place du Capitole, an immense open square lined with arcaded cafés and shops. (It is next door to the regional tourist office, at Donjon du Capitole; phone:

61-23-32-00.) Nearby are two of the city's loveliest Renaissance structures: Hôtel de Bernuy, at 1 Rue Gambetta, and farther south, off the broad shopping street Rue de Metz, Hôtel d'Assézat. The latter was built in the 1550s by Toulouse's-greatest Renaissance architect, Nicolas Bachelier, for one of the city's wealthy *pastel* merchants. On Rue Lakanal are the church, cloister, and convent of Les Jacobins; the church is an example of the unusual Gothic style of the region with four single rows of tall supporting pillars across the middle of the nave, its spacious interior a wonderful polychrome play of light and color. The remains of St. Thomas Aquinas were brought here in 1974, the 700-year anniversary of his death, and are on exhibit. Continue on to Rue du Taur, where you'll pass the Church of Notre-Dame-du-Taur, said to have been constructed on the spot where, in 250, the body of the martyred St. Sernin was left after he had been dragged through the streets by a bull until he died. At the end of Rue du Taur is Toulouse's gem, the magnificent Basilique St-Sernin, the largest and most beautiful Romanesque church in the south of France, some say in the Western world. Begun in 1080 on the foundation of a 4th-century basilica, consecrated in 1096, and completed in the middle of the 14th century, it is laid out in the form of a Latin cross. Notice the nine chapels surrounding the apse, the superb 12th-century 5-story bell tower, and the Renaissance Miègeville Gate with its magnificently carved marble figures that include Christ, St. Peter, King David, and Adam and Eve.

The second district centers around Cathédrale St-Etienne (Pl. St-Etienne, off Allée François-Verdier). In comparison to the exquisitely harmonious St. Sernin, it appears jarringly lopsided and disparate. Constructed from the 13th through the 17th century, it incorporates many styles. Not to be missed by even the most hurried visitor is the *Musée des Augustins* (closed Tuesdays), where Rue de Metz and Rue d'Alsace-Lorraine intersect. It is filled with paintings and sculpture from all periods and, most noteworthy, the richest collection of chiseled stonework in France, all in the pleasing medieval setting of the old Augustinian convent. The *Notre-Dame-de-Grace* here is one of the most celebrated medieval sculptures of the Virgin and Child. *Musée Paul-Dupuy* (13 Rue de la Pleau) is devoted to applied arts from the Middle Ages to the present; the displays include clocks, coins, metalwork, and stamps. It is closed on Tuesdays and Sunday mornings. The *Musée du Vieux-Toulouse* (7 Rue du May, off Rue St-Rome) contains regional art and information about the history and traditions of the city (closed daily except Thursday afternoons in the winter and Sundays in the summer); the *Musée d'Histoire Naturelle* (closed Tuesdays), in the Jardin Botanique, has a significant prehistoric collection. Also in this district are the law courts, the residence of the Counts of Toulouse, and, along Rue de la Dalbade, the Eglise Notre-Dame-la-de-Dalbade, which has a lovely Renaissance doorway, the Hôtel de Clary, with its 17th-century stone façade, and the 16th-century houses of members of Parliament. At the end of Pont Neuf is a 1822 water tower which is now a museum and photography gallery (*Château d'Eau;* closed Tuesdays). Don't leave Toulouse without strolling through one of its many delightful small parks or tasting its cassoulet, the hardy white bean, duck (or goose), and sausage dish that it (along with two other Languedocian cities, Carcassonne and Castelnaudry) claims as its own. If you want to buy various duck products, stop by *Ducs de Gascogne* (60 Bd. Carnot; phone: 61-62-28-00). Part of a nationwide chain, this store specializes in foie gras, *magret* and *confit de canard,* all from Gascony, Languedoc and Périgord. Oenophiles might be interested in *Domaine de Lastours* (44 Rue de Languedoc; phone: 61-52-05-20), the oldest wine merchant in town, which carries more than 3,000 different kinds of wine.

CHECKING IN: *Altéa Wilson* – What this modern hotel lacks in old-fashioned charm it makes up for in modern comforts and efficiency. It has 95 rooms with color TV sets, mini-bars, and luxurious baths. Major credit cards accepted. 7 Rue Labéda, Toulouse (phone: 61-21-21-75; fax: 61-22-77-64; telex: 530550). Expensive.

Crowne Plaza Holiday Inn – Opened in 1989, it offers contemporary comfort in the center of the city. There are also a number of rooms reserved for nonsmokers. Major credit cards accepted. 7 Pl. du Capitole, Toulouse (phone: 61-61-19-19; fax: 61-23-79-96; telex: 520348). Expensive.

Grand Hôtel de l'Opéra – This gracious 17th-century edifice, once a convent and then quarters for opera students, has been completely renovated and transformed into what is now one of the most charming and comfortable hostelries in town. Its entrance is secluded in a tranquil courtyard, and its 15 suites and 63 contemporary rooms have air conditioning and television sets. Its restaurant, *Les Jardins de l'Opéra* (see *Eating Out*), has earned two Michelin stars. Major credit cards accepted. 1 Pl. du Capitole, Toulouse (phone: 61-21-82-66; fax: 61-23-41-04; telex: 521998). Expensive.

Chaumont – Small and charming, overlooking a lovely garden, it offers 28 comfortable rooms. Visa accepted. 19 Rue Lafayette, Toulouse (phone: 61-21-86-42). Moderate to inexpensive.

EATING OUT: *Darroze* – On a small back street, this bistro is full of rustic regional charm, as is the very well-prepared traditional fare that has earned it one Michelin star. Sample the foie gras with purée of truffles or *canette* (duckling) *du Gers*. Closed Saturday lunch and Sundays. Major credit cards accepted. 19 Rue Castellane, Toulouse (phone: 61-62-34-70). Expensive.

Les Jardins de l'Opéra – Dominique Toulousy, one of France's most promising young chefs (he has earned two Michelin stars), concocts such heavenly specialties as *raviolis de foie gras frais* (ravioli filled with fresh foie gras) and *feuilleté au chocolat et écorces d'oranges confites* (chocolate-filled puff pastry with glazed orange peel), all served amid the flowers of the lovely winter and summer garden dining rooms of the *Grand* hotel. Closed Sundays, the first week of January, and 2 weeks in August. Major credit cards accepted. 1 Pl. du Capitole, Toulouse (phone: 61-23-07-76). Expensive.

Vanel – Lucien Vanel was the venerable gastronomic light of Toulouse. The new chef, Pierre Yves LaMaison is trying to maintain the Vanel tradition, and his efforts have earned him a Michelin star. In summer, try his salad of melon, Bayonne ham, and artichokes or his fish dishes with delicate sauces; in winter, his hardy variations on Gascon specialties. The surroundings are modern and refined but pleasingly relaxed. Closed Sundays, holidays, 10 days in July. Major credit cards accepted. 22 Rue Maurice-Fonvielle, Toulouse (phone: 61-21-51-82). Expensive to moderate.

Colombier – A pleasingly unpretentious restaurant near the train station, it is reputed to serve the best cassoulet in town. Closed weekends, *Easter, Christmas* week, and 3 weeks in August. Major credit cards accepted. 14 Rue Bayard, Toulouse (phone: 61-62-40-05). Moderate.

Pavillon d'Argent – In the region of hearty cuisine, this Vietnamese eatery with an interior garden offers delicate cooking from old Saigon. Its speciality is light spring rolls stuffed with crab. Closed Sundays and Monday mornings. Major credit cards accepted. 43 Rue du Taur, Toulouse (phone: 61-23-36-48). Moderate.

La Grillothèque – You might mistake this modern eatery, with its limited, standard menu, for a transplanted American steakhouse; but you'll know it's completely French once you've tasted the ample entrecôte, the house specialty. And you'll understand why it's always busy. Open daily until 10:30 PM. Visa accepted. 16 Bd. de Strasbourg, Toulouse (phone: 61-62-87-31). Inexpensive.

En Route from Toulouse – Parallel to the road from Toulouse to Carcassonne is France's engineering masterpiece from the Louis XIV era — the Canal du Midi. Completed in 1680, the 150-mile waterway linking Toulouse to the Mediterranean port at

Sète was the main connection between the Atlantic Ocean and the Mediterranean Sea. Boats transported wine, wheat, sand, wood, and passengers until the railroad, built during the second half of the 19th century, cut the trip from 9 days to 12 hours. Today vacation houseboats and wine barges ply the waters. Route A61 makes a wide sweep southeast to the great fortified city of Carcassonne, passing Castelnaudary on the way. Both of these cities lay claim to the quintessential cassoulet, challenging Toulouse. So, if you like to make gastronomic comparisons, a lunchtime stop at Castelnaudary is a must. *Les Palmes* (10 Rue Maréchal-Foch, Castelnaudary; phone: 68-83-17-10) and *Fourcade* (14 Rue des Carmes, Castelnaudary; phone: 68-23-02-08) come highly recommended, though you'll find cassoulet on nearly every menu in town. Major credit cards accepted.

CARCASSONNE: Thus satisfied with Castelnaudary's cassoulet, you'll be ready for a long ramble through the meandering streets of the walled city of Carcassonne, about 17 miles (27 km) southeast on A61. One of the largest fortified cities in Europe, it stands like a turreted Walt Disney creation high on a plateau overlooking the Aude River. Its imposing ramparts are even more impressive at night when illuminated. The city is made up of two parts, "Ville Nouvelle," the new city established by Louis IX in the 13th century on the river's left bank, and the old fortified city on top of a 1,500-foot hill on the right bank. Leave your car in the lot on the city's east side and walk through the lovely Narbonne gate and across the drawbridge into the oldest part of the city, La Cité. The medieval mood inside is jarred somewhat by the inevitable scores of souvenir stalls, but the city's curving streets and half-timbered and stone dwellings retain enough charm to allow one to look past the kitsch and drift back into the time of Raymond-Roger Trencavel, Viscount of Carcassonne, under whose dynasty many of its grandest structures, including the walled Château Comtal and the Basilique St-Nazaire, were constructed. Long before the reign of Roger and the Trencavels, the Romans had fortified this spot in the 1st century, and in the 5th century the Visigoths added their share of stones to the ramparts of this strategic site, for centuries the border between the lands of what are now France and Spain.

Charlemagne besieged the city for 5 years in the 9th century and eventually was outwitted, according to legend, by Dame Carcas, a clever townswoman said to have tossed the city's last remaining pig, stuffed with everyone's last rations of wheat, over the ramparts of the town, thereby giving Charlemagne the impression that their larders still were well stocked and their spirit unbroken. Discouraged, Charlemagne retreated, his departure announced by Dame Carcas's trumpet call and the townspeople's jubilant cries of "Carcas sonne" ("Carcas sounds the horn"). It's an amusing tale of how the city got its name, although historians generally discredit it as no more than a romantic invention of the troubadours.

During the Albigensian Crusade of the 13th century the Trencavel dynasty and the city fell to Simon de Montfort, who subsequently established this fort as his base in the south. Later, Louis IX (St. Louis) and then his son Philip III (Philip the Bold) further strengthened the city with a second series of ramparts encircling the first, making it, they believed, impregnable. The strength of this double-walled system was never tested, however, because the city lost its strategic importance when the Treaty of the Pyrénées established that mountain range as the new boundary between France and Spain in 1659. The new city then became a major textile manufacturing center while the fortress was neglected and in danger of falling into ruin until 1835, when a resident brought it to the attention of the French government and Prosper Mérimée, the inspector of historical monuments (and author of the short story from which the opera *Carmen* was drawn). In 1844 the famous architect Eugène Viollet-le-Duc was commissioned to restore the city. His work was criticized by purists, since his efforts resulted in a very personal vision of how the city was supposed to look during the Middle Ages.

The tour of 12th-century Château Comtal, its museum, and the surrounding ramparts is a must, as is a visit to Basilique St-Nazaire, with its lovely Gothic windows, considered among the most interesting in the Midi. The city's winding streets are alive with cafés and pleasant restaurants, many featuring the cassoulet in which this town also excels. In summer there are frequent concerts in the open-air amphitheater. The city is particularly spectacular during traditional fireworks on July 14 (*Bastille Day*). For 2 weeks in August, the city organizes various shows on medieval life. For information, contact the tourist office (15 Bd. Camille-Pelletan; phone: 68-25-07-04 or 68-25-41-32). There is also another office (Porte Narbonnaise; phone: 68-25-68-81) that is open March through October only.

CHECKING IN: *La Cité* – This elegant former pope's palace within the ramparts sustains the medieval mood with wonderful carved wood and appropriately heavy and grand decor. Its 23 large, renovated gracious rooms and 3 suites have high ceilings and balconies and are the most comfortable accommodations in La Cité. A garden overlooks the ramparts. Its restaurant is considered the best in town, and the new chef, Michel Del Burgo, whips up delicious local and Mediterranean dishes. Major credit cards accepted. Pl. de l'Eglise, Carcassonne (phone: 68-25-03-34; fax: 68-71-50-15; telex: 505296). Expensive.

***Domaine D'Auriac* –** Just 2½ miles (4 km) south of Carcassone and in a charming 23-room hotel, this is the best restaurant in the region. A Michelin star justly compensates Bernard Rigaudis's efforts in the kitchen. His foie gras, done in salt, is a must, as well as cow's cheek with pig's ear *à la carcassonaise*. Trust us! Closed Sunday evenings and Monday lunch from November to *Easter,* and January 10–31. Major credit cards accepted. Rte. de St-Hilaire, Auriac (phone: 68-25-72-22; fax: 68-47-35-54; telex: 500385). Expensive.

***Donjon* –** A small, pleasing hotel in the heart of La Cité, it has a light, airy mood, a particularly pleasant manager, and 36 simply decorated rooms, some with small balconies. It was scheduled to undergo renovation as we went to press. A nice garden restaurant is open only in the evenings, and closed on Sundays. 2 Rue du Comte-Roger, Carcassonne (phone: 68-71-08-80; fax: 68-25-06-60; telex: 505012). Expensive to moderate.

***Pont Vieux* –** There are 20 rooms in this charming hotel, located between the Pont Vieux and La Cité's walls. Closed 2 weeks in January. Major credit cards accepted. 32 Rue Trivalle (phone: 68-25-24-99; fax: 68-47-62-71). Moderate.

EATING OUT: *Château St. Martin Trencavel* – It's worth a trip outside the ramparts of La Cité, via N113, to this rustic 16th-century *auberge* with its large, welcoming terrace. It is reputed to serve the best cassoulet in Carcassonne (one Michelin star) — no small claim, and also offers a wide choice of other tempting and creative specialties. A member of the Relais & Châteaux group. Closed Wednesdays. Major credit cards accepted. 290 Av. Général-Leclerc, Carcassonne (phone: 68-71-09-53). Moderate.

***La Crémade* –** This light and cheery dining spot offers well-prepared regional specialties and relaxed, gracious service. Closed Sunday nights and Mondays off-season, as well as 1 week in November and all of January. Major credit cards accepted. 1 Rue du Plo, Carcassonne (phone: 68-25-16-64). Moderate.

***Le Plo* –** Stone walls enclose this curious, cozy little shell of a restaurant in La Cité, with nothing overhead but a vine-covered trellis and the stars. It has a simple, limited menu of salads, pâtés, and grilled items cooked over aromatic vines. Closed from November 15 to March 15. No credit cards accepted. Rue du Plo, Carcassonne (phone: 68-25-51-85). Inexpensive.

En Route from Carcassonne – Traveling north on D118, you'll soon drive into the Montagne Noire. These gentle mountains are the extreme southeastern limit of the

Massif Central. Their southern slopes are arid, almost Mediterranean, while on the other side, where rainfall is extremely heavy, they are cloaked with lush, deep forests so thick and dark that they have earned this range the name Black Mountains. Its highest peak is the 3,699-foot Pic de Nore. Its northern slopes roll down into the Parc Régional du Haut Languedoc, an area dotted with lakes and beautiful scenery too often overlooked by visitors. The traveler with time and a love of nature will want to make a small circuit of the small, often unnumbered roads of the Montagne Noire and the regional park. The town of Mazamet, the regional center of France's wool industry since the 18th century, makes a convenient base for excursions. For information, stop at the tourist office, Rue des Caserne (phone: 63-61-27-07).

From Mazamet head northwest on N112 to Castres, the birthplace of the socialist leader Jean Jaurès, which has a museum in his honor as well as the *Musée Goya* (closed Mondays), with a collection of paintings that span 50 years of the artist's life. There's also the Hôtel de Ville (Town Hall), formerly a bishop's palace, with an elegant, sculpted garden, Jardin de L'Evêché; it is the 1676 work of André Le Nôtre, most celebrated for designing the gardens of Versailles. For information, contact the tourist office, Pl. de la République (phone: 65-59-92-44).

Before continuing north to Albi, take a short detour east on D622 to the area known as the Sidobre, a granite plateau with strange and fascinating rock formations. The site is cut with grottoes and deep gorges of the Agout and Durenque rivers and there also are gigantic granite quarries. At first, the great round boulders piled precariously on top of one another seem to be the work of human hands, stacked, perhaps, for some mysterious ritual. In fact, the picturesque curiosities, with names like "the Priest's Hat," "the Rock of the Goose," "the Trembling Rock," and "the Three Cheeses," are the work of nature.

ALBI: Pick up N112 north again to Albi, a city on the northern edge of the Languedoc, therefore somewhat off the tourist route and sometimes omitted from itineraries. The first glimpse of this enchanting pink city and its powerful brick cathedral above the Tarn River should make you glad to be here. Like Toulouse, Albi la Rouge, as it is called, is built of terra cotta brick and red roof tiles, and the tones and moods of the city change with the movement of the sun.

Albi was an important religious center during the 12th and 13th centuries, not only for the church but also for the Cathari, the religious "heretics" also known as Albigensians, named after this city where they found refuge and gathered strength early in their movement. They were later chased south by Simon de Montfort, the warrior who led Pope Innocent III's fierce crusade against them. Albi's great Cathédrale Ste-Cécile was built at the end of the 13th century after the martyrdom of the last of the Cathari, a symbol of the restored strength and irrefutability of the Catholic church. It stands like a fortress with high towers, sheer brick walls, and narrow windows; in fact, it was built to serve as a fortress as well as a place of worship and has an unusual exterior design. The main entrance, added in the 15th century, is on the south side, a wonderfully ornate and frilly contrast to the stark simplicity of the walls. The richly ornamented interior is considered one of the purest examples of the Gothic style of the Midi, with its superb carvings of biblical characters and saints around and inside the choir and an almost surrealistic 15th-century fresco of the Last Judgment behind the altar. In addition, you can climb a narrow staircase up into the tower for a view of the rooftops of Albi and the surrounding countryside. Next door is the 13th-century Palais de la Berbie, formerly the archbishop's palace and now the *Musée Toulouse-Lautrec* (see "Memorable Museums" in *For the Mind,* DIVERSIONS). It has the most important collection in France of the artist's work — more than 500 paintings, posters, sketches, and lithographs assembled by his mother. It is in itself reason enough for a visit to this city.

Toulouse-Lautrec was born here in 1864, and you can visit some of the rooms in his birthplace, now the Hôtel du Bosc, on Rue Toulouse-Lautrec in Old Albi. This section of town is filled with charmingly lopsided, half-timbered houses, craftsmen's workshops, and cozy little restaurants. The plaques of the Circuit Pourpré (the Crimson Circuit) mark a self-guided tour of Old Albi, which passes by the beautiful Church and Cloister of St-Salvy, created in several styles over several centuries (the 12th through the 15th). During the summer Albi holds several festivals, including the *Festival de Musique* in August. Stop in at the Palais de la Berbie (Pl. Ste-Cécile; phone: 63-54-22-30) for information and schedules.

CHECKING IN: *Hostellerie St-Antoine* – Though this establishment, founded in 1739 and half hidden on a quiet street near the center of Albi, claims to be one of the oldest hostelries in France, it looks relatively modern because it was rebuilt in the 1960s. Its lobby is studded with antiques and flowers, its tranquil garden where guests take breakfast is lovely, its 42 rooms and 8 suites are pleasant and comfortable, and its restaurant is very good. The Rieux family, which has managed the hotel for 5 generations, also operates *La Réserve* (below). The restaurant is closed Saturdays and Sundays for lunch, and Sunday dinner off-season. Major credit cards accepted. 17 Rue St-Antoine, Albi (phone: 63-54-04-04; fax: 63-47-10-47; telex: 520850). Expensive.

La Réserve – A plush 24-room country hotel, recently named a member of the Relais & Châteaux group, just outside town at the edge of the Tarn Gorge. A swimming pool and tennis courts are on the property. Reservations are necessary at its fine restaurant. Both the hotel and restaurant are closed from November 1 to March 31. Reservations essential. Major credit cards accepted. Rte. de Cordes; phone: 63-60-79-79; fax: 63-47-63-60). Expensive.

Relais Gascon – At the edge of the Old City and just off a large *place* with ample parking, this 17-room inn also is a good value; it houses the *Auberge Landaise* (see *Eating Out*). Major credit cards accepted. 1 Rue Balzac, Albi (phone: 63-54-26-51). Moderate.

Parc – There are 20 simple but very comfortable rooms in this small hotel, just around the corner from the city's lush Rochegude Park. The rooms offer particularly good value for the money. 3 Av. du Parc, Albi (phone: 63-54-12-80). Inexpensive.

EATING OUT: *Auberge Landaise* – The flavor and spirit of Gascony live in this cozy, wood-beamed *auberge,* where you can dine on foie gras, *magret de canard* (breast of duck), and other hearty, satisfying specialties of the Landes and Gers regions. Closed Sunday evening and Monday afternoon. Major credit cards accepted. 3 Rue Balzac, Albi (phone: 63-54-26-51). Moderate.

La Viguière d'Alby – A tiny, homey place in the old part of town, it is filled with lace-draped tables, grandfather clocks, and vases of flowers. The food is simple and good — like dining at Grandma's or a favorite aunt's house. Closed Wednesdays. Visa accepted. 7 Rue Toulouse-Lautrec, Albi (phone: 63-54-76-44). Inexpensive.

CORDES: Travel about 16 miles (26 km) northwest on D600 through pastoral countryside to the medieval town of Cordes, often called Cordes-sur-Ciel (Cordes on the Sky) because of its dramatic location on the crest of a steep hill. It's also called La Dame en Pierre ("The Woman in Stone") because of the lovely stone structures that line its steep, narrow streets. The city is surrounded by five sets of protective walls. The Counts of Toulouse built their hunting lodges on this hill in the early 13th century. Later, Count Raymond VII fortified the town, making it a stronghold against the advances of Simon de Montfort and a place of refuge for the Cathari. After the turmoil of the Albigensian Crusade, the city prospered and grew into a center for leatherwork and weaving. During the 16th century it again offered refuge, this time to the Catholics, who in 1568 were attacked and overrun by the Protestants here. In later centuries, as a result of the bubonic plague and several wars, the town was virtually abandoned until Prosper Mérimée, the inspector of historical monuments under Louis-Philippe, ordered its restoration. Among its structures are some of the finest examples of Gothic civil architecture in France. Particularly beautiful are the old hunting lodges and the grand façades of homes built during the city's heyday. Today, a handful of artists and craftspeople have boutiques here, and there are pleasant cafés and hotels. Although you can drive into the city, the streets are very narrow and maneuvering is difficult. It's best to leave your car in one of the lots near the entrance to the city and explore on foot. For information, stop by the tourist office (Town Hall; phone: 63-56-00-52); closed from mid-September to *Easter*.

CHECKING IN: *Le Grand Ecuyer* – This magnificent medieval edifice, once the hunting lodge of Count Raymond VII of Toulouse, has 12 large, elegant rooms, some with fireplaces and all furnished with antiques. The warmly lighted lounge and restaurant with their carved wood pieces and stone walls are grand and welcoming, and Yves Thuries's creative cuisine has won him a Michelin star. Closed mid-October to mid-March; restaurant closed Mondays off-season. Major credit cards accepted. On the tiny, unnamed, cobblestone main street, Cordes (phone: 63-56-01-03; fax: 63-56-16-99; telex: 530955). Expensive.

Cité – A very small hotel (only 8 rooms) but also very quiet and comfortable. Major credit cards accepted. On the main street, Cordes (phone: 63-56-03-53). Moderate.

En Route from Cordes – Return to Albi and take D999 east toward Millau. You'll see a gradual change in the scenery from the vineyards, green farmland, and hills around Albi as you move into the region known as Les Causses, roughly translated as "the chalky lands." Here the land has been pushed up by the same cataclysmic shifting of continents that produced the Pyrénées, forming in this area great plateaus and mesas not unlike those in Arizona and New Mexico. The Causses dominate the landscape, rising dramatically above the surrounding valleys and gorges. There are many caves here that once were inhabited by prehistoric man. The limestone plateaus are arid and largely uninhabited except for herds of about 1 million *brebis,* the sheep whose rich milk produces flavorful cheeses such as the famous roquefort. The road passes near Roquefort-sur-Soulzon, a dreary, minuscule town huddled against a gigantic mass of fallen rock known as Mount Combalou, whose caves' unique atmosphere produces the only blue-veined cheese in the world allowed to be called roquefort. Cheese is the town's only product, the huge, rather glum factory its main tourist attraction. The factory tour is somewhat anticlimactic, however, as the cheese is only aged here; it is fabricated in small lots throughout the region. Since there usually is a very long line to get into the caves, this stop might well be bypassed by all but the true *fromage*-ophile. If you do decide to visit, turn off D999 onto D23 just after St-Affrique, about 50 miles (80 km) from Albi.

CHECKING IN/EATING OUT: *Grand Hôtel* – The wonderful (one Michelin star) restaurant merits a stay at this 16-room hotel with a rustic decor. Try the *filet de caneton dans le jus de truffes* (duckling in truffle sauce). Closed Sunday dinner and Monday in off-season and from November through March. Major credit cards accepted. Roquefort-sur-Soulzon (phone: 65-59-90-20). Moderate.

MILLAU: Millau sits placidly at the confluence of the Tarn and the Dourbie rivers in a rich green valley rimmed with the limestone walls and forested slopes of the Causses. The largest city in the Causses and the western gateway to the magnificent Gorges du Tarn, it is an excursion center filled with a holiday spirit in summer. The Romans settled here in 121 BC near a rich bed of very fine clay that ancient craftspeople fashioned into the pottery known as Graufesenque, famous throughout the Roman world. Digs in the area have turned up many examples of this red glazed pottery, which also has been found in Italy (near Pompeii), Germany, and Scotland. Since the 12th century Millau has been known for fine leatherwork, particularly gloves made from the skins of the mountain sheep that produce the cheeses of the area. The city still produces about a third of the gloves made in France as well as a vast array of other leather goods that can be purchased in the many shops that line Millau's commercial streets. Although there are some sights of interest — the Eglise Notre-Dame, the 12th-century Gothic belfry, the archaeological museum with a collection of Graufesenque pottery, and the quaint old section of town — Millau's real appeal is its scenic location, its pleasant arcaded squares, and its unhurried pace of life. For more information, contact the tourist office, 1 Av. Alfred-Merle (phone: 65-60-02-42).

CHECKING IN: La Musardière – This 120-year-old hotel, a former *maison particulière,* truly retains the atmosphere of an elegant private home, with a grand central stairway and 12 large, individually furnished bedrooms. The lively patroness, Mme. Giselle Canac, completes the "at home" feeling. Her plush dining room offers traditional fare. Closed from November to *Easter.* Major credit cards accepted. 34 Av. de la République, Millau (phone: 65-60-20-63; fax: 65-61-02-05). Expensive to moderate.

L'International – Although this establishment has more than 100 rooms, service is very personalized. Rooms on higher floors have breathtaking views. The restaurant (closed Sunday afternoons in off-season and Mondays) features typically French dishes. Major credit cards accepted. 1 Pl. de la Tine, Millau (phone: 65-60-20-66; fax: 65-59-11-78; telex: 520629). Moderate.

Château de Creissels – On a hill overlooking Millau (a mile/1.6 km or so west via D992) is this old château with a crenelated tower, 30 rooms, comfortable lounges, and a garden where guests take breakfast. The dining room is under the warm stone vaulting of the oldest part of the castle, which dates from the 8th century. The rooms are simply furnished but quite comfortable and a particularly good value. Closed January and February; restaurant is closed on Tuesdays. Major credit cards accepted. Creissels (phone: 65-60-16-59; fax: 65-61-02-05). Moderate to inexpensive.

EATING OUT: Buffet de France – Next to the train station in what at first appears to be a cafeteria (it was once the *buffet de la gare*), this restaurant is a diamond in the rough, serving carefully prepared specialties such as *coufidou de boeuf millavoise* (Millau-style braised beef), *ris de veau à la rouergate* (veal sweetbreads Rouergue-style), *foie frais de canard aux raisins* (duck liver with grapes), and *truite meunière* (sautéed trout). It's much more than what one might expect from the "buffet" appellation. There is a pleasant covered dining terrace in back. Closed Tuesdays — except in July and August. Most major credit cards accepted. Pl. de la Gare, Millau (phone: 65-60-09-04). Moderate to inexpensive.

En Route from Millau – Follow D110 northeast about 9 miles (14 km) to the Chaos de Montpellier-le-Vieux, an extraordinary group of bizarre rock formations built up over centuries by the slow dripping of water on the surface of the Causse Noir. This rock forest in the middle of nowhere looks, from a distance, somewhat like a city in ruins; it once was feared by the inhabitants of the area as a cursed place haunted by the devil. Signs for the Chaos lead from the main road to the Auberge du Maubert, in a clearing, where one can purchase tickets before driving a couple of miles (3 km) farther to a parking lot at the entrance. A walk through this rock labyrinth takes about 1½ hours. Signposts guide you past these masses of tall rocks shaped (at least to some eyes) like bears, sphinxes, and other creatures. One is even labeled Queen Victoria, although it takes some imagination to see the resemblance. This area is open to visitors from *Easter* through November 1.

GORGES DU TARN: From Montpellier-le-Vieux travel northeast on D110 to D29, to Le Rozier. There pick up D907 north, which for the next 30 miles (48 km) or so winds its way through the Gorges du Tarn, one of the most extraordinarily scenic stretches of country in all of France. Like the Causses, these gorges probably were formed at the same time as the Pyrénées, the gigantic shifting of land causing this limestone plateau at the southern extreme of the Massif Central to split apart. The River Tarn, flowing down from Mont-Lozère in the Cévennes range, ran into the giant fissure and over millions of years carved its deep dramatic path through these canyons. The road snakes along the Tarn in the shadow of sheer limestone cliffs and magnificent rock formations towering high above the riverbed. A number of quaint villages are nestled amid these canyons, lost in another time, with rustic *auberges* and cozy restaurants. Some of the most beautiful rock formations are found around Les Vignes, one of the first villages you'll encounter. For a magnificent vista of the gorges, take the small side road at the village up a hill to Point Sublime, some 1,320 feet above the river. A little farther is the town of La Malène, the starting point for one of several boat trips through the gorges; this one leads through the beautiful *détroits* (straights) and the Cirque des Baumes, a circular rock formation inaccessible by car. A couple of miles past La Malène on D907 is one of the loveliest hotels in the gorges, the 15th-century *Château de la Caze* (see *Checking In/Eating Out*), worth a look even if you don't plan to spend the night.

At a northern loop in the river a bit farther along D907 is the medieval village of Ste-Enimie, a particularly picturesque place with lively cafés and shops. There is an ancient convent with a Romanesque chapel, said to have been built by Ste-Enimie, a young noblewoman who was cured of leprosy at this spot and thereafter devoted her life to God. See the Burle Fountain, whose waters cured the saint, and the grotto chapel in the rocks above the village. There also is a small medieval museum.

From Ste-Enimie, a short southern detour via D986 (about 16 miles/26 km) leads to the grottoes of Aven Armand, whose exceptional stalagmites reaching as high as 99 feet are said to be the most magnificent in this grotto-rich area. Then return to Ste-Enimie to complete the circuit of the Gorges du Tarn, following the windings of the river, along D907 and N106, to Florac, the eastern gateway to the gorges. From here follow the sinuous N106 down through the Cévennes range, the beautiful, wild, green mountains that Robert Louis Stevenson traveled through on a donkey more than 100 years ago. Continue southeast on N106 to Nîmes, about 60 miles (96 km) away.

CHECKING IN/EATING OUT: *Château de la Caze* – This wonderful, pale stone château, built in the 15th century, sits in a low meadow on the banks of the Tarn under the shadow of a tremendous looming rock. The mood is late medieval and tranquil, the large rooms are decorated with antiques, and the restaurant's food is very good. The hotel is closed from October 30 to May 1; restaurant closed on Thursdays. Major credit cards accepted. La Malène (phone: 66-48-51-01; fax: 66-48-55-75). Expensive.

NÎMES: Although this appealing southern city lies in the area still generally considered to be the Languedoc, its mood and pace are much like that of neighboring Provence. There is a certain sweetness of life here, heightened by the physical beauty of the city, with its wide tree-lined boulevards and its remarkable monuments. Nîmes often is called the French Rome, and for good reason: Two Roman emperors were born here, and the city is generously endowed with magnificent remnants — most notably an imposing stone temple called the Maison Carrée and a 21,000-seat amphitheater — of the prosperous Roman settlement that grew up around a sacred spring here a century before Christ. This spring was said to have been frequented by the god Nemausus — whence the city's name was derived.

The first glimpse of Nîmes's double-arched stone amphitheater in the center of town is arresting, recalling chariot races and gladiator games. Built early in the 1st century AD, it looks very much like a smaller version of the Colosseum in Rome. It is one of the best preserved of the some 70 amphitheaters known to have been built by the Romans and ranks 20th in size in that group. Visitors can ramble at will through the galleries of the arena, which still is used for bullfights in May and September, during the town's two most colorful annual festivals, and for other public events. In the winter months the arena is covered with a rather ugly inflated plastic roof. Sporting matches and various shows are offered in the air conditioned atmosphere.

Not far away on the Place de la Comédie is the *Maison Carrée,* built in the 1st century AD; the temple is in exceptionally good condition, perhaps the best preserved of its style in existence. It now is a museum containing Roman artifacts, including a statue of Apollo, found during excavations of the area. The square around the *Maison Carrée* is constantly being dug up and new Roman and post-Roman artifacts found. Less well preserved but no less evocative of Roman times is the Temple of Diana in the beautiful Jardin de la Fontaine (Fountain Garden). The name of this crumbling remnant of what was a much larger structure is unfounded, as there is no proof to whom it was dedicated or even for what it was used, though many chroniclers feel it was part of the city's public baths, where there are some interestingly graphic 17th- and 18th-century stone carvings high up on the walls. To the north is the Tour Magne, a watchtower, on Mont-Cavalier; climbing the 140 steps to the top offers not only a good workout but also a splendid view of the city and its environs. This was the biggest of the towers built into the walls surrounding the Roman city and dates from about the 1st century BC. The Porte d'Auguste (Gate of Augustus), also called Porte d'Arles, and other remnants of the old ramparts — the longest in Gaul, they extend more than 4 miles — are visible around the city. The Castellum (Roman water tower), which received the town's water supply via an aqueduct from Uzès, is on Rue Lampeze, east of Mont-Cavalier. The graceful Pont du Gard, 13 miles (21 km) northeast of Nîmes, is all that remains of the aqueduct.

In addition to these awesome Roman souvenirs, the city has numerous monuments to more modern times: the Jardin de la Fontaine, the Eglise St-Perpétue, the Palais de Justice built by Gaston Bourbon, and the Esplanade, with a fountain designed by Jacques Pradier. All date from around the mid-19th century. Place d'Assas has been rebuilt, giving Nîmes a small and curious sculpture garden. In the 18th and 19th centuries, Nîmes was famous for its textile production and "bleu de Nîmes," a sturdy cloth now known as denim. Nîmes also has some fine museums, including a fine arts museum, a natural history museum, an archaeological museum, and the *Musée du Vieux-Nîmes* (Pl. de la Cathédrale), formerly the episcopal palace, which displays a fine collection of 17th- and 18th-century furniture. Colorful parades, dancing in the streets, and corridas (bullfights) take place in May and September during the city's annual spring and harvest festivals, and in July there are opera and jazz festivals. A *Festival des Santons* (the quaint clay figurines of Provence used in creating *Christmas* crèches) takes place during the second and third weeks of November in the nearby town of Garons. For information, contact the tourist office (6 Rue Auguste; phone: 66-67-39-11; or 3 Pl. des Arènes; phone: 66-21-02-51)..

CHECKING IN/EATING OUT: *Imperator* – An elegant dowager facing the lovely Jardin de la Fontaine, there are 2 suites and 59 large rooms, a gracious lobby, and a delightful garden where guests can dine in the summer. Its restaurant, *Enclos de la Fontaine,* one of the city's most highly rated, serves fine and inventive fare — for example, *rouget* (red mullet) with leeks and thyme, and lightly sauced *feuilleté de légumes* (vegetable-filled pastry) — all in plush surroundings. Major credit cards accepted. Quai de la Fontaine, Nîmes (phone: 66-21-90-30; fax: 66-67-70-25; telex: 490635). Expensive.

Le Vieux Castillon – This member of the Relais & Châteaux group offers 33 splendid guestrooms and 2 suites in a medieval setting overlooking the impressive Pont-du-Gard. Its dining room serves first-rate fare, such as roasted lamb with garlic, and fresh cod served in lime. There is a beauty salon on the premises, as well as a pool, tennis courts, and nearby golf facilities. Closed from early January through early March. Pont-du-Gard, on D228, Remoulins (phone: 66-37-00-77). Expensive to moderate.

Cheval Blanc – This traditional 40-room hotel has a restaurant with a pleasant shrub-enclosed dining terrace facing the Roman amphitheater. The traditional one-star menu includes specialties of the Landes and Gers regions: *magret de canard* (breast of duck), *confit* (preserved duck), and, in summer, light fish dishes. 1 Pl. des Arènes, Nîmes (phone: 66-67-20-03). Moderate.

Le Louvre – Located on a lovely little square in a 17th-century building, this 36-room hotel also has a restaurant that offers a variety of traditional dishes. Restaurant closed most Sundays. Major credit cards accepted. 2 Pl. de la Couronne (phone: 66-67-22-75). Moderate.

En Route from Nîmes – Before continuing southeast to Montpellier via A9, take a short northeastern detour on N86 to the Pont du Gard aqueduct near Remoulins. This remarkable piece of Roman architecture was built in the 1st century BC to carry Nîmes's water supply from a spring in the medieval town of Uzès, about 12 miles (19 km) north. Visitors can walk across all levels of the 3-tiered, arched stone structure that spans the Gardon River. Those afraid of heights should definitely avoid walking on the roof of the top tier. The bottom tier has 6 arches, the middle tier 11, and the top tier, which carried the water, has 35 arches. Weekdays, stop and have a drink of Perrier at Vergéze, 10 miles (16 km) from Nîmes (phone: 66-87-62-00).

MONTPELLIER: The capital of Bas Languedoc and an important university town, Montpellier is a busy and animated metropolis whose wide avenues, tree-lined promenades, and superb 17th-century public monuments give it a grace and charm unmatched by other cities in the region. In recent years, ultramodern structures such as the multilevel *Polygone Shopping Center,* on Place de la Comédie, have added a new dimension to this vital city. The area was settled in the 9th and 10th centuries by spice merchants engaged in trade with the East, and it remained a dominant Mediterranean trading center until Provence, with its major port of Marseilles, became part of France in 1481. The first French medical school was established here around the beginning of the 13th century, an outgrowth of the herb and spice trade, whose merchants were aware of the therapeutic qualities of their plants and who nurtured a curiosity about medicine. One of the school's most famous graduates was François Rabelais, who studied here in the 1530s. Some of the original buildings, dating to the 14th century, are still in use (Rue de l'Université).

The university area is the oldest section of town, and its crooked streets are lined with ancient stone dwellings and the elaborately decorated *hôtels particuliers* of wealthy 17th- and 18th-century merchants. Near the medical school is the former chapel, now the Cathédrale St-Pierre, the only church in Montpellier not completely demolished during the devastating Wars of Religion. The cathedral was built in 1364 and, though restored in the 17th and 19th centuries, it retains a fortress-like façade, with romantic stone towers and a vaulted entrance. Next door, in a 14th-century structure, is the *Musée Atger,* which has a collection of baroque drawings.

Across Boulevard Henri-IV from the cathedral and the museum is the Jardin des Plantes, France's first botanical garden (1593). The boulevard leads to the Promenade du Peyrou, the exquisite 17th-century public garden and promenade that sit at the crest of the hill on which the city was built. At one end is the Arc de Triomphe, built in 1691 to honor Louis XIV; an equestrian statue of the Sun King stands in the center of the gardens; and at the opposite end is the Corinthian-columned Château d'Eau de Peyron, a superb decorative structure perched on the highest point of the promenade like the crowning flourish on an ornate wedding cake. It cleverly conceals the tank in which the city's water supply was stored after being transported via an aqueduct from a spring 9 miles (14 km) away. From this point, the view of Montpellier and the surrounding area is superb. On a clear day, the sparkling Mediterranean coast is visible. On Tuesdays there is a colorful flower market under the arches of the aqueduct beside the Promenade du Peyrou.

The town's center of activity is the Place de la Comédie, a giant marble plaza surrounded by outdoor cafés. Nearby is the tree-lined Esplanade and the *Musée Fabre*, with a rich collection of paintings and sculpture, including the works of Ingres, David, Delacroix, Courbet, Houdon, and Barye. Among the many beautiful *hôtels particuliers* that stud the old sections of town, the 18th-century Hôtel de Rodez-Bénavent is perhaps the loveliest. A 5-minute walk from the Place de la Comédie brings you to Montpellier's link to the past — Antigone. A 60-acre re-created metropolis, Antigone is being built by Spanish architect Ricardo Bofill in somewhat oversized classic architectural style, using modern materials. The last sections are scheduled for completion in 1994, when it will house various cultural institutions and will accommodate 10,000 people. For more information, contact the tourist office at Triangle, a modern structure just off Place de la Comédie (78 Av. du Pirée; phone: 67-58-67-58). There also are several beaches within a couple of miles of Montpellier, and sparkling new resorts are just a short drive east. Other sites worth an excursion include Pic St-Loup, 14 miles (22 km) north via D986 to D113, and the Grotte des Demoiselles (Grotto of the Fairies), 12 miles (19 km) farther along D986. St. Loup Peak rises 2,171 feet at the end of a long, stark ridge and provides a stunning panorama of the area. The grotto, discovered in 1770, is filled with white calcite stalactites and stalagmites; one formation, "La Vierge et l'Enfant," is said to resemble the Virgin, and the largest cavern, with just a short leap of the imagination, could be a huge cathedral with a ceiling that soars 165 feet overhead. The cave is open daily.

 CHECKING IN: *Noailles* – This romantic hostelry, a former 17th-century *hôtel particulier,* is a treasure, not only for its vaulted stone lobby and lounge and its delightfully furnished rooms (some overlooking the Esplanade) but also for its extremely reasonable rates. It's on a tiny street in the charming Aiguillerie quarter of Old Montpellier. Closed December 22 to January 18. Major credit cards accepted. 2 Rue des Ecoles-Centrales, Montpellier (phone: 67-60-49-80; fax: 67-66-08-26). Moderate.

 EATING OUT: *Chandelier* – Wonderful seafood specialties are featured at this very pleasant, often-recommended restaurant that has earned one Michelin star. Closed Sundays and Monday lunch. Major credit cards accepted. 3 Rue Leenhardt, Montpellier (phone: 67-92-61-62). Moderate.

Le Vieil Ecu – A warm, homey little place tucked away on a small square in the old part of the city. The tables and chairs are all moved outdoors in summer. Its varied but simple menu includes many fish and seafood dishes. Closed Sundays, Monday lunch, and February. Visa accepted. 1 Rue des Ecoles-Laiques, Montpellier (phone: 67-66-39-44). Moderate.

En Route from Montpellier – Before traveling south along the Languedoc coast, take a short detour east via D21 and D62 to the resorts of the lagoon area known as the Camargue (see *Provence,* DIRECTIONS). Most of this region was mosquito-infested swampland until the 1960s, when the government, hoping to reduce pressure on the overcrowded Riviera, decided to dredge these lagoons and create eight new resorts at the southwest corner. La Grande-Motte, 12 miles (19 km) from Montpellier, is the most famous of these developments; its beaches now are lined with the futuristic pyramidal hotels and apartment buildings that have come to symbolize the project. Although the architecture is somewhat jarring, the beaches here are wide and sandy and very crowded in July and August. Some of the dried-up swamps have been refilled to conserve their unique flora and fauna.

Continue east on D62 another 9 miles (14 km) to Aigues-Mortes, a medieval remnant in sharp contrast to the modern development. This western edge of swampy Camargue Regional Natural Park stands out against a flat background. Visitors can walk around the massive ramparts and towers of this fortified city founded by Louis IX (St-Louis), who set off on his first crusade in 1248 from this port. Up to the middle of the 14th century, the city rivaled nearby Marseilles, but the receding sea and development of Sète Port turned Aigues-Mortes into only a local agricultural center. As it was not near major roads, it escaped the destruction of war and is one of the most authentic remnants of the Middle Ages. The largest tower, Tour de Constance, was used as a prison.

Return to Montpellier and travel west on N109, then north on D32 and D27 (about 25 miles/40 km) to another fascinating antiquity, St-Guilhem-le-Desert, a small village of warm yellow stone houses and narrow streets curiously wedged into the mouth of the Gorges de l'Hérault. The town, somewhat reminiscent of Les Baux-de-Provence, is grouped around a beautiful old abbey, part of the cloisters of which were dismantled by the American sculptor George Grey Barnard in 1906 and re-created as the *Cloisters* (a museum) in New York City overlooking the Hudson River. Nearby is the Grotte de Clamouse, with its dramatically lighted interior.

SÈTE: Take A9 south from Montpellier to Sète, a delightful fishing port and resort on a spit of land reached by a narrow causeway. Curiously set on and around Mont-St-Clair and lined with canals, it once was Montpellier's access to the sea. Sète was granted free trade status by Louis XIV in the 17th century and prospered as the fifth most important port in France until the mid-19th century. Today Sète is both an important port for car-ferry crossings to North Africa and a fishing center. The seafood in its restaurants is renowned. It's definitely worth a stop for a meal or simply a plate of oysters in any of the simple, outdoor open fish restaurants that line the Quai de Bosc. For more refined ambience and more elaborate presentation, try *Palangrotte* (1 Rampe Paul-Valéry; phone: 67-74-80-35). Closed January, 1 week in November, Sunday evenings, and Mondays in off-season. Moderate.

Route A9 continues south to Narbonne.

NARBONNE: In Roman times, this peaceful, slow-paced city was a key Mediterranean port and the capital of Gallia Narbonensis, a large and flourishing Roman province that stretched all along the coast and inland toward Carcassonne. Later it served as a base for the Visigoth kings. When its port silted up in the 14th century, the city's fortunes waned, but it remained an important religious center, evidenced by its beautiful cathedral and archbishop's palace. The building of the Cathédrale St-Just, Narbonne's most impressive monument, began in 1272, but the interior never was completed. Nonetheless, its high Gothic choir is, at 135 feet, one of the tallest in France, surpassed only by those in the cathedrals in Amiens and Beauvais. A 14th-century cloister connects the cathedral to the archbishop's palace, which today has two museums, one of art and history, another of archaeology, as well as the Hôtel de Ville (Town Hall) that was rebuilt by Viollet-le-Duc in 1840. The beautifully ornamented palace was built between the 10th and the 17th century. The lapidary museum (on Pl. Lamourguier) is also worth a visit. Stop at the tourist office (Pl. R. Salengro; phone: 68-65-15-60) for information.

Narbonne vies with nearby Béziers for supremacy on the rugby field and as the center of the region's flourishing wine trade; the Maison Vigneronne (a former Dominican church), near the cathedral, has regular exhibits on wine production. The wide boulevards, pleasant parks, and Mediterranean mood make the city an appealing stop on the route south. Narbonne-Plage, a sandy beach lined with small hotels and holiday homes, is about 8 miles (13 km) east via D168 through the rugged hills of the coast. Autoroute A9 continues south from Narbonne to Perpignan.

CHECKING IN/EATING OUT: _Relais du Val d'Orbieu_ – A charming 15-room country inn with a fine restaurant. Hotel closed in February; restaurant closed Sunday evenings; both the hotel and restaurant are closed from December 27 through March 1. Major credit cards accepted. Ornaisons (phone: 68-27-10-27; fax: 68-27-52-44). Expensive.

En Route from Narbonne – About 9 miles (14 km) southwest via N113, D613, and a small unmarked road is the solitary late-11th-century Cistercian abbey of Fontfroide. This harmonious ensemble of Romanesque church, beautiful cloister, and stone abbey is hidden away in a grove of cypresses and poplars surrounded by a wild, deserted valley. The stained glass windows are a modern addition. Farther south on N9, near the town of Sigean, is the Réserve Africaine de Sigean, a drive-in wildlife park with Tibetan bears, white rhinoceroses, prides of lions, birds, and other animals living on the edge of a saltwater lagoon.

PERPIGNAN: The last important metropolis before the Spanish border, Perpignan is a city whose heart, soul, and history are divided. Culturally, linguistically, and to a certain extent commercially, it is tied to Catalonia, the distinctive region that encompasses both sides of the border from Perpignan to Barcelona. Its loyalties, in fact, seem stronger to Catalonia than to France, and though certainly not totally Spanish in character, the city cannot be said to be totally French either.

Perpignan and the surrounding Roussillon territory, of which it was the fortified capital, bounced back and forth between France and Spain for hundreds of years. It wasn't until the Peace of the Pyrénées, signed by Louis XIV in 1659, that they shifted permanently into the French domain.

The 20th century has brought a new prosperity to this once poor and war-torn area. Since 1914, the city of Perpignan has almost tripled in population (now 115,000). Its economic vitality comes chiefly from the orchards and vineyards of the surrounding plains and coastal area, which now supply a significant share of France's fruit and table wines. Though the area's fertile valleys have produced wine for centuries, during the past few decades local cooperatives have made great strides in dispelling their image as producers of "plonk" by making wines of considerable quality. Perpignan also has renewed its past academic glories. In 1954, its 600-year-old university was reopened after being closed for almost 200 years.

Throughout Perpignan the Spanish influence is apparent, from the orange and yellow Catalonian flag that flies proudly throughout the city to the clean white stucco dwellings with bougainvillea-laced wrought-iron balconies. But the most stunning souvenir of Spanish rule is the immense Palais des Rois de Majorque (Palace of the Kings of Majorca) on the right bank of the River Têt, and a tour of the city might well start at this formidable Gothic fortress enclosed by ramparts. A long, curving ramp under brick vaulting leads to the upper level, where a lovely garden and an elegant arcaded inner courtyard are surrounded by great meeting halls and two Gothic chapels. The top of the palace keep offers a lovely view of the city.

From the palace, it's only a short walk north to the heart of the Old City. The tourist association gives a walking tour of this area every afternoon from June to September, starting from its offices at Palais des Congrès (Pl. A.-Lanoux; phone: 68-66-30-30). The first stop is the Castillet, an elegant red brick fort-like château built in 1368, originally the gateway to the town and later a prison. Today it houses the _Casa Païral,_ a museum devoted to the arts and traditions of the Catalan culture. Nearby is the paved pink marble Place de la Loge, the animated center of the old city, still a favored meeting place and the spot where on summer nights residents dance the traditional Catalonian *sardana.* Here also is the lovely 14th-century Gothic Loge de Mer; once the trade exchange, it now has a lively café. Next door is the Hôtel de Ville, a beautiful 18th-century edifice (sections date from the 14th and 16th centuries) whose courtyard shelters Aristide Maillol's graceful bronze statue *The Mediterranean.* Ask the concierge for permission to see the marriage hall, with its magnificent 15th-century Moorish wood ceiling and 19th-century wall paintings. See also the façade of the small 15th-century Palais de la Députation. On a small back street nearby, at 2 Rue des Fabriques d'en Nabot, is the Maison Julia, an exquisite private residence with an interior courtyard encircled by 14th-century Gothic arches and a gallery.

Take Rue St-Jean to Place Gambetta and the Cathédrale St-Jean, founded in 1324 by Sanche, the second King of Majorca. Particularly noteworthy here is a truly lovely treasure in a small chapel near the right entrance, the *Devout Christ,* a haunting wood carving of Christ on the cross, believed to have been made in Germany in the 14th century and brought here 2 centuries later. In this poignant work, Christ's head hangs very near his shoulders and is said to move infinitesimally closer each year. According to legend, when the head touches his shoulders, the world will come to an end.

Perpignan also has the *Musée d'Histoire Naturelle* (Rue Emile-Zola) and the *Musée Hyacinthe Rigaud,* a block southeast of Place Arago; the latter exhibits paintings of early Catalonian and Spanish masters from the 14th, 15th, and 16th centuries as well as several works by Rigaud, a native of Perpignan who was a 17th-century portrait painter and an official artist for Louis XIV and Louis XV. Ask the tourist association or go to the tourist office (Palais de Congrès; phone: 68-66-30-30) for information about weekly bus tours of the surrounding vineyards. The best way to see them, though, is by car, driving into the valleys of the Têt, the Tech, and the Agley rivers. These lush areas of gently rolling vine-covered hills are among the loveliest sights in the Languedoc. Springs and summers are lively in Perpignan; especially colorful is a procession of Pénitents de la Sanch on *Good Friday,* and during the annual modern dance festival in July.

CHECKING IN: *Park* – This modern hotel with 67 rooms offers comfort and hospitality. Its restaurant, *Le Chapon Fin,* is the best in the city and the only one with a Michelin star. It has a noisy Mediterranean atmosphere and inventive French and Catalan dishes. Restaurant closed Saturday evenings, Sundays, August 1 to September 1, and the first 3 weeks in January. Reservations essential. Major credit cards accepted. 18 Bd. J. Bourrat, Perpignan (phone: 68-35-14-14; fax: 68-35-48-18; telex: 506161). Expensive to moderate.

Aragon – A small, modern hotel near the Palais des Rois de Majorque, it may lack regional charm, but it does have 33 contemporary air conditioned rooms. Visa accepted. 17 Av. Gilbert-Brutus, Perpignan (phone: 68-54-04-46). Moderate.

France – A comfortable, established hotel, it overlooks the Basse River and is only a few feet from the Castillet. The style is traditional French, and the rooms are large and well furnished, some with luxurious, big, beautiful baths. The restaurant here, *L'Echanson,* is highly regarded for traditional brasserie fare. Restaurant closed Saturday evenings and Sundays in July and August. Visa accepted. 16 Quai Sadi-Carnot, Perpignan (phone: 68-34-92-81). Moderate.

EATING OUT: *L'Apero* – An appealing Belle Epoque bistro that serves sophisticated contemporary cooking. Closed Mondays. Visa accepted. 42 Rue de la Fusterie, Perpignan (phone: 68-51-21-14). Moderate.

L'Hostal – This bucolic restaurant definitely is worth the 9-mile (14 km) detour southwest of Perpignan for both the food and the setting. In the fortified hilltop outpost of Castelnou, surrounded by the wild and romantic Roussillon landscape, it is reached via D612 (toward Thuir) and tiny, winding D48. The food is as authentically Catalonian as you'll find in France, featuring the traditional *cargolade,* a feast consisting of snails, local sausages, lamb chops, and *boles de picolat* (spicy meatballs), all grilled outside over aromatic vine branches. After lunch, wander through the winding streets of this walled village, a pedestrians-only unspoiled treasure reminiscent of St-Paul-de-Vence without the crowds. Closed Mondays, Wednesday evenings, January through March 28. Reservations essential. No credit cards accepted. Castelnou (phone: 68-53-45-42). Moderate.

Le Vauban – Simple, well-prepared fare — at very reasonable prices — is served at this brasserie. Closed Sundays. Visa accepted. 29 Quai Vauban, Perpignan (phone: 68-51-05-10). Moderate.

Provence

Quintessentially Mediterranean in landscape, temperament, and culture, the essence of Provence is often more like that of Italy and Spain than that of the rest of France.

Some geographers like to define the northern limits of the Mediterranean region by the latitude where the olive stops growing. Certainly the silver-leaved and gnarled old olive trees are dominant features of the Provençal landscape. So, too, are the umbrella pines and cypresses, almond groves and shady *micocoulier de Provence,* the vineyards, and the arid but fragrant scrubland of wild lavender, thyme, rosemary, and the other familiar *herbes de Provence,* the stone buildings, pastel colors, and Roman tiles. All are characteristic of the Mediterranean's celebrated backcountry. There also is the mistral, the famous northerly wind, which keeps the skies blue and forces farmers to grow cypress ash hedges to protect their fruit trees and vegetable gardens.

The sunny climate, brilliant blue skies, siesta-inducing afternoons, and mellow evenings make for an easygoing folk who, for many visitors, provide a welcome change from the more sober and abrupt temperaments of Paris and the rest of the north of France. Even the leisurely lilt of the Provençal accent seems imbued with the warmth of the climate. The cultural kinship is clear. Beneath the plane trees on a village square in, say, St-Rémy, it's not hard to imagine a Neapolitan *boccie* buff trying to hustle in on the locals' lazy game of *pétanque* — and losing. And if the bullfights at Arles or Nîmes lack some of the elegance of a corrida in Madrid, they make up for it in the grandiose setting of their Roman arenas.

Provence owes much of its Mediterranean flavor to the Romans. While the Celts and Germanic tribes were settling the rest of France, Rome colonized Provence (Provincia Romana) in 125 BC after Marseilles, which was then a Greek trading port, had asked them for help against Ligurian pirates and Gallic tribes in its hinterland. With the first Roman foothold at Aix (Aquae Sextiae), Provence became a vital communications link between Rome's Spanish possessions and Italy.

Emperor Augustus intensified the Roman presence by giving the town of Nîmes to the war veterans who had defeated Anthony and Cleopatra, and the town's coat of arms still bears a symbol of that victory: an enchained Egyptian crocodile. Orange was a center of Roman commercial prosperity, and Emperor Constantine made Arles his home.

Something of a backwater in the Middle Ages, Provence reemerged in the 14th century as a congenial alternative home for the popes, who had fled the turmoils of Italy to set up headquarters at Avignon. While the French kingdom acquired most of the region in 1486, Avignon and the papal lands of the Comtat Venaissin (including Apt, Carpentras, and Cavaillon) remained independent until the French Revolution. During World War II, Provence was part of the *zone libre* (unoccupied zone) until the Germans invaded at the end of 1942.

Even the sunlight figures in the history of the region. The dazzling Provençal light, which drives sane locals into the shade, was the inspiration for Paul Cézanne's most mature realizations. Disgusted with the uncomprehending Parisian art world, he returned to his native Aix-en-Provence and found in the surrounding countryside the inspiration for the powerful and intense colors of his greatest landscapes. For the modern visitor, there's a special joy in seeking out the original locations depicted on those canvases, most notably around the Montagne Ste-Victoire area east of Aix. (Unfortunately, fires during the past several summers, particularly those in 1990, destroyed much of the pine forest here, as in most of southern France).

At the same time, over in Arles, the sun was having its effect on Van Gogh, for whom the contrast with the cooler light of his native Holland was creatively explosive. In his work, the light bursts all over the streets and squares of Arles, the fields outside of town, and the country road to Tarascon. Again, with his famous images in your head, it is a wonderful adventure to try to track down his subjects or their equivalents. All over Provence, even when you're indoors and the morning sun invades your hotel room, you'll be tempted to exclaim "That's a Van Gogh" or, outside in the ocher glow at the end of the afternoon, "Look, pure Cézanne!"

Away from the main roads, the most characteristic Provençal landscapes abound around the lovely Luberon hill villages east and southeast of Avignon and the spectacular springs of Fontaine-de-Vaucluse. Stop for the sweet and indolent life of Gordes, Roussillon, Bonnieux, Ménerbes, and Oppède-le-Vieux, and you may never want to move on.

South of St-Rémy the terrain becomes wilder, more rugged — with stark outcroppings reminiscent of Arizona or New Mexico. These are the last splutterings of the Alpilles, the western end of the Alpine mountain range that begins its great arc on the Adriatic coast of Yugoslavia. The most dramatic spot in the region is the formidable Les-Baux-de-Provence, a medieval fortress high atop a ravine that was held for centuries by robber barons.

While driving around Provence, it's easy to imagine what the Roman Empire must have looked like in its heyday. Ruins are often better preserved here than in Italy: the magnificent theater and triumphal arch at Orange, the grand arenas of Nîmes and Arles, the gigantic aqueduct at Pont du Gard, the ruined houses of Vaison-la-Romaine and St-Rémy. And every now and again you will find yourself trundling along a stretch of original paving from the Via Aurelia, the ancient precursor of a freeway linking Rome and Arles via Genoa, Nice, Aix, and farther west toward Spain.

But summer in Provence is a region-wide celebration of modern culture, attracting the top international stars to the tiniest villages. Apart from the great theater and music festivals in Avignon and Aix, there's opera, ballet, photographic, and choral works in Carpentras, in the amphitheaters of Orange and Vaison, and in the arenas at Nîmes and Arles. In addition to the attraction of first class performances, the settings and atmosphere of a balmy Provençal evening lend a particular magic to the experience.

The festivals usually are held during July and early August, but for the best seats, book tickets (and hotel rooms) by early March, since many European art lovers come here to sunbathe and indulge in culture. Fervent music lovers usually rent a house in one of those Luberon villages for the entire month in order to make the rounds of all the festivals.

While the region's cuisine may lack some of the sophistication and finesse of Lyons's or the richness of Périgord's, it is nonetheless admirably adapted to the sunny, outdoor life found here, with enough "high temples" of gastronomy and examples of innovative culinary arts to satisfy even the most demanding palate.

At almost every table, garlic and ónions dominate — but they're sweet garlic and young onions — joined by tomatoes, green peppers, zucchini, eggplant, and the ubiquitous olives, all marvelously enhanced by the aromatic local herbs. Ratatouille is a hot or cold stew of the whole kit and caboodle. The salads are heaven, and the whole of France swears by the melons of Cavaillon. Fig jam makes a wonderful spread on a breakfast brioche.

Of the seafood coming up fresh from the coast, go for the *daurade* (gilt head), the delicate *rouget* (red mullet), or the royal *loup de mer* (sea bass) served with fennel, or — not to be snubbed — a plate of grilled sardines. Lamb, with the local rosemary, takes pride of place over beef.

The wines have none of the aristocratic pretensions of Burgundy or Bordeaux, but as you come down the Rhône Valley, you'll come across some great croze hermitage and châteauneuf-du-pape reds and some refreshing tavel rosés. In Provence proper, beware of the punch of the splendid gigondas reds before nightfall. A less lethal mid-afternoon drink is a glass of Pernod mixed with plenty of water. When sipped slowly it quenches the thirst and helps conversation.

If you're coming down from Paris, you'll find Provence a strong contrast. Hence we've chosen an itinerary that eases you into the region gently. First, stop just south of Lyons at Valence, then take a 20-mile (32-km) trip down the west bank of the Rhône to a fine hostelry at Baix before taking the aptly named Autoroute du Soleil to the Provençal gateway town of Orange. From there head southeast to the Fontaine-de-Vaucluse, then across to the Lubéron and a circuit covering a couple of hundred miles or so, around Avignon, St-Rémy, the Alpilles, and Les Baux, southwest to Arles, and then slightly southeast again via Salon-de-Provence to end up at Aix in grand style.

The price of a double room in places we list as expensive is around $100 and up; moderate (the large majority), $50 to $100; inexpensive, under $50. The price of dinner for two, with a good local wine, in a restaurant we list as expensive is about $100 and up; in a moderate restaurant, from $50 to $100; and inexpensive, under $50. Service usually is included.

VALENCE: An ideal break in the journey from Paris (the *TGV* will whisk you south of the perpetual traffic jams of Lyons where you can rent a car), this market town is the distribution point for the great fruit and vegetables of the Rhône Valley. Valence provides the first whiff of the good life of the south. François Rabelais spent his student days here in the 15th century, and Valence today pays fitting homage to the gargantuan appetite celebrated in his lusty writings. In a civilization where restaurants rival cathedrals and palaces as national monuments, the town boasts the much revered gastronomic sanctuary, *Pic* (see *Eating Out*).

From the esplanade of the Champ de Mars, there's a fine view across the Rhône River to a ruined château atop the white stone Crussol Mountain, a challenge to any climber — not least of all to Napoleon Bonaparte, who is said to have scaled it when he was a cadet at the Valence Artillery School in 1785. Valence is also the home of l'Arsenal, one of France's oldest gunpowder factories.

At the town museum (*Musée des Beaux-Arts*), south of the austere and over-restored cathedral, there's a fine collection of 18th-century *sanguines* (red chalk drawings) by Hubert Robert that will set the mood of your Provençal trip. His studies of Rome's ancient ruins evoke something of the wistfulness of Provence's imperial monuments.

CHECKING IN: *Hôtel 2000* – Of the town's hotels where efficiency wins out over charm, this one is modern and clean, with the asset of a quiet east side location and breakfast served in the garden. It has 31 rooms, good service, and a restaurant, the *Des Lys* (closed Sundays from November to March). Major credit cards accepted. Av. de Romans, Valence (phone: 75-43-73-01; fax: 75-55-00-95; telex: 345 873). Moderate.

Château d'Urbilhac – Worth the drive to reach this pretty, romantic hideaway that exudes a somewhat faded Provençal charm. All 13 guestrooms are tastefully appointed and unusually cozy, and there is access to nearby tennis courts. Restaurant closed Tuesdays and Thursdays for lunch. Reservations necessary. Major credit cards accepted. Twenty one miles (41 km) northwest of Valence, Rte. de Vernoux, Lamastre (phone: 75-06-42-11). Expensive to moderate.

Hostellerie Beau Rivage – Also worth a drive: A lovely 24-room inn beautifully appointed with French country antiques. Patrons gaze upon the picturesque Rhône river as they dine upon such classic regional dishes as *fleur de courgettes à la mousse de brochet* (zucchini blossoms sautéed in butter) and *côte de boeuf casserole aux échalotes confites* (beef casserole with pickled shallots). Open year-round. Reservations advised. Major credit cards accepted. 2 Rue du Beau-Rivage, 40 miles (60 km) north of Valence on A 7, Condrieu (phone: 74-59-52-24). Expensive to moderate.

EATING OUT: *Chabran* – In an age where fanciful sauces supercede the simple joy of a good meal prepared with finesse, this small establishment deserves more than faint praise. Chef Michel Chabran's artful cooking has recently earned two Michelin stars. From the mouthwatering lobster salad to the braised duck simmered in wine to the terrine of foie gras accompanied by artichokes and zucchini, each dish lingers on as a delicious memory. There is also a creditable wine list. Open year-round. Reservations necessary. Major credit cards accepted. Fifteen miles (25 km) north of Valence, Av. du 45e Parallèle, Pont-de-l'Isère (phone: 75-06-42-11). Expensive.

Pic – For many it's the only, but also a totally justifiable, reason for stopping in or making a trip to Valence. If you can't get a table in the charming shady garden, the dining room is elegant without being overdone in exactly the same way that Jacques Pic's three-Michelin-star cuisine manages to be sumptuous without losing its delicacy and subtlety. There is no routine of "specialties," but langouste salad, sea bass, veal sweetbreads, and ingenious desserts are some of the triumphs of his repertoire. The local côtes du rhône wines are excellent. If you're staying overnight at this member of the Relais et Châteaux group or have time for a siesta, risk the cornucopia of the *menu Rabelais.* Reserve a month or two in advance if you wish to stay in one of the house's 2 beautiful bedrooms or 2 suites. Closed Sunday evenings, Wednesdays, February, and August. Reservations necessary. Major credit cards accepted. 285 Av. Victor-Hugo, Valence (phone 75-44-15-32; fax: 25-40-96-03). Expensive.

En Route from Valence – Before entering Provence proper, coast along the west bank of the Rhône, up in the wooded Vivarais hills of the Col de Ayes and Col de Rôtisson. Take the N532 west over the river to winding D279 and D479, connect with D232 and D266 till you rejoin the N86 highway past orchards of apricot, pear, and peach trees to the pretty little village of Baix. (From there, back up 4 miles/6 km to get on the Autoroute du Soleil, A7, near Le Pouzin, for the 45-minute drive to Orange.)

CHECKING IN/EATING OUT: *Hostellerie la Cardinale* – This charming hotel-restaurant, a member of the Relais & Châteaux group, offers a delightful Rhône view from the flowery waterside terrace while you try the house specialties of *cassolette d'escargots* (snails stewed out of their shells), *lotte* (angler fish) *à l'orange,* and chicken fricassee in tarragon. Besides 5 comfortable rooms in the 17th-century manor house above the restaurant, there are 10 more secluded rooms in an attractive property with a swimming pool in the hills just 2 miles (3 km) up the N86 highway. Open daily; restaurant and hotel closed from the beginning of November to mid-March. Major credit cards accepted. Quai du Rhône, Baix (phone: 75-85-80-40; fax: 75-85-82-07). Expensive to moderate.

***La Beaugravière* –** An unpretentious haven for regional cooking, over which chef Guy Jullien presides. All of the fine fare prepared here is based on classic Provençal recipes, such as *pieds et paquets* (lambs' feet and tripe stuffed with pork, garlic, and parsley) and lamb stew steeped in wine, accompanied by anchovies, capers, and *cornichons*. Jullien's foremost pride is his fine collection of reasonably priced Rhône wines, which only the most stringent teetotalers can avoid. Open year-round. Reservations advised. Most major credit cards accepted. 7 National Route, Mondragon (phone: 90-40-82-54). Moderate.

ORANGE: This is the true beginning of Provence. Cheerful as its name — with a few orange trees in the gardens to legitimize it — the town historically has nothing at all to do with that bright citrus fruit. The name is a corruption of the pre-Roman town of Arausio, which was once dedicated to the Celtic god of the local water source. Orange is charmingly sleepy today, but sleep often is broken by the noise of jet planes flying in and out of a nearby military base. Its magnificently preserved monuments recall its ancient role as a major center of Roman trade. Orange was (and still is) an important agricultural center. For a panoramic view, drive up the Colline St-Eutrope south of town to the park where first Celtic, then Roman, armies had encampments.

On the northern side of town, the Arc de Triomphe dates from 20 BC. Its sculpted reliefs from AD 26-27 on the northern façade commemorate Roman Emperor Tiber's victories over local Gallic tribes and the Greek merchant ships of Marseilles. It stands astride the old Via Agrippa (at this point the N7 highway), once the link between Arles and Rome's Gallic capital at Lyons.

At the foot of the hill, the *Théâtre Antique* (Amphitheater) is a few decades older than the arch and is revered by scholars as the most handsome and best preserved of its kind in the Empire. It is the only one with its monumental scenic wall still standing, complete with a heroic statue of Augustus Caesar at its center. Today, it offers opera lovers a magical backdrop for the summer festival that attracts the world's greatest singers. The acoustics are stunning. Reservations for the July and August festival — opera, symphony concerts, and lieder recitals — begin in mid-January, and tickets are often gone by May; get details and ticket order forms from *Chorégies d'Orange* (Pl. Frères-Mounet; phone: 90-34-24-24) or the tourist office (Cours A.-Briand; phone: 90-34-70-88).

CHECKING IN: *Château de Rochegude* – Eight miles (13 km) from town this small hotel was once a castle that was remodeled in the 18th century and is now a member of the prestigious Relais & Châteaux group. It has 25 rooms, 4 suites, a park, a tennis court, and a swimming pool. Its one-star Michelin restaurant offers regional fare cooked with local herbs as well as Rhône wines. Closed January through February. Major credit cards accepted. Rochegude (phone: 75-04-81-88; fax: 75-04-89-87; telex: 345661). Expensive.

Arène – Terrific value for the money, this hotel is in the center of town and miraculously quiet. The service is intelligent and considerate, and most of the 30 air conditioned, comfortable little rooms have balconies. Closed November to mid-December. Major credit cards accepted. Pl. de Langes, Orange (phone: 90-34-10-95; fax: 90-34-91-62). Moderate.

En Route from Orange – Archaeology buffs may like to head 20 miles (32 km) northeast along the D975 to Vaison-la-Romaine, where the ruins do not have the dramatic impact of the great monuments of Orange or Arles, but the excavated sites do resemble the layout of a Roman town. You'll see its houses and streets, together with a little museum where the more valuable finds are displayed and an explanation of the ruins given. Concerts and operas are held during the summer months in the amphitheater. For information, contact the tourist office (Pl. Abbé-Sautel; phone: 90-36-02-11). Vaison is worth a visit just for the cobblestone Haute Ville medieval quarter huddled around a 12th-century fortress atop the hill above the little Ouvèze River. A 2,000-year-old Roman bridge connects it to the rest of the town. The *Galerie du Vieux Marché* (Haute Ville, Vaison-la-Romaine; phone: 90-36-16-05) sells superb olivewood kitchenware and sculpture by a man with the most un-Provençal name of Niels Christiansen. Closed from mid-November through February.

CHECKING IN: *Domaine de Cabasse* – While the 9 lovely guestrooms of this appealing little inn are quite comfortable, the dining room is considered the main attraction. Chef Nadine Latour prepares succulent selections that range from the classic *bouef en daube* to boiled chicken served with escargot, salted cod, and garlic aioli. Closed Mondays, except in July and August. Reservations advised. Most major credit cards accepted. Rte. de Sablet, 14 miles (22 km) northeast of Orange, Séguret (phone: 90-46-91-12). Moderate.

La Table du Comtat – In a fairy-tale setting amidst medieval stone houses set high on a hill, this tiny establishment houses 8 prettily furnished rooms and a first-tier, one-star restaurant. Among the finer offerings on the menu are truffles with pheasant's eggs and filet mignon and lamb served with peppercorns. Closed Tuesdays and Wednesdays in off-season, and from November 24 to December 4. Reservations advised. Major credit cards accepted. Le Village, Séguret (phone: 90-46-91-49). Moderate.

From Vaison travel on D938 20 miles (32 km) south to Carpentras, home of France's oldest synagogue (signposted near the Hôtel de Ville). The 14th-century structure still has the ritual bath (*mikvah*) in its basement, a baking oven for matzos on the ground floor, and a fine paneled hall of worship upstairs. Before the French Revolution, 20% of the town's population was Jewish; they lived in a walled ghetto and were forced to wear yellow hats.

FONTAINE-DE-VAUCLUSE: This is one of those beautiful natural wonders, like Niagara Falls or Yellowstone's geysers, that have become so popular that they can only really be enjoyed out of season. The mob scene surrounding the gushing springs of the Sorgue River can be hard to take in summer. If possible, visit during the spring or winter, when the waters are both higher and more spectacular. Among lush trees, at a rate of up to 7,000 cubic feet per second, they pour out of a great cavern at the base of a 750-foot-high cliff in marvelous emerald green cascades. The site is a 15-minute walk from the parking lot along the river, which unfortunately is cluttered by a rather ugly collection of restaurants. The Italian poet, Francesco Petrarca (Petrarch), lived in the valley on and off for 25 years. It was here that he wrote of his love for Laura (De Noves) from nearby Avignon.

Nearby, to the west and slightly south of Fontaine-de-Vaucluse, is Ile sur la Sorgue, an island village in the middle of the Sorgue River, noteworthy for its picturesque location and Saturday flea market/antiques fair. The market takes place along the western riverbank every Saturday (in season) and offers some of the best Art Deco pieces to be found in France.

CHECKING IN: *La Maison aux Fruits* – Each of the 4 rooms in this cozy inn has murals that were painted by the owner. The building gets its name from its façade, which sports reliefs of painted fruits. No restaurant. No credit cards. Fontaine-de-Vaucluse (phone: 90-20-39-15). Inexpensive.

LUBÉRON: These rugged mountains at the southern end of the Vaucluse plateau, the villages with their pretty gardens and tasteful boutiques, and a surrounding countryside of fragrant heathland blend to form the classic Provençal landscape, protected here as a national park. It's an area where visitors should get out of the car and walk. Stock up on melons and other picnic goodies at Cavaillon's street market before heading east on the D2. First stop: Gordes. The village's spotless houses, solid *bastides*, and drystone *bories* (stone huts intricately constructed without mortar) hug the hill, which is topped by a medieval and Renaissance château. There is a museum in the château with five rooms devoted to the Hungarian artist Vasarely. (The elongated farmhouses, called *mas*, are seen mainly in the valleys.) The *Musée du Vitrail*, a museum devoted to stained glass (particularly from the Middle East), is nearby on Route de St-Pantaleon (open daily from 10 AM to noon and from 2 to 7 PM; phone: 90-72-22-11). From Gordes, drive a couple of miles north along the winding D177 to a valley of lavender fields and the exquisitely restored 12th-century Cistercian Abbey of Sénanques, now a striking setting for two permanent exhibitions: Symbolism and Architecture; and Desert and Man, Sahara of the Nomads (closed Sunday mornings; phone: 90-75-88-34). Behind the abbey are fragrant and colorful fields of lavender.

Back on the D2, go 7 miles (11 km) east to Roussillon, a provocation for any painter as it rises rust-colored from its wreath of ocher quarries and red cliffs dotted with Mediterranean pines and green oaks. The little D149 heads south across a main road to Bonnieux, again perched on a hill with a terrace behind the Town Hall, from which there's a panorama back across to Roussillon and Gordes. For a good view back at Bonnieux, take the D3 west toward the 15th-century hilltop citadel of Ménerbes (with a pretty 14th-century church on its outskirts), then continue on to the strange but beautiful ruined village of Oppède-le-Vieux, abandoned at the turn of the century, but gradually being restored by painters. Writers come here from all over France for a little peace of mind; the dilapidated 12th-century castle is a melancholy poem all to itself.

CHECKING IN: *Domaine de l'Enclos* – On the northern outskirts of Gordes, this luxurious hotel which changed owners in 1990, comprises a collection of houses clustered around a restaurant. Each of the 9 rooms and 5 apartments is airy and brightly furnished, with its own little garden in front of the window. The view over the Lubéron alone is worth half of the considerable price. The restaurant serves a very sophisticated cuisine using classic Provençal ingredients and those from the nearby sea. There's a tennis court and swimming pool to help work off the considerable calories. Reservations necessary. Major credit cards accepted. Rte. de Sénanque, Gordes (phone: 90-72-08-22; fax: 90-72-03-03; telex: 432119). Expensive.

Mas de Garrigon – Two miles (3 km) north of Roussillon, this inn has only 7 small, very comfortable rooms, charmingly decorated in traditional Provençal style. The big fireplace in the lounge creates the ambience of a large country house. Other features: a swimming pool, horseback riding, a library, and a good restaurant with a nonsmoking section, and lovely view of the countryside from the terrace. Closed Sunday evenings, Mondays, and from mid-November to December 27. Reservations necessary. Major credit cards accepted. Rte. de St-Saturnin-d'Apt, Roussil-lon (phone: 90-05-63-22; fax: 90-05-70-01). Expensive.

Mas des Herbes Blanches – In the very heart of Provence, between Lubéron and Ventoux, this traditional stone house (a member of the Relais & Châteaux group) has 16 rooms and 2 suites, a swimming pool, tennis courts, and a delightful restaurant that offers both nouvelle and classic cuisines. Closed from January 4 to March 8. Reservations necessary. Major credit cards accepted. 1½ miles (2 km) on D102A/Rte. de Murs (phone: 90-05-79-79; fax: 90-05-71-96; telex: 432045). Expensive.

 EATING OUT: La Tarasque – A pleasant bistro in Roussillon proper, with an accent on herb-scented Provençal specialties. Closed Wednesdays and from mid-February to mid-March. Reservations necessary during the week in winter. Major credit cards accepted. Rue Richard-Casteau, Roussillon (phone: 90-05-63-86). Expensive to moderate.

En Route from Luberon: Route N100 takes you west to Avignon (for a detailed report on the city, its sights, hotels, and restaurants, see *Avignon* in THE CITIES).

ST-RÉMY-DE-PROVENCE: The village is one of those Provençal market towns with great charm and more than a little cultural interest in its nearby Roman ruins that is, above all, a simple pleasure in which to relax. Charm has its price, however, and celebrities and international royalty have taken a liking to the region, and frequently congregate here on vacation. It's worth planning at least a couple of days (more, if you get hooked) just to soak up the atmosphere of the carefree daily life: Watch the world go by over a coffee or *pastis* at the *Brasserie du Commerce* on Place de la République; check out the local goat cheeses, olives, almonds, freshest of fruits and vegetables at the market; toss a *boule* or two in a game of *pétanque* with the locals; become, for a brief moment, a St-Rémois. The town's annual *Festival de Musique* begins in mid-July and lasts until the end of September. For more information, contact the tourist office, Pl. Jaurès (phone: 90-92-05-22).

On the southern outskirts of town, down the D5, is the ruined Greco-Roman city of Glanum (signposted as Les Antiques), which dates back to the town's colonization by the Greek merchants of Marseilles in the 3rd century BC. Buildings in the town were constructed using perfectly chiseled stones that were held together by their fit and not by mortar. The city was destroyed by Germanic tribes 600 years later. Its two most important monuments are the mausoleum erected to the memory of Augustus Caesar's grandson and an older, more dilapidated (but still impressive) triumphal arch from the end of the 1st century BC. The rest of the site shows the layout of the town — houses, forum, fountains, and bathhouse. Glanum became St-Rémy after Franc kings gave it to a monastery, St-Rémy de Reims, as a token for the Catholic church's help in obtaining Provence in the 9th century. Back in St-Rémy, in the Hôtel de Sade on Rue du Parage, there's a museum housing the town's sculptural treasures and an archaeological account of Glanum's daily life. The famous astrologist Michel de Nostredame (known as Nostradamus) was born here in 1503. In his work *Centuries* he predicted correctly, among other things, the way in which Henry II of France would die and that a non-Italian would become the pope.

Near the ruins, look for the medieval monastery of St-Paul-de-Mausole, now converted into a sanatorium; self-confined Van Gogh was its most celebrated patient. Visit the graceful Romanesque cloister for a contemplative moment out of the sun.

 CHECKING IN: Château des Alpilles – Five minutes west of town you'll find the peace and quiet of a tastefully modernized country manor on tree-shaded grounds — 16 rooms and 2 suites, with tennis courts, swimming pool, sauna, and a poolside barbecue. Closed mid-January to mid-March and mid-November to December 21. Major credit cards accepted. Rte. D31, St-Rémy-de-Provence (phone: 90-92-03-33; fax: 90-92-45-17; telex: 431487). Expensive.

Le Castelet des Alpilles – No relation to the *Château des Alpilles,* this old, formerly private mansion is a stone's throw from the central square but seems in a world of its own, thanks to tranquil rooms that overlook a soothing garden surrounding the house. Hotel closed from November 1 through March 31; restaurant closed on Mondays and Tuesdays for lunch. Major credit cards accepted. Pl. Mireille, St-Rémy-de-Provence (phone: 90-92-07-21). Moderate to inexpensive.

EATING OUT: *Le Bistrot des Alpilles* – Also not related to the *Château,* this unpretentious old-style eatery offers the best of simple, unadorned Provençal cuisine, with top honors going to that pungent celebration of garlic, the *brandade de morue* — cod cooked in olive oil with garlic, mashed and stirred until it's the texture of mashed potatoes. Two grilled dishes also are excellent — salmon and calf's liver with raisins. There is live jazz on weekend nights. Closed Sundays. Major credit cards accepted. 15 Bd. Mirabeau, St-Rémy-de-Provence (phone: 90-92-09-17). Moderate.

Café des Arts – Not at all fancy, this is a lively local rendezvous for what once might have been described as the town's bohemians. Its walls are decorated with the works of local artists (for sale). The wise stick to the steaks, chops, salads, and omelettes. There also are 17 serviceable rooms upstairs. Closed Wednesdays, the first 2 weeks in November, and February. Major credit cards accepted. 30 Bd. Victor-Hugo, St-Rémy-de-Provence (phone: 90-92-08-50). Moderate to inexpensive.

En Route from St-Rémy-de-Provence – The vineyards, olive, and almond groves around St-Rémy, against the backdrop of the craggy Alpilles mountains, make this great cycling — and hiking — country. (Rent a bike at *Agence Florelia,* 35 Av. de la Libération, St-Rémy; phone: 90-92-10-88.) The St-Rémy Syndicat d'Initiative (tourist office at Pl. Jean-Jaurès; phone: 90-92-05-22) can propose several ambitious tours for experienced cyclists, but for an easy 10-mile (16-km) circuit, head northwest on D5 to Maillane (an exquisite little village and the birthplace of Provençal poet and Nobel Prize winner Frédéric Mistral), returning on D27 across the main N99 highway toward Les Baux, then cutting back east on the Chemin de Roussan to St-Rémy.

By car, drive 2½ miles (4 km) south along the winding D5 south toward Les Baux; make a little detour east to the observation point of La Caume (near a TV relay station) for a magnificent view of the mountains and the Camargue plain west of Marseilles.

LES-BAUX-DE-PROVENCE: This ruined medieval citadel, with an astonishing position high on a promontory of sheer rock ravines, has caves that were first inhabited in 3,000 BC, and overlooks the Provençal plain and the Val d'Enfer (Valley of Hell); it has long been a privileged tourist destination — so much so that, like the Fontaine-de-Vaucluse, it is now a tiresome crush in midsummer. But don't hesitate to visit in spring or autumn — and in winter when it is even more spectacularly desolate. Even in summer, hedonists make the pilgrimage just for the gastronomic indulgences of *L'Oustaù de Baumanière* and its companion *La Cabro d'Or* (see *Romantic French Hostelries* and *Haute Gastronomie,* DIVERSIONS).

This splendid feudal redoubt was defended for centuries by robber barons against French kings and the Avignon popes. As the star of Christ's Nativity on their coat of arms proudly indicates, the original Lords of Les Baux claimed descendance from Balthazar, one of the Three Kings who traveled to Bethlehem. From the 11th to the 15th century, they ruled more than 80 Provençal townships and their court was a center of medieval chivalry. When it became a focus of rebellion for the region's Protestants in the 17th century, Cardinal Richelieu, head of Louis XIII's government council, decided quite simply to do away with the citadel, rubbing salt into the wound by making the residents pay for the demolition of the fortress and ramparts on top of a heavy fine of 100,000 gold coins.

This footnote may partly explain why the job was never completed and why, today, large sections of the baron's 13th-century castle and its chapels are still visible outside the main village, in what is known as the Ville Morte (dead town). Each structure affords superb vantage points overlooking the Val d'Enfer to the east or the Vallon de la Fontaine to the west. The hill on which the fortress stands contains the bauxite mineral to which the town gave its name. Bauxite was discovered in 1822 as raw material for aluminum. The nearby bauxite mine was closed down in 1991. The bottom slopes on the southern side are covered with thousands of olive trees — some planted by the Greeks and Romans — and the oil they produce is considered the best in France.

The "modern" village is in fact a delightful maze of Renaissance houses, with hidden courtyards and gardens. Besides the unavoidable souvenir junk, the myriad boutiques and galleries have their fair share of genuine craftsmanship in olivewood items and patchwork quilts.

CHECKING IN: *L'Oustaù de Baumanière* – Far more elegant than the *Cabro d'Or* (and also a Relais & Châteaux member), this venerable old manor house (a must stop on any well-heeled itinerary) tucked into the rocky crags of the gleaming limestone Alpilles foothills boasts accommodations befitting a prince: fireplaces, vaulted ceilings, tapestries, and four-poster beds in its 11 rooms and 13 suites. In regal settings guests are presented some of the most highly reputed food in France — Michelin has awarded it two stars. *Filets de rougets au vinaigre* (fish filets in a vinegar sauce) and *gigot d'agneau en croûte* (leg of lamb in pastry crust) are among the two-star restaurant's specialties. Closed from mid-January to March; restaurant also closed Wednesdays and for lunch Thursdays during the off-season. Reservations necessary. Major credit cards accepted. Les Baux-de-Provence (phone: 90-54-33-07; in the US, 800-372-1323; fax: 90-54-40-46; telex: 420203). Very expensive.

Cabro d'Or – Despite its fairy-tale setting at the foot of the ancient Cité des Baux, this member of the Relais & Châteaux group offers modern amenities, including TV sets and telephones in each of its 22 rooms; there also is a one-Michelin-star restaurant which serves traditional Provençal food. Closed November 12 through December 21; restaurant closed Tuesday afternoons, and Mondays October 31 through March 31. Reservations necessary. Major credit cards accepted. Les-Baux-de-Provence (phone: 90-54-33-21; fax: 90-54-45-98; telex: 401810). Expensive.

La Benvengudo – A perfectly respectable alternative to the *Cabro d'Or* in a superb secluded setting southwest of the town, this classic Provençal country house offers 17 traditionally furnished rooms and 3 suites with good, big bathrooms. The restaurant does an admirable job with regional products on a rich and varied menu — the bass with *cèpe* mushrooms is a special treat. Restaurant closed Sunday evenings and from November to February. Reservations essential. Visa accepted. Rte. D78F, Les Baux-de-Provence (phone: 90-54-32-54; fax: 90-54-42-58). Expensive to moderate.

Bautezar – If the town is not overcrowded, try this attractive little place with 10 comfortable rooms and a stupendous dining room view past the terrace to the Val d'Enfer and the Vallon de la Fontaine. Closed January and February. Reservations essential. Grande-Rue Frédéric-Mistral, Les Baux-de-Provence (phone: 90-54-32-09). Moderate.

EATING OUT: *Le Bistro du Paradou* – A short drive from Les Baux (east on D17) stands a white house with blue shutters that Jean-Louis and Mireille Pons have transformed into a genuine country bistro-café featuring one daily menu, one wine, and one price — about $20. Daily specials include *lapin à l'ail* *nouveau* (rabbit with fresh garlic) and *gigot d'agneau* served with *gratin de pommes de terre* (leg of lamb with potatoes gratin). Lunch only in off-season. Dinner served July through September. Closed Sundays during school holidays. Visa accepted. Rte. D17, Le Paradou (phone: 90-54-32-70). Inexpensive.

ARLES: A major link in Rome's chain of communications with its Spanish colonies, Arles today uses its imposing ancient arena for colorful bullfights that recall the more brutal sports of the Romans. If you don't visit during the summer bullfight season, be sure to climb the tower beside the entrance for a walk along the roofs of the arena's arches. Imagine the roar of the spectators (capacity 26,000) cheering on the gladiators or taking sides when the lions met the Christians.

Southwest of the arena and a century older, the amphitheater is less well preserved than the one at Orange since it was in great part dismantled in the Middle Ages to build the city's churches. But it still serves as a striking setting for open-air theater, an international photo festival at the beginning of July — when there also are outdoor slide presentations in the Place de Forum — and dance and folklore festivals in the summer.

There is a rare jewel of Provençal Romanesque architecture in the Church of St-Trophime (Pl. de la République), with its beautifully sculpted portal depicting the Last Judgment. Don't miss the church's cloister and the richly carved pillars of the arcade, especially those on the northwest and northeast corners.

Arles was also the home of Vincent Van Gogh in the late 1880s. (The town commemorated his arrival with *Centenaire Van Gogh,* a year-long festival, in 1988.) The artist's house has disappeared, and only the noonday sun baking the surrounding countryside reminds you of his ghost, though one of his subjects remains: the melancholy alley of sarcophagi at the Roman cemetery of Les Alyscamps, in the southwest corner of town.

Picasso loved the town so much that he gave it 57 drawings that are now housed in the *Musée Réattu* (10 Rue du Grand Trieure). The view of the Rhône River from the museum's windows is breathtaking, particularly when the strong mistral is blowing. But perhaps the best time one can have is at Place de Forum: It is a natural place to start the day with morning coffee; the best place to have a light lunch, an obvious spot for a pre-dinner drink, and just about the only watering hole for a nightcap. It's the rendezvous of choice and *tous Arles* comes here to see and be seen at one of the cafés, under the heavy shade of 100-year-old plane trees.

CHECKING IN: *Grand Hôtel Nord-Pinus* – After being closed down for almost a decade, this establishment that used to host toreadors before they went to meet bulls at the arena is again a focal point of bullfighting fans. On its walls stand one of the finest collection of bullfighting posters. Closed from November 15 to March 1. Reservations essential. Major credit cards accepted. Pl. Forum, Arles (phone: 90-93-34-00; fax: 90-93-34-00). Expensive.

Jules César – A large 52-room, 3-suite hotel (a Relais & Châteaux member) converted from a 17th-century convent — complete with a baroque chapel — makes a comfortable old-fashioned stop near the center of town. Besides the room of the Mother Superior, the most coveted are those overlooking the cloister. Its restaurant, the *Lou Marquès,* does fine scrambled eggs with an anchovy and olive *tapenade* and *gigot* of baby lamb. Closed November to December 22. Major credit cards accepted. Bd. des Lices, Arles (phone: 90-93-43-20; fax: 90-93-33-47; telex: 400239). Expensive.

D'Arlatan – Amazingly quiet in the center of town — 30 exquisitely furnished rooms and 11 suites in a medieval and Renaissance building overlook a lovely garden or the swimming pool. Be sure to reserve well in advance during the summer festival months. Major credit cards accepted. 26 Rue du Sauvage, Arles (phone: 90-93-56-66; fax: 90-49-68-45; telex: 441203). Expensive to moderate.

Le Cloître – This modest little place is centrally located, quiet, comfortable, and clean. Several of the 33 rooms face the Cloister of St-Trophime. Major credit cards accepted. 18 Rue du Cloître, Arles (phone: 90-96-29-50; telex: 440096). Inexpensive.

EATING OUT: *Mas de Curé Bourse* – Chef Françoise Donzé serves up tasty fare such as grouper in a red wine sauce, eggplant with tomato *coulis,* and a delectable pear tart in this converted farmhouse. Closed Sundays evenings and Mondays. Reservations advised. Major credit cards accepted. Carrefour de Velorgues, Isle-sur-la Sorgue (phone: 90-38-16-58). Moderate.

Les Vaccarés – Picturesque views overlooking a charming square, a statue of native poet Frédéric Mistral, and a row of stalwart plane trees are some of the delights at this intimate establishment. The fine fare found here is hardly an afterthought; classic dishes such as lamb with garlic and basil and guinea hen with new potatoes crown the menu. And the reasonably priced and handsome wine list only enhances the food. Open daily. Closed Sundays. Reservations advised. Major credit cards accepted. Pl. du Forum, Arles (phone: 90-96-06-17). Moderate.

En Route from Arles – South of Arles on D570 is Camargue National Park, one of Europe's most important wildlife preserves. There are almost 200,000 acres of swamps, shallow lakes, sand dunes, and natural and artificial canals, spread across the estuary of the Rhône. Although summer visitors disturb the various wildlife — pink flamingos, wild horses, Camargue bulls, birds, and fish — they still manage to thrive in these lowlands. Two cities dominate the Camargue swamps — Saintes-Marie-de-la-Mer in the south and Aigues-Mortes in the southwestern corner (see *The Languedoc,* DIRECTIONS).

Legend has it that the three Marys — Mary Magdalene, Mary Jacob, Mary Salome — and Sarah, their Egyptian servant — landed in this area in a boat with no sails or oars, steered by the divine hand. In the 15th century, a chapel was built and the local Gypsies began to worship the three Marys and Sarah. Twice a year — at the end of May and the end of October — Gypsies from all over Europe gather here to pay homage to Sarah, their patron saint. Contact the tourist office (Av. Van-Gogh; phone: 90-97-82-55) for information.

Return to Arles. Heading east toward Aix on N113 to the autoroute, stop at Salon-de-Provence, which commands the expressway entrance. Though in many ways it's an unexceptional southern town, it is interesting to see how the region's handsome ocher sandstone has been ingeniously used to blend the modern architecture of its boutiques, cafés, and apartments with the old castle towering above them, Empéri, first built in the 10th century and rebuilt several times up to the 19th century to incorporate each era's architectural style. Drink a fresh fruit milkshake on the terrace of the *St-Michel* brasserie (Pl. de la Salomenque). Military buffs will want to visit *L'Empéri,* the castle museum built between the 10th and 16th centuries, for the collection of French army uniforms and weapons from the 17th century to World War I. Nostradamus lived and wrote *Centuries* here and is buried at Eglise St-Laurent.

Take the autoroute toward Aix-en-Provence — the perfect climax to any tour in the south of France. (For a detailed report on the city, its sights, hotels, and restaurants, see *Aix-en-Provence* in THE CITIES.)

CHECKING IN/EATING OUT: *Abbaye de Sainte-Croix* – A 12th-century Romanesque abbey converted, with considerable taste, into a luxury hostelry — a member of the Relais & Châteaux group — with a grand view over the Salon plain (3 miles/5 km northeast of town). Its 24 rooms and suites each are named after a saint, but the comfort is far from monastic. It has a great swimming pool set among wild shrubs in the hillside, and the hotel can arrange temporary membership in the exclusive tennis club just down the road. The one-Michelin-star restaurant serves regional cuisine with great subtlety, notably bass with basil and purées of garlicked zucchini and pumpkin and côtes de provence and palette wines. The chef could lay claim to the best apple pie in Provence. Closed Monday lunch and from November to March. Reservations necessary. Major credit cards accepted. Rte. D16, Val de Cuech, Salon-de-Provence (phone: 90-56-24-55; fax: 90-56-31-12; telex: 401247). Expensive.

The Côte d'Azur

The term "Côte d'Azur" can be confusing. It usually describes that privileged part of the Mediterranean coastline from Menton in the east to just beyond St-Tropez in the west, embracing part of the Riviera (which extends from La Spezia in Italy to Cannes in France) and forming part of the ancient province of Provence. But ask the French themselves exactly how far west the Côte d'Azur stretches and you're likely to get half a dozen answers because it is not an official administrative *département*. Purists (especially natives of Nice) insist that the true Côte d'Azur is the coastal region of the Alpes-Maritimes *département*, which ends at Miramar, 15 miles (24 km) west of Cannes. But most people agree that it reaches into Var, the neighboring *département*, and some say as far as Les Lecques, 6 miles (10 km) west of Bandol.

It is an area of spectacular beauty, with dazzling white or red cliffs rising from the soothing blue sea, gracefully curved bays, and rich varieties of conifer trees. The translucent quality of light gives a special spark to the colors and the smells of the salt water and fragrant flowers and pine trees all add to the splendor of the Côte d'Azur. There also are some of the most luxurious and palatial hotels in the world. The past decade has seen the urbanization of most of the coastline. Except for parts of the bottom slopes of the Massif de l'Esterel, east of Cannes, it is difficult to find spots that are not filled with vacation retreats. Yet, this is the place for sunning, swimming, gambling, eating, nightclubbing, and for seeing some of the finest collections of modern paintings in France (many of the most prominent figures in 20th-century art lived here at one time or another, drawn by the beauty of the terrain and the extraordinary quality of the light). Besides urbanization, another plague hit the area about 10 years ago — the summer forest fire. Every year from May to September, hundreds of fires burn thousands of acres of forest. In 1990, half of the Massif des Maures, the spectacular forest behind St-Tropez, was destroyed.

The statues of Queen Victoria in Menton and of Lord Brougham (a Victorian aristocrat and politician) in Cannes are reminders that the Côte d'Azur was discovered and developed by upper-crust English during the last part of the 19th century. In those days it was the exclusive resort of the rich and leisured who were attracted by the mild climate, a result of the warming influence of the Mediterranean and the screen of mountains to the north. (In January, the average temperature in Nice is 48F and it can reach the high 70s on a sunny day. Winter nights, though, can be cold, and it's much colder inland.) For many years, no self-respecting monarch, cabinet minister, or business tycoon (not to mention the crowds of swindlers and fortune hunters), would miss spending a part of the winter in one of the elegant, wedding cake hotels of Menton, Monte Carlo, or Nice, or in an Edwardian villa tucked away behind the bougainvillea and frangipani along the splendid Cap d'Antibes.

More recently, especially since the 1950s, visitors have begun to forsake the sedateness of these towns for the frivolity and frenzy of St-Tropez and the Ile de Porquerolles. And, although the coast is lively year-round, nowadays the high season is July and August, when the French themselves as well as people from all over the world flock here for vacation. (Indeed, the mass influx of people can be something of a nightmare; for example, the traffic in St-Tropez becomes so congested that entering the town is virtually impossible.)

One happy result of this burgeoning of tourism is that despite the Côte d'Azur's reputation as a playground of the rich and famous (which indeed it is), you'll find a remarkably wide spread of prices and a fairly reliable level of quality. This is because the vacationing French (who are, after all, the most demanding of people) have contrived to keep standards high across all price ranges, from simple bistros and *auberges* to the most haute restaurants and luxury hotels. Thus, whatever your taste and however deep your pocket, the simple pleasures of the Mediterranean — food, wine, sun, and the sea — will prove enormously satisfying.

Many beaches are rocky or pebbly, but there are plenty of sandy beaches, especially between Antibes and St-Tropez. Some beaches are public and free of charge, others are "private," which usually means they belong to a restaurant or hotel. But it's worth renting an air mattress and a beach umbrella at one of them for around $5 a day. Topless sunbathing (said to have originated at Tahiti Plage near St-Tropez in the early 1970s) is ubiquitous but hardly the rule. One of the great delights of the Côte d'Azur is that everyone does his or her own thing — the French are consummate individualists. So relax.

Of course, there's more to do than just sit on the beach. If you feel the need to escape wall-to-wall people, take a day trip to Grasse, the famous perfume center, or to any of the other villages in the mountains. It will be cooler in the higher elevations than down on the coast. Or indulge in some lazy people watching: Seek out the heart of any Provençal village and its charming central square, which usually is graced by a fountain, shaded by plane trees, and often edged by small cafés. At the end of the afternoon, sit on a café terrace with a *kir* (white wine with a dash of black currant brandy, deliciously cooling in summer) or a *pastis* (a very potent anise-flavored drink) and watch the residents play the traditional *boules* (lawn bowls). Or, if you're feeling energetic, visit one of the abundant fruit, vegetable, or flower markets or perhaps an art museum, a special treat on the Côte d'Azur. The work of the modern masters is exhibited in delightful settings — Renoir's paintings at his house in Cagnes-sur-Mer, where his simple studio is still set up just as he left it; Picasso's ceramics (a new medium he explored after World War II) in the Château Grimaldi in Antibes or at Vallauris; Matisse's drawings and paintings, a selection of which spans his whole life, in a museum in his native Nice.

There are gastronomic masterpieces to sample as well: bouillabaisse, the classic fish stew made with onions, tomatoes, garlic, olive oil, and saffron; rouille, a fiery mayonnaise made with red chili pepper; aioli, also a mayonnaise but based on olive oil and garlic; and *pissaladière,* a kind of pizza topped with onions, anchovies, and black olives. Provence is not one of France's great wine regions, but there are several local vintages. Try the dry whites from Cassis, the bandol red, or the bellet reds or whites. The côtes de provence rosés are light and fruity and can be enjoyed with most fish or meat dishes.

In an effort to provide the quintessential Provençal experience, we have suggested three complementary tour routes that either can be followed separately or combined, depending on the amount of time available. Motorists might find it useful to buy the Michelin green map No. 195, Côte d'Azur–Alpes Maritimes, or the Michelin yellow map No. 245 Provence–Côte d'Azur, which extends slightly farther west. The first route explores Les Corniches, between Nice and Menton, three roads that hug the coast and provide spectacular views of the sea and mountains for a distance of 17 miles (27 km). The second route is from Nice to Cannes and back, venturing slightly inland to Grasse and to St-Paul and Vence as well as visiting Antibes on the coast. Our third route is from Cannes to St-Tropez, a distance of 47 miles (75 km), and takes in St-Raphaël, Ste-Maxime, Port Grimaud, and other beach resorts.

Although our narrative assumes that the reader is driving a car, it is possible to cover the Côte d'Azur by train. The railway line, squeezed between the beach and the coast road, burrows through cliffs and sweeps past bays, offering some pretty remarkable views. The trains also are inexpensive, and they stop at dozens of little stations, which are clean and well-kept with wrought-iron canopies and tubs of flowers. An unexpected plus is that you never have far to walk; Cannes's station, for example, is only 5 minutes from the luxury resorts and beaches of the Croisette.

Despite the Côte d'Azur's extravagant reputation, there is a wide range of accommodations at various prices (except in Monaco, which caters mostly to the well-heeled tourist). In general, you can expect to pay $100 and up (occasionally way up) for a double room in hotels listed as expensive; $60 to $100 in moderate; and under $60 in an inexpensive one. (It is possible to find perfectly decent rooms for as little as $80, especially in Nice.) The tab for dinner for two is $200 and up in the restaurant listed as very expensive; from $100 to $200 in expensive places; from $50 to $100 in the moderate range; and under $50 in the inexpensive category. A few last caveats: Price ranges do not include wine or drinks (though service usually is included); set *menus* are always more economical than ordering à la carte; and in high season you may need to buy lunch or dinner in order to get a room, called "pension complète" for both meals and "demi-pension" for just one (plus breakfast in both cases).

LES CORNICHES

NICE: For a detailed report on the city, its sights, hotels, and restaurants, see *Nice* in THE CITIES. To start this tour, drive east along the Corniche Inférieure, which skirts the coast and offers many grand views of the sea.

VILLEFRANCHE-SUR-MER: The first stop is a town full of steep, old streets with a magnificent backdrop of soaring mountains. Its deep harbor is a safe anchorage for fleets of oceangoing cruise ships and naval warships that frequently arrive on courtesy visits (you're quite likely to rub shoulders with sailors from the giant carriers *Nimitz* and *Kennedy* in the town's bars and restaurants). Not to be missed is the 16th-century Citadelle Ste-Elme, which was used by the military until 1965, and the Chapelle St-Pierre, which was decorated in 1957 by Jean Cocteau, the French painter and poet.

CHECKING IN: *Welcome* – Across from the St-Pierre chapel, it has a restaurant, *Le St-Pierre,* with food prepared in the Escoffier tradition and served on an open terrace overlooking the sea. 32 rooms and parking available. Closed from November 20 through December 20. Major credit cards accepted. 1 Quai Courbet, Villefranche-sur-Mer (phone: 93-76-76-93; fax: 93-01-88-81; telex: 470281). Expensive to moderate.

Riviera – A comfortable, pleasant hotel where all the rooms have private baths, telephones, and some have terraces overlooking the sea. Major credit cards accepted. 2 Av. Albert-I, Villefranche-sur-Mer (phone: 93-76-62-76). Moderate in summer and inexpensive in winter.

ST-JEAN-CAP-FERRAT: Across the water from Villefranche-sur-Mer is the wooded peninsula of St-Jean-Cap-Ferrat, which is reached by turning right onto D25. Cap-Ferrat, an old fishing port now taken over by pleasure craft, is worth visiting for a look at the *Villa Ephrussi de Rothschild,* a museum (on the former property of the late King Leopold II of Belgium) containing the family's collection of paintings, china, tapestries, and furniture. Closed Mondays. Also notable are the botanic garden and zoo. Bd. Denis-Semeria (phone: 93-01-33-09).

 CHECKING IN: *Bel'Air Cap Ferrat* – A luxury 59-room hotel right on the water, with lovely grounds, a beach, tennis, and a one-Michelin-star restaurant. Its "Club Dauphin" on the sea has a spectacular pool, sauna, restaurant (perfect for lunch), and a funicular to take guests back up to the hotel. Isolated and exquisitely remodeled, this member of the Relais & Châteaux group is arguably the finest hostelry on the Riviera. Open year-round. Major credit cards accepted. (See also "Romantic French Hostelries" in *For the Experience,* DIVERSIONS.) Bd. Général-de-Gaulle, St-Jean-Cap-Ferrat (phone: 93-76-00-21; fax: 93-01-62-49; telex: 470184). Very expensive.

Voile d'Or – This elegant property (though a bit on the stuffy side) on the harbor with a fine restaurant (one Michelin star) features fish specialties, a heated pool, and superb views of the port. Demi-pension is required in season. Closed from November through February. Major credit cards accepted. Port de St-Jean, St-Jean-Cap-Ferrat (phone: 93-01-13-13; fax: 93-76-11-17; telex: 470317). Expensive.

 EATING OUT: *Cappa* – A good yet reasonably priced (for this area) seafood restaurant overlooking the port. Closed Wednesdays, and from November through January. Visa accepted. Av. Jean-Mermoz, St-Jean-Cap-Ferrat (phone: 93-76-03-91). Expensive.

Le Provençal – The specialties of this beautiful dining spot that has been awarded one Michelin star are the light nouvelle cuisine dishes. Closed Sunday evenings, Mondays in off-season, and in February. Visa accepted. 2 Av. D.-Semeria, St-Jean-Cap-Ferrat (phone: 93-76-03-97). Expensive to moderate.

BEAULIEU-SUR-MER: Leaving St-Jean-Cap-Ferrat, turn right onto D125, which takes you into Beaulieu. Protected by the surrounding hills from the cold north winds, this village is one of the warmest spots on the Riviera and deserving of its name which means beautiful place. Among the many glamorous homes built here by wealthy visitors is Villa Kerylos, a beautiful reconstruction of an ancient Greek dwelling. The villa, which dates from 1900 and has a small sculpture museum, is open to the public (except Mondays). It sits on a promontory overlooking the Baie des Fournis, and has magnificent views of Cap-Ferrat, Eze, and Cap-d'Ail (phone: 93-01-01-44).

 CHECKING IN/EATING OUT: *Le Métropole* – Reminiscent of an Italian palazzo, this luxurious, 50-room, 3-suite member of the Relais & Châteaux group has a heated swimming pool, an excellent restaurant that boasts one

Michelin star, and a private helicopter landing pad. Closed November 1 to December 20. Major credit cards accepted. 15 Bd. du Maréchal-Leclerc, Beaulieu-sur-Mer (phone: 93-01-00-08; fax: 93-01-18-51; telex: 470304). Expensive.

La Réserve – Once one of France's top luxury hotels, it had experienced a decline in recent years. Now under new management, it seems well on the way to regaining some of its former glory. Set right on the sea, it has a heated swimming pool. Parking is available. Major credit cards accepted. 5 Bd. du Maréchal-Leclerc, Beaulieu-sur-Mer (phone: 93-01-00-01; fax: 93-01-28-99; telex: 470301). Expensive.

MONACO: For a complete report on the principality, its sights, hotels, and restaurants, see *Monaco (and Monte Carlo)* in THE CITIES. Leaving Monaco, follow the signs to Cap-Martin. The road climbs gently, the mountainside becomes more densely wooded, and it's worth stopping for a moment at one of the bends to look back for some marvelous views of Monaco and the bay to Cap-d'Ail. Around the cape the road is flanked by handsome villas with luxuriant gardens of pines, palms, and olive trees. There are fine views of the bay of Menton on your right as you swing toward Roquebrune.

ROQUEBRUNE: This town and its peninsula, Cap Martin, merge in to Menton as you follow D52 along the beachfront. Roquebrune and Menton are also linked historically: They date from about the 10th century and have been held successively by the Counts of Provence, the republic of Genoa, and the Grimaldis of Monaco before electing to become part of France in 1793, following the French Revolution. They reverted to the Princes of Monaco under the Treaty of Paris in 1814, and after a short period as free towns, they finally joined France in 1861. The medieval village of Roquebrune is particularly worth a visit, with its steep, narrow passageways and carefully restored 15th-century castle. At Rue de la Fontaine and Route de Menton, about 200 yards from the village, is a thousand-year-old olive tree said to be one of the oldest trees in the world. In 1467, survivors of the bubonic plague held performances of a Passion Play here. The town continues that tradition on its esplanade every August 5.

CHECKING IN/EATING OUT: *Vista Palace* – This luxurious, renovated 42-room and 6-suite hotel beautifully set on a cliff has exceptional views of Roquebrune and the French and Italian coast. A fine restaurant, a pool, gardens, and parking complete the amenities. Open daily, year-round. Major credit cards accepted. About 2 miles (3 km) from the center of Roquebrune on the Grande Corniche (phone: 93-35-01-50; fax: 93-35-18-94; telex: 461021). Expensive.

Reine d'Azur – A good, simple hotel with 32 rooms. Guests who take their meals here are in for a bargain. Most major credit cards accepted. 29 Promenade Cap-Martin (phone: 93-35-76-84; fax: 93-28-02-91). Moderate.

MENTON: Like Beaulieu, Menton is protected from the cold northern winds by mountains and as a result has the mildest climate on the Côte d'Azur. Menton's average winter temperature is about 54F (compare 46F for Cannes). Thanks to its warm and sunny climate, Menton and the surrounding region is famous for a profusion of flowers and citrus fruit, especially lemons. The delicate lemon tree (which dies if it freezes) produces fruit year-round; this fecundity is celebrated in the charming *Fêtes du Citron* during February.

Also due to its mild weather, Menton, a town of 25,000 inhabitants, for many years was considered the traditional winter resort for older people; although the character of the town has changed somewhat, it's still a good deal more sedate than Cannes and

Nice. Since 1949, Menton has become something of a cultural center, with a *Chamber Music Festival* held in August. (For details, inquire at the tourist office at the Palais de l'Europe, Av. Boyer; phone: 93-57-57-00.)

A good way to start a visit is to stroll along the Promenade du Soleil, which runs along the beaches and is lined with luxury hotels (it's a slightly more decorous version of Nice's famous Promenade des Anglais). At the end of the promenade is the *Musée Cocteau* with drawings, paintings, and tapestries by Jean Cocteau. (Closed Mondays and Tuesdays; phone: 93-57-72-30.) Continue past the museum along the Quai Napoléon-III for a magnificent view of the Old Town. In the heart of the Old Town, among its many narrow streets, is the 17th-century Eglise St-Michel, the finest baroque church in the region, with a beautiful Italianate square in front.

The Rue St-Michel leads into the pedestrian precinct, just behind the Promenade du Soleil. Close by is the Hôtel de Ville (Town Hall), which has a "marriage room" decorated with murals by Cocteau. The ticket for this includes admission to the *Musée Cocteau.* Not to be missed is the indoor market, which is housed in an old wrought-iron building reminiscent of a Victorian train station.

The centerpiece of the modern town is the turn-of-the-century Jardin Biovès. With your back to the *Casino Municipal,* the garden is an impressive sight — bordered with plane and palm trees, interspersed with lemon trees. Among the fountains and statues is a memorial commemorating the annexation of Menton and Roquebrune to France in 1793. On the right is the vast Palais d'Europe, which houses the tourist office and is the center of the town's many cultural activities.

CHECKING IN: *Alexandra* – Quiet, and its wonderful view of the mountains and sea that stretches all the way to Italy make this 1950s hotel one of the best places to stay in town. Early risers will be rewarded by the extraordinary sunrises. Located at the entrance of the charming Cap Martin Peninsula at the western end of Menton Bay. Major credit cards accepted. 93 Av. Sir Winston Churchill, Roquebrune Cap Martin (phone: 93-35-65-45). Moderate.

Chambord – Here is a pleasant 40-room hostelry overlooking the Jardin Biovès. No restaurant. Major credit cards accepted. 6 Av. Boyer, Menton (phone: 93-35-94-19; fax: 93-41-30-55). Moderate.

Pin Doré – A charming 18-room hotel, it has a pool, a bar, and a garden, but no restaurant. Closed from November 11 to December 20. Major credit cards accepted. 16 Av. Félix-Faure, Menton (phone: 93-28-31-00). Moderate to inexpensive.

EATING OUT: *Petit Port* – This family-run place offers a variety of fish cooked on a wood stove, and is one of the rare eateries to serve grilled sardines. Caen-style tripe is on the menu, reflecting the origins of the owner. Closed Wednesdays in off-season. Reservations necessary on Saturday evenings. Visa accepted. Pl. de Port (phone: 93-35-82-62). Moderate.

STE-AGNÈS: Take D22 out of Menton and head north, following the signs to Ste-Agnès. The road climbs rapidly and tortuously, offering a magnificent view of the valley. From higher still, you'll see the whole of the Bay of Menton spread out below. After 9 miles (14 km) of this serpentine ascent, you'll enter the medieval village of Ste-Agnès, which clings precariously to the mountainside. At an altitude of 2,262 feet, it claims to be the highest coastal village in Europe.

This is one of the most unaffected places on the Côte d'Azur. Its steep, cobbled streets contain many shops in which genuine bargains in woolens, ceramics, and leather goods may be found. Essences of lemon and lavender, which are distilled locally, are also sold. As in Menton, Ste-Agnès has a "marriage room" decorated by Jean Cocteau, located at the *Mairie* (City Hall). Also worth visiting in the town's 16th-century Notre-Dame des Neiges church.

En Route from Ste-Agnès – Continue on D22. This is not a road for inexperienced drivers; you'll often have to stop to let other cars get past as the road winds up to an elevation of 2,600 feet at the Col de la Madone. Turn right at D53 into Peille. This town is not as interesting as Ste-Agnès, but it's worth visiting the 11th-century ramparts and the chapels of St. Joseph and St. Antoine. From the lower part of the village, you have to backtrack the way you came. Don't follow the signs to Nice but continue on D53, which winds down to La Turbie.

LA TURBIE: At 1,575 feet, this is the highest point of the Grande Corniche. The town is best known for its Roman relic, the Trophée des Alpes (Tropea Augusti in Latin), which was built in the 6th century BC to commemorate Augustus Caesar's victory over the Gallic tribes of the region. There are only two structures of this kind still standing (the other is in Romania). The round pillar originally stood 160 feet high and on the base was engraved a list of the 44 conquered tribes. Above, between Doric columns, were statues of the generals who took part in the campaign. The top was surmounted by a statue of Augustus himself, flanked by two prisoners. A large part of the monument was destroyed by the Lombards in the 6th century, and villagers took much of the fallen stone for their houses. From the ruins you can catch some spectacular views (particularly at night) of Monaco and down the coast as far as Bordighera in Italy. The adjacent museum has interesting photographs of the restoration of the area, done some 40 years ago. Both the monument and museum are open daily except Tuesdays and holidays (phone: 93-41-10-11). On the side of the mountain below the Old City there is an image of a dog's head, known as "Le Tête de Chien." From there, a once spectacular view of the Riviera has been marred by blackened tree trunks from the recent summer fires. In January, the final stages of the *Monte Carlo Rally* twist around Turbic's treacherous roads.

 CHECKING IN/EATING OUT: *Le Napoléon* – A comfortable, modernized hotel with 24 rooms, bar, restaurant, and flowered terrace. Hotel closed mid-February to mid-March; restaurant closed Tuesdays from October to April. Major credit cards accepted. 7 Av. de la Victoire, La Turbie (phone: 93-41-00-54). Moderate.

Césarée – Modest but pleasant, it has 11 rooms and a terrace restaurant with a panoramic view. No credit cards accepted. 16 Av. Albert-I, La Turbie (phone: 93-41-16-08). Inexpensive.

EZE: Follow the signs to the Moyenne Corniche and the village of Eze. Perched like an eagle's nest (1,300 feet) on the mountainside, this ancient settlement is famous for its vertiginous views of the sea — you can even see Corsica on a very clear day. Aside from its breathtaking setting, Eze is mostly notable for its 14th-century Chapelle des Penitents-Blancs, which contains a fine Catalan crucifix dating to 1258 as well as several paintings and enamels of the crucifixion. There also is an exotic garden with a rich collection of cacti.

This completes the first route on the Côte d'Azur.

CHECKING IN/EATING OUT: *Château de la Chèvre d'Or* – This restored medieval manor house, in the heart of the village with splendid views of the sea, is a member of the Relais & Châteaux group. It has 12 rooms (6 of them are in a separate building perched on the edge of the cliff) and 3 suites, 2 pools, and a dining room that offers classic French cuisine rating one Michelin star. Hotel closed from December to March; restaurant closed Wednesdays in off-season and from December to March. Major credit cards accepted. (See also "Romantic Hostelries" in *For the Experience,* DIVERSIONS.) Rue du Barri, Eze (phone: 93-41-12-12; fax: 93-41-06-72; telex: 970839). Expensive.

Château Eza – Once the residence of Prince William of Sweden, this 5-room and

3-suite hostelry offers splendid views of the Mediterranean (you actually can see St-Tropez on a clear day) and a luxurious decor that more than make up for the overpriced food at its one-Michelin-star restaurant. All of the rooms have private baths, mini-bar, and color TV; there also are 2 suites with fireplaces. Beware the less-than-adequate double beds that seem diminutive compared to their American counterparts. Hotel and restaurant are closed from November 1 to March 31. Major credit cards accepted. Rue du Barri, Eze (phone: 93-41-12-24; fax: 93-41-16-64; telex: 490382). Expensive.

NICE-CANNES ROUND TRIP

The next portion of this route is a loop between Nice and Cannes. Turn right out of Eze on D46, which winds up the mountain to rejoin the Grande Corniche. From here descend back into Nice. Leave Nice by the Promenade des Anglais and follow the coast road (N98) west to Cros-de-Cagnes (just past the airport and *Cap 3000,* a vast shopping center which is worth a visit). Follow the signs through Cagnes-Ville (the modern town) to Haut-de-Cagnes.

CAGNES-SUR-MER: This includes the medieval village of Haut-de-Cagnes, perched on a hillside covered with olive, citrus, cypress, and palm trees, a mile back from the sea; Cros-de-Cagnes, the somewhat tacky coastal strip; and Cagnes-Ville, the mundane modern neighborhood.

Head straight for the castle in the old village, which dates from the early 14th century and whose history has been dominated by the ubiquitous Grimaldi family. The castle museum (phone: 93-20-85-57) — an old olive oil mill — has rooms devoted to several dissimilar subjects: the history and cultivation of the olive tree; a trompe l'oeil ceiling fresco of the *Fall of Phaeton* by the Genoese artist Carlone; and paintings by 20th-century artists who lived near the Mediterranean, including Marc Chagall and Raoul Dufy. The museum (closed Tuesdays and from October 15 through November 15) also is the home of the *Cagnes International Festival of Painting,* held during July, August, and September. In the castle precincts are a number of bars and restaurants, one of which, *Jimmy's,* is a good place to stop for a refreshing drink or snack. In Haut-de-Cagnes there are some interesting nightclubs (both gay and straight).

Les Collettes, the house where Pierre-Auguste Renoir lived for the last 12 years of his life, is on Avenue des Collettes in Cagnes-Ville (phone: 93-20-61-07). His studio on the first floor has been left just as it was and in the garden is his magnificent bronze statue of Venus. There also are more than 6 acres of beautiful trees and flower gardens. (Closed Tuesdays and from October 15 to November 15.) There also is a race track, *Hippodrome de la Côte d'Azur,* near the sea, that is open from December to March and in August and September (Bd. Kennedy, Cagnes sur Mer; phone: 93-20-30-30). Six miles (10 km) south of Cagnes is Ville Neuve-Loubet, where August Escoffier (1847-1935) was born. His former childhood home now houses a museum of culinary art. Open daily except on Mondays and in November. 3 Rue Escoffier, Ville Neuve-Loubet (phone: 93-20-80-51).

ST-PAUL-DE-VENCE: From Cagnes-sur-Mer follow D36 and D2 to St-Paul. Half-way between Cagnes and Vence, it is set in olive groves with splendid views on all sides: to the north are the Alps, and to the south, the Mediterranean and Cap-d'Antibes. The town is enclosed by massive ramparts arranged in the form of an acropolis. A single cannon, which guards the entrance, is named Lacan and dates from the battle of Cerisilles in 1544.

The town is something of an artists colony (Modigliani, Bonnard, Soutine, and Chagall lived here) and is filled with studios, boutiques, and galleries. Don't miss the

Fondation Maeght (phone: 93-32-81-63), a museum with one of the finest collections of contemporary art in France. Within the house, courtyard, and garden are beautifully displayed works by Braque, Chagall, Kandinsky, Miró, Giacometti, Bonnard, Dérain, Matisse, Bazaine, and many other artists. Special exhibitions featuring various other artists are also presented during the year as well as films, ballet, and poetry recitals. The building itself is worth a visit. For details, contact the tourist office on Rue Grande (phone: 93-32-86-95).

Also worth a stop is the Eglise St-Paul-de-Vence, a 12th- and 13th-century church whose collection includes such treasures as a painting of St. Catherine of Alexandria attributed to Tintoretto and a 16th-century alabaster Madonna.

CHECKING IN: *La Colombe d'Or* – Famous for its remarkable art collection — works by Miró, Calder, Picasso, Chagall, and others — this once sumptuous small hotel has begun to show its age. It has 24 rooms and suites, a pool, and a terrace restaurant. Closed from mid-November to mid-December. Major credit cards accepted. 1 Pl. du Général-de-Gaulle, St-Paul-de-Vence (phone: 93-32-80-02; fax: 93-32-77-78; telex: 970607). Expensive.

Mas d'Artigny – This modern luxury hotel (a member of the Relais & Châteaux group) has 59 balconied bedrooms and 25 villas, each with a private patio and a pool, as well as tennis courts, air conditioning, parking, and even a helicopter pad. The restaurant, with one Michelin star, serves fine seafood; try the *bourride de baudroie provençale.* Visa accepted. Rte. de la Colle, D7, and des Hauts de St-Paul, St-Paul-de-Vence (phone: 93-32-84-54; fax: 93-32-95-36; telex: 470601). Expensive.

Le Hameau – A pleasant hostelry in a garden setting, it has 16 reasonably priced rooms but no restaurant. Closed from mid-November through mid-December, and mid-January to mid-February. Major credit cards accepted. 528 Rte. de la Colle, D7, St-Paul-de-Vence (phone: 93-32-80-24; telex: 970846). Expensive to moderate.

VENCE: This picturesque Roman town on a plateau at 1,400 feet is separated from the sea by low, wooded hills and has fine views of the mountains. Unlike St-Paul, Vence has spread out into a complex tangle of suburbs, but don't be put off: Head straight for the old walled town, which was one of the most important religious centers in southern France until the French Revolution. Take note of the 10th-century cathedral with a 19th-century rococo façade, with handsomely carved choir stalls and a Chagall mosaic of Moses parting the waters; the urn-shaped fountain in the Place du Peyra, on the site of the old Roman Forum; and the Chapelle du Rosaire, which was cleverly designed by Matisse so that the sunlight streaming through its luminous stained glass windows creates striking patterns on the white ceramic walls. Open Tuesdays and Thursdays; closed November to mid-December (phone: 93-58-03-26). For tourist information, stop in at Place Grand-Jardin (phone: 93-58-06-38).

CHECKING IN: *Château du Domaine St-Martin* – A posh place (a Relais & Châteaux member) filled with antique furniture and tapestries, it is perched on a hillside amid 35 acres of parkland and has 17 bedrooms and 10 villas, a pool, and tennis courts. Its restaurant was awarded one Michelin star. Restaurant closed Wednesdays in off-season and both hotel and restaurant closed mid-November to mid-March. Major credit cards accepted. Rte. de Coursegoules, Vence (phone: 93-58-02-02; fax: 93-24-08-91; telex: 470282). Expensive.

Auberge des Seigneurs – This comfortable and atmospheric old Provençal inn has 9 rooms and a good restaurant. Closed from mid-November through December 15; restaurant closed Sunday dinner and Mondays. Major credit cards accepted. Pl. du Frene, Vence (phone: 93-58-04-24). Moderate.

Closerie des Genets – It's small (11 rooms and 2 suites) and quiet, with a terrace, garden, and restaurant. Restaurant closed Sunday dinner and Tuesdays in off-season. Visa accepted. 4 Av. M.-Maurel, Vence (phone: 93-58-33-25). Moderate.

La Roseraie – A restored 12-room manor house that is comfortably furnished in Provençal style, with gardens, a swimming pool, and a restaurant featuring the cuisine of southwest France, which is only available to hotel guests. Closed Tuesdays, Wednesday lunch, and the month of January. Major credit cards accepted. Av. Henri-Girard, Vence (phone: 93-58-02-20; fax: 93-58-99-31). Moderate.

EATING OUT: *Les Portiques* – This small bistro in the Old Town has a reputation for fine food and service. Open daily. Reservations necessary. Most major credit cards accepted. 6 Rue St-Véran, Vence (phone: 93-58-81-99). Moderate.

En Route from Vence – Take D2210, which winds west through lushly wooded countryside with views of the Gorges du Loup unfolding on your right. Stop at the medieval village of Tourrette-sur-Loup to visit the 15th-century church for its triptych by Bréa and the Chapelle St-Jean for its frescoes rendered in the naïf style by Ralph Soupault. As you approach Pont-du-Loup, there's a fabulous view of the waterfalls streaming from the heart of the mountain hundreds of feet above. The town has many artists and artisans' shops. The road climbs out of Pont-du-Loup past the ruins of the old railroad viaduct, which was destroyed in 1944. Two miles (3 km) farther is the village of Le Bar-sur-Loup, (with its 14th-century dungeon) set among orange terraces and jasmine and violet fields, which supply ingredients for the perfume factory on your right. A fine view of the Gorges du Loup and the hills behind Vence can be seen from the porch of the Eglise St-Jacques. At Le Pré du Lac, at the junction of D2210 and D2085, turn right for Grasse, 4 miles (6 km) down the road.

GRASSE: The very name of this city (since the 17th century) is synonymous with perfume. Three out of four bottles of perfume sold in the world contain essences distilled here. Ten thousand tons of flowers (jasmine, mimosa, and lavender) are used every year by the three major manufacturers, Fragonard, Galimard, and Molinard. Guided factory tours are given; visitors may observe how perfumes are still made in the traditional manner and watch the master perfumer (usually called *le nez* — the nose) blending essences. Each factory has its own museum and welcomes visitors. Details are available from the tourist office on Place de la Foux, on your right as you enter town (phone: 93-36-03-56) or call the factories direct: Fragonard, 93-36-44-65; Galimard, 93-09-20-00; Molinard, 93-36-01-62; or the *International Museum of Perfumes* (8 Pl. du Cour; phone: 93-36-80-20).

Also of interest is the Old Town, which has hardly changed since the 18th century. Here is the Cathédrale Notre-Dame-du-Puy, which dates from the 12th century and contains paintings by Rubens as well as a fine tryptych by Louis Bréa; the *Fragonard Villa,* a museum honoring the painter Jean-Honoré Fragonard (closed Mondays and November; phone: 93-36-01-61); and the *Musée d'Art et Histoire de Provence,* which is housed in an 18th-century mansion and contains exhibits on the art and history of Provence from prehistory to the end of the 19th century (closed Saturdays, the second and third Sundays of each month, and November; phone: 93-36-01-61). The *Musée de la Marine* (Hôtel Particulier Pontèves–Morel; phone: 93-09-10-71) has an interesting collection of 18th-century model boats. Closed Saturdays and Sundays, and the month of November.

EATING OUT: *Maître Boscq* – Authentic regional cuisine and M. Boscq's warm welcome await diners at this small eatery in the Old Town. Closed Sundays and Mondays, holidays in off-season, and 2 weeks in November. Visa accepted. 13 Rue de la Fontette, Grasse (phone: 93-36-45-76). Inexpensive.

MOUGINS: This quiet old village (12,000 people) perched on a hilltop retains little of its early fortifications except a 15th-century gate. During medieval times it was an important agricultural center and more important as a town than nearby Cannes. At nearby Notre-Dame-de-Vie is the house where Picasso spent his last years. Mougins is known mostly for its fine restaurants (which have a total of six Michelin stars), so it's the place to stop if you've a taste for some rich and elaborate food. Three miles (5 km) from Mougins on the road to Cannes (N85) is an interesting vintage car museum, *Musée de l'Automobile,* 722 Chemin de Font-de-Currault (phone: 93-69-27-80).

EATING OUT: *Le Moulin de Mougins* – Also set in a 16th-century olive oil mill, accented with exotic plants outside and paintings within, this is one of the most famous restaurants in France, with three Michelin stars. Chef Roger Vergé's specialties include zucchini stuffed with truffles, lobster and artichoke salad, fresh *palangre* (a Mediterranean fish) in a light tomato and basil sauce, noisettes of Alpine lamb, and filet of duck in margaux wine. Desserts make delicious use of fresh fruit: peaches and melon, cold wild strawberry soufflé, and lavender ice cream. There is also an excellent wine list. The restaurant also has 5 delightful suites (book ahead) and a cooking school (see *Learning the Culinary Arts,* DIVERSIONS). Closed Mondays in off-season, Thursday lunch, and February to *Easter.* Reservations necessary. Major credit cards accepted. Notre-Dame-de-Vie, southeast 1 mile (1.6 km) via D3, Mougins (phone: 93-75-78-24; fax: 93-90-18-55; telex: 970732). Very expensive.

L'Amandier de Mougins – Roger Vergé's "other" restaurant, which serves simpler and somewhat less expensive food worthy of one Michelin star, is in a former olive oil mill. The standouts here are the appetizers — foie gras with raisins, marinated salmon and sea bass with dill and coriander, and an array of courses incorporating the delicious local cheeses and fruits. Closed Wednesdays, and Saturday lunch. Reservations necessary. Major credit cards accepted. Pl. du Commandant-Lamy, Mougins (phone: 93-90-00-91; fax: 93-90-18-55; telex: 970732). Expensive.

Le Bistrot de Mougins – Good food at reasonable prices is the keynote at this cheery little bistro, which once enjoyed lesser fame as a 17th-century stable. Closed Tuesdays, Wednesday lunch in off-season, and from December 3 through January 18. Major credit cards accepted. Pl. du Village, Mougins (phone: 93-75-78-34). Moderate.

CANNES: For a detailed report on the city, its sights, hotels, and restaurants, see *Cannes* in THE CITIES.

En Route from Cannes – A pleasant excursion would be to the nearby Iles de Lérins. Boats leave from Cannes (phone: 93-39-11-82 or 93-99-62-01) and from Golfe-Juan and Antibes; information on boat service may be obtained by calling 93-63-81-31. The trip takes half a day, including stops at Ile Ste-Marguerite, fragrant with eucalyptus and pine forests, and at Ile St-Honorat, the site of an ancient fortified monastery. It is said that the legendary "Man in the Iron Mask" was imprisoned on Ste-Marguerite in the Fort de l'Ile; however, his identity remains the subject of much debate.

Another possible excursion is to Vallauris (take D803), known as a pottery center and the home of the *Biennial International Festival of Ceramic Art.* (For details, contact the tourist office at Pl. 8 Mai; phone: 93-63-82-58 or the *Palais des Festivals et des Congrès* at 93-39-24-53.) Picasso spent several years here working in clay and in 1952 was asked by the town council to decorate the chapel of the local priory. The resulting fresco, called *War and Peace,* can be seen at the *Musée National La Guerre et La Paix* (phone: 93-64-18-05). Along the Avenue Georges Clemenceau, there are a number of pottery shops, including the *L'Atelier Madoura,* that still sell some of Picasso's ceramics.

A mile (1.6 km) down the road (D135) from Vallauris is the old fishing port of Golfe-Juan, now mostly given over to pleasure craft and popular for water sports of all kinds. It has good, sandy beaches; there's a sailing school and club that holds regular regattas; and wind surfing and water skiing are easily arranged. The town-has historical as well as sporting associations. A 1932 plaque on the quayside commemorates Napoleon's landing here on March 1, 1815. He chose this spot for his return from exile on Elba because Cap d'Antibes and the headland of the Croisette provided protection from the guns of the forts of Antibes and Cannes. The South of France was Royalist territory, so Napoleon quickly headed north, on what later became known as the famous Route Napoléon, with his small army of 1,200 men.

Along the seafront, Golfe Juan merges imperceptibly into Juan-les-Pins, which comes alive in the summer, its cafés and discos throbbing with activity and young people. The nightlife centers mostly around the casino, which is in a cool garden just set back from the sea. In July, a *World Jazz Festival* is held in the Palace of Congresses and outside among the pine trees. For details on this and other events, contact the tourist office at 51 Bd. Guillaumont (phone: 93-61-04-98).

CHECKING IN: *Juana* – An excellent location just 100 yards from the beach affords most of the 45 rooms and 5 suites of this elegant hotel lovely sea views. It also has a heated swimming pool, a private beach, and 2 bars. Its restaurant, *La Terrasse,* has two Michelin stars. Open for dinner only in July and August. Closed from November until 10 days before *Easter* each year. No credit cards accepted. Av. G.-Gallice, Juan-les-Pins (phone: 93-61-08-70; fax: 93-67-10-40). Expensive.

***Astoria* –** This renovated, comfortable 55-room hotel right near the shore is one of the few in the area that is open all year. Major credit cards accepted. 15 Av. Maréchal-Joffre, Juan-les-Pins (phone: 93-61-23-65; fax: 93-61-76-60; telex: 470900). Moderate.

***Mimosas* –** A small (36 rooms), pleasant hostelry in a garden setting. There is a swimming pool, and parking is available. Closed October through March. Visa accepted. Rue Pauline, Juan-les-Pins (phone: 93-61-04-16). Moderate.

EATING OUT: *Tétou* – Grilled lobster and bouillabaisse are good choices at this eatery that has been awarded one Michelin star. Closed Wednesdays, for dinner from December 20 to *Easter,* and from October 15 through December 20. No credit cards accepted. Bd. des Frères-Roustan, on the beach, Golfe-Juan (phone: 93-63-71-16). Expensive.

***Le Bistro du Port* –** A great place for steaks or broiled fish. Closed Sunday evenings and Mondays except in season, and December through January. Visa accepted. 53 Bd. des Frères-Roustan, Golfe-Juan (phone: 93-63-70-64). Expensive to moderate.

On the seafront in Juan-les-Pins, there are restaurants and cafés every few yards, each with its own section of beach.

CAP D'ANTIBES: Cap d'Antibes is one of the most exclusive spots on the Côte d'Azur, where the sun is worshiped in utter luxury. For a beautiful drive, follow D2559 around the cape from Juan-les-Pins and ignore the "direct to Antibes" signs. Lovely villas line the approach to Cap d'Antibes, a peninsula covered with lush pine forests and rocky creeks (*calanques*). Take a few minutes to walk around the *Hôtel du Cap d'Antibes* (see *Checking In*) or enjoy a drink on the terrace or swim at the leafy pool of the *Hôtel Résidence du Cap;* the experience will convince you that Cap d'Antibes deserves its romantic reputation. After your feet touch the ground again, the *Musée Naval et Napoléonien* (Batterie du Grillon; phone: 93-61-45-32) is worth a look for its memorabilia of Napoleon's landing at Golfe-Juan, as is the Jardin Thuret, a 10-acre botanic garden established in 1856 to introduce tropical vegetation to the surrounding area.

CHECKING IN: *Cap d'Antibes* – Over the years this grand and exclusive luxury hotel (also known as the *Hôtel du Cap*) has welcomed many celebrities and is said to be the hotel described by F. Scott Fitzgerald in *Tender Is the*

Night. Set above the rocks, it has gorgeous grounds and views, 130 handsomely decorated bedrooms, a swimming pool, a tennis court, and a well-known restaurant, the *Pavillon Eden Roc.* (See also *Romantic French Hostelries,* DIVERSIONS.) Closed mid-October to the end of March. Visa accepted. Bd. Kennedy, Cap d'Antibes (phone: 93-61-39-01; fax: 93-67-76-04; telex: 470763). Very expensive.

Saint Paul – This pleasant 30-room hotel overlooks the sea. Open year-round. Major credit cards accepted. Chemin de la Garoupe, Cap d'Antibes (phone: 93-61-70-12; fax: 93-67-33-55). Expensive to moderate.

Gardiole – This simple, quiet hostelry set among the pines has 21 rooms, some of which face the sea, as well as a charming wisteria-draped terrace. Closed November 5 to February 28. Major credit cards accepted. Chemin de la Garoupe, Cap d'Antibes (phone: 93-61-35-03; fax: 93-67-61-87). Moderate.

EATING OUT: *Bacon* – Here on a terrace overlooking the sea, diners may choose bouillabaisse or excellent fresh fish from a menu that has been awarded one Michelin star. Closed Sunday evenings in off-season and from mid-November through January. Reservations necessary. Major credit cards accepted. Bd. de Bacon, Cap d'Antibes, right on the northeastern point of the cape as you approach the town of Antibes (phone: 93-61-50-02). Expensive.

ANTIBES: Antibes is one of the oldest settlements on the Côte d'Azur. Originally called Antipolis, the city was founded by the Greeks in the 5th century BC and quickly developed into an important port of trade between Marseilles and Italy and an important stop on Via Aurelia, which once extended from Rome to Spain. Several centuries later, Antibes proved valuable to the Kings of France for its strategic military position on the border of Savoy, and from the 15th to the 17th century they built and rebuilt its fortifications. (Of these efforts, only Fort Carré, just to the north of the harbor, and some of the ramparts along the seafront remain.) Still later, during the French Revolution, the city was Napoleon's base when as general he was made responsible for the defense of the southern coast; after the downfall of Robespierre in 1794, Napoleon was imprisoned at Fort Carré.

Nowadays, Antibes has a more tranquil reputation as a center for commercial flower production; primarily roses and carnations are cultivated. The town also is notable for its *Musée Picasso,* a collection of some of the artist's best paintings and drawings as well as a fabulous selection of his ceramics. The museum is in the Château Grimaldi, a castle in the Old Town built in the 12th century and rebuilt in the 16th century. (Closed Tuesdays and November; no admission charge on Wednesdays; details from the tourist office at 11 Pl. Général-de-Gaulle; phone: 93-33-95-64.) Just behind the Château Grimaldi is the marketplace (Cours Masséna), where the townspeople buy their fish, cheese, fruit, and vegetables — a walk through here and the Old Town, which buzzes with activity all year, and along the city ramparts are a must.

CHECKING IN/EATING OUT: *La Bonne Auberge* – The fine Provençal cuisine and attentive service have won this elegant restaurant two Michelin stars. There is a no smoking room. Closed Monday lunch from April to September, Wednesday lunch in season, and from mid-November to mid-December. Reservations necessary. Major credit cards accepted. On the left-hand side of N7, en route to Nice, Antibes (phone: 93-33-36-65; fax: 93-33-48-52; telex: 470989). Expensive.

L'Armoise – A tiny, utterly charming restaurant serving inventive fare. Closed Wednesday nights during off-season, and from mid-November to mid-December. Most major credit cards accepted. 2 Rue de la Touraque, Antibes (phone: 93-34-71-10). Expensive to moderate.

Chez Paul le Pêcheur – Possibly the best fish soup on the whole Côte d'Azur is served here. The owner sometimes goes all the way to Marseilles to get the freshest possible delicacies from the sea. His grilled and fried fish also are delicious and the portions more than generous. Closed Wednesdays off-season. Reservations necessary. Major credit cards accepted. 42 Bd. d'Aiguillon (phone: 93-34-59-42). Expensive to moderate.

Mas Djoliba – This small, quiet hotel with 13 rooms and a swimming pool has a beautiful park setting right in the center of town. Half board is required during the summer. Major credit cards accepted. 29 Av. de Provence, Antibes (phone: 93-34-02-48; fax: 93-34-05-81; telex: 461686). Expensive to moderate.

La Famiglia – Authentic Italian dishes excellently prepared in a friendly atmosphere. Closed Wednesdays and in November. Major credit cards accepted. 34 Av. Thiers, Antibes (phone: 93-34-60-82). Inexpensive.

L'Oursin – Although its setting is rather plain, this popular little eatery has the best seafood in the downtown area. Closed Sunday evenings, Mondays, and July 23 to August 26. Reservations necessary. Visa accepted. 16 Rue de la République, Antibes (phone: 93-34-13-46). Moderate to inexpensive.

En Route from Antibes – A few miles along the coast (N7 or N98), perched on a hilltop, is Biot, a village renowned for its ceramics. It was founded by Greeks and Romans, and in the 13th century was fortified by Templars. At the Biot Glassworks (reached via D4; phone: 93-65-03-00), visitors can watch glass blowing or buy the finished article. Also off D4 and worth visiting is the *Musée Fernand Léger,* devoted entirely to the work of this artist — paintings, mosaics, and sculptures (phone: 93-65-63-61). Route N98 will take you back to Nice via the coast.

CANNES–ST-TROPEZ ROUND TRIP

As you drive along the coast between Cannes and St-Tropez, the seascapes become incredibly vast and beautiful. It's a good idea to take the autoroute (A8) west through the mountains and then to return to Cannes along the coast road, stopping at the beach resorts of Ste-Maxime, Fréjus, and St-Raphaël along the way. With the sea on your right, the views are even more magnificent. From A8, exit at Le Muy and cross the Massif des Maures via D25 to Ste-Maxime, or stay on A8 for another 12 miles (19 km), take the exit at Le Cannet des Maures, and strike south on D558. This road climbs up the steep mountains to La Garde-Freinet, then winds down through the delightful village of Grimaud and connects with the coast road to St-Tropez.

LA GARDE-FREINET: Surrounded by cork forests and perched on the crest of the Massif des Maures, this little town is notable for its ruined, allegedly Saracen castle, abandoned in the 10th century. From here there's a fine view out to sea.

EATING OUT: *La Faücado* – This attractive terrace restaurant has a magnificent view of the wooded valley below and offers a fine set menu at lunchtime. Classic dishes are standard here. Closed Tuesdays in off-season, and from mid-January to mid-March. Major credit cards accepted. 31 Bd. de l'Esplanade, La Garde-Freinet (phone: 94-43-60-41). Moderate.

PORT GRIMAUD: Stop here for a look at this modern replica of an old-fashioned Provençal fishing village designed by François Spoerry. The architect's grand concept provided for the traditional main square; connecting canals; privately owned homes, each with its own mooring; the usual complement of shops, a church, and such.

CHECKING IN/EATING OUT: *Giraglia* – A comfortable lodging in a seaside setting, it has a private beach and a fine restaurant, *L'Amphitrite.* Closed October to April. Major credit cards accepted. Pl. du 14-Juin, Port Grimaud (phone: 94-56-31-33; fax: 94-56-33-77; telex: 470494). Expensive.

ST-TROPEZ: For a detailed report on the city, its sights, hotels, and restaurants, see *St-Tropez* in THE CITIES.

En Route from St-Tropez – Although the heart of the Côte d'Azur more or less ends at St-Tropez, the scenery found in the region to the west is still quite dazzling. Before you start back to Cannes, we suggest a short detour in this direction along the coast road or a visit to Ramatuelle, 8 miles (12 km) from St-Tropez, a picturesque medieval village with a magnificent view of the whole St-Tropez peninsula. To head for the coast, drive west on N98 and D559 toward Cavalaire-sur-Mer for a view of its dramatic high cliffs and expansive seascapes. Farther west on D559 is Le Lavandou, a former fishing village that is now a resort with fine sandy beaches. From here, a boat may be taken to the Iles d'Hyères — Porquerolles, Port Cros, and Levant — where you may swim, sunbathe, picnic, bicycle, or walk among the fragrant pine and eucalyptus. (For details about boat schedules, call 94-71-01-02.) Still farther west (N559 to D41) is Bormes-les-Mimosas, a charming old village set on a steep hill among pine and mimosa and overlooking the sea; it's another departure point for the Iles d'Hyères as well as offering sandy beaches and a marina. From here, turn right on the mountain road, N98, and go back to St-Tropez.

STE-MAXIME: Ten miles (16 km) east along the coast road (N98) from St-Tropez (which can be seen across the gulf) is Ste-Maxime, a quiet seaside resort popular with young families. It has a 16th-century fortress and a fine sand beach, plenty of water sports, and the marina is always busy with pleasure craft. Follow the signs 1 mile (1.6 km) north (via Bd. Bellevue) to the Sémaphore, at an altitude of 400 feet, for a sensational view of the coast and the mountains. East of Ste-Maxime, past the Cap des Sardinaux, is La Nartelle, where the Allies landed in August 1944. From here to St-Aygulf are a number of small beach resorts, including Vald'Esquières, San Peïre, Les Calanques, and Les Issambres.

CHECKING IN: *Calidianus* – A simple hotel with 33 comfortable rooms, beach, tennis courts, and 2 pools, but no restaurant. Closed January 8 to February 8. Most major credit cards accepted. Bd. Jean-Moulin, Ste-Maxime (phone: 94-96-23-21; fax: 94-49-12-10). Moderate.

EATING OUT: *La Gruppi* – Excellently prepared fish and seafood dishes, and friendly service. Closed Mondays in off-season and major holidays. Most major credit cards accepted. Av. Charles-de-Gaulle, Ste-Maxime (phone: 94-96-03-61). Expensive to moderate.

FRÉJUS: Founded by Julius Caesar in 49 BC, as Forum Julii, Fréjus was an important Roman naval base, with a population of 40,000 and a large inland harbor connected to the sea by canal. By the Middle Ages the port had declined in importance and gradually became occluded from the sea. Outbreaks of plague in the 14th century and endemic malaria caused the inhabitants to abandon the Roman site, and by 1780 the population had declined to 2,000. Today, Fréjus consists of two entities: Fréjus Plage, 3 miles of magnificent sandy beach that blend into that of St-Raphaël; and the Old Town, which is now about a mile from the sea and a treasure trove of both Roman remains and medieval buildings, all of which can be visited. Among the former are some fortifications, houses, and baths as well as a huge amphitheater with space for 10,000 people (there are bullfights here in July and August; closed Tuesdays). Also noteworthy is the Episcopal quarter, which was built in the Middle Ages on a small area of the Roman site; it consists of a cathedral with a 5th-century baptistry (one of the oldest ecclesiastical buildings in France) and magnificent 12th-century cloisters. Try to visit the *Museé Archéologique* just behind the cloisters; it contains some splendid Roman mosaics, a marble statue of the god Hermès, and a 1st-century BC bust of Jupiter. For details on hours and tours, contact the tourist office at 325 Rue Jean Jaurès (phone: 94-17-19-19) or from *Easter* to September at Fréjus-Plage (Bd. Libération; phone: 94-51-48-42).

CHECKING IN/EATING OUT: *Vieux Four* – There are 8 moderately priced rooms and regional cuisine is stylishly served at its restaurant in an old wine cellar close to the cathedral. Closed Sunday lunch in season, Mondays off-season, and from November 15 to December 15. Major credit cards accepted. 57 Rue de Grisolle, Fréjus (phone: 94-51-56-38). Expensive to moderate.

Les Résidences du Colombier – It's a modern quiet hotel with individual bunga-lows designed in the Provençal style and set among pine trees in a private park of 8 acres. It has a restaurant, beach, and tennis facilities. Restaurant open daily. Major credit cards accepted. Rte. de Bagnols, Fréjus (phone: 94-51-45-92 or 94-51-46-57; fax: 94-53-82-85; telex: 470328). Moderate.

ST-RAPHAËL: The sister town to Fréjus, it also was founded by the Romans, although no ruins of their occupation remain. A pyramid on the harbor (Av. Comman-dant-Guilbaud) commemorates Napoleon's return to France from his Egyptian cam-paign; he landed here in 1790 and was dispatched from here in 1814 to exile on Elba. It was a favorite vacation spot for Berlioz, Alexandre Dumas, du Maupassant, and many others during the late 19th century. From the promenade along the water can be seen the reddish, offshore twin rocks called Lion de Terre and Lion de Mer (Land Lion and Sea Lion).

While less frenetic than St-Tropez, St-Raphaël is a very pretty and popular resort. In addition to its splendid beach and marina, the town has a full and varied program of cultural and sports events from February right through to November. Visit the tourist information office near the train station for details (on Rue Rousseau; phone: 94-95-16-87 or 94-95-19-70). The *Museum of Underwater Archaeology* (Av. de Vales-cure; phone: 94-95-64-99) has an important collection of amphorae dug up in the area by diving club members. Closed Sundays off-season and Tuesdays in-season.

CHECKING IN: *La Potinière* – This quiet, modern hotel set in a garden has 25 rooms with balconies, is near the beach, and has a swimming pool and tennis court. Its restaurant is closed on Thursdays for lunch during off-season. Major credit cards accepted. Av. des Plaines, at Boulouris, 3 miles (5 km) along the N98 to Cannes (phone: 94-95-21-43; fax: 94-95-29-10). Expensive to moderate.

En Route from St-Raphaël – During this last leg east along the Corniche de l'Esterel to Cannes (some 27 miles/43 km) the views are breathtaking, so drive slowly. You'll pass through the resorts of Boulouris, Le Dramont, Camp Long, Agay, Anthéor, Le Trayas, Miramar, Théoule, and La Napoule, all with marvelous sand beaches. You even might discover some tiny hidden strands if you scramble down the rocky cliffs from the road. As you pass the Pointe de l'Aiguille, just before Théoule, the coastline softens into the magnificent Gulf of Napoule, with Cannes to the northeast.

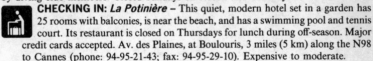
CHECKING IN: *Royal Hôtel Casino* – A luxury establishment right on the beach in the town of La Napoule, it has a heated pool, an impressive casino, and a good restaurant, *Chez Loulou,* done up as a yacht. Be sure to ask for accommodations facing the beach as rooms overlooking the road are somewhat noisy. Open all year. Major credit cards accepted. Bd. Henri-Clews, La Napoule (phone: 92-97-70-00; fax: 93-49-51-50; telex: 470878). Expensive.

St-Christophe – Just a few miles from Miramar and Théoule-sur-Mer, this recently renovated, 40-room hostelry is isolated among pine trees and red rocks on the Esterel Corniche. Rooms have TV sets, a balcony or a terrace, with garden or sea view. It has 2 restaurants specializing in fish, a private beach, a small pool, and a spectacular view. Major credit cards accepted. Corniche d'Or, 47 Av. de Miramar, Miramar par Théoule (phone: 93-75-41-36; fax: 93-75-44-83; telex: 470878). Expensive.

EATING OUT: *L'Orangerie* – A kitschy turn-of-the-century dining room, with an excellent menu, a Provence wine list, and lots of flowers. Closed Sunday dinner and Mondays. Major credit cards accepted. Promenade R. Coty, St-Raphaël (phone: 94-83-10-50). Moderate to inexpensive.

Pastorel – Considered by most to be the best in St-Raphaël, this charming place has consistently good food, nice wines, and great service. Closed Sunday dinner, Mondays, mid-February to mid-March, mid-November to mid-December, and for lunch during August. Major credit cards accepted. 54 Rue de la Liberté, St-Raphaël (phone: 94-95-02-36). Moderate to inexpensive.

The Alps

Waterfalls crashing over rocks, glacial streams racing through valleys enclosed by snow-capped mountains, pine forests alluring as sirens, meadows of gentian and edelweiss, a dizzying array of breathtaking vistas and of pass after vertiginous pass — rev up those eyes and fasten those seatbelts, you're in the Alps.

Most travelers in the Alps find little need for volumes on culture and history. Goggling at the magnificent scenery, skiing, fishing, swimming, and pursuing other pastimes usually replace any preoccupation with Roman ruins, medieval ramparts, and the like. However, there is more to this region than just wildflowers and ski resorts, even if it is known to most people as the home of the Mont-Blanc, Western Europe's highest peak (15,771 feet).

Made up of two ancient provinces, Dauphiné and Savoie, the French Alps are bordered by Italy and Switzerland and, to the north and west for about 200 miles, by the Rhône River. The Dauphiné, occupying the southern half of the high Alps and taking in the offical *départements* of Hautes-Alpes, Isère, and Drôme, belonged first to the kingdoms of Provence and Arles and then to the Holy Roman Empire. It came under French control without violence fairly early, when it was sold to France by the pious and profligate King Humbert II of Dauphiné in 1349.

Savoie, on the other hand, because of its position astride many militarily and commercially important mountain passes, was the object of repeated assaults by countries who wanted to control the area not so much for its own sake but for the potential access to the land of the enemy. Ruled first by the kingdom of Burgundy, then Arles, then made part of the Holy Roman Empire, in the 11th century it was consolidated with other fiefdoms under Humbert the White-handed, who founded the House of Savoie. Over the years, through marriage and acquisition, Savoie became a powerful duchy that governed parts of France, Italy, and Switzerland. In the 16th century, the ducal seat was moved to Turin, making Savoie Italian rather than French, and in the 18th century, it became part of the kingdom of Sardinia. A plebiscite was held in 1860 to determine if the Savoyards wished to be returned to France or stay with Italy. The vote was overwhelming: 130,533 for France, 235 for Italy; and the subsequent Treaty of Turin ceded the region to France.

Today the French Alps have a very special character of their own. The people are feisty, industrious, and laconic — the Gallic equivalent of New Englanders. You might still hear the older generation speak the regional *patois* (dialect) that can confound the unsuspecting traveler: they pronounce words ending in *oz* or *az* as if the last two letters didn't exist; for example, Sierroz becomes *Sierre* and Clusaz is pronounced *Cluse*.

The Alpine cuisine is straightforward, hearty, healthy. Regional menus feature many kinds of freshwater fish — trout, pike, carp — as well as ham, sausage, and wild game. Crayfish and wild mushrooms (*morilles*) are two favorite delicacies. Several excellent cheeses are produced, including *chèvre* (goat cheese); *reblochon,* a creamy, mild cheese; *tomme de Savoie,* also mild; and *beaufort,* a type of gruyère. The wines of the region marry well with the cuisine; the sparkling white wine seyssel is considered one of the best. The liqueurs, gentian (flavored with the flower) and the famous chartreuse, are interesting finales to dinner; also try the local marc de Savoie, made from the residue that remains after brandy is pressed. (But beware, this is a sneaky potion, much like tequila in its aftereffects.)

The Alps have two important seasons — both summer and winter — when thousands of tourists come to enjoy the beauty and majesty of the mountains. At the risk of stating the obvious, winter is not a time for touring but rather for skiing, hiking, and other Alpine sports. The major mountain passes generally are closed, the weather is unpredictable, and the roads can be treacherous; however, tremendous improvement to the roads and highways in the Tarentaise Valley in Savoie were made to facilitate access to the *1992 Winter Olympics* sites. Although the tour that's laid out here is designed for summertime, when most of the highest roads are open, we have included some winter highlights as well. (Even in July, some mountain passes such as the Col de l'Iseran can be closed, so be sure to inquire before you set out.)

Another precaution would be to check your car, especially its tire pressure and suspension. On the road, you'll notice that when people are asked for distance and directions, they answer in hours, not miles (or kilometers); mileage is irrelevant on these winding mountain roads that require special attention and careful driving. Also be aware of the peculiar French habit of occasionally ignoring center lines in taking hairpin curves. One more caveat: the region's growing popularity has been known to produce bumper-to-bumper traffic.

The suggested tour of the French Alps forms an extended oval, starting in the extreme north at Lake Geneva (Lac Léman), going through the eastern side of the Alps, passing along the southern part of Dauphiné through Gap. It then moves back up the western ridge of the Alps, through the parks of Vercors and Chartreuse, through Grenoble, and ends up in the idyllic lakeside city of Annecy. Lovely villages and spectacular views are so abundant that it is impossible to begin to capture them all; if you take an alternate route, you can hardly go wrong.

The French Alps is the only area in the world to have hosted the *Winter Olympics* three times — the first games were held in Chamonix in 1924; Grenoble welcomed them in 1968; and Albertville, in the Tarentaise Valley, home of some of the region's most famous ski resorts (Val-d'Isère, Tignes, and Les Trois Vallées), was the location of last year's games. For the first time in the games' history, the events were spread out over 13 sites.

Visitors to the Alps will benefit from the improvements that were made for the *Olympics* — in addition to expanding the road and highway system, other transportation improvements to the area include the extension of the *TGV* "Bullet" train's route to the Tarentaise Valley, and the construction of a second runway at the Lyons-Satolas Airport, which now can accommodate twice as many visitors. New hotels have been built and existing properties have been redesigned and renovated with both short- and long-term results; immediately, for the more than 1 million spectators who attended the games, and after the *Olympics* for the many travelers who return here to vacation in this spectacular region.

A warning: In a way, the Alps are too beautiful. They attract hordes of tourists, and during the high season, it is easy to be put off by the disappointing lack of tranquillity and by the sheer volume of people just like yourself. The best way to deal with this is to visit off-season or to seek out the lesser-known areas. For example, Vercors, on the western side of the Alps, is not as famous as Chamonix or Val-d'Isère, but it is also very beautiful.

The Alps traditionally have been heavily developed for the tourist trade, so there's a plethora of hotel rooms in every price range (although in some resorts, such as Courchevel, rates are sky high). In general, you can expect to pay $220 and up for a double room listed as very expensive; between $150 and $220 in the expensive category; from $100 to $150 for a moderate room; and under $100 for an inexpensive one. Dinner for two with wine in a restaurant listed as very expensive will cost $200 or more; from $120 to 200, expensive; from $75 to $120, moderate, and below $70, inexpensive. Prices do not include aperitifs or after-dinner drinks, but service usually is included.

EVIAN-LES-BAINS: About two-thirds of the southern coast of Lake Geneva or Lake Léman belongs to France, and Evian-les-Bains, on its lakeshore, has a familiar name because of the drinking water that takes its name from the town. Before the discovery of the health-restoring properties of its waters in the 19th century, Evian-les-Bains was a tiny fortified city. While traces of the pre-spa city remain (three towers, remnants of the city walls, a few old buildings), what Evian really has to offer is not the quaintness of the Middle Ages but the grandeur of the Belle Epoque. Though no longer only for the very rich, it looks as if it were, with an elegant casino (made famous by Ian Fleming in his James Bond book, *Casino Royale*), opulent hotels, exquisitely manicured gardens, and a long lakefront promenade. Every May the *Rencontres Musicales d'Evian,* a well-known music festival, takes place at the casino. The festival includes a competition for string quartets (phone: 50-75-03-78).

Stroll along the boulevards or the promenade, treat yourself to a drink or dinner in one of the hotels, perhaps the *Royal Evian* (see *Checking In*), and drift into Marcel Proust's world of idleness and wealth. Proust, who stayed at the now-defunct *Splendid* at the turn of the century, fashioned his "Balbec baths" after Evian's, and his train that runs from Paris to Brittany is in fact the train from Geneva to Evian. Some 60 years later, the negotiations that led to the independence of Algeria took place in one of Evian's grand hotels.

Numerous short outings can be taken from Evian. Thonon-les-Bains, some 5½ miles (9 km) to the west, also is a spa, but more bustling and modern, and is a good place for shopping. About a mile (1.6 km) north of Thonon is the Château de Ripaille, which the Savoyard King Amadeus VIII made his home two times, once after abdicating his throne in 1434 and again, 15 years later, after renouncing his papal (or rather anti-papal) title as Félix V. Lake Geneva, which is shaped like a giant boomerang sailing across Europe, lends itself to innumerable boat trips. A tour of the entire lake takes about 10 hours; an alternative is to take a boat into Switzerland, to the lakeside cities of Lausanne-Ouchy, directly across the lake, for instance, or to Montreux, 23 miles (37 km) to the east and the site of the Château de Chillon, a 13th-century medieval fortress virtually built on the lake where Byron was imprisoned.

If fitness, health, and beauty rank high among your preoccupations, you can take advantage of your stay in Evian for some à la carte treatment. For more information, get in touch with the tourist office (Pl. d'Allinges; phone: 50-75-04-26; fax: 50-75-61-08) or the *Centre Evian Equilibre* (phone: 50-75-02-30).

The most efficient way to get to Chamonix from Evian is through Switzerland. Head east along the lake on N5 to the French border town of St-Gingolph, then south on route 21 through Vouvry and Monthey. At Martigny, take the Col de la Forclaz back into France; the border town is Vallorcine. Route N506 leads to Chamonix.

CHECKING IN: *Royal Club Evian* – Built in 1907 for King Edward VII of England, this "palace" offers both refinement and modern comforts in its 158 suites, rooms and spa facilities. Guests staying a minimum of 2 days have free access to the property's 18-hole golf course — located 2 miles (3 km) away. It has 5 restaurants, including one that offers a dietetic gastronomic menu. The hotel provides a complimentary bus nightly to the casino. Closed mid-December to mid-February. Major credit cards accepted. Rte. du Mateirons, Evian-les-Bains (phone: 50-26-85-00; fax: 50-75-38-40). Very expensive, although discounted rates available off-season.

La Verniaz et Ses Chalets – Set in gardens overlooking Lake Geneva, this elegant and lovely member of the Relais & Châteaux group has 35 rooms and 5 private chalets as well as a swimming pool, tennis courts, and a first class restaurant. Closed December and January. Major credit cards accepted. Rte. Abondance, Evian-les-Bains (phone: 50-75-04-90; fax: 50-70-78-92). Expensive.

Terrasse – A much humbler hotel but also attractive, it has 29 renovated rooms. Open year-round. Major credit cards accepted. 10 Rue B.-Moutardier, Evian-les-Bains (phone: 50-75-00-67). Moderate.

EATING OUT: *Bourgogne* – At a place that serves fine, traditional fare (one Michelin star). The *omble chevalier* (blackened fish) is especially good. Other specialties include duck foie gras or veal kidney and sweetbread casserole. There also are 29 comfortable rooms for those who want to stay the night. Closed on Sunday evenings and Mondays during the winter and in November. Reservations necessary. Major credit cards accepted. 73 Rue Nationale, Evian-les-Bains (phone: 50-75-01-05; fax: 50-75-04-05). Expensive.

La Toque Royale – Excellent cooking, rating one Michelin star, is featured on an extensive menu, and it's easy to spend any money left after the meal since the restaurant is in the casino. Specialties include roasted king prawn with spices and local fish in butter sauce. Open all year. Reservations advised. Major credit cards accepted. At the casino, Evian-les-Bains (phone: 50-75-03-78; fax: 50-75-38-40). Expensive.

CHAMONIX: At the base of 15,771-foot Mont-Blanc, the highest mountain in Western Europe, Chamonix is probably Europe's most important center for serious alpinism. Compared to nearby neighbors such as Megève and Val-d'Isère, it is a no-frills town: Chic is out in Chamonix; in its bustling, hyperactive downtown, along with the inevitable hordes of sedentary types, the streets are thronged with determined alpinists loaded down with pitons, carabiners, and the other accoutrements of mountaineering. The town is sandwiched into a narrow valley with the Mont-Blanc range on one side and the Aiguilles-Rouges on the other, an awe-inspiring setting. Cable cars pass on slender cables between peaks many thousands of feet above the ground. An ancient glacier descends to less than 1,000 feet above a major thoroughfare, and avalanches, with accompanying cracks and rumbles, occur periodically. In Chamonix, perhaps more than anywhere else in the Alps, the mountain gods make their intimidating presence felt.

A multitude of activities demand attention in Chamonix. Visits to nearby peaks, which can be accomplished via cog railway or cable car, are a must. A relatively tame trip is the one taken by train from the Gare du Montenvers to the Mer de Glace (Sea of Ice), a glacier 6,313 feet high. Farther up, at the summit of Montenvers, you'll find an ice grotto and a small museum. On the other side of the valley, there is the trip up Le Brévent to an altitude of 8,285 feet. The most spectacular excursion of all, however, is undoubtedly to the summit of the Aiguille du Midi, alongside the great Mont-Blanc itself. This trip is accomplished in two stages, first with a relatively normal cable car, picked up at the end of Avenue Aiguille-du-Midi, that takes you up to 7,500 feet, and then by a second one, which takes what seems like an almost vertical route to the summit of the Aiguille, an altitude of close to 12,600 feet. This is heart-stopping indeed, especially when distances of more than 1,600 feet separate you from good old terra firma.

Those who prefer more land-based activities will find more than enough to do in the valley. *Les Praz*, an 18-hole golf course designed by Robert Trent Jones, is just outside town (phone: 50-53-06-28), and there's also swimming, tennis, riding, and ice skating. A fitness center offers a good selection of the usual facilities as well as Turkish baths and a wall to practice mountain climbing. The serious alpinist, of course, can spend a lifetime in Chamonix without getting bored. For more information, contact the tourist office (Pl. Triangle de l'Amitié; phone: 50-53-00-24; fax: 50-53-58-90).

Some 22 miles (35 km) down the road from Chamonix, via N205, D902, D909, and N212, lies Megève, another major resort.

CHECKING IN/EATING OUT: Aiglons – Recently opened, this 42-room and 13-suite hostelry offers modern amenities in an Old World setting. It is conveniently located near the Aiguille-du-Midi cable car station. There is a restaurant, fitness center, Jacuzzi, and solarium. Open year-round. Major credit cards accepted. Av. de Courmayeur, Chamonix (phone: 50-55-90-93; fax: 50-53-51-08). Expensive.

Auberge du Bois-Prin – An 11-room Savoyard chalet, it offers a view of Mont-Blanc and an opportunity to use the pool and tennis courts at the *Albert I,* almost a mile (1.6 km) away (see below). Member of the Relais & Châteaux group. Closed the last 2 weeks in May and in November. Major credit cards accepted. 69 Chemin de l'Hermine, Les Moussoux, Chamonix (phone: 50-53-33-51; fax: 50-53-4875). Expensive.

Mont Blanc – Centrally located, this hostelry has 31 rooms and 13 suites, a swimming pool, and an attractive garden. Closed in April and from mid-October to mid-December. Major credit cards accepted. Pl. de l'Eglise, Chamonix (phone: 50-53-05-64; fax: 50-53-41-39). Expensive.

Albert I – This hostelry has 29 rooms and apartments, a pool and tennis courts, a flower garden with a children's play area, and a splendid view of the peaks. Its restaurant has been awarded one Michelin star, and offers such well-prepared specialties as duck sausage with cabbage or roasted lamb with Savoie potato fritters. Closed the last 2 weeks in May and in November. Reservations necessary. Major credit cards accepted. 119 Impasse du Montenvers, Chamonix (phone: 50-53-05-09; fax: 50-55-95-48). Expensive to moderate.

Alpina – The amount of luxury and the price of each of the 134 rooms is determined by whether it faces Mont-Blanc. The seventh-floor restaurant offers a panoramic view. Closed mid-October to mid-December and May. Major credit cards accepted. 79 Av. du Mont-Blanc, Chamonix (phone: 50-53-47-77; fax: 50-55-98-99). Expensive to moderate.

Labrador – This 32-room hotel is right on *Les Praz* golf course. Its restaurant, *La Cabane,* is closed Thursdays for lunch and Wednesdays from *Christmas* through April. The hotel is closed the first 2 weeks of April, and mid-November to mid-December. Major credit cards accepted. Rte. du Golf, Chamonix (phone: 50-55-90-09; fax: 50-53-15-85). Moderate.

Beausoleil – Amid cow-filled pastures at the foot of Chamonix's peaks, this hotel has 15 rooms, a restaurant, and a tennis court. The owner, M. Bossonney, also is a high-mountain guide and willing to help you explore the rocky terrain. Closed mid-September to mid-December. Visa accepted. 60 Allée Peupliers, Le Lavancher (phone: 50-54-00-78; fax: 50-54-17-34). Moderate to inexpensive.

Richemond – Centrally located, this is a comfortable 53-room hostelry with a restaurant surrounded by a garden. Closed mid-April through May and November. Major credit cards accepted. 228 Rue Docteur-Paccard, Chamonix (phone: 50-53-08-85; fax: 50-55-91-69). Inexpensive.

Roma – Each of the 33 rooms in this hostelry has a mountain view. It has a lovely garden, but no restaurant. Closed the second half of June and from mid-October to mid-December. Major credit cards accepted. 289 Rue Ravanel-le-Rouge, Chamonix (phone: 50-53-00-62; fax: 50-53-50-31). Inexpensive.

MEGÈVE: Compared to Chamonix, Megève is effete, but this is not to say that it is unattractive. It has a lovely little downtown area bisected by a mountain stream and filled with appealing but expensive boutiques and outdoor cafés. On Fridays there is a market in the town's center, where mountain farmers sell their cheese, smoked ham, and other local produce. Like Chamonix, it is a center for outdoor sports, with fine skiing. Among the many hikes and Alpine tours in the area, the prime attraction is probably the cable car ride to the top of Mont-d'Arbois, where you have a view of the surrounding ranges of Mont-Blanc, Fiz, and Aravis. The point of departure is Petit Bois, 2 miles (3 km) north of town on Route du Mont-d'Arbois. In late August, a tournament is held at *Golf du Mont-d'Arbois* (phone: 50-21-29-79), an 18-hole golf course. At night, join Paris's jet set at the bar of the *Les Enfants Terribles* restaurant (see *Loges du Mont-Blanc Hotel* below) for live music and a look at Jean Cocteau's frescoes. Or try the cozy *Le Club des 5 Rues* (Pl. des 5 Rues; phone: 50-21-24-36) for exotic cocktails and live jazz.

CHECKING IN: Chalet–Mont-d'Arbois – A splendid 20-room chalet and a member of the Relais & Châteaux group, it is located in a tranquil setting. Closed mid-April to mid-June and in November. Major credit cards accepted. It's 3 miles (5 km) up the road to Mont-d'Arbois, on Rte. de Mont-d'Arbois, Megève (phone: 50-21-25-03; fax: 50-21-24-79). Very expensive.

Parc des Loges – This luxury hotel, a pension before its renovation in Art-Deco style, has 51 rooms, suites, and apartments, many of them with a fireplace. The 2 restaurants, *La Rotonde* and *Le Grand Café*, are under the supervision of five well-known chefs. There is an outdoor swimming pool, Jacuzzi, sauna, solarium, and massage available. Half or full board only. Open year-round. Major credit cards accepted. 100 Rte. d'Arly, Megève (phone: 50-93-05-03; fax: 50-93-09-52). Very expensive.

Les Loges du Mont-Blanc – There are 44 pricey rooms (including 3 suites) from which to choose and the hotel's fine restaurant features frescoes by Jean Cocteau and a bar, *Les Enfants Terribles*, where you can nibble on caviar along with a glass of champagne. There is a swimming pool and sauna as well. Open year-round. Major credit cards accepted. Pl. de l'Eglise, Megève (phone: 50-21-20-02; fax: 50-93-09-52). Hotel, very expensive; restaurant, expensive.

Les Fermes de Marie – A group of old farmhouses was brought here in pieces and then put back together to make up this hostelry with 42 luxurious rooms. The owner also is an artist who has decorated the place with her paintings of the surrounding Alpine scenery. There's a swimming pool, Turkish baths, and a fitness center. Closed mid-April to July and November. Major credit cards accepted. Chemin de Riante-Colline, Megève (phone: 50-93-03-10; fax: 50-93-09-84). Expensive.

Au Coin du Feu – Run by the same folks who own *Les Fermes de Marie*, this little gem has 23 cozy rooms furnished with 19th-century antiques. There is also a small restaurant that proffers fine traditional fare. Closed mid-April to mid-July and September to mid-December. Major credit cards accepted. Rte. de Rochebrune, Megève (phone: 50-21-04-94). Moderate.

Idéal-Mont-Blanc – Only 3 miles (5 km) from Megève, this hotel has 28 rooms, and a breathtaking view of Mont-Blanc. Closed October, November, and mid-May to mid-June. Major credit cards accepted. Combloux (phone: 50-58-60-54; fax: 50-58-64-50). Moderate.

La Prairie – This 32-room hostelry enjoys a wonderful mountain view. There is a restaurant and garden. Closed mid-April to July and October to mid-December. Major credit cards accepted. Av. Ch.-Feige, Megève (phone: 50-21-48-55; fax: 50-21-42-13). Moderate.

St-Jean – An attractive place, it has 15 comfortable rooms. Closed mid-September to mid-December, May, and June. No credit cards accepted. Chemin du Maz, Megève (phone: 50-21-24-45; fax: 50-58-78-50). Inexpensive.

Les Sapins – There are 19 rooms in this hotel with a garden. Its restaurant has a terrace for outdoor dining. Closed *Easter* to July and mid-September to mid-December. Visa accepted. Rte. de Rochebrune, Megève (phone: 50-21-02-79; fax: 50-93-07-54). Inexpensive.

EATING OUT: Auberge Les Griottes – This fine restaurant features a good choice of fish dishes. Closed Mondays from *Easter* to mid-May, and November. Reservations advised. Visa accepted. Rte. Nationale, Megève (phone: 50-93-05-94). Moderate.

Le Chamois – Located in the center of the village, this popular dining spot specializes in regional fare such as fondue, raclette, and smoked ham. Open daily. Reservations advised. Visa accepted. Megève (phone: 50-21-25-01). Moderate.

En Route from Megève – Head southwest on N212 toward Flumet, Ugine, and Albertville, which was the main site of the *1992 Winter Olympics*. For the games, the city built a 30,000-seat stadium for the opening and closing ceremonies, as well as an "ice hall" which was the scene of figure skating and short track speed skating events.

Directly across the river from Albertville, you might want to pay a quick visit to the pleasingly restored walled village of Conflans, with buildings dating back as far as the 14th century. Leaving Albertville, head south on N90 to D915A south (which becomes D117) to Val-Thorens — one of the resorts of Les Trois Vallées — a ski area that is said to be largest in the world.

CHECKING IN/EATING OUT: Million – This 29-room hotel houses one of the best kitchens in France, rating two Michelin stars, and includes on its menu snail soup and veal *fricandeau* in sorrel sauce, and numerous fish dishes, as well as many Savoie specialties. The restaurant is closed Sunday evenings and Mondays, and the last 2 weeks in September. A member of the Relais & Châteaux group. Reservations advised. Major credit cards accepted. 8 Pl. Liberté, Albertville (phone: 79-32-25-15; fax: 79-32-25-36). Expensive.

La Berjann – Attractively furnished, this 11-room hostelry also offers good cooking. Restaurant closed Sunday evenings from October to July. Visa accepted. 33 Rte. Tours, Albertville (phone: 79-32-47-88; fax: 79-37-74-09). Moderate to inexpensive.

VAL-THORENS: What you first notice as you approach Val-Thorens is its breathtaking, stark landscape, which is totally treeless. Because it is the highest resort in Western Europe (slopes reach heights of between 6,000 and 11,500 feet), Val Thorens is colder than other places. There is always fine skiing (even when there is little snow in other parts of the Alps) on its north slopes, and glacier skiing is popular in the summer.

Nearly 90% of the skiing here is *off-piste,* allowing the adventurous to go off on their own to ski on the fantastic powder snow.

Most hotels are located right on the runs, enabling serious skiers to roll out of bed onto the slopes. And unique to Val-Thorens is that no parking is allowed within the resort during high season. After being greeted at the 24-hour welcome booths by tourist office staff who provide general information about the area, visitors park in garages at the resort's entrance and then take free shuttle buses to their lodgings. The tourist office, located at the Maison de Val-Thorens (phone: 79-00-08-08; fax: 79-00-00-04), has information on the resort's activities.

 CHECKING IN/EATING OUT: *Fitz Roy* – An indoor glass elevator carries guests to the 33 rooms and 3 suites (with fireplaces) in this exquisite member of the Relais & Châteaux group. All rooms have balconies and are decorated in pastels and wood (each one has a beautiful painted plaque with the room number). The hair salon and beauty treatment center is the only one in Val-Thorens. There is a restaurant (serving haute cuisine), tearoom, bar, pool, fitness center, sauna, Jacuzzi, and meeting room. Half or full board. Closed mid-May through November. Major credit cards accepted. Val-Thorens (phone: 79-00-04-78; fax: 79-00-06-11). Very expensive.

Le Bel Horizon – Right on the slopes, each of the 31 rooms in this hostelry has a balcony, television set, and direct-dial phone. There is a restaurant, bar, fitness center, sauna, and meeting room. Closed May through mid-December. Visa accepted. Val-Thorens (phone: 79-00-04-77; fax: 79-00-06-08). Moderate.

Le Val Thorens – All 74 rooms surround an interior courtyard where the flags of many countries are displayed. Most have a view of the slopes (from the room or balcony) and the wood furniture is built into the walls. The restaurant offers both à la carte and prix fixe menus; the fitness center is free for guests. There also is a bar and ski shop. Closed beginning of May to end of November. Major credit cards accepted. Val-Thorens (phone: 79-00-09-40). Moderate.

En Route from Val-Thorens – Take D117 northwest toward Moûtiers, stopping at Les Menuires, site of last winter's *Olympics* men's slalom race. Although it isn't as developed as nearby Val-Thorens, Les Menuires offers quite good skiing on its numerous downhill and cross-country trails and is the training ground for the French national ski teams. Summertime here is ideal for families — there's tennis, mountain biking, swimming, and horseback riding — and accommodations in residences and condominiums are easily found. There also are a few hotels. The tourist office is next to the new stadium (phone: 79-00-73-00).

Continue on D117 to the village of St-Martin-de-Belleville. Before arriving at this picturesque town of 2,150 people, be sure to stop at the 17th-century baroque Church of Notre Dame de la Vie on the side of the road — it is a startling contrast to the mountain backdrop.

ST-MARTIN-DE-BELLEVILLE: This village offers vacationers a Savoie farm village — complete with traditional homes made of stone, wood, and slate, and narrow and steep streets — and access to the ski slopes. Though not as high as the other resorts in the Belleville Valley (Val-Thorens and Les Menuires), St-Martin has lifts that carry skiers up to the slopes of Les Trois Vallées. Its tourist office is located near the *Alp Hotel* (phone: 79-08-93-09).

Take D117 north to Moûtiers, follow D915 east, and then D91 south to the ritzy resort of Courchevel.

 CHECKING IN: *Latitudes* – All 95 rooms in this hotel have a balcony and a south view of the Belleville Valley; 2 rooms are designed for guests with disabilities. There are 2 restaurants, and the community pool and skating rink next door are free for guests' use. Jazz is played every night in the bar. Half or full board. Closed mid-April through mid-December. Major credit cards accepted. Reberty, Les Menuires (phone: 79-00-75-10; fax: 79-00-70-70). Expensive.

Alp – Located in St-Martin-de-Belleville, this 30-room inn offers quiet relaxation and, right outside, a ski lift to the summit. All rooms have a balcony with a spectacular view. There is a restaurant, sauna, Jacuzzi, and solarium. Closed mid-April through mid-December. MasterCard and Visa accepted. St-Martin-de-Belleville (phone: 79-08-92-82; fax: 79-08-94-61). Inexpensive.

L'Ours Blanc – Recently opened, this hostelry's 53 rooms (including 2 suites and 2 apartments) all are decorated in pastel colors and have balconies. Special care was taken in constructing this place — the owner's father built all the wood furniture, beams, and doors. It faces La Masse Mountain, and after a day on the slopes (right outside), skiers can enjoy a steambath and/or solarium. There's a day-care center run by an English nanny, a restaurant, bar, and meeting rooms. Half or full board. Closed in May, June, September, and November. Major credit cards accepted. Reberty, Les Menuires (phone: 79-00-61-66; fax: 79-00-63-67). Inexpensive.

EATING OUT: *La Marmite de Géant* – Right next to the *Latitude* hotel, this restaurant serves typical Savoie fare including *salade campagnarde* (salad with tomatoes, eggs, croutons, and ham), raclette, and *fondue bourguignonne*. Open daily for lunch and dinner. Reservations necessary. Major credit cards accepted. Reberty, Les Menuires (phone: 79-00-74-75). Moderate.

COURCHEVEL: One of the first ski resorts in France, Courchevel is well known for its luxury hotels and as the place where celebrities (including the Aga Khan, the King of Spain, and Princess Caroline of Monaco, as well as many French stars) go. Its prices are much higher than other areas in Savoie, although ironically Courchevel was originally conceived as a working class resort back in the 1940s!

Courchevel is really four resorts — Courchevel 1300 (Le Praz), 1550, 1650, and 1850 (the number corresponds to each area's height in meters). From La Saulire peak at 1850, there is a spectacular view of Mont-Blanc as well as other surrounding mountains. The brilliant sun in Courchevel makes for pleasant skiing — though the slopes are not terribly challenging — but skiers also have the option of zooming downhill around the rest of the 375 miles of slopes of Les Trois Vallées. Just before arriving at 1850 (where a large sports complex, *The Forum*, has been built), you'll pass a 119-foot-high pinnacle of ice — used for climbing — that adds to the exotic nature of the landscape. Homesick pangs will subside after seeing a sign just in front of the icicle saying that Courchevel is a twin city to Park City, Utah.

Summer activities — swimming, mountain biking, golf, tennis, hiking, paragliding, and canoeing — have become more prominent in recent years. The tourist office in 1850 (phone: 79-08-00-29) can provide details about all kinds of sports.

For those folks looking for a more tranquil resort, take D91 north, then D91A west, and D90 south to attractive Méribel.

CHECKING IN: *Les Airelles* – In the lobby of this totally renovated hostelry, a heated pillar surrounded by seats offers immediate warmth from a day on the slopes right outside. All 56 luxurious rooms (including suites and apartments) have hand-painted tiles, hand-crafted wood, mini-bar, cable television, VCR, and heated towel racks. France's high society is comfortable here. There is a restaurant, piano bar, swimming pool, fitness center, Jacuzzi, steamroom, tanning beds, beauty salon, and 3 meeting rooms. Half or full board required. Closed *Easter* to *Christmas*. Major credit cards accepted. Jardin Alpin, Courchevel 1850 (phone: 79-09-38-38; fax: 79-08-38-69). Very expensive.

Bellecôte – Decorated with a mixture of traditional regional furniture and antiques brought back from Afghanistan (take a look at the precious 17th-century carved doors), this 53-room hotel (plus 2 suites and 1 apartment) is directly on the slopes. It has a restaurant, piano bar, bridge and meeting rooms, pool, fitness center, sauna, Jacuzzi, sun lamps, and hair salon. All rooms have balconies. Half or full board. Closed mid-May through November. Major credit cards accepted. Bellecôte, Courchevel 1850 (phone: 79-08-10-19; fax: 79-08-17-16). Very expensive.

Byblos des Neiges – Like its sister hotel in St-Tropez, the oldest hostelry in Courchevel was built with lavishness in mind. The 75 elegant rooms and suites all face south (the best view of the slopes) and have cable television and mini-bars. There are 2 restaurants (*Les Arches* specializes in fish), bar, pool, fitness center, sauna, boutiques, and hair salon. Half or full board. Closed mid-April to mid-December. Major credit cards accepted. Jardin Alpin, Courchevel 1850 (phone: 79-08-12-12; fax: 79-08-19-38). Very expensive.

Les Grandes Alpes – Completely renovated, all 37 rooms have balconies in this hotel that is in the center of town, yet next to the ski lifts. There is a restaurant, an American bar (with a full range of liquors), garage, pool, fitness center, steamroom, and Jacuzzi (suites and the VIP room have their own). Unique in Courchevel, it also is open in summer. Closed mid-May to June, and September through November. Major credit cards accepted. Courchevel 1850 (phone: 79-08-03-35; fax: 79-08-12-52). Expensive.

De la Loze – Same owners as *Les Airelles,* but smaller, simpler, and much less costly. Located in town, across from the cable cars, each of its 26 rooms has cable television, radio, mini-bar, balcony, and terrycloth bathrobes. No restaurant, but breakfast is included. Closed May to November. Major credit cards accepted. Courchevel 1850 (phone: 79-08-28-25; fax: 79-08-39-29). Expensive.

La Sivolière – Quaint, cozy, and exquisitely kept, this hotel has 28 rooms and a good restaurant. Visitors can munch on succulent pastries in front of the fireplace at teatime after a long day of careening down the mountainside. Closed mid-April to December. Visa accepted. 1850 Courchevel (phone: 79-08-08-33; fax: 79-08-15-73). Expensive to moderate.

EATING OUT: *Le Bateau Ivre* – Rating two Michelin stars, this restaurant has a panoramic view of the Vanoise chain of mountains. Those who revel in panoramic vistas will appreciate the view of the Vanoise from this splendid dining room. Specialties include lobster tails in herb butter, roasted filet of pike, and frozen chocolate truffles with gingerbread. Closed mid-April to mid-December. Reservations advised. Major credit cards accepted. In the *Hôtel Pomme-de-Pin,* Courchevel 1850 (phone: 79-08-02-46; fax: 79-08-38-72). Expensive.

La Cendrée – If you are tired of fondue and raclette, this fine Italian restaurant (the owner is from Calabria, the chef from Sicily) is the place to go. It is frequented by Courchevel's jet set, perhaps because of its extensive wine selection. The fare ranges from pizza baked in a brick oven to pasta such as *spaghetti alla carbonara* (with *pancetta* bacon) or *penne alla foie gras* (quill-shaped pasta with pâté) to various meat and fish dishes. Open daily for lunch and dinner. Closed May through July. Reservations necessary. Major credit cards accepted. Courchevel 1850 (phone: 79-08-29-38 or 79-08-34-36). Expensive.

La Bergerie – This rustic eatery on the slope of Pralong is in a former shepherd's dwelling, the oldest house in Courchevel. Choose from typical Savoyarde fare such as raclette or *fondue bourguignonne* or traditional French dishes like salmon filet with vegetables. The first floor turns into a disco at night. Closed June through mid-December. Reservations necessary for dinner. American Express accepted. Jardin Alpin, Courchevel 1850 (phone: 79-08-24-70). Moderate.

MÉRIBEL: After the German invasion of Austria in 1938, the British looked for a place to ski and chose Méribel. It started as a pastoral village and was built up slowly over the years — adding chalets and few hotels. It now has spread out to cover five different areas. Méribel's strict zoning code requires that everything be constructed following the Alpine architectural design — double-slanted roofs atop chalets with wood and stone façades and balconies. This is one place where the arrival of last year's *Olympics* created a boom in hotel construction.

Méribel's east-west exposure affords lots of sunshine, making it an ideal place to ski. In the heart of Les Trois Vallées, Méribel was the site of last year's *Olympics* women's alpine races and ice hockey games. In addition to hotels, new construction included a complex with a skating rink.

In summer when the snow melts, families often come here for a variety of sports — tennis, mountain biking, hiking, rock climbing, swimming, rafting, and golfing at an 18-hole course. Cultural events include the *Tarentaise Baroque Music Festival* every August. Méribel's tourist office is in the center of the resort (phone: 79-08-60-01).

CHECKING IN: *Allodis* – Each of the 41 rooms (including 12 suites) is decorated in a different style. All 3 of its restaurants face the slopes and there is a fitness center, pool, sauna, and conference room. Half board. Closed May, June, October, and November. Major credit cards accepted. Le Belvédère, Méribel (phone: 79-00-56-00; fax: 79-00-59-28). Very expensive.

***Le Chalet* –** One of Méribel's newer hotels, it has 35 rooms (including 6 suites) and is beautifully decorated. Sports-oriented, it is right next to the cable cars and close to a golf course; there is a Jacuzzi, steamroom, sauna, indoor/outdoor pool, and fitness equipment. The restaurant has an open grill and the bar has a piano and fireplace. There also is a meeting room and children's playroom, as well as a garage. Half or full board. Closed May, June, and September to mid-December. Major credit cards accepted. Le Belvédère, Méribel (phone: 79-00-55-71; fax: 79-00-56-22). Very expensive.

***Mont Vallon* –** In addition to the usual fitness amenities of hotels in this region, this 63-room and 7-suite hostelry has 2 restaurants — one offering traditional French cuisine and the other an informal lunch area with a terrace which can be enjoyed when the sun is really hot. Half or full board. Closed May to mid-December. Major credit cards accepted. Mottaret, Méribel (phone: 79-00-44-00; fax: 79-00-46-93). Expensive.

***Le Grand Coeur* –** The oldest hotel in the resort, this member of the Relais & Châteaux group has 42 rooms — all with balconies — and direct access to the slopes. There is a restaurant, piano bar, gameroom, fitness center, sauna, and steambath. Half or full board. Closed May through November. Major credit cards accepted. Méribel (phone: 79-08-60-03; fax: 79-08-58-38). Expensive.

En Route from Méribel – Head back toward Moûtiers; just before you reach it, detour onto N915 to Pralognan-la-Vanoise, which hosted the *Olympics* curling matches. Pralognan is one of the gateways to the Vanoise, the first national park created in France (1963). With its outlying areas, this wonderland for hikers and campers encompasses some 80,000 acres of spectacular mountains and meadows. Automobile traffic is barred in the park itself, and indigenous mountain animals such as the ibex and chamois roam unthreatened.

Other access points also lead to the Vanoise. The road back from Pralognan (the only way out except by foot) branches off toward Champagny-en-Vanoise; follow it through the village and on to its very end to cross a lovely high valley that passes through rugged mountainscapes and arrives at a much less populated jumping-off point for the Vanoise.

For an unexpectedly breathtaking bit of shunpiking (taking side roads) on the way back to Moûtiers from Champagny-en-Vanoise and neighboring Champagny-en-Haut, take the serpentine back road that leads up to Feissons-sur-Salins (D89E). This is the real Savoie: tiny tourist-empty hamlets clinging to the sides of steep hills, and successions of spectacular views. Back in Moûtiers, pick up N90 heading northeast for the summer and winter sports center of Bourg-St-Maurice, and then follow lovely, winding D902 south (and up) to the remarkable resort of Tignes.

CHECKING IN: *Petite Auberge* – An appealing inn slightly off the main road, it offers 15 comfortable rooms, a pleasant terrace restaurant, and a family atmosphere. Closed Sunday evenings, Wednesdays from September to June, the last week of September, and from mid-December to mid-January. Visa accepted. Rte. de Moûtiers, Le Reverset, on the outskirts of Bourg-St-Maurice (phone: 79-07-05-86). Inexpensive.

TIGNES: With the construction of a hydroelectric dam in the 1950s, the old village of Tignes was displaced and reestablished some 1,000 feet higher, by a small natural lake. You'll know you've reached the resort when you come upon a mural of Hercules, painted on the wall of the dam. Said to be the largest fresco in the world, it represents both the strength of the ancient world and the energy of the modern one. There is something unbelievable about the new town (Tignes is actually three villages), where even the oldest buildings date back only 40 years — surely a phenomenon in France. Apartments, boutiques, and restaurants are strung together in an oddly mechanical, modern style that, while undeniably unattractive, manages somehow to blend in perfectly with the imposing moonlike landscape.

Grotesque yet oddly appropriate, Tignes is pure resort, offering superb skiing with 90 miles of runs. New areas have been prepared for the *Olympics* events hosted here — ballet, aerial, moguls, and free-style skiing. The almost 12,000-foot-high Grande Motte glacier dominates the valley — the construction of an underground funicular has made it possible to get almost to the top in just 6 minutes. Together with Val-d'Isère — 8 miles (13 km) away — the area is known as "L'Espace Killy," because most of the runs were designed by Jean-Claude Killy, the French skiing champion.

The resort offers 32 miles of summer skiing, an entry into the Vanoise, water sports on the lake, an 18-hole golf course (the highest in Europe), tennis, and a variety of other activities about which the tourism office (right on the lake; phone: 79-06-15-55) will provide more details. Leaving Tignes, continue on D902 south to Val-d'Isère.

CHECKING IN: *Ski d'Or* – At this particularly pleasant member of the Relais & Châteaux group, all 22 inviting rooms face the new *Olympics* area. It has a good restaurant, fitness center, Jacuzzi, and meeting room. Ski pass included in December, January, and April with a 6-day minimum stay. Closed from May to December. Visa accepted. Val-Claret, Tignes (phone: 79-06-51-60; fax: 79-06-45-49). Expensive.

***Curling* –** All 35 rooms in this hostelry near the *Olympic* stadium have balconies. There is a breakfast room, bar, and meeting room. Breakfast included. Closed June, September, and October. Major credit cards accepted. Val-Claret, Tignes (phone: 79-06-34-34; fax: 79-06-46-14). Moderate.

***Gentiana* –** The restaurant of this 20-room hotel serves a fine meal for the money. Closed September, October, May, and June. Demi-pension is required. Visa accepted. Tignes-le-Lac, Tignes (phone: 79-06-52-46; fax: 79-06-35-61). Hotel, inexpensive; restaurant, moderate.

***Campanules* –** Each of the 36 rooms in this comfortable hostelry has a view of the mountains; there also is a restaurant. Closed September through November and from *Easter* through June. Visa accepted. Tignes-le-Lac, Tignes (phone: 79-06-34-36). Inexpensive.

EATING OUT: *La Troïka* – The delicious fish soup here is served *à la marseillaise* (with garlic mayonnaise, cheese, and croutons). There also is brick-oven pizza in addition to many traditional French appetizers and main dishes. Open daily from December through May; closed Sundays the rest of the year. Reservations advised. Major credit cards accepted. Rue de la Poste, Tignes le Lac, Tignes (phone: 79-06-30-24). Moderate.

VAL-D'ISÈRE: Physically, this town is not as picturesque as Megève or as imposing as Chamonix, but its nightlife is renowned, and the surrounding landscapes provide their own magic. Unlike Tignes, Val-d'Isère is a centralized resort. It is thought by many to feature the best skiing in the world. There are innumerable slopes for every level of skier, and one can whoosh along at altitudes of well over 11,000 feet. Before or after skiing down the Tête de Solaise, stop at the cafeteria at the beginning of the mountain's ascent for something warm to eat or drink. Even in the coldest weather, it's a good spot for relaxing on recliners and enjoying the strong sun.

Jean-Claude Killy, who was born here, designed a difficult track on the side of Rocher de Bellevarde for the 1992 *Olympics* men's downhill events. Killy, the hero of the 1968 Grenoble games, has commented, "It will be very impressive. I'm glad I don't have to run anymore." Maintaining the area's ecological balance was a factor in laying out the trails and stadium — five times more trees were planted next to the stadium than were cut down. At La Daille, 1½ miles (3 km) down the road from Val-d'Isère, a new funicular that goes both above- and underground takes people to the summit of Bellevarde.

In addition to the almost 200 miles of ski runs, Val-d'Isère offers parasailing, gliding, snowshoeing, and the "Renault Passion," a school (phone: 79-06-21-40) where you can learn how to drive on ice and snow (very useful here). Stroll around the old village to look at the small stone houses and the 11th-century church. For après-ski, the *Sofitel* hotel's fitness and water therapy center (see *Checking In*) offers many activities, including an indoor/outdoor pool.

Nightlife plays an important role in Val-d'Isère. Popular spots include pubs such as the *Ginger-man* (phone: 79-06-02-01), where all kinds of Caribbean and Mexican cocktails are served and soft music is played, and clubs like *Club 21* in the *Park* hotel (phone: 79-06-04-93), where the dancing doesn't get started until midnight.

Summer provides a wide variety of outdoor activities, too. Val-d'Isère is in the heart of the Vanoise and offers any number of hikes and excursions. Particularly memorable outings include the cable car ride to the Rocher de Bellevarde and the ascent to the Tête de Solaise. Summer skiing is possible on the 10,000-foot-high Grand Pissaillas glacier. In August, the resort hosts the *International 4-Wheel Drive Motor Show*. For more information, check at the tourist office, at Maison de Val-d'Isère, close to the town center (phone: 79-06-10-83).

Most of the area around Val-d'Isère has become very touristic; those hankering for a taste of the real Savoie can find it in out-of-the-way villages such as La Gurraz and Les Masures.

CHECKING IN: *Christiania* – Totally renovated and enlarged, this comfortable hostelry has a fitness center, swimming pool, restaurant, bar, and circular fireplace in its lobby. Each of the 72 rooms (including 6 suites) has a balcony. Breakfast included. Closed May through November. MasterCard and Visa accepted. Val-d'Isère (phone: 79-06-08-25; fax: 79-41-11-10). Expensive.

Latitudes – One of the newest hotels in town, it has 94 modern rooms, each with cable television. There are 2 restaurants, a piano bar (with a fireplace), nightclub, day-care center, meeting room, and a fitness center for guests only. Closed May to July and September to December. Major credit cards accepted. Val-d'Isère (phone: 79-06-18-88; fax: 79-06-18-87). Expensive.

Sofitel – Known for its *Centre de Balneothérapie* (Health and Fitness Center), its 53 rooms are all decorated in the ubiquitous wood. There are 2 restaurants (one buffet-style), and a lovely bar in the lobby. Closed May to July and September to December. Major credit cards accepted. Val-d'Isère (phone: 79-06-08-30; fax: 79-06-04-41). Expensive.

Savoyarde – Decorated in traditional chalet-style, most of the 44 rooms and 2 suites in this hostelry have terraces. It has a restaurant, bar, sauna, Jacuzzi, and ski room with lockers for each room. Closed May through November except the last 2 weeks of August. Major credit cards accepted. Val-d'Isère (phone: 79-06-01-55; fax: 79-41-11-29). Expensive to moderate.

Altitude – This 41-room hotel has a restaurant with a terrace, bar, and an outdoor swimming pool. Closed mid-May to July and September to December. Master-Card and Visa accepted. Val-d'Isère (phone: 79-06-12-55; fax: 79-41-11-09). Moderate.

Kern – Antiques abound in this charming 19-room inn. Closed May through November. Visa accepted. Val-d'Isère (phone: 79-06-06-06; fax: 79-06-26-31). Inexpensive.

EATING OUT: *La Pedrix Blanche* – Bountiful portions of oysters, mussels, snails, lobster, and crab are served at this casual restaurant. It also has an excellent wine list. Closed May through November. MasterCard and Visa accepted. Val-d'Isère (phone: 79-06-12-09). Moderate.

En Route from Val-d'Isère – Head almost due south (as the crow flies, anyhow) to Briançon, the next major town on the itinerary and 98 miles (157 km) away; follow D902 to N6-E70, to D902, to N91.

For those who love the high, high Alps, this route offers everything a traveler could hope for, including two unbelievably beautiful mountain passes. (Incidentally, the French seem to have a good time crossing these passes on bicycles, a pastime that may strike the four-wheeled visitor as tinged with lunacy.)

The first pass is the Col de l'Iseran, whose summit is about 9,000 feet above sea level. Historically, it was so hard to get to until the mid-19th century, cartographers simply guessed at its location on their maps. And it was only in 1937 that the first road over the pass was opened. As might be expected, the air here is bracing, the views spectacular, and the road, with its intermittent railings, cause for occasional palpitations of the heart.

Properly equipped and experienced (this trail is not for the inexperienced or easily frightened), climbers can hike from the summit of the Col de l'Iseran to the Pointe des Lessières, about 1,000 feet higher, for a magnificent Alpine panorama. Before setting out, make sure conditions are favorable.

The Col de l'Iseran descends into the Maurienne Valley, through which the Arc River courses. This relatively industrial yet nonetheless pleasant route goes through the towns of Bonneval-sur-Arc, Lanslevillard, Termignon, Modane, and St-Michel-de-Maurienne. Bonneval is particularly attractive; its ambience arises mostly out of the delightfully unpretentious Alpine architecture of its buildings. Another especially pleasing village, about 25 miles (40 km) farther, is Aussois. In addition to the attractions of the town itself, there are a couple of interesting sites in the immediate neighborhood: the Monolith of Sardières, a spectacular, isolated rock face that was first scaled in 1960, and the massive fortress of the Esseillon, which was constructed at great labor and expense in 1815 by the Sardinian regime to protect against a French invasion and then was never used.

After St-Michel-de-Maurienne, the road starts to climb steeply; the Col du Télé-graphe is some 2,500 feet above St-Michel, and the slowly expanding resort of Valloire, a little farther down the road, is close to a mile above sea level. For those for whom altitude is everything, this whole strip, valley and pass included, is a lovely preparation for the second great pass of the tour, the Col du Galibier, which takes you from the Maurienne to the Briançonnais, the area surrounding the town of Briançon. Rising to 8,500 feet above sea level, the Col du Galibier is fully as spectacular as the Col de l'Iseran. A magnificent view awaits those who leave their car at the road's high point and climb to the viewing station.

Taking on the Col de l'Iseran and the Col du Galibier in a single day is possible but taxing. Fortunately, a number of attractive places offer lodging along the way, and there is a splendid stopover just south of Col du Galibier.

CHECKING IN: *Auberge du Choucas* – This completely renovated 1770 farmhouse, nestles in an Alpine village just beyond the Col du Galibier. The inn has 8 rooms and 4 independent studios, and easy access to Ecrins National Park and the skiing area of Serre-Chevalier, just 500 yards away. Closed mid-November to *Christmas*. Visa accepted. Le Monêtier-les-Bains (phone: 92-24-42-73; fax: 92-24-51-60). Expensive to moderate.

***Club Les Carrettes* –** Here you'll find 30 modern, comfortable rooms, a swimming pool, a restaurant, and an owner with a sense of humor; he doubles as a nightclub performer in his hotel. Closed mid-April through June and September to mid-December. Visa accepted. Valloire (phone: 79-59-00-99; fax: 79-59-05-60). Expensive to moderate.

***Le Choucas* –** Some 28 comfortable, simple rooms are available here. There is a perfectly tended little garden and an outdoor terrace for dining. Closed May, October, and November. Major credit cards accepted. Aussois (phone: 79-20-32-77). Inexpensive.

***La Marmotte* –** Attractively situated and reasonably priced, it offers 28 rooms. Closed May to mid-June and mid-September to mid-December. Major credit cards accepted. Bonneval-sur-Arc (phone: 79-05-94-82). Inexpensive.

BRIANÇON: Poised at an entry point into Italy and at the foot of several mountain passes, Briançon has long been an important military and commercial center. Today its excellent climate (it is one of Europe's largest healing centers for asthma and also has an international center for sports training in high altitudes) and beautiful location — at 4,333 feet, it is supposedly the highest town in Europe — make it a major tourist center, but unlike many of the more ski-based Alpine resort villages, Briançon has a palpable historical foundation. This city has been lived in. While the newer part of the town is attractive, the real highlight is the Old Town, called Ville Haute or Briançon-Vauban, for the engineer who controlled its reconstruction in the late 17th and 18th centuries after a fire had destroyed the village. Briançon-Vauban is positively redolent with a sense of the past. With no traffic and surrounded by ramparts, cute but not kitschy, it invites the visitor to stroll, to explore, to relax. Leave the car at the Champ de Mars and enter by the Pignerol gate, next to the tourist office (phone: 92-21-08-50). The Grande-Rue is relatively broad and bustling, and each of its numerous side streets has its own special charm. The graceful, twin-towered Eglise Notre-Dame, built by Vauban from 1703 to 1718, is just off Grande-Rue, and beyond it is a lovely view. From the citadel above the old city, there is an excellent panorama of the surrounding peaks and the Durance Valley. The Pont d'Asfeld, constructed in 1754, arcs audaciously over the river gorge at a height of 17 feet; those who can get there (by footpath) can walk across.

Those who wish to stay in the most "alpish" part of the Alps should head back up to the Col de Lautaret, via N91, and continue on to Grenoble, 73 miles (118 km) away. Consider stopping at a major ski resort such as Les Deux-Alpes or L'Alpe-d'Huez.

CHECKING IN: *Vauban* – There are 44 very comfortable rooms in this hostelry with a garden. Closed mid-November to mid-December. Visa accepted. 13 Av. Général-de-Gaulle, Briançon (phone: 92-21-12-11). Inexpensive.

EATING OUT: *Le Péché Gourmand* – Poultry and fish dishes served with exquisite sauces are the specialties at this restaurant. Be sure to save room for the wonderful desserts. Closed the last 2 weeks in November, Sunday evenings and Mondays during May and June and from October to January. Major credit cards accepted. 2 Rte. de Gap, Briançon (phone: 92-20-11-02). Moderate.

En Route from Briançon – The southern route to Grenoble is much more extensive, covering, with its various windings, well over 200 miles (320 km). It is worth the detour, however, and in no case should spectacular Vercors Regional Park be missed, be it along this route or as a day trip from Grenoble. The whole area can be covered in a day, but only by going at such a pace that much of the pleasure of the low mountains, steep buttes, and small villages is lost. It is best to follow this route in a leisurely fashion over a few days.

South of Briançon, the terrain begins to change. With some noteworthy exceptions, the mountains grow tamer, the views become longer and flatter. The area is less majestic somehow, and more subdued, but filled with beauties of its own. Route N94 and then D994 take the traveler through the Vallouise, an area named after the 15th-century King Louis XI. Nearby Queyras Regional Park, attainable by D902 out of Briançon, benefits from excellent weather and a wide variety of flora and fauna; Château-Queyras, a 13th-century fortress, is at its heart.

Route D902 meanders through the park and on to Guillestre, a lively market and resort town; a couple of miles (3 km) west, pick up N94 for a trip through the Durance Valley. About 12 miles (19 km) down N95, just before the enormous (7,410-acre) artificial lake of Serre-Ponçon, is the town of Embrun. As Eburodunum under the Romans, then as a major ecclesiastical center, Embrun was for many years a town of major importance. Now it is little more than a village, with a lovely church, Eglise Notre-Dame, well worth visiting, and a commanding view of the Durance Valley.

After the magnificent lakes of the Alps, the sprawling, mountain-splayed Serre-Ponçon is something of a letdown. Nonetheless, it is a popular sports center and on some summer days seems filled with windsurfers.

Just before the hamlet of La Bâtie-Neuve, about 7 miles (11 km) beyond the lake, D942 branches south off N94. Shortly thereafter, a small road heads north (right) toward Ancelle, St-Léger-les-Mélèzes, Chabottes, and then to Chaillol. This little roundabout offers a wide assortment of scenery: pine forests, farm country, Alpine views — all lovely and definitely off the beaten track.

Pick up N94 again and continue west to Gap, a bustling commercial center with an attractive downtown area. It is also a center from which some serious trout (not to mention perch, chub, and barbel) fishing can be done. For more information about the area's mountain streams and lakes as well as more general information, write to the *Comité Départemental du Tourisme des Hautes-Alpes* (BP 46, Gap 05002), or contact the tourist office (phone: 92-51-57-03). From Gap, pick up the famous and much-traveled Route Napoléon (now N85) and head north. Corps, an especially comely little town perched above Lake Sautet, lies 25 miles (40 km) on N85 north of Gap. If you prefer to bypass Gap, head for St-Bonnet from Chaillol.

A special treat awaits the traveler who leaves N85 at Corps and takes off on back roads through the villages of La Croix-de-la-Pigne, Mens (D66 west of Corps), Lavars (D34A off D34), and Clelles (D526 west of Mens). Far more bucolic than the high Alps, the scenery — pastures, rock faces, and pine forests — is nonetheless splendid in its own right. With each new turn, it appears utterly changed, as if the voyager was looking through a kaleidoscope.

Clelles is at the edge of Vercors Regional Park, a marvelous agglomeration of buttes, boulders, and ravines reminiscent of the scenery in movie westerns. By heading from Clelles to Châtillon-en-Diois on the D7 and D120 and thence to the distressingly mistitled town of Die (actually pronounced *Dee*), on D539 and D93, one gets not only a beautiful tour through Vercors but also a glimpse of the narrow, lavender-planted valley of the Drôme. Die is lovely and renowned for its bubbly white wine, clairette de Die. The main road back into Vercors from Die, D518, scales the Col de Rousset and passes through the resort town of St-Agnan-en-Vercors and on to another resort, St-Eulalie-en-Royans, where D531 leads to yet another resort, Villard-de-Lans (phone: 76-95-10-38), then on to Grenoble.

 CHECKING IN: *Eterlou* – There are 24 rooms in this very pleasant hostelry located in the northern part of Villard-de-Lans. It also has a restaurant, outdoor pool and tennis courts. Closed September to mid-December and April to mid-June. Major credit cards accepted. Villard-de-Lans (phone: 76-95-17-65). Moderate.

Grand Hôtel de Paris – A stately old hotel, it is in Vercors Regional Park in an attractive private park of its own. There is something vaguely and pleasingly anachronistic about this place, which has 54 rooms, a tennis court, a swimming pool, and a small dining room. Closed in April and November. Visa accepted. Villard-de-Lans (phone: 76-95-10-06). Moderate.

Les Barnières I and II – These two hotels, one beside the other, have 82 rooms furnished with all the modern amenities and offer tennis and swimming as well as a superb view of the Durance Valley. Full board required during July and August. *Barnières I* is closed from October through May; *Barnières II* is closed from mid-October to mid-December. Visa accepted. Guillestre (phone: 92-45-04-87 and 92-45-05-07). Inexpensive.

Ferrat – On the doorstep of Vercors park and at the foot of the striking and legendary Mont-Aiguille (legendary because until it was first climbed in the 15th century, supernatural creatures reportedly populated it), this 16-room hotel is handsomely furnished and well managed. There also is a swimming pool. The only problem is its proximity to the much-traveled N75. While extremely accessible, it also is quite noisy. Closed mid-November through February and Tuesdays off-season. Visa accepted. Clelles (phone: 76-34-42-70). Inexpensive.

La Louzière – This mountain-modern, 29-room hostelry nestles in a small resort just above the village of Chaillol, not far from Gap. It affords a spectacular view. Closed mid-April through June and October to mid-December. No credit cards. Chaillol (phone: 92-50-48-44). Inexpensive.

EATING OUT: La Petite Auberge – Across from the train station, this restaurant has good food for the prices; there are 11 rooms as well. Closed Sunday evenings, Wednesdays from September to June, the last week in September, and from mid-December to mid-January. Reservations advised. Visa accepted. Av. Sadi-Carnot, Die (phone: 75-22-05-91). Hotel, inexpensive; restaurant, moderate to inexpensive.

La Poste – A popular and excellent eatery with a terrace, it also has 20 rooms. Closed December and January. Reservations necessary. Visa accepted. Bordering Rte. Napoléon, Corps (phone: 76-30-00-03). Moderate to inexpensive.

GRENOBLE: Grenoble, which has been around since the year 1 BC and is the French Alps' major urban center, claims a population approaching 400,000. The host of the *1968 Winter Olympics,* it is a thriving commercial and intellectual center and handsome as well as historical (it was in Grenoble, for example, that the French Revolution really began). The University of Grenoble was founded in 1339; today it has some 35,000 students.

A walk through the bustling downtown area, with its elegant squares, well-designed parks, and old buildings, gives you a good sense of the city's attractions. Pick up a map at the tourist office (14 Rue de la République; phone: 76-54-34-36). For a bird's-eye view, however, take the little *téléphérique* at Quai Stéphane-Jay and rise across the Isère River to Fort de la Bastille. From the fort, it's possible to explore the neighboring Parc Guy-Pape and the Jardin des Dauphins, sip a cup of coffee or have a bite to eat, and, above all else, gaze ad infinitum at the city and mountain spires (Mont-Blanc included on clear days).

Grenoble has a number of interesting museums, foremost among them the *Musée des Beaux-Arts* (Pl. de Verdun), which has an excellent collection of paintings, including works by Corot, Renoir, Monet, Picasso, Modigliani, and Tanguy. The *Musée Stendhal* (in the old Hôtel de Ville — Town Hall — on Rue Beyle-Stendhal) contains memorabilia pertaining to the author of *Le Rouge et Le Noir* (The Red and the Black) and *La Chartreuse de Parme* (The Charterhouse of Parma), who was born in Grenoble in

1783. Devotees of the writer will find a visit here entertaining (though others may be less enthusiastic). The *Centre National d'Art Contemporain* ("Le Magasin"), a contemporary art museum, is in a former factory at 155 Cours Berriat. The small *Musée de la Résistance et de la Déportation* (Museum of the Resistance and Deportation; 14 Rue Jean-Jacques-Rousseau) is a moving tribute to the heroes and martyrs of World War II; it was built on the site of the birthplace of Stendhal.

Grenoble is undeniably a clean, modern city that has seen tremendous growth in the last few decades, but historic enclaves remain amid the proliferating new buildings. Make your way to Place Grenette in the old part of town and wander among the streets and gardens around it. Across the river, on Quai Xavier-Jouvin, is Eglise St-Laurent, which contains one of the oldest crypts in France.

The Dauphiné region may be best known for its skiing, but it also is abundantly rich in fishing. In every direction from Grenoble, well-stocked rivers, streams, and lakes await visiting anglers. For specific information, write to the *Fédération de la Pêche de l'Isère* (1 Rue Cujas, Grenoble 38000; phone: 76-44-28-39). Follow A41-E712 north to Chambéry, 34 miles (54 km) away.

CHECKING IN: *Park* – This newly renovated hotel is conveniently situated downtown with 40 cheerful rooms and a cozy, wood-paneled lobby and restaurant. Closed the first 2 weeks in August and during *Christmas*. Major credit cards accepted. 10 Pl. Paul Mistral, Grenoble (phone: 76-87-29-11; fax: 76-46-49-88). Expensive.

Le Manoir des Dauphins – While the accommodations here may never win a coveted spread in *Architectural Digest,* all 10 rooms are simply yet handsomely furnished. Its restaurant, however, has caught the attention of the Michelin guide, which has awarded it one star for such dishes as young rabbit with prunes. Closed on Sunday evenings, Tuesdays, and in August. Major credit cards accepted. 48 Cours de la Libération, Grenoble (phone: 76-48-00-06; fax: 76-48-43-04). Expensive.

Lesdiguières – This 36-room hotel is actually located in a park, and is very comfortable. Perhaps because it is a hotel school, the staff is particularly attentive. Closed August and the last 2 weeks in December. Major credit cards accepted. 122 Cours Libération, Grenoble (phone: 76-96-55-36; fax: 76-48-10-13). Moderate.

Les Oiseaux – Six miles (10 km) due south of Grenoble via D269, this hostelry offers an especially appealing setting, 20 pleasant rooms, and a swimming pool. Closed January. Major credit cards accepted. 8 Rue des Perouses, Claix (phone: 76-98-07-74). Moderate.

Skieurs – In a pleasant little village about 10 miles (16 km) north of Grenoble on N512, this hostelry has 18 clean, simple rooms and a swimming pool. Closed April, November, and December. Visa accepted. Le Sappey-en-Chartreuse (phone: 76-88-80-15; fax: 76-88-85-76). Inexpensive.

EATING OUT:

Chavant – Among the more elegant restaurants in the area and a few miles south of Grenoble via D264. The service is good and the menu, which is vast, features traditional as well as more creative fare. There also are 8 rooms and an outdoor swimming pool. Closed Saturday lunch and Wednesdays. Reservations advised. Major credit cards accepted. Bresson (phone: 76-25-15-14; fax: 76-51-18-02). Expensive to moderate.

Poularde Bressane – Specialties at this dining spot include fresh and smoked salmon. Closed Saturday lunch, Sundays, and in August. Major credit cards accepted. 12 Pl. Mistral, Grenoble (phone: 76-87-08-90). Expensive to moderate.

L'Antarctique – This eatery specializes in exotic and traditional fish dishes. Open daily until midnight. Reservations advised. Visa accepted. 9 Bd. Gambetta, Grenoble (phone: 76-46-63-64). Moderate to inexpensive.

L'Epicurien – Ham cooked in hay is the specialty of this fine dining spot. Closed Saturday afternoons and Sundays. Reservations advised. Visa accepted. 1 Pl. Aux Herbes, Grenoble (phone: 76-51-96-06). Moderate to inexpensive.

Au Petit Vatel – A first-rate if simple bistro, it takes its name from a famous French chef who committed suicide when a fish dish turned out to be a failure. Closed Sunday evenings and Mondays. Reservations advised. Visa accepted. 3 Pl. de Gordes, Grenoble (phone: 76-44-68-26). Inexpensive.

En Route from Grenoble – Due north lies the Chartreuse mountain range, one of the highest in France. One of its tranquil valleys harbors a unique history, reason enough to bypass the autoroute to Chambéry and head into the thick of the forest via D512 over the Col de Porte.

In 1084, St. Bruno and seven followers bushwhacked their way 16 miles (26 km) into these unruly hills to found the Carthusian order of monks, which has been there ever since (with the exception of the years 1903 to 1941, when they were expelled). For the past several hundred years the monks, who are isolated not only from the world but from each other most of the time, have been making a well-known green (also yellow) liqueur, chartreuse, whose formula has always remained a secret to all but three of them. The charterhouse of the monks, La Grande Chartreuse, is not open to the public, although in an outbuilding about a mile away is a small museum devoted to the daily life of these recluses. Called La Correrie, off D520-B, it is open from *Palm Sunday* to *All Saints' Day* (November 1). It is possible to hike to the charterhouse gate, but no farther. Those interested in seeing the liqueur distilled may do so in Voiron, 19 miles (30 km) northwest of Grenoble on N75. The proceeds from the million bottles of chartreuse sold annually, half of them to the French, support 460 Carthusian monks in 24 monasteries worldwide.

An easy exit out of the Chartreuse is D520-B west to St-Laurent-du-Pont; then continue to Chambéry on D520 to N6.

CHAMBÉRY: An appealing little city of 57,000, the namesake of a pale vermouth, and the capital of Savoie from the 13th to the 17th century, it exists today as a compact assemblage of squares and boulevards, arcades and alleyways. Marking the bull's-eye of a map of Chambéry, the Fontaine des Eléphants is a charming tribute to the Count of Boigne, commemorating this local hero's (and benefactor's) trip to India; ensconced where Rue de Boigne and Boulevard de la Colonne merge, the four bronze behemoths date from 1838. The ancient château of the Dukes of Savoie still stands, and Rue de Boigne and Rue Juiverie lead pleasantly to it; the large, oblong Place St-Léger, filled with fountains and lampposts, is nearby. Located at the other end of the Boulevard de la Colonne from Fontaine des Eléphants, the tourist office can provide information on the guided tours of the city and its environs (phone: 79-33-42-47). A little over a mile (1.6 km) out of town via D4 is Les Charmettes, where Jean-Jacques Rousseau lived blissfully with Madame de Warens for 6 years; the place is filled with his memorabilia. Try to taste some of the luscious wild raspberries and strawberries that grow on the surrounding mountainsides.

Autoroute A41 continues from Chambéry 31 miles (50 km) north and east to Annecy.

CHECKING IN: Hôtel du Château – Just 3½ miles (6 km) out of Chambéry, this 10-acre property was the home of the Counts of Challes in the 15th century. Now a 63-room Best Western hotel, it features a restaurant serving regional fare, tennis courts, a swimming pool, a casino, and meeting facilities. Open year-round. Major credit cards accepted. Challes-Les-Eaux (phone: 79-72-86-71; fax: 79-72-83-83). Expensive.

Ombremont – This secluded 27-room hotel is ideally located in a park on Lac du

Bourget. A member of the Relais & Châteaux group, it also has a swimming pool and a good restaurant that has earned one Michelin star — specialties include salad of duck and foie gras, king prawns with wild mushrooms, and saddle of lamb cooked in a crust of salt. Closed mid-November to February. Restaurant closed Saturday for lunch and Wednesdays during the low seasons. Major credit cards accepted. One mile (2 km) north of Le Bourget-du-Lac via N504 (phone: 79-25-00-23; fax: 79-25-25-77). Expensive.

Château de Trivier – A quick 4 miles (6 km) east of Chambéry via N6, this lovely 27-room hotel, the ancestral home of the Seigneurs de Trivier, is a pocket of tranquillity. It is surrounded by a small park complete with its own pond. Closed April and December. Major credit cards accepted. Challes-les-Eaux (phone: 79-72-82-87). Moderate.

La Cérisaie – Perched on a height above Lac du Bourget, just off the N504, about 9 miles (14 km) north of Chambéry, it offers a relaxing stay. The 7 rooms offer only the bare comforts, but a pleasant view of the lake and mountains adds to its appeal. Closed Mondays and February through mid-March. Visa accepted. Rte. Dent-du-Chat, just north of the village of Bourget-du-Lac (phone: 79-25-01-29). Inexpensive.

Princes – Located in the center of town is a comfortable 45-room hotel. Its adjoining eatery specializes in fish dishes. Restaurant closed Sunday evenings and the last 2 weeks in July. Major credit cards accepted. 4 Rue Boigne, Chambéry (phone: 79-33-45-36; fax: 79-70-31-47). Hotel inexpensive, restaurant moderate.

EATING OUT: _Roubatcheff_ – This popular and oft-heralded eating spot with one Michelin star makes every dish a delicacy. Besides Russian-inspired dishes such as _blinis de saumon fumé_ (small pancakes packed with smoked salmon), other specialties include pâté of pigeon and foie gras, and _escargot_ in wine sauce. The prix fixe meals are decidedly less expensive. Open daily year-round. Reservations necessary. Major credit cards accepted. Esplanade Curial, Chambéry (phone: 79-33-24-91). Expensive.

En Route from Chambéry – A lovely road heads north toward St-Jean d'Arvey, then through La Feclaz, a local winter sports center, and over Mont-Revard to Aix-les-Bains. This grand old spa is on Lac du Bourget, the lake that inspired the romantic poet Lamartine's tragic lament, "Le Lac." A stroll through Aix's elegant streets or on its long, handsome promenade is well worth the time. Across the lake is the Abbaye de Hautecombe, which deserves a visit, either by boat from Aix or by car. On Sundays at 9:15 AM and weekdays at 9:30 AM, mass includes Gregorian chants.

CHECKING IN: _L'Orée du Lac_ – A jewel close to both Aix-les-Bains and Le Bourget du Lac, this small (10 rooms) but complete hotel with a restaurant (for guests only) boasts its own park, a pool, and tennis courts. Closed from mid-November to mid-January. Major credit cards accepted. La Croix Verte (phone: 79-25-24-19; fax: 79-25-08-51). Expensive.

EATING OUT: _Le Bateau Ivre_ – Set in a former 17th-century barn that was used to store salt, and now surrounded by a garden full of flowers, this restaurant has earned two Michelin stars. Member of the Relais & Châteaux group. Closed Tuesdays and October through April. Reservations necessary. Major credit cards accepted. La Croix Verte (phone: 79-25-02-66; fax: 79-25-25-03). Expensive.

Auberge Lamartine – Named after the famous poet, this dining spot overlooking the lake specializes in game. Try their chartreuse-flavored ice cream with chocolate sauce for dessert. Closed Sunday evenings and Mondays, and in December and January. Visa accepted. 3-5 kms north of Le-Bourget-du-Lac via N504 (phone: 79-25-01-03). Moderate.

ANNECY: Annecy has boomed into a major urban center in the last 20 years for several reasons, not the least of which is a sage town government that has encouraged industry while recognizing the importance of the city's physical setting. Its tourist office is housed in the very modern *Centre Bonlieu,* a shopping mall that also includes a theater (1 Rue Jean-Jaurès; phone: 50-45-00-33).

Annecy is also a city of the past. It was the home of St-François de Sales (1567–1622), the Savoyard nobleman, missionary, and writer who was canonized in 1665. Annecy also played an important part in the life of Jean-Jacques Rousseau (he lost his heart to Madame de Warens here). Today the Old City of Annecy is charming and well preserved, with a number of attractive churches, including the Eglise St-Maurice and the Eglise St-François. The château, the former residence of the Counts of Geneva and the Dukes of Savoie-Nemours, also deserves a visit.

If you are in Annecy the last Saturday of any month, stop at the flea and antiques market that takes place on the streets of the Old City. Other times, try *Atelier du Sarvan* (7 Rue Perrière; phone: 50-45-75-68) and *Art-Chipel* (24 Pl. Ste-Claire; phone: 50-45-65-25) for local handicrafts and Alpine crystals and stones.

The lakefront at Annecy is popular, crowded, and active, but you can get quite a different sense of the lake by taking its east coast around to Talloires. This little village, nestled behind a point and across from the striking (and privately owned) château of Duingt at the foot of the Aravis mountain range, is a model of elegance, tranquillity, and taste. A picnic lunch at the lakeside here is a pleasure, as is the water, at an ideal temperature for swimming. A few miles beyond the south end of the lake is the village of Faverges, a good starting point for some pleasant meandering; take a right at the junction here and head toward Tertenoz and perhaps beyond it for a sense of the real Savoyard countryside, an enticing blend of gently rolling pastures and soul-stirring Alpine vistas.

CHECKING IN: *L'Impérial Palace* – A turn-of-the-century Belle Epoque palace, this enchanting establishment has recently been renovated, refurbished, and reopened. It cachet is further enhanced by its location on the Annecy lakeshore, and the extraordinary mountain views might just literally make you gasp in amazement. All 91 rooms and 8 suites are meticulously appointed, and there are tennis courts, a private beach, 2 restaurants, and a casino, should you feel the need to bet a few francs. Open all year round. Major credit cards accepted. 32 Av. d'Albigny, Annecy (phone: 50-09-30-00; fax: 50-09-33-33). Very expensive.

Abbaye – On the east side of Lake Annecy, this former 17th-century Benedictine abbey (and more recently the refuge of Haiti's Jean-Claude "Baby Doc" Duvalier) has a handsome decor. The 30 rooms were originally monks' cells, but fortunately for visitors, the modern decor is far from spartan. Located right on the lakeshore, there is also a shaded garden and a terrace. Member of the Relais & Châteaux group. Closed mid-December to mid-January. Major credit cards accepted. Talloires, 8 miles (13 km) south of Annecy (phone: 50-60-77-33; fax: 50-60-78-81) Expensive.

Beau-Site – One of the more unique features of this luxurious 15-room hotel annex is its stunning lakefront views. Open from mid-February to November. Visa accepted. Talloires (phone: 50-60-76-11; fax: 50-60-73-42). Expensive to moderate. The main hotel has 29 well-appointed rooms and a private beach that looks out on Lac Annecy. A charming canopy of century-old trees grace the property. Open mid-May to mid-October (phone: 50-60-71-04; fax: 50-60-79-22). Moderate.

Pavillon de l'Ermitage – Seafood lovers should seek out this one-Michelin-star establishment overlooking the lake, midway between Annecy and Talloires. Specialties include *omble chevalier* (salmon fresh from the lake) and *soufflé de brochet* (pike soufflé). After a filling dinner, it's possible to retire to one of 11 rooms. Closed

November through February. Reservations necessary. Major credit cards accepted. Chavoires (phone: 50-60-11-09). Expensive to moderate.

Marceau – Perched on a hilltop, this 16-room hostelry is quiet and restful, and there is a tennis court and garden. Closed mid-December to mid-January. Major credit cards accepted. Doussard, just south of Lake Annecy's southern shore (phone: 50-44-30-11; fax: 50-44-39-44). Moderate.

Florimont – This 27-room hotel also has a terrace garden. Its 2 restaurants offer quality food at reasonable prices. Open daily year-round. Major credit cards accepted. Faverges, 2 miles (3 km) toward Albertville on N508 (phone: 50-44-50-05). Moderate to inexpensive.

Gay Séjour – Aptly called "gay sojourn," this family-run enterprise off the beaten track offers 11 rooms with lovely mountain views. Closed Mondays and Sundays evenings and during January. Major credit cards accepted. Tertenoz, just south of Faverges, which lies 16 miles (26 km) south of Annecy on N508; go 2 miles (3 km) toward the Col de Tamie on the D12 (phone: 50-44-52-52; fax: 50-44-49-52). Inexpensive.

EATING OUT: Auberge de l'Eridan – This place sets the best table in Annecy (two Michelin stars), if not in the French Alps — maybe because the chef seasons his fare with fresh Alpine herbs that he picks himself (try the rosemary and oregano sorbet). Those who savor unusual and innovative fare should make a beeline for some of the specialties of this member of the Relais & Châteaux group, such as tomatoes stuffed with *lotte* (monkfish) in verbena juice or veal-kidney with blue-gentian sauce. The dining room features sumptuous floral displays. Little wonder the establishment is a favorite of French President François Mitterrand. Closed the last 2 weeks in August, *Christmas,* and in February. Reservations necessary. Major credit cards accepted. 7 Av. de Chavoires, Annecy-le-Vieux (phone: 50-66-22-04). Very expensive.

Auberge du Père Bise – This restaurant, on the eastern shore of Lake Annecy, is renowned throughout France for the quality and richness of its cuisine; Michelin gives it two stars. Duck is a specialty here, as witnessed by the *tourte de canard* (duck pie) and the *pot-au-feu de canard* (duck stew), among other dishes. Count on a meal you won't forget, but expect to pay for the pleasure. Reservations necessary. Closed mid-November to mid-Janaury. Major credit cards accepted. Some 20 rooms and 10 suites also are available at this member of the Relais & Châteaux group. Talloires, 8 miles (13 km) south of Annecy (phone: 50-60-72-01; fax: 50-60-73-05). Very expensive.

Le Grand Alexandre – Excellent traditional French fare is served at this eatery. One of the prix fixe meals includes a different wine to go with each dish. Open daily year-round. Reservations advised. Major credit cards accepted. Faubourg des Annonciades, Annecy (phone: 50-51-32-35). Moderate.

Burgundy

When most people hear "Burgundy," they think of wine. But while it is true that the wines of this region are world-renowned, Burgundy offers much more than the pleasures of wine to the visitor. Its countryside is remarkably varied, ranging from the bucolic rolling pastures of Aix-en-Othe to the rough and striking hill country around Cluny to the lakes and forests of the Morvan. Burgundian villages seem to be caught in an enchanting time warp: Driving along a pleasant, winding country road, visitors suddenly find themselves among beflowered stone buildings that date from the 16th century. However, Burgundy's unchanging, timeless quality is due not only to the landscape, with its cathedrals, châteaux, and abbeys, but also to its people. Like so many agrarian folk, they are profoundly conservative, rooted to their land, and suspicious of the city and modern ways. Though Paris is only a few hours' drive away on the autoroute, it is a trip that not a few Burgundians have made only once, if at all. And it may well be that the quietude and tranquillity of today's Burgundy is due to a collective, subconscious memory of past glories. Some 5 centuries ago, the power and influence of the Dukes of Burgundy rivaled that of any crowned head in Europe. Whatever the reason, Burgundy is now a land in semiretirement, ripe with age and leaning back in its rocking chair, enjoying its repose after a most successful career.

Burgundy's history is as long as it is rich. At Solutré, a village at the foot of an imposing precipice in the Mâconnais region, archaeologists came upon the skeletons of 100,000 horses. Their theory is that the horses were herded together and then driven over the cliff, probably by fire, about 15,000 years ago, at the same time that Egypt's New Kingdom was reigning supreme in the so-called cradle of civilization many thousands of miles to the east. Some 10,000 years later, Burgundy was a center of Celtic civilization and subsequently of Celtic resistance to Rome's northern expansion. It was at Bibracte, the present Autun, that Vercingétorix held a war council of tribes committed to contest Rome's drive into Burgundy, and at Alésia (Alise Ste-Reine), Vercingétorix with his 250,000 troops went down in defeat at the hands of Julius Caesar. With the fall of the Roman Empire, the area changed in character and in name. The Burgund tribe originally was from the Baltic Sea. They gradually emigrated south and west, and in the 5th century AD, Aetius, a general charged with defending the crumbling Roman Empire, invited them to settle in Sapaudia (Savoie). The Burgundians soon extended their hegemony to west of the Saône, and the kingdom of Burgundy was born.

It was not until the 14th century, however, that Burgundy's halcyon days began. Philip the Bold, John the Fearless, Philip the Good, Charles the Bold — this succession of dukes had enough power to challenge that of the Kings of France. Palace life in Dijon was opulent, and the Burgundian

Renaissance preceded the French one by several decades. During the 1470s, this power was sharply reduced, with Burgundy itself being annexed by Louis XI and the remaining provinces of Flanders, Artois, and Franche-Compte going over to Austria by marriage. By then, though, the legacy already had been established; the century of glory had lent to Burgundy the luxurious sheen of royalty. It is an aura that remains today.

Burgundian cuisine is part and parcel of its history. It was one of the central luxuries in the life of the grand Dukes of Burgundy, and today Dijon still enjoys a reputation as a gastronomic capital. It is a cuisine for gourmands as well as gourmets, with the servings as generous as they are delicious. Burgundian dishes are hearty and based on the region's produce, including carefully bred chickens from Bresse, lean beef from Charolais, and freshwater fish from the Saône and Rhône rivers. Four universally recognized Burgundian specialties include *coq au vin* (chicken in wine sauce), *escargots* (snails) cooked in their shells with garlic butter, *oeufs en meurette* (poached eggs in red wine sauce), and *boeuf bourguignon* (beef in red wine sauce). Cassis, the local liqueur made from black currant, is well worth sampling; try a *kir* (*aligoté,* a dry white wine, with cassis), a *kir royal* (made with champagne), or the sweeter *suze cassis* (a combination of cassis and suze, the gentian-derived liqueur). Naturally, every visitor should sample the famous Burgundian wines, which include the dry white made in Chablis, the full-bodied and aromatic reds and whites produced along the Côte d'Or south of Dijon, and the light, fruity reds made in the Beaujolais. Burgundian wine lists are a pleasure to the connoisseur and novice alike, although the latter may find the *vins de table* far less expensive and eminently satisfactory.

The best way to see Burgundy is by car — put it into gear, start traveling the byways, and you will have great trouble being bored. The route outlined below starts in the Pays d'Othe, in the northern tip of Burgundy, and works its way south, culminating with visits to Beaune, home of the Hôtel-Dieu, and to Cluny, the seat of the ancient abbey. For those who seek a change of pace, there is an alternative to the automobile — the boat. More than 600 miles of navigable canals run through Burgundy, and you can tour them on day cruises, on boats you rent and pilot yourself, or on luxurious barge "hotels." These floating cruise craft operate from April to November at costs ranging from about $1,000 up to $3,000 per person per week, meals included. Reservations are made through *Continentale de Croisières* (9 Rue Jean Renaud; phone: 80-30-49-20; fax: 80-30-27-01) or by contacting *Continental Waterways/Abercrombie and Kent* (1420 Kensington Rd., Oakbrook, Illinois; phone: 708-954-2944; fax: 708-954-3324). Write to the Comité Régional du Tourisme de Bourgogne (BP 1602, Dijon 21035; phone: 80-50-10-20; fax: 80-30-59-45) for their brochure *Boating Holidays in Burgundy,* which details a wide variety of regional cruising possibilities.

Accommodations, as throughout France, are pretty uniformly comfortable and clean. There are numerous château- and mill-hotels, which are surprisingly moderate in price and provide a special experience. In general, you can expect to pay $90 and up for a double room in hotels listed as expensive; $60 to $90 in moderate; and under $60 at inexpensive places. Meals in general tend to be fairly expensive; however, dinner for two with wine costs about $100 and up in a restaurant listed as expensive; from $75 to $100 in moderate; and below $75 in one considered inexpensive. Service usually is included.

SENS: Originally called Agendicum, this was one of the most important towns in Roman Gaul. Made a regional capital in AD 395, the boundaries of its domain were soon adopted by the church, and Sens became a major archbishopric. It was split up in 1622, after which Sens began its slow decline to its present status as a modest provincial town.

Sens's centerpiece, as in so many Burgundian towns, is the Cathédrale St-Etienne, a prime example of early Gothic architecture. Particularly noteworthy are the stained glass windows, constructed between the 12th and 17th centuries. Be sure to visit the Trésor (Treasure); it's one of the richest in France, offering a unique collection of fabrics, liturgical vestments, shrouds, tapestries, and holy reliquaries. The Palais Synodal was the seat of the Officialité, a major ecclesiastical tribunal. It is architecturally elegant and historically grisly: Included in the tour is a visit to the dungeon where heretics and sinners awaited trial. The Synodal Palace was restored in the 19th century by the famous Eugène Viollet-le-Duc, an architect whose name crops up frequently in the cathedrals of Burgundy.

A stroll through Sens is imperative if you want a real sense of the town. In particular, look for the two interesting old buildings, called Abraham's House and the House of the Pillar, which sit beside each other at the intersection of Rue de la République and Rue Jean-Cousin.

CHECKING IN/EATING OUT: *Manoir de l'Onde* – An idyllic small hotel in the countryside around five miles north of Sens by the D58 road. Ask for a room that looks out on the Yvonne River. There is also a restaurant with very reasonable prices. Open all year; closed Sundays and Mondays from September to April. Major credit cards accepted. 33 Rue Barrage, Villeperrot 89140 (phone: 86-67-05-93; fax: 86-96-37-25). Moderate.

Le Palais – A local favorite for two reasons: good cooking and good prices. Closed Sunday evenings, Mondays, 2 weeks in January, and 2 weeks in June. Major credit cards accepted. 18 Pl. de la République, in front of the cathedral, Sens (phone: 86-65-13-69). Moderate to inexpensive.

En Route from Sens – South on the N77 is the Pontigny Abbey, built between 1150 and 1212, and considered one of Burgundy's finest examples of Cistercian architecture. Then head south on N6 to Joigny, the "gateway to Burgundy," worth a stop for its three-star restaurant, *La Côte St-Jacques* (see *Checking In/Eating Out*) as well as for its streets lined with half-timbered houses and two picturesque churches, St. Thibault and St. Jean. Leave Joigny via D943 traveling east, then turn south toward château country to visit two indisputably fine châteaux near each other, Tanlay and Ancy-le-Franc. Tanlay, 5½ miles (9 km) to the east of Tonnerre on D965, was built in the 16th century, and its stately elegance reflects the spirit of Louis XIII. The Little Château, as it is called, is most notable for its frescoes, but a tour of the interior reveals a fine display of antique furniture as well. A few miles farther east via D965, in the town of Châtillon-sur-Seine, is a fine museum with exhibits from the Treasure of Vix, a sepulcher from the 6th century BC. Among the most striking of many impressive artifacts is an enormous bronze vase — almost 5½ feet tall and weighing well over 400 pounds.

Ancy-le-Franc, which can be reached from Tanlay via Pimelles, was built a few years before Tanlay by Antoine de Clermont, Earl of Tonnerre, according to plans drawn up by the famed Italian architect Sebastiano Serlio. Among the many impressive rooms in the palace, the most striking is the Guards Hall, an immense space of almost 3,000 square feet.

From Ancy-le-Franc, take D905 and D965 toward Auxerre; along the way you'll pass through Chablis, home of the famous wine. Cellars in the area usually allow visitors, so ask around if you're interested in wine tasting.

CHECKING IN/EATING OUT: *La Côte St-Jacques* – An 18th-century former *maison bourgeoise* that won its third star from Michelin in 1986 and is now the weekend destination of connoisseurs from Paris and beyond, who come to savor such specialties as sea bass in caviar cream sauce, an ethereal *poularde à la vapeur de champagne* (chicken with a delicate champagne sauce) or truffle ravioli. Many of the 25 rooms and suites of this member of the Relais & Châteaux group have been redecorated in Flamboyant style — with prices to match. Closed January. Major credit cards accepted. 14 Faubourg de Paris, Joigny (phone: 86-62-09-70; fax: 86-91-49-70). Expensive.

La Vaudeurinoise – A 6-room hostelry, praiseworthy for the tranquillity of its surroundings and a tradition of gracious service and excellent cuisine. Nearby are tennis courts and horseback riding. Hotel and restaurant closed in February; restaurant closed Wednesday evenings and Thursdays off-season. Major credit cards accepted. Rte. de Grange-Sèche, Vaudeurs (phone: 86-96-28-00; fax: 86-96-28-03). Moderate.

AUXERRE: This attractive and bustling city on the left bank of the River Yonne has been the home of a number of French celebrities, including Germain, the famed bishop of the 5th century AD, and Marie-Noël, the 20th-century "poetess of love."

With its sculpted portals and elegant nave, the Cathédrale St-Etienne is a first class example of 13th-century Flamboyant Gothic architecture. Be sure to visit the Romanesque crypt; hauntingly beautiful, it features a rare and remarkable 11th-century fresco titled *Christ on Horseback.* Also impressive are the frescoes in the crypts of the Abbaye St-Germain, which was established in the 6th century by Queen Clothilde on the spot where that saint was buried in AD 448. Numerous old houses are notable, including the Coche d'Eau, at the foot of the Abbaye St-Germain in the Marine quarter, and the buildings at 16-18 Place de l'Hôtel; 3-5 Place Charles-Surugue; 14-16 Rue Sous-Murs; and 21 Rue de Paris.

EATING OUT: *Jean-Luc Barnabet* – An old building on the river quai, fitted out in post-modern decor, is one of the newest spots for local *becs fins.* The young chef, formerly found in the kitchens of *La Petite Auberge* in nearby Vaux, shows considerable promise (Michelin has awarded him one star). Specialties include *sandre en meurette bourguignonne* (pickerel in red burgundy sauce), and *vis de veau poêles aux champignons de bois* (veal sweetbreads sautéed with wild mushrooms). Closed Sunday night and Mondays and from December 22 to early January. Reservations advised. Major credit cards accepted. 14 Quai République, Auxerre (phone: 86-51-68-88). Expensive to moderate.

La Chamaille – An ancient 7-room manor house on the edge of a little stream, where the one-star cooking is traditional Burgundian (a meat terrine is brought to your table while you are reading the menu). The hosts are friendly, and the chablis and other local wines are superb. Closed Mondays, Tuesdays, *Christmas,* mid-January to mid-February, and 1 week in September. Major credit cards accepted. 4 Rte. de Boiloup, Chevannes, 5 miles (8km) southwest of Auxerre via N151 and D1 (phone: 86-41-24-80; fax: 86-46-42-96).

En Route from Auxerre – Head toward Noyers-sur-Serein via St-Bris-le-Vineux and D956. (Incidentally, the wine of St-Bris-le-Vineux is less well known than that of Chablis, but it's thought by many Burgundians to be superior.) Noyers is a special treat:

It's a very well preserved little medieval town that sees surprisingly few tourists. Not far away, via D86 and D11, Montréal is another pretty medieval town; at the crest of the hill on which it sits is a small church, from the back of which appears a superb panorama of the surrounding countryside.

CHECKING IN/EATING OUT: *Moulin de Ste-Vertu* – The kind of place you hear about only in legend: a 7-room country inn where you can have a six-course meal for almost nothing. It's an old farmhouse with antique furnishings. Open year-round. No credit cards accepted. Ste-Vertu (phone: 86-75-90-09). Inexpensive.

AVALLON: High on a hill above the Vallée du Cousin, Avallon was a major stronghold during the Middle Ages. As weaponry became more sophisticated, however, its military significance declined until Louis XIV finally sold the ramparts to the citizens of the town.

Though an attractive city in its own right, as far as tourism is concerned, Avallon is resigned forever to play second fiddle to its near neighbor, Vézelay, whose cathedral is widely considered the gem of Burgundy. Nonetheless, Avallon has much to offer. The Eglise St-Lazare is an ancient edifice dating from the 4th century AD. Around AD 1000, the church received a relic of St. Lazarus, the patron saint of lepers, and pilgrimages to the church by lepers began en masse. The church was too small — it proved always to be too small — and was expanded a number of times through the following centuries. Its most interesting features are the two Romanesque portals, with varied sculptures showing musicians of the Apocalypse, signs of the zodiac, wine, acanthus leaves, and more. No visit to Avallon is complete, however, without a leisurely stroll of the ramparts and a look at the 15th-century clock tower on the Butcher's Gate.

CHECKING IN/EATING OUT: *Hostellerie de la Poste* – A recently renovated, atmospheric little inn with only 23 rooms, it dispenses consistently fine food and wines. Open year-round. Major credit cards accepted. 13 Pl. Vauban, Avallon (phone: 86-34-06-12). Expensive.

Relais Fleuri – Modern amenities, including tennis courts and a swimming pool, are a definite plus for this well-managed, 48-room hotel in a pleasant setting at the edge of Avallon. Another draw is its fine restaurant that serves traditional Burgundian specialties. Open daily. Major credit cards accepted. Rte. Saulieu, Avallon (phone: 86-34-02-85; fax: 86-34-09-98). Moderate.

En Route from Avallon – Head southwest toward Vézelay via the Vallée du Cousin, a lovely, shaded road that wends its way beside the Cousin River. There are numerous places where you can pull off the road for an undisturbed, feet-in-the-water picnic. Turn left at Pontaubert and follow D957 into Vézelay. Or, if you're in the mood for something exotic, pick up N6 out of Avallon or after the Vallée du Cousin and head for the Grottes d'Arcy-sur-Cure, some 12 miles (19 km) north of Vézelay. There are approximately 1½ miles of subterranean grottoes here, about half of which can be explored; it's a fantastic underground world of stalactites, stalagmites, and lakes.

CHECKING IN/EATING OUT: *Château de Vault de Lugny* – Surrounded by a moat in a bucolic setting, this 16th-century château has 11 charmingly appointed rooms with private bathrooms. There is a small dining room which is only open to guests of the château. Open from mid-March to mid-November. Major credit cards accepted. Avallon (phone: 86-34-07-86; fax: 86-34-16-36). Expensive to moderate.

Moulin des Ruats – This converted mill on the banks of the River Cousin has 26 simply decorated rooms and a restaurant. It's a soothing place to sojourn, with the stillness of the glade disturbed only by the rush of water through the millrace. The inn is closed from mid-November to mid-December and January to February

15. Major credit cards accepted. Vallée du Cousin, Avallon (phone: 86-34-07-14; fax: 86-31-65-47). Hotel, moderate; restaurant, expensive.

Moulin des Templiers – Well managed and tiny (14 rooms), this place has an eccentric country charm — its owner keeps a small menagerie (goats, turkeys, and so on) across the road. Breakfast served on a terrace next to the Cousin river. Closed November through mid-March. No credit cards accepted. Vallée du Cousin, Avallon (phone: 86-34-10-80). Moderate.

VÉZELAY: About 9 miles (14 km) up the road from Avallon is Vézelay, a town famous for that jewel of Romanesque architecture, the Basilique Ste-Madeleine. The basilica has a long history. It is part of the Abbey of Vézelay, which was founded in the 9th century, according to popular memory, by the legendary Girart de Rousillon, an early Count of Burgundy, and was consecrated by Pope John VIII in AD 878. In the 11th century, the abbey was taken over by the powerful Abbey of Cluny. A multitude of miracles were reported to have taken place thanks to the relics of Mary Magdalene that were housed here, and so began an onslaught of pilgrimages to the church. In 1122, this precipitated a disaster. A massive fire broke out and the church collapsed, burying thousands of pilgrims alive. But the church soon was rebuilt, this time with a narthex (a vestibule leading to the nave) added to provide overnight lodging for the many pilgrims. Some years later, other relics of the saint were found in Provence, and this decreased Vézelay's appeal. Later still, the basilica suffered destruction during the religious wars and then the French Revolution; eventually, it went into decline. It was the poet Prosper Mérimée, working in his capacity as inspector of historical monuments, who "discovered" the beauty of the basilica and undertook an immense restoration of the building that lasted from 1840 till 1859. Again, the architect Viollet-le-Duc played a leading role in the restoration.

Today, the church is a masterpiece of light and space. As the novelist André Malraux wrote, "Romanesque architecture, in its organization of interior space, is not striving after decorative effects, but . . . to release a feeling of sacredness, to express the inexpressible." The Basilique Ste-Madeleine accomplishes these goals admirably. Note particularly the tympanum over the central entryway and the sculpted details of the interior columns. For energetic visitors, a hike to the top of the tower is well worth the effort. The view of the surrounding countryside is nothing short of magnificent. In the village of St-Père-sous-Vézelay is an often-overlooked Gothic jewel, Eglise de Nôtre-Dame de Saint-Père, whose human scale and delicate architecture are especially appealing.

CHECKING IN: *L'Espérance* – A quintessentially elegant 17-room hotel, and a member of the Relais & Châteaux group, that's furnished with antiques and overlooks a flower garden. Its glass-enclosed restaurant, ranked by many as Burgundy's finest, is almost as great a magnet as Ste-Madeleine, and has been awarded three Michelin stars. (See "Romantic Hostelries" in *For The Experience,* DIVERSIONS.) Closed during January. Restaurant closed Tuesdays and Wednesday lunch. Major credit cards accepted. St-Père-sous-Vézelay (phone: 86-33-20-45; fax: 86-33-26-15). Very expensive.

Le Pontot – Classified as a "historic private home," this 15th-century residence in the Town Hall Square offers 7 rooms and 3 suites, each uniquely appointed. A large Louis XVI–style room has canopy beds, a fireplace, and a dressing room; another apartment has stone floors, a 16th-century beamed ceiling, and antique peasant furniture. All have modern baths. Breakfast is served in the paneled Louis XVI Salon or in a walled garden. No restaurant, since *L'Espérance* (see above) is nearby, but boat trips and even balloon rides can be arranged. Major credit cards accepted. Town Hall Square, Vézelay (phone: 86-33-24-40). Expensive to moderate.

En Route from Vézelay – Head south toward Autun through the Morvan, the northern reaches of France's Massif Central and of Burgundy's hill country. *Morvan* is derived from the Celtic for "black mountain," and it captures the spirit of the region well. Less prosperous and less bucolic than the rest of Burgundy, like so many backwoods areas it is looked down upon as something of a poor sister by many Burgundians. Nonetheless, with its many lakes and forests, it is a regional center for sports lovers and a popular weekend spot for Parisians.

There are innumerable ways to cut through the Morvan, almost any of which will yield a host of striking vistas. A good midway point is Château-Chinon, the capital of the area. A hike to the top of Calvary hill in Château-Chinon provides an excellent view of the surrounding landscape. South of Château-Chinon is the High Morvan, the more mountainous part of the region. Take D27 through the Forêt de la Gravelle, then head toward St-Léger, 5 miles (8 km) to the east of which is Mont-Beuvray; from there, on clear days, one can see as far as Mont-Blanc, hundreds of miles to the east.

AUTUN: This city owes its name to Augustus Caesar; originally called Augustodonum, it was a major Roman garrison and served as a base of operations for the destruction of the Bibracte. In Gallo-Roman times, it became an important commercial center on the route between Lyons and Boulogne. Autun's prominence made it a popular military target, and after many invasions, the city went into decline.

However, Autun enjoyed a renaissance in the 15th century, thanks largely to the efforts of Nicolas Rolin, Philip the Good's chancellor and a native of Autun, and his son, the Cardinal Rolin, who made Autun a major church center.

Today, Autun is a thriving provincial town of some 20,000 inhabitants, with several sights of interest. The Cathédrale St-Lazare, built between 1120 and 1146, is most celebrated for the tympanum over the central portal. Rendered by the sculptor Gislebertus, it portrays the Last Judgment and is less gloomy than many such depictions; heaven occupies the greatest portion of the tympanum, with hell confined to a small corner on the right. Just a few steps away is the *Musée Rolin* (3 Rue de Bancs; phone: 85-52-09-76), in a house built for Nicolas Rolin; it has a fine collection of Gallo-Roman artifacts as well as of 14th- and 15th-century sculpture and paintings (open daily except Tuesdays from 10 AM to noon and 2 to 4 PM; in the summer, it stays open until 6 PM). Among the latter are two depictions of Old Autun that seem to combine the qualities of map and painting, which gives the viewer a good sense of what the city was like. La Porte St-André (St. Andrew's Gate), on the north side of town, is a remnant of the ancient Roman walls that used to surround Autun; this great edifice has two large arches through which vehicles may pass and two smaller ones for pedestrians.

Between June and August every year, Autun celebrates its Roman past with an *Augustodunum Festival* in which 600 costumed Autun citizens take part. Check with the city's tourism office for details; 3 Ave. Charles de Gaulle (phone: 85-52-20-34).

CHECKING IN/EATING OUT: *Hostellerie de Vieux Moulin* – A lovely waterside garden distinguishes this 16-room hotel and its dining room. Closed mid-December through March; restaurant also closed Sunday evenings and Mondays off-season. Major credit cards accepted. Porte d'Arroux, Autun (phone: 85-52-10-90). Hotel, moderate to inexpensive; restaurant, expensive to moderate.

Les Ursulines – A hotel and restaurant located in a former convent, with 32 comfortable and (as one might imagine) very quiet rooms and 5 suites surrounding a well-manicured garden. In fine weather you can dine on the restaurant's terrace, which overlooks the city. 14 rue Rivault, Autun (phone: 85-52-68-00). Open every day all year. Expensive to moderate.

En Route from Autun – The surrounding area offers many short excursions. La Cascade de Brisecou (Breakneck Waterfall) is about 1½ miles (2 km) south of Autun via D256. Leave the car at the church at Couhard and take the 20-minute walk to the waterfall. On the return trip, note the odd, pyramidal Pierre de Couhard, believed to date from Roman times. Also of interest is the Château de Sully. Built in the 15th century, it was the birthplace of Marshal MacMahon, President of the French Republic from 1873 to 1879. To visit the château, take D973 out of Autun, then make a left onto D326 at Creusefond. (Unfortunately, visitors may enjoy only the exterior of the château; the interior is closed to the public.) Head back northwest along the eastern edge of the Parc Régional du Morvan to the town of Saulieu.

CHECKING IN/EATING OUT: *Château de Chailly* – A Renaissance castle in the midst of calm and greenery (owned by a Japanese consortium), this elegant structure was transformed into a 45-room hostelry and opened in 1990. Its grounds include an 18-hole golf course and tennis courts. The accommodations rank among the most luxurious in the region. Closed the month of January. Major credit cards accepted. Pouilly-en-Auxois (phone: 80-90-89-61; fax: 80-90-89-78). Expensive.

La Côte d'Or – Awarded a third star from Michelin last year, Bernard Loiseau finally figures among the elite of France's chefs, after several years of aspiring, perfecting, and remodeling to meet the test. In addition to the celestial dining room, the 22-room hostelry, which is a member of the Relais & Châteaux group, has two sections — an old part dating from the 19th century, and a more modern wing of rooms with garden views. (Rumor has it that this is a favorite stopover for French President Mitterand). Closed 2 weeks in March and from late November to early December. Major credit cards accepted. 2 Rue d'Argentine, Saulieu (phone: 80-64-07-66; fax: 86-34-09-98). Expensive.

La Tour d'Auxois – It has 30 modest but clean and comfortable rooms, somewhat reminiscent of those found in a college dormitory. The restaurant is more appealing, with a small terrace for aperitifs and very tasty prix fixe meals. Closed December to January 15; restaurant also closed Sunday evenings and Mondays. 10 Rue Sallier, Saulieu (phone: 80-64-13-30). Inexpensive.

SEMUR-EN-AUXOIS: Just a few miles southeast of Montréal via D11 and D954 is the lovely town of Semur-en-Auxois. During the Middle Ages, it enjoyed a reputation as a virtually impregnable fortress, and it still has all the lineaments of its past might. The approach to Semur via the flower-lined Pont Joly gives the visitor a striking first glimpse of this medieval town, although a walking tour is probably the best way to enjoy it. You might stroll along the ramparts for a look at the many attractive old buildings and a view of the surrounding countryside, or stop in at Eglise Notre-Dame, which originally was built in the 11th century but contains elements added from the 13th to the 16th century. The church also underwent restoration under the direction of the 19th-century architect Viollet-le-Duc.

Not far from Semur, and within a few miles of each other, are a number of unusually interesting places. The first of these, some 12 miles (19 km) due east of Semur and more than a little reminiscent of Montréal, is Flavigny-sur-Ozerain. This medieval walled city at the top of a hill and surrounded on three sides by water is very appealing for its sleepy, scarcely trafficked streets, pretty old houses, and ancient ramparts. Flavigny was a fortification of some significance during the Middle Ages, but it's mostly notable these days for the popular lozenges produced by a nearby abbey.

About 4½ miles (7 km) from Flavigny via D29 is the town of Alise-Ste-Reine, the site of ancient Alésia, where the 250,000-strong army of Vercingétorix succumbed to the siege of the amassed Roman legions in 52 BC. The saga of Vercingétorix's defeat is tragic. He was taken as a prisoner to Rome, kept there for 6 years, forced to participate in Caesar's triumphal march, and, after that humiliation, summarily executed. In the 19th century, Napoleon III had an enormous statue of Vercingétorix built at the site of ancient Alésia, where it still stands in all its kitschy glory.

A few miles down the road from Alise-Ste-Reine is the Château de Bussy-Rabutin, small (by château standards), handsome, and positively bubbling over with effrontery. The château reflects the spirit of its irrepressible owner, the soldier and writer Roger de Rabutin, Comte de Bussy, whose barbed verses incurred the wrath of Louis XIV. He was sent into exile at Bussy-Rabutin, where he continued his literary endeavors and wrote *An Amorous History of the Gauls*. For this effort, which mocked members of Louis's court, Roger de Rabutin landed in the Bastille; upon his release, he found much to his dismay that his mistress, for whom he had written his splendid lines, had lost patience and left him.

The château at Bussy-Rabutin was known to contemporaries of the count as the Temple of Impertinence, and it deserved the title. A typically irreverent touch is the series of moons at the entrance, a not-so-subtle counterpoint to that glorious symbol so often used to represent the Sun King, Louis XIV, in Paris.

A quite different experience is found at the Abbaye de Fontenay, north of Bussy-Rabutin toward Montbard. This 12th-century Cistercian monastery has gone through a number of changes since its heyday. It first was abused by avaricious abbots, then converted into a paper factory after the French Revolution. Nonetheless, most of the buildings are intact, and a visit to the tranquil, elegant site gives a fine sense of the monastic life some 800 years ago. The guides at Fontenay can be prim to the point of schoolmarmishness — a point against the abbey, especially after a tour given by the lighthearted guides at Bussy-Rabutin. If one is prepared to wear a fittingly pious expression, however, the visit is worth it.

About 3 miles (5 km) south of Semur-en-Auxois (on the D103) is the Lac de Pont, a large artificial lake with its own sandy beach surrounded by a forest. A lovely hiking trail circles the lake, making this a perfect place to picnic or swim. West of Semur (on the D954) is the sleepy town of Epoisses, whose local château, owned by the same family since the 17th century, has welcomed such noble visitors as Henri IV, Madame de Sévigné, and Chateaubriand. Built over several centuries, the château has the remains of a 7th-century moat, a lovely 15th-century *pigeonnier* (pigeon tower), a 13th-century church and tower, and a Renaissance well. The château's gardens are open every day from *Easter* to September from 9 AM to 7 PM; the interior of the château is open to visitors in July and August, from 10 AM to noon and 3 to 6 PM. Closed Tuesday. In spite of its noble past, Epoisses is now known primarily for its local cheese, a tangy, runny, unpasteurized cow's milk cheese with an orange-red exterior achieved by bathing the cheese in sage and *marc de Bourgogne* (grape brandy) as it ages.

CHECKING IN/EATING OUT: *Hostellerie du Val-Suzon* – It has a tranquil atmosphere, a pleasant little garden, a fine kitchen, and 17 rooms, 10 of them in a neighboring chalet. Hotel closed January to mid-February; restaurant also closed Wednesdays and Thursdays for lunch off-season. Major credit cards accepted. Rte. N71, Val-Suzon (phone: 80-35-60-15; fax: 80-35-61-36). Hotel, moderate; restaurant, expensive to moderate.

***Auberge Chez Guite* –** Part of a functioning farm, this *gîte* offers 11 rooms, all clean and simple; meals are similarly unpretentious but hearty and good. The owners are M. and Mme. Frelet. Open year-round. Visa cards accepted. St-Seine-l'Abbaye (phone: 80-35-01-46). Inexpensive.

***Le Moulin de Lamargelle* –** An appealing *ferme auberge* where M. and Mme. Froidevaux welcome guests to dine in a stone enclave built around an old mill. Freshly fished trout and many farm-raised products figure on their menus. There also are 4 simple rooms. Restaurant open only on weekends in winter. Reservations advised. No credit cards accepted. Lamargelle (phone: 80-35-15-06). Inexpensive.

En Route from Semur-en-Auxois – From Saulieu, travel east along D977, then pick up the autoroute east, which leads to the capital and true heart of Burgundy, Dijon.

DIJON: For a detailed report on the city, its sights, hotels, and restaurants, see *Dijon* in the CITIES section.

En Route from Dijon – Just south is the part of Burgundy with which most people are familiar — the famed Côte d'Or (Golden Slope). Here the grapes are grown for several wines — le montrachet, for example — whose very names set oenophiles' palates a-tingling. Leave Dijon via D122, known as the Route des Grands Crus, and follow it south until it rejoins N74 at Vougeot; follow this road to Beaune and beyond. Along the way you'll pass through some of the great wine producing villages, among them Gevrey-Chambertin, Morey-St-Denis, Chambolle-Musigny, Vougeot, Vosne-Romanée, Nuits-St-Georges, Pernand-Vergelesses, Aloxe-Corton, Savigny-les-Beaune, Pommard, Volnay, Meursault, Puligny-Montrachet, Chassagne-Montrachet, and Santenay; you might stop to visit their vineyards. The people at Morin et Fils, in Nuits-St-Georges, are particularly friendly and offer a broad selection of wines for tasting.

One highly recommended stop on the Côte d'Or is the Château du Clos de Vougeot, completely surrounded by its priceless vineyards. This ancient building houses the Confrérie des Chevaliers du Tastevin, the Burgundian wine tasting society. Tours of the château, along with descriptions of the activities of the Confrérie (which include the promotion of burgundy wines), are given on a regular basis. Although the tour devotes too much time to hailing the glories of the rather Elk-ish Confrérie, it also takes the visitor through rooms full of ancient wine making apparatus, and this aspect of the visit is fascinating.

For those who can tear themselves away from the famous vineyards for a day, two narrow-gauge trains operate from March to November along the picturesque valley of the Ouche River and the Canal de Bourgogne southwest of Dijon. The *Chemin de Fer de la Vallée de l'Ouche,* with a steam engine, departs from Bligny-sur-Ouche. For information, contact the *Association du Rail de la Vallée de l'Ouche* (4 Rue Pasumot; phone: 80-22-86-35). The second train, *Le Petit Train de la Côte-d'Or,* leaves from Plombières Canal station in Plombières-les-Dijon. Contact the *Association du Petit Train de la Côte-d'Or* (phone: 80-23-83-75).

CHECKING IN: *Château de Gilly* – Located midway between Dijon and Beaune at the edge of the Citeaux forest, this palatial medieval abbey, extensively and opulently remodeled in the 17th century into an aristocratic family's residence, has been transformed into a luxurious 37-room hostelry. The romantic complex has vaulted hallways, Gothic dining rooms, elaborately painted beams, and Louis XV bedrooms, as well as more contemporary amenities, such as conference facilities for up to 100. A member of the prestigious Relais & Châteaux group. Closed February. Major credit cards accepted. Gilly Les Citeaux, Vougeot (phone: 80-62-89-98; fax: 80-62-82-34). Expensive.

Domaine Comtesse Michel Loisy – This dignified manor house with 4 rooms is situated between the vines where a spirited countess welcomes overnight guests into her privileged world. A certified oenologue (wine expert), the *comtesse* also offers weekend tasting seminars. Open year-round. Reserve well in advance. No credit cards accepted. 28 Rue Général-de-Gaulle, Nuits-St-George (phone: 80-61-02-72; fax: 80-61-36-14). Expensive.

EATING OUT: *La Rôtisserie du Chambertin* – About a 20-minute drive from Dijon in the quaint town of Gevrey-Chambertin, this restaurant, which remains wonderful (despite the loss of its Michelin star) thanks to the talents of chef Jean-Pierre Nicolas, who turns out such dishes as *fricassée des grenouilles et escargots* and *pigeonneau rôti aux épices et au miel* (young squab roasted with spices and honey). The town is famous for its powerful red wine and its semisoft cow's milk cheese — be sure to try them both here. The wine list is extraordinary.

Closed Sunday evenings, Mondays, February, and the first week of August. Major credit cards accepted. Gevrey-Chambertin, 7 miles (11 km) south of Dijon on N74 (phone: 80-34-33-20; fax: 80-34-12-30). Expensive.

BEAUNE: This thriving city of 20,000 is renowned not only as the heart of Burgundy's wine country but also for its many fine treasures of art and architecture. By far and away Beaune's most famous structure is the Hôtel-Dieu, built in the 15th century by the Chancellor (and tax collector) of Burgundy, Nicolas Rolin. This striking example of Flemish-Burgundian architecture, though somewhat somber overall, is topped by an eye-catching roof of colorful ceramic tiles laid out in an intricate geometric pattern. The Hôtel-Dieu, which was founded by Rolin to provide care and comfort for the poor, sick, and aged, functioned as a hospital right up through 1971; today it is an old age home. (One story, perhaps apocryphal, has it that King Louis XI thought it only fitting that Rolin, who had made so many people poor, should then found a charity hospital.)

The tour of the Hôtel-Dieu includes a visit to its museum, which contains some very beautiful tapestries as well as the remarkable polyptych, *The Last Judgment,* painted by the 15th-century Flemish artist Rogier van der Weyden. The painting is a masterpiece of color and detail, which viewers can best appreciate by using a special magnifying mirror. A sound-and-light show is held in the courtyard of the Hôtel Dieu duirng the summer.

Nicolas Rolin also bequeathed to the hospital his vineyards, the wine from which is sold at the annual wine auction held at Beaune's marketplace. Although these wines frequently command a fairly high price because the proceeds go to the hospital and other charities, they also usually set the trend for the sale of other Burgundian wines. Thus, if this year's prices for Hospice wines are generally bid up, so too will the prices be for other wines. The auction, held on the third Sunday in November, draws buyers and wine lovers from all over the world.

Near the Hôtel-Dieu is the *Musée du Vin de Bourgogne* (Rue d'Enfer; phone: 80-22-08-19), in the old mansion of the Dukes of Burgundy, which documents the history of wine making and the cultivation of the grape. Guided tours in English are given every hour; closed on Tuesdays, *Christmas,* and *New Year's Day.* Open daily from 9 AM to 12:30 PM and 2 to 6 PM, *Easter* to November; open daily except Tuesdays from 10 AM to noon and 2 to 5:30 PM in winter. Of interest to summer visitors is Beaune's annual music festival, held during the first 2 weeks of July.

The Beaune Tourist Office (Office du Tourisme de Beaune; Rue de l'Hotel Dieu; phone: 80-22-24-51) is one of Burgundy's most active and efficient. The friendly staff helps to arrange hotel accommodations and has a wide assortment of brochures on Beaune's attractions, including special events. .

The *Marché aux Vins* on the Rue Nicolas-Rolin near the tourist office has one of the most instructive independent wine-tasting setups around. About 40 wines are set out on barrels (less expensive ones in a *cave* and others on the main floor); visitors "buy" a wine glass (for about $8; 40F) and wander around tasting at their discretion, marking their responses on a card listing all the wines on display. (There are small wooden buckets on the floor next to the barrels, where the taste is supposed to be spat out rather than drunk.) The choice of wines usually include most of the main types of burgundies, or various vintages. The idea, of course, is that visitors will buy a bottle or case of their favorite at the end of the tour, but there is no pressure from the staff to do so. Open 9 to 11:30 AM and 2 to 7:30 PM all year; closed in January.

For informative presentations and free *dégustations* (tastings), visit one of the following: L'Ambassade du Vin (20-22 Rue du Faubourg-Madeleine; phone: 80-24-79-88), where the tastings are accompanied by a wine expert's commentary (in French, although most commentators also speak English; call ahead or contact the tourist office to confirm times); the Caves des Cordeliers in the Couvent des Cordeliers (6 Rue de l'Hôtel Dieu; phone: 80-22-14-25); Patriarche Père et Fils (7 Rue du Collège; phone: 80-22-23-20), a venerable house, founded in 1780, offering around 20 wines in its *dégustation;* Caves du Chancelier (1 Rue Ziem; phone: 80-22-50-29); and La Reine Pédauque (2 Rue Faubourg Saint-Nicolas; phone: 80-22-23-11).

Golfers who would like a chance to tee up in the lush countryside should visit the 18-hole *Golf de Beaune* in the nearby village of Levermois, open all year (phone: 80-24-10-29).

CHECKING IN/EATING OUT: *Bernard Morillon* – Trained in Lyons and the recipient of accolades from critics and consumers alike, chef Bernard Morillon offers light traditional *bourguignon* fare, with a heavy accent on fish. Guests dine in a covered outdoor garden. One Michelin star. Closed Mondays, Tuesday afternoons, and the month of February. Major credit cards accepted. 31 Rue Maufoux, Beaune (phone: 80-24-12-06). Expensive.

Hostellerie du Vieux Moulin – There are 27 rooms with TV sets in this inn. Chef Jean-Pierre Silva made big news on the Côte d'Or last year when the Michelin guide awarded him a second star for such creations as *bar rôti au jus de homard* (roasted sea bass with lobster essence) and *pigeonneau rôti dans son jus* (young squab roasted in its juices). Closed Thursday afternoons, Wednesdays (except holidays), mid-December to mid-January, and usually for 2 weeks during February or March. Major credit cards accepted. About 10 miles (16 km) outside of Beaune in Bouilland (phone: 80-21-51-16; fax: 80-21-59-90). Expensive.

Béléna – Beaune's newest hotel offers fine accommodations in its 34 comfortable rooms, which overlook an interior courtyard. The adjoining restaurant, named for its chef Jacques Lainé, has already earned one Michelin star. Specialties include Burgundian classics as well as dishes with an innovative used of herbs and spices, such as *sandre* (pickerel) with cardamom. Closed Tuesdays and for lunch on Wednesdays, with an annual closing in winter. Major credit cards accepted. 10-12 Bd. Foch (phone: 80-24-76-10; fax: 80-22-77-78). Expensive to moderate.

Hôtellerie de Levernois – Set in a 10-acre park just 2 miles (3 km) outside of Beaune, this gracious 12-room hotel-restaurant, a Relais & Châteaux member, was opened by Jean Crotet, former chef-owner of the highly rated *Côte d'Or* in nearby Nuits-St. Georges. The rooms, furnished by Mme. Crotet, are spacious and very comfortable, and the inviting, terraced dining room offers the same excellent food for which Crotet gained two Michelin stars at his previous residence. Closed Tuesday and Wednesday lunch from the end of July to mid-August, and from December 20 to January 10. Major credit cards accepted. Rte. de Combertault, Levernois (phone: 80-24-73-58; fax: 80-22-78-00). Expensive.

La Poste – At this old favorite with 30 comfortable rooms and 8 suites, with a view of vineyards and Beaune's ramparts, travelers will find tasty regional cuisine prepared by well-known Burgundian chef Allain Billrad and a good list of local wines. Hotel open all year; restaurant closed Wednesdays and Thursday afternoons. Major credit cards accepted. 1 Bd. Clemenceau, Beaune (phone: 80-22-08-11; fax: 80-24-19-71). Expensive.

En Route from Beaune – Although the Côte d'Or ends at Chagny, 9 miles (14 km) south, this is not the end of Burgundy's wine country. Between Chagny and Chalon-sur-Saône is the area known as the Côte Chalonnais, which has four more wine villages — Rully (where a fruity Rully *blanc* now popular in Paris wine bars is produced), Mercurey, Givry, and Montagny. And, about 35 miles (54 km) south of Chalon, is the town of Mâcon and the surrounding Mâconnais wine country. Still farther south is that area known as the Beaujolais.

EATING OUT: *Lameloise* – At this atmospheric, 15th-century country mansion, which has been given three Michelin stars, Burgundian cooking is raised to a high art. The prices are pretty high, too, but the gustatory experience is worth it, and there are 24 rooms in case you need to sleep it off. A member of the Relais & Châteaux group. Closed Wednesdays, Thursday lunch, and most of January. Major credit cards accepted. 36 Pl. d'Armes, Chagny (phone: 85-87-08-85; fax: 85-87-03-57). Expensive.

Moulin d'Hauterive – A bit more off the beaten track is this restaurant in a restored mill on the edge of a sleepy stream. The isolated setting and tranquil surroundings only enhance the kitchen's fine renditions of nouvelle cuisine. Closed Sunday evenings and Mondays off-season and from November to February. Take D62 from Chagny to Chaublanc and follow signs to the tiny hamlet of St-Gervais-en-Vallière (phone: 85-91-55-56; fax: 85-91-89-65). Moderate.

TOURNUS: At the northern edge of the Mâconnais is the city of Tournus, the home of an ancient abbey and church, Eglise St-Philibert. The abbey was built on the spot where Valerian, an early Christian, was martyred in the 2nd century AD. Begun in the 10th and continued over the next several centuries, the church is a marvel of Romanesque architecture as exemplified by its plain façade and simple, heavy narthex. Its nave, though devoid of decoration, is nonetheless handsome and uplifting, suffused with light from high windows toward which reach tall, slender columns made of beautiful rosy stone quarried in Préty, near Tournus.

CHECKING IN/EATING OUT: *Greuze* – Fine, traditional Burgundian food and beaujolais wines are offered at this charming country inn named for Jean-Baptiste Greuze, an 18th-century artist born in Tournus. Chef Jean Ducloux's efforts have earned him two Michelin stars. There are 21 rooms in the nearby *Hôtel de Greuze* (5 Pl. de l'Abbaye) which Ducloux opened in 1986. Closed the first 10 days of December. Major credit cards accepted. 1 Rue Thibaudet, Tournus (phone: 85-51-13-52). Expensive.

MÂCON: About 18 miles (29 km) south of Tournus and also on the Saône is the village of Mâcon. Its famous native son is Alphonse de Lamartine, a 19th-century poet and politician. Lamartine wrote several volumes of poetry, the most successful of which was *Méditations Poétiques;* his work is generally characterized as being in the romantic tradition. To learn more about his life, visit the *Musée Lamartine* (Rue Sigorgne, Hôtel Senece; phone: 85-38-81-18). Open daily except Sundays from 10 AM to noon and 2 to 6 PM from March through December. The house where the poet was raised (15 Rue Lamartine, Hôtel d'Ozenay) is not open to the public. There's also the Circuit Lamartine, a 40-mile (64-km) drive through the environs of Mâconnais. Among the high points of the circuit are the Château de Monceau, now an old age home, one of Lamartine's favorite residences, and Milly-Lamartine, the town where Lamartine lived as a child and where he wrote his first meditation, *L'Isolement.*

The vineyards of the Mâconnais region begin at Tournus and extend south past Mâcon to the northern reaches of the Beaujolais. Perhaps the best known of the Mâconnais wines is the pouilly-fuissé, produced in the villages of Solutré-Pouilly, Davayé, and Fuissé. All three are in the lovely hills west of Mâcon, in the general direction of the Rock of Solutré and the Rock of Vergisson. After a visit to these vineyards, head up to Solutré for a look at the precipice over which thousands of wild horses were stampeded 10,000 years ago.

En Route from Mâcon – The region between Mâcon and Villefranche-sur-Saône is known as the Beaujolais, and vineyards are found in many of the villages here. However, those that consistently produce first class wines are referred to as the Beaujolais-

Villages and include St-Amour, Juliénas, Chénas, Moulin-à-Vent, Fleurie, Chiroubles, Morgon, Brouilly, Côtes de Brouilly, and Regnie, the latest *cru* to be promoted to Villages status.

CHECKING IN/EATING OUT: *Château de Fleurville* – This quiet 15-room hotel and its restaurant are part of a group of fortified buildings that were built by the Counts of Fleurville and later belonged to the Counts of Talleyrand-Périgord. Hotel closed mid-November to mid-December, and one week in February; restaurant closed Monday lunches. Major credit cards accepted. Fleurville (phone: 85-33-12-17). Expensive to moderate.

CLUNY: Northwest of Mâcon on routes N79 and D980 is the ancient city of Cluny, home of the once very powerful Abbey of Cluny. Founded in 910, the Cluniac order was unique in that its constitution provided for freedom from secular supervision as well as from that of the local bishop. As a result, the abbey became a wellspring of spiritual influence and religious reform throughout Europe. Numerous small priories were opened, with as many as 10,000 monks in different countries under the authority of the abbot at Cluny. During the 14th century, the power of the order began to decline, and in the aftermath of the French Revolution many of the abbey's buildings at Cluny were torn down (including a magnificent cathedral, which until the construction of St. Peter's in Rome was the largest in the world). Today, only the south part of the transepts remains, and a visit to Cluny is rather like visiting many prehistoric ruins. One is forced to imagine how things must have been but are no longer. Nonetheless, the tour is stimulating, and the journey up to Cluny, through surprisingly rough hill country, is quite enjoyable. You might stop at one of the many goatherds' huts along the way to pick up some homemade *chèvre* (goat cheese).

CHECKING IN: *Bourgogne* – Near the abbey, it has 12 comfortable rooms, 3 suites, and a dining room rating one Michelin star. Room rates include breakfast and dinner. Closed mid-November to mid-February; restaurant also closed Mondays and Wednesday lunch. Major credit cards accepted. Pl. de l'Abbaye, Cluny (phone: 85-59-00-58). Expensive.

Château d'Igé – An enchanting 13th-century château set in its own park, this member of the Relais & Châteaux group has 6 luxurious rooms, 6 suites, and excellent service. The restaurant offers traditional Burgundian cuisine in elegant surroundings. Closed from December to March. Visa accepted. About 8 miles southeast of Cluny on the road from Mâcon (phone: 85-33-33-99; fax: 85-33-47-41). Expensive to moderate.

Moderne – Another small hotel with 15 rooms. Its restaurant, with a charming dining room overlooking the Grosne river, specializes in traditional Burgundian dishes such as *oeufs en meurette* (poached eggs in red burgundy wine sauce). Demi-pension (breakfast and 1 other meal) required in high season for guests. Closed Wednesdays, Thursdays for lunch, February, and 2 weeks in November (phone: 85-59-05-65; fax: 85-59-19-43). Pont-de-l'Etang, Cluny (phone: 85-59-05-65). Moderate.

EATING OUT: *Potin Gourmand* – A local favorite for fresh, often inspired, and affordably priced *cuisine marché* (the chef uses products bought at the market that day). Closed Sunday evenings, Mondays, and January to late March. Visa accepted. 4 Pl. du Champs de Foire, Cluny (phone: 85-59-02-06). Moderate.

Café du Nord – A friendly little bistro, with bar and terrace looking out over the abbey, it has checkered tablecloths and serves simple, hearty fare. It's delightfully unaffected considering its touristy locale. No credit cards accepted. Pl. du Marché, Cluny (phone: 85-59-09-96). Inexpensive.

En Route from Cluny – About 25 miles (40 km) west on N79 is Paray-le-Monial, worth a stop for its Basilique du Sacré-Coeur. Modeled after the cathedral in Cluny, no longer extant, it is a fine example of Romanesque architecture. Simple yet elegant, the church has two square towers over the narthex and an octagonal tower over the transept. Inside, the edifice is striking for its height and, again, its simplicity. Just next door in what was formerly the priory is a museum devoted to the faïence of Charolais, a decorative earthenware made in the region. In addition to exhibiting a collection of over 2,000 pieces, the oldest of which date from 1836, the museum contains a section devoted to pottery making tools and an archive of designs used for Charolaise faïence. Av. Jean-Paul II (phone: 85-88-83-07); open from 2 PM to 6 PM daily, except Thursdays, from March 20 to October 20.

About 35 miles (56 km) east of Cluny, technically located outside the Burgundy region in the département of Ain, but nevertheless sharing much of its character, is Bourg-en-Bresse. This busy city, which does not feel totally Burgundian — traces of neighboring Savoie are already detectable — is noted for the remarkable monastic enclave of Brou. Behind it is a story of conjugal devotion and familial obligation. In the 15th century, the Count of Bresse had a hunting accident. His wife vowed that if he recovered, she would convert the priory of Brou into an abbey. He recovered, but she never fulfilled her vow. This failure haunted her all her life, and on her deathbed she expressed her regrets to her son and husband. More time passed and still nothing was done until the death of the count's son, Philibert le Beau. This event was interpreted by the daughter-in-law, Marguerite, as divine punishment; concerned that her husband's soul would suffer eternal damnation, she began work on Brou at last. The resulting church is a magnificent example of Flamboyant Gothic architecture, with a skillfully carved triangular façade and sculpted tympanum over the doorway. The vagaries of history have taken their toll on the adjacent monastery. Over the years it has been a pig farm, a prison, and a mental hospital. Today, at last, it is simply a monument to the past.

Alsace

The green strip that is Alsace lies between the Vosges Mountains and the Rhine Valley. Much of it is hilly and some parts are actually mountainous. Natives say that the mountains act as umbrellas, protecting their vine-covered hillsides from too much rain. And so much is covered with vineyards — principally the area from Marlenheim to Thann, in the valleys of the Thur and the Bruche rivers — and orchards that Louis XIV is reported to have exclaimed "What a beautiful garden!" upon seeing this verdant region. The many varieties of fruit grown here are used to make the prized Alsatian eaux-de-vie — some 25 different dry, colorless, fruit-flavored alcohols — and the grapes are turned into fresh, fruity, mostly white wines quite unlike those from Bordeaux and Burgundy.

Alsace comprises two *départements,* the Bas-Rhin and the Haut-Rhin, which are bordered by Germany and Switzerland as well as the Rhine River. Paradoxically, the Haut-Rhin (Upper Rhine) *département* is south of the Bas-Rhin (Lower Rhine).

Alsace has been inhabited since prehistoric days, but it was the Celts, in the 8th century BC, who really settled it. Like most of Europe, it was annexed by the Romans, who were thrown out in AD 352. In the 8th century, under Charlemagne, it was near the center of power while remaining an independent province, not actually part of France. Alsace was officially annexed to France under the terms of the Treaty of Westphalia, in 1648, but was then ceded to Germany after the Franco-Prussian War, in 1871. The desire to reclaim Alsace became part of the growing French nationalism prior to World War I, and it was a joyful day for the entire country when in 1918 the region was returned to France. Later, when France fell to Hitler, in 1940, Alsace was occupied by Germany until the Liberation, in 1945.

Today, the relationship between this very singular region and France and Germany is rightfully complex. Perhaps because of its seesaw history — Alsace was bandied between the two nations four times in 75 years — it has clung ferociously to its own, albeit mixed, culture, architecture, and traditions. Some of its villages, its wines, and its people have German names, and until a couple of years ago, most of the street names were in German. Alsatian architecture often is reminiscent of that found in northern European Rhenish villages, with Hansel and Gretel confections of white, geranium-trimmed, half-timbered houses with steeply pitched roofs. (Visitors will be delighted to happen upon villages little changed since the Renaissance.) However, in certain cultural aspects — art, music, and hospitality — Alsace is most resolutely French. This dichotomy of history and culture has given the region much of its charm and quirkiness.

To preserve its natural parks and villages while allowing for 20th-century advances, the Alsatians have organized several preservation groups. Architects are paid by the state to consult with developers, striving for harmony between new buildings and old. Entire sections of Strasbourg and Colmar, two of the three major cities, have been restored to their original condition and closed to automobile traffic.

The region boasts a first-rate opera company and a good symphony orchestra, which both travel from Strasbourg to Colmar and Mulhouse, the third major city. Cultural activity in these three centers is brisk: Each has a local theater and many visiting troupes.

Strasbourg and Mulhouse are easily reached by plane, train, and car from nearly every major European city. Alsace is very well organized for tourism, with *Syndicats d'Initiative* in most towns. There is a seemingly endless supply of maps and brochures on every aspect of tourism, from mountain climbing and camping to visiting châteaux, all conveniently published in French, English, and German.

The Bas-Rhin is appealing for its forests and national parks, which have a complex pattern of meticulously marked hiking trails, maps of which are available at most tourist offices. Short-term rentals of rustic farms and houses also are possible through an association called the *Gîte Rural de France.* The Haut-Rhin region gave birth to the idea of *fermes auberges* — working farms that give adventurous tourists an alternative to traditional hotels and inns. Travelers can dine and spend the night with families of the many *fermes auberges* scattered throughout the region, a great many located in the Vosges Mountains. To receive information about the Bas-Rhin, write to the *Relais Départemental des Gîtes Ruraux de France* (7 Place des Meuniers, Strasbourg; phone: 88-75-56-50); for the Haut-Rhin, contact the *Association Départmentale du Tourisme du Haut-Rhin* (Hôtel du Département, BP 371, Colmar 68007; phone: 89-20-10-68).

Like other French regions, Alsace has its own style of cooking, which borrows several ingredients from its German and Swiss neighbors. Its basic character is homey, simple, and lusty, although there are many refined, elegant restaurants. Basically, visitors can expect to find pork and goose variations, with potatoes and cabbage the main vegetables.

It is wise to become familiar with some specialties, such as *tarte à l'oignon* and *tarte flambée:* the former with onions and cream, the latter a type of thin pizza with cream, cheese, onion, and bacon. *Coq au riesling* is chicken cooked in the regional white wine. *Schiefala,* smoked pork shoulder, often is served with warm potato salad. *Baeckaeoffe,* a long-simmered stew of pork, lamb, and veal with onions and potatoes, often must be ordered in advance. The best-known specialty is *choucroute,* sauerkraut cooked in wine and served with a vast variety of sausage and ham. Desserts are simple fruit tarts, light *tarte au fromage* (cheese tart), and *kugelhopf,* a sweet yeast bread studded with raisins and dusted with sugar and almonds.

Alsatian wines, primarily white, constitute 20% of French production and are a source of great pride. They take their names from the vine plants, not from the regions where they are grown, as in the rest of France. Sylvaner is a fresh and fruity dry wine; pinot blanc has more body. The best-known, riesling, gets better with age and can be full-bodied and dry, an elegant wine. Tokay d'Alsace, or pinot gris, is an excellent accompaniment to fowl or white meat. Gewürztraminer is a spicy, fruity wine, to be drunk with rich foods; it's a good choice with foie gras, the fattened goose livers that are another prized regional specialty. Pinot noir is the Alsatian red, lightweight but fruity, and sometimes resembling a rosé. Muscat is a dry white wine usually served as an aperitif.

The suggested route is divided into two parts. The first itinerary makes a circle through the northernmost portion of Alsace; it begins in the cosmopolitan yet charming city of Strasbourg and then tours the countryside, giving the traveler a look at the several national parks and forests of the region as well as its many lovely villages. The second itinerary, the 90-mile (145-km) Route du Vin (Wine Road), extends from Marlenheim to Mulhouse, near the Swiss border, and includes a number of typical villages whose well-ordered fields produce the popular Alsatian wines. This route also includes Colmar, noted for its architectural beauty. The entire route is covered by the Michelin map No. 87.

Although this area generally has not been discovered by Americans, it does see a fair amount of tourism. Reservations are advised in high season (summer). Hotel listings include a very expensive category, over $130 for a double room with bath; expensive, from $95 to $130; moderate, $65 to $95; and inexpensive, under $65. Restaurants that charge more than $95 for two people are listed as expensive; from $65 to $95, moderate; and under $65, inexpensive. Prices do not include wine or drinks; service usually is included. Good restaurants are full even off-season, so make reservations when you can.

STRASBOURG: For a detailed report on the city, its sights, hotels, and restaurants, see *Strasbourg* in THE CITIES. To start this tour, take D41 northwest from Strasbourg to Saverne.

SAVERNE: A small town perched on a hill, Saverne has the enormous and elegant Château de Rohan, named after the powerful family of princes and bishops. Its façade of pink sandstone overlooks the Canal de la Marne au Rhin; inside is a small archaeology and history museum. About every 2 years (usually even-numbered, but it depends on the budget) on August evenings, the town's cultural service puts on ambitious theatrical performances, which animate historical subjects. In alternate years, there is a folkloric festival in the first 2 weeks of August. For dates and information, contact the *Services Culturels de la Ville de Saverne* (phone: 88-91-18-52). Other local attractions include a nearby outdoor market that bustles on Thursday mornings on the Place du Général-de-Gaulle, and a flea market in May and September. On Grande-Rue, the main pedestrian street, is the Hôtel de Ville (Town Hall), flanked by the Maison Katz, dating from 1605, with its lovely mullioned windows. *Muller Oberling,* at 66-68 Grande-Rue, is a good tearoom.

CHECKING IN/EATING OUT: *Chez Jean* – Here you'll find 30 clean, rustic rooms and a restaurant that serves hearty food, including an immense *choucroute* and good steaks, and Alsatian wines by the carafe. The latest addition to this operation is a *winstub* next door. Closed Sunday evenings and Mondays, and December 22 to January 10. Major credit cards accepted. 3 Rue Gare, Saverne (phone: 88-91-10-19). Moderate.

Auberge de Kochersberg – This *auberge* has a casual restaurant that serves as a lunchtime canteen for employees of the nearby Adidas sneaker factory, as well as a more gastronomic restaurant. Both are open to the public, after 12:30 PM for lunch and after 7 PM for dinner. Closed Sunday evenings, Mondays, and late July to mid-August. Major credit cards accepted. Landersheim, 8 miles (13 km) outside Saverne on D4l (phone 88-69-91-58). Inexpensive.

En Route from Saverne – Follow the signs to the Col de Saverne. Along the way is the Jardin des Roses, which has some 2,000 plants and is open from May to September. The forest here, filled with footpaths and picnic tables, is a tempting place to stop for lunch.

Take D122, D133, and D178 to La Petite-Pierre, where a fortified château dominates the mountaintop. From La Petite-Pierre, D7 leads east to Weiterswiller, a pretty Alsatian village notable for its 17th-century houses with exposed beams. Next, take D7 and D6 to Ingwiller and D28 northeast to Niederbronn-les-Bains, and enjoy the gorgeous scenery, rolling hills, and tiny villages of the Parc National des Vosges du Nord. Niederbronn is a spa, prized for its mountain waters used in the treatment of arthritis and rheumatism. The town's municipal museum also has a small collection of medieval artifacts.

From Niederbronn, follow the zigzagging roads to Wissembourg, passing the ruins of centuries-old châteaux on the way. North on D653, then left on D53, are the Châteaux de Windstein, two castles built in 1212 and 1340, right next to each other. The ruins can be reached only on foot.

Back on N62, go northwest to the Château de Falkenstein, which was founded in 1128 and destroyed in 1564; only ruins remain. They also may be reached only by foot. From the ruins one has a view of the northern Vosges. Follow the small road of N62 to Etang de Hanau; link up with D3 and travel east through Obersteinbach and on to the Château de Fleckenstein. This stretch passes a large, curious, and beautiful Alsatian farm, with crooked rooftops and windows crazily askew. The château, another ruin, overlooks the German border. Inside, the rooms are cut directly from the rock.

CHECKING IN: *Auberge de l'Imsthal* – The management of this 23-room hotel, located in a calm setting next to a large pond, has added a fitness center with Jacuzzi, sauna, steambath, and solarium. There also is a restaurant that serves several Alsatian specialties, such as ham, game, and *pot-au-feu* (a hearty meat and vegetable stew). Hotel open year-round; restaurant closed Monday evenings, Tuesdays, and from November 25 to December 20. Major credit cards accepted. Rte. Forestière, La Petite-Pierre (phone: 88-70-45-21; fax: 88-70-40-26). Expensive to moderate.

Les Trois Roses – A fine view, an indoor pool, and a tennis court enhance this 48-room hotel. Closed January. Major credit cards accepted. 19 Rue Principale, La Petite-Pierre (phone: 88-70-45-02; fax: 88-70-41-28). Moderate.

Des Vosges – This hotel faces the valley and has 30 charming rooms; the restaurant serves fine Alsatian food. Closed mid-November to mid-December. Major credit cards accepted. 30 Rue Principale, La Petite-Pierre (phone: 88-70-45-05; fax: 88-70-41-13). Moderate to inexpensive.

EATING OUT: *Bristol* – A sophisticated dining spot that is run by a young chef. Menu offerings change regularly but generally include a mouth-watering cabbage tart, tasty turbot with tomatoes and basil, and sumptuous desserts. Closed Wednesdays and during January. Major credit cards accepted. 4 Pl. Hôtel-de-Ville, Niederbronn-les-Bains (phone: 88-09-61-44; fax: 88-09-01-20). Moderate to inexpensive.

WISSEMBOURG: The doorway between France and Germany during the last two wars, this village fortunately remains beautifully preserved. On the main square, the Place du Marché-aux-Choux (Cabbage Market), an outdoor market, is held on Sunday mornings. On the Rue de la République is the Hôtel de Ville (Town Hall), built in the mid-18th century. A tiny street leads to the Lauter River, with its small bridge and view of the old houses along it.

The Eglise St-Pierre et St-Paul, built in the 13th century, is Alsace's largest church after the Strasbourg Cathedral. It has an ornate Gothic interior of pink stone, with the vestiges of frescoes (that of St. Christopher, near the apse, is perhaps the largest portrait in France) and 13th-century stained glass windows. Across the river, on Quai Anselman, is a richly decorated house dated 1540.

Five miles (8 km) west of Wissembourg on the D3, near Lembach, are the Maginot Line fortifications built by the French between the world wars to protect their north-eastern border with Germany. In the town of Lembach, take D65 south to the Valley of Sauer where almost 2 miles of shops await visitors (open daily from March 15 to November 20).

Follow D263 south to Haguenau.

CHECKING IN: *Au Cygne* – Choose one of the 5 pretty rooms in the annex next door to the main hotel, which has 16 modest rooms. The restaurant is closed Thursday lunch, Wednesdays, February, and 2 weeks in July. Major credit cards accepted. 3 Rue du Sel, Wissembourg (phone 88-94-00-16; fax: 88-54-38-28). Inexpensive.

EATING OUT: *L'Ange* – This restaurant in a 16th-century house that is more picturesque outside than in, was taken over by new management. There are several prix fixe menus as well as many à la carte selections. Closed Tuesday evenings and Wednesdays. Reservations advised. Major credit cards accepted. 2 Rue de la République, Wissembourg (phone 88-94-12-11). Moderate.

En Route from Wissembourg – Halfway to Haguenau, on village-dotted D263, you can detour onto D243 to visit Betschdorf, known for its pretty blue and white pottery. A museum in the village at 4 Rue de Kehlendorf (phone: 88-54-48-00; closed Tuesdays, and November to May) is devoted to it, and several shops sell it.

HAGUENAU: With its modern buildings, the city itself is of little interest, but it does have a worthwhile museum and church. The *Musée Alsatien* is in a restored 15th-century building (1 Pl. Joseph Thierry; phone: 88-73-30-41; closed Saturday, Sunday, and Tuesday mornings). On the first floor are beautiful furniture collections as well as pottery and metal household objects. Upstairs is a re-created potter's studio and some examples of Betschdorf pottery. There's also the *Historical Museum* (9 Rue du Maréchal Foch; phone: 88-93-79-22; closed Saturday mornings) which houses important archaeological collections including items from Bronze and Iron Age tombs in the Haguenau Forest as well as bronze objects from the Roman period, books printed in the 15th and 16th centuries, and an exhibit devoted to the history of the town.

The Eglise St-Nicolas boasts magnificent 18th-century woodwork on the organ and choir stalls; the chapels have several intriguing woodcarvings of religious subjects.

EATING OUT: *Barberousse* – Robust regional cuisine characterizes this family-run restaurant. Meat dishes such as *salade de langue d'agneau*, and *tête de veau ravigote*, as well as fresh fish from the local market get equal billing on the menu, and the Lorentz family serves it with a smile. Outdoor terrace dining during the warmer months. Closed Sunday evenings, Mondays, 2 weeks in February, and the first 2 weeks in August. Reservations advised. Major credit cards accepted. 8 Pl. Barberousse (phone: 88-73-31-09). Moderate.

From here, take N63 to return to Strasbourg; then take N4 due west to Marlenheim, where the Wine Road begins.

MARLENHEIM and the ROUTE DU VIN: The Route du Vin begins at Marlenheim, about 12 miles (19 km) from Strasbourg on N4. The scenery changes as the road nears, then veers from, the mountains. The villages along the way, with similar architecture of half-timbered façades and quirky roofs, all have their charms. The road, which is very well marked, winds south, zigzagging back and forth across N422, which joins N83 north of Sélestat. The wine villages are completely hidden from these main arteries.

Alsace's vineyards bear little resemblance to France's other wine producing regions, primarily because the area is mountainous. The wineries welcome visitors, and all along the road wine stands offer free tastings and sell bottled wines to travelers. (Note that the wines of Alsace are unusual in that they are known by the name of the grape — riesling, for example — rather than by the name of the town in which they are grown.)

Journey west, then south, from Marlenheim through Wangen and Westhoffen to Molsheim; these are typical wine villages, with old houses and winding, narrow streets that climb the hillsides.

CHECKING IN/EATING OUT: *Hostellerie du Cerf* – This comfortable hotel has a fine restaurant that has earned two Michelin stars. Imaginative adaptations of many regional favorites are served, including game, foie gras, and several stews of fish and fowl. Closed Tuesdays and Wednesdays. Major credit cards accepted. 30 Rue du Général-de-Gaulle, Marlenheim (phone 88-87-73-73; fax: 88-87-68-08). Hotel, moderate; restaurant, expensive.

MOLSHEIM: A lovely town, it clings to the left bank of the Bruche River, at the foot of the Vosges. Visit the Metzig, a Renaissance building on Place de l'Hôtel-de-Ville with typical Rhenish architecture of a steeply pitched roof with dormer windows. A double staircase leads to a central door surmounted by a fanciful clock tower; built in the 16th century by the local butchers' corporation, it now houses a museum. On Place de l'Eglise is a former Jesuit seminary, built in 1618; inside are elaborate stucco decorations and a richly sculpted pulpit. Lovely houses line the Rue de Strasbourg: One is decorated with sculpted heads representing people and animals.

Routes D422 and D35 lead to Rosheim.

CHECKING IN/EATING OUT: *Père Benoît* – A family-run hotel on the site of an 18th-century farmhouse just east of Molsheim via A352 and only 5 minutes from the Strasbourg airport. Alsatian specialties such as *tarte flambée* are served in front of a log fire under the vaulted ceiling of the former farmhouse's cellar. Closed Sunday lunch, Mondays, 2 weeks in January, and 2 weeks in June. Major credit cards accepted. 34 Rte. de Strasbourg, Entzheim (phone: 88-68-98-00; fax: 88-68-64-56). Moderate.

ROSHEIM: This Romanesque village nestles in a verdant, sweeping valley. On Rue du Général-de-Gaulle are some of Alsace's oldest houses, made of gray stone with curious, tiny windows. The oldest house, nicknamed "House of the Heathen," dates from around 1170. The ancient gateways to the town remain, as do some of the ramparts. The town also produces rouge aottrott, one of Alsace's few red wines.

Obernai lies 4 miles (6 km) south of Rosheim.

OBERNAI: This is the most beautiful village, completely preserved, in this part of the Route du Vin. The ramparts and towers date from the Middle Ages, the Town Hall and belfry from the Renaissance. The Hôtel de Ville (Town Hall), built of the local golden stone, marks the beginning of a passageway lined with galleries. The old Wheat Market is topped by a huge stork's nest. *Urban,* a pastry shop on the Place du Marché, has windows full of *kugelhopf,* the buttery circular cake so popular in this region. Three hundred feet down Route du Général-Gouraud is *Gross,* another fine pastry shop. Local celebrations include the *Obernai C'est la Fête,* an annual folkloric festival held the third weekend of July, and the yearly harvest festival that takes place the third weekend of October. Every year on December 13, the *Festival of St. Odilia,* patron saint of Alsace, attracts pilgrims from all over the region.

CHECKING IN: *A La Cour d'Alsace* – An elegant addition to Obernai's accommodations, this 30-room country hotel is housed in an ensemble of 16th- and 17th-century structures and filled with antiques. Major credit cards accepted. 3 Rue de Gail, Obernai (phone: 88-95-07-00; fax: 88-95-19-21). Expensive.

Le Parc – This property not only has roomy accommodations but saunas, a gymnasium, and indoor and outdoor pools to recommend it. Try its restaurant for a sumptuous Sunday lunch buffet or, any day, the many updated Alsatian specialties. There's an unparalleled selection of eaux-de-vie, the passion of the owner, Marc Wucher. Hotel and restaurant closed the first week of July; restaurant closed Sunday evenings and Mondays. Major credit cards accepted. 169 Rue Général-Gouraud, Obernai (phone: 88-95-50-08; fax: 88-95-37-29). Hotel, moderate; restaurant, expensive.

La Diligence – Really three hotels in a series of old, picturesque buildings in the center of town. Open all year round. No restaurant. Major credit cards accepted. 23 Pl. Mairie, Obernai (phone: 88-95-55-69; fax: 88-95-42-46). Moderate to inexpensive.

Les Vosges – This small place offers convenient but modest lodgings. The rooms are clean, and the price is right. Hotel open year-round; restaurant closed 2 weeks in January, 2 weeks in June, and Sunday evenings and Mondays off-season. Visa accepted. 5 Pl. de la Gare, Obernai (phone: 88-95-53-78). Moderate to inexpensive.

EATING OUT: *A l'Etoile* – A simple *winstub* — a bistro serving regional food and wines, often by the glass. Closed Mondays, Tuesday lunch in autumn, and from early January to early March. Visa accepted. 6 Pl. de l'Etoile, Obernai (phone: 88-95-50-57). Moderate to inexpensive.

La Halle aux Blés – Perhaps the prettiest restaurant in town; in the old Wheat Market, it has a brasserie on the main floor and a more elegant restaurant upstairs. Visa accepted. Pl. du Marché, Obernai (phone 88-95-56-09). Moderate to inexpensive.

En Route from Obernai – Proceed south to Sélestat, stopping off at Barr, where an annual wine fair is held in July and a harvest fair in October. For information, inquire at the *Syndicat d'Initiative* (Pl. Hôtel-de-Ville; phone: 88-08-66-66). Also stop off at Andlau, whose mostly 12th-century church is sculpted with fantastical figures.

Continue south on D35 to Châtenois, then southwest on N59 to Haut-Koenigsbourg. The road to this town climbs through two parks: Monkey Mountain and Eagle's Park. The castle in Haut-Koenigsbourg, which belonged to a family of Swiss counts, is one of the most visited in Alsace; it dates from feudal times but was completely restored in 1908, a bit heavy-handedly. As a result, some of the present architecture suggests the early 20th century rather than the Middle Ages. The castle sits high — some 2,000 feet — above the Rhine plain on a rocky outcrop and thus commands a fine view of the surrounding vineyards and neighboring Germany.

Route D159 leads back to Sélestat.

CHECKING IN/EATING OUT: *Arnold* – About halfway between Obernai and Sélestat is this appealing Tudor-style, 28-room inn with antique furnishings and a good restaurant, all set beautifully in the middle of vineyards. The hotel has recently been refurbished, but the lovely antiques have been retained. Restaurant closed Sunday evenings and Mondays. Major credit cards accepted. Route D422, Itterswiller (phone: 88-85-50-58; fax: 88-85-55-54). Expensive to moderate.

SÉLESTAT: A mostly modern town on the left bank of the Ill River, Sélestat does have two lovely churches. The 12th-century pink sandstone Eglise Ste-Foy, in the center of town, is considered one of the best examples of Romanesque churches in Alsace. Next to it is the Eglise St-Georges (dating from the 13th to the 15th century), which displays a mélange of styles with stained glass windows that show angels playing 16th-century musical instruments. The stained glass windows were executed by Max Ingrand. Sélestat was once the seat of a flourishing university, and the Bibliothèque Humaniste, founded in 1452, is rich in rare manuscripts, such as a 7th-century Merovingian dictionary and some 2,000 15th-century Humanist works. The name "America" was born in the Alsace town of St-Dié. It first appeared in print in 1507, to identify the Western Hemisphere, named after Amerigo Vespucci. The historic document, *Cosmographiae Introductio*, is on view in Sélestat's Humanist Library.

The second leg of the Route du Vin begins south of Sélestat, on the way to Ribeauvillé.

En Route from Sélestat – Detour briefly off the Route du Vin (Wine Road) by crossing the Ill River on D424 and heading 9 miles (14 km) southeast to Marckolsheim, where the *Mémorial-Musée de la Ligne Maginot du Rhin* (Memorial Museum of the Maginot Line) is installed in a World War II bunker. Among the exhibits here are a Sherman tank, French and German arms, and maps of the area showing the French defense strategy. Closed mid-November to mid-March; open daily from mid-June to mid-September from 8 AM to noon and 2 to 6 PM; open weekends only from mid-March to mid-June and mid-September to mid-November. Rte. du Rhin (phone: 88-92-51-70.)

To rejoin the Route du Vin, head west on D10 and D106 to Ribeauvillé. On the way, in Illhaeusern, is the region's best (and best-known) restaurant.

EATING OUT: *Auberge de l'Ill* – On the bank of the Ill, with a sweeping green lawn bordered by feathery willow trees, this three-star restaurant is a romantic spot indeed. The dining room is serene and filled with flowers, sparkling with old silver collected by the owners, the Haeberlin brothers, Paul and Jean-Pierre. Some specialties are flan of frogs' legs with watercress, venison in a light pepper sauce, and salmon soufflé. The wine list has the best Alsatian vintages as well as a large selection from other regions. Book well in advance. Closed Mondays, Tuesdays, most of February, and the first week of July. Major credit cards accepted. (See also *Haute Gastronomie,* DIVERSIONS.) Rue de Collanges, Illhaeusern (phone: 89-71-83-23; fax: 89-71-82-83). Expensive.

RIBEAUVILLÉ: This bustling wine town is filled with old houses and picturesque public buildings. Two towers of the ancient fortifications are left, now topped with storks' nests. Leave your car at the entrance to town, where there is a statue of a wine maker. Grande-Rue, the main street, is lined with old buildings. *Zum Pfifferhüs,* a *winstub,* or bistro, from the 16th century, is in one of the oldest (see *Eating Out*). One house, inscribed "Ave Maria," has a central oriel window flanked by two caryatids, one representing an angel, the other representing the Virgin Mary, portraying the Annunciation.

The Wheat Market, a 16th-century Gothic building with two arches, leads to the tiny Rue des Tanneurs, bordered with lovely houses. The Chapelle de l'Hôpital dates from the 14th century.

At 58 Grande-Rue, *John,* a pastry shop, sells *kugelhopf* by the slice. Don't miss the outlet store of the *Manufacture d'Impression sur Etoffes* (19 Rte. de St-Marie-aux-Mines; phone: 89-73-64-64) which produces extraordinarily beautiful fabrics. The street widens at the Hôtel de Ville (Town Hall), a lovely 18th-century structure. Opposite is the Eglise des Augustins, with its multicolored tile roof. At the square's edge is the Tour des Bouchers, a 13th-century belfry. The street, and the town, ends at the Place de la République, with a Renaissance fountain bearing the coat of arms of the town. *Pfifferday* (Pipers Day), a folklore festival, is held the first week in September. There's also a wine festival on the next to last weekend in July, and a village music festival on the last Sunday in August.

Aficionados of eaux-de-vie — the clear, fiery brandies — might want to stop at one of the region's many distilleries. One worth a visit in Ribeauvillé is that of Jean-Paul Metté (9 Rue des Tanneurs; phone: 89-73-65-88). It is open Mondays through Fridays from 2 to 7 PM; Saturdays and Sundays for 1 hour only, from 6 to 7 PM. The Syndicat d'Initiative in the nearby town of Villé (Hôtel de Ville; phone: 88-57-11-57) can supply a list of other distilleries. In Lapoutroie, west of Kayersberg on Route N415, there even is a museum dedicated to these liqueurs — the *Musée des Eaux de Vie* (Rue de Général-Dufieux; phone: 89-47-50-26). It is open daily from 9 AM to noon and 2 to 7 PM.

From Ribeauvillé, travel south to Riquewihr. This road, and beyond it as far as Kaysersberg, which was the scene of intense fighting during World War II, is dotted with memorials and gravesites.

CHECKING IN: *Clos St-Vincent* – A lovely place with 8 rooms and 3 suites, and a restaurant, it is set in the vineyards above Ribeauvillé. Hotel and restaurant closed mid-November to mid-March. Restaurant closed Tuesdays and Wednesdays. Visa accepted. Rte. de Bergheim, Ribeauvillé (phone: 89-73-67-65; fax: 89-73-32-20). Very expensive.

Le Ménestrel – Alsace's gently sloping vineyards surround this modern, flower-studded inn just outside Ribeauvillé, opened in 1989 by a pastry chef and his wife. Closed mid-January to mid-February. Major credit cards accepted. 27 Av. du Général-de-Gaulle, Ribeauvillé (phone: 89-73-80-52; fax: 89-73-32-39). Moderate.

Les Signeurs de Ribeaupierre – A fine bargain, this family-run 17th-century inn offers 10 rooms — large, pretty, and spotless. Closed February and March. 11 Rue du Château, Ribeauvillé (phone: 89-73-70-31; fax: 89-73-71-21). Moderate.

La Tour – This charming place is run by a wine family who has turned an old winery into a 34-room hotel. Closed January to mid-March. Major credit cards accepted. 1 Rue de la Mairie, Ribeauvillé (phone 89-73-72-73). Moderate to inexpensive.

EATING OUT: *Les Vosges* – Clean and modern, this restaurant (with one Michelin star) features an extensive menu with a three-course, reasonably fixed-price meal. Also has 18 guestrooms. Restaurant closed Tuesday lunch and Mondays from July through October; also closed along with the hotel for the last 2 weeks in January, the end of February to mid-March, and one week in June. Major credit cards accepted. 2 Grande-Rue, Ribeauvillé (phone 89-73-61-39; fax: 89-73-34-21). Hotel, moderate; restaurant, expensive to moderate.

Zum Pffiferhüs – An appealing *winstub* in a landmark building, this one has excellent *choucroute.* Closed Wednesdays, Thursdays, and during February. Visa accepted. 14 Grande-Rue, Ribeauvillé (phone: 89-73-62-28). Inexpensive.

En Route from Ribeauvillé – Continuing on D3 toward Riquewihr, you'll pass a stork preserve near Hunawihr. Generally regarded as the symbol of Alsace, the stork has been threatened with extinction due to the disappearance of the marshes, its natural habitat. The preserve is part of a program to restock the area with these harbingers of good fortune. Domestic birds are mated with wild ones, and the stork couples then are returned to the wild for their annual migration.

RIQUEWIHR: It's almost too much, this picture-postcard town resembling a stage set. In fact, some of it is only façade; the Hugel winery, for example, occupies two 16th-century houses that have been gutted to make room for its equipment. The entire village is a historical monument.

The town's Société d'Archéologie publishes an excellent map showing 33 buildings of interest; ask for it in tourist offices (there's one on Place Voltaire), bookstores, and hotels. At the beginning of the cobblestoned main street, the Grande-Rue, the *Musée des Postes et Télécommunications* (formerly the castle of the Dukes of Montbéllard-Wurtemberg) has an exhibit that explains that the mail system was created by the Roman emperor Augustus to transmit his orders throughout the Roman Empire, which included Alsace. Beautiful wrought-iron signs, old wagons, telephones, and mailmen's costumes are other attractions (closed during the winter; phone: 89-47-93-80).

The Grande-Rue is lined with extraordinary houses, completely preserved; many are now restaurants and tearooms. One, 18 Grande-Rue, dating from 1535, has a courtyard surrounded by a sculpted balcony. Vaulted passageways lead to tiny streets and hidden courtyards. In the Cour des Vignerons, the old Wine Makers' Guildhall is decorated with a dazzling array of windowboxes brimming with flowers. The Rue des Cerfs, marked by a stag's head, has many signs welcoming guests to bed and breakfast accommodations.

The Dolder, a 13th-century guard tower set into the city walls, houses a museum of old money and arms. The walls themselves formed a double ring of protection for the town, and the old gates and iron doors are perfectly preserved (phone: 89-47-92-15).

Many wineries are open for tastings. Because Riquewihr attracts so many tourists, avoid it during the summer, except in the early morning and late afternoon, and the entire month of August.

Continue south, then west, to Kaysersberg.

CHECKING IN: *St. Nicolas* – Actually an old Alsatian house, it is now a comfortable hotel. Closed mid-January to mid-March. Major credit cards accepted. 2 Rue St-Nicolas, Riquewihr (phone: 89-49-01-51; fax: 89-49-04-36). Inexpensive.

EATING OUT: *Auberge de Schoenenbourg* – Enjoy one-star Alsatian food with nouvelle cuisine touches and gaze out at the vineyard stretching behind the restaurant. The wines served are made from grapes grown here. Open daily. Major credit cards accepted. 2 Rue de la Piscine, Riquewihr (phone: 89-47-92-28; fax: 89-47-95-88). Expensive.

Au Tire Bouchon – Hearty local food is served amid lovely decor. Closed the first 2 weeks in March, and late November to early December. Major credit cards accepted. 29 Rue du Général-de-Gaulle, Riquewihr (phone: 89-47-91-61). Moderate to inexpensive.

En Route from Riquewihr – The road through Beblenheim to Kaysersberg climbs into the hillier vineyards and is marked with military cemeteries and memorials to the two world wars. In Mittelwihr, the Mur des Fleurs was covered in red, white, and blue flowers during the Occupation as a symbol of Alsatian fidelity to France. The National Cemetery at Sigolsheim, which looks out over the vine-covered hills, is a burial ground for French soldiers who died in World War II.

The church in Kientzheim has a gravestone for Lazare de Schwendi, who supposedly imported the tokay grape to Alsace from Hungary.

KAYSERSBERG: Known mainly as the birthplace of Albert Schweitzer (in 1875), the town is also a delightful wine village filled with medieval houses and bustling farm activity. The southern bank of the meandering Weiss River affords a good view of the ruins of the ancient castle perched above the town, the Hôtel de Ville (Town Hall), an elegant 16th-century building, and the Romanesque Eglise de la Ste-Croix, hugged by tiny streets (Rues Eglise, Hôpital, Gendarmerie) bordered with ancient houses. Rue du Général-de-Gaulle, also called Grande-Rue, has its fair share of lovely old houses as well. The quirky architecture here is silhouetted against a pine forest. Cross over on the fortified bridge that dates from 1511 and has a minuscule chapel built into it.

The tourist office is immediately behind Ste-Croix, and next door is tiny St-Michel chapel, which dates from 1463. To visit, knock on the door of house No. 43, to the left of the chapel; once inside, make a point to see the interesting 14th-century crucifix in the choir.

Schweitzer's birthplace is now a museum in his honor (126 Rue du Général-de-Gaulle; phone: 89-47-36-55; closed *Easter* to November). There is also the *Historical Museum* (62 Rue du Général-de-Gaulle; phone: 89-78-22-78; open daily in July and August and weekends only from *Easter* to November), featuring some notable works of religious art, regional archaeological finds, and documents of Kayserberg's famous sons, including Jean Geiler and Mathias Zell.

Other local festivals include the *Fêtes des Vendanges* (Harvest Festival) held the last weekend in September (a small version of the festival that formerly took place every 5 years), and *Noël à Kayserberg,* the annual *Christmas* fete held 4 weekends before December 25.

CHECKING IN/EATING OUT: *Résidence Chambard* – A comfortable, modern 20-room hotel, it has conveniences that include direct-dial telephones. Its classic restaurant with one Michelin star offers a gracious dining room and specialties such as foie gras cooked in cabbage leaves. Hotel closed at *Christmas* and for most of March; restaurant closed Mondays and Tuesday lunch. Major credit cards accepted. *Résidence Chambard* is just behind the *Chambard* restaurant at 13 Rue du Général-de-Gaulle, Kayserberg (phone: 89-47-10-17; fax: 89-47-35-03). Hotel, expensive to moderate; restaurant, expensive.

Château – This simple but acceptable 10-room lodging is near the *Schweitzer Museum* and has a restaurant. Closed Wednesday evenings, Thursdays, and January. Visa accepted. 38 Rue du Général-de-Gaulle, Kayserberg (phone: 89-78-24-33). Inexpensive.

En Route from Kayserberg – Through Ammerschwihr and Niedermorschwihr, the Wine Road overlooks the entire plain of Alsace and passes through lovely villages. At the *Caveau Morakopf,* a fine *winstub* in Niedermorschwihr, the bill comes with the handwritten message "Thank you and see you soon." Nearby, at the pastry shop *Au Relais des Trois Epis* (La Barroche; phone: 89-49-83-67), Maurice Ferber makes what is probably the best *kugelhopf* in Alsace.

In the town of Turckheim, a few miles farther south, a watchman in Renaissance costume patrols the streets in summer, sword in one hand, lantern in the other. The three ancient entries into town remain: France Gate, with its huge tower, and Munster Gate, both just off the quay beside the Fecht River, and the Brand Gate, on Rue des Vignerons.

Go west on D10 to Munster, where the famous cheese is made. From here, the well-marked Route des Crêtes, sinuous and lovely, offers some spectacular views. Scattered nearby are *fermes auberges,* farms open to the public that serve simple meals for low prices. Some also offer rooms and other amenities such as horseback riding and skiing. An excellent guide to the Vallée de Munster is available free at most tourist offices in the area.

From Munster, take D417 to Colmar.

CHECKING IN/EATING OUT: *Aux Armes de France* – Run with impressive efficiency by chef Gaertner, this restaurant's traditional French cuisine has earned it one Michelin star. The foie gras is outstanding. It also offers 8 moderately priced rooms. Closed Wednesdays, Thursday lunch, and the month of January. Major credit cards accepted. 1 Grand-Rue, Ammerschwihr (phone: 89-47-10-12; fax: 89-47-38-12). Expensive.

COLMAR: Unquestionably Alsace's most beautiful city, now lovingly restored, Colmar was once the royal residence of Charlemagne. Since the Middle Ages, it has housed artists and artisans, and its graceful streets and often spectacular architecture still reflect this past.

Begin at La Petite Venise (Little Venice), a restored neighborhood of half-timbered houses, shops, and artist's studios perched along the banks of the Lauch River. Pont St-Pierre overlooks the tranquil scene. Wander along any of the picturesque streets toward the Ancienne Douane (Ancient Custom House), a large, 15th-century arcaded building with a roof tiled in a colorful diamond pattern; also known as the Koifhus, its inscription ("In 1480 was the house built") is in German. This landmark now is a local conference center.

Directly north, the Quartier des Tanneurs, where leatherworkers once labored, is another neighborhood that has been restored and converted to a pedestrian zone (as has most of Old Colmar). Many distinguished buildings are crammed into the tiny streets, and all are well marked in French and German. The tourist office (4 Rue Unterlinden; phone: 89-41-02-29) and bookshops can provide excellent maps and guides in English.

Maison Pfister, built midway along lovely Rue des Marchands in 1537 and restored in 1971, displays an imaginatively painted exterior of emperors, allegorical figures, and animals. Five swooping arches grace the ground level, and a spiral staircase leads to the upper floors. An especially large oriel window looks onto the outdoor café in the plaza below, and the third-floor balcony overflows with pink, purple, and red impatiens. A jaunty green turret caps the impressive creation. Across the street is the Maison Schongauer; the house once belonged to the family of the 15th-century artist Martin Schongauer.

Maison des Têtes (19 Rue des Têtes), now a brasserie, dates from 1608 and takes its name from the dozens of tiny carved heads of people and animals that ornament its façade (see *Eating Out*).

The Eglise des Dominicains, built in the 14th century of warm, golden stone, houses a magnificent altar painting by Martin Schongauer, *The Virgin of the Rose Bush* (1473); the stained glass windows deserve special attention, as well (open mid-March to mid-November). The restored, 14th-century Eglise St-Martin, has a pink stone exterior with an intricately sculpted portal showing the Last Judgment.

Entire books have been written on France's *Musée d'Unterlinden,* the most visited museum outside of Paris, and its two major treasures, the Issenheim altarpiece by Matthias Grünewald and the 24-panel series of the Passion by Schongauer. The altar is an artistic curiosity, its paintings alternately expressionist and surrealist. Chamber pots and dirty linen are depicted next to angels and virgins. The altar's central panel is flanked by side panels that open in an intricate design. A *maquette* (model) in the gallery demonstrates how the work looks both open and closed. The museum, in a 13th-century convent with a vine-covered cloister, has a delightful collection of Alsatian folk art on the second floor: peasant scenes of old farms, folk costumes, unique musical instruments, arms, and ceramics. Ask the guard to turn on the sophisticated animated toys. The museum is at Place de la Sinn (phone: 89-41-89-23). There are plans for a new municipal museum — the *Rhine Museum of the Manuscript and the Ancient Book* — that will be located in the Convent of the Dominicans. It will house some 1,200 manuscripts and a rare collection of early printed books. For information, call 89-41-02-29.

Scattered throughout the squares in this town are statues by Auguste Bartholdi, the sculptor of the Statue of Liberty, who was born here in 1834. A museum in his family's home at 30 Rue des Marchands displays many of his works. Open Saturdays and Sundays from 10 AM to noon and 2 to 5 PM. (phone: 89-41-90-60).

From mid-April to mid-October, the tourist office sponsors a mini-train that travels a 50-minute route to the city's main attractions. It leaves several times a day from the Hôtel de Ville (Town Hall). For information, call the tourist office.

Every year the town holds a week-long wine festival that encompasses the *Feast of the Assumption* holiday (August 15). A newer annual tradition is the *Festival International de Colmar,* held in early July and featuring a week of classical concerts by *Les Virtuoses de Moscou* and other visiting groups and soloists. For information, contact the tourist office. Colmar's biennial *International Festival of Gastronomy* is held in March in even-numbered years and hosts chefs and participants from all over France as well as other countries. Call 89-41-22-78 for information.

Shopping in Colmar can be a distinct pleasure. Although there is a smattering of international clothing boutiques, the best buys are local comestibles. Rue des Boulangers has the greatest concentration of food shops, including *Glasser* (No. 18) and *Sigmann* (No. 6), both *charcuteries,* and *Alou* (No. 16), which carries fresh produce as well as Alsatian wines and eaux de vie. On nearby Rue des Têtes are *La Ferme* (No. 34), a cheese shop; and *Au Bon Nègre* (No. 9), which stocks exotic coffees and teas, along with their appropriate pots and cups.

The third leg of the journey along the Wine Road begins due west of Colmar, in Wintzenheim.

CHECKING IN: *Terminus-Bristol* – A large, old-fashioned hotel that remodeled several of its rooms a few years ago. Ask for a deluxe room to experience the best of these high-style *chambres.* Its one-star restaurant, *Rendez-vous de Chasse* (phone: 89-41-10-10), has a talented young chef who offers one of the town's most refined and inventive menus. (A second, less formal restaurant next door, *L'Auberge,* has traditional fare.) Open daily. Major credit cards accepted. 7 Pl. de la Gare, Colmar (phone: 89-23-59-59; fax: 89-23-92-26). Expensive.

Le Maréchal – At the water's edge in the Little Venice quarter of Colmar, this sprawling collection of half-timbered houses with flower-strewn balconies and crooked stairways has a special, quirky charm. Its 30 rooms, which recently have been remodeled, are named for composers — Mozart, Wagner, Beethoven — and each is decorated differently. The paneled, candlelit restaurant overlooks the water and has earned one Michelin star. Open daily. Major credit cards accepted. 4-6 Pl. des Six-Montagnes-Noires, Colmar (phone: 89-41-60-32; fax: 89-24-59-40). Expensive to moderate.

L'Amiral – This former factory at the edge of town has been converted into a pleasant, modern hotel with a military theme. Adjoining it is *Le Best Bar* with piano playing nightly. Major credit cards accepted. 11A Bd. du Champ-de-Mars, Colmar (phone: 89-23-26-25; fax: 89-23-83-64). Moderate.

St. Martin – In the center of the old town of Colmar, this residence with its superb Renissance staircase has expanded across the courtyard, adding 11 modern rooms to its original simple but comfortable 12 *chambres.* Closed during January and February. Major credit cards accepted. 38 Grand-Rue, Colmar (phone: 89-24-11-51). Moderate.

EATING OUT: *Au Fer Rouge* – Tucked into a charming house in the center of town and run by a young chef full of inventive ideas that have won him one Michelin star, it has a good wine list and a luxurious but still cozy atmosphere. Closed Sunday evenings, Mondays, the last week of February, and most of August. Major credit cards accepted. 52 Grande-Rue, Colmar (phone: 89-41-37-24; fax: 84-24-28-87). Expensive.

Schillinger – Enjoy caring service and regional specialties and game, such as partridge on a bed of *choucroute,* foie gras, and sumptuous desserts, which have been given two Michelin stars. Closed Sunday evenings, Mondays, late February to early March, and most of July. Major credit cards accepted. 16 Rue Stanislas, Colmar (phone: 89-41-43-17; fax: 89-24-28-87). Expensive.

Maison des Têtes – A simple brasserie in an extraordinary 17th-century landmark building, where heads of people and mythical animals adorn the façade, imploring you to enter. Closed Sunday evenings, Mondays, and mid-January to mid-February. Major credit cards accepted. 19 Rue des Têtes, Colmar (phone: 89-24-43-43). Expensive to moderate.

Le Boulevard 15 – This trendy restaurant, with expansive sloping picture windows reminiscent of an ocean liner, is docked on the main thoroughfare. Its nouvelle cuisine is served in a club-like atmosphere. Open until midnight; closed Sundays. Major credit cards accepted. 15 Bd. du Champ de Mars (phone: 89-24-24-44). Moderate.

Chez Hansi – Alsatian specialties form the mainstay of the menu here, including the best *choucroute* found in Colmar. And the ambience complements the traditional menu, right down to the waitresses wearing an elephantine headdress called a *Schlupkapp.* Closed Wednesday dinner, Thursdays, and in January. Reservations advised. Major credit cards accepted. 23 Rue des Marchands (phone: 89-41-37-84). Moderate.

Le Petit Bouchon – Tucked away on a small square, this tiny upstairs eatery is decorated in pink tones and with flowers, and serves Lyonnais and Alsatian fare that is carefully prepared. Portions are generous and prices reasonable. Closed mid-July through mid-August. Visa accepted. 11 Rue d'Alspach (phone: 89-23-45-57). Moderate.

Caveau St-Pierre – From this *winstub,* smack on the water in La Petite Venise, you can admire the scene, fill up on reasonably priced fare, and imbibe at leisure. Closed Sunday evenings and Mondays. Visa accepted. 24 Rue de la Herse, Colmar (phone: 89-41-99-33) Moderate to inexpensive.

S'Pariser Stewele – The most atmospheric *winstub* or tavern in town, decorated with etchings by Hansi, the Norman Rockwell of Alsace. A lively crowd of upscale locals comes to imbibe or indulge in Alsatian classics and such dishes as *bibeleskäs,* an herbed cheese. Closed Tuesdays, 3 weeks in February, the last week in June, and the last week in September. Reservations unnecessary. No credit cards accepted. 4 Pl. Jeanne-d'Arc (phone: 89-41-42-33). Moderate to inexpensive.

Unterlinden – Across from Colmar's eponymous museum, this restaurant offers a classic menu of all the Alsatian dishes from *tarte à l'oignon* to hot Munster cheese, all prepared under the careful guidance of Madame Stockel. Closed Sunday evenings, Tuesdays, and the first 2 weeks in January. Reservations unnecessary. No credit cards accepted. 2 Rue Unterlinden (phone: 89-41-18-73). Moderate to inexpensive.

En Route from Colmar – Take the Wine Road from Wintzenheim and Wettolsheim to Eguisheim, another perfectly preserved wine village set into the vine-crested hills. The main square, with a lovely Renaissance fountain, is the center of a web of circular streets and alleys crammed full of old houses. The imposing pink sandstone towers, ruins of the castle built 7 centuries ago, dominate the hill. Shops line the main square. The best buys here are in cooking equipment: pottery for preparing Alsatian specialties and copper utensils. The village of Husseren-les-Châteaux, the highest point on the Wine Road, has an excellent view of the entire valley and of Eguisheim, to the north. Hattstatt, once a fortified town, has an interesting church that comprises Romanesque, Renaissance, and baroque styles.

Continue south, through Gueberschwihr and Pfaffenheim, to Rouffach.

EATING OUT: *Caveau d'Eguisheim* – Renowned for its *choucroute,* frogs' legs, onion tart, *kugelhopf,* and other regional specialties, this warm, homey dining place is especially welcoming to visitors. It recently lost its Michelin star, but the quality of the fare served here is still good. It also features wines of the village, namely those from Léon Beyer. The building itself dates from 1603. Closed Tuesday evenings, Wednesdays, and mid-January to March. Major credit cards accepted. 3 Pl. du Château-St-Léon, Eguisheim (phone: 89-41-08-89; fax: 89-23-79-99). Expensive to moderate.

ROUFFACH: The Eglise Notre-Dame de l'Assomption, begun in the Romanesque style in the 11th century and completed a number of centuries later, was built in the same pink stone as the Strasbourg Cathedral. Plan to visit at the end of the day, when the western sunlight filters through its lovely rose window. On the square outside the church is the 16th-century Wheat Market and an old Hôtel de Ville (Town Hall) with a charming Renaissance façade. The crenelated Tour des Sorcières (Witches' Tower) dates from the 13th century and wears a stork's nest headdress.

From Rouffach, take N83 south to Guebwiller.

CHECKING IN/EATING OUT: *Château d'Isenbourg* – This luxurious, spacious, and utterly hospitable Relais & Châteaux inn sits above the village in the midst of a vineyard and is gracefully landscaped. Its 37 rooms and 3 suites are decorated with antiques, and some offer a view of the valley. Other amenities include a swimming pool, tennis courts, and a good restaurant, *Les Tommeries*, in a vaulted room dating from the 13th century. Closed mid-January to March. Visa accepted. Rouffach (phone: 89-49-63-53; fax: 89-78-53-70). Expensive.

GUEBWILLER: Many remarkable old Alsatian houses — 107 Rue Théodore-Deck with its 3-story oriel window, for instance — grace this town, the gateway to the Florival, the flower-filled Lauch River Valley. The Hôtel de Ville has a lovely protruding window with geraniums cascading from it as well as a 16th-century carved Virgin. Next door, note the outstanding Art Nouveau building with winding plant motifs.

The triple-towered Eglise St-Léger, just off Rue de la République, was built during the 12th and 13th centuries and has an elegant portal with ribbed arches and bays. The choir is carved ornately in wood.

Routes 430 and 431 lead in a roundabout fashion from Guebwiller into the mountains past the Grand Ballon peak to Cernay. Called the Route des Crêtes (roughly, the crest or ridge road), this is perhaps the loveliest trip: steep, forested, and spectacularly colored in autumn. Route N66 leads west to Thann.

En Route from Guebwiller – Due east, across N83 via D4, lies Ungersheim, the site of *Ecomusée,* an open-air museum. It includes old farms, peasant houses, and other examples of Alsatian architecture that were destined for demolition until a group of students got the idea of dismantling, moving, and carefully reassembling them here.

THANN: This village marks the southern end of the Route du Vin. The soaring, yellow stone Collégiale St-Thiébault (Collegiate Church of St. Theobald) dominates the town, its elegant spire piercing the sky. Nicknamed "the Cathedral," it was built in stages from 1351 to the end of the 15th century and was restored in 1989. Although the exterior is obscured by scaffolding, this remains the most beautiful Gothic structure in all of Alsace. Inside, the vaults are joined by painted keys. The extraordinary carved wooden choir stalls display sculptures of monsters and humans in minute detail. Small angels peer from the ceiling, painted at the cross of the vaults' ribs.

From Thann, take N66 east to Mulhouse (pronounced Mu-*looz*), almost at the Swiss border.

MULHOUSE: Compared with the delightful wine villages and the seductive architecture of Colmar, this is an ugly, predominantly modern city (pronounced mul-*ooze*). Once the center of a prosperous textile industry, it is now mainly a border town with thriving chemical plants. Yet travelers may prefer to stay here rather than next door in pricier Switzerland. Mulhouse has several modern, comfortable, and moderately priced hotels that welcome families with children. At least five other good reasons to pay a visit are its five museums — of fine arts, history, textiles, railroad cars, and automobiles (one of the world's best collections of old cars). For information, stop by the tourist office, 9 Av. Maréchal Foch (phone: 89-45-68-31).

The *Musée Historique,* in the beautifully restored 16th-century Hôtel de Ville, at Place de la Réunion, is a lovable blend of the past and present. The town council still meets here in a room decorated with the portraits of all the mayors since 1347. The museum is filled with costumes and musical instruments, a charming postcard collection, playing cards, dolls, toy soldiers, and *kugelhopf* molds. Several rooms depict bourgeois living in the late 19th century and are furnished with household utensils. The entrance is at ground level to the right of the stairs; admission includes access to the other parts of the Hôtel de Ville (closed Tuesdays). Pl. de la Réunion (phone: 89-32-59-46).

The *Musée de l'Impression des Etoffes* (closed Tuesdays; 3 Rue des Bonnes-Gens; phone: 89-45-51-20) is devoted to the art of fabric printing. Several Rube Goldberg–esque presses function during the summer, showing various printing techniques. The archives contain some 8 million samples of fabric and original designs and are an important reference point for designers and couturiers. There's also an outstanding collection of handkerchiefs; the gift shop sells copies.

Nearby, at the corner of Rue du Sauvage and Rue de Sinne, *Charcutière Alsacienne* beckons museumgoers with 12 varieties of homemade sausage.

On the edge of town, the *Musée Français du Chemin de Fer* (open daily; 2 Rue Alfred-de-Glehn; phone: 89-42-25-67) is in a huge train station where old locomotives rest on six tracks. All the railroad cars, some dating from the 1800s, have been beautifully restored and painted. Three kinds of steam engines are on display along with the first electric train, from 1900. One car, from the prestigious *Train Bleu,* has gleaming brass and crystal figures. Another, from 1856, was used by Napoleon's aides and was decorated by the architect Viollet-le-Duc.

Also at the edge of town, the *Musée National de l'Automobile* (closed Tuesdays in winter; 192 Av. de Colmar; phone: 89-42-29-17) is perhaps the town's greatest attraction. Once the private collection of two Swiss industrialists and claimed by the French government in payment of taxes, this vast building is crammed with Bugattis, Mercedes-Benzes, Rolls-Royces, and Hispano Suizas. A Rolls-Royce Silver Ghost, from 1910, has silver-plated fittings. The Dion Bouton, with facing seats and no roof, gaily painted in blue and red, resembles an open stagecoach on wheels. A Bugatti T16 Garros, built for the French aviator Roland Garros, is one of only two ever made; its transparent plastic body reveals the motor.

CHECKING IN: *Parc* – Recently restored to its Art Deco splendor, this 76-room establishment in downtown Mulhouse offers luxurious surroundings and attentive service. Many of the nicely appointed guestrooms overlook Steinbach Park. Just off the hotel lobby, *Charlie's Bar* attracts a lively crowd of locals. There is also a restaurant, *Le Park's,* which serves classic regional French cooking. Major credit cards accepted. 26 Rue de la Sinne, Mulhouse (phone: 89-66-12-22; fax: 89-66-42-44). Expensive.

Altéa Mulhouse – A modern hotel, with 96 rooms and a restaurant, the *Alsace.* Its convenience makes up for its lack of charm. Major credit cards accepted. 4 Pl. Charles-de-Gaulle, Mulhouse (phone: 89-46-01-23; fax: 89-56-59-98). Moderate.

Auberge de Froeningen – This quiet, 7-room inn is in Froeningen, just 4 miles (7 km) southwest of Mulhouse. Lovingly run by the Renner family, its homey touches include cheery flower arrangements, an herb garden, and a restaurant that serves one of the most succulent and ample breakfasts served in the area. Closed 3 weeks in January and the last 2 weeks in August. Major credit cards accepted. 2 Rte. d'Illfurth, Froeningen (phone: 89-25-48-48). Moderate.

Novotel Mulhouse-Sausheim – In Sausheim, 3 miles (5 km) northeast of Mulhouse, this contemporary 77-room hotel offers a grill-type restaurant, a buffet breakfast, a bar, and an especially pleasant outdoor swimming pool. Major credit cards accepted. Rue de l'Ile-Napoléon, Sausheim (phone: 89-61-84-84; fax: 89-61-77-99). Moderate.

EATING OUT: *Wir* – Perfect for busy sightseers, it provides a straightforward menu, quickly served. Closed Fridays and July. Major credit cards accepted. 1 Porte de Bâle, Mulhouse (phone: 89-56-13-22). Expensive to moderate.

La Bucherie – A good choice for excellent grilled meat and local fruit tarts. Closed Saturday lunch, Sundays, and during February and July. Visa accepted. 2 Av. du Président-Kennedy, Mulhouse (phone: 89-42-12-51). Moderate.

Winstub Henriette – Mulhouse's *winstub* (tavern) is an oasis of Alsatian tradition: warm wood walls and furnishings are a charming backdrop for hearty servings of *choucroute* and other regional specialties. More adventurous folks can try the *tête de veau vinaigrette,* better known as calf's head accompanied by a vinaigrette dressing. Closed Saturday evenings, Sundays, and holidays. Reservations unnecessary. Major credit cards accepted. 9 Rue Henriette (phone: 89-46-27-83). Moderate.

Auberge du Vieux Mulhouse – Well-located, this place offers a variety of prix fixe menus. Closed Sundays. Major credit cards accepted. Pl. de la Réunion, Mulhouse (phone: 89-45-84-18). Inexpensive.

Lorraine

Lorraine is a land of quiche, quetsch (a variety of plum), and crystal. It contains forests and farms, factories and shops, and two proud and prominent cities: Metz and Nancy. It is inextricably linked in people's minds with Alsace, its sister province with which part of it switched back and forth between French and German rule in recent centuries, but it is profoundly different in its geography, architecture, cuisine, and temperament. Indeed, the many parts of Lorraine are strikingly different from one another. Although Lorraine has a historical and artistic unity, it is a region of enormous diversity — perhaps one of its chief appeals to visitors.

Lorraine is by no means a magnet attracting tourists from abroad. The northeastern corner, with its famous and severely depressed mining (coal and iron) and steel industries, often is bleak. But Lorraine does have beauty and points of interest. French campers head for popular sites in forests and by rivers and lakes throughout the region. In the southeast, the countryside of predominantly gently rolling hills rises to the Vosges Mountains, where winter and summer resorts attract French vacationers. The health spas of its south also have a strong French following, especially the notable watering spots of Vittel and Contrexéville. Moreover, remnants of Lorraine's rich history, from Roman times through the world wars, provide some broadly appealing attractions — churches, châteaux, artworks, and war memorials — and its splendid chief cities genuinely merit attention. In short, although Lorraine lacks the reputation and the high spots of a major tourist area, it provides the traveler with a variety of richly rewarding stops.

"Traveler" is a word to bear in mind when contemplating a visit, because Lorraine is a time-established crossroads of Europe. It is bordered on the north by Belgium and Luxembourg and on the northeast by Germany; Switzerland is not far from its southeastern corner. In addition, three of France's most celebrated provinces are next to or near it: Besides Alsace to the east, Champagne is its western boundary, and Burgundy is just a short way across the tip of Champagne to the south. Its role as a major European crossroads is enhanced by an excellent highway system and by its railroad lines, which are trunk routes to the east and west of Europe.

Lorraine first came into prominence as a center of trade and communication between the Mediterranean and northern Europe after the conquest of Gaul by the Romans. Its name, however, dates from the 9th century. In 843, the Treaty of Verdun divided Charlemagne's huge empire among his three grandsons, one of whom, Lothair, received a portion consequently known as Lotharingia and in due course simply as Lorraine. Lothair's original allotment included the present Netherlands, Belgium, Luxembourg, Lorraine, Alsace, and parts of Germany, but during the Middle Ages, as the fates of the German ruling families in the area rose and fell and divisions and subdivisions took place, a much-reduced entity known as the duchy of Lorraine emerged, pockmarked by various independent fiefs — such as the duchy of Bar and the three bishoprics of Metz, Toul, and Verdun — which the dukes were unable to control.

The French domination of Lorraine dates only from the 16th century, and the formal annexation of Lorraine to France did not take place until 1766, with the death of Stanislas Leszczynski, the former Polish king who was given the duchy by his son-in-law Louis XV. A century later, as a result of the French defeat in the Franco-Prussian War in 1870–71, part of Lorraine passed to Germany with Alsace as Alsace-Lorraine but was returned to France after the German defeat in World War I; it has remained French except for 4 years of German occupation during World War II. Throughout these vicissitudes, the sympathies of the people of Lorraine have tended strictly toward Paris (it's no accident that two of the most potent symbols of French patriotism — Joan of Arc and the Cross of Lorraine — are native to the region), and the reality of German rule caused many Lorrainers to resettle in more western areas of France. In their place are new Lorrainers, i.e., the many foreign workers from Mediterranean and North African countries who came to take advantage of the post–World War II boom in Lorraine's industrial areas and settled here permanently.

The route outlined below begins just across the border of Champagne, in Verdun, and tours the World War I battlefields and war memorials surrounding the town before presenting the option of detouring to Bar-le-Duc or continuing directly east to Metz, an attractive city with a splendid cathedral. Via A4, the drive to Metz takes an hour and passes through the farmland and forests of the huge Parc Naturel Régional de Lorraine, but it is possible to take in a few towns and a few more glimpses of the inhabited countryside by skipping the fast pay road and following the slower D903. Then it's south to Nancy, an elegant commercial and intellectual center and the base for side trips to such places as the old town of Toul and the birthplace of Joan of Arc in Domrémy-la-Pucelle, or to the town famous for its small-scale version of Versailles, Lunéville, and the town synonymous with crystal, Baccarat. (Although it is Lorraine's most famous name in crystal, Baccarat is not the only place in the region where crystal is made and sold.) The final leg of the tour is farther south, to the resort-spas of Vittel and Contrexéville to sample the waters as well as their other offerings, and east, to Gérardmer, a winter-summer lake resort on the western slopes of the Vosges. In Gérardmer, you are merely a mountain's crest away from Alsace. Michelin maps No. 57 and No. 62 cover the area.

Though there are no world class restaurants in Lorraine, you'll find lots of good ones, and there will be plenty of opportunities to taste the local specialties — including quiche par excellence. The traditional and hospitable people of Lorraine especially love bacon and pork and mix them beautifully with cream and butter. For desserts there are the famous *madeleines* of Commercy, the macaroons of Boulay and Nancy, and many fresh fruits and berries, including quetsch plums and *mirabelles,* the small yellow plums that are a particular specialty of Metz. The same fruits are distilled into a potent eau-de-vie, the universal digestif of the region, and for those who like their fruits sweet and without alcohol, there are always the special jams of Bar-le-Duc, made of local *groseilles* (red currants).

Hotel accommodations should present no problem. For a double room (private bath and toilet are standard) without breakfast ($5 to $10 extra per person for the continental fare), expect to pay $100 or more at places we list as expensive; $75 to $100 for those in the moderate range; and below $75 for inexpensive lodgings. It's about the same for meals — but depending on your eyes, stomach, and will power — your final tally could go into a category higher than the one intended. A full meal for two, excluding wine and drinks (service usually is included), will run about $100 or more in an expensive restaurant; $70 to $100 in a moderate one; and under $70 in an inexpensive one.

VERDUN: Built on the banks of the Meuse River, this former fortified town has played a strategic role in French history. Approached from the west, from Paris through Champagne, it is the gateway to Lorraine, to its principal cities of Metz and Nancy, and to areas of Germany, Luxembourg, and Alsace that lie beyond. Invaders, however, historically have approached it from the east, seeing it as a gateway of a different sort. Verdun was already a fortress in Gallic and Roman times and it has a huge underground citadel from the reign of Louis XIV, but it was following a siege by the Prussians in 1870 that a string of forts was built around the town to make it France's most formidable bulwark against the Germans. In 1916, then, Verdun became the site of the longest and perhaps the bloodiest battle of the First World War.

The battle of Verdun began in February with a massive German assault along an 8-mile front to the north and east of town. The first of the outlying forts fell almost instantly, General Pétain organized the French resistance to the cry of "They shall not pass!" (which became the French slogan for the rest of the war), and fighting of the most brutal kind, characterized by the use of poison gas and flame throwers, went on for 11 months. By December, Verdun's defenders had recovered most of the territory lost and the Germans — whose aim was to "bleed France white" — had been driven back approximately to the same positions held before the attack. In the meantime, the city had been destroyed, nearly 350,000 French soldiers and an almost equal number of Germans had lost their lives, and Verdun had become a symbol of the most horrific and pointless aspects of war.

Despite further heavy damage in 1944, Verdun (pop. 24,000) is today a pleasant administrative center, busy and modern, though with more than a few architectural hints of its past. The Meuse divides it into a lower town of residential and commercial areas (the tourist office is near the river at Place de la Nation; phone: 29-84-18-85) and an upper town, which overlooks the valley and contains the restored Cathédrale Notre-Dame and the Citadelle Souterraine, both worth a visit. The cathedral, built on the highest spot in town, is an interesting blend of Romanesque and Gothic styles; it dates back largely to the 11th and 12th centuries, and its cloister dates from the 14th to the 16th century. Not far away, the Citadelle — the work of the 17th-century military engineer Sébastien Vauban — contains several miles of subterranean galleries in which troops defending the city were fed and housed (open to the public from February through mid-December). The Unknown Soldier who lies under the Arc de Triomphe in Paris was selected in a ceremony here in 1920.

The Monument de la Victoire, a war memorial with books listing the names of all who fought in Verdun's defense, is in town, but most of what makes Verdun a place of pilgrimage is in the surrounding countryside. Several circuits lead through the battlefields and commemorative monuments, but the visit to the right bank of the

Meuse is by far the most concentrated and moving; the circuit of the left bank is distinguished perhaps only by the 14,000 marble crosses of the American cemetery in Romagne-sous-Montfaucon.

For the right circuit, an approximately 20-mile (32-km) drive, take N3 out of Verdun toward Etain, passing the 5,000 graves of the Cimetière National du Faubourg-Pavé. Farther along, take the turnoff for Fort de Vaux (left onto D913, right onto D913A). The Germans laid siege to this fort on March 9, 1916, but did not overcome a heroic defense by the garrison until June 7. Five months later, the fort was recaptured. Guided tours (from February to mid-December) take visitors through the fort, and from the top there is an impressive panorama of the surrounding landscape and war memorials. From Fort de Vaux, return to D913 and follow it toward Douaumont. The *Memorial-Musée de la Bataille de Verdun* (closed from mid-December to mid-January) is where the village of Fleury once stood. Farther along, the Ossuaire de Douaumont (open all year) is the most important French memorial to the dead of 1914–18. The remains of 100,000 unidentified soldiers lie in this long, low necropolis; in the Cimetière National in front of it, 15,000 crosses on a carpet of green mark another 15,000 graves. In the center of the ossuary is a Catholic chapel, where mass is held at 10:30 AM on Sundays (earlier on other days), and at the top of the tower rising above it, orientation tables pick out the various sectors of the battlefield. The nearby Fort de Douaumont, which fell on February 25, 1916 (only 4 days after the surprise German attack began), and was not retaken until late in October, also is open to visitors. From the heights of this multilevel fortification (guided tours take place from *Easter* through October), there is a full view of the battlefield, surrounding forest, and the ossuary. To reach the next monument of the right circuit, the Tranchée des Baïonnettes (Trench of Bayonets), where an infantry section was buried alive following violent bombing on June 10, 1916, return from Fort de Douaumont toward the ossuary and follow the signs. After the visit, the winding road down the "Ravin de la Mort" to Bras and then D964 will return you to Verdun.

CHECKING IN/EATING OUT: *Hostellerie Coq Hardi* – Near the center of town, there are 40 rooms and 3 apartments in this comfortable, Lorraine house, old-fashioned but for color television sets. Its family-run restaurant is an opulent-looking dining room. The chef turns out superb sauces and a "light" cuisine that has earned one Michelin star. It can be tasted to maximum effect in such dishes as *salade Coq Hardi,* foie gras with fresh noodles, or wild salmon with parsley and flamed *mirabelles.* Hotel closed late December through January; restaurant closed Fridays. Major credit cards accepted. 8 Av. de la Victoire, Verdun (phone: 29-86-36-36; fax: 29-86-09-21). Hotel, moderate; restaurant, expensive.

Bellevue – Operated by the owners of the *Coq Hardi,* it has 75 rooms in all, with color television sets, some with lovely views of Verdun's Botanical Garden. Another garden is in back, there is a restaurant, and a garage is available. Closed November through March, except January. Major credit cards accepted. 1 Rond-point du Maréchal-de-Lattre-de-Tassigny, Verdun (phone: 29-84-39-41; fax: 29-86-09-21). Moderate.

En Route from Verdun – Proceed 48 miles (77 km) east on A4 to Metz, or detour southwest via N35 to the town of Bar-le-Duc. The 35-mile (56-km) stretch of road between Verdun and Bar-le-Duc is known as the Voie Sacrée (Sacred Way), so called because it was the crucial supply route for men and matériel coming to bolster the defense of Verdun following the surprise German attack in 1916.

BAR-LE-DUC: This busy commercial center of 20,500 people was once the capital of the important duchy of Bar, which was united to the duchy of Lorraine late in the

15th century. It occupies a picturesque spot on the Ornain River and contains a remarkable group of 16th-to-18th-century houses as well as the 15th-century Gothic Eglise St-Etienne, which has a famous and decidedly macabre statue by Ligier Richier, a distinguished regional artist of the 16th century. Called *Le Squelette* (The Skeleton), the statue is a likeness of René de Châlon, Prince of Orange, who is pictured, according to his wishes, as he would appear after death. Another work by Richier is a wooden statue of Christ in the town's Eglise Notre-Dame.

Bar-le-Duc is known well beyond Lorraine for its currant preserves (*confiture de groseilles*), the production of which is a flourishing cottage industry following centuries of tradition. The currant harvest begins in July, preparation is well under way by August, and though it isn't possible to visit the places where the preserves are made, if you come to town in early September, you can witness the annual *Fête de la Groseille,* an old-fashioned country fair and antiques show that celebrates the Barisien delicacy. Bar-le-Duc's tourist office is in the Hôtel de Ville (Town Hall), 5 Rue Jeanne d'Arc (phone: 29-45-16-03; fax: 29-79-11-13).

EATING OUT: *La Meuse Gourmande* – This very popular restaurant in a former convent serves good regional cuisine — mushrooms, snails, eels, blood sausage — and good local wines, particularly the côtes-de-meuse. Avoid any nouvelle dishes. Closed Sunday evenings, Mondays, and holidays. Major credit cards accepted. 1 Rue François-de-Guise, Bar-le-Duc (phone: 29-79-28-40). Moderate.

METZ: Set at the confluence of the Seille and Moselle rivers, Metz (pronounced *Mess*) is a thriving regional administrative, political, commercial, and economic center, the home of some 118,500 Messins. Though it was the scene of violent fighting and much destruction in World War II, the rebuilt city is today an attractive blend of old and new architecture. Streets in the heart of town have been closed to traffic and turned into appealing pedestrian shopping malls; riverside parks and an esplanade are filled with flowers, terraces, views, and recreational facilities; sailing and other boating activities are popular along the Moselle.

Metz was an important city of Roman Gaul from the time of Caesar to the time of the Frankish King Clovis. Later, during the reign of Charlemagne (768–814), it became the intellectual cradle of the Carolingian Empire (Charlemagne favored Metz so much that he chose to bury his wife, Hildegarde, here). In the 12th century, it became a free city, a rival to the great Flemish, German, and Italian cities of the time and strong enough to repel the frequent attempts of the Dukes of Lorraine to annex it. Instead, along with the other two independent bishoprics of Verdun and Toul, it was captured by Henry II of France in 1552 and its status as part of France was confirmed in 1648 by the Treaty of Westphalia.

The city's one touristic "must" is the soaring Gothic Cathédrale St-Etienne, built largely from the mid-13th to the early 16th century on the site of two previous, adjoining churches: an ancient oratory dedicated to St. Stephen, which miraculously escaped the devastation of Attila and the Huns in the 5th century, and a later church, Notre-Dame la Ronde. The height of St-Etienne's nave (131 feet) and aisles (44 feet) makes it one of the loftiest cathedrals in France, and, at 372 feet, it also is one of the longest, but it is most noted for its sublime stained glass windows. The rose window above the central doorway is the work of Hermann of Munster (1384–92); the great window of the left transept in Flamboyant Gothic, that of Theobald of Lyxheim (1504); the great window of the right transept in Renaissance style, that of Valentin Bousch (1521–27). The latter two windows, said to be the largest in the world (each covers about 4,140 square feet), bathe the transept in a glorious symphony of colored light. Many of the cathedral's other stained glass windows were lost in wartime, but there are splendid modern replacements, including those done in the 1960s by Marc Chagall.

Not far away, the city's exemplary *Musée d'Art et d'Histoire* (2 Rue du Haut-Poirier; phone: 87-75-10-18) also merits a visit. Its contents, covering 1,700 years of history, are housed in ancient structural remains ranging from the marble-covered sandstone walls of Roman baths to the façade of a Renaissance mansion built in 1529. Exhibits include a collection of Merovingian artifacts excavated in Metz over the last 150 years and, particularly interesting, objects belonging to the legendary Charlemagne. Incorporated in the museum is a 5-story, 15th-century granary, the only one of its kind in Europe, which houses the extensive Gothic collection as well as ambitious programs of Gothic art and artisanship; for example, pottery, porcelain, and glassware workshops. The museum is open daily except Tuesdays from 10 AM to noon and 2 to 5 PM.

Among Metz's other notable buildings is its enormous train station, built from 1905 to 1908 in the massive Roman Rhenan style; across from it, the post office, built in the same style in 1911 in red sandstone from the Vosges; the large 18th-century Hôtel de Ville (Town Hall); the Porte des Allemands, a 13th-century château-fort on the Seille River; and the Eglise St-Pierre-aux-Nonnains. This church, which dates from the 4th century and is reportedly the oldest in France, is closed to visitors, however, and is not overly impressive from the outside. There is useful information on Metz, some in English, at the Office du Tourisme, Pl. d'Armes (phone: 87-75-65-21).

CHECKING IN: *Altéa St. Thiébault* – This modern hotel with 120 large, well-equipped rooms is on a beautiful square near the city center. Major credit cards accepted. 29 Pl. St-Thiébault, Metz (phone: 87-36-17-69; fax: 87-75-48-18). Expensive.

Novotel Metz Centre – Right downtown, near the main shopping area and the heart of the St-Jacques commercial center, this hotel has 98 comfortable, air conditioned rooms, a piano bar, and an outdoor pool. Major credit cards accepted. Pl. des Paraiges, Metz (phone: 87-37-38-39; fax: 87-36-10-00). Expensive.

Royal-Concorde – A turn-of-the-century choice in the residential area near the train station; the 70 rooms are large and comfortable. Major credit cards accepted. 23 Av. Foch, Metz (phone: 87-66-81-11; fax: 87-56-13-16). Expensive.

Cécil – Also near the train station, it's a small, sound, but undistinguished hotel with 39 modern, functional rooms in an old building. Major credit cards accepted. 14 Rue Pasteur, Metz (phone: 87-66-66-13; fax: 87-56-96-02). Moderate to inexpensive.

Ibis – In the Pontiffroy quarter on the outskirts of town, this small modern hostelry caters to French businesspeople and families. The 79 rooms are functional and well-kept. Major credit cards accepted. 47 Rue Chambière, Metz (phone: 87-31-01-73; fax: 87-31-25-46). Moderate to inexpensive.

Foch – Between the town center and the train station, this pretty 1920s building now houses an old-style hostelry offering 38 comfortable rooms with modern baths and television sets. Major credit cards accepted. 8 Pl. R.-Mondon, Metz (phone: 87-75-56-42; fax: 87-74-49-90). Inexpensive.

EATING OUT: *La Dinanderie* – The best restaurant in the city, and overall a good one, in a contemporary and elegant setting. Expect fine produce and diverse dishes with light sauces that show off the chef's masterful touch. The fish dishes are good. Closed Sundays, Mondays, August 8–31, and *Christmas* to early January. Major credit cards accepted. 2 Rue de Paris, Metz (phone: 87-30-14-40). Expensive.

Le Crinouc – A trendy, one-star restaurant that caters to the same clientele as *La Goulue* (below). The cuisine is a successful blend of tradition and innovation, and the sauces are perfection. Closed Sunday evenings, Mondays, and the first 2 weeks of January. Major credit cards accepted. 79 Rue du Général-Metman, Metz (phone: 87-74-12-45). Expensive to moderate.

La Goulue – A lovely bistro with an emphasis on fish, it also has excellent produce.

Closed Sundays, Mondays, and from *Christmas* to after *New Year's*. Major credit cards accepted. 24 Pl. St-Simplice, Metz (phone: 87-75-10-69). Expensive to moderate.

A La Ville de Lyon – Where the Messins (locals) eat. The cuisine is traditional, regional, and consistently good. Closed Sunday evenings, Mondays, and during August. Major credit cards accepted. 7 Rue des Piques, Metz (phone: 87-36-07-01). Expensive to moderate.

NANCY: Thirty-five miles (56 km) south of Metz, this city of about 100,000 inhabitants is another regional hub of government and commerce, a center of finance, mining, metallurgy, and engineering, and the seat of the third largest scientific university in France. It also is a city of classic French culture and elegance, with an astonishing group of 18th-century buildings at its core to testify to a notable past.

As the capital of the duchy of Lorraine from the 12th to the 18th century, the city was the creation of its dukes, and particularly of its last duke, who was not French at all but Polish. By an arrangement that ended the War of the Polish Succession, François III, Duke of Lorraine, exchanged his duchy for that of Tuscany. In his place, Louis XV installed Stanislas Leszczynski, his own father-in-law and the deposed King of Poland, on the throne of Nancy in 1737, with the proviso that on his death (which occurred in 1766), Nancy and Lorraine would become part of France.

The last Duke of Lorraine set about beautifying and developing the city, and the huge, regal square now named Place Stanislas was his showplace. The work of architect Emmanuel Héré and ironmaster Jean Lamour, this beautifully proportioned ensemble of palaces and gilded wrought-iron grillwork — in gateways, fountains, railings, and balconies — is considered a supreme achievement of 18th-century art. The largest building on the square, now the Hôtel de Ville (Town Hall), contains a magnificent wrought-iron staircase leading to salons from which the rest of Stanislas's urban plan is visible in all its refined harmony. Four larger and two smaller buildings ornamented with imposing arcades flank the Hôtel de Ville; directly in front of it is the Arc de Triomphe in honor of Louis XV. Behind that is a second square, Place de la Carrière, which dates from the 16th and 17th centuries but was transformed by Héré. This long rectangle is surrounded by 18th-century townhouses, embellished by more fountains and grillwork and closed off, at its far end, by a colonnade and the Palais du Gouvernement, once the residence of the Governors of Lorraine.

Pass to the left of the Palais du Gouvernement and take the Grande-Rue to two more sites of merit: the Palais Ducal, the palace where the dukes and their courts once resided, and the Eglise des Cordeliers, the now deconsecrated church where most of the dukes are buried. The palace as it stands today was built principally by Duke Antoine in the 16th century (on the site of an earlier structure) but restored considerably following damage in the 18th century. Of particular interest is the famous Porterie, an elaborate doorway in the Grande-Rue façade surmounted by an equestrian statue of Duke Antoine topped with a Flamboyant Gothic gable. Adjoining the palace, the Eglise des Cordeliers was the final stop of funeral ceremonies for the dukes that were long enough (they took weeks) and showy enough to compare with the coronations of emperors at Frankfurt and the investitures of kings at Reims, according to an old French proverb. The church (open from 10 AM to noon and 2 to 5 PM except Tuesdays) contains numerous ducal tombs, including the notable 16th-century tombs of René II and his wife, Philippa de Gueldre, the tomb of the latter a work of Ligier Richier. However, Duke Stanislas and his wife, Catherine Opalinska, are buried in another church, the Eglise Notre-Dame-de-Bon-Secours, somewhat southeast of the center on Avenue de Strasbourg.

Nancy also has some museums of considerable distinction. The *Musée Historique Lorrain,* in the ducal palace, has a rich collection pertaining to the history of Nancy and the region. An archaeological garden displays Celtic, Gallo-Roman, and Frankish artifacts; there's an almost complete collection of the engravings of Jacques Callot (a native of Nancy), a sampling of paintings by Georges de la Tour (a native of Lorraine), a floor full of the furniture and folk art of the area, Judaica, and a museum of pharmacology. (64 Grande-Rue; phone: 83-32-18-74; open daily except Tuesdays from 10 AM to noon and 2 to 5 PM.) The *Musée des Beaux-Arts*, in one of the palaces off Place Stanislas, is devoted to European paintings from the 14th century to modern times, including works by Perugino, Tintoretto, Rubens, Delacroix, Manet, Bonnard, Utrillo, and Modigliani, among others. (3 Pl. Stanislas; phone: 83-37-65-01; open daily except Monday morning and Tuesdays from 10:30 AM to 6 PM.) Southwest of the city's center, a third museum of interest is the *Musée de l'Ecole de Nancy* (36-38 Rue Sergent-Blandan; phone: 83-40-14-86; hours as above), with furniture, glassware, and ceramics by artists of Nancy's own school of Art Nouveau, including objects from the workshop of Emile Gallé, who was its inspiration.

Nancy is a fine city for walking, and not just in its 18th-century core. Just a short walk from Place Stanislas is the factory and showroom for Daum, a fine French crystal less well known than Baccarat, whose factory also is nearby (see *Baccarat*, below). Daum's workrooms can be visited Mondays through Saturdays from 9:30 AM to 12:30 PM and Saturday afternoons from 2:30 to 6 PM (17 Rue des Cristalleries; phone: 83-32-14-55). There are shop-lined streets and shopping arcades for browsing and buying, university areas, pleasant squares with fountains, and numerous parks for sitting and strolling, notably the large Parc de la Pépinière off Place de la Carrière.

CHECKING IN: Grand Hôtel de la Reine – A fine hotel (a member of the Relais & Châteaux group) in one of the landmark 18th-century buildings right on Place Stanislas. Marie-Antoinette may have once resided here, but now all 50 rooms have modern conveniences, including color TV sets; there's a good restaurant, the *Stanislas*, with a wonderful fixed-price menu and a very talented chef. Major credit cards accepted. 2 Pl. Stanislas, Nancy (phone: 83-35-03-01; fax: 83-32-86-04). Expensive.

Altéa Thiers – The 192 rooms of this member of the reliable chain are comfortable (with TV sets and air conditioning), effectively decorated, and in a perfect location near Place Stanislas. There's a good restaurant and bar as well. Major credit cards accepted. 11 Rue Raymond-Poincaré, Nancy (phone: 83-39-75-75; fax: 83-32-78-17). Expensive to moderate.

Albert Ier–Astoria – A quiet, comfortable stop with 120 rooms near the train station, it was recently renovated by new owners who added conference rooms and other conveniences. No restaurant. 3 Rue de l'Armée-Patton, Nancy (phone: 83-40-31-24; fax: 83-28-47-78). Moderate.

EATING OUT: Le Capucin Gourmand – There's delicious food here at the city's finest restaurant, which has been given one Michelin star, and the decor features some shining examples of Nancy's own Art Nouveau. Traditional cuisine is limited to a few outstanding choices (try the fresh foie gras), supplemented by a half dozen or so of the chef's varied specials (notable are the *feuilleté* of oysters and the pigeon *kefta*). The cheese tray is outstanding, and the desserts, such as apple *galette* perfumed with *bergamote* — the local bonbon — unusual. Closed Sundays, Mondays, 2 weeks in January, and August; reservations advised. Visa accepted. 31 Rue Gambetta, Nancy (phone: 83-35-26-98). Expensive.

Le Goéland – The only place in town with a really luxurious, contemporary dining room. The specialties are "products of the sea" prepared with inventiveness and subtlety, and there's a nice wine list. One Michelin star. Closed Sunday evenings, Mondays, holidays, and 2 weeks in August. Reservations advised. Major credit cards accepted. 27 Rue des Ponts, Nancy (phone: 83-35-17-25). Expensive.

Excelsior – A classic, Art Nouveau brasserie that boasts high, ornate ceilings, leaded stained glass, and graceful fixtures. It offers a varied choice of reasonably priced specialties. Service can be slow. Open daily, with drinks and snacks served between meal times. Reservations advised. Major credit cards accepted. 50 Rue Henri-Poincaré, Nancy (phone: 83-35-24-57). Moderate.

La Gentilhommière – This charming provincial restaurant has excellent meat, poultry (veal, squab, duck), and refined sauces. Closed Saturdays, Sundays, most of August, and at *Christmas*. Reservations advised. Major credit cards accepted. 29 Rue des Maréchaux, Nancy (phone: 83-32-26-44). Moderate.

Le Comptoir de Gastrolatre – A charming bistro offering simple and delicious country food at bargain prices. Closed Sundays, Monday lunch, *Easter Week,* and the first half of September. Reservations advised. No credit cards accepted. Pl. Vaudemont, Nancy (phone: 83-35-51-94). Inexpensive.

En Route from Nancy – Several points of interest south of Nancy are arranged in a manner that allows you to visit them easily in a series of excursions using Nancy as a base. Domrémy-la-Pucelle, the birthplace of Joan of Arc, is southwest of the city, via Toul, once an important town and worth an excursion in its own right. Southeast of the city, there is a splendid 18th-century château at Lunéville; after a visit, fanciers of fine crystal often proceed to Baccarat. Directly south of Nancy, the spa towns of Vittel and Contrexéville and then the summer and winter resort of Gérardmer farther east can be the objects of a pleasant day's outing from Nancy or stops on the way to Burgundy or Alsace.

TOUL: Take A33 west from Nancy; this old town is only 14 miles (22 km) away. Toul, along with Metz and Verdun, was one of the three bishoprics that emerged as independent cities during the Middle Ages and remained free until captured for France by Henry II in the mid-16th century. Much damaged during World War II, the town is the site of the battered yet still fascinating Cathédrale St-Etienne, built from the 13th to the 16th century. The church has a Flamboyant Gothic façade that is especially magnificent and a beautiful cloister.

DOMRÉMY-LA-PUCELLE: From Toul, it's another 24 miles (38 km; N74 south, then D19 west) to Domrémy — or Domrémy-la-Pucelle (Domrémy-the-Maid), as the village has been renamed in honor of its most famous daughter. Joan of Arc was born to two pious peasants (in 1411 or 1412) in a starkly simple house here (open daily April through mid-September; closed Tuesdays in winter) and baptized in the local church, which, though much changed, contains a few objects of her time, including the baptismal font. Next door, a small museum is devoted to her life.

LUNÉVILLE: The center of attraction in this town 22 miles (35 km) southeast of Nancy is a château known as "little Versailles." Lunéville was the favorite residence of Léopold, Duke of Lorraine, who commissioned the château as a modest replica of the great palace of Versailles in 1703. Later, Stanislas Leszczynski, the last duke and the inspired developer of Nancy, was instrumental in decorating it and in laying out the beautiful gardens of the adjoining Parc des Bosquets, now the setting for a summer sound and light show. Lunéville became Stanislas's favorite residence, too, and it was here that he died, but not before contributing to the reputation of the "petit Versailles" by the quality of his guests, who included such notables as Voltaire and Diderot. Designed by architect Germain Boffrand (a student of Jules Hardouin-Mansart, the architect of Louis XIV's royal buildings), the château has a huge, majestic court on the west side, two small wings separated from the great halls by porticoes, and a chapel modeled on that at Versailles. A small museum established early in the 18th century displays furniture, engravings, historical documents, and an especially distinguished collection of Lunéville faïences.

 EATING OUT: *Château d'Adoménil* – This delightful mansion (a member of the Relais & Châteaux group) and its well-tended park are in a lovely country setting 3 miles (5 km) outside Lunéville. The menu, rating one Michelin star, features seasonal fish and game specialties, and the service is excellent. Closed Sunday evenings, Mondays, Tuesdays for lunch, and weeks in February. Major credit cards accepted. South of Lunéville in Réhainviller-à-Doménil (phone: 83-74-04-81; fax: 83-74-21-78). Expensive to moderate.

BACCARAT: Southeast from Lunéville down N59, it's 15 miles (24 km) to Baccarat, a name synonymous with fine crystal since the founding of its factory in 1764. During the summer, tourists throng the small town to marvel at antique and modern crystal works in the *Musée du Crystal* (Rue de Cristalleries; for information on when it's open, call the tourist office, phone: 83-75-10-46 or 83-75-10-01), thence to acquire souvenirs in glass — at comparatively good prices — in any number of accommodating shops along the main street. The best is *Baccarat-Magasin de Vente* (Rue des Cristalleries; phone: 83-75-12-47), which ships all over the world. Open daily from 10 AM to 12:30 PM and 2:30 to 7 PM; from 8:30 AM to 12:30 PM and 1:30 to 7 PM on Sundays. The crystal decorations in the little town church, built in 1957, also are worth a stop.

VITTEL: South of Nancy, in the woods of southern Lorraine, is an area known for its mineral and thermal springs and consequently for its spa resorts. The town of Vittel, 43 miles (69 km) from Nancy via D413, is the largest and one of the best known of these spa towns. Its cold-water springs were familiar to the Romans, then forgotten, then rediscovered in the mid-19th century. Today, Vittel water at its source is used internally and externally to treat a variety of illnesses (including liver and kidney diseases, gout, and rheumatism), and bottled Vittel water is much more likely to be found on French tables than Perrier water. Besides the thermal establishment, in a large park, the town is well equipped to attract the health-conscious visitor. Facilities for amusements — golf, tennis, swimming, and riding, among them — are in good supply, there's a good selection of hotels and restaurants, and there's a gambling casino.

CONTREXÉVILLE: Like Vittel, its neighbor 3 miles (5 km) away, Contrexéville is known for its mineral water, which also springs cold from its source and which also is bottled and popular all over France. Both resorts are low-key places, and Contrexéville, too, has a casino, but it is the smaller of the two and has the nicer accommodations.

CHECKING IN: *Cosmos* – This hotel with a restaurant and 81 beautifully furnished rooms is in a lovely and quiet park. Closed from October through April. Major credit cards accepted. 13 Rue de Metz, Contrexéville (phone: 29-08-15-90; fax: 29-08-68-67). Moderate.

Grand Hôtel Etablissement – A charming old hotel inside the thermal park, it has 29 rooms and a restaurant. Closed from mid-September to April. Major credit cards accepted. Cour d'Honneur, Contrexéville (phone: 29-08-01-31; fax: 29-08-17-30). Moderate.

EATING OUT: *L'Aubergade* – A warm welcome greets all who enter this lovely, small dining room. Specialties include salmon in puff pastry, mousse of frogs, steaks with mushrooms, and a few daring but successful experimental dishes. The homemade desserts use such local fruits as peaches and *mirabelles* (yellow plums) and are delicious. Adjoining is a 9-room hotel added 6 years ago. Closed Sunday evenings and Mondays. Major credit cards accepted. 265 Av. de Tilleul, Vittel (phone: 29-08-04-39). Expensive to moderate.

En Route from Vittel or Contrexéville – You can take a trip southeast through the lovely forest of Darney, then go on to the nearby hot water spas of Bains-les-Bains and Plombières-les-Bains, both of them in use in Roman times. From Plombières, it is 26 miles (42 km) to Gérardmer, the main resort of the Vosges Mountains, which separate Lorraine from Alsace.

GÉRARDMER: This popular resort occupies a magnificent site in the midst of evergreen forests on the western slopes (the Lorraine side) of the Vosges and at the eastern end of the largest of the range's many lakes, Lac de Gérardmer. It is an excellent spot for skiing and skating in winter and for swimming, boating, fishing, and hiking in summer. Sightseeing possibilities include a look at the local church, made of Vosges sandstone; a circuit of the lake, which can be done by motorboat or car (a 4-mile/6-km drive partly through forest that opens up to views of water and encircling mountains); and any number of excursions — to neighboring slopes, to Lac de Longemer and Lac de Retournemer, and along the road to Colmar in Alsace, which crosses the panoramic Route des Crêtes running north and south along the ridge of the Vosges 9 miles (14 km) east of Gérardmer. The town is well equipped for visitors, with the oldest tourist office in France, hotels, restaurants, and a gambling casino.

CHECKING IN/EATING OUT: *Bragard –* In town, this nicely furnished hotel has 61 rooms plus a swimming pool, a sauna, and an exercise room. It's restaurant, *Au Grand Cerf,* offers fine traditional local dishes and nouvelle cuisine. Open year-round. Major credit cards accepted. Pl. du Tilleul, Gérardmer (phone: 29-63-06-31). Expensive to moderate.

Hostellerie Bas-Rupts – This modern, chalet-style hostelry of 32 rooms is on a quiet mountainside approximately 2½ miles (4 km) south of Gérardmer via D486. There are tennis courts and instruction is offered, the hotel is only a short distance from ski resorts, and a new swimming pool has been added. The restaurant, *Les Bas-Rupts,* is a luxurious dining room done in rustic Louis XIII decor. It boasts a chef trained by France's masters, exquisite service, and a refined menu of light, delicious dishes that merits one Michelin star. In good weather you can eat outdoors on the terrace. Major credit cards accepted. Bas-Rupts, just south of Gérardmer (phone: 29-63-09-25; fax: 29-63-00-40). Expensive to moderate.

Champagne

Champagne. The word is magical, as charged with rich associations as the bottles of sparkling wine that bear it on their labels. The world's most famous wine takes its name from the region 90 miles (145 km) east of Paris that produces it, though La Champagne, the region, is much less known outside France than *le champagne,* the celebrated bubbly product.

An elongated oval stretching 100 miles from north to south, Champagne nevertheless offers visitors a surprising wealth of sights; foremost among them are its glorious Romanesque and Gothic churches, including the incomparable Cathedral of Reims; its great champagne houses, with miles of cellars housing millions of bottles of champagne in the making; and, of course, the vineyards themselves, more than 75,000 fertile acres spread across the landscape. Yet perhaps the greatest charm of the region lies in the villages scattered throughout the countryside. An hour and a half from Paris, less than 10 minutes outside urban Reims, and beyond the often uninteresting, even bleak views afforded by the region's highways, it is possible to sample French provincial life, to step back, it seems, into the 19th century in villages crowded around medieval churches, and to drive along narrow, nearly deserted roads through fields and vineyards looking as if time had cradled them ever so gently.

This serene aspect is an illusion. The word "champagne" comes from the Latin *campania,* meaning "open, level, unforested land," and despite undulating hills, rivers, and lakes — despite, even, numerous forests — such it is. The entire area is a plateau seldom exceeding 600 feet in altitude, and this topographical fact, combined with the region's geographical location, shaped its destiny. Civilized since the neolithic era, Champagne has been a crossroads of Europe, a route of invasion, and a battlefield for 2,000 years. It has been ravaged repeatedly, and Epernay alone was destroyed close to 2 dozen times.

Julius Caesar brought his Roman legions to Champagne when he conquered Gaul between 58 and 51 BC. The region flourished under the subsequent Roman occupation, and Reims, then a city of 80,000-plus inhabitants, far exceeded Paris in size and importance. In AD 451, Attila the Hun and half a million barbarian soldiers stormed into Roman Gaul and made their camp on the plains of Champagne. What ensued was one of the fiercest and bloodiest battles in history, a monumental encounter between Orient and Occident in which 1 million soldiers fought, 200,000 died, and Attila was defeated. This saga of war and destruction continued, and before the end of the 10th century Champagne had been the scene of numerous invasions and annexations, and Reims had been razed to the ground seven times. A few centuries of peace and prosperity followed: Champagne became a center of commerce between the textile regions of the north and the Mediterranean (to this day, Troyes and Reims are textile centers), and the great Champagne fairs of the Middle

Ages attracted merchants from all over Europe six times a year. Prosperity led to a flowering of culture, which culminated in the poetry of Chrétien de Troyes and in the Gothic cathedral at Reims. This peaceful interlude was only temporary, however: Champagne was one of the principal battlegrounds of the bloody Hundred Years War (1337–1453) and the site of many other conflicts through the centuries, including some during the French Revolution, the Napoleonic Wars of the late 18th and early 19th centuries, and during the Franco-Prussian War of 1870–71.

In our century, the region was spared nothing during the two world wars. In World War I, the Champagne district was the scene of the nightmare battles of the Marne (1914 and 1918), and it was in 1914 that the Germans committed an outrage never forgotten by the people of Champagne: the shelling of Reims Cathedral at the onset of more than 1,000 days of bombardment of the city. Not for the first time, the Champenois took to the relative safety of the champagne cellars to live and work. Throughout the war, fighting took place in the vineyards, and at the war's end, the countryside was scorched and the large towns heavily damaged. The Champenois had it little better during World War II. In 1940, Nazi tanks stormed into France via Champagne, and during the next 5 years, only Normandy suffered greater devastation in France. Afterward, accounts emerged of the powerful underground resistance movement that had operated in German-occupied Champagne — accounts of walled-off champagne cellars hiding precious stocks from the Germans, of rerouted trains, of remarkable individual heroics. Today the two wars are part of the Champenois soul, and monuments, cemeteries, and rebuilt towns throughout the region are poignant reminders of its recent ordeals.

A remarkable indicator of the Champenois character is that throughout both world wars, throughout all the shelling of the vineyards and the towns, the vines were tended and harvested, and each year champagne was bottled in the cellars (albeit not in prewar quantities). When there were few men available, the women and children stepped in, and some lost their lives while working. The battle currently being fought here, however, is economic: decline in champagne sales, particularly in the United States, and rising production costs are plaguing even the major houses, some of which have closed. The Champenois have been known throughout history as hard-working, sensible, thrifty, and honorable. If, after centuries of war, they also are a rather serious and reserved people, it is understandable.

Since champagne is the region's lifeblood and since a stretch of vineyards and at least one champagne cellar are sure to be on your itinerary, a brief introduction to the king of wines (and the wine of kings) is indispensable. Ever since the Romans planted vines in the 1st century, Champagne has been known for its wine. By the Middle Ages, the wine was being exported, and there are clear indications that according to the standards of the day, its quality was outstanding. But it was not sparkling wine. The techniques that gave birth to the foaming wine were developed only at the end of the 17th century, the same century that saw the wines of Champagne — still and sparkling — become the wines of aristocrats and connoisseurs. In the next century, the sparkling wine became supreme, welcomed and praised widely at all the best tables. This in turn led to the mystique of champagne, to the industry's expansion, and to the exportation of the wine in the 19th and 20th centuries. Meanwhile, a significant change in the character of the wine was occurring. At first the sparkling wine was sweet, but as tastes changed, particularly in this century, most champagne was made drier and drier. Today, 85% of the approximately 200 million bottles produced annually are *brut* champagne and can be characterized as bone dry.

Champagne is the northernmost vine-growing region in France — essentially, in Europe (exceptions are the more northerly Rheingau and Mosel vineyards of Germany). This climate is one of the factors that guarantees the uniqueness and quality of the most imitated wine in the world. Others are the chalky soil; the type, characteristics, and quality of the grapes (by law, only chardonnay, pinot noir, and pinot meunier may be used); and time-honored, meticulous, and painstaking techniques of vine cultivation and wine making. The making of champagne is the most regulated and legislated wine producing process anywhere.

Strictly speaking, champagne is a blend of many wines that have been caused to ferment a second time in a stoppered bottle. The grapes, which come from 250 villages, are pressed according to rigorous standards and are fermented in vats into still wines at the region's 110 champagne houses (only 2 dozen of which are large and widely known). The still wines are then married to wines from other vine stocks, other sources, and even other years, according to the taste of the cellar master, resulting in a harmonious blend known as the *cuvée.* Most champagnes contain wines from several years and are classified as non-vintage. If the wines are all from the same year, an exceptional year, the champagne will be vintage and will bear the year on its label.

Up to this point, the blend still is simply white wine. Now it is bottled, and special yeasts and a small quantity of sugar are added to cause the second fermentation, which takes place in the champagne house's old labyrinthine chalk cellars, where the wines are left to mature for at least a year, usually 3 to 5 years. A few steps remain. The sediment thrown off by the second fermentation is eliminated by tilting the bottle neck downward and rotating it frequently, thus collecting the sediment on the cork. This process, usually done by hand, can take 3 months and is known as riddling, or *remuage.* The *dégorgement* process follows, whereby the neck is frozen and the cork is removed, allowing the pressure in the bottle to expel the ice pellet with the sediment. The bottle is then topped off with the *dosage,* a reserve wine with cane sugar added to establish the desired sweetness, and corked. *Et voilà,* champagne.

From north to south, the Champagne region has four vine-growing areas — the Mountain of Reims, the Valley of the Marne, the Côte des Blancs (Slope of the Whites), and the Region of the Aube — and the three centers of Reims, Epernay, and Troyes. The route we suggest begins in the cathedral city and champagne center of Reims and circles south through the hilly vineyards and small villages of the Montagne de Reims before reaching Epernay. Next, it follows the Valley of the Marne, which stretches east and west of Epernay, then turns south through the villages and vineyards of the

Côte des Blancs. After a visit to the historic crossroads town of Châlons-sur-Marne, it continues south to Troyes, the former capital of Champagne as well as an art center, and from there proceeds southeast through the remaining Aube vineyard area to end at the threshold of yet another famous wine region, Burgundy. If you want detailed maps, Michelin No. 56 covers the entire Champagne Road area (and the northern leg of our route) and map No. 61 covers the remaining area beyond Châlons-sur-Marne.

Since a good deal of what you will want to see lies in and around Reims and Epernay, which are only 16 miles (26 km) apart (by the direct, not the scenic, route), doubling back to hotels, restaurants, villages, and other sites presents little inconvenience. There are many inviting restaurants in this part of France, but the hotels are not as appealing; though Reims has an ample supply of beds, there are some charming small hotels in the country, and there generally is good value for money throughout the region. If you hope to stay in a small hotel or to visit during the harvest (usually beginning the second half of September and lasting 2 to 3 weeks), reservations are a good idea. For a double room (private bath and toilet are standard) without breakfast ($6 to $10 extra per person for the continental kind), expect to pay $125 or more at places we list as expensive, $75 to $125 for those in the moderate range, and below $75 for those listed as inexpensive. It's about the same for food. A full meal for two, excluding wine and drinks, will run about $125 or more in an expensive restaurant, $75 to $125 in a moderate one, and less than $75 in an inexpensive one. Service usually is included.

REIMS: This historic city straddles autoroute A4 (which runs between Paris and Lorraine and Germany) and is on the main train route connecting Paris and northern Europe. Hence, it is the logical starting point for a visit to Champagne. For a detailed report on the city, its sights, hotels, and restaurants, see *Reims,* in THE CITIES.

En Route from Reims – The Montagne de Reims, the first of the wine growing areas of Champagne, is a gentle, wooded rising between Reims and the valleys of the Vesle and the Ardre to the north and Epernay and the Valley of the Marne to the south. Route N51 cuts across it from north to south — between what is known as the *petite montagne* to the west and the *grande montagne* to the east — and connects the two cities somewhat as the crow flies, but the vineyards and wine villages, lying against the slopes, lead from one city to the other by a more circuitous route. To begin, take N380 from Reims toward Château-Thierry, then turn left onto D26 — the road to follow for the next 23 miles (37 km), as far as the village of Ambonnay.

On D26 you will first follow the flank of the "small" mountain whose vineyards are the most acidic in the region. Leave the road briefly to see the beautiful church with a square steeple and lovely interior in Ville-Dommange and, nearby, the small 12th-to-16th-century chapel of St-Lié, surrounded by a quiet cemetery marked with two World War I casemates (bombproof shelters with openings for the guns). Pause for the view of Reims and its cathedral, the Reims plain, and the Tardenois woods, then drive on to Sacy, which has a beautiful 12th-century church, and follow D26 through Ecueil, Chamery, and Sermiers (there's a nice statue-fountain dated 1900 near its church) until you come to Montchenot, which has a splendid view of the flatland and also of Reims.

CHECKING IN: Hostellerie du Château – Though slightly off the route, this Renaissance château set in a 14-acre park northwest of Reims is worth a detour — not only for its luxurious rooms, but also for its fish and other specialties served in its one-star (Michelin) dining room. Reservations necessary. Major credit cards accepted. Between the towns of Château-Thierry and Fismes in the village of Fère-en-Tardenois (phone: 23-82-21-13; fax: 23-82-37-81). Expensive.

EATING OUT: *Auberge du Grand Cerf* – With one Michelin star, this restaurant is one of the best in the area, with a chef who tends to avoid traditional dishes in favor of more inventive nouvelle ones. For a perfect marriage with champagne, try the warm oysters or the scallops in puff pastry. Any fish dish is recommended, as well as the beautiful salads made of whatever is freshest in the market, and a remarkable lobster risotto. The prix fixe menus give a good sampling. Closed Sunday evenings, Wednesdays, and 2 weeks in February and August. Reservations advised. Major credit cards accepted. On N51, Montchenot (phone: 26-97-60-07; fax: 26-97-64-24). Expensive to moderate.

En Route from Montchenot – After crossing N51, D26 begins to follow the flank of the "big" mountain. Villers-Allerand, which contains a church from the 13th and 14th centuries, is the first village down the road; then comes Rilly-la-Montagne, which counts a number of champagne producers among its 1,000 inhabitants. Fittingly, the town's church has sculptured stalls depicting *vignerons* (vine growers). Rilly is the starting point for walks on 900-foot-high Mt. Joli, one of the few places where the Montagne de Reims comes to a point and thus one that affords a wonderful panorama of the plain of Reims.

Next on D26 is Chigny-les-Roses, where there's an interesting Renaissance door to the sanctuary of the church, and Ludes, whose 15th-to-16th-century church has a statue of the Virgin and Child holding a bunch of grapes. Ludes also has the champagne cellars of Canard-Duchêne (phone: 26-61-10-96; fax: 26-61-13-90), which can be visited. These beautiful, long, and scrupulously clean chalk cellars with attractively arched galleries are open weekdays (10 AM to noon and 2 to 4 PM) year-round except August and holidays. Tours in English are available; call or fax 2 weeks ahead.

An area of first-rate vineyards begins at Mailly-Champagne, where you can visit the champagne cellar of the village's cooperative Société des Producteurs (phone: 26-49-41-10). It is open year-round for visits weekdays from 9 AM to noon and 2 to 5 PM, from 9 to 11 AM and 3 to 5:30 PM on Saturdays, and 3 to 5:30 PM on Sundays. There is a charge for the visit and tasting. The vineyards of Verzenay, less than 2 miles (3 km) away, produce exceptional wine, but the town also is well known for its old windmill, probably the only one left in Champagne, which was used as an observation tower during World War I. In nearby Verzy, follow the road on the right (D34) into the forest, leave the car in the parking lot, and walk to the observatory of Mt. Sinaï. From this very panoramic spot, the highest point in the Montagne de Reims (928 feet), General Gouraud watched the progress of the battle of Reims in 1918. For an interesting — and unusual — sight, take the forest road to the left of the modern chapel of St-Basles on D34 to reach the Faux de Verzy, a bizarre landscape of twisted beech trees with corkscrew-like branches, many over 500 years old.

Beyond Verzy is Villers-Marmery, where you can detour 3 miles (5 km) off D26 — crossing highways A4 and N44 and the village of Les Petites Loges — to Sept-Saulx, the site of a fine restaurant and hotel.

CHECKING IN/EATING OUT: *Cheval Blanc* – In the middle of a quiet village, this charming, vine-covered inn offers views of a park and of the Vesle River. There are 2 suites and 19 well-equipped rooms (all with color TV sets and decorated with antique furniture), as well as a tennis court. The large and comfortable dining room has an elegant country look and even a fireplace for broiling meat over an open flame. The atmosphere is friendly and cordial, the service attentive, and the food rates (and earns) stars (one from Michelin). Try the fish dishes or the lamb with fresh mint. The wine list is among the area's best. Closed from mid-January to mid-February. Reservations necessary. Demi-pension (breakfast and one other meal) required in high season (July and August). Major credit cards accepted. Rue du Moulin, Sept-Saulx (phone: 26-03-90-27; fax: 26-03-97-09). Expensive to moderate.

En Route from Sept-Saulx – Continuing on D26, you come to Trépail, where the small church has columns decorated with sculptured animals, before reaching villages that are known for their fruity red wines. One of these, Ambonnay, is picturesquely set amid the vines with a church that has an elegant Romanesque steeple and a pure, well-preserved interior. Another, Bouzy — reached by switching from D26 to D19 at Ambonnay — is famous for its non-sparkling bouzy *rouge* (as well as for the particularly suggestive sound of its name to speakers of English). Louvois, with a 12th-century church, lies just northwest of Bouzy. Here, where the vineyards end, you can look through 18th-century wrought-iron gates and be rewarded with the classic prospect of an impressive château standing in the midst of a vast park. Much of Château Louvois, which belonged to a chancellor of France and the father of one of Louis XIV's ministers, was destroyed during the French Revolution, so, except for its outbuildings, most of what you see dates from post-revolutionary days.

From Louvois to Epernay on D9, you drive through farmland and woods and the villages of Tauxières, Mutry, Fontaine-sur-Ay, and Avenay-Val-d'Or. This last is worth a stop to see the Flamboyant Gothic portal and rich interior of St-Trésain, a beautiful church built in the 12th and 16th centuries. Then you'll be among lovely vineyards again, but by now belonging to the Vallée de la Marne. Following D9, D1, and D201, you will shortly be in Ay, a small town that is the home of champagne houses, then Epernay, with even more champagne houses; its importance in the production of champagne belies its size. You can stop to visit Ay at this point, but since it is an appropriate starting place for a tour of the villages and vineyards of the Marne, stretching east and west of here, you may want to visit Epernay first, returning to Ay as you take to the road later.

EPERNAY: In the heart of the vineyards, strongly provincial in character, and dotted with parks and gardens, Epernay rivals Reims as the capital of the king of wines. It is small (pop. 29,000) compared to Reims, and it lacks the other city's architectural richness — lovers of "old stones" are reminded that often during its history, Epernay was in the path of invading armies sweeping along the Marne. The great champagne firms established here are its main attractions. Miles and miles of champagne cellars (*caves*), where millions of bottles of bubbly now are aging, have been hewn out of the chalky soil under Epernay, and the major champagne houses offer tours of their facilities. The Office du Tourisme (7 Av. de Champagne; phone: 26-55-33-00) distributes a brochure giving the firms' hours; several of the most famous houses are right on the Avenue de Champagne. Remember that the cellars have a constant temperature of 45F to 50F, so bring a jacket or warm sweater. Appropriate shoes also are recommended, in part because some cellars are damp and may be slippery, in part because the tours usually involve a bit of walking underground, occasionally in rather dark surroundings. All tours are free, and it is not unusual for them to end with a taste of the product, though this is unpredictable. Tours in English are offered by most firms, but if you are traveling in the off-season, it might be best to call ahead to make sure a guide is available.

Of the major houses open to the public in Epernay, Moët & Chandon (20 Av. de Champagne; phone: 26-54-71-11) is the largest and has the most extensive cellars — 17 miles of galleries. Although they are not the most beautiful cellars, Moët's explanation of the making of champagne is extremely good, hence it is one of the most popular tourist spots in all of France. The cellars are open weekdays (10 AM to 12:30 PM and 2 to 5:30 PM) year-round, and also on Saturdays (10 AM to noon and 2 to 5:30 PM) and Sundays (9:30 AM to noon and 2 to 4 PM) between April 1 and October 31. Nearby, Mercier (70 Av. de Champagne; phone: 26-54-75-26) conducts the tour of its 11 miles of cellars aboard an electric train. The cellars are open from 9:30 to 11:30 AM and from 2 to 5:30 PM from April to November (to 4:30 PM in March and November). Closed Sundays and December. Neither Moët & Chandon nor Mercier requires an appointment, but at Perrier-Jouët (26 Av. de Champagne; phone: 26-55-20-53), which has 6 miles of brick, chalk, and stone cellars, an appointment is requested. It is open from May 1 to September 15, weekdays from 9 AM to noon and 2 to 5 PM only. The 6 miles of cellars at De Castellane (57 Rue de Verdun; phone: 26-55-15-33) can be seen weekdays except holidays and August from 10 AM to noon and 2 to 6 PM; and the dark and spacious cellars of Pol Roger (1 Rue Henri-Lelarge; phone: 26-55-41-95) also are open weekdays, except August, by appointment only.

Other points of interest in Epernay include the colorful *Musée du Champagne et de Préhistoire* (13 Av. de Champagne; phone: 26-51-90-31; closed Tuesdays and November 30 to March 1). Set up in the 19th-century Château Perrier, it contains maps of the region, agricultural tools, winepresses, and a collection of labels and old bottles. (Open from 9 AM to noon and from 2 to 6 PM except on Sundays, when the hours are 10 AM to noon and 2 to 5 PM; closed Tuesdays and from December through February.) The Hôtel de Ville (Town Hall), at the Place de la République end of Avenue de Champagne, is an imposing building in the center of a 19th-century garden. The Renaissance stained glass windows in the Eglise St-Martin are worth a look, too. Finally, the governing body of the champagne industry, Comité Interprofessionnel du Vin de Champagne, is headquartered in Epernay (5 Rue Henri-Martin; phone: 26-54-47-20), the place for anyone with a serious interest in champagne to ask unanswered questions.

A pleasant way to view the surrounding countryside is to take a short cruise on the Marne River. Boats leave daily from Cumières, about 2 miles (3 km) north of Epernay. Cruise on *La Champagne* (phone: 26-54-49-51) or *Le Coche d'Eau,* which offer meals and music (phone: 26-74-05-85) from May to September. Afterward, stop in at the *Boulangerie Bressy* on the corner of Rue Jean-Pierrot and the Rue St-Thibault, which has delicious *biscuits de Reims* (to munch with champagne) and warm *chaussons aux pommes* (apple turnovers).

CHECKING IN: *Champagne –* This small hotel near the center of town has 35 modern, functional rooms, each with a color TV set and direct-dial phone. No restaurant, but there is a generous buffet-style breakfast. Parking is available. Major credit cards accepted. 30 Rue Eugène-Mercier, Epernay (phone: 26-55-30-22; fax: 26-51-94-63). Inexpensive.

EATING OUT: There is no temple of haute cuisine in Epernay, but a number of small, unpretentious restaurants offer good meals at reasonable prices.

Les Berceaux – This old establishment, built in 1889 on the town's former ramparts, has a restaurant with the atmosphere of a country dining room. Try the turbot in champagne sauce or veal with *chanterelles* (wild mushrooms). There are also 29 comfortable guestrooms. Closed Sunday evenings, also Mondays from November to March. Major credit cards accepted. 13 Rue des Berceaux, Epernay (phone: 26-55-28-84). Expensive to moderate.

La Terrasse – The menu is limited, but it represents good value. Closed Sunday evenings and Mondays. Major credit cards accepted. 7 Quai de la Marne, Epernay (phone: 26-55-26-05). Moderate to inexpensive.

Le Chapon Fin – It can't claim the most elegant dining room, but it's a nice place to try a few local dishes such as *andouillette* (small sausages made with chitterlings) *au champagne.* Closed Wednesdays and the last 2 weeks in August. Visa accepted. 2 Pl. Mendès-France, Epernay (phone: 26-55-40-03). Inexpensive.

Le Palmier – If you feel like eating a fine couscous, this is the place; try it with a local red wine. The restaurant is run by native Moroccans. Closed Mondays. Reservations advised. Major credit cards accepted. 2 Pl. Carnot, Epernay (phone: 26-54-54-71). Inexpensive.

En Route from Epernay – You can tour the vine-laden slopes and graceful landscapes of the winding Marne Valley by taking D201 directly into Ay, crossing the Marne and the canal that runs along it. Or, for a more comprehensive trip, take N3 east, crossing the Marne some miles down the road via D19 into Tours-sur-Marne, and return west toward Ay via D1. If you opt for the detour you will see several towns: Tours-sur-Marne, a town with an old priory and, near the tree-lined canal, the headquarters of Laurent-Perrier, whose ancient·cellars and collection of rare, large champagne bottles are open weekdays, except August, by appointment only (phone: 26-58-91-22); Bisseuil, famous for its red wines and with a church worth visiting for the beauty of its vaults and fine columns (ask for the key at the house next door); and Mareuil-sur-Ay, which offers a good view of the vineyards, a 12th-century church, and the headquarters of Philipponnat, whose cellars also can be visited weekdays, except August, by appointment (phone: 26-52-60-43).

AY: This quiet town of 5,000 stands on the banks of the canal across the Marne almost 2 miles (3 km) north of Epernay. Because the vineyards of the area are on slopes of undulating ground in a particularly felicitous position, its wine has been renowned for centuries and was supplied in earlier days to the Kings of France and England and to a Renaissance pope. Ay (pronounced Ah-*ee*) suffered serious damage during the war, but it still has some preserved 15th- and 16th-century churches and several half-timbered houses, including a wood paneled one on Rue St-Vincent that is described as once having been the press house of Henri IV. The champagne cellars of Bollinger (4 Bd. Maréchal de Lattre; phone: 26-55-21-31), Deutz (16 Rue Jeanson; phone: 26-55-15-11), and Ayala (2 Bd. du Nord; phone: 26-55-15-44) can be visited by appointment on weekdays only. There also is a museum containing a collection of tools relating to the cultivation of the vine.

En Route from Ay – As you head west on D1, celebrated vineyards are on your right; the left is dominated by a developing suburb of Epernay. In Dizy, turn right onto N51 (the main road to Reims) and drive up the rising road to Champillon. Here, amid hilly landscape, is a splendid, not-to-be-missed panorama of the Marne Valley vineyards. Nearby Hautvillers can be reached directly from D1 back at Dizy via N386 or through the tiniest of back roads from Champillon.

CHECKING IN/EATING OUT: *Royal Champagne* – Set high in the countryside, this outstanding small hotel (a Relais et Châteaux member) looks down on the vineyards, the Marne Valley, and Epernay. Its 24 rooms and 2 suites, set off from the main building — formerly an 18th-century coaching house — are furnished beautifully, and most of them have a terrace with a vineyard view. Apart from *Boyer "Les Crayères"* in Reims, the *Royal Champagne* is probably the region's best hotel, so book ahead, especially during the summer and around harvest time. Its celebrated one-star restaurant offers a mix of traditional and nouvelle dishes, particularly fish dishes that go splendidly with champagne as well as such specialties as veal *grenadin* and chicken fricassee. There is a nice selection of local cheeses and an extensive wine list from which a competent and friendly sommelier will help you select a champagne or local still wine not normally found outside France. Expect to see producers entertaining their guests in the comfortable and tastefully decorated dining room with a lovely view of the vine-covered hills. Closed for 3 weeks in January. Reservations advised. Major credit cards accepted. On N51, Champillon (phone: 26-52-87-11; fax: 26-52-89-69). Expensive.

HAUTVILLERS: This tiny hilltop village has old, half-timbered houses with arched doorways and interesting wrought-iron signs depicting the various tasks of the *vigneron* (vine grower), but it is the Abbaye de St-Pierre d'Hautvillers that always has been the focus for travelers. Of all the medieval abbeys in Champagne — and the abbeys of the Middle Ages were powerful, both as intellectual centers and as the owners of vast properties, including vineyards — none was better known than Hautvillers, which for nearly 12 centuries from the time of its founding in 660 was one of the most famous in France. The continuing fame of the abbey (though not much of it remains) is due to the Benedictine monk Pierre Pérignon, its cellar master from the late 1660s to the end of his life, in 1715. Dom Pérignon revolutionized local wine making by developing the technique of the second fermentation in the bottle that gives champagne its sparkle, by creating the *cuvée* (blend) that in part is champagne's guarantee of quality and consistency, and by making other innovations. Dom Pérignon is said to have exclaimed to his fellow monks, "Come quickly! I am drinking stars!" on the occasion of the world's first champagne tasting.

The abbey site, above the village, is now owned by Moët & Chandon, whose attractive *Musée Dom Pérignon,* filled with historical documents and artifacts relating to champagne making, is open only by appointment from March to November; closed weekends (phone: 26-54-71-11). Not to be missed is the spectacular view from the abbey's broad stone terrace — the same spot is sometimes used for celebrations and *fêtes* relating to champagne. Then visit the little church, with its fine woodcarvings and organ, where Dom Pérignon and his uncle and friend, Dom Thierry Ruinart, are buried.

En Route from Hautvillers – Return to D1 and turn right to reach Cumières, a village known for its delicate red wine. The picturesque road continues along the right bank of the Marne through Damery, which has a fine 12th-to-16th-century church, and then through Venteuil, Reuil, and Binson, which has an old priory with a restored 12th-century chapel. A little farther west and just off D1 is Châtillon-sur-Marne, with a large statue of Pope Urban II, the remains of a castle, and a good view of the Marne. Go through Verneuil and Vincelles — the limit of the Marne *département* — and cross the river to Dormans, a picturesque old town considerably damaged by the war but still endowed with a beautiful church dating from the 13th century and a 17th-century château. From the Chapelle de la Reconnaissance (Chapel of Gratitude), built in the middle of a large park to commemorate the battles of the Marne (1914 and 1918), there is a fine view over the valley.

Dormans is the turnaround point for the stretch of the Champagne route leading through the vineyards of the Marne Valley. You can return to Epernay along the southern side of the river by staying on N3 the whole way or, for a better view from a higher road, by going part of the way on D222 (reached by taking D226 uphill out of Port-à-Binson) and passing through Oeuilly, Boursault, and Vauciennes before dropping down again to N3.

The vineyards of the Côte des Blancs, where the aristocratic white chardonnay grapes grow, are traversed by D10 and D9 south of Epernay. The excursion — as far as Bergères-les-Vertus — is a peaceful and leisurely morning or afternoon drive begun by leaving Epernay on N51 and turning left onto D10 at Pierry.

CHECKING IN/EATING OUT: *La Briqueterie* – A quiet place surrounded by gardens and vineyards, this hotel is in one of the area's nicest spots. Since it is only about 4 miles (6 km) from Epernay (off N51 beyond Pierry), it can be a convenient base for touring. Its 42 rooms and public areas have undergone extensive renovation, and brought the comfort level in line with the French government's four-star rating. A swimming pool, sauna, workout room, conference facilities, and a restaurant were added. Pleasant and inviting, the one-star (Michelin) dining room is the sort of place where French families take their midday meal on Sundays. The continental breakfast is wonderful. During the summer, have a drink outside on the lovely terrace. Open daily. Major credit cards accepted. 4 Rte. de Sézanne, Vinay (phone: 26-59-99-99; fax: 26-59-92-10). Expensive.

En Route from Vinay – Heading south on D10, you come to the boundary of the black grape area at Cuis, where a 12th-century Romanesque church built on a terrace dominating the village affords a pretty view. The next town, Cramant, is one of the most renowned in the region for the quality of its grapes, which are white only. Cramant is a charming village, and if you detour up through its vineyards you'll see the elegant and finely maintained Château Saran set imposingly on the hillside. South of Cramant, Avize, in the heart of the Côte des Blancs, has an interesting church, mostly 12th-century Romanesque but with a 15th-century Gothic transept and choir. Next comes Oger, also with an early church, and then Le Mesnil-sur-Oger, another village producing famous *blanc de blancs* with another interesting church. Note particularly the 17th-century paneling inside and the Renaissance door. Pierre Moncuit, a local producer whose champagnes (especially his 1989 vintage) have won many awards, gives tours of his cellars by appointment. Open all year. 11 Rue Persault Maheu, Le-Mesnil-sur-Oger (phone: 26-57-52-65; fax: 26-57-97-89).

Vertus lies on D9 after it merges with D10. This quiet little town with irregular streets and charming squares was once a fortified city. A medieval gate remains as does the church of St. Martin, a remarkable example of the transition from Romanesque to Gothic style. Walk around the church to see "the wells of St. Martin," where springs form a mirrorlike pond. Nearby is Champagne Guy Larmandier (30 Rue Général Koënig; phone: 26-52-12-41), a small champage operation offering a friendly welcome in a flower-covered house; the bubbly is excellent and reasonably priced.

CHECKING IN/EATING OUT: *Hostellerie de la Reine Blanche* – Looking something like a streamlined Alpine ski lodge, this 23-room hotel is well equipped and comfortable and includes a restaurant. Closed 2 weeks in February. Major credit cards accepted. 18 Av. Louis-Lenoir, Vertus (phone: 26-52-20-76; fax: 26-52-16-59). Hotel, moderate; restaurant, moderate to inexpensive.

La Commédia – This restaurant (guestrooms are no longer available) provides a chance to meet the people and try the local food — veal kidney and fish with champagne sauce are good choices. Three very inexpensive prix fixe menus are offered. Major credit cards accepted. 4 Rue de Châlons, Vertus (phone: 26-52-12-20). Inexpensive.

En Route from Vertus – Between Vertus and Bergères-les-Vertus, the Côte des Blancs ends and black grapes are seen again. Beyond Bergères, Mont-Aimé, the site of prehistoric, Roman, and feudal remains, offers a splendid view back over the Côte des Blancs vineyards and forward toward Châlons-sur-Marne, 18 miles (29 km) northeast on N33.

CHECKING IN/EATING OUT: *Mont-Aimé* – All 11 rooms overlook a charming garden, and are simply yet tastefully furnished. This establishment's restaurant has a highly touted reputation with the locals, who come to feast on the excellent duck breast with bouzy sauce. 4-6 Rue Vertus, Bergères-les-Vertus. Open all year. Major credit cards accepted (phone: 26-52-21-31; fax: 26-52-21-39). Expensive to moderate.

CHÂLONS-SUR-MARNE: Built on both sides of the Marne, this ancient crossroads town of 54,300 is an administrative center for the Marne *département.* Attila the Hun was defeated on the plain of Châlons in AD 451, and the town has played a significant role in military history ever since, especially under Napoleon III and during the two world wars. It is still the home of an important military school. Châlons has, in part, a bourgeois look, with 17th- and 18th-century townhouses, tree-lined riverbanks, and 16th-century bridges (Pont de l'Arche-Mauvillan, Pont des Viviers, Pont des Mariniers) crossing canals formed by Marne tributaries. A tourist office is at 3 Quai des Arts (phone: 26-65-17-89).

Two of Châlons's many churches stand out. The Cathédrale St-Etienne is known for the pure Gothic style of its northern façade and for its beautiful stained glass windows, which span the 12th to the 16th century — a veritable survey of the development of the art. Its 17th-century western portal is massive and impressive, and there also is superb artwork in various other sections — in chapels, the northern transept, and in the treasury. The Eglise Notre-Dame en Vaux shows characteristics of the Romanesque-Gothic transition period and is a masterpiece of 12th-century *champenoise* architecture. The interior is harmoniously proportioned and illuminated by beautiful 16th-century stained glass windows, and its carillon of 56 bells chimes out ancient melodies. Just north is the *Musée du Cloître* (Rue Nicolas-Durand; phone: 26-64-03-87) which contains some 50 recently excavated carved columns, marvels of 12th-century art. (Open daily except Tuesdays from 10 AM to noon and from 2 to 6 PM.)

Two other medieval churches in Châlons — St-Jean and St-Alpin — also are noteworthy, particularly for their stained glass windows. The 18th-century Préfecture (County Hall) is of architectural interest, and the *Musée Municipal,* containing artifacts from the Stone Age to the Gallo-Roman era, is of archaeological interest (Rue Carnot; phone: 26-64-38-42; open from 2 to 6 PM daily except Tuesdays and holidays). The Bibliothèque Municipale (Town Library), in an 18th-century residence (Passage Vendel; phone: 26-68-54-44), has a rich collection of antiquarian books and illuminated manuscripts, including *The Confessions of St. Augustine,* the *Romance of the Rose,* and the *Book of Hours.* (Open from 9 AM to noon and 2 to 6 PM except Sundays, Mondays, and holidays.)

Before driving the 48 miles (77 km) via N77 directly to Troyes, a short detour on N3 to L'Epine, 6 miles (10 km) east, is well worth the time.

CHECKING IN/EATING OUT: *Angleterre* – In the center of town, this charming hotel has 19 recently renovated rooms and a garden where you may lunch or dine. Named after its chef, *Jacky Michel,* the restaurant offers three attractive prix fixe menus, a wine list that changes monthly, and good values — especially on champagne. It is considered by many to be the best in town; Michelin has awarded it one star. Closed Saturdays at lunch, Sundays, and with the hotel from late December to early January and the second half of July. Reservations advised. Major credit cards accepted. 19 Pl. Monseigneur-Tissier, Châlons-sur-Marne (phone: 26-68-21-51). Moderate.

L'EPINE: This village is famous for the Basilique Notre-Dame-de-l'Epine, built in the 15th and early 16th centuries and one of the special sights of the region. As you drive toward L'Epine, the large church suddenly rises majestically in the midst of the flatlands of Champagne and calls to mind the Cathedral of Reims, though on a reduced scale. The Flamboyant Gothic façade, graced with three sculptured doorways depicting Christ's birth, passion, and resurrection, is its glory, but note also the realistic, sometimes racy, gargoyles found all around the exterior (they symbolize the vices and evil spirits chased from the sanctuary by divine power). From the beginning and continuing to this day, each May pilgrims make their way to Notre-Dame-de-l'Epine to venerate its statue of the Virgin. A laser, light, and music show is offered here on Friday and Saturday nights at 10:30 PM from mid-June to mid-September. For information, contact City Hall (phone: 26-66-96-99).

CHECKING IN/EATING OUT: *Aux Armes de Champagne* – You can see the basilica from the neo-rustic dining room of this charming, recently renovated, 40-room hotel. The rooms are lovely, as is the garden, which has a miniature golf course. The cuisine, which already has earned one Michelin star and is getting better every year, includes both nouvelle dishes and regional specialties such as pigeon with bouzy wine, *sandre* (pickerel) from the Marne prepared in various ways, and snails with champagne. The sommelier won France's "best young sommelier of the year" award in 1991, and the *cave* is worthy of his talent. The cheese tray is a must if you want to try the local products; sample the native red wine, too. If you are stopping for lunch only, the prix fixe menus are a good idea. Closed mid-January to mid-February. Major credit cards accepted. Pl. de la Basilique, L'Epine (phone: 26-66-96-79; fax: 26-66-92-31). Moderate.

TROYES: The southern part of Champagne is all too often ignored by visitors, especially Troyes, the region's former capital. This was not so in the Middle Ages, when the city was a center of international commerce and one of the sites of the annual champagne trade fairs (troy weight, one of the standards of measurement set by the fairs, persists today). Troyes was an equally famous center of the arts in medieval times and remained so even after its commercial importance had begun to decline. As the Renaissance replaced the Gothic age, the influence of a uniquely Troyen school of architecture spread over the entire region and into Burgundy, Troyen sculptors approached their finest hour, and Troyen stained glass craftsmen were well on their way to filling the city's churches with kaleidoscopic light. Today, Troyes remains at once one of the great art towns of France, with a delightful old section of narrow streets and half-timbered houses, and a modern, bustling, prosperous town of 64,800 inhabitants, many employed in the manufacture of textiles — as their ancestors were since the 16th century. There's an Office du Tourisme near the station (16 Bd. Carnot; phone: 25-73-00-36) and another one near the cathedral (24 Quai Dampierre; phone: 25-72-34-30) that is open only from early June to mid-September.

Troyes's churches were the main beneficiaries of its artists' outpouring of sculpture and stained glass, and the Cathédrale St-Pierre-et-St-Paul is endowed with a wealth of it. Built from the 13th to the 17th century, the church has a richly decorated 16th-century Flamboyant Gothic façade with a rose window above the central portal (carvings and statues missing from the tympana of the doors were destroyed during the French Revolution). Walk around to the doorway of the north transept — the 13th-century "Beau Portail" — for another rose window and four rosettes. Inside, the stained glass is stunning, from the earlier, 13th-century windows of the choir to the mainly 16th-century windows of the nave, including the Tree of Jesse window. The treasury of the church has a collection of beautiful 16th-century enamels, and the church tower provides a fine view of the town. Friday and Saturday evenings from early June through September, a spectacular *Cathédral de Lumière* show featuring laser images and sound is performed here, as in the cathedrals of nearby Reims and L'Epine. At press time, it was still uncertain whether the show would continue. For information, call City Hall (phone: 25-42-33-33).

The Basilique St-Urbain, built in the 13th century by Pope Urban IV on the spot where his father had a cobbler's shop, also is known for its splendid stained glass windows — which here occupy so much wall space, you'll wonder how the edifice stays upright. It also is known for its many noteworthy statues, especially the "Vierge au raisin," a beautiful example of local 16th-century sculpture. A third church, Eglise Ste-Madeleine, dates from the 12th century. Though it is Troyes's oldest church, the marvelous stained glass in its choir is from the 16th century, as are its sculptured masterpieces: the intricately Flamboyant rood screen and the statue of St. Martha.

You'll see the picturesque old section of town, full of restored 16th-century houses, if you wander around in the vicinity of the Eglise St-Jean. Do walk along Rue Champeaux, and don't miss Rue des Chats, where the cantilevered gables of the houses almost touch each other across the narrow street. Troyes also has several interesting small museums. The *Musée des Beaux-Arts et d'Histoire Naturelle* (1 Rue Chrétien de Troyes), in the 18th-century Abbaye St-Loup, has a varied collection of art and artifacts including a nice collection of 15th-to-16th-century paintings. (Open from 10 AM to noon and 2 to 6 PM daily except Tuesdays.) The *Musée Historique de Troyes et de Champagne,* with good sculptures, drawings, and paintings from the region, and the *Musée de la Bonneterie,* which traces the history of the region's textile industry, are both in the Hôtel de Vauluisant (4 Rue de Vauluisant; phone: 25-42-33-33 for both museums), a 16th-century building with an interesting façade. (Its hours are the same as those of the *Musée des Beaux-Arts,* with which there is a reciprocal entry arrangement.) There also is the *Maison de l'Outil et de la Pensée Ouvrière* (7 Rue de la Trinité; phone: 25-73-28-26), which has tools and craftsmen's implements. (Open daily except Tuesdays from 9 AM to noon and 2 to 7 PM, closing an hour earlier in winter.) The *Musée de Pharmacie* (Hôtel Dieu le Comte, Quai des Comtes de Champagne) is a beautiful old pharmacy that remains as it was at the beginning of the 18th century. It includes collections of tools, faïence, and other objects used in the original pharmacy. For information about this and other museums in Troyes, call 25-80-49-84. But to many, the city's most interesting museum is the *Musée d'Art Moderne* (Pl. St-Pierre; phone: 25-80-57-30). Located to the right of the cathedral in the former episcopal palace, this collection featuring some 1,500 works by Braque, Bonnard, Cézanne, Gauguin, Matisse, Picasso, and other artists is one of Europe's most important gatherings of contemporary art. (Open from 11 AM to 6 PM, except Tuesdays and holidays.)

CHECKING IN: *Grand Hôtel* – This traditional establishment near the train station has 100 pleasant rooms, the majority with color TV sets. Two restaurants — the moderately priced *Le Champagne* and inexpensive *Le Croco* — make it convenient for meals, too. Major credit cards accepted. 4 Av. Maréchal-Joffre, Troyes (phone: 25-79-90-90; fax: 25-78-48-93). Moderate to inexpensive.

***La Poste* –** Its 34 rooms, also with television sets, are within striking distance of the old quarter of St-Jean, Basilique St-Urbain, and other sights. The elegant restaurant, *La Table Gourmande,* is in the moderate range with some agreeable prix fixe menus and a wine list offering many great *crus* at reasonable rates. Major credit cards accepted. 35 Rue Emile-Zola, Troyes (phone: 25-73-05-05; fax: 25-73-80-76). Moderate to inexpensive.

EATING OUT: *Valentino* – The city's finest place to eat, and its prettiest, is in the old part of town. The emphasis is on fish, and although all the dishes are commendable, the sea bass preparations are remarkable. And don't skip dessert. Closed Sunday evenings, Mondays, mid-August to September 6, and early February. Major credit cards accepted. 11 Cour de la Rencontre, Troyes (phone: 25-73-14-14). Expensive.

***La Chanoine Gourmand* –** A tiny dollhouse of an eatery located just behind the cathedral where the bright young chef-owner Heriot Christian turns out inventive and delicate dishes such as langoustine with hot lime vinaigrette and *coq rouge* (a rare fish) in red wine sauce. In summer, a pleasant garden behind the restaurant expands the seating capacity. Closed Sunday evenings and Mondays, 1 week in mid-March, 1 week in mid-August, and *Christmas* to early January. Major credit cards accepted. 32 Rue de la Cité, Troyes (phone: 25-80-42-06). Expensive to moderate.

***Le Bourgogne* –** This is a safe address in Troyes, meaning that the dishes are well prepared but not very innovative, and that the wine list is nice but limited. (A further disappointment is that the restaurant recently lost its one Michelin star.)

The service, however, is impeccable. Closed Sundays, Monday evenings, and August. Reservations advised. Major credit cards accepted. 40 Rue Général-de-Gaulle, Troyes (phone: 25-73-02-67). Moderate.

En Route from Troyes – Because the fourth vine growing area of Champagne — the region of the Aube — actually is less esteemed in the making of champagne than the three areas described above, many visitors take N71 southeast directly into Burgundy. Our route, however, traces a final loop eastward to encompass the Aube vineyards and picks N71 farther along, at Bar-sur-Seine.

Leaving Troyes on N19, you'll soon come (13 miles/21 km) to the Lac et Forêt d'Orient, part of a large regional park and recreation area that includes reserves for birds and animals as well as water sports facilities for Troyens on weekend outings. Mesnil-St-Père, on the south side of the lake just off N19, and Géraudot, on the north side on D1, are tiny villages with sand beaches. From Géraudot, it is 15 miles (24 km; via D1 and D11) northeast to Brienne-le-Château, the birthplace of Jean de Brienne, who made a name for himself in the Crusades; but it is better known through Napoleon Bonaparte, who went to the military academy here from 1779 to 1784. A small museum, *Musée Napoléon Premier* (phone: 25-92-82-41), contains souvenirs of the young Napoleon as well as mementos of his nearby battles during the campaign of 1814. (Open from 9 AM to noon and 2 to 5:30 PM, except Tuesdays and holidays, and December 1 to March 1.)

Another 15 miles (24 km), this time to the southeast (via D396 and N19), and you'll be in Bar-sur-Aube, in the center of one section of the Aube vineyards. On the right bank of the river, this little town of 7,000 people already was famous in the Middle Ages, at the time of the great fairs of Champagne, and it is now bordered by boulevards instead of ramparts. See the churches of St-Pierre and St-Maclou, the former built in the 12th, 14th, and 16th centuries and surrounded by picturesque wooden galleries, the latter built in the 13th and 15th centuries.

CHECKING IN/EATING OUT: *Relais des Gouverneurs* – Halfway between the town's two historic churches is this establishment with 15 recently renovated guestrooms and a good restaurant. Try the foie gras with sauterne, the salad of sea scallops with truffle juice, or the smoked salmon crêpes — and with them drink one of the local still wines. Closed during January. Major credit cards accepted. 38 Rue Nationale, Bar-sur-Aube (phone: 25-27-08-76; fax: 25-27-20-80). Expensive to moderate.

Hostellerie de Pont-Ste-Marie – In spite of the grand-sounding name, this is a simple place (which nevertheless makes some nouvelle efforts) that the locals call "Chez Jules." If you feel in the mood for *salade tiède de cuisses de grenouilles* (warm frogs' legs salad), *pied de cochon* (pig's feet), and chocolate mousse, all served in a friendly atmosphere, this is the place. Closed Sunday evenings, Mondays, and mid-January to mid-February. Major credit cards accepted. In Pont-Sainte-Marie, around 1½ miles (3km) northeast of Troyes by the N77 (phone: 25-81-13-09; fax: 25-73-80-76). Moderate to inexpensive.

En Route from Bar-sur-Aube – A detour 9 miles (14 km) east via N19 will take you to the quiet village of Colombey-les-Deux-Eglises. Charles de Gaulle is buried here, and part of his private residence, La Boisserie, which he maintained from 1933 to his death in 1970, is open to visitors. From Bar, you also can take a brief excursion south to Bayel, well known for its Cristalleries de Champagne glassworks (you'll see lots of crystal for sale) and of interest for several beautiful sculptures in the village church, including a 14th-century Virgin and Child and a 16th-century Pietà attributed to the same hand as the St. Martha in the Eglise Ste-Madeleine in Troyes.

From Bar-sur-Aube, head southwest, winding 23 miles (37 km) on D4 across the region to pick up N71 at Bar-sur-Seine, the central town of the remaining section of the Aube vineyards and the end of the champagne route. Besides some interesting 15th- and 16th-century houses, Bar-sur-Seine has the Eglise St-Etienne, whose stained glass windows and paintings representing the life of the Virgin are noteworthy. There also are a number of interesting, typical villages to the south of Bar-sur-Aube. Chaource, well known for its cheese, has some old houses on wooden stilts and a 16th-century Entombment, possibly from the *atelier* (studio) of the St. Martha master, in its church. Les Riceys, a holiday resort, turns out a tasty rosé wine and has several 16th-century churches. Essoyes is associated with Renoir, who used to live here, and Mussy-sur-Seine, finally, is a nice town with numerous historical buildings. At Mussy, you are back on N71, a main route into the heart of Burgundy.

Corsica

Corsica, France's largest island and the third-largest in the Mediterranean, lies southeast of the Côte d'Azur some 100 miles from Nice, a 6-hour boat trip or 35 minutes by air. But there the promixity ends; in just about every other way, Corsica and the Côte d'Azur are worlds apart. While the chic, opulent Côte is where the beautiful people go to see and be seen, Corsica, with its wild, rugged terrain and vast, uninhabited stretches, is where people come to get away from it all. And on Corsica, wealth and good looks are not a prerequisite for fitting in; the only beauty that's seriously worshiped here is that of the landscape.

Corsica has been described as a mountain growing out of the sea. Except for the eastern coast, with its 190-mile stretch of white and gold sand beaches, the island is covered with mountains, from its coastal hills to the towering peaks of the central range (Monte Cinto is the highest, at 8,900 feet). Much of the mountainous center and northwest is deeply forested, though there are treeless, barren stretches as well, including the Agriates Desert in the north. Some of the most dramatic scenery anywhere can be found on the rocky western coast between Calvi and Ajaccio, with deep wooded gorges, sparkling gulf waters, and jagged mountain precipices diving straight into the sea. Equally beautiful, though not quite so dramatic, are the mountains and seascapes of Cap Corse, a 30-mile peninsula projecting fingerlike from St-Florent and Bastia in the northwest.

The sun shines year-round in Corsica and in the summer can be unrelentingly hot. Spring is the gentler season, when the island becomes green and vivid with flowers: mostly wild roses and, everywhere, acres of *maquis* — the wild, white heather that covers the island with a thick underbrush.

Abundant in natural beauty, Corsica in many other ways is quite barren. There is very little culture or nightlife, and the island's 300 Romanesque churches from the 11th and 12th centuries constitute the only architecture of any significance. Even the population has dwindled over the years — it's just under 300,000 today — making this 3,369-square-mile island the least densely populated in the Mediterranean. Part of the reason for this widespread emigration is the mechanization of farming on an island where tobacco growing supports roughly one-fourth of the economy. Another factor was the arrival of the French from Algeria after it gained its independence in 1962. Many of the Corsicans, claiming that the outsiders obtained land unjustly, fled the island in anger.

But this is a minor incident in Corsica's long, embattled history. Over the centuries it has absorbed countless invasions; nearly every major city was once a fortress. Occupied by Greece in 560 BC, Corsica later became a colony of Rome, then Pisa. The Genoese came in the 13th century and held the island until 1768 (a year before Napoleon's birth here), when it was sold to France.

And except for a brief British takeover — quashed by Napoleon and his troops in 1796 — it has been under French rule ever since.

The centuries of political occupation as well as the hard and isolated life imposed by the terrain have had a powerful influence on the character of Corsica's inhabitants. Generally speaking, they are an insular and fiercely independent people, despite the numerous outside attempts to crush that independence. During the past few decades, the issue of separatism has reared its head, with Corsica demanding — sometimes violently — cultural recognition and greater autonomy. After a series of attacks by separatists in early 1991, the French government promised to give the island more self-determination. For years the French government tried to suppress the Corsican language (a form of Italian) by banning it in the schools; however, it always was spoken in the home, and though most residents do speak French, Corsican remains the preferred tongue.

Many Corsicans, particularly those who live in the isolated valleys of the central region, still practice what's known as "a politics of the clan," with loyalties to leaders that often go back centuries. The island's past, perhaps even its present, is filled with feuds between families and regions. It's no accident that the word "vendetta" is Corsica's sole contribution to the English language.

 TOURIST INFORMATION: Although prices generally are higher between June and September, tourist services on the island also are more plentiful then, so plan your trip accordingly. Here is a list of major tourist offices in Corsica:

Ajaccio: 17 Bd. Roi Jérôme (phone: 95-21-56-56); Hôtel de Ville, 1 Pl. Foch, by the harbor (phone: 95-21-40-87 or 95-21-53-39)
Bastia: 3 Pl. St-Nicolas (phone: 95-31-00-89)
Bonifacio: Rue Longue (phone: 95-73-11-88)
Calvi: Port de Plaisance (phone: 95-65-16-67 or 95-65-05-87)
Corte: *Hôtel de la Paix* (phone: 95-46-24-20)
Ile-Rousse: Rue J.-Galizi (phone: 95-60-04-35)
Porto: 9 Rte. de la Marine (phone: 95-26-10-55)
Porto Vecchio: 2 Rue Maréchal-Juin (phone: 95-70-09-58)
Propriano: 17 Rue du Général-de-Gaulle (phone: 95-76-01-49)
Sartène: Cours Saranelli (phone: 95-77-15-40)

Numerous free guides are available in English from the local tourist offices. An excellent one is *Guide to Corsica,* an illustrated index of hotels, restaurants, camping sites, and bungalows and apartments to rent. Supplement this with the Guide to Hotels, published by the Corsican Tourist Office, which lists hotels by region, including prices and amenities. For information before visiting, write the C.R.T. de Corse (17 Bd. Roi-Jérôme, 20000 Ajaccio; phone: 95-51-00-22 or 95-21-56-56; fax: 95-51-14-14). The best map of Corsica is the Michelin yellow map No. 90, available at any newsstand.

 TELEPHONE: The area code for Corsica is 95, which is incorporated into all local 8-digit numbers. When calling a number in Corsica from the Paris region (including Ile-de-France), dial 16, then the 8-digit number. When calling a number from outside Paris, dial only the 8-digit number. When calling from the US, dial 33 (which is the country code), followed by the 8-digit number.

 FOOD AND WINE: While Corsican cuisine can't compete with the gastronomic wonders of a city like Paris, there are still some delicious specialties. The good charcuterie here includes *prisuttu,* smoked raw ham, and *figatellus,*

smoked liver sausage. *Brocciu* is a soft cheese used in all sorts of dishes; often it's served with *fiandonu,* pastries made of chestnut flour. Main dishes include *aziminu,* Corsica's version of the Provençal fish stew bouillabaisse, and lamb kebabs in which the meat is skewered on myrtle twigs and barbecued over an aromatic wood fire. The island offers a wide variety of game in season and fresh fish year-round.

Corsican wines are greatly underestimated by the French. The best come from the vineyards of Patrimonio and Sartenais — robust reds and dry, aromatic whites and rosés.

GETTING AROUND: *Air France* offers daily flights to Ajaccio and Bastia from Paris, Nice, and Marseilles, and there are weekly flights from Amsterdam and Brussels. *Air France*'s domestic carrier, *Air Inter,* also flies from Paris, Nice, and Marseilles to Ajaccio, Bastia, and Calvi. From May through October, *Air Alpes* flies from Nice and Hyères to Ajaccio, Bastia, Propriano, and Figari, near Bonifacio. *TAT* also has regular flights to Figari, Ajaccio, Calvi, and Bastia.

Once you're here, a car is by far the most practical way to explore the island. But be extra careful; though roads generally are well paved, they're also tortuous. Allow plenty of time to reach your destination — 100 miles (160 km) through the mountains is a hard day's drive. Since some villages have neither garage nor gas station, it's not a bad idea to carry a spare steel container (safer than plastic) of gas in the trunk.

Bus – There is regular and inexpensive bus service to most villages, generally once a day. Numerous bus tours of the island, ranging from a half day to 7 days, are organized by the *Service d'Autocars de la SNCF* (phone: 95-21-14-08) and by local firms in Ajaccio, Bastia, Ile-Rousse, and Calvi. Contact the Gare Routière (phone: 95-21-28-01) or the local tourist office for details.

Car Rental – Ajaccio: *Avis* (4 Av. de Paris; phone: 95-21-01-86; and at the airport; phone: 95-23-25-14); *Europcar* (16 Cours Grandval; phone: 95-21-05-49; and at the airport; phone: 95-23-18-73); *Hertz* (8 Cours Grandval; phone: 95-21-70-94; and at the airport; phone: 95-23-24-17); and *Inter-Rent* (5 Montée St-Jean; phone: 95-22-61-79; and at the airport; phone: 95-23-19-42). Bastia: *Avis* (9 Av. M. Sebastiani; phone: 95-31-11-71; and at the airport; phone: 95-36-03-56); *Europcar* (1 Rue du Nouveau Port; phone: 95-31-59-29; and at the airport; phone: 95-36-03-55); *Hertz* (Sq. St-Victor; phone: 95-31-14-24; and at the airport; phone: 95-36-02-46); and *Inter-Rent* (2 Rue Notre Dame de Lourdes; phone: 95-31-03-11). Calvi: *Avis* (6 Av. de la République; phone: 95-65-06-74); *Europcar* (Av. de la République; phone: 95-65-10-35; and at the airport; phone: 95-65-10-19); *Hertz* (2 Rue Mal-Joffre; phone: 95-65-06-64; and at the airport; phone: 95-65-02-96); and *Inter-Rent* (Pl. Christophe-Colombe; phone: 95-65-02-13).

Ferry – *SNCM* (*Société Nationale Corse Maritime*) serves the following ports: *Ajaccio:* Quai l'Herminier (phone: 95-21-90-70); *Bastia:* Nouveau Port, BP 40 (phone: 95-313663); *Calvi:* Quai Landry (phone: 95-65-01-38); *Ile-Rousse:* Av. J.-Calizi (phone: 95-60-09-56); *Propriano:* Quai Commandant-l'Herminier (phone: 95-76-04-36). You also can make a ferry connection from Marseilles (61 Bd. des Dames; phone: 91-56-62-05), Nice (3 Av. Gustave-V; and Gare Maritime, Quai du Commerce; phone: 93-89-89-89 or 93-13-66-66), and Toulon (21 and 49 Av. de l'Infantène-de-Marine; phone: 94-41-25-76 and 94-41-01-76). The crossing takes from 5 to 12 hours, depending on the route you choose.

Tours – In addition to bus tours of the island organized by the *Service d'Autocars de la SNCF* (phone: 95-21-14-08), the following agencies offer tours: *SAIB Bus Tours* (2 Rue Maréchal Ornano, Ajaccio; phone: 95-21-53-74); *Autocars Bastiais* (40 Bd. Paoli, Bastia; phone: 95-31-01-79); *Autocars Balesi* (Rte. de Bastia, Porto-Vecchio; phone: 95-70-15-55); and *Corse Voyage Autocars Mariani* (Quai Landry, Calvi; phone: 95-46-00-35). Daily boat excursions run from Ajaccio, Bonifacio, Calvi, Ile-Rousse, Porto, and Propriano, ranging from 1-hour to day trips. One of the most popular is a 3-hour cruise from Ajaccio to the Iles-Sanguinaires (literally "the bloody islands," so named because at sunset they're suffused with the blood red glow of the sun). The cruise leaves from Ajaccio Harbor (phone: 95-21-41-31 or 95-21-06-95).

Train – A scenic railway links Ajaccio, Corte, Bastia, Ile-Rousse, and Calvi, a distance of 145 miles (233 km). And a special tramway-train service runs 30 shuttles a day between the ports of Calvi and Ile-Rousse — a good way to visit the many beaches along this part of the coast. Ajaccio station (Pl. de la Gare; phone: 95-23-11-03); Bastia station (Av. Mal-Sebastiani; phone: 95-32-60-06); Calvi station (Av. de la Gare; phone: 95-65-00-61); Corte station (Pl. de la Gare; phone: 95-46-00-97). For general train information on Corsica, call 95-23-11-03.

 SPECIAL EVENTS: One of the best-known religious ceremonies on Corsica is the *Catenacciu* procession, held on *Good Friday*. Penitents dressed in red hoods and shackled with heavy chains bear a large wooden cross through the cobbled streets of Sartène. A more festive occasion, blending religion and folklore, is the *Santa di u Niulu,* held on September 8 in Casamaccioli to celebrate the birth of the Virgin. After a procession, in which a painted, wooden statue of the Virgin is carried through the street, the celebrants — largely mountain folk and shepherds — recite poetry and improvise songs.

Perhaps the biggest cultural event on the island is the *Milleli,* a festival of music, theater, and poetry held during July and August in Ajaccio. For more information, contact the local tourist office.

 SPORTS: Boating – Sailors insist that the best way to see Corsica is from the sea. Certainly, some of the most beautiful parts of the coast as well as certain beaches are accessible only by boat. The following are some of the places where you can rent vessels ranging from sailboats to windsurfers: *Balagne Sport,* Ile-Rousse (phone: 95-60-05-17); *Cap Corse Voile,* Macinaggio, on the northeast of Cap Corse (phone: 95-35-41-47); *Europe Yachting,* Ajaccio (phone: 95-21-00-57), Porto-Vecchio (phone: 95-70-18-69); *Scim Corse,* Bonifacio (phone: 95-73-03-13).

To find out about the island's many sailing schools and clubs, contact *Ligue Corse de Voile* (Corsican Sailing League), Villa Suspirata, Bastelicaccia CP, Ajaccio 20000 (phone: 95-21-90-33).

Fishing – The waters of Corsica teem with some 200 species of fish. Trout can be caught in the fast-running mountain streams. Some rivers and parts of the coast are restricted, however. For more fishing information, contact *Fédération Départementale de Pêche et de Pisciculture* (7 Bd. Paoli, Bastia; phone: 95-31-47-31). If you find yourself in a port town and speak some French, you probably can find a fisherman who will be a guide by inquiring in the port cafés.

Hiking, Climbing, and Skiing – Corsica is a hiker's dream. The Regional National Park (phone: 95-21-56-54) is a fine place to start, and is accessible to pedestrians via GR20. In the park and its environs, you can explore the Col de Vergio (Vergio Pass), Gorges de Resontica (Resontica Gorges), Forêt de Bavella (Bavella Forest), and Scala di Santa Regina (St. Regina's "Staircase"). On the west coast, good hiking can be found around the gulfs of Girolata and Valinco and along the stunning Calanques of Piana, natural rock formations that resemble immense Henry Moore sculptures.

If you're serious about mountaineering or cross-country skiing, the island has 50 peaks above 6,500 feet, snow-covered from November through May. For information, contact the *Comité Corse de Ski* (1 Bd. Auguste Gandin, Bastia 20200). Local clubs for climbing and cross-country skiing include the ones in Ajaccio (phone: 95-22-09-86) and Bastia (phone: 95-31-17-32). The main resorts for downhill skiing are at Asco (phone: 95-31-02-04), Ghisoni (phone: 95-57-61-28, 95-56-02-72, or 95-56-12-12), and Col de Vergio (phone: 95-48-00-01). For cross-country skiing, the main resorts are at Val d'Ese (phone: 95-28-71-73) and the region of Coscione (Quenza, phone: 95-78-60-97 or 95-78-62-85; Zicavo, phone: 95-24-40-05 or 95-24-42-13).

Scuba Diving – The average sea temperature ranges from 55F in March to 74F in August, and the clear water abounds with grouper, multicolored rockfish, and red coral. Two diving schools on the island are the *Harpoon Club* at Ajaccio (phone: 95-22-23-78, 95-22-04-83, or 95-21-64-80) and the *Neptune Club* at Bastia (phone: 95-31-69-02). There also are a number of diving clubs in most of the main port cities. For more information contact *Centre d'Etudes Sous-Marines* (28 Rue du Four, Paris 75006; phone: 42-22-52-66), *La Fédération Française d'Etude et des Sports Sous-Marins* (50 Ter. Av. Général-Graziani, Bastia; phone: 95-31-03-32), or the *Comité Corse de Plonger* (phone: 95-20-26-79).

Swimming – The island has countless beaches and the choice is yours. The east coast offers long stretches of golden sand. On the west there's more variety: large bays and small creeks; beaches that are half rock, half sand; and some spots where you can be alone even at the height of the season.

AJACCIO-BONIFACIO-CALVI

The route outlined below begins on the western coast in Ajaccio, then dips south through coastal resorts and mountains to Bonifacio, at the island's southern tip. From there it runs along the eastern coast, with its miles and miles of beaches, then travels inland to the ancient capital, Corte. After a swing west to the port of Calvi, the route ends back in Ajaccio — a distance of some 340 miles (547 km). Allow yourself at least 3 or 4 days to make the trip.

Prices on Corsica generally are lower than those on the mainland of France. Expect to pay $80 and up for a double room in hotels listed as expensive; $55 to $80 in those listed as moderate; and under $55 in the inexpensive ones. Booking ahead isn't essential, even during the height of vacation season. A meal for two in an expensive restaurant costs $80 and up; $55 to $80 in a moderate establishment; and less than $55 at one that's inexpensive. These prices include tax, service charge, and in some cases, wine. Fresh seafood, which usually is delicious on Corsica, is by far the best bargain when dining out.

AJACCIO: Founded in the 15th century by the Genoese, Ajaccio is the capital of Corsica's southern district (Corse du Sud); it and Bastia are the island's two largest cities. Ajaccio perhaps is best known as the birthplace of Napoleon Bonaparte. The 3-story Maison Bonaparte, where Napoleon entered the world on August 15, 1769, can be seen in a guided tour starting from the Hôtel de Ville (Town Hall; Pl. Maréchal-Foch; phone: 95-21-40-87). A gold mine of Napoleona, the tour encompasses the 16th-century baroque cathedral where Napoleon was baptized; the Chapelle Impériale, which served as a mausoleum for members of the Bonaparte family; and the *Musée Fesch.* The tour also takes you through the picturesque alleys of Ajaccio's old town, near the fishing port with its splendid bay. If you prefer to just take it easy, there's a pleasant beach along Boulevard Lantivy.

Reinaugurated in July 1990 after several years of extensive renovation, the *Musée Fesch* (50 Rue Fesch; phone: 95-21-48-17) — first opened in 1852 — now ranks among France's finest. The early 19th-century palace that belonged to Cardinal Fesch, Napoleon's uncle, houses the best of about 16,000 paintings collected by this man of the cloth who had a passion for art (particularly from Italy). Some of the finest Italian primitive and Renaissance paintings found outside the *Uffizi* and *Pitti Palace* museums in Florence and the *Louvre* are now displayed to their best advantage in a white, modern setting. Among the most valuable works are Botticelli's *Madonna and Child,* and Tura's *Madonna and Child with St. Jerome.* The paintings are interspersed among huge arched windows that overlook the blue bay of Ajaccio. There also is a collection of Napoleon memorabilia. Open daily except Tuesdays from 9:30 AM to noon and 3 to 6 PM; in winter, from 2:30 to 5 PM. Admission charge.

CHECKING IN: Cala di Sole – On the beach, with a superb view of the Gulf of Ajaccio, this small, 30-room, air conditioned luxury hotel is 4 miles (6 km) out of town on D111. There is a pool, water sports, and tennis. Closed mid-October to April. Major credit cards accepted. Rte. de Sanguinaires, Ajaccio (phone: 95-52-01-36). Expensive.

Campo dell'Oro – A comfortable, modern hostelry in a garden setting, 2 minutes from the airport and the beach. Open year-round. Major credit cards accepted. Ajaccio (phone: 95-22-32-41; fax: 95-20-60-21). Expensive.

Eden Roc – Sleek, modern elegance and comfort characterize this recently remodeled resort hotel with 37 balconied rooms and suites, all overlooking the sea. A state-of-the-art saltwater spa facility, an outdoor pool, a sheltered beach, tennis courts, and a restaurant and piano bar with a panoramic view make this garden paradise complete. Open year-round. Major credit cards accepted. Rte. des Iles-Sanguinaires, Ajaccio (phone: 95-52-01-47).

Le Maquis – Hidden away on a sandy beach in Porticcio, 11 miles (17 km) south of Ajaccio, this white stucco retreat is perhaps the most charming and romantic to be found on the island. All 30 rooms, some with large terraces, have views of the sea. There are indoor and outdoor pools, a Jacuzzi, solarium, and an excellent restaurant overlooking the gulf and Ajaccio. Open year-round. Restaurant closed in February. Major credit cards accepted. Porticcio (phone: 95-25-05-55; fax: 95-25-11-70). Expensive.

Sofitel – Another modern luxury hotel, this one has 100 rooms, a heated pool, fine sandy beaches, and a very good restaurant serving French and Corsican fare. A few miles south of town on the D55, close to the Thalassa baths and spa. Open year-round. Major credit cards accepted. Porticcio (phone: 95-29-40-40; fax: 95-25-00-63). Expensive.

Hôtel du Golfe – Centrally located in the heart of Ajaccio overlooking the port, market, and the Hôtel de Ville, is this simple, old, 50-room hotel. It has a certain appeal, even though it could use some freshening up. Ask for one of the rooms with a terrace that overlooks the bay. There also are mini-bars, television sets, air conditioning, and double-glazed windows to shut out noise. Closed in February. Major credit cards accepted. 5 Bd. Roi-Jérôme, Ajaccio (phone: 95-21-47-64). Expensive to moderate.

Albion – Quiet and relaxed, with air conditioned rooms. In the residential area. Closed February and March. Major credit cards accepted. 15 Av. Général-Leclerc, Ajaccio (phone: 95-21-66-70). Moderate.

Fesch – This traditional hotel is in the heart of the Old Town. Closed mid-December to mid-January. Major credit cards accepted. 7 Rue Fesch, Ajaccio (phone: 95-21-50-52). Moderate.

EATING OUT: L'Amore Piattu – A local favorite, where chef-owner Marie-Louise Maestracci prepares contemporary versions of Corsican specialties such as skate, grilled mussels with peppers, a *gâteau* (cake) of lamb and eggplant, and Middle Eastern–style chicken fricassee. Closed Sunday evenings and October. Reservations advised. Major credit cards accepted. 8 Pl. de Gaulle, Diamant II, Ajaccio (phone: 95-51-00-53). Moderate.

Auberge du Prunelli – A cozy fireplace and rustic antique furnishings make this eatery a particularly appealing spot to try traditional Corsican dishes such as roast baby goat, hearty peasant soups, and *brocciu*. Closed for lunch in the summer, Tuesdays, October, and November. Reservations advised. No credit cards accepted. Six miles (10 km) south of Ajaccio on the old Rte. de Sartène (phone: 95-20-02-75). Moderate.

Auberge Seta – This ultramodern restaurant serving typical Corsican fare rises like a monolith in the heart of the tiny village of Bastelicaccia. The 2-story glass and beam structure is actually an architect's clever expansion upward of the Seta family's old 1-story *auberge.* Closed Wednesdays and January. Reservations advised. Major credit cards accepted. Just 7 miles (11 km) south of Ajaccio on the road to Porticcio, Bastelicaccia (phone: 95-20-00-16). Moderate.

Côte d'Azur – Traditional French cuisine is served here. Closed Sundays and from June 21 through July 20. Reservations advised. Major credit cards accepted. 12 Cours Napoléon, Ajaccio (phone: 95-21-50-24). Moderate.

En Route from Ajaccio – Route N196 heads east before dipping south, through the ubiquitous mountains and charming villages like Petreto-Bicchisano and Olmeto. The road is winding, and at nearly every turn there are views of deep, forested gorges. For a more panoramic view, stop at the Col de Celaccia, a mountain pass 38 miles (61 km) from Ajaccio. From there you can take D57 6 miles (10 km) to the archaeological site of Filitosa (open *Easter* until late October; phone: 95-74-00-91), where stone monoliths carved with human faces stare out to sea. Back on the main road, it's a short drive to Propriano, a family resort with fine sand beaches. If you're inclined to stay overnight, the best hotel in town is the *Miramar* (see *Checking In*).

Leaving Propriano, stay on N196 inland to Sartène. The writer Prosper Mérimée, who was a government official in Corsica in the 1860s, called Sartène "the most Corsican of Corsican towns." He considered it severe and somber; perhaps he also was thinking of the town's 19th-century history of bloody vendettas among the feudal barons who controlled it. Today, however, Sartène is neither severe nor embattled; in fact, it would be difficult to find a more peaceful city. The oldest part of town is especially picturesque, with its narrow steps and alleyways, and the surrounding region is rich in prehistoric finds.

As you drive from Roccapina to Bonifacio, the terrain becomes flatter and more rugged, with rocky creeks and sandy beaches off to the right, private enough for nude swimming and sunbathing.

CHECKING IN: *Miramar* – Perched on a hill overlooking the Gulf of Valinco, this cool stucco hotel amidst palm trees and gardens is Propriano's most luxurious hostelry. All 28 rooms face the sea and most have terraces. There is a swimming pool. Closed late October through March. Major credit cards accepted. Rte. de la Corniche, Propriano (phone: 95-76-06-13; fax: 95-76-13-14). Expensive.

Lido Beach – Just a few steps from the beach, this hotel has 18 large rooms, each with a small terrace overlooking the bay. Nearby, its sister establishment, the *Lido,* has a restaurant where seafood specialties including lobster are served. Open year-round. Major credit cards accepted. Av. Napoléon, Propriano (phone: 95-76-17-74). Moderate.

EATING OUT: *Auberge Santa Barbara* – Corsican-born Mme. Lovichi and her husband returned here after a decade of operating a successful restaurant in Versailles. Her rendition of Corsican specialties, served in the homey, beamed dining room or the flowered garden, have won laurels. Forty guestrooms with panoramic valley views have been added this year. Closed November to *Easter.* Major credit cards accepted. Propriano (no phone). Moderate.

La Rascasse – A simple spot about a block from the port, featuring fresh fish and the local version of bouillabaisse. Reservations unnecessary. Closed Sunday evenings and Mondays from October to April 15 and December 23 through January. Major credit cards accepted. Rue des Pêcheurs, Propriano (phone: 95-76-13-84). Moderate.

La Chaumière – A charming and cozy place to sample regional specialties. Closed

Monday evenings except June through September, and January and February. Reservations advised. Major credit cards accepted. 39 Rue Capitaine-Benedetti (phone: 95-77-07-13). Inexpensive.

BONIFACIO: Set on a peninsula of sheer limestone cliffs overlooking the port, this town at the southern tip of Corsica boasts one of the most dramatic sites in the Mediterranean. Bonafacio, founded as a fortress, is actually a town of two levels. Atop the cliffs, rising more than 200 feet above the sea, are the houses and churches of the *haute ville,* or upper town, as well as the citadel, the ancient fortress that is now garrisoned by the French Foreign Legion. The Marine (port) below can be reached from the *haute ville* by descending the Aragonese Steps, a long stairway carved from the rocky cliffs; most of Bonifacio's hotels, restaurants, and other tourist facilities are on this level.

The cliffs are full of caves and grottoes, and boat excursions can be arranged through a boat owners' association (phone: 95-73-05-43 or 95-73-03-76). The same group offers excursions to the nearby islands of Cavallo and Lavezzi, with their excellent beaches. *Tirrenia* (phone: 95-73-00-96) runs boats to the island of Sardinia, 8 miles away, another good spot for a day trip.

If you turn right on D58 out of Bonifacio, you'll soon reach the Sémaphore Phare de Pertusato, a lighthouse that provides a sweeping coastal view.

CHECKING IN: *La Caravelle* – A venerable old establishment with 30 comfortable rooms, overlooking the Lower Town's quaint port. The ground floor restaurant of the same name is known for its high-quality seafood. Closed November through *Easter.* Reservations advised. Major credit cards accepted. 11 Quai Comparetti, Bonifacio (phone: 95-73-00-03). Expensive.

Le Genovese – This 14-room salmon stucco hotel was formerly a barracks set into the ramparts of the upper town (dating back to the 13th century when the Genoans controlled the town). A luxurious hostelry, with a covered pool, solarium, nearby golf course, and conference rooms. Open year-round. Major credit cards accepted. Quartier de la Citadelle, Hauteville, Bonifacio (phone: 95-73-12-34; fax: 95-73-09-03). Expensive.

EATING OUT: *L'Albatros* – Excellent fish is served at this portside restaurant. Open year-round. Reservations advised. Major credit cards accepted. Quai du Port, Bonifacio (phone: 95-73-01-97). Moderate.

Le Voilier – Breezy white, sea-blue, and wicker decor makes this portside seafood restaurant among the Lower Town's most inviting dining spots. Closed Sunday evenings and Mondays from October through December, and January and February. Reservations advised. Major credit cards accepted. La Marine, Quai Comparetti, Bonifacio (phone: 95-73-07-06). Moderate.

En Route from Bonifacio – Driving north, the road (N198) becomes straighter. Take it 17 miles (27 km) to Porto-Vecchio, a popular resort with great beaches along the gulf. In summer, the water is crammed with sailboats and other pleasure craft.

Continue north until you reach the town of Ghisonaccia. From Ghisonaccia, head inland 4 miles (6 km) on D344, approaching the gorges of Inzecca and Strette, and their striking overhangs of rock. At nearby Ghisoni, pick up D69, which winds through some glorious mountain scenery to join the main Ajaccio-Bastia road (N193). Turn right to reach Corte, 12 miles (19 km) north.

CHECKING IN: *Grand Hôtel de Cala Rossa* – In a pine wood on a beach, this 50-room luxury establishment is 6 miles (10 km) north of Porto-Vecchio. Its fine restaurant has been awarded one Michelin star. Open from mid-April through October. Reservations necessary. Major credit cards accepted. On D468 via D568 and N198, Porto-Vecchio (phone: 95-71-61-51; fax: 95-71-60-11). Expensive.

Shegara – Rugged stone and wrought-iron terraces overlooking the sea mark this old 30-room establishment. It offers simple comforts and easy access to the sea, as well as an open-air restaurant featuring lobster, fish, and grilled meat. Closed December through February. Major credit cards accepted. Porto-Vecchio (phone: 95-70-04-31; fax: 95-70-23-38). Moderate.

EATING OUT: L'Orée du Maquis – Gérard and Danille Carteaud gave up their city life and respective professions to transform this villa near Porto-Vecchio into an intimate restaurant. Mme. Carteaud's cooking, perfected in the kitchens of such gastronomic stars as Roger Vergé and Alain Passard, is delicate and refined — specialties include langoustines in a sweet-and-sour sauce and scallops in port butter with asparagus. Open daily for dinner except Sundays and 2 weeks in February. Reservations advised. Major credit cards accepted. Rte. de la Lézardière, Trinité de Porto-Vecchio (phone: 95-70-22-21). Expensive.

Le Bistrot du Port – Offering slightly fancier seafood fare (and higher prices) than the average bistro, this restaurant has a terrace overlooking the sea. Open year-round. Reservations advised. Major credit cards accepted. Quai Paoli, Porto-Vecchio (phone: 95-70-22-06). Expensive to moderate.

CORTE: The stillness of this hilltop town in the heart of the central mountains belies its somewhat rocky history. Occupied intermittently since ancient times, Corte became the capital of Corsica during the island's 18th-century War of Independence, fought against the ruling Genoese. No longer the capital, it's now quiet and slumberous, with little to do save excellent hiking in the gorges and forests of Tavignano and Restonica, just southwest of the city on D623.

CHECKING IN: Auberge de la Restonica – Staying in this rustic, wood-beamed retreat surrounded by nature is like being a guest in a Corsican country house. Family run and friendly, a cat in every armchair, a library full of books available to guests, and a rambling dining room with a river view add to the ambience. Though the food can be disappointing and the 6 guestrooms could use some sprucing up, the warm welcome and the secluded, peaceful location are memorable. Thirty rooms built in an adjoining wing were added last year. Hotel open year-round; restaurant closed November to December 15 and *Christmas* through March. Reservations advised in season. Major credit cards accepted. Rte. de la Restonica, Corte (phone: 95-46-09-58). Moderate.

Paix – A pleasantly located place, on a tree-lined square. Open from *Easter* through October. Pl. du Général-de-Gaulle, Corte (phone: 95-46-06-72). Moderate to inexpensive.

EATING OUT: Pascal Paoli – Named for the great 18th-century Corsican leader who established Corte as the capital, this is a relaxed, friendly place on the main square. Weather permitting (almost always), you can sit at a sidewalk table and watch the world pass slowly by. Open from *Easter* through October 15. Pl. Paoli, Corte (phone: 95-46-13-48). Inexpensive.

U Palazziunu – Stop by this breezy café/restaurant for a simple meal of quiche, salad, or the daily special after a visit to the nearby Citadel in the Upper Town. Open daily except Sundays and 2 weeks in February. Reservations unnecessary. Major credit cards accepted. 3 Rue du Palais-National, Corte (phone: 95-46-03-87). Inexpensive.

En Route from Corte – Follow N193 north for 15 miles (24 km) to Ponte Leccia, where you pick up N197 headed northwest. As you get closer to the sea, the mountains become more rounded and wooded. At Lozari, head south on the coastal road, N197, for 16 miles (26 km) — through Ile-Rousse, a yachting port with good beaches — to Calvi.

CHECKING IN: *Isola Rossa* – Located just a few steps from the beach, this simple, white stucco, 23-room establishment is clean and homey. Ask for a room overlooking the bay, preferably one with a small balcony. Open year-round. Major credit cards accepted. Rte. Port, Ile-Rousse (phone: 95-60-01-32). Moderate.

Napoléon Bonaparte – This old seaside hotel, once the grandest in the area, has recently undergone a much-needed makeover. Seventy of the 106 rooms have been renovated, and work on the common areas includes restoring the sweeping corridors, palatial pillars, and high-ceiling rooms to their former elegance. Open year-round. Major credit cards accepted. Ile-Rousse (phone: 95-60-06-09). Moderate.

CALVI: Corsica's chicest and most popular resort, Calvi is also a fortress town with a military history that goes back centuries. Occupied through the Roman era and the Middle Ages, it was settled in the 15th century by the Genoese, who built the town's Citadel on an immense rock towering above the sea. During the Napoleonic wars, Calvi was taken by the British after 2 months of incessant combat in which Admiral Nelson lost his eye.

At the Citadel you can see the ruins of the house where Christopher Columbus was born in 1441. Also worth a visit is the *Oratoire St-Antoine,* within the walls of the fortified part of town. Built in the 15th century, it's now a museum of ancient and medieval religious art.

History aside, Calvi boasts some enticing long, white beaches. You also can take a boat trip on the *Colombo* line (phone: 95-65-03-40 or 95-65-32-10) to Grotte des Veaux Marins, the well-known caves on nearby Peninsula de la Revelata (phone: 95-65-28-16 or 95-65-29-65). Boats leave daily at 9:15 AM and 4:30 PM April to October. For guided walks of the caves, call to make reservations (phone: 95-50-56-14). South of Calvi lies some of the island's most magnificent coastline, best appreciated when viewed from the sea, so the boat ride is a treat in itself.

CHECKING IN: *Caravelle* – A pleasant 34-room beach hotel. Open from May through September. Major credit cards accepted. On N197, just north of Calvi (phone: 95-65-01-21). Moderate.

Clos des Amandiers – A charming place with guest bungalows in a garden setting and a pool and tennis facilities. Closed from November through April. Major credit cards accepted. A mile (1.6 km) south of Calvi on Rte. Pietra-Major, via N197 (phone: 95-65-08-32). Moderate.

Le Magnolia – Formerly the home of a countess, this 19th-century mansion, laced with white wrought iron and graced by a luscious garden where bougainvillea, hibiscus, and an immense magnolia tree bloom, emanates a Belle Epoque, antebellum, and Florentine aura all at once. Each of the 14 rooms — named for writers such as George Sand and Racine — are quaint and comfortable. Most overlook the garden, though one has a view of the bay. Closed January and February. Major credit cards accepted. Pl. du Marché, Calvi (phone: 95-65-19-16). Moderate.

EATING OUT: *Comme Chez Soi* – On the lively waterfront strip, this place serves delicious fish. Open year-round. Reservations necessary. Major credit cards accepted. Quai Landry, Calvi (phone: 95-65-00-59). Expensive.

Ile de Beauté – Also on the waterfront, this excellent spot specializes in lobster dishes; the oysters with lime are popular, too. Closed Wednesdays and October to May. Reservations necessary. Major credit cards accepted. Quai Landry, Calvi (phone: 95-65-00-46). Expensive.

En Route from Calvi – Heading south on D81, the road soon ascends to 400 feet above the sea, providing a final panoramic view of the Peninsula de la Revelata, its caves, and its lighthouse. Driving by the peninsula, on the left is the belvedere of Notre-Dame-de-la-Serra, a tiny chapel that's the site of *Santa di u Niuli,* Calvi's annual pilgrimage celebrating the birth of the Virgin.

The next 40-mile (64-km) stretch is, quite simply, breathtaking, even for an island where spectacular scenery is abundant. Driving along the rugged cliff road you see mountains and rocky headlands on your left, the sea on the right, visible from almost every bend. From atop the Col de Bassa, 850 feet high and 17 miles (27 km) from Calvi, you can see the long, isolated beach at Galeria; or climb the nearby Col de Palmarella for a look at the Gulf of Girolata.

Porto, 10 miles (16 km) on, is a small beach resort where you can take a boat excursion to Girolata or, to the south, visit the famous Calanques of Piana. These are red-brown rock formations, the texture of giant coral, molded by nature into phantasmagorical shapes, that plunge into bays of sparkling green and black water. From the road out of Porto, rising to 870 feet, the Calanques can be seen in all their glory. The village of Piana, 8 miles (13 km) from Porto, has a fine beach, Ficajola; it's a 2-mile (3-km) descent down D624 — well paved but with a wicked hairpin turn.

From Piana, D81 strikes inland to rejoin the coast at Cargèse, a small Greek Orthodox community north of the Gulf of Sagone, 70 miles (113 km) from Calvi. The road from Cargèse back to Ajaccio is 32 miles (54 km); for half the distance it hugs the Gulf coast before plunging you into the mountains.

CHECKING IN: *Auberge de la Signoria* – Reached via the airport road and a few miles from the beach, this pretty 17th-century estate (formerly a relay station) sits well back from the road amidst eucalyptus trees and a garden-rimmed pool. There's a calm and peacefulness here not found in the hotels closer to bustling Calvi. There are 11 comfortable rooms and a good restaurant serving such delicate dishes as salad of warm turbot with truffle vinaigrette. Closed October to April. Restaurant closed for lunch except weekends in July and August. Major credit cards accepted. Rte. de l'Aéroport, Calvi (phone: 95-65-23-73; fax: 95-65-33-20). Expensive.

Marina – A modern hotel with a pool, a sun deck, and a fine view of the sea and mountains. Open from May through September. Porto-Marine, Porto (phone: 95-26-10-34; fax: 95-26-13-04). Expensive.

Capo Rosso – A luxury property overlooking the *calanques* (creeks) and the gulf. Sunning yourself by the pool, you feel as though you're part of this glorious landscape. A good restaurant serves fresh fish from the gulf. Closed from mid-October through March. Major credit cards accepted. Rte. des Calanches, Piana (phone: 95-27-82-40; fax: 95-27-80-00). Expensive to moderate.

Dolce Vita – Also between Calvi and Porto, this is a fine hostelry on a hilltop, 2 miles (3 km) from a good sand beach. Open from April through October. Major credit cards accepted. Col de la Croix, Osani (phone: 95-27-31-86; fax: 95-27-31-57). Moderate.

Auberge de Ferayola – Midway between Calvi and Porto; a quite comfortable hotel. The view from every room is splendid, the restaurant is good, and there's a beach a mile (1.6 km) away at Argentella. Closed October to June. Major credit cards accepted. D81, Ferayola (phone: 95-65-25-25). Moderate to inexpensive.

EATING OUT: *U Campanile* – Crayfish and other specialties from the gulf are served on a terrace overlooking the village square. Open from April through September. Reservations unnecessary. Major credit cards accepted. Pl. de l'Eglise, Piana (phone: 95-27-81-71). Inexpensive.

CAP CORSE

A much shorter alternate route covers the Cap Corse, a narrow peninsula on the northeast that offers some of the island's most beautiful coastal and mountain scenery. It's an 80-mile (129-km) round trip from Bastia, on the eastern heel of the cape.

A Genoese fortress from the 15th to the 18th century, Bastia today is the capital of Corsica's northern district (Haute-Corse) and the island's industrial center. In Terra-Vecchia, the 17th-century neighborhood north of the old port, is Bastia's landmark, the 17th-century Eglise St-Jean-Baptiste, with its simple, pretty façade. From here you can climb from the Quai du Sud up to Terra-Nova, the Genoese citadel in Bastia's Vieux Port. Just inside the citadel's main gate is the *Musée d'Ethnographie Corse* (phone: 95-31-09-12). It's an excellent introduction to Corsica, with artifacts spanning the island's history from prehistoric to medieval times. Several exhibitions portray Corsican customs, handicrafts, and folklore as well as 19th-century photographs and collections of Napoleona. More artifacts, including the emperor's death mask, are displayed on the second floor. Open daily from 9 AM to noon and 2 to 6 PM, Saturdays and Sundays from 10 AM to noon and 2 to 6 PM.

Drive inland on D81, a mountain road that twists and curls its way across the base of the peninsula. At the midpoint is the Col de Teghime, the site of a major battle during Corsica's liberation in World War II. Eventually you will reach the port of St-Florent, now a beach resort. Just to the east, and worth a look, is a 13th-century Pisan cathedral, practically all that remains of the medieval city of Nebbio. Some very good fish restaurants can be found in the port's Old Town, among them *Gaffe* (phone: 95-37-00-12; closed Mondays and from November to mid-December). In St-Florent, you can take a motorboat across the gulf to explore the solitary beaches of the Agriates Desert and the salt lakes of Mortella.

Heading north, D81 swings inland to the vineyards of Patrimonio and then back to the coast. Twelve miles (19 km) from St-Florent is the village of Nonza, with its sand beach and medieval fortress on a cliff. At the northwest corner of the cape is tiny Centuri-Port, where you can get decent food and lodging. From Centuri take D80 across the cape to the marina at Macinaggio. Driving the eastern length of the cape back to Bastia, the beaches aren't as attractive as those on the west, but the sight of the sea will sustain you.

 CHECKING IN: *Pietracap* – A modern hotel set in a park of olive trees; its heated pool offers a view of the sea. Closed December through February. Major credit cards accepted. Rte. de San Martino, 2 miles (3 km) north of Bastia on the coast at Pietranera (phone: 95-31-64-63; telex: 460254). Expensive to moderate.

Thalassa – This small, quiet, 30-room hotel on the beach has an excellent restaurant serving regional specialties. Closed December through February. Major credit cards accepted. Rte. du Cap, Pietranera (phone: 95-31-56-63; fax: 95-32-32-79). Moderate.

 EATING OUT: *Le Bistrot du Port* – Small and friendly, this restaurant is in an alley off the quai. Try the gratin of mussels with spinach. Closed Sundays and October. Reservations unnecessary. No credit cards accepted. Right off the Quai Martyrs-de-la-Libération on Rue Posta-Vecchia, Bastia (phone: 95-32-19-83). Expensive to moderate.

Le Vieux Moulin – A dining spot where you also can spend the night. Closed from November to February. Major credit cards accepted. On the port, Centuri-Port (phone: 95-35-60-15). Moderate.

INDEX

Index

NOTES

NOTES